Encyclopedia of Parallel Computing

David Padua (Ed.)

Encyclopedia of Parallel Computing

Volume 4

Q–Z

With 880 Figures and 98 Tables

Editor-in-Chief
David Padua
University of Illinois at Urbana-Champaign
Urbana, IL
USA

ISBN 978-0-387-09765-7   e-ISBN 978-0-387-09766-4
DOI 10.1007/978-0-387-09766-4
Print and electronic bundle ISBN: 978-0-387-09844-9
Springer New York Dordrecht Heidelberg London

Library of Congress Control Number: 2011935063

© Springer Science+Business Media, LLC 2011

All rights reserved. This work may not be translated or copied in whole or in part without the written permission of the publisher (Springer Science+Business Media, LLC, 233 Spring Street, New York, NY 10013, USA), except for brief excerpts in connection with reviews or scholarly analysis. Use in connection with any form of information storage and retrieval, electronic adaptation, computer software, or by similar or dissimilar methodology now known or hereafter developed is forbidden.
The use in this publication of trade names, trademarks, service marks, and similar terms, even if they are not identified as such, is not to be taken as an expression of opinion as to whether or not they are subject to proprietary rights.

Printed on acid-free paper

Springer is part of Springer Science+Business Media (www.springer.com)

Preface

Parallelism, the capability of a computer to execute operations concurrently, has been a constant throughout the history of computing. It impacts hardware, software, theory, and applications. The fastest machines of the past few decades, the supercomputers, owe their performance advantage to parallelism. Today, physical limitations have forced the adoption of parallelism as the preeminent strategy of computer manufacturers for continued performance gains of all classes of machines, from embedded and mobile systems to the most powerful servers. Parallelism has been used to simplify the programming of certain applications which react to or simulate the parallelism of the natural world. At the same time, parallelism complicates programming when the objective is to take advantage of the existence of multiple hardware components to improve performance. Formal methods are necessary to study the correctness of parallel algorithms and implementations and to analyze their performance on different classes of real and theoretical systems. Finally, parallelism is crucial for many applications in the sciences, engineering, and interactive services such as search engines.

Because of its importance and the challenging problems it has engendered, there have been numerous research and development projects during the past half century. This Encyclopedia is our attempt to collect accurate and clear descriptions of the most important of those projects. Although not exhaustive, with over 300 entries the Encyclopedia covers most of the topics that we identified at the outset as important for a work of this nature. Entries include many of the best known projects and span all the important dimensions of parallel computing including machine design, software, programming languages, algorithms, theoretical issues, and applications.

This Encyclopedia is the result of the work of many, whose dedication made it possible. The 25 Editorial Board Members created the list of entries, did most of the reviewing, and suggested authors for the entries. Colin Robertson, the Managing Editor, Jennifer Carlson, Springer's Reference Development editor, and Editorial Assistants Julia Koerting and Simone Tavenrath, worked for 3 long years coordinating the recruiting of authors and the review and submission process. Melissa Fearon, Springer's Senior Editor, helped immensely with the coordination of authors and Editorial Board Members, especially during the difficult last few months. The nearly 400 authors wrote crisp, informative entries. They include experts in all major areas, come from many different nations, and span several generations. In many cases, the author is the lead designer or researcher responsible for the contribution reported in the entry. It was a great pleasure for me to be part of this project. The enthusiasm of everybody involved made this a joyful enterprise. I believe we have put together a meaningful snapshot of parallel computing in the last 50 years and presented a believable glimpse of the future. I hope the reader agrees with me on this and finds the entries, as I did, valuable contributions to the literature.

David Padua
Editor-in-Chief
University of Illinois at Urbana-Champaign
Urbana, IL
USA

Editors

David Padua
Editor-in-Chief
University of Illinois at Urbana-Champaign
Urbana, IL
USA

Sarita Adve
Editorial Board Member
University of Illinois at Urbana-Champaign
Urbana, IL
USA

Colin Robertson
Managing Editor
University of Illinois at Urbana-Champaign
Urbana, IL
USA

Gheorghe S. Almasi
Editorial Board Member
IBM T. J. Watson Research Center
Yorktown Heights, NY
USA

Srinivas Aluru
Editorial Board Member
Iowa State University
Ames, IA
USA

Gianfranco Bilardi
Editorial Board Member
University of Padova
Padova
Italy

David Bader
Editorial Board Member
Georgia Tech
Atlanta, GA
USA

Siddharta Chatterjee
Editorial Board Member
IBM Systems & Technology Group
Austin, TX
USA

Luiz DeRose
Editorial Board Member
Cray Inc.
St. Paul, MN
USA

José Duato
Editorial Board Member
Universitat Politècnica de València
València
Spain

Jack Dongarra
Editorial Board Member
University of Tennessee
Knoxville, TN
USA
Oak Ridge National Laboratory
Oak Ridge, TN
USA
University of Manchester
Manchester
UK

Paul Feautrier
Editorial Board Member
Ecole Normale Supérieure de Lyon
Lyon
France

María J. Garzarán
Editorial Board Member
University of Illinois at Urbana Champaign
Urbana, IL
USA

William Gropp
Editorial Board Member
University of Illinois Urbana-Champaign
Urbana, IL
USA

Michael Gerndt
Editorial Board Member
Technische Universitaet Muenchen
Garching
Germany

Thomas Gross
Editorial Board Member
ETH Zurich
Zurich
Switzerland

James C. Hoe
Editorial Board Member
Carnegie Mellon University
Pittsburgh, PA
USA

Hironori Kasahara
Editorial Board Member
Waseda University
Tokyo
Japan

Laxmikant Kale
Editorial Board Member
University of Illinois at Urbana Champaign
Urbana, IL
USA

Christian Lengauer
Editorial Board Member
University of Passau
Passau
Germany

José E. Moreira
Editorial Board Member
IBM Thomas J. Watson Research Center
Yorktown Heights, NY
USA

Keshav Pingali
Editorial Board Member
The University of Texas at Austin
Austin, TX
USA

Yale N. Patt
Editorial Board Member
The University of Texas at Austin
Austin, TX
USA

Markus Püschel
Editorial Board Member
ETH Zurich
Zurich
Switzerland

Ahmed H. Sameh
Editorial Board Member
Purdue University
West Lafayette, IN
USA

Pen-Chung Yew
Editorial Board Member
University of Minnesota at Twin Cities
Minneapolis, MN
USA

Vivek Sarkar
Editorial Board Member
Rice University
Houston, TX
USA

List of Contributors

DENNIS ABTS
Google Inc.
Madison, WI
USA

SARITA V. ADVE
University of Illinois at Urbana-Champaign
Urbana, IL
USA

GUL AGHA
University of Illinois at Urbana-Champaign
Urbana, IL
USA

JASMIN AJANOVIC
Intel Corporation
Portland, OR
USA

SELIM G. AKL
Queen's University
Kingston, ON
Canada

HASAN AKTULGA
Purdue University
West Lafayette, IN
USA

JOSÉ I. ALIAGA
TU Braunschweig Institute of Computational Mathematics
Braunschweig
Germany

ERIC ALLEN
Oracle Labs
Austin, TX
USA

GEORGE ALMASI
IBM
Yorktown Heights, NY
USA

SRINIVAS ALURU
Iowa State University
Ames, IA
USA
and
Indian Institute of Technology Bombay
Mumbai
India

PATRICK AMESTOY
Université de Toulouse ENSEEIHT-IRIT
Toulouse cedex 7
France

BABA ARIMILLI
IBM Systems and Technology Group
Austin, TX
USA

ROGER S. ARMEN
Thomas Jefferson University
Philadelphia, PA
USA

DOUGLAS ARMSTRONG
Intel Corporation
Champaign, IL
USA

DAVID I. AUGUST
Princeton University
Princeton, NJ
USA

CEVDET AYKANAT
Bilkent University
Ankara
Turkey

DAVID A. BADER
Georgia Institute of Technology
Atlanta, GA
USA

MICHAEL BADER
Universität Stuttgart
Stuttgart
Germany

DAVID H. BAILEY
Lawrence Berkeley National Laboratory
Berkeley, CA
USA

RAJEEV BALASUBRAMONIAN
University of Utah
Salt Lake City, UT
USA

UTPAL BANERJEE
University of California at Irvine
Irvine, CA
USA

ALESSANDRO BARDINE
Università di Pisa
Pisa
Italy

MUTHU MANIKANDAN BASKARAN
Reservoir Labs, Inc.
New York, NY
USA

CÉDRIC BASTOUL
University Paris-Sud 11 - INRIA Saclay Île-de-France
Orsay
France

AARON BECKER
University of Illinois at Urbana-Champaign
Urbana, IL
USA

MICHAEL W. BERRY
The University of Tennessee
Knoxville, TN
USA

ABHINAV BHATELE
University of Illinois at Urbana-Champaign
Urbana, IL
USA

SCOTT BIERSDORFF
University of Oregon
Eugene, OR
USA

GIANFRANCO BILARDI
University of Padova
Padova
Italy

ROBERT BJORNSON
Yale University
New Haven, CT
USA

GUY BLELLOCH
Carnegie Mellon University
Pittsburgh, PA
USA

ROBERT BOCCHINO
Carnegie Mellon University
Pittsburgh, PA
USA

HANS J. BOEHM
HP Labs
Palo Alto, CA
USA

ERIC J. BOHM
University of Illinois at Urbana-Champaign
Urbana, IL
USA

MATTHIAS BOLLHÖFER
Universitat Jaume I
Castellón
Spain

DAN BONACHEA
Lawrence Berkeley National Laboratory
Berkeley, CA
USA

PRADIP BOSE
IBM Corp. T.J. Watson Research Center
Yorktown Heights, NY
USA

MARIAN BREZINA
University of Colorado at Boulder
Boulder, CO
USA

JEFF BROOKS
Cray Inc.
St. Paul, MN
USA

HOLGER BRUNST
Technische Universität Dresden
Dresden
Germany

HANS-JOACHIM BUNGARTZ
Technische Universität München
Garching
Germany

MICHAEL G. BURKE
Rice University
Houston, TX
USA

ALFREDO BUTTARI
Université de Toulouse ENSEEIHT-IRIT
Toulouse cedex 7
France

ERIC J. BYLASKA
Pacific Northwest National Laboratory
Richland, WA
USA

ROY H. CAMPBELL
University of Illinois at Urbana-Champaign
Urbana, IL
USA

WILLIAM CARLSON
Institute for Defense Analyses
Bowie, MD
USA

MANUEL CARRO
Universidad Politécnica de Madrid
Madrid
Spain

ÜMIT V. ÇATALYÜREK
The Ohio State University
Columbus, OH
USA

LUIS H. CEZE
University of Washington
Seattle, WA
USA

BRADFORD L. CHAMBERLAIN
Cray Inc.
Seattle, WA
USA

ERNIE CHAN
NVIDIA Corporation
Santa Clara, CA
USA

RONG-GUEY CHANG
National Chung Cheng University
Chia-Yi
Taiwan

BARBARA CHAPMAN
University of Houston
Houston, TX
USA

DAVID CHASE
Oracle Labs
Burlington, MA
USA

DANIEL CHAVARRÍA-MIRANDA
Pacific Northwest National Laboratory
Richland, WA
USA

NORMAN H. CHRIST
Columbia University
New York, NY
USA

MURRAY COLE
University of Edinburgh
Edinburgh
UK

PHILLIP COLELLA
University of California
Berkeley, CA
USA

SALVADOR COLL
Universidad Politécnica de Valencia
Valencia
Spain

GUOJING CONG
IBM
Yorktown Heights, NY
USA

JAMES H. COWNIE
Intel Corporation (UK) Ltd.
Swindon
UK

ANTHONY P. CRAIG
National Center for Atmospheric Research
Boulder, CO
USA

ANTHONY CURTIS
University of Houston
Houston
TX

H. J. J. VAN DAM
Pacific Northwest National Laboratory
Richland, WA
USA

FREDERICA DAREMA
National Science Foundation
Arlington, VA
USA

ALAIN DARTE
École Normale Supérieure de Lyon
Lyon
France

RAJA DAS
IBM Corporation
Armonk, NY
USA

KAUSHIK DATTA
University of California
Berkeley, CA
USA

JIM DAVIES
Oxford University
UK

JAMES DEMMEL
University of California at Berkeley
Berkeley, CA
USA

MONTY DENNEAU
IBM Corp., T.J. Watson Research Center
Yorktown Heights, NY
USA

JACK B. DENNIS
Massachusetts Institute of Technology
Cambridge, MA
USA

MARK DEWING
Intel Corporation
Champaign, IL
USA

VOLKER DIEKERT
Universität Stuttgart FMI
Stuttgart
Germany

JACK DONGARRA
University of Tennessee
Knoxville, TN
USA

DAVID DONOFRIO
Lawrence Berkeley National Laboratory
Berkeley, CA
USA

RON O. DROR
D. E. Shaw Research
New York, NY
USA

IAIN DUFF
Science & Technology Facilities Council
Didcot, Oxfordshire
UK

MICHAEL DUNGWORTH

SANDHYA DWARKADAS
University of Rochester
Rochester, NY
USA

RUDOLF EIGENMANN
Purdue University
West Lafayette, IN
USA

E. N. (MOOTAZ) ELNOZAHY
IBM Research
Austin, TX
USA

JOEL EMER
Intel Corporation
Hudson, MA
USA

BABAK FALSAFI
Ecole Polytechnique Fédérale de Lausanne
Lausanne
Switzerland

PAOLO FARABOSCHI
Hewlett Packard
Sant Cugat del Valles
Spain

PAUL FEAUTRIER
Ecole Normale Supérieure de Lyon
Lyon
France

KARL FEIND
SGI
Eagan, MN
USA

WU-CHUN FENG
Virginia Tech
Blacksburg, VA
USA
and
Wake Forest University
Winston-Salem, NC
USA

JOHN FEO
Pacific Northwest National Laboratory
Richland, WA
USA

JEREMY T. FINEMAN
Carnegie Mellon University
Pittsburgh, PA
USA

JOSEPH A. FISHER
Miami Beach, FL
USA

CORMAC FLANAGAN
University of California at Santa Cruz
Santa Cruz, CA
USA

JOSÉ FLICH
Technical University of Valencia
Valencia
Spain

CHRISTINE FLOOD
Oracle Labs
Burlington, MA
USA

MICHAEL FLYNN
Stanford University
Stanford, CA
USA

JOSEPH FOGARTY
University of South Florida
Tampa, FL
USA

PIERFRANCESCO FOGLIA
Università di Pisa
Pisa
Italy

TRYGGVE FOSSUM
Intel Corporation
Hudson, MA
USA

GEOFFREY FOX
Indiana University
Bloomington, IN
USA

MARTIN FRÄNZLE
Carl von Ossietzky Universität
Oldenburg
Germany

FRANZ FRANCHETTI
Carnegie Mellon University
Pittsburgh, PA
USA

STEFAN M. FREUDENBERGER
Freudenberger Consulting
Zürich
Switzerland

HOLGER FRÖNING
University of Heidelberg
Heidelberg
Germany

KARL FÜRLINGER
Ludwig-Maximilians-Universität München
Munich
Germany

EFSTRATIOS GALLOPOULOS
University of Patras
Patras
Greece

ALAN GARA
IBM T.J. Watson Research Center
Yorktown Heights, NY
USA

PEDRO J. GARCIA
Universidad de Castilla-La Mancha
Albacete
Spain

MICHAEL GARLAND
NVIDIA Corporation
Santa Clara, CA
USA

KLAUS GÄRTNER
Weierstrass Institute for Applied Analysis and Stochastics
Berlin
Germany

ED GEHRINGER
North Carolina State University
Raleigh, NC
USA

ROBERT A. VAN DE GEIJN
The University of Texas at Austin
Austin, TX
USA

AL GEIST
Oak Ridge National Laboratory
Oak Ridge, TN
USA

THOMAS GEORGE
IBM Research
Delhi
India

MICHAEL GERNDT
Technische Universität München
München
Germany

AMOL GHOTING
IBM Thomas. J. Watson Research Center
Yorktown Heights, NY
USA

JOHN GILBERT
University of California
Santa Barbara, CA
USA

Robert J. van Glabbeek
NICTA
Sydney
Australia
and
The University of New South Wales
Sydney
Australia
and
Stanford University
Stanford, CA
USA

Sergei Gorlatch
Westfälische Wilhelms-Universität Münster
Münster
Germany

Kazushige Goto
The University of Texas at Austin
Austin, TX
USA

Allan Gottlieb
New York University
New York, NY
USA

Steven Gottlieb
Indiana University
Bloomington, IN
USA

N. Govind
Pacific Northwest National Laboratory
Richland, WA
USA

Susan L. Graham
University of California
Berkeley, CA
USA

Ananth Y. Grama
Purdue University
West Lafayette, IN
USA

Don Grice
IBM Corporation
Poughkeepsie, NY
USA

Laura Grigori
Laboratoire de Recherche en Informatique Universite
Paris-Sud 11
Paris
France

William Gropp
University of Illinois at Urbana-Champaign
Urbana, IL
USA

Abdou Guermouche
Université de Bordeaux
Talence
France

John A. Gunnels
IBM Corp
Yorktown Heights, NY
USA

Anshul Gupta
IBM T.J. Watson Research Center
Yorktown Heights, NY
USA

John L. Gustafson
Intel Corporation
Santa Clara, CA
USA

Robert H. Halstead
Curl Inc.
Cambridge, MA
USA

Kevin Hammond
University of St. Andrews
St. Andrews
UK

James Harrell

ROBERT HARRISON
Oak Ridge National Laboratory
Oak Ridge, TN
USA

JOHN C. HART
University of Illinois at Urbana-Champaign
Urbana, IL
USA

MICHAEL HEATH
University of Illinois at Urbana-Champaign
Urbana, IL
USA

HERMANN HELLWAGNER
Klagenfurt University
Klagenfurt
Austria

DANNY HENDLER
Ben-Gurion University of the Negev
Beer-Sheva
Israel

BRUCE HENDRICKSON
Sandia National Laboratories
Albuquerque, NM
USA

ROBERT HENSCHEL
Indiana University
Bloomington, IN
USA

KIERAN T. HERLEY
University College Cork
Cork
Ireland

MAURICE HERLIHY
Brown University
Providence, RI
USA

MANUEL HERMENEGILDO
Universidad Politécnica de Madrid
Madrid
Spain
IMDEA Software Institute
Madrid
Spain

OSCAR HERNANDEZ
Oak Ridge National Laboratory
Oak Ridge, TN
USA

PAUL HILFINGER
University of California
Berkeley, CA
USA

KEI HIRAKI
The University of Tokyo
Tokyo
Japan

H. PETER HOFSTEE
IBM Austin Research Laboratory
Austin, TX
USA

CHRIS HSIUNG
Hewlett Packard
Palo Alto, CA
USA

JONATHAN HU
Sandia National Laboratories
Livermore, CA
USA

THOMAS HUCKLE
Technische Universität München
Garching
Germany

WEN-MEI HWU
University of Illinois at Urbana-Champaign
Urbana, IL
USA

François Irigoin
MINES ParisTech/CRI
Fontainebleau
France

Ken'ichi Itakura
Japan Agency for Marine-Earth Science and Technology (JAMSTEC)
Yokohama
Japan

Joseph F. Jaja
University of Maryland
College Park, MD
USA

Joefon Jann
T. J. Watson Research Center, IBM Corp.
Yorktown Heights, NY
USA

Karl Jansen
NIC, DESY Zeuthen
Zeuthen
Germany

Pritish Jetley
University of Illinois at Urbana-Champaign
Urbana, IL
USA

Wibe A. de Jong
Pacific Northwest National Laboratory
Richland, WA
USA

Laxmikant V. Kalé
University of Illinois at Urbana-Champaign
Urbana, IL
USA

Ananth Kalyanaraman
Washington State University
Pullman, WA
USA

Amir Kamil
University of California
Berkeley, CA
USA

Krishna Kandalla
The Ohio State University
Columbus, OH
USA

Larry Kaplan
Cray Inc.
Seattle, WA
USA

Tejas S. Karkhanis
IBM T.J. Watson Research Center
Yorktown Heights, NY
USA

Rajesh K. Karmani
University of Illinois at Urbana-Champaign
Urbana, IL
USA

George Karypis
University of Minnesota
Minneapolis, MN
USA

Arun Kejariwal
Yahoo! Inc.
Sunnyvale, CA
USA

Maleq Khan
Virginia Tech
Blacksburg, VA
USA

Thilo Kielmann
Vrije Universiteit
Amsterdam
The Netherlands

Gerry Kirschner
Cray Incorporated
St. Paul, MN
USA

Christof Klausecker
Ludwig-Maximilians-Universität München
Munich
Germany

KATHLEEN KNOBE
Intel Corporation
Cambridge, MA
USA

ANDREAS KNÜPFER
Technische Universität Dresden
Dresden
Germany

GIORGOS KOLLIAS
Purdue University
West Lafayette, IN
USA

K. KOWALSKI
Pacific Northwest National Laboratory
Richland, WA
USA

QUINCEY KOZIOL
The HDF Group
Champaign, IL
USA

DIETER KRANZLMÜLLER
Ludwig-Maximilians-Universität München
Munich
Germany

MANOJKUMAR KRISHNAN
Pacific Northwest National Laboratory
Richland, WA
USA

CHI-BANG KUAN
National Tsing-Hua University
Hsin-Chu
Taiwan

DAVID J. KUCK
Intel Corporation
Champaign, IL
USA

JEFFERY A. KUEHN
Oak Ridge National Laboratory
Oak Ridge, TN
USA

V. S. ANIL KUMAR
Virginia Tech
Blacksburg, VA
USA

KALYAN KUMARAN
Argonne National Laboratory
Argonne, IL
USA

JAMES LA GRONE
University of Houston
Houston, TX
USA

ROBERT LATHAM
Argonne National Laboratory
Argonne, IL
USA

BRUCE LEASURE
Saint Paul, MN
USA

JENQ-KUEN LEE
National Tsing-Hua University
Hsin-Chu
Taiwan

CHARLES E. LEISERSON
Massachusetts Institute of Technology
Cambridge, MA
USA

CHRISTIAN LENGAUER
University of Passau
Passau
Germany

RICHARD LETHIN
Reservoir Labs, Inc.
New York, NY
USA

ALLEN LEUNG
Reservoir Labs, Inc.
New York, NY
USA

John M. Levesque
Cray Inc.
Knoxville, TN
USA

Michael Levine

Jean-Yves L'Excellent
ENS Lyon
Lyon
France

Jian Li
IBM Research
Austin, TX
USA

Xiaoye Sherry Li
Lawarence Berkeley National Laboratory
Berkeley, CA
USA

Zhiyuan Li
Purdue University
West Lafayette, IN
USA

Calvin Lin
University of Texas at Austin
Austin, TX
USA

Heshan Lin
Virginia Tech
Blacksburg, VA
USA

Hans-Wolfgang Loidl
Heriot-Watt University
Edinburgh
UK

Rita Loogen
Philipps-Universität Marburg
Marburg
Germany

Pedro López
Universidad Politécnica de Valencia
Valencia
Spain

Geoff Lowney
Intel Corporation
Husdon, MA
USA

Victor Luchangco
Oracle Labs
Burlington, MA
USA

Piotr Luszczek
University of Tennessee
Knoxville, TN
USA

Olav Lysne
The University of Oslo
Oslo
Norway

Xiaosong Ma
North Carolina State University
Raleigh, NC
USA
and
Oak Ridge National Laboratory
Raleigh, NC
USA

Arthur B. Maccabe
Oak Ridge National Laboratory
Oak Ridge, TN
USA

Kamesh Madduri
Lawrence Berkeley National Laboratory
Berkeley, CA
USA

Jan-Willem Maessen
Google
Cambridge, MA
USA

Konstantin Makarychev
IBM T.J. Watson Research Center
Yorktown Heights, NY
USA

Junichiro Makino
National Astronomical Observatory of Japan
Tokyo
Japan

Allen D. Malony
University of Oregon
Eugene, OR
USA

Madha V. Marathe
Virginia Tech
Blacksburg, VA
USA

Alberto F. Martín
Universitat Jaume I
Castellón
Spain

Glenn Martyna
IBM Thomas J. Watson Research Center
Yorktown Heights, NY
USA

Eric R. May
University of Michigan
Ann Arbor, MI
USA

Sally A. McKee
Chalmers University of Technology
Goteborg
Sweden

Miriam Mehl
Technische Universität München
Garching
Germany

Benoit Meister
Reservoir Labs, Inc.
New York, NY
USA

Phillip Merkey
Michigan Technological University
Houghton, MI
USA

José Meseguer
University of Illinois at Urbana-Champaign
Urbana, IL
USA

Michael Metcalf
Berlin
Germany

Samuel Midkiff
Purdue University
West Lafayette, IN
USA

Kenichi Miura
National Institute of Informatics
Tokyo
Japan

Bernd Mohr
Forschungszentrum Jülich GmbH
Jülich
Germany

José E. Moreira
IBM T.J. Watson Research Center
Yorktown Heights, NY
USA

Alan Morris
University of Oregon
Eugene, OR
USA

J. Eliot B. Moss
University of Massachusetts
Amherst, MA
USA

Matthias Müller
Technische Universität Dresden
Dresden
Germany

Peter Müller
ETH Zurich
Zurich
Switzerland

Yoichi Muraoka
Waseda University
Tokyo
Japan

Anca Muscholl
Université Bordeaux 1
Talence
France

Ravi Nair
IBM Thomas J. Watson Research Center
Yorktown Heights, NY
USA

Stephen Nelson

Mario Nemirovsky
Barcelona Supercomputer Center
Barcelona
Spain

Ryan Newton
Intel Corporation
Hudson, MA
USA

Rocco De Nicola
Universita' di Firenze
Firenze
Italy

Alexandru Nicolau
University of California Irvine
Irvine, CA
USA

Jarek Nieplocha[†]
Pacific Northwest National Laboratory
Richland, WA
USA

[†]deceased

Allen Nikora
California Institute of Technology
Pasadena, CA
USA

Robert W. Numrich
City University of New York
New York, NY
USA

Steven Oberlin

Leonid Oliker
Lawrence Berkeley National Laboratory
Berkeley, CA
USA

David Padua
University of Illinois at Urbana-Champaign
Urbana, IL
USA

Scott Pakin
Los Alamos National Laboratory
Los Alamos, NM
USA

Bruce Palmer
Pacific Northwest National Laboratory
Richland, WA
USA

Dhabaleswar K. Panda
The Ohio State University
Columbus, OH
USA

Sagar Pandit
University of South Florida
Tampa, FL
USA

Yale N. Patt
The University of Texas at Austin
Austin, TX
USA

OLIVIER PÈNE
University de Paris-Sud-XI
Orsay Cedex
France

PAUL PETERSEN
Intel Corporation
Champaign, IL
USA

BERNARD PHILIPPE
Campus de Beaulieu
Rennes
France

MICHAEL PHILIPPSEN
University of Erlangen-Nuremberg
Erlangen
Germany

JAMES C. PHILLIPS
University of Illinois at Urbana-Champaign
Urbana, IL
USA

ANDREA PIETRACAPRINA
Università di Padova
Padova
Italy

KESHAV PINGALI
The University of Texas at Austin
Austin, TX
USA

TIMOTHY M. PINKSTON
University of Southern California
Los Angeles, CA
USA

ERIC POLIZZI
University of Massachusetts
Amherst, MA
USA

STEPHEN W. POOLE
Oak Ridge National Laboratory
Oak Ridge, TN
USA

WILFRED POST
Oak Ridge National Laboratory
Oak Ridge, TN
USA

CHRISTOPH VON PRAUN
Georg-Simon-Ohm University of Applied Sciences
Nuremberg
Germany

FRANCO P. PREPARATA
Brown University
Providence, RI
USA

COSIMO ANTONIO PRETE
Università di Pisa
Pisa
Italy

TIMOTHY PRINCE
Intel Corporation
Santa Clara, CA
USA

JEAN-PIERRE PROST
Morteau
France

GEPPINO PUCCI
Università di Padova
Padova
Italy

MARKUS PÜSCHEL
ETH Zurich
Zurich
Switzerland

ENRIQUE S. QUINTANA-ORTÍ
Universitat Jaume I
Castellón
Spain

PATRICE QUINTON
ENS Cachan Bretagne
Bruz
France

Ram Rajamony
IBM Research
Austin, TX
USA

Arun Raman
Princeton University
Princeton, NJ
USA

Lawrence Rauchwerger
Texas A&M University
College Station, TX
USA

James R. Reinders
Intel Corporation
Hillsboro, OR
USA

Steven P. Reinhardt

John Reppy
University of Chicago
Chicago, IL
USA

María Engracia Gómez Requena
Universidad Politécnica de Valencia
Valencia
Spain

Daniel Ricciuto
Oak Ridge National Laboratory
Oak Ridge, TN
USA

Rolf Riesen
IBM Research
Dublin
Ireland

Tanguy Risset
INSA Lyon
Villeurbanne
France

Yves Robert
Ecole Normale Supérieure de Lyon
France

Arch D. Robison
Intel Corporation
Champaign, IL
USA

A. W. Roscoe
Oxford University
Oxford
UK

Robert B. Ross
Argonne National Laboratory
Argonne, IL
USA

Chris Rowen
CEO, Tensilica
Santa Clara, CA, USA

Duncan Roweth
Cray (UK) Ltd.
UK

Sukyoung Ryu
Korea Advanced Institute of Science and Technology
Daejeon
Korea

Valentina Salapura
IBM Research
Yorktown Heights, NY
USA

Joel H. Saltz
Emory University
Atlanta, GA
USA

Ahmed Sameh
Purdue University
West Lafayette, IN
USA

Miguel Sanchez
Universidad Politécnica de Valencia
Valencia
Spain

Benjamin Sander
Advanced Micro Device Inc.
Austin, TX
USA

Peter Sanders
Universitaet Karlsruhe
Karlsruhe
Germany

Davide Sangiorgi
Universita' di Bologna
Bologna
Italy

Vivek Sarin
Texas A&M University
College Station, TX
USA

Vivek Sarkar
Rice University
Houston, TX
USA

Olaf Schenk
University of Basel
Basel
Switzerland

Michael Schlansker
Hewlett-Packard Inc.
Palo-Alto, CA
USA

Stefan Schmid
Telekom Laboratories/TU Berlin
Berlin
Germany

Martin Schulz
Lawrence Livermore National Laboratory
Livermore, CA
USA

James L. Schwarzmeier
Cray Inc.
Chippewa Falls, WI
USA

Michael L. Scott
University of Rochester
Rochester, NY
USA

Matous Sedlacek
Technische Universität München
Garching
Germany

Joel Seiferas
University of Rochester
Rochester, NY
USA

Frank Olaf Sem-Jacobsen
The University of Oslo
Oslo
Norway

André Seznec
IRISA/INRIA, Rennes
Rennes
France

John Shalf
Lawrence Berkeley National Laboratory
Berkeley, CA
USA

Meiyue Shao
Umeå University
Umeå
Sweden

David E. Shaw
D. E. Shaw Research
New York, NY
USA
and
Columbia University
New York, NY
USA

Xiaowei Shen
IBM Research
Armonk, NY
USA

SAMEER SHENDE
University of Oregon
Eugene, OR
USA

GALEN M. SHIPMAN
Oak Ridge National Laboratory
Oak Ridge, TN
USA

HOWARD JAY SIEGEL
Colorado State University
Fort Collins, CO
USA

DANIEL P. SIEWIOREK
Carnegie Mellon University
Pittsburgh, PA
USA

FEDERICO SILLA
Universidad Politécnica de Valencia
Valencia
Spain

BARRY SMITH
Argonne National Laboratory
Argonne, IL
USA

BURTON SMITH
Microsoft Corporation
Redmond, WA
USA

MARC SNIR
University of Illinois at Urbana-Champaign
Urbana, IL
USA

LAWRENCE SNYDER
University of Washington
Seattle, WA
USA

MARCO SOLINAS
Università di Pisa
Pisa
Italy

EDGAR SOLOMONIK
University of California at Berkeley
Berkeley, CA
USA

MATTHEW SOTTILE
Galois, Inc.
Portland, OR
USA

M'HAMED SOULI
Université des Sciences et Technologies de Lille
Villeneuve d'Ascq cédex
France

WYATT SPEAR
University of Oregon
Eugene, OR
USA

EVAN W. SPEIGHT
IBM Research
Austin, TX
USA

MARK S. SQUILLANTE
IBM
Yorktown Heights, NY
USA

ALEXANDROS STAMATAKIS
Heidelberg Institute for Theoretical Studies
Heidelberg
Germany

GUY L. STEELE, JR.
Oracle Labs
Burlington, MA
USA

THOMAS L. STERLING
Louisiana State University
Baton Rouge, LA
USA

TJERK P. STRAATSMA
Pacific Northwest National Laboratory
Richland, WA
USA

PAULA E. STRETZ
Virginia Tech
Blacksburg, VA
USA

THOMAS M. STRICKER
Zürich, CH
Switzerland

JIMMY SU
University of California
Berkeley, CA
USA

HARI SUBRAMONI
The Ohio State University
Columbus, OH
USA

SAYANTAN SUR
The Ohio State University
Columbus, OH
USA

JOHN SWENSEN
CPU Technology
Pleasanton, CA
USA

HIROSHI TAKAHARA
NEC Corporation
Tokyo
Japan

MICHELA TAUFER
University of Delaware
Newark, DE
USA

VINOD TIPPARAJU
Oak Ridge National Laboratory
Oak Ridge, TN
USA

ALEXANDER TISKIN
University of Warwick
Coventry
UK

JOSEP TORRELLAS
University of Illinois at Urbana-Champaign
Urbana, IL
USA

JESPER LARSSON TRÄFF
University of Vienna
Vienna
Austria

PHILIP TRINDER
Heriot-Watt University
Edinburgh
UK

RAFFAELE TRIPICCIONE
Università di Ferrara and INFN Sezione di Ferrara
Ferrara
Italy

MARK TUCKERMAN
New York University
New York, NY
USA

RAY TUMINARO
Sandia National Laboratories
Livermore, CA
USA

BORA UÇAR
ENS Lyon
Lyon
France

MARAT VALIEV
Pacific Northwest National Laboratory
Richland, WA
USA

NICOLAS VASILACHE
Reservoir Labs, Inc.
New York, NY
USA

MARIANA VERTENSTEIN
National Center for Atmospheric Research
Boulder, CO
USA

Jens Volkert
Johannes Kepler University Linz
Linz
Austria

Yevgen Voronenko
Carnegie Mellon University
Pittsburgh, PA
USA

Richard W. Vuduc
Georgia Institute of Technology
Atlanta, GA
USA

Gene Wagenbreth
University of Southern Califorina
Topanga, CA
USA

Dali Wang
Oak Ridge National Laboratory
Oak Ridge, TN
USA

Jason Wang
LSTC
Livermore, CA
USA

Gregory R. Watson
IBM
Yorktown Heights, NY
USA

Roger Wattenhofer
ETH Zürich
Zurich
Switzerland

Michael Wehner
Lawrence Berkeley National Laboratory
Berkeley, CA
USA

Josef Weidendorfer
Technische Universität München
München
Germany

Tong Wen
University of California
Berkeley, CA
USA

R. Clint Whaley
University of Texas at San Antonio
San Antonio, TX
USA

Andrew B. White
Los Alamos National Laboratory
Los Alamos, NM
USA

Brian Whitney
Oracle Corporation
Hillsboro, OR
USA

Roland Wismüller
University of Siegen
Siegen
Germany

Robert W. Wisniewski
IBM
Yorktown Heights, NY
USA

David Wohlford
Reservoir Labs, Inc.
New York, NY
USA

Felix Wolf
Aachen University
Aachen
Germany

David Wonnacott
Haverford College
Haverford, PA
USA

Patrick H. Worley
Oak Ridge National Laboratory
Oak Ridge, TN
USA

SUDHAKAR YALAMANCHILI
Georgia Institute of Technology
Atlanta, GA
USA

KATHERINE YELICK
University of California at Berkeley and Lawrence Berkeley National Laboratory
Berkeley, CA
USA

PEN-CHUNG YEW
University of Minnesota at Twin-Cities
Minneapolis, MN
USA

BOBBY DALTON YOUNG
Colorado State University
Fort Collins, CO
USA

CLIFF YOUNG
D. E. Shaw Research
New York, NY
USA

GABRIEL ZACHMANN
Clausthal University
Clausthal-Zellerfeld
Germany

FIELD G. VAN ZEE
The University of Texas at Austin
Austin, TX
USA

LIXIN ZHANG
IBM Research
Austin, TX
USA

GENGBIN ZHENG
University of Illinois at Urbana-Champaign
Urbana, IL
USA

HANS P. ZIMA
California Institute of Technology
Pasadena, CA
USA

JAROSLAW ZOLA
Iowa State University
Ames, IA
USA

Q

QCD apeNEXT Machines

OLIVIER PÈNE
University de Paris-Sud-XI, Orsay Cedex, France

Definition

apeNEXT is a massively, fully custom, parallel computer conceived and designed by an Italian–German–French collaboration and delivered since 2006. It is the latest computer of the APE series. It is a 3D array of computing nodes with periodic boundary conditions. It is dedicated to the calculations of lattice quantum chromodynamics, which is the "ab initio" computational method for the theory of the strong interactions in subnuclear matter.

Discussion

Introduction

All the matter surrounding us is made of atoms, which are made up of electrons surrounding an atomic nucleus. The latter nuclei are made up of protons and neutrons, which themselves are made up of quarks. The force responsible for binding quarks into protons, neutrons, and many other such particles, generically named "hadrons," is the "strong interaction" of subnuclear matter. The same strong force binds the protons and neutrons together to form atomic nuclei. This force is so strong that quarks are "confined" into hadrons, which means that one cannot find in nature free quarks, not bound into hadrons. Only at incredibly high temperature the quarks become deconfined.

The theory of this force was discovered in the 1970s and this discovery was awarded by the Nobel Prize of physics in 2004. It is called "quantum chromodynamics (QCD)." This theory demonstrates that the strong force is mediated by new fundamental particles named "gluons." However, computing within his theory is a formidable task. The most rigorous method uses a four dimensional lattice which provides a discretised description of space-time. This technique is called lattice QCD (LQCD). It allows to compute ab initio the masses of particles such as the proton, the neutron, the pion, etc., and their properties. This method is the best since it relies uniquely on the theory itself. However it is highly demanding in terms of needed computing power.

This is why the LQCD community has developed since the mid-1980s a series of dedicated computers, in order to be able to perform these computations at an affordable price. This has been done in the USA, in Japan, in Europe. There have been several generations of these computers. The last generation is the QCDOC designed by a US–Britain collaboration with IBM. This is the ancestor of the BlueGene series of IBM. In continental Europe, the APE series started in Italy in 1984. Nicola Cabbibo [1] and Giorgio Parisi were among the iniators of APE. The first APE was operative in 1986. The next generation, the apecento, started in 1993. The APEmille, the third generation, became operative in 2001. The APE series has been supported in Italy by the Italian institute for nuclear and particle physics (INFN). The third generation of APE, APEmille, was done in collaboration with a German group in DESY-Zeuthen. The fourth APE was named apeNEXT with the additional participation of a French group (Université Paris-sud and IRISA/Rennes). The apeNEXT collaboration has published a series of paper or conference contributions [2–7]. More details can be found on the documentation Web sites [8, 9].

The apeNEXT Hardware

The Computing Node

Since the operations performed in LQCD are mainly multiplicatons of complex matrices, the computing units are harware devised to work on complex numbers.

David Padua (ed.), *Encyclopedia of Parallel Computing*, DOI 10.1007/978-0-387-09766-4,
© Springer Science+Business Media, LLC 2011

For every clock cycle, the arithmetic unit performs the APE normal operation:

$$a * b + c \qquad (1)$$

where a, b, c are complex numbers. Expressed in terms of floating point operations it corresponds to eight flops per clock cycle. The peak computing power is thus eight times the clock frequency per processor. This allows for a low clock frequency (about 140 MHz) for a peak performance of 1.2 Gflop per processor, and consequently a low power consumption and a reasonable heat dissipation: Air cooling is enough. It uses intensively "Very Large Scale Integration." A word of 128 bits is processed every clock cycle, corresponding either to a double precision complex number or to a very long instruction word. There are no cache, but there role is provided by a large register file (256 words of 128 bits).

Each processor is fully independent with its private memory bank of 256–1024 Mbytes based on standard DDR-SDRAM. The memory stores both data and program. The memory controller receives the input from an address generation unit that allows to perform integer operations independently of the arithmetic unit. Error correction is implemented. The memory access has a latency of 15 clock cycles. Since most often the calculation proceeds via large matrices, i.e., in large arrays, the call for numbers in an array is pipe-lined in such a way that, after the arrival of the first complex number of the array, which costs the latency, the following ones come at the speed of one per cycle. A data buffer close to the arithmetic unit allows for a prefetch of the data, thus minimizing the effect of the latency.

Since both data and instructions are imported from memory there is a risk of conflict. This is minimized by a compression of the microcode containing the instructions, and by an instruction buffer allowing prefetch and storing the critical kernels for repeated operations. Instruction decompression is performed on the flight by the hardware.

The Torus Network

The network is a custom one, designed for apeNEXT. The computing nodes are organized according to a 3D torus. Every node is directly connected to six neighbors, up and down in three directions. The last one along one direction is connected to the first one, thus producing a circle. This is fully adapted to LQCD. Indeed the LQCD calculations are performed on a discrete lattice which is a 4D torus. Every lattice site communicates with its eight neighbors and the last one along one line communicates with the first one. Thus it is natural to decompose the LQCD lattice into sublattices located on every computing node. For example, let us consider a LQCD lattice of size $32^3 * 64$ (where 64 is in the time direction). An apeNEXT rack has 512 processors organized in a 8^3 3D torus. It is thus possible to decompose the LQCD lattice into sublattices of size $4^3 * 64$. Other combinations are of course possible. Thus every lattice site is located on one computing node, and its neighbors are either on the same computing node or on neighbouring ones.

The hardware allows an access to the memory banks located on the considered computing nodes and to those of the neighboring computing nodes. Each link is bidirectional and moves one byte per clock cycle and the start-up latency is about 20 cycles, i.e., about 150 ns, which is very short. To minimize the effect of the latency via a prefetch of the data from neighboring nodes, six dedicated buffers are used for the data from the six neighboring nodes. The maximum throughput of the network is reached for rather small bursts of 12 words (200 bytes) of data. This is convenient for the LQCD algorithms.

This torus organization allows for a high scalability when the number of processors increases. The parallel implementation is Single Program Multiple Data (SPMD) which means that all the computing nodes perform the same operations simultaneously, including their communication with neighbors. There is no data transfer bottleneck during the computation except for a limited number of cases (e.g., when a global sum has to be performed).

The Global Features

Every board contains 16 computing nodes. A crate contains 16 boards assembled thanks to a backplane which provides all the communication links. A crate thus contains 256 nodes. A rack contains two crates. It has a peak performance of 0.6 Tflop, a footprint of 1 m^2 only, a power consumption less than 10 kW which allows for air cooling. The apeNEXT system is accessed from a master front-end PC which controls slave PCs (typically one for two boards). The PCs communicate via custom designed host-interface PCI boards. It uses a simple I2C network for operating system requests, to know the state of the machine, handle errors and exceptions. Input/output operations are handled via a highspeed link, called "7th link," and proceed via the PCs. Several racks can also be connected together for a large scale calculation.

The apeNEXT Software

The TAO Language

Details on the software can be found on the Web site [9]. The series of APE computers use a special high-level language named "TAO." It is a rather simple language, somehow in the spirit of Fortran. It contains some improvements. For example one can define a mathematical object which is a $SU(3)$ matrix (i.e., a 3*3 unitary complex matrix of determinant 1). Once defined all the operations on these matrices, one can overload the "multiply" symbol:

$$C = A * B \qquad (2)$$

where C, B, A are $SU(3)$ matrices, means that C is the matrix product of A and B. This is extremely useful, knowing that the $SU(3)$ matrices are basic objects in LQCD.

TAO language contains a few additional commands related to the SPMD parallelism. For example, an "if" is different whether it applies to the full system (in which case it induces a branching) or to one node (in which case it will go through both branches with an appropriate mask). The transfer of data between nodes is simply performed by address numbers which are understood as being on the remote node.

Finally TAO is associated with a preprocessing language, "ZZ." It allows to define new data types, operations between these types and to write loops which are unrolled at compile time.

The Compiler

The compiler also has been written by the apeNEXT collaboration. It contains several successive modules. The Tao code is first translated into the user level Assembly language named SASM. The latter is then converted into the microcode level Assembly, MASM. An optimizer named SOFAN [10] then eliminates the useless instructions or combines several instructions. It turns the original MASM code into an improved MASM code. The "shaker," then, converts the MASM into the microcode and reorganizes the program to eliminate, as much as possible, useless cycles, e.g., while waiting for data from memory.

The compiler decides how to use the register files in order to minimize the latency of data retrieval from memory or from other nodes. The programmer can also take some decisions concerning the use of the registers, e.g., demanding some often reused data to stay in registers.

More generally it is noticeable that, the architecture being rather simple and transparent, the programmer can know very exactly what happens during a calculation including every step of data transfer. Having thus a complete and clear understanding of how the computing time is used, one can efficiently improve the code's efficiency. It also helps when debugging.

Of course, the software also contains a custom operating system which is adapted to the architecture.

The Theoretical Physics Research Thanks to apeNEXT

The apeNEXT is the latest computer of the APE series, after APE, APEcento, and APEmille. The apeNEXT racks have been installed in 2006 in three places: In an international computational laboratory in the university of Rome "La Sapienza" (13 racks belonging to the INFN and used by the majority of Italian LQCD groups, plus 2 racks supported by the French CNRS and National Research Agency (ANR)). Six racks are in the Bielefeld university in Germany and four racks in DESY-Zeuthen (close to Berlin).

During these 3 years, the apeNEXT computers have been intensively used for research in theoretical physics. The major difficulty in LQCD calculations is the presence of very light quarks in nature. The computing time increases very fast when the quarks become lighter. apeNEXT and other computers of that generation allowed the LQCD community to really perform calculation with quarks significantly lighter than what was possible before, although, it was not enough to reach a quark mass as light as in nature. This is left to the next generation of computers.

The LQCD group in Bielefeld has used its apeNEXT's to study the properties of QCD at finite temperature, a situation which has existed after the big bang and is still observable in accelerators in which very heavy ions collide at very large energy. They have among other quantities, computed at which temperature a phase transition takes place which deconfines the quarks and gluons, i.e., liberates them from being bound into hadrons.

The apeNEXT computers in Zeuthen and Rome have been mainly devoted to the zero temperature case. They have studied the properties of the proton, neutron, and the pion which constitute the atomic nuclei and represent more than 90% of the visible mass of our universe. They have also devoted many studies to states containing the heavy quarks named "charm quarks" and "beauty quarks." These quarks are not frequent in our everyday surrounding, they have to be produced by accelerators of particles. They have been extensively studied experimentally in dedicated accelerators because they allow an accurate test of the standard model of particle physics, which is our present understanding of the fundamental laws of nature. They also open a window toward an understanding of the laws of nature at still smaller scales than the ones we already understand. These experiments in combination with theoretical studies, mainly based on LQCD, have confirmed the "Cabbibo–Kobayashi–Maskawa (CKM)" model which describes the mixing between different quark species and a mechanism for CP violation (asymmetry between particles and their antiparticles). Thanks to this vast experimental and theretical work, the CKM model has been awarded by the Nobel Prize in 2008.

It is impossible of course to quote all the publications stemming from calculations performed thanks to the apeNEXT computer. They have provided a great help to LQCD in continental Europe. In Italy, they are still today the major tool to perform the heavy LQCD calculations. In France, it was so until fall 2008 when a BlueGene was installed in the CNRS computing center, but they are still under very active use.

Conclusion

The apeNEXT, the latest computer of the APE series, was, during the last years, the only fully custom high-power computer designed and produced in Europe. All APE computers were created without the help of any major computer company. The Italian SME "Eurotech" company has built the prototypes of apeNEXT and the market products. The apeNEXT team was essentially an accademic collaboration of physicists and computer scientists from Italy, Germany, and France. The funding came from different scientific institutions in these three countries.

This created a rich know-how which was recently reused in the QPACE project building a LQCD dedicated supercomputer using IBM-CELL [11, 12] processors and an apeNEXT inspired network. This know-how is also used in the recent Aurora project [13, 14] of a supercomputer using Intel/Nehalem processors. It is finally used in the petaQCD project of the "Agence Nationale de la Recherche" about software and hardware problems of the petaflop era for LQCD [15]. Beyond the know-how, the community which was created around the apeNEXT project is still alive and may be fruitful in the future.

Finally, the apeNEXT computers played an essential role in allowing the European LQCD community to enter really in the era of lattice calculations with light dynamical quarks.

Related Entries

▶IBM Blue Gene Supercomputer
▶QCDSP and QCDOC Computers

Bibliographic Notes and Further Reading

A popular and deep presentation of QCD can be found in Frank Wilczek's Nobel lecture [16] or paper in Physics Today named "QCD made simple" [17].

The history of the APE series has been recently summarized by Nicola Cabbibo [1].

The apeNEXT collaboration has published a series of paper or conference contributions [2–7]. More details can be found on the documentation Web sites [8, 9] and [18, 19].

Bibliography

1. http://www.ba.infn.it/~apenext/PRESENTATIONS_FILES/Cabibbo.pdf
2. Bodin F et al (2002) Nucl Phys Proc Suppl 106:173, arXiv:hep-lat/0110197
3. Alfieri R et al. APE Collaboration, arXiv:hep-lat/0102011

4. Ammendola R et al (2003) Nucl Phys Proc Suppl 119:1038, arXiv:hep-lat/0211031
5. Bodin F et al (2003) In: The proceedings of 2003 conference for computing in high-energy and nuclear physics (CHEP 03), La Jolla, 24–28 Mar 2003, pp THIT005, arXiv:hep-lat/0306018
6. Bodin F et al (2003) ApeNEXT collaboration. In: The proceedings of 23rd international conference on physics in collision (PIC 2003), Zeuthen, 26–28 Jun 2003, pp FRAP15, arXiv:hep-lat/0309007
7. Bodin F et al (2005) ApeNEXT collaboration. Nucl Phys Proc Suppl 140:176
8. http://www.fe.infn.it/fisicacomputazionale/ricerca/ape/NXTPROJECT/dcc/root.html
9. http://apegate.roma1.infn.it/APE/index.php?go=/documentation.tpl
10. http://hpc.desy.de/ape/software/sofan/
11. Baier H et al (2009) Pos LAT 2009:001. http:arxiv.org/abs/0911.2174
12. Baier H et al. arXiv:0810.1559, hep-lat
13. Aurora Science Collaboration (2010) Pos LATTICE 2010:225
14. Abramo A et al. Tailoring petascale computing. In: Proceedings of ISC09, June 200923–26 (Hamburg)
15. https://www.petaqcd.org/
16. http://nobelprize.org/nobelprizes/physics/laureates/2004/wilczek-lecture.html
17. http://www.frankwilczek.com/Wilczek_Easy_Pieces/
18. Belletti F et al (2006) ApeNEXT collaboration. Nucl Instrum Meth A 559:90
19. Belletti F et al (2006) ApeNEXT collaboration. Comput Sci Eng 8:8

QCD (Quantum Chromodynamics) Computations

Karl Jansen
NIC, DESY Zeuthen, Zeuthen, Germany

Definition

Quantum Chromodynamics (QCD) is the prime and generally accepted theory of the strong interactions between quarks and gluons. In QCD, there appear intrinsically nonperturbative effects such as the confinement of quarks, chiral symmetry breaking, and topology. These effects can be analyzed by formulating the theory on a four-dimensional space-time lattice and solving it by large-scale numerical simulations. An overview of the present simulation landscape, a physical example and a description of simulation and parallelization aspects of QCD on the lattice is given.

Discussion

Introduction

When experiments at large accelerators such as HERA at DESY and LEP and LHC at CERN are performed, in the detectors one observes hadrons such as pions, protons, or neutrons. On the other hand, from the particular signature of these particles as seen in the detectors, it is known that the hadrons are not fundamental particles but that they must have an inner structure.

It is strongly believed nowadays that the constituent particles of all hadrons are the quarks with the gluons being the interaction particles that "glue" the quarks together to perform the bound hadron states, i.e., the particles that are seen in the experiments. The force that binds the quarks and gluons together – the strong interaction – is theoretically described by quantum chromodynamics (QCD). The postulation of QCD is that at very short distances much below 1 fm, the quarks behave as almost free particles that interact only very weakly, a phenomenon called asymptotic freedom. On the other hand, at large distances, at the order of 1 fm, the quarks interact extremely strongly, in fact so strong that they will never be seen as free particles but rather form the observed hadron-bound spectrum. The latter phenomenon is called confinement.

Since the interaction between quarks becomes so strong at large distances, analytical methods such as perturbation theory fail to analyze QCD. A method to nevertheless tackle the problem is to formulate QCD on a four-dimensional, euclidean space-time lattice [1] with a nonzero lattice spacing a. This setup first of all allows for a rigorous definition of QCD and to address theoretical questions in a conceptually clean and fundamental way. On the other hand, the lattice approach enables theorists to perform numerical simulations [2] and therefore to investigate also problems of nonperturbative nature.

In the past, lattice physicists had to work with a number of limitations when performing numerical simulations because these simulations are extremely computer time expensive, needing petaflop computing and even beyond, a regime of computing power which is just reached today. Therefore, for a long time the quarks were treated as infinitely heavy, since in this situation the computational costs are orders of magnitude smaller. However, this is a crude approximation given

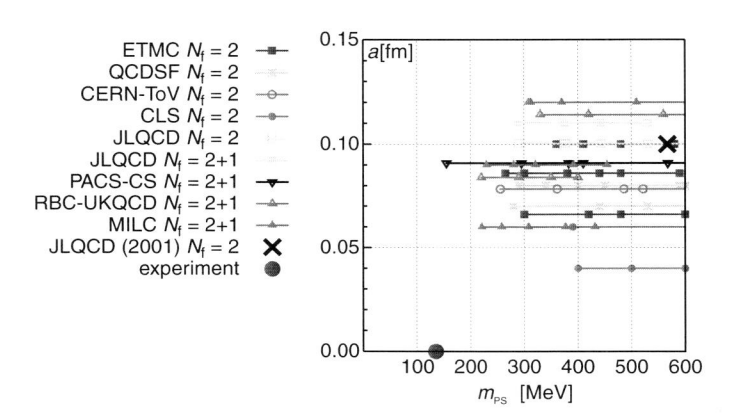

QCD (Quantum Chromodynamics) Computations. Fig. 1 The values of the lattice spacing a and pseudo scalar masses m_{PS} as employed in typical QCD simulations by various collaborations as (incompletely) listed in the legend. The *blue dot* indicates the physical point where in the continuum limit the pseudo scalar meson assumes its experimentally measured value of m_{PS} = 140 MeV. The *black cross* represents a state of the art simulation by the JLQCD collaboration in 2001

that the up and down quarks have masses of only O(MeV). In a next step, only the lightest quark doublets, the up and down quarks, were taken into consideration, although their mass values as used in the simulation have been unphysically large, about two to three times their physical values.

Nowadays, besides the up and down quarks, also the strange quark is included in the simulations. In addition, these simulations are performed in almost physical conditions, having the quark masses close to their physical values, large lattices with about 3 fm linear extent and small values of the lattice spacing such that a continuum limit can be performed. The situation [3] of the change of the simulation landscape is illustrated in Fig. 1. In the figure, the blue dot indicates the physical point, i.e., a zero value of the lattice spacing and a pion mass reaching its physical value of 140 MeV. The black cross represents a state-of-the-art simulation in the year 2001. As can be seen in the graph, most of the simulations currently go well beyond what could be reached in 2001, clearly demonstrating the progress in performing realistic simulations.

This quite significant change in the situation is due to three main developments: (a) algorithmic breakthroughs [4–7]; (b) machine development; the computing power of the present BlueGene P systems of about 1 Petaflops is even outperforming Moore's law (c) conceptual developments, such as the use of improved actions which reduce lattice artefacts and the development of nonperturbative renormalization.

As one example of a physics result, the computation of the light hadron spectrum from first principles using lattice simulations [8] is shown in Fig. 2. Using only two input masses, the ones for the pion and the Kaon, all other masses are a result from these ab initio calculations. Note that the lattice data reach in general a few percent accuracy while the experimentally obtained values are partly at the sub-percent level. In addition, some of the states are resonances which would need a special treatment on the lattice. Nevertheless, the good agreement between the experimentally observed and the numerically computed spectrum is thus a nice confirmation that QCD is indeed the correct theoretical description of the strong interaction, although further tests using more physical observables are necessary to eventually consolidate and verify this result.

Results of lattice computations, the progress in the field, and a discussion of many technical aspects are documented in the proceedings of the lattice symposia taking place worldwide on a yearly basis.

The Principle of Lattice Gauge Theory Calculations

The main target of lattice calculations is to compute expectation values $\langle \mathcal{O} \rangle$ of physical observables $\mathcal{O}$, the hadron masses discussed above being one example. The general problem of such calculations is to solve a specific, high-dimensional integral ($O(10^{\text{several thousand}})$).

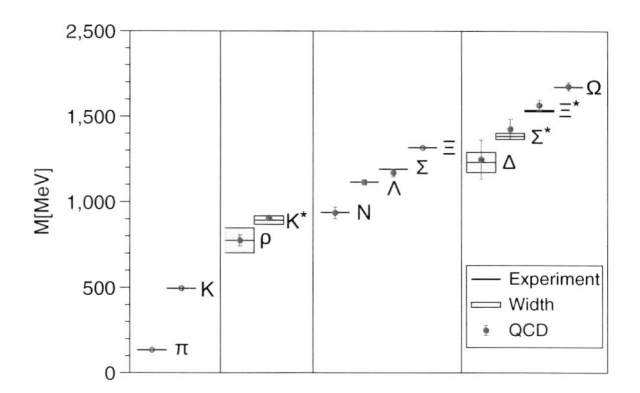

QCD (Quantum Chromodynamics) Computations. Fig. 2
The light hadron spectrum as obtained in ref. [8]

Here, field $\Psi^{(i,\alpha)}(x)$ is equipped with internal indices $i = 1, 2, 3$ representing colour and $\alpha = 1, 2, 3, 4$ representing the Dirac structure. The so-called gauge field $U^{(i,j)}(x, \mu)$ is a SU(3)-matrix describing the gluon degrees of freedom. It goes beyond the scope of this article to discuss in detail the physical motivation and interpretation of this coupling structure of neighbouring fields and for our purposes it is more important to just look at the mathematical structure of this coupling. Let us remark also that the gauge fields U interact with themselves which can be expressed through another action $S_g(U)$ the particular form of which is not important here.

The expectation value of a physical observable corresponds now to solving the integral

$$\langle \mathcal{O} \rangle = \int \mathcal{D}\Psi \mathcal{D}\bar{\Psi} \mathcal{D}U \mathcal{O} e^{-S(U,\bar{\Psi},\Psi)} \quad (2)$$

where the integration is to be performed over all quark and gluon fields and where the action is given by

$$S(U, \bar{\Psi}, \Psi) = S_g(U) + \sum_{(x,y)} \bar{\Psi}(x) M(x, y) \Psi(y). \quad (3)$$

The action in Eq. 3 contains two free parameters, the quark mass and the gauge coupling. These parameters have to be tuned in order to achieve a particular physical situation.

Before proceeding, another technical difficulty has to be discussed. The quark fields are not represented by normal, commuting numbers but by so-called Grassmann variables which *anti-commute*. As a consequence, the quark fields cannot be dealt with on a computer directly since computers deal with normal numbers only. However, the Grassmann fields can be integrated over leading to an expression (assuming that the matrix M is such that all the integrations discussed here can be performed, which is, of course, the case for real lattice QCD)

$$\langle \mathcal{O} \rangle = \int \mathcal{D}U \mathcal{O} \det[M(U)] e^{-S_g(U)}. \quad (4)$$

However, given the large size of the matrix M, computing its determinant is hopeless. The solution of this difficulty is to integrate the determinant in again using ordinary, bosonic fields Φ leading to our final expression for a physical observable,

$$\langle \mathcal{O} \rangle = \int \mathcal{D}\Phi^\dagger \mathcal{D}\Phi \mathcal{D}U \mathcal{O} e^{-S(U,\Phi^\dagger,\Phi)} \quad (5)$$

To illustrate the problem, let us consider a one-dimensional problem in only one variable x. The eventual aim is the computation of the "expectation value" $\langle f(x) \rangle$ of a function $f(x)$. In analogy to QCD, this amounts to calculate the integral $\int dx f(x) e^{-S(x)}$ where $S(x)$ is the so-called action which defines the physical system under consideration. If a very simple form of such an action is taken, namely, $S(x) = \frac{1}{2}x^2$ then the integral can be solved by generating Gaussian random numbers of unit variance as integration points x_i. This is the principle of "importance sampling." With this choice of integration variables x_i, $\langle f(x) \rangle$ is simply given by the sum over all x_i, $\langle f(x) \rangle \approx \frac{1}{N} \sum_i f(x_i)$ where N is the total number of integration points.

In lattice QCD the same principle of importance sampling is used to compute physical observables but the action used is much more complicated. The form of the action is given as $S = \sum_{(x,y)} \bar{\Psi}(x) M(x, y) \Psi(y)$. Here (x, y) denotes four-dimensional, integer lattice points and the quark fields Ψ (anti-quark fields $\bar{\Psi}$) are defined at these discrete lattice points. The matrix $M(x, y)$ describes the interaction between the quark fields. It has to be remarked already at this point that M is a very large matrix of the order of a hundred million times a hundred million for most advanced simulations nowadays.

However, a big advantage is that the general structure of the matrix M is such that only quark fields at nearest neighbour points are coupled. The general form of the interaction is

$$\bar{\Psi}^{(i,\alpha)}(x) U^{(i,j)}(x, \mu) \Gamma^{\alpha,\beta} \Psi^{(j,\beta)}(x + a\hat{\mu}). \quad (1)$$

with

$$S(U, \Phi^\dagger, \Phi) = S_g(U) + \Phi^\dagger M^{-1} \Phi. \qquad (6)$$

This shows that for the evaluation of the action $S(U, \Phi^\dagger, \Phi)$ the vector $X = M^{-1}\Phi$ is needed. The basic numerical problem in lattice QCD is thus to solve a set of linear equations

$$MX = \Phi \qquad (7)$$

with the fermion matrix M having the particular interaction form given in Eq. 1 with the mentioned size of hundred million times hundred million. Since M connects only nearest neighbor points on the lattice, it is a sparse matrix with only the diagonal and a few $O(10)$ sub-diagonals occupied and the techniques to solve such sparse systems of linear equations [9] can be applied. Moreover, what is actually (hard-) coded is only the application of the fermion matrix M on a vector and hence M need not be stored in memory. Nevertheless, the matrix M is large and a solver, such as, e.g., conjugate gradient (CG) [9], needs several hundred to thousands of iterations to converge to the solution with the desired accuracy of about 10^{-14} (relative precision). Moreover, the computation of the integral of Eq. 5 over the gauge fields U needs several thousands of these gauge fields and hence Eq. 7 needs to be solved hundred thousands of times to obtain just one physical result at just one value of the action parameters, i.e., the quark mass and the gauge coupling. In order to have a complete result, simulations at many of these action parameters have to be performed.

Parallelization

The description of the computational elements given above leads to a very high total computational cost. For example, if a moderately sized lattice of $24^3 \cdot 48$ is taken, on one rack of a BG/P system, corresponding to 4096 processors, one would get about 200 gauge field configurations per day. A simulation leading to a sufficiently precise estimate of $\langle \mathcal{O} \rangle$ requires about 5,000 of such configurations and would thus need about 1 month. Clearly, without any parallelization, it would be totally unrealistic to solve this problem.

Fortunately, the structure of the fermion interaction with only nearest neighbor couplings renders the problem of parallelization rather easy. There are essentially two approaches. The first is to use MPI. Here, the total lattice is distributed over the number of desired processors (domain decomposition). The total lattice is then divided into local sub-lattices of size $l_t \cdot l_x \cdot l_y \cdot l_z$ on a $N_t \cdot N_x \cdot N_y \cdot N_z$ processor grid. The parallelization strategy is then to equip the fields on the sub-lattice with "borders" which will take the neighboring lattice points needed for the sub-lattice on a particular processor. Before any computation is performed, each processor

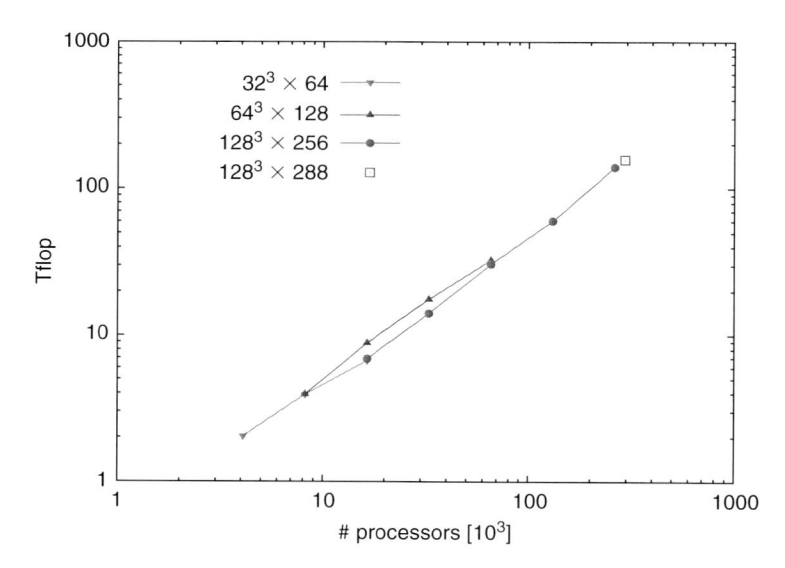

QCD (Quantum Chromodynamics) Computations. Fig. 3 Strong scaling of the lattice fermion matrix on the Jugene BG/P system at the Jülich supercomputer center for three different global lattice volumes

sends the necessary neighbor points to corresponding adjacent processors where these points are then stored in the borders. This concept works well for machines with a very fast communication network with, however, a rather large latency.

Another concept is a direct memory access to neighboring processors. Here, a single datum is sent to a neighboring processor whenever it is needed. In an application code this looks like $\Phi(x + a\hat{\mu} + mn)$ where "mn" stands for a so-called magic number which addresses the memory location of the field $\Phi(x + a\hat{\mu})$ but on a neighbouring processor. Realizations of this concept have been made on the dedicated lattice QCD machines APE [10] and QCDOC [11].

Other, new developments are machines with multi-core processors [12] and GPUs. Here, new parallelization concepts have to be developed and the problem of working efficiently on many GPUs in general is still under investigation.

Figure 3 represents an example of the (strong) scaling behaviour of a certain implementation of a lattice QCD code [13]. The total performance in Teraflops is shown for the application of the fermion matrix on three different volumes – a $32^3 \cdot 64$, a $64^3 \cdot 128$, and a $128^3 \cdot 256$. The performance is shown as a function of the number of processors in a double log plot. A clear linear scaling is observed for all volumes used. The single point in Fig. 3 represents the performance measurement for a $128^3 \cdot 288$ volume which was chosen to use the full 72-rack installation of the BG/P system at the supercomputer center in Jülich. The graph shows that lattice QCD is very well suited for massively parallel machines and shows an almost perfect strong scaling behaviour. Note that lattice QCD applications typically reach 20–30% of the peak performance of the supercomputers used.

The total simulation cost depends strongly on the volume, the pion mass, and the lattice spacing used in the simulations. For a discussion on the scaling of the algorithm employed in lattice QCD applications, I refer to refs. [3, 14]. For quantities, such as some of the hadron masses and decay constants, it can be expected that machines in the multi-Petaflops regime are sufficient to match the experimental accuracy. For other more complicated observables for example connected to scattering states or unstable particles, clearly exaflops computing capabilities are required.

Bibliography

1. Wilson KG (1974) Confinement of quarks. Phys Rev D10:2445–2459
2. Creutz M (1980) Monte Carlo study of quantized SU(2) Gauge theory. Phys Rev D21:2308–2315
3. Jansen K (2008) POSCI LATTICE2008, 010, Lattice QCD: a critical status report. [arXiv:0810.5634 [hep-lat]].
4. Lüscher M (2005) Schwarz-preconditioned HMC algorithm for two-flavour lattice QCD. Comput Phys Commun 165:199
5. Urbach C, Jansen K, Shindler A, Wenger U (2006) HMC algorithm with multiple time scale integration and mass preconditioning. Comput Phys Commun 174:87–98
6. Clark MA, Kennedy AD (2007) Accelerating dynamical fermion computations using the rational hybrid Monte Carlo (RHMC) algorithm with multiple pseudofermion fields. Phys Rev Lett 98:051601
7. Luscher M (2007) Deflation acceleration of lattice QCD simulations. JHEP 12:011
8. Dürr S et al (2008) Ab initio determination of light hadron masses. Science 322:1224–1227
9. Saad Y (2003) Iterative methods for sparse linear systems, 2nd edn. SIAM, Philadelphia, PA
10. Belletti F et al (2006) Computing for LQCD: apeNEXT. Comput Sci Eng 8:18–29
11. Boyle PA et al (2005) QCDOC: project status and first results. J Phys Conf Ser 16:129–139
12. Baier H et al QPACE – a QCD parallel computer based on Cell processors, arXiv:0911.2174
13. Jansen K, Urbach C (2009) tmLQCD: a program suite to simulate Wilson Twisted mass Lattice QCD. Comput Phys Commun 180:2717–2738
14. Jung C (2009) POSCI LAT2009, 002, Status of dynamical ensemble generation. [arXiv:1001.0941 [hep-lat]].

QCD Machines

NORMAN H. CHRIST
Columbia University, New York, NY, USA

Definition

QCD machines are parallel computers whose design and construction are specially tailored to efficiently carry out lattice QCD calculations. Quantum chromodynamics (QCD) is that part of the standard model of particle physics which describes the interactions of quarks and gluons. Lattice QCD is a discrete formulation of this theory which permits its study by numerical methods.

Discussion

Introduction

The neutrons and protons which compose the atomic nucleus are themselves made of quarks and gluons which are accurately described by the fundamental theory of quantum chromodynamics (QCD). QCD is a natural generalization of Maxwell's theory of electromagnetism. To a large degree, the theory of electromagnetism can be understood using classical physics with quantum phenomena appearing as important refinements of the classical theory, revealing quantum granularity when only a few quanta are present. This theory is well described by Maxwell's four partial differential equations with quantum corrections that can be computed using quantum perturbation theory.

In contrast, the phenomena of QCD have no relevant classical limit and must be understood by solving the full quantum mechanical problem without recourse to perturbation theory. This challenging theory is best formulated as a Feynman sum over histories or a Wiener integral, which in present applications requires the evaluation of an integral over 100 million variables – a problem that demands the power of highly parallel computing. This large number of variables is only an approximation to the infinite number that would be needed if an integration variable were assigned to each point in the space-time continuum. By approximating the space-time continuum by a four-dimensional grid or lattice of points, the number of integration variables is made finite. Lattice QCD exploits such a grid and evaluates the resulting integral by Monte Carlo methods.

While many important problems require the enormous computing power that potentially results from a large degree of parallelism, lattice QCD has particular features which make it a natural first target for parallelization and support the construction of parallel computers specialized for its solution. In order of importance, these features are:

Homogeneity. As a fundamental description of the physics of quarks and gluons in space-time, QCD offers enormous natural parallelism. Since each lattice site must be treated symmetrically, the parallel computation that must be performed on the variables at one site must be the same for every other. This high degree of homogeneity makes the code simple and leads to perfect load balancing if each processor in a parallel system is assigned the same number of lattice sites.

Locality. An important consequence of Einstein's theory of special relativity is that all interactions are local. Only nearby variables in space-time are coupled, and long-range effects come about as changes propagate from one site to the next, finally crossing many sites. Thus, communication between the homogenous processes described in the previous paragraph need only be provided between neighboring processes. This vastly simplifies the needed communication in a parallel computer and supports the simplest of mesh communication fabrics.

Simplicity. The basic algorithms needed to stochastically evaluate the QCD path integral are intrinsically simple. The code needed for the early study of only the gluon variables requires a simple heat bath or Metropolis update and takes only a few hundred lines. If the quarks are included in the calculation, then the Dirac matrix must be inverted. This sparce matrix acts on variables defined at each lattice site and connects only neighboring sites. Its inverse can be efficiently calculated using the conjugate gradient algorithm, again with a few hundred lines of code. In this situation, rewriting QCD code to target special floating point units is a manageable task.

Stability. The most effective algorithms for lattice QCD calculations have evolved very slowly. While algorithmic improvements have provided spectacular gains in performance, often outstripping the gains coming from computer technology, these improvements have involved little change to the fundamental structure of the computational method. There is reasonable expectation that a computer architecture that is presently efficient for QCD will also be efficient in a few years.

Over the past 30 years, the computing resources available for lattice QCD have increased by more than six orders of magnitude, from one million floating point additions or multiplications per second (1 Mflops) to more than one trillion (1 Tflops). Combined with substantial advances in algorithms, this has allowed the size of a typical space-time volume to increase from perhaps $8^3 \times 16$ to $32^3 \times 64$ or more. With this substantial increase, QCD becomes a "multi-scale" problem in which substantial advantage follows from using increasingly sophisticated methods to treat differently those parts of the calculation which are physical with a scale of 10–20 lattice spacings and unphysical, cut-off effects associated with distances of 1–4 lattice spacings. These new methods are not simple and are evolving quickly. Thus, the simplicity and stability of QCD code is less evident now that it was 15 or 20 years ago.

These four features of lattice QCD have made this application an attractive target for the construction of specialized parallel computers. The first of these were the Cosmic Cube at Caltech, the Columbia 16-node machine, and the APE machine in Rome in the 1984–1986 period. The next generation of machine, constructed in the 1987–1993 period, were the 64- and 256-node Columbia machines, the ACPMAPS machine at Fermilab, the GF11 at IBM, and the APE-100 in Rome. Finally, the most recent group of QCD machines, completed in the 1993–2010 time frame, are QCDSP, APEmille, QCDOC, apeNEXT, and QPACE computers. QCDSP, QCDOC, and apeNEXT are treated in separate entries in this volume; the others are described below. These special purpose machines have both made important contributions to the study of QCD and served as examples and inspiration for the development of commercial parallel computers.

First Examples

The story of QCD machines begins in 1980, a time when three important opportunities converged: (1) the physics potential offered by large-scale lattice QCD calculations, (2) the possibility to exploit large-scale parallelism, and (3) the availability of complex functionality in highly integrated, easily interconnected and inexpensive VLSI (very large scale integration) computer chips. The first machine to exploit these three possibilities was the Cosmic Cube of Fox and Seitz at Caltech [1]. This machine was constructed both to perform lattice QCD calculations and to provide a platform on which parallel implementations of many computational science problems could be mounted. Therefore, a very general hypercube communication network was constructed. The first machine had 64 nodes. The network was constructed to treat these nodes as the 64 corners of a six-dimensional cube with each node connected to its six neighboring nodes in the cube. The individual nodes were built from Intel 8086 and 8087 chips. The 8087 contained floating point hardware with a peak speed of 50 Kflops. The performance for QCD on the 64-node cosmic cube was ~2 Mflops [2], and interesting physics results for the heavy quark potential were published in 1984 [3].

A similar effort to construct special purpose computers for lattice QCD was started by Christ and Terrano in the Physics Department of Columbia University at the same time. Here the focus was on providing high-performance floating point capability while constructing the simplest communications network required to support this floating point capability. Thus, the first Columbia QCD machine was a single floating point accelerator which was attached to a DEC PDP11 computer and used to perform the six triples of 3×3 matrix multiplication and accumulation that are required for the Monte Carlo sampling of the Feynman path integral for the theory of gluons alone [4]. This machine used a TRW 16-bit integer multiplier, cascaded four-bit adders, and increased the performance of the PDP11 code by a factor of 20 for a performance twice that of a VAX 11/780.

Following this successful demonstration of the ease with which standard components could be combined to provide fast floating point arithmetic, this same team constructed the Columbia 16-node machine [5, 6]. This machine contained 16 nodes, each on a single-large printed circuit board with wire-wrap connections, arranged as a 4×4 mesh. The right and left edges of this mesh were joined as were the top and bottom edges changing the two-dimensional topology from a square to a torus. Each node was composed of Intel 80286 and 80287 chips, providing easily programmable control, address generation, and floating point capability. However, the real power of the node was provided by a vector processor composed of a pair of TRW chips, a floating point adder, and an integer multiplier enhanced by extra circuitry to perform floating point operations. This unit performed long sequences of pipelined, floating point additions and multiplications with the specific operations and operand addresses determined by the 56 bits in a sequence of microcode words stored in a $4K \times 56$-bit wide memory. Running at 8 MHz, this unit had a peak speed of 16 Mflops, and the entire machine a peak speed of 256 Mflops.

By modern standards, the nearest-neighbor communication provided in this machine were somewhat primitive. Each node was connected to its four nearest neighbors by 16 bidirectional data wires. If we locate each node with x and y coordinates running between 0 and 3, then these data paths expand the memory of the node with coordinates (x,y) to include the memories of the two nodes with coordinates $((x+1)\%4, y)$ and $(x,(y+1)\%4)$, where % indicates the usual mod operation. No address lines were included in these network connections, and off-node communication was carried out in a synchronous SIMD (single instruction multiple data) mode in which all nodes functioned in lock-step and the needed data in the off-node memories was addressed by the local processors (either micro- or vector processor) on those nodes.

The programming model for this machine followed naturally from the homogenous character of both lattice QCD and the computer's architecture. The code was written from the perspective of a single node with an off-node access treated no differently from one which was local. Such single-node code was loaded and run on each node. Those portions of the code that were strictly local could run in MIMD (multiple instruction multiple data) mode without synchronization. Metropolis accept–reject decisions could be easily made in this mode. However, during off-node communications, all code had to be executing the same branch and the Intel 80286 processors had to be synchronous on a cycle-by-cycle level.

Creating code for the 80286/80287 processors was straightforward with good compiler support. This single-node execution model and memory-mapped nearest neighbor communication is relatively easy to understand and follow. Programming the vector unit was more difficult even with a rudimentary assembler. Perhaps the greatest software challenge was created by the heterogenous character of the computer node. Much effort was required to reach an optimal balance between slow but easily created and modified code running on the microprocessors and that executing on the vector processor. Performance improved as bottle necks in the 80286/80287 portions of the code were identified and replaced by vector processor routines.

This machine executed QCD code at a speed 20% faster than its Cray 1 contemporary, sustaining ~50 Mflops or 20% efficiency for critical codes. It began physics production in March of 1985 and was used primarily to study the QCD phase transition for a theory of only gluons. Calculations on this machine were able to reach far enough into the weak coupling regime to verify the dependence of the transition temperature on the coupling strength expected in perturbation theory [7].

The third of these early QCD machines was the APE computer designed and built by an Italian group lead by Parisi and centered at Rome [8]. The first physics results [8] were obtained on a machine of four relatively powerful nodes connected in a one-dimensional ring. This machine later grew into the full APE computer with a larger ring of 16 of these nodes. In contrast to the two machines described above, the APE architecture was entirely designed by the APE collaboration and used no commercial microprocessor. The machine was driven by complier-generated microcode, which controlled the floating point units (eight Weitek chips on each node), and a sequencer, which determines the next microcode instruction that will be executed. The ring architecture was highly programmable. If nodes are numbered 0 through 15 and the separate memory units, also labeled 0–15, then in a given cycle, processor number k could be joined to access memory number $k+l\%16$ for all $0 \leq k < 16$ with a fixed value of l determined by program control.

The machine operated in SIMD mode with all nodes controlled by common microcode. Because of the homogeneous character of the machine, a high-level compiler was created to support a Fortran-like "APE language." The output of the compiler could directly control the computer and could also be written out as symbolic tables which could inform further hand optimization of the input code. A four-node APE computer had a peak speed of 256 Mflops and boasted a 70% efficiency. Two 4-node machines and a later 16-node machine enabled the extensive and influential physics program of the APE collaboration during the late 1980s.

Second Generation QCD Machines

This next period of QCD machines spans the 1987–1992 time frame and includes significant evolutions in the Caltech and Columbia projects. The full 16-node, 1 Gflops peak (10^9 floating point operations per second) APE machine was brought into operation in 1988 [9]. In addition, new QCD machines were built in Japan, at Fermilab, and by IBM.

The Cosmic Cube described above lead to a sequence of larger hypercube machines at Caltech.

The 32-node Mark IIIfp computer added a Weitek chip set to each node and achieved a 150 Mflops performance on QCD code. While the principal purpose of this machine was to enable parallel computation for a broad range of scientific applications, an interesting state-of-the-art study of the static quark potential was performed on this machine [10]. This series of Caltech machines was instrumental in stimulating Intel to begin producing parallel computers targeting the scientific market.

The Columbia 16-node machine was followed by a 64-node machine which began operation in August of 1987 with a peak speed of 1 Gflops and sustained performance of ~200 Mflops. This machine used the same Intel microprocessor, mesh architecture, and host computer communication as did its 16-node predecessor. The only change was an increased memory size (from 1 Mbyte to 2 Mbytes/node) and a change to 32-bit IEEE Weitek floating point chips. Thus, only the microcode needed to be refreshed. This was followed in 1989 by a third, 256-node machine. Again the same microprocessor was used, the network bandwidth was doubled, and a large enhancement to the floating point unit was realized by using a pair of more advanced Weitek chips each with two external Weitek registers files all running at 16 instead of 8 MHz. This gave an increase in performance of 16× over the 64-node machine for a peak performance of 16 Gflops and a sustained QCD performance of 6.5 Gflops for SU(3) conjugate gradient inversion. It should be recognized that this performance was greater or equal to the fastest commercially available machines. For example, a sustained speed of 6.23 Gflops was achieved a year later on a 64K node CMII machine [11].

The new project begun at Fermilab, called ACPMAPS (Advanced Computer Program Multiarray Processor System) [12], targeted a machine of 256 nodes based on a unified processor architecture constructed from a Weitek chip set. This provided a peak speed of 20 Mflops per node and 5 Gflops for the full machine. The Fermilab approach was crafted to give both cost-effective performance for QCD codes as well as a user-friendly programming environment that would be well suited to the development of new algorithms. The communications network was a hierarchy of 16 × 16 crossbar switches, providing a greater degree of interconnectivity than the one-dimensional and two-dimensional networks of the APE and Columbia machines. Each of the 32 crates contained eight processor boards interconnected with one crossbar switch. The 32 crates were themselves interconnected as the nodes in a 2^5 hypercube. The first physics results from ACPMAPS were reported at the 1991 Lattice Field Theory Symposium in Japan [13, 14]. This machine was upgraded to one of 50 Gflops peak speed in 1992 with a substantial enhancement to the node architecture (the Weitek chip set was replaced by a pair of Intel i860 processors) but with no change in the network [15]. The flexibility of this machine was supported by an innovative software environment which included C-level programming for the individual nodes and a system called Canopy [12] which provided a grid-aware framework that allowed parallel programs to be created with the details of grid communication managed by the software.

During this same time frame, the QCDPAX computer was designed [16] and put into operation [17] at Tsukuba in Japan. This machine contained 480 nodes arranged in a two-dimensional mesh with the edges connected to form a torus. The individual nodes were constructed from a Motorola 68020 processor and a gate-array controlled LSI Logic L64133 floating point chip. The 480 node machine had a peak speed of 14 Gflops and sustained speed of 2.6 Gflops, with 4–5 Gflops for the inversion of the Wilson Dirac operator. First physics results were presented in 1991 [18].

The last of the machines built during this period is the IBM GF11 of Beetham, Deneau, and Weingarten [19]. This had begun in 1983 and first physics results were presented in 1991 [20]. Like the APE machines, the GF11 was microcode controlled by a standard computer, in this case a RT/PC, and the resulting sequence of microcoded instructions was broadcast to the 566 processors in the system as well as to inputs that controlled a large 576 × 576 switch, which could realize an arbitrary permutation between its 576 data inputs and outputs. During actual program execution, the microcode instructions could choose between 1,024 preloaded switch configurations. The extra 10 ports on the switch were connected to 10 disks, so this switch also provided a very flexible connection between the 566 processors and these 10 disks. Each processor contained a hierarchy of memory (2 MB DRAM, 16K SRAM, and

256 word register file) and a Weitek floating point adder and multiplier, giving each node a peak speed of 20 Mflops. The typical sustained performance reported on a 440-node version of the machine was 6.9 Gflops [21].

While the 8-year time-to-completion suggests the difficult struggle needed to complete the GF11, once online, this machine was very successful. It produced the first calculation, in which a systematic effort was made to remove the errors associated with finite lattice spacing, large quark mass, and finite volume [22]. Later influential work studied the masses and widths of the lightest glueball states (particles formed from gluons rather than quarks) [23].

Toward One Teraflops

The projects described above succeeded in bringing a few Gigaflops of sustained computational speed to bear on the problems of lattice QCD. During the period 1992–1998, these speeds were dramatically increased by projects in the USA, Italy, and Japan. The APE collaboration developed the APE-100 which enlarged the one-dimensional architecture of the original APE machine to a three-dimensional mesh and incorporated an integrated arithmetic chip which contained the entire original APE node. The first 128-node, 6 Gflops APE100 machines were operational in 1992 and the 2048-node, 100 Gflops version by 1995. This was constructed commercially, and commercial machines, with the name "Quadrics," were purchased by other groups in Europe to support their own lattice QCD calculations.

This was followed by a still faster APE machine: APEmille. Begun in 1994 [24], this machine replaced the single central controller of the earlier APE machine with an array of controllers with one per eight nodes, all mounted on a single PC board along with memory and communications. APEmille benefited from substantial board-level integration and a 2× faster processor chip. Separate installations of this machine in Germany, France, Italy, and Wales were producing interesting results by 2000.

The group at Columbia began designing a new QCD machine in 1993 [25]. This machine, called QCDSP (QCD with Digital Signal Processors), followed a different architecture than the earlier Columbia machines, being built from credit card–size nodes interconnected in a four-dimension network. Machines with 8K and 12K nodes, sustaining 120 and 180 Gflops, were built at Columbia and the RIKEN BNL Research Center (RBRC). This machine and the follow-on QCDOC computer are described in a related entry.

Finally, in this period, the Tsukuba group, working with the Hitachi company, constructed CP-PACS (Computational Physics Parallel Array Computer System) [26]. Begun in 1992, this machine was complete in 1996 and sustained 200 Gflops [27]. It was constructed as a three-dimension array of Hewlett Packard RISC processors. These were a version of a commercial HP chip modified to include four times the usual 32 floating point registers that were accessed through a sliding window architecture. The network was more powerful than a simple nearest neighbor mesh. While arranged on a three-dimensional Cartesian grid, each node was joined to three crossbar switches which allowed direct communication with any node whose (x, y, z) coordinates differed in only one variable. This was a fully asynchronous machine with communication performed by message passing. The machine contained 2,048, 300 Mflops nodes for a peak speed of 614 Gflops. A commercial version of this machine was then sold by Hitachi.

Beyond One Teraflops

Three projects have succeeded in creating QCD machines capable of sustained performance in excess of 1 Tflops. Two of these are described in related entries. The first is the QCDOC machines designed and constructed by a collaboration of Columbia University, the RBRC, and UKQCD. Begun in 1999 and completed in 2005 three QCDOC machines, each with a sustained performance of 4 Tflops were installed at the RBRC, Edinburgh, and the Brookhaven National Laboratory. The second, apeNEXT, was begun in 2000 and led to large machines in Bielefeld, DESY/Zeuten, and Rome with peak speeds of 3.6, 2.4, and 8 Tflops, respectively.

The third machine in this multi-teraflops class is the QPACE machine. This was constructed by a collaboration centered at the University of Regensburg with significant involvement from IBM. Four racks were installed in 2009 at the University of Wuppertal and four more at the Jülich Supercomputing Centre. The aggregate peak speed of the eight racks is 200 Tflops [28] with a sustained performance of 20–30% of peak. The machine is based on an IBM/Sony CELL processor similar to that used in the Playstation 3 but upgraded to perform double-precision arithmetic.

The nodes are interconnected in a three-dimensional mesh network which is connected to each node by a field programmable gate array (FPGA). This machine had a remarkably short design and construction time which was achieved in part by avoiding the design of a special purpose chip (as was done in the QCDOC and apeNEXT projects) and using instead an FPGA in which initial errors could be easily corrected. Physics calculations are expected to begin on this hardware in January 2010.

Conclusion

The theory of quantum chromodynamics is a computationally simple but highly demanding application area in which the strategy for parallelization is obvious. It is therefore a natural target for parallel computing and, as described above, a natural target for application-specific, highly parallel machines. During the period 1983 through the late nineties QCD machines lead or rivaled the most powerful parallel machines available commercially. For example, the 1 Tflops aggregate peak speed of the QCDSP machines put into operation in 1998 was comparable 3.1 Tflops of the Intel ASCII Red installed at Sandia in 1999.

The later QCD machines were built at costs ranging between $1 and $15 million, as might be expected for large research instruments. During the present 2000–2010 period, the 10–20 times larger sums spent on commercial supercomputers and their increasingly effective architectures (inspired in some cases by QCD machines) have lead commercial machines to outstrip by an order of magnitude or more the power available from special purpose machines. Thus, at present (2010), with the possible exception of the QPACE machine, the most challenging QCD problems are run on commercial computers.

Because of the necessary investment of effort and money, machines built for QCD targeted important research goals requiring the largest possible computer capability to achieve. However, beginning in the late 1990s, smaller QCD problems began to be tackled with what were known as Beowulf clusters, collections of 10–100 standard workstations connected by a commercial network [29]. While these machines, often configured in a fashion optimized for lattice QCD, are not able to efficiently manage the small lattice volumes per computer node that are required to mount the most demanding lattice QCD problems on a very large number of processors, they have become increasingly capable, are highly cost effective, and can be easily upgraded every year. These cluster machines are now enjoying a further increase in performance by incorporating the latest graphics processing units (GPU), which provide enormous performance boosts when a very large local volume can be used on each node. In the USA, the great majority of lattice QCD research is now performed on workstation clusters and the IBM BlueGene computers.

To an even greater extent than in 1980, the deeper study of the physics of quarks, gluons, and new strongly interacting particles likely to be discovered at the Large Hadron Collider at CERN requires vast computational resources not available from current computers. In fact, many important problems require computing performance on the exaflops (10^{18} flops) scale. Given the experienced and talented research groups in Germany, Great Britain, Italy, Japan, and the USA, we may hope that new technologies will be recognized that can provide this needed computational power and that can be exploited by new generations of specially built QCD machines.

Related Entries
▶QCD apeNeXT Machines
▶QCD (Quantum Chromodynamics) Computations
▶QCDSP and QCDOC Computers

Bibliographic Notes and Further Reading

The plans, progress, and first results from the QCD machines described here were usually reported in the annual International Symposia on Lattice Field Theory which provide many of the bibliographic citations here. An early volume describing both QCD and other special purpose machines of B. Alder [1] may be of interest. Further detailed information about the first QCD machines can be found in the workshop proceedings of Li, Qiu, and Ren [30], and more recent machines in those of Iwasaki and Ukawa [31]. The theoretical foundations of these lattice methods are described in many monographs and textbooks, for example, those of Creutz [32], Montvay and Muenster [33], Smit [34], Rothe [35], and Degrand and Detar [36].

Bibliography

1. ALder BJ (ed) (1988) Special purpose computers. Academic, Boston
2. Otto SW (1984) Lattice gauge theories on a hypercube computer. In: Proceedings, gauge theory on a lattice, Argonne, pp 12–20
3. Otto SW, Stack JD (1984) The SU(3) Heavy quark potential with high statistics. Phys Rev Lett 52:2328
4. Christ NH, Terrano AE (1984) Hardware matrix multiplier / accumulator for lattice gauge theory calculations. Nucl Instr Meth A222:534–539
5. Christ NH, Terrano AE (1984) A very fast parallel processor, IEEE T Comput C-33:344–350
6. Christ NH, Terrano AE (1986) A micro-based supercomputer. Byte 11:145–160
7. Christ NH, Terrano AE (1986) The deconfining phase transition in lattice QCD. Phys Rev Lett 56:111
8. APE Collaboration, Albanese M et al (1987) The APE computer: an array processor optimized for lattice gauge theory simulations. Comput Phys Commun 45:345–353
9. APE Collaboration, Remiddi E (1988) From APE to APE100. In: Proceedings, lattice 88, Batavia, pp 562–565
10. Ding HQ, Baillie CF, Fox GC (1990) Calculation of the heavy quark potential at large separation on a hypercube parallel computer. Phys Rev D41:2912
11. Liu WC. Fast QCD conjugate gradient solver on the connection machine. In: Proceedings, lattice 90, Tallahassee, pp 149–152 (see High Energy Physics Index 29 (1991) No. 11041)
12. Fischler M et al (1989) The Fermilab lattice supercomputer project. Nucl Phys Proc Suppl 9:571–576
13. Mackenzie PB (1992) Charmonium with improved Wilson fermions. 1. A determination of the strong coupling constant. Nucl Phys Proc Suppl 26:369–371
14. El-Khadra AX (1992) Charmonium with improved Wilson fermions. 2. The spectrum. Nucl Phys Proc Suppl 26:372–374
15. Fischler M, Gao M, Hockney G, Isely M, Uchima M (1993) Reducing communication inefficiencies for a flexible programming paradigm. Nucl Phys Proc Suppl 30:301–304
16. PAX Collaboration, Iwasaki Y, Hoshino T, Shirakawa T, Oyanagi Y, Kawai T (1988) QCD-PAX: a parallel computer for lattice QCD simulation. Comput Phys Commun 49:449–455
17. QCDPAX Collaboration, Iwasaki Y et al (1991) QCDPAX: present status and first physical results. Nucl Phys Proc Suppl 20:141–144
18. QCDPAX Collaboration, Kanaya K et al (1991) Pure QCD at finite temperature: results from QCDPAX. Nucl Phys Proc Suppl 20:300–304
19. Beetem J, Denneau M, Weingarten D (1985) The gf11 supercomputer. In: The 12th annual international symposium on computer architecture, Boston, pp 108–115
20. Butler F, Chen H, Sexton J, Vaccarino A, Weingarten D (1992) Volume dependence of the valence Wilson fermion mass spectrum. Nucl Phys Proc Suppl 26:287–289
21. Weingarten DH (1992) Parallel QCD machines. Nucl Phys Proc Suppl 26:126–136
22. Butler F, Chen H, Sexton J, Vaccarino A, Weingarten D (1994) Hadron masses from the valence approximation to lattice QCD. Nucl Phys B430:179–228, hep-lat/9405003
23. Sexton J, Vaccarino A, Weingarten D (1995) Numerical evidence for the observation of a scalar glueball. Phys Rev Lett 75: 4563–4566, hep-lat/9510022
24. Bartoloni A et al (1995) The new wave of the APE project: APEmille. Nucl Phys Proc Suppl 42:17–20
25. Arsenin I et al (1994) A 0.5-teraflops machine optimized for lattice QCD. Nucl Phys Proc Suppl 34:820–822
26. Oyanagi Y (1993) New parallel computer project in Japan dedicated to computational physics. Nucl Phys Proc Suppl 30:299–300
27. CP-PACS Collaboration, Iwasaki Y (1998) The CP-PACS project. Nucl Phys Proc Suppl 60A:246–254, hep-lat/9709055
28. Baier H et al. QPACE – a QCD parallel computer based on Cell processors. arXiv:0911.2174
29. Gottlieb SA (2001) Comparing clusters and supercomputers for lattice QCD. Nucl Phys Proc Suppl 94:833–840, hep-lat/0011071
30. Li X-Y, Qiu Z-M, Ren H-C (eds) (1987) Lattice gauge theory using parallel processors. In: Proceedings, CCAST (world laboratory) symposium/workshop, Peking, 21 May–2 June, 1987. Gordon & Breach, New York, 644 p (proceedings of the CCAST symposium/workshop, 1)
31. Iwasaki Y, Ukawa A (eds) Lattice QCD on parallel computers. In: Proceedings, international workshop, Tsukuba, 10–15 Mar 1997. Prepared for international workshop on lattice QCD on parallel computers, Tsukuba, 10–15 Mar 1997
32. Creutz M (1983) Quarks, gluons and lattices. Cambridge University Press Cambridge, 169 p (Cambridge monographs on mathematical physics)
33. Montvay I, Munster G (1994) Quantum fields on a lattice. Cambridge University Press Cambridge, 491 p (Cambridge monographs on mathematical physics)
34. Smit J (2002) Introduction to quantum fields on a lattice: a robust mate. Camb Lect Notes Phys 15:1–271
35. Rothe HJ (2005) Lattice gauge theories: an introduction. World Sci Lect Notes Phys 74:1–605
36. DeGrand T, Detar CE (2006) Lattice methods for quantum chromodynamics. World Scientific, New Jersey, 345 p

QCDSP and QCDOC Computers

NORMAN H. CHRIST
Columbia University, New York, NY, USA

Definition

QCDSP (quantum chromodynamics on digital signal processors) and QCDOC (quantum chromodynamics on a chip) are two computer architectures optimized for large-scale calculations in lattice QCD, a first-principles, numerical formulation of the theory which describes the interactions of quarks and gluons. Both are mesh machines with a communication network arranged as a four- and six-dimensional torus, respectively. Completed in 1998 the largest QCDSP machine had a peak speed of 0.6 Tflops while three QCDOC machines were completed in 2004/2005, each with a peak speed of 10 Tflops. Both architectures delivered a sustained performance for QCD of about 30% of peak.

Discussion

Overview

The QCDSP and QCDOC machines represent a second generation of massively parallel computers optimized for QCD. Earlier QCD machines constructed at Columbia University had exploited single-board computers to assemble large machines with 64 or 256 nodes, where each node was a large printed circuit board containing a microprocessor and much support electronics including memory, internode communications and substantial added floating point hardware. By the early 1990s, all of these functions could be contained in a very few chips. In particular, if one of those chips was a custom-designed ASIC (applications specific integrated circuit) then even the "glue" or interface logic special to the particular design could be integrated into this small number of chips.

This large increase in integration capability made it possible to shrink one of the large node boards, for example, a 45 × 33 cm board making up one node in the Columbia 256-node machine, to the small, credit-card size, 6.7 × 4.5 cm, QCDSP node shown in Fig. 1. While the size of the node was drastically reduced, the floating point performance remained nearly the same. The 50 Mflops peak speed of this new DSP chip compared well with the 64 Mflops peak speed of the two 16 MHz Weitek chips used on the earlier node. Thus, a large increase in computational power could be achieved if this minaturization was exploited to achieve a substantial increase in the number of nodes. In fact, compact packaging allowed 12,288 QCDSP nodes to be accommodated in a 5 m² footprint, very similar to the area occupied by the 256 nodes of the earlier machine. The result was a nearly 40× increase in performance.

Such a large increase in the number of nodes required a change in the way the nodes were interconnected. If the two-dimensional torus interconnection

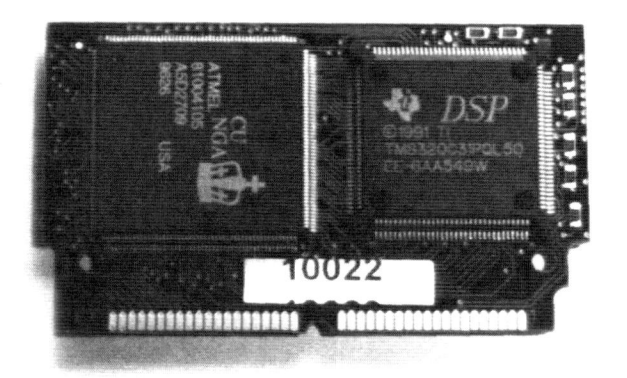

QCDSP and QCDOC Computers. Fig. 1 A single node of the QCDSP computer. The chip on the right is the Texas Instruments TMS320C31 DSP. That on the left is the ASIC which provides the interface connecting the DSP and memory and manages internode communication over the four-dimensional network interconnecting the nodes. Five memory chips (which are not visible) are mounted on the opposite side of this 6.7 × 4.5 cm DIMM card

were simply expanded from the 16 × 16 mesh of the earlier 256 node machine the result would be 64 × 64 mesh for even a 4K node partition of a 12K node machine. Since the difficulty of the typical lattice QCD calculation increases at least as fast as the seventh power of the linear size of the system under study, the 40× increase in computer power would only allow a $40^{1/7}$ = 1.7 times increase in problem size, far smaller than the increase in mesh size from 16 to 64. Of course, the linear size of a mesh of 4,096 processors can be easily reduced by increasing the dimension of the mesh. For QCDSP a four-dimensional mesh was used because this nicely matches the four-dimensional space-time mesh of sites used in lattice QCD. With such an interconnect and the onboard wiring adopted for QCDSP, 4,096 nodes can be configured as a 16 × 16 × 4 × 4 mesh allowing the full processing power of such a ten times more powerful 4K node partition to be applied to the same size problem as could be mounted on the earlier 256-node machine. The QCDOC network was further expanded to a six-dimensional mesh in order to allow a more flexible mapping of four- or five-dimensional problems onto a fixed partition geometry as discussed below.

Networks

Typically such massively parallel machines require a variety of networks. In addition to the mesh network which provides high-bandwidth data communication, a combining and broadcast network is needed to perform global sums or to identify the largest or smallest case of a variable appearing across all nodes and then to distribute the result to all nodes. A third network, often distributing interrupt signals, is needed to implement barriers for synchronization among the nodes. This or a similar network is needed to announce errors and bring all nodes to a halt as quickly as possible so that a malfunctioning node can be easily identified. Finally a control network is needed to boot the machine and perform and report the results of power-on diagnostics.

The network most important for high computational performance is that transmitting the data between nodes as the calculation progresses. As discussed above for the QCDSP and QCDOC computers, this network is a four- or six-dimensional toroidal mesh. A four-dimensional lattice QCD problem can be easily mapped onto the four-dimensional network of QCDSP. Each processor node in an $N_x \times N_y \times N_z \times N_t$ network can be assigned an $n_x \times n_y \times n_z \times n_t$ local volume so the resulting space-time volume contained in the entire machine is an $N_x \cdot n_x \times N_y \cdot n_y \times N_z \cdot n_z \times N_t \cdot n_t$ volume assembled by juxtaposing these smaller local volumes in the obvious way. The standard interactions between neighboring sites in this $N_x \cdot n_x \times N_y \cdot n_y \times N_z \cdot n_z \times N_t \cdot n_t$ mesh of physical space-time points can then be accomplished either within a processing node or by communication between adjacent nodes in the $N_x \times N_y \times N_z \times N_t$ network of nodes.

While this four-dimension mesh worked very well, the rigid coupling between the problem size and the machine size required frequent reconfiguration of the QCDSP partitions as the size of problem changed. This reconfiguration was accomplished by a physical reconnection of the communications cables, a significant impediment that often delayed making needed changes in problem size.

In the QCDOC computer, this coupling between problem size and partition geometry was weakened by increasing the number of dimensions of the network from four to six. For both QCDSP and QCDOC each motherboard held 64 nodes. For QCDSP this was wired as a $4 \times 4 \times 2 \times 2$ mesh with the first "4" connected back to itself to form a one-dimensional torus within the motherboard. The other six faces of this four-dimensional cube were wired to six external connectors. Multi-conductor ribbon cables then joined the corresponding faces between logically adjacent motherboards connecting the other three, off-board dimensions of the four-dimensional torus.

For QCDOC the 64 nodes are interconnected on a motherboard as a $2 \times 2 \times 2 \times 2 \times 2 \times 2$ mesh. For this machine a daughter card, shown in Fig. 2 contains two nodes to accommodate the long dual inline memory modules (DIMM) provided for each node. The two nodes on a daughter card are connected in a two-dimensional torus and the other network connections made to the motherboard. The motherboard is wired to join these 32 daughter cards into a 2^5 cube. Two additional dimensions of this 2^5 cube are connected as two-node torii and connections to the remaining six faces of the 2^6 cube of nodes are carried to 6 connectors leaving the motherboard. Thus, as in QCDSP, external cables join the motherboards to assemble a three-dimensional torus of motherboards.

Since it is easy to map a lower dimensional torus within one of higher dimension, the six-dimensional network of QCDOC can be used to allow a single six-dimensional QCDOC partition to support a greater variety of four-dimensional mesh geometries than can be accommodated in a single four-dimensional QCDSP partition. This is illustrated in Fig. 3 which shows the example of a two-dimensional network in which a subset of the links are used to realize a one-dimensional mesh. Used in this way, the three-dimensional $2 \times 2 \times 2$ QCDOC network that is wired on the motherboard can be combined with the more distributed $2N_x \times 2N_y \times 2N_z$ network connecting $N_x N_y N_z$ motherboards in a variety of ways. For example, these extra eight processors can be wired into an added one-dimensional torus in the time dimension of size 8 giving a $2N_x \times 2N_y \times 2N_z \times 8$ torus. Alternatively only two of these dimension could be used to form a one-dimensional torus of size 4 and the third dimension could be combined with the x-direction to double its length giving a $4N_x \times 2N_y \times 2N_z \times 4$ torus.

Neither QCDSP and QCDOC has a separate/combining broadcast network. Instead hardware features are added to the mesh communications network which identify particular paths though the mesh network that can be used to combine or broadcast

QCDSP and QCDOC Computers. Fig. 2 A single daughter board of the QCDOC computer. This card holds two QCDOC nodes (the two silver colored chips), an Ethernet five-port hub (the rectangular Altima chip visible on the left), four Ethernet "PHY" chips (identifiable as the four small square Altima chips) and two DIMM sticks which varied in size between 128 and 512 MB

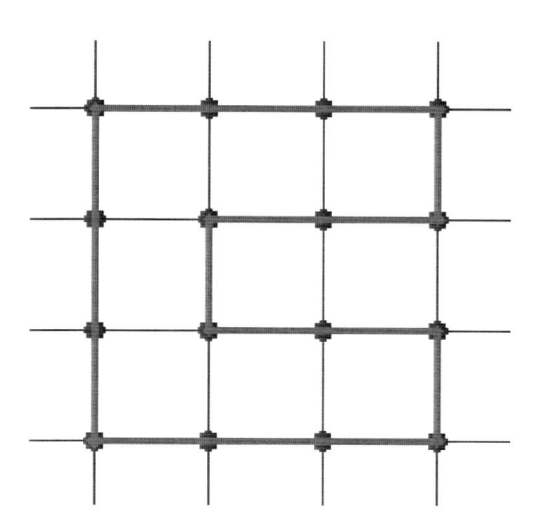

QCDSP and QCDOC Computers. Fig. 3 An example of mapping a one-dimensional 16-site torus into a two-dimensional 4 × 4 torus

data. For example, additional hardware was provided that allows data passed from one or more neighboring nodes into a given node to be added or compared to local data and then the sum or maximum or minimum to be passed on with minimal latency to a specially designated neighbor. The QCDSP design had a separate interrupt network which allows the implementation of barriers and the transmission of interrupts. For QCDOC this network is realized in two ways. First a simple network of three interrupt lines was connected throughout the machine which allows a signal sent by one processor to be seen by all others which is used during boot-up and to signal fatal errors. A larger and more flexible system of interrupts is provided by the distribution of 8-bit interrupt packets over the six-dimensional mesh network.

The networks used for booting, diagnostics, and file transfer for QCDSP and QCDOC were quite different. For QCDSP a tree whose individual links used the commercial SCSI bus conventions connected the host workstation, typically a SUN, to each of the motherboards. For QCDOC this host communication and control function is provided by standard Ethernet connections. In fact each node has two Ethernet ports. The first is connected directly to the JTAG control of the processor allowing JTAG commands embedded in Ethernet packets to load boot code and boot the QCDOC Power PC 440 processor. The second port is configured as a standard Ethernet device, supporting conventional remote procedure call (RPC) communication with the host and a standard NFS client which runs on each node and provides access to networked disk servers. This Ethernet hardware is likely the greatest source of difficulty with the QCDOC design with frequent hang-ups requiring elaborate software work-arounds.

Mechanical Design

As shown in Fig. 1, the individual QCDSP nodes were mounted on small printed circuit boards with the form factor of a standard DIMM card. This design provided very reliable. Sixty three of these daughter cards were socketed on a QCDSP motherboard. The 64th node was soldered directly to the mother board and supplied with added connections giving it more memory, access to two SCSII interface chips and an EEPROM. This modular design allowed easy repair of faulty daughter cards and was continued for QCDOC. In this case two nodes are mounted on a daughter card as shown in Fig. 2. A QCDOC motherboard is shown in Fig. 4.

For both machines eight motherboards are mounted in a backplane that makes up a crate as shown for QCDOC in Fig. 5. Two crates are stacked to form a rack. The racks are water cooled with a heat exchanger installed below each crate followed by a tray of muffin fans pushing the air upward. The return path for the air is provided inside the cabinet holding the two crates. The racks can then be lined up in a row with cables running from one rack to the next. If desired, these racks can also be stacked two high with a final "top hat" added which contains the Ethernet switches. Figure 6 shows the largest QCDOC installation at the Brookhaven National Laboratory.

Both machines are remarkably low power with a single QCDSP node consuming about 3 W and a QCDOC node slightly more. Thus, QCDSP achieved about 5 Gflops/KW while QCDOC achieves 60 Gflops/KW. Both machines were also highly economical at the time they were finished. The price per sustained performance for QCDSP was $13/Mflops while for QCDOC this number falls to a little more than $1/Mflops.

Software

The software for these two machines is composed of application code which performs the lattice QCD calculation and the operating system (OS) which boots the machine, responds to error conditions, loads and passes arguments to the application code, and provides network and file system support. On both machines the custom OS is divided between the nodes of the parallel machine and the host computer. At boot-up the OS on the host is active, loading the operating system on each node, carrying out extensive diagnostic tests of the parallel machine and loading the user code. Control is then passed to the OS on each node which starts the application code and provides the services requested by that code. The OS running on each node is designed to provide a "C" and "C++" environment for the application code with much of the standard UNIX functionality supported. To the extent that resources beyond those available on the node are required, for example data from a remote disk file or the ability to print to the user's screen, the node component of the OS requests these services from the OS running on the host computer. Now the host component of the OS acts as the slave to the OS running on each node.

The simple and lean structure of the node OS is critical to the high performance of these machines. No multitasking or asynchronous behavior interefers with the application code on any of the nodes. The node OS ceases to execute when the application code starts running.

QCDSP and QCDOC Computers. Fig. 4 A QCDOC motherboard holding 31 daughter cards with the 32nd daughter card removed. The three large edge connectors are wired directly through the backplane to three groups of eight cable connectors. Each cable is a bundle of 20 twisted, differential pairs, 16 of which provides uni-directional communications for the QCDOC mesh network

QCDSP and QCDOC Computers. Fig. 5 Front and rear views of a QCDOC crate. The bundles of black cables carry the mesh communications while the gray cables leaving the lower right provide the 64 Ethernet connections to the eight motherboards

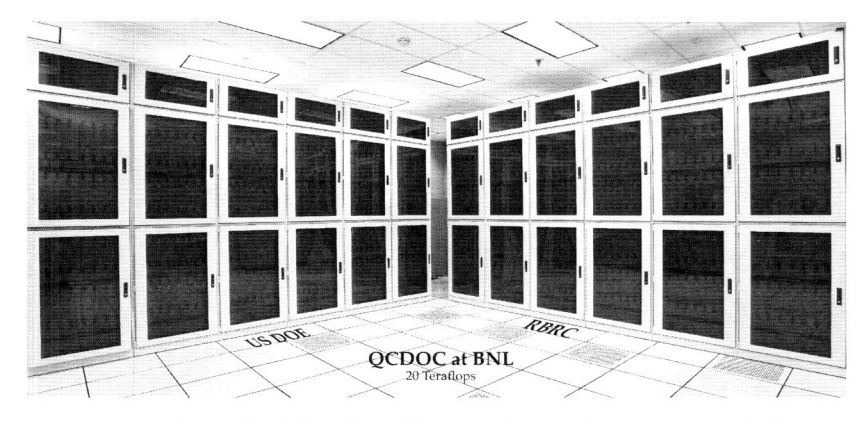

QCDSP and QCDOC Computers. Fig. 6 The QCDOC installation at the Brookhaven National Laboratory (BNL). The RIKEN-funded RBRC QCDOC makes up the 12 racks on the right while the DOE-funded USQCD QCDOC computer appears on the left. Each machine contains 12,288 nodes, has a peak speed of 10 Tflops and a sustained speed in excess of three Tflops for lattice QCD

Both machines were typically used in a mode where the same code is executing on each node. Since there was no requirement for precise synchronization, the programs on different nodes can execute different branches. However, if one node runs ahead of the rest and begins communications with its slower neighbors, that faster node will wait until needed data is sent by its neighbors or the data it has sent to its neighbors has been removed from the neighbor's input buffer and this action acknowledged so that further data can be sent. This self-synchronization provided by the communications hardware is automatic and requires no action from the user program.

The QCDSP DSP chip came with "C" and "C++" compilers although the "C++" compiler quickly became out-of-date. Given the lack of a data cache, standard "C" code gave poor performance (typically a few percent of peak) so that frequently used routines had to ultimately be written in assembler. The PowerPC core in QCDOC is much more efficient with its 32 KB instruction and data caches. With reasonable precautions "C" code might achieve 10 or even 20% of peak. The most critical code was best written in assembler, a process greatly aided by the Boyle assembler generation library (BAGEL) which was used to generate much of the assembler used in the QCD code.

Such single node code can be run directly on QCDSP or QCDOC machines with thousands of nodes if this many-node environment is kept in mind when that code is written. For example, if data is sent to a neighboring node in the $+\mu$ direction, then the corresponding action of the neighbor in the $-\mu$ direction must be anticipated and a matching $-\mu$ direction receive instruction invoked as well. If a sum across all lattice sites is to be performed, this must be done by a call to a global sum routine which returns the sum performed across all nodes in the machine. The sends and receives of data in a particular direction are initiated by "C" function calls which begin the transmissions and test to see if they are complete.

On QCDOC in addition to these special function calls, internode communications can also be accomplished by using the quantum message passing (QMP) library. This software was produced with SciDAC support by the USQCD collaboration. QMP provides communication routines which overlap in functionality with the standard message passing interface (MPI). Code which incorporates QMP calls can be run on many platforms including workstation clusters and other massively parallel supercomputers allowing portable code to be run on QCDOC. This QMP support was highly successful and resulted in most of the code used by groups in the USA studying lattice QCD being run on the QCDOC machines at BNL.

QCDSP Architecture

A mesh architecture permits essentially all of the computing hardware of the parallel computer (with the exception of the network wires and perhaps some transceivers) to be built into the computing node. This was realized in the QCDSP machines. Essentially all of the computer's functions were carried out by the three basic components on the daughter card shown in Fig. 1. Thus, the remaining parts of the computer, the motherboard and backplane, were to a large degree passive, providing a clock signal and power to the daughter cards and routing the communication wires.

This concentration of functionality on the QCDSP daughter board was achieved with the custom-designed ASIC (referred to here as the "node gate array" or NGA) that was the third component, beyond the DSP and memory, which was mounted on the daughter board. Figure 7 shows the organization of the daughter card. The NGA provided the interface between the DSP and

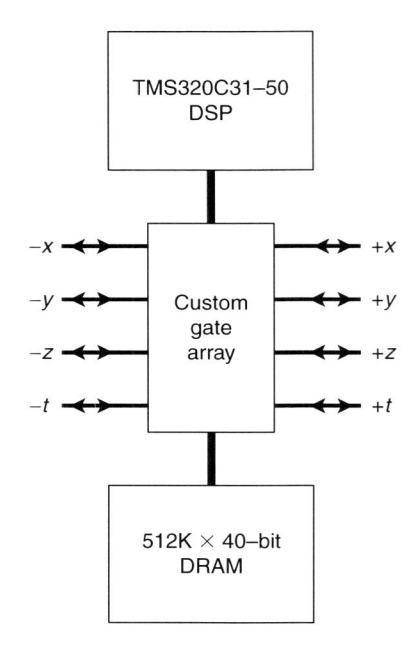

QCDSP and QCDOC Computers. Fig. 7 A block diagram showing a QCDSP node. The central block is the node gate array (NGA) which provided the interface between the upper DSP chip and the lower DRAM chips. It also provided serial communications to each of the eight nearest neighbors connected to this node by the four-dimensional QCDSP mesh network

the dynamic random access memory (DRAM), supplying the periodic refresh signal and error checking and correction (ECC) required by this dense, economical memory technology.

The NGA also contained a 32-location circular buffer which prefetched and stored DRAM data according to commands from the DSP. Thus, when the DSP began to multiply an 18-element link matrix by a 12 component fermion spinor, the circular buffer could be instructed by the DSP to load the next 32-bit data word from memory followed by the additional 17 sequential locations corresponding to the link matrix. These data were held in the circular buffer, available for later, low-latency DSP access.

The NGA also sent and received data to and from the eight neighbors of the node. It managed the low-level protocol needed to serialize and transmit the data to be sent, or receive and deserialize incoming data. The NGA would also send an acknowledgment packet after 32 bits of data had been received and the receive buffer had been cleared so that a further 32-bits could be received. Received data with bad parity was acknowledged with an error packet and would be retransmitted.

The data being sent or received was fetched or stored directly from/to memory by an independent, direct memory access (DMA) controller, one for each of the eight directions. The DSP needed only load the starting address for such a transfer and a start command in order to begin the transfer. Additional preloaded control bits determined how much data was to be transferred and if the data should be fetched from or stored to memory as a series of blocks of fixed length separated by a fixed stride. Thus, the DSP could quickly start such a data transfer and then resume calculation using data not involved in the transfer. All eight directions could be active simultaneously at 50 MHz for a total off-mode transfer rate of 50 MB/s.

QCDOC Architecture

The QCDOC architecture is a natural evolution of that described above for QCDSP, exploiting the much higher degree of integration that was available in 1999 when the QCDOC design was begun. Here the PowerPC processor is an IBM ASIC library component and was combined with the serial communications unit (SCU) into the single chip that makes up nearly all of a QCDOC node. The entire 2 MB memory of the QCDSP chip was doubled and included in the QCDOC chip as embedded DRAM (EDRAM), again exploiting IBM technology. In addition two Ethernet controllers, a synchronous DRAM controller, and an 0.8 Gflops double precision attached floating point unit were incorporated in this QCDOC chip as shown in Fig. 8.

These improvements give the QCDOC machine more than ten times the capability of QCDSP. The processor has increased from 50 to 400 MHz and the peak performance from 50 to 800 Mflops. The memory bandwidth has grown from 25 MB/s to 2.1 GB/s while the total off-node bandwidth increased from 0.025 to 0.6 GB/s for send and for receive. Finally the limited DSP with its non-IEEE compliant single precision has been replaced by the IEEE, 64-bit precision of the IBM FPU, making QCDOC a highly capable and convenient-to-program computer.

Conclusion

Both the QCDSP and QCDOC machines have been used for a wide range of influential physics calculations. The large QCDSP machines at Columbia and the RBRC began operation in 1998 and continued until January 31, 2006. A smaller 2-crate machine was also installed at the Supercomputer Computations Research Institute of Florida State University. The first 12,288-node QCDOC machine began operation in December of 2004 at the University of Edinburgh which was followed in a few months by the RBRC and DOE 12,288-node machines at BNL. The two large machines at BNL are still operating at full capacity at the time of this writing (May 2011).

The QCDSP machines were used to develop and exploit the chiral, domain wall fermion (DWF) formalism [1, 2]. This approach to lattice calculations with spin-1/2 particles preserves the independent symmetry of the left- and right-handed quarks in the limit of vanishing quark mass by adding a fifth dimension to the usual four-dimensional space-time lattice. The substantial increase in capability provided by QCDSP allowed the study of these new five-dimensional lattices with lattice extent varying between 16 and 128 in this fifth dimension. Among the more notable results achieved with these machines were a through quenched study of low-energy QCD using DWF [3], the application of this new method to the weak decays of the K meson including results for the complex, CP violating amplitudes A_0 and A_2 [4], the successful application of RI/MOM techniques to non-perturbatively renormalize the seven four-Fermi operators which appear in this calculation [4, 5], and the development of methods to include the effects of DWF quark loops in lattice QCD calculations at both zero [6] and nonzero [7] temperatures.

This inclusion of quark loops, a step necessary for consistency, was at the limit of the capabilities of QCDSP. However, this preliminary work set the stage for much larger scale calculations enabled by the QCDOC machines. Thus, the RIKEN, BNL, Columbia (RBC) and UKQCD collaborations, which had worked together on the design and construction of QCDOC began a joint program of large-scale DWF calculations using the completed QCDOC computers to study a wide range of questions important in particle and nuclear physics on $16^3 \times 32$ and $24^3 \times 64$ grids. Among

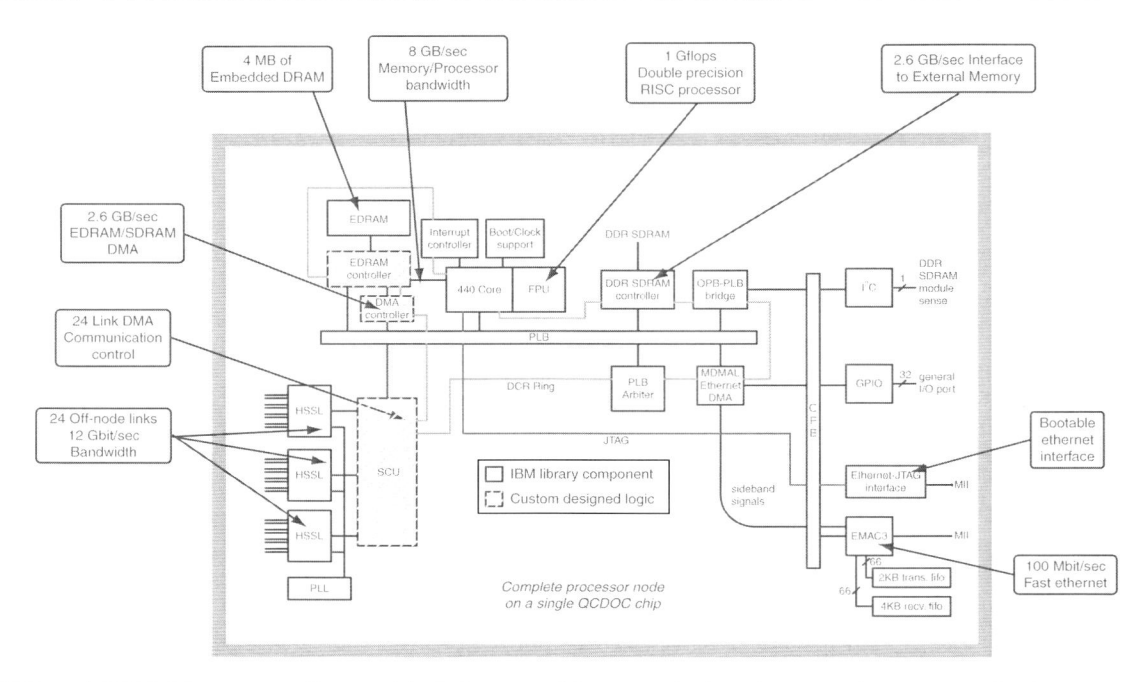

QCDSP and QCDOC Computers. Fig. 8 A block diagram of the ASIC which makes up each QCDOC node. The cross-hatched blocks are those designed by the team which built the computer while the open boxes represent standard IBM ASIC library components

the many results obtained one might note those for the neutral K meson mixing parameter B_K [8], the nucleon axial coupling g_A [9] and the decay amplitude f_+ of a K meson into a pion and lepton pair [10], to mention a few examples. In addition a wide range of topics have been studied by members of the USQCD collaboration using the DOE-funded QCDOC.

The QCDSP and QCDOC machines have also exerted influence on high-performance computing technology. The award of the Gordon Bell prize for cost performance at SC98 to the BNL QCDSP machine helped attract attention to this economical, low power, and yet broadly applicable architecture. This visibility together with the recruiting by IBM of four physicists closely involved with QCDSP and earlier Columbia University machines, lead to a collaboration between IBM, Columbia University, Edinburgh University, and the RIKEN laboratory in Japan on the QCDOC computer and at the same time, the start of the separate Blue Gene Light project at IBM. Blue Gene Light evolved into the present IBM Blue Gene series of commercial computers which have transformed high-performance computing and dominated the top 500 list.

Related Entries

▶QCD apeNeXT Machines
▶QCD (Quantum Chromodynamics) Computations
▶QCD Machines

Bibliographic Notes and Further Reading

A thorough account of these two computer architectures can be found in Ref. [11], written after both machines were complete. Addition information about QCDSP appears in Ref. [12]. Earlier accounts of the design and construction these computers appear in the proceedings of the annual International Symposia on Lattice Field Theory and other HPC conferences. For QCDSP see Refs. [13–16] and for QCDOC Refs. [17–22].

Bibliography

1. Kaplan DB (1992) A method for simulating chiral fermions on the lattice. Phys Lett B288:342–347 [hep-lat/9206013]
2. Shamir Y (1993) Chiral fermions from lattice boundaries. Nucl Phys B406:90–106 [hep-lat/9303005]
3. Blum T et al (2004) Quenched lattice qcd with domain wall fermions and the chiral limit. Phys Rev D69:074502 [hep-lat/0007038]

4. RBC Collaboration, Blum T et al (2003) Kaon matrix elements and cp-violation from quenched lattice qcd. i: the 3-flavor case. Phys Rev D68:114506 [hep-lat/0110075]
5. Blum T et al (2002) Non-perturbative renormalisation of domain wall fermions: quark bilinears. Phys Rev D66:014504 [hep-lat/0102005]
6. Aoki Y et al (2005) Lattice QCD with two dynamical flavors of domain wall fermions. Phys Rev D72:114505 [hep-lat/0411006]
7. Chen P et al (2001) The finite temperature qcd phase transition with domain wall fermions. Phys Rev D64:014503, [arXiv:hep-lat/0006010]. 13
8. RBC Collaboration, Antonio DJ et al (2008) Neutral kaon mixing from 2 + 1 flavor domain wall QCD. Phys Rev Lett 100:032001 [hep-ph/0702042]
9. RBC+UKQCD Collaboration, Yamazaki T et al (2008) Nucleon axial charge in 2 + 1 flavor dynamical lattice QCD with domain wall fermions. Phys Rev Lett 100:171602 [0801.4016]
10. Boyle PA et al (2008) Kl3 semileptonic form factor from 2 + 1 flavour lattice QCD. Phys Rev Lett 100:141601 [0710.5136]
11. Boyle P et al (2005) Overview of the qcdsp and qcdoc computers. IBM Res J 49:351–350
12. Mawhinney RD (1999) The 1 teraflops qcdsp computer. Parallel Comput 25:1281 [hep-lat/0001033]
13. Arsenin I et al (1994) A 0.5-teraflops machine optimized for lattice QCD. Nucl Phys Proc Suppl 34:820–822
14. Chen D et al (1998) The qcdsp project: a status report. Nucl Phys Proc Suppl 60A:241–245
15. Chen D et al (1999) Status of the qcdsp project. Nucl Phys Proc Suppl 73:898 [hep-lat/9810004]
16. Christ NH (2000) Computers for lattice qcd. Nucl Phys Proc Suppl 83:111–115 [hep-lat/9912009]
17. Chen D et al (2001) QCDOC: a 10-teraflops scale computer for lattice QCD. Nucl Phys Proc Suppl 94:825–832 [hep-lat/0011004]
18. Boyle PA et al (2002) Status of the QCDOC project. Nucl Phys Proc Suppl 106:177–133 [hep-lat/0110124]
19. Boyle PA et al (2003) Status of and performance estimates for QCDOC. Nucl Phys Proc Suppl 119:1041–1043 [hep-lat/0210034]
20. QCDOC Collaboration, Boyle PA, Jung C, Wettig T (2003) The qcdoc supercomputer: hardware, software, and performance. ECONF C0303241:THIT003 [hep-lat/0306023]
21. Boyle PA et al (2004) Hardware and software status of QCDOC. Nucl Phys Proc Suppl 129:838–843 [hep-lat/0309096]
22. Boyle PA et al (2005) Qcdoc: project status and first results. J Phys Conf Ser 16:129–139

QsNet

▶Quadrics

Quadrics

Salvador Coll
Universidad Politécnica de Valencia, Valencia, Spain

Synonyms
QsNet

Definition
Quadrics was a company that produced hardware and software for high-performance interconnection networks used in cluster-based supercomputers. Their main product was QsNet, a high-speed interconnection network that was referred to as Quadrics interconnection network. Quadrics, and QsNet, played a significant role in the supercomputing field from 1996, when the company was created, until 2009, when it was officially closed.

Discussion

Introduction
Quadrics was created in 1996 as a subsidiary of Finmeccanica, a large Italian industrial group, under the name Quadrics Supercomputers World (QSW). The new company inherited the architecture of the Quadrics parallel computer and the Meiko CS-2 supercomputer [2]. The Quadrics computer was originally developed at the Istituto Nazionale di Fisica Nucleare (IFNF) and later commercialized by Alenia Spazio (another Finmeccanica subsidiary). The Meiko CS-2 was a massively parallel supercomputer based on Sun or Fujitsu processors connected by a multistage fat-tree network. The network was implemented by two hardware building blocks, a programmable network interface, called Elan and an 8-way crossbar switch called Elite. That technology was later developed into QsNet by QSW, whose name was shortened to be simply Quadrics on 2002. QsNet proved very successful reaching its peak on June 2003 when six out of the ten fastest supercomputers in the world used the Quadrics interconnect. During 2004, the second generation of the Quadrics network, QsNetII, was deployed. Finally, very close to the completion of the third-generation Quadrics network, QsNetIII, the company was closed on June 2009 and the support was transferred to Vega UK Ltd.

The Quadrics Interconnection Network

The Quadrics network surpassed contemporary high-speed interconnects – such as Gigabit Ethernet [23], GigaNet [26], the Scalable Coherent Interface (SCI) [13], the Gigabyte System Network (HiPPI-6400) [25], and Myrinet [4] – in functionality with an approach that integrated a node's local virtual memory into a globally shared, virtual-memory space; provided a programmable processor in the network interface that allowed the implementation of intelligent communication protocols; delivered integrated network fault detection and fault tolerance; and supported collective communication operations at hardware level.

The Quadrics interconnection network is a bidirectional multistage interconnection network with a connection pattern among stages known as butterfly. It is based on 4×4 switches, and can be viewed as a quaternary fat tree [14]. QsNet is based on two custom ASICs: a communication coprocessor called Elan, integrated into a network interface card, and a high-bandwidth, low-latency, communication switch called Elite. It uses wormhole switching with two virtual channels per physical link, source-based routing and adaptive routing. The main specifications of the two commercialized QsNet generations are summarized in Table 1 for the network interface card, and in Table 2 for the network switches.

QsNet connects Elite switches in a quaternary fat-tree topology, which belongs to the more general class of k-ary n-trees [18, 19]. A quaternary fat-tree of dimension n is composed of 4^n processing nodes and $n \times 4^{n-1}$ switches interconnected as a butterfly network (see below); it can be recursively built by connecting four quaternary fat trees of dimension $n - 1$.

Fat-Tree (k-ary n-tree)

A k-ary n-tree is composed of two types of vertices: $N = k^n$ processing nodes and nk^{n-1} $k \times k$ communication switches (a k-ary n-tree of dimension $n = 0$ is composed of a single processing node). Each node is an n-tuple $\{0, 1, ..., k - 1\}^n$, while each switch is defined as an ordered pair (w, l), where $w \in \{0, 1, ..., k - 1\}^{n-1}$ and $l \in \{0, 1, ..., n - 1\}$.

- Two switches $(w_0, w_1, ..., w_{n-2}, l)$ and $(w'_0, w'_1, ..., w'_{n-2}, l')$ are connected by an edge if and only if $l' = l + 1$ and $w_i = w'_i$ for all $i \neq l$. The edge is labeled

Quadrics. Table 1 Quadrics NIC specifications

QsNet	QsNetII
32-bit RISC thread processor	64-bit RISC thread processor
32-bit virtual addressing	64-bit virtual addressing
16Kbytes data cache	32Kbytes data cache
64 Mbytes ECC SDRAM	64 Mbytes DDR SDRAM
PCI 64 bit/66 MHz	PCI-X 64 bit/133 MHz
2×400 MHz byte-wide links	2×1.33 GHz byte-wide links

Quadrics. Table 2 Quadrics switch specifications

QsNet	QsNetII
8 links $\times$ 2 virtual channels	8 links $\times$ 2 virtual channels
35 ns unblocked latency	20 ns unblocked latency

with w'_l on the level l vertex and with w_l on the level l' vertex.

- There is an edge between the switch $(w_0, w_1, ..., w_{n-2}, n - 1)$ and the processing node $p_0, p_1, ..., p_{n-1}$ if and only if $w_i = p_i$ for all $i \in \{0, 1, ..., n - 2\}$. This edge is labeled with p_{n-1} on the level $n - 1$ switch.

The labeling scheme shown makes the k-ary n-tree a delta network [8, 9]: any path starting from a level 0 switch and leading to a given node $p_0, p_1, ..., p_{n-1}$ traverses the same sequence of edge labels $(p_0, p_1, ..., p_{n-1})$. An example of such labeling is shown in Fig. 1, for a 64-node QsNet network, that is a 4-ary 3-tree. The above-defined connection pattern among levels is also referred to as butterfly.

First Generation, QsNet

The Elan3 network interface connects the high-performance, multistage Quadrics network to a processing node containing one or more CPUs. In addition to generating and accepting packets to and from the network, the Elan provides substantial local processing power to implement high-level, message-passing protocols such as MPI. The internal functional structure of the Elan3, shown in Fig. 2, centers around two primary processing engines: the microcode processor and thread processor.

The 32-bit microcode processor supports four threads of execution, where each thread can independently issue pipelined memory requests to the memory system. Up to eight requests can be outstanding at

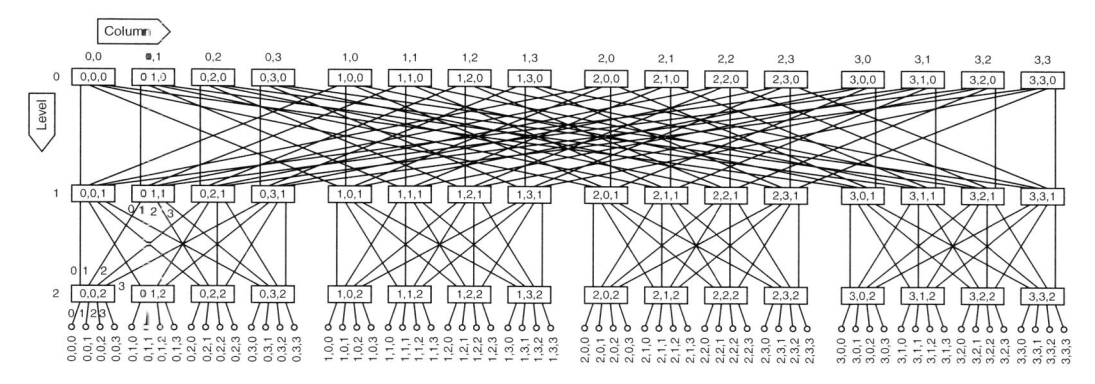

Quadrics. Fig. 1 4-ary 3-tree node, switch, and edge labels

any given time. The scheduling for the code processor enables a thread to wake up, schedule a new memory access on the result of a previous memory access, and go back to sleep in as few as two system-clock cycles.

The four code threads are for

- The inputter, which handles input transactions from the network
- The DMA engine, which generates DMA packets to write to the network, prioritizes outstanding DMAs, and time slices large DMAs to prevent adverse blocking of small DMAs
- Processor-scheduling, which prioritizes and controls the thread processor's scheduling and descheduling
- The command processing, which handles requested operations (commands) from the host processor at the user level

The thread processor is a 32-bit RISC processor that helps implement higher-level messaging libraries without explicit intervention from the main CPU. To better support the implementation of high-level, message-passing libraries without the main CPU's explicit intervention, QsNet augments the instruction set with extra instructions. These extra instructions help construct network packets, manipulate events, efficiently schedule threads, and block save and restore a thread's state when scheduling.

The memory management unit (MMU) translates 32-bit virtual addresses into either 28-bit local SDRAM physical addresses or 48-bit peripheral component interconnect (PCI) physical addresses. To translate these addresses, the MMU contains a 16-entry, fully associative, translation look-aside buffer (TLB) and a small data-path and state machine used to perform table walks to fill the TLB and save trap information when the MMU experiences a fault.

The Elan contains routing tables that translate every virtual processor number into a sequence of tags that determine the network route.

Elan has an 8-Kbyte memory cache (organized as 4 sets of 2Kbytes) and 64-Mbyte SDRAM memory. The cache line size is 32 bytes. The cache performs pipelined fills from SDRAM and can issue multiple cache fills and write backs for different units while still being servicing accesses for units that hit on the cache. The SDRAM interface is 64 bits in length with eight check bits added to provide error-correcting code. The memory interface also contains 32-byte write buffer and read buffers.

The link logic transmits and receives data from the network and generates 9 bits and a clock signal on each half of the clock cycle. Each link provides buffer space for two virtual channels with a 128-entry, 16-bit FIFO RAM for flow control.

The Elite provides the following features:

- Eight bidirectional links supporting two virtual channels in each direction
- An internal 16 × 8 full crossbar switch (the crossbar has two input ports for each input link to accommodate two virtual channels)
- Packet error detection and recovery with cyclic-redundancy check-protected routing and data transactions
- Two priority levels combined with an aging mechanism to ensure fair delivery of packets in the same priority level

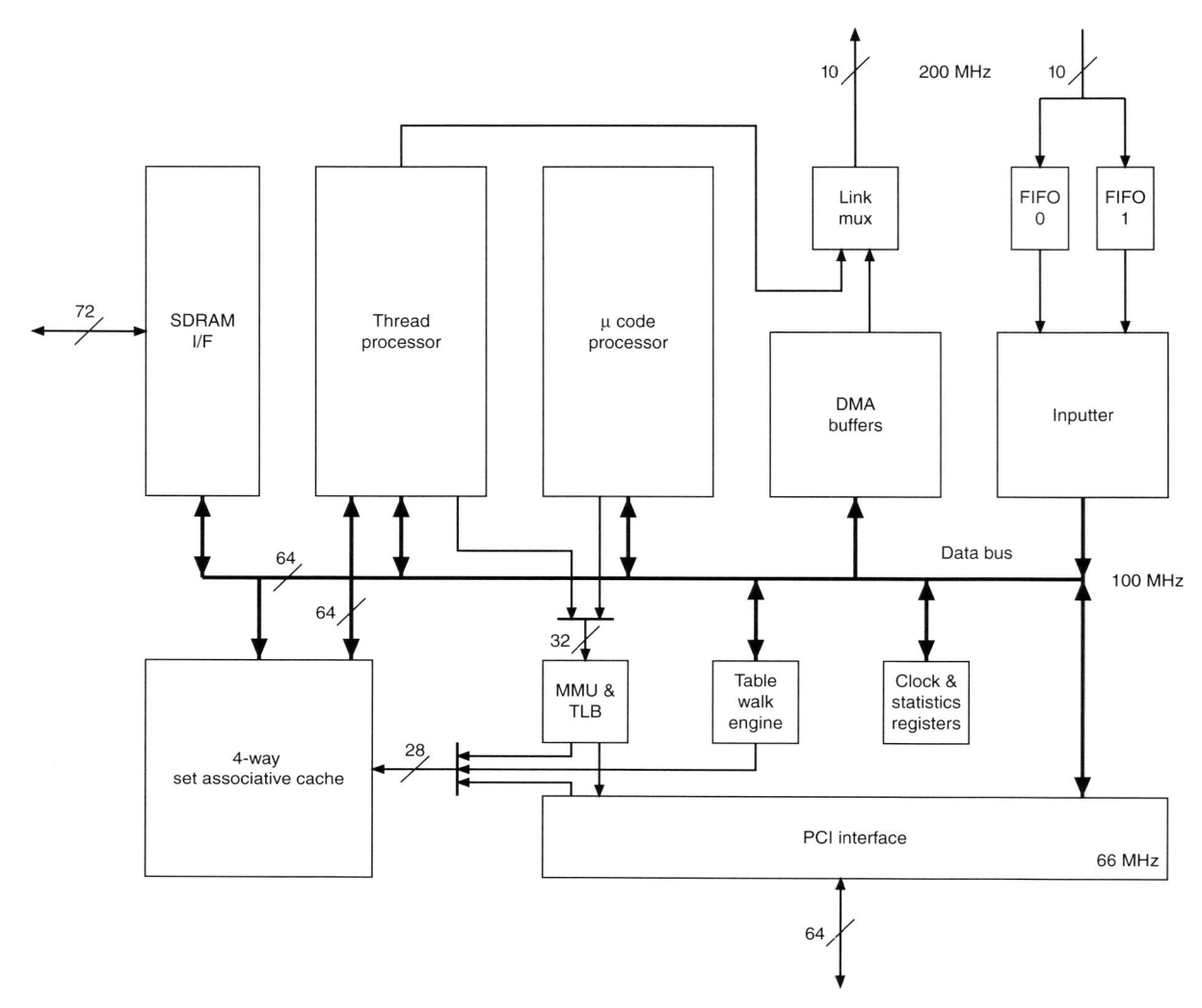

Quadrics. Fig. 2 Elan3 functional units

- Hardware support for collective communication
- Adaptive routing

Multiple Network Rails

One novel solution exploited by Quadrics-based systems to the issues of limited bandwidth availability in network connections, and of fault tolerance, is the use of multiple independent networks (also known as rails) [6]. Support for multirail networks has been included for all the QsNet products. In a multirail system, the network is replicated. In this way, each node can be connected to two or more networks through multiple network interface cards.

Packet Routing and Flow Control

Each user- and system-level message is chunked in a sequence of packets by the Elan. An Elan packet contains three main components. The packet starts with the (1) routing information, which determines how the packet will reach the destination. This information is followed by (2) one or more transactions consisting of some header information, a remote memory address, the context identifier and a chunk of data, which can

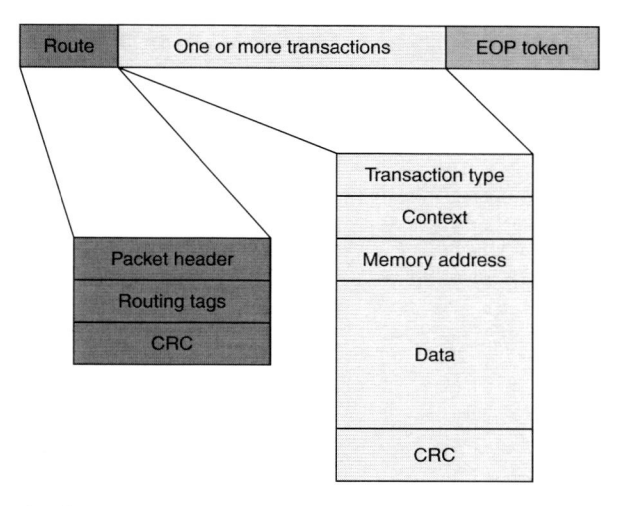

Quadrics. Fig. 3 Packet transaction format

be up to 64 bytes in the current implementation. The packet is terminated by (3) an end of packet (EOP) token, as shown in Fig. 3.

Transactions fall into two categories: write block transactions and non-write block transactions. The purpose of a write block transaction is to write a block of data from the source node to the destination node, using the destination address contained in the transaction immediately before the data. A DMA operation is implemented as a sequence of write block transactions, partitioned into one or more packets (a packet normally contains five write block transactions of 64 bytes each, for a total of 320 bytes of data payload per packet). The non-write block transactions implement a family of relatively low-level communication and synchronization primitives. For example, non-write block transactions can atomically perform remote test-and-write or fetch-and-add and return the result of the remote operation to the source, and can be used as building blocks for more sophisticated distributed algorithms.

Elite networks are source routed. The Elan network interface, which resides in the network node, attaches route information to the packet header before injecting the packet into the network. The route information is a sequence of Elite link tags. As the packet moves inside the network, each Elite switch removes the first route tag from the header and forwards the packet to the next Elite switch in the route or to the final destination. The routing tag can identify either a single link (used for point-to-point communication) or a group of adjacent links (used for collective communication).

The Elan interface pipelines each packet transmission into the network using wormhole flow control. At the link level, the Elan interface partitions each packet into smaller 16-bit units called flow control digits or *flits* [7]. Every packet closes with an end-of-packet token, but the source Elan normally only sends the end-of-packet token after receipt of a packet acknowledgment token. This process implies that every packet transmission creates a virtual circuit between source and destination. It is worth noting that both acknowledgment and EOP can be tagged to communicate control information. So, for example, the destination can notify the successful completion of a remote non-write block transaction without explicitly sending an extra packet.

Minimal routing between any pair of nodes is accomplished by sending the message to one of the nearest common ancestor switches and from there to the destination [9]. In this way, each packet experiences two routing phases: an adaptive ascending phase (in forward direction) to get to a nearest common ancestor, where the switches forward the packet through the least loaded link; and a deterministic descending phase (in backward direction) to the destination.

Network nodes can send packets to multiple destinations using the network's broadcast capability. For successful broadcast packet delivery, the source node must receive a positive acknowledgment from all the broadcast group recipients. All Elan interfaces connected to the network can receive the broadcast packet but, if desired, the sender can limit the broadcast set to a subset of physically contiguous Elans.

Global Virtual Memory

Elan can transfer information directly between the address spaces of groups of cooperating processes while maintaining hardware protection between these process groups. This capability (called virtual operation) is a sophisticated extension to the conventional virtual memory mechanism that is based on two concepts: Elan virtual memory and Elan context.

Elan virtual memory. Elan contains an MMU to translate the virtual memory addresses issued by the various on-chip functional units (thread processor, DMA engine, and so on) into physical addresses. These physical memory addresses can refer to either Elan local memory (SDRAM) or the node's main memory. To support main memory accesses, the configuration tables for the Elan MMU are synchronized with the main processor's MMU tables so that Elan can access its virtual address space. The system software is responsible for MMU table synchronization and is invisible to programmers.

The Elan MMU can translate between virtual addresses in the main processor format (e.g., a 64-bit word, big-endian architecture, such as that of the AlphaServer) and virtual addresses written in the Elan format (a 32-bit word, little-endian architecture). A processor with a 32-bit architecture (e.g., an Intel Pentium) requires only one-to-one mapping. Figure 4 shows a 64-bit processor mapping. The 64-bit addresses starting at 0x1FF0C808000 are mapped to the Elan's 32-bit addresses starting at 0xC808000. This means that the main processor can directly access virtual addresses in the range 0x1FF0C808000 to 0x1FFFFFFFFFF, and Elan can access the same memory with addresses in the 0xC808000 to 0xFFFFFFFF range. In our example, the user can allocate main memory using `malloc`, and the process heap can grow outside the region directly accessible by the Elan, which is delimited by 0x1FFFFFFFFFF. To avoid this problem, both the main and Elan memory can be allocated using a consistent memory allocation mechanism.

As shown in Fig. 4, the MMU tables can map a common region of virtual memory called the memory allocator heap. The allocator maps, on demand, physical pages (of either main or Elan memory) into this virtual address range. Thus, using allocation functions provided by the Elan library, the user can allocate portions of virtual memory either from main or Elan memory, and the main processor and Elan MMUs can be kept consistent.

Elan context. In a conventional virtual-memory system, each user process has an assigned process identification number that selects the MMU table set and, therefore, the physical address spaces accessible to the user process. QsNet extends this concept so that the user address spaces in a parallel program can intersect. Elan replaces the process identification number value with a context value. User processes can directly access an exported segment of remote memory using a context value and a virtual address. Furthermore, the context value also determines which remote processes can access the address space via the Elan network and where those processes reside. If the user process is multithreaded, the threads will share the same context just as they share the same main-memory address space. If the node has multiple physical CPUs, then different CPUs can execute the individual threads. However, the threads will still share the same context.

Network Fault Detection and Fault Tolerance

QsNet implements network fault detection and tolerance in hardware. (It is important to note that this fault detection and tolerance occurs between two communicating Elans). Under normal operation, the source Elan transmits a packet (i.e., route information for source routing followed by one or more transactions). When the receiver in the destination Elan receives a transaction with an ACK Now flag, it means that this transaction is the last one for the packet. The destination Elan then sends a packet acknowledgment token back to the source Elan. Only when the source Elan receives the packet acknowledgment token does it send an end-of-packet token to indicate the packet transfer's completion. The fundamental rule of Elan network operation

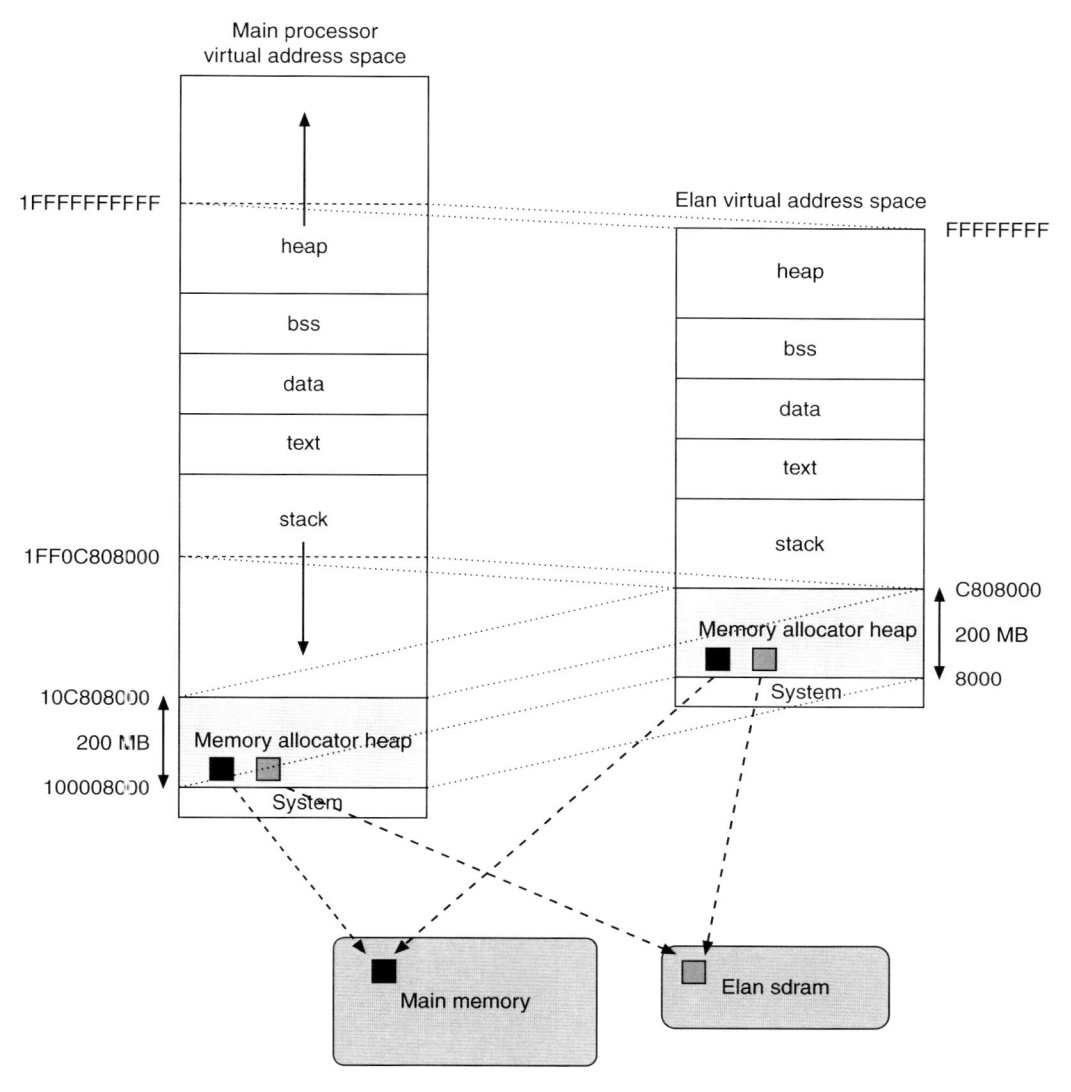

Quadrics. Fig. 4 Virtual address translation. The *dotted lines* in the figure signify that a segment of memory from one address space maps onto an equally sized segment of memory in another address space

is that for every packet sent down a link, an Elan interface returns a single packet-acknowledgment token. The network will not reuse the link until the destination Elan sends such a token.

If an Elan detects an error during a packet transmission over QsNet, it immediately sends an error message without waiting for a packet-acknowledgment token. If an Elite detects an error, it automatically transmits an error message back to the source and the destination. During this process, the source and destination Elans and the Elites between them isolate the faulty link and/or switch via per-hop fault detection [21]; the source receives notification about the faulty component and can retry the packet transmission a default number of times. If this is unsuccessful, the source can appropriately reconfigure its routing tables to avoid the faulty component.

Communication Libraries

With respect to software, QsNet provides several layers of communication libraries that trade off performance with machine independence and programmability. Figure 5 shows the different programming libraries for the Elan network interface. The Elan3lib provides the

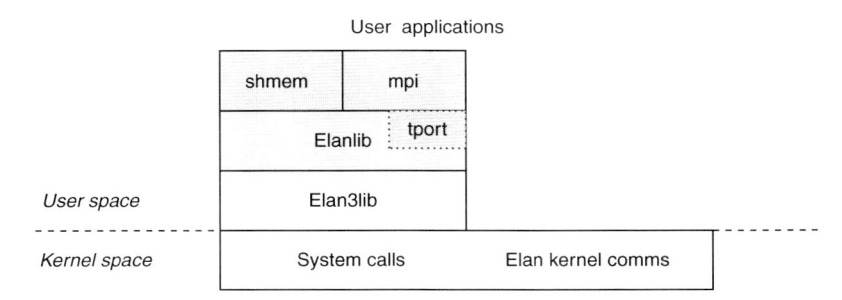

Quadrics. Fig. 5 Elan programming libraries

lowest-level, user space programming interface to the Elan3. At this level, processes in a parallel job can communicate through an abstraction of distributed, virtual, shared memory. Each process in a parallel job is allocated a virtual process identification (VPID) number and can map a portion of its address space into an Elan. These address spaces, taken in combination, constitute a distributed, virtual, shared memory. A combination of a VPID and a virtual address can provide an address for remote memory (i.e., memory on another processing node belonging to a process). The system software and the Elan hardware use VPID to locate the Elan context when they perform a remote communication. Since Elan has its own MMU, a process can select which part of its address space should be visible across the network, determine specific access rights (e.g., write or read only), and select the set of potential communication partners.

Elanlib is a higher-level interface that releases the programmer from the revision-dependent details of Elan and extends Elan3lib with collective communication primitives and point-to-point, tagged message-passing primitives (called tagged message ports or Tports). Standard communication libraries such as that of the MPI-2 standard [12, 24] or Cray SHMEM are implemented on top of Elanlib.

Elan3lib

The Elan3lib library supports a programming environment where groups of cooperating processes can transfer data directly, while protecting process groups from each other in hardware. The communication takes place at the user level, with no copy, bypassing the operating system. The main features of Elan3lib are the memory mapping and allocation scheme (described previously), event notification, and remote DMA transfers.

Events provide a general-purpose mechanism for processes to synchronize their actions. Threads running on Elan and processes running on the main processor can use this mechanism. Processes, threads, packets, etc. can access events both locally and remotely. In this way, intranetwork synchronization of processes is possible, and events can indicate the end of a communication operation, such as the completion of a remote DMA. QsNet stores events in Elan memory to guarantee atomic execution of the synchronization primitives. (The current PCI bus implementations cannot guarantee atomic execution, so it is not possible to store events in main memory). Processes can wait for an event by busy-waiting, or polling. In addition, processes can tag an event as block copy. The block-copy mechanism works as follows: A process can initialize a block of data in Elan memory to hold a predefined value. An equivalent-sized block is located in main memory, and both blocks are in the user's virtual address space. When the specified event is set, for example when a DMA transfer has completed, a block copy takes place. That is, the hardware in the Elan, the DMA engine, copies the block in Elan memory to the block in main memory. The user process polls the block in main memory to check its value (by, e.g., bringing a copy of the corresponding memory block into the level-two cache) without polling for this information across the PCI bus. When the value is the same as that initialized in the source block, the process knows that the specified event has occurred.

The Elan supports remote DMA transfers across the network, without any copying, buffering, or operating system intervention. The process that initiates the DMA fills out a DMA descriptor, which is typically allocated on the Elan memory for efficiency. The DMA descriptor contains source and destination process VPIDs, the amount of data, source and destination addresses, two event locations (one for the source and the other for the destination process), and other information that enhances fault tolerance. Figure 6 outlines the typical steps of remote DMA. The command processor referred to in the figure is an Elan microcode thread that processes user commands; it is not a specific microprocessor.

Elanlib

Elanlib is a machine-independent library that integrates the main features of Elan3lib with higher-level collective communication primitives and Tports.

Tports provide basic mechanisms for point-to-point message passing. Senders can label each message with a tag, sender identity, and message size. This information is known as the envelope. Receivers can receive their messages selectively, filtering them according to the sender's identity and/or a tag on the envelope. The Tports layer handles communication via shared memory for processes on the same node. The Tports programming interface is very similar to that of MPI.

Tports implement message sends (and receives) with two distinct function calls: a non-blocking send that posts and performs the message communication, and a blocking send that waits until the matching start send is completed, allowing implementation of different flavors of higher-level communication primitives.

Tports can deliver messages synchronously and asynchronously. They transfer synchronous messages from sender to receiver with no intermediate system buffering; the message does not leave the sender until the receiver requests it. QsNet copies asynchronous messages directly to the receiver's buffers if the receiver has requested them. If the receiver has not requested them, it copies asynchronous messages into a system buffer at the destination.

Collective Communication Support

The basic hardware mechanism that supports collective communication is provided by the Elite switches. The Elite switches can forward a packet to several output ports, with the only restriction that these ports must be contiguous. In this way, a group of adjacent nodes can be reached by using a single hardware multicast transaction. When the destination nodes are not contiguous, this hardware mechanism is not usable. Instead, a software-based implementation which uses a tree and point-to-point messages, exchanged by the Elans without interrupting their processing nodes, is used. These mechanisms constitute the basic blocks to implement collective communication patterns such as barrier synchronization, broadcast, reduce, and reduce-to-all.

Hardware-Based Multicast

The routing phases for multicast packets differ from those defined for unicast packets. With multicast, during the ascending phase the nearest common ancestor switch for the source node and the destination group is reached. After that, the turnaround routing step is performed and, during the second routing phase, the packet spans the appropriate links to reach all the destination nodes.

The operation of the hardware-based multicast is outlined in Fig. 7. A process in a node injects a multicast packet into the network (see Fig. 7(a)). In Fig. 7(b) the packet reaches the nearest common ancestor switch, and then multiple branches are propagated in parallel. All nodes are capable of receiving a multicast packet, as long as the multicast set is physically contiguous. For a multicast packet to be successfully delivered, a positive acknowledgment must be received from all the recipients of the multicast group. The Elite switches combine the acknowledgments, as pioneered by the NYU Ultracomputer [3, 20], returning a single one to the source (see Figs. 7(c) and 7(d)). Acknowledgments are combined in a way that the worst ack wins (a network error wins over an unsuccessful transaction, which on its turn wins over a successful one), returning a positive acknowledgment only when all the partners in the collective communication complete the distributed transaction with success.

The network hardware guarantees the atomic execution of the multicast: either all nodes successfully complete the operation or none. It is worth noting that the multicast packet opens a set of circuits from the source to the destination set, and that multiple transactions (up to 16 in the current implementation) can be pipelined

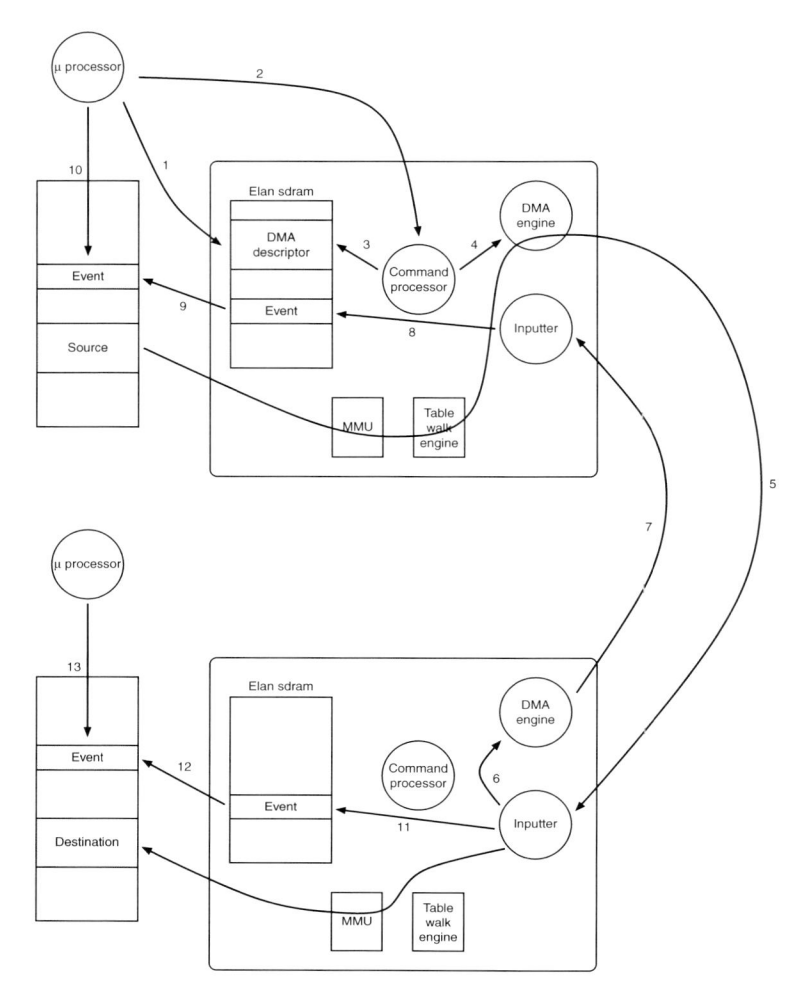

Quadrics. Fig. 6 Execution of a remote DMA. The sending process initializes the DMA descriptor in the Elan memory (1) and communicates the address of the DMA descriptor to the command processor (2). The command processor checks the correctness of the DMA descriptor (3) and adds it to the DMA queue (4). The DMA engine performs the remote DMA transaction (5). Upon transaction completion, the remote inputter notifies the DMA engine (6), which sends an acknowledgment to the source Elan's inputter (7). The inputters or the hardware in the Elan can notify source (8, 9, 10) and destination (11, 12, 13) events, if needed

within a single packet. For example, it is possible to conditionally issue a transaction based on the result of a previous transaction. This powerful mechanism allows the efficient implementation of sophisticated collective operations and high-level protocols [10, 11].

Second Generation, QsNetII

The QsNetII network has been designed to optimize the interprocessor communication performance in systems constructed from standard server building blocks. The organization of the network remains the same while outperforming what it was achieved with QsNet. The network is based on two building blocks: Elan4, a communication processor for the network interface and Elite4, an 8-way high-performance crossbar switch. The network interface incorporates a number of innovative features to minimize latency for short messages, and achieve the maximum bandwidth from a standard PCI-X interface. The network interface has a full 64-bit virtual addressing capability and can perform RDMA operation from user space to user space in 64-bit architectures. As in the QsNet an embedded I/O processor,

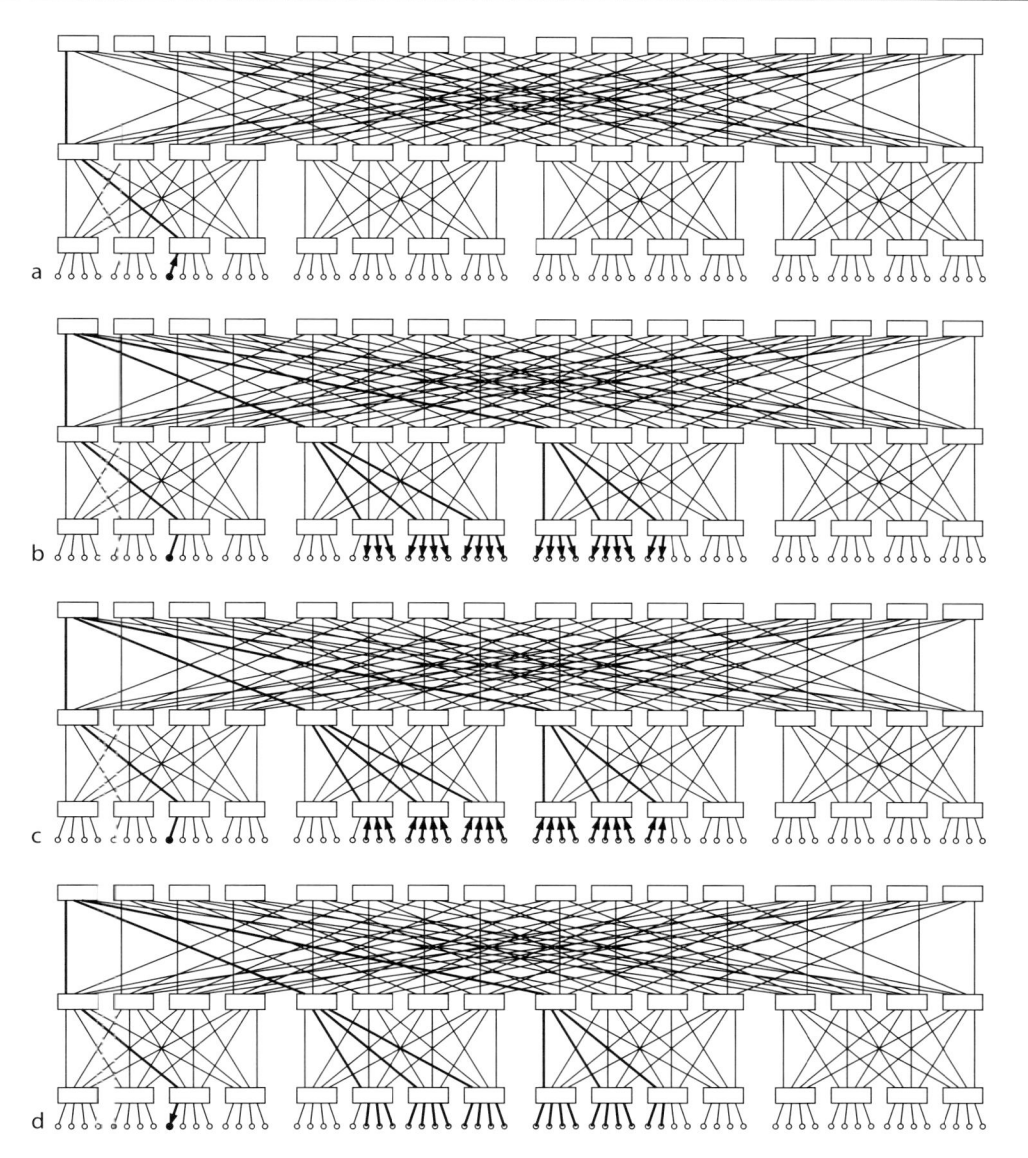

Quadrics. Fig. 7 Hardware-based multicast quadrics. (**a**) A process in node injects a packet into the network (the ascending routing phase in shown); (**b**) The packet reaches the destinations passing through a nearest common ancestor switch (descending routing phase shown); (**c**) The acknowledgments are combined; (**d**) The issuing process receives a single acknowledgment

which is user programmable can be used to offload asynchronous protocol handling tasks.

As an improvement from the first generation, apart from the technology evolution summarized in Table 1 and Table 2, QsNetII includes specific hardware at Elan level for processing short reads and writes and protocol control to provide very low latencies. Elan4 architecture allows data flow from the PCI-X bus directly to the output link, thus providing very low latency and high bandwidth.

Related Entries

- ▶ All-to-All
- ▶ Broadcast
- ▶ Buses and Crossbars
- ▶ Clusters

- ►Collective Communication
- ►Collective Communication, Network Support for
- ►Flow Control
- ►Interconnection Networks
- ►Meiko
- ►MPI (Message Passing Interface)
- ►Myrinet
- ►Network Interfaces
- ►Network of Workstations
- ►Networks, Fault-Tolerant
- ►Networks, Multistage
- ►OpenSHMEM - Toward a Unified RMA Model
- ►Routing (Including Deadlock Avoidance)
- ►SCI (Scalable Coherent Interface)
- ►Scheduling Algorithms
- ►Shared-Memory Multiprocessors
- ►Switch Architecture
- ►Switching Techniques
- ►Top500
- ►Ultracomputer, NYU

Bibliographic Notes and Further Reading

As indicated in the introduction, QsNet inherited the architecture of the Meiko CS-2 supercomputer whose design is described in [2]. Many of the performance characteristics of QsNet rely on the fat-tree topology used in the network implementation. Fat-tree networks were first introduced by Charles E. Leiserson in 1985 [14], and later used in the Connection Machine CM5 supercomputer [15]. In [18], Fabrizio Petrini and Marco Vanneschi presented the first formal model of k-ary n-trees based on a recursive definition of fat-tree networks built with constant arity switches.

A description and evaluation of point-to-point communication in QsNet is reported in [16], while extensions of the previous paper with an evaluation of permutation patterns, scalability of uniform traffic, analysis of I/O traffic, and collective communication are presented in [5, 17]. In [11], the QsNet high-performance collective communication primitives are shown to be a key factor to provide resource-management functions, orders of magnitude faster than previously reported results.

A novel technique introduced by Quadrics is the use of independent network rails to overcome bandwidth limitations and enhance fault tolerance. In [6], various venues of exploiting multiple rails are presented and analyzed.

Finally, QsNetII is presented and evaluated in [1] while QsNetIII, that was never commercialized, is described in [22].

Bibliography

1. Beecroft J, Addison D, Hewson D, McLaren M, Roweth D, Petrini F, Nieplocha J (2005) QsNetII: defining high-performance network design. IEEE Micro 25(4):34–47
2. Beecroft J, Homewood M, McLaren M (1994) Meiko cs-2 interconnect elan-elite design. Parallel Comput 20(10–11):1627–1638
3. Bell G (1992) Ultracomputers: a teraflop before its time. Communications of the ACM 35(8):27–47
4. Boden NJ, Cohen D, Felderman RE, Kulawik AE, Seitz CL, Seizovic JN, Su W-K (1995) Myrinet: a gigabit per-second local area network. IEEE Micro 15(1):29–36
5. Coll S, Duato J, Mora F, Petrini F, Hoisie A (2003) Collective communication patterns on the Quadrics network. In: Getov V, Gerndt M, Hoisie A, Malony A, Miller B, (eds) Performance analysis and grid computing, Chapter 1, Kluwer Academic, Norwell, MA, pp 93–107
6. Coll S, Frachtenberg E, Petrini F, Hoisie A, Gurvits L (2003) Using multirail networks in high-performance clusters. Concurrency Computat Pract Exper 15(7–8):625–651
7. Dally WJ, Seitz CL (1987) Deadlock-free message routing in multiprocessor interconnection networks. IEEE Trans Comput C-36(5):547–553
8. Dally WJ, Towles B (2004) Principles and practices of interconnection networks. Morgan Kaufmann, San Francisco, CA
9. Duato J, Yalamanchili S, Ni L (2002) Interconnection networks: an engineering approach. Morgan Kaufmann, San Francisco, CA
10. Fernández J, Frachtenberg E, Petrini F (2003) BCS-MPI: a new approach in the system software design for large-scale parallel computers. In: ACM/IEEE SC2003, Phoenix, Arizona
11. Frachtenberg E, Petrini F, Fernandez J, Pakin S, Coll S (2002) Storm: lightning-fast resource management. In: IEEE/ACM SC2002, Baltimore, MD
12. Gropp W, Huss-Lederman S, Lumsdaine A, Lusk E, Nitzberg B, Saphir W, Snir M (1998) MPI - the complete reference, vol 2, the MPI extensions. The MIT Press, Cambridge, London
13. Hellwagner H (1999) The SCI Standard and Applications of SCI. In: Hellwagner H, Reinfeld A (eds) SCI: scalable coherent interface, vol 1291 of lecture notes in computer science. Springer, Berlin, pp 95–116
14. Leiserson CE (1985) Fat-Trees: universal networks for hardware efficient supercomputing. IEEE Trans Comput C-34(10):892–901
15. Leiserson CE et al (1996) The network architecture of the connection machine CM-5. J Parallel Distrib Comput 33(2):145–158
16. Petrini F, Vanneschi M (1997) k-ary n-trees: high performance networks for massively parallel architectures. In: Proceedings of the 11th international parallel processing symposium, IPPS'97, Geneva, Switzerland, pp 87–93 April 1997

17. Petrini F, Vanneschi M (1998) Performance analysis of wormhole routed k-ary n-trees. Int J Found Comput Sci 9(2):157–177
18. Petrini F, Feng W-C, Hoisie A, Coll S, Frachtenberg E (2002) The Quadrics network: high-performance clustering technology. IEEE Micro, 22(1):46–57
19. Petrini F, Frachtenberg E, Hoisie A, Coll S (2003) Performance evaluation of the quadrics interconnection network. Cluster Comput 6(2):125–142
20. Pfister GF, Norton VA (1985) "Hot Spot" contention and combining in multistage interconnection networks. IEEE Trans Comput C-34(10):943–948
21. Quadrics Supercomputers World Ltd (1999) Elan programming manual. Bristol, England, UK
22. Roweth D, Jones T (2008) QsNetIII an adaptively routed network for high performance computing. In: Proceedings of the 2008 16th IEEE symposium on high performance interconnects, HOTI '08 Washington, DC, pp 157–164
23. Seifert R (1998) Gigabit ethernet: technology and applications for high speed LANs. Addison-Wesley Boston, MA
24. Snir M, Otto S, Huss-Lederman S, Walker D, Dongarra J (1998) MPI - the complete reference, vol 1, the MPI core. The MIT Press, Cambridge, London
25. Tolmie D, Boorman TM, DuBois A, DuBois D, Feng W, Philp I (1999) From HiPPI-800 to HiPPI-6400: a changing of the guard and gateway to the future. In: Proceedings of the 6th international conference on parallel interconnects (PI'99), Anchorage, AK
26. Vogels W, Follett D, Hsieh J, Lifka D, Stern D (2000) Tree-saturation control in the AC3 velocity cluster. In: Proceedings of the eighth symposium on high performance interconnects (HOTI'00), Stanford University, Palo Alto CA

Quantum Chemistry

▶NWChem

Quantum Chromodynamics (QCD) Computations

▶QCD (Quantum Chromodynamics) Computations

Quicksort

▶Sorting

R

Race

▶ Race Conditions

Race Conditions

CHRISTOPH VON PRAUN
Georg-Simon-Ohm University of Applied Sciences, Nuremberg, Germany

Synonyms
Access anomaly; Critical race; Determinacy race; Harmful shared-memory access; Race; Race hazard

Definition
A race condition occurs in a parallel program execution when two or more threads access a common resource, e.g., a variable in shared memory, and the order of the accesses depends on the timing, i.e., the progress of individual threads.

The disposition for a race condition is in the parallel program. In different executions of the same program on the same input access events that constitute a race can occur in different order, which may but does not generally result in different program behaviors (non-determinacy).

Race conditions that can cause unintended non-determinacy are programming errors. Examples of such programming errors are violations of atomicity due to incorrect synchronization.

Discussion

Introduction
Race conditions are common on access to shared resources that facilitate inter-thread synchronization or communication, e.g., locks, barriers, or concurrent data structures.

Such structures are called *concurrent objects* [7], since they operate correctly even when being accessed concurrently by multiple threads.

The term *concurrent* refers to the fact that the real-time order in which accesses from different threads execute is not predetermined by the program. Concurrent may but does not necessarily mean *simultaneous*, i.e., that the execution of accesses overlaps in real time.

Concurrent objects can be regarded as *arbiters* that decide on the outcome of race conditions. Threads that participate in a race when accessing a concurrent object will find agreement about the outcome of the race; hence access to concurrent objects is a form of inter-thread *synchronization*.

A common and intuitive correctness criterion for the behavior of a concurrent object is *linearizability* [8], which informally means that accesses from different threads behave as if the accesses of all threads were executed in some total order that is compatible with the program order within each thread and the real-time order.

Linearizability is not a natural property of concurrent systems. Ordinary load and store operations on weakly-ordered shared memory, e.g., can expose many more behaviors than permitted by the strong rules of linearizability. Hence when implementing concurrent objects on such systems, specific algorithms or hardware synchronization instructions are required to ensure correct, i.e., linearizable, operation.

Race conditions on access to resources that are not designed as concurrent objects, e.g., shared memory locations with ordinary load and store operations, are commonly considered as programming errors. An example of such errors are *data races*. Informally, a data race occurs when multiple threads access the same variable in shared memory; the accesses may occur simultaneously and at least one access modifies the variable.

David Padua (ed.), *Encyclopedia of Parallel Computing*, DOI 10.1007/978-0-387-09766-4,
© Springer Science+Business Media, LLC 2011

Model and Formalization

The definition and formalization of the terminology is adopted from Netzer and Miller [18].

Events An *event* represents an execution instance of a statement or statement sequence in the program. Every event specifies the set of shared memory locations that are read and/or written. In this entry, events typically refer to individual read or write operations that access a single shared memory location.

Simultaneous events Events do not necessarily occur instantaneously, and in parallel programs, events can be unordered.

A simple model that relates the occurrence of events to wall clock time is as follows: The timing of an event is specified by its *start* and *end* instants. Events e_1, e_2 are *simultaneous* if the start of e_1 occurs after the start of e_2 but before the end of e_2, or vice versa. Figure 1 illustrates the concept.

Temporal ordering relation Events that are not simultaneous are ordered by a *temporal ordering relation* $\xrightarrow{T}$, such that $e_1 \xrightarrow{T} e_2 :\Leftrightarrow end(e_1) < start(e_2)$. In the execution of a sequential program $\xrightarrow{T}$ is a total order, for parallel programs $\xrightarrow{T}$ is typically a partial order.

For clarity of the presentation and without limiting generality, the temporal ordering relations in the examples of this entry are total orders.

Shared data dependence relation Another relation among events is the *shared data dependence relation* $\xrightarrow{D}$ that specifies how events communicate through memory. $e_1 \xrightarrow{D} e_2$ holds if e_2 reads a value that was written by e_1. This relation serves to distinguish executions that have the same temporal ordering but differ in the communication among simultaneous events.

Program execution A *program execution* is a triplet $P = \langle E, \xrightarrow{T}, \xrightarrow{D} \rangle$.

Feasible program executions To characterize a race condition in a program execution P, it is necessary to contrast P with other possible executions P' of the same program on the same input. P' can differ from P in the temporal ordering or shared data dependence relation (or both). Moreover, P' should be a *prefix* of P, which means that each thread in P' performs the same or an initial sequence of events as the corresponding thread in P. In other words, the projection for each thread in P' is the same or a prefix of the projection of the corresponding thread in P. The set of such program executions P' is called the set of *feasible program executions* X_f. A feasible execution is one that adheres to the control and data dependencies prescribed by the program.

It is reasonable to contrast P with execution prefixes P', since the focus of interest is on the earliest point of the program execution P where a race condition occurred and thus non-determinacy may have been introduced. The execution that follows from that point on may contain further race conditions or erroneous program behavior but these may merely be a consequence of the initial race condition.

X_f contains, e.g., program executions P' that differ from P only in the temporal ordering relation. In other words, the timing in P' can deviate from the timing in P but not such that any shared data dependencies among events from different threads are resolved differently. Thus P and P' have the same functional behavior. An execution that differs from P in Fig. 2 in such a way is, e.g., $P' = \langle \{e_1, e_2, ..., e_5\}, e_4 \xrightarrow{T'} e_1 \xrightarrow{T'} e_2 \xrightarrow{T'} e_3 \xrightarrow{T'} e_5, \emptyset \rangle$: Reordering the read of shared variable x does not alter the shared data dependence relation.

A somewhat more substantial departure from P but still within the scope of feasible program executions, are executions where shared data dependencies among events from different threads are resolved differently. An execution that differs from P in Fig. 2 in such a way is, e.g., $P'' = \langle \{e_1, e_2, e_3, e_4\}, e_1 \xrightarrow{T''} e_2 \xrightarrow{T''} e_3 \xrightarrow{T''} e_4, e_3 \xrightarrow{D''} e_4 \rangle$: The update of x (event e_3) occurs in this execution before the read of x in event e_4. This induces a new data

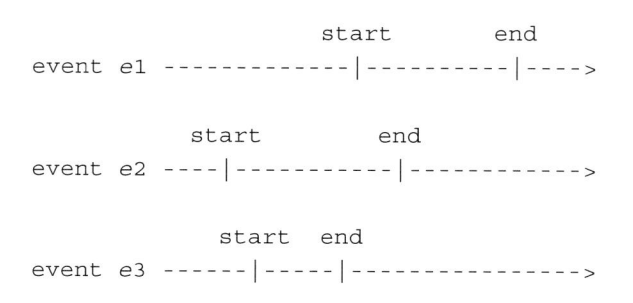

```
                         start           end
      event e1  -------------|-----------|---->

                    start        end
      event e2  ----|-----------|--------------->

                      start  end
      event e3  ------|-----|------------------->
```

Race Conditions. Fig. 1 e_2 is simultaneous to e_1 and e_3

```
initially x = 0
thread-1                    thread-2

(1)   r1 = x                (4)   r2 = x
(2)   if (r1 == 0)          (5)   x = r2 + 1
(3)   x = r1 + 1
```

Race Conditions. Fig. 2 Feasible execution: $P = \langle \{e_1, e_2, ..., e_5\}, e_1 \overset{i}{\to} e_4 \overset{T}{\to} e_2 \overset{T}{\to} e_3 \overset{T}{\to} e_5, \varnothing \rangle$. Events e_i correspond to the execution of statements marked (i). There are no shared data dependencies in this execution

dependence. It is sufficient that P'' specifies a prefix of P, namely, up to the event where the change in the shared data dependence manifests.

Finally, an execution of the program in Fig. 2 that is not feasible: $P''' = \langle \{e_1, e_2, e_3, e_4, e_5\}, e_4 \overset{T'''}{\to} e_5 \overset{T'''}{\to} e_1 \overset{T'''}{\to} e_2 \overset{T'''}{\to} e_3, e_5 \overset{D'''}{\to} e_1 \rangle$. This execution is not possible, since e_3 would not be executed if e_0 read a value different from 0.

Conflicting events A pair of events is called *conflicting*, if both events access the same shared resource and at least one access modifies the resource [21].

General Races and Data Races

Given a program execution $P = \langle E, \overset{T}{\to}, \overset{D}{\to} \rangle$, let X_f be the set of feasible executions corresponding to P.

General race A *general race* exists between conflicting events $a, b \in E$, if there is a $P' = \langle E', \overset{T'}{\to}, \overset{D'}{\to} \rangle \in E$, such that $a, b, \in E'$ and

1. $b \overset{T'}{\to} a$ if $a \overset{T}{\to} b$, or
2. $a \overset{T'}{\to} b$ if $b \overset{T}{\to} a$, or
3. $a \not\to b$.

In other words, there is some order among events a and b but the order is not predetermined by the program (cases 1 and 2), or executions are feasible where a and b occur simultaneously (case 3).

Data race A *data race* is a special case of a general race. A data race exists between conflicting memory accesses $a, b \in E$, if there is a $P' = \langle E', \overset{T'}{\to}, \overset{D'}{\to} \rangle \in X$, such that $a, b, \in E'$ and $a \overset{T'}{\not\to} b$. In other words, executions are feasible where a and b occur simultaneously.

Programmers commonly use *interleaving semantics* when reasoning about concurrent programs. Interleaving semantics mean that the possible behaviors of a parallel program correspond to the sequential execution of events interleaved from different threads. This property of an execution is also called *serializability* [3]. The resulting intuitive execution model is also known as sequential consistency [9].

The motivation for the distinction between data races and general races is to explicitly term those race conditions, where the intuitive reasoning according to interleaving semantics may fail; these are the data races. A common situation where interleaving semantics fails in the presence of data races are concurrent accesses to shared memory in systems that have a memory consistency model that is weaker than sequential consistency [1].

A data race $\langle a, b \rangle$ means that events a and b have the potential of occurring simultaneously in some execution. Simultaneous access can be prevented by augmenting the access sites in the program code with some form of explicit concurrency control. That way, every data race can be turned into a general race that is not a data race.

Race conditions and concurrent objects For linearizable concurrent objects, the distinction between data races and general races among events is immaterial. This is because linearizability requires that events on concurrent objects that are simultaneous behave as if they occurred in some order.

Feasible and Apparent Races

Feasible races So far, the definition of a race condition in P is based on the set of *feasible* program executions X_f. Thus, locating a race condition requires that the feasibility of a program execution P', i.e., $P' \in X_f$, is assessed and that in turn requires a detailed analysis of shared data and control dependencies. This problem NP-hard [16, 17]. Race conditions defined on the basis of feasible program executions are called *feasible general races* and *feasible data races* respectively.

Apparent races Due to the difficulty of verifying the feasibility of a program execution P, common race detection methods widen the set of program executions to consider. The set $X_a \supseteq X_f$ contains all executions

```
initially x,y = 0
thread-1              thread-2

(1)    x = 1          (3)    r1 = y
(2)    y = 1          (4)    if (r1 == 1)
                      (5)    r2 = x
```

Race Conditions. Fig. 3 This program does not have explicit synchronization that would restrict the temporal ordering $\stackrel{T'}{\to}$. Thus the execution $P' = \langle \{e_1, ..., e_5\}, e_3 \stackrel{T}{\to} e_4 \stackrel{T}{\to} e_5 \stackrel{T}{\to} e_1 \stackrel{T}{\to} e_2, \emptyset \rangle$ is in X_a. P' is however not feasible, since control dependence does not allow execution of e_5 if the read in e_3 returns 0

```
initially x,y = 0
thread-1              thread-2

(1)    r1 = x         (4)    r2 = y
(2)    if (r1 == 1)   (5)    if (r2 == 1)
(3)    y = 1          (6)    x = 1
```

Race Conditions. Fig. 4 Program with read and write accesses to shared variables that does neither have a feasible nor an apparent data race

P' that are prefixes of P with the following restriction: The temporal ordering $\stackrel{T'}{\to}$ obeys the program order and inter-thread dependencies due to explicit synchronization; such relation is also known as the happened-before relation [8]. It is not required that P' be feasible with respect to shared data dependencies or control dependencies that result from those. Figure 3 gives an example.

Race conditions that are determined using a superset of feasible program executions, e.g., X_a, are called *apparent general races* and *apparent data races* respectively. Note that this definition of race conditions depends on the specifics of the synchronization mechanism.

The notion of feasible races is more restricting than the notion of apparent races. This means that an algorithm that detects apparent races considers executions that are not feasible and therefore may report race conditions that could never occur in a real program execution. Such reports are called *spurious races*.

Figure 4 shows another example to illustrate the notion of apparent races further. This program does not have explicit synchronization and has read and write accesses to shared variables x and y.

Perhaps surprisingly, the program in Fig. 4 does neither have an apparent nor a feasible data race. The reason is that there is no program execution P that contains event e_3 or e_6. Hence the sets X_f or X_a, which are defined based on P, cannot contain those events either and hence neither X_f nor X_a would lead us to determine a feasible respectively apparent race condition.

Some of the literature does not explicitly distinguish apparent and feasible races, i.e., the term "race" may refer to either of the two definitions, depending on the context.

Actual data races An *actual data race* exists in execution $P = \langle E, \stackrel{T}{\to}, \stackrel{D}{\to} \rangle$, if events $a, b \in E$ are conflicting and both events occur simultaneously, i.e., $a \not\stackrel{T'}{\to} b$.

Race Conditions as Programming Errors

Some race conditions are due to programming errors and some are part of the intended program behavior. The distinction between the two is commonly made along the distinction of data races and general races: data races are programming errors, whereas general races that are not data races are considered as "normal" behavior. While such distinction is oftentimes true, exceptions exist and are common.

First, there are correct programs that entail the occurrence of data races at run time. In non-blocking concurrent data structures [13], e.g., data races are intended and considered by the algorithmic design. The development and implementation of such algorithms that "tolerate" race conditions is extremely difficult, since it requires a deep understanding of the shared memory consistency model. Moreover, the implementation of such algorithms is typically not portable, since different platforms may have different shared memory semantics (see ▶"Data-Race-Free Programs").

Data races that are not manifestations of program bugs are called *benign data races*.

Second, there are incorrect programs that have executions with general races that are not data races. An example for such programming error is a *violation of atomicity* [6]: Accesses to a shared resource occur in separate critical sections, although the programmer's intent was to have the accesses in the same atomicity scope.

Non-determinacy Race conditions can but do not necessarily introduce non-determinacy in parallel programs. For a detailed discussion of this aspect, refer to the entry on ▶"Determinacy".

Data-Race-Free Programs

Data races are an important concept to pinpoint certain behaviors of parallel programs that are manifestations of programming errors. But beyond this role, the concept of data races is also important for system architects who design shared *memory consistency models*.

Intuitively, a shared memory consistency model defines the possible values that a read may return considering prior writes. Consider the program execution in Fig. 5.

Despite the fact that this execution is correct according to the memory consistency model of common multiprocessor architectures [23], such program behavior is difficult to analyze and explain. The reason is, that the program execution is not *serializable*, i.e., there is no interleaving of events from different threads that obeys program order and that would justify the results returned by the reads [3].

Why should such behavior be permitted? For optimization of the memory access path, a processor or compiler can reorder and overlap the execution of memory accesses such that the temporal ordering relation $\xrightarrow{T}$, and with it the shared data dependence relation $\xrightarrow{D}$, can differ from the program order. For the program in Fig. 5, one of the processors hoists the read before the writes, thus permitting the result.

To allow such optimization on the one hand and to give programmers an intuitive programming abstraction on the other hand, computer architects have phrased a minimum guarantee that shared memory consistency models should adhere to: *Data-race-free programs* should only have executions that could also occur on sequentially consistent hardware. In other words, the behavior of parallel programs that are *data-race-free* follows the intuitive interleaving semantics. So what means *data-race-free*?

Data-race-free in computer architecture Adve and Hill [2] define a data race as a property of a single program execution: A pair of conflicting accesses participates in a data race, if their execution is not ordered by the happened-before relation [8]. The happened-before relation is defined as the combination of program order and the synchronization order due to synchronization events from different threads. This definition allows, unlike the definition according to Netzer and Miller [18], to validate the presence or absence of data race by inspecting a single program execution. An execution is *data-race-free*, if it does not have a data race. A program is data-race-free, if all possible executions are data-race-free. "Possible executions" are thereby implicitly defined as any executions permitted by the processor, for which the memory model is defined.

Data-race-free in parallel programming languages The developers of parallel programming languages also specify the semantics of shared memory using a memory model [10, 15]. Like memory models at the hardware level, the minimum requirement is that *data-race-free programs* can only have behaviors that could result from sequentially consistent executions.

The definition of what constitutes a data race is however more complex, since building the model entirely around the happened-before relation is not sufficient. This is because the starting point for the definition of data races are programs, not program executions. It is necessary to explicitly define which executions are *feasible* for a given program.

Causality Manson et al. [10] define a set requirements called *causality* that a program execution has to meet to be *feasible*. As an example, consider the program in Fig. 4. The *causality* requirement serves to rule out the feasibility of executions that contain events e_3 or e_6. Intuitively, causality requires that there is a noncyclic

```
    thread-1            thread-2

(1) write(x, 1)     (4) write(y, 5)
(2) write(x, 2)     (5) write(y, 7)
(3) read(y, 5)      (6) read(x, 1)
```

Race Conditions. Fig. 5 Program execution with a data race. This execution is not serializable

chain of "facts" that justify the execution of a statement. The writes e_3, e_6 may only execute if the reads e_1, e_4 returned the value 1. That in turn requires, that the writes executed. This kind of cyclic justification order is forbidden by the Java memory model. This program is hence data-race-free since executions that include the writes e_3, e_6 are not feasible due to a violation of the causality rule.

More generally, the causality requirement reflects on the overall definition of "data-race-free" as follows: Programs that have no data races *in sequentially consistent* executions are called data-race-free. Execution of such programs are always sequentially consistent.

Alternatives to causality Causality has led to significant complexity in the description of the Java memory model and it is not evident that the rules for causality are complete. Hence alternative proposals have been made to specify feasible program executions, e.g., by Saraswat et al. [20].

Effects of Data Races on Program Optimization

Midkiff and Padua [14] observed that program transformations that preserve the semantics of sequential programs may not be correct for parallel programs with data races. Thus, the presence of data races inhibits the optimization potential of compilers for parallel programs.

Race Conditions in Distributed Systems

Race conditions can also occur in distributed systems, e.g., when multiple client computers communicate with a shared server. Conceptually, the shared server is a concurrent object that gives certain guarantees on the behavior of concurrent accesses. Typically, concurrency control at the level of the communication protocol or at the level of the server implementation will ensure that semantics follow certain intuitive and well-understood correctness conditions such as linearizability.

In MPI programs [12], e.g., a race condition may occur at a receive operation (`MPI_Recv`) where the source of the message to be received can be arbitrary (`MPI_ANY_SOURCE`). The order in which concurrent messages from different sources are received can be different in different program runs. The receive operation serializes the arrival of consecutive messages and hence exercises concurrency control.

Related Entries
▶ Determinacy
▶ Memory Models
▶ Race Detection Techniques

Bibliographic Notes and Further Reading

Race conditions and data races have been discussed in early literature about the analysis and debugging of parallel programs [4, 5, 11, 19, 22]. An informal characterization of the term "race" was, e.g., given by Emrath and Padua [5]: *A race exists when two statements in concurrent threads access the same variable in a conflicting way and there is no way to guarantee execution ordering.*

A formal definition is given by Netzer and Miller [18], which is based on the existence of program executions with certain properties as discussed by this entry. This definition however does not lend itself to the design of a practical algorithm that validates the presence or absence of a race condition in a given program execution (see the related entry on Race Detection Techniques).

Hence for practical applications, slightly different definitions of data races are common.

In the context of shared memory models, the interest is mainly in characterizing the absence of data races, hence the definition of data-race-free program executions and data-race-free programs in [2, 10, 15].

Most definitions for data races in the context of static analysis tools make a conservative approximation of the program's data-flow and control-flow and thus are akin to Netzer and Miller's concept of apparent data races. For dynamic data-race detection, the approximations made for the definition of what constitutes a data race may not be conservative any longer: While the goal of dynamic race detection tools is to detect all feasible races on the basis of a single-input-single-execution (SISE) [4], there are feasible data races according to [18] that may be overlooked according to these definitions.

Bibliography

1. Adve S, Gharachorloo K (1996) Shared memory consistency models: a tutorial. IEEE Comput 29:66–76

2. Adve S, Hill M (June 1993) A unified formalization of four shared-memory models. IEEE Trans Parallel Distrib Syst 4(6):613–624
3. Arvind, Maessen J-W (2006) Memory model = instruction reordering + store atomicity. SIGARCH Comput Archit News 34(2):29–40
4. Dinning A, Schonberg E (December 1991) Detecting access anomalies in programs with critical sections. In: Proceedings of the ACM/ONR workshop on parallel and distributed debugging, pp 85–96
5. Emrath PA, Padua DA (January 1989) Automatic detection of nondeterminacy in parallel programs. In: Proceedings of the ACM workshop on parallel and distributed debugging, pp 89–99
6. Flanagan C, Freund SN (2004) Atomizer: a dynamic atomicity checker for multithreaded programs. In: POPL'04: Proceedings of the 31st ACM SIGPLAN-SIGACT symposium on principles of programming languages, ACM, New York, pp 256–267
7. Herlihy MP, Wing JM (July 1990) Linearizability: a correctness condition for concurrent objects. ACM Trans Program Lang Syst (TOPLAS) 12:463–492
8. Lamport L (July 1978) Time, clock and the ordering of events in a distributed system. Commun ACM 21(7):558–565
9. Lamport L (July 1997) How to make a correct multiprocess program execute correctly on a multiprocessor. IEEE Trans Comput 46(7):779–782
10. Manson J, Pugh W, Adve S (2005) The Java memory model. In: Proceedings of the symposium on principles of programming languages (POPL'05), ACM, New York, pp 378–391
11. Mellor-Crummey J (May 1993) Compile-time support for efficient data race detection in shared-memory parallel programs. In: Proceedings of the workshop on parallel and distributed debugging. ACM, New York, pp 129–139
12. Message Passing Interface Forum (June 1995) MPI: a message passing interface standard. http://www.mpi-forum.org/
13. Michael MM, Scott ML (1996) Simple, fast, and practical non-blocking and blocking concurrent queue algorithms. In: PODC'96: Proceedings of the 15th annual ACM symposium on principles of distributed computing. ACM, New York, pp 267–275
14. Midkiff S, Padua D (August 1990) Issues in the optimization of parallel programs. In: Proceedings of the international conference on parallel processing, pp 105–113
15. Nelson C, Boehm H-J (2007) Sequencing and the concurrency memory model (revised). The C++ Standards Committee, Document WG21/N2171 J16/07-0031
16. Netzer R, Miller B (1990) On the complexity of event ordering for shared-memory parallel program executions. In: Proceedings of the international conference on parallel processing, Pennsylvania State University, University Park. Pennsylvania State University Press, University Park, pp 93–97
17. Netzer R, Miller B (July 1991) Improving the accuracy of data race detection. Proceedings of the ACM SIGPLAN symposium on principles and practice of parallel programming PPOPP, published in ACM SIGPLAN NOTICES 26(7):133–144
18. Netzer R, Miller B (March 1992) What are race conditions? Some issues and formalizations. ACM Lett Program Lang Syst 1(1):74–88
19. Nudler I, Rudolph L (1988) Tools for the efficient development of efficient parallel programs. In: Proceedings of the 1st Israeli conference on computer system engineering
20. Saraswat VA, Jagadeesan R, Michael M, von Praun C (2007) A theory of memory models. In: PPoPP'07: Proceedings of the 12th ACM SIGPLAN symposium on principles and practice of parallel programming. ACM, New York, pp 161–172
21. Shasha D, Snir M (April 1988) Efficient and correct execution of parallel programs that share memory. ACM Trans Program Lang Syst 10(2):282–312
22. Sterling N (January 1993) WARLOCK: a static data race analysis tool. In: USENIX Association (ed) Proceedings of the USENIX winter 1993 conference, San Diego, pp 97–106
23. Weaver DL, Germond T (1991) The SPARC architecture manual (version 9)

Race Detection Techniques

CHRISTOPH VON PRAUN
Georg-Simon-Ohm University of Applied Sciences, Nuremberg, Germany

Synonyms
Anomaly detection

Definition
Race detection is the procedure of identifying race conditions in parallel programs and program executions. Unintended race conditions are a common source of error in parallel programs and hence race detection methods play an important role in debugging such errors.

Discussion

Introduction
The following paragraphs summarize the notion of race conditions and data races. An elaborate discussion and detailed definitions are given in the corresponding related entry on "▶race conditions."

Race conditions. A widely accepted definition of race conditions is given by Netzer and Miller [47]: A *general race*, or *race* for short, is a pair of conflicting accesses to a shared resource for which the order of accesses is not guaranteed by the program, i.e., the accesses may execute in either order or simultaneously. A subclass of general races are *data races*, for which conflicting memory accesses may occur simultaneously.

Data races. The bulk of literature on *race detection* discusses methods for the detection of *data races*. Most data races are programming errors, typically due to *omitted synchronization*. Data races can potentially cause the atomicity of critical sections to fail.

Violations of atomicity. Race conditions that are not data races are common in parallel program executions. Some of such races are however programming errors related to *incorrect use of synchronization*. A common example are accesses to a shared resource that occur in separate critical sections, although the programmer's intent was to have the accesses in the same atomicity scope. Such programming errors are commonly called *violations of atomicity* [23]. Taken literally, this terminology seems perhaps too general, since data races, which are non implied by this term, can also cause the atomicity of a critical section to fail.

Detection accuracy. An ideal race detection should have two properties: (1) A race condition is reported if the program or a program execution, whatever is checked, has some race condition. This property is called *soundness*. Notice that if there are several race conditions, soundness does not require that all of them are reported. (2) Every reported race condition is a genuine race condition in a feasible program execution. This property is called *completeness* [24].

Detection methods. *Static methods* analyze the program code and do not require that the program executes. Sound and complete detection of feasible race conditions in a parallel program by static analysis is in general undecidable due to a theoretical result by Ramalingam [56].

Dynamic methods. analyze the event stream from a single program execution, and thus determine the occurrence of a race condition in one program execution. Such analysis can be sound and complete. Naturally, dynamic methods cannot make general statements about the disposition of a race condition in a program. However, the accuracy of a dynamic analysis can be more or less sensitive to the timing of threads. Ideally, a dynamic race detection algorithm has the *single input, single execution* (SISE) property [16], which means that *"A single execution instance is sufficient to determine the existence of an anomaly (data race) for a given input."* In other words, the detection accuracy should be oblivious to the timing of the execution.

When designing a static or dynamic race detection method, trade-offs between performance, resource usage, and accuracy are made. In practice, it is not uncommon that useful tools are unsound, incomplete, or both with respect to the detection of feasible race conditions.

Data Race Detection

There are two principal approaches to detect data races: *happened-before-based* (HB-based) and *lockset-based* methods.

HB-Based Data Race Detection

HB-based data race detection operates typically at runtime, thus validating the occurrence of data races in a program execution.

Data race definition. A data race $\langle a, b \rangle$ is deemed to have occurred in a program execution, if a and b are conflicting accesses to the same resource, and the accesses are *causally unordered*. The causal order among run-time events in a concurrent systems is thereby defined through the *happened-before relation* by Lamport [31].

This definition assesses the existence of a data race on one particular program execution and its HB-relation. Note that this is different from the definition of feasible and apparent data races by Netzer and Miller [47], since their definition assesses the occurrence of a data race on a set of program executions. Thus, it is possible that an execution is classified as "data-race-free" according to the above (HB-based) defintion but it is not data-race-free according to Netzer and Miller's defintion [47]. An example of such a program execution, which is detailed in a later paragraph, is given in Fig. 1.

Happened-before relation. A pair of events $\langle a, b \rangle$ is ordered according to the happened-before relation (HB-relation), if a and b occur in the same thread and are ordered according to the sequential execution of that thread, or a and b are synchronization events in different threads that are ordered due to the synchronization order. Overall, the happened-before relation is a transitive partial order.

The notion of synchronization order depends on the underlying programming model and has been originally described for point-to-point communication in

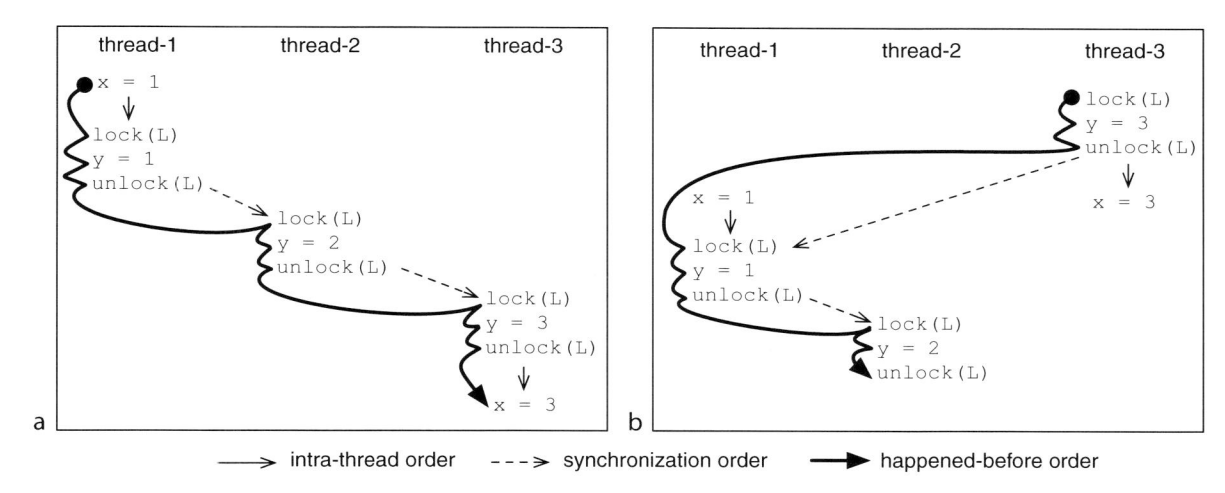

Race Detection Techniques, Fig. 1 In execution (**a**), the assignments to variable x in thread-1 and thread-3 are ordered by the HB-relation. There is however a feasible data race, since these assignments may occur simultaneously as, e.g., in execution (**b**)

distributed systems [31]. The synchronization order has also been defined for synchronization operations on multiprocessor architectures [2, 60], for fork-join synchronization [36], and critical sections [16].

Algorithmic principles. HB-based race detectors perform three tasks: (1) track the HB-relation within each thread; (2) keep an access history as sequence of logical timestamps for each shared resource; (3) validate that, for every resource, critical accesses are ordered by the HB-relation.

Various HB-based race detection algorithms have been proposed; they differ in the precise methods and run-time organization of computing the three tasks.

Accuracy. If the HB-relation is recorded precisely, HB-based data race detection on a specific program execution can be complete and also sound according to the HB-based definition of data races. However, HB-based data race detection is not sound with respect to data races according to Netzer and Miller's definition [45]: Fig. 1 illustrates two executions of the same program, one where the assignments to x are ordered by the HB-relation (a), and one where the assingments occur simultaneously (b). An HB-based race detector applied to execution (a) would not report the data race. In other words, HB-based race detection does not have the SISE property.

Encodings and algorithms for computing the HB-relation. The HB-relation can be represented and recorded precisely during a program execution with standard *vector clocks* [19, 33]. Race detectors that build on standard vector clocks are, e.g., the family of Djit detectors by Pozniansky and Schuster [52, 53]. The algorithm requires that maximum number of threads is specified in advance.

A theoretical result from Charron-Bost [11] implies that the precise computation of vector clocks values for n events in an execution with p processors requires $O(np)$ time and space. Due to this result, the encoding of the HB-relation with vector clocks is considered to be impractical [48].

Performance optimizations. There are two main sources of overhead in HB-based race detection: First, the tracking of logical time, usually by vector clocks or variations. Second, access operations to shared memory and synchronization operations are instrumented to record access histories and verify orderings.

Flanagan and Freund [22] optimize vector clocks with an adaptive representation of timestamps as follows: The majority of memory accesses target thread-local, lock-protected or shared-read data; for such "safe" access patterns a very efficient and compact timestamp representation is used. This representation is adaptively enhanced to a full vector clock when the access patterns deviate from the safe ones; then, access ordering can be validated according to the HB-relation.

Variants of vector clocks with alternative encodings of the HB-relation have been developed to improve the efficiency of tracking logical time and checking the ordering among pairs of accesses. Examples for such encodings are the *English-Hebrew labeling* (EH) by Nudler and Rudolph [50], *task recycling* (TR) by Dinning and Schonberg [15], and *offset-span labeling* (OS) by Mellor-Crummey [36]. These algorithms make trade-offs at different levels: For example, OS does, unlike TR, avoid global communication when computing the timestamps; this makes the algorithm practical for distributed environments. However, OS is limited to nested fork-join synchronization patterns.

The implementation of encodings can be optimized further for efficiency, sometimes however at the cost of reducing the accuracy of the detection. Dinning and Schonberg [15], e.g., limit the size of access histories per variable. Some data races may not be reported due to this optimization, which seemed to occur infrequently in their experiments.

A similar optimization is described by Choi and Min [13]: Their algorithm records only the most recent read and write timestamp for a shared variable; as a concequence, data races that occurred in an execution may not be not reported. They argue however that this optimization preserves the soundness of the detection, i.e., if there is some data race according to the HB-definition, it is reported. An iterative debugging process based on deterministic replay will eventually identify all data races and thus lead to a program execution that is data-race-free (again according to the HB-definition). The significant contribution of Choi and Min [13] is their systematic and provably correct debugging methodology for data races.

Compilers can reduce the overhead of race detection by pruning the instrumentation of accesses that are provably not involved in data races, such as access to thread-local data. Moreover, accesses that lead to *redundant access events* [7, 37] at run-time may also be recognized by a compiler. Static analyses of concurrency properties support this process (see "Static Analysis").

Even if redundant accesses cannot be safely recognized by a compiler, techniques have been developed by Choi et al. [14] to recognize and filter redundant access events at run-time.

Another run-time technique to reduce the overhead of dynamic data race detection is to include only small fractions of the overall program execution (sampling) in the checking process [34]. Perhaps surprisingly, the degradation of accuracy due to an incomplete event trace is moderate and acceptable in the light of significant performance gains.

Race detection in distributed systems. Race detection in distributed systems refers to HB-based data race detection in distributed shared memory (DSM) systems. Perkovic and Keleher, e.g., [51] present an optimized DSM protocol where the tracking of HB-information is piggybacked on the coherence protocol. Another DSM race detection technique is presented by Richards and Larus [57].

Lockset-Based Data Race Detection

Lockset-based data race detection is a technique tailored to programs that use critical sections as their primary synchronization model. Instead of validating the absence of data races directly, the idea of lockset-based data race detection is to validate that a program or program execution adheres to a certain programming policy, called *locking discipline* [59].

Locking discipline. A simple locking policy could, e.g., state that threads that access a common memory location must hold a mutual exclusion lock when performing the access. Compliance with this locking discipline implies that executions are data-race-free. The validation of the locking discipline is done with static or dynamic program analysis, or combinations thereof.

The key ideas of lockset-based data race detection are due to Savage et al. [59], although the concept of *lock covers*, which is related to locksets is discussed earlier by Dinning and Schonberg [16].

Algorithmic principles. Checking a locking discipline works as follows: Each thread tracks at run-time the set of locks it currently holds. Conceptually, each variable in shared memory has a shadow location that holds a lockset. On the first access to a shared variable, the shadow memory is initialized with the lockset of the current thread. On subsequent accesses, the lockset in shadow memory is updated by intersecting it with the lockset of the accessing thread. If the intersection is empty and the variable has been accessed by different threads, a potential data race is reported.

Accuracy. Lockset-based detection is sound. In fact, the validation of a locking discipline has the SISE property, i.e., all race conditions that occur in a certain execution are reported. The detection is however incomplete, since accesses that violate the locking discipline, may be ordered by other means of synchronization.

The principles of lockset-based race detection have been refined with two goals in mind: To increase the accuracy (reduce overreporting) and to improve the performance of dynamic checkers.

Increasing the accuracy. There are several common parallel programming idioms that are data-race-free but violate the simple locking discipline stated before. Examples are initialization without lock protection, read-sharing, or controlled data handoff. To accommodate these patterns, the simple locking policy can be extended as follows: An abstract state machine is associated with each shared memory location. The state machine is designed to identify safe programing idioms in the access stream and to avoid overreporting.

For example, read and write accesses of the initializing thread can proceed safely, even without locking. If other threads read the variable and only read accesses follow, a read-sharing pattern is deemed to have occurred and no violation of the locking policy is reported, even if the accessing threads do not hold a common lock at the time of the accesses [59]. Subsequent work has picked up these ideas and refined the state model to capture more elaborate sharing patterns that are safe [29, 67].

The state model can introduce unsoundness, namely, in cases where the timing of threads in an execution lets an access sequence look like a safe programming idiom, where indeed an actual data race occurred. In practice, the benefits of reduced overreporting outweigh the drawback due to potential unsoundness.

Hybrid data race detection. Some methods for dynamic data race detection [16, 50, 52, 70] combine the lockset algorithm [59] with checks of Lamport's happened-before relation. Such a procedure mitigates the shortcomings of either approach and improves the accuracy of the detection.

Performance optimizations. Dynamic tools can be supported by a compiler that reduces instrumentation and thus the frequency of run-time checks. For example, accesses that are known at compile-time not to participate in data races don't have to be instrumented [14, 50, 67].

Another strategy to reduce the run-time overhead is to track the lockset and state information in shadow memory not per fixed-size variable but at a larger granularity, e.g., at the granularity of programming language objects [67] or minipages [71].

Application to non-blocking synchronization models. Although most work has studied programs with blocking synchronization (locks), the principles are also applicable to optimistic synchronization[55, 69].

Dynamic Methods

So far, data race detection has been described as a dynamic program analysis. Dynamic methods are also called *trace-based*, since subject of the analysis is an execution trace.

Architecture. There are different styles for organizing the data collection and analysis phase:

- *Post-mortem methods* record a complete set of relevant run-time events in a persistent trace for *offline analysis*. This method was common in early race detection systems, e.g., by Allan and Padua [4]. Due to the possibly large size of the trace, this method is limited to short program runs.
- *Online methods*, also called *on-the-fly detection*, record events temporarily and perform the data race analysis entwined with the actual program execution. Much of the recorded information can be discarded as the analysis proceeds. Depending on the algorithm, this may but does not necessarily compromise the accuracy of the detection. Most dynamic data race tools choose this architecture, e.g., Mellor-Crummey [36] for an HB-based analysis and Savage et al. [59] for a method based on locksets. In distributed systems, online methods are also the preferred analysis architecture.

Implementation techniques. Dynamic race detection is an aspect that is crosscutting and orthogonal to the remaining functionality of a software. Several techniques have been used to incorporate race detection in a software system:

- *Program instrumentation* augments memory and synchronization accesses with checking code. Instrumentation can occur at compile-time [59], or at run-time [14].
- Race detection as part of a software-based *protocol implementation* in distributed shared memory systems [48, 51, 57].
- *Hardware extensions* for HB-based [3, 40, 42, 54] or lock-set-based [72] race detection.

Limitations. An inherent limitation of dynamic race detection is that it is based on information from a single program execution.

This limitation is twofold. First, not all possible control paths may have been exercised on the given input. Second, possible race conditions may have been covert in the specific thread schedule of the execution trace, as e.g., in example in Fig. 1. This second limitation, called *scheduling dependence*, can be mitigated or entirely avoided by so-called *predictive analyses* [12, 25, 61, 68]. The key idea of predictive (dynamic) analyses is to consider not only the order of events recorded in a specific execution trace but also permutations thereof. This technique increases the coverage of the dynamic analysis of concurrent program executions, since it is capable to expose thread interleavings (event orders) that have not been exercised.

Static Methods

Static program analysis, does not require that the program is executed.

Pragmatic methods. A pragmatic approach to find programming errors is to identify situations in the source code, where the program deviates from common programming practice. Naturally, this approach lends itself to find deviations from common programming idioms in concurrent programs that may lead to unintended race conditions. This approach is called pragmatic, since the analysis is neither sound nor complete with respect to identifying data races. In practice, pragmatic analysis methods have turned out to be very effective with the additional benefit that in most cases, analyses do not require sophisticated data-flow or concurrency analysis and hence can be very efficient.

Findbugs by Ayewah et al. [5] is a tool for pragmatic analyses of Java programs. Hovenmeyer and Pugh [28] describe numerous analyses for concurrency related errors. One programming idiom for concurrent program in Java is, e.g., that accesses to a shared mutable variable are consistently protected by synchronized blocks. Violations of this programming practice are described as *bug pattern* called "inconsistent synchronization." Inconsistent synchronization occurs, if a class contains mixed (synchronized and unsynchronized) accesses to a field variable and no more than one third of the accesses (writes weighed higher than reads) occur outside a synchronized block.

RacerX [18] is a static data race and deadlock detection system targeted to check large operating system codes. The tool builds a call graph and verifies a locking discipline along a calling context sensitive traversal of the code. The system does however not have a pointer analysis and approximates aliasing through variable types. Moreover, the system uses a heuristic to classify sections of code that are sequential and those that are concurrent. These approximations facilitate the analysis of very large codes (>500 K lines of code). As the analysis issues a significant number of spurious reports, a clever ranking scheme is used to prioritize the large numbers of reports according to their likelihood of being an actual bug.

Methods based on data-flow analysis. May-happen-in-parallel analysis (MHP) is the foundation of many compile-time analyses for concurrent programs. MHP analysis approximates the order of statements executed by different threads and computes the may-happen-in-parallel relation among statements. MHP analysis in combination with a compile-time model of program data can serve as the foundation of compile-time data race detection.

Bristow [9] used an *inter-process precedence graph* for determining anomalies in programs with post-wait synchronization. Taylor [65] and Duesterwald and Soffa [17] extend this work and define a model for parallel tasks in Ada programs with rendez-vous synchronization. The program representation in [17] is modular and enables an efficient analysis of programs with procedures and recursion based on a data-flow framework. Masticola and Ryder [35] generalize and improve the approach of [17]. Naumovic et al. [44] compute the potential concurrency in Java programs at the level of statements. The authors have shown that the precision of their data-flow algorithm is optimal for most of the small applications that have been evaluated. The approach requires that the number of real threads in the system is specified as input to the analysis. The combination of MHP information with a model of program data (heap shape and reference information) could be used to determine conflicting data accesses. This approach is discussed by Midkiff, Lee, Padua, and Sura [38, 64].

Static race detection for Java programs has been developed, e.g., by Choi et al. [14] and Naik et al. [43]. Both systems are based on a whole program analysis to determine an initial set of potentially conflicting object accesses. This set is pruned (refined) by several successive analysis steps, which are alias analysis, thread escape analysis, and lockset analysis. The Chord checker by Naik et al. [43] is object context-sensitive [32, 39], and this feature is found to be essential, in combination with a precise, inclusion-based alias analysis, to achieve a high detection accuracy; object context sensitivity incurs however a significant scalability cost. Chord sacrifices soundness since it approximates lock identity through *may alias* information when determining common lock protection.

Type-based methods. Type systems can model and express data protection and locking policies in data and method declarations. Compliance of data access and method invocations with the declared properties can be checked mostly statically. The main advantage of the type-based approach is its modularity, which makes it, in contrast to a whole program analysis, well amenable to treat incomplete and large programs. The type systems that can prove data-race-freedom have either been proposed as extensions to existing programming languages by Bacon at al. [6] or Boyapati and Rinard [8]. Flanagan and Freund [1, 20] present a type system that is able to specify and check lock-protection of individual variables. In combination with an annotation generator [21], they applied the type checker to Java programs of up to 450 KLOC. The annotation generator is able to recognize common locking patterns and further uses heuristics to classify as benign certain accesses without lock protection. The heuristics are effective in reducing the number of spurious warnings; some are however unsound, which has not been a problem for the benchmarks investigated in [21].

Model checking. The principle of model checking is to explore every possible control flow-path and variable value assignment for undesired program behavior. Since this procedure is obviously intractable, models of data and program are explored instead. An additional source of complexity in parallel versus sequential programs is the timing of threads resulting in myriads of possible interleaving of actions from different threads.

The main challenge of model checking for concurrency errors, such as data races, is hence to reduce the state space to be explored. One idea is to consider only those states and transitions of individual threads that operate on shared data, and are thus visible to other threads. Another idea is to aggregate the possible interleavings, e.g., by modeling multiple threads and their transitions in one common state transition space.

Model checking has been applied to the detection of access anomalies in concurrent programs, e.g., in [27, 30, 41, 62, 63, 66]. Stoller's model checker [63] verifies adherence to a locking policy. Henzinger et al. [27] describe a model checker that identifies conflicting accesses that are not ordered according to the HB-relation. Both works assume an underlying sequentially consistent execution platform. Model checking for executions on weakly-ordered memory systems have been conceived as well by [10], though not particularly for the purpose of data race detection.

Detection of Determinacy and Atomicity Violations

The emphasis of this entry is on the detection of race conditions that are data races. Related to race conditions are also *violations of determinacy* and *violations of atomicity*. Techniques for their detection are discussed in the corresponding essays on ▶determinacy and atomicity.

Complexity

Netzer and Miller [47] characterize race conditions in terms of feasible programs executions. A program execution is feasible, if the control flow and shared data-dependencies in the execution could actually occur at run-time in accordance with the semantics of the program.

The problem of detecting a race condition is at least as hard as determining if a feasible program execution exists, where a pair of suspect statements occurs concurrently. Netzer and Miller [46] found that problem to be intractable even if shared data-dependencies are ignored. Helmbold and McDowell [26] confirm and refine this result by restricting programs to certain control-flow and synchronization models. For unrestricted programs, if data-dependencies are not ignored, the problem of deciding if two conflicting statement participate in a race is as hard as the halting problem [26].

In practice, most dynamic and also static data-flow-based race detection analyses have a complexity that is quasi-linear in the number of synchronization and shared resource accesses.

Related Entries

▶Determinacy
▶Formal Methods–Based Tools for Race, Deadlock, and Other Errors
▶Race Conditions

Bibliography

1. Abadi M, Flanagan CE, Freund SN (2006) Types for safe locking: static race detection for Java. Trans Program Lang Syst (TOPLAS) 28(2):207–255
2. Adve S, Hill M (June 1990) Weak ordering — A new definition. In: Proceedings of the annual international symposium on computer architecture (ISCA'90), pp 2–14
3. Adve S, Hill M, Miller B, Netzer R (May 1991) Detecting data races on weak memory systems. In: Proceedings of the annual international symposium on computer architecture (ISCA'91), pp 234–243
4. Allen TR, Padua DA (August 1987) Debugging fortran on a shared memory machine. In: Proceedings of the international conference on parallel processing, pp 721–727
5. Ayewah N, Hovemeyer D, Morgenthaler JD, Penix J, Pugh W (2008) Using static analysis to find bugs. IEEE Softw 25(5):22–29
6. Bacon D, Strom R, Tarafdar A (October 2000) Guava: a dialect of Java without data races. In: Proceedings of the conference on object-oriented programming, systems, languages, and applications (OOPSLA'00), pp 382–400
7. Balasundaram V, Kennedy K (1989) Compile-time detection of race conditions in a parallel program. In: Proceedings of the international conference on supercomputing (ISC'89), pp 175–185
8. Boyapati C, Lee R, Rinard M (November 2002) Ownership types for safe programming: preventing data races and deadlocks. In: Proceedings of the conference on object-oriented programming, systems, languages, and applications (OOPSLA'02), pp 211–230
9. Bristow G, Dreay C, Edwards B, Riddle W (1979) Anomaly detection in concurrent programs. In: Proceedings of the international conference on software engineering (ICSE'79), pp 265–273
10. Burckhardt S, Alur R, Martin MMK (2007) CheckFence: checking consistency of concurrent data types on relaxed memory models. In: PLDI'07: Proceedings of the 2007 ACM SIGPLAN conference on programming language design and implementation. ACM, New York, pp 12–21
11. Charron-Bost B (1991) Concerning the size of logical clocks in distributed systems. Inf Process Lett 39(1):11–16
12. Chen F, Serbanuta TF, Rosu G (2008) jpredictor: a predictive runtime analysis tool for java. In: ICSE'08: Proceedings of the 30th international conference on software engineering. ACM, New York, pp 221–230
13. Choi J-D, Min SL (1991) Race frontier: reproducing data races in parallel program debugging. In: PPOPP'91: Proceedings of the third ACM SIGPLAN symposium on principles and practice of parallel programming. ACM, New York, pp 145–154
14. Choi J-D, Lee K, Loginov A, O'Callahan R, Sarkar V, Sridharan M (June 2002) Efficient and precise datarace detection for multithreaded object-oriented programs. In: Conference on programming language design and implementation (PLDI'02), pp 258–269
15. Dinning A, Schonberg E (1990) An empirical comparison of monitoring algorithms for access anomaly detection. In: PPOPP'90: Proceedings of the second ACM SIGPLAN symposium on principles & practice of parallel programming. ACM, New York, pp 1–10
16. Dinning A, Schonberg E (December 1991) Detecting access anomalies in programs with critical sections. In: Proceedings of the ACM/ONR workshop on parallel and distributed debugging, pp 85–96
17. Duesterwald E, Soffa M (1993) Concurrency analysis in the presence of procedures using a data-flow framework. In: Proceedings of the symposium on testing, analysis, and verification (TAV4), pp 36–48
18. Engler D, Ashcraft K (October 2003) RacerX: Effective, static detection of race conditions and deadlocks. In: Proceedings of the symposium on operating systems principles (SOSP'03), pp 237–252
19. Fidge CJ (1988) Timestamp in message passing systems that preserves partial ordering. In: Proceedings of the 11th Australian computing conference, pp 56–66
20. Flanagan C, Freund SN (June 2000) Type-based race detection for Java. In: Proceedings of the conference on programming language design and implementation (PLDI'00), pp 219–229
21. Flanagan C, Freund SN (June 2001) Detecting race conditions in large programs. In: Proceedings of the workshop on program analysis for software tools and engineering (PASTE'01), pp 90–96
22. Flanagan C, Freund SN (2009) FastTrack: Efficient and precise dynamic race detection. In: PLDI'09: Proceedings of the 2009 ACM SIGPLAN conference on programming language design and implementation. ACM, New York, pp 121–133
23. Flanagan C, Qadeer S (June 2003) A type and effect system for atomicity. In: Proceedings of the conference on programming language design and implementation (PLDI'03), pp 338–349
24. Flanagan C, Leino R, Lillibridge M, Nelson G, Saxe J, Stata R (June 2002) Extended static checking for Java. In: Proceedings of the

conference on programming language design and implementation (PLDI'02), pp 234–245

25. Flanagan C, Freund SN, Yi J (2008) Velodrome: a sound and complete dynamic atomicity checker for multithreaded programs. In: PLDI'08: Proceedings of the 2008 ACM SIGPLAN conference on programming language design and implementation. ACM, New York, pp 293–303

26. Helmbold DP, McDowell CE (September 1994) A taxonomy of race detection algorithms. Technical Report UCSC-CRL-94-35, University of California, Santa Cruz, Computer Research Laboratory

27. Henzinger TA, Jhala R, Majumdar R (2004) Race checking by context inference. In: PLDI'04: Proceedings of the ACM SIGPLAN 2004 conference on programming language design and implementation. ACM, New York, pp 1–13

28. Hovemeyer D, Pugh W (July 2004) Finding concurrency bugs in java. In: Proceedings of the PODC workshop on concurrency and synchronization in Java programs

29. Jannesari A, Bao K, Pankratius V, Tichy WF (2009) Helgrind+: An efficient dynamic race detector. In: Proceedings of the 23rd international parallel & distributed processing symposium (IPDPS'09). IEEE, Rome

30. Kidd N, Reps T, Dolby J, Vaziri M (2009) Finding concurrency-related bugs using random isolation. In: VMCAI'09: Proceedings of the 10th international conference on verification, model checking, and abstract interpretation. Springer-Verlag, Heidelberg, pp 198–213

31. Lamport L (July 1978) Time, clock and the ordering of events in a distributed system. Commun ACM 21(7):558–565

32. Lhoták O, Hendren L (March 2006) Context-sensitive points-to analysis: is it worth it? In: Mycroft A, Zeller A (eds) International conference of compiler construction (CC'06), vol 3923 of LNCS. Springer, Vienna, pp 47–64

33. Mattern F (1988) Virtual time and global states of distributed systems. In: Proceedings of the Parallel and distributed algorithms conference. Elsevier Science, Amsterdam, pp 215–226

34. Marino D, Musuvathi M, Narayanasamy S (2009) Literace: effective sampling for lightweight data-race detection. In: PLDI'09: Proceedings of the 2009 ACM SIGPLAN conference on programming language design and implementation. ACM, New York, pp 134–143

35. Masticola S, Ryder B (1993) Non-concurrency analysis. In: Proceedings of the symposium on principles and practice of parallel programming (PPoPP'93), pp 129–138

36. Mellor-Crummey J (November 1991) On-the-y detection of data races for programs with nested fork-join parallelism. In: Proceedings of the supercomputer debugging workshop, pp 24–33

37. Mellor-Crummey J (May 1993) Compile-time support for efficient data race detection in shared-memory parallel programs. In: Proceedings of the workshop on parallel and distributed debugging, pp 129–139

38. Midkiff S, Lee J, Padua D (June 2001) A compiler for multiple memory models. In: Rec. Workshop compilers for parallel computers (CPC'01)

39. Milanova A, Rountev A, Ryder BG (2005) Parameterized object sensitivity for points-to analysis for Java. ACM Trans Softw Eng Methodol 14(1):1–41

40. Min SL, Choi J-D (1991) An efficient cache-based access anomaly detection scheme. In: ASPLOS-IV: Proceedings of the 4th international conference on architectural support for programming languages and operating systems. ACM, New York, pp 235–244

41. Musuvathi M, Qadeer S, Ball T, Basler G, Nainar PA, Neamtiu I (2008) Finding and reproducing heisenbugs in concurrent programs. In: OSDI'08: Proceedings of the 8th USENIX conference on operating systems design and implementation. USENIX Association, Berkeley, pp 267–280

42. Muzahid A, Suárez D, Qi S, Torrellas J (2009) Sigrace: signature-based data race detection. In: ISCA'09: Proceedings of the 36th annual international symposium on computer architecture. ACM, New York, pp 337–348

43. Naik M, Aiken A, Whaley J (June 2006) Effective static race detection for Java. In: Proceedings of the conference on programming language design and implementation (PLDI'06), pp 308–319

44. Naumovich G, Avrunin G, Clarke L (September 1999) An efficient algorithm for computing MHP information for concurrent Java programs. In: Proceedings of the European software engineering conference and symposium on the foundations of software engineering, pp 338–354

45. Netzer R, Miller B (August 1990a) Detecting data races in parallel program executions. Technical report TR90-894, Department of Computer Science, University of Wisconsin, Madison

46. Netzer R, Miller B (January 1990b) On the complexity of event ordering for shared-memory parallel program executions. Technical report TR 908, Computer Sciences Department, University of Wisconsin, Madison

47. Netzer R, Miller B (March 1992) What are race conditions? Some issues and formalizations. ACM Lett Program Lang Syst 1(1):74–88

48. Netzer R, Brennan T, Damodaran-Kamal S (1996) Debugging race conditions in message-passing programs. In: SPDT'96: Proceedings of the SIGMETRICS symposium on parallel and distributed tools. ACM, New York, pp 31–40

49. Nudler I, Rudolph L (1988) Tools for the efficient development of efficient parallel programs. In: Proceedings of the 1st Israeli conference on computer system engineering

50. O'Callahan R, Choi J-D (June 2003) Hybrid dynamic data race detection. In: Symposium on principles and practice of parallel programming (PPoPP'03), pp 167–178

51. Perkovic D, Keleher PJ (October 1996) Online data-race detection via coherency guarantees. In: Proceedings of the 2nd symposium on operating systems design and implementation (OSDI'96), pp 47–57

52. Pozniansky E, Schuster A (June 2003) Efficient on-the-y data race detection in multi-threaded c++ programs. In: Proceedings of the symposium on principles and practice of parallel programming (PPoPP'03), pp 179–190

53. Pozniansky E, Schuster A (2007) Multirace: efficient on-the-y data race detection in multithreaded c++ programs: research articles. Concurrency Comput: Pract Exper 19(3):327–340

54. Prvulovic M, Torrellas J (2003) Reenact: using thread-level speculation mechanisms to debug data races in multithreaded codes. SIGARCH Comput Archit News 31(2):110–121
55. Rajwar R, Goodman JR (2001) Speculative lock elision: enabling highly concurrent multithreaded execution. In MICRO 34: Proceedings of the 34th annual ACM/IEEE international symposium on microarchitecture. IEEE Computer Society, Washington, DC, pp 294–305
56. Ramalingam G (2000) Context-sensitive synchronization-sensitive analysis is undecidable. ACM Trans Program Lang Syst (TOPLAS) 22:416–430
57. Richards B, Larus JR (1998) Protocol-based data-race detection. In SPDT'98: Proceedings of the SIGMETRICS symposium on parallel and distributed tools. ACM, New York, pp 40–47
58. Savage S, Burrows M, Nelson G, Sobalvarro P, Anderson T (October 1997a) Eraser: a dynamic data race detector for multi-threaded programs. In: Proceedings of the symposium on operating systems principles (SOSP'97), pp 27–37
59. Savage S, Burrows M, Nelson G, Sobalvarro P, Anderson T (1997b) Eraser: a dynamic data race detector for multithreaded programs. ACM Transactions on computer systems 15(4):391–411
60. Scheurich C, Dubois M (June 1987) Correct memory operation of cache-based multiprocessors. In: Proceedings of 14th annual symposium on computer architecture, Computer Architecture News, pp 234–243
61. Sen K, Rosu G, Agha G (2003) Runtime safety analysis of multithreaded programs. In: ESEC/FSE-11: Proceedings of the 9th European software engineering conference held jointly with 11th ACM SIGSOFT international symposium on foundations of software engineering. ACM, New York, pp 337–346
62. Shacham O, Sagiv M, Schuster A (2005) Scaling model checking of dataraces using dynamic information. In: PPoPP'05: Proceedings of the tenth ACM SIGPLAN symposium on principles and practice of parallel programming. ACM, New York, pp 107–118
63. Stoller SD (October 2002) Model-checking multi-threaded distributed Java programs. Int J Softw Tools Technol Transfer 4(1):71–91
64. Sura Z, Fang X, Wong C-L, Midkiff SP, Lee J, Padua DA (June 2005) Compiler techniques for high performance sequentially consistent Java programs. In: Proceedings of the symposium principles and practice of parallel programming (PPoPP'05), pp 2–13
65. Taylor RN (May 1983) A general purpose algorithm for analyzing concurrent programs. Commun ACM 26(5):362–376
66. Visser W, Havelund K, Brat G, Park S (2000) Model checking programs. In: ASE'00: Proceedings of the 15th IEEE international conference on automated software engineering. IEEE Computer Society, Washington, p 3
67. von Praun C, Gross T (October 2001) Object race detection. In: Conference on object-oriented programming, systems, languages, and applications (OOPSLA'01), pp 70–82
68. Wang L, Stoller SD (2006) Accurate and efficient runtime detection of atomicity errors in concurrent programs. In: PPoPP'06: Proceedings of the eleventh ACM SIGPLAN symposium on Principles and practice of parallel programming. ACM, New York, pp 137–146
69. Welc A, Jagannathan S, Hosking AL (June 2004) Transactional monitors for concurrent objects. In: Proceedings of the European conference on object-oriented programming (ECOOP'04), pp 519–542
70. Yu Y, Rodeheffer T, Chen W (October 2003) RaceTrack: Efficient detection of data race conditions via adaptive tracking. In: Proceedings of the symposium on operating systems principles (SOSP'03), pp 221–234
71. Yu Y, Rodeheffer T, Chen W (2005) Racetrack: efficient detection of data race conditions via adaptive tracking. In SOSP'05: Proceedings of the 20th ACM symposium on operating systems principles. ACM, New York, pp 221–234
72. Zhou P, Teodorescu R, Zhou Y (2007) Hard: hardware-assisted lockset-based race detection. In: HPCA'07: Proceedings of the 2007 IEEE 13th international symposium on high performance computer architecture. IEEE Computer Society, Washington, DC, pp 121–132

Race Detectors for Cilk and Cilk++ Programs

JEREMY T. FINEMAN[1], CHARLES E. LEISERSON[2]
[1]Carnegie Mellon University, Pittsburgh, PA, USA
[2]Massachusetts Institute of Technology, Cambridge, MA, USA

Synonyms

Cilkscreen; Nondeterminator

Definition

The Nondeterminator race detector takes as input an ostensibly deterministic Cilk program and an input data set and makes the following guarantee: it will either determine at least one location in the program that is subject to a determinacy race when the program is run on the data set, or else it will certify that the program always behaves the same on the data set, no matter how it is scheduled. The Cilkscreen race detector does much the same thing for Cilk++ programs. Both can also detect data races, but the guarantee is somewhat weaker.

Discussion

Introduction

Many Cilk programs are intended to be deterministic, in that a given program produces the same behavior no matter how it is scheduled. The program may behave nondeterministically, however, if a *determinacy race* occurs: two logically parallel instructions update the same location, where at least one of the two instructions writes the location. In this case, different runs of the program on the same input may produce different behaviors. Race bugs are notoriously hard to detect by normal debugging techniques, such as breakpointing, because they are not easily repeatable. This article describes the *Nondeterminator* and *Cilkscreen* race detectors, which are systems for detecting races in Cilk and Cilk++ programs, respectively.

Determinacy races have been given many different names in the literature. For example, they are sometimes called *access anomalies* [12], *data races* [24], *race conditions* [22], *harmful shared-memory accesses* [32], or *general races* [31]. Emrath and Padua [15] call a deterministic program *internally deterministic* if the program execution on the given input exhibits no determinacy race and *externally deterministic* if the program has determinacy races but its output is deterministic because of the commutative and associative operations performed on the shared locations. The Nondeterminator program checks whether a Cilk program is internally deterministic. Cilkscreen allows for some internal nondeterminism in a Cilk++ program, specifically, nondeterminism encapsulated by "reducer hyperobjects" [18].

To illustrate how a determinacy race can occur, consider the simple Cilk program shown in Fig. 1. The parallel control flow of this program can be viewed as the directed acyclic graph, or *dag*, illustrated in Fig. 2. The vertices of the dag represent parallel control constructs, and the edges represent *strands*: serial sequences of instructions with no intervening parallel control constructs. In Fig. 2, the strands of the program are labeled to correspond to code fragments from Fig. 1, and the subdags representing the two instances of foo() are shaded. In this program, both of the parallel instantiations of the procedure foo() update the shared variable x in the x = x + 1 statement. This statement actually causes the processor executing the strand to

```
int x;

cilk void foo()
{
    x = x + 1;
    return;
}

cilk int main()             /* F  */
{
    x = 0;                  /* e_0 */
    spawn foo();            /* F_1 */
                            /* e_1 */
    spawn foo();            /* F_2 */
                            /* e_2 */
    sync;
    printf("x is %d\n", x); /* e_3 */
    return 0;
}
```

Race Detectors for Cilk and Cilk++ Programs. Fig. 1 A simple Cilk program that contains a determinacy race. In the comments at the right, the Cilk strands that make up the procedure main() are labeled

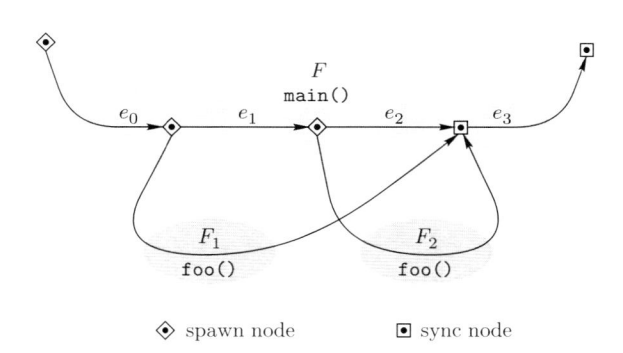

Race Detectors for Cilk and Cilk++ Programs. Fig. 2 The parallel control-flow dag of the program in Fig. 1. A spawn node of the dag represents a spawn construct, and a sync node represents a sync construct. The edges of the dag are labeled to correspond with code fragments from Fig. 1

perform a read from x, increment the value, and then write the value back into x. Since these operations are not atomic, both might update x at the same time. Figure 3 shows how this determinacy race can cause x to take on different values if the strands comprising the two instantiations of foo() are scheduled simultaneously.

The Nondeterminator

The Nondeterminator [16] determinacy-race detector takes as input a Cilk program and an input data set and either determines at least one location in the program that is subject to a determinacy race when the program is run on the data set, or else it certifies that the program always behaves the same when run on the data set. If a determinacy race exists, the Nondeterminator localizes the bug, providing variable name, file name, line number, and dynamic context (state of runtime stack, heap, etc.).

The Nondeterminator is not a program verifier, because the Nondeterminator cannot certify that the program is race-free for all input data sets. Rather, it is a debugging tool. The Nondeterminator only checks a program on a particular input data set. What it verifies is that every possible scheduling of the program execution produces the same behavior. If the program relies on any random choices or runtime calls to hardware counters, etc., these values should also be viewed as part of the input data set.

The Nondeterminator is a serial program that operates *on-the-fly*, meaning that it detects races as it simulates the execution of the program, rather than by logging and subsequent analysis. As it executes, it maintains various data structures for determining the existence of determinacy races. An "access history" maintains a subset of strands that access each particular memory location. An "SP-maintenance" data structure maintains the series-parallel (*SP*) relationships among strands. Specifically, the race detector must determine whether two strands (that access the same memory location) operate logically in parallel (i.e., whether it is possible to schedule both strands at the same time), or whether there is some serial relationship between the strands.

The Nondeterminator was implemented by modifying the ordinary Cilk compiler and runtime system. Each read and write in the user's program is instrumented by the Nondeterminator's compiler to perform determinacy-race checking at runtime. The Nondeterminator then takes advantage of the fact that any Cilk program can be executed as a C program. Specifically, if the Cilk keywords are deleted from a Cilk program, a C program results, called the Cilk program's *serialization* (also called *serial elision* in the literature), whose semantics are a legal implementation of the semantics of the Cilk program [19]. The Nondeterminator executes the user's program as the serialization would execute, but it performs race-checking actions when reads, writes, and parallel control statements occur.

Since the Nondeterminator was implemented by modifying the Cilk compiler, it is unable to detect races that occur in precompiled library code. In contrast, the Cilk++ race detector, called Cilkscreen, uses binary instrumentation [5, 23, 27]. Cilkscreen dynamically replaces memory accesses in a Cilk++ program binary with instrumented memory accesses, and thus it can operate on executable binaries for which no source code is available. Cilkscreen employs much the same algorithmic technology as the Nondeterminator, however.

Detecting Races in Programs that Use Locks

The original Nondeterminator [16] is designed to detect determinacy races in a Cilk program. Typically a programmer may add locks to the program to protect against the externally nondeterministic interleaving given in Fig. 3, thus intending and sanctioning nondeterministic executions. Thus, it may not make sense to test the program for determinacy races, but some weaker form of race detection may be desired.

Case 1			Case 2		
F_1	F_2	e_3	F_1	F_2	e_3
read x = 0			read x = 0		
write x = 1				read x = 0	
	read x = 1		write x = 1		
	write x = 2			write x = 1	
		"x is 2"			"x is 1"

Race Detectors for Cilk and Cilk++ Programs. Fig. 3 An illustration of a determinacy race in the code from Fig. 1. The value of the shared variable x read and printed by strands e_3 can differ depending on how the instructions in the two instances F_1 and F_2 of the foo() procedure are scheduled

The Nondeterminator-2 [7] detects *data races*, which occur when two logically parallel strands holding no locks in common update the same location, where at least one of the two instructions modifies the location. Although the Nondeterminator and Nondeterminator-2 test for different types of races, a significant chunk of the implementations and algorithms used (notably, the SP-maintenance algorithm) remains the same in both debugging tools. This article focuses on determinacy-race detection.

Series-Parallel Parse Trees

The structure of a Cilk program can be interpreted as a *series-parallel (SP) parse tree* rather than a series-parallel dag. Figure 5 shows a parse tree for the dag in Fig. 2. In the SP parse tree, each internal node is either an *S-node*, denoted by S, or a *P-node*, denoted by P, and each leaf is a strand of the dag. If two subtrees are children of the same S-node, then the strands in the left subtree *logically precede* the strands in the right subtree, and (the subcomputation represented by) the left subtree must execute before (that of) the right subtree. If two subtrees are children of the same P-node, then the strands in the left subtree operate *logically in parallel* with those in the right subtree, and no ordering holds between (the subcomputations represented by) the two subtrees. For two strands e and e', the notation $e \parallel e'$ means that e and e' operate logically in parallel, and the notation $e < e'$ means that e logically precedes e'.

A canonical SP parse tree for a Cilk dag, shown in Fig. 4, can be constructed as follows: First, build a parse tree recursively for each child of the root procedure. Each sync block of the root procedure contains a series of spawns with strands of intervening C code (some of which may be empty). Then, create a parse tree for the sync block alternately applying series and parallel composition to the child parse trees and the root strands. Finally, string the parse trees for the sync blocks together into a *spine* for the procedure by applying a sequence of series compositions to the sync blocks. Sync blocks are composed serially, because a sync statement is never passed until *all* previously spawned subprocedures have completed. The only ambiguities that might arise in the parse tree occur because of the associativity of series composition and the commutativity of parallel composition. If, as shown in Fig. 4, the alternating S-nodes and P-nodes in a sync block always place strands and subprocedures on the left, and the series compositions of the sync blocks are applied in order from last to first, then the parse tree is unique. Figure 5 shows such a *canonical* parse tree for the Cilk dag in Fig. 2.

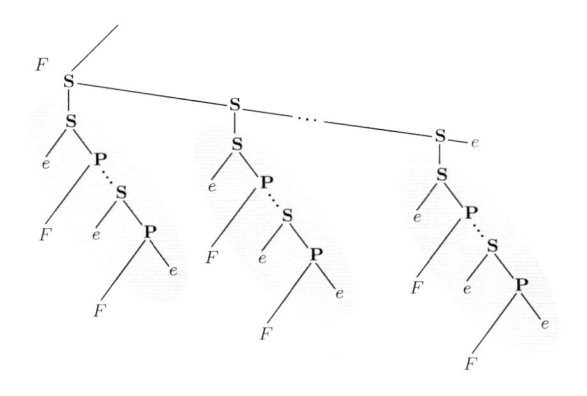

Race Detectors for Cilk and Cilk++ Programs. Fig. 4 The canonical series-parallel parse tree for a generic Cilk procedure. The notation F represents the SP parse tree of any subprocedure spawned by this procedure, and e represents any strand of the procedure. All nodes in the shaded areas belong to the procedure, and the nodes in each oval belong to the same sync block. A sequence of S-nodes forms the spine of the SP parse tree, composing all sync blocks in series. Each sync block contains an alternating sequence of S-nodes and P-nodes. Observe that the left child of an S-node in a sync block is always a strand, and that the left child of a P-node is always a subprocedure

One convenient feature of the SP parse tree is that the logical relationship between strands can be determined by looking at the least common ancestor (lca) of the strands in the parse tree. For example, consider the parse tree in Fig. 5. The least common ancestor of strands e_0 and e_3, denoted by $\text{lca}(e_0, e_3)$, is the root S-node, and hence $e_0 < e_3$. In contrast, $\text{lca}(F_2, F_2)$ is a P-node, and hence $F_1 \parallel F_2$. To see that the dag and the parse tree represent the same control structure requires only observing that $\text{lca}(e_i, e_j)$ is an S-node in the parse tree if and only if there is a directed path from e_i to e_j in the corresponding dag. A proof of this fact can be found in [16].

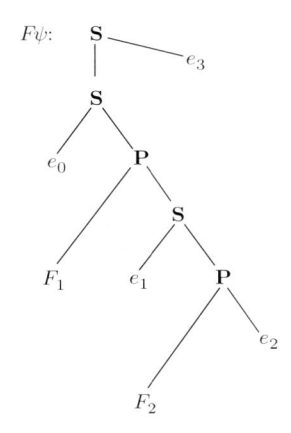

Race Detectors for Cilk and Cilk++ Programs. Fig. 5 The canonical series-parallel parse tree for the Cilk dag in Fig. 2

```
write a shared location ℓ by strand e:
    if reader[ℓ] ∥ e or writer[ℓ] ∥ e
        then a determinacy race exists
    writer[ℓ] ← e

read a shared memory location ℓ by strand e:
    if writer[ℓ] ∥ e
        then a determinacy race exists
    if reader[ℓ] ≺ e
        then reader[ℓ] ← e
```

Race Detectors for Cilk and Cilk++ Programs. Fig. 6 Pseudocode describing the implementation of read and write operations for a determinacy-race detector. The access history is updated on these operations

An execution of a Cilk program can be interpreted as a walk or traversal of the corresponding SP parse tree. The order in which nodes are traversed depends on the scheduler. A partial execution must obey series-parallel relationships, namely, that the tree walk cannot enter the right subtree of an S-node until the left subtree has been fully executed. Both subtrees of a P-node, however, can be traversed in arbitrary order or in parallel. The canonical parse tree is such that an ordinary, left-to-right, depth-first tree walk visits strands in the same order as the program's serialization visits them.

Access History

The Nondeterminator and Cilkscreen race detectors execute a Cilk program in serial, depth-first order while maintaining two data structures. The SP-maintenance data structure, described later in this article, is used to query the logical relationships among strands. The access history maintains information as to which strands have accessed which memory locations.

At a high level, an *access history* maintains for each shared-memory location two sets of strands that have read from and written to the location. As the Nondeterminator executes, strands are added to and removed from the access history. Whenever an access of memory location *v* occurs, each of the strands in *v*'s access history are compared against the currently executing strand. If any of these strands operates logically in parallel with the currently executing strand, and one of the accesses is a write, then a race is reported. This query of logical relationships is determined by the SP-maintenance data structure described in section "Series-Parallel Maintenance." The main goal when designing an access history is to reduce the number of strands stored; the larger the access history the more series-parallel queries need to be performed.

For a serial determinacy race detector, an access history of size $O(1)$ per memory location suffices. In particular, the access history associates with each memory location ℓ two values $reader[\ell]$ and $writer[\ell]$, each storing a single strand that has previously read from or written to ℓ, respectively. Specifically, $writer[\ell]$ stores a unique runtime ID of the strand that has most recently written to ℓ. Similarly, $reader[\ell]$ stores the ID of some previous reader of ℓ, although it need not be the most recent reader.

The Nondeterminator updates the access history as new memory accesses occur. Each read and write operation of the original program is instrumented to update the access history and discover determinacy races. Figure 6 gives pseudocode describing the instrumentation of read and write operations. A race occurs if a strand e writes a location ℓ and discovers that either the previous reader or the previous writer of ℓ operates logically in parallel with e. Similarly, a race occurs whenever e reads a location ℓ and discovers that the previous writer operates logically in parallel with e. Whenever a location ℓ is written, the access history $writer[\ell]$ is updated to be the current strand e. The read history $reader[\ell]$ is updated to e when a read occurs, but only if the previous reader operates logically in series with e.

The cost of maintaining the access history is $O(1)$ plus the cost of $O(1)$ series-parallel queries, for each memory access. A correctness proof of the access history can be found in [16]. The proof involves showing that an update (or lack of an update) to $reader[\ell]$ does not discard any important information. Specifically, consider three strands e_1, e_2, and e_3 that occur in that order in the serial execution, where e_1 is the current value of $reader[\ell]$, e_2 is the currently executing strand reading ℓ, and e_3 is some future strand. If $e_1 \prec e_2$ and $e_1 \parallel e_3$, then $e_2 \parallel e_3$. Thus, a test for a conflict between e_2 and e_3 produces the same result as a test for a conflict between e_1 and e_3. On the other hand, if $e_1 \parallel e_2$ and $e_2 \parallel e_3$, then $e_1 \parallel e_3$, and so keeping e_1 gives at least as much information as e_2. Since updates to $reader[\ell]$ do not lose information, the access history properly detects a race whenever the current writer operates logically in parallel with any previous reader. The full proof considers the other two race cases separately (the current writer operates logically in parallel with a previous writer, or the current reader operates logically in parallel with a previous writer), showing that either a race is reported on the access or an earlier writer-writer race was reported.

Data-Race Detection

In contrast to the Nondeterminator, which detects determinacy races, the Nondeterminator-2 [7] and Cilkscreen can also detect data races. The difference between the Nondeterminator and these other two debugging programs lies in how they deal with the access history. The Nondeterminator-2 and Cilkscreen tools report data races for locking protocols in which every lock is acquired and released within a single strand and cannot be held across parallel control constructs. Strands may hold multiple locks at one time, however. These tools do not detect deadlocks, but only whether during a serial left-to-right depth-first execution, two logically parallel strands holding no locks in common access a shared variable, where at least one of the strands modifies the location.

The *lock set* of an access (`read` or `write`) is the set of locks held by the strand performing the access when the access occurs. If the lock sets of two parallel accesses to the same location have an empty intersection, and at least one of the accesses is a `write`, then a data race exists. To simplify the race-detection algorithm, a small trick avoids the extra condition that "at least one of the

$\text{ACCESS}(\ell)$ in strand e with lock set H:
   for each $\langle e', H' \rangle \in lockers[\ell]$
     do if $e' \parallel e$ and $H' \cap H = \emptyset$
        then a data race exists
   $redundant \leftarrow \text{FALSE}$
   for each $\langle e', H' \rangle \in lockers[\ell]$
     do if $e' \prec e$ and $H' \supseteq H$
        then $lockers[\ell] \leftarrow lockers[\ell] - \{\langle e', H' \rangle\}$
       if $e' \parallel e$ and $H' \subseteq H$
        then $redundant \leftarrow \text{TRUE}$
   if $redundant = \text{FALSE}$
     then $lockers[\ell] \leftarrow lockers[\ell] \cup \{\langle e, H \rangle\}$

Race Detectors for Cilk and Cilk++ Programs. Fig. 7
Pseudocode describing the implementation of read and write operations for a data-race detector. The access history is updated on these operations using the lock-set algorithm

accesses is a `write`." The idea is to introduce a *fake lock* for read accesses called the R-LOCK, which is implicitly acquired immediately before a `read` and released immediately afterward. The R-LOCK behaves from the race detector's point of view just like a normal lock, but during an actual computation, it is never actually acquired and released (since it does not actually exist). The use of R-LOCK allows the condition for a data race to be stated more succinctly: *If the lock sets of two parallel accesses to the same location have an empty intersection, then a data race exists.* By this condition, a data race (correctly) does not exist for two read accesses, since their lock sets both contain the R-LOCK.

The access history for the algorithm for detecting data races records a set of readers and writers for each memory location and their lock sets. For a given location ℓ, the entry $lockers[\ell]$ stores a list of *lockers*: strands that access ℓ, each paired with the lock set that was held during the access. If $\langle e, H \rangle \in lockers[\ell]$, then location ℓ is accessed by strand e while it holds the lock set H. Figure 7 gives pseudocode for the data-race-detection algorithm employed by the Nondeterminator-2 and Cilkscreen.

This algorithm for data-race detection does not provide as strong a guarantee as the algorithm for determinacy-race detection. Programming with locks introduces intentional nondeterminism which may not be exposed during a serial left-to-right depth-first execution. Thus, although the algorithm always finds a data race if one is exposed, some data races may not be exposed. Nevertheless, for *abelian* programs, where critical sections protected by the same lock "commute" – produce the same effect on memory no matter in which order they are executed – a guarantee can be provided. For a computation generated by a deadlock-free abelian program running on a given input, the algorithm guarantees to find a data race if one exists, and otherwise guarantee that all executions produce the same final result. A proof of the correctness of this assertion can be found in [7].

The cost of querying the access history for data-race detection is much more than the $O(1)$ cost for determinacy-race detection. There are at most n^k entries for each memory location, where n is the number of locks in the program and $k \leq n$ is the number of locks held simultaneously. Thus, the running time of the data-race detector may increase proportionally to n^k in the worst case. In practice, however, few locks are held simultaneously, and the running time tends to be only slightly worse than for determinacy-race detection.

Series-Parallel Maintenance

The main structural component of the two Nondeterminator programs and Cilkscreen is their algorithm for maintaining series-parallel (SP) relationships among strands. These race detectors execute the program in a left-to-right depth-first order while maintaining the logical relationships between strands. As new strands are encountered, the SP-maintenance data structure is updated. Whenever the currently executing strand accesses a memory location, the Nondeterminator queries the SP-maintenance data structure to determine whether the current strand operates in series or in parallel with strands (those in the access history) that made earlier accesses to the same memory location.

Figure 8 compares the serial space and running times of several SP-maintenance algorithms. The SP-bags and SP-order algorithms, described in this section, are employed by various implementations of the Nondeterminator. The English-Hebrew [32] and Offset-Span [24] algorithms are used in different race detectors and displayed for comparison. The modified SP-bags entry reflects a different underlying data structure than the SP-bags entry, but the algorithm for both is the same. As the number of queries performed by a determinacy race detector can be as large as $O(T)$ for a program that runs serially in T time, keeping the query time small

Algorithm	Space per node	Time per Strand creation	Time per Query
English-Hebrew [32]	$\Theta(f)$	$\Theta(1)$	$\Theta(f)$
Offset-Span [24]	$\Theta(d)$	$\Theta(1)$	$\Theta(d)$
SP-bags [16]	$\Theta(1)$	$\Theta(\alpha(v,v))^*$	$\Theta(\alpha(v,v))^*$
Modified SP-bags [17]	$\Theta(1)$	$\Theta(1)^*$	$\Theta(1)$
SP-order [4]	$\Theta(1)$	$\Theta(1)$	$\Theta(1)$
f = number of forks/spawns in the program d = maximum depth of nested parallelism v = number of shared locations being monitored			

Race Detectors for Cilk and Cilk++ Programs. Fig. 8 Comparison of serial, SP-maintenance algorithms. An asterisk (*) indicates an amortized bound. The function α is Tarjan's functional inverse of Ackermann's function

is desirable, and hence SP-bags and SP-order are more appealing algorithms for serial race detectors. The situation is exacerbated in a data-race detector where the number of queries can be larger than T.

SP-Bags

Since the logical relationship between strands can be determined by looking at their least common ancestor in the SP parse tree, a straightforward approach for SP-maintenance would maintain this tree explicitly. Querying the relationship between strands can then be implemented naively by climbing the tree starting from each strand until converging at their least common ancestor. This approach yields expensive queries, as the worst-case cost is proportional to the height of the tree, which is not bounded.

SP-bags [16] is indeed based on finding the least common ancestor, but it uses a clever algorithm that yields far better queries. The algorithm itself is an adaptation of Tarjan's offline least-common-ancestors algorithm.

The SP-bags algorithm maintains a collection of disjoint sets, employing a "disjoint sets" or "union-find" data structure that supports the following operations:

1. MAKE-SET(x) creates a new set whose only member is x.
2. UNION(x, y) unites the sets containing x and y.
3. FIND(x) returns a representative for the set containing x.

A classical disjoint-set data structure with "union by rank" and "path compression" heuristics [9, 34, 35] supports m operations on n elements in $O(m\alpha(m,n))$ time, where α is Tarjan's functional inverse of Ackermann's function [9, 35].

As the program executes, for each active procedure, the SP-bags algorithm maintains two *bags* (unordered sets) with the following contents at any given time:

- The *S-bag* S_F of a procedure F contains the descendant procedures of F that logically precede the currently executing strand. (The descendant procedures of F include F itself.)
- The *P-bag* P_F of a procedure F contains the completed descendant procedures of F that operate logically in parallel with the currently executing strand.

The S- and P-bags are represented using a disjoint sets data structure as described above.

The SP-bags algorithm is given in Fig. 9. As the Cilk program executes in a serial, depth-first fashion, the SP-bags algorithm performs additional operations whenever one of the three following actions occurs: spawn, sync, return, resulting in updates to the S- and P-bags. Whenever a new procedure F (entering the left subtree of a P-node) is spawned, new bags are created. The bag S_F is initially set to contain F, and P_F is set to be empty. Whenever a procedure F' returns to its parent procedure F (completing the walk of the left subtree of a P-node), the contents of $S_{F'}$ are unioned into P_F, since the descendants of F' can execute in parallel with the remainder of the sync block in F. When a *sync* occurs (traversing a spine node in the parse tree) in F, the bag P_F is emptied into S_F, since all of F's executed descendants precede any future strands in F.

As a concrete example, consider the program given in Fig. 5. The execution order of strands and procedures is $e_0, F_1, e_1, F_2, e_2, e_3$. Figure 10 shows the state of the S- and P-bags during each step of the execution. As the S- and P-bags are only specified for active procedures, the number of bags changes during the execution.

To determine whether a previously executed procedure (or strand) F is logically in series or in parallel with the currently executing strand, simply check whether F belongs to an S-bag by looking at the identity of FIND-SET(F).

Figure 10 illustrates the correctness of SP-bags for the program Fig. 1. For example, when executing F_2, all previously executed instructions in F (namely, e_0 and e_1) serially precede F_2, and F does indeed belong to an S-bag S_F. Moreover, the procedure F_1 operates logically in parallel with F_2, and F_2 belongs to the P-bag P_F. For a proof of correctness, which is omitted here, refer to [16].

Combining SP-bags with the access history yields an efficient determinacy race detector. Consider a Cilk program that executes in time T on one processor and references v shared memory locations. The SP-bags algorithm can be implemented to check this program for determinacy races in $O(T\alpha(v,v))$ time.

A proof of this theorem, which is provided in [16], is conceptually straightforward. The number of MAKE-SET, UNION, and FIND-SET operations is at most $O(T)$, yielding a total running time of $O(T\alpha(m,n))$ for some value of m and n. It turns out that these values can be reduced to v when garbage collection is employed.

The theoretical running time of SP-bags can be improved by replacing the underlying disjoint sets data structure. Since the UNIONs are structured nicely, Gabow and Tarjan's data structure [20], which features $O(1)$ amortized time per operation, can be employed. The SP-bags algorithm can be implemented to check a program for determinacy races in $O(T)$ time, where the program executes in time T on one processor. A full discussion of this improvement appears in [17].

spawn a procedure F:
　　$S_F \leftarrow$ MAKE-SET(F)
　　$P_F \leftarrow \emptyset$

return from a procedure F' to parent F:
　　$P_F \leftarrow$ UNION($P_F, S_{F'}$)
　　$S_{F'} \leftarrow \emptyset$

sync in a procedure F:
　　$S_F \leftarrow$ UNION(S_F, P_F)
　　$P_F \leftarrow \emptyset$

Race Detectors for Cilk and Cilk++ Programs. Fig. 9 The SP-bags algorithm. Whenever one of three actions occurs during the serial, depth-first execution of a Cilk parse tree, the operations in the figure are performed. These operations cause SP-bags to manipulate the disjoint sets data structure

Execution step	State of the Bags			
e_0	$S_F = \{F\}$	$P_F = \emptyset$		
F_1	$S_F = \{F\}$	$P_F = \emptyset$	$S_{F_1} = \{F_1\}$	$P_{F_1} = \emptyset$
e_1	$S_F = \{F\}$	$P_F = \{F_1\}$		
F_2	$S_F = \{F\}$	$P_F = \{F_1\}$	$S_{F_2} = \{F_2\}$	$P_{F_2} = \emptyset$
e_2	$S_F = \{F\}$	$P_F = \{F_1, F_2\}$		
e_3	$S_F = \{F, F_1, F_2\}$	$P_F = \emptyset$		

Race Detectors for Cilk and Cilk++ Programs. Fig. 10 The state of the SP-bags algorithm when run on the parse tree from Fig. 5

SP-Order

SP-order uses two total orders to determine whether strands are logically parallel, an *English order* and a *Hebrew order*. In the English order, the nodes in the *left* subtree of a P-node precede those in the *right* subtree of the P-node. In the Hebrew order, the order is reversed: the nodes in the *right* subtree of a P-node precede those in the *left*. In both orders, the nodes in the left subtree of an S-node precede those in the right subtree of the S-node.

Figure 11 shows English and Hebrew orderings for the strands in the parse tree from Fig. 5. Notice that if x belongs in the left subtree of an S-node and y belongs to the right subtree of the same S-node, then $E[x] < E[y]$ and $H[x] < H[y]$. In contrast, if x belongs to the left subtree of a P-node y belongs to the right subtree of the same P-node, then $E[x] < E[y]$ and $H[x] > H[y]$.

The English and Hebrew orderings capture the SP relationships in the parse tree. Specifically, if one strand x precedes another strand y in both orders, then $x \prec y$, since lca(x, y) is an S-node, and hence there is a directed path from x to y in the dag. If x precedes y in one order but x follows y in the other, then $x \parallel y$, since lca(x, y) is a P-node, and hence there is no directed path from one to the other in the dag. For example, in Fig. 11, the fact e_0 precedes e_2 can be determined by observing $E[e_0] < E[e_2]$ and $H[e_0] < H[e_2]$. Similarly, it follows that F_1 and F_2 are logically parallel since $E[F_1] < E[F_2]$ and $H[F_1] > H[F_2]$. The following lemma, proved in [4], shows that this property always holds.

Lemma 1 *Let E be an English ordering of strands of an SP-parse tree, and let H be a Hebrew ordering. Then, for any two strands x and y in the parse tree, $x \prec y$ if and only if $E[x] < E[y]$ and $H[x] < H[y]$. Equivalently, $x \parallel y$ if and only if $E[x] < E[y]$ and $H[x] > H[y]$, or if $E[x] > E[y]$ and $H[x] < H[y]$.*

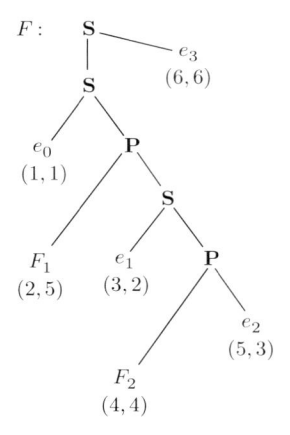

Race Detectors for Cilk and Cilk++ Programs. Fig. 11 An English ordering E and a Hebrew ordering H for strands in the parse tree of Fig. 5. Under each strand/procedure e is an ordered pair $(E[e], H[e])$ giving its rank in each of the two orders. Equivalently, the English order is $e_0, F_1, e_1, F_2, e_2, e_3$ and the Hebrew order is $e_0, e_1, e_2, F_2, F_1, e_3$

Labeling a static SP parse tree with an English-Hebrew ordering is straightforward. To compute the English ordering, perform a depth-first traversal visiting left children of both P-nodes and S-nodes before visiting right children (an *English walk*). Assign label i to the ith strand visited. To compute the Hebrew ordering, perform a depth-first traversal visiting right children of P-nodes before visiting left children but left children of S-nodes before visiting right children (a *Hebrew walk*). Assign labels to strands as before, in the order visited.

In race-detection applications, however, these orderings must be generated on-the-fly before the entire parse tree is known. If the parse tree unfolds according to an English walk, as in the Nondeterminator, then computing the English ordering is trivial. Unfortunately, computing the Hebrew ordering during an English walk is problematic. In a Hebrew ordering, the label of a strand in the left subtree of a P-node depends on the number of strands in the right subtree. This number is unknown, while performing an English walk, until the right subtree has unfolded completely.

Nudler and Rudolph [32], who introduced English-Hebrew labeling for race detection, addressed this problem by using large static strand labels. In particular, the number of bits in a label in their scheme can grow linearly in the number of P-nodes in the SP parse tree. Although they gave a heuristic for reducing the size of labels, manipulating large labels is the performance bottleneck of their algorithm.

The solution in SP-order is to employ order-maintenance data structures [3, 10, 11, 37] to maintain the English and Hebrew orders dynamically rather than using the static labels described above. An order-maintenance data structure is an abstract data type that supports the following operations:

- OM-PRECEDES(L, x, y): Return TRUE if x precedes y in the ordering L. Both x and y must already exist in the ordering L.
- OM-INSERT($L, x, y_1, y_2, \ldots, y_k$): In the ordering L, insert new elements $y_1, y_2, \ldots, y_k$, in that order, immediately after the existing element x. Any previously existing elements that followed x now follow y_k.

The OM-PRECEDES operation can be supported in $O(1)$ worst-case time. The OM-INSERT operation can be supported in $O(1)$ worst-case time for each node inserted. In the efficient order-maintenance data structures, labels are assigned to each element of the data structure, and the relative ordering of two elements (OM-PRECEDES) is determined by comparing these labels. Keeping the labels small guarantees good query cost. The labels change dynamically as insertions occur.

The SP-order data structure consists of two order-maintenance data structures to maintain English and Hebrew orderings. (In fact, the English ordering can be maintained implicitly during a left-to-right tree walk. For conceptual simplicity, however, both orderings are represented with the data structure here.) With the data structure chosen, the implementation of SP-order is remarkably simple. When first traversing an S-node S with left child x and right child y, perform OM-INSERT(Eng, S, x, y) to insert x then y after S in the English ordering Eng. Also perform OM-INSERT(Heb, S, x, y) to insert these children in the same order after S in the Hebrew ordering Heb. When first traversing a P-node P with left child x and right child y, also perform OM-INSERT(Eng, P, x, y) as before, but perform OM-INSERT(Heb, P, y, x) to insert these children in the opposite order in the Hebrew ordering.

To determine whether a previously executed strand e' is logically in series or in parallel with the currently executing strand e, simply check whether OM-PRECEDES(Heb, e', e). (It is always the case that OM-PRECEDES(Eng, e', e), as the program executes in the order of an English walk.) If OM-PRECEDES(Heb, e', e), then $e' \prec e$. If not, then $e' \parallel e$.

While the preceding description of SP-order with respect to the parse tree fully describes the algorithm, it is somewhat opaque with respect to the effect on Cilk code and the Cilk compiler. Figure 12, which is analogous to Fig. 9 for the SP-bags algorithm, describes the SP-order algorithm with respect to Cilk keywords. The main point of this figure is to show that, like SP-bags, incorporating SP-order into a Cilk program is fairly lightweight. In contrast to SP-bags, whose data structural elements are procedures, SP-order builds data structures over strands. As such, new objects or IDs are created whenever new strands are encountered. On a

```
spawn a child procedure F' of F:
    create strand IDs for:
        e_0: the first strand in F'
        e_c: the continuation strand in F
    OM-INSERT(Eng, current[F], e_0, e_C)
    OM-INSERT(Heb, current[F], e_c, e_0)

return from a procedure F' to parent F:
    nothing

following a spawn of procedure F or a sync in F:
    create strand ID for:
        e_S: the strand following the next sync in F
    OM-INSERT(Eng, current[F], e_S)
    OM-INSERT(Heb, current[F], e_S)
```

Race Detectors for Cilk and Cilk++ Programs. Fig. 12 The SP-order algorithm. Whenever a `spawn`, `sync`, or `return` occurs during the serial, depth-first execution of the Cilk parse tree, the operations in the figure are performed. These operations cause SP-order to manipulate the order maintenance data structures. The value *current*[F] denotes the currently executing strand in procedure F

spawn, strands are created for both the spawned procedure and the continuation strand within the parent procedure. These strands are then inserted into *Eng* and *Heb* in opposite orders, as they operate logically in parallel. Whenever beginning to execute a sync block in procedure F, either after spawn'ing F or sync'ing within F, a new strand e_S is created to represent the start of the next sync block. This e_S is then inserted after the currently executing strand in both *Eng* and *Heb*, as it operates logically after the currently executing strand. Unlike SP-bags, no data structural changes occur in SP-order when return'ing from a procedure.

One interesting feature of SP-order is that elements (strands) are only added to the data structure. No elements are ever reordered once added. Unreferenced elements may be removed as part of garbage collection. The (incomplete) English and Hebrew orderings at any time are thus consistent with the *a posteriori* orderings, with not-yet-encountered strands removed. The correctness of SP-order, the proof of which is given in [4], is arguably easier to convince oneself of than the proof of SP-bags.

Making the Nondeterminator Run in Parallel

The two Nondeterminators and Cilkscreen are serial race detectors. Even though these are debugging tools intended for parallel programs, they themselves run serially. This section discusses how to make these race detectors run in parallel. Both the access history and SP-maintenance algorithms must be augmented to permit a parallel algorithm. Moreover, contention due to concurrent updates to these data structures needs to be addressed.

A Parallel Access History

The access history described in section "Access History" is appealing because it requires only a single reader and writer for a determinacy-race detector, thus keeping the cost of maintaining and querying against the access history low. This strategy, however, is inherently serial. If only a single reader and writer are recorded, a parallel race detector may not discover certain races in the program [17]. Fortunately, Mellor-Crummey [24] shows that recording two readers and writers suffices to guarantee correctness in a parallel execution, which increases the number of SP-maintenance queries by only a factor of 2. A full description of such a parallel access history and its correctness can be found in [17, 24].

The other challenge in parallelizing the access history is in performing concurrent updates to the data structure. Specifically, two parallel readers may attempt to update the same $reader[\ell]$ at the same time. (If the goal is to just report a single race in the program, updating $writer[\ell]$ in parallel is not as much of an issue, as discovering such a parallel update indicates a race on its own. If the goal is to report one race for each memory location, as in the Nondeterminator, then concurrent updates to $writer[\ell]$ also matter here.) Some extra machinery is required to guarantee the correct value is recorded when concurrent updates occur. As discussed by Fineman [17], concurrent updates by P processors can be resolved in $O(t \lg P)$ worst-case time, where t is the serial cost of an access-history update: $t = O(1)$ for a determinacy-race detector, and $t = O(n^k)$ for a data-race detector.

Parallel SP-Maintenance

The SP-bags algorithm is inherently serial, as the correctness relies on an execution order corresponding to an English walk of the parse tree. Correctness of SP-order, on the other hand, does not rely on any particular execution order. SP-order thus appears like a natural choice for a parallel algorithm. The main complication arises in performing concurrent updates to the underlying order-maintenance data structures of SP-order. The obvious approach for parallelizing SP-order directly requires locking the order-maintenance data structures whenever performing an update. As with the access history, a lock may cause all the other $P - 1$ processors to waste time waiting for the lock, thus causing a $\Theta(P)$ overhead per lock acquisition. For programs with short strands, a $\Theta(P)$ overhead per strand creation results in no improvement as compared to a serial execution.

The SP-ordered-bags algorithm, previously called SP-hybrid [4, 17], uses a two-tiered algorithm with a global tier and a local tier to overcome the scalability problems with lock synchronization. The global tier uses a parallel SP-order algorithm with locks, and the local tier uses the serial SP-bags algorithm without locks. By bounding the number of updates to the global tier, the locking overhead is reduced.

SP-ordered-bags leverages the fact that the Cilk scheduler executes a program mostly in an English order. The only exception occurs on steals when the thief processor causes a violation in the English ordering. The thief then continues executing its local subtree serially in an English order. Thus, any serial SP-maintenance algorithm, like SP-bags, is viable within each of these local serially executing subtrees. (SP-bags is also desirable as it interacts well with the global tier; details are omitted here.) Moreover, each local SP-bags data structure is only updated by the single processor executing that subtree, and thus no locking is required. The local tier permits SP queries within a single local subcomputation.

The global tier is responsible for arranging the local subcomputations to permit SP-queries among these subcomputations. SP-ordered-bags employs the parallel SP-order algorithm to arrange the subcomputations. Although the global tier is locked whenever an update occurs, updates occur only when the Cilk scheduler causes a steal. Since the Cilk scheduler causes at most $O(PT_\infty)$ steals, where T_∞ is the span of the program being executed, updates to the global tier add only $O(PT_\infty)$ to the running time of the program.

Combining the local and global tiers together into SP-ordered-bags yields a parallel SP-maintenance algorithm that runs in $O(T_1/P + PT_\infty)$ time on P processors, where T_1 and T_∞ are the work and span of the underlying program being tested. A detailed discussion of SP-ordered-bags, including correctness and performance proofs, can be found in [4, 17].

Related Entries
▶Cilk
▶Race Conditions
▶Race Detection Techniques

Bibliographic Notes and Further Reading

Static race detectors [1, 2, 6, 15, 25, 36] analyze the text of the program to determine whether a race occurs. Static analysis tools may be able to determine whether a memory location can be involved in a race for any input. These tools are inherently conservative, however, sometimes reporting races that do not exist, since the static debuggers cannot fully understand the control-flow and synchronization semantics of a program. For example, dynamic control-flow constructs (e.g., a fork statement) inside if statements or loops are particularly difficult to deal with. Mellor-Crummey [25] proposes using static tools as a way of pruning the number of memory locations being monitored by a dynamic race detector.

Dynamic race detectors execute the program given a particular input. Some dynamic race detectors perform a post-mortem analysis based on program-execution logs [8, 14, 21, 26, 28–30], analyzing a log of program-execution events after the program has finished running. On-the-fly race detectors, like the Nondeterminators and Cilkscreen, report races during the execution of the program. Both dynamic approaches are similar and use some form of SP-maintenance algorithm in conjunction with an access history. On-the-fly race detectors benefit from garbage collection, thereby reducing the total space used by the tool. Post-mortem tools, on the other hand, must keep exhaustive logs.

Netzer and Miller [31] provide a common terminology to unify previous work on dynamic race detection. A *feasible* data race is a race that can actually occur in an execution of the program. Netzer and Miller show that locating feasible data races in a general program is NP-hard. Instead, most race detectors, including the ones in this article, deal with the problem of discovering *apparent* data races, which is an approximation of the races that may actually occur. These race detectors typically ignore data dependencies that may make some apparent races infeasible, instead considering only explicit coordination or control-flow constructs (like forks and joins). As a result, these race detectors are conservative and report races that may not actually occur.

Dinning and Schonberg's "lock-covers" algorithm [13] detects apparent races in programs that use locks. Cheng et al. [7] generalize this algorithm and improve its running time with their All-Sets algorithm, which is the one used in the Nondeterminator-2 and Cilkscreen.

Savage et al. [33] give an on-the-fly race detector called Eraser that does not use an SP-maintenance algorithm, and hence would report races between strands that operate in series if applied to Cilk. Their Eraser tool works on programs that have static threads (i.e., no nested parallelism) and enforces a simple locking discipline. A shared variable must be protected by a particular lock on every access, or they report a race. The Brelly algorithm [7] employs SP maintenance while enforcing an "umbrella" locking discipline, which generalizes Eraser's locking discipline. Brelly was incorporated into the Nondeterminator-2, but although it theoretically runs faster than the All-Sets algorithm in the worst case, most users preferred the All-Sets algorithm for the completeness of coverage, and the typical running time of All-Sets is not onerous.

Nudler and Rudolph [32] introduced the English-Hebrew labeling scheme for their SP-maintenance algorithm. Each strand is assigned two static labels, similar to the labeling described for SP-order. They do not, however, use a centralized data structure to reassign labels. Instead, label sizes grow proportionally to the maximum concurrency of the program. Mellor-Crummey [24] proposed an "offset-span labeling" scheme, which has label lengths proportional to the maximum nesting depth of forks. Although it uses shorter label lengths than the English-Hebrew scheme, the size of offset-span labels is not bounded by a constant as it is SP-order. Both of these approaches perform local decisions on strand creation to assign static labels. Although these approaches result in no locking or synchronization overhead for SP-maintenance, and are inherently parallel algorithms, the large labels can drastically increase the work of the race detector.

Dinning and Schonberg's "task recycling" algorithm [12] uses a centralized data structure to maintain series-parallel relationships. Each strand (block) is given a unique task identifier, which consists of a task and a version number. A task can be reassigned (recycled) to another strand during the program execution, which reduces the total amount of space used by the algorithm. Each strand is assigned a parent vector that contains the largest version number, for each task, of its ancestor strands. To query the relationship between an active strand e_1 and a strand e_2 recorded in the access history, task recycling simply compares the version number of e_2's task against the version number stored in the appropriate slot in e_1's parent vector, which is a constant-time operation. The cost of creating a new strand, however, can be proportional to the maximum logical concurrency. Dinning and Schonberg's algorithm also handles other coordination between strands, like barriers, where two parallel threads must reach a particular point before continuing.

Bibliography

1. Appelbe WF, McDowell CE (1985) Anomaly reporting: a tool for debugging and developing parallel numerical algorithms. In: Proceedings of the 1st international conference on supercomputing systems. IEEE, pp 386–391
2. Balasundaram V, Kennedy K (1986) Compile-time detection of race conditions in a parallel program. In: Proceedings of the 3rd international conference on supercomputing, ACM Press, New York, pp 175–185
3. Bender MA, Cole R, Demaine ED, Farach-Colton M, Zito J (2002) Two simplified algorithms for maintaining order in a list. In: Proceedings of the European syposium on algorithms, pp 152–164
4. Bender MA, Fineman JT, Gilbert S, Leiserson CE (2004) On-the-fly maintenance of series-parallel relationships in fork-join multi-threaded programs. In: Proceedings of the sixteenth annual ACM symposium on parallel algorithms and architectures, Barcelona, Spain, June 2004, pp 133–144
5. Bruening D (2004) Efficient, transparent, and comprehensive runtime code manipulation. Ph.D. thesis, Department of Electrical Engineering and Computer Science, Massachusetts Institute of Technology
6. Callahan D, Sublok J (1988) Static analysis of low-level synchronization. In: Proceedings of the 1988 ACM SIGPLAN and SIGOPS workshop on parallel and distributed debugging, ACM Press, New York, pp 100–111
7. Cheng G-I, Feng M, Leiserson CE, Randall KH, Stark AF (1988) Detecting data races in Cilk programs that use locks. In: Proceedings of the ACM symposium on parallel algorithms and architectures, June 1998, pp 298–309
8. Choi J-D, Miller BP, Netzer RHB (1991) Techniques for debugging parallel programs with flowback analysis. ACM Trans Program Lang Syst 13(4):491–530
9. Cormen TH, Leiserson CE, Rivest RL, Stein C (2009) Introduction to algorithms, 3rd edn. MIT Press, Cambridge
10. Dietz PF (1982) Maintaining order in a linked list. In: Proceedings of the ACM symposium on the theory of computing, May 1982, pp 122–127
11. Dietz PF, Sleator DD (1987) Two algorithms for maintaining order in a list. In: Proceedings of the ACM symposium on the theory of computing, May 1987, pp 365–372
12. Dinning A, Schonberg E (1990) An empirical comparison of monitoring algorithms for access anomaly detection. In: Proceedings of the ACM SIGPLAN symposium on principles and practice of parallel programming, pp 1–10
13. Dinning A, Schonberg E (1991) Detecting access anomalies in programs with critical sections. In: Proceedings of the ACM/ONR workshop on parallel and distributed debugging, May 1991, ACM Press, pp 85–96
14. Emrath PA, Ghosh S, Padua DA (1989) Event synchronization analysis for debugging parallel programs. In: Proceedings of the 1989 ACM/IEEE conference on supercomputing, November 1989, pp 580–588
15. Emrath PA, Padua DA (1988) Automatic detection of nondeterminacy in parallel programs. In: Proceedings of the workshop

on parallel and distributed debugging, Madison, Wisconsin, May 1988, pp 89–99
16. Feng M, Leiserson CE (1997) Efficient detection of determinacy races in Cilk programs. In: Proceedings of the ACM symposium on parallel algorithms and architectures, June 1997, pp 1–11
17. Fineman JT (2005) Provably good race detection that runs in parallel. Master's thesis, Massachusetts Institute of Technology Department of Electrical Engineering and Computer Science, August 2005
18. Frigo M, Halpern P, Leiserson CE, Lewin-Berlin S (2009) Reducers and other cilk++ hyperobjects. In: Proceedings of the twenty-first annual symposium on parallelism in algorithms and architectures, pp 79–90
19. Frigo M, Leiserson CE, Randall KH (1998) The implementation of the Cilk-5 multithreaded language. In: Proceedings of the ACM SIGPLAN conference on programming language design and implementation, pp 212–223
20. Gabow HN, Tarjan RE (1985) A linear-time algorithm for a special case of disjoint set union. J Comput System Sci 30(2):209–221
21. Helmbold DP, McDowell CE, Wang J-Z (1990) Analyzing traces with anonymous synchronization. In: Proceedings of the 1990 international conference on parallel processing, August 1990. pp II70–II77
22. Steele GL Jr (1990) Making asynchronous parallelism safe for the world. In: Proceedings of the seventeenth annual ACM symposium on principles of programming languages, ACM Press, pp 218–231
23. Luk C-K, Cohn R, Muth R, Patil H, Klauser A, Lowney G, Wallace S, Reddi VJ, Hazelwood K (2005) Pin: building customized program analysis tools with dynamic instrumentation. In: Proceedings of the 2005 ACM SIGPLAN conference on programming language design and implementation, ACM Press, New York, pp 190–200
24. Mellor-Crummey J (1991) On-the-fly detection of data races for programs with nested fork-join parallelism. In: Proceedings of supercomputing, pp 24–33
25. Mellor-Crummey J (1993) Compile-time support for efficient data race detection in shared-memory parallel programs. In: Proceedings of the ACM/ONR workshop on parallel and distributed debugging, San Diego, California, May 1993. ACM Press, pp 129–139
26. Miller BP, Choi J-D (1988) A mechanism for efficient debugging of parallel programs. In: Proceedings of the 1988 ACM SIGPLAN conference on programming language design and implementation, Atlanta, Georgia, June 1988, pp 135–144
27. Nethercote N, Seward J (2007) Valgrind: A framework for heavyweight dynamic binary instrumentation. In: Proceedings of the ACM SIGPLAN 2007 conference on programming language design and implementaion, ACM, San Diego, June 2007, pp 89–100
28. Netzer RHB, Ghosh S (1992) Efficient race condition detection for shared-memory programs with post/wait synchronization. In: Proceedings of the 1992 international conference on parallel processing, St. Charles, Illinois, August 1992
29. Netzer RHB, Miller BP (1990) On the complexity of event ordering for shared-memory parallel program executions. In: Proceedings of the 1990 international conference on parallel processing, August 1990. pp II:93–97
30. Netzer RHB, Miller BP (1991) Improving the accuracy of data race detection. In: Proceedings of the third ACM SIGPLAN symposium on principles and practice of parallel programming, New York, NY, USA. ACM Press, pp 133–144
31. Netzer RHB, Miller BP (1992) What are race conditions? ACM Lett Program Lang Syst 1(1):74–88
32. Nudler I, Rudolph L (1986) Tools for the efficient development of efficient parallel programs. In: Proceedings of the first Israeli conference on computer systems engineering, May 1986
33. Savage S, Burrows M, Nelson G, Sobalvarro P, Anderson T (1997) Eraser: a dynamic race detector for multi-threaded programs. In: Proceedings of the sixteenth ACM symposium on operating systems principles (SOSP), ACM Press, New York, pp 27–37
34. Tarjan RE (1975) Efficiency of a good but not linear set union algorithm. J ACM 22(2):215–225
35. Tarjan RE (1983) Data structures and network algorithms. Society for Industrial and Applied Mathematics, Philadelphia
36. Taylor RN (1983) A general-purpose algorithm for analyzing concurrent programs. Commun ACM 26(5):361–376
37. Tsakalidis AK (1984) Maintaining order in a generalized linked list. Acta Inform 21(1):101–112

Race Hazard

▶ Race Conditions

Radix Sort

▶ Sorting

Rapid Elliptic Solvers

EFSTRATIOS GALLOPOULOS
University of Patras, Patras, Greece

Synonyms
Fast poisson solvers

Definition
Direct numerical methods for the solution of linear systems obtained from the discretization of certain partial

differential equations, typically elliptic and separable, defined on rectangular domains in d dimensions, with sequential computational complexity $O(N \log_2 N)$ or less, where N is the number of unknowns.

Discussion

Mathematical models in many areas of science and engineering are often described, in part, by elliptic partial differential equations (PDEs), so their fast and reliable numerical solution becomes an essential task. For some frequently occurring elliptic PDEs, it is possible to develop solution methods, termed Rapid Elliptic Solvers (RES), for the linear systems obtained from their discretization that exploit the problem characteristics to achieve (almost linear) complexity $O(N \log N)$ or less (all logarithms are base 2) for systems of N unknowns. RES are direct methods, in the sense that in the absence of roundoff they give an exact solution and require about the same storage as iterative methods. When well implemented, RES can solve the problems they are designed for faster than other direct or iterative methods [7, 32]. The downside is their limited applicability; since RES impose restrictions on the PDE, the domain of definition and their performance and ease of implementation may also depend on the boundary conditions and the size of the problem.

Major historical milestones were the paper [27], by Hyman, where Fourier analysis and marching were proposed to solve Poisson's equation as a precursor of methods that were analyzed more than a decade later; and the paper by Bickley and McNamee [3, Sect. 3], where the inverse of the special block tridiagonal matrices occurring when solving Poisson's equation and a first version of the Matrix Decomposition algorithm were described. Reference [22] by Hockney with its description of the FACR(l) algorithm and the solution of tridiagonal systems with cyclic reduction (in collaboration with Golub) is widely considered to mark the beginning of the modern era of RES. That and the paper by Buzbee, Golub, and Nielson [9], with its detailed analysis of the major RES were extremely influential in the development of the field. The evolution to methods of low sequential complexity was enabled by two key developments: the advent of the FFT and fast methods for the manipulation of Toeplitz matrices.

Interest in the design and implementation of parallel algorithms for RES started in the early 1970s, with the papers of Buzbee [10] and Sameh et al. [45] and has been attracting the attention of computational scientists ever since. These parallel RES can solve the linear systems under consideration in $O(\log N)$ parallel operations on $O(N)$ processors instead of the fastest but impractical algorithm for general linear systems that requires $O(\log^2 N)$ parallel operations on $O(N^4)$ processors. Parallel implementations were discussed as early as 1973 for the Illiac IV (see ▶Illiac IV) [14] and subsequently for most important high-performance computing platforms, including vector processors, vector multiprocessors, shared memory symmetric multiprocessors, distributed memory multiprocessors, SIMD and MIMD processor arrays, clusters of heterogeneous processors, and in Grid environments. References for specific systems can be found for the Cray-1 [49, 51]; the ICL DAP [25]; Alliant FX/8 [18, 31]; Caltech and Intel hypercubes [13, 36, 41, 50]; Thinking Machines CM-2 [35]; Denelcor HEP [8]; the University of Illinois Cedar machine [16, 20]; Cray X-MP [49]; Cray Y-MP [12]; Cray T3E [21, 42]; Grid environments [52]; Intel multicore processors and processor clusters [28]; GPUs [43]. Regarding the latter, it is worth noting the extensive studies conducted at Yale on an early GPU, the FPS-164 [38]. Proposals for special-purpose hardware are in [53]. RES were included in the PELLPACK parallel problem-solving environment for elliptic PDEs [26]. More information can be found in the annotated bibliography provided in [17]. As will become clear, RES are an important class of structured matrix computations whose design and parallelization depends on special mathematical transformations not usually applicable when dealing with direct matrix computations. This is a topic with many applications and the subject of intensive investigation in computational mathematics.

Problem Formulation

RES are primarily applicable for solving numerically separable elliptic PDEs whose discretization (cf. [5, 29, 55]) leads to block Toeplitz tridiagonal linear systems of order $N = mn$,

$$\mathcal{A}U = F, \text{ where } \mathcal{A} = \text{trid}_n[W, T, W], \text{ and } W, T \in \mathbb{R}^{m \times m}, \quad (1)$$

where W, T are symmetric, simultaneously diagonalizable and thus $WT = TW$. Symbol $\text{trid}_n[C, A, B]$ denotes block Toeplitz tridiagonal or Toeplitz tridiagonal matrices, where C, A, B are the (matrix or scalar) elements along the subdiagonals, diagonals, and superdiagonals, respectively, and n is their number.

A simple but very common problem is Poisson's equation on a rectangular region. After suitable discretization, e.g., using an $m \times n$ rectangular grid, (1) becomes

$$\begin{pmatrix} T & -I & & & \\ -I & T & -I & & \\ & \ddots & \ddots & \ddots & \\ & & -I & T & -I \\ & & & -I & T \end{pmatrix} \begin{pmatrix} U_1 \\ U_2 \\ \vdots \\ \vdots \\ U_n \end{pmatrix} = \begin{pmatrix} F_1 \\ F_2 \\ \vdots \\ \vdots \\ F_n \end{pmatrix}, \quad (2)$$

where $T = \operatorname{trid}_m[-1, 4, -1]$ is Toeplitz symmetric and tridiagonal. Vectors $U_i = [U_{i,1}, \ldots, U_{i,m}]^\top \in \mathbb{R}^m$ for $i = 1, \ldots, n$ contain the unknowns at the ith grid row, and $F_i = [F_{i,1}, \ldots, F_{i,m}]^\top$ the values of the right-hand side F including the boundary terms and scalings related to the discretization. This is the problem for which RES are eminently applicable and mostly discussed in the literature of RES, hence the term "fast Poisson solvers." The homogeneous case, $f \equiv 0$, is Laplace's equation, that lends itself to even more specialized fast methods (not discussed here). RES can also be designed to solve the general separable problem

$$-(a(x)u_{xx} + b(x)u_x) - (d(y)u_{yy} + e(y)u_y) + (c(x) + \tilde{c}(y))u = f(x, y) \quad (3)$$

whose discrete form is

$$\begin{pmatrix} T + \alpha_1 I & -\beta_1 I & & & \\ -\gamma_2 I & T + \alpha_2 I & -\beta_2 I & & \\ & \ddots & \ddots & \ddots & \\ & & -\gamma_{n-1} I & T + \alpha_{n-1} I & -\beta_{n-1} I \\ & & & -\gamma_n I & T + \alpha_{n-1} I \end{pmatrix} \begin{pmatrix} U_1 \\ U_2 \\ \vdots \\ \vdots \\ U_n \end{pmatrix} = \begin{pmatrix} F_1 \\ F_2 \\ \vdots \\ \vdots \\ F_n \end{pmatrix}, \quad (4)$$

for scalars $\alpha_j, \beta_j, \gamma_j$. This is no longer block Toeplitz, but the diagonal and off diagonal blocks have special structure.

Once the equations become nonseparable and/or the domain irregular, RES are not directly applicable and other methods are preferred. All is not lost, however, because frequently RES could be used as building blocks of more general solvers, e.g., in domain decomposition and preconditioning.

Sequential RES are much faster than direct solvers such as sparse Cholesky elimination (see ▶ Sparse Direct Methods). This advantage carries over to parallel RES. Other methods that can be used but are addressed elsewhere in this volume are multigrid methods (see ▶ Algebraic Multigrid) and preconditioned conjugate gradients (see ▶ Iterative Methods) that are the basis for software PDE packages such as PETSc.

Mathematical Preliminaries and Notation

The following concepts from matrix analysis are essential to describe and analyze RES.

1. Kronecker products of matrices and their properties.
2. Chebyshev polynomials (first and second kind) C_d, S_d, and modified Chebyshev polynomials (second kind) $\tilde{C}_d$.
3. The analytic expression for the eigenvalues and eigenvectors of the symmetric tridiagonal Toeplitz matrix $T = \operatorname{trid}_m[-1, \alpha, -1]$: Specifically

$$\lambda_j = \alpha - 2\cos\left(\frac{\pi j}{m+1}\right), \quad q_j = \sqrt{\frac{2}{m+1}} \left[\sin\left(\frac{\pi j}{m+1}\right), \ldots, \sin\left(\frac{\pi j m}{m+1}\right)\right]^\top. \quad (5)$$

If $Q = [q_1, \ldots, q_m]$ then the product Qy for any $y \in \mathbb{R}^m$ has elements $\sqrt{\frac{2}{m+1}} \sum_{j=1}^m \sin\left(\frac{\pi i j}{m+1}\right)$ for $i = 1, \ldots, m$ and so is the *discrete sine transform* (DST) of y times a scaling factor. Also $Q^\top = Q$ and $Q^\top Q = I$. The DST can be computed in $O(m \log m)$ operations using FFT-type methods. Similar results for the eigenstructure also hold for slightly modified matrices that occur when the boundary conditions for the continuous problem are not strictly Dirichlet.

4. The fact (see [1, 3, 37]) that for any nonsingular $T \in \mathbb{R}^{m \times m}$, the matrix $\mathcal{A} = \operatorname{trid}_n[-I, T, -I]$ is nonsingular and $\mathcal{A}^{-1}$ can be written as a block matrix with general term

$$(\mathcal{A}^{-1})_{ij} = \begin{cases} S_n^{-1}(T) S_{i-1}(T) S_{n-j}(T), & j \geq i, \\ S_n^{-1}(T) S_{j-1}(T) S_{n-i}(T), & i \geq j. \end{cases} \quad (6)$$

5. The vec operator and its inverse, unvec_n. Also the *vec-permutation* matrix $\Pi_{m,n} \mathbb{R}^{mn \times mn}$, that is the

unique matrix such that $\text{vec}(A) = \Pi_{m,n}\text{vec}(A^\top)$, where $A \in \mathbb{R}^{m \times n}$. The matrix is orthogonal and $\Pi_{m,n}(I_n \otimes \tilde{T}_m) = (\tilde{T}_m \otimes I_n)\Pi_{m,n}$.

Algorithmic Infrastructure

Most RES make use of the finite difference analogue of a key idea in the separation of variables method for PDEs, namely, that under certain conditions, some multidimensional problems can be solved by solving several one-dimensional problems [34]. In line with this, it turns out that RES for (2) make extensive use of and their performance greatly depends on two basic kernels: (1) Tridiagonal linear system solvers and (2) fast Fourier and trigonometric transforms. These kernels are also used extensively in collective form, that is for given tridiagonal $T \in \mathbb{R}^{m \times m}$ and any $Y \in \mathbb{R}^{m \times s}$, solve $TX = Y$ for $s \geq 1$. In many cases, shifted or multiply shifted tridiagonal systems with one or multiple right-hand sides must be solved. Also if the $m \times m$ matrix Q represents the discrete sine, cosine or Fourier transform of length m, then RES call for the fast computation of QY as well as the inverse transforms $Q^{-1}Y$. The best known parallel techniques for solving tridiagonal systems are *recursive doubling*, *cyclic reduction*, and *parallel cyclic reduction*, that all need $O(\log m)$ parallel arithmetic operations on $O(m)$ processors, e.g., [23, 30, 56]. For more flexibility, it is possible to combine those or Gaussian elimination with *divide-and-conquer* methods. Fourier-based RES also require fast implementations of the discrete cosine transform and the discrete Fourier transform to handle Neumann and periodic boundary conditions. Many publications on RES (e.g., [23, 38, 45, 47]) include extensive discussion of these building blocks. It is common for the tridiagonal matrices to have additional properties that can be used for faster processing. They are usually symmetric positive definite, Toeplitz, and have the form $\text{trid}_m[-1, \tau, -1]$, where $\tau \geq 2$. When $\tau > 2$, they are diagonally dominant in which case it is possible to terminate early Gaussian elimination (as implemented by O'Donnell et al. in [38]) and cyclic reduction (as proposed by Hockney in [22]), at negligible error. ScaLAPACK includes efficient tridiagonal and narrow-banded solvers, but the Toeplitz structure is not exploited (see ▶ScaLAPACK). A detailed description of the fast Fourier and other discrete transforms used in RES can be found in [54].

Chapter (see ▶FFTW) documents very efficient algorithms for the single and multiple FFTs needed for kernels of type (2). Parallel algorithms for the fast transforms required in the context of the RES have $O(\log m)$ complexity on m processors.

Matrix Decomposition

MD refers to a large class of methods to solve systems with matrices such as (4). As Buzbee noted in [10]: "It seldom happens that the application of L processors would yield an L-fold increase in efficiency relative to a single processor, but that is the case with the MD algorithm." Sameh et al. in [45] provided the first detailed study of parallel MD for Poisson's equation. MD can be succinctly described, as shown early on by Lynch et al. and Egerváry, using the compact Kronecker product representation of $\mathcal{A}$ (see [34] and extensive discussion and references in [2]). Of greatest relevance here is the case that $\mathcal{A} = (I_n \otimes \tilde{T}_m + \tilde{T}_n \otimes I_m)$, where any of $\tilde{T}_m, \tilde{T}_n$ is diagonalizable using matrices expressed by Fourier or trigonometric transforms. Denoting by $Q_x \in \mathbb{R}^{m \times m}$ (resp. $Q_y \in \mathbb{R}^{n \times n}$) the matrix of eigenvectors of $\tilde{T}_m$ (resp. $\tilde{T}_n$), then $\mathcal{A}U = F$ can be rewritten as

$$\left(I_n \otimes Q_x^\top\right)\left(I_n \otimes \tilde{T}_m + \tilde{T}_n \otimes I_m\right)\left(I_n \otimes Q_x\right)$$
$$\left(I_n \otimes Q_x^\top\right) U = \left(I_n \otimes Q_x^\top\right) F$$

and equivalently as

$$\left(I_n \otimes \tilde{\Lambda}_m + \tilde{T}_n \otimes I_m\right)\left(I_n \otimes Q_x^\top\right) U = \left(I_n \otimes Q_x^\top\right) F.$$

Applying the similarity transformation with the vec-permutation matrix $\Pi_{m,n}$, the system becomes

$$\underbrace{\left(\tilde{\Lambda}_m \otimes I_n + I_m \otimes \tilde{T}_n\right)}_{\mathcal{B}}\left(\Pi_{m,n}\left(I_n \otimes Q_x^\top\right) U\right) = \Pi_{m,n}\left(I_n \otimes Q_x^\top\right) F.$$

Matrix $\mathcal{B}$ is block diagonal, so these are m independent tridiagonal systems of order n each. Thus

$$U = (I_n \otimes Q_x)\Pi_{m,n}^\top \mathcal{B}^{-1}\Pi_{m,n}\left(I_n \otimes Q_x^\top\right) F. \quad (7)$$

When either of $\tilde{T}_m$ of $\tilde{T}_n$ is diagonalizable with trigonometric or Fourier transforms, as in the matrix of (2) for the Poisson equation, where they both are of the form $\text{trid}[-1, 2, -1]$, and matrix (4) when the coefficients are constant in one direction, MD will also be called Fourier MD and can be applied at total cost $O(N \log N)$. For example, if Q_x can be applied in $O(m \log m)$ operations, the overall cost becomes $O(nm \log m)$ for Fourier MD. From (7) emerge the three major computational phases of Fourier MD for (2). In phase (I), the term $(I_n \otimes Q_x^\top)F$ is computed, which amounts to the DST of n vectors $F_i, i = 1, \ldots, n$ to compute the $\hat{F}_i = Q_x^\top F_i$. In phase (II), m independent tridiagonal systems with coefficient matrices $B_j = \text{trid}_n\left[-1, \lambda_j^{(m)}, -1\right]$ are solved, where $\lambda_j^{(m)}$ is the jth eigenvalue of T in (2). The right-hand sides are the m columns of $[\hat{F}_1, \ldots, \hat{F}_n]^\top$. In terms of the vec- constructs, these are the m contiguous, length-n subvectors of the mn length vector $\Pi_{m,n}\text{vec}[\hat{F}_1, \ldots, \hat{F}_n]$. The respective solutions $\hat{U}_j, j = 1, \ldots, m$ are stacked and reordered into $\tilde{U} = \Pi_{m,n}^\top \text{vec}[\hat{U}_1, \ldots, \hat{U}_m]$ so that phase (III) consists of independent application of a scaled, length m DST of each column of $[\tilde{U}_1, \ldots, \tilde{U}_n] = \text{unvec}_n \tilde{U}$. Opportunities for parallelism abound, and if mn processors are available and each tridiagonal system is solved using a parallel algorithm of logarithmic complexity, then MD can be accomplished in $O(\log mn)$ parallel operations. There are several ways of organizing the computation. When there are $n = m$ processors, phases (I) and (III) can be performed independently in $m \log m$ steps. This will leave the data in the middle phase distributed across the processors so that the multiple tridiagonal systems will be solved with a parallel algorithm that would require significant data movement. Instead, one can transpose the output data from phase (I) and also at the end of phase (II) so that all data is readily accessible from any processor that needs it. This approach has the advantage that it builds on mature numerical software for uniprocessors. It requires, however, the use of efficient algorithms for matrix transposition.

MD algorithms have been designed and implemented on vector and parallel architectures and are frequently used as the baseline in evaluating new Poisson solvers; cf. [10, 12–14, 21, 25, 35, 36, 38, 41, 45, 51] and [17] for more details. More applications of MD can be found in the survey [2] by Bialecki et al.

Complete Fourier Transform

The idea of CFT was discussed by Hyman in [27] and described in the context of the tensor product methods of Lynch et al. (cf. [5, 34]). For low cost, this requires that both $\tilde{T}_m$ and $\tilde{T}_n$ are diagonalizable with Fourier or trigonometric transforms, as is the case for (2). Then the solution of (2) is

$$U = (Q_y \otimes Q_x)(I_n \otimes \tilde{\Lambda}_m + \tilde{\Lambda}_n \otimes I_m)^{-1}(Q_y^\top \otimes Q_x^\top)F,$$

where matrix $(I_n \otimes \tilde{\Lambda}_m + \tilde{\Lambda}_n \otimes I_m)$ is diagonal. Multiplication by $Q_y^\top \otimes Q_x^\top$ amounts to performing n independent DSTs of length m and m independent DSTs of length n; similarly for $Q_y \otimes Q_x$. The middle phase is an element-by-element division by the diagonal of $I_n \otimes \tilde{\Lambda}_m + \tilde{\Lambda}_n \otimes I_m$ that contains the eigenvalues of $\mathcal{A}$.

The parallel computational cost is $O(\log m + \log n)$ operations on $O(mn)$ processors. Hockney and Jesshope [23], Swarztrauber and Sweet [47], among others, studied CFT for various parallel systems. In the latter, CFT was found to have lower computational and communication complexity than MD and BCR for systems with $O(mn)$ processors connected in a hypercube. Specific parallel implementations were described by O'Donnel et al. in [38] for the FPS-164 attached array processor where CFT had lower performance than MD and FACR(1), by Cote in [13] for Intel hypercubes; see also [17].

Block Cyclic Reduction

BCR is a solver for (1) that generalizes the (scalar) cyclic reduction of Hockney and Golub. It is also more general than Fourier MD because it does not require knowledge of the eigenstructure of T neither uses fast transforms. A detailed analysis is found in [9]. BCR was key to the design of FISHPAK, the influential numerical library by Swarztrauber, Sweet, and Adams.

It is outlined next for $n = 2^k - 1$ blocks, though, as shown by Sweet, the method can be modified to handle any n. For steps $r = 1, \ldots, k - 1$, adjacent blocks of equations are combined in groups of three to eliminate two blocks of unknowns; in the first step, for instance, unknowns from even-numbered blocks are eliminated and a reduced system $\mathcal{A}^{(1)} = \text{trid}_{2^{k-1}-1}[-I, A^2 - 2I, -I]$, containing approximately half the blocks remains. Setting $T^{(0)} = T$, and $T^{(r)} = (T^{(r-1)})^2 - 2I$, at the rth step the reduced system is

$$\text{trid}_{2^{k-r}-1}[-I, T^{(r)}, -I]\mathbf{U}^{(r)} = \mathbf{F}^{(r)},$$

where $\mathbf{F}^{(r)} = \text{vec}[F_{2^r \cdot 1}, \ldots, F_{2^r \cdot (2^{k-r}-1)}]$. These are computed by

$$F_{2^r \cdot j} = F_{2^{r-1}(j-1)} + F_{2^{r-1}(j+1)} + T^{(r-1)}F_{2^{r-1}j}. \quad (8)$$

Matrix $T^{(r)}$ can be written in terms of Chebyshev polynomials, $T^{(r)} = 2C_{2^r}\left(\frac{T}{2}\right) = \tilde{C}_{2^r}(T)$. The roots are known analytically, $\rho_i^{(r)} = 2\cos\left(\frac{(2i-1)}{2^{r+1}}\pi\right)$, therefore the product form of $T^{(r)}$ is also available.

After $r = k - 1$ steps, only the system $T^{(k)} U_{2^{k-1}} = F^{(r)}_{2^{k-1}}$ remains. After this is solved, a back substitution phase recovers the remaining unknowns. Each reduction step requires $2^{k-r} - 1$ independent matrix-vector multiplications with $T^{(r-1)}$. All multiplications with $T^{(r-1)}$ are done using its product form so that the total cost is $O(nm \log n)$ operations without recourse to fast transforms. Even with unlimited parallelism, the systems composing $T^{(r)}$ must be solved in sequence, which creates a parallelization bottleneck. Also the algorithm as stated (sometimes called CORF [9]) is not numerically viable because the growing discrepancy in the magnitude of the terms in (8) leads to excessive roundoff.

Both problems can be overcome. Stabilization is achieved by means of a clever modification due to Buneman and analyzed in detail in [9], in which the unstable recurrence (8) is replaced with a coupled recurrence for a pair of new vectors, that can be computed stably, by exchanging tridiagonal matrix-vector multiplications with tridiagonal linear system solves. The number of sequential operations remains $O(mn \log n)$.

The parallel performance bottleneck can be resolved using *partial fractions*, a versatile tool for parallel processing first used, ingeniously, by H.T. Kung in [33] to enable the evaluation of arithmetic expressions such as x^n, $\prod_{i=1}^{n}(x + \rho_i)$ and Chebyshev polynomials in few parallel divisions and $O(\log n)$ parallel additions. For scalars, these findings are primarily of theoretical interest since the expressions can also be computed in $O(\log n)$ multiplications. The idea becomes much more attractive for matrices (the problem of computing powers of a matrix is mentioned in [33] but not pursued any further) as is the case of BCR in the CORF or the stable variants of Buneman. Specifically, the parallelization bottleneck that occurs when solving

$$T^{(r)} X_r = Y_r, \text{ where } T^{(r)} = \prod_{i=1}^{2^r}\left(T - \rho_i^{(r)} I\right) \text{ and}$$

$$X_r, Y_r \in \mathbb{R}^{m \times (2^{k-r}-1)}$$

for large r is resolved because, for each r, the roots $\rho_i^{(r)}, i = 1, \ldots, 2^r$ are distinct and so for any right-hand side $f \in \mathbb{R}^m$,

$$(T^{(r)})^{-1} f = \sum_{i=1}^{2^r} \alpha_i^{(r)} \left(T - \rho_i^{(r)} I\right)^{-1} f, \qquad (9)$$

where the $\alpha_i^{(r)}$ are the corresponding partial fraction coefficients that can be easily computed from the values of the derivative of $\tilde{C}_{2^r}(z)$ at $z = \rho_i^{(r)}$. This was described by Sweet (see [48]) and also by Gallopoulos and Saad in [18]. Moreover, when BCR is applied for more general values of n or other boundary conditions that lead to more general matrix rational functions, partial fractions eliminate the need for operations with the numerator. Expression (9) can be evaluated independently for each right-hand side. Therefore, solving with coefficient matrix $T^{(r)}$ and $2^{k-r} - 1$ right-hand sides for $r = 1, \ldots, k - 1$ can be accomplished by solving 2^r independent tridiagonal systems for each right-hand side and then combining the partial solutions by multiplying $2^{k-r} - 1$ matrices, each of size $m \times 2^r$ with the vector of 2^r partial fraction coefficients.

The algorithm has parallel complexity $O(\log n \log m)$. Even though this is somewhat inferior to parallel MD and CFT, BCR has wider applicability; cf. the survey of Bini and Meini in [4] for many additional uses and parallelization. References [18, 20, 31, 47] discuss the application of partial fraction based parallel BCR and evaluate its performance on vector processors and multiprocessors, multicluster vector multiprocessors, and hypercubes. As shown by Calvetti et al. in [11], the use of partial fractions above is numerically safe for the polynomials that occur when solving Poisson's equation, but caution is required in the general case.

The above techniques for parallelizing MD and BCR were implemented in CRAYFISHPAK, a package that contains most of the functionality of FISHPAK (results for the Cray Y-MP listed in [49]). Beyond BCR, partial fractions can also be used to parallelize the computation important matrix functions, e.g., the matrix exponential.

FACR

This method, proposed in [22], is based on the fact that at any step of the reduction phase of BCR, the coefficient matrix is $\mathcal{A}^{(r)} = \text{trid}_{2^{k-r}-1}[-I, T^{(r)}, -I]$, and that because $T^{(r)} = 2C_{2^r}(\frac{T}{2})$ has the same eigenvectors as T and eigenvalues $2C_{2^r}(\frac{\lambda_j^{(m)}}{2})$, the reduced system can be solved using Fourier MD. FACR(l) (acronym for Fourier Analysis Cyclic Reduction) is a hybrid algorithm consisting of the following phases: (1) Perform l steps of BCR to obtain $\mathcal{A}^{(l)}$ and $F^{(l)}$. (2) Use MD to solve $\mathcal{A}^{(l)} U^{(l)} = F^{(l)}$. (3) Use l steps of back substitution to obtain the remaining subvectors of U. Research of Hockney, Swarztrauber, and Temperton has shown that a value $l \approx \log \log m$ reduces the number of sequential operations down to $O(mnl)$. Therefore, properly designed FACR is faster than MD and BCR. In practice, the best choice for l depends on the relative performance of the underlying kernels and other characteristics of the computer platform. The selection for vector and parallel architectures has been studied at length by Hockney (cf. [23] and references therein) and Jesshope and by Briggs and Turnbull [8]. A general conclusion is that l is typically very small (so that BCR can be applied in its simplest CORF form), especially for high levels of parallelism, and that it is worth determining it empirically.

The parallel implementation of all steps can proceed using the techniques deployed for BCR and MD; in fact, FACR(l) can be viewed as an alternative to partial fractions to avoid the bottleneck to parallelization that was observed after a few steps of reduction in BCR. For example, one can monitor the number of systems that can be solved in parallel in BCR, and before the number of independent computations is small and no longer acceptable, switch to MD. This approach was analyzed by Briggs and Turnbull in [8] on a shared-memory multiprocessor. Corroborating the complexity estimates above, FACR is frequently found to be faster than MD and CFT; see, e.g., [38] for results on an attached array processor.

Marching and Other Methods

Marching methods are RES that can be used to solve Poisson's equation as well as general separable PDEs. The idea was already mentioned in [27] and by 1980, as recounted by Hockney [24], a marching algorithm by Lorenz was cautiously cited as the fastest performing RES for Poisson's equation on uniprocessors, provided that it is "used sensibly." The caution is due to numerical instability that can have deleterious effects on accuracy. Bank and Rose in [1] proposed *Generalized Marching (GM)* methods that are stable with operation count $O\left(n^2 \log \frac{n}{k}\right)$ when $m = n$, where k is determined by the sought accuracy, instead of the theoretical $O(n^2)$ for simple but unstable marching.

The key idea in marching methods is that if one knows U_n in (2), then the remaining $U_{n-1}, \ldots, U_1$ could be computed from this and the boundary values U_{n+1} by the recurrence $U_{j-1} = F_j + U_{j+1} - TU_j$ in $O(mn)$ operations. Vector U_n can also be computed in $O(mn)$ operations in the course of block LU of a reordering of (2) by solving a linear system with a matrix rational function of Chebyshev polynomials like S_n.

The process is not numerically viable for large n, thus in GM the domain is partitioned into k strips that are small enough so that sufficient accuracy is maintained when marching is used to compute the solution in each. This is a form of *domain decomposition*, whose merits for parallel processing are discussed in the next section. The interface values of U necessary to start the independent marches can be computed independently extending the process described above. Additional parallelism is available from using partial fractions.

When the right-hand-side F of (1) is sparse and one is interested in only few values of U, then the cost of computing such a solution with MD is reduced. Based on an idea of Banegas, Vassilevski and Kuznetsov designed variants of cyclic reduction that generate systems where a *partial solution method* is deployed to build the final solution. Parallel algorithms using these ideas were implemented by Petrova (on a workstation cluster) [39] and by Rossi and Toivanen (algorithm PSCR on a Cray T3E) who also showed a radix-q version of cyclic reduction that eliminates a factor of $q \geq 2$ blocks at a time. As with other RES (e.g., [46]), to solve the general separable system (4), these methods require additional preprocessing to compute eigenvalues and eigenvectors that are not available analytically.

The special form of the inverse blocks of (2) in (6) shows that both the matrix and its inverse are "data sparse," a property that is used to design effective approximate algorithms to solve elliptic equations using an integral equation formulation; cf. [6, 15]. The explicit formula for the inverse and partial fractions can be combined to solve (2) for any rows of the grid in $O(\log N)$ parallel operations, as proposed in [19]. Marching can also be parallelized by diagonalizing T. Description of this and other methods are found in the monograph [53] by Vajteršic.

Domain Decomposition

Domain decomposition (DD) is a methodology for solving elliptic PDEs in which the solution is constructed by partitioning and solving the problem on subdomains (when these do not overlap, DD is called substructuring) and synthesizing the solution by combining the partial solutions, usually iteratively, until a satisfactory solution is obtained. Whenever the equations and subdomains are suitable, RES can be used as building blocks for DD methods; the algorithm outlined by Buzbee et al. in [9, Sect. 9] is a case in point and confirms that RES were an early motivation behind the development of DD. In some cases, one can dispense of the iterative process altogether and compute the solution to the PDE at sequential cost $O(N \log N)$, thus extending RES to irregular domains. DD naturally lends itself for parallel processing (see ▶Domain Decomposition), introducing another layer of parallelism in the RES described so far and thus providing greater flexibility in their mapping on parallel architectures, e.g., when processors are organized in loosely coupled clusters, for better load balancing on heterogeneous processors, etc. One such method based on Fourier MD was proposed in [44] and can be viewed as a special case of the Spike banded solver method developed by Sameh and collaborators (cf. [40]) (▶Spike).

A slightly different formulation of this DD solver is based on reordering the equations in (2) combined with block LU. This was investigated by Chan and Resasco and then at length with hypercube implementations (cf. [41] and references therein) and by Chan and Fatoohi for vector multiprocessors in [12]. The interface values in domain decomposition can also be computed using the partial solution methodology, e.g., in combination with GM as suggested by Vassilevski and studied by Bencheva in the context of parallel processing (cf. [17]). DD was also used by Barberou to increase the performance of the partial solution method of Rossi and Toivanen on a computational Grid of high-performance systems [52].

Extensions

The above methods can be extended to solve Poisson's equation in three dimensions. The corresponding matrix will be multilevel Toeplitz: It is block Toeplitz tridiagonal with each block being of the form (2). Sameh in [44] proposed a six phase parallel MD-like algorithm that combines independent FFTs in two dimensions and tridiagonal system solutions along the third dimension. Similar parallel RES for the Intel hypercube were described in [41, 50] and in [21] for the Cray T3E. The partial solution method was also extended to three-dimensional problems, e.g., [52, cf. comments on solver PDC3D].

The parallel RES methods above can be extended to handle other types of boundary conditions (Dirichlet, Neumann and periodic) and operators (e.g., biharmonic) and provide a blueprint for the design of parallel RES of higher order of accuracy, e.g., the FACR-like method FFT9 of Houstis and Papatheodorou (see [5, 17]).

Related Entries
▶Algebraic Multigrid
▶Domain Decomposition
▶FFTW
▶Illiac IV
▶Preconditioners for Sparse Iterative Methods
▶ScaLAPACK
▶Sparse Direct Methods
▶Spike

Bibliography

1. Bank RE, Rose DJ (1977) Marching algorithms for elliptic boundary value problems. Part I: the constant coefficient case. Part II: the variable coefficient case. SIAM J Numer Anal 14(5):792–829 (Part I); 950–969 (Part II)
2. Bialecki B, Fairweather G, Karageorghis A (2010) Matrix decomposition algorithms for elliptic boundary value problems: a survey. Numer Algorithms. http://www.springerlink.com/content/g66527532724p607/fulltext.pdf
3. Bickley WG, McNamee J (1960) Matrix and other direct methods for the solution of systems of linear difference equations. Philos Trans R Soc Lond A: Math Phys Sci 252(1005):69–131
4. Bini DA, Meini B (2008) The cyclic reduction algorithm: from Poisson equation to stochastic processes and beyond. Numer Algorithms 51(1):23–60
5. Birkhoff G, Lynch RE (1984) Numerical solution of elliptic problems. SIAM, Philadelphia
6. Börm S, Grasedyck L, Hackbusch W (2006) Lecture notes 21/2003: hierarchical matrices. Technical report, Max Planck Institut fuer Mathematik in den Naturwissenschaften, Leipzig
7. Botta EFF et al (1997) How fast the Laplace equation was solved in 1995. Appl Numer Math 24(4):439–455
8. Briggs WL, Turnbull T (1988) Fast Poisson solvers for MIMD computers. Parallel Comput 6:265–274
9. Buzbee B, Golub G, Nielson C (1970) On direct methods for solving Poisson's equation. SIAM J Numer Anal 7(4):627–656 (see also the comments by Buzbee in Current Contents, 36, September 1992)

10. Buzbee BL (1973) A fast Poisson solver amenable to parallel computation. IEEE Trans Comput C-22(8):793–796
11. Calvetti D, Gallopoulos E, Reichel L (1995) Incomplete partial fractions for parallel evaluation of rational matrix functions. J Comput Appl Math 59:349–380
12. Chan TF, Fatoohi R (1989) Multitasking domain decomposition fast Poisson solvers on the Cray Y-MP. In: Proceedings of the fourth SIAM conference on parallel processing for scientific computing. SIAM, Philadelphia, pp 237–244
13. Cote SJ (1991) Solving partial differential equations on a MIMD hypercube: fast Poisson solvers and the alternating direction method. Technical report UIUCDCS-R-91-1694, University of Illinois at Urbana-Champaign, Urbana
14. Ericksen JH (1972) Iterative and direct methods for solving Poisson's equation and their adaptability to Illiac IV. Technical report UIUCDCS-R-72-574, Department of Computer Science, University of Illinois at Urbana-Champaign
15. Ethridge F, Greengard L (2001) A new fast-multipole accelerated Poisson solver in two dimensions. SIAM J Sci Comput 23(3):741–760
16. Gallivan KA, Heath MT, Ng E, Ortega JM, Peyton BW, Plemmons RJ, Romine CH, Sameh AH, Voigt RG (1990) Parallel algorithms for matrix computations. SIAM, Philadelphia
17. Gallopoulos E. An annotated bibliography for rapid elliptic solvers. http://scgroup.hpclab.ceid.upatras.gr/faculty/stratis/Papers/myresbib
18. Gallopoulos E, Saad Y (1989) Parallel block cyclic reduction algorithm for the fast solution of elliptic equations. Parallel Comput 10(2):143–160
19. Gallopoulos E, Saad Y (1989) Some fast elliptic solvers for parallel architectures and their complexities. Int J High Speed Comput 1(1):113–141
20. Gallopoulos E, Sameh AH (1989) Solving elliptic equations on the Cedar multiprocessor. In: Wright MH (ed) Aspects of computation on asynchronous parallel processors. North-Holland, Amsterdam, pp 1–12
21. Giraud L (2001) Parallel distributed FFT-based solvers for 3-D Poisson problems in meso-scale atmospheric simulations. Int J High Perform Comput Appl 15(1):36–46
22. Hockney R (1965) A fast direct solution of Poisson's equation using Fourier analysis. J Assoc Comput Mach 12:95–113
23. Hockney R, Jesshope C (1983) Parallel computers. Adam Hilger, Bristol
24. Hockney RW (1980) Rapid elliptic solvers. In: Hunt B (ed) Numerical methods in applied fluid dynamics. Academic, London, pp 1–48
25. Hockney RW (1983) Characterizing computers and optimizing the FACR(l) Poisson solver on parallel unicomputers. IEEE Trans Comput C-32(10):933–941
26. Houstis EN, Rice JR, Weerawarana S, Catlin AC, Papachiou P, Wang K-Y, Gaitatzes M (1998) PELLPACK: a problem-solving environment for PDE-based applications on multicomputer platforms. ACM Trans Math Softw 24(1):30–73
27. Hyman MA (1951–1952) Non-iterative numerical solution of boundary-value problems. Appl Sci Res B 2:325–351
28. Intel Cluster Poisson Solver Library – Intel Software Network. http://software.intel.com/en-us/articles/intel-cluster-poisson-solver-library/
29. Iserles A (1996) Introduction to numerical methods for differential equations. Cambridge University Press, Cambridge
30. Johnsson L (1987) Solving tridiagonal systems on ensemble architectures. SIAM J Sci Statist Comput 8:354–392
31. Jwo J-S, Lakshmivarahan S, Dhall SK, Lewis JM (1992) Comparison of performance of three parallel versions of the block cyclic reduction algorithm for solving linear elliptic partial differential equations. Comput Math Appl 24(5–6):83–101
32. Knightley JR, Thompson CP (1987) On the performance of some rapid elliptic solvers on a vector processor. SIAM J Sci Statist Comput 8(5):701–715
33. Kung HT (1976) New algorithms and lower bounds for the parallel evaluation of certain rational expressions and recurrences. J Assoc Comput Mach 23(2):252–261
34. Lynch RE, Rice JR, Thomas DH (1964) Tensor product analysis of partial differential equations. Bull Am Math Soc 70:378–384
35. McBryan OA (1989) Connection machine application performance. Technical report CH-CS-434-89, Department of Computer Science, University of Colorado, Boulder
36. McBryan OA, Van De Velde EF (1987) Hypercube algorithms and implementations. SIAM J Sci Stat Comput 8(2):s227–s287
37. Meurant G (1992) A review on the inverse of symmetric tridiagonal and block tridiagonal matrices. SIAM J Matrix Anal Appl 13(3):707–728
38. O'Donnell ST, Geiger P, Schultz MH (1983) Solving the Poisson equation on the FPS-164. Technical report YALE/DCS/TR293, Yale University
39. Petrova S (1997) Parallel implementation of fast elliptic solver. Parallel Comput 23(8):1113–1128
40. Polizzi E, Sameh AH (2007) SPIKE: A parallel environment for solving banded linear systems. Comput Fluids 36(1):113–120
41. Resasco DC (1990) Domain decomposition algorithms for elliptic partial differential equations. Ph.D. thesis, Yale University, Department of Computer Science
42. Rossi T, Toivanen J (1999) A parallel fast direct solver for block tridiagonal systems with separable matrices of arbitrary dimension. SIAM J Sci Stat Comput 20(5):1778–1796
43. Rossinelli D, Bergdorf M, Cottet G-H, Koumoutsakos P (2010) GPU accelerated simulations of bluff body flows using vortex particle methods. J Comput Phys 229(9):3316–3333
44. Sameh AH (1984) A fast Poisson solver for multiprocessors. In: Birkhoff G, Schoenstadt A (eds) Elliptic problem solvers II. Academic, New York, pp 175–186
45. Sameh AH, Chen SC, Kuck DJ (1976) Parallel Poisson and biharmonic solvers. Computing 17:219–230
46. Swarztrauber PN (1974) A direct method for the discrete solution of separable elliptic equations. SIAM J Numer Anal 11(6):1136–1150
47. Swarztrauber PN, Sweet RA (1989) Vector and parallel methods for the direct solution of Poisson's equation. J Comput Appl Math 27:241–263

48. Sweet RA (1988) A parallel and vector cyclic reduction algorithm. SIAM J Sci Statist Comput 9(4):761–765
49. Sweet RA (1992) Vectorization and parallelization of FISHPAK. In: Dongarra J, Kennedy K, Messina P, Sorensen DC, Voigt RG (eds) Proceedings of the fifth SIAM conference on parallel processing for scientific computing. SIAM, Philadelphia, pp 637–642 (see also http://www.cisl.ucar.edu/softlib/CRAYFISH.html)
50. Sweet RA, Briggs WL, Oliveira S, Porsche JL, Turnbull T (1991) FFTs and three-dimensional Poisson solvers for hypercubes. Parallel Comput 17:121–131
51. Temperton C (1979) Fast Fourier transforms and Poisson solvers on Cray-1. In: Hockney RW, Jesshope CR (eds) Infotech state of the art report: supercomputers, vol 2. Infotech, Maidenhead, pp 359–379
52. Tromeur-Dervout D, Toivanen J, Garbey M, Hess M, Resch MM, Barberou N, Rossi T (2003) Efficient metacomputing of elliptic linear and non-linear problems. J Parallel Distrib Comput 63(5):564–577
53. Vajteršic M (1993) Algorithms for elliptic problems: efficient sequential and parallel solvers. Kluwer, Dordrecht
54. Van Loan C (1992) Computational frameworks for the fast Fourier transform. SIAM, Philadelphia
55. Widlund O (1978) A Lanczos method for a class of nonsymmetric systems of linear equations. SIAM J Numer Anal 15(4):801–812
56. Zhang Y, Cohen J, Owens JD (2010) Fast tridiagonal solvers on the GPU. In: Proceedings of the 15th ACM SIGPLAN PPoPP 2010, Bangalore, India, pp 127–136

Reconfigurable Computer

▶Blue CHiP

Reconfigurable Computers

Reconfigurable computers utilize reconfigurable logic hardware – either standalone, as a part of, or in combination with conventional microprocessors – for processing. Computing using reconfigurable logic hardware that can adapt to the computation can attain only some level of the performance and power efficiency gain of custom hardware but has the advantage of being retargetable for many different applications.

Bibliography

1. Hauck S, DeHon A (2008) Reconfigurable computing: the theory and practice of FPGA-based computing. Morgan Kaufmann, Burlington

Reconstruction of Evolutionary Trees

▶Phylogenetics

Reduce and Scan

MARC SNIR
University of Illinois at Urbana-Champaign, Urbana, IL, USA

Synonyms
Parallel Prefix Sums; Prefix; Prefix Reduction

Definition
Given n inputs $x_1, \ldots, x_n$, and an associative operation $\otimes$, a *reduction* algorithm computes the output $x_1 \otimes \cdots \otimes x_n$. A *prefix* or *scan* algorithm computes the n outputs $x_1, x_1 \otimes x_2, \ldots, x_1 \otimes \cdots \otimes x_n$.

Discussion
The reduction problem is a subset of the prefix problem, but as we shall show, the two are closely related. The reduction and scan operators are available in APL [8]: Thus +/3 7 1 computes the value 11 and +\3 7 1 computes the vector 3 10 11. The two primitives appears in other programming languages and libraries, such as MPI [10].

There are two interesting cases to consider:

Random access: The inputs $x_1, \ldots, x_n$ are stored in consecutive location in an array.
Linked list: The inputs $x_1, \ldots, x_n$ are stored in consecutive locations in a linked list; the links connect each element to its predecessor.

We analyze these two cases using a circuit or PRAM model, and ignoring communication costs.

Random-Access Reduce and Scan
The sequential circuit for a reduction computation is shown in Fig. 1; the corresponding sequential code is shown in Algorithm 1. This circuit has $W = n - 1$ operations and depth $D = n - 1$. It also computes a scan.

One can take advantage of associativity in order to change the order of evaluation, so as to reduce the parallel computation time. An optimal parallel reduction

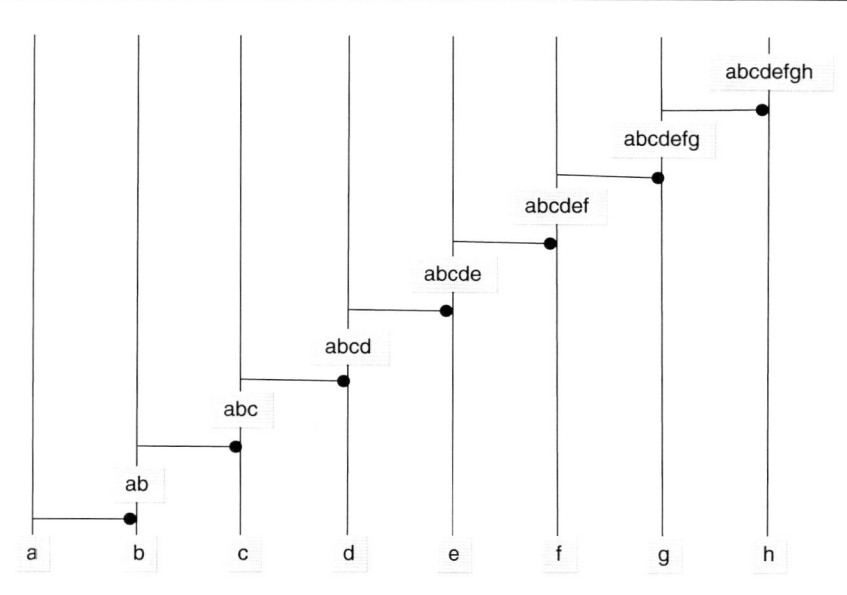

Reduce and Scan. Fig. 1 Sequential prefix circuit

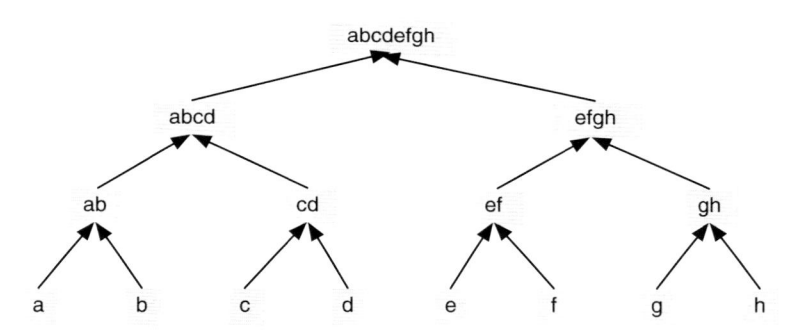

Reduce and Scan. Fig. 2 Binary tree reduction

algorithm is achieved by using a balanced binary tree for the computation, as shown in Figs. 2 and 3, for $n = 8$. The corresponding algorithm is shown in Algorithm 2.

Algorithm 1 Sequential reduction and scan
---
for $(i = 2;\ i \leq n;\ i{+}{+})$
  $x_i = x_{i-1} \otimes x_i;$

Algorithm 2 Binary tree reduction
---
for $(i = 1;\ i \leq k;\ i{+}{+})$
  forall $(j = 2^i;\ j \leq 2^k;\ j{+}{=}\ 2^i)$
    $x_j = x_{j-2^{i-1}} \otimes x_j;$

The algorithm has $W = n - 1$ operations and depth $D = \lceil \log n \rceil$, which is optimal; it requires $\lfloor n/2 \rfloor$ processes. If the number p of processes is smaller, then the inputs are divided into segments of $\lceil n/p \rceil$ consecutive inputs; a sequential reduction is applied to each group, followed by a parallel reduction of p values; we obtain a running time of $\lceil n/p \rceil - 1 + \log p$. In particular, the reduction of n values can be computed in $O(\log n)$ time, using $n/\log n$ processes.

Given a tree that computes the reduction of n inputs, one can build from it a parallel prefix circuit, as shown in Figs. 4 and 5, for $n = 8$: The reduction is computed when values move up the tree, while the remaining prefix values are computed when values move down the tree. The algorithm is shown in Algorithm 3, for $n = 2^k$. This

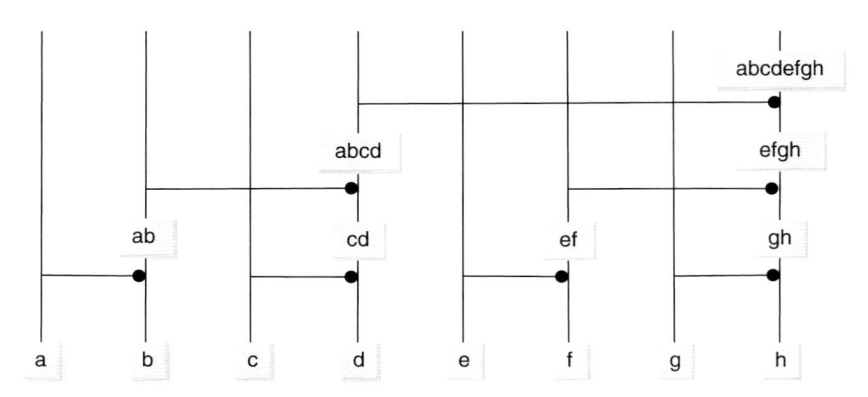

Reduce and Scan. Fig. 3 Binary tree reduction

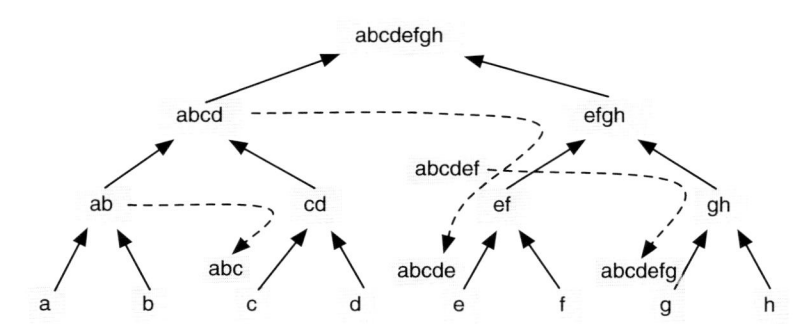

Reduce and Scan. Fig. 4 Tree prefix computation

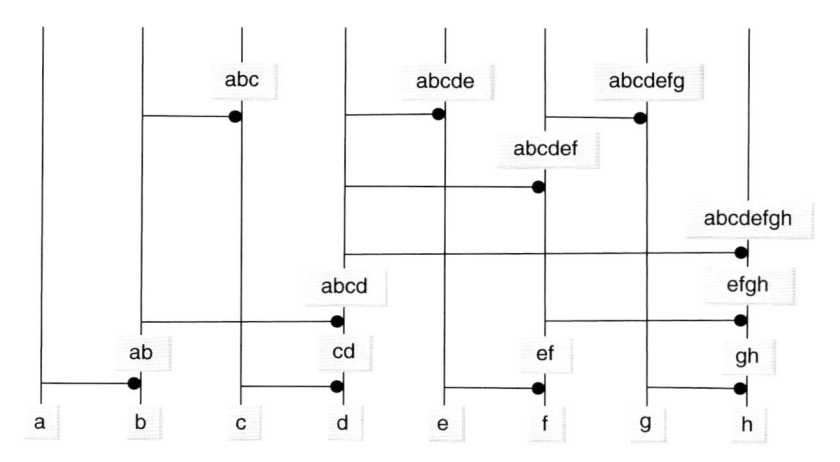

Reduce and Scan. Fig. 5 Parallel prefix circuit

algorithm performs $2n - 2\lfloor \lg n \rfloor - 2 \leq W \leq 2n - \lfloor \lg n \rfloor - 2$ operations and requires $2\lfloor \lg n \rfloor - 1 \leq D \leq 2\lfloor \lg n \rfloor$ steps, with $n/2$ processors.

If we have $p \leq n/2$ processes, then one can compute the parallel prefix using the algorithm shown in Algorithm 4: One computes prefix products sequentially for each sublist, combine the sublist products to compute a global parallel prefix, and then update sequentially elements in each sublist by the product of the previous sublists. The running time is

Algorithm 3 Parallel prefix algorithm

for $(i = 1; i \leq k; i++)$
    forall $(j = 2^i; j \leq 2^k; j += 2^i)$
        $x_j = x_{j-2^{i-1}} \otimes x_j;$
for $(i = k - 1; i \geq 1; i--)$
    forall $(j = 2^i + 2^{i-1}; j \leq 2^k; j += 2^i)$
        $x_j = x_{j-2^{i-1}} \otimes x_j;$

Algorithm 4 Parallel prefix with limited number of processes

// We assume that p divides n
forall $(i = 0; i < p; i++)$
    for $(j = i \times n/p + 1; j \leq (i+1) \times n/p; j++)$
        $x_j = x_{j-1} \otimes x_j;$
parallel prefix$(x_{n/p}, x_{2n/p}, \ldots, x_n);$
forall $(i = 1; i < p; i++)$
    for $(j = i \times n/p + 1; j \leq (i+1) \times n/p; j++)$
        $x_j = x_{i \times n/p} \otimes x_j;$

$D = 2n/p + 2\lg p + O(1)$ and the number of operations is $W = (2 - 1/p)n + O(1)$.

It follows that the parallel prefix computation can be done in time $O(\log n)$ using $n/\log n$ processes.

The last circuit can be improved: Snir shows in [11] that any parallel prefix circuit must satisfy $W + D \geq 2n - 2$ and that this bound can be achieved for any $2 \log n - 2 \leq D \leq n - 1$. Constructions for D in the range $\log n \leq D \leq 2 \log n - 2$ are given by Ladner and Fisher in [10]; they achieve $D = \lceil \log n \rceil + k$ and $W = (2 + 2^{\{1-k\}})n - o(n)$. Thus, it is possible to have parallel prefix circuits of optimal depth and linear size.

The upper and lower bounds hold for circuits that only use the operation $\otimes$. Bilardi and Preparata study prefix computations in a more general Boolean network model [1]. In this model, prefix can be computed in time T by a network of size $S = \Theta((n/T) \lg(n/T))$, in general, or size $S = \Theta(n/T)$ if the operation $\otimes$ satisfies some additional properties, for any T in a range $[c \lg n, n]$.

Applications

Parallel reduction is a frequent operation in parallel algorithms: It is required for parallel dot products, parallel matrix multiplications, counting, etc.

The parallel prefix algorithm has many applications, too. Blelloch shows in [2] how to use parallel prefix for sorting (quicksort and radix sort) and merging, graph algorithms (minimum spanning trees, connected components, maximum flow, maximal independent set, biconnected components), computational geometry (convex hull, K-D tree building, closest pair in plane, line of sight), and matrix operations. These algorithms use parallel prefix with the operations + and max. Other usages are listed in [3]: addition in arbitrary precision arithmetic, polynomial evaluation, recurrence solution, solution of tridiagonal linear systems, lexical analysis, tree operations, etc. Greenberg et al. show how the use of parallel prefix can speed up discrete event simulations [5].

A few other examples are shown below.

Enumeration and packing: One has n processes and wants to enumerate all processes that satisfy some condition. Process i sets x_i to 1 if it satisfies the condition, 0 otherwise. A scan computation will enumerate the processes with a 1, giving each a distinct ordinal number. The same approach can be used to pack all nonzero entries of a vector into contiguous locations. Enumeration is used in radix-sort and quicksort to bin keys.

Segmented scan: A segmented parallel prefix operation computes parallel prefix within segments of the full list, rather than on the entire list. Thus $+\backslash [3\ 5\ |\ 2\ 4\ 1\ |\ 7]$ yields $[3\ 8\ |\ 2\ 6\ 7\ |\ 7]$.

Let $<S, \otimes>$ be a semi-ring (S is a set closed under the associative binary operator $\otimes$). Define a new semi-ring $<\hat{S}, \hat{\otimes}>$ whose elements are $S \cup \{|s : s \in S\}$ and the operation $\hat{\otimes}$ is defined as follows:

$a \hat{\otimes} b = a \otimes b$ if $a, b \in S$
$|a \hat{\otimes} b = |c$, where $c = a \otimes b;$
$a \hat{\otimes} |b = |a \hat{\otimes} |b = |b.$

The new operation is associative; a parallel prefix computation with the new operation computes segmented parallel prefixes for the old operation.

Carry-lookahead adder: Consider the addition of two binary numbers $a_n, \ldots, a_1$ and $b_n, \ldots, b_1$. Let c_i be the carry bit at position i. Then the addition result is

$s_{n+1}, \ldots, s_0$, where $s_{n+1} = c_n$, and $s_i = a_i \oplus b_i \oplus c_{i-1}$, for $i = 1, \ldots, n$.

Define $p_i = a_i \vee b_i$ (carry propagate) and $s_i = a_i \wedge b_i$ (carry set). The carry bits for the adder are defined by the recursion

$c_0 = 0;$
$c_i = p_i c_{i-1} \vee s_i.$

This can be written, in matrix form, as

$$\begin{pmatrix} c_0 & 0 \\ 1 & 0 \end{pmatrix} = \begin{pmatrix} 0 & 0 \\ 1 & 0 \end{pmatrix}$$

$$\begin{pmatrix} c_i & 0 \\ 1 & 0 \end{pmatrix} = \begin{pmatrix} p_i & s_i \\ 0 & 1 \end{pmatrix} \begin{pmatrix} c_{i-1} & 0 \\ 1 & 0 \end{pmatrix}$$

with addition being $\vee$ (or) and multiplication being $\wedge$ (and). Thus, if

$$M_0 = \begin{pmatrix} 0 & 0 \\ 1 & 0 \end{pmatrix}, M_i = \begin{pmatrix} p_i & s_i \\ 0 & 1 \end{pmatrix}, \text{ for } i = 1, \ldots n,$$

we can compute the carry bits by computing the prefixes $M_i \cdot \cdots \cdot M_0$, for $i = 1, \ldots, n$; any parallel prefix circuit can be used to build a carry-lookahead adder.

Linear recurrences: Consider an order one linear recurrence, of the form

$$x_i = a_i x_{i-1} + b_i.$$

The can be written as

$$\begin{pmatrix} x_i & 0 \\ 1 & 0 \end{pmatrix} = \begin{pmatrix} a_i & b_i \\ 0 & 1 \end{pmatrix} \begin{pmatrix} x_{i-1} & 0 \\ 1 & 0 \end{pmatrix},$$

with the usual interpretation of addition and multiplication. This has the same formal structure as the previous recursion.

The same approach extends to higher-order linear recurrences: A recurrence of the form $x_i = \sum_{j=1}^{k} a_{ij} x_{i-j} + b_i$ can be solved in parallel by computing the parallel prefix of the product of $(k+1) \times (k+1)$ matrices.

Function composition: Given n functions $f_1, \ldots, f_n$ consider the problem of computing $f_1, f_2 \cdot f_1, \ldots, f_n \cdot \cdots \cdot f_1$. Since function composition is associative, then a parallel prefix algorithm can be used. This is a generalization of the usual formulation for prefix: Define

$f_1 : x \to a_1,$
$f_i : x \to x \otimes a_i, \text{ for } i = 2, \ldots, n$

then $f_i \cdot \cdots \cdot f_1 = a_1 \otimes \cdots \otimes a_i.$

In this formulation, one has a set $\mathcal{F}$ of functions that is closed under composition. This general formulation leads to a practical algorithm if functions in $\mathcal{F}$ have a representation such that function composition is easily computed in that representation. The linear recurrence example is such a case: The affine functions $x \to ax + b$ is represented by the matrix

$$\begin{pmatrix} a & b \\ 0 & 1 \end{pmatrix}$$

and function composition corresponds, in this representation, to matrix product.

Another example is provided by deterministic finite state transducers: The sequence of outputs generated by the automaton can be computed in logarithmic time from the sequence of inputs.

Finally, consider a sequence of accesses to a memory location that are either loads, stores, or fetch&adds. Then the values returned by the loads and fetch&adds can be computed in logarithmic time [8]. (*Fetch&add(address, increment)* is defined as the atomic execution of the following code: {temp = &address; &address += increment; return temp}; the operation increments a shared variable and returns its old value.)

Linked List Reduce and Scan

The previous algorithms are not easily applied in the case where elements are in a linked list, as the rank of the elements is not known (indeed, computing the ranks is a parallel prefix computation!): It is not obvious which elements should be involved in the computation at each stage.

One approach is the *recursive-doubling* algorithm shown in Algorithm 5, The algorithm has $\lceil \lg n \rceil$ stages and uses n processes, one per node in the linked list; at stage i, each process computes the product of the (up

---

Algorithm 5 Recursive doubling algorithm

for $(i = 1; i \leq \lceil \log n \rceil; i++)$
   forall v *in linked list*
      if $v.next \neq$ **NULL** {
         $v.x = (v.next \to x) \otimes v.x;$
         $v.next = v.next \to next;$
      }

---

to) 2^i values at consecutive nodes in the list ending with the process' node, and links that node to the node that is 2^i positions down the list. This algorithm performs $W = n\lceil \log n \rceil - 2^{\lceil \log n \rceil} + 1$ operations and requires $D = \lceil \log n \rceil$ steps. The $\lceil \log n \rceil$ depth is optimal, but this algorithm is not *work-efficient,* as it uses $\Theta(n \log n)$ operations, compared to $\Theta(n)$ for the sequential algorithm.

Algorithm 6 Generic linked list reduce algorithm

Reduce(list L) {
  if $(L.head = \&v) \&\& (v.next = $ **NULL**$)$ return $v.x$; // list has only one element
  else {
    pick an indepedendent subset V of active nodes from L;
    forall $v \in V$ {
      // delete predecessor of v from the list
      $ptr = v.next$;
      $(v.x = ptr \rightarrow x) \otimes v.x$;
      $v.next = ptr \rightarrow next$;
    }
  }
  barrier;
  Reduce(L);
}

Algorithm 7 Generic linked list scan algorithm

Scan(list L) {
  if $((L.head = \&v) \&\& (v.next = $ **NULL**$))$ return $v.x$; // list has only one element
  else {
    pick an indepedendent subset V of active nodes from L;
    forall $v \in V$ {
      // delete predecessor of v from the list
      $ptr = v.next$;
      $v.x = (ptr \rightarrow x) \otimes v.x$;
      $v.next = ptr \rightarrow next$;
    }
  }
  barrier;
  Scan(L);
  barrier;
  forall $v \in V$ {
    // reinsert predecessor of v in list
    if $(ptr.next \neq $ **NULL**$)$ $ptr.x = ptr.next \rightarrow x \otimes ptr.x$;
    $v.next = ptr$;
  }
  barrier;
}

A set of nodes of the linked list is *independent* if each node in the set has a predecessor outside the set. A linked list reduction algorithm that performs no superfluous products has the generic form shown in Algorithm 6. At each step of this parallel algorithm one replaces nonoverlapping pairs of adjacent nodes with one node that contains the product of these two nodes, until we are left with a single node. Given such reduction algorithm, we can design a parallel prefix algorithm, by "climbing back" the reduction tree, as shown in Algorithm 7. The reduction is illustrated, for a possible schedule, on the top of Fig. 6, while the unwinding of the recursion tree that computes the remaining prefix values is shown on the bottom of Fig. 6.

The problem, then, is to find a large independent subset and schedule the processes to handle the nodes in the subset at each round.

One possible approach is to use randomization for symmetry breaking: At each round, active processes choose randomly, with probability 1/2, whether to participate in this round; if a process decided to participate and its successor also decided to participate, it drops from the current round. The remaining processes form an independent set. On average, 1/4 of the processes that are active at the beginning of a round participate in the round. With overwhelming probability, the algorithm will require a logarithmic number of rounds.

Deterministic "coin-tossing" algorithms have been proposed by various authors. Cole and Vishkin are

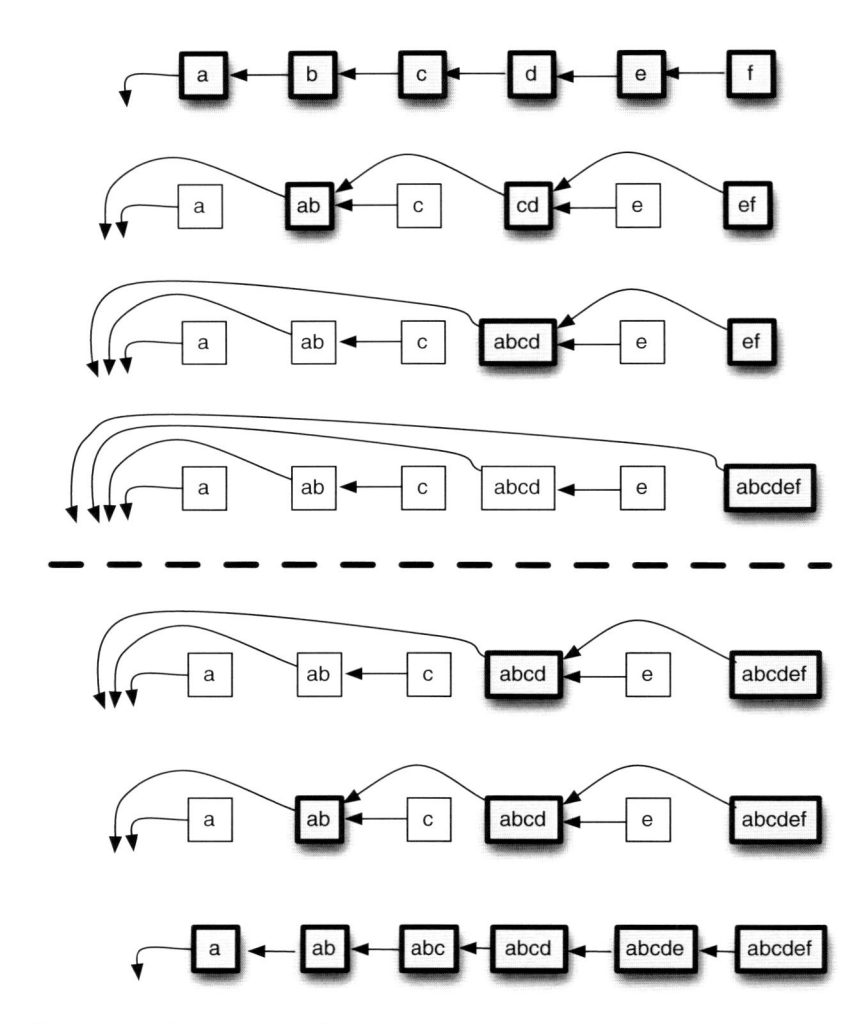

Reduce and Scan. Fig. 6 Linked list parallel prefix

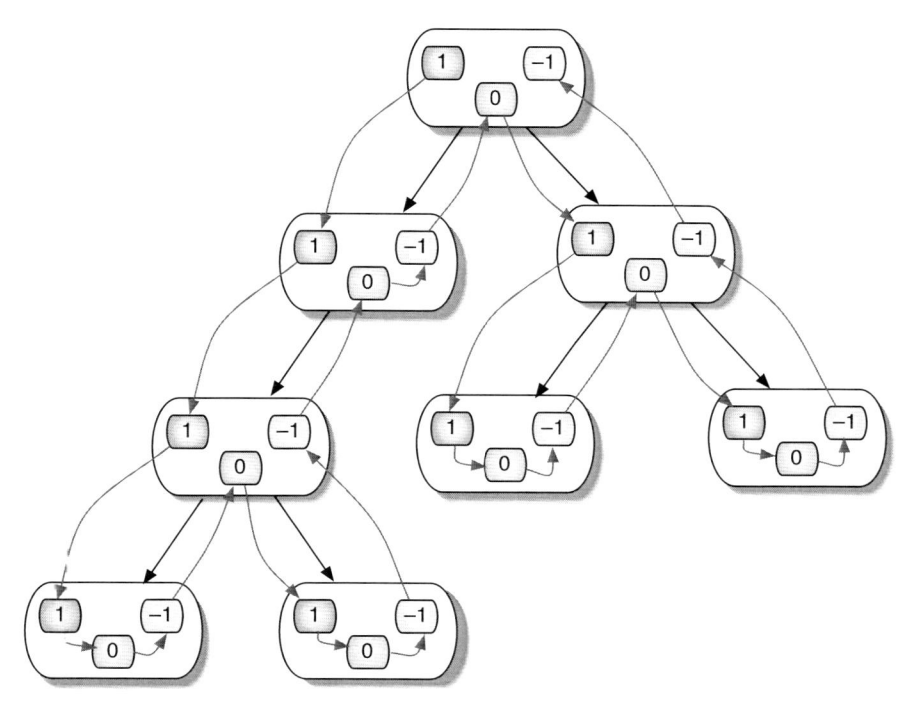

Reduce and Scan. Fig. 7 Tree depth computation

showing in [4] how to solve deterministically the linked list parallel prefix problem in time $O(\log n \log^* n)$ using $n/\log n \log^* n$ processes.

Applications

Linked list prefix computations can be used to solve a variety of graph problems, such as computing spanning forests, connected components, biconnected components, and minimum spanning trees [9].

A simple example is shown below.

Tree depth computation: Given a tree, one wishes to compute for each node the distance of that node from the root. One builds an Euler tour of the tree, as shown in Fig. 7. Each tree node is replaced by three nodes in the tour, with value 1 (moving down), 0 (moving right), and −1 (moving up). One can easily see that a prefix sum on the tour will compute the depth of each node. A variant of this algorithm (with −1 replaced by 0) will number the nodes in preorder [12].

Related Entries

▶ Array Languages
▶ Collective Communication
▶ Connection Machine
▶ MapReduce
▶ NESL
▶ Ultracomputer, NYU

Bibliography

1. Bilardi G, Preparata FP (1989) Size-time complexity of Boolean networks for prefix computations. J ACM 36:362–382
2. Blelloch GE (1989) Scans as primitive parallel operations. IEEE Tram Comp 38:1526–1538
3. Chatterjee B, Blelloch GE, Zagha M (1990) Scan primitives for vector computers. In: Proceedings of supercomputing conference. IEEE Computer Society Press, New York
4. Cole R, Vishkin U (1986) Deterministic coin tossing with applications to optimal parallel list ranking. Inform Control 70:32–53
5. Greenberg AG, Lubachevsky BD, Mitrani I (1996) Superfast parallel discrete event simulations. ACM Trans Model Comput Simul 6:107–136
6. Iverson KE (1962) A Programming language. Wiley, New York
7. Kruskal CP, Rudolph L, Snir M (1986) Efficient synchronization on multiprocessors with shared memory. ACM TOPLAS 10:579–601
8. Kruskal CP, Rudolph L, Snir M (1990) Efficient parallel algorithms for graph problems. Algorithmica 5:43–64
9. Ladner RE, Fischer MJ (1980) Parallel prefix computation. J Assoc Comput Mach 27:832–838

10. Message Passing Interface Forum (1994) MPI: a message-passing interface standard. Int J Supercomput Appl High Perform Comput 8:165–416
11. Snir M (1986) Depth-size trade-offs for parallel prefix computation. J Algorithms 7:185–201
12. Tarjan RE, Vishkin U (1985) An efficient parallel biconnectivity algorithm. Siam J Comput 14:862–874

Relaxed Memory Consistency Models

▶ Memory Models

Reliable Networks

▶ Networks, Fault-Tolerant

Rendezvous

▶ Synchronization

Reordering

MICHAEL HEATH
University of Illinois at Urbana-Champaign, Urbana, IL, USA

Definition

Reording for parallelism is a technique for enabling or enhancing concurrent processing of a list of items by determining an ordering that removes or reduces serial dependencies among the items.

Discussion

Ordered lists are ubiquitous and seem entirely natural in many aspects of daily life. But the specific order in which items are listed may be irrelevant, or even counterproductive, to the purpose of the list. In making a shopping list, for example, we usually list items in the order we happen to think of them, but rarely will such an order coincide with the most efficient path for locating the items in a store. Even for a structure that may have no natural linear ordering, such as a graph, we nevertheless typically number its nodes in some order, which may or may not facilitate efficient processing. In general, finding an optimal ordering is often a difficult combinatorial problem, as famously exemplified by the traveling salesperson problem.

Similarly, in programming when we write a *for* loop, we specify an ordering that may or may not have any significance for the successive tasks to be done inside the loop, yet the semantics of most programming languages usually require the compiler to schedule the tasks in the specified sequential order, even if the tasks are totally independent and could validly be done in any order. This constraint often goes unnoticed in serial computation, but it can seriously inhibit parallel processing of sequential loops. If each successive task depends on the result of the immediately preceding one, then the given sequential order must be honored in order for the program to execute correctly. But if the tasks have no such interdependence, for example, in a loop initializing all the elements of an array to zero, then the element assignments could be done in any order, or simultaneously in parallel.

Unfortunately, conventional programming languages offer no mechanism for indicating when tasks are independent, which has motivated the development of compiler techniques for discovering and exploiting loop-based parallelism, as well as compiler directives, such as those provided by OpenMP, that enable programmers to specify parallel loops. It has also motivated the development of higher-level languages in which structures such as arrays are first-class objects that can be referenced as a whole without having to enumerate array elements sequentially. Although smart compilers, compiler directives, and higher-level objects can help identify and preserve potential parallelism, it may still be difficult to determine how best to exploit the parallelism, especially if the ordering affects the total amount of work required. In such cases, the necessary reordering may be considerably deeper than it is reasonable to expect any compiler or automated system to identify or exploit.

These issues are well illustrated by computational linear algebra. When we write a vector in coordinate notation, we implicitly specify an ordering of the coordinate basis for the vector space that is generally arbitrary. Similarly, when we write a system of n linear equations in n unknowns, $Ax = b$, where A is an $n \times n$ matrix, b is a given n-vector, and x is an n-vector to be determined, the ordering of the rows of A is arbitrary, as each equation in the system must be satisfied individually, irrespective of the order in which they happen to be listed. Consequently, the rows of the matrix A can be permuted arbitrarily without affecting the solution x. The column ordering of A is also arbitrary in the sense that it corresponds to the arbitrary ordering chosen for the entries of x, so that permuting the columns of A affects the solution only in that it correspondingly permutes the entries of x. To summarize, the solution to the system $Ax = b$ is given by $x = Qy$, where y is the solution to the permuted system $PAQy = Pb$, and P and Q are any permutation matrices, so in this sense the original and permuted systems are mathematically equivalent, although the computational resources required to solve them may be quite different. This freedom in choosing the ordering can be exploited to enhance numerical stability (e.g., partial or complete pivoting) or computational efficiency, or a combination of these.

The order in which the entries of a matrix are accessed can have a dramatic effect on the performance of matrix algorithms, in part because of the memory hierarchy (registers, multiple levels of cache, main memory, etc.) typical of modern microprocessors. A dense matrix is usually stored in a two-dimensional array, whose layout in memory (typically row-wise or column-wise) strongly affects the cache behavior of programs that access the matrix entries. Many matrix algorithms, such as matrix multiplication and matrix factorization, systematically access the entries of the matrix using nested loops whose indices can validly be arranged in any order, so the order can be chosen to make optimal use of data residing in the most rapidly accessible level of the memory hierarchy. In addition, the order in which matrix rows or columns (or both, in the case of a two-dimensional decomposition) are assigned to processors may strongly affect parallel efficiency. Assignment by contiguous blocks, for example, tends to reduce communication but inhibits concurrency and can yield a poor load balance, whereas assigning rows or columns to processors in a cyclic manner (like dealing cards) has the opposite effects. Optimizing the tradeoff between these extremes may suggest a hybrid block-cyclic assignment, with smaller blocks of tunable size assigned cyclically.

These issues are further complicated for matrices that are *sparse*, meaning that the entries are mostly zeros, so that it is advantageous to employ data structures that store only the nonzero entries (along with information indicating their locations within the matrix) and algorithms that operate on only nonzero entries. For a sparse matrix, the ordering of the rows and columns strongly affects the total amount of work and storage required to compute a factorization of the matrix. Sparsity can also introduce additional parallelism into the factorization process, beyond the substantial parallelism already available in the dense case.

To illustrate the effects of ordering for sparse systems, we focus on systems for which the sparse matrix A is symmetric and positive definite, so that we will not have the additional complication of ordering to preserve numerical stability as well. In this case, for a direct solution we compute the *Cholesky factorization* $A = LL^T$, where L is lower triangular, so that the solution x to the system $Ax = b$ can be computed by solving the lower triangular system $Ly = b$ for y by forward substitution and then the upper triangular system $L^T x = y$ for x by back substitution.

To see how the ordering of the sparse matrix affects the work, storage, and parallelism, we need to take a closer look at the Cholesky algorithm, shown in Fig. 1, in which only the lower triangle of the input matrix A is accessed, and is overwritten by the Cholesky factor L. The outer loop processes successive columns of the matrix. The first inner loop, labeled $cdiv(k)$, scales column k by dividing it by the square root of its diagonal entry, while the second inner loop, labeled $cmod(j,k)$, modifies each subsequent column j by subtracting from it a scalar multiple, a_{jk}, of column k.

The first important observation to make about the Cholesky algorithm is that a given $cmod(j,k)$ operation may introduce new nonzero entries, called *fill*, into column j in locations that were previously zero. Such fill entries require additional storage and work to process, so we would like to limit the amount of fill, which is dramatically affected by the ordering of the matrix, as

```
for k = 1 to n
    a_kk = √a_kk
    for i = k + 1 to n
        a_ik = a_ik / a_kk                 {cdiv(k)}
    end
    for j = k + 1 to n
        for i = j to n
            a_ij = a_ij − a_ik a_jk        {cmod(j,k)}
        end
    end
end
```

Reordering. Fig. 1 Cholesky factorization algorithm

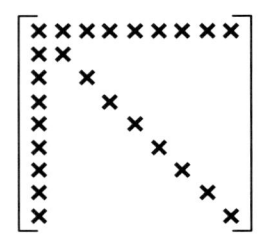

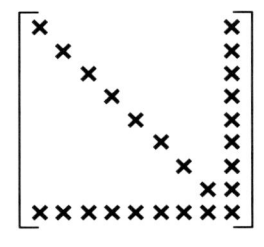

Reordering. Fig. 2 *"Arrow"* matrix example illustrating dependence of fill on ordering. Nonzero entries indicated by ×

illustrated for an extreme case by the "arrow" matrix whose nonzero pattern is shown for a small example in Fig. 2 with two different orderings. The ordering on the left results in a dense Cholesky factor (complete fill), whereas the ordering on the right results in no new nonzero entries (no fill). In general, we would like to choose an ordering for the matrix A that minimizes fill in the Cholesky factor L, but this problem is known to be NP-complete, so instead we use heuristic ordering strategies such as *minimum degree* or *nested dissection*, which effectively limit fill at reasonable cost.

A second important observation is that the *cdiv* operation that completes the computation of a given column of L cannot take place until the modifications (*cmod*s) by all previous columns have been done. Thus, the successive *cdiv* operations appear to require serial execution, and this is indeed the case for a dense matrix. But a given $cmod(j,k)$ operation has no effect, and hence need not be done, if $a_{jk} = 0$, so a sparse matrix may therefore enable additional parallelism that is not available in the dense case. Once again, however, this potential benefit depends critically on the ordering chosen for the rows and columns of the sparse matrix.

Even if the *cdiv* operations must be performed serially, however, multiple *cmod* operations can still be performed in parallel, and this is the principal source of parallelism for a dense matrix.

The interdependence among the columns of the Cholesky factor L is precisely characterized by the *elimination tree*, which has one node per column of A, with the parent of node j being the row index of the first subdiagonal nonzero in column j of L. In particular, each column of L depends only on its descendants in the elimination tree. For a dense matrix, this potential source of additional parallelism is of no help, as the elimination tree is simply a linear chain. But for a sparse matrix, more advantageous tree structures are possible, depending on the ordering chosen.

A small example is shown in Fig. 3, in which a two-dimensional mesh $G(A)$, whose edges correspond to nonzero entries of matrix A, is ordered row-wise, resulting in a banded matrix A and Cholesky factor L. With this ordering, the elimination tree $T(A)$ is a linear chain, implying sequential execution of the corresponding *cdiv* operations, as each column of L depends on all preceding columns.

An alternative ordering is shown in Fig. 4, in which the same two-dimensional mesh is ordered by *nested dissection*, where the graph is recursively split into pieces with the nodes in the *separators* at each level numbered last. In this example, numbering the "middle" nodes last, that is, 7, 8, and 9, leaves two disjoint pieces that are in turn split by their "middle" nodes, numbered 3 and 6, leaving four isolated nodes, numbered 1, 2, 4, and 5. The absence of edges between the separated pieces of the graph induces blocks of zeros in the matrix A that are preserved in the Cholesky factor L, which accordingly suffers fewer fill entries than with the banded ordering, and hence requires less storage and work to compute. Equally important, the elimination tree now has a hierarchical structure, with multiple leaf nodes corresponding to *cdiv* operations that can be executed simultaneously in parallel at each level of the tree up to the final separator. The lessons from this small example apply much more broadly: with an appropriate ordering, sparsity can enable additional parallelism that is unavailable for dense matrices. A divide-and-conquer approach, exemplified by nested dissection, is an excellent way to identify and exploit such parallelism, and it typically also reduces the overall

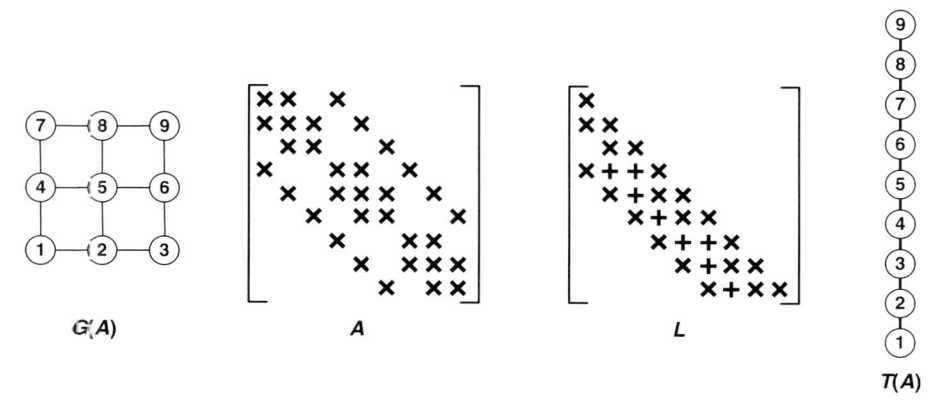

Reordering. Fig. 3 Two-dimensional mesh $G(A)$ ordered row-wise, with corresponding matrix A, Cholesky factor L, and elimination tree $T(A)$. Nonzero entries indicated by × and fill entries by +

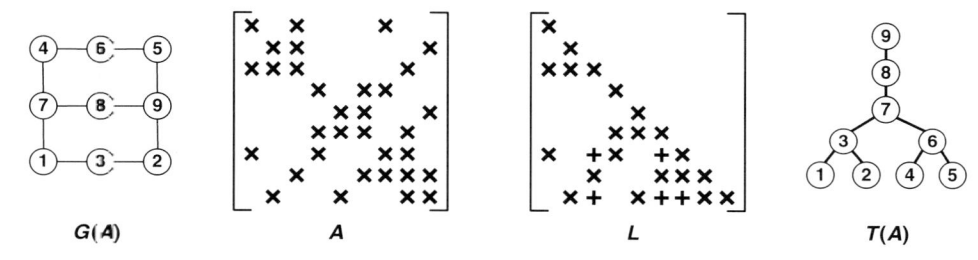

Reordering. Fig. 4 Two-dimensional mesh $G(A)$ ordered by nested dissection, with corresponding matrix A, Cholesky factor L, and elimination tree $T(A)$. Nonzero entries indicated by × and fill entries by +

work and storage required for sparse factorization by reducing fill.

In addition to direct methods based on matrix factorization, reordering also plays a major role in parallel implementation of iterative methods for solving sparse linear systems. For example, reordering by nested dissection can be used to reduce communication in parallel sparse matrix-vector multiplication, which is the primary computational kernel in Krylov subspace iterative methods such as conjugate gradients. Another example is in parallel implementation of the Gauss-Seidel or Successive Overrelaxation (SOR) iterative methods. These methods repeatedly sweep through the successive rows of the matrix, updating each corresponding component of the solution vector x by solving for it based on the most recent values of all the other components. This dependence of each component update on the immediately preceding one seems to require strictly serial processing, as illustrated for a small example in Fig. 5, where a two-dimensional mesh is numbered in a natural row-wise ordering, with the corresponding matrix shown, and indeed only one row can be processed at a time.

By reordering the mesh and corresponding matrix using a *red-black* ordering, in which the nodes of the mesh alternate colors in a checkerboard pattern as shown in Fig. 6, with the red nodes numbered before the black ones, solution components having the same color no longer depend directly on each other, as can be seen both in the graph and by the form of the reordered matrix. Thus, all of the components corresponding to red nodes can be updated simultaneously in parallel, and then all of the black nodes can similarly be done in parallel, so the algorithm proceeds in alternating sweeps between the two colors with ample parallelism. For an arbitrary sparse matrix, the same idea still works, but more colors may be required to color its graph, and hence the resulting parallel implementation will have as many successive parallel phases as the number of colors. One cautionary note, however, is that the convergence

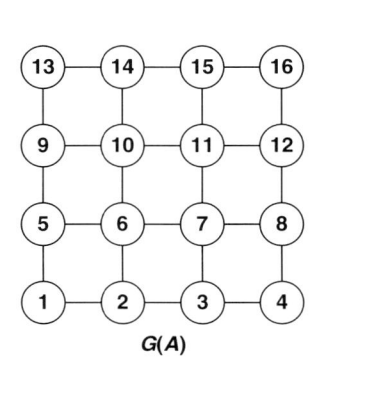

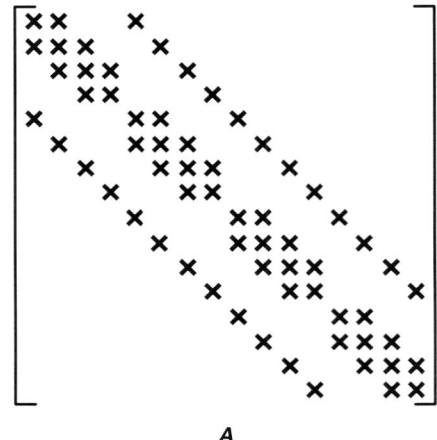

Reordering. Fig. 5 Two-dimensional mesh $G(A)$ ordered row-wise, with corresponding matrix A. Nonzero entries indicated by $\times$

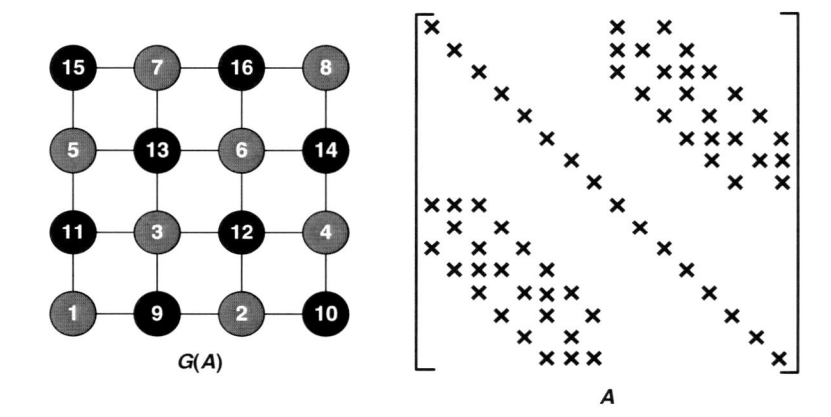

Reordering. Fig. 6 Two-dimensional mesh $G(A)$ with red-black ordering and corresponding reordered matrix A. Nonzero entries indicated by $\times$

rate of the underlying iterative method may depend on the particular ordering, so the gain in performance per iteration may be offset somewhat if an increased number of iterations is required to meet the same convergence tolerance.

In this brief article we have barely scratched the surface of the many ways in which reordering can be used to enable or enhance parallelism. We focused mainly on computational linear algebra, but additional examples abound in many other areas, such as the use of multicolor reordering to enhance parallelism in solving ordinary differential equations using waveform relaxation methods or in solving partial differential equations using domain decomposition methods. Yet another example is in the parallel implementation of the Fast Fourier Transform (FFT), where reordering can be used to optimize the tradeoff between latency and bandwidth for a given parallel architecture.

Related Entries

▶Dense Linear System Solvers
▶Graph Partitioning
▶Layout, Array
▶Loop Nest Parallelization
▶Linear Algebra, Numerical
▶Loops, Parallel
▶Scheduling Algorithms
▶Sparse Direct Methods
▶Task Graph Scheduling

Bibliographic Notes and Further Reading

For a broad overview of parallelism in computational linear algebra, see [2–4]. For a general discussion of sparse factorization methods, see [1, 5]. For specific discussion of reordering for parallel sparse elimination, see [6–8].

Bibliography

1. Davis TA (2006) Direct methods for sparse linear systems. SIAM, Philadelphia, PA
2. Demmel JW, Heath MT, van der Vorst HA (1993) Parallel numerical linear algebra. Acta Numerica 2:111–197
3. Dongarra JJ, Duff IS, Sorenson DC, van der Vorst HA (1998) Numerical linear algebra for high-performance computers. SIAM, Philadelphia
4. Gallivan KA, Heath MT, Ng E, Ortega JM, Peyton BW, Plemmons RJ, Romine CH, Sameh AH, Voigt RG (1990) Parallel algorithms for matrix computations. SIAM, Philadelphia
5. George A, Liu JW-H (1981) Computer solution of large sparse positive definite systems. Prentice Hall, Englewood Cliffs
6. Liu JW-H (1986) Computational models and task scheduling for parallel sparse Cholesky factorization. Parallel Comput 3:327–342
7. Liu JW-H (1989) Reordering sparse matrices for parallel elimination. Parallel Comput 11:73–91
8. Liu JW-H (1990) The role of elimination trees in sparse factorization. SIAM J Matrix Anal Appl 11:134–172

Resource Affinity Scheduling

▶ Affinity Scheduling

Resource Management for Parallel Computers

▶ Operating System Strategies

Rewriting Logic

▶ Maude

Ring

▶ Networks, Direct

Roadrunner Project, Los Alamos

Don Grice[1], Andrew B. White, Jr.[2]
[1]IBM Corporation, Poughkeepsie, NY, USA
[2]Los Alamos National Laboratory, Los Alamos, NM, USA

Synonyms

Petaflop barrier

Definition

The Los Alamos Roadrunner Project was a joint Los Alamos and IBM project that developed the first supercomputer to break the Petaflop barrier on a Linpack run for the Top500 list.

Discussion

Introduction

In 2002, Los Alamos and IBM began to explore the potential of a new class of power-efficient high-performance computing systems based on a radical view of the future of supercomputing. The resulting LANL Roadrunner project had three primary roles: (1) an advanced architecture which presaged the primary components of next generation supercomputing systems; (2) a uniquely capable software and hardware environment for investigation and solution of science and engineering problems of importance to the US Department of Energy (DOE). Section 5.1 describes some of the key LANL applications that were studied; and (3) achievement of the first sustained petaflops.

A significant point in the thinking surrounding petascale and now exascale computing, is that the challenge is not just "solving the same problem faster" but rather "solving a better problem" by harnessing the leap in computing performance; that is, the key to better predictive simulations in national nuclear security, in climate and energy simulations, and in basic science is increasing the fidelity of our computational science by using better models, by increasing model resolution, and imbedding uncertainty quantification within the solution itself.

The computing capability of the supercomputer on the top of the Top500 list continues to grow at a staggering rate. In 2008, Roadrunner broke the sustained petaflops boundary on the list for the first time. This represented a performance improvement of over a factor of 1,000 in just 11 years. As a result of the availability of such large machines, and the accompanying price and performance improvements for smaller machines, HPC solutions are now moving into markets that were previously considered beyond the reach of computing technology.

More comprehensive drug simulations, car crash simulations, and climate models are advances one might have easily predicted, but the impacts of HPC on movie making, games, and even remote surgery are things that might not have been so easy to see on the horizon. Today even financial institutions are using real-time modeling to guide investment choices. The growth of HPC opportunities in markets that did not involve traditional HPC users is what is driving the business excitement around the improvements in computing capability.

However, these opportunities do not come without their own technical challenges. The total amount of power and cooling required to drive some large systems, the programming complexity as hundreds of thousands of threads need to be harnessed into a single solution, and overall system reliability, availability, and serviceability (RAS) are the biggest hurdles. It was important to address the fundamental technology challenges facing further advances in application performance.

Designed and developed for the US Department of Energy (DOE) and Los Alamos National Laboratory (LANL), the DOE/LANL Roadrunner project was a joint venture between LANL and IBM to address computing challenges with a range of technical solutions that are opening up new opportunities for business, scientific, and social advances. The Roadrunner project is named after the state bird of New Mexico where the Roadrunner system has been installed at LANL.

To address the power and performance issues, a fundamental design decision was made to use a hybrid programming approach that combines standard x86-architecture processors and Cell BE–based accelerators. The Cell BE accelerators provide a much denser and power-efficient peak performance than the standard processors, but introduce a different dimension in programming complexity because of the hybrid architecture and the necessity to explicitly manage memory on the Cell processor. When the project first started, this approach was considered radical, but now these attributes are widely accepted as necessary components of next generation systems leading to exascale. The Roadrunner program was targeted at getting a head start on the software issues involved in programming these architectures.

Roadrunner Hardware Architecture

As shown in Fig. 1 and described in the Sect. "Management for Scalability," the Roadrunner system

Roadrunner Project, Los Alamos. Fig. 1 Overall roadrunner structure

is a cluster of over 3,000 *triblade* nodes (described in detail below). The nodes are organized in smaller clusters called *connected units* (CUs). Each CU is composed of 180 computational triblade nodes, 12 I/O nodes, and a service node. Each CU has its own 288-port Voltaire Infiniband (IB) switch. [2] These CUs are then connected to each other with a standard second level switch topology where each of the first level switches has connections to each of the second level switches. There are 17 of these CUs in the overall system.

The triblade node architecture and implementation described in the Sect. "Triblade Architecture" were chosen in order to use existing hardware-building blocks and to capitalize on the RAS characteristics of the IBM Blade Center [8] infrastructure. Ease of construction and service were critical requirements because of the short schedule and the large number of parts in the final system. Since the compute nodes make up the bulk of the system hardware, they were the focus of the hardware and software design efforts.

Management for Scalability

The management configuration of the Roadrunner system was designed for scalability from the beginning. The primary concern was the ability to use and control individual CUs without impacting the operation of the other CUs. That was the fundamental reason for having a first level IB switch dedicated to each CU. One can reboot the nodes in a CU, and even replace nodes in a CU, without impacting the operation of the other CUs, or applications running in those CUs. It is possible to isolate the first level switches from the second level switches with software commands so that other CUs do not route data to a CU that is under debug or repair.

The I/O nodes are dedicated to use by nodes within the CU which allows file system traffic to stay within a CU and not utilize any second level switch bandwidth. This also allows for file system connectivity and performance measurements to be done in isolation, including rebooting the CU, at the CU level. Actually, there are two sets of six I/O nodes for each CU which each serve half of the compute nodes, thus providing further performance isolation and greater performance consistency for applications.

Triblade Architecture

As described in the Sect. "Heterogeneous Cores and Hybrid Architecture," a fundamental innovation in the Roadrunner design was the use of heterogeneous core types to maximize the energy efficiency of the system. Having cores designed for specific purposes allows for energy efficiency by eliminating circuits in the cores that will not be used. The three core types in the Roadrunner system are all programmable and not hardwired algorithmic cores, such as a cryptography engine, but the circuits are optimized for the type of code that will run on each core type.

There are two computational chips in the system: the PowerXCell 8i 3.2GHz chip which is packaged on the QS22 [5] blade and the AMD Opteron dual core 1.8GHz chip that is packaged on the LS21 [4] blade.

The PowerXCell 8i has eight specialized SPEs (Synergistic Processing Elements) that run the bulk of the application floating point operations but do not need the circuits nor the state to run the OS. It also has a PowerPC core that is neither as space nor energy efficient as the SPEs but it does run the OS on the QS22 and controls the program flow for the SPEs.

The AMD chip runs the MPI stack and controls the communications between the triblades in the system. It also controls the overall application flow and does application work for sections of the code that are not floating point intensive. The LS21 blade has its own address space, separate from the QS22, which introduces another level of hybridization into the node structure.

The triblades, as shown in Fig. 2, are the compute nodes that contain these computational chips and the heart of the system. They consist of three computational blades: one LS21 and two QS22s and a fourth expansion blade that handles the connectivity among the three computational blades as well as the connection to the CU IB switch.

The LS21 is a dual socket, dual core AMD based blade, so there are four AMD cores per triblade. The QS22 is a dual socket PowerXCell 8i (Cell BE chip) blade, so there are four Cell BE chips in the triblade to pair with the four AMD cores. The software model most commonly used is one MPI (message passing interface) task per AMD core-Cell BE chip pair. There is 16 GB of main storage on the LS21 and a total of 16 GB of main storage on the pair of QS22s. Having matched storage of 4 GB on each AMD core and each Cell BE chip simplifies designing and coding the applications that share data structures on each processing unit in the pair, since there can be duplicate copies kept on each side and only updates to the structures need to be communicated between the process running on the AMD core and the process running on the partner Cell BE chip.

Since the triblade structure presents dual address spaces, (one on the LS21 and one on the QS22) to each of the MPI tasks, as shown in Fig. 3, having bandwidth and latency efficient methods for transferring data between these address spaces is critical to the scaling success of the applications.

A significant architectural feature of the triblade is the set of four dedicated peripheral component interconnect express (PCIe)-x8 links that connect the four AMD cores on the LS21 to their partner Cell BE chips on the QS22s. All four links can transmit data in both directions simultaneously for moving Cell BE data structures up to the Opteron processors and Opteron structures down to the Cell BE chips.

A common application goal, not surprisingly, was to maximize the percentage of the work done by the Cell BE synergistic processing elements (SPEs) [6]. When the SPEs need to communicate boundary information with their logical neighbor SPEs in the problem space, that are located in physically different triblades, they need to send the data up to their partner AMD core, which in turn will send it, usually using MPI, to the AMD core that is the partner of the actual target SPE. The receiving AMD will then send the data down to the actual target SPEs. Having the four independent

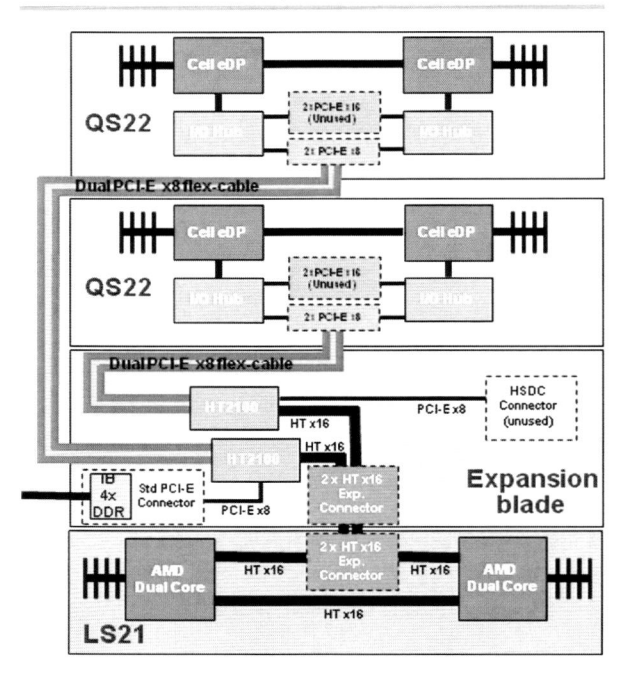

Roadrunner Project, Los Alamos. Fig. 2 Triblade architecture

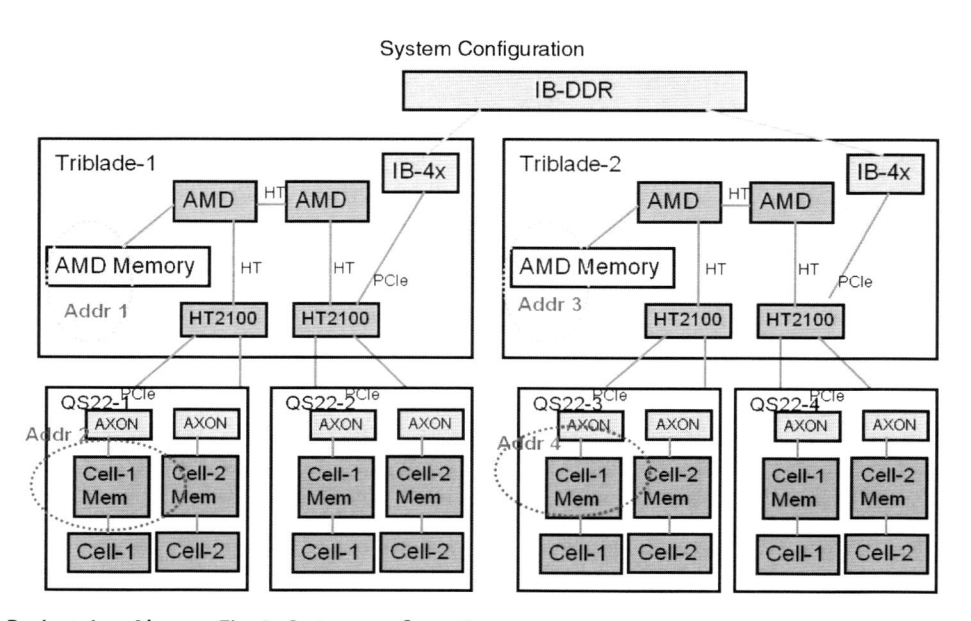

Roadrunner Project, Los Alamos. Fig. 3 System configuration

PCIe links allows all four Cell BE chips to send the data to and from their partner AMD cores at the same time.

Figure 3 shows a logical picture of two triblades connected together with their IB link to show the different address spaces that exist and need to be managed by the application data flow. What is shown is one of the four pairs of address spaces on each of the triblades. Each AMD core and each Cell BE chip has its own logical address space. Since each AMD core is paired with its own Cell BE chip, there are four pairs of logical address spaces on a triblade. Address space 1 is the AMD address space for Core 0 in the AMD chip on the left of triblade 1. That core is partnered with Cell BE-1 on QS22-1 which owns address space 2. There are corresponding address spaces 3 and 4 on triblade 2. There is a set of library functions that can be called from the application on the AMD or the Cell BE to transfer data between address spaces 1 and 2, and 3 and 4. OpenMPI is used to transfer data between the AMD address spaces 1 and 3 using typical MPI and IB methods. The difference between the standard MPI model and the triblade MPI model is that in the triblade model, an MPI task controls both a standard Opteron core and the heterogeneous Cell BE chip. This is similar in some ways to having multiple threads running under a single MPI task except that the address spaces need to be explicitly controlled and the cores are heterogeneous.

The ability to control the data flow both between the hybrid address spaces and within the Cell BE address space allows the application to optimize the utilization of the memory bandwidths in the system. As chip densities increase, but circuit and pin frequencies do not, utilizing pin bandwidths (both memory bandwidth and communication bandwidth) efficiently will become increasingly important. The Cell BE chip local stores, which act like software controlled cache structures, allow for some very efficient computational models. As an example, the DGEMM (double-precision general matrix multiply) routine that ran in the hybrid Linpack application [7], was over 99% efficient, and was the heart of the computational efficiency that led to the sustained petaflops achievement. The same software cache model applies to the separate address spaces that exist in the AMD and Cell BE chips within the MPI task.

Technology Drivers

The ongoing reduction in the rate of processor frequency improvement has led to three fundamental issues in development to achieve dramatically better application performance: (1) Software complexity which is caused by the growing number of cores needed for ever greater performance, (2) Energy requirements driven by the increased number of cores and chips needed for performance improvements, and (3) RAS requirements driven by the ever increasing number of circuits and components in the larger systems. All three of these issues were important features of the Roadrunner project overall design and implementation.

Software Complexity

For the last several decades, lithographic technology improvements guided by Dennard's CMOS Scaling Theory [14] in accordance with Moore's law [10] have not only provided circuit density improvements, but the shrinkage in the vertical dimension also provided an accompanying frequency increase. This meant that for applications to scale in performance, one did not need to modify the software to utilize additional cores or threads, since system performance improved simply because of the frequency scaling.

The elimination of future frequency scaling puts the burden of application performance improvement on the application software and programming environment, and requires a doubling of the number of cores applied to a problem in order to achieve a doubling of the peak performance available to the application. Since sustained application performance for strong scaling, and to a lesser extent weak scaling, is likely to be less than linear in the number of cores available, more than double the number of cores will usually be required to achieve double the sustained application performance.

At a nominal 1 GHz, effectively a million functional units are required for petascale sustained performance, and the number of cores will continue to grow as greater sustained performance is desired. Finding ways to cope with this fundamental issue, in a way that is tenable for both algorithm development and code maintenance, while still achieving reasonable fractions of nominal peak performance for the sustained performance on real (as opposed to test or benchmark) applications, was a major goal of the project. Since application scaling going to petascale and beyond was such a major focus, considerable time and energy were spent on making sure that real applications would scale on the machine.

While high-level language constructs and advances, in and of themselves were not a major focus of the project, rethinking the applications themselves was. The LANL application and performance modeling teams, as well as the IBM application and performance modeling teams, analyzed how the construction of the base algorithm flow and the interaction with the projected hardware would work.

The IBM Linpack team modified Linpack to operate in the hybrid environment and modeling was done to optimize the structure of the code around the anticipated performance characteristics of the system. The workhorse of the sustained petaflops performance was the DGEMM algorithm on the Cell BE chip since it provided over 99% of the computation required by the overall solution of the Linpack problem. The AMD core provided the overall control flow for the application, performed the OpenMPI communication, and did some of the algorithmic steps that could be overlapped with the Cell BE DGEMM calculations. The final structure of the solutions was both hybrid (between the x86 and Cell BE) units and heterogeneous on the Cell BE itself [7].

Linpack was only one of the codes that were studied in great detail, and had the machine only been useful for a Linpack run, and not for critical science and DOE codes, it would not have been built. A full year was spent analyzing and testing pieces of several applications prior to making the decision to go forward with the actual machine manufacture and construction.

Los Alamos National Laboratory revamped several applications to the Roadrunner architecture. These applications represent a wide variety of workload types. Among the applications ported are [11]:

- VPIC – full relativistic, charge-conserving, 3D explicit particle-in-cell code.
- SPaSM – Scalable Parallel Short-range Molecular Dynamics code, originally developed for the Thinking Machines Connection Machine model CM-5.
- Milagro – Parallel, multidimensional, object-oriented code for thermal x-ray transport via implicit Monte Carlo methods on a variety of meshes.
- Sweep3D – Simplified 1-group 3D Cartesian discrete ordinates kernel representative of a neutron transport code.

The different applications employed multiple methods to exploit the capabilities of Roadrunner. Milagro used a host-centric accelerator offload model where the majority of the application was unchanged, (except for the control code which was modified due to the new hybrid structure of the triblade,) and selected computationally intensive portions were modified to move their most performance critical sections to the accelerator (Cell BE). VPIC employed an accelerator-centric approach where the majority of the program logic was migrated to the accelerator and the host systems and the InfiniBand interconnect served primarily to provide accelerator to accelerator message communications.

Early performance results on the applications showed speed-ups over an unaccelerated cluster in the range of 4–9 times depending on how much work could be moved to the Cell. Between 2 KLOC (thousand lines of code) and 33 KLOC needed to be modified to achieve these speed-ups. Some of the applications had obvious compute kernels that could be transferred to the Cell BE and those applications required fewer changes to the code than the cases where the compute parts were more distributed or where the control code itself had to be restructured, as was the case with Milagro. But, even in the case of Milagro, it was a small percentage of the code that was changed.

Understanding of how to construct applications and lay out data structures to achieve reasonable sustained scaled performance will be important to future machine designs as well as provide input and examples for the translation of high-level language constructs into operational code. One example of a hardware feature in the base architecture of the QS22 is the ability for software to control the Local Store memory traffic [5, 6]. Since memory bandwidth will be an important commodity to optimize around in the future processor designs, understanding how best to do data pipelining from an application point of view is important base data to have. Hardware controlled flow of memory pre-fetching (cache) is a good feature for processors to have in general, but optimal efficiency will require explicit application tuning of bandwidth utilization. Automating the software control based on algorithms, hints, or language constructs is something that can be added later to take some of the burden off of the software developers but for now, understanding how best to use features like these is more important.

Energy

As was stated earlier, energy consumption and cooling of IT facilities are an increasing critical problem. The business-as-usual technology projections in 2010 indicate that by 2020 large-scale systems will be more expensive to operate than to acquire [12]. Due to the increase in power requirements as ultra-scale computing systems grow in computing capability, it is often the case that new facilities need to be built to house the anticipated supercomputing machines.

Another innovation in the Roadrunner project was minimizing the overall power required by using heterogeneous core types that optimize the power utilization, not by lowering the thread performance (frequency) but by eliminating unnecessary circuits in the SPEs themselves. As was discussed previously, this presents a different set of issues to the programmer. The Roadrunner system, using heterogeneous core types, uses fewer overall threads for the same performance than a homogeneous core machine using the same amount of power, but the core types need separate compiled code, and more explicit thought about where each piece of the algorithm should run.

Heterogeneous Cores and Hybrid Architecture

Using heterogeneous core types on the PowerXCell8i was a way of dealing with the computational density and power efficiency. Using a hybrid node architecture that included a combination of the QS22s for computational efficiency and the LS21 for the general purpose computations and communications control was a way of overcoming the limitations of the PowerPC core on the Cell BE chip. One can easily imagine future supercomputers based on SoC designs that do not required the additional level of heterogeneity utilized in Roadrunner.

The PowerXCell8i has two core types, a general purpose embedded PowerPC core (the power processing element, PPE) which handles all of the operating system and hybrid communication tasks and eight specialized compute cores (the synergistic processing elements, SPEs). The SPEs take up significantly less chip area than the PowerPC core since they only need the facilities and instruction set to handle the intense computational tasks. This adds to the software complexity of the application algorithms because tasks must be assigned appropriately to the cores, and additional memory space management is required, but the results are well worth it [6]. Software tools such as OpenMP and OpenCL are emerging which will help hide the heterogeneity from the application user, but the complexity will still exist in the system itself.

The Roadrunner solution was not only the first to break the sustained petaflops Linpack barrier and therefore first on the Top500 list in June 2008 but it was third on the June 2008 Green500 as well. The first and second places on that Green500 list went to QS22 only based systems, so the energy efficiency of using the heterogeneous core approach is obvious. It is a trend that will continue into the future as the industry works to figure out the best utilization of the increasing number of circuits available on chips while also making the computational efficiency of the circuits at the application level improve.

Reliability, Availability, and Serviceability

As machines grow in size and complexity, and applications scale to use increasing amounts of hardware for long run times, the reliability and availability characteristics become increasingly important. For an application to make forward progress, it needs to either checkpoint its progress often enough or have a mechanism for migrating processes running on failing parts of the system onto other working hardware. The Roadrunner system chose to use the checkpoint/restart approach since it seemed the most generally practical for a machine of its size and for the types of applications that it would be running. High availability (HA) through failover system design, at the node or even cluster level, was not a cost-effective approach for the technologies that are employed, and checkpointing could be tolerated.

Of course, there are certainly parts of the system, like the memory DIMMs (dual in-line memory modules), that have error-correcting facilities as well as memory sparing capabilities, and these increase the inherent overall node availability. But making the nodes themselves redundant or failover capable outside of the checkpoint/restart process was not an objective.

Three technology developments whose impact on service were very critical to the overall success, and in particular the ability to build the entire system in a short time, are IBM BladeCenter technology, the Roadrunner triblade mechanical design, and the integrated optical cable that was used for the IB subsystem [9].

The IBM BladeCenter was designed from the outset to maximize serviceability and ease of upgradability. The modular nature of the BladeCenter chassis with the ability to just slide new blades into an existing and pretested infrastructure that has the system management and power management built in, and I/O connections that can stay in place as the blades are slid in and out, provides a very robust base for building large-scale systems. This was proven in practice when the petaflop barrier was broken only four days after the triblades for the final CU were delivered to the lab from manufacturing. They were plugged in, verified to be good, integrated in with the other CUs, and then the entire system turned over to the applications group in less than 48 h.

Conclusion

Roadrunner has achieved each and every one of its original goals, and more. First and foremost, fully capable simulations from fluid mechanics to radiation transport, from molecular to cosmological scale, are running routinely and efficiently on this system. The development of these new capabilities provides a roadmap for developing exascale applications over the next decade.

While there will always be challenges to getting to the next orders of magnitude in computing performance, the Roadrunner project collaboration between LANL and IBM was the first to recognize that a new paradigm was necessary for high-performance computing and to address the energy efficiency and computational performance of a new generation of these systems.

There was concentrated effort on the software algorithm structures needed to implement heterogeneous and hybrid computing models at this scale. It has shown that Open Source components can be used to advantage when the technical challenges attract interested and motivated participants.

The use of a modular building block approach to hardware design, including the BladeCenter management and control infrastructure, provided a very stable base for doing the software experimentation. With some of the breakthroughs that this program produced, the HPC community is now well positioned to solve, or help solve, the scaling issues that will produce major breakthroughs in business, science, energy, and social arenas.

The HPC community needs to be thinking "Ultra Scale" computing in order to harness the emerging technological advances and head into the exascale arena with the momentum that IBM and LANL built crossing the petaflops boundary.

Bibliography

1. Los Alamos National Laboratory, LANL Roadrunner. http://www.lanl.gov/roadrunner/
2. Voltaire Inc. Infiniband Products. http://www.voltaire.com/Products/Infiniband
3. xCAT: Extreme Cloud Administration Tool 2.0. http://xcat.sourceforge.net/
4. IBM Corporation, IBM BladeCenter LS21. http://www-03.ibm.com/systems/bladecenter/hardware/servers/ls21/index.html
5. Vogt J-S, Land R, Boettiger H, Krnjajic Z, Baier H (2009) IBM BladeCenter QS22: design, performance and utilization in hybrid computing systems. IBM J Res Dev 53(5) Paper 3:1–14
6. Gschwind M (2009) Integrated execution: a programming model for accelerators. IBM J Res Dev 53(5) Paper 4:1–14
7. Kistler M, Gunnels J, Brokenshire D, Benton B (2009) Programming the Linpack benchmark for Roadrunner. IBM J Res Dev 53(5) Paper 9:1–11
8. IBM Corporation, IBM BladeCenter. http://www-03.ibm.com/systems/bladecenter/
9. EMCORE Corporation, Infiniband Optics Cable. http://www.emcore.com/fiber_optics/emcoreconnects
10. Moore G (1965) Cramming more components onto integrated circuits. Electronics 38(8):114–117
11. Los Alamos National Laboratory, LANL Applications. http://lanl.gov/roadrunner/rrseminars.shtml
12. Humphreys J, Scaramella J IDC 'The Impact of Power and Cooling on Data Center Infrastructure,' Document #201722, May 2006. http://www-03.ibm.com/systems/resources/systems_z_pdf_IDC_ImpactofPowerandCooling.pdf
13. Green500 List. http://www.green500.org/
14. Dennard R, Gaensslen F, Rideout V, Bassous E, LeBlanc A (1974) Design of ion-implanted MOSFETs with very small physical dimensions. IEEE J Solid State Circuits SC-9(5):256–268
15. IBM Corporation, IBM Deep Computing. http://www-03.ibm.com/systems/deepcomputing/

Router Architecture

▶Switch Architecture

Router-Based Networks

▶ Networks, Direct
▶ Networks, Multistage

Routing (Including Deadlock Avoidance)

PEDRO LÓPEZ
Universidad Politécnica de Valencia, Valencia, Spain

Synonyms
Forwarding

Definition
The routing method used in an interconnection network defines the path followed by packets or messages to communicate two nodes, the source or origin node, which generates the packet, and the destination node, which consumes the packet. This method is often referred to as the routing algorithm.

Discussion

Introduction
Processing nodes in a parallel computer communicate by means of an interconnection network. The interconnection network is composed of switches interconnected by point to point links. Topology is the representation of how these switches are connected. Direct or indirect regular topologies are often used. In direct topologies every network switch has an associated processing node. In indirect topologies, only some switches have processing nodes attached to them. The k-ary n-cube (which includes tori and meshes) and k-ary n-tree (an implementation of fat-trees) are the most frequently used direct and indirect topologies, respectively. In the absence of a direct connection among all network nodes, a routing algorithm is required to select the path packets must follow to communicate every pair of nodes.

Taxonomy of Routing Algorithms
Routing algorithms can be classified according to several criteria. The first one considers the place where decisions are made. In source routing, the full path is computed at the source node, before injecting the packet into the network. The path is stored as a list of switch output ports in the packet header, and intermediate switches are configured according to this information. On the contrary, in distributed routing, each switch computes the next link that will be used by the packet while the packet travels across the network. By repeating this process at each switch, the packet reaches its destination. The packet header only contains the destination node identifier. The main advantage of source routing is that switches are simpler. They only have to select the output port for a packet according to the information stored in its header. However, since the packer header itself must be transmitted through the network, it consumes network bandwidth. On the other hand, distributed routing has been used in most hardware routers for efficiency reasons, since packet headers are more compact. Also, it allows more flexibility, as it may dynamically change the path followed by packets according to network conditions or in case of faults.

Routing algorithms can be also classified as deterministic or adaptive. In deterministic routing, the path followed by packets exclusively depends on their source and destination nodes. In other words, for a given source-destination pair, they always choose the same path.

On the contrary, in adaptive routing, the path followed by packets also depends on network status, such as node or link occupancy or other network load information. Adaptive routing increases routing flexibility, which allows for a better traffic balance on the network, thus improving network performance.

Deterministic routing algorithms are simpler to implement than adaptive ones. On the other hand, adaptive routing introduces the problem of out of order delivery of packets, as two consecutive packets sent from the same source to the same destination may follow different paths. An easy way of increasing the number of routing options is virtual channel multiplexing [2]. In this case, each physical link is decomposed into several virtual channels, each one with its own buffer, which can be separately reserved. Physical link is shared among all the virtual channels using time division multiplexing. Adaptive routing algorithms may provide all the feasible routing options to forward the packet towards its destination (fully adaptive routing) or only a subset (partially adaptive routing).

If adaptive routing is used, the selection function chooses one of the feasible routing options according to some criteria. For instance, in case of distributed adaptive routing, the selection function may select the link with the lowest buffer occupation or with the lowest number of busy virtual channels.

A routing algorithm is minimal if the paths it provides are included in the set of shortest or minimal paths from source to destination. In other words, with minimal routing, every link crossed by a packet reduces its distance to destination. On the contrary, a non-minimal routing algorithm allows packets to use paths longer than the shortest ones. Although these routing algorithms are useful to circumvent congested or faulty areas, they use more resources than strictly needed, which may negatively impact on performance. Additionally, paths having an unbounded number of allowed non-minimal hops might result in packets never reaching their destination, situation that is referred to as livelock.

Routing algorithms can be implemented in several ways. Some routers use routing tables with a number of entries equal to the number of destinations. With source routing, these tables are associated with each source node, and each entry contains the whole path towards the corresponding destination. With distributed routing, these tables (known as forwarding tables) are associated to each network switch, and contain the next link a packet destined to the corresponding entry must follow. With a single entry per destination, only deterministic routing is allowed. The main advantage of table-based routing is that any topology and any routing algorithm can be used in the network. However, routing based on tables suffers from a lack of scalability. The size of the table grows linearly with network size ($O(N)$ storage requirements), and, most important, the time required to access the table also depends on network size.

An alternative to tables is to place a specialized hardware at each node that implements a logic circuit and computes the output port to be used as a function of the current and destination nodes and the status of the output ports. The implementation is very efficient in terms of both area and speed, but the algorithm is specific to the topology and to the routing strategy used on that topology. This is the approach used for the fixed regular topologies and routing algorithms used in large parallel computers.

There are hybrid implementations, such as the Flexible Interval Routing (FIR) [11] approach, which defines the routing algorithm by programming a set of registers associated to each output port. The strategy is able to implement the most commonly-used deterministic and adaptive routing algorithms in the most widely used regular topologies, with $O(\log(N))$ storage requirements.

Deadlock Handling

A deadlock in an interconnection network occurs when some packets cannot advance toward their destination because all of them are waiting on one another to release resources (buffers or links). In other words, the involved packets request and hold resources in a cyclic fashion. There are three strategies for deadlock handling: deadlock prevention, deadlock avoidance, and deadlock recovery.

Deadlock prevention incurs in a significant overhead and is only used in circuit switching. It consists of reserving all the required resources before starting transmission. In deadlock avoidance, resources are requested as packets advance but routing is restricted in such a way that there are no cyclic dependencies between channels. Another approach consists of allowing the existence of cyclic dependencies between channels while providing some escape paths to avoid deadlock, therefore increasing routing flexibility. Deadlock recovery strategies allow the use of unrestricted fully adaptive routing, potentially outperforming deadlock avoidance techniques. However, these strategies require a deadlock detection mechanism [13] and a deadlock recovery mechanism [1, 12] that is able to recover from deadlocks. If a deadlock is detected, the recovery mechanism is triggered, resolving the deadlock. Progressive recovery techniques deallocate buffer resources from other "normal" packets and reassign them to deadlocked packets for quick delivery. Disha [1] and software-based recovery [12] are examples of this approach. Regressive techniques deallocate resources from deadlocked packets by killing and later re-injecting them at the original source router (i.e., abort-and-retry).

In deadlock-avoidance, the routing algorithm restricts the paths allowed by packets to only those ones that keep the global network state deadlock-free. Dally [2] proposed the necessary and sufficient condition for a deterministic routing algorithm to be deadlock-free. Based on this condition, he defined a channel dependency graph (CDG) and established a total order among channels. Routing is restricted to visit channels in order, to eliminate cycles in the CDG. The CDG associated to a routing algorithm on a given topology is a directed graph, where the vertices are the network links and the edges join those links with direct dependencies between them, i.e., those adjacent links that could be consecutively used by the routing algorithm. The routing algorithm is deadlock free if and only if the CDG is acyclic. To design deadlock-free routing algorithms based on this idea while keeping network connectivity, it may be required that physical channels are split into several virtual channels, and the ordering is performed among the set of virtual channels. Although this idea was initially proposed for deterministic routing, it has been also applied to adaptive routing. For instance, in the turn model [10], a packet produces a turn when it changes direction, usually changing from one dimension to another in a mesh. Turns are combined into cycles. Prohibiting just enough turns to break all the cycles prevents deadlock.

Although imposing an acyclic CDG avoids deadlock, it results in poor network performance, as routing flexibility is strongly constrained. Duato [5] demonstrates that a routing algorithm can have cycles in the CDG while remaining deadlock-free. This allows the design of deadlock-free routing algorithms without significant constraints imposed on routing flexibility. The key idea that supports deadlock freedom despite the existence of cyclic dependencies is the concept of escape path. Packets can be routed without restrictions, provided that there exists a subset of network links – the escape paths – without cyclic dependencies, which allow every packet to escape from a potential cycle. An important characteristic of the escape paths is that it must be possible to deliver packets from any point in the network to their corresponding destination using the escape paths alone. However, this does not imply that a packet that used an escape path at some router must continue using escape paths until delivered. Indeed, packets are free to leave the escape paths at any point in the network and continue using full routing flexibility until delivered.

These ideas can be stated more formally as follows. A routing subfunction R1 associated to the routing function R supplies a subset of the links provided by R (the set of escape channels), therefore restricting its routing flexibility, while still being able to deliver packets from any valid location in the network to any destination. The concept of indirect dependency between two escape channels is defined as follows. A packet may reserve a set of adjacent channels c_i, c_{i+1},..., c_{k-1}, c_k, where only c_i and c_k are provided by R1, but c_{i+1},... c_{k-1} are not. The extended CDG for R1 has as vertices the escape channels, and as edges both the direct and indirect dependences between escape channels.

The theory states that a routing function R is deadlock-free if there exists a routing subfunction R1 without cycles in its extended CDG. A simple way to design adaptive routing algorithms based on the theory is to depart from a well-known deterministic deadlock-free routing function, adding virtual channels in a regular way. The new additional channels can be used for fully adaptive routing. As mentioned above, when a packet uses an escape channel at a given node, it can freely use any of the available channels supplied by the routing function at the next node.

Duato also developed necessary and sufficient conditions for deadlock-free adaptive routing under different switching techniques, and for different sets of input data for the routing function. All of those theoretical extensions are based on the principle described above.

Routing in *k*-ary *n*-cubes

A *k*-ary *n*-cube is a *n*-dimensional network, with k nodes in each dimension, connected in a ring-fashion. Every node is connected to $2n$ neighbors. The number of nodes is $N = k^n$. This topology is often referred to as a *n*-dimensional torus, and it has been used in some of the largest parallel computers, such as the Cray T3E or the IBM BlueGene (both of them use a 3D-torus). The *n*-dimensional mesh is a particular case where the nodes of each dimension are connected as a linear array (i.e., there are not wraparound connections). The symmetry and regularity of the *k*-ary *n*-cube simplify network implementation and packet routing as the movement of a packet along a given network dimension does not modify the number of remaining hops in any other dimension toward its destination.

In a mesh, dimension-order routing (DOR) avoids deadlocks (and livelocks) by allowing only the use of minimal paths that cross the network dimensions in some total order. That is, the routing algorithm does not allow the use of links of a given dimension until no other links are needed by the packet in all of the preceding dimensions to reach its destination. In a 2D-mesh, this is easy to achieve by crossing dimensions in XY order.

This simple routing algorithm is not deadlock-free in a torus. The wraparound links create a cycle among the nodes of each dimension. This is easily solved by multiplexing each physical channel into two virtual channels (H -high- and L -low-), and restricting routing in such a way that H channels can only be used if the coordinate of the destination node in the corresponding dimension is higher than the current one and vice versa. Consider a 4-node unidirectional ring (a 4-ary 1-cube) with nodes n_i, $i = 0, 1, 2, 3$ and two channels connecting each pair of adjacent nodes. Let c_{Hi} and c_{Li}, $i = 0, 1, 2, 3$ be output channels of node n_i. Figure 1 shows the CDG corresponding to the routing algorithm presented above. As there are not cycles in the channel dependency graph, it is deadlock free.

An adaptive routing algorithm for tori can be easily defined by merely adding a new virtual channel to each physical channel (the A -adaptive- channel). This new channel can be freely used, even to cross network dimensions in any order, thus providing fully adaptive routing on the k-ary n-cube. In this routing algorithm, the H and L channels belong to the set provided by the routing subfunction. Figure 2 shows the extended CDG for this routing algorithm in a 4-node unidirectional ring, which is acyclic, and thus the routing algorithm is deadlock-free. This routing algorithm will provide several routing options, depending on the relative locations of the node that currently stores the packet and the destination node. For instance, in a 2D-torus, if both X and Y channels remain to be crossed, two adaptive virtual channels in both dimensions and one escape channel (the H or L in the X dimension) will be provided. The selection function is in charge of making the final choice, selecting one of the links also considering network status. A simple selection function may be based on assigning static priorities to virtual channels, returning the first free channel according to this order. Priorities could be assigned to give more preference to adaptive channels. More sophisticated selection functions could be also used, such as selecting a channel of the least multiplexed physical channel to minimize the negative effects of virtual channel multiplexing.

Routing in *k*-ary *n*-trees

Clusters of PCs are being considered as a cost-effective alternative to small and medium scale parallel computing systems. These machines use any of the commercial high-performance switch-based point-to-point interconnects. Multistage interconnection networks (MINs) are the most usual choice. In particular, fat-trees have risen in popularity in the past few years (for instance, Myrinet, InfiniBand, Quadrics).

A fat-tree is based on a complete tree that gets thicker near the root. Processing nodes are located at the leaves. However, assuming constant link bandwidth, the number of ports of the switches increases as we approach the root, which makes the physical implementation unfeasible. For this reason, some alternative implementations have been proposed in order to use switches with fixed arity. In k-ary n-trees, bandwidth is increased as we approach the root by replicating switches. A k-ary n-tree (see Fig. 3) has n stages, with k (arity) links connecting each switch to the previous or to the next stage. A k-ary n-tree is able to connect $N = k^n$ processing nodes using nk^{n-1} switches.

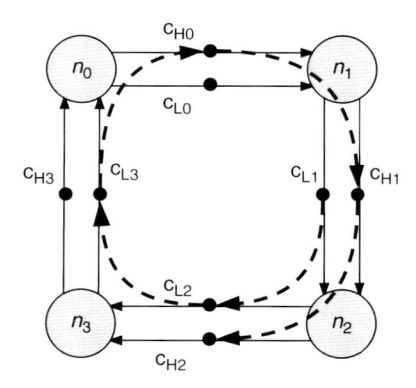

Routing (Including Deadlock Avoidance). Fig. 1 Channel dependency graph for a 4-ary 1-cube

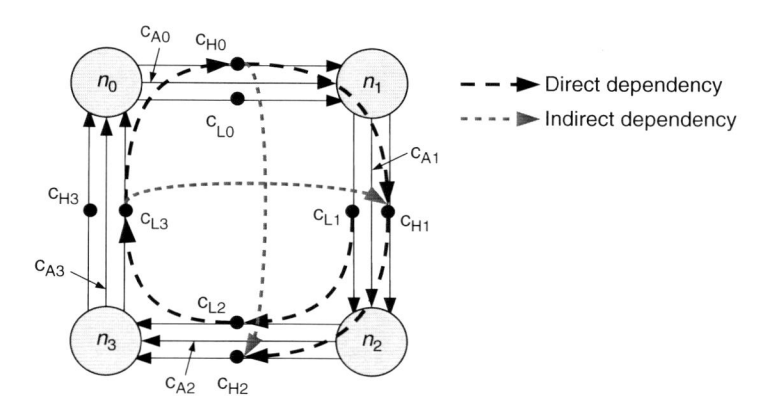

Routing (Including Deadlock Avoidance). Fig. 2 Extended channel dependency graph for a 4-ary 1-cube

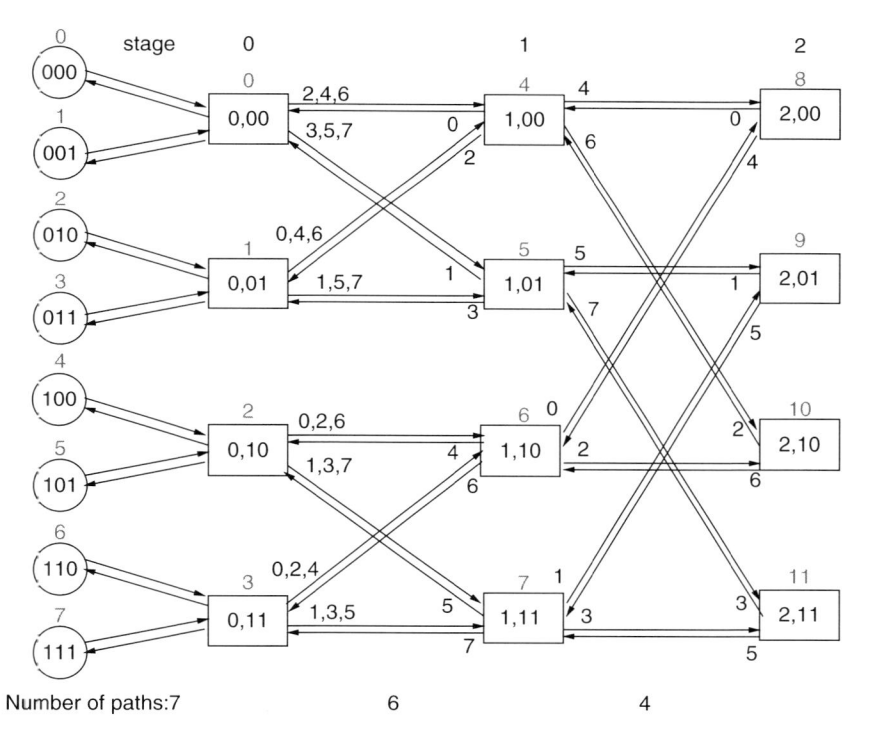

Routing (Including Deadlock Avoidance). Fig. 3 Load-balanced deterministic routing in a 2-ary n-tree

In a k-ary n-tree, minimal routing from a source to a destination can be accomplished by sending packets upwards to one of the nearest common ancestors of the source and destination nodes and then, from there, downwards to destination. When crossing stages in the upward direction, several paths are possible, thus providing adaptive routing. In fact, each switch can select any of its up output ports. Once a nearest common ancestor has been reached, the packet is turned around and sent downwards to its destination and just a single path is available.

A deterministic routing algorithm for k-ary n-trees can be obtained by reducing the multiple ascending paths in a fat-tree to a single one for each source-destination pair. The path reduction should be done trying to balance network link utilization. That is, all the links of a given stage should be used by a similar number of paths. A simple idea is to shuffle, at each switch, consecutive destinations in the ascending phase [8]. In other words, consecutive destinations in a given switch are distributed among the different ascending links, reaching different switches in the next stage. Figure 3 shows the destination node distribution in the ascending and descending links of a 2-ary 3-tree following this idea. In the figure, each ascending link has been labeled with the destinations it can forward to. As can be seen, packets destined to the same node reach the same switch at the last stage, independently of their source node. Each switch of the last stage receives packets addressed only to two destinations, and packets destined to each one are forwarded through a different descending link (as there are two descending links per switch). Therefore, this mechanism efficiently distributes the traffic destined to different nodes, and balances load across the links.

Routing in Irregular Networks. Agnostic Routing

As stated above, direct topologies and multistage networks are often used when performance is the primary concern. However, in the presence of some switch or link failures, a regular network will become an irregular one. In fact, most of the commercially available interconnects for clusters support irregular topologies. An alternative for tolerating faults in regular networks without requiring additional logic is the use of generic or topology agnostic routing algorithms. These routing algorithms can be applied to any topology and provide a valid and deadlock free path for every source-destination pair of nodes in the network (if they are physically connected). Therefore, in the presence of any possible combination of faults, a topology agnostic routing algorithm provides a valid solution for routing.

An extensive number of topology agnostic routing strategies have been proposed. They differ in their goals and approaches (e.g., obtaining minimal paths, fast computation time) and the resources they need (typically virtual channels). The oldest topology agnostic routing algorithm is up*/down* [14], being the most popular topology agnostic routing scheme used in cluster networks. Routing is based on an assignment of direction labels (up or down) to the links in the network by building a breadth first spanning tree (BFS). Cyclic channel dependencies are avoided by prohibiting messages to traverse a link in the up direction after having traversed one in the down direction. Although simple, this approach generates a network unbalance because a high percentage of traffic is forced to cross the root node. Derived from up*/down*, some improvements were proposed, such as assigning directions to links by computing a depth first spanning tree (DFS), the Flexible Routing scheme, which introduced unidirectional routing restrictions to break cycles in each direction at different positions, or the Segment-based Routing algorithm, which splits a topology into subnets, and subnets into segments. This allows placing bidirectional turn restrictions locally within a segment, which results in a larger degree of freedom.

Most of these routing algorithms do not guarantee that all packets will be routed through a minimal path. This causes an increment in the packet latency and an inefficient use of network resources, affecting the overall network performance. The Minimal Adaptive routing algorithm, which is based on Duato's theory, adds a new virtual channel which provides minimal routing, keeping the paths provided by up*/down* as escape paths. The In-Transit Buffers mechanism [7] also provides minimal routing for all the packets. To avoid deadlocks, packets are ejected from the network, temporarily stored in the network interface card at some intermediate hosts and later re-injected into the network. However, this mechanism requires some support at NICs and at least one host to be attached to every switch in the network, which cannot always be guaranteed. Other approaches make use of virtual channels to route all the packets through minimal paths while still guaranteeing deadlock freedom. For instance, Layered Shortest Path (LASH) guarantees deadlock freedom by dividing the physical network into a set of virtual networks using separate virtual channels. Minimal paths between every source-destination pair of hosts are spread onto these layers, such that each layer becomes deadlock free. In Transition Oriented Routing (TOR), unlike the LASH routing, up*/down* is used as a baseline routing algorithm in order to decide when to change to a new virtual net work (when a forbidden transition down→up appears). To remove cyclic channel dependencies, virtual networks are crossed in increasing order, thus guaranteeing deadlock freedom. However, due to the large number of routing restrictions imposed by up*/down*, providing minimal paths among every pair of hosts may require a high number of virtual channels.

Related Entries
- ►Clusters
- ►Deadlocks
- ►Flow Control
- ►Infiniband
- ►Interconnection Networks
- ►Myrinet
- ►Network of Workstations
- ►Networks, Direct
- ►Networks, Fault-Tolerant
- ►Networks, Multistage
- ►Switch Architecture
- ►Switching Techniques

Bibliographic Notes and Further Reading

Dally's [4] and Duato's [6] books are excellent textbooks on Interconnection Networks and contain abundant material about routing. The sources of the theories about deadlock-free routing can be found in [2] and [5]. Although virtual channels where introduced in [2], they were formally proposed in [3] as "virtual channel flow control." The Turn-model, which allows adaptive routing in tori without virtual channels was proposed in [10]. The selection function has some impact on network performance. Several selection functions have been proposed. For instance, [9] proposed a set of possible selection functions in the context of fat-trees. Deadlock-recovery strategies are based on the assumption that deadlocks are rare. This assumption was evaluated in [15], were the frequency of deadlocks was measured. Disha and software-based recovery, two progressive deadlock-recovery mechanisms, were proposed in [1] and [12], respectively. To make deadlock-recovery feasible, an efficient deadlock detection mechanism that matches the low deadlock occurrence must be used, such as the FC3D deadlock-detection mechanism proposed in [13]. FIR [11] is an alternative implementation to algorithmic and table-based routing that could be used in commercial switches. The load-balanced deterministic routing algorithm described for fat-trees can be found in [8]. Up*/down* routing was initially proposed for Autonet [14]. The ITB mechanism [7] was proposed to improve performance of source routing in the context of Myrinet networks.

Bibliography

1. Anjan KV, Pinkston TM (1995) DISHA: a deadlock recovery scheme for fully adaptive routing. In: Proceedings of the 9th international parallel processing symposium, Santa Barbara, CA, pp 537–543
2. Dally WJ (1992) Virtual-channel flow control. IEEE Trans Parallel Distributed Syst 3(2):194–205
3. Duato J (1993) A new theory of deadlock-free adaptive routing in wormhole networks. IEEE Trans Parallel Distributed Syst 4(12):1320–1331
4. Dally WJ, Seitz CL (1987) Deadlock-free message routing in multiprocessor interconnection Networks. IEEE Trans Comput C-36(5):547–553
5. Dally WJ, Towles B (2004) Principles and practices of interconnection networks. Morgan Kaufmann, San Francisco, CA
6. Duato J, Yalamanchili S, Ni LM (2003) Interconnection networks: an engineering approach. Morgan Kaufmann, San Francisco, CA
7. Flich J, López P, Malumbres MP, Duato J (2002) Boosting the performance of myrinet networks. IEEE Trans Parallel Distributed Syst 13(11):1166–1182
8. Gómez C, Gilabert F, Gómez ME, López P, Duato J (2007) Deterministic vs. adaptive routing in fat-trees. In: Proceedings of the 2007 international parallel and distributed processing symposium, IEEE Computer Society Press, Long Beach, CA
9. Gilabert F, Gómez ME, López P, Duato J (2006) On the influence of the selection function on the performance of fat-trees. Lecture Notes in Computer Science 4128, Springer, Berlin
10. Glass CJ, Ni LM (1992) The turn model for adaptive routing. In: Proceedings of the 19th international symposium on computer architecture, ACM, New York, pp 278–287
11. Gómez ME, López P, Duato J (2006) FIR: an efficient routing strategy for tori and meshes. J Parallel Distributed Comput-Elsevier 66(7):907–921
12. Martínez JM, López P, Duato J (2001) A cost-effective approach to deadlock handling in wormhole networks. IEEE Trans Parallel Distributed Syst 12(7):716–729
13. Martínez JM, López P, Duato J (2003) FC3D: flow control based distributed deadlock detection mechanism for true fully adaptive routing in wormhole networks. IEEE Trans Parallel Distributed Syst 14(8):765–779
14. Schroeder MD et al (1990) Autonet: a high-speed, self-configuring local area network using point-to-point links. Technical report SRC research report 59, DEC, April 1990

15. Warnakulasuriya S, Pinkston TM (1997) Characterization of deadlocks in interconnection Networks. In: Proceedings of the 11th international parallel processing symposium, IEEE Computer Society, Washington, DC, pp 80–86

R-Stream Compiler

BENOIT MEISTER, NICOLAS VASILACHE, DAVID WOHLFORD, MUTHU MANIKANDAN BASKARAN, ALLEN LEUNG, RICHARD LETHIN
Reservoir Labs, Inc., New York, NY, USA

Definition

R-Stream (R-Stream is a registered trademark of Reservoir Labs, Inc.) is a source-to-source, auto-parallelizing compiler developed by Reservoir Labs, Inc. R-Stream compiles programs in the domains of high-performance scientific (HPC) and high-performance embedded computing (HPEC), where loop nests, dense matrices, and arrays are the common idioms. It generates *mapped* programs, i.e., optimized programs for parallel execution on the target architecture. R-Stream targets modern, heterogeneous, multi-core architectures, including multiprocessors with caches, systems with accelerators, and distributed memory architectures that require explicit memory management and data movement. The compiler accepts the C language as input. Depending on the target platform, the compiled output program can be in C with the appropriate target APIs or annotations for parallel execution, other data parallel languages such as CUDA for GPUs, or dataflow assembly for FPGA targets.

History

DARPA funded R-Stream development in the Polymorphous Computer Architecture (PCA) research program, starting in 2002. The PCA program developed new programmable computer architectures for approaching the energy efficiency of application-specific fixed function processors, particularly those for advanced signal processing in radars. These new PCA chips included RAW [36], TRIPS [34], Smart Memories [26], and Monarch [32]; these chips innovated architecture features for energy efficiency, such as manycores, heterogeneity, mixed execution models, and explicit memory communications management. DARPA wanted R-Stream for programming the architectural space spanned by these chips from a single high-level and target-independent source. Since the PCA architectures uniformly presented a very high ratio of on-chip computational rates to off-chip bandwidth, R-Stream research prioritized transformations that increased arithmetic intensity (the ratio of computation to communication) in concert with parallelization, and on creating mappings that executed the program in a streaming manner – hence the name of the compiler, R-Stream (the "R" stands for Reservoir).

As the R-Stream compiler team refined the mapping algorithms, the conception of what the high-level, machine independent programming language should be also evolved. Streaming as an *execution model* had been well established for many decades, as the dominant execution paradigm for programming digital signal processors (DSPs): software-pipelining of computation with direct memory access (DMA). The PCA research program investigated whether streaming should be considered as the *programming model*. Initially, two streaming-based research programming languages, Stanford Brook [9] and MIT StreamIt [21], were supported in the PCA program. These languages provide means for expressing computations as aggregate operations (Brook calls them *kernels*; StreamIt calls them *filters*) on linear streams of data. However, as more understanding of the compilation process was acquired, the R-Stream compiler team started to move away from streaming as being the right expression form for algorithms for several reasons:

1. The expressiveness of the streaming languages was limited. They were biased toward one-dimensional streams, but radar signal processing involves multi dimensional data "cubes" processed along various dimensions [33].
2. Transformations for compiling streaming languages are isomorphic to common loop transformations – e.g., parallelization, tiling, loop fusion, index set splitting, array expansion/contraction, and so forth.
3. While streaming notations were found to sometimes be a good shorthand for expression of a particular mapping of an algorithm to a particular architecture, that particular mapping would not run well

on another architecture without significant transformation. The notation and idioms of the streaming languages actually frustrate translation, because a compiler would have to undo them to extract semantics for re mapping.

Consequently, the R-Stream team moved away from streaming as a programming paradigm to instead supporting input programs (mainly loops) written in the C language: C can more succinctly express the multidimensional radar algorithms (compared to the streaming languages); the basic theory of loop optimization for C was well understood; and C can be written in a textbook manner with the semantics plain. However, the compilation challenges coming from the architectural features in the PCA chips were open problems. To attack these problems, the R-Stream team adopted and extended the powerful polyhedral framework for loop optimization.

PCA features are now in commercial computing chips. Programming such chips is complex, requiring more than just parallelization. Thus, the R-Stream compiler is being used by programmers and researchers to map C to chips such as Cell, GPGPUs, Tilera, and many-core SMP. It is also being extended in research on compilation to ExaScale supercomputers. R-Stream is available commercially and also licensed in source form to research collaborators.

Design Principles

R-Stream performs high-level automatic parallelization. The high-level mapping tasks that R-Stream performs include parallelism extraction, locality improvement, processor assignment, managing the data layout, and generating explicit data movements. R-Stream takes as input sequential programs written in C, with the kernels to be optimized marked with a simple pragma, but with all mapping decisions for the target automated.

Low-level or machine-level optimizations, such as instruction selection, instruction scheduling, and register allocation, are left to an external *low-level compiler* that takes the mapped source produced by R-Stream.

R-Stream currently performs mostly static mapping for all its target architectures. Resource and scheduling decisions are computed statically at compile time, with very little dynamic decisions done at runtime. For all architectures, the mapping is also "bare-metal," with only a small dedicated runtime layer that is specialized to each architecture.

Using R-Stream

Programmers write succinct loop nests in sequential ANSI C. The loop nest can be imperfect but must fit within an *extended static control program* form. That is, the loops have affine parametric extents and static integer strides. Multidimensional array references must be affine functions of loop index variables and parameters. Certain dynamic control features are allowed, such as conditionals that are affine functions of index variables and parameters. Programs that are not directly within the affine static control program form can be handled by wrapping the code in an abstraction layer and providing a compliant image function in C that models the effects of the wrapped function.

The programmer indicates the region to be mapped with a simple single pragma. Again, R-Stream does not require the programmer to indicate *how* this mapping should proceed: not through any particular idiomatic correspondence of the loop nest to particular hardware features, nor through detailed specifications encoded in pragma. R-Stream *automatically* determines the mapping, based on the target machine and emits transformed code. For example, a loop nest expressed in ANSI C can be rendered into optimized CUDA [1].

Architecture

R-Stream is built on a set of independent and reusable optimizations on two intermediate representations (IRs). Unlike many source-to-source transformation tools, R-Stream shuns ad hoc pattern-matching-based transformations in favor of mathematically sound transformations, in particular dependence- and semantics-based transformations in the polyhedral model. The two intermediate representations are designed to support this view. The first intermediate representation, called Sprig, is used in the scalar optimizer. It is based on static single assignment (SSA) form [14], similar to Click's graph-based IR [13], augmented with operators from value dependence graph [41] for expressing state dependencies. The second intermediate representation is the *generalized dependence graph* (GDG), the representation used in the polyhedral mapper. Conversions from the SSA representation to the GDG representation are performed by the *raising* phase,

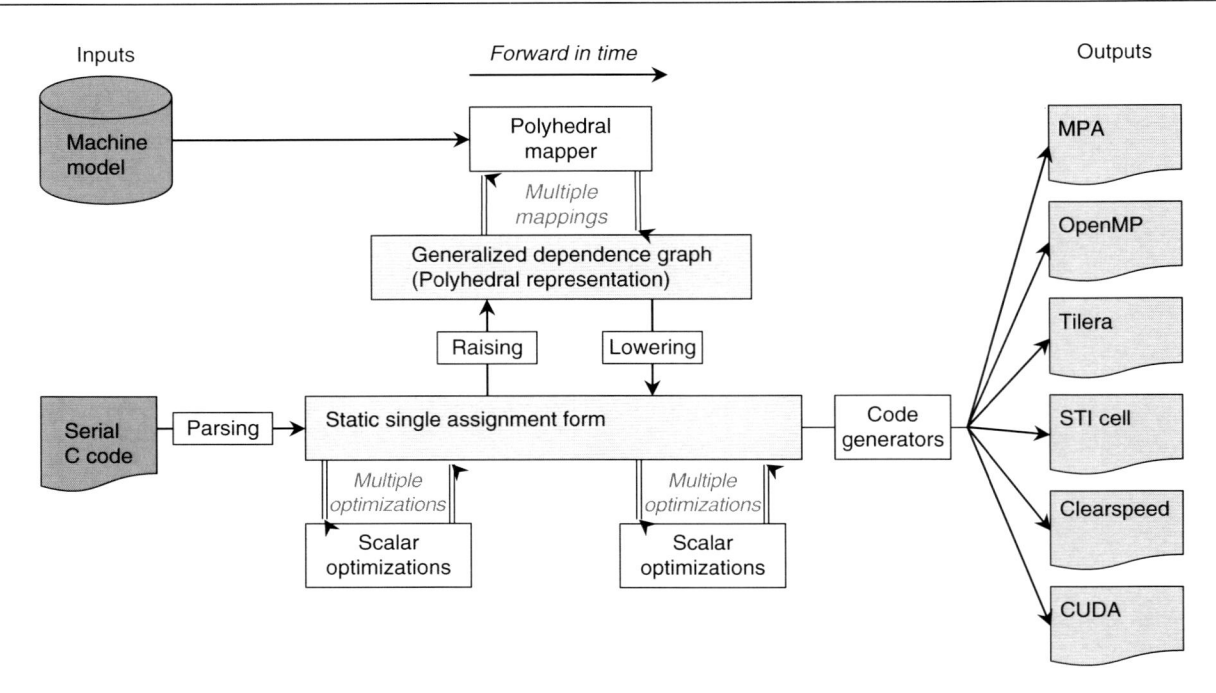

R-Stream Compiler. Fig. 1 R-Stream's architecture

and the converse by the *lowering* phase. These components are shown as different parts of the R-Stream compiler flow in Fig. 1.

Scalar Optimizer

The main task of the scalar optimizer is to simplify and normalize the input source so that subsequent analysis of the program in the raising phase can proceed. The scalar optimizer also runs after mapping and lowering, to remove redundancies and simplify expressions that result from the polyhedral scanning phases. The scalar optimizer provides traditional optimizations.

Syntax Recovery

The output of R-Stream has to be processed by low-level compilers corresponding to the target architectures. These low-level compilers often have trouble compiling automatically generated programs, even if the code is semantically legal, because they pattern-match optimizations to the code idioms that humans typically write. For example, many low-level compilers cannot perform loop optimizations on loops that are expressed using gotos and labels. Thus, to ensure that the output code can be effectively optimized by the low-level compiler, R-Stream's code generation back-end performs syntax recovery to convert a program in the scalar representation into idioms that look human-like. The engineering challenge is that R-Stream is designed to represent and transform programs in semantics-based IRs, far from the original syntax and language. Source reconstruction is more complex than simple unparsing. R-Stream uses an algorithm using early coalescing of ϕ-functions to exit SSA, extensions to Cifuentes [10, 11] to detect high-level statement forms, and then localized pattern matching to generate syntax. Sprig also represents types in terms of the input source language, to allow for faithful reproduction of those types at output.

Machine Model

R-Stream supports Cell, Tilera, GPUs, ClearSpeed, symmetric multiprocessors, and FPGAs as targets. These are rendered and detailed in machine models (MM), expressed in an XML-based description language. The target description is an entity graph connecting physical components that implicitly encodes the system capabilities and execution models that can be exploited by the mapper.

The nodes in the entity graph are processors, memories, data links, and command links. Processor entities are computation engines, including scalar processors, SIMD processors, and multiprocessors. These are structured as a multi dimensional grid geometry. Memory entities are data-caches, instruction-caches, combined data and I-caches, and main and scratchpad memories. There are two types of edges in the graph. Data-link edges stand for explicit communication protocols that require software control, such as DMA. Command-link edges stand for instructions that one processor can send to another entity, such as thread spawning or DMA initiation.

The final ingredient in an MM is the morph. A morph is a parallel computer, or a part of one, on which the mapping algorithms are focused. The term morph derives from the polymorphous aspect of the DARPA PCA program for efficient chips that could be reconfigured; a morph would describe one among many configurations of a polymorphous architecture. R-Stream also uses the term "morph" to describe the single configuration for a non-reconfigurable portion of a target.

Each morph in a MM contains a *host processor* and a set of *processing elements* (PEs), plus its entity graph. The host processor and the PEs are allowed to be identical, e.g., in a SMP environment. Associated with the hosts and PEs is its *topology* and a list of submorphs.

A machine model is subdivided into a set of morphs. This mechanism allows a mapping problem for a complex machine to be decomposed into a set of smaller problems, each concentrating on one morph of the machine. In hierarchical mapping, the set of morphs form a tree, with sub-morphs representing submapping problems after the high-level mapping problems have been completed.

The Generalized Dependence Graph

The GDG is the IR used by the mapper. All phases of the mapper take a set of GDGs as an input and produce a set of modified GDGs as output. Thus, mapping proceeds strictly in this IR.

Initially, the input to the mapper is a single GDG that represents the part of the program that the programmer has indicated should be mapped. Mapping phases annotate and rewrite this graph, essentially choosing a projection of the GDG into the target machine space (across processors) and time (schedule), and then find a good description of that projection in terms of the target machine execution model. That is, the mapper finds a schedule of execution of computation, memory use, and communication.

As the mapping process proceeds, the GDG may be split into multiple GDGs, for submapping problems to portions of a hierarchical or heterogeneous machine.

The GDG (defined below) uses polyhedra to model the computations, dependences, and memory references of the part of the program being mapped. The polyhedral description provides *compactness* and *precision*, for a broad set of useful loop nest structures, and enables tractable analytical formulations of concepts like "dataflow analysis" and "coarse-grained parallelization."

A GDG is a multigraph, where the nodes represent statements (called *polyops*), and the edges represent the dependences between the statements. The basic information attached to each polyop node includes:

- Its iteration domain, represented as a polyhedral set
- A list of array references, each represented as an affine function from the iteration space, to the data space of the corresponding array
- A predicate function indicating under what conditions the statement should be executed
- Data-dependent conditionals are supported through the predicates.

Attached to each edge of the GDG is its dependence polyhedron, a polyhedral set that encodes the dependence between the iterations of the edge's nodes.

The polyhedral sets used in the GDG are unions of intersections of integer lattices with parametric polyhedra, called Z-Domains. Z-Domains are the essence of the mathematical language of polyhedral compilation. The use of unions allows for describing a broad range of "shapes" of programs, the integer lattices provide precision through complex mappings. Using parametric polyhedra also provides a richness of description; it enables parametrically specified families of programs to be optimized at once and it enables describing loop nests and array references that depend on iteration variables from enclosing loop nests. R-Stream includes a ground-up implementation of a library for manipulating Z-Domains that provides performance and functionality that we could not obtain had we used Loechner's Polylib [25].

Mapping Flow

The basic mapping flow in R-Stream is through the following mapper phases:

- Perform *raising* to convert mappable regions into the polyhedral form.
- Perform dependence analysis and/or dependence removal optimizations such as array expansion.
- Perform affine scheduling to extract parallelism.
- Perform task formation (a generalization of tiling) and processor placement. Also perform thread partitioning to split the mapped region among the host processor and the co-processing elements.
- Perform memory promotion to improve locality. If necessary, also perform data layout transformations and insert communications.
- Perform *lowering* to convert the mapped program back into the scalar IR, Sprig.

These phases are mixed and matched and can be recursively called for different target architectures. For example, for SMP targets, it is not necessary to promote memory and insert explicit communications, since such machines have caches. (However, in some cases-explicit copies also help on cache-based machines by compacting the footprint of the data accessed by a task; we call such efforts "virtual scratchpad.") For a target machine with a host processor and multiple GPUs, R-Stream will first map coarsely across GPUs (inserting thread controls and explicit communictions) and then recursively perform mapping for parts of the code that will be executed within the GPUs.

Raising

The raising phase is responsible for converting loop nests inside mappable regions into the polyhedral form. R-Stream's raising process is as follows:

1. Mappable regions are identified by the programmer via pragmas. Mappable regions can also be expanded by user-directed inlining pragmas.
2. Perform loop detection and if/then/else region detection.
3. Perform if-conversion [3] to convert data dependent predicates into predicated statements.
4. Perform induction variable detection using the algorithm of Pop [30]. The algorithm has been extended to detect inductions based on address arithmetic. Affine loop bounds and affine address expressions can be converted into the iteration domains and access functions in the GDG.
5. Within each basic block, partition the operators into maximal subsets of operators connected via value flow such that the partitions can be sequentially ordered. These maximal subsets are made into individual polyops.
6. Finally, convert the loop iteration domains and access functions into constraints form in the GDG.

Dependence Analysis and Array Expansion

R-Stream provides a more advanced covering dependence analysis from Vasilache [39] to remove transitively implied dependencies, which improves upon the algorithms from Feautrier [18].

R-Stream provides a novel *corrective array expansion* based on Vasilache's violated dependence analysis [37, 38]. Corrective array expansion essentially fuses array expansion phases into scheduling phases.

A "violated" dependence is a relationship between a source and a target instruction of the program that exhibit a memory-based dependence in the original program that is not fulfilled under a chosen schedule. A violation arises when the target statement is scheduled before the source statement in the transformed program.

Such a violation can be corrected by either recomputing a new schedule or by changing the memory locations read and written. This allows for better schedules with as small a memory footprint as possible by performing the following steps:

1. Provide a subset of the original dependencies in the program to the affine scheduler phase so that it determines an aggressive schedule with maximum parallelism.
2. When the schedule turns out to be incorrect with regards to the whole set of dependencies, perform a correction of the resulting schedule by means of renaming and array expansion.
3. Perform lazy corrections targeting only the very causes of the semantics violations in the aggressively scheduled program.

Unlike previous array expansion algorithms in the literature by Feautrier [16], Barthou et al. [5], and Offner et al. [29], which tend to expand all arrays fully and render the program in dynamic single assignment form, the above algorithm only expands arrays by need – i.e., only if the parallelism exposed by the scheduling algorithm requires the array to be expanded.

Affine Scheduling

Under the exact affine representation of dependences in the GDG, it was known that useful scheduling properties of programs can be optimized such as maximal fine-grained parallelism using Feautrier's algorithm [20], maximal coarse-grained parallelism using Lim and Lam's algorithm [24], or maximal parallelism given a (maximal) fusion/distribution structure using Bondhugula's et al.'s algorithm [8]. R-Stream improved on these algorithms by introducing the concept of affine fusion and this enables a single seamless formulation of the joint optimization of cost functions representing trade-offs between amount of parallelism and amount of locality at various depths in the loop nest hierarchy. Scheduling algorithms in R-Stream search an optimization space that is either constructed on a depth-by-depth basis as solutions are found, or based on the convex space of all legal multi dimensional schedules as had been illustrated by Vasilache [39]. R-Stream allows direct optimization of the tradeoff function using Integer Linear Programming (ILP) solvers as well as iterative exploration of the search space. Redundant solutions in the search space are implicitly pruned out by the combined tradeoff function as they exhibit the same overall cost. In practice, a solution to the optimization problem represents a whole class of equivalent scheduling functions with the same cost.

Building upon the multi dimensional affine fusion formulation, R-Stream also introduced the concept of joint optimization of parallelism, locality, and amount of contiguous memory accesses. This additional metric is targeted at memory hierarchies where accessing a contiguous set of memory references is crucial to obtain high performance. Such hardware features include hardware and software prefetchers, and explicit vector load and store into and from registers, and coalescing hardware in GPUs. R-Stream defines the cost of contiguous memory accesses up to an affine data layout transformation.

To support hierarchical/heterogeneous architectures, the scheduling algorithm can be used hierarchically. Different levels of the hardware hierarchy are optimized using very different cost functions. At the outermost levels of the hierarchy, weight is put on obtaining coarse-grained parallelism with minimal communications that keep as many compute cores busy. At the innermost levels, after communications have been introduced, focus is set to fine-grained parallelism, contiguity and alignment to enable hardware features such as vectorization. Tiling also separates mapping concerns between different levels of the hierarchy.

Task Formation and Placement

The streaming execution model that R-Stream targets is as follows:

- A bulk set of input data D_i is loaded into a memory M that is close to processing element P.
- A set of operations T, called "task," works on D_i.
- A live-out data set D_o produced by T is unloaded from M to make room for the next task's input data.

The role of task formation is to partition the program's operations into such tasks in a way that minimizes the program execution time. Since computing is much faster than transferring data, one of the goals of task formation is to obtain a high computation-per-communication ratio for the tasks. The memory M may be a local or scratchpad memory, which holds a fixed number of bytes. This imposes a capacity constraint: the working data set of a task should not overflow M's capacity. Finally, the considered processing element P could be composite, in the sense that it may be itself formed of several processing elements. Task formation also ensures that enough parallelism is provided to such processing elements.

R-Stream's task formation algorithm improves on prior algorithms for tiling by Ancourt et al. [4], Xue [42], and Ahmed et al. [2]. The algorithm is enabled by using Ehrhart polynomial techniques developed by Clauss et al. [12], Verdoolage et al. [40], and Meister et al. [28]. The Ehrhart polynomials are used to quickly count the volume (number of integer points) in Z-Domains that model the data footprint implied by prospective iteration tilings. The R-Stream task formation algorithm directly tiles imperfect loop nests independently. The prior work requires perfect loop nests or expanded imperfect loop nests into a perfect form that forced all sections of code, even vastly unrelated ones into the same tiling structure.

The R-Stream task formation algorithm uses *evaluators* and *manipulators*, which can be associated with task groups, loops or the whole function. Evaluators are a function of the elements of the entity they are associated with. They can be turned into a constraint (implicitly: evaluator must be nonnegative) or an objective function. Manipulators enforce constraints on the entity they are associated with. For instance, the tile size of a loop can be made to be a multiple of a certain size, or a power of two, and a set of loops can be set to have the same tile size. Evaluators and manipulators can be combined (affine combination, sequence, conditional sequence) to produce a custom tiling problem.

The task formation algorithm addresses whether the task can be executed in parallel or sequentially; it uses heuristics that walk the set of operations of the GDG and groups the operations based on fusion decisions made by the scheduler, data locality considerations, and the possibility of executing the operations on the same processor.

The task formation algorithm also can detect a class of reductions and mark such loops. It then uses associativity of the scanned operations to relax polyhedral dependence constraints when computing the loop's tiling constraints.

Memory Promotion

R-Stream performs memory promotion for architectures with fast but limited scratch-pad memories on distributed memory architectures. When data are migrated from one memory to another, the compiler also performs a reorganization of the data layout to improve storage utilization, or locality of reference, or to enable other optimizations. Such data layout reorganization often comes "for free," especially if it can be overlapped with computation via hardware support, such as DMA. This technique is a generalization of Schreiber et al. [35].

Communication Generation and DMA Optimizations

When the data set is promoted from a source memory to a target memory, R-Stream generates data transfer from the source array to the target array and back. Those transfers are represented as a element-wise copy loop nest with additional information that identifies which innermost loops transfer the data required for one task. When there is explicit bulk communication hardware between the source and target memories, R-Stream concatenates element-wise transfer operations into strided transfer (e.g., DMA) commands.

Target-Specific Optimizations: GPU

While R-Stream can target many different architectures, the GPU target is an illustrative case. GPUs are many-core architectures that have multiple levels of parallelism with outer coarse-grained MIMD parallelism and inner finer-grained SIMT (Single Instruction Multiple Threads) parallelism. Furthermore, they have complex memory hierarchy with memories of varied latencies and varied characteristics. To achieve high performance on such architectures, it is very important to exploit all levels of parallelism and utilize appropriate memories in an efficient manner. There are three important aspects to be addressed by an automatically parallelizing high-level compiler for GPUs, namely,

- To identify and utilize outer coarse-grained and inner fine-grained parallelism
- To make GPU DRAM ("global memory") accesses to be contiguous and aligned in the parallel loop
- To make proper utilization of the on-chip memories, namely "shared memory" and "registers"

R-Stream exploits the affine scheduling algorithm mentioned earlier, to have, whenever possible, coarse-grained parallelism at outer level and fine-grained parallelism at inner level with contiguously aligned memory accesses. The affine scheduler tries to find a right mix of parallelism, data locality, and data contiguity. As a result, not all global memory array accesses can be made contiguous by the schedule. In such cases, and also in cases where global memory accesses are used multiple times, R-Stream generates data transfers from global DRAM to shared memory (which resides on chip and is shared by all threads in a multiprocessor) as a element-wise copy loop nest such that the global memory accesses are contiguous in the transfer. The global memory accesses are then appropriately replaced by the shared memory accesses. As a result, R-Stream achieves data contiguity in global memory and also improves data reuse across threads.

```
#pragma rstream map
void gaussseidel2D_9points(real_t (*A)[N], int pT, int pN) {
  int i, j, t;
  for (t=0; t<pT; t++) {
    for (i=1; i<pN-1; i++) {
      for (j=1; j<pN-1; j++) {
        A[i][j] = C0*A[i][j] +
          C1*(A[i-1][j-1] + A[i-1][j]   + A[i-1][j+1] +
              A[i  ][j-1] +               + A[i  ][j+1] +
              A[i+1][j-1] + A[i+1][j]   + A[i+1][j+1]);
      }
    }
  }
}
```

R-Stream Compiler. Fig. 2 R-Stream's input: Gauss-Seidel nine-point stencil

```
#pragma unroll
 for (i1 = (__maxs_32(__maxs_32(-480 * j + -64 * k + -16 * (int)blockIdx.x + -
       (int)threadIdx.y + 7 >> 3, - (int)threadIdx.y + 7 >> 3), __maxs_32(-64 *
       i + -1440 * j + -32 * k + -48 * (int)blockIdx.x + - (int)threadIdx.y + 31 +
       7 >> 3, 480 * j + 64 * k + 16 * (int)blockIdx.x + - (int)threadIdx.y +
       -2076 + 7 >> 3))); i1 <= _t3; i1++) {
   int _t6; int j1;
   _t6 = (__mins_32(__mins_32(480 * j + 64 * k + -8 * i1 + 16 * (int)blockIdx.x +
       - (int)threadIdx.x + - (int)threadIdx.y + 66 >> 4, -64 * i + -960 * j + 32
       * k + -32 * (int)blockIdx.x + - (int)threadIdx.x + 2078 >> 4), __mins_32(-
       (int)threadIdx.x + 2047 >> 4, __mins_32(480 * j + 64 * k + 8 * i1 + 16 *
       (int)blockIdx.x + - (int)threadIdx.x + (int)threadIdx.y + 2 >> 4, 480 * j +
       64 * k + 16 * (int)blockIdx.x + - (int)threadIdx.x + 33 >> 4))));
#pragma unroll
   for (j1 = (__maxs_32(__maxs_32(480 * j + 64 * k + -8 * i1 + 16 * (int)blockIdx.x
       + - (int)threadIdx.x + - (int)threadIdx.y + -31 + 15 >> 4, __maxs_32(-64 *
       i + -960 * j + 32 * k + -32 * (int)blockIdx.x + - (int)threadIdx.x + -30 +
       15 >> 4, 64 * i + 1920 * j + 96 * k + 64 * (int)blockIdx.x + -
       (int)threadIdx.x + -2107 + 15 >> 4)), __maxs_32(- (int)threadIdx.x + 15 >>
       4, __maxs_32(480 * j + 64 * k + 8 * i1 + 16 * (int)blockIdx.x + -
       (int)threadIdx.x + (int)threadIdx.y + -63 + 15 >> 4, 480 * j + 64 * k + 16
       * (int)blockIdx.x + - (int)threadIdx.x + -46 + 15 >> 4)))); j1 <= _t6; j1++)
   {
     A_l_1[8 * i1 + (int)threadIdx.y][46 + (-480 * j + -64 * k) + (16 * j1 + (-16 *
         (int)blockIdx.x + (int)threadIdx.x))] = A_l[-31 + (64 * i + 1440 * j) + (32
         * k + 8 * i1 + (48 * (int)blockIdx.x + (int)threadIdx.y))][16 * j1 +
         (int)threadIdx.x];
   }
 }
 syncthreads();
```

R-Stream Compiler. Fig. 3 Excerpt of R-Stream's CUDA output: Gauss-Seidel nine-point stencil

Example

Figure 2 shows input code to R-Stream. The input code is ANSI C, for a simple nine point Gauss Seidel stencil operated on a 2D array. The input style that can be raised is succinct and the user does not give directives describing the mapping, only the indication that the compiler should map the function. The compiler determines the mapping structure automatically. The total output code for this important kernel must be hundreds of lines long to achieve performance in CUDA and on GPUs; a small excerpt of the output from R-Stream in CUDA from this example is in Fig. 3. One can see that the compiler has formed parallelism that is implicit in the CUDA thread and block structure. The chosen schedule balances parallelism, locality, and in particular contiguity, to enable coalescing of loads. Also illustrated is the creation of local copies of the array, the generation of explicit copies into the CUDA scratchpad "shared memories."

Related Entries

▶Parallelization, Automatic

Bibliographic Notes and Further Reading

The final report on R-Stream research for DARPA is Lethin et al. [22]. More information on R-Stream is available from various subsequent workshop papers by Leung et al. [23], Meister et al. [27], and Bastoul et al. [7]. Several US and International patent applications by this encyclopedia entry's authors are pending and will publish with even more detail on the optimizations in R-Stream.

Feautrier is credited with defining the polyhedral model in the late 1980s and early 1990s [17, 19, 20]. Darte et al. provided a detailed comparison of polyhedral techniques to classical techniques, in terms of the benefits of the exact dependence relations, in 2000 [15]. Much theoretical work accumulated on the polyhedral model in the decades after its invention, but it took the work of Quillere, Rajopadhye, and Wilde to unlock the technique for application by showing effective code generation algorithms [31]; these were later improved by Bastoul [6] and Vasilache [39] (the latter thesis also providing a good bibliography on the polyhedral model).

Bibliography

1. nVidia CUDA Compute Unified Device Architecture Programming Guide (Version 2.0), June 2008
2. Ahmed N, Mateev N, Pingali K (2000) Tiling imperfectly-nested loop nests. In: Supercomputing '00: proceedings of the 2000 ACM/IEEE conference on supercomputing (CDROM), IEEE Computer Society, Washington, DC, pp 60–90
3. Allen JR, Kennedy K, Porterfield C, Warren J (1983) Conversion of control dependence to data dependence. In: Proceedings of the 10th ACM SIGACT-SIGPLAN symposium on principles of programming languages, New York, pp 177–189
4. Ancourt C, Irigoin F (1991) Scanning polyhedra with DO loops. In: Proceedings of the 3rd ACM SIGPLAN symposium on principles and practice of parallel programming, Williamsburg, VA, pp 39–50, Apr 1991
5. Barthou D, Cohen A, Collard JF (1998) Maximal static expansion. In: Proceedings of the 25th ACM SIGPLAN-SIGACT symposium on principles of programming languages, New York, pp 98–106
6. Bastoul C (2003) Efficient code generation for automatic parallelization and optimization. In: Proceedings of the international symposium on parallel and distributed computing, Ljubjana, pp 23–30, Oct 2003
7. Bastoul C, Vasilache N, Leung A, Meister B, Wohlford D, Lethin R (2009) Extended static control programs as a programming model for accelerators: a case study: targetting Clearspeed CSX700 with the R-Stream compiler. In: First workshop on Programming Models for Emerging Architectures (PMEA)
8. Bondhugula U, Hartono A, Ramanujan J, Sadayappan P (2008) A practical automatic polyhedral parallelizer and locality optimizer. In: ACM SIGPLAN Programming Languages Design and Implementation (PLDI '08), Tucson, Arizona, June 2008
9. Buck I (2003) Brook v0.2 specification. Technical report, Stanford University, Oct 2003
10. Cifuentes C (1993) A structuring algorithm for decompilation. In: Proceedings of the XIX Conferencia Latinoamericana de Informatica, Buenos Aires, Argentina, pp 267–276
11. Cifuentes C (1994) Structuring decompiled graphs. Technical Report FIT-TR- 1994–05, Department of Computer Science, University of Tasmania, Australia, 19. Also in Proceedings of the 6th international conference on compiler construction, 1996, pp 91–105
12. Clauss P, Loechner V (1996) Parametric analysis of polyhedral iteration spaces. In: IEEE international conference on application specific array processors, ASAP'96. IEEE Computer Society, Los Alamitos, Calif, Aug 1996
13. Click C, Paleczny M (1995) A simple graph-based intermediate representation. ACM SIGPLAN Notices, San Francisco, CA
14. Cytron R, Ferrante J, Rosen BK, Zadeck FK (1991) Efficiently computing static single assignment form and the control dependence graph. ACM Trans Program Lang Syst 13(4):451–490
15. Darte A, Schreiber R, Villard G (2005) Lattice-based memory allocation. IEEE Trans Comput 54(10):1242–1257
16. Feautrier P (1988) Array expansion. In: Proceedings of the 2nd international conference on supercomputing, St. Malo, France

17. Feautrier P (1988) Parametric integer programming. RAIRO-Recherche Opérationnelle, 22(3):243–268
18. Feautrier P (1991) Dataflow analysis of array and scalar references. Int J Parallel Prog 20(1):23–52
19. Feautrier P (1992) Some efficient solutions to the affine scheduling problem. Part I. One-dimensional time. Int J Parallel Prog 21(5):313–348
20. Feautrier P (1992) Some efficient solutions to the affine scheduling problem. Part II. Multidimensional time. Int J Parallel Prog 21(6):389–420
21. StreamIt Group (2003) Streamit language specification, version 2.0. Technical report, Massachusetts Institue of Technology, Oct 2003
22. Lethin R, Leung A, Meister B, Szilagyi P, Vasilache N, Wohlford D (2008) Final report on the R-Stream 3.0 compiler DARPA/AFRL Contract # F03602-03-C-0033, DTIC AFRL-RI-RS-TR-2008-160. Technical report, Reservoir Labs, Inc., May 2008
23. Leung A, Meister B, Vasilache N, Baskaran M, Wohlford D, Bastoul C, Lethin R (2010) A mapping path for multi-GPGPU accelerated computers from a portable high level programming abstraction. In: Third Workshop on General-Purpose Computation on Graphics Processing Units, GPGPU-3, Mar 2010
24. Lim AW, Lam MS (1997) Maximizing parallelism and minimizing synchronization with affine transforms. In: Proceedings of the 24th annual ACM SIGPLAN-SIGACT symposium on principles of programming languages, Paris, France, pp 201–214
25. Loechner V (1999) Polylib: a library for manipulating parametrized polyhedra. Technical report, University of Louis Pasteur, Strasbourg, France, Mar 1999
26. Mai K, Paaske T, Jayasena N, Ho R, Dally W, Horowitz M (2000) Smart memories: a modular reconfigurable architecture. In: Proceedings of the international symposium on Comuter architecture, pp 161–171, June 2000
27. Meister B, Leung A, Vasilache N, Wohlford D, Bastoul C, Lethin R (2009) Productivity via automatic code generation for PGAS platforms with the R-Stream compiler. In: Workshop on asynchrony in the PGAS programming model, June 2009
28. Meister B, Verdoolaege S (2008) Polynomial approximations in the polytope model: bringing the power of quasi-polynomials to the masses. In: ODES-6: 6th workshop on optimizations for DSP and embedded systems, Apr 2008
29. Offner C, Knobe K (2003) Weak dynamic single assignment form. Technical Report HPL-2003-169, HP Labs
30. Pop S, Cohen A, Silber G (2005) Induction variable analysis with delayed abstractions. In: Proceedings of the 2005 international conference on high performance embedded architectures and compilers, Barcelona, Spain
31. Quilleré F, Rajopadhye S, Wilde D (2000) Generation of efficient nested loops from polyhedra. Int J Parallel Prog 28(5):469–498
32. Rettberg RD, Crowther WR, Carvey PP, Tomlinson RS (1990) The Monarch parallel processor hardware design. Computer 23:18–30
33. Richards MA (2005) Fundamentals of radar signal processing. McGraw-Hill, New York
34. Sankaralingam K, Nagarajan R, Gratz P, Desikan R, Gulati D, Hanson H, Kim C, Liu H, Ranganathan N, Sethumadhavan S, Sharif S, Shivakumar P, Yoder W, McDonald R, Keckler SW, Burger DC (2006) The distributed microarchitecture of the TRIPS prototype processor. In: 39th international symposium on microarchitecture (MICRO), Los Alamitos, Calif, Dec 2006
35. Schreiber R, Cronquist DC (2004) Near-optimal allocation of local memory arrays. Technical Report HPL-2004-24, Hewlett-Packard Laboratories, Feb 2004
36. Taylor MB, Kim J, Miller J, Wentzlaff D, Ghodrat F, Greenwald B, Hoffmann H, Johnson P, Lee JW, Lee W, Ma A, Saraf A, Seneski M, Shnidman N, Strumpen V, Frank M, Amarasinghe S, Agarwal A (2002) The raw microprocessor: a computational fabric for software circuits and general purpose programs. Micro, Mar 2002
37. Vasilache N, Bastoul C, Cohen A, Girbal S (2006) Violated dependence analysis. In: Proceedings of the 20th international conference on supercomputing (ICS'06), Cairns, Queensland, Australia. ACM, New York, NY, USA, pp 335–344
38. Vasilache N, Cohen A, Pouchet LN (2007) Automatic correction of loop transformations. In: 16th international conference on parallel architecture and compilation techniques (PACT'07), IEEE Computer Society Press, Brasov, Romania, pp 292–304, Sept 2007
39. Vasilache NT (2007) Scalable program optimization techniques in the polyhedral model. PhD thesis, Université Paris Sud XI, Orsay, Sept 2007
40. Verdoolaege S, Seghir R, Beyls K, Loechner V, Bruynooghe M (2004) Analytical computation of Ehrhart polynomials: enabling more compiler analyses and optimizations. In: Proceedings of the 2004 international conference on compilers, architecture, and synthesis for embedded systems, ACM Press, New York, pp 248–258
41. Weise D, Crew R, Ernst M, Steensgaard B (1994) Value dependence graph: representation without taxation. In: ACM symposium on principles of programming languages, New York, pp 297–310
42. Xue J (1997) On tiling as a loop transformation. Parallel Process Lett 7(4):409–424

Run Time Parallelization

Joel H. Saltz[1], Raja Das[2]
[1]Emory University, Atlanta, GA, USA
[2]IBM Corporation, Armonk, NY, USA

Synonyms
Parallelization

Irregular array accesses arise in many scientific applications including sparse matrix solvers, unstructured mesh partial differential equation (PDE) solvers, and particle methods. Traditional compilation techniques require that indices to data arrays be symbolically analyzable at compile time. A common characteristic of irregular applications is the use of indirect indexing to represent relationships among array elements. This means that data arrays are indexed through values of other arrays, called *indirection arrays*. Figure 1 depicts a simple example of a loop with indirection arrays. The use of indirection arrays prevents compilers from identifying array data access patterns. Inability to characterize array access patterns symbolically can prevent compilers from generating efficient code for irregular applications.

The inspector/executor strategy involves using compilers to generate code to examine and analyze data references *during program execution*. The results of this execution-time analysis may be used (1) to determine which off-processor data needs to be fetched and where the data will be stored once it is received and (2) to reorder and coordinate execution of loop iterations in problems with irregular loop carried dependencies, as seen in the example in Fig. 2. The initial examination and analysis phase is called the *inspector*, while the phase that uses results of analysis to optimize program execution is called the *executor*.

Irregular applications can be divided into two subclasses: static and adaptive. Static irregular applications are those in which each object in the system interacts with a predetermined fixed set of objects. The indirection arrays, which capture the object interactions, do not change during the course of the computation (e.g., unstructured mesh PDE solver). In adaptive irregular applications, each object interacts with an evolving list of objects (e.g., molecular dynamics codes). This causes

```
for i = 1 to n do
  x(ia(i)) + = y(ib(i))
end do
```

Run Time Parallelization. Fig. 1 Example of a loop involving indirection arrays

```
for i = 1 to n do
   y(i) + = y(ia(i)) + y(ib(i)) + y(ic(i))
end do
```

Run Time Parallelization. Fig. 2 Example of loop-carried dependencies determined by a subscript array

the indirection array, which is the object interaction list, to slowly change over the life of the computation. Figure 3 shows an example of an adaptive code. In this figure, ia, ib, and ic are the indirection arrays. Arrays x and y are the data arrays containing properties associated with the objects of the system.

The inspector/executor strategy can be used to parallelize static irregular applications targeted for distributed parallel machines and can achieve high performance. Additional optimizations are required to achieve high performance when adaptive irregular applications are parallelized using inspector/executor approach. The example adaptive code in Fig. 3 shows that the indirection array ic does not change its value for every iteration of the outer loop. It typically has to be regenerated every few iterations of the outer loop, providing the opportunity for optimization.

Inspector/executor strategies have also been adopted to optimize I/O performance when applications need to carry out large numbers of small non-contiguous I/O requests. The inspector/executor strategy was initially articulated in the late 1980s and early 1990s, as described in Mirchandaney [20], Saltz [25], Koelbel [13], Krothapalli [14], and Walker [32]. This article addresses use of inspector/executor methods to optimize retrieval and management of off-processor data and in parallelization of loops with loop-carried dependencies created by indirection arrays. Use of inspector/executor methods and related compiler frameworks to optimize I/O has also been described.

Inspector/Executor Methods and Distributed Memory

The inspector/executor strategy works as follows: During program execution, the inspector examines data references made by a processor and determines (1) which off-processor data elements need to be obtained and (2) where the data will be stored once it is received. The executor uses the information from the inspector to gather off-processor data, carry out the actual computations, and then scatter results back to their home processors after the computational phase is completed. A central strategy of inspector/executor optimization is to identify and exploit situations that permit reuse of information obtained by inspectors. As discussed below, it is often possible to relocate preprocessing outside a set of loops or to carry out interprocedural analysis and

```
for t = 1, step                         //outer step loop
   for i = 1, n                         //inner loop
      x(ia(i)) = x(ia(i)) + y(ib(i))
   endfor                               //end inner loop
   if (required) then
      regenerate ic(:)
   endif
   for i = 1, n                         //inner loop
      x(ic(i)) = x(ic(i)) + y(ic(i))
   endfor                               //end inner loop
endfor                                  //end outer step loop
```

Run Time Parallelization. Fig. 3 Example loop from adaptive irregular applications

`for i = 1, n do`
`   x(ia(ib(i))) = ....`
`end do`
	`for i = 1, n do`
	`   if (ic(i)) then`
	`      x(ia(i)) = ...`
	`   end if`
	`end do`
		`for I =1, n do`
		`   do j = ia(i), ia(i + 1)`
		`      x(ia(j)) = ...`
		`   end do`
		`end do`

Run Time Parallelization. Fig. 4 Examples of loops with complex access functions

transformation so that results from an inspector can be reused many times.

A variety of program analysis methods and transformations have been developed to generate programs that can make use of inspector/executor strategies. In loops with simple irregular access patterns such as those in Fig. 1, a single inspector/executor pair can be generated by the straightforward method described in [31]. Many application codes contain access patterns with more complex access functions such as those depicted in Fig. 4. Subscripted subscripts and subscripted guards can make indexing of one distributed array dependent on values in another. To handle this kind of situation, an inspector must itself be split into an inspector-executor pair as described in [10]. A dataflow framework was developed to help place executor communication calls, determine when it is safe to combine communications statements, move them into less frequently executed code regions, or avoid them altogether in favor of reusing data that is already buffered locally.

Communication Schedules

A communication schedule is used to fetch off-processor elements into a local buffer before the computation phase and to scatter computed data back to home processors. Communication schedules determine the volume of communication and number of communication startups. A variety of approaches to schedule generation have been taken. In the CHAOS system [12], a hash table data structure is used to support a two-phase schedule generation process. The index analysis phase examines data access patterns to determine which references are off-processor, remove duplicate off-processor references, assign local buffers for off-processor references, and translate global indices to local indices. The results of index analyses are managed in a hash table data structure. The schedule generation phase then produces communication schedules based on hash table information. The CHAOS hash table contains a bit array used to identify which indirection arrays entered each element into the hash table. This approach facilitates efficient management and coordination of analysis information derived from programs with multiple indirection arrays and provides support for building incremental and merged communication schedules.

In some cases it can be advantageous to employ communication schedules that carry out bounding box or entire-array bulk read or write operations rather than using schedules that only communicate accessed array elements. These approaches differ in costs associated with both the inspector and the executor phases. The bounding box approach requires only that the inspector compute a bounding box containing all the necessary elements and no inspector is required to retrieve the entire array. A compiler and runtime system using performance models to choose between element-wise gather, bounding box bulk read, and entire-array retrieval were implemented by the Titanium group discussed in [28].

A variety of techniques have been incorporated into CHAOS and into efficiently supported applications such as particle codes, which manifest access patterns that change from iteration to iteration. The crucial observation is that in many such codes, the communication-intensive loops are actually carrying out a generalized reduction in which it is not necessary to control the order of elements stored. Hwang [12] demonstrates that order-independence can be used to dramatically reduce schedule generation overhead.

Runtime Parallelization

A variety of runtime parallelization techniques have been developed for indirectly indexed loops with data dependencies among iterations, as shown in Figs. 2 and 5. Most of this work has targeted shared memory architectures due to the fine grained concurrency that typically results when such codes are parallelized. One of the earliest techniques for runtime parallelization of loops involves the use of a key field associated with each indirectly indexed array element to order accesses. The algorithm repeatedly sweeps over all loop iterations in alternating analysis and computation phases. An iteration is allowed to proceed only if all accesses to array elements y(ia(i)) and y(ib(i)) by iterations j < i have completed. These sweeps have the effect of partitioning the computation into wavefronts. Key fields are used to ensure that dependences are taken into account. This is discussed further in [19]. This strategy is extended by allowing concurrent reads to the same entry, as Midkiff explains, and through development of a systematic dependence analysis and program transformation framework for singly nested loops. Intra-procedural and interprocedural analysis techniques are presented in an article by Lin [15] to analyze the common and

```
for i = 1 to n do
        y(ia(i)) = ...
        ...
        ... = y(ib(i))
end do
```

Run Time Parallelization. Fig. 5 Subscript array-determined loop carried dependences with output dependence

important cases of irregular single-indexed accesses and simple indirect array accesses.

An inspector/executor approach, applicable to loops without output dependencies, can be carried out through generation of an inspector that identifies *wavefronts* of concurrently executable loop iterations followed by an executor that transforms the original loop L into two loops, L_1 and L_2. The new outer loop L_1 is sequential and the new inner loop L_2 involves all loop indexes assigned to each wavefront, as described in Saltz [25]. This is analogous to *loop skewing*, as described by Wolfe [33], except that the identification of parallelism is carried out during program execution.

A doacross loop construct can also be used as an executor. The wavefronts generated by the inspector are used sort indices assigned to each processor into ascending wavefront order. Full/empty bit or busy-waiting synchronization enforces true dependencies; computation does not proceed until the array element required for the computation is available. A doacross executor construct was introduced in [25], and this concept has been greatly refined through a variety of schemes that support operation level synchronization in the work of Chen and Singh [6, 26]. A very fine-grained data flow inspector/executor scheme that also employed operation level synchronization was proposed and tested on the CM-5, as described in Chong's work [7].

Many situations occur in which runtime information might demonstrate that: (1) all loop iterations are independent and could execute in parallel or (2) that cross-iteration dependences are reductions. A kind of inspector/executor technique has been developed that involves (1) carrying out compiler transformations that assume parallelism or reduction parallelism, (2) running the generated speculative loop, and then (3) invoking tests to assess correctness of the speculative parallel execution, as discussed in Rauchwerger [23]. The compilation and runtime support framework generate tests and recovery code that need to be invoked if the tests demonstrate that the speculation was unsuccessful.

Structural Abstraction

Over the course of a decade Baden explored three successive runtime systems to treat data-dependent communication patterns and workload distributions: LPAR, LPAR-X, and KeLP [1, 2]. The libraries were used in various applications including: structured adaptive mesh refinement for first principles simulation of real materials, genetic algorithms, cluster identification for spin models in statistical mechanics, turbulent flow, and cell microphysiology. This effort contributed the notion of structural abstraction which supports user-level geometric meta-data that admit data-dependent decompositions used in irregular applications. These also enable communication to be expressed in a high level geometric form which may be manipulated at runtime to optimize communication. KeLP was later extended to handle more general notions of sparse sets of data that logically communicate within rectangular subspaces of Zd, even if the data does not exist as rectangular sets of data, e.g., particles, as noted by Baden. A multi-tier variant of KeLP, KeLP2, subsequently appeared to treat hierarchical parallelism in the then-emerging SMP cluster technologies, with support to mask communication delays [1].

Loop Transformation

The compiler parallelizes the loop shown in Fig. 6 by generating the corresponding inspector/executor pair. Assume that all arrays are aligned and distributed in blocks among the processors, and the iterations of the *i*-loop are likewise block-partitioned. The resulting computation mapping is equivalent to that produced by the "owner computes" rule, a heuristic that maps the computation of an assignment statement to the processor that owns the left-hand-side reference. Data array *y* is indexed using array ia, causing a single level of indirection.

The compiler generates a single executable: a copy of this executable runs on each processor. The program running on each processor determines what processor

```
for i = 1 to n do
   x(i) = y(ia(i)) + z(i)
end do
```

Run Time Parallelization. Fig. 6 Simple irregular loop

it is running on, and uses that information to figure out where its data and iteration fit in the global computation. Let my_elements represent the number of iterations assigned to a processor and also the number of elements of data arrays x, y, z and indirection array ia assigned to the processor. The code generated by the compiler and executed by each processor is shown in Fig. 7.

Compiler Implementations

Inspector/executor schemes have been implemented in a variety of compilers. Initial inspector/executor implementations in the early 1990s were carried out in the ARF [24], [31] and Kali [13] compilers as discussed by Saltz and Koelbel, respectively. Inspector/executor schemes were subsequently implemented in Fortran D; Fortran 90D [21, 30]; the Polaris compiler discussed by Lin [15]; the SUPERB [5] compiler; the Vienna Fortran compiler [29]; the Titanium Java compiler [28]; compilation systems designed to support efficient implementation of OpenMP on platforms that support MPI, discussed by Basumallik [3]; to platforms that support Global Arrays, discussed by Liu [16]; and in HPF compilers described in examples by Benkner and Merlin [4, 18]. Many of these compiler frameworks support user-specified data and iteration partitioning methods. A framework that supports compiler based analysis about runtime data and iteration reordering transformations is described in [27].

Speculative parallelization techniques have been proposed to effectively parallelize loops with complex data access patterns. Various software [8, 11, 23] and hardware [9, 22] techniques have been proposed. The hardware techniques involve increased hardware complexity but can catch cross-iteration data dependencies immediately with minimal overheads. On the other hand, full software solutions do not require new hardware but in certain cases can lead to significant performance penalties. The first known work on speculative parallelization techniques to parallelize loops

```
//inspector code
for i = 1, my_elements
   index_y(i) = ia(i)
endfor
sched_ia = generate_schedule(index_y)//call the inspector schedule
   generation codes
call gather(y(begin_buffer), y, sched_ia)
//executor code
for i = 1, my_elements
   x(i) = y(index_y(i)) + z(i)
endfor
```

Run Time Parallelization. Fig. 7 Transformed irregular loop

with complex data access pattern was proposed by Rauchwerger et al. [23]. Instead of breaking loops into inspector/executor computations, they do a speculative execution of the loop as a doall with a runtime check (the LRPD test) to assess whether there are any cross-iteration dependencies. The scheme supports back-tracking and serial re-execution of the loop if the runtime check fails. The biggest advantage of this technique is that the access pattern of the data arrays does not have to be analyzed separately and the runtime tests are performed during the actual computation of the loop. They used this technique on loops, which cannot be parallelized statically, from the PERFECT Benchmark and showed that in many cases, it leads to code that performs better than the inspector/executor strategy. The scheme can be used for automatic parallelization of complex loops, but its main limitation is that dependency violations are detected after the computation of the loop, and a severe penalty has to be paid in terms of rolling back the computation and executing it serially. Gupta et al. [11] proposed a number of new runtime tests that improve the techniques presented in [23]; thus significantly reducing the penalties associated with misspeculation. Dang et al. [9] proposed a new technique that transforms a partially parallel loop into a sequence of fully parallel loops. It is a recursive technique where in each step all remaining iterations of the irregular loop are executed in parallel. After the execution, the LRPD test is done to detect dependencies. The iterations that were correct are committed, and the recursive process starts with the remaining iterations. The limitation of the technique is that the loop iterations have to be statically block-scheduled in increasing order of iterations between the processors, possibly causing work imbalance.

Bibliography

1. Baden SB, Fink SJ (2000) A programming methodology for dual-tier multicomputers. IEEE Trans Softw Eng 26(3):212–226
2. Baden SB, Kohn SR (1995) Portable parallel programming of numerical problems under the LPAR system. J Parallel Distrib Comput 27(1):38–55
3. Basumallik A, Eigenmann R (2006) Optimizing irregular shared-memory applications for distributed-memory systems. In: Proceedings of the eleventh ACM SIGPLAN symposium on principles and practice of parallel programming (PPoPP'06), New York, 29–31 Mar 2006. ACM, New York, pp 119–128
4. Benkner S, Mehrotra P, Van Rosendale J, Zima H (1998) High-level management of communication schedules in HPF-like languages. In: Proceedings of the 12th international conference on supercomputing (ICS'98), Melbourne. ACM, New York, pp 109–116
5. Brezany P, Gerndt M, Sipkova V, Zima HP (1992) SUPERB support for irregular scientific computations. In: Proceedings of the scalable high performance computing conference (SHPCC-92), Williamsburg, 26–29 Apr 1992, pp 314–321
6. Chen DK, Torrellas J, Yew PC (1994) An efficient algorithm for the run-time parallelization of DOACROSS loops. In: Proceedings of the 1994 ACM/IEEE conference on supercomputing, Washington, DC, pp 518–527
7. Chong FT, Sharma SD, Brewer EA, Saltz JH (1995) Multiprocessor runtime support for fine-grained, irregular DAGs. Parallel Process Lett 5:671–683
8. Cintra M, Martinez J, Torrellas J (2000) Architectural support for scalable speculative parallelization in shared-memory multiprocessors. In: Proceedings of 27th annual international symposium on computer architecture, Vancouver, pp 13–24
9. Dang F, Yu H, Rauchwerger L (2002) The R-LRPD test: speculative parallelization of partially parallel loops. In: Proceedings of the international parallel and distributed processing symposium (IPDPS02), Ft. Lauderdale

10. Das R, Saltz J, von Hanxleden R (1994) Slicing analysis and indirect accesses to distributed arrays. Lecture notes in computer science, vol 768. Springer, Berlin/Heidelberg
11. Gupta M, Nim R (1998) Techniques for speculative run-time parallelization of loops. In: Proceedings of the 1998 ACM/IEEE conference on supercomputing (SC'98), pp 1–12
12. Hwang YS, Moon B, Sharma SD, Ponnusamy R, Das R, Saltz JH (1995) Runtime and language support for compiling adaptive irregular programs. Softw Pract Exp 25(6):597–621
13. Koelbel C, Mehrotra P, Van Rosendale J (1990) Supporting shared data structures on distributed memory machines. In: Symposium on principles and practice of parallel programming. ACM, New York, pp 177–186
14. Krothapalli VP, Sadayappan P (1990) Dynamic scheduling of DOACROSS loops for multiprocessors. In: International conference on databases, parallel architectures and their applications (PARBASE-90), Miami, pp 66–75
15. Lin Y, Padua DA (2000) Compiler analysis of irregular memory accesses. In: Proceedings of the ACM SIGPLAN 2000 conference on programming language design and implementation. Vancouver, pp 157–163
16. Liu Z, Huang L, Chapman BM, Weng TH (2004) Efficient implementation of OpenMP for clusters with implicit data distribution. WOMPAT, Houston, pp 121–136
17. Lusk EL, Overbeek RA (1987) A minimalist approach to portable, parallel programming. In: Jamieson L, Gannon D, Douglass R (eds) The characteristics of parallel algorithms. MIT Press, Cambridge, MA, pp 351–362
18. Merlin JH, Baden SB, Fink S, Chapman BM (1999) Multiple data parallelism with HPF and KeLP. Future Gener Comput Syst 15(3):393–405
19. Midkiff SP, Padua DA (1987) Compiler algorithms for synchronization. IEEE Trans Comput 36(12):1485–1495
20. Mirchandaney R, Saltz JH, Smith RM, Nicol DM, Crowley K (1988) Principles of runtime support for parallel processors. In: Proceedings of the second international conference on supercomputing (ICS'88), St. Malo, pp 140–152
21. Ponnusamy R, Hwang YS, Das R, Saltz JH, Choudhary A, Fox G (1995) Supporting irregular distributions using data-parallel languages. Parallel Distrib Technol Syst Appl 3(1):12–24
22. Prvulovic M, Garzaran MJ, Rauchwerger L, Torrellas J (2001) Removing architectural bottlenecks to the scalability of speculative parallelization. In: Proceedings, 28th annual international symposium on Computer architecture, pp 204–215
23. Rauchwerger L, Padua D (1995) The LRPD test: speculative run-time parallelization of loops with privatization and reduction parallelization. In: Proceedings of the ACM SIGPLAN 1995 conference on programming language design and implementation (PLDI'95), La Jolla, 18–21 June 1995. ACM, New York, pp 218–232
24. Saltz JH, Berryman H, Wu J (1991) Multiprocessors and run-time compilation. Concurr Pract Exp 3(6):573–592
25. Saltz JH, Mirchandaney R, Crowley K (1991) Run-time parallelization and scheduling of loops. IEEE Trans Comput 40(5):603–612
26. Singh DE, Martín MJ, Rivera FF (2003) Increasing the parallelism of irregular loops with dependences. In: Euro-Par, Klagenfurt, pp 287–296
27. Strout M, Carter L, Ferrante J (2003) Compile-time composition of run-time data and iteration reordering. Program Lang Des Implement 38(5):91–102
28. Su J, Yelick K (2005) Automatic support for irregular computations in a high-level language. In: Proceedings, 19th IEEE International Parallel and distributed processing symposium, Atlanta, pp 53b, 04–08 Apr 2005
29. Ujaldon M, Zapata EL, Chapman BM, Zima HP (1997) Vienna-Fortran/HPF extensions for sparse and irregular problems and their compilation. IEEE Trans Parallel Distrib Syst 8(10):1068–1083
30. von Hanxleden R, Kennedy K, Koelbel C, Das R, Saltz J (1993) Compiler analysis for irregular problems in Fortran D. In: Proceedings of the fifth international workshop on languages and compilers for parallel computing. Springer, London, pp 97–111
31. Wu J, Das R, Saltz J, Berryman H, Hiranandani S (1995) Distributed memory compiler design for sparse problems. IEEE Trans Comput 44(6):737–753
32. Walker D (1989) The implementation of a three-dimensional PIC Code on a hypercube concurrent processor. In: Conference on hypercubes, concurrent computers, and application, Pasadena
33. Wolfe M (1989) More iteration space tiling. In: Proceedings of the 1989 ACM/IEEE conference on supercomputing (Supercomputing'89), pp 655–664

Runtime System

▶Operating System Strategies

S

Scalability

▶ Metrics
▶ Single System Image

Scalable Coherent Interface (SCI)

▶ SCI (Scalable Coherent Interface)

ScaLAPACK

Jack Dongarra, Piotr Luszczek
University of Tennessee, Knoxville, TN, USA

Definition
ScaLAPACK is a library of high-performance linear algebra routines for distributed-memory message-passing MIMD computers and networks of workstations supporting PVM [1] and/or MPI [2, 3]. It is a continuation of the LAPACK [4] project, which designed and produced analogous software for workstations, vector supercomputers, and shared-memory parallel computers.

Discussion
Both LAPACK and ScaLAPACK libraries contain routines for solving systems of linear equations, least squares problems, and eigenvalue problems. The goals of both projects are efficiency (to run as fast as possible), scalability (as the problem size and number of processors grow), reliability (including error bounds), portability (across all important parallel machines), flexibility (so users can construct new routines from well-designed parts), and ease of use (by making the interface to LAPACK and ScaLAPACK look as similar as possible). Many of these goals, particularly portability, are aided by developing and promoting standards, especially for low-level communication and computation routines. These goals have been successfully attained, limiting most machine dependencies to two standard libraries called the BLAS, or Basic Linear Algebra Subprograms [5–8], and BLACS, or Basic Linear Algebra Communication Subprograms [9, 10]. LAPACK will run on any machine where the BLAS are available, and ScaLAPACK will run on any machine where both the BLAS and the BLACS are available.

The library is written in Fortran 77 (with the exception of a few symmetric eigenproblem auxiliary routines written in C to exploit IEEE arithmetic) in a Single Program Multiple Data (SPMD) style using explicit message passing for interprocessor communication. The name ScaLAPACK is an acronym for Scalable Linear Algebra PACKage, or Scalable LAPACK.

ScaLAPACK can solve systems of linear equations, linear least squares problems, eigenvalue problems, and singular value problems. ScaLAPACK can also handle many associated computations such as matrix factorizations or estimating condition numbers.

Like LAPACK, the ScaLAPACK routines are based on block-partitioned algorithms in order to minimize the frequency of data movement between different levels of the memory hierarchy. The fundamental building blocks of the ScaLAPACK library are distributed-memory versions of the Level 1, Level 2, and Level 3 BLAS, called the Parallel BLAS or PBLAS [11, 12], and a set of Basic Linear Algebra Communication Subprograms (BLACS) [9, 10] for communication tasks that arise frequently in parallel linear algebra computations. In the ScaLAPACK routines, the majority of interprocessor communication occurs within the PBLAS. So the source code of the top software layer of ScaLAPACK looks similar to that of LAPACK.

ScaLAPACK contains *driver routines* for solving standard types of problems, *computational routines* to perform a distinct computational task, and *auxiliary routines* to perform a certain subtask or common

David Padua (ed.), *Encyclopedia of Parallel Computing*, DOI 10.1007/978-0-387-09766-4,
© Springer Science+Business Media, LLC 2011

low-level computation. Each driver routine typically calls a sequence of computational routines. Taken as a whole, the computational routines can perform a wider range of tasks than are covered by the driver routines. Many of the auxiliary routines may be of use to numerical analysts or software developers, so the Fortran source for these routines have been documented with the same level of detail used for the ScaLAPACK computational routines and driver routines.

Dense and band matrices are provided for, but not general sparse matrices. Similar functionality is provided for real and complex matrices. However, not all the facilities of LAPACK are covered by ScaLAPACK yet.

ScaLAPACK is designed to give high efficiency on MIMD distributed-memory concurrent supercomputers, such as the older ones like Intel Paragon, IBM SP series, and the Cray T3 series, as well as the newer ones, such IBM Blue Gene series and Cray XT series of supercomputers. In addition, the software is designed so that it can be used with clusters of workstations through a networked environment and with a heterogeneous computing environment via PVM or MPI. Indeed, ScaLAPACK can run on any machine that supports either PVM or MPI.

The ScaLAPACK strategy for combining efficiency with portability is to construct the software so that as much as possible of the computation is performed by calls to the Parallel Basic Linear Algebra Subprograms (PBLAS). The PBLAS [11, 12] perform global computation by relying on the Basic Linear Algebra Subprograms (BLAS) [5–8] for local computation and the Basic Linear Algebra Communication Subprograms (BLACS) [9, 10] for communication.

The efficiency of ScaLAPACK software depends on the use of block-partitioned algorithms and on efficient implementations of the BLAS and the BLACS being provided by computer vendors (and others) for their machines. Thus, the BLAS and the BLACS form a low-level interface between ScaLAPACK software and different machine architectures. Above this level, all of the ScaLAPACK software is portable.

The BLAS, PBLAS, and the BLACS are not, strictly speaking, part of ScaLAPACK. C code for the PBLAS is included in the ScaLAPACK distribution. Since the performance of the package depends upon the BLAS and the BLACS being implemented efficiently, they have not been included with the ScaLAPACK distribution. A machine-specific implementation of the BLAS and the BLACS should be used. If a machine-optimized version of the BLAS is not available, a Fortran 77 reference implementation of the BLAS is available from Netlib [13]. This code constitutes the "model implementation" [14, 15]. The model implementation of the BLAS is not expected to perform as well as a specially tuned implementation on most high-performance computers – on

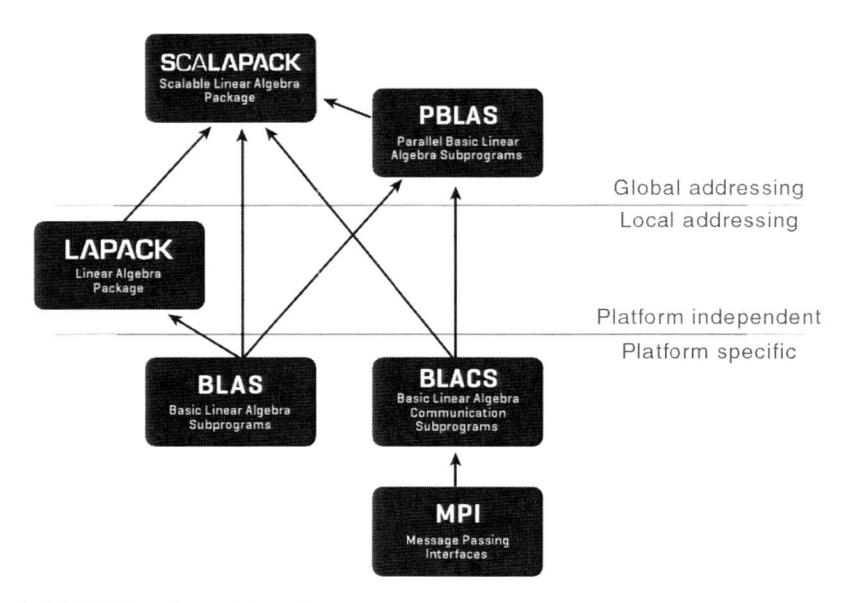

ScaLAPACK. Fig. 1 ScaLAPACK's software hierarchy

some machines it may give much worse performance – but it allows users to run ScaLAPACK codes on machines that do not offer any other implementation of the BLAS.

If a vendor-optimized version of the BLACS is not available for a specific architecture, efficiently ported versions of the BLACS are available on Netlib. Currently, the BLACS have been efficiently ported on machine-specific message-passing libraries such as the IBM (MPL) and Intel (NX) message-passing libraries, as well as more generic interfaces such as PVM and MPI. The BLACS overhead has been shown to be negligible [10]. Refer to the URL for the blacs directory on Netlib for more details: http://www.netlib.org/blacs/index.html

Figure 1 describes the ScaLAPACK software hierarchy. The components below the line, labeled *local addressing*, are called on a single processor, with arguments stored on single processors only. The components above the line, labeled *global addressing*, are synchronous parallel routines, whose arguments include matrices and vectors distributed across multiple processors.

LAPACK and ScaLAPACK are freely available software packages provided on the World Wide Web on Netlib. They can be, and have been, included in commercial packages. The authors ask only that proper credit be given to them which is very much like the modified BSD license.

Related Entries
▶LAPACK
▶Linear Algebra, Numerical

Bibliography
1. Geist A, Beguelin A, Dongarra J, Jiang W, Manchek R, Sunderam V (1994) Parallel Virtual Machine. A Users' Guide and Tutorial for Networked Parallel Computing. MIT Press, Cambridge, MA, 1994
2. MPI Forum, MPI: A message passing interface standard, International Journal of Supercomputer Applications and High Performance Computing, 8 (1994), pp 3–4. Special issue on MPI. Also available electronically, the URL is ftp://www.netlib.org/mpi/mpi-report.ps
3. Snir M, Otto SW, Huss-Lederman S, Walker DW, Dongarra JJ (1996) MPI: The Complete Reference, MIT Press, Cambridge, MA
4. Anderson E, Bai Z, Bischof C, Blackford LS, Demmel JW, Dongarra J, Du Croz J, Greenbaum A, Hammarling S, McKenney A, Sorensen D, LAPACK Users' Guide, SIAM, 1992
5. Hanson R, Krogh F, Lawson CA (1973) A proposal for standard linear algebra subprograms, ACM SIGNUM Newsl, 8
6. Lawson CL, Hanson RJ, Kincaid D, Krogh FT (1979) Basic Linear Algebra Subprograms for Fortran Usage, ACM Trans Math Soft 5:308–323
7. Dongarra JJ, Du Croz J, Hammarling Richard S, Hanson J (March 1988) An Extended Set of FORTRAN Basic Linear Algebra Subroutines, ACM Trans Math Soft 14(1):1–17
8. Dongarra JJ, Du Croz J, Duff IS, Hammarling S (March 1990) A Set of Level 3 Basic Linear Algebra Subprograms, ACM Trans Math Soft 16(1):1–17
9. Dongarra J, van de Geijn R (1991) Two dimensional basic linear algebra communication subprograms, Computer Science Dept. Technical Report CS-91-138, University of Tennessee, Knoxville, TN (Also LAPACK Working Note #37)
10. Dongarra J, Whaley RC (1995) A user's guide to the BLACS v1.1, Computer Science Dept. Technical Report CS-95-281, University of Tennessee, Knoxville, TN (Also LAPACK Working Note #94)
11. Choi J, Dongarra J, Ostrouchov S, Petitet A, Walker D, Whaley RC (May 1995) A proposal for a set of parallel basic linear algebra subprograms, Computer Science Dept. Technical Report CS-95-292, University of Tennessee, Knoxville, TN (Also LAPACK Working Note #100)
12. Petitet A (1996) Algorithmic Redistribution Methods for Block Cyclic Decompositions, PhD thesis, University of Tennessee, Knoxville, TN
13. Dongarra JJ, Grosse E (July 1987) Distribution of Mathematical Software via Electronic Mail, Communications of the ACM 30(5): 403–407
14. Dongarra JJ, du Croz J, Duff IS, Hammarling S (1990) Algorithm 679: A set of Level 3 Basic Linear Algebra Subprograms, ACM Trans Math Soft 16:18–28
15. Dongarra JJ, DU Croz J, Hammarling S, Hanson RJ (1998) Algorithm 656: An extended set of FORTRAN Basic Linear Algebra Subroutines, ACM Trans Math Soft 14:18–32

Scalasca

Felix Wolf
Aachen University, Aachen, Germany

Synonyms
The predecessor of Scalasca, from which Scalasca evolved, is known by the name of KOJAK.

Definition
Scalasca is an open-source software tool that supports the performance optimization of parallel programs by

measuring and analyzing their runtime behavior. The analysis identifies potential performance bottlenecks – in particular those concerning communication and synchronization – and offers guidance in exploring their causes. Scalasca targets mainly scientific and engineering applications based on the programming interfaces MPI and OpenMP, including hybrid applications based on a combination of the two. The tool has been specifically designed for use on large-scale systems including IBM Blue Gene and Cray XT, but is also well suited for small- and medium-scale HPC platforms.

Discussion

Introduction

Driven by growing application requirements and accelerated by current trends in microprocessor design, the number of processor cores on modern supercomputers is expanding from generation to generation. As a consequence, supercomputing applications are required to harness much higher degrees of parallelism in order to satisfy their enormous demand for computing power. However, with today's leadership systems featuring more than a hundred thousand cores, writing efficient codes that exploit all the available parallelism becomes increasingly difficult. Performance optimization is therefore expected to become an even more essential software-process activity, critical for the success of many simulation projects. The situation is exacerbated by the fact that the growing number of cores imposes scalability demands not only on applications but also on the software tools needed for their development.

Making applications run efficiently on larger scales is often thwarted by excessive communication and synchronization overheads. Especially during simulations of irregular and dynamic domains, these overheads are often enlarged by wait states that appear in the wake of load or communication imbalance when processes fail to reach synchronization points simultaneously. Even small delays of single processes may spread wait states across the entire machine, and their accumulated duration can constitute a substantial fraction of the overall resource consumption. In particular, when trying to scale communication-intensive applications to large processor counts, such wait states can result in substantial performance degradation.

To address these challenges, Scalasca has been designed as a diagnostic tool to support application optimization on highly scalable systems. Although also covering single-node performance via hardware-counter measurements, Scalasca mainly targets communication and synchronization issues, whose understanding is critical for scaling applications to performance levels in the petaflops range. A distinctive feature of Scalasca is its ability to identify wait states that occur, for example, as a result of unevenly distributed workloads.

Functionality

To evaluate the behavior of parallel programs, Scalasca takes performance measurements at runtime to be analyzed *postmortem* (i.e., after program termination). The user of Scalasca can choose between two different analysis modes:

- Performance overview on the call-path level via profiling (called runtime summarization in Scalasca terminology)
- In-depth study of application behavior via event tracing

In profiling mode, Scalasca generates aggregate performance metrics for individual function call paths, which are useful for identifying the most resource-intensive parts of the program and assessing process-local performance via hardware-counter analysis. In tracing mode, Scalasca goes one step further and records individual performance-relevant events, allowing the automatic identification of call paths that exhibit wait states. This core feature is the reason why Scalasca is classified as an automatic tool. As an alternative, the resulting traces can be visualized in a traditional time-line browser such as ►VAMPIR to study the detailed interactions among different processes or threads. While providing more behavioral detail, traces also consume significantly more storage space and therefore have to be generated with care.

Figure 1 shows the basic analysis workflow supported by Scalasca. Before any performance data can be collected, the target application must be instrumented, that is, probes must be inserted into the code which carry out the measurements. This can happen at different levels, including source code, object code, or library.

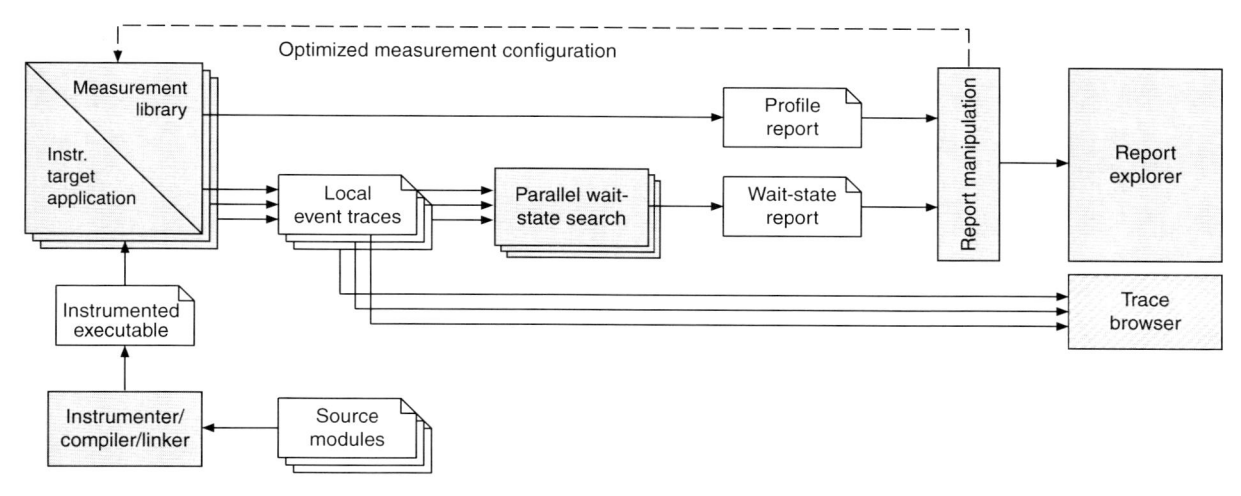

Scalasca. Fig. 1 Schematic overview of the performance data flow in Scalasca. *Gray rectangles* denote programs and *white rectangles* with the upper right corner turned down denote files. *Stacked symbols* denote multiple instances of programs or files, in most cases running or being processed in parallel. *Hatched boxes* represent optional third-party components

Before running the instrumented executable on the parallel machine, the user can choose between generating a profile or an event trace. When tracing is enabled, each process generates a trace file containing records for its process-local events. To prevent traces from becoming too large or inaccurate as a result of measurement intrusion, it is generally recommended to optimize the instrumentation based on a previously generated profile report. After program termination, Scalasca loads the trace files into main memory and analyzes them in parallel using as many cores as have been used for the target application itself. During the analysis, Scalasca searches for wait states, classifies detected instances by category, and quantifies their significance. The result is a wait-state report similar in structure to the profile report but enriched with higher-level communication and synchronization inefficiency metrics. Both profile and wait-state reports contain performance metrics for every combination of function call path and process/thread and can be interactively examined in the provided analysis report explorer (Fig. 2) along the dimensions of performance metric, call tree, and system. In addition, reports can be combined or manipulated to allow comparisons or aggregations, or to focus the analysis on specific extracts of a report. For example, the difference between two reports can be calculated to assess the effectiveness of an optimization or a new report can be generated after eliminating uninteresting phases (e.g., initialization).

Instrumentation

Preparation of a target application executable for measurement and analysis requires it to be *instrumented* to notify the measurement library, which is linked to the executable, of performance-relevant execution events whenever they occur at runtime. On all systems, a mix of manual and automatic instrumentation mechanisms is offered. Instrumentation configuration and processing of source files are achieved by prefixing selected compilation commands and the final link command with the Scalasca instrumenter, without requiring other changes to optimization levels or the build process, as in the following example for the file foo.c:

```
> scalasca -instrument mpicc -c foo.c
```

Scalasca follows a *direct instrumentation* approach. In contrast to interrupt-based sampling, which takes periodic measurements whenever a timer expires, Scalasca takes measurements when the control flow reaches certain points in the code. These points mark performance-relevant events, such as entering/leaving a function or sending/receiving a message. Although instrumentation points have to be chosen with care to minimize intrusion, direct instrumentation offers advantages for the global analysis of communication and synchronization operations. In addition to pure direct instrumentation, future versions of Scalasca will combine direct instrumentation with sampling in

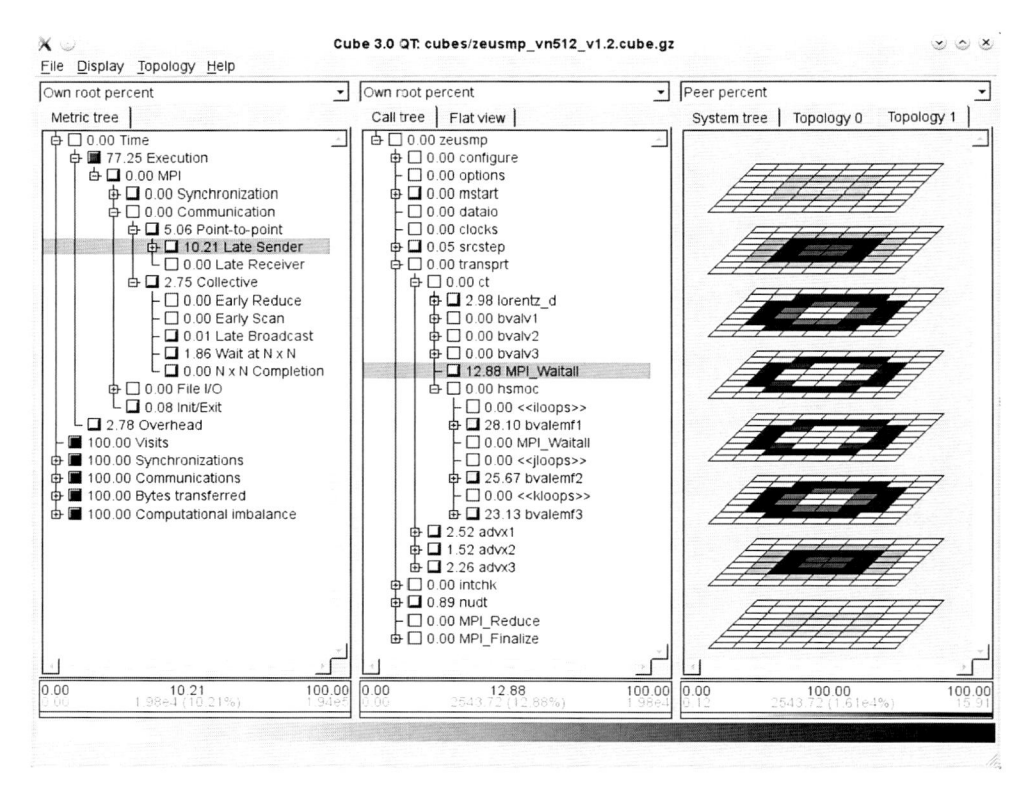

Scalasca. Fig. 2 Interactive performance-report exploration for the Zeus MP/2 code [8] with Scalasca. The *left pane* lists different performance metrics arranged in a specialization hierarchy. The selected metric is a frequently occurring wait state called *Late Sender*, during which a process waits for a message that has not yet been sent (Fig. 3a). The number and the color of the icon to the *left* of the label indicate the percentage of execution time lost due to this wait state, in this case 10.21%. In the *middle pane*, the user can see which call paths are most affected. For example, 12.88% of the 10.21% is caused by the call path `zeusmp() → transprt() → ct() → MPI_Waitall()`. The *right pane* shows the distribution of waiting times for the selected combination of wait state and call path across the virtual process topology. The display indicates that most wait states occur at the outer rim of a spherical region in the center of the three-dimensional Cartesian topology

profiling mode to better control runtime dilation, while still supporting global communication analyses [15].

Measurement

Measurements are collected and analyzed under the control of a workflow manager that determines how the application should be run, and then configures measurement and analysis accordingly. When tracing is requested, it automatically configures and executes the parallel trace analyzer with the same number of processes as used for measurement. The following examples demonstrate how to request measurements from MPI application `bar` to be executed with 65,536 ranks, once in profiling and once in tracing mode (distinguished by the use of the "-t" option).

```
> scalasca -analyze mpiexec \
  -np 65536 bar <arglist>
> scalasca -analyze -t mpiexec \
  -np 65536 bar <arglist>
```

Call-Path Profiling

Scalasca can efficiently calculate many execution performance metrics by accumulating statistics during measurement, avoiding the cost of storing them with events for later analysis. For example, elapsed times and hardware-counter metrics for source regions (e.g., routines or loops) can be immediately determined and the differences accumulated. Whereas trace storage requirements increase in proportion to the number of events (dependent on the measurement duration), summarized statistics for a call-path profile per thread have a fixed storage requirement (dependent on the number of threads and executed call paths).

In addition to call-path visit counts, execution times, and optional hardware counter metrics, Scalasca profiles include various MPI statistics, such as the numbers of synchronization, communication and file I/O operations along with the associated number of bytes transferred. Each metric is broken down into collective versus point-to-point/individual, sends/writes versus receives/reads, and so on. Call-path execution times separate MPI message-passing and OpenMP multithreading costs from purely local computation, and break them down further into initialization/finalization, synchronization, communication, file I/O and thread management overheads (as appropriate). For measurements using OpenMP, additional thread idle time and limited parallelism metrics are derived, assuming a dedicated core for each thread.

Scalasca provides accumulated metric values for every combination of call path and thread. A call path is defined as the list of code regions entered but not yet left on the way to the currently active one, typically starting from the main function, such as in the call chain `main()` → `foo()` → `bar()`. Which regions actually appear on a call path depends on which regions have been instrumented. When execution is complete, all locally executed call paths are combined into a global dynamic call tree for interactive exploration (as shown in the middle of Fig. 2, although the screen shot actually visualizes a wait-state report).

Wait-State Analysis

In message-passing applications, processes often require access to data provided by remote processes, making the progress of a receiving process dependent upon the progress of a sending process. If a rendezvous protocol is used, this relationship also applies in the opposite direction. Collective synchronization is similar in that its completion requires each participating process to have reached a certain point. As a consequence, a significant fraction of the time spent in communication and synchronization routines can often be attributed to wait states that occur when processes fail to reach implicit or explicit synchronization points in a timely manner. Scalasca provides a diagnostic method that allows the localization of wait states by automatically searching event traces for characteristic patterns.

Figure 3 shows several examples of wait states that can occur in message-passing programs. The first one is the *Late Sender* pattern (Fig. 3a), where a receiver is blocked while waiting for a message to arrive. That is, the receive operation is entered by the destination process before the corresponding send operation has been entered by the source process. The waiting time lost as a consequence is the time difference between entering the send and the receive operations. Conversely, the *Late Receiver* pattern (Fig. 3b) describes a sender that is likely to be blocked while waiting for the receiver when a rendezvous protocol is used. This can happen for several reasons. Either the MPI implementation is working in synchronous mode by default, or the size of the message to be sent exceeds the available MPI-internal buffer space and the operation is blocked until the data is transferred to the receiver. The *Late Sender / Wrong Order* pattern (Fig. 3c) describes a receiver waiting for a message, although an earlier message is ready to be received by the same destination process (i.e., messages received in the wrong order). Finally, the *Wait at N×N* pattern (Fig. 3d) quantifies the waiting time due to the inherent synchronization in n-to-n operations, such as `MPI_Allreduce()`. A full list of the wait-state types supported by Scalasca including explanatory diagrams can be found online in the Scalasca documentation [11].

Parallel Wait-State Search

To accomplish the search in a scalable way, Scalasca exploits both distributed memory and parallel processing capabilities available on the target system. After the target application has terminated and the trace data have been flushed to disk, the trace analyzer is launched with one analysis process per (target) application process and loads the entire trace data into its distributed memory address space. Future versions of Scalasca may exploit persistent memory segments available on systems such as Blue Gene/P to pass the trace data to the analysis stage without involving any file I/O. While traversing the traces in parallel, the analyzer performs a replay of the application's original communication. During the replay, the analyzer

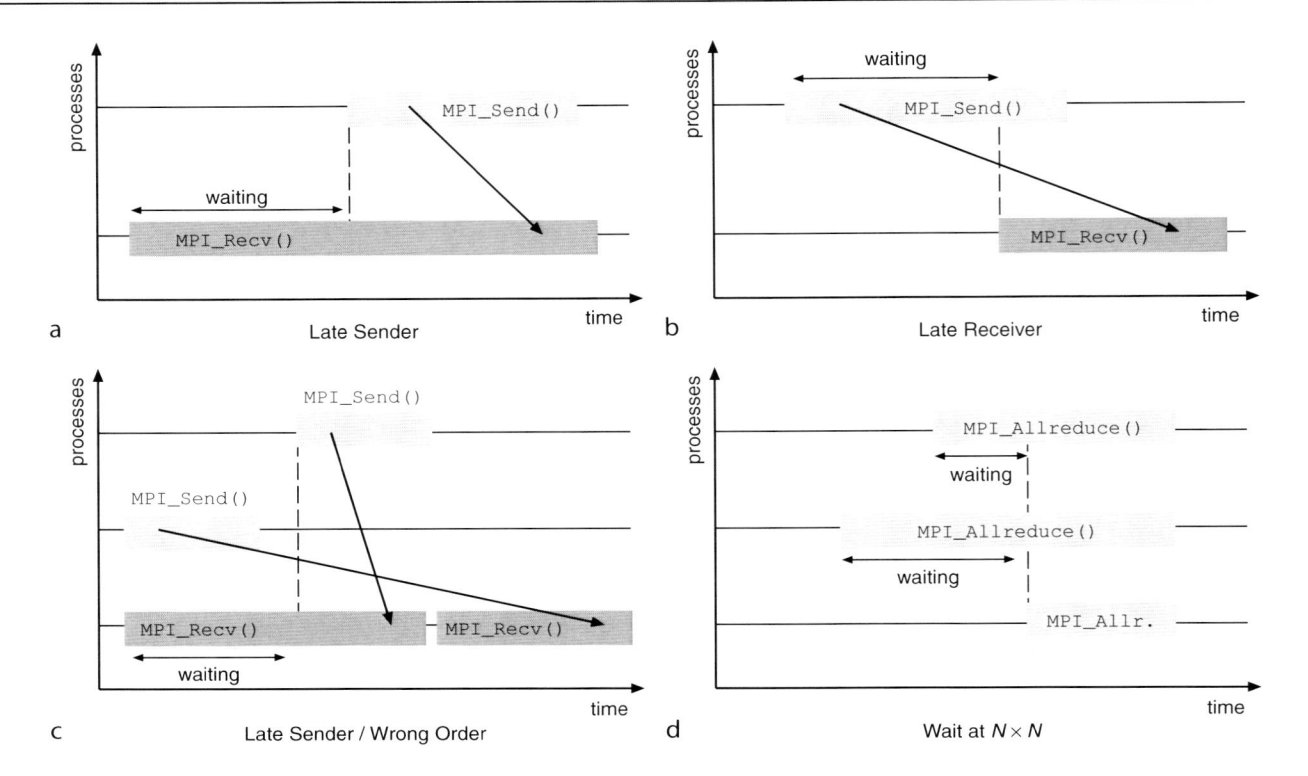

Scalasca. Fig. 3 Four examples of wait states (**a–d**) detected by Scalasca. The combination of MPI functions used in each of these examples represents just one possible case. For instance, the blocking receive operation in wait state (**a**) can be replaced by a non-blocking receive followed by a wait operation. In this case, the waiting time would occur during the wait operation

identifies wait states in communication and synchronization operations by measuring temporal differences between local and remote events after their time stamps have been exchanged using an operation of similar type. Detected wait-state instances are classified and quantified according to their significance for every call path and system resource involved. Since trace processing capabilities (i.e., processors and memory) grow proportionally with the number of application processes, good scalability can be achieved even at previously intractable scales. Recent scalability improvements allowed Scalasca to complete trace analyses of runs with up to 294,912 cores on a 72-rack IBM Blue Gene/P system [23].

A modified form of the replay-based trace analysis scheme is also applied to detect wait states occurring in MPI-2 RMA operations. In this case, RMA communication is used to exchange the required information between processes. Finally, Scalasca also provides the ability to process traces from hybrid MPI/OpenMP and pure OpenMP applications. However, the parallel wait-state search does not yet recognize OpenMP-specific wait states, such as barrier waiting time or lock contention, previously supported by its predecessor.

Wait-State Search on Clusters without Global Clock

To allow accurate trace analyses on systems without globally synchronized clocks, Scalasca can synchronize inaccurate time stamps postmortem. Linear interpolation based on clock offset measurements during program initialization and finalization already accounts for differences in offset and drift, assuming that the drift of an individual processor is not time dependent. This step is mandatory on all systems without a global clock, such as Cray XT and most PC or compute blade clusters. However, inaccuracies and drifts varying over time can still cause violations of the logical event order that are harmful to the accuracy of the analysis. For this reason, Scalasca compensates for such violations by shifting communication events in time as much as needed to restore the logical event order while trying to preserve the length of intervals between local events. This logical synchronization is currently optional and should be performed if the trace analysis reports (too many) violations of the logical event order.

Future Directions

Future enhancements of Scalasca will aim at further improving both its functionality and its scalability. In addition to supporting the more advanced features of OpenMP such as nested parallelism and tasking as an immediate priority, Scalasca is expected to evolve toward emerging programming models and architectures including partitioned global address space (PGAS) languages and heterogeneous systems. Moreover, optimized data management and analysis workflows including in-memory trace analysis will allow Scalasca to master even larger processor configurations than it does today. A recent example in this direction is the substantial reduction of the trace-file creation overhead that was achieved by mapping large numbers of logical process-local trace files onto a small number of physical files [4], a feature that will become available in future releases of Scalasca.

In addition to keeping up with the rapid new developments in parallel hardware and software, research is also undertaken to expand the general understanding of parallel performance in simulation codes. The examples below summarize two ongoing projects aimed at increasing the expressive power of the analyses supported by Scalasca. The description reflects the status of March 2011.

Time-Series Call-Path Profiling

As scientific parallel applications simulate the temporal evolution of a system, their progress occurs via discrete points in time. Accordingly, the core of such an application is typically a loop that advances the simulated time step by step. However, the performance behavior may vary between individual iterations, for example, due to periodically reoccurring extra activities or when the state of the computation adjusts to new conditions in so-called adaptive codes. To study such time-dependent behavior, Scalasca can distinguish individual iterations in profiles and event traces. Figure 4 shows the distribution of point-to-point messages across the iteration-process space in the MPI-based PEPC [7] particle simulation code. Obviously, during later stages of the simulation the majority of messages are sent by only a small collection of processes with time-dependent

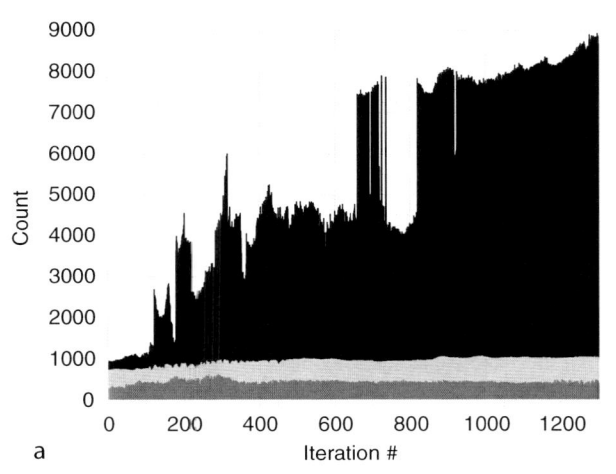

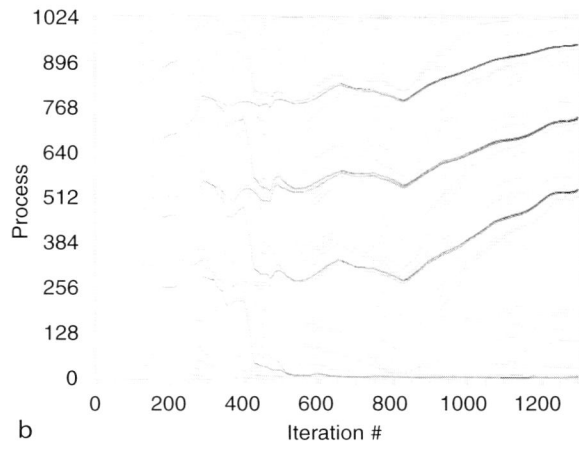

Scalasca. Fig. 4 Gradual development of a communication imbalance along 1,300 timesteps of PEPC on 1,024 processors. (**a**) Minimum (*bottom*), median (*middle*), and maximum (*top*) number of point-to-point messages sent or received by a process in an iteration. (**b**) Number of messages sent by each process in each iteration. The higher the number of messages the *darker the color* on the value map

constituency, inducing wait states on other processes (not shown).

However, even generating call-path profiles (as opposed to traces) separately for thousands of iterations to identify the call paths responsible may exceed the available buffer space – especially when the call tree is large and more than one metric is collected. For this reason, a runtime approach for the semantic compression of a series of call-path profiles based on incrementally clustering single-iteration profiles was developed that scales in terms of the number of iterations without sacrificing important performance details [16]. This method, which will be integrated in future versions of Scalasca, offers low runtime overhead by using only a condensed version of the profile data when calculating distances and accounts for process-dependent variations by making all clustering decisions locally.

Identifying the Root Causes of Wait-State Formation

In general, the temporal or spatial distance between cause and symptom of a performance problem constitutes a major difficulty in deriving helpful conclusions from performance data. Merely knowing the locations of wait states in the program is often insufficient to understand the reason for their occurrence. Building on earlier work by Meira, Jr. et al. [12], the replay-based wait-state analysis was extended in such a way that it attributes the waiting times to their root causes [3], as exemplified in Fig. 5. Typically, these root causes are intervals during which a process performs some additional activity not performed by its peers, for example as a result of insufficiently balancing the load.

However, excess workload identified as the root cause of wait states usually cannot simply be removed. To achieve a better balance, optimization hypotheses drawn from such an analysis typically propose the redistribution of the excess load to other processes instead. Unfortunately, redistributing workloads in complex message-passing applications can have surprising side effects that may compromise the expected reduction of waiting times. Given that balancing the load statically or even introducing a dynamic load-balancing scheme constitute major code changes, such procedures should ideally be performed only if the prospective performance gain is likely to materialize. Other recent work [10] therefore concentrated on determining the savings we can realistically hope for when redistributing a given delay – before altering the application itself. Since the effects of such changes are hard to quantify analytically, they are simulated in a scalable manner via a parallel real-time replay of event traces after they have been modified to reflect the redistributed load.

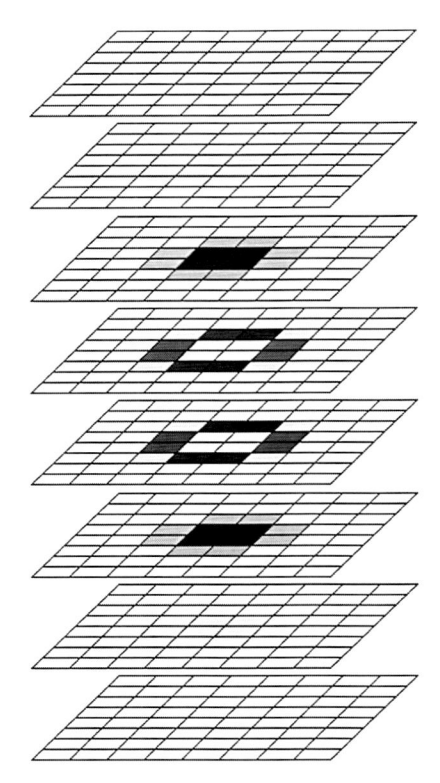

Scalasca. Fig. 5 In the lorentz_d() subroutine of the Zeus MP/2 code, several processes primarily arranged on a small hollow sphere within the virtual process topology are responsible for wait states arranged on the enclosing hollow sphere shown earlier in Fig. 2. Since the inner region of the topology carries more load than the outer region, processes at the rim of the inner region delay those farther outside. The darkness of the color indicates the amount of waiting time induced by a process but materializing farther away. In this way, it becomes possible to study the root causes of wait-state formation

Related Entries
▶ Intel® Thread Profiler
▶ MPI (Message Passing Interface)
▶ OpenMP

▶OpenMP Profiling with OmpP
▶Performance Analysis Tools
▶Periscope
▶PMPI Tools
▶Synchronization
▶TAU
▶Vampir

Bibliographic Notes and Further Reading

Scalasca is available for download including documentation under the New BSD license at www.scalasca.org.

Scalasca emerged from the KOJAK project, which was started in 1998 at the Jülich Supercomputing Centre in Germany to study the automatic evaluation of parallel performance data, and in particular, the automatic detection of wait states in event traces of parallel applications. The wait-state analysis first concentrated on MPI [20] and later on OpenMP and hybrid codes [21], motivating the definition of the POMP profiling interface [13] for OpenMP, which is still used today even beyond Scalasca by OpenMP-enabled profilers such as ompP (▶OpenMP Profiling with OmpP) and ▶TAU. A comprehensive description of the initial trace-analysis toolset resulting from this effort, which was publicly released for the first time in 2003 under the name KOJAK, is given in [19].

During the following years, KOJAK's wait-state search was optimized for speed, refined to exploit virtual process topologies, and extended to support MPI-2 RMA communication. In addition to the detection of wait states occurring during a single run, KOJAK also introduced a framework for comparing the analysis results of different runs [14], for example, to judge the effectiveness of optimization measures. An extensive snapshot of this more advanced version of KOJAK including further literature references is presented in [22]. However, KOJAK still analyzed the traces sequentially after the process-local trace data had been merged into a single global trace file, an undesired scalability limitation in view of the dramatically rising number of cores employed on modern parallel architectures.

In 2006, after the acquisition of a major grant from the Helmholtz Association of German Research Centres, the Scalasca project was started in Jülich as the successor to KOJAK with the objective of improving the scalability of the trace analysis by parallelizing the search for wait states. A detailed discussion of the parallel replay underlying the parallel search can be found in [6]. Variations of the scalable replay mechanism were applied to correct event time stamps taken on clusters without global clock [1], to simulate the effects of optimizations such as balancing the load of a function more evenly across the processes of a program [10], and to identify wait states in MPI-2 RMA communication in a scalable manner [9]. Moreover, the parallel trace analysis was also demonstrated to run on computational grids consisting of multiple geographically dispersed clusters that are used as a single coherent system [2]. Finally, a very recent replay-based method attributes the costs of wait states in terms of resource waste to their original cause [3].

Since the enormous data volume sometimes makes trace analysis challenging, runtime summarization capabilities were added to Scalasca both as a simple means to obtain a performance overview and as a basis to optimally configure the measurement for later trace generation. Scalasca integrates both measurement options in a unified tool architecture, whose details are described in [5]. Recently, a semantic compression algorithm was developed that will allow Scalasca to take time-series profiles in a space-efficient manner even if the target application performs large numbers of timesteps [16].

Major application studies with Scalasca include a survey of using it on leadership systems [24], a comprehensive analysis of how the performance of the SPEC MPI2007 benchmarks evolves as their execution progresses [17], and the investigation of a gradually developing communication imbalance in the PEPC particle simulation [18]. Finally, a recent study of the Sweep3D benchmark demonstrated performance measurements and analyses with up to 294,912 processes [23].

From 2003 until 2008, KOJAK and later Scalasca was jointly developed together with the Innovative Computing Laboratory at the University of Tennessee. During their lifetime, the two projects received funding from the Helmholtz Association of German Research Centres, the US Department of Energy, the US Department of Defense, the US National Science Foundation, the German Science Foundation, the German Federal Ministry of Education and Research, and the European Union. Today, Scalasca is a joint project between Jülich and the German Research School for Simulation Sciences in nearby Aachen.

The following individuals have contributed to Scalasca and its predecessor: Erika Ábrahám, Daniel Becker, Nikhil Bhatia, David Böhme, Jack Dongarra, Dominic Eschweiler, Sebastian Flott, Wolfgang Frings, Karl Fürlinger, Christoph Geile, Markus Geimer, Marc-André Hermanns, Michael Knobloch, David Krings, Guido Kruschwitz, André Kühnal, Björn Kuhlmann, John Linford, Daniel Lorenz, Bernd Mohr, Shirley Moore, Ronal Muresano, Jan Mußler, Andreas Nett, Christian Rössel, Matthias Pfeifer, Peter Philippen, Farzona Pulatova, Divya Sankaranarayanan, Pavel Saviankou, Marc Schlütter, Christian Siebert, Fengguang Song, Alexandre Strube, Zoltán Szebenyi, Felix Voigtländer, Felix Wolf, and Brian Wylie.

Bibliography

1. Becker D, Rabenseifner R, Wolf F, Linford J (2009) Scalable timestamp synchronization for event traces of message-passing applications. Parallel Comput 35(12):595–607
2. Becker D, Wolf F, Frings W, Geimer M, Wylie BJN, Mohr B (2007) Automatic trace-based performance analysis of metacomputing applications. In: Proceedings of the international parallel and distributed processing symposium (IPDPS), Long Beach, CA, USA. IEEE Computer Society, Washington, DC
3. Böhme D, Geimer M, Wolf F, Arnold L (2010) Identifying the root causes of wait states in large-scale parallel applications. In: Proceedings of the 39th international conference on parallel processing (ICPP), San Diego, CA, USA. IEEE Computer Society, Washington, DC, pp 90–100
4. Frings W, Wolf F, Petkov V (2009) Scalable massively parallel I/O to task-local files. In: Proceedings of the ACM/IEEE conference on supercomputing (SC09), Portland, OR, USA, Nov 2009
5. Geimer M, Wolf F, Wylie BJN, Ábrahám E, Becker D, Mohr B (2010) The Scalasca performance toolset architecture. Concurr Comput Pract Exper 22(6):702–719
6. Geimer M, Wolf F, Wylie BJN, Mohr B (2009) A scalable tool architecture for diagnosing wait states in massively-parallel applications. Parallel Comput 35(7):375–388
7. Gibbon P, Frings W, Dominiczak S, Mohr B (2006) Performance analysis and visualization of the n-body tree code PEPC on massively parallel computers. In: Proceedings of the conference on parallel computing (ParCo), Málaga, Spain, Sept 2005 (NIC series), vol 33. John von Neumann-Institut für Computing, Jülich, pp 367–374
8. Hayes JC, Norman ML, Fiedler RA, Bordner JO, Li PS, Clark SE, ud-Doula A, Mac Low M-M (2006) Simulating radiating and magnetized flows in multiple dimensions with ZEUS-MP. Astrophys J Suppl 165(1):188–228
9. Hermanns M-A, Geimer M, Mohr B, Wolf F (2009) Scalable detection of MPI-2 remote memory access inefficiency patterns. In: Proceedings of the 16th European PVM/MPI users' group meeting (EuroPVM/MPI), Espoo, Finland. Lecture notes in computer science, vol 5759. Springer, Berlin, pp 31–41
10. Hermanns M-A, Geimer M, Wolf F, Wylie BJN (2009) Verifying causality between distant performance phenomena in large-scale MPI applications. In Proceedings of the 17th Euromicro international conference on parallel, distributed, and network-based processing (PDP), Weimar, Germany. IEEE Computer Society, Washington, DC, pp 78–84
11. Jülich Supercomputing Centre and German Research School for Simulation Sciences. Scalasca parallel performance analysis toolset documentation (performance properties). http://www.scalasca.org/download/documentation/
12. Meira W Jr, LeBlanc TJ, Poulos A (1996) Waiting time analysis and performance visualization in Carnival. In: Proceedings of the SIGMETRICS symposium on parallel and distributed tools (SPDT'96), Philadelphia, PA, USA. ACM
13. Mohr B, Malony A, Shende S, Wolf F (2002) Design and prototype of a performance tool interface for OpenMP. J Supercomput 23(1):105–128
14. Song F, Wolf F, Bhatia N, Dongarra J, Moore S (2004) An algebra for cross-experiment performance analysis. In: Proceedings of the international conference on parallel processing (ICPP), Montreal, Canada. IEEE Computer Society, Washington, DC, pp 63–72
15. Szebenyi Z, Gamblin T, Schulz M, de Supinski BR, Wolf F, Wylie BJN (2011) Reconciling sampling and direct instrumentation for unintrusive call-path profiling of MPI programs. In: Proceedings of the international parallel and distributed processing symposium (IPDPS), Anchorage, AK, USA. IEEE Computer Society, Washington, DC
16. Szebenyi Z, Wolf F, Wylie BJN (2009) Space-efficient time-series call-path profiling of parallel applications. In: Proceedings of the ACM/IEEE conference on supercomputing (SC09), Portland, OR, USA, Nov 2009
17. Szebenyi Z, Wylie BJN, Wolf F (2008) SCALASCA parallel performance analyses of SPEC MPI2007 applications. In: Proceedings of the 1st SPEC international performance evaluation workshop (SIPEW), Darmstadt, Germany. Lecture notes in computer science, vol 5119. Springer, Berlin, pp 99–123
18. Szebenyi Z, Wylie BJN, Wolf F (2009) Scalasca parallel performance analyses of PEPC. In: Proceedings of the workshop on productivity and performance (PROPER) in conjunction with Euro-Par, Las Palmas de Gran Canaria, Spain, August 2008. Lecture notes in computer science, vol 5415. Springer, Berlin, pp 305–314
19. Wolf F (2003) Automatic Performance Analysis on Parallel Computers with SMP Nodes. PhD thesis, RWTH Aachen, Forschungszentrum Jülich. ISBN 3-00-010003-2
20. Wolf F, Mohr B (2001) Specifying performance properties of parallel applications using compound events. Parallel Distrib Comput Pract 4(3):301–317
21. Wolf F, Mohr B (2003) Automatic performance analysis of hybrid MPI/OpenMP applications. J Syst Archit 49(10–11):421–439
22. Wolf F, Mohr B, Dongarra J, Moore S (2007) Automatic analysis of inefficiency patterns in parallel applications. Concurr Comput Pract Exper 19(11):1481–1496

23. Wylie BJN, Geimer M, Mohr B, Böhme D, Szebenyi Z, Wolf F (2010) Large-scale performance analysis of Sweep3D with the Scalasca toolset. Parallel Process Lett 20(4):397–414
24. Wylie BJN, Geimer M, Wolf F (2008) Performance measurement and analysis of large-scale parallel applications on leadership computing systems. Sci Program 16(2–3):167–181

Scaled Speedup

▶Gustafson's Law

Scan for Distributed Memory, Message-Passing Systems

Jesper Larsson Träff
University of Vienna, Vienna, Austria

Synonyms

All prefix sums; Prefix; Parallel prefix sums; Prefix reduction

Definition

Among a group of p consecutively numbered processing elements (nodes) each node has a data item x_i for $i = 0, \ldots p - 1$. An associative, binary operator $\oplus$ over the data items is given. The nodes in parallel compute all p (or $p - 1$) *prefix sums* over the input items: node i computes the *inclusive prefix sum* $\oplus_{j=0}^{i} x_j$ (or, for $i > 0$, the *exclusive prefix sum* $\oplus_{j=0}^{i-1} x_j$).

Discussion

For a general discussion, see the entry on "▶Reduce and Scan."

For distributed memory, message-passing parallel systems, the scan operation plays an important role for load-balancing and data-redistribution operations. In this setting, each node possesses a local data item x_i, typically an n-element vector, and the given associative, binary operator $\oplus$ is typically an element-wise operation. The required prefix sums could be computed by arranging the input items in a linear sequence and "scanning" through this sequence in order, carrying along the corresponding inclusive (or exclusive) prefix sum. In a distributed memory setting, this intuition would be captured by arranging the nodes in a linear array, but much better algorithms usually exist. The inclusive scan operation is illustrated in Fig. 1.

The scan operation is included as a collective operation in many interfaces and libraries for distributed memory systems, for instance MPI [5], where both an inclusive (MPI_Scan) and an exclusive (MPI_Exscan) general scan operation is defined. These operations work on vectors of consecutive or non-consecutive elements and arbitrary (user-defined) associative, possibly also commutative operators.

Algorithms

On distributed memory parallel architectures parallel algorithms typically use tree-like patterns to compute the prefix sums in a logarithmic number of parallel communication rounds. Four such algorithms are described in the following. Algorithms also exist for hypercube and mesh- or torus-connected communication architectures [1, 4, 8].

The p nodes are consecutively numbered from 0 to $p - 1$. Each node i has an input data item x_i. Nodes must communicate explicitly by send and receive operations. For convenience a fully connected model in which each node can communicate with all other nodes at the same cost is assumed. Only one communication operation per node can take place at a time. The data items x_i are assumed to all have the same size $n = |x_i|$. For scalar items, $n = 1$, while for vector items n is the number of elements. The communication cost of transferring a data item of size n is assumed to be $O(n)$ (linear).

Linear Array

The simplest scan algorithm organizes the nodes in a linear array. For $i > 0$ node i waits for a *partial sum*

Before			After		
Node 0	Node 1	Node 2	Node 0	Node 1	Node 2
$x^{(0)}$	$x^{(1)}$	$x^{(2)}$	$\oplus_{j=0}^{0} x^{(j)}$	$\oplus_{j=0}^{1} x^{(j)}$	$\oplus_{j=0}^{2} x^{(j)}$

Scan for Distributed Memory, Message-Passing Systems. Fig. 1 The inclusive scan operation

$\oplus_{j=0}^{i-1} x_j$ from node $i-1$, adds its own item x_i to arrive at the partial sum $\oplus_{j=0}^{i} x_j$, and sends this to node $i+1$, unless $i = p-1$. This algorithm is strictly serial and takes $p-1$ communication rounds for the last node to finish its prefix computation, for a total cost of $O(pn)$. This is uninteresting in itself, but the algorithm can be pipelined (see below) to yield a time to complete of $O(p+n)$. When n is large compared to p this easily of implementable algorithm is often the fastest, due to its simplicity.

Binary Tree

The *binary tree* algorithm arranges the nodes in a balanced binary tree T with in-order numbering. This numbering has the property that the nodes in the subtree $T(i)$ rooted at node i have consecutive numbers in the interval $[s, \ldots, i, \ldots, e]$, where s and e denote the first (start) and last (end) node in the subtree $T(i)$, respectively. The algorithm consists of two phases. It suffices to describe the actions of a node in the tree with parent, right and left children. In the *up-phase*, node i first receives the *partial result* $\oplus_{j=s}^{i-1} x_j$ from its left child and adds its own item x_i to get the partial result $\oplus_{j=s}^{i} x_j$. This value is stored for the down-phase. Node i then receives the partial result $\oplus_{j=i+1}^{e} x_j$ from its right child and computes the partial result $\oplus_{j=s}^{e} x_j$. Node i sends this value upward in the tree without keeping it. In the *down-phase*, node i receives the partial result $\oplus_{j=0}^{s-1} x_j$ from its parent. This is first sent down to the left child and then added to the stored partial result $\oplus_{j=s}^{i} x_j$ to form the final result $\oplus_{j=0}^{i} x_j$ for node i. This final result is sent down to the right child.

With the obvious modifications, the general description covers also nodes that need not participate in all of these communications: Leaves have no children. Some nodes may only have a leftmost child. Nodes on the path between root and leftmost leaf do not receive data from their parent in the down-phase. Nodes on the path between rightmost child and root do not send data to their parent in the up-phase.

Since the depth of T is logarithmic in the number of nodes, and data of size n are sent up and down the tree, the time to complete the scan with the binary tree algorithm is $O(n \log p)$. This is unattractive for large n. If the nodes can only either send or receive in a communication operation but otherwise work simultaneously, the number of communication operations per node is at most 6, and the number of communication rounds is $6 \lceil \log_2 p \rceil$.

Binomial Tree

The *binomial tree* algorithm likewise consists of an *up-phase* and a *down-phase*, each of which takes k rounds where $k = \lfloor \log_2 p \rfloor$. In round j for $j = 0, \ldots, k-1$ of the up-phase each node i satisfying $i \wedge (2^{j+1} - 1) \equiv 2^{j+1} - 1$ (where $\wedge$ denotes "bitwise and") receives a partial result from node $i - 2^j$ (provided $0 \leq i - 2^j$). After sending to node i, node $i - 2^j$ is inactive for the remainder of the up-phase. The receiving nodes add the partial results, and after round j have a partial result of the form $\oplus_{\ell=i-2^{j+1}+1}^{i} x_\ell$. The down-phase counts rounds downward from k to 1. Node i with $i \wedge (2^j - 1) \equiv 2^j - 1$ sends its partial result to node $i + 2^{j-1}$ (provided $i + 2^{j-1} < p$) which can now compute its final result $\oplus_{\ell=0}^{i+2^{j-1}} x_\ell$. The communication pattern is illustrated in Fig. 2.

The number of communication rounds is $2\lfloor \log p \rfloor$, and the time to complete is $O(n \log p)$. Each node is either sending or receiving data in each round, with no possibility for overlapping of sending and receiving due to the computation of partial results.

Simultaneous Trees

The number of communication rounds can be improved by a factor of two by the *simultaneous binomial tree* algorithm. Starting from round $k = 0$, in round k, node i sends a computed, partial result $\oplus_{j=i-2^k+1}^{i} x_j$ to node $i + 2^k$ (provided $i + 2^k < p$) and receives a likewise computed, partial result from node $i - 2^k$ (provided $i - 2^k \geq 0$). Before the next round, the previous and received partial

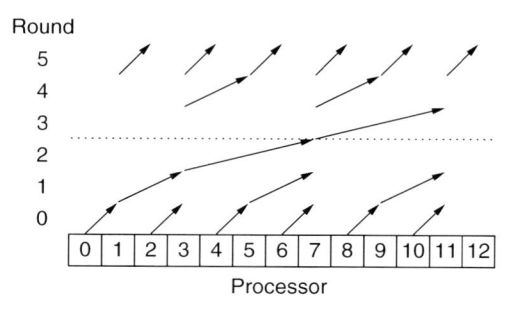

Scan for Distributed Memory, Message-Passing Systems. Fig. 2 The communication pattern for the binomial tree algorithm for $p = 13$

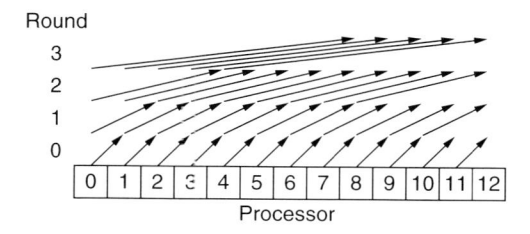

Scan for Distributed Memory, Message-Passing Systems. Fig. 3 The communication patterns for the simultaneous binomial tree algorithm for $p = 13$

results are added. It is easy to see that after round k, node i's partial result is $\oplus_{j=\max(0,i-2^{k+1}+1)}^{i} x_j$. Node i terminates when both $i - 2^k < 0$ (nothing to receive) and $i + 2^k \geq p$ (nothing to send). Provided that the nodes can simultaneously send and receive an item in the same communication operation this happens after $\lceil \log_2 p \rceil$ communication rounds for a total time of $O(n \log p)$. This is again not attractive for large n. This algorithm dates back at least to [2] and is illustrated in Fig. 3.

For large n the running time of $O(n \log p)$ is not attractive due to the logarithmic factor. For the binary tree algorithm pipelining can be employed, by which the running time can be improved to $O(n + \log p)$. Neither the binomial nor the simultaneous binomial tree algorithms admit pipelining. A pipelined implementation breaks each data item into a certain number of blocks N each of roughly equal size of n/N. As soon as a block has been processed and sent down the pipeline, the next block can be processed. The time of such an implementation is proportional to the depth of the pipeline plus the number of blocks times the time to process one block. From this an optimal block size can be determined, which gives the running time claimed for the binary tree algorithm. For very large vectors relative to the number of nodes, $n \gg p$, a linear pipeline seems to be the best practical choice due to very small constants. Pipelining can only be applied if the binary operator can work independently on the blocks. This is trivially the case if the items are vectors and the operator works element-wise on these.

Related Entries
▶Collective Communication
▶Message Passing Interface (MPI)
▶Reduce and Scan

Bibliographic Notes and Further Reading

The parallel prefix problem was early recognized as a fundamental parallel processing primitive, and its history goes back at least as far as the early 1970s. The simultaneous binomial tree algorithm is from [2], but may have been discovered earlier as well. The binary tree algorithm easily admits pipelining but has the drawback that leaf nodes are only using either send or receive capabilities, and that simultaneous send-receive communication can be only partially exploited. In [6] it was shown how to overcome these limitations, yielding theoretically almost optimal scan (as well as reduce and broadcast) algorithms with (two) binary trees. Algorithms for distributed systems in the *LogP* performance model were presented in [7]. An algorithm for multiport message-passing systems was given in [3]. For results on meshes and hypercubes see, for instance [1, 4, 8].

Bibliography

1. Akl SG (1999) Parallel computation: models and methods. Prentice-Hall, Upper Saddle River
2. Daniel Hillis W, Steele GL Jr (1986) Data parallel algorithms. Commun ACM 29(12):1170–1183
3. Lin Y-C, Yeh C-S (1999) Efficient parallel prefix algorithms on multiport message-passing systems. Inform Process Lett 71:91–95
4. Mayr EW, Plaxton CG (1993) Pipelined parallel prefix computations, and sorting on a pipelined hypercube. J Parallel Distrib Comput 17:374–380
5. MPI Forum (2009) MPI: A message-passing interface standard. Version 2.2. www.mpiforum.org. Accessed 4 Sept 2009
6. Sanders P, Speck J, Träff JL (2009) Two-tree algorithms for full bandwidth broadcast, reduction and scan. Parallel Comput 35:581–594
7. Santos EE (2002) Optimal and efficient algorithms for summing and prefix summing on parallel machines. J Parallel Distrib Comput 62(4):517–543
8. Ziavras SG, Mukherjee A (1996) Data broadcasting and reduction, prefix computation, and sorting on reduces hypercube parallel computer. Parallel Comput 22(4):595–606

Scan, Reduce and

▶Reduce and Scan

Scatter

▶Collective Communication

Scheduling

▶Job Scheduling
▶Task Graph Scheduling
▶Scheduling Algorithms

Scheduling Algorithms

PATRICE QUINTON
ENS Cachan Bretagne, Bruz, France

Synonyms
Execution ordering

Definition
Scheduling algorithms aim at defining when operations of a program are to be executed. Such an ordering, called a *schedule*, has to make sure that the dependences between the operations are met. Scheduling for parallelism consists in looking for a schedule that allows a program to be efficiently executed on a parallel architecture. This efficiency may be evaluated in term of total execution time, utilization of the processors, power consumption, or any combination of this kind of criteria. Scheduling is often combined with *mapping*, which consists in assigning an operation to a resource of an architecture.

Discussion

Introduction
Scheduling is an essential design step to execute an algorithm on a parallel architecture. Usually, the algorithm is specified by means of a program from which dependences between statements or operations (also called *tasks*) can be isolated: an operation A depends on another operation B if the evaluation of B must precede that of A for the result of the algorithm to be correct.

Assuming the dependences of an algorithm are already known, scheduling has to find out a partial order, called a *schedule*, which says when each statement can be executed. A schedule may be resource-constrained, if the ordering must be such that some resource – for example, processor unit, memory, etc. – is available for the execution of the algorithm.

Scheduling algorithms are therefore classified according to the precision of the dependence analysis, the kind of resources needed, the optimization criteria considered, the specification of the algorithm, the granularity size of the tasks, and the kind of parallel architecture that is considered for execution.

Scheduling can also happen at run-time – *dynamic scheduling* – or at compile-time – *static scheduling*.

In the following, basic notions related to task graphs are first recalled, then scheduling algorithms for loops are presented. The presentation separates mono-dimensional and higher-dimensional loops. *Task Graph scheduling*, a topic that is covered in another essay of this site, is not treated here.

Task Graphs and Scheduling
Task graphs and their scheduling is the basis of many situations of parallel computations and has been the subject of a number of researches. Task graphs are a means of representing dependences between computations of a program: vertices V of the graph are elementary computations, called tasks, and oriented edges E represent dependences between computations. A task graph is therefore an acyclic, directed multigraph.

Assume that each task T has an estimated integer value $d(T)$ representing its execution duration. A schedule for a task graph is a function σ from the vertex set V of the graph to the set of positive integers, such that $\sigma(u) + d(u) \leq \sigma(v)$, where d represents the duration associated to the evaluation of task u, and v depends on u. Since it is acyclic, a task graph always admits a schedule.

Scheduling a task graph may be constrained by the number of processors p available to run the tasks. It is assumed that each task T, when ready to be evaluated, is allocated to a free processor, and occupies this processor during its duration $d(T)$, after which the processor is released and becomes idle. When p is unlimited, we say that the schedule is *resource free*, otherwise, it is *resource constrained*.

The total computation time for executing a task graph on p processors, is also called its *makespan*. If the number of processors is illimited, that is, $p = +\infty$, it can be shown that finding out the makespan amounts to a simple traversal of the task graph.

When the number of processors is bounded, that is, $p < +\infty$, it can be shown that the problem becomes NP-complete. It is therefore required to rely on heuristics. In this case, a simple *greedy* heuristics is efficient: try to schedule at a given time as many tasks as possible on processors that are available at this time.

A *list schedule* is a schedule such that no processor is deliberately kept idle; at each time step t, if a processor P is available, and if some task T is *free*, that is to say, when all its predecessors have been executed, then T is scheduled to be executed on processor P. It can be shown that a list schedule allows a solution within 50% of the optimal makespan to be found.

List scheduling plays a very important rôle in scheduling theory and is therefore worth mentioning. A generic *list scheduling* algorithm looks as follows:

1. Initialization
   a. Assign to all free tasks a priority level (the choice of the priority function depends on the problem at hand).
   b. Set the time step t to 0.
2. While there remain tasks to execute:
   a. If the execution of a task terminates at time t, suppress this task from the predecessor list of all its successors. Add those tasks whose predecessor tasks has become empty to the free tasks, and assign them a priority.
   b. If there are q available processors, and r free tasks, execute the $\min(q, r)$ tasks of highest priority.
   c. Increase the time step t by one.

Scheduling One-Dimensional Loops

A particular field of interest for scheduling is how to execute efficiently a set of computations that re-execute a large amount of time, also called *cyclic scheduling*.

Such a problem is encountered when scheduling a one-dimensional loop. Consider for example, the following loop:

do $k = 0$, **step** 0, **to** $N - 1$

A : $a(k) = c(k - 1)$

B : $b(k) = a(k - 2) \times b(k - 1)$

C : $c(k) = b(k) + 1$

endo

This loop could be modeled as a task graph where tasks would be A(k), B(k), and C(k), $k = 0, \ldots, N - 1$. But if N is large, this graph becomes difficult to handle, hence the idea of finding out a generic way to schedule the operations by following the stucture of the loop.

Scheduling such a loop consists in finding out a time instant for each instruction to be executed, while respecting the dependences between these instructions. Call *operation* the execution of an instruction for a given value of index k, and denote A(k), B(k), and C(k) these operations. Notice that A(k) depends on the value $c(k - 1)$, which is computed by operation C($k - 1$) during the previous iteration of the loop. Similarly, B(k) depends on B($k - 1$) and A($k - 2$); finally, C(k) depends on B(k), an operation of the same loop iteration. To model this situation, the notion of *reduced dependence graph*, which gather all information needed to schedule the loop, is introduced: its vertices are operation names (e.g., A, B, C etc.), and its edges represent dependences between operations. To each vertex v, associate an integer value $d(v)$ that represents its execution duration, and to each edge, associate a positive integer w that is 0 if the dependence lies within an iteration, and the difference between the iterations number otherwise. Fig. 1 represents the reduced dependence graph of the above loop.

With this representation, a schedule becomes a function σ from $V \times \mathbf{N}$ to $\mathbf{N}$, where $\mathbf{N}$ denotes the set of integers; $\sigma(v, k)$ gives the time at which instruction v of iteration k can be executed. Of course, a schedule must meet the dependence constraints, which can be expressed in the following way: for all edge $e = (u, v)$ of the dependence graph, it is needed that $\sigma(v, k + w(e)) \geq \sigma(u, k) + d(u)$.

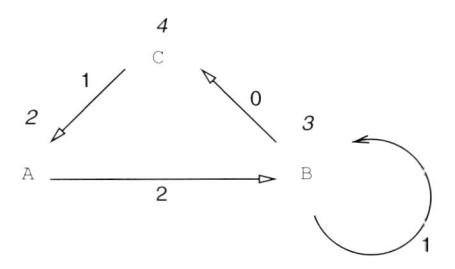

Scheduling Algorithms. Fig. 1 Reduced dependence graph of the loop

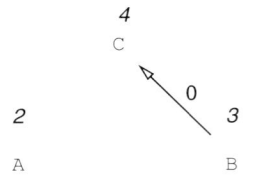

Scheduling Algorithms. Fig. 2 Reduced dependence graph without nonzero edges. This graph is necessarily acyclic, and a simple traversal provides a schedule

For this kind of problem, the performance of a schedule is defined as the *average cycle time* λ defined as

$$\lambda = \lim_{N \to \infty} \frac{\max\{\sigma(v,k) + d(v) \mid v \in V, 0 \le k < N\}}{N}.$$

In order to define a *generic* schedule for such a loop, it is interesting to consider schedules of the form $\sigma(v,k) = \lambda k + c(v)$ where λ is a positive integer and $c(v)$ is a constant integer associated to instruction v. Constant λ is called the *initiation interval* of the loop, and it represents the number of cycles between the beginning of two successive iterations.

Finding out a schedule is quite easy: by restricting the reduced dependence graph to the intra-iteration dependences (i.e., dependences whose value w is 0), one obtains an acyclic graph that can be scheduled using a list scheduling algorithm. Let then λ be the makespan of such schedule, and let $ls(v)$ be the schedule assigned to vertex v by the list scheduling; then, a schedule of the form $\sigma(v,k) = \lambda k + ls(v)$ is a solution to the problem. Fig. 2 shows, for example, the task graph obtained when removing nonzero inter-iteration dependencies. One can see that the makespan of this graph is 7, and therefore, a schedule of the form $\sigma(v,k) = 7k + ls(v)$ is a solution. Figure 3 shows a possible execution, on two processors, with an initiation interval of 7.

However, one can do better in general, as shall be seen. Again, the *cyclic scheduling* problem can be stated with or without resources. Assuming, for the sake of simplicity, that instructions are carried out by a set of p identical processing units, the number of available processors constitutes a resource limit.

First, one can give a lower bound for the *initiation interval*. Let C be a cycle of the reduced dependence graph, and let $d(C)$ be its duration (the sum of the durations of its instructions) and $w(C)$ be its iteration weight, i.e., the sum of the iteration weights of its edges.

Then, $\lambda \ge \frac{d(C)}{w(C)}$. The intuition behind this bound is that the duration of the tasks of the cycle have to be spread on the number of iterations spanned by this cycle, and as cycles have all the same duration λ, one cannot do better than this ratio. Applying this bound to this example, it can be seen that $\lambda \ge \frac{9}{3} = 3$ (cycle A → B → C → A) and $\lambda \ge 3$ (self dependence of B). Can the value $\lambda = 3$ be reached?

The answer depends again on the resource constraints. When an unlimited number of processors is available, one can show that the lower bound can be reached by solving a polynomial algorithm (essentially, Belman-Ford longest path algorithm). For this example, this would lead to the schedule $\sigma(\text{B},k) = 3k$, $\sigma(\text{C},k) = 3k+3$, and $\sigma(\text{A},k) = 3k+4$, which meets the constraints and allows the execution of the loop on 4 processors (see Fig. 4).

Solving the problem for limited resources is NP-complete. Another lower bound is related to the number of processors available. If p processors are available, then $p\lambda \ge \sum_{v \in V} d(v)$. Intuitively, the total execution time available during one iteration on all processors ($p\lambda$) cannot be less than the total execution time needed to evaluate all tasks of an iteration.

Several heuristics have been proposed in the literature to approach this bound: loop compaction, loop shifting, modulo scheduling, etc. All these methods rely upon list scheduling, as presented in the Sect. "Task graphs and Scheduling". Notice, finally, that there exits *guaranteed heuristics* for solving this problem. One such heuristics combines loop compaction, loop shifting and retiming to obtain such a result.

Scheduling Multidimensional Loops

Scheduling unidimensional loops is based on the idea of avoiding unrolling the loop and therefore, of keeping

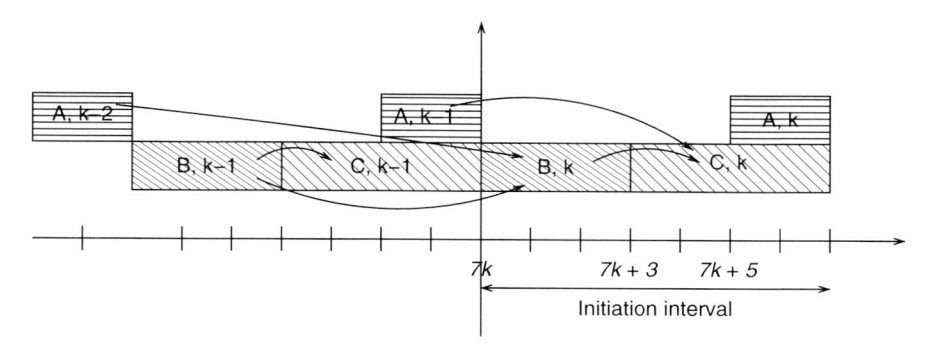

Scheduling Algorithms. Fig. 3 Execution of the loop with an initiation interval of 7. The corresponding schedule is $\sigma(A,k) = 7k+5$, $\sigma(B,k) = 7k$, and $\sigma(C,k) = 7k+3$

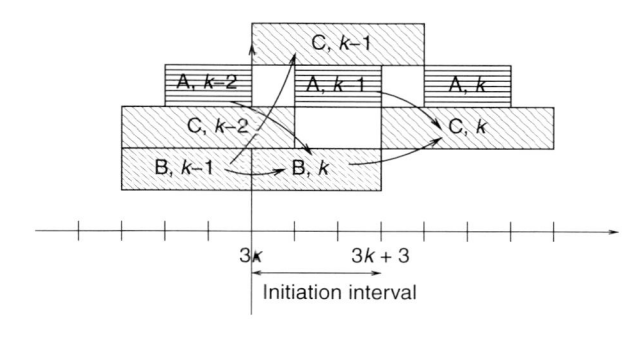

Scheduling Algorithms. Fig. 4 Execution of the loop with an optimal initiation interval of 3. The corresponding schedule is $\sigma(A,k) = 3k+4$, $\sigma(B,k) = 3k$, and $\sigma(C,k) = 3k+3$

the model compact and tractable, independently on the loop bound N. To this end, the schedule is chosen to be a linear expression of the loop index. The same idea can be pushed further: instead of unrolling a multiple index loop, one tries to express the schedule of an operation by a linear (or affine) function of the loop indexes. This technique can be applied to imperative loops, but it interacts deeply with the detection of dependences in the loop, making the problem more difficult. Another way of looking at this problem is to consider algorithms expressed as recurrence equations, where parallelism is directly exposed.

Consider the following recurrences for the matrix multiplication algorithm $C = AB$ where A, B, and C are square matrices of size N:

$$1 \leq i,j,k \leq N \rightarrow C(i,j,k) = C(i,j,k-1) + a(i,k) \times b(k,j) \quad (1)$$
$$1 \leq i,j \leq N \rightarrow c(i,j) = C(i,j,N). \quad (2)$$

Each one of these equations is a single assignment, and it expresses a recurrence, whose indexes belong to the set defined by the left-hand inequality. The first recurrence (1) defines how C is computed, where k represents the iteration index; the second recurrence (2) says that value $c(i,j)$ is obtained as the result of the evaluation of $C(i,j,k)$ for $k = N$.

An easy way to schedule these computations for parallelism is to find out a schedule t that is an affine function of all the indexes of these calculations. Assume that C has a schedule of the form $t(i,j,k) = \lambda_1 i + \lambda_2 j + \lambda_3 k + \alpha$; also, assume that the evaluation of equations take at least one cycle, one must have, from Eq. 1:

$$t(i,j,k) > t(i,j,k-1), \quad \forall i,j,k \text{ s.t. } 1 \leq i,j,k \leq N$$

or once simplified, $\lambda_3 > 0$. This defines a set of possible values for t, with simplest form $t(i,j,k) = k$ (coefficient α can be chosen arbitrarily equal to 0.) Once a schedule is found, it is possible to allocate the computations of a recurrence equation on a parallel architecture. A simple way of doing it is to use a linear allocation function: for the matrix multiplication example, one could take i and j as the number of the processors, which would result in a parallel matrix multiplication executed on a square grid-connected array of size N. But many other allocations are possible.

This simple example contains all the ingredients of loop parallelization techniques, as will be seen now.

First, notice that this kind of recurrence is particular: it is said to be *uniform*, as left-hand side operations depend uniformly on right-hand side expressions through a dependence of the form $(0,0,1)$ (such a dependence is a simple translation of the left-hand side index). In general, one can consider *affine recurrences* where any right-hand side index is an affine function of the left-hand side index.

Second, the set where the indexes must lie is an *integral convex polyhedron*, whose bounds may be parameterized by some symbolic values (here N for example).

This is not surprising: most of the loops that are of interest for parallelism share the property that array indexes are almost always affine, and that the index space of a loop can be modeled with a polyhedron.

Scheduling affine recurrences in general can be also done by extending the method. Assume that a recurrence has the form

$$\forall z \in P, V(z) = f(U(a(z)), ...)$$

where U and V are variables of a program, z is a n-dimensional integer vector, P is a polyhedron, and $a(z)$ is an affine mapping of z. The difference with the previous case is that the number of dependences may now be infinite: depending on the a function and the size of P, one may have a large, potentially infinite, number of dependences between instances of $V(z)$ and $U(a(z))$, for which the schedule t must meet $t(V(z)) > t(U(a(z)))$. However, properties of polyhedra may be used. A given polyhedron P may be represented equivalently by a set of inequalities, or by its set of generators, that is to say, its vertices, rays, and lines. Generators are in finite number, and it turns out that it is necessary and sufficient to check the property of t on vertices and rays, and this leads to a finite set of linear inequalities involving the coefficients of the t function. This is the basis of the so-called *vertex method* for scheduling recurrences. Another, equivalent method, called the *Farkas method*, involves directly the inequalities instead of the generator system of the polyhedron. In general, such methods lead to high complexity algorithms, but in practice, they are tractable: a typical simple algorithm leads to a few hundreds of linear constraints.

Without going into the details, these methods can be extended to cover interesting problems. First of all, it is not necessary to assume that all variables of the recurrences have the same schedule. One may instead suppose that variable V is scheduled with a function $t_V(i, j, ...) = \lambda_{V,1} i + \lambda_{V,2} j + ... + \alpha_V$ without making the problem more difficult. Secondly, one may also suppose that the schedule has several dimensions: if operation $V(z)$ is scheduled at time $\begin{pmatrix} t_{V,1}(z) \\ t_{V,2}(z) \end{pmatrix}$, then the time is understood as a lexicographical ordering. This allows modeling situations where more than one dimension of the index space are evaluated sequentially on a single processor, thus allowing architectures of various dimensions to be found.

Very few researches have yet explored scheduling loops under constraints, as was the case for cyclic scheduling.

A final remark: cyclic scheduling is a particular case of multidimensional scheduling, where the function has the form $\sigma(v, k) = \lambda k + \alpha_v$. Indeed, the α constant describes the relative time of execution of operation $v(k)$ during an iteration. In a similar way for higher-level recurrences, α_V plays the same rôle and allows one to refine the pipeline structure of one processor.

From Loops to Recurrences

The previous section (Sect. Scheduling Multi-Dimensional Loops) has shown how a set of recurrence equations can be scheduled using linear programming techniques. Here it is sketched how loops expressed in a some imperative language can be translated into single-assignment form that is equivalent to recurrence equations. Consider the following example:

```
for i := 0 to 2n do
    {S1}:  c[i] := 0.;
for i :=0 to n do
    for j := 0 to n do
        {S2}:  c[i+j] := c[i+j] +
               a[i]*b[j];
```

which computes the product of two polynomials of size $n+1$, where the coefficients of the input polynomials are in arrays a and b and the result in c. This program contains two loops, each one with one statement, labeled S1 and S2 respectively.

Each statement represents as many elementary *operations* as loop indexes surrounding it. Statement S1 corresponds to $2n + 1$ operations, denoted by $(S1, (i))$, and statement S2 corresponds to operations denoted $(S2, (i, j))$.

The left-hand side element of statement S2, c[i+j], writes several times in the same memory cell and its right-hand side makes use of the content of the same memory cell. In order to rewrite these loops as recurrence equations, one need to carry out a *data flow analysis* to find out which statement made the last modification to c[i+j]. Since both statement modify c, it may be either S2 itself, or S1.

Consider first the case when S2 is the source of the operation that modifies c[i+j] for operation (S2, (i,j)). Then this operation is (S2, (i',j')) where $i' + j' = i + j$, and indexes i' and j' must satisfy the limit constraints of the loops, that is, $0 \leq i' \leq n$ and $0 \leq j' \leq n$. There is another condition, also called *sequential predicate*: (S2, (i',j')) must be the operation that was the last to modify cell c[i+j] before (S2, (i,j)) uses it. But (i',j') is smaller than (i,j) in lexicographic order, and thus, (i',j') is the lexical maximum of (i,j). All these conditions being affine inequalities, it turns out that finding out the source index can be done using *parameterized linear programming*, resulting in a so-called *quasi-affine selection tree* (quast) whose conditions on indices are also linear. One would thus find out that

$(i', j') =$ if $i > 1 \wedge j < n$ then $(i-1, j+1)$ else $\bot$

where $\bot$ represents the situation when (i',j') was defined by a statement that precedes the loops.

Now if S1 is the source of the operation, this operation is (S1, i') where $i' = i + j$, and index i' must lay inside the bounds, thus $0 \leq i' \leq 2n$. Moreover, this operation must be executed before, which is obviously always true. Thus, it can be seen that $(i') = (i + j)$. Combining both expressions, one finds that the source of (i,j) is given by

if $i > 1 \wedge j < n$ then (S2, $i-1, j+1$) else (S1, $i+j$).

Once the source of each operation is found, rewriting the program as a system of recurrence equations is easy. For each statement S, a variable $S(i,j,\ldots)$ with as many indexes as surrounding loops is introduced, and the right hand side equation is rewritten by replacing expressions by their source translation. An extra equation can be provided to express the value of output variables of the program, here, c for example.

$$0 \leq i \leq 2n \rightarrow S1(i) = 0. \quad (3)$$

$$0 \leq i \leq n \wedge 0 \leq j \leq n \rightarrow S2(i,j) = \text{if } i > 1 \wedge j < n \quad (4)$$
$$\text{then } S1(i-1, j+1) + a(i) * b(j)$$
$$\text{else } S1(i+j) + a(i) * b(j) \quad (5)$$

$$0 \leq i \leq 2n \rightarrow c(i) = \text{if } j = 0 \text{ then } S2(i,j) \text{ else } S2(n,j) \quad (6)$$

The exact data flow analysis is a means of expressing implicit dependences that result from the encoding of the algorithm as loops. Although other methods exist in order to schedule loops without single assignement, this method is deeply related to scheduling techniques.

Scheduling Today and Future Directions

Loop scheduling is a central process of autoparallelization techniques, either implicit – when loops are rewritten after dependence analysis and then compiled, – or explicit, when the scheduling function is calculated and explicitly used during the parallelization process. Compilers incorporate more and more often sophisticated dependence and analysis tools to produce efficient code for target parallel architecture. Mono-dimensional loop scheduling is both used to massage loops for instruction-level parallelism, but also to design special-purpose hardware for embedded calculations. Finally, multi-dimensional scheduling is included in some autoparallelizers to produce code for parallel processors.

The need to produce efficient compilers is a limitation to the use of complex scheduling methods, as it has been shown that most practical problems are NP-complete. Progress in the knowledge of scheduling algorithms has made more and more likely for methods, previously rejected because of their complexity, to become common ingredients of parallelization tools. Moreover, the design of parallel programs tolerates a slightly longer production time than compiling everydays' program does, in particular because many applications of parallelism target embedded systems. Thus, the spreading of parallel computers – for example, GPU or multi-core – will certainly make these techniques useful.

Bibliographic Notes and Further Reading

Darte, Robert, and Vivien [2] wrote a reference book on scheduling for parallelism; it provides an in-depth coverage of the techniques presented here, in particular task scheduling and cyclic scheduling. It also provides a survey and comparison of various methods for dependence analysis. This entry borrows a large part of its material from this book.

El-Rewini, Lewis, and Ali give in [3] a survey on scheduling in general and task scheduling in particular. In [1], Benoit and Robert give complexity results for scheduling problems that are related to recent parallel platforms.

Lam [9] presents *software pipelining*, one of the most famous applications of cyclic scheduling to loops. Theoretical results on cyclic scheduling can be found in [7].

Karp, Miller, and Winograd [8] were among the first authors to consider scheduling for parallel execution, in a seminal paper on recurrence equations. Lamport [10] published one of the most famous papers on loop parallelization. Loop dependence analysis and loop transformations for parallelization are extensively presented by Zima and Chapman in [12]. Mauras, Quinton, Rajopadhye, and Saouter presented in [11] the vertex method to schedule affine recurrences, whereas Feautrier ([5] and [6]) describes the Farkas method for scheduling affine loop nests.

Data flow analysis is presented in great detail by Feautrier in [4].

Bibliography

1. Benoit A, Robert Y (Oct 2008) Complexity results for throughput and latency optimization of replicated and data-parallel workflows. Algorithmica 57(4):689–724
2. Darte A, Robert Y, Vivien F (2000) Scheduling and automatic parallelization. Birkhäuser, Boston
3. El-Rewini H, Lewis TG, Ali HH (1994) Task scheduling in parallel and distributed systems. Prentice Hall, Englewood Cliffs, New Jersey
4. Feautrier P (February 1991) Dataflow analysis of array and scalar references. Int J Parallel Program 20(1):23–53
5. Feautrier P (Oct 1992) Some efficient solutions to the affine scheduling problem, Part I, one dimensional time. Int J Parallel Program 21(5):313–347
6. Feautrier P (December 1992) Some efficient solutions to the affine scheduling problem, Part II, multidimensional time. Int J Parallel Program 21(6):389–420
7. Hanen C, Munier A (1995) Cyclic Scheduling on parallel processors: An overview. In: Chrétienne P, Coffman EG Jr, Lenstra K, Lia Z (eds) Scheduling theory and its applications. John Wiley & Sons
8. Karp RM, Miller RE, Winograd S (July 1967) The organization of computations for uniform recurrence equations. J Assoc Comput Machin 14(3):563–590
9. Lam MS (1988) Software pipelining: an effective scheduling technique for VLIW Machines. In: SIGPLAN'88 conference on programming language, design and implementation, Atlanta, GA. ACM Press, pp 318–328
10. Lamport L (Feb 1974) The parallel execution of DO loops. Commun ACM 17(2):83–93
11. Mauras C, Quinton P, Rajopadhye S, Saouter Y (September 1990) Scheduling affine parameterized recurrences by means of variable dependent timing functions. In: Kung SY, Schwartzlander EE, Fortes JAB, Przytula KW (eds) Application Specific Array Processors, Princeton University, IEEE Computer Society Press, pp 100–110
12. Zima H, Chapman B (1989) Supercompilers for Parallel and Vector Computers. ACM Press, New York

SCI (Scalable Coherent Interface)

HERMANN HELLWAGNER
Klagenfurt University, Klagenfurt, Austria

Synonyms

International standard ISO/IEC 13961:2000(E) and IEEE Std 1596, 1998 edition

Definition

Scalable Coherent Interface (SCI) is the specification (standardized by ISO/IEC and the IEEE) of a high-speed, flexible, scalable, point-to-point-based interconnect technology that was implemented in various ways to couple multiple processing nodes. SCI supports both the message-passing and shared-memory communication models, the latter in either the cache-coherent or non-coherent variants. SCI can be deployed as a system area network for compute clusters, as a memory interconnect for large-scale, cache-coherent, distributed-shared-memory multiprocessors, or as an I/O subsystem interconnect.

Discussion

Introduction

SCI originated in an effort of bus experts in the late 1980s to define a very high performance computer bus ("Superbus") that would support a significant degree of multiprocessing, i.e., number of processors. It was soon realized that backplane bus technology would not be able to meet this requirement, despite advanced concepts like split transactions and sophisticated implementations of the latest bus standards and products. The committee thus abandoned the bus-oriented view and developed novel distributed solutions to overcome the shared-resource and signaling problems of buses, while retaining the overall goal of defining an interconnect that offers the convenient services well known from centralized buses [3, 6].

The resulting specification of SCI, approved initially in 1992 [8] and finally in the late 1990s [9], thus describes hardware and protocols that provide processors with the shared-memory view of buses. SCI also specifies related transactions to read, write, and lock memory locations without software protocol involvement, as well as to transmit messages and interrupts. Hardware protocols to keep processor caches coherent are defined as an implementation option. The SCI interconnect, the memory system, and the associated protocols are fully distributed and scalable: an SCI network is based on point-to-point links only, implements a distributed shared memory (DSM) in hardware, and avoids serialization in almost any respect.

Goals of SCI's Development

Several ambitious goals guided the specification process of SCI [3, 5, 8].

High performance. The primary objective of SCI was to deliver high communication performance to parallel or distributed applications. This comprises:

- High sustained throughput;
- Low latency;
- Low CPU overhead for communication operations.

The performance goals set forth were in the range of Gbit/s link speeds and latencies in the low microseconds range in loosely-coupled systems, even less in tightly-coupled multiprocessors.

Scalability. SCI was devised to address scalability in many respects, among them [4]:

- Scalability of *performance* (aggregate bandwidth) as the number of nodes grows;
- Scalability of interconnect *distance*, from centimeters to tens of meters, depending on the media and physical layer implementation, but based on the same logical layer protocols;
- Scalability of the *memory system*, in particular of the *cache coherence protocols*, without a practical limit on the number of processors or memory modules that could be handled;

- *Technological scalability*, i.e., use of the same mechanisms in large-scale and small-scale as well as tightly-coupled and loosely-coupled systems, and the ability to readily make use of advances in technology, e.g., high-speed links;
- *Economic scalability*, i.e., use of the same mechanisms and components in low-end, high-volume and high-end, low-volume systems, opening the chance to leverage the economies of scale of mass production of SCI hardware;
- No short-term practical limits to the *addressing capability*, i.e., an addressing scheme for the DSM wide enough to support a large number of nodes and large node memories.

Coherent memory system. Caches are crucial for modern microprocessors to reduce average access time to data. This specifically holds for a DSM system with NUMA (non-uniform memory access) characteristics where remote accesses can be roughly an order of magnitude more expensive than local ones. To support a convenient programming model as known, e.g., from symmetric multiprocessors (SMPs), the caches should be kept coherent in hardware.

Interface characteristics. The SCI specification was intended to describe a standard interface to an interconnect to enable multiple devices from multiple vendors to be attached and to interoperate. In other words, SCI should serve as an "open distributed bus" connecting components like processors, memory modules, and intelligent I/O devices in a high-speed system.

Main Concepts of SCI

In the following, the main concepts and features of SCI will be summarized and the achievements, as represented by several implementations of SCI networks, will be assessed.

Point-to-point links. An SCI interconnect is defined to be built only from unidirectional, point-to-point links between participating nodes. These links can be used for concurrent data transfers, in contrast to the one-at-a-time communication characteristics of buses. The number of the links grows as nodes are added to the system, increasing the aggregate bandwidth of the network. The links can be made fast and their performance can scale with improvements in the underlying technology. They can be implemented in a bit-parallel manner (for small distances) or in a bit-serial fashion (for larger distances), with the same logical layer protocols. Most implementations use parallel links over distances of a few centimeters or meters.

Sophisticated signaling technology. The data transfer rates and lengths of shared buses are inherently limited due to signal propagation delays and signaling problems on the transmission lines. The unidirectional, point-to-point SCI links avoid such signaling problems. Since there is only a single transmitter and a single receiver rather than multiple devices, the signaling speed can be increased significantly. High speeds are also fostered by low-voltage differential signals.

Furthermore, SCI strictly avoids back-propagating signals, even reverse flow control on the links, in favor of high signaling speeds and scalability. Flow control information becomes part of the normal data stream in the reverse direction, leading to the requirement that an SCI node must at least have one outgoing link and one incoming link.

Already in the mid 1990s, SCI link implementation speeds reached 500 Mbyte/s in system area networks (distances of a few meters, 16-bit parallel links) and 1 Gbyte/s in closely-coupled, cache-coherent shared-memory multiprocessors; transfer rates of 1 Gbyte/s have also been demonstrated over a distance of about 100 m, using parallel fiber-optic links; see [6].

Nodes. SCI was designed to connect up to 64 k nodes. A node can be a complete workstation or server machine, a processor and its associated cache only, a memory module, I/O controllers and devices, or bridges to other buses or interconnects, as illustrated exemplarily in Fig. 1. Each node is required to have a standard interface to attach to the SCI network, as described in [3, 5, 8]. In most SCI systems implemented so far, nodes are complete machines, often even multiprocessors.

Topology independence. In principle, SCI networks with complex topologies could be built; investigations into this area are described in several chapters of [6]. However, the standard anticipates simple topologies to be used. For small systems, for instance, the preferred topology is a small ring (a so-called *ringlet*); for larger systems, topologies like a single switch connecting multiple ringlets, rings of rings, or multidimensional tori are feasible; see Fig. 1. Most SCI systems implemented used single rings, a switch, multiple rings, or two-dimensional tori.

Fixed addressing scheme. SCI uses the 64-bit fixed addressing scheme defined by the Control and Status

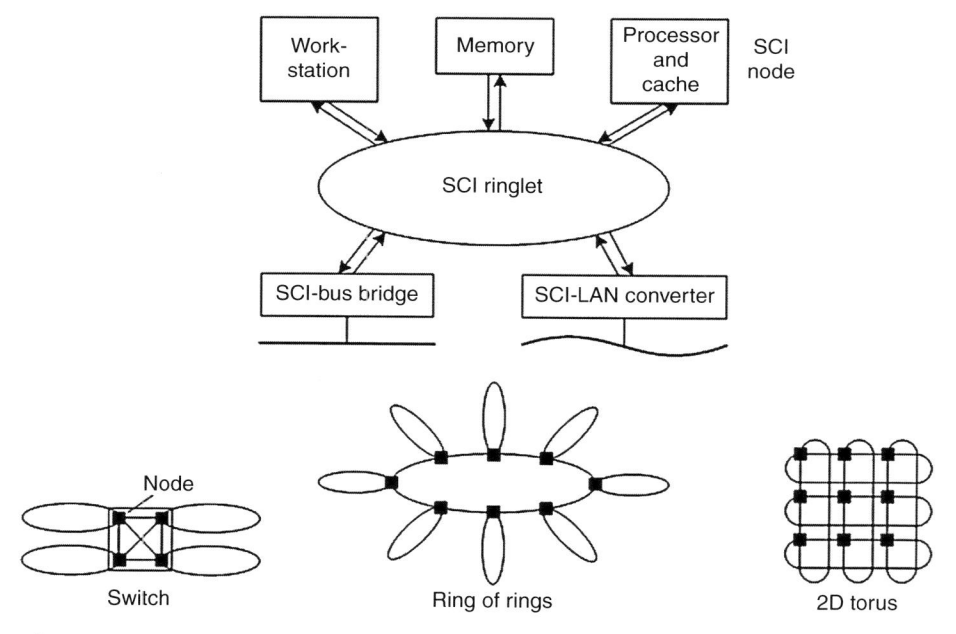

SCI (Scalable Coherent Interface). Fig. 1 Simple SCI network topologies

Register (CSR) Architecture standard (IEEE Std 1212-1991) [7]. The 64-bit SCI address is divided into two fixed parts: the most significant 16 address bits specify the node ID (node address) so that an SCI network can comprise up to 64 k nodes; the remaining 48 bits are used for addressing within the nodes, in compliance with the CSR Architecture standard.

Hardware-based distributed shared memory (DSM). The SCI addressing scheme spans a global, 64-bit address space; in other words, a physically addressed, distributed shared memory system. The distribution of the memory is transparent to software and even to processors, i.e., the memory is logically shared. A memory access by a processor is mediated to the target memory module by the SCI hardware.

The major advantage of this feature is that internode communication can be effected by simple load and store operations by the processor, without invocation of a software protocol stack. The instructions accessing remote memory can be issued at user level; the operating system need not be involved in communication. This results in very low latencies for SCI communication, typically in the low microseconds range.

A major implementation challenge, however, is how to integrate the SCI network (and, thus, access to the system-wide SCI DSM) with the memory architecture of a standard single-processor workstation or a multiprocessor node. The common solutions, attaching SCI to the I/O bus or to the memory bus, will be outlined below.

Bus-like services. To complete the hardware DSM, SCI defines transactions to read, write, and lock memory locations, functionality well-known from computer buses. In addition, message passing and global time synchronization are supported, both as defined by the CSR Architecture; interrupts can be delivered remotely as well. Broadcast functionality is also defined.

Transactions can be tagged with four different priorities. In order to avoid starvation of low-priority nodes, fair protocols for bandwidth allocation and queue allocation have been developed. Bandwidth allocation is similar in effect to bus arbitration in that it assigns transfer bandwidth (if scarce) to nodes willing to send. Queue allocation apportions space in the input queues of heavily loaded, shared nodes, e.g., memory modules or switch ports, which are targeted by many nodes simultaneously. Since the services have to be implemented in a fully distributed fashion, the underlying protocols are rather complex.

Split transactions. Like multiprocessor buses, SCI strictly splits transactions into *request* and *response* phases. This is a vital feature to avoid scalability impediments; it makes signaling speed independent of the distance a transaction has to travel and avoids monopolizing network links. Transactions therefore have to be self-contained and are sent as packets, containing a transaction ID, addresses, commands, status, and data as needed. A consequence is that multiple transactions can be outstanding per node. Transactions can thus be pumped into the network at a high rate, using the interconnect in a pipeline fashion.

Optional cache coherence. SCI defines distributed cache coherence protocols, based on a distributed-directory approach, a multiple readers – single writer sharing regime, and write invalidation. The memory coherence model is purposely left open to the implementer. The standard provides optimizations for common situations such as pair-wise sharing that improve performance of frequent coherence operations.

The cache coherence protocols are designed to be implemented in hardware; however, they are highly sophisticated and complex. The complexity stems from a large number of states of coherent memory and cache blocks, correspondingly complex state transitions, and the advanced algorithms that ensure atomic modifications of the distributed-directory information (e.g., insertions, deletions, invalidations). The greatest complication arises from the integration of the SCI coherence protocols with the snooping protocols typically employed on the nodes' memory buses. An implementation is highly challenging and incurs some risks and potentially high costs. Not surprisingly, only a few companies have done implementations, as described below.

The cache coherence protocols are provided as options only. A compliant SCI implementation need not cover coherence; an SCI network even cannot participate in coherence actions when it is attached to the I/O bus as is the case in compute clusters. Yet, a common misconception was that cache coherence was required functionality at the core of SCI. This misunderstanding has clearly hindered SCI's proliferation for non-coherent uses, e.g., as a system area network.

Reliability in hardware. In order to enable high-speed transmission, error detection is done in hardware, based on a 16-bit CRC code which protects each SCI packet. Transactions and hardware protocols are provided that allow a sender to detect failure due to packet corruption, and allow a receiver to notify the sender of its inability to accept packets (due to a full input queue) or to ask the sender to re-send the packet. Since this happens on a per-packet basis, SCI does not automatically guarantee in-order delivery of packets. This may have a considerable impact on software which would rely on a guaranteed packet sequence. An example is a message passing library delivering data into a remote buffer using a series of remote write transactions and finally updating the tail pointer of the buffer. Some SCI hardware provides functionality to enforce a certain memory access order, e.g., via memory barriers [6].

Various time-outs are provided to detect lost packets or transmission errors. Hardware retry mechanisms or software recovery protocols may be implemented based on transmission-error detection and isolation mechanisms; these are however not part of the standard. As a consequence, SCI implementations differed widely in the way errors are dealt with.

The protocols are designed to be robust, i.e., they should, e.g., survive the failure of a node with outstanding transactions. Among other mechanisms, error containment and logging procedures, ringlet maintenance functions and a packet time-out scheme are specified. Robustness is particularly important for the cache coherence protocols which are designed to behave correctly even if a node fails amidst the modification of a distributed-directory entry.

Layered specification. The SCI specification is structured into three layers.

At the *physical layer*, three initial physical link models are defined: a parallel electrical link operating at 1 Gbyte/s over short distances (meters); a serial electrical link that operates at 1 Gbit/s over intermediate distances (tens of meters); and a serial optical link that operates at 1 Gbit/s over long distances (kilometers).

Although the definitions include the electrical, mechanical, and thermal characteristics of SCI modules, connectors, and cables, the specifications were not adhered to in implementations. SCI systems typically used vendor-specific physical layer implementations, incompatible to others. It is fair to say, therefore, that SCI has not become the open, distributed interconnect system that the designers had envisaged to create.

The *logical layer* specifies transaction types and protocols, packet types and formats, packet encodings, the standard node interface structure, bandwidth and queue allocation protocols, error processing, addressing and initialization issues, and SCI-specific CSRs.

The *cache coherence layer* provides concepts and hardware protocols that allow processors to cache remote memory blocks while still maintaining coherence among multiple copies of the memory contents. Since an SCI network no longer has a central resource (i.e., a memory bus) that can be snooped by all attached processors to effect coherence actions, distributed-directory-based solutions to the cache coherence problem had to be devised.

At the core of the cache coherence protocols are the distributed sharing lists shown in Fig. 2. Each shared block of memory has an associated distributed, doubly-linked sharing list of processors that hold a copy of the block in their local caches. The memory controller and the participating processors cooperatively and concurrently create and update a block's sharing list, depending on the operations on the data.

C code. A remarkable feature of the SCI standard is that major portions are provided in terms of a "formal" specification, namely, C code. Text and figures are considered explanatory only, the definitive specification are the C listings. Exceptions are packet formats and the physical layer specifications. The major reasons for this approach are that C code is (largely) unambiguous and not easily misunderstood and that the specification becomes executable, as a simulation. In fact, much of the specification was validated by extensive simulations before release.

Implementations and Applications of SCI

SCI was originally conceived as a shared-memory interconnect, but SCI's flexibility and performance potential

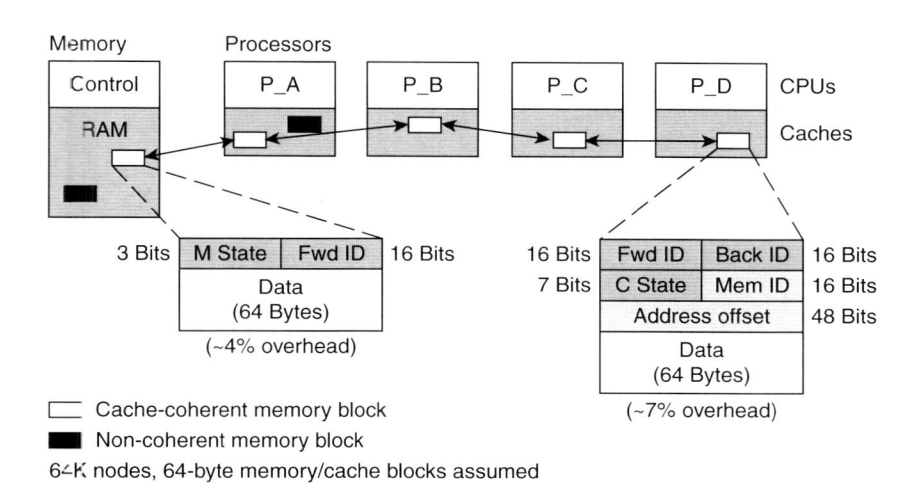

SCI (Scalable Coherent Interface). Fig. 2 Sharing list and coherence tags of SCI cache coherence protocols

also for other applications was soon realized and leveraged by industry. In the following, a few of these "classical" applications of SCI are introduced and examples of commercial systems that exploited SCI technology are provided.

System Area Network for Clusters

In compute clusters, an SCI system area network can provide high-performance communication capabilities. In this application, the SCI interconnect is attached to the I/O bus of the nodes (e.g., PCI) by a peripheral adapter card, very similar to a LAN; see Fig. 3. In contrast to "standard" LAN technology and most other system area networks, though, the SCI cluster network, by virtue of the common SCI address space and associated transactions, provides hardware-based, *physical* distributed shared memory. Figure 4 shows a high-level view of the DSM. An SCI cluster thus is more tightly coupled than a LAN-based cluster, exhibiting the characteristics of a NUMA parallel machine.

The SCI adapter cards, together with the SCI driver software, establish the DSM as depicted in Fig. 4. (This description pertains to the solutions taken by the pioneering vendor, Dolphin Interconnect Solutions, for their SBus-SCI and PCI-SCI adapter cards [2, 6].) A node that is willing to share memory with other nodes (e.g., *A*), creates shared memory segments in its physical memory and exports them to the SCI network (i.e., SCI address space). Other nodes (e.g., *B*) import these DSM segments into their I/O address space. Using on-board address translation tables (ATTs), the SCI adapters maintain the mappings between their local I/O addresses and the global SCI addresses. Processes on the nodes (e.g., *i* and *j*) may further map DSM segments into their virtual address spaces. The latter mappings are conventionally being maintained by the processors' MMUs.

Once the mappings have been set up, inter-node communication may be performed by the participating processes at *user level*, by simple CPU load and store operations into DSM segments mapped from remote memories. The SCI adapters translate I/O bus transactions that result from such memory accesses into SCI transactions, and vice versa, and perform them on behalf of the requesting processor. Thus, remote memory accesses are both transparent to the requesting processes and do not need intervention by the operating system. In other words, no protocol stack is involved in remote memory accesses, resulting in low communication latencies.

In the 1990s, the prevailing commercial implementations of such SCI cluster networks were the SBus-SCI and PCI-SCI adapter cards (and associated switches) offered by Dolphin Interconnect Solutions [2]. These cluster products were used by other companies to build key-turn cluster platforms; examples were Sun Microsystems, offering high-performance, high-availability server clusters, and Scali Computers and Siemens providing clusters for parallel computing based on MPI; see [6]. Similar SCI adapters are still offered at the time of writing and are being used in embedded systems, e.g., medical devices such as CT scanners [2].

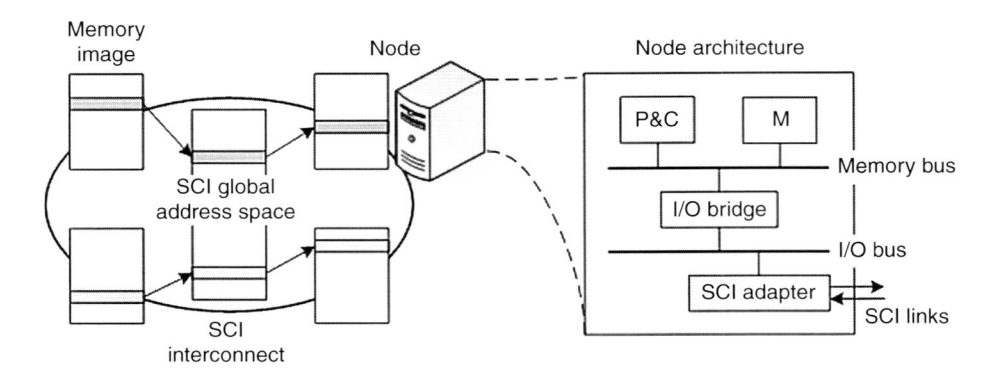

SCI (Scalable Coherent Interface). Fig. 3 SCI cluster model

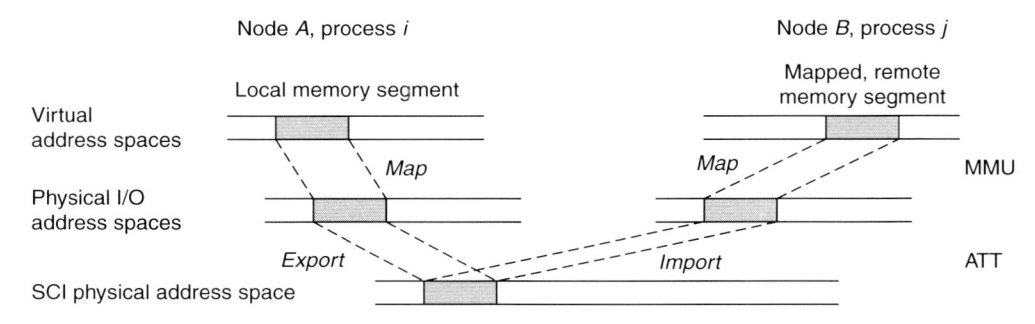

SCI (Scalable Coherent Interface). Fig. 4 Address spaces and address translations in SCI clusters

In addition, there were research implementations of adapter cards, among them one developed at CERN as a prototype to investigate SCI's feasibility and performance for demanding data acquisition systems in high-energy physics, i.e., in one of the LHC experiments; see [6].

The description of an SCI cluster interconnect given above does not address many of the low-level problems and functionality that the implementation has to cover. For instance, issues like the translation of 32-bit node addresses to 64-bit SCI addresses and vice versa, the choice of the shared segment size, error detection and handling, high-performance data transfers between node hardware and SCI adapter, and the design and implementation of low-level software (SCI drivers) as well as message-passing software (e.g., MPI) represent a spectrum of research and development problems. Several contributions in [6] describe these problems and corresponding solutions in some detail.

An important property of such SCI cluster interconnect adapters is worth pointing out here. Since an SCI cluster adapter attaches to the I/O bus of a node, it cannot directly observe, and participate in, the traffic on the memory bus of the node. This therefore precludes caching and coherence maintenance of memory regions mapped to the SCI address space. In other words, remote memory contents are basically treated as non-cacheable and are always accessed remotely. Standard SCI cluster interconnect hardware does not implement cache coherence capabilities therefore. This property raises a performance concern: remote accesses (round-trip operations such as reads) must be used judiciously since they are still an order of magnitude more expensive than local memory accesses (NUMA characteristics).

The basic approach to deal with the latter problem is to avoid remote operations that are inherently round-trip, i.e., reads, as far as possible. Rather, remote writes are used which are typically buffered by the SCI adapter and therefore, from the point of view of the processor issuing the write, experience latencies in the range of local accesses, several times faster than remote read operations. Again in [6], several chapters describe how considerations like this influence the design and implementation of efficient message-passing libraries on top of SCI.

Finally, several contributions in [6] deal with how to overcome the limitations of non-coherent SCI cluster hardware, in particular for the implementation of shared-memory and shared-object programming models. Techniques from software DSM systems, e.g., replication and software coherence maintenance, are applied to provide a more convenient abstraction, e.g., a common virtual address space spanning all the nodes in the SCI cluster.

Memory Interconnect for Cache-Coherent Multiprocessors

The use of SCI as a cache-coherent memory interconnect allows nodes to be even more tightly coupled than in a non-coherent cluster. This application requires SCI to be attached to the memory bus of a node, as shown in Fig. 5. At this attachment point, SCI can participate in and "export," if necessary, the memory and cache coherence traffic on the bus and make the node's memory visible and accessible to other nodes. The nodes' memory address ranges (and the address mappings of processes) can be laid out to span a global (virtual) address space, giving processes transparent and coherent access to memory anywhere in the system. Typically, this approach is adopted to connect multiple bus-based commodity SMPs to form a large-scale, cache-coherent (CC) shared-memory system, often termed a CC-NUMA machine.

There were three notable examples of SCI-based CC-NUMA machines: the HP/Convex Exemplar series [1], the Sequent NUMA-Q multiprocessor [10], and the Data General AViiON scalable servers (see [6]). The latter two systems comprised bus-based SMP nodes with Intel processors, while the Exemplar used HP PA-RISC processors and a non-blocking crossbar switch within the nodes. The inter-node memory interconnects were proprietary implementations of the SCI standard, with specific adaptations and optimizations incorporated to ease implementation and integration with the node architecture and to foster overall performance.

The major challenge in building a CC-NUMA machine is to bridge the cache coherence mechanisms on the intra-node interconnect (e.g., the SMP bus running a snooping protocol) and the inter-node network (SCI). Since it is well documented, the Sequent NUMA-Q machine is used as a case study in [6] to illustrate the essential issues in building such a bridge and making the protocols interact correctly.

I/O Subsystem Interconnect

SCI can be used to connect one or more I/O subsystems to a computing system in novel ways. The shared SCI address space can include the I/O nodes which then are enabled to directly transfer data between the peripheral devices (in most cases, disks) and the compute nodes' memories using DMA; software needs not be involved in the actual transfer. Remote peripheral devices in a cluster, for instance, thus can become accessible like local devices, resulting in an I/O model similar to SMPs; remote interrupt capability can also be provided via SCI. High bandwidth and low latency, in addition to the direct remote memory access capability, make SCI an interesting candidate for an I/O network.

There were two commercial implementations of SCI-based I/O system networks. One was the GigaRing channel from SGI/Cray [12], the other one the

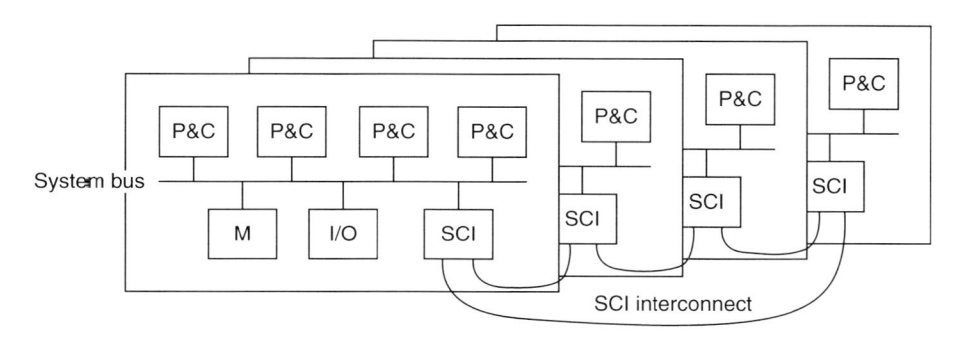

SCI (Scalable Coherent Interface). Fig. 5 SCI based CC-NUMA Multiproccessor Model

external I/O subsystem interconnect of the Siemens RM600 Enterprise Servers, based on Dolphin's cluster technology; see again [6].

Concluding Remarks

SCI addresses difficult interconnect problems and specifies innovative distributed structures and protocols for a scalable DSM architecture. The specification covers a wide spectrum of bus, network, and memory architecture problems, ranging from signaling considerations up to distributed directory-based cache coherence mechanisms.

In fact, this wide scope of SCI has raised criticism that the standard is actually "several standards in one" and difficult to understand and work with. This lack of a clear profile and the wide applicability of SCI have probably contributed to its relatively modest acceptance in industry. Furthermore, the SCI protocols are complex (albeit well devised) and not easily implemented in silicon. Thus, implementations are quite complex and therefore expensive.

In an attempt to reduce complexity and optimize speed, many of the implementers adopted the concepts and protocols which they regarded as appropriate for their application, and left out or changed other features according to their needs. This use of SCI led to a number of proprietary, incompatible implementations.

As a consequence, the goal of economic scalability has not been satisfactorily achieved in general. Further, SCI has clearly also missed the goal of evolving into an "open distributed bus" that multiple devices from different vendors could attach to and interoperate.

However, in terms of the technical objectives, predominantly high performance and scalability, SCI has well achieved its ambitious goals. The vendors that have adopted and implemented SCI (in various flavors), offered innovative high-throughput, low-latency interconnect products or full-scale cache-coherent shared-memory multiprocessing systems, as described above.

SCI had noticeable influence on further developments, e.g., interconnect standard projects like Sync-Link, a high-speed memory interface, and Serial Express (SerialPlus), an extension to the SerialBus (IEEE 1394) interconnect. SCI also played a role in the debate on "future I/O systems" in the late 1990s, which then led to the InfiniBand™ Architecture. The latest developments on SCI are explored in more detail in the final chapter of [6].

Related Entries

▶Buses and Crossbars
▶Cache Coherence
▶Clusters
▶Distributed-Memory Multiprocessor
▶InfiniBand
▶Myrinet
▶NOW
▶Nonuniform Memory Access (NUMA) Machines
▶Quadrics
▶Shared-Memory Multiprocessors

Bibliographic Notes and Further Reading

SCI was standardized and deployed in the 1990s. David B. Gustavson, one of the main designers, provides first-hand information on SCI's origins, development, and concepts [3, 4, 5]; even the standard document is stimulating material [8, 9]. Gustavson also maintained a Website that actively traced and documented the activities around SCI and related standards [11].

In the late 1990s, the interest in SCI largely disappeared. However, [6] was published as a comprehensive (and somehow concluding) summary of the technology, research and development projects, and achievements around SCI. For many projects and products, the corresponding chapters in [6] are the only documentation still available in the literature; in particular, information on products has disappeared from the Web meanwhile, but is still available to some extent in this book for reference.

This entry of the encyclopedia is a condensed version of the introductory chapter of [6].

Bibliography

1. Brewer T, Astfalk G (1997) The evolution of the HP/Convex Exemplar. In: Proceedings of COMPCON, San Jose
2. Dolphin Interconnect Solutions (2009) http://www.dolphinics.com. Accessed October 2009
3. Gustavson DB, (1992) The Scalable Coherent Interface and related standards projects. IEEE Micro 12(1):10–22

4. Gustavson DB (1994) The many dimensions of scalability. In: Proceedings of the COMPCON Spring, San Francisco
5. Gustavson DB Li Q (1996) The Scalable Coherent Interface (SCI). IEEE Comm Mag 348:52–63
6. Hellwagner H, Reinefeld A (eds) (1999) SCI: Scalable Coherent Interface. Architecture and software for high-performance compute clusters. LNCS vol 1734, Springer, Berlin
7. IEEE Std 1212-1991 (1991) IEEE standard Control and Status Register (CSR) Architecture for microcomputer buses
8. IEEE Std 1596-1992 (1993) IEEE standard for Scalable Coherent Interface (SCI)
9. International Standard ISO/IEC 13961:2000(E) and IEEE Std 1596, 1998 Edition (2000) Information technology - Scalable Coherent Interface (SCI). ISO/IEC and IEEE
10. Lovett T, Clapp R (1996) STiNG: a CC-NUMA computer system for the commercial marketplace. In: Proceedings of the 23rd Internationl Symposium on Computer Architecture (ISCA), May 1996, Philadelphia
11. SCIzzL: the local area memory port, local area multiprocessor, Scalable Coherent Interface and Serial Express users, developers, and manufacturers association. http://www.scizzl.com. Accessed October 2009
12. Scott S (1996) The GigaRing channel. IEEE Micro 16(1):27–34

Semantic Independence

Martin Fränzle[1], Christian Lengauer[2]
[1]Carl von Ossietzky Universität, Oldenburg, Germany
[2]University of Passau, Passau, Germany

Definition

Two program fragments are semantically independent if their computations are mutually irrelevant. A consequence for execution is that they can be run on separate processors in parallel, without any synchronization or data exchange. This entry describes a relational characterization of semantic independence for imperative programs.

Discussion

Introduction

The most crucial analysis for the discovery of parallelism in a sequential, imperative program is the dependence analysis. This analysis tells which program operations must definitely be executed in the order prescribed by the source code (see the entries on dependences and dependence analysis). The conclusion is that all others can be executed in either order or in parallel.

The converse problem is that of discovering independence. Program fragments recognized as independent may be executed in either order or in parallel, all others must be executed in the order prescribed by the source code.

The search for dependences is at the basis of an automatic program parallelizer (see the entries on autoparallelization and on the polyhedron model). The determination of the independence of two program fragments is a software engineering technique that can help to map a specific application program to a specific parallel or distributed architecture or it can tell something specific about the information flow in the overall program.

While the search for dependences or independences has to be based on some form of analysis of the program text, the criteria underlying such an – in any Turing-complete programming language necessarily incomplete – analysis should be semantic. The reason is that the syntactic form of the source program will make certain (in)dependences easy to recognize and will occlude others. It is therefore much wiser to define independence in a model which does not entail such an arbitrary bias. An appropriate model for the discovery of independence between fragments of an imperative program is the relation between its input states and its output states.

Central Idea and Program Example

Program examples adhere to the following notational conventions:

- The value sets of variables are specified by means of a declaration of the form var $x, y, \ldots : \{0, \ldots, n\}$, for $n \geq 1$ (that is, they are finite).
- If the value set is $\{0, 1\}$, Boolean operators are used with their usual meaning, where the number 0 is identified with false and 1 with true.
- Boolean operators bind more tightly than arithmetic ones.

The initial paper on semantic independence [2] contains a number of illustrative examples. The most complex one, Example 4, shall serve here as a guide:

$$\text{var } x, y, z : \{0, 1\};$$
$$\alpha_1 : \quad (x, y) := (x \wedge z, y \wedge \neg z)$$
$$\alpha_2 : \quad (x, y) := (x \wedge \neg z, y \wedge z)$$

The question is whether the effect of these two distinct multiple assigments can be achieved by two independent operations which could be executed mutually in parallel. At first glance, it does not seem possible, since x and y are subject to update and are both shared by both statements. However, this is due to the particular syntactic form of the program. One should not judge independence by looking at the program text but by looking at a semantic model.

One suitable model is a graph of program state transitions. The graph for the program above is depicted in Fig. 1. The nodes are program states. A program state consists of the three binary values of variables x, y, and z. State transitions are modelled by arrows between states. Solid arrows depict transitions of statement α_1, dashed arrows transitions of statement α_2.

The question to be answered in order to determine independence on any platform is: is there a transformation of the program's state space which leads to variables that can be accessed independently? It is not sufficient to require updates to be independent but allow reading to be shared, because the goal is to let semantically independent program fragments access disjoint pieces of memory. This obviates a cache coherence protocol in a multiprocessor system and improves the utilization of the cache space. Some special-purpose platforms, for example, systolic arrays, disallow shared reading altogether; see the entry on systolic arrays. Consequently, all accesses – writing and reading – must be independent.

For the example, there is such a transformation of the variables x, y, and z to new variables V and W:

$$\text{var } V : \{0,1\},\ W : \{0,1,2,3\};$$
$$V = (x \wedge \neg z) \vee (y \wedge z)$$
$$W = 2 * z + (x \wedge z) \vee (y \wedge \neg z)$$

The transformation is depicted in Fig. 2. The figure shows the same state graph as Fig. 1 but imposes two partitionings on the state space. The set ρ_1 of the two amorphously encased partitions yields the two-valued variable V. As denoted in the figure, each partition models one distinct value of the variable. The set ρ_2 of the four rectangularly encased partitions yields the four-valued variable W. The partitionings must – and do – satisfy certain constraints to be made precise below.

The semantically equivalent program that results is:

$$\text{var } V : \{0,1\},\ W : \{0,1,2,3\};$$
$$\alpha'_1 : \quad V := 0$$
$$\alpha'_2 : \quad W := 2 * (W \,\text{div}\, 2)$$

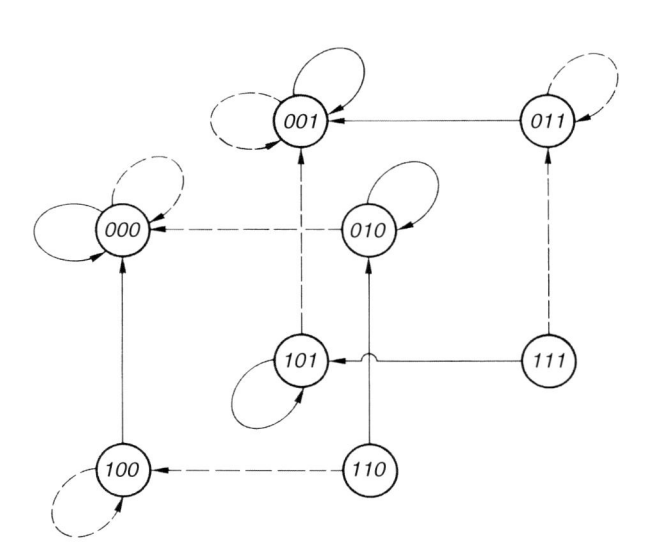

Semantic Independence. Fig. 1 State relations of the program example

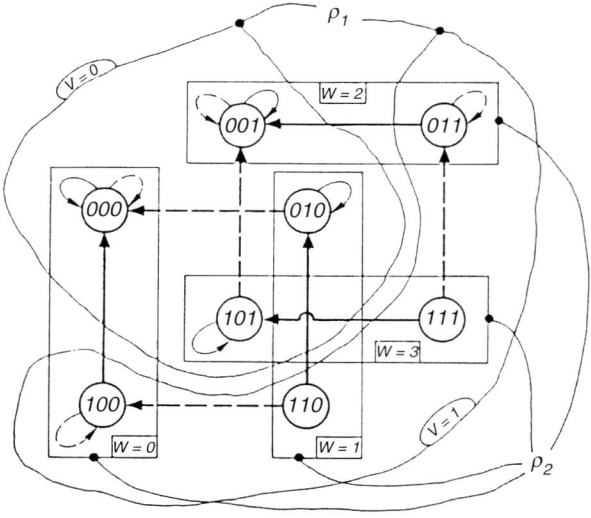

Semantic Independence. Fig. 2 State relations of the program example, partitioned

As is plainly evident, the new statements α'_1 and α'_2 access distinct variable spaces and are, thus, trivially independent. In Fig. 2, this property is reflected by the fact that α_1 (and, thus, α'_1) transitions are exclusively inside partitions of partitioning ρ_2 and α_2 (and, thus, α'_2) transitions exclusively inside partitions of partitioning ρ_1.

The notion of semantic independence illustrated above and formalized below specifies a transformation of the state space that induces two partitionings, each covering one update in the transformed state space, such that both updates can be performed in parallel, without any need for shared access to program variables: they are completely independent in the sense that no information flows between them.

If the parallel updates depend on a common context, that is, they constitute only a part of the overall program, the transformations between the original and the transformed state space must become part of the implementation. Then, the transformation from the original to the transformed space may require multiple read accesses to variables in the original state space and the backtransformation may require multiple read accesses to variables in the transformed state space. Depending on the abilities of the hardware, the code for these transformations may or may not be parallelizable (see the section on disjoint parallelism and its limitations).

Formal Definition

The first objective of this subsection is the independence of two imperative program fragments, as illustrated in the example. The generalization to more than two program fragments as well as to the interior of a single fragment follows subsequently.

Independence Between Two Statements

A transformation of the state space can be modelled as a function

$$\eta : X \to Y$$

from a state space X to a state space Y. In this subsection, consider two program fragments, R and S, which are modelled as relations on an arbitrary (finite, countable, or uncountable) state space X:

$$R \subseteq X \times X \text{ and } S \subseteq X \times X.$$

η is supposed to expose binary independence. This leads to a partitioning of state space Y, that is, Y should be the Cartesian product of two nontrivial, that is, neither empty nor singleton state spaces A and B:

$$Y = A \times B.$$

Desired are two new program fragments $R' \subseteq Y \times Y$ and $S' \subseteq Y \times Y$, such that R' operates solely on A and S' operates solely on B. Given two relations

$$r \subseteq A \times A \text{ and } s \subseteq B \times B$$

denote their product relation as follows:

$$r \otimes s = \{((a,b),(a',b')) \mid (a,a') \in r, (b,b') \in s\}$$
$$\subseteq (A \times B) \times (A \times B)$$

Also, write I_M for the identity relation on set M, that is, the relation $\{(m,m) \mid m \in M\}$. Then, the above requirement that R' and S' operate solely on A and B, respectively, amounts to requiring that

$$R' = (r \otimes I_B) \text{ and } S' = (I_A \otimes s).$$

for appropriate relations $r \subseteq A \times A$ and $s \subseteq B \times B$.

Furthermore, the composition of R' and S' should exhibit the same input–output behavior on the image $\eta(X) \subseteq Y$ of the transformation η as the composition of R and S on X. Actually, this requirement has been strengthened to a mutual correspondence in order to avoid useless parallelism in which either R' or S' does the full job of both R and S: R' must behave on its part of $\eta(X)$ like R on X and S' like S. With relational composition denoted as left-to-right juxtaposition, that is,

$$r\,s = \{(x,y) \mid \exists z : (x,z) \in r \land (z,y) \in s\},$$

the formal requirement is:

$$R\,\eta = \eta\,R' \text{ and } S\,\eta = \eta\,S'.$$

In order to guarantee a correspondence between the resulting output state in Y and its equivalent in X, there is one more requirement: η's relational inverse $\eta^{-1} = \{(y,x) \mid y = \eta(x)\}$, when applied to $\eta(X)$, must not incur a loss of information of a poststate generated by program fragments R or S. This is expressed by the two equations:

$$R = \eta\,R'\,\eta^{-1} \text{ and } S = \eta\,S'\,\eta^{-1}$$

Figure 3 depicts the previous two requirements as commuting diagrams, on the left for relation R and on the right for relation S. The dashed arrows represent the former and the dashed-dotted arrows the latter requirement. Together they imply:

$$R = R\eta\eta^{-1} \quad \text{and} \quad S = S\eta\eta^{-1}.$$

It is neither a consequence that η^{-1} is a function when confined to the images of R or S, nor that it is total on these images. However, if $\eta\eta^{-1}$ contains two states (x, y) and (x, y'), then y and y' are R-equivalent (and S-equivalent) in the sense that $(z, y) \in R$ iff $(z, y') \in R$, for each $z \in X$ (and likewise for S), that is, y and y' occur as poststates of exactly the same prestates. If R (or S) is a total function, which is the case for deterministic programs, then η^{-1} restricted to the image of R (or S, respectively) must be a total function.

Putting all requirements together, one arrives at the following definition of semantic independence between two imperative program fragments.

Definition 1 (Semantic independence [4]) *Two relations R and S on the state set X are called* semantically independent *if there are nontrivial (i.e., cardinality > 1) sets A and B, relations r on A and s on B, and a function $\eta : X \to A \times B$ such that*

$$R\eta = \eta(r \otimes I_B), \quad R\eta\eta^{-1} = R, \quad \text{and}$$
$$S\eta = \eta(I_A \otimes s), \quad S\eta\eta^{-1} = S. \qquad (1)$$

Under the conditions of Eq. 1, R is simulated by r in the sense that

$$R = R\eta\eta^{-1} = \eta(r \otimes I_B)\eta^{-1}$$

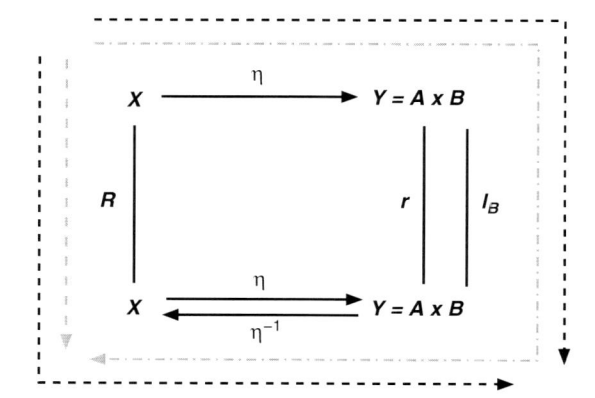

and, likewise, S by s due to

$$S = S\eta\eta^{-1} = \eta(I_A \otimes s)\eta^{-1}.$$

That is, after applying state transformation η, an effect equivalent to R can be obtained by executing r, with the result to be extracted by transforming the state space back via η^{-1}. The gain is that r only operates on the first component A of the transformed state space, not interfering with s which, in turn, simulates S on the second component B.

An immediate consequence of Definition 1 is that semantically independent relations commute with respect to relational composition, which models sequential composition in relational semantics. Take again R and S:

$$\begin{aligned}
&& R\,S \\
&=& R\,S\,\eta\,\eta^{-1} \\
&=& R\,\eta\,(I_A \otimes s)\,\eta^{-1} \\
&=& \eta\,(r \otimes I_B)(I_A \otimes s)\,\eta^{-1} \\
&=& \eta\,(I_A \otimes s)\,(r \otimes I_B)\,\eta^{-1} \\
&=& S\,\eta\,(r \otimes I_B)\,\eta^{-1} \\
&=& S\,R\,\eta\,\eta^{-1} \\
&=& S\,R
\end{aligned}$$

However, the converse is not true: semantic independence is more discriminative than commutativity. Intuitively, it has to be, since semantic independence

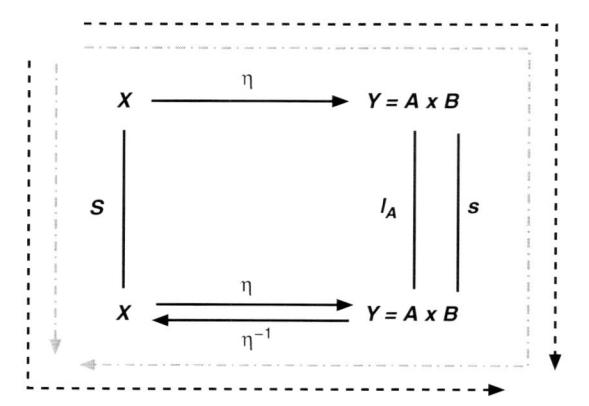

Semantic Independence. **Fig. 3** Two requirements on semantic independence

must ensure truly parallel execution, without the risk of interference, while commutativity may hold for interfering program fragments. A case of two program fragments which commute but are not semantically independent was provided as Example 5 in the initial paper [2]:

var $x : \{0,1,2,3\}$;
$\alpha_1 :\quad x := (x+1) \mod 4$
$\alpha_2 :\quad x := (x+2) \mod 4$

To prove the dependence, consider the projection of a Cartesian product to its first component:

$\downarrow_1 : A \times B \to A$
$\downarrow_1 ((a,b)) = a$

Since α_1 corresponds to a transition relation that is a total and surjective function on $X = \{0,1,2,3\}$, $\eta \downarrow_1$ is necessarily a bijection between X and A whenever η satisfies Eq. 1. Consequently, relation S', which implements α_2 in the transformed state space, cannot leave the first component A of the transformed state space $A \times B$ unaffected, that is, it cannot be of the form $(I_A \otimes s)$, since α_2 is not the identity on X.

As pointed out before, the example in Fig. 1 is semantically independent in the sense of Definition 1. Taking $A = \{0,1\}$, that is, as the domain of variable V from the transformation on page 2, and $B = \{0,1,2,3\}$, that is, as the domain of variable W, and taking

$\eta(x,y,z) = ((x \wedge \neg z) \vee (y \wedge z), 2*z + (x \wedge z) \vee (y \wedge \neg z))$,

the two relations

$s = \{(a,0) \mid a \in A\}$ and $r = \{(b, 2*(b \text{ div } 2)) \mid b \in B\}$

satisfy Eq. 1. These two relations s and r are the relational models of the assignments α_1' and α_2' on page 4.

Mutual Independence Between More than Two Fragments

Semantic independence is easily extended to arbitrarily many program fragments. To avoid subscripts, consider only three program fragments given as relations R, S, T on the state set X, which illustrates the general case sufficiently. These relations are called semantically independent if they correspond to relations r, s, t on three nontrivial sets A, B, C, respectively, such that there is a function

$\eta : X \to A \times B \times C$

that can be used to represent R, S and T by the product relations

$r \otimes I_B \otimes I_C, \quad I_A \otimes s \otimes I_C, \quad I_A \otimes I_B \otimes t$

respectively. For R, this representation has the form

$R\eta = \eta(r \otimes I_B \otimes I_C)$.

As before, the requirement is that $R\eta\eta^{-1} = R$. Relations S and T are represented analogously and are subject to corresponding requirements.

These conditions are considerably stronger than requiring the three pairwise independences of R with ST, of S with RT, and of T with RS. The individual checks of the latter may use up to three different transformations η_1 to η_3 in Eq. 1. This freedom of choice does not capture semantic independence adequately.

Independence Inside a Single Statement

Up to this point, an underlying assumption has been that a limit of the granularity of parallelization is given by the imperative program fragments considered. At the finest possible level of granularity, these are individual assigment statements. If some such assignment statement contains an expression whose evaluation one would like to parallelize, one must break it up into several assignments to intermediate variables and demonstrate their independence.

One can go one step further and ask for the potential parallelism within a single statement. The question then is whether there exists a transformation that permits a slicing of the statement into various independent ones in order to obtain a parallel implementation.

An appropriate condition for semantic independence within a single statement given as a relation $R \subseteq X \times X$ is that X can be embedded into a nontrivial Cartesian product $A \times B$ via a mapping $\eta : X \to A \times B$ such that

$$R\eta = \eta(r \otimes s), \quad R\eta\eta^{-1} = R \qquad (2)$$

for appropriate relations $r \subseteq A \times A$ and $s \subseteq B \times B$. The generalization to more than two slices is straightforward.

Disjoint Parallelism and Its Limitations

One notable consequence of the presented notion of semantic independence is that, due to accessing disjoint pieces of memory, the concurrent execution of the transformed statements neither requires shared reading nor shared writing. These operations are eliminated by the transformation or, if the context requires a state space representation in the original format X rather than the transform Y, localized in code preceding the fork of the concurrent statements or following their join. This is illustrated with our initial example, where the shared reading and writing of x and y as well as the shared reading of z present in the original statements

$$\alpha_1: \quad (x,y) := (x \wedge z, y \wedge \neg z)$$
$$\alpha_2: \quad (x,y) := (x \wedge \neg z, y \wedge z)$$

disappear in the semantically equivalent form

$$\alpha_1': \quad V := 0$$
$$\alpha_2': \quad W := 2 * (W \text{ div } 2)$$

If the context requires the format of X, one will have to include the transformations η and η^{-1} in the implementation. For the example, this means that the code

$$\text{var } V : \{0,1\},\ W : \{0,1,2,3\};$$
$$\beta_1: \quad V := (x \wedge \neg z) \vee (y \wedge z)$$
$$\beta_2: \quad W := 2 * z + (x \wedge z) \vee (y \wedge \neg z)$$

(or any alternative code issuing the same side effects on V and W) has to be inserted before the concurrent statements α_1' and α_2' and that the code

$$\gamma_1: \quad x := \text{if } (W \text{ div } 2) = 1 \text{ then } (W \text{ mod } 2) \text{ else } V$$
$$\gamma_2: \quad y := \text{if } (W \text{ div } 2) = 0 \text{ then } (W \text{ mod } 2) \text{ else } V$$
$$\gamma_3: \quad z := W \text{ div } 2$$
$$\text{endvar } V,\ W$$

has to be appended behind their join. The keyword endvar indicates that, after the backtransformation, variables V and W are irrelevant to the remainder of the program. (The backtransformation γ_3 of z from the transformed to the original state space could be omitted, since the original statements do not have a side effect on z, that is, γ_3 turns out not to modify z).

Whether implementations such as β_1 and β_2 of the projections $\eta \downarrow_1$ and $\eta \downarrow_2$, which prepare the state spaces for the two parallel statements to be sparked, can themselves be executed in parallel depends on the ability to perform shared reading. Since these transformations have no side effects on the common state space X and only local ones on A or B, respectively, yet require shared reading on X, they can be executed in parallel if and only if the architecture supports shared reading on X – yet not necessarily on A or B, which need not be accessible to the respective statement executed in parallel. Conversely, a parallel execution of the reverse transformation does, in general, require shared reads on A and B, yet no shared reads or writes of the individual variables spanning X, as illustrated by the statements γ_1, γ_2, and γ_3 above.

Practical Relevance

In the parallelization of algorithms, the mapping η transforming the state space is often fixed, depending on the application, and, thus, left implicit. This leads to fixed parallelization schemes which can be applied uniformly, which makes the search for η and the calculation of the simulating relations r and s from the original state transformers R and S unnecessary. Instead, it suffices to justify the parallelization scheme once and for all. It is worth noting that, for many practical schemes, this can be done via the concept of semantic independence. Examples are the implementation of $*$-LISP on the Connection Machine [5] and Google's closely related MapReduce framework [3], which are based on a very simple transformation, or the use of residue number systems (RNS) in arithmetic hardware and signal processing [8], which exploits a much more elaborate transformation.

In the former two cases, transformation η maps a list of elements to the corresponding tuple of its elements, after which all elements are subjected to the same mapping, say f, in parallel. The implementation of η distributes the list elements to different processors. Then, f is applied independently in parallel to each list element and, finally, by the implementation of η^{-1}, the local results are collected in a new list.

In contrast, RNS, which has gained popularity in signal processing applications during the last two decades, transforms the state space rather intricately following the Chinese remainder theorem of modular arithmetic. In its simplest form, one considers assignments of the form $x := y \odot z$, where the variables are bounded-range, nonnegative integers and the operation $\odot$ can be addition, subtraction, or multiplication. RNS transforms the variables in such assignments to vectors of remainders with co-primal bases as follows. (The numbers of a co-primal base have no common positive factors other than 1.)

Let x, y, z be variables with ranges $\mathbb{N}_{<k}$, where k is a nonzero natural number and $\mathbb{N}_{<k}$ denotes the natural numbers up to $k-1$ and let $f_1, \ldots, f_n \ll k$ be co-primal natural numbers with $\prod_{i=1}^{n} f_i \geq k$. Then, each variable v of x, y, z is transformed to a vector $(v_1, \ldots, v_n)$ of variables such that v_i ranges over $\mathbb{N}_{<f_i}$ and $v_i = v \bmod f_i$. Consequently,

$$\eta(x, y, z) = (x \bmod f_1, y \bmod f_1, z \bmod f_1, \ldots,$$
$$x \bmod f_n, y \bmod f_n, z \bmod f_n).$$

The independence of the slices of assignment $x := y \odot z$, one for each f_i, follows from the fact that

$$(y \odot z) \bmod f_i$$
$$= ((y \bmod f_i) \odot (z \bmod f_i)) \bmod f_i$$
$$= (y_i \odot z_i) \bmod f_i$$

for each of the three operations that can be substituted for $\odot$. This allows a parallel implementation in which the assignment $x := y \odot z$ is replaced by n semantically independent assignments

$$x_i := (y_i \odot z_i) \bmod f_i \quad \text{for} \quad i = 1, \ldots, n.$$

These are executed in parallel without any need for information exchange. A significant speedup results from the reduced bit width of the arithmetic operations involved, which shrinks from $\lceil \log_2 k \rceil$ to $\lceil \log_2(\max_{i=1}^{n} f_i) \rceil$. If chains of assignments are performed, the speedup can easily amortize the computational effort involved in the transformations η and η^{-1}. Then this parallelization scheme remains attractive even when the data are supplied and expected in standard binary encoding, as is normally the case in signal processing.

Related Entries

▶Connection Machine
▶Dependences
▶Dependence Analysis
▶Parallelization, Automatic
▶Polyhedron Model
▶Systolic Arrays

Bibliographic Notes and Further Reading

Semantic independence is a generalization of the syntactic independence criterion proposed by Arthur J. Bernstein in 1966 [1]. This criterion states that independent program fragments are allowed to read shared variables at any time but must not update any shared variable.

Lengauer introduced a notion of independence based on Hoare logic in the early 1980s [6, 7]. It combines a semantic with a syntactic requirement. The semantic part of the independence relation is called full commutativity and permits an arbitrary interleaving of the program fragments at the statement level, the syntactic part is called non-interference and ensures the absence of shared updates within each statement.

The independence relation based on a program state graph, as proposed by Best and Lengauer in 1989 [2], is entirely semantic. Von Stengel [9] ported the model to universal algebra and Fränzle et al. [4] generalized it shortly thereafter to the notion presented here. Whether a general, automatic, and efficient method of finding η and constructing r and s in any practical programming language exists remains an open question.

Zhang [10] has ported the above notion of semantic independence to security. He adopts Definition 1 as the definition of a set of mutually secure transitions. Transformation η defines the local views of users and r and s are the locally visible effects of the globally secure transitions R and S.

The transformations of the state space, which make independence visible, reflect the same principle as the coordinate transformations of the iteration space in polyhedral loop parallelization. There are other correspondences between the two models, for example, the way in which one exposes parallelism in a single assignment statement. For a more detailed comparison, see the entry on the polyhedron model.

Bibliography

1. Bernstein AJ (1966) Analysis of programs for parallel processing. IEEE Trans Electr Comput EC-15(5):757–763
2. Best E, Lengauer C (1989) Semantic independence. Sci Comput Program 13(1):23–50
3. Dean J, Ghemawat S (2008) MapReduce: simplified data processing on large clusters. Commun ACM, 51(1):107–113, January 2008
4. Fränzle M, von Stengel B, Wittmüss A (1995) A generalized notion of semantic independence. Info Process Lett 53(1):5–9
5. Hillis WD (1986) The connection machine. MIT Press, Cambridge, MA

6. Lengauer C (1982) A methodology for programming with concurrency: the formalism. Sci Comput Program 2(1):19–52
7. Lengauer C, Hehner ECR (1982) A methodology for programming with concurrency: an informal presentation. Sci Comput Program 2(1):1–18
8. Omondi A, Premkumar B (2007) Residue number systems – theory and implementation, volume 2 of Advances in computer science and engineering. Imperial College Press, United Kingdom
9. von Stengel B (1991) An algebraic characterization of semantic independence. Info Process Lett 39(6):291–296
10. Zhang K (1997) A theory for system security. In: 10th IEEE computer security foundations workshop. IEEE Computer Society Press, June 1997, pp 148–155

Semaphores

▶Synchronization

Sequential Consistency

▶Memory Models

Server Farm

▶Clusters
▶Distributed-Memory Multiprocessor

Shared Interconnect

▶Buses and Crossbars

Shared Virtual Memory

▶Software Distributed Shared Memory

Shared-Medium Network

▶Buses and Crossbars

Shared-Memory Multiprocessors

Luis H. Ceze
University of Washington, Seattle, WA, USA

Synonyms

Multiprocessors

Definition

A shared-memory multiprocessor is a computer system composed of multiple independent processors that execute different instruction streams. Using Flynns's classification [1], an SMP is a multiple-instruction multiple-data (MIMD) architecture. The processors share a common memory address space and communicate with each other via memory. A typical shared-memory multiprocessor (Fig. 1) includes some number of processors with local caches, all interconnected with each other and with common memory via an interconnection (e.g., a bus).

Shared-memory multiprocessors can either be symmetric or asymmetric. Symmetric systems implies that all processors that compose the system are identical. Conversely, asymmetric systems have different types of processors sharing memory. Most multicore chips are single-chip symmetric shared-memory multiprocessors [2] (e.g., Intel Core 2 Duo).

Discussion

Communication between processors in shared-memory multiprocessors happens implicitly via read and write operations to common memory address. For example, a data producer processor writes to memory location A, and a consumer processor reads from the same memory location:

```
P1        P2
------    -----
...       ...
A = 5     ...
...       ...
...       tmp = A
...       ...
```

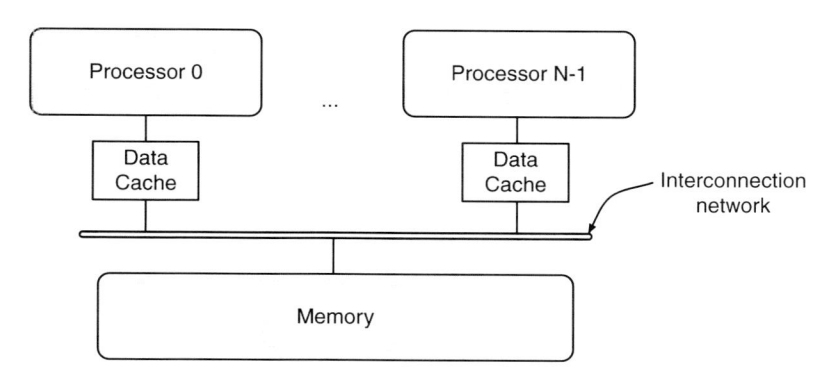

Shared-Memory Multiprocessors. Fig. 1 Conceptual overview of a typical shared-memory multiprocessor

Processor P1 wrote to location A and later processor P2 read from A and therefore read the value "5" into local variable "tmp," written by P1. One way to think about the execution of a parallel program in a shared-memory multiprocessor is as some global interleaving of the memory operations of all threads. This global interleaving of instructions is nondeterministic, as there are no guarantees that if a given program is executed multiple times with the same input will lead to the same interleaving and therefore the same result.

Since communication happens nondeterministic, programs need to explicitly ensure that when communication happens, the data communicated is in a consistent state. This is done via synchronization, e.g., using mutual exclusion to prevent two threads from manipulating the same piece of data simultaneously.

One of the key components of a shared-memory multiprocessor is the cache coherence protocol. The cache coherence protocol ensures that all caches in each processor hold consistent data. The main job of the coherence protocol is to keep track of when cache lines are written to and propagating changes when that happens. Therefore, the granularity of data movement between processors is a cache line. There are many trade-offs in how cache coherence protocols are implemented. For example, whether updates should be propagated as they happen or if they should only be propagated when a remote processor tries to read the corresponding data. Another very important aspect of shared-memory multiprocessors is the memory consistency model, which determines when (what order) memory operations are made visible to processors in the system [3].

For the actual physical memory organization (and the interconnection network), it is common to have multiple partitions physically spread over the processors. This means that each partition is closer to some processors than others. Therefore, some regions of memory have faster access than others. Such organization is called non-uniform memory access, or NUMA. ccNUMA refers to NUMA multiprocessors with private caches per processor and cache coherence.

Given the general slower improvement in single-thread performance, processor manufacturers are now scaling raw compute performance in the forms of more cores (or processors) on a single chip, forming a symmetric shared-memory multiprocessor. Another recent trend points towards using specialized processors to further improver performance and energy efficiency, leading towards asymmetric shared-memory multiprocessor system.

Related Entries
▶ Cache Coherence
▶ Cedar Multiprocessor
▶ Locality of Reference and Parallel Processing
▶ Memory Models
▶ Race Conditions
▶ Race Detection Techniques

Bibliographic Notes and Further Reading

There are many notable shared-memory multiprocessor systems worth reading about, starting from mainframes in the 60s (e.g., Burroughs B5500), many machines built in academia (e.g., UIUC CEDAR, Stanford Flash, Stanford DASH), and many systems manufactured and sold by Sequent and DEC (now defunct), as well as IBM, Sun, SGI, Fujitsu, HP, among several others.

Bibliography

1. Flynn M (1972) Some computer organizations and their effectiveness. IEEE Trans Comput C-21:948
2. Olukotun et al (1996) The case for a single-chip multiprocessor. In: Proceedings of the 7th international symposium architectural support for programming languages and operating systems (ASPLOS VII), Cambridge, MA, October 1996
3. Adve S, Gharachorloo K (1996) Shared memory consistency models: a tutorial. IEEE Comput Soc 29(12):66–76

SHMEM

▶OpenSHMEM - Toward a Unified RMA Model

SIGMA-1

KEI HIRAKI
The University of Tokyo, Tokyo, Japan

Synonyms

Dataflow supercomputer

Definition

SIGMA-1 is a large-scale computer based on fine-grain dataflow architecture designed to show feasibility of fine-grain dataflow computer to highly parallel computation over conventional von Neumann computers. SIGMA-1 project was stated on 1984 and the 128 processing element (PE) started working on 1988. SIGMA-1 was design and built at the Electrotechnical Laboratory (ETL for short), Ministry of International Trade and Industry, Japan. SIGMA-1 is still the largest scale dataflow computer so far built and it achieved more 100 Mflops as a maximum measured performance of the total system. As for the language for SIGMA-1, ETL developed Dataflow-C language as a subset of C programming language. Dataflow-C is a single assignment language that can compile C-like source programs to highly parallel executable dataflow machine codes (Fig. 1).

Architecture

Organization

The global organization of the SIGMA-1 is shown in Fig. 2. The SIGMA-1 consists of 128 processing elements, 128 structure elements, 32 local networks, a global network, 16 maintenance microprocessors, a service processor, and a host computer (Figs. 3 and 4). The processing elements and structure elements are divided into 32 groups, each of which consists of four processing elements, four structure elements, and a local network. All groups are connected via the global network. The global network consists of a two-stage omega network with a new adaptive load distribution mechanism. Its transfer rate is 2G bytes per second. A local network is a ten-by-ten crossbar packet switching network, eight ports of which are used for communication between processing elements and structure elements within a group and two to interface the global network. The transfer rate of a local network is 600M bytes per second. The whole system is synchronous and operates under a single clock (Fig. 5).

Figure 6 illustrates a processing element and a structure element. A processing element consists of an input buffer, a matching memory with a waiting matching function, an instruction memory, and a link register file. A processing element executes all the SIGMA-1 instructions except structure-handling instructions such as read, white, allocate, and deallocate used to access the structure memory in a structure element. A processing element works as a two-stage pipeline: the firing stage and the execution stage. In the firing stage, operand matching and instruction fetching are performed simultaneously. Input packets, stored in the input buffer, are sent to the matching memory. The matching memory enables the execution of instructions with two input operands. Successfully matched packets are sent to the execution stage with the instructions fetched from the instruction memory. If the match fails, the packet is stored in the matching memory and the instruction fetched is discarded. Chained hashing

SIGMA-1. Fig. 1 SIGMA-1 system

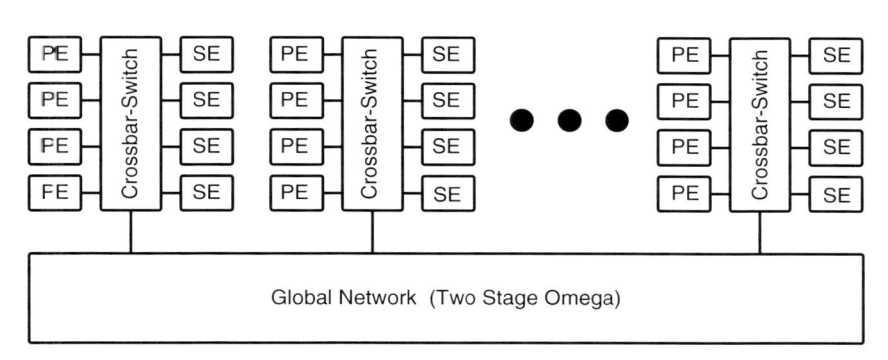

SIGMA-1. Fig. 2 Global architecture of the SIGMA-1

PE an instruction-level dataflow processing element
SE a structure processing element

hardware is used to speed up the operand matching operation, where a first-in-first-out queue is attached to each key to enable multiple entries with the same key Table 1.

The link register is used to identify a parallel activity in a program and hold a base address of a procedure. In the execution stage, instructions are executed in parallel with packet identifier generation, where a packet identifier keeps the destination address (next instruction address) as well as a parallel activity identifier (a procedure identifier and an iteration counter). These operations are similar to those in a conventional computer. After combining the result value of the execution unit with the packet identifier, an output packet is produced and sent to the input buffer of the same or another processing element via the local network. If an array is treated as a set of scalar values, the matching memory provides automatic synchronization and space management. However, heavy packet traffic causes a serious bottleneck at the matching memory, since each element of the array must be handled separately. This is the reason additional structure elements

SIGMA-1. Fig. 3 SIGMA-1 Processing element (optional)

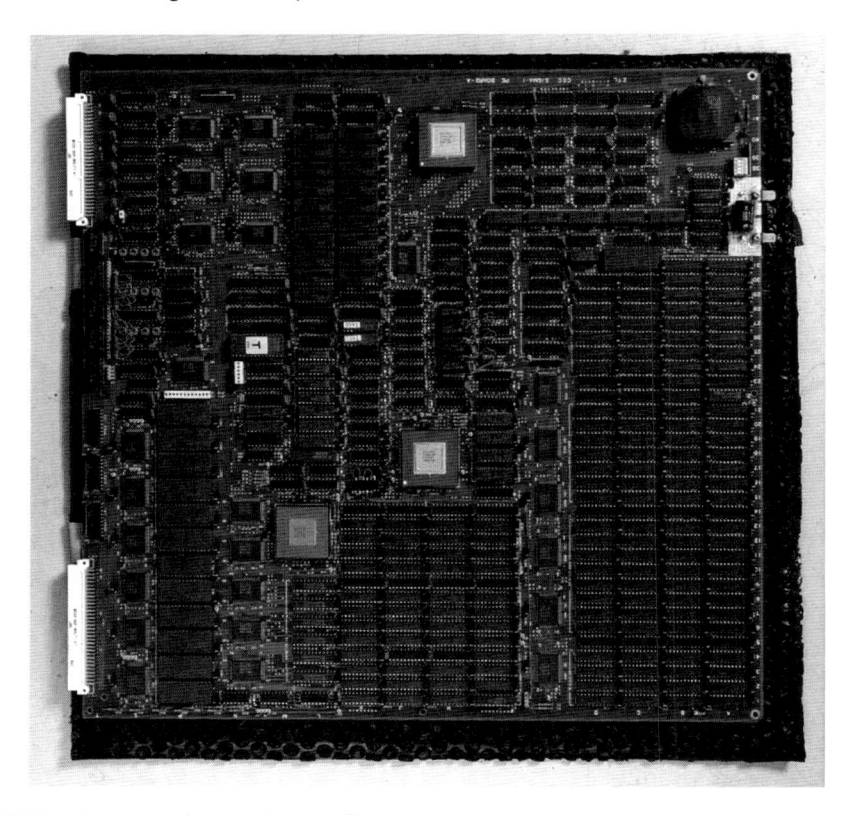

SIGMA-1. Fig. 4 SIGMA-1 Structure element (optional)

SIGMA-1. Fig. 5 SIGMA-1 Local network (optional)

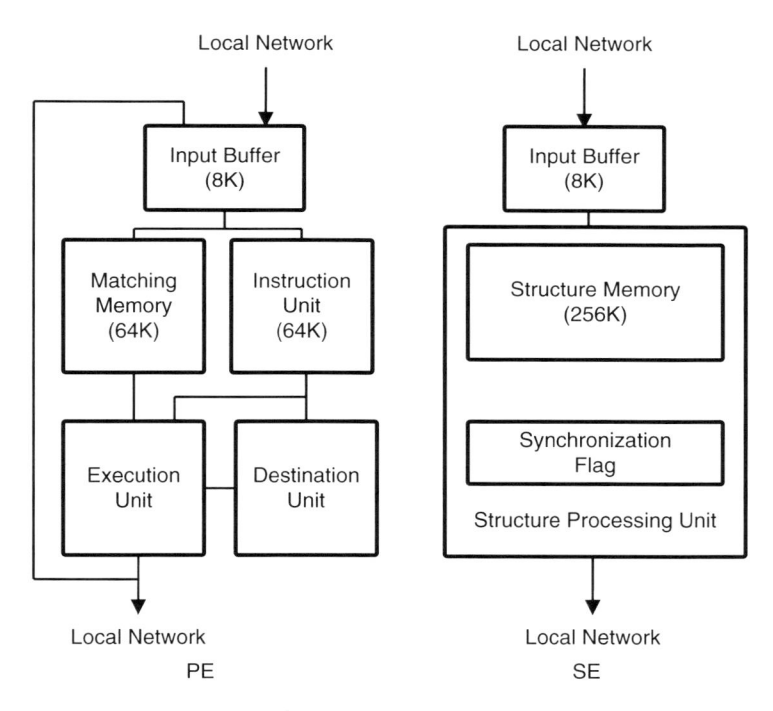

SIGMA-1. Fig. 6 Processing element (PE) and SE of the SIGMA-1

are introduced in the SIGMA-1. A structure element consists of an input buffer, a structure memory, two flag logic functions, and a structure controller with a register file. The flag logic function is capable of test and setting all flags in an area arbitrarily specified in a single clock. The structure controller is responsible for waiting queue control and memory management. A structure element handles arrays, which are the most

SIGMA-1. Table 1 Hardware specification of the SIGMA-1

Technology:	CMOS Gate-array, SRAM, DRAM
Clock	10 MHz
Input buffer	8 K words(80bits/word)
Matching memory	64 K words(80bits/word)
Instruction memory	64 K words(40bits/word)
Structure memory	256 K words(40bits/word)
Total amount of memory	326 M Byte
Total no. of gates	19,013,447 gates
Total no. of ICs	91,029
Total no. of PE/SE	128 + 128

important data structure involved in numerical computations. Each structure cell is composed of a 40-bit data (data type and payload data) word and two flag bits used for read and write synchronization. Multiple read before write operations are realized by a waiting queue attached to each cell. The buddy system implemented in microprogramming is used to increase the speed of allocating and deallocating structures.

The architectural features of the SIGMA-1 are designed to achieve high speed by decreasing the parallel processing overheads in dataflow computers. For example, the short pipeline architecture enables quick response to small-sized programs with low parallelism. It was anticipated that the matching memory and the communication network would play a significant role in the system design from the viewpoint of synchronization and data transmission overhead. Besides the newly proposed mechanisms, high-speed and compact gate-array LSI elements have been developed for this purpose.

Testing, debugging, and maintenance are performed by a special purpose parallel architecture [6]. This maintenance architecture uses a set of conventional von Neumann microprocessors, since maintenance operations generally need history sensitivity utilizing side effects.

The architectural features of the SIGMA-1 are summarized as follows:

1. A short (two-stage) pipeline in a processing element, reducing the gap between the maximum and average performance
2. Chained hashing hardware for the matching memory, giving efficient and high-speed synchronization
3. An array-oriented structure element, minimizing structure handling overhead
4. A hierarchical network with a dynamic load distribution function, reducing performance degradation caused by load imbalance
5. A maintenance architecture for testing and debugging, providing high-speed input and output operations and performing precise performance measurements

Packet and Instruction Architecture

The SIGMA-1 adopts packet communication architecture. Processing elements and structure elements communicate using fixed length packets. Input and output to the host computer and maintenance system are also in packet form. Therefore, hardware initialization and hardware maintenance are carried out in packet form. As shown in Fig. 7, a packet contains a destination processing element number, a packet identifier and tagged data, and miscellaneous control information.

The 89-bit packet is divided into two 40-bit segments, a processing element number field (8 bits), and a cancel bit. A packet is transferred in two consecutive segments; the first segment contains a processing element or structure element number, a destination address in the processing element or structure element (32 bits), and packet type (8 bits). The second segment consists of data (32 bits), data type (8 bits), and one cancel bit. The cancel bit is used for canceling the preceding segment when a malfunction occurs. When the cancel bit is on, the whole packet becomes invalid.

A destination address consists of a procedure identifier (8 bits) for specifying a parallel activity, a relative instruction address (10 bits) within the activity, an iteration counter (10 bits), and some control information determining the firing rule in the matching memory (4 bits). The iteration counter is utilized to implement the loop construct efficiently. As in the ordinary model of dynamic dataflow, the concatenation of the procedure identifier and iteration counter is used to distinguish parallel activities in a program. The types of packets used are: result of instruction, procedure call and return, interrupt handling and system management, structure operation, and system initiation and maintenance for system resources.

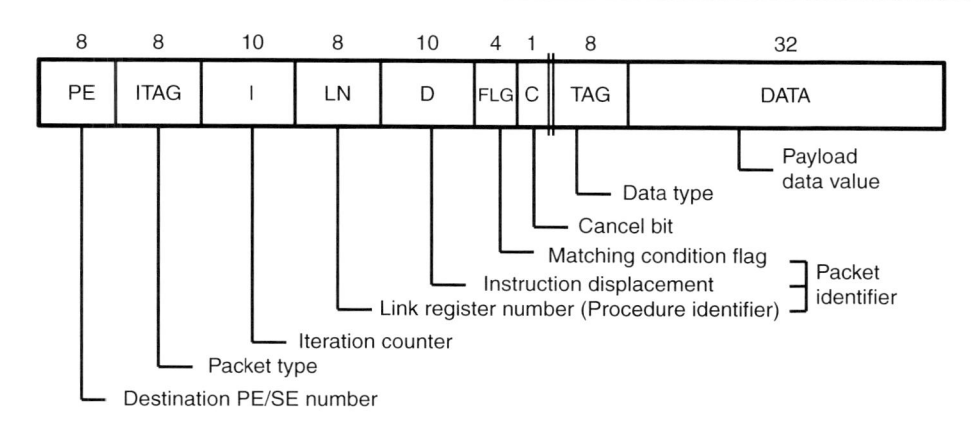

```
  8    8    10   8    10   4  1  8         32
┌────┬────┬────┬────┬────┬───┬─┬────┬──────────────┐
│ PE │ITAG│ I  │ LN │ D  │FLG│C│TAG │     DATA     │
└────┴────┴────┴────┴────┴───┴─┴────┴──────────────┘
```

- Payload data value (DATA)
- Data type (TAG)
- Cancel bit (C)
- Matching condition flag (FLG)
- Instruction displacement (D) — Packet identifier
- Link register number (Procedure identifier) (LN) — Packet identifier
- Iteration counter (I)
- Packet type (ITAG)
- Destination PE/SE number (PE)

SIGMA-1. Fig. 7 Packet format

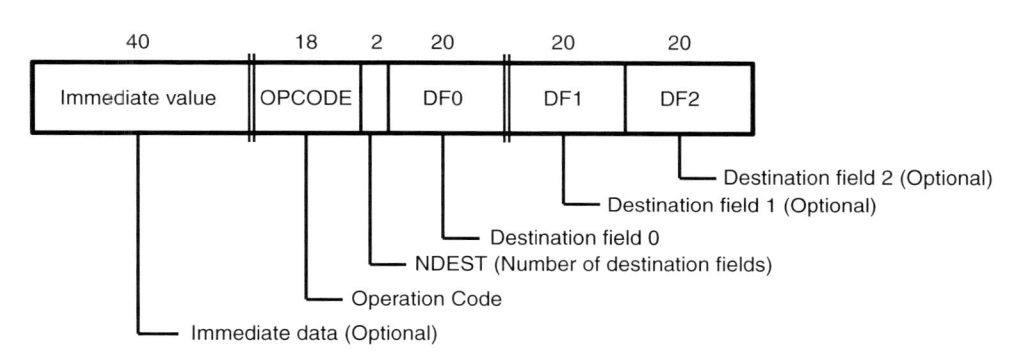

```
    40              18     2    20        20        20
┌────────────────┬────────┬───┬──────┬─────────┬─────────┐
│ Immediate value│ OPCODE │   │ DF0  │  DF1    │  DF2    │
└────────────────┴────────┴───┴──────┴─────────┴─────────┘
```

- Destination field 2 (Optional) (DF2)
- Destination field 1 (Optional) (DF1)
- Destination field 0 (DF0)
- NDEST (Number of destination fields)
- Operation Code (OPCODE)
- Immediate data (Optional)

SIGMA-1. Fig. 8 Instruction format

The minimum length of an instruction is 40 bits (one word) as illustrated in Fig. 8. The first 20 bits indicate the operation to be performed (18 bits) and the number of destination address fields (2 bits). The next 20 bits indicate the destination address of the result, which does not contain dynamically assigned information such as a procedure identifier and iteration counter. An immediate data operand can be located at the header part of each instruction. The maximum number of destination address fields is three, using two words. When an instruction contains an immediate data (constant) operand, another word is required.

The objective of the SIGMA-1 instruction set design is to execute efficiently application programs that cannot be efficiently executed on a vector-type supercomputer or a parallel von Neumann computer. Low efficiency in these program executions is caused by frequent procedure calls and returns, large amount of scalar arithmetic operations, and wide fluctuations of parallelism. Fine-grain parallelism has the advantage over coarse-grain parallelism to overcome this inefficiency. As a result, 200 instructions on a processing element and 97 instructions on a structure element have been implemented (Fig. 9).

Software

The DataFlow C (DFC) compiler is implemented using the language development tools of the UNIX operating system. The emphasis was not on efficiency but on ease of implementation. Efficiency and compactness are still to be considered. Basically, DFC is a subset of the C language with a single assignment rule. Therefore, assignment to a variable is generally allowed only once in each procedure. However, the loop construct, realized by the *for* statement, is an exception. A non-single assignment expression can be written as the third argument of the *for* statement as shown in the following summation program. The argument n of the main program is given by a trigger packet invoking the program.

SIGMA-1. Fig. 9 SIGMA-1 PEs and SEs (optional)

```
#define N 10
main(n)
int n;
{int i; float a[N], retval, sigma();
for(i=0;i<5;i=I + 1) a[i] = i;
retval=sigma(n, a); print(retval);}

float sigma(n, a)
int n; float a[];
{int i; float s;
for (i=0, s=0; i<n; s=s+a[i],i=i+1);
return(s);}
```

DFC may have multiple return values as an extension to the C language. DFC programs without multiple return values can be compiled by a C compiler. The advantage is that DFC programs can be verified by a C compiler on a host computer. The DFC compiler comprises approximately 7,000 steps in C. A nested structure of *for* or *if* statements is not implemented and is inhibited. The DFC compiler generates a macro-assembly language program. This corresponds to a dataflow graph with no restriction on the number of arcs.

System Performance

The whole system operates synchronously at a 10 MHz clock frequency. The execution time of an instruction is determined by the maximum execution time of the two pipeline stages. Single operand instructions are executed every two cycles and two operand instructions every three cycles. The firing stage normally takes three cycles. Since non-division arithmetic operations take at most two cycles, the execution stage completes most of the instruction execution in two cycles. This consideration implies that the maximum speed of a processing element is about 5 MIPS and 3 MFLOPS. For a structure element, each read and write instruction is carried out in two cycles. Since instructions for allocating and deallocating structures are implemented by a microprogrammed buddy system, the execution times estimated are between 10 and 340 cycles. The network transfers a packet every two cycles. Therefore, structure elements can utilize maximum performance of the network.

Performance is measured in terms of program execution time rather than raw machine cycles. The measurement study proved that there is no difference in computing ability of a single processing element between dataflow architecture and von Neumann architecture, in case of constructing them using the same device technology.

1. A speed degradation of 30% occurs when structure elements are adopted. This is due to the extra index and address calculation for structure handling.
2. The single processing element performance is almost constant over the vector length, because of the short pipeline architecture.
3. The speedup ratio for a single processing element to four processing element organization is 3.9 without structure elements and 3.5 with structure elements.

This performance evaluation shows that the average performance of the 128 processing element organization is more than 100 MFLOPS. For example, SIGMA-1 compute matrix multiplies at 117 Mflops.

Discussion

Table 2 shows development history of major MIMD parallel computers and dataflow computers.

SIGMA-1. Table 2 History of dataflow parallel processors

Year[a]	System name	#PE	Word length	Architecture
1976	DDM1	1 PE	4	Static dataflow
1978	TI DDP	4 PE	16	Static dataflow
1979	LAU	32 PE	32	Static dataflow
1981	Manchester dataflow machine	1 PE	24	Dynamic dataflow
1982	OKI DDDP	4 PE	16	Dynamic dataflow
1982	NTT Eddy	16 PE	16	Simulated dynamic dataflow
1984	NEC NEDIPS	8 PE	32	Static dataflow
1983	Q-p	1 PE	16	Static dataflow, Asyncronous
1984	**SIGMA-1 Prototype**	**1PE**	**32**	**Dynamic dataflow**
1988	**SIGMA-1**	**128 PE**	**32**	**Dynamic dataflow**
1988	MIT monsoon prototype	1 PE	64	Dynamic dataflow
1990	ETL EM-4	80 PE	32	Dynamic/Hybrid dataflow
1991	MIT monsoon	8 PE	64	Dynamic dataflow
1996	ETL EM-X	80 PE	32	Dynamic/Hybrid dataflow

[a]Year denote the date start working in its full configuration

As shown in Table 2, SI-1 is the largest dataflow computer so far built.

Illustrations, diagrams, and code examples.

Bibliography

1. Hiraki K, Nishida K, Sekiguchi S, Shimada T (1986) Maintenance architecture and its LSI implementation of a dataflow computer with a large number of processors. Proceedings of International Conference on Parallel Processing, IEEE Computer Society, University Park, pp 584–591
2. Hiraki K, Sekiguchi S, Shimada T (1987) System architecture of a dataflow supercomputer. Proceedings of 1987 IEEE Region 10 Conference, IEEE computer Society, Los Alamitos, pp 1044–1049
3. Hiraki K, Shimada T, Nishida K (1984) A hardware design of the SIGMA-1—A data flow computer for scientific computations. Proceedings of 1984 International Conference on Parallel Processing, IEEE Computer Society, Los Alamitos, pp 524–531
4. Hiraki K, Shimada T, Sekiguchi S (1993) Empirical study of latency hiding on a fine-grain parallel processor. Proceedings of International Conference on Supercomputing, ACM, Tokyo, pp 220–229
5. Sekiguchi S, Shimada T, Hiraki K (1991) Sequential description and parallel execution language DFCII dataflow supercomputers. Proceedings of International Conference on Supercomputing, ACM, New York, pp 57–66
6. Shimada T, Hiraki K, Sekiguchi S, Nishida K (1986) Evaluation of a single processor of a prototype data flow computer SIGMA-1 for scientific computations. Proceedings of 12th Annual International Symposium on Computer Architecture, IEEE Computer Society, Chicago, pp 226–234

SIMD (Single Instruction, Multiple Data) Machines

▶ Cray Vector Computers
▶ Floating Point Systems FPS-120B and Derivatives
▶ Flynn's Taxonomy
▶ Fujitsu Vector Computers
▶ Illiac IV
▶ MasPar
▶ MPP
▶ NEC SX Series Vector Computers
▶ Vector Extensions, Instruction-Set Architecture (ISA)

SIMD Extensions

▶ Vector Extensions, Instruction-Set Architecture (ISA)

SIMD ISA

▶ Vector Extensions, Instruction-Set Architecture (ISA)

Single System Image

Rolf Riesen[1], Arthur B. Maccabe[2]
[1]IBM Research, Dublin, Ireland
[2]Oak Ridge National Laboratory, Oak Ridge, TN, USA

Synonyms
Distributed process management

Definition
A Single System Image (SSI) is an abstraction that provides the illusion that a multicomputer or cluster is a single machine. There are individual instances of the Operating Systems (OSs) running on each node of a multicomputer, processes working together are spread across multiple nodes, and files may reside on multiple disks. An SSI provides a unified view of this collection to users, programmers, and system administrators. This unification makes a system easier to use and more efficient to manage.

Discussion

Introduction
Multicomputers consist of nodes, each with its own memory, CPUs, and a network interface. In the case of clusters, each node is a stand-alone computer made of commodity, off-the-shelf parts. Instead of viewing this collection of computers as individual systems, it is easier and more economical if users, programmers, and system administrators can treat the collection as a single machine. For example, users want to submit a single job to the system, even if it consists of multiple processes working in parallel.

The task of an SSI is to provide the illusion of a single machine under the control of the users and system administrators. The SSI is a layer of abstraction that provides functions and utilities to use, program, and manage the system. An SSI consists of multiple pieces. Some of them are implemented as individual utilities, other pieces are found in system libraries, there are additional processes running to hold up the illusion, OSs are modified, and in some systems hardware enables some of the abstraction. No SSI provides a complete illusion. There are always ways to circumvent the abstraction, and sometimes it is necessary to interact with specific components of the system directly. Many SSI in daily use provide a limited abstraction that is enough to make use of the system practical, but do not add too much overhead or impede scalability.

An OS consists of a kernel, such as Linux, and a set of utilities and tools, such as a graphical user interface and tools to manipulate files. On a single computer, for example, a desktop workstation, the OS manages resources, such as CPUs, memory, disks, and other peripherals. It does that by providing a set of abstractions such as processes and files that allow users to interact with the system in a consistent manner independent of the specific hardware used in that system. For everyday tasks, it should not matter what particular CPU is installed, or whether files reside on a local or a network-attached disk drive. The goal of an SSI is to provide a similar experience to users of a parallel system.

That is not that difficult to achieve in a Symmetric Multi-Processor (SMP) where all memory is shared and all CPUs have, more or less, equally fast access to it. The OS for an SMP has additional features to manage the multiple CPUs, but the view it presents to a user is mostly the same that a user of a single-CPU system sees. For example, when launching an application, a user of an SMP does not need to specify which CPU should run it. The OS will select the least busy CPU and schedules the process to run there. There are additional functions that an SMP OS provides, for example, to synchronize processes, pin them to specific CPUs, and allow them to share memory. Nevertheless, the abstraction is still that of a single, whole machine.

In contrast, in a distributed memory system, such as a large-scale supercomputer or a cluster, each node runs its own copy of the OS. It is possible that not all nodes have the same capabilities; some may have access to a Graphic Processing Unit (GPU), the CPUs and memory sizes may be different, and some nodes may have connections to wide-area networks that are not available to all nodes in the system. The task of an SSI is to unify these individual components and present them to the user as if they were a single computer. This is difficult and sometimes not desired. Accessing data in the memory or disk of a remote node is much more time consuming than accessing data locally. It therefore makes sense for a user to specify that a process be run on the node where the data currently resides. It also makes sense to give users the ability to specify that a process be run on a node that meets minimum memory requirements or has a certain type of CPU or GPU installed. On the other hand, for many tasks, or in a homogeneous system, the SSI should hide the complexity of the underlying system and present a view that lets users interact with it as if it were a large SMP.

An SSI is meant to make interaction with a parallel system easier and more efficient for three different groups of users: Application users who use the system to run applications such as a database or a simulation, programmers who create applications for parallel systems, and administrators who manage these systems. Each group has its own requirements for, and uses of, an SSI; and the view an SSI presents to each group is different. Of course, there is some overlap since there are tasks that need to be done by members of more than one group. The following sections discuss an SSI from these three different viewpoints. Functions that overlap are discussed in earlier viewpoints.

Application User's View

A user of a parallel system uses it for an application such as computing the path of an asteroid, the weekly payroll, or maintaining the checking accounts of a bank. This type of user does this by running an application which provides the necessary functionality. In some cases, like the banking example, the user never directly interacts with the system. Those users only see the application interface, for example, the banking application that presents information about customers and their account balances. Parallel systems used in science and engineering cater to users who each have their own applications to solve their particular scientific problems. These users do interact with the system and an SSI assists them in making these interactions smooth and reliable.

Large systems that are shared among many users usually dedicate several nodes as login nodes. Smaller clusters sometimes let users log into any of the nodes, though this is less efficient for running parallel applications. An SSI gathers these login nodes under the umbrella of a single address. Users remotely log into that address and the SSI chooses the least busy node as the actual login node.

Once logged in, users need the ability to launch serial or parallel jobs (applications) and control them.

An SSI chooses the nodes to run the individual processes on and provides utilities to the user to obtain status information, stop, suspend, and resume jobs.

While an application is running, users need to interact with it. The SSI transparently directs user input to the application, independent of which node it is running on. Similarly, output from the application is funneled (if it comes from multiple processes) back to the user. This is the same as on any computing system. However, in a distributed system, the SSI needs to provide that functionality even if a process migrates to another node.

Input and output data for an application is often stored in files. Users must have the ability to see these files and manipulate them, for example, copy, move, and delete them. This requires a shared file system, since the application must be able to access the same files. Since the user, the application, and the files themselves may all reside on different nodes, a distributed file system is needed that presents a single root to all nodes in the system. That means the full path name of a file, that is, the hierarchy of directories (folders) above it and the file name itself, must be the same when viewed from any node.

Peripherals should be visible as if they were connected to the local node. The SSI must provide a view of that peripheral and transfer data to and from it, if the device is not local.

Programmer's View

Programmers of parallel applications have many of the same requirements as application users. They also need to launch applications, to test them for example, and need access to the file system. The same is true for writing and compiling applications.

For debugging, the SSI may need to route requests from the debugger to processes on another node to suspend them and to inspect their memory and registers. If this functionality is embedded in the debugger itself, then this is no longer a requirement for the SSI, but it does require services that are part of the OS.

Programmers do have additional requirements that an SSI provides. The programs they write need to access low-level system services provided by the OS. That is done through system calls that allow applications to trap into an OS kernel to obtain a specific service. Typical services provided are calls to open a file for reading and writing, creating and starting a new process, and interact through Inter-Process Communication (IPC) with another process. In a distributed system, these functions become more complex.

A process creation request in a desktop system is an operation carried out by the local OS. In a distributed system managed by an SSI, process creation may mean interaction with the OS of another node. If the original process and the new process need to communicate, then data has to move between nodes instead of just being copied locally into another memory location. For an application that is not aware of the distributed nature of the system it is running on, the SSI must provide this functionality so that it is transparent to the application.

Many applications consist of multiple processes that work together by sharing memory locations. On a single system, that is an efficient way to move data from one process to another and lets multiple processes read the same data. If these processes, in a distributed system, do not have access to the same memory anymore, this becomes more difficult and expensive, than it was before. Some SSI provide the illusion of a shared memory space. This is enabled by specialized hardware or through Distributed Shared Memory (DSM) implemented in software.

Administrator's View

An administrator of a parallel system is responsible for managing user accounts, keeping system software up to date, replacing failed components, and in general have the system available for its intended use. Many of the administrators tasks are similar to the ones a user performs, for example, manipulating files, but with a higher privilege level.

In addition, an SSI should provide a single administrative domain. That means once the system administrator has logged in and has been authenticated by the system, the administrator should be able to perform all tasks for the entire system from that node. The SSI enables killing, suspending, and resuming any process, independent of its location. A system administrator further has the ability to trigger the migration of a process. This is sometimes necessary to vacate a portion of the system so it can be taken down for maintenance or repair. To do this, it must be possible to "down" network links, disks, CPUs, and whole nodes. Once down, they wont be allocated and used again until they have been fixed or are done with maintenance.

System administrators also need the ability to monitor nodes and links to troubleshoot problems or look for early signs of failures. An SSI can help with these tasks by providing utilities to search, filter, and rotate logs as an aggregate so an administrator does not need to login or access each node individually.

Often, each node has its own copy of system files, libraries, and the OS installed on a local disk. This increases performance and enhances scalability. An SSI provides functions to keep the versions of all these files synchronized and allows a system administrator to update the system software on all nodes with a single command.

Implementation of an SSI

The previous section looked at the functionality an SSI provides to users, programmers, and system administrators. This section provides a little bit more detail on how these abstractions are implemented and at what level of the system hierarchy. Figure 1 shows the layers of a system that contain SSI functions. User level is a CPU mode of operation where hardware prevents certain resource accesses. Applications and utilities run at this level. At the kernel level, all (local) resources are fully accessible. The OS kernel runs at this privilege level and manages resources on behalf of the applications running above it.

At the bottom of the hierarchy is the hardware. Some SSI features can only be implemented at that level. If the necessary hardware is missing, that feature will not be available or only very inefficiently in the form of a software layer. Shared memory on a system without hardware support for it is such an example.

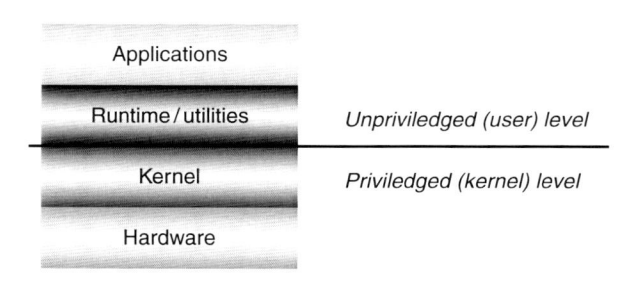

Single System Image. Fig. 1 Privilege and abstraction layers in a typical system

One level above the hardware resides the OS kernel. Some SSI functionality, for example, process migration, needs to be implemented at that level. Above the OS is the runtime layer and system utilities. This layer is sometimes called middle-ware. A batch and job control system which determines when and were (on which nodes) a job should run can be found at this level. Of course, utilities at that layer need the support of the OS and ultimately the underlying hardware to do their job.

Above that are the applications that make use of the system. Some SSI functionality, for example, application-level checkpoint and restart can be implemented at that level, for example, in a library. Table 1 shows various SSI features and at what level they are implemented. Some can be implemented at more than one level. Only the levels that have been traditionally used, and where a feature is most efficient, are marked.

Shared Memory

Sharing memory that is distributed among several nodes requires hardware support to work well. Implementations in software of so-called Distributed Shared Memory (DSM) systems have been done, but they all suffer from poor performance and scalability.

Single System Image. Table 1 Features of an SSI and at what layer of the system hierarchy they are most commonly implemented

Feature	Implementation layer			
	HW	Kernel	Runtime	App.
Shared memory	●			
Up/down sys components	●	●	●	
Debugger support		●	●	
Process migration		●		
Stdin/stdout		●		
File system		●		
System calls		●		
Checkpoint/restart		●	●	●
Batch system			●	
Login load leveling			●	
Sys log management			●	
SW maintenance			●	

Management of System Components

In larger systems, it is desirable to mark components as being down so they wont be used anymore. Marking a node down, for example, should prevent the job scheduling system from allocating that node. In some systems, it is possible to mark links as being down and have the system route messages around that link. This is useful for system maintenance. Components that need repair wont be used until the system is brought down during the regular maintenance period, when all failed components can be repaired at the same time. Depending on the sophistication of this management feature, it requires hardware and kernel support. Simply telling the node allocator to avoid certain nodes can be done at user level in the runtime system.

Debugger Support

A debugger is a user-level program like any other application. However, in order to signal and control processes, and to inspect their memory and registers, the debugger needs support from the OS. Some SSI modify kernels such that standard Unix facilities, for example, signals and process control, are extended to any process in the system; independent of which node they are currently running on. In that case, the debugger does not need to change, although adding support to debug multiple processes at the same time makes it a more useful tool.

If the OS is not capable of providing these services, they can be implemented in the debugger with the help of runtime system features such as daemons and remote procedure calls (RPC).

Process Migration

Migrating a process to another node is useful for load balancing and as a precautionary measure before a node is marked down. Migrating a process requires that all data structures, such as the Process Control Block (PCB), which the OS maintains for this process, migrate in addition to the code and user-level data structures the process has created. A completely transparent migration also requires that file handles to open files and those used for IPC are migrated as well. That, in return, requires that some information remains in the local OS about where the process has migrated to. (Or that all connections to the migrating process are updated before the migration.) For example, another process on the local node which was communicating with the migrated process via IPC will continue to do so. When data arrives for the migrated process, the OS needs to forward the data to the new location. If a process migrates multiple times, forwarding becomes more expensive and convoluted.

Stdin/Stdout

The default channels for input to and output from a process under UNIX are called stdin and stdout. If a user is logged into one node and starts a process on another, then the OS transfers data between these two nodes on behalf of the user. If an application consists of multiple processes, the OS ensures that output from all of them gets funneled through the stdout channel to the user. Data from the stdin channel usually does not get replicated and only the first process that reads it, will receive a copy. The OS must maintain these data channels even if processes migrate to other nodes, otherwise the illusion of a single system image would be broken.

File System

In a system managed by an SSI, all processes should see the same directory (folder) and file hierarchy. This feature, called shared root, is what is available on a desktop system where multiple processes can access files on the local disk. In a parallel system, files are often distributed among multiple disks to enhance performance and scalability. Distributing files like that complicates things, since metadata (information about files and directories) may not be located on the same device as the files themselves. Yet, metadata must be kept up-to-date to preserve file semantics. For example, two processes appending data to the end of a file must not overwrite each other's data. That requires that the file pointer always points to the true end of the file.

Some files which the OS frequently accesses should be local to the node. However, some files, such as/etc/passwd, should be the same on all nodes and a system administrator should have the ability to update only one of them and then propagate the changes to all copies. On the other hand, some (pseudo) files that describe local devices for example, need to be unique on each node. If a process migrates and had one of these files open, it must continue to interact with the device on the original node, even though a file with the same name exists on the new node as well. Yet for other files, temporary files for example, it may be desirable that they are only visible locally. File systems that can handle all these cases are complex and need to be tightly integrated with the OS.

System Calls

System calls are functions an application uses to interact with the OS. Calls for opening, closing, reading, and writing a file are typical. So are calls to create and control other processes. An SSI that wants to maintain these calls unchanged in a distributed system requires changes to the OS kernel. For example, process creation may not be strictly local anymore, if the system tries to balance load by creating new processes on less busy nodes.

Checkpoint/Restart

Long-running applications often do not finish, due to an interruption by a faulty component or a software problem. This is especially true for parallel applications, where it is more likely that at least one of the many nodes it runs on will fail. To combat this problem, an application occasionally writes intermediate data and its current state to disk. When a failure occurs, the application is restarted on a different node, or on the same node after it has been rebooted or repaired. The application then reads the checkpoint data written earlier and continues its computation.

This can be done by the application itself, in the runtime system, or in the OS kernel. The latter has the nice property that application writers do not need to worry about it, but it has the potential for waste, since the kernel cannot know what data the application will need to restart. Therefore, it has to checkpoint the complete application state and all of its data. Checkpoint/restart needs to be integrated with the SSI system, even if checkpointing is done at the application level.

Batch System

Many parallel systems use a batch scheduler to increase throughput of jobs through the system and to allow it to continue processing unattended, for example, at night or on weekends. Users submit scripts that describe the application they want to run, how much time they require, and how many nodes the application needs. The batch scheduler uses the job priority and knowledge about available nodes to select and run the jobs currently enqueued for processing.

A batch system is one of the most common SSI components in a cluster. It allows the user to treat the collection of machines as a single system and use a single command to submit jobs to it. A batch system provides additional commands to view status information about the currently enqueued and running jobs and to manage them. All these commands treat jobs as if they were a single process on the local system.

Login Load Leveling

Parallel systems usually have more than one node where users can log in. In a partitioned system, there is a service partition comprised of the nodes dedicated to user login and common tasks such as editing files and compiling applications. Parallel jobs are then run on nodes that have been assigned to the compute partition. Often, nodes in the service partition are of a different type; they may have more memory or local disks attached. Smaller clusters may not use partitioning, though that is less efficient. In either case, the SSI should present a single address to the outside world. When a user logs in at that address, the SSI picks one of the service nodes for that user to log in. The choice is usually made based on the current work load of each node in the service partition. As far as the user is concerned, there is only one login node.

System Log Management

A lot of information about the current state of the system is stored in log files that are unique to each node of a parallel system. System administrators consult these logs to diagnose problems and to detect and prevent faults before they occur (e.g., warnings about the rising temperature inside a CPU). An SSI should provide functions to aggregate these individual files and let system administrators search through, purge, or archive them with a single command.

Software Maintenance

The software versions of the system utilities, libraries, and applications installed on each node must be the same system-wide or at least be compatible with each other. As with system log management, an SSI should provide functions to system administrators that allow them to upgrade and check software packages on multiple nodes with a single command.

Imperfect SSI

The previous sections listed the features an SSI must provide and a glance at what implementing them entails. Many of these features are independent components and useful even when none of the other components are available. In fact, no SSI running on more than a couple hundred of nodes implements all features described thus far. The reason for that is scalability. Some features work well when used on eight nodes, but become unusably slow when extended much beyond that number.

Among the most costly features described earlier is process migration, especially if an SSI tries to achieve complete transparency. Once a process starts interacting with other processes on a node and obtains file handles to node-local resources, it becomes difficult to migrate that process. After migration, a forwarding mechanism must be in place to route information to the new location of the migrated process. If the original node retains information about the new location of the migrated process, a failure of that node will disrupt the flow of information. If no information is kept at the original location, then all processes that are communicating with the migrated process must be told about the new location. If migration is frequent, and interaction among processes is high, this becomes very costly. Furthermore, it does not always work, for example, if the migrated process was using a peripheral that is only available on the original node. Another high-cost SSI item is shared memory. Even when supported by hardware, the illusion of a single, large memory starts to fall apart as the number of nodes (CPUs) increases.

Not all is lost, though. Some systems deploy additional hardware to assist with some SSI features. For example, some systems have an additional network and disks dedicated to system software maintenance. Furthermore, complete transparency is not always required, and users are willing to use different commands and utilities when dealing with parallel processes, in return for better performance and scalability. For example, using a command such as qsub to submit a parallel job does not seem a high burden compared to the transparent method of just naming the application on the command line to start it. The UNIX command ps is used to obtain process status information. In a transparent SSI system, it would return that information even if the process is not local, or return information about many processes, if they are part of a parallel application.

In contrast, users often only want to know whether their job is running and whether it is making progress. The batch system has a command that can answer at least the former question and a `ps` output for hundreds of processes scattered throughout the system would not provide any additional useful information.

Therefore, even a partial SSI can be of benefit. Application users benefit most from a batch scheduling system. This also assists system administrators who also need a way to efficiently manage the hardware and software of the system. Most other functionality, especially less scalable features, are not strictly necessary to make a parallel system useful. That may mean additional utilities that expose the distributed aspects of the system and modifications to applications to allow them to work in parallel and with greater efficiency.

Future Directions

Desktop systems with two or four CPU cores are common now. High-performance systems will be the first to receive CPUs with tens of cores, but those CPUs will soon be common. Desktop OSs will adapt to these systems and provide SSI features to manage and use the cores in a single system. Users will expect to see these features in parallel systems as well, which will drive the development of SSI features and integration into parallel OSs.

At the very high-end, exascale systems are on the horizon. Implementing SSI for these systems will be a challenge due to the size of these systems. Displaying the status of a hundred-thousand nodes in a readable fashion without endless scrollbars is only feasible with intelligent software that zooms in on interesting events and features of the system. Commercial tools for applications that span that many nodes do not exist yet. Simple tools have a better chance at scaling to these future systems, but managing and debugging such large applications and systems will remain a challenge.

Related Entries

▶ Checkpointing
▶ Clusters
▶ Fault Tolerance
▶ Operating System Strategies
▶ Scalability

Bibliographic Notes and Further Reading

Overviews of SSI are presented in [3], Chapter 11 of [13], and [8]. The descriptions of actual systems are out of date or the systems are not in use anymore. Nevertheless, the fundamental features and issues described are still valid.

Many papers discuss specific aspects of SSI. For example, [5] and [4] discuss partitioning and present job launch mechanisms. In [12], the authors discuss specific SSI challenges for petascale systems. SSI tools to make system administration easier are presented in [2, 7, 15].

Process migration is discussed in detail in [10] and specific implementations appear in MOSIX [1], BProc [6], and IBM's WPAR [9], among others. The survey in [16] is a little bit dated, but it gives a good description of so-called worms, which are processes specifically designed to migrate.

Implementations of SSI, most of them partial, abound even before the term SSI was coined. Examples include LOCUS [17], Plan 9 [14], MOSIX [1], and Kerrighed [11].

Bibliography

1. Barak A, La'adan O (1998) The MOSIX multicomputer operating system for high performance cluster computing. Future Gener Comput Syst 13(4–5):361–372
2. Brightwell R, Fisk LA, Greenberg DS, Hudson T, Levenhagen M, Maccabe AB, Riesen R (2000) Massively parallel computing using commodity components. Parallel Comput 26(2–3):243–266
3. Buyya R, Cortes T, Jin H (2001) Single system image. Int J High Perform Comput Appl 15(2):124–135
4. Frachtenberg E, Petrini F, Fernandez J, Pakin S, Coll S (2002) STORM: lightning-fast resource management. In: Supercomputing '02: proceedings of the 2002 ACM/IEEE conference on supercomputing, Baltimore. IEEE Computer Society, Los Alamitos, pp 1–26
5. Greenberg DS, Brightwell R, Fisk LA, Maccabe AB, Riesen R (1997) A system software architecture for high-end computing. In: SC'97: high performance networking and computing: proceedings of the 1997 ACM/IEEE SC97 conference, San Jose, Raleigh, 15–21 Nov 1997. ACM/IEEE Computer Society, New York
6. Hendriks E (2002) BPROC: the Beowulf distributed process space. In: ICS '02: proceedings of the 16th international conference on supercomputing, pp 129–136. ACM, New York
7. Hendriks EA, Minnich RG (2006) How to build a fast and reliable 1024 node cluster with only one disk. J Supercomput 36(2):171–181
8. Hwang K, Jin H, Chow E, Wang C-L, Xu Z (1999) Designing SSI clusters with hierarchical check pointing and single I/O space. IEEE Concurr 7(1):60–69

9. Kharat S, Mishra R, Das R, Vishwanathan S (2008) Migration of software partition in UNIX system. In: Compute '08: proceedings of the first Bangalore annual compute conference, Bangalore. ACM, New York, pp 1–4
10. Milojičić DS, Douglis F, Paindaveine Y, Wheeler R, Zhou S (2000) Process migration. ACM Comput Surv 32(3):241–299
11. Morin C, Gallard P, Lottiaux R, Vallée G (2004) Towards an efficient single system image cluster operating system. Future Gener Comput Syst 20(4):505–521
12. Ong H, Vetter J, Studham RS, McCurdy C, Walker B, Cox A (2006) Kernel-level single system image for petascale computing. SIGOPS Oper Syst Rev 40(2):50–54
13. Pfister GF (1998) In search of clusters: the ongoing battle in lowly parallel computing, 2nd edn. Prentice-Hall, Upper Saddle River
14. Pike R, Presotto D, Thompson K, Trickey H, Winterbottom P (1993) The use of name spaces in Plan 9. SIGOPS Oper Syst Rev 27(2):72–76
15. Skjellum A, Dimitrov R, Angaluri SV, Lifka D, Coulouris G, Uthayopas P, Scott SL, Eskicioglu R (2001) Systems administration. Int J High Perform Comput Appl 15(2):143–161
16. Smith JM (1988) A survey of process migration mechanisms. SIGOPS Oper Syst Rev 22(3):28–40
17. Walker B, Popek G, English R, Kline C, Thiel G (1983) The LOCUS distributed operating system. In: SOSP '83: proceedings of the ninth ACM symposium on operating systems principles, Bretton Woods. ACM, New York, pp 49–70

Singular-Value Decomposition (SVD)

▶ Eigenvalue and Singular-Value Problems

Sisal

JOHN FEO
Pacific Northwest National Laboratory, Richland, WA, USA

Definition

Streams and Iterations in a Single Assignment Language (Sisal) was a general-purpose applicative language developed for shared-memory and vector supercomputer systems. It provided an hierarchical intermediate form, parallel runtime system, optimizing compiler, and programming environment. The language was strongly typed. It supported both array and stream data structures, and had both iterative and parallel loop constructs.

Discussion

Introduction

Streams and Iterations in a Single Assignment Language (Sisal) was a general-purpose applicative language defined by Lawrence Livermore National Laboratory, Colorado Sate University, University of Manchester and Digital Equipment Corporation in the early 1980s [1]. Lawrence Livermore and Colorado State developed the language over the next 2 decades. They maintained the language definition, compiler and runtime system, programming tools, and provided education and user support services. The language version used widely in the 1980s and 1990s was Sisal 1.2 [2]. Three Sisal user conferences were held in 1991, 1992, and 1993 [3, 4].

The Sisal Language Project had four major accomplishments: (1) IF1, an intermediate form used widely in research [5]; (2) OSC, an optimizing compiler that preallocated memory for most data structures and eliminated unnecessary coping and reference count operations [7]; (3) a highly efficient, threaded runtime system that supported most shared-memory, parallel computer systems [6], and (4) execution performance and scalability equivalent to imperative languages [1, 8].

Language Definition

Sisal's applicative semantics and keyword-centric syntax proved to be a simple, easy-to-use, easy-to-read parallel programming language that facilitated algorithm development and simplified compilation. Since the value of any expression depended only on the values of its subexpressions and not on the order of evaluation, Sisal programs defined the data dependencies among operations, but left the scheduling of operations, the communication of data values, and the synchronization of concurrent operations to the compiler and runtime system.

Sisal was strongly typed. Programmers specified the types of only function parameters; the compiler inferred all other types. All functions were mathematically sound. A function had access to only its arguments and there were no side effects. Each function invocation was independent and functions did not retain state between invocations. Sisal programs were referentially transparent and single-assignment. Since a name was bound to one value and not a memory location, there was no aliasing. In general, a Sisal program defined a set of mathematical expressions where names stood for specific values, and computations progressed without state making the transformation from source code to dataflow graph trivial.

Sisal supported the standard scalar data types: boolean, character, integer, real, and double precision. It also included the aggregate types: array, stream, record, and union. All arrays were one-dimensional; multidimensional arrays were arrays of arrays. The type, size, and lower bound of an array was not defined explicitly, rather it was a consequence of execution. Arrays were created by gathering elements, "modifying" existing arrays, or catenations.

A stream was a sequence of values of uniform type. In Sisal, stream elements were accessible in order only; there was no random access. A stream could have only one producer, but many consumers. By definition, Sisal streams were nonstrict – each element was available as soon as it was produced. The Sisal runtime system supported the concurrent execution of the producer and consumer(s).

The two major language constructs were *for initial* and *for* expressions. The former expression substituted for sequential iteration in conventional languages, but retained single assignment semantics. The rebinding of loop names to values was implicit and occurred between iterations. Loop names prefixed with *old* referred to previous values. A returns clause defined the results and arity of the expression. Each result was either the final value of some loop name or a reduction of the values assigned to a loop name during loop execution. The following *for initial* expression returns the prefix sum of A

```
for initial
    i := 0;
    x := A[i]
while i < n repeat
    i := old i + 1;
    x := old x + A[i]
returns array of x
end for
```

Sisal supported seven intrinsic reductions: *array of*, *stream of*, *catenate*, *sum*, *product*, *least*, and *greatest*. The order of reduction was determinate.

The *for* expression provided a way to specify independent iterations. The semantics of the expression did not allow references to values defined in other iterations. The expression was controlled by a range expression that could be simple, a dot product of ranges, or a cross product of ranges. The next two expressions compute the dot and cross product of two arrays of size n and m

```
for i in 0 to n - 1 dot j
     in 0 to m - 1
  x := A[i] * B[j]
returns sum of x
end for
for i in 0 to n - 1 cross j
     in 0 to m - 1
  x := A[i] * B[j]
returns array of x
end for
```

Note that the expression does not indicate how the parallel iterations should be scheduled. The management of parallel threads was the responsibility of the compiler and runtime systems and was highly tuned for each architecture. This separation of responsibility greatly simplified Sisal programs, improved portability, and made the language easy to use.

Build-in-Place Analysis

The Sisal compile process comprised eight phases shown in Fig. 1. The two most important phases concerned build-in-place (IF2MEM) and update-in-place analysis (IF2UP). IF2 was a superset of IF1. It was not applicative as it included operations (AT-nodes) that directly referenced and manipulated memory.

Prior to Sisal, functional programming languages were considered very inefficient. Since the size and structure of aggregate data types are a consequence of execution, without analysis aggregates must be built one element at a time possibly requiring elements to be copied many times as the aggregate grows in size. Moreover, strict adherence to single-assignment semantics requires construction of a new array whenever a single element is modified.

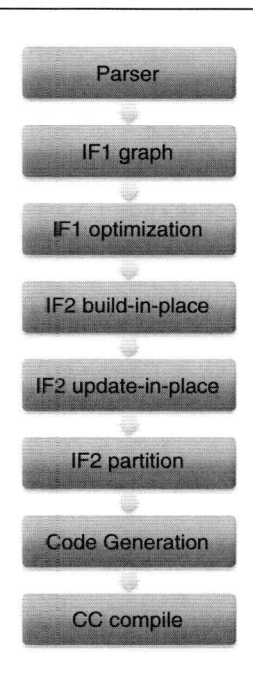

Sisal. Fig. 1 OSC phases

(Flowchart: Parser → IF1 graph → IF1 optimization → IF2 build-in-place → IF2 update-in-place → IF2 partition → Code Generation → CC compile)

Build-in-place analysis attacked the incremental construction problem [6]. The algorithm had two passes. Pass 1 visited nodes in data flow order, and built, where possible, an expression to calculate an array's size at run time. The expression was a function of the semantics of the array constructor and the size expressions of its inputs. Determining the size of an array built during loop execution required an expression to calculate the number of loop iterations before the loop executes. Deriving this expression was not possible for all loops. Pass 1 concluded by pushing, in the order of encounter, the nodes for the size expression onto a stack.

Pass 2 removed nodes from the stack, inserted them into the data flow graph, and appropriately wired memory references among them by inserting edges transmitting pointers to memory. If a node was the parent of an already converted node, it could build its result directly into the memory allocated to its child, thus eliminating the intermediate array. If the node was not the parent of an already converted node, it built its result in a new memory location. Note that the ordering of nodes on the stack guaranteed processing of children before parents.

Update-in-Place Analysis

Update-in-place analysis attacked the aggregate update problem [7]. OSC introduced dependences in the data flow graph to schedule readers of an aggregate object before writers. It used reference counts to identify the last use of an object. If the last use was a write, then the write was executed in place. By re-ordering nodes and aggregating reference copy operations, OSC eliminated up to 98% of explicit reference count operations in larger programs without reducing parallelism. Consequently, the inefficiencies of reference counting largely disappeared and the benefits of updating aggregate objects were fully enjoyed by Sisal programs.

OSC considered an array as two separately reference-counted objects: a dope vector defining the array's logical extent and the physical space containing its constituents. As array elements are computed and stored, dope vectors cycle between dependent nodes to communicate the current status of the regions under construction. As a result, multiple dope vectors might reference the same or different regions of the physical space and the individual participants in the construction would produce new dope vectors to communicate the current status of the regions to their predecessors. Without update-in-place optimization, each stage in construction would copy a dope vector.

Runtime System

The runtime software supported the parallel execution of Sisal programs, provided general purpose dynamic storage allocation, implemented operations on major data structures, and interfaced with the operating system for input/output and command line processing [7].

The Sisal runtime made modest demands of the host operating system. At program initiation a command line option specified the number of operating system processes (workers) to instantiate for the duration of the program. The runtime system maintained two queues of threads: the For Pool and the Ready List. A worker was always in one of three modes of operation: executing a thread from the For Pool, executing a thread from the Ready Pool, or idle. The runtime system allocated stacks for threads on demand, but every effort was made to reuse previously allocated stacks and thus reduce allocation and deallocation overhead.

The For Pool maintained slices of *for* expressions. A worker would pick up a slice, execute it, and return to the pool for another slice. The worker that executed the last slice of an expression placed the parent thread on the Ready List, and returned to the For Pool to look for slices from other expressions. By persisting in executing slices of *for* expressions, a worker avoided deallocating and allocating its stack.

The Ready List maintained all other threads made executable by events, such as the main program or function calls. If a worker found no work on either Pool, it examined the Storage Deallocation List for deferred storage deallocation work.

Sisal relied on dynamic storage allocation for many data values such as arrays and streams, and for internal objects such as thread descriptors and execution stacks. It used a two-level allocation mechanism that was fast, efficient, and parallelizable. A standard boundary tag scheme was augmented with multiple entry points to a circular list of free blocks. Both the free list search and deallocation of blocks were parallelized, even though the former sometimes completely removed blocks from the list and the latter coalesced physically adjacent but logically distant blocks. To increase speed, an exact-fit caching mechanism was interposed before the boundary tag scheme. It used a working set of different sizes of recently freed blocks.

Performance

As noted above, most Sisal programs executed as fast as their imperative language counterparts. Consequently, Sisal attracted a wide user community that developed many different types of parallel applications, including benchmark codes, mathematical methods, scientific simulations, systems optimization, and bioinformatics.

Table 1 lists the execution times of four applications and Table 2 gives compilation statistics for each program. Columns 2–4 give the number of static arrays built, preallocated, and built-in-place; columns 5–8 list the number of copy, conditional copy and reference count operations after optimization, and the number of artificial dependency edges introduced by the compiler.

It is instructive to examine two of the applications. SIMPLE was a two-dimensional Lagrangian hydrodynamics code developed at Lawrence Livermore National Laboratory to simulate the behavior of a fluid in a sphere. The hydrodynamic and heat condition equations are solved by finite difference methods. A tabular ideal gas equation determines the relation between state variables. The implementation of SIMPLE in Sisal 1.2 was straightforward and highly parallel.

The compiler preallocated and built all arrays in place (261 of them), eliminated all absolute copy operations, marked 19 copy operations for run time check, and eliminated 2,005 out of 2,066 reference count operations. The 19 conditional copy operations were a result of row sharing. Since they always tested false at runtime, no copy operations actually occured. For 62 iterations of a 100 × 100 grid problem, the Sisal and Fortran versions of SIMPLE on one processor executed in 3,099.3 and 3,081.3 s, respectively. On ten processors, the Sisal code realized a speedup of 7.3. An equivalent of 1.5 processors

Sisal. Table 1 Execution times

Program	Fortran	Sisal (#p)	Sisal (#p)	Speedup
GaussJordan	54.0 s	54.5 s (1)	8.8 s (10)	6.2
RICARD	30.6 h	31.0 h	3.5 h (10)	9.0
SIMPLE	3081.3 s	3099.3 s(1)	422.0 (10)	7.3
Simulated annealing	476.6 s	956.2 s (1)	267.8 s (5)	3.6

Sisal. Table 2 OSC optimizations

Program	Arrays	PreAllocated	Built inplace	Copy	CCopy	Ref counts	Artificial edges
GaussJordan	7	7	7	0	0	1	9
RICARD	29	29	28	0	6	7	5
SIMPLE	261	261	261	0	19	61	347
Simulated annealing	46	46	42	0	4	41	168

was lost in allocating and deallocating two-dimensional arrays. The implementation of true multi-dimensional arrays was proposed in both Sisal 2.0 [9] and Sisal 90. [These language definitions were defined near the end of the project, but never implemented.]

Simulated annealing is a generic Monte Carlo optimization technique for solving many difficult combinatorial problems. In the case of the school timetable problem, the objective is to assign a set of tuples to a fixed set of time slots (periods) such that no critical resource is scheduled more than once in any period. Each tuple is a record of four fields: class, room, subject, and teacher. Classes, rooms, and teachers are critical resources; subjects are not. At each step of the procedure, a tuple is chosen at random and moved to another period. If the new schedule has equivalent or lower cost, the move is accepted. If the new schedule has higher cost, the move is accepted with a certain exponential probability. If the move is not accepted, the tuple is returned to its original period. The procedure can be paralleilized by simultaneously choosing one tuple from each nonempty period and applying the move criterion to each. The accepted moves are then carried out one at a time.

OSC preallocated memory for all the arrays, and built all but four of the arrays in place. It removed all absolute copy operations, marked four copy operations for run time check, and removed all but 41 reference count operations. The four arrays not built in pace resulted from adding a tuple to a period. Although the compiler did not mark the new periods for build-in-place, the periods were rarely copied. When an element was removed from the high-end of an array, the array's logical size shrunk by one, but its physical size remained constant. Thus, when an element was added to a period, there was often space to add the element without copying. Whenever copying occurred, extra space was allocated to accommodate future growth. This foresight saved over 15,000 copies in this application at the cost of a few hundred bytes of storage.

Bibliographic Notes and Further Reading

For a summary of the project and details on the compiler and runtime system see [1]. The language definition can be found in [2]. IF1 is described [5].

Build-in-place analysis and update-in-place analysis are described in more detail in [6] and [7], respectively.

In 1991 and then again in 1992 two new versions of the language, Sisal 2.0 and Sisal 90, were defined. These versions included: higher-order functions, user-defined reductions, parameterized data types, foreign language modules, array syntax, and rectangular arrays. While compilers for the version were never released there is some information available on the web.

Bibliography

1. Feo JT, Cann D, Oldehoeft R (1990) A report of the Sisal Language Project. J Parallel Distrib Comput 10(4):349–366
2. McGraw J et al (1985) Sisal: streams and iterations in a single-assignment language, reference manual version 1.2. Lawrence Livermore National Laboratory Manual M-146, Livermore, CA, September 1985
3. Feo J (ed) Proceedings of the 2nd Sisal User Conference. Lawrence Livermore National Laboratory, CONF-9210270, San Diego, CA, October 1992
4. Feo J (ed) Proceedings 3rd Sisal User Conference. Lawrence Livermore National Laboratory, CONF-9310206, San Diego, CA, October 1993
5. Skedzielewski S, Glauert J (1985) IF1 – an intermediate form for applicative languages. Lawrence Livermore National Laboratory Manual M-170, Livermore National Laboratory, Livermore, CA, September 1985
6. Ranelletti J (1996) Graph transformation algorithms for array memory optimization in applicative languages. PhD dissertation, University of California at Davis, CA, May 1996
7. Cann D (1998) Compilation techniques for high performance applicative computation. PhD dissertation, Colorado State University, CO, May 1998
8. Cann D (1992) Retire Fortran?: A debate rekindled. Commun ACM 35(8):81–89
9. Oldehoeft R et al (1991) The Sisal 2.0 reference manual. Lawrence Livermore National Laboratory, Technical Report UCRL-MA-109098, Livermore, CA, December 1991

Small-World Network Analysis and Partitioning (SNAP) Framework

▶SNAP (Small-World Network Analysis and Partitioning) Framework

SNAP (Small-World Network Analysis and Partitioning) Framework

KAMESH MADDURI
Lawrence Berkeley National Laboratory, Berkeley, CA, USA

Synonyms

Graph analysis software; Small-world network analysis and partitioning (SNAP) framework

Definition

SNAP (Small-world Network Analysis and Partitioning) is a framework for exploratory analysis of large-scale complex networks. It provides a collection of optimized parallel implementations for common graph-theoretic problems.

Discussion

Introduction

Graphs are a fundamental abstraction for modeling and analyzing data, and are pervasive in real-world applications. Transportation networks (road and airline traffic), socio-economic interactions (friendship circles, organizational hierarchies, online collaboration networks), and biological systems (food webs, protein interaction networks) are a few examples of data that can be naturally represented as graphs. Understanding the dynamics and evolution of real-world network abstractions is an interdisciplinary research challenge with wide-ranging implications. Empirical studies on networks have led to a variety of models to characterize their topology and evolution. Quite surprisingly, it has been shown that graph abstractions arising from diverse systems such as the Internet, social interactions, and biological networks exhibit common structural features such as a low diameter, unbalanced degree distributions, self-similarity, and the presence of dense subgraphs [1, 11, 14]. Some of these topological features are captured by what is known as the *small-world* model or phenomenon.

The analysis of large graph abstractions, particularly small-world complex networks, raises interesting computational challenges. Graph algorithms are typically highly memory intensive, make heavy use of data structures such as lists, sets, queues, and hash tables, and exhibit a combination of data and task-level parallelism. On current workstations, it is infeasible to do exact in-core computations on graphs larger than 100 million vertex/edge entities (*large* in general refers to the typical problem size for which the graph and the associated data structures do not fit in 2–4 GB of main memory). In such cases, parallel computers can be utilized to obtain solutions for memory and compute-intensive graph problems quickly. Due to power constraints and diminishing returns from instruction-level parallelism, the computing industry is rapidly converging towards widespread use of multicore chips and accelerators. Unfortunately, several known parallel algorithms for graph-theoretic problems do not easily map onto clusters of multicore systems. The mismatch arises due to the fact that current systems lean towards efficient execution of regular computations with low memory footprints and working sets, and heavily penalize memory-intensive applications with irregular memory accesses; however, parallel graph algorithms in the past were mostly designed assuming an underlying, well-balanced compute-memory platform. The small-world characteristics of real networks, and the load-balancing constraints they impose during parallelization, represent an additional challenge to the design of scalable graph algorithms.

SNAP [2, 10] is an open-source computational framework for graph-theoretic analysis of large-scale complex networks. It is intended to be an optimized collection of computational kernels (or algorithmic building-blocks) that the end-user could readily use and compose to answer higher-level, ad-hoc graph analysis queries. The target platforms for SNAP are shared-memory multicore and symmetric multiprocessor systems. SNAP kernels are implemented in C and use OpenMP for parallelization. On distributed memory systems, SNAP can be used for intra-node parallelization, and the user has to manage inter-node communication, and also identify and implement parallelism at a coarser node-level granularity.

The parallel graph algorithms in SNAP are significantly faster than alternate implementations in other open-source graph software. This is due to a combination of the use of memory-efficient data structures, preprocessing kernels that are tuned for small-world

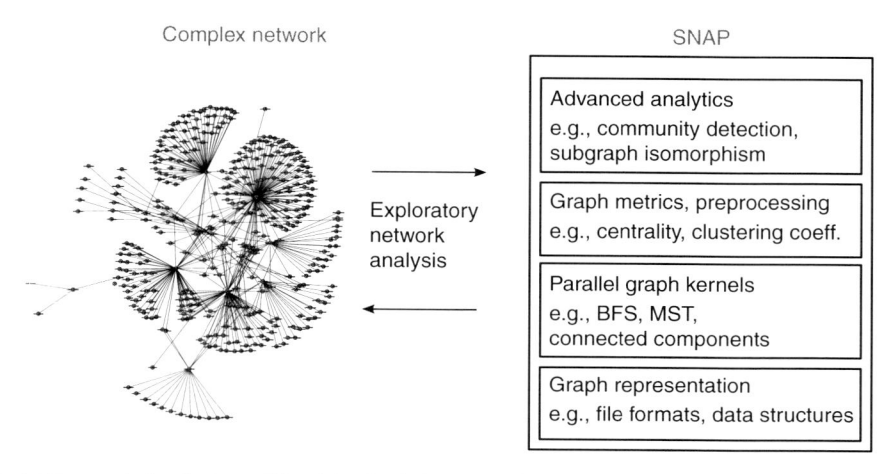

Complex network → Exploratory network analysis → SNAP

SNAP:
- Advanced analytics
  e.g., community detection, subgraph isomorphism
- Graph metrics, preprocessing
  e.g., centrality, clustering coeff.
- Parallel graph kernels
  e.g., BFS, MST, connected components
- Graph representation
  e.g., file formats, data structures

SNAP (Small-World Network Analysis and Partitioning) Framework. Fig. 1 A schematic of the SNAP graph analysis framework [8]

networks, as well as algorithms that are designed to specifically target cache-based multicore architectures. These issues are discussed in more detail in the following sections of this article.

As the project title suggests, the initial design goals of SNAP were to provide scalable parallel solutions for community structure detection [4], a problem variant of graph partitioning that is of great interest in social, and in general, small-world network analysis. Community structure detection is informally defined as identifying densely connected sets of vertices in the network, thereby revealing latent structure in a large-scale network. It is similar to the problem of graph partitioning in scientific computing, as is usually formulated as a graph clustering problem. SNAP includes several different parallel algorithms for solving this problem of community detection.

Graph Representation

The first issue that arises in the design of graph algorithms is the use of appropriate in-memory data structures for representing the graph. The data to be analyzed typically resides on disk in a database, or in multiple files. As the data is read from disk and loaded into main memory, a graph representation is simultaneously constructed. The minimal layout that would constitute an in-memory graph representation is a list of edge tuples with vertex identifiers indicating the source and destination vertices, and any attributes associated with the edges and vertices. However, this does not give one easy access to lists of edges originating from a specific vertex. Thus, the next commonly used representation is to sort the edge tuple list by the source vertex identifier, and store all the adjacencies of a particular vertex in a contiguous array. This is the primary *adjacency list* representation of graphs that is supported in SNAP. Edges can have multiple attributes associated with them, in which case they can either be stored along with the corresponding adjacency vertex identifier, or in separate auxiliary arrays. This representation is space-efficient, has a low computational overhead for degree and membership queries, and provides cache-friendly access to adjacency iterators.

In cases where one requires periodic structural updates to the graph, such as insertions and deletions of edges, SNAP uses alternate graph representations. An extension to the static representation is the use of dynamic, resizable adjacency arrays. Clearly, this would support fast insertions. Further, parallel insertions can be supported using non-blocking atomic increment operations on most of the current platforms. There are two potential parallel performance issues with this data structure. Edge deletions are expensive in this representation, as one needs to scan the entire adjacency list in the worst case to locate the required tuple. The scan is particularly expensive for high-degree vertices. Second, there may be load-balancing issues with parallel edge insertions (for instance, consider the case where there are a stream of insertions to the adjacency list of a single vertex). These problems can be alleviated by batching the updates, or by randomly shuffling the updates before scheduling the insertions. If one uses sorted adjacency lists to address the deletion problem, then the cost of insertions goes up due to the overhead of maintaining the sorted order.

An alternative to arrays is the use of tree structures to support both quick insertions and deletions. Treaps are binary search trees with a priority (typically a random number) associated with each node. The priorities are maintained in heap order, and this data structure supports insertions, deletions, and searching in average-case logarithmic time. In addition, there are known efficient parallel algorithms for set operations on treaps such as union, intersection, and difference. Set operations are particularly useful to implement kernels such as graph traversal and induced subgraphs, and also for batch-processing updates.

To process both insertions and deletions efficiently, and also given the power-law degree distribution for small-world networks, **SNAP** supports a hybrid representation that uses dynamically resizable arrays to represent adjacencies of *low-degree* vertices, and treaps for *high-degree* vertices. The threshold to determine low and high-degree vertices can be varied based on the data set characteristics. By using dynamic arrays for low-degree vertices (which will be a majority of vertices in the graph), one can achieve good performance for insertions. Also, deletions are fast and cache-friendly for low-degree vertices, whereas they take logarithmic time for high-degree vertices represented using treaps. Madduri and Bader [9] discuss the parallel performance and space-time trade-offs involved with each of these representations in more detail.

Parallelization Strategies

There is a wide variety in the known approaches for exploiting parallelism in graph problems. Some of the easier ones to implement and analyze are computations involving iterations over vertex and edge lists, without much inter-iteration dependencies. For instance, queries such as determining the top-k high-degree vertices, or the maximum-weighted edge in the graph, can be easily parallelized. However, most parallel algorithms require the use of data structures such as priority queues and multisets. Further, one needs support for fast parallel operations on these structures, such as parallel insertions, membership queries, and batched deletions. Fine-grained, low overhead synchronization is an important requirement for several efficient parallel implementations. Further, the notion of *partitioning* a graph is closely related to several parallel graph algorithms. Given that inter-processor communication is expensive on distributed memory systems (compared to computation on a single node), several parallel graph approaches rely on a graph partitioning and vertex reordering preprocessing step to minimize communication in subsequent algorithm executions. Graph partitioning is relevant in the context of shared-memory **SNAP** algorithms as well, since it reduces parallel synchronization overhead and improves locality in memory accesses.

Consider the example of breadth-first graph traversal (BFS) as an illustration of more complex paradigms for parallelism in graph algorithms. Several **SNAP** graph kernels are designed to exploit fine-grained thread-level parallelism in graph traversal. There are two common parallel approaches to breadth-first search: *level-synchronous* graph traversal, where the adjacencies of vertices at each level in the graph are visited in parallel; and *path-limited searches*, where multiple searches from vertices that are *far apart* are concurrently executed, and the independent searches are aggregated. The level-synchronous approach is particularly suited for small-world networks due to their low graph diameter. Support for fine-grained efficient synchronization is critical in both these approaches. The **SNAP** implementation of BFS aggressively reduces locking and barrier constructs through algorithmic changes as well as architecture-specific optimizations. For instance, the **SNAP** BFS implementation uses a lock-free approach for tracking visited vertices and thread-local work queues, significantly reducing shared memory contention. While designing fine-grained algorithms for small-world networks, it is also important to take the unbalanced degree distributions into account. In a level-synchronized parallel BFS where vertices are statically assigned to multiple threads of execution, it is likely that there will be phases with severe work imbalance (due to the imbalance in vertex degrees). To avoid this, the **SNAP** implementation first estimates the processing work to be done at each vertex, and then assigns vertices accordingly to threads. Several other optimization techniques, and their relative performance benefits, are discussed by Bader and Madduri in more detail [2].

Graph algorithms often involve performance trade-offs associated with memory utilization and parallelization granularity. In cases where the input graph instance is small enough, one could create several replicates of the graph or the associated data structures for multiple threads to execute concurrently, and thus reduce synchronization overhead. SNAP utilizes this technique for the exact computation of betweenness centrality, which requires a graph traversal from each vertex. The fine-grained implementation parallelizing each graph traversal requires space linear in the number of vertices and edges, whereas the coarse-grained approach (the traversals are distributed among p threads) incurs a p-way multiplicative factor memory increase. Depending on the graph size, one could choose an appropriate number of replicates to reduce the synchronization overhead.

SNAP Kernels for Exploratory Network Analysis

Exploratory graph analysis often involves an iterative study of the structure and dynamics of a network, using a discriminating selection of topological metrics. SNAP supports fast exact and approximate computation of well-known social network analysis metrics, such as average vertex degree, clustering coefficient, average shortest path length, rich-club coefficient, and assortativity. Most of these metrics have a linear or sub-linear computational complexity, and are straightforward to implement. When used appropriately, they not only provide insight into the network structure, but also help speed up subsequent analysis algorithms. For instance, the average neighbor connectivity metric is a weighted average that gives the average neighbor degree of a degree-k vertex. It is an indicator of whether vertices of a given degree preferentially connect to high- or low-degree vertices. Assortativity coefficient is a related metric, which is an indicator of community structure in a network. Based on these metrics, it may be possible to say whether the input data is representative of a specific common graph class, such as bipartite graphs or networks with pronounced community structure. This helps one choose an appropriate community detection algorithm and also the right clustering measure to optimize for. Other preprocessing kernels that are beneficial for exposing parallelism in the problem include computation of connected and biconnected components of the graph. If a graph is composed of several large connected components, it can be decomposed and individual components can be analyzed concurrently. A combination of these preprocessing kernels before the execution of a compute-intensive routine often lead to a substantial performance benefit, either by reducing the computation by pruning vertices or edges, or by exposing more coarse-grained concurrency and locality in the problem.

Community Identification Algorithms in SNAP

Several routines in SNAP are devoted to solving the community identification problem in small-world networks. Graph partitioning and community identification are related problems, but with an important difference: the most commonly used objective function in partitioning is minimization of edge cut, while trying to *balance the number of vertices* in each partition. The number of partitions is typically an input parameter for a partitioning algorithm. Clustering, on the other hand, optimizes for an appropriate application-dependent measure, and the number of clusters is unknown beforehand. Multilevel and spectral partitioning algorithms (e.g., Chaco [6] and Metis [7]) have been shown to be very effective for partitioning graph abstractions derived from physical topologies, such as finite-element meshes arising in scientific computing. However, the edge cut when partitioning small-world networks using these tools is nearly two orders of magnitude higher than the corresponding edge cut value for a nearly-Euclidean topology, for graph instances that are comparable in the number of vertices and edges. Clearly, small-world networks lack the topological regularity found in scientific meshes and physical networks, and current graph partitioning algorithms cannot be adapted as-is for the problem of community identification.

The parallel community identification algorithms in SNAP optimize for a measure called modularity. Let $C = (C_1, \ldots, C_k)$ denote a partition of the set of vertices V such that $C_i \neq \phi$ and $C_i \cap C_j = \phi$. The cluster $G(C_i)$ is identified with the induced subgraph $G[C_i] := (C_i, E(C_i))$, where $E(C_i) := \{\langle u, v \rangle \in E : u, v \in C_i\}$. Then, $E(C) := \cup_{i=1}^{k} E(C_i)$ is the set of intra-cluster edges and $\tilde{E}(C) := E - E(C)$ is the set of inter-cluster edges. Let $m(C_i)$ denote the number of inter-cluster edges in C_i. Then, the modularity measure $q(C)$ of a clustering C is defined as

$$q(C) = \sum_i \left[\frac{m(C_i)}{m} - \left(\frac{\sum_{v \in C_i} deg(v)}{2m} \right)^2 \right].$$

Intuitively, modularity captures the idea that a *good division* of a network into communities is one in which the inter-community edge count is less than what is expected by random chance. This measure does not try to minimize the edge cut in isolation, nor does it explicitly favor a balanced community partitioning. The general problem of modularity optimization has been shown to be $\mathcal{NP}$-complete, and so there are several known heuristics to maximize modularity. Most of the known techniques fall into one of the two broad categories: *divisive* and *agglomerative* clustering. In the agglomerative scheme, each vertex initially belongs to a singleton community, and communities whose amalgamation produces an increase in the modularity score are typically merged together. The divisive approach is a top-down scheme where the entire network is initially in one community, and the network is iteratively broken down into subcommunities. This hierarchical structure of community resolution can be represented using a tree (referred to as a dendrogram). The final list of the communities is given by the leaves of the dendrogram, and internal nodes correspond to splits (joins) in the divisive (agglomerative) approaches.

SNAP includes several parallel algorithms for community identification that use agglomerative and divisive clustering schemes [2]. One divisive clustering approach is based on the greedy betweenness-based algorithm proposed by Newman and Girvan [12]. In this approach, the community structure is resolved by iteratively filtering edges with high *edge betweenness centrality*, and tracking the modularity measure as edges are removed. The compute-intensive step in the algorithm is repeated computation of the edge betweenness scores in every iteration, and SNAP performs this computation in parallel. SNAP also supports several greedy agglomerative clustering approaches, and the main strategy to exploit parallelism in these schemes is to concurrently resolve communities that do not share intercommunity edges. Performance results on real-world networks indicate that the SNAP parallel community identification algorithms give substantial performance gains, without any loss in community structure (given by the modularity score) [2, 8].

Related Entries
▶ Chaco
▶ Graph Algorithms
▶ Graph Partitioning
▶ METIS and ParMETIS
▶ PaToH (Partitioning Tool for Hypergraphs)
▶ Social Networks

Bibliographic Notes and Further Reading

The community detection algorithms in SNAP are discussed in more detail in [3, 8]. Other popular libraries and frameworks for large-scale network analysis include Network Workbench [13], igraph [3], and the Parallel Boost Graph Library [5].

Bibliography

1. Amaral LAN, Scala A, Barthélémy M, Stanley HE (2000) Classes of small-world networks. Proc Natl Acad Sci USA 97(21): 11149–11152
2. Bader DA, Madduri K (April 2008) SNAP: Small-world Network Analysis and Partitioning: an open-source parallel graph framework for the exploration of large-scale networks. In: Proceedings of the 22nd IEEE International Parallel and Distributed Processing Symposium (IPDPS 2008), IEEE, Miami, FL
3. Csárdi G, Nepusz T (2006) The igraph software package for complex network research. InterJournal Complex Systems 1695. http://igraph.sf.net. Accessed May 2011
4. Fortunato S (Feb 2010) Community detection in graphs. Physics Reports 486(3–5):75–174
5. Gregor D, Lumsdaine A (July 2005) The Parallel BGL: a generic library for distributed graph computations. In: Proceedings of the Parallel/High-Performance Object-Oriented Scientific Computing (POOSC '05), IOS Press, Glasgow, UK
6. Hendrickson B, Leland R (Dec 1995) A multilevel algorithm for partitioning graphs. In: Proceedings of the 1995 ACM/IEEE Conference on Supercomputing (SC 1995), ACM/IEEE Computer Society, New York
7. Karypis G, Kumar V (1999) A fast and high quality multilevel scheme for partitioning irregular graphs. SIAM J Sci Comput 20(1):359–392
8. Madduri K (July 2008) A high-performance framework for analyzing massive complex networks. Ph.D. thesis, Georgia Institute of Technology
9. Madduri K, Bader DA (May 2009) Compact graph representations and parallel connectivity algorithms for massive dynamic

network analysis. In Proceedings of the 23rd IEEE International Parallel and Distributed Processing Symposium (IPDPS 2009), IEEE Computer Society, Rome, Italy
10. Madduri K, Bader DA, Riedy EJ (2011) SNAP: Small-world Network Analysis and Partitioning v0.4. http://snap-graph.sf.net. Accessed May 2011
11. Newman MEJ (2003) The structure and function of complex networks. SIAM Rev 45(2):167–256
12. Newman MEJ, Girvan M (2004) Finding and evaluating community structure in networks. Phys Rev E 69:026113
13. NWB Team (2006) Network Workbench Tool. Indiana University, Northeastern University, and University of Michigan, http://nwb.slis.indiana.edu. Accessed May 2011
14. Watts DJ, Strogatz SH (1998) Collective dynamics of small world networks. Nature 393:440–442

SoC (System on Chip)

Tanguy Risset
INSA Lyon, Villeurbanne, France

Definition

A System on Chip (SoC) refers to a single-integrated circuit (chip) composed of all the components of an electronic system. A SoC is heterogeneous, in addition to classical digital components: processor, memory, bus, etc.; it may contain analog and radio components. The SoC market has been driven by embedded computing systems: mobile phones and handheld devices.

Discussion

Historical View

Gordon Moore predicted in 1965 the exponential growth of silicon integration and its consequences on the application of integrated circuits. Following this growth, known as *Moore's Law*, the number of transistor integrated on a single silicon chip has doubled every 18 months, leading to a constant growth in the semi conductor industry for over 30 years. This technological evolution implied constant changes in the design of digital circuits, with, for instance, the advent of gate level simulation and logic synthesis. Amongst these changes, the advent of System on Chip (SoC) represented a major technological shift.

The term SoC became increasingly widespread in the 1990s and is used to describe chips integrating on a single silicon die what was before spread on several circuits: processor, memory, bus, hardware device drivers, etc. SoC technology did not fundamentally change the functionality of the systems built, but drastically enlarged the *design space*: choosing the best way to assemble a complete system from beginning (system specification) to end (chip manufacturing) became a difficult task. In 1999, a book entitled *Surviving the SoC Revolution: A guide to plateform-based design* was published. It was written by a group of people from Cadence Design System, an important computer-aided design tool company: SoC was driving a revolution of the *design methodologies* for digital systems.

The production of SoC has been driven by the emerging market of embedded systems, more precisely *embedded computing systems*: cellular phones, PDA, digital camera, etc. Embedded computing systems require strong integration, computing power and energy saving, features that were provided by SoC integration. Moreover, most of these systems required radio communication features; hence, a SoC integrates digital components and analog components: the radio subsystem. The success of mobile devices has increased the economic pressure on SoCs, design cost and time-to-market have become major issues, leading to new design methodologies such as IP-based design and hardware/software codesign.

Another consequence of integration is the exponential growth of embedded software, shifting the complexity of SoC design from hardware to software. Emulation, simulation at various level of precision, and high level design techniques are used because nowadays SoC are incredibly complex: hundreds of millions of gates and millions of lines of code. Increasing digital computing power enables software radio, providing everything everywhere transparently. SoCs are now used to provide convergence between computing, telecommunication, and multimedia. Pervasive environments will also make extensive use of embedded "intelligence" with SoCs.

What Is a SoC?

A system on chip or SoC is an integrated circuit composed of many components including: one or several processors, on-chip memories, hardware accelerators, devices drivers, digital/analog converters, and analog components. It was initially named SoC because all the features of a complete "system" were integrated together on the same chip. At that time, a system was dedicated to a single application: video processing or wireless communication for instance. Thanks to the increasing role of software, SoCs are no longer specific, in fact many of them are reused in several different telephony or multimedia devices.

Processors

The processor is the core of the SoC. Unlike desktop machine processors, a wide variety of processors is integrated in the SoC: general purpose processors, digital signal processors, micro-controllers, application specific processors, FPGA based soft cores, etc. The International Technology Road-Map for Semiconductors (ITRS) indicated that, in 2005, more than 70% of application specific integrated circuit (ASICs) contained a processor. Until 2010, most SoCs were composed of a single processor, responsible for the control of the whole system, associated with hardware accelerators and direct memory access components (DMA). In 2008, the majority of SoCs were built around a processor of one of the following form of processor architectures: ARM, MIPS, PowerPC, or x86. Multi-processor SoCs (MPSoC) are progressively appearing and making use of the available chip area to keep performance improvements. MPSoC appears to be a new major technological shift and MPSoC designers are facing problem traditionally associated with super-computing.

Busses

The bus, or more generally the interconnection medium, is also a major component of the SoC. Many SoCs contain several busses, including a fast system bus connecting the major SoC components (processor, memory, hardware accelerator) and a slower bus for other peripherals. For instance, the Advanced Microcontroller Bus Architecture (Amba) proposes the AHB specification (Advanced High-performance Bus), and the APB (Advanced Peripheral Bus), STBus (ST-Microelectronics), and CoreConnect (IBM) are other examples of SoC busses. The use of commercial bus protocol has been a major obstacle to SoC standardization: a bus comes with a dedicated communication protocol which might be incompatible with other busses. Networks on Chip (NoC) are progressively used with MPSoC, the major problem of NoCs today is their considerable power consumption.

Dedicated Components

A SoC will include standard control circuits such as UART for the serial port, USB controller, and control of specific devices: GPS, accelerometer, touch pad, etc. It might also include more compute intensive dedicated *intellectual properties* (IPs) usually targeted to signal or image processing: FFT, turbo decoder, H.263 coder, etc. Choosing between a dedicated component or a software implementation of the same functionality is done in early stages of the design, in the so-called *hardware/software partitioning*. A hardware IP will save power and execution time compared to a software implementation of the same functionality. Dedicated IPs are often mandatory to meet the performance requirements of the application (radio or multimedia), but they increase SoC price, complexity, and also reduce its flexibility.

Other Components

Analog and mixed signal components may be included to provide radio connexion: audio front-end, radio to baseband interfaces, analog to digital converters. Other application domains may require very specific components such as microelectromechanical systems (MEMS), optical computing, biochips, and nanomaterials.

Quality Criteria

The only objective indicator of the quality of a SoC is its economical success, which is obviously difficult to predict. Among the quality criteria, the most important are: power consumption, time to market, cost, and reusability.

Power consumption has been a major issue for decades. Integrating all components on the same chip reduces power consumption because inter chip wires have disappeared. On the other hand, increasing clock rate, program size, and number of computations has a negative impact on power consumption. Moreover, it is very difficult to statically predict the power consumption of a SoC as it heavily depends on low-level technological details. A precise electrical simulation of a SoC is extremely slow and cannot be used in practice for a complete system. Minimizing memory footprint and memory traffic, gating clocks for idle components, and dynamically adapting clock rate are techniques used to reduce power consumption in SoCs. In recent submicronic technologies, static power consumption is significant, leading to power consumption for idle devices.

It is usually said that, for a given product, the first commercially available SoC will capture half of the market. Hence, reducing the design time is a critical issue. Performing hardware and software design in parallel is a designer's dream: it becomes possible with virtual prototyping, that is, simulation of software on the virtual hardware. High-level design and refinement are also widely used: a good decision at a high level may save weeks of design.

The cost of a SoC is divided into two components: the nonrecurring engineering (NRE) cost which corresponds to the design cost and the unit manufacturing cost. Depending on the number of units manufactured and the implementation technology, a complex trade-off between the two can be made, bearing in mind that some technological choices can shorten the time to market such as field programmable gate arrays (FPGA) for instance. NRE cost integrates, in addition to the design cost of the hardware and software part of the SoC, the cost of computer-aided design tools, computing resource for simulation/emulation, and development of tools for the SoC itself: compilers, linkers, debuggers, simulation models of the IPs, etc. To give a very rough idea, in 2008, the development cost of a complex SoC could reach several million dollars and could need more than one hundred man years. In this context, is seems obvious that the reuse of IPs, tools, and SoCs is a major issue because it shrinks both NRE costs and time to market.

An Example

Figure 1 shows the architecture of the Samsung S3CA400A01 SoC, designed to be associated with another chip containing processor and memory through the Cotulla interface. The Cotulla interface is associated with Xscale processor (strong ARM processor architecture manufactured by Intel). This chip was used for instance in association with the PXA250 chip of Intel in the PDA of Hewlett Packard iPaQ H5550. This SoC illustrates the different device driver components that can be found, one can also observe the hierarchy of busses mentioned before. It also shows that there is no *standard SoC*, this one has no processor inside. Thanks to the development of the open source software community, many SoC architectures have been detailed and Linux ports are available for many of them.

Why Is It a SoC "Revolution"?

Although its advent was predicted, SoC really caused a revolution in the semiconductor industry because it changed design methods and brought many software design problems in the microelectronics community.

Hardware design has been impacted by the arrival of SoCs. The complexity of chip mechanically increases with the number of gates on the chip. But the design and verification effort increases more than linearly with the number of gates. This is known as the *design gap*: How can the designer efficiently use the additional gates available without breaking design time and design reliability? A SoC requires different technologies to be integrated on the same silicon die (standard cells, memory, FPGA). The clock distribution tree is a major source of power dissipation leading to the advent of globally asynchronous, locally synchronous systems (GALS). Routing wires became a real problem partially solved by using additional metal layers.

Hardware design methods have drastically changed with the constant arrival of new Electronic Design Automation (EDA) tools. RTL design methods (RTL stands for *register transfer level*) have become the standard for hardware developers replacing transistor-level circuit design. The hardware description languages VHDL and Verilog are widely used for hardware specification before synthesis. However, higher-level hardware description language are needed, partly because SoC simulation time became prohibitive, requiring huge FPGA based emulators. In addition, the networked nature of embedded applications, and the non-determinism introduced by parallelism in MPSoC greatly complicates SoC simulation. As mentioned before, cost and time to market imposes pressure on engineers productivity, leading managers to new management methods. The hardware/software nature of a SoC requires a constant dialog between hardware and software engineers.

Embedded software has been introduced in circuit design, this is, in itself, a revolution. In 2006, the Siemens company employed more software developers than Microsoft did, and since the mid-2000s, more than half of the SoC design efforts were spent in software development. Originally composed of a very basic infinite loop waiting for interrupts, embedded software has evolved by adding many device drivers, standard or real time operating system services: tasks or

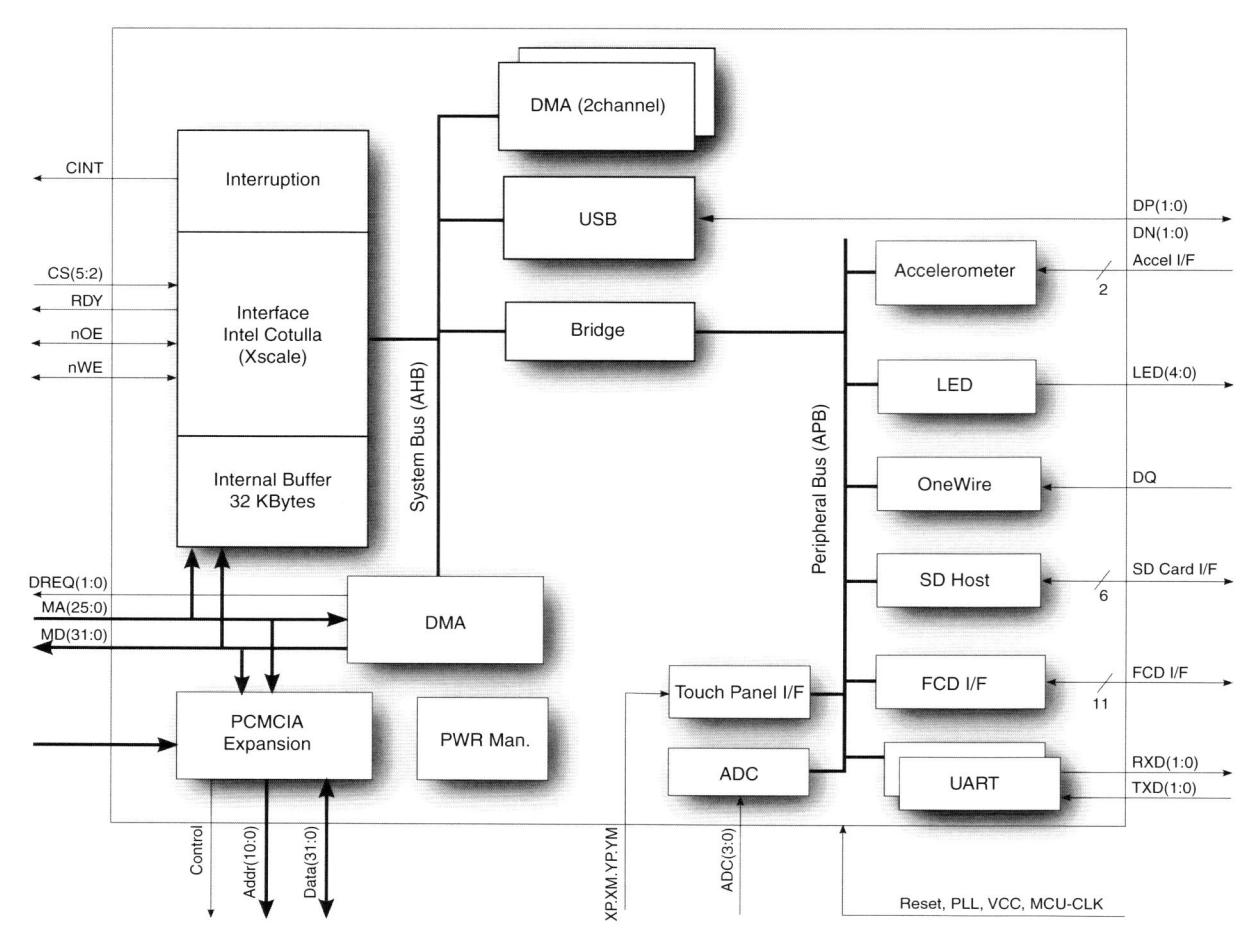

SoC (System on Chip). Fig. 1 Architecture of the Samsung S3CA400A01 SoC

threads, resource management, shared memory, communication protocols, etc. Even if an important part of embedded code is written in C, there is a trend to use component based software design methodologies that reduces the conceptual difference between hardware and software objects. Verifying software reliability is very difficult, even if an important effort is dedicated to that during the design process, complete formal verification is impossible because of the complexity of the software. This explains the bugs that everybody has experienced on their mobile devices.

Both hardware and software design methods have been drastically modified, but the most important novelty concerns the whole SoC design methodology that tries to associate in a single framework hardware and software design.

SoC Design Methodology

There are many names associated with SoC design methodologies, all of them refer more or less to the same goal: designing hardware and software in the same framework such that the designer can quickly produce the most efficient implementation for a given system specification. The term frequently used today is *system level design*, the generic scheme of system level design is the following: (1) derive hardware components and software components from the specification, (2) map the software part on the hardware components, (3) prototype the resulting implementation, and (4) possibly provide changes at some stage of the design if the performance or cost is not satisfactory.

There is a global agreement on the fact that high-level specifications are very useful to reduce the design time. Many design frameworks have been proposed for system level SoC design. The idea of refinement of the original specification down to hardware is present in many frameworks, high level synthesis (HLS) was once seen as the solution but appears to be a very difficult problem in general. In HLS, the hardware is completely derived from the initial specifications. During the 1990s, the arrival of Intellectual Properties (IP) introduced a clear distinction between circuit fabrication and circuit design, leading some companies to concentrate on IP design (ARM for instance). On the other hand, IP-based design and later *platform-based design* propose to start from fixed (or parameterizable) hardware library to reduce the design space exploration phase. Improvement in simulation techniques permits, with the use of systemC language, to have an approach between the two by using virtual prototypes: cycle true simulation of complete SoC before hardware implementation.

MPSoC and Future Trends

An open question remains at the present time: What will be the dominant model for MPSoCs that are predicted to include more than one hundred processors? There are two main trends: heterogeneous MPSoCs following actual heterogeneous SoC architecture or homogeneous SPMD-like multiprocessors on a single chip.

A heterogeneous MPSoC includes different types of processors with different instruction set architectures (ISA): general purpose processors, DSPs, application specific instruction set processors (ASIP). It also contains dedicated IPs that might not be considered as processors, DMAs, and memories. All these components are connected together through a network on chip.

Heterogeneous MPSoCs are a natural evolution of SoC, their main advantage is that they are more energy efficient than homogeneous MPSoCs. They have been driven by specific application domains such as software radio or embedded video processing. But, for the future, they suffer from many drawbacks. As they are usually tuned for a particular application, they are difficult to reuse in another context. Because of incompatibility between ISAs, tasks cannot migrate between processors inducing a much less flexible task mapping. Moreover, in the foreseen transistor technology, integrated circuits will have to be fault tolerant because of electronics defaults. Heterogeneous MPSoC are not fault tolerant by nature. Finally, their scalability is not obvious and code reuse between different heterogeneous platforms is impossible. However, because heterogeneous MPSoCs provide better performance with lower power consumption and lower cost, there are lots of commercial activities on this model.

Homogeneous MPSoC are more flexible, they can implement well known operating system services such as code portability between different architectures, dynamic task migration, virtual shared memory. Homogeneity can help in being fault tolerant, as any processor can be replaced by another. However, with more than a hundred processor on a chip in 2020, the MPSoC architecture cannot be completely homogeneous, it has to be hierarchical: clusters of processors tightly linked, these clusters being interconnected with a network on chip. Memory must be physically distributed with non-uniform access.

Ensuring cache coherency and providing efficient compilation and parallelization tools for these architectures are real challenges. In 2009, the ITRS road-map predicted for 2013 the advent of a concurrent software compiler that will "Enable compilation and software development in highly parallel processing SoC," this will be a critical step towards the advent of homogeneous MPSoC. However, many unknowns remain concerning the programming model to use, the ability of compilation tools to efficiently use the available resources, the reusability of the chip and the reusability of the embedded code between platforms, and the real power consumption of these homogeneous multiprocessors on chip.

A trade-off would be a homogeneous SoC with some level of heterogeneity: dedicated IPs for domain-specific treatments. New technological techniques, such as 3D VLSI packaging technology or more generally the arrival of so-called *system in package*, mixing various nanotechnologies on a single chip might also open a new road to embedded computing systems. But, whatever will be the successful MPSoC model, it will bring highly parallel computing on a chip and should lead to a revival of parallel computing engineering.

Bibliographic Notes and Further Reading

A number of books have been published on SoC, we have already talked about "surviving the SOC revolution" [1]. Many interesting ideas were also present in the Polis project [4]. Daniel Gajski [9] worked on SoC from the beginning. Wayne Wolf published a general presentation [13]. More recently, Chris Rowen [11] proposed an interesting view of SoC design.

A good overview of the status of high-level synthesis can be found in Coussy and Moraviec book [2]. More practical details can be found on the Steve Furber book on ARM [8].

A number of useful information are present on the web, from the International Technology Roadmap for Semiconductors (ITRS [7]), from analyst or engineer [3] or open source software developer for embedded devices [5, 6]. A simple introduction to semiconductor industry can be found in Jim Turley's book [12].

A good introduction on MPSoC is presented in [10], but most of the interesting work on this subject are presented in the proceedings of the international conferences on the subject: Design Automation Conference (DAC), Design automation and Test in Europe (DATE), International Forum on Embedded MPSoC and Multicore (MPSOC), etc.

Bibliography

1. Chang H, Cooke L, Hunt M, Martin G, McNelly AJ, Todd L (1999) Surviving the SOC revolution: a guide to platform-based design. Kluwer Academic Publishers, Norwell, MA
2. Coussy P, Morawiec A (eds) (2008) High-level synthesis: from algorithm to digital circuit. Springer, Berlin, Germany
3. Embedded System Design (2009) http://www.embedded.com/
4. Balarin F et al (1997) Hardware-software co-design of embedded systems: the POLIS approach. Kluwer Academic Press, Dordrecht
5. Linux for device (2009) http://www.linuxfordevices.com/
6. Open Embedded: framework for embedded Linux (2009) http://wiki.openembedded.net
7. International Technology Roadmap for Semiconductors (2009) http://www.itrs.net/
8. Furber S (2000) ARM system-on-chip architecture. Addison Wesley, Boston, MA
9. Gajski DD, Abdi S, Gerstlauer A, Schirner G (2009) Embedded system design: modeling, synthesis and verification. Kluwer Academic Publishers, Dordrecht
10. Jerraya A, Wolf W (2004) Multiprocessor systems-on-chips (The Morgan Kaufmann Series in Systems on Silicon). Morgan Kaufmann, San Francisco, CA
11. Rowen C (2004) Engineering the complex SOC: fast, flexible design with configurable processors. Prentice-Hall Press, Upper Saddle River, NJ
12. Turley J (2002) The essential guide to semiconductors. Prentice Hall Press, Upper Saddle River, NJ
13. Wolf W (2002) Modern VLSI design: system-on-chip design. Prentice Hall Press, Upper Saddle River, NJ

Social Networks

MALEQ KHAN, V. S. ANIL KUMAR, MADHA V. MARATHE, PAULA E. STRETZ
Virginia Tech, Blacksburg, VA, USA

Introduction

Networks are pervasive in today's world. They provide appropriate representations for systems comprised of individual agents interacting locally. Examples of such systems are urban regional transportation systems, national electrical power markets and grids, the Internet, ad-hoc communication and computing systems, public health, etc. According to Wikipedia, *A social network is a social structure made of individuals (or organizations) called "nodes," which are tied (connected) by one or more specific types of interdependency, such as friendship, kinship, financial exchange, dislike, sexual relationships, or relationships of beliefs, knowledge or prestige.* Formally, a social network induced by a set V of agents is a graph $G = (V, E)$, with an edge $e = (u, v) \in E$ between individuals u and v, if they are interrelated or interdependent. Here, we use a more general definition of nodes and edges (that represent interdependency). The nodes represent living or virtual individuals. The edges can represent information flow, physical proximity, or any feature that induces a potential interaction. For example, the social contact networks, an edge signifies some form of physical co-location between the individuals – such a contact may either capture physical proximity, an explicit physical contact or a co-location in the virtual world, e.g., Facebook. Socio-technical networks are a generalization of social networks and consist of a large number of interacting physical, technological, and human/societal agents. The links in socio-technical networks can be physically real or a matter of convention such as those imposed by law or social norms, depending on the specific system being represented. This entry primarily deals with social networks.

Social networks have been studied for at least 100 years; see [9] for a detailed account of the history and development of social networks and the analytical tools that followed them. Scientists have used social networks to uncover interesting insights related to societies and social interactions. Social networks, their structural analysis, and dynamics on these networks (e.g., spread of diseases over social contact networks) are now a key part of social, economic, and behavioral sciences. Importantly these concepts and tools are also becoming popular in other scientific disciplines such as public health epidemiology, ecology, and computer science due to their potential applications. For example, in computer science, interest in social networks has been spurred by web search and other online communication and information applications. Google and other search engines crucially use the structure of the web graph. Social networking sites, such as Facebook and Twitter, and blogging sites have grown at an amazing rate and play a crucial role in advertising and the spread of fads, fashion, public opinion, and politics. The growing importance of social networks in the scientific community can be gauged by a report from the National Academies [18] as well as a recent issue of Science [21]. The proliferation of Facebook, MySpace, Twitter, Blogsphere, and other online communities has made social networking a pervasive and essential part of our lingua.

An important and almost universal observation is that the network structure seems to have a significant impact on these systems and their associated dynamics. For instance, many infrastructure networks (such as the Internet) have been observed to be highly vulnerable to targeted attacks, but are much more robust to random attacks [2]. In contrast, social contact networks are known to be very robust to all types of attacks [7]. These robustness properties have significant implications for control and policies on such systems - for instance, protecting high degree nodes in Internet-like graphs has been found to be effective in stopping the spread of worms [19]. For many processes, e.g., the SIS model of diffusion (which models "endemic" diseases, such as Malaria and Internet malware), the dynamics have been found to be characterized quite effectively by the spectral properties of the underlying network [19]. Similarly, classical and new graph theoretic metrics, e.g., centrality (which, informally, determines the fraction of shortest paths passing through a node), have been found to be useful in identifying "important" nodes in networks and community structure. Therefore, computing the properties of these graphs, and simulating the dynamical processes defined on them are important research areas.

Most networks that arise in practice are very large and heterogeneous, and cannot be easily stored in memory - for instance, the social contact graph of a city could have millions of nodes and edges [13], while the web graph has over 11 billion nodes [7] and several billion edges. Additionally, these networks change at very short time scales. They are also naturally labeled structures, which adds to the memory requirements. Consequently, simple and well-understood problems such as finding shortest paths, which have almost linear time algorithms, become challenging to solve on such graphs. High-performance computing has been successfully used in a number of scientific applications involving large data sets with complex processes, and is, therefore, a natural and necessary approach to overcome such resource limitations.

Most of the successful applications of high-performance computing have been in physical sciences, such as molecular dynamics, radiation transport, n-body dynamics, and sequence analysis, and researchers routinely solve very large problems using massive distributed systems. Many techniques and general principles have been developed, which have made parallel computing a crucial tool in these applications. Social networks present fundamentally new challenges for parallel computing, since they have very different structure, and do not fit the paradigms that have been developed for other applications. As we discuss later, some of the key issues that arise in parallelization of social network problems include highly irregular structure, poor locality, variable granularity, and data-driven computations. Most social contact networks have a scale-free and "small world" structure (described formally below), which is very different from regular structures such as grids. As a result, social network problems often cannot be decomposed easily into smaller independent sub-problems with low communication, making traditional parallel computing techniques very inefficient.

The goal of this article is to highlight the challenges for high-performance computing posed by the growing area of social networks. New paradigms are needed at all levels of hardware architecture, software methodologies, and algorithmic optimization.

Section "Background and Notation" presents some background into social networks, their history, and important problems. Section "Petascale Computing Challenges for Social Network Problems" identifies the main challenges for parallel computing. We discuss some recent developments in Section "Techniques" and conclude in section "Conclusions".

Background and Notation

Many of the results in sociology that have now become folklore have been based on insights from social network analysis. One of such classic results is the "six-degree of separation" experiment, in which Stanley Milgram [22] asked 296 randomly chosen people to forward a letter to a stock broker in Boston, by sending it to one of their acquaintances, who is most likely to know the target. Milgram found that the median length of chains that successfully reached the target was about 6, suggesting that the global social contact network was very highly connected. Attempts to explain this phenomenon have led to the "small-world" graph models, which show that a small fraction of long-range contacts to individuals spatially located far away is adequate to bring the diameter of the network down. Another classic result is Granovetter's concept of the "strength of weak ties" [13], which has become one of the most influential papers in sociology. He examined the role of information that individuals obtain as a result of their position in the social contact network, and found that information from acquaintances (weak ties), and not close friends, was the most useful, during major lifestyle changes, e.g., finding jobs. This finding has led to the notions of "homophily" (i.e., nodes with similar attributes form contacts) and "triadic closure" (i.e., nodes with a common neighbor are more likely to form a link), and the idea that weak ties form bridges that span different parts of the network.

Concepts such as these have been refined and formalized using graph theoretic measures; see [5, 19] for a formal discussion. Some of the key graph measures are: (1) *(Weighted) Degree distribution*: The degree of a node is the number of contacts it has, and the degree distribution is the frequency distribution of degrees. This measure is commonly used to characterize and distinguish various families of graphs. In particular, it has been found that many real networks have power law or lognormal degree distributions, instead of Poisson, which has been used to develop models to explain the construction and evolution of these networks. (2) The *Clustering coefficient*, $C(v)$, of a node v is the probability that two randomly picked neighbors of node v are connected, and models the notion of triadic closure, and its extensions. (3) *Centrality*: Let $f(s,t)$ denote the number of shortest paths from s to t, and let $f_v(s,t)$ denote the number of shortest paths from s to t that pass through node v. The centrality of node v is defined as $bc(v) = \sum_{s,t} f_v(s,t)/f(s,t)$, and captures its "importance". (4) *Robustness to node and edge deletions*, which is quantified in terms of the giant component size, as a result of node and edge deletions, and has been found to be a useful measure to compare graphs. (5) *Page Rank and Hubs* have been used to identify "important" web pages for search queries, but have been extended to other applications. The Page Rank of a node is, informally, related to the stationary probability of a node in a random walk model of a web surfer. (6) A *community* or a *cluster* is a "loosely connected" set of nodes with similar attributes, which are different from nodes in other communities. There are many different methods for identifying communities, including modularity and spectral structure [19, 22].

In applications such as epidemiology and viral marketing, the network is usually associated with a diffusion process, e.g., the spread of disease or fads. There are many models of diffusion, and some of the most widely used classes of models are *Stochastic cascade models* [11, 19]. In these models, we are given a probability $p(e)$ for each edge $e \in E$ in a graph $G = (V, E)$. The process starts at a node s initially. If node v becomes active at time t, it activates each neighbor w with probability $p(v,w)$, independently (and also independent of the history); no node can be reactivated in this process. In the case of viral marketing, active nodes are those that adopt a certain product, while in the SIR model of epidemics, the process corresponds to the spread of a disease, and the active nodes are the ones that get infected. Another class of models that has been studied extensively involves *Threshold functions*; one of the earliest uses of threshold models was by Granovetter and Schelling [10], who used it for modeling segregation. The *Linear Threshold Model* [14] is at the core of many of these models. In this model, each node v has a threshold Θ_v (which may be chosen randomly), and each edge (v, w) has a weight $b_{v,w}$. A node v becomes active at time t, if $\sum_{w \in N(v) \cap A_t} b_{v,w} \geq \Theta_v$, where $N(v)$ denotes the set of neighbors of v and A_t denotes the set of active nodes at time t (in this model, an active node remains active throughout). Such diffusion processes are instances of more general models of dynamical systems, called *Sequential Dynamical Systems (SDSs)* [7, 19], which generalize other models, such as cellular automata, Hopfield networks, and communicating finite state machines. An SDS S is defined as a tuple (G, F, π), where: (a) $G = (V, E)$ is the underlying graph on a set V of nodes, (b) $F = (f_v)$ denotes a set of local functions for each node $v \in V$, on some fixed domain. Each node v computes its state by applying the local function f_v on the states of its neighbors. (c) π denotes a permutation (or a word) on V, and specifies the order in which the node states are to be updated by applying the local functions. One update of the SDS involves applying the local functions in the order specified by π. It is easy to see that the above diffusion models can be captured by suitable choice of the local functions f_v and the order π. It is easy to extend the basic definition of SDS to accommodate local functions that are stochastic, the edges that are dynamic, and the graph that is represented hierarchically (to capture organizational structure).

Fundamental questions in social networks include (1) understanding the structure of the networks and the associated dynamics, especially how the dynamics is affected by the network properties; (2) techniques to control the dynamics; (3) identifying the most critical and vulnerable nodes crucial for the dynamics; and (4) coevolution between the network and dynamics – this issue brings in behavioral changes by individuals as a result of the diffusion process. The above mentioned problems require large-scale simulations, and parallel computing is a natural approach for designing them.

Petascale Computing Challenges for Social Network Problems

Lumsdaine et al. [15] justifiably assert that traditional parallel computing techniques (e.g., those developed in the context of applications such as molecular dynamics and sequencing) are not well suited for large-scale social network problems because of the following reasons: (1) Graph algorithms chiefly involve data driven computations, in which the computations are guided by the graph structure. Therefore, the structure and sequence of computations are not known in advance and are hard to predict, making parallelization difficult. (2) Social networks are typically very irregular and strongly connected, which makes partitioning into "independent" sub-problems difficult [15]. As observed by many researchers, these networks usually have a small-world structure with high clustering, and such graphs have low diameter and large separators (unlike regular graphs such as grids, which commonly arise in other applications). (3) Locality is one of the key properties that helps in parallelization; however, computations on social networks tend to give low locality because of the irregular structure, leading to computations and data access patterns with global properties. (4) As noted in [15, 16], graph computations often involve exploration of the graph structure, which are highly memory intensive and there is very little computation to hide the latency to memory accesses. Thus, the performance of memory subsystem, rather than the memory clock frequency, dominates the performance of graph algorithms.

Traditional parallel architectures have been developed for applications that do not have these constraints, and therefore, are not completely suited for social network algorithms. The most common paradigm of distributed computing, the distributed memory architectures with message-passing interface (MPI), leads to high message passing, because of the lack of locality and high data access to computation ratio. The shared memory model is much more suited for the kinds of data-driven computations that arise in graph algorithms, and multithreaded approaches have been found to be more effective in exploiting the parallelism that arises. Some of the main hardware and software challenges that arise are as follows: (1) In many graph problems, e.g., shortest paths, parallelism can be found at a fairly fine level of granularity, though in other problems, e.g., computing centrality, there is coarse grained granularity, where each path computation is an independent task. (2) While multithreading is crucial for graph algorithms, the unstructured nature of these graphs implies that there are significant memory contention and cache-coherence problems. (3) It is difficult to achieve load balancing on graph computations, where the level of parallelism varies with time, e.g., as in breadth-first search.

Techniques

Parallel algorithms for social network problems is an active area of research and we now discuss some of the key techniques that have been found to be effective for some problems that arise in analyzing social networks. These techniques are still application specific, and developing general paradigms is still an active research area.

Massive Multithreading Techniques

In [12], Hendrickson and Berry discussed how massively multithreaded architectures, such as the Cray MTA-2 and its successor the XMT, can be used to boost the performance of parallel graph algorithms. Instead of trying to reduce latency for single-memory access, the MTA-2 tolerates it by ensuring that the processor has other work to do while waiting for a memory request to be satisfied by supporting many concurrent threads in a single processor and switching between them in a single clock cycle. When a thread issues memory request, the processor immediately switches to another ready-to-execute thread. MTA-2 supports fast and dynamic thread creation and destruction allowing the program to dynamically determine the number of threads based on the data to be processed. Support of virtualization of threads allows adaptive parallelism and dynamic load balancing. MTA-2 also supports word-level locking of the data items, which decreases access contention and minimizes impact on the execution of other threads.

Drawbacks of massively multithreaded machines include higher price and much slower clock rate than mainstream systems, and the difficulty in porting to other architectures. Hendrickson and Berry [12], using the massively multithreaded architectures, extended a small subset of the Boost Graph Library (BGL) into the Multithreaded Graph Library (MTGL). This library, which is their ongoing current work, retains the BGL's look and feel, yet encapsulates the use of nonstandard features of massively multithreaded architectures. Madduri et al. [16] also discussed architectural features of the massively multithreaded Cray XMT system and present implementation details and optimization of betweenness centrality computations. They further showed how the parallel algorithm for betweenness centrality can be modified so that locking is not necessary to avoid concurrent access to a memory unit, which they call lock-free parallel algorithm.

Distributed Streaming Algorithms

Data streaming is a useful approach to deal with memory constraints, in which processors keep a "sketch" of the data, while making one or more passes through the entire data (or stream), which is assumed to be too big to store. Streaming is usually sequential, and Google's MapReduce [6] and Apache's Hadoop [1] provide a generic programming framework for distributed streaming. MapReduce/Hadoop provide a transparent implementation which takes care of issues like data distribution, synchronization, load balancing, and processor failures. It can, thus, greatly simplify computation over large-scale data sets, and has been proven to be a useful abstraction for solving many problems, especially those related to web applications.

We briefly describe the MapReduce framework here. In the map step, the master node takes a task, partitions it into smaller *independent subtasks* and passes them down to the worker nodes. The worker nodes may recursively do the same, or process the subtask and pass it back to the master node. The master node then collects the solutions to each subtask that it had assigned and processes these solutions to obtain the final solution for the original task. More formally, the input to the MapReduce system is represented as a set of (key, value) pairs, which can be defined in a completely general manner. There are two functions: *Map* and *Reduce*, which need to be specified by the user. A Map function processes a key/value pair (k_1, v_1) and produces a list of zero or more intermediate key/value pairs (k_2, v_2). Once the Map function completes processing of the input key/value pairs, the system groups the intermediate pairs by each key k_2 and makes a list of all values associated with k_2. These lists are then provided as input to the Reduce function. The Reduce function is then applied independently to each key/value-list pair to obtain a list of final values. The whole sequence can be repeated as needed.

Programs written in this functional style are automatically parallelized and executed on a large cluster of machines, insulating users from all the run-time issues. The MapReduce framework is quite powerful, and can be used to efficiently compute any symmetric order-invariant function [8], a large subclass of problems that can be solved by streaming algorithms. This class includes many stream statistics that arise in web applications. Kang et al. [13] use this approach to estimate the diameter of a massive instance of the web graph with over 10 billion edges. The (key, value) pairs in their algorithm capture adjacencies of nodes and estimates of the number of nodes within a d-neighborhood of a node; the algorithm is run in multiple stages in order to keep the keys and associated values simple and small, and also uses efficient sketches for representing set unions. The uniqueness of a MapReduce framework lies in its ability to hide the underlying computing architecture from the end-user. Thus, the user can compute using a MapReduce framework on parallel clusters as well as loosely coupled machines in a cloud or over volunteer computing resources comprised of independent, heterogeneous machines.

Dynamical Processes on Social Networks

So far, much of the discussion has focused on computational considerations related to social network structure. But many more interesting questions arise when one studies dynamical processes on these networks; in fact, it is fair to say that social networks exist to serve the function of one or more dynamical processes on them. While researchers have worked extensively on structural properties of social networks, the literature on the study of dynamical processes on social networks is relatively sparse. When it does exist, it is usually in the context of very small networks or stylized and regular networks. Unfortunately, many of these results do not scale or apply to large and realistic social networks. In [3], the authors discuss new algorithms and their implementations for modeling certain classes of dynamical processes on large social networks. In general, the problem is *hard* computationally; it becomes even harder when the social network structure, the dynamical processes and individual node behavior coevolve. For certain class of dynamical processes that capture a number of interesting social, economic, and behavioral theories of collective behavior, it is possible to develop fast parallel algorithms. Intuitively, such dynamical processes can be expressed as SDSs with a certain symmetry condition imposed on local transition functions.

Conclusions

As our society is becoming more connected, there is an increasing need to develop innovative computational tools to synthesize, analyze, and reason about large and progressively realistic social networks. Applications of social networks for analyzing real-world problems will require the study of multi-network, multi-theory systems – systems composed of multiple networks among agents whose behavior is governed by multiple behaviors. Advances in computing and information are also giving rise to new classes of social networks. Two examples of these networks are: (1) botnet networks in which individual nodes are software agents (bots) and (2) wireless-social networks in which social networks between individuals are being supported by wireless devices that allow them to communicate and interact anytime and anywhere. As the society becomes more connected, these applications require support for real-time individualized decision making over progressively larger evolving social networks. This same technology will form the basis of new modeling and data processing environments. These environments will allow us to leverage the next generation computing and communication resources, including cloud computing, massively parallel peta-scale machines and pervasive wireless sensor networks. The dynamic models will generate new synthetic data sets that cannot be created in any other way (e.g., direct measurement). This will enable social scientists to investigate entirely new research questions about functioning societal infrastructures and the individuals interacting with these systems. Together, these advances also allow scientists, policy makers, educators, planners, and emergency responders unprecedented opportunities for multi-perspective reasoning.

Acknowledgments

This work has been partially supported by NSF Grant CNS-0626964, SES-0729441, CNS-0831633, and OCI-0904844, and DTRA Grant HDTRA1-0901-0017 and HDTRA1-07-C-0113.

Bibliography

1. Apache hadoop. Code and documentation are available at http://developer.yahoo.com/hadoop/
2. Barabasi A, Albert R (1999) Emergence of scaling in random networks. Science 286:509–512

3. Barrett C, Bisset K, Marathe A, Marathe M (2009) An integrated modeling environment to study the co-evolution of networks, individual behavior and epidemics. AI Magazine, 2009
4. Barrett C, Eubuank S, Marathe M (2005) Modeling and simulation of large biological, information and socio-technical systems: an interaction based approach interactive computation. In: Goldin D, Smolka S, Wegner P (2005) The new paradigm, Springer, Berlin, Heidelberg, New York
5. Baur M, Brandes U, Lerner J, Wagner D (2009), Group-level analysis and visualization of social networks. In: Lerner J, Wagner D, Zweig K (eds) Algorithmics of large and complex networks, vol 5515, LNCS. Springer, Berlin, Heidelberg, New York, pp 330–358
6. Dean J, Ghemawat S (2004) Mapreduce: Simplified data processing on large clusters. In: Proceedings of the sixth symposium on operating system design and implementation (OSDI), San Francisco, December 2004
7. Eubank S, Guclu H, Anil Kumar VS, Marathe MV, Srinivasan A, Toroczkai Z, Wang N (2004) Modelling disease outbreaks in realistic urban social networks. Nature 429(6998):180–184
8. Feldman J, Muthukrishnan S, Sidiropoulos A, Stein C, Svitkina Z (2008) On distributing symmetric streaming computations. In: Proceedings of the nineteenth annual ACM-SIAM symposium on Discrete algorithms (SODA), San Francisco, pp 710–719
9. Freeman L (2004) The development of social network analysis: a study in the sociology of science. Empirical Press, Vancouver
10. Granovetter M (1978) Threshold models of collective behavior. Am J Sociology 83(6):1420–1443
11. Grimmett G (1999) Percolation. Springer, New York
12. Hendrickson B, Berry J (2008) Graph analysis with high-performance computing. Comput Sci Eng 10:14–19
13. Kang U, Tsourakakis CE, Appel AP, Faloutsos C, Leskovec J (2008) Hadi: fast diameter estimation and mining in massive graphs with hadoop. Technical Report CMU-ML-08-117, Carnegie Mellon University
14. Kempe D, Kleinberg JM, Tardos E (2003) Maximizing the spread of influence through a social network. In: SIGKDD '03, Washington
15. Lumsdaine A, Gregor D, Hendrickson B, Berry J (2007) Challenges in parallel graph processing. Parallel Process Lett 17:5–20
16. Madduri K, Ediger D, Jiang K, Bader DA, Chavarra-Miranda DG (2009) A faster parallel algorithm and efficient multithreaded implementations for evaluating betweenness centrality on massive datasets. In: Proceedings of the 3rd Workshop on Multi-threaded Architectures and Applications (MTAAP), Miami, May 2009
17. Mortveit HS, Reidys CM (2000) Discrete sequential dynamical systems. Discrete Math 226:281–295
18. National Research Council of the National Academies (2005) Network Science. The National Academies Press, Washington, DC
19. Newman M (2003) The structure and function of complex networks. SIAM Rev 45:167–256
20. Newman MEJ (2004) Detecting community structure in networks. European Phy J B, 38:321–330
21. Special issue on complex systems and networks, Science, 24 July 2009, 325 (5939):357–504
22. Travers J, Milgram S (1969) An experimental study of the small world problem. Sociometry 32(4):425–443

Software Autotuning

▶ Autotuning

Software Distributed Shared Memory

Sandhya Dwarkadas
University of Rochester, Rochester, NY, USA

Synonyms

Implementations of shared memory in software; Shared virtual memory; Virtual shared memory

Definition

Software distributed shared memory (SDSM) refers to the implementation of shared memory in software on systems that do not provide hardware support for data coherence and consistency across nodes (and the memory therein).

Discussion

Introduction

Executing an application in parallel requires the coordination of computation and the communication of data to respect dependences among tasks. Historically, multiprocessor machines provide either a shared memory or a message passing model for data communication in hardware (with models such as partitioned global address spaces that fall in between the two extremes). In the message passing model, communication and coordination across processes is achieved via explicit messages. In the shared memory model, communication and coordination is achieved by directly reading and writing memory that is accessible by multiple processes and mapped into their address space. Either model can be emulated in software if the hardware does not directly implement it. This entry focuses on implementations of shared memory in software on machines that do not support shared memory in hardware across all nodes.

In the shared memory model, data communication is implicitly performed when shared data is accessed. Programmers (or compilers) must still ensure, however, that shared data users synchronize (coordinate) with each other in order to respect program dependencies. The message passing model typically requires explicit communication management by the programmer or compiler – software must specify *what* data to communicate, with *whom* to communicate the data, and *when* the communication must be performed (typically on both the sender and the receiver). Coordination is often implicit in the data communication. While parallel programming has proven inherently more difficult than sequential programming, shared memory is considered conceptually easier as a parallel programming model than message passing. In contrast to message passing, the shared memory model hides the need for explicit data communication from the user, thereby avoiding the need to answer the "*what, when, and whom*" questions.

In terms of implementation, typical shared memory-based hardware requires support for coherence – ensuring that any modifications made by a processor propagate to all copies of the data — and consistency – ensuring a well-defined ordering in terms of when and in what order modifications are visible to other processors. Such support and the need for access to the physically shared memory impacts the scalability of the design. In contrast, message-based hardware is typically easier to build and to scale to large numbers of processors.

Software distributed shared memory (SDSM) attempts to combine the conceptual appeal of shared memory with the scalability of distributed message-based communication by allowing shared memory programs to run on message-based machines. SDSM systems target the knee of the price-performance curve by using commodity components as the nodes in a network of machines. SDSM provides processes with the illusion of shared address spaces on machines that do not physically share memory. Kai Li's [27, 28] pioneering work in the mid-1980s was the first to consider implementing SDSM on a network of workstations. Since then, there has been a tremendous amount of work exploring the state space of possible implementations and programming models, targeted at reducing the software overheads required and hiding the larger communication overheads of message-based hardware.

Implementation Issues

In order to implement coherence, accesses to shared data must be detected and controlled. Implementing coherence in software can typically be accomplished either using virtual memory hardware [8, 23, 28], using instrumentation [34], or using language-level hooks [3, 18]. The former two approaches assume that memory is a linear untyped array of bytes. The latter approach takes advantage of object- and type-specific information to optimize the protocol. The trade-offs are discussed below.

Implementations Using Virtual Memory

The virtual memory mechanisms available on general-purpose processors may be used to implement coherence [8, 23, 28]. The virtual memory framework combines protection with address translation at a granularity of a page, which is typically on the order of a few (e.g., 4) KBytes on today's machines. Hardware protection modes can be exercised to ensure that read or write accesses to pages that are shared are trapped if protection is violated. Software handlers installed by the runtime can then determine the necessary actions required to maintain coherence. The advantage of the virtual memory approach is that there is no overhead for data that is private or already cached. The disadvantage is the large sharing granularity, which can result in data being falsely (i.e., different processors reading and writing to independent locations that are colocated on the same page) shared, and the large cost of handling a miss.

Implementations Using Instrumentation

An alternative approach is to instrument the program in order to monitor every load and store operation to shared data. The advantage of this approach is that coherence can be maintained at any desired granularity [35], resulting in lower miss penalties. The disadvantage is that overhead is incurred regardless of whether data is actually shared, resulting in higher hit latency. Optimizations that identify and instrument accesses to only shared data and that hide the instrumentation behind existing program computation [34] help reduce this overhead. Alternatively, hardware support, such as ECC (error-correcting code) bits in memory [35], can be leveraged to eliminate the software instrumentation by using the ECC bits to raise an exception when the data is not valid. However, complications do arise if these exceptions are not precise.

Language-Level Implementations
Language-level programming systems (e.g., [3, 18]) provide the opportunity to use objects and types to improve the efficiency of recognizing accesses to shared data. Coherence is usually maintained at the granularity of an object, providing application developers with control over how data is managed. The DOSA system [18] shows how a handle-based implementation (an implementation in which all object references are redirected through a handle) enables efficient fine- and coarse-grain data sharing. Handle-based implementations work transparently when used in conjunction with safe languages (ones in which no pointer arithmetic is allowed). The handles make it easy to relocate objects in memory, making it possible to use virtual memory techniques for access and modification detection and control. They also interact well with the garbage collection algorithms used in these type-safe languages, allowing good performance for these systems. The redirection allows the implementation to avoid false sharing for fine-grained access patterns.

Single- Versus Multiple-Writer Protocols
Traditional hardware-based cache coherence usually maintains the coherence invariant of allowing only a single writer for each coherence granularity unit of data. This approach has the advantage of simplicity, works well under the intuitive assumption that two processes will not intentionally write to the same location concurrently without some form of coordination, and makes it easy to ensure write serialization. However, coherence granularities are often larger than a single word. Even with hardware coherence, it is possible for a cache line to bounce ("ping-pong") between caches because processes modify logically disjoint regions of the same cache line. This problem is further exacerbated by the larger coherence granularities of software coherence, particularly when using a virtual memory implementation.

In order to combat the resulting performance penalties caused by such false sharing, multiple-writer protocols have been proposed [8]. In these protocols, the single writer state invariant of traditional hardware coherence no longer holds. At any given time, multiple processes may be writing to the same coherence unit. Write serialization is ensured by making sure that modifications (determined by keeping track of exactly what locations in the coherence unit were written) are propagated to all valid copies or that these copies are invalidated. Modified addresses can be determined as in the previous section, either by using instrumentation or virtual memory techniques. In the latter case, a *twin* or copy of the virtual memory page is made prior to modification, which is subsequently used to compare to the modified page in order to create a *diff* or an encoding of only the data that has changed on the page. Multiple-writer protocols work particularly well when combined with a more relaxed memory consistency model that allows coherence actions to be delayed to program synchronization points (elaborated on in the next section).

Memory Models
In order to help hide long communication latencies, SDSM systems typically use some form of relaxed consistency model, which enable aggregation of coherence traffic. In release consistency [16], ordinary accesses to shared data are distinguished from synchronization. Synchronization is further split into acquires and releases. An acquire roughly corresponds to a request for access to data, such as a lock operation. A release roughly corresponds to making such data available, such as an unlock operation. SDSM systems leverage the release consistency model to delay coherence actions on writes until the point of a release [8]. This enables both aggregation of coherence messages and a reduction in the false sharing penalty. The former is beneficial because of the high per message costs on typical network-based platforms. The latter is a result of data "ping-ponging" between sharers due to the fact that logically differentiated data resides in the same coherence

unit. By delaying coherence actions to the release point, the number of such "ping-pongs" is reduced.

Release consistency mandates, however, that before the release is visible to *any* other process, all ordinary data accesses made prior to the release are visible at *all* other processes. This results in extra messages between processes at the time of a release. The TreadMarks system [2] proposed the use of a lazy release consistency model [22] by making the observation that for data race free [1] programs, such ordinary data accesses need only be visible at the time of an acquire. Communication can thus be further aggregated and limited to between an acquirer and a releaser.

While lazy release consistency reduces the number of coherence messages used to the minimum possible, it comes at a cost in terms of implementation complexity. Since data accesses are not made visible everywhere at the time of a release, the runtime system must keep track of the ordering of such coherence events and transmit this information when a process eventually performs an acquire. TreadMarks accomplishes this via the use of vector timestamps. The execution of each process is divided into intervals delineated by synchronization operations (either an acquire or a release). Each interval is assigned a monotonically increasing number. Intervals of different processes are partially ordered: Intervals on a single process are totally ordered by program order and intervals on different processes are ordered by acquire–release causality. This partial order is what is captured by assigning a vector timestamp to each interval. Write notices for all data written in an interval are associated with its vector timestamp. This information is piggybacked on release messages to ensure coherence. Each process must then ensure that write notices from all intervals that precede its current interval are applied prior to execution of the current interval.

On system area networks such as Infiniband [21], where the latency and CPU occupancy of communication is an order of magnitude lower than on traditional networks, it can sometimes be beneficial to overlap communication with computation. Cashmere [25] leverages this observation in a moderately lazy release consistent implementation on the Memory Channel [16] network. Write notices are pushed to all processes at the time of a release. They are only applied at the time of the next acquire, thereby avoiding the need to interrupt the remote process. Another advantage of this implementation is that it removes the need to maintain vector timestamps along with the associated metadata management complexity.

An alternative consistency model, *entry consistency*, was defined by Bershad and Zekauskas [5]. All shared data are required to be explicitly associated with some synchronization (lock) variable. On a lock acquisition, only the shared data associated with the lock is guaranteed to be made coherent. This model has some implementation and efficiency advantages. However, the cost is a change to the programming model, requiring explicit association of shared data with synchronization and additional synchronization beyond what is usually required for data race free programs. Scope consistency [20] provides a model similar to entry consistency, but helps eliminate the burden of explicit binding by implicitly associating data with the locks under which they are modified.

Data and Metadata Location

In order to get an up-to-date copy of data, the runtime system must determine the location of the latest version/s. Most implementations fall into two categories – ones in which the information is distributed across all nodes at the time of synchronization, and ones in which each coherence and metadata unit has a *home* that keeps track of where the latest version resides, similar to a hardware directory-based protocol. The former implies that every process knows where the latest version is or has the latest version of the data propagated directly to them. The latter implies a level of indirection (through the home) in order to locate the latest version of the data or owner of the metadata. Variations of the latter protocol include making sure that the home node is kept up to date so that any process requesting a copy can retrieve it directly from the home, and allowing migration of the home to (one of) the most active user/s.

Leveraging Hardware Coherence

As multiprocessor desktop machines become more common, and with the advent of multicore chips, a cluster of multicore multiprocessor machines is a fairly common computing platform. In implementing shared memory on these platforms, the challenge is to take advantage of hardware-based sharing whenever possible and ensure that software overhead is incurred *only* when actively sharing data across nodes in a cluster.

SoftFLASH [12] is a kernel-level implementation of a two-level coherence protocol on a cluster of symmetric multiprocessors (SMPs). SoftFLASH implements coherence using virtual memory techniques, which implies that coherence is implemented by changing read/write permissions in the process's page table. These permissions are normally cached in the translation lookaside buffer (TLB) in each of the processors of a single node. Since the TLB is not typically hardware coherent, in order to ensure that all threads/processes on a single node have appropriate levels of permission to access shared data, the TLBs in each processor within a node must be examined and flushed if necessary. This process, called TLB shootdown, is usually accomplished with costly inter-processor interrupts.

Cashmere-2L [36] avoids the need for these expensive TLB shootdowns through a combination of a relaxed memory model and the use of a novel two-way diffing technique. Leveraging the observation that in a data race free model, accesses by different processes between two synchronization points will be to different memory locations, Cashmere-2L avoids the need to interrupt other processes during a software coherence operation. Updates to a page are applied through a reverse diffing process that identifies and updates only the bytes that have changed, allowing concurrent processes to continue accessing and modifying unrelated data. Invalidations are applied individually by each process and once again leverage the use of diffing in order to avoid potential conflicts with concurrent writers on the node.

Shasta [33] uses instrumentation to implement a finer granularity coherence protocol across SMP nodes. The lack of atomicity of coherence state checks with respect to the actual load or store (the two actions consist of multiple instructions) results in protocol race conditions that require extra overhead when data is shared by processes within an SMP node. A naive solution would involve sufficient synchronization to avoid the race. Shasta avoids this costly synchronization through the selective use of explicit messages. Since protocol metadata is visible to all processes, per-process state tables are used to determine processes that are actively sharing data. Messages are sent only to these processes and overhead incurred only with active sharing.

Leveraging Additional Hardware Support

Systems such as Ivy, TreadMarks, and Munin are implemented under the assumption that memory on remote machines is not directly accessible and must be read/accessed by requesting service from a handler on the remote machine. This is typically accomplished by sending a message over the network, which can be detected and received at the responding end either by periodically polling or by using interrupts. On traditional local area networks, interrupts are typically expensive because of the need for operating system intervention. However, the advantage is that overhead is incurred only when communication is required. Polling (periodically checking the status of the network interface), on the other hand, is relatively cheap (on the order of a few tens of processor cycles), but because the runtime system has no knowledge of when communication will occur, the frequency of checks can result in a significant overhead that is incurred regardless of whether or not data is actively shared. TreadMarks attempted to minimize the number of messages using a lazy protocol on the assumption that the per message costs (both network and processor occupancy as well as the cost to interrupt a remote processor in order to elicit a response) are at least two orders of magnitude higher than memory read and write latencies.

High-performance network technologies, such as those that conform to the Infiniband [21] standard (as well as research prototypes such as Princeton's Shrimp [7] and earlier commercial offerings such as DEC's Memory Channel, Myrinet, and Quadrics QsNet), provide low latency and high bandwidth communication. These networks achieve low latency by virtualizing the network interface. Issues of protection are separated from actual data communication. The former involves the operating system and is performed once at setup time. The latter is performed at user level, thereby achieving lower latency. The majority of these networks allow the possibility of direct access (reads and/or writes) to remote memory, changing the equation in terms of the trade-off in the number of messages used and the eagerness and laziness of the protocol. Protocols such as Cashmere and HLRC [6] leverage such direct access to perform protocol actions eagerly without the need to interrupt the remote processor.

Sharing in the Wide Area

As "computing in the cloud," i.e., taking advantage of geographically distributed compute resources, becomes more ubiquitous, the ability to seamlessly share information across the wide area will improve programmability. Several projects [3, 10, 14, 26, 31, 37] have examined techniques to allow data sharing in the wide area. Most enforce a strongly object-oriented programming model. Specifically, InterWeave [9] supports both language and machine heterogeneity, using an intermediate format to provide persistent data storage and to communicate seamlessly across heterogeneous machines. InterWeave leverages existing hardware and network characteristics (including support for coherence in hardware) whenever possible. The memory model is further relaxed to incorporate application-specific tolerances for delays in consistency. Writes are, however, serialized using a centralized approach (per object) for coordination.

Compiler and Language-Level Support

Early work in incorporating compiler support with SDSMs [11] examined techniques by which data communication could be aggregated or eliminated entirely by understanding the specific access patterns of the application. In particular, the shortcomings of a generalized runtime system for shared memory relative to a program written for message passing is that in order to minimize the volume of data communicated, data communication is often separated from synchronization and data is fetched on demand at the granularity of the coherence unit. Compile-time analysis can identify data that will be accessed and inform the runtime system so that the data can be explicitly prefetched. Similarly, by using appropriate directives to the runtime to identify when entire coherence units are being written without being read, coherence communication can be eliminated entirely. Subsequently, several efforts have examined the use of SDSM as a back end for programming models such as OpenMP [17, 29]. They discuss the trade-offs between using a threaded (with a default of sharing the entire address space) versus a process model (with a default of private address spaces with shared data being specifically identified). Their work shows that naive implementations can perform poorly, and that identification of shared data is important to the feasibility and scalability of using programming environments such as OpenMP on SMP clusters.

Future Directions

Despite intense research and significant advances in the development of SDSM systems in the 1980s and 1990s, they remain in limited use due to their trade of scalability for the platform transparency they achieve. As multicore platforms become more ubiquitous, and as the number of cores increases, the scalability of pure hardware-based coherence is also in question, and SDSM systems may see a bigger role. Several researchers continue to explore the possibility of combining hardware and software coherence, in terms of hardware assists for a software-based coherence implementation [13] and in terms of alternating between automatic hardware coherence and software-managed incoherence based on application or compiler knowledge [24]. There is also renewed interest in the use of SDSM techniques in order to support heterogeneous platforms composed of a combination of general-purpose CPUs and accelerators [4, 32].

Related Entries

▶ Cache Coherence
▶ Distributed-Memory Multiprocessor
▶ Linda
▶ Memory Models
▶ Network of Workstations
▶ POSIX Threads (Pthreads)
▶ Processes, Tasks, and Threads
▶ Shared-Memory Multiprocessors
▶ SPMD Computational Model
▶ Synchronization

Bibliographic Notes and Further Reading

Protic et al. [30] published a compendium of works in the area of distributed shared memory circa 1994. Iftode and Singh [19] wrote an excellent survey article that encompasses both network interface advances and the incorporation of multiprocessor nodes.

Acknowledgment

This work was supported in part by NSF grants CCF-1016902, CCF-0702505, CNS-0834451, and CNS-0509270. Any opinions, findings, and conclusions or recommendations expressed in this material are those of the author and do not necessarily reflect the views of the granting agencies.

Bibliography

1. Adve S, Hill M (1990) Weak ordering: a new definition. In: Proceedings of the 17th annual international symposium on computer architecture, May 1990. ACM, New York, pp 2–14
2. Amza C, Cox A, Dwarkadas S, Keleher P, Lu H, Rajamony R, Zwaenepoel W (1996) Tread-marks: shared memory computing on networks of workstations. IEEE Comput 29(2):18–28
3. Bal H, Kaashoek M, Tanenbaum A (1992) Orca: a language for parallel programming of distributed systems. IEEE Trans Softw Eng 18(3):190–205
4. Becchi M, Cadambi S, Chakradhar S (2010) Enabling legacy applications on heterogeneous platforms. Poster paper, 2nd USENIX workshop on hot topics in parallelism (HOTPAR), Berkley, June 2010
5. Bershad B, Zekauskas M (1991) Midway: shared memory parallel programming with entry consistency for distributed memory multiprocessors. Technical Report CMU-CS-91-170, Carnegie-Mellon University, Sept 1991
6. Bilas A, Jiang D, Singh JP (2001) Accelerating shared virtual memory via general-purpose network interface support. ACM Trans Comput Syst 19:1–35
7. Blumrich M, Li K, Alpert R, Dubnicki C, Felten E, Sandberg J (1994) Virtual memory mapped network interface for the SHRIMP multicomputer. In: Proceedings of the 21st annual international symposium on computer architecture. ACM, New York, pp 142–153
8. Carter J, Bennett J, Zwaenepoel W (1991) Implementation and performance of Munin. In: Proceedings of the 13th ACM symposium on operating systems principles, ACM Press, New York, pp 152–164
9. Chen D, Tang C, Chen X, Dwarkadas S, Scott ML (2001) Beyond S-DSM: shared state for distributed systems. Technical report 744, University of Rochester, Mar 2001
10. Chen D, Tang C, Chen X, Dwarkadas S, Scott ML (2002) Multi-level shared state for distributed systems. In: International conference on parallel processing, Aug 2002, Vancouver
11. Dwarkadas S, Cox A, Zwaenepoel W (1996) An integrated compile-time/run-time software distributed shared memory system. In: Proceedings of the 7th symposium on architectural support for programming languages and operating systems, pp 186–197, Oct 1996
12. Erlichson A, Nuckolls N, Chesson G, Hennessy J (1996) SoftFLASH: analyzing the performance of clustered distributed virtual shared memory. In: Proceedings of the 7th symposium on architectural support for programming languages and operating systems, Oct 1996. ACM Press, New York, pp 210–220
13. Fensch C, Cintra M (2008) An OS-based alternative to full hardware coherence on tiled CMPs. In: Proceedings of the fourteenth international symposium on high-performance computer architecture symposium, February 2008, Phoenix
14. Foster I, Kesselman C (1997) Globus: a metacomputing infrastructure toolkit. Int J Supercomputer Appl 11(2):115–128
15. Gharachorloo K, Lenoski D, Laudon J, Gibbons P, Gupta A, Hennessy J (1990) Memory consistency and event ordering in scalable shared-memory multiprocessors. In: Proceedings of the 17th annual international symposium on computer architecture, May 1990. ACM, New York, pp 15–26
16. Gillett R (1996) Memory channel: an optimized cluster interconnect. IEEE Micro 16(2):12–18
17. Hu Y, Lu H, Cox AL, Zwaenepoel W (1999) OpenMP for networks of SMPs. In: Proceedings of the 13th international parallel processing symposium (IPPS/SPDP), Apr 1999. IEEE, New York, pp 302–310
18. Hu YC, Yu W, Cox AL, Wallach D, Zwaenepoel W (2003) Runtime support for distributed sharing in sage languages. ACM Trans Comput Syst 21(1):1–35
19. Iftode L, Singh JP (1999) Shared virtual memory: progress and challenges. Proceedings of the IEEE 87(3):498–507
20. Iftode L, Singh JP, Li K (1996) Scope consistency: a bridge between release consistency and entry consistency. In: ACM symposium on parallelism in algorithms and architectures, June 1996. ACM Press, New York, pp 277–287
21. Association (2010) InfiniBand. http://www.infinibandta.org
22. Keleher P, Cox AL, Zwaenepoel W (1992) Lazy release consistency for software distributed shared memory. In: Proceedings of the 19th annual international symposium on computer architecture, May 1992. ACM Press, New York, pp 13–21
23. Keleher P, Dwarkadas S, Cox A, Zwaenepoel W (1994) Treadmarks: distributed shared memory on standard workstations and operating systems. In: Proceedings of the 1994 winter Usenix conference, Jan 1994. USENIX Association, Berkeley, pp 115–131
24. Kelm JH, Johnson DR, Tuohy W, Lumetta SS, Patel SJ (2010) Cohesion: a hybrid memory model for accelerators. In: Proceedings of the international symposium on computer architecture (ISCA), June 2010, St Malo
25. Kontothanassis L, Hunt G, Stets R, Hardavellas N, Cierniak M, Parthasarathy S, Meira W, Dwarkadas S, Scott M (1997) VM-based shared memory on low-latency, remote-memory-access networks. In: 24th international symposium on computer architecture, June 1997. ACM Press, New York, pp 157–169
26. Lewis M, Grimshaw A (1996) The core legion object model. In: Proceedings of the 5th high performance distributed computing conference, Aug 1996, Syracuse
27. Li K (1986) Shared virtual memory on loosely coupled multiprocessors. Ph.D. thesis, Yale University
28. Li K, Hudak P (1989) Memory coherence in shared virtual memory systems. ACM Trans Comput Syst 7(4):321–359
29. Min S-J, Basumallik A, Eigenmann R (2003) Optimizing openmp programs on software distributed shared memory systems. Int J Parallel Prog 31:225–249
30. Protic J, Tomasevic M, Milutinovic V (1998) Distributed shared memory: concepts and systems. IEEE Computer Society Press, Piscataway, p 365

31. Rogerson D (1997) Inside COM. Microsoft Press, Redmond
32. Saha B, Zhou X, Chen H, Gao Y, Yan S, Rajagopalan M, Fang J, Zhang P, Ronen R, Mendelson (2009) A Programming Model for a Heterogeneous x86 Platform. In Proceedings of the ACM SIGPLAN 2009 Conference on Programming Language Design and Implementation, June 2009
33. Scales D, Gharachorloo K, Aggarwal A (1998) Fine-grain software distributed shared memory on smp clusters. In: Proceedings of the fourth international symposium on high-performance computer architecture symposium, Feb 1998. ACM, New York, pp 125–136
34. Scales D, Gharachorloo K, Thekkath C (1996) Shasta: A low overhead, software-only approach for supporting fine-grain shared memory. In: Proceedings of the 7th symposium on architectural support for programming languages and operating systems, Oct 1996, pp 174–185
35. Schoinas I, Falsafi B, Lebeck AR, Reinhardt SK, Larus JR, Wood DA (1994) Fine-grain access control for distributed shared memory. In: Proceedings of the 6th symposium on architectural support for programming languages and operating systems, Oct 1994. ACM, New York, pp 297–306
36. Stets R, Dwarkadas S, Hardavellas N, Hunt G, Kontothanassis L, Parthasarathy S, Scott M (1997) Cashmere-2L: software coherent shared memory on a clustered remote-write network. In: Proceedings of the 16th ACM symposium on operating systems principles, Oct 1997. ACM, New York, pp 170–183
37. van Steen M, Homburg P, Tanenbaum AS (1999) Globe: a wide-area distributed system. IEEE Concurr 7(1):70–78

Sorting

LAXMIKANT V. KALÉ[1], EDGAR SOLOMONIK[2]
[1]University of Illinois at Urbana-Champaign, Urbana, IL, USA
[2]University of California at Berkeley, Berkeley, CA, USA

Definition

Parallel sorting is a process that given n keys distributed over p processors (numbered 0 through $p-1$), migrates the keys so that all keys on processor k, for $k \in [0, p-2]$, are sorted locally and are smaller than or equal to all keys on processor $k+1$.

Discussion

Introduction

Parallel sorting algorithms have been studied in a variety of contexts. Early studies in parallel sorting addressed the theoretical problem of sorting n keys distributed over n processors, using fixed interconnection networks. Modern parallel sorting algorithms focus on the scenario where n is much larger than the number of processors, p. However, even contemporary algorithms need to satisfy an array of use-cases and architectures, so various parallel sorting techniques have been analyzed for GPU-based sorting, shared memory sorting, distributed memory sorting, and external memory sorting. On most if not all of these architectures, parallel sorting is typically dominated by communication, in particular, the movement of data values associated with the keys.

Parallel sorting has a wide breadth of practical applications. Some scientific applications in the field of high-performance computing (e.g., ChaNGa) perform sorting each iteration, placing high demand on good scalability and adaptivity of parallel sorting algorithms. Parallel sorting is also utilized in the commercial field for processing of numeric as well as nonnumeric data (i.e., parallel database queries). Moreover, Integer Sort is one of the NAS parallel benchmarks.

Parallel Sorting Algorithms

There are a few important parallel sorting algorithms that dominate multiple use-cases and serve as building blocks for more specialized sorting algorithms. The algorithms will be described for the distributed memory paradigm, though most are also applicable to other architectures and models.

Parallel Quicksort

Parallelization of Quicksort can be done in a variety of ways. A simplified, recursive version is described below. A more thorough analysis can be found in [1] or [2].

1. A processor broadcasts a pivot element to all p processors.
2. Each processor then splits its keys into two sections (smaller keys and larger keys) according to the pivot.
3. Two prefix sums calculate the total number of smaller keys and larger keys on the first k processors, for $k \in [0, p-1]$. If, $small_k$ and $large_k$ are, respectively, the total numbers of smaller and larger keys on processors 0 through k, then, after this operation, processor k knows $small_{k-1}$ and $large_{k-1}$ as well as $small_k$ and $large_k$.
4. Processor $p-1$ knows the total sums, $small_{p-1}$ and $large_{p-1}$. It can therefore divide the set of processors

in proportion with $small_{p-1}$ and $large_{p-1}$, thus determining two sets of processors (P_s and P_l) that should be given the smaller and larger keys. This processor should also broadcast the average number of keys these two sets of processors should receive ($small_{avg}$ and $large_{avg}$).

5. Each processor k can now decide where its keys need to be sent. For example, the smaller keys should go to processor $\left\lfloor \frac{small_{k-1}}{small_{avg}} \right\rfloor$ through processor $\left\lfloor \frac{small_k}{small_{avg}} \right\rfloor$.
6. After the communication, it is sufficient for the Parallel Quicksort procedure to recurse on the two processor sets (P_s and P_l) until all data values are on the correct processors and can be sorted locally.

This algorithm generally achieves good load balance by determining the correct portions of processors that should receive smaller and larger keys. However, the necessity of moving half the data for every iteration is costly on large distributed systems. In the average case, Parallel Quicksort necessitates $\Theta(n \log p)$ data movement. Moreover, both the quality of load balance achieved for small processor sets and the total number of recursive levels are dependent on pivot selection. Efficient implementations of Parallel Quicksort typically use more complex pivoting techniques and multiple pivots [2]. Nevertheless, Parallel Quicksort is easy to implement and can achieve good performance on some shared memory and smaller distributed systems. Additionally, the number of messages sent by each processor in step 5 is constant – typically no more than four. Therefore, Parallel Quicksort has a relatively small message latency cost of $\Theta(p \log p)$ messages.

Bitonic Sort

Introduced in 1968 by Batcher [3], Bitonic Sort is one of the oldest parallel sorting algorithms. This algorithm is based on the sorting of *bitonic sequences*. A *bitonic sequence* is a sequence S or any cyclic shift of S, such that $S = S_1 S_2$ where S_1 is monotonically nondecreasing and S_2 is monotonically nonincreasing. Further, any unsorted sequence can be treated as a series of bitonic subsequences of length two. A *bitonic merge* turns a bitonic subsequence into a fully sorted subsequence. Bitonic Sort works by application of a series of bitonic merges until the entire sequence is sorted. Applying bitonic merges on a series of bitonic subsequences effectively doubles the length of each sorted subsequence and cuts the number of bitonic subsequences in half.

Therefore, for an unsorted sequence of length k, where k is a power of two, Bitonic Sort requires $\log k$ merges.

The main insight of Bitonic Sort is in the bitonic merge operation. A bitonic merge recursively slices a bitonic sequence into two bitonic sequences, with all elements in one sequence larger than all elements in the other. When the bitonic sequence is sliced into pieces of unit length, the entire input is sorted. Given a bitonic sequence of length s, where s is a power of two, every slice operation compares and swaps each element k, where $k \in [0, s/2)$ with element $k + s/2$. These swaps result in two bitonic sequences of length $s/2$, with the elements in one being larger than the elements of the other. Thus, if s is a power of two, a bitonic merge requires $\log s$ slices, which amounts to $\log s$ comparison operations on every element.

In the case of $n = p$ on a hypercube network, a bitonic merge requires $\Theta(\log n)$ swaps, one swap in each hypercube dimension. The algorithm requires $\log n$ merges on such a network, for a composed running time of $\Theta(\log^2 n)$. Adaptive Bitonic Sorting [4] avoids the redundant comparisons in Bitonic Sort and achieves a runtime complexity of $\Theta(\log n)$. Further, Bitonic Sort is also asymptotically optimal on mesh connected networks [5].

As proposed by Blelloch [6], Bitonic Sort can be extended for the case of $n \geq p$, by introducing virtual hypercube dimensions within each processor. Alternatively, a more efficient sequential sorting algorithm can be used for the sequential sorting work. Though historically significant and elegant in nature, Bitonic Sort is not widely used on modern supercomputers, since the algorithm requires data to be migrated through the network $\Theta(\log^2 p)$ times or, in the case of Adaptive Bitonic Sorting, $\Theta(\log p)$ times. Nevertheless, Bitonic Sort has been used in a wide variety of applications, ranging from network router hardware to sorting on GPUs [7–9]. A more thorough analysis and justification of correctness of this algorithm can be found in the Bitonic Sort article.

Parallel Radix Sort

Radix Sort is a counting-based sorting algorithm that relies on the bitwise representation of keys. An r-bit radix looks at r bits of each key at a time and permutes the keys to move to one of the 2^r buckets, where the r-bit value of each key corresponds to its destination bucket. If each key has b bits, by looking at the r least-significant bits first, Radix Sort can sort the entire dataset in $\lceil \frac{b}{r} \rceil$ permutations. Therefore, this algorithm has a complexity of $\Theta\left(\frac{b}{r}n\right)$. Notably, this complexity is linear with respect to n, a feature that cannot be matched by comparison-based sorting algorithms, which must do at least $\Theta(n \log n)$ comparison operations. However, Radix Sort is inherently cache-inefficient since each key may need to go to any one of the 2^r buckets for each iteration, independent of which bucket it resided in the previous iteration [10]. A further limitation on Radix Sort is its reliance on the bitwise representation of keys, which is satisfied for integers and requires a simple transformation for floats, but is not necessarily possible or simple for strings and other data types.

Parallel Radix Sort is implemented by assigning a subset of the buckets to each processor [6]. Thus, each of $\lceil \frac{b}{r} \rceil$ permutations would result in a step of all-to-all communication. Load balancing is also achieved relatively easily by computing a histogram of the number of keys headed for each bucket at the beginning of each step. These histograms can be computed using local data on each processor first, then summed up using a reduction. Given a summed-up histogram, a single processor can then adaptively decide the set of buckets to assign to each processor and broadcast this information to all other processors. Each processor then sends all of its keys to the processor that owns the appropriate bucket for each key, using all-to-all communication.

A good way to improve the efficiency of local histogram computation in Radix Sort is to use an auxiliary set of low-bit counters [11]. Given a large r, it is unlikely that an array of 2^r 32-bit counters can fit into the L1 cache. However, by using an array of 2^r 8-bit counters and incrementing the 32-bit counter array only when the 8-bit counters are about to overflow, cache performance can be significantly improved.

The simplicity of Radix Sort as well as its relatively good all-around performance and scalability have made it a popular parallel sorting algorithm in a variety of contexts. However, Radix Sort still suffers from cache-efficiency problems and requires multiple steps of all-to-all communication, which can be an extremely costly operation on a large enough system.

Sample Sort

Sample Sorting is a *splitter-based* method which performs data partitioning by collecting a sample of the entire dataset [12]. *Splitter-based* parallel sorting algorithms determine the destinations for each key by determining a range bounded by two *splitters* for each processor. These *splitters* are simply values meant to subdivide the entire key range into p approximately equal chunks, so that each processor can be assigned a roughly even-sized chunk. After the splitters have been determined and broadcasted to all processors, a single all-to-all communication step suffices in giving each processor the correct data.

Parallel Sorting by Regular Sampling is a Sample Sorting algorithm introduced by Shi and Schaeffer [13]. This algorithm determines the correct splitters by collecting a sample of data from each processor. Sorting by Regular Sampling uses a regular sample of size $p-1$ and generally operates as follows:

1. Sort local data on each processor.
2. Collect sample of size $p-1$ on each processor with the kth element of each sample as element $\frac{n}{p} \times \frac{k+1}{p}$ of the local data.
3. Merge the p samples to form a combined sorted sample of size $p \times (p-1)$.
4. Define $p-1$ splitters with the kth splitter as element $p \times \left(k + \frac{1}{2}\right)$ of the sorted sample.
5. Broadcast splitters to all processors.
6. On each processor, subdivide the local keys into p chunks (numbered 0 through $p-1$) according to the splitters. Send each chunk to equivalently numbered processor.
7. Merge the incoming data on each processor.

Collecting a regular sample of size $p-1$ from each processor has been proven to guarantee no more than $\frac{2n}{p}$ elements on any processor [14] and shown to achieve almost perfect load balance for most practical distributions. The algorithm has also been shown to be asymptotically optimal as long as $n \geq p^3$.

Regular Sample Sort is easy to implement, insensitive to key distribution, and optimal in terms of the data movement required (there is a single all-to-all step, so each key gets moved only once). The algorithm has been shown to perform very well for $n \gg p$ and has been the parallel sorting algorithm of choice for many modern applications. One important issue with the traditional Sorting by Regular Sampling technique is the requirement of a combined sample of size $\Theta(p^2)$. For a small-enough p this is not a major cost; however, for high-performance computing applications running on thousands of processors, this cost begins to overwhelm the running time of the sorting algorithm and the $n \geq p^3$ assumption crumbles.

Sorting by Random Sampling [6] is a parallel sorting technique that can potentially alleviate some of the drawbacks of Parallel Sorting by Regular Sampling. Instead of selecting an evenly distributed sample of size $p - 1$ from each processor, random samples of size s are collected from the initial local datasets to form a combined sample of size $s \times p$. The s parameter has to be carefully chosen, but sometimes sufficient load balance can be achieved for $s < p$. Additionally, Sorting by Random Sampling allows for better potential overlap between computation and communication since the sample can be collected before the local sorting is done.

Another interesting variation of Sample Sort was introduced by Helman et al. [15]. Instead of collecting a sample, this sorting procedure first permutes the elements randomly with a randomized data transpose, then simply selects the splitters on one processor. To execute the transpose, each processor randomly assigns each of its local keys to one of the p buckets, then sends the jth bucket to the jth processor. With high probability, this permutation guarantees that any processor's elements will be representative of the entire key set. Thus, this algorithm avoids the cost of collecting and analyzing a large sample on a single processor. One processor still needs to select and broadcast splitters but this is a relatively cheap operation. The main disadvantage of this technique is the extra all-to-all communication round, which is very expensive on a large system. Additionally, as p scales to n/p, the load balance achieved by the algorithm deteriorates.

Histogram Sort

Histogram Sort [16] is another splitter-based method for parallel sorting. Like Sample Sort, Histogram Sort determines a set of $p - 1$ splitters to divide the keys into p evenly sized sections. However, it achieves this task by taking an iterative guessing approach rather than simply collecting one big sample. Each set of splitter-guesses, called the *probe*, is matched up to the data then adjusted, until *satisfactory values* for all splitters have been determined. A *satisfactory value* for the kth splitter needs to divide the data so that approximately $\frac{k+1}{p} \times n$ keys are smaller than the splitter value. Typically, a threshold range is established for each splitter so that the splitter-guesses can converge quicker. The kth splitter must divide the data within the range of keys, $\left(\frac{nk}{p} - \frac{nT}{p}, \frac{nk}{p} + \frac{nT}{p}\right)$, where T is the given threshold. A basic implementation of Histogram Sort operates as follows:

1. Sort local data on each processor.
2. Define a probe of $p - 1$ splitter-guesses distributed evenly over the key data range.
3. Broadcast the probe to all processors.
4. Produce local histograms by determining how much of each processor's local data fits between each key range defined by the splitter-guesses.
5. Sum up the histograms from each processor using a reduction to form a complete histogram.
6. Analyze the complete histogram on a single processor, determining any splitter values satisfied by a splitter-guess, and bounding any unsatisfied splitter values by the closest splitter-guesses.
7. If any splitters have not been satisfied, produce a new probe and go back to step 3.
8. Broadcast splitters to all processors.
9. On each processor, subdivide the local keys into p chunks (numbered 0 through $p - 1$) according to the splitters. Send each chunk to equivalently numbered processor.
10. Merge the incoming data on each processor.

This iterative technique can refine the splitter-guesses to an arbitrarily narrow threshold range. Quick convergence can be guaranteed by defining each new probe to contain a guess in the middle of the bounded range for each unsatisfied splitter.

Like any splitter-based sort, Histogram Sort is optimal in terms of the data movement required. However, unlike all previously described sorting algorithms, the running time of Histogram Sort depends on the distribution of the data through the data range. The iterative approach employed by this sorting procedure guarantees desired level of load balance which Sample Sort and Radix Sort cannot. Additionally, the probing technique is flexible and does not require that local data be sorted immediately [17]. This advantage allows an excellent opportunity for the exploitation of communication and computation overlap. However, Histogram Sort is generally more difficult to implement than common alternatives such as Radix Sort or Sample Sort.

Architectures and Theoretical Models

Parallelism is exhibited by a variety of computer architectures. Shared memory multiprocessors, distributed systems, supercomputers, sorting networks, and GPUs are all fundamentally different parallel computing constructions. As such, parallel sorting algorithms need to be designed and tuned for each of these architectures specifically.

Sorting Networks and Early Theoretical Models

Traditional parallel sorting targeted the problem of sorting n numbers on n processors using a fixed interconnection network. Bitonic Sort [3] was an early success as it provided a $\Theta(\log^2 n)$-depth sorting network. The bitonic sorting network also yielded a practical algorithm for sorting n keys in parallel using n processors in $\Theta(\log^2 n)$ time on network topologies such as the hypercube and shuffle-exchange. In 1983, Ajtai et al. [18], introduced an $\Theta(\log n)$-depth sorting network capable of sorting n keys in $\Theta(\log n)$ time using $\Theta(n \log n)$ comparators. However, this construction was shown to lead to less-efficient networks than Bitonic Sort for reasonable values of n. Leighton [19] introduced the Column Sort algorithm. He showed that, based on Column Sort, for any sorting network with $\Theta(n \log n)$ comparators and $\Theta(\log n)$ depth, one can construct a corresponding constant-degree network of n processors that can sort in $\Theta(\log n)$ time.

Much work has targeted the complexity of parallel sorting on the less-restrictive PRAM model where each processor can access the memory of all other processors in constant time. In 1986, Cole [20] introduced an efficient and practical parallel sorting algorithm with versions for the CREW (concurrent read only) and EREW (no concurrent access) PRAM models. This algorithm was based on a simple tree-based Mergesort, but was elegantly pipelined to achieve a $\Theta(\log n)$ complexity for sorting n keys using n processors. Cole's merge sort used a $\Theta(\log n)$ time merging algorithm, which naturally leads to a $\Theta(\log^2 n)$ sorting algorithm. However, his sorting algorithm used results from lower levels of the merge tree to partially precompute the merging done in higher levels of the merge tree. Thus, the sorting algorithm was designed so that at every node of the merge tree only a constant amount of work needed to be done, yielding a $\Theta(\log n)$ overall sorting complexity.

Sorting networks have also been extensively studied for the VLSI model of computation. The VLSI model focuses on area-time complexity, that is, the area of the chip on which the network is constructed and the running time. A good analysis of lower bounds for the complexity of such VLSI sorters can be found in [21].

These theoretical methods have been studied intensively in literature and have yielded many elegant parallel sorting algorithms. However, the theoretical machine models they were designed for are no longer representative or directly useful for current parallel computer architectures. Nevertheless, these studies provide valuable groundwork for modern and future parallel sorting algorithms. Moreover, sorting networks may prove to be useful for emerging architectures such as GPUs and chip multicores.

GPU-Based Sorting

Early GPU-based sorting algorithms utilized a limited graphics API which, among other restrictions, did not allow scatter operations and made Bitonic Sort the dominant choice. GPUTeraSort [7] is an early efficient hybrid algorithm that uses Radix Sort and Bitonic Sort. GPUTeraSort was designed for GPU-based external sorting, but is also general to in-memory GPU-based sorting. A weakness of the GPUTeraSort algorithm is its $\Theta(n \log^2 n)$ running time, typical of parallel sorting algorithms based on Bitonic Sort. GPU-ABiSort [8] improved over GPUTeraSort by using Adaptive Bitonic Sorting [4], lowering the theoretical complexity to $\Theta(n \log n)$ and often demonstrating a lower practical running time.

Newer GPUs, assisted by the CUDA software environment, allow for efficient scan primitives and a much broader set of parallel sorting algorithms. Efficient versions of Radix Sort and a parallel Mergesort are presented by Satish et al. [9]. Newer GPU-based sorting algorithms also exploit instruction-level parallelism by performing steps such as merging using custom vector operations. An array of various other GPU-based sorting algorithms, which are not detailed here, can be found in literature.

Current results on modern GPUs suggest that Radix Sort typically performs best, particularly when the key size is small [9]. Radix Sort is well fit for GPU execution since keys can be processed independently and synchronization is almost purely in the form of prefix sums, which can be executed with high efficiency on GPUs. Radix Sort also requires few or no low-level branches, unlike comparison-based sorting algorithms. Finally, the cache inefficiency of Radix Sort has been less costly on GPUs since most GPUs have no cache. However, newer GPUs, such as the NVIDIA GPUs of compute capability 2.0, already have small caches and are rapidly evolving. It is hard to predict whether Radix Sort or a different sorting algorithm will prove most efficient on emerging GPU and accelerator architectures.

Shared Memory Sorting

Parallel merging techniques have commonly been used to produce simple shared memory parallel sorting algorithms. Francis and Mathieson [22] present a k-processor merge that allows for all processors to participate in a parallel merge tree, with two processors participating in each merge during the first merging stage and all processors participating in the final merge at the head of the tree. Good performance is achieved by subdividing each of the two arrays of size a and b being merged into k sections, where k is the number of processors participating in the merge. The subdivisions are selected so that the ith processor merges the ith section of each of the two arrays and produces elements $\frac{i}{k}(a+b)$ through $\frac{i+1}{k}(a+b)$ of the merged array.

Merge-based algorithms, such as the one detailed above, as well as parallel versions of Quicksort and Mergesort, are predominant on contemporary shared memory multiprocessor architectures. However, with the advent of increased parallelism in chip architectures, techniques such as sampling and histogramming may become more viable.

Distributed Memory Sorting

Parallel Sorting algorithms for distributed memory architectures are typically used in the high-performance computing field, and often require good scaling on modern supercomputers. In the 1990s Radix Sort and Bitonic Sort were widely used. However, as architectures evolved, these sorting techniques proved insufficient. Modern machines have thousands of cores, so, to achieve good scaling interprocessor communication needs to be minimized. Therefore, splitter-based algorithms such as Sample Sort and Histogram Sort are now more commonly used for distributed memory sorting. Splitter-based parallel sorting algorithms have minimal communication since they only move data once.

Future Directions

Despite the extraordinarily large amount of literature on parallel sorting, the demand for optimized parallel sorting algorithms continues to motivate novel algorithms and more research on the topic. Moreover, the continuously changing and, more recently, diverging nature of parallel architectures has made parallel sorting an evolving problem.

High-performance computer architectures are rapidly growing in size, creating a premium on parallel sorting algorithms that have minimal communication and good overlap between computation and communication. Since parallel sorting necessitates communication between all processors, the creation and optimization of topology-aware all-to-all personalized communication strategies is extremely valuable for many splitter-based parallel sorting algorithms. As previously mentioned, algorithms similar to Sample Sort and Histogram Sort are the most viable candidates for this field due to the minimal nature of the communication they need to perform.

Shared memory sorting algorithms are beginning to face a challenge that most modern sequential algorithms have to endure. The demand for good cache efficiency is now a key constraint for all algorithms due to the increasing relative cost of memory accesses. Parallel sorting is being studied under the cache-oblivious model [23] in an attempt to reevaluate previously established algorithms and introduce better ones.

Currently, parallel sorting using accelerators, such as GPUs, is probably the most active of all parallel sorting research areas due to the rapid changes and advances happening in the accelerator architecture field. Little can be said about which algorithms will dominate this field in the future, due to the influx of novel GPU-based sorting algorithms and newer accelerators in recent years.

The wide use of sorting in computer science along with the popularization of parallel architectures and parallel programming necessitates the implementation of parallel sorting libraries. Such libraries can be difficult to standardize, however, especially for the efficiency-sensitive field of high-performance computing. Nevertheless, these libraries are quickly emerging, especially under the shared memory computing paradigm.

Related Entries
▶Algorithm Engineering
▶All-to-All
▶Bitonic Sort
▶Bitonic Sorting, Adaptive
▶Collective Communication
▶Data Mining
▶NAS Parallel Benchmarks
▶PRAM (Parallel Random Access Machines)

Bibliographic Notes and Further Reading

The literature on parallel sorting is very large and this entry is forced to cite only a select few. The sources cited are a mixture of the largest impact publications and the most modern publications. A few of the sources also give useful information on multiple parallel sorting algorithms. Blelloch et al. [6] provide an in-depth experimental and theoretical comparative analysis of a few of the most important distributed memory parallel sorting algorithms. Satish et al. [9] provide good analysis of a few of the most modern GPU-sorting algorithms. Vitter [24] presents a good analysis of external memory parallel sorting.

Bibliography
1. Kumar V, Grama A, Gupta A, Karypis G (1994) Introduction to parallel computing: design and analysis of algorithms. Benjamin-Cummings, Redwood City, CA
2. Sanders P, Hansch T (1997) Efficient massively parallel quicksort. In: IRREGULAR '97: Proceedings of the 4th International Symposium on Solving Irregularly Structured Problems in Parallel, pp 13–24. Springer-Verlag, London, UK
3. Batcher K (1968) Sorting networks and their application. Proc. SICC, AFIPS 32:307–314
4. Bilardi G, Nicolau A (1986) Adaptive bitonic sorting: an optimal parallel algorithm for shared memory machines. Technical report, Ithaca, NY
5. Thompson CD, Kurg HT (1977) Sorting on a mesh-connected parallel computer. Commun ACM 20(4):263–271
6. Blelloch G et al. (1991) A comparison of sorting algorithms for the Connection Machine CM-2. In: Proceedings of the Symposium on Parallel Algorithms and Architectures, July 1991
7. Govindaraju N, Gray J, Kumar R, Manocha D (2006) Gputerasort: high performance graphics co-processor sorting for large database management. In: SIGMOD '06: Proceedings of the 2006 ACM SIGMOD international conference on Management of data, pp 325–336. ACM, New York
8. Greb A, Zachmann G (2006) Gpu-abisort: optimal parallel sorting on stream architectures. In: Parallel and Distributed Processing Symposium, 2006. IPDPS 2006, 20th International, pp 45–54, April 2006
9. Satish N, Harris M, Garland M (2009) Designing efficient sorting algorithms for manycore gpus. Parallel and Distributed Processing Symposium, International, Rome, pp 1–10
10. LaMarca A, Ladner RE (1997) The influence of caches on the performance of sorting. In: SODA '97: Proceedings of the eighth annual ACM-SIAM symposium on Discrete algorithms, pp 370–379. Society for Industrial and Applied Mathematics, Philadelphia, PA
11. Thearling K, Smith S (1992) An improved supercomputer sorting benchmark. In: Proceedings of the Supercomputing, November 1992.
12. Huang JS, Chow YC (1983) Parallel sorting and data partitioning by sampling. In: Proceedings of the Seventh International Computer Software and Applications Conference, November 1983
13. Shi H, Schaeffer J (1992) Parallel sorting by regular sampling. J Parallel Distrib Comput 14:361–372
14. Li X, Lu P, Schaeffer J, Shillington J, Wong PS, Shi H (1993) On the versatility of parallel sorting by regular sampling. Parallel Comput 19(10):1079–1103
15. Helman DR, Bader DA, JáJá J (1998) A randomized parallel sorting algorithm with an experimental study. J Parallel Distrib Comput 52(1):1–23
16. Kale LV, Krishnan S (1993) A comparison based parallel sorting algorithm. In: Proceedings of the 22nd International Conference on Parallel Processing, pp 196–200, St. Charles, IL, August 1993
17. Solomonik E, Kale LV (2010) Highly scalable parallel sorting. In: Proceedings of the 24th IEEE International Parallel and Distributed Processing Symposium (IPDPS). Urbana, IL, April 2010
18. Ajtai M, Komlós J, Szemerédi E (1983) Sorting in c log n parallel steps. Combinatorica 3(1):1–19
19. Leighton T (1984) Tight bounds on the complexity of parallel sorting. In: STOC '84: Proceedings of the sixteenth annual ACM symposium on Theory of computing, pp 71–80. ACM, New York
20. Cole R (1986) Parallel merge sort. In: SFCS '86: Proceedings of the 27th Annual Symposium on Foundations of Computer Science, pp 511–516. IEEE Computer Society, Washington, DC
21. Bilardi G, Preparata FP (1986) Area-time lower-bound techniques with applications to sorting. Algorithmica 1(1):65–91
22. Francis RS, Mathieson ID (1988) A benchmark parallel sort for shared memory multiprocessors. Comput IEEE Trans 37(12):1619–1626

23. Blelloch GE, Gibbons PB, Simhadri HV (2009) Brief announcement: low depth cache-oblivious sorting. In: SPAA '09: Proceedings of the twenty-first annual symposium on Parallelism in algorithms and architectures, pp 121–123. ACM, New York
24. Vitter JS (2001) External memory algorithms and data structures: dealing with massive data. ACM Comput Surv 33(2):209–271

Space-Filling Curves

Michael Bader[1], Hans-Joachim Bungartz[2], Miriam Mehl[2]
[1]Universität Stuttgart, Stuttgart, Germany
[2]Technische Universität München, Garching, Germany

Synonyms

FASS (space-**f**illing, self-**a**voiding, **s**imple, and self-**s**imilar)-curves

Definition

A space-filling curve is a continuous and surjective mapping from a 1D parameter interval, say $[0,1]$, onto a higher-dimensional domain, say the unit square in 2D or the unit cube in 3D. Although this, at first glance, seems to be of a purely mathematical interest, space-filling curves and their recursive construction process have obtained a broad impact on scientific computing in general and on the parallelization of numerical algorithms for spatially discretized problems in particular.

Discussion

Introduction

Space-filling curves (SFC) were presented at the end of the nineteenth century – first by Peano (1890) and Hilbert (1891), and later by Moore, Lebesgue, Sierpinski, and others. The idea that some curves (i.e., something actually one-dimensional) may completely cover an area or a volume sounds somewhat strange and formerly caused mathematicians to call them "topological monsters." The construction of all SFC follows basically the same principle: start with a *generator* indicating an order of traversal through the similar first-level substructures of the initial domain (the unit square, unit cube, etc.), and produce the next iterates by successively subdividing the domain in the same way as well as placing and connecting shrinked, rotated, or reflected versions of the generator in the next-level subdomains. This has to happen in an appropriate way, ensuring the two properties *neighborhood* (neighboring subintervals are mapped to neighboring subdomains) and *inclusion* (subintervals of an interval are mapped to subdomains of the interval's image). If all is done properly, it can be proven that the limit of this recursive process in fact defines a curve that completely fills the target domain and, hence, results in an SFC.

While the SFC itself as the asymptotical result of a continuous limit process is more a playground of mathematics, the iterative or recursive construction or, to be precise, the underlying mapping can be used for sequentializing higher-dimensional domains and data. Roughly speaking, these higher-dimensional data (elements of a finite element mesh, particles in a molecular dynamics simulation, stars in an astrophysics simulation, pixels in an image, voxels in a geometric model, or even entries in a data base, e.g.) now appear as pearls on a thread. Thus, via the locality properties of the SFC mapping, clusters of data can be easily identified (interacting finite elements, neighboring stars, similar data base entries, etc.). This helps for the efficient processing of tasks such as answering data base queries, defining hardware-aware traversal strategies through adaptively refined meshes or heterogeneous particle sets, and, of course, subdividing the data across cores or processors in the sense of (static or dynamic) load distribution in parallel computing. The main idea for the latter is that the linear (1D) arrangement of the data via the mapping basically reduces the load distribution problem to the sorting of indices.

Construction

Space-filling curves are typically constructed via an iterative or recursive process. The source interval and the target domain are recursively substructured into smaller intervals and domains. From each level of recursion to the next, a mapping between subintervals and subdomains is constructed, where the child intervals of a subinterval are typically mapped to the children of the image of the parent interval. The SFC is then defined as the image of the limit of these mappings.

Figure 1 illustrates this recursive construction process for the 2D Hilbert curve. From each level to the next, the subintervals are split into four congruent

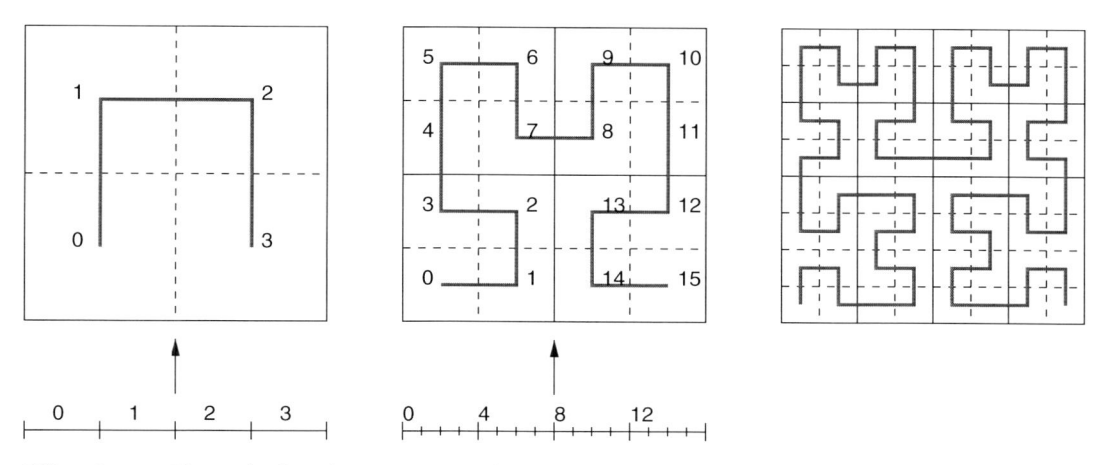

Space-Filling Curves. Fig. 1 The first three iterations of the Hilbert curve

subintervals. Likewise, the square subdomains are split into four subsquares. In the nth iteration, an interval $[i \cdot 4^{-n}, (i+1) \cdot 4^{-n}]$ is mapped to the ith subsquare, as indicated in the figure. The curves in Fig. 1 connect the subsquares of the nth level according to their source intervals and are called *iterations* of the Hilbert curve. For the limit $n \to \infty$, the iterations shall, in an intuitive sense, converge to the Hilbert curve.

More formal: for any given parameter $t \in [0,1]$, there exists a sequence of nested intervals $[i_n \cdot 4^{-n}, (i_n + 1) \cdot 4^{-n}]$ that all contain t. The corresponding subsquares converge to a point $h(t) \in [0,1]^2$. The image of the mapping h defined by that construction is called the Hilbert curve. h shall be called the Hilbert mapping.

Computation of Mappings

Figure 1 shows that the nth Hilbert iteration consists of the connection of four $(n-1)$th Hilbert iterations, which are scaled, rotated, and translated appropriately. For $n \to \infty$, this turns into a fix-point argument: the Hilbert curve consists of the connection of four suitably scaled, rotated, and translated Hilbert curves. The respective transformations shall be given by operations H_q, where $q \in \{0, 1, 2, 3\}$ determines the relative position of the transformed Hilbert curve. This leads to the following recursive equation:

$$h(0_4.q_1 q_2 q_3 q_4 \ldots) = H_{q_1} \circ h(0_4.q_2 q_3 q_4 \ldots). \quad (1)$$

If the parameter t is given as a quarternary fraction, i.e., $t = 0_4.q_1 q_2 q_3 \cdots = \sum_n q_n \frac{1}{4^n}$, then the interval numbers i_n and the relative position of subintervals within their parent can be obtained from the quarternary digits q_n.

For finite quarternary fractions, successive application of Eq. 1 leads to the following formula to compute h:

$$h(0_4.q_1 q_2 \ldots q_n) = H_{q_1} \circ H_{q_2} \circ \ldots \circ H_{q_n} \circ h(0). \quad (2)$$

For the Hilbert curve, the operators H_q are defined as:

$$H_0 := \begin{pmatrix} x \\ y \end{pmatrix} \to \begin{pmatrix} \frac{1}{2}y \\ \frac{1}{2}x \end{pmatrix}$$

$$H_1 := \begin{pmatrix} x \\ y \end{pmatrix} \to \begin{pmatrix} \frac{1}{2}x \\ \frac{1}{2}y + \frac{1}{2} \end{pmatrix}$$

$$H_2 := \begin{pmatrix} x \\ y \end{pmatrix} \to \begin{pmatrix} \frac{1}{2}x + \frac{1}{2} \\ \frac{1}{2}y + \frac{1}{2} \end{pmatrix}$$

$$H_3 := \begin{pmatrix} x \\ y \end{pmatrix} \to \begin{pmatrix} -\frac{1}{2}y + 1 \\ -\frac{1}{2}x + \frac{1}{2} \end{pmatrix}$$

Equations 1 and 2 may be easily turned into an algorithm to compute the image point $h(t)$ from any given parameter t.

Inverting this process leads to algorithms that find a parameter t that is mapped to a given point $p = h(t)$. However, note that the Hilbert mapping h is not bijective; hence, an inverse mapping h^{-1} does not exist. Still, it is possible to construct mappings $\bar{h}^{-1}$ that return a uniquely defined parameter $t = \bar{h}^{-1}(p)$ with $p = h(t)$. Note that for practical applications, only the discrete orders induced by h are of interest. These orders are usually bijective – for example, the relation between subsquares and subintervals during the construction of the Hilbert mapping is a bijective one. Bijectivity is only lost with $n \to \infty$.

Examples of Space-Filling Curves

Figure 2 illustrates the construction of different SFC. All of them are constructed in a similar way as the Hilbert curve and can be computed via an analogous approach. The Hilbert-Moore curve combines four regular, scaled-down Hilbert curves to a closed curve. The $\beta\Omega$-curve is a Hilbert-like curve that uses nonuniform refinement patterns throughout the iterations. Similar to the Hilbert-Moore curve, it is a closed curve. Morton order and the Z-curve result from a bit-interleaving code for 2D grids. They lead to discontinuous mappings from the unit interval to the unit square. However, the Lebesgue curve uses the same construction, but maps the Cantor set to the unit square in order to obtain continuity.

The Sierpinski curve is a curve that is generated via recursive substructuring of triangles. The combination of two triangle-filling Sierpinski curves leads to a curve that fills the unit square. The H-index follows a construction compatible to that for the Sierpinski curve, but generates a discrete order on Cartesian grids. Infinite refinement of the H-index, then, leads to the Sierpinski curve. The Peano curve, finally, as well as its variant, the Peano-Meander curve, are square-filling curves that are based on a recursive 3×3-refinement of the unit square.

Figure 3 provides snapshots of the construction processes of 3D Hilbert and Peano curves.

Locality Properties of Space-Filling Curves

The recursive construction of SFC leads to locality properties that can be exploited for efficient load distribution and load balancing. The Hilbert curve, for example,

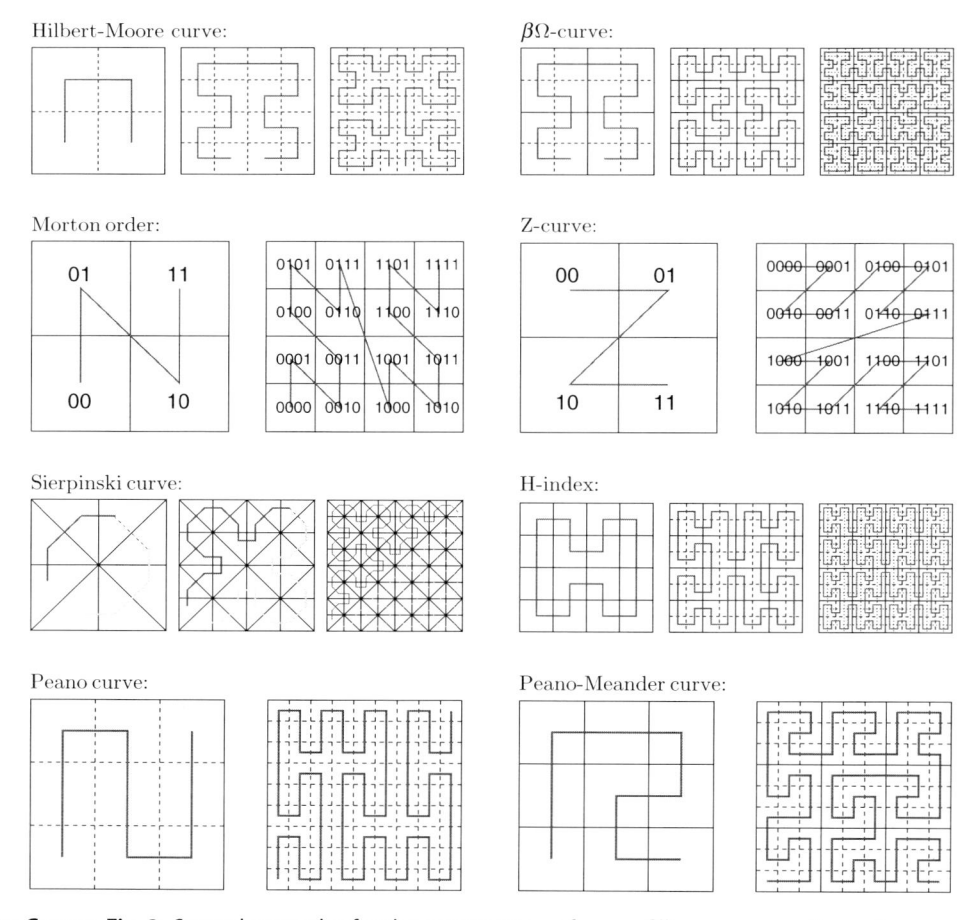

Space-Filling Curves. Fig. 2 Several examples for the construction of space-filling curves on the unit square

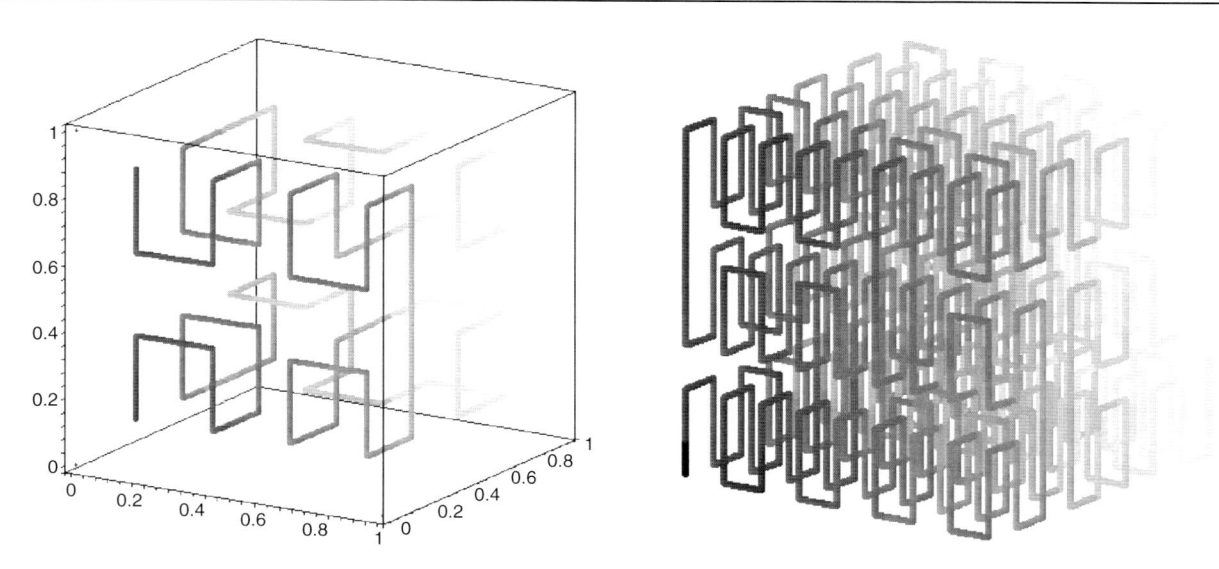

Space-Filling Curves. Fig. 3 Second iterations of three-dimensional Hilbert and Peano curves

and curves that follow a similar construction, can be shown to be Hölder continuous, i.e., for two parameters t_0 and t_1, the distance of the images $h(t_0)$ and $h(t_1)$ is bounded by

$$\|h(t_0) - h(t_1)\|_2 \leq C |t_0 - t_1|^{1/d}, \qquad (3)$$

where d denotes the dimension. As $|t_0 - t_1|$ is also equal to the area covered by the space-filling curve segment defined by the parameter interval $[t_0, t_1]$ (i.e., h is parameterized by area or volume), Eq. 3 gives a relation between the area covered by a curve segment and the distance between the end points of the curve. It is thus a measure for the compactness of partitions defined by curve segments. For d-dimensional objects such as spheres or cubes, the volume typically grows with the dth power of the extent (diameter, e.g.,) of the object. Hence, an exponent of d^{-1} is asympotically optimal, and the constant C characterizes the compactness of an SFC.

High Performance Computing and Load Balancing with Space-Filling Curves

The ability of recursively substructuring and linearizing high-dimensional domains is mainly responsible for the revival of SFC – or their arrival in computational applications – starting in the 1960s of the last century. As some milestones, the Z-order (Morton-order) curve has been proposed for file sequencing in geodetic data bases in 1966 by G.M. Morton [15]; *quadtrees* (nothing else than 2D Lebesgue SFC) were introduced in image processing [9, 19]; *octrees*, their 3D counterparts, marked the crucial idea for breakthroughs in the complexity of particle simulations, the *Barnes Hut* [3] as well as the *Fast Multipole* algorithms [11]. Octrees were also successfully used in CAD [10, 12], as well as for organizational tasks such as grid generation [20, 21] or steering volume-oriented simulations [16], and the portfolio of SFC of practical relevance is still widening.

The locality properties of SFC yield a high locality of data access and, therewith, a high efficiency of cache-usage for various kinds of applications. This will be a crucial aspect for future computing architectures, in particular multi-core architectures, where the memory bottleneck will become even more severe than already for today's high-performance computers. For example, the Peano curve is used for highly efficient block-structured matrix–matrix products [2], and it can serve as a general paradigm for PDE frameworks, where all the steps of geometry representation, adaptive grid generation, grid traversal, data structure design, and parallelization follow an SFC-based strategy [8, 13]. While all the SFC discussed so far refer to structured Cartesian grids or subdomain structures, the Sierpinski curve is defined on a triangular master domain and has been recently used to benefit from SFC characteristics also in the context of managing, traversing, and distributing triangular finite element meshes [1].

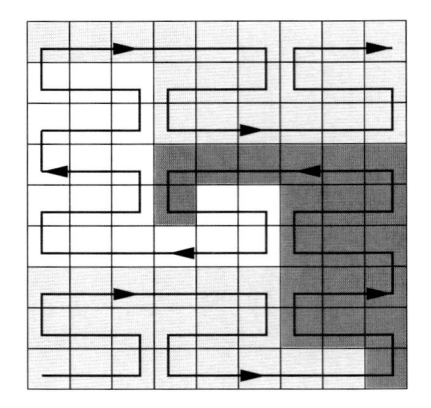

Space-Filling Curves. Fig. 4 Partitioning of a triangulation according to the Sierpinski curve and a Cartesian grid according to the Peano curve

Hilbert or Hilbert-Peano curves were probably the first SFC to see a broad application for load distribution and load balancing [6, 17]. Meanwhile, SFC-based strategies have become a well-established tool frequently outperforming alternatives such as graph partitioning. The classical SFC-based load-balancing approach is to queue up grid elements like pearls on a thread and to cut this queue into pieces with equal workload [4, 6, 7, 17, 18, 22, 24]. Fig. 4 shows examples for the partitioning of a triangulation according to the Sierpinski curve and a Cartesian grid according to the Peano curve. This reduces the load balancing problem to a problem of sorting data according to their positions on a space-filling curve. The locality properties of SFC yield connected partitions with quasi-minimal surfaces that is quasi-minimal communication costs. However, the constants involved in the quasi-optimality statement can be rather large [24].

More recent approaches combine the space-filling curve ordering with a tree-based domain decomposition [5, 14, 23]. This approach has the advantage that already the domain decomposition itself as well as dynamical rebalancing can easily be done fully parallel and that it fits in a natural way with highly efficient multilevel numerical methods such as multigrid solvers.

Summarizing, it is obvious that although load balancing is the most attractive application of SFC in the context of parallel computing, the scope of SFC has become much wider with their parallelization characteristics often just being one side effect.

Related Entries
▶ Domain Decomposition
▶ Hierarchical data format

Bibliographic Notes and Further Reading
1. Sagan H (1994) Space-filling curves, Springer, New York.
2. Bader M Space-filling curves – an introduction with applications in scientific computing, Texts in Computational Science and Engineering, Springer, submitted.

Bibliography
1. Bader M, Schraufstetter S, Vigh CA, Behrens J (2008) Memory efficient adaptive mesh generation and implementation of multigrid algorithms using Sierpinski curves. Int J Comput Sci Eng 4(1):12–21
2. Bader M, Zenger Ch (2006) Cache oblivious matrix multiplication using an element ordering based on a Peano curve. Linear Algebra Appl 417(2–3):301–313
3. Barnes J, Hut P (1986) A hierarchical O(n log n) force-calculation algorithm. Nature 324:446–449
4. Brázdová V, Bowler DR (2008) Automatic data distribution and load balancing with space-filling curves: implementation in conquest. J Phy Condens Matt 20
5. Brenk M, Bungartz H-J, Mehl M, Muntean IL, Neckel T, Weinzierl T (2008) Numerical simulation of particle transport in a drift ratchet. SIAM J Sci Comput 30(6):2777–2798
6. Griebel M, Zumbusch GW (1999) Parallel multigrid in an adaptive PDE solver based on hashing and space-filling curves. Parallel Comput 25:827–843

7. Günther F, Krahnke A, Langlotz M, Mehl M, Pögl M, Zenger Ch (2004) On the parallelization of a cache-optimal iterative solver for PDES based on hierarchical data structures and space-filling curves. In: Recent Advances in Parallel Virtual Machine and Message Passing Interface: 11th European PVM/MPI Users Group Meeting Budapest, Hungary, September 19–22, 2004. Proceedings, vol 3241 of Lecture Notes in Computer Science. Springer, Heidelberg
8. Günther F, Mehl M, Pögl M, Zenger C (2006) A cache-aware algorithm for PDEs on hierarchical data structures based on space-filling curves. SIAM J Sci Comput 28(5):1634–1650
9. Hunter GM, Steiglitz K (1979) Operations on images using quad trees. IEEE Trans Pattern Analy Machine Intell PAMI-1(2): 145–154
10. Jackings C, Tanimoto SL (1980) Octrees and their use in representing three-dimensional objects. Comp Graph Image Process 14(31):249–270
11. Rokhlin V, Greengard L (1987) A fast algorithms for particle simulations. J Comput Phys 73:325–348
12. Meagher D (1980) Octree encoding: A new technique for the representation, manipulation and display of arbitrary 3d objects by computer. Technical Report, IPL-TR-80-111
13. Mehl M, Weinzierl T, Zenger C (2006) A cache-oblivious self-adaptive full multigrid method. Numer Linear Algebr 13(2–3):275–291
14. Mitchell WF (2007) A refinement-tree based partitioning method for dynamic load balancing with adaptively refined grids. J Parallel Distrib Comput 67(4):417–429
15. Morton GM (1966) A computer oriented geodetic data base and a new technique in file sequencing. Technical Report, IBM Ltd., Ottawa, Ontario
16. Mundani R-P, Bungartz H-J, Niggl A, Rank E (2006) Embedding, organisation, and control of simulation processes in an octree-based cscw framework. In: Proceedings of the 11th International Conference on Computing in Civil and Building Engineering, Montreal, pp 3208–3215
17. Patra A, Oden JT (1995) Problem decomposition for adaptive hp finite element methods. Comput Syst Eng 6(2):97–109
18. Roberts S, Klyanasundaram S, Cardew-Hall M, Clarke W (1998) A key based parallel adaptive refinement technique for finite element methods. In: Proceedings of the Computational Techniques and Applications: CTAC '97, Singapore, pp 577–584
19. Samet H (1980) Region representation: quadtrees from binary arrays. Comput Graph Image Process 13(1):88–93
20. Saxena M, Finnigan PM, Graichen CM, Hathaway AF, Parthasarathy VN (1995) Octree-based automatic mesh generation for non-manifold domains. Eng Comput 11(1):1–14
21. Schroeder WJ, Shephard MS (1988) A combined octree/delaunay method for fully automatic 3-d mesh generation. Int J Numer Methods Eng 26(1) 37–55
22. Sundar H, Sampath RS, Biros G (2008) Bottom-up construction and 2:1 balance refinement of linear octrees in parallel. SIAM J Sci Comput 30(5):2675–2708
23. Weinzierl T (2009) A framework for parallel PDE solvers on multiscale adaptive Cartesian grids. Verlag Dr. Hut
24. Zumbusch GW (2001) On the quality of space-filling curve induced partitions. Z Angew Math Mech 81:25–28

SPAI (SParse Approximate Inverse)

Thomas Huckle, Matous Sedlacek
Technische Universität München, Garching, Germany

Synonyms
Sparse approximate inverse matrix

Definition
For a given sparse matrix A a sparse matrix $M \approx A^{-1}$ is computed by minimizing $\|AM - I\|_F$ in the Frobenius norm over all matrices with a certain sparsity pattern. In the SPAI algorithm the pattern of M is updated dynamically to improve the approximation until a certain stopping criterion is reached.

Discussion

Introduction
For applying an iterative solution method like the conjugate gradient method (CG), GMRES, BiCGStab, QMR, or similar algorithms, to a system of linear equations $Ax = b$ with sparse matrix A, it is often crucial to include an efficient preconditioner. Here, the original problem $Ax = b$ is replaced by the preconditioned system $MAx = Mb$ or $Ax = A(My) = b$. In a parallel environment a preconditioner should satisfy the following conditions:

- M can be computed efficiently in parallel.
- Mc can be computed efficiently in parallel for any given vector c.
- The iterative solver applied on $AMx = b$ or $MAx = Mb$ converges much faster than for $Ax = b$ (e.g., it holds $cond(MA) \ll cond(A)$).

The first two conditions can be easily satisfied by using a sparse matrix M as approximation to A^{-1}. Note, that the inverse of a sparse A is nearly dense, but in many cases the entries of A^{-1} are rapidly decaying, so most of the entries are very small [11].

Benson and Frederickson [4] were the first to propose a sparse approximate inverse preconditioner in a static way by computing

$$\min_{M} \|AM - I\|_F \quad (1)$$

for a prescribed a priori chosen sparsity pattern for M. The computation of M can be split into n independent subproblems $\min_{M_k} \|AM_k - e_k\|_2$, $k = 1, \ldots, n$ with M_k the columns of M and e_k the k-th column of the identity matrix I. In view of the sparsity of these Least Squares (LS) problems, each subproblem is related to a small matrix $\hat{A}_k := A(I_k, J_k)$ with index set J_k which is given by the allowed pattern for M_k and the so-called shadow I_k of J_k, that is, the indices of nonzero rows in $A(:, J_k)$. These n small LS problems can be solved independently, for example, based on QR decompositions of the matrices $\hat{A}_k$ by using the Householder method or the modified Gram-Schmidt algorithm.

The SPAI Algorithm

The SPAI algorithm is an additional feature in this Frobenius norm minimization that introduces different strategies for choosing new profitable indices in M_k that lead to an improved approximation. Assume that, by solving (1) for a given index set J, an optimal solution $M_k(J_k)$ has been already determined resulting in the sparse vector M_k with residual r_k. Dynamically there will be defined new entries in M_k. Therefore, (1) has to be solved for this enlarged index set $\tilde{J}_k$ such that a reduction in the norm of the new residual $\tilde{r}_k = A(\tilde{I}_k, \tilde{J}_k)M_k(\tilde{J}_k) - e_k(\tilde{I}_k)$ is achieved.

Following Cosgrove, Griewank, Díaz [10], and Grote, Huckle [13], one possible new index $j \in J_{new}$ out of a given set of possible new indices J_{new} is tested to improve M_k. Therefore, the reduced 1D problem

$$\min_{\lambda_j} \|A(M_k + \lambda_j e_j) - e_k\| = \min_{\lambda_j} \|\lambda_j A_j + r_k\| \quad (2)$$

has to be considered. The solution of this problem is given by

$$\lambda_j = -\frac{r_k^T A e_j}{\|A e_j\|^2}$$

which leads to an improved squared residual norm

$$\rho_j^2 = \|r_k\|^2 - \frac{(r_k^T A e_j)^2}{\|A e_j\|^2}.$$

Obviously, for improving M_k one has to consider only indices j in rows of A that are related to the nonzero entries in the old residual r_k; otherwise they do not lead to a reduction in the residual norm. Thus, the column indices j have to be determined that satisfy $r_k^T A e_j \neq 0$ with the old residual r_k. Let the index set of nonzero entries in r_k be denoted by L. Furthermore, let $\tilde{J}_i$ denote the set of new indices that are related to the nonzero elements in the i-th row of A, and let $J_{new} = \cup_{i \in L} \tilde{J}_i$ denote the set of all possible new indices that can lead to a reduction of the residual norm. Then, one or more indices J_c are chosen as a subset of J_{new} that corresponds to a large reduction in r_k. For this enlarged index set $J_k \cup J_c$ the QR decomposition of the related LS submatrix has to be updated and solved for the new column M_k.

Inside SPAI there are different parameters that steer the computation of the preconditioner M:

- How many entries are added in one step
- How many steps of adding new entries are allowed
- Start pattern
- Maximum allowed pattern
- What residual $\|r_k\|$ should be reached
- How to solve the LS problems

Modifications of SPAI

A different and more expensive way to determine a new profitable index j with $\tilde{J}_k := J_k \cup \{j\}$ considers the more accurate problem

$$\min_{M_k(\tilde{J}_k)} \|A(:, \tilde{J}_k)M_k(\tilde{J}_k) - e_k\|$$

introduced by Gould and Scott [12]. For $\tilde{J}_k$ the optimal reduction of the residual is determined for the full minimization problem instead of the 1D minimization in SPAI.

Chow [9] showed ways to prescribe an efficient static pattern a priori and developed the software package PARASAILS.

Holland, Shaw, and Wathen [17] have generalized this ansatz allowing a sparse target matrix on the right side in the form $\min_M \|AM - B\|_F$. This approach is useful in connection with some kind of two-level preconditioning: First compute a standard sparse preconditioner B for A and then improve this preconditioner by an additional Frobenius norm minimization with target B. From the algorithmic point of view the minimization with target matrix B instead of I introduces no additional difficulties. Only the pattern of M should be chosen more carefully with respect to A and B.

Zhang [23] introduced an iterative form of SPAI where in each step a thin M is derived starting with $\min_{M_1} \|AM_1 - I\|_F$. In the second step the sparse matrix AM_1 is used and $\min_{M_2} \|(AM_1)M_2 - I\|_F$ is solved, and so on. The advantage is, that because of the very sparse patterns in M_i the Least Squares problems are very cheap.

Chan and Tang [8] applied SPAI not to the original matrix but first used a Wavelet transform W and computed the sparse approximate inverse preconditioner for WAW^T that is assumed to be more diagonal dominant.

Yeremin, Kolotilina, Nikishin, and Kaporin [19, 20] introduced factorized sparse approximate inverses of the form $A^{-1} \approx LU$. Huckle generalized the factorized preconditioners adding new entries dynamically like in SPAI [14].

Grote and Barnard [2] developed a software package for SPAI and also introduced a block version of SPAI.

Huckle and Kallischko [15] generalized SPAI and the target approach. They combined SPAI with the probing method [7] in the form

$$\min_M \left(\|AM - I\|_F^2 + \rho^2 \|e^T AM - e^T\|^2 \right)$$

for probing vectors e on which the preconditioner should be especially improved. Furthermore, they developed a software package for MSPAI.

Properties and Applications
Advantages of SPAI:

- Good parallel scalability.
- SPAI allows modifications like factorized approximation or including probing conditions to improve the preconditioner relative to certain subspaces, for example, as smoother in Multigrid or for regularization [16].
- It is especially efficient for preconditioning dense problems (see Benzi [1] et al.).

Disadvantages of SPAI:

- SPAI is sequentially more expensive, especially for denser patterns of M.
- Sometimes it shows poor approximation of A^{-1} and slow convergence as preconditioner.

Related Entries
▶Preconditioners for Sparse Iterative Methods

Bibliographic Notes and Further Reading

Books
1. Axelsson O (1996) Iterative solution methods. Cambridge University Press, Cambridge
2. Saad Y (2003) Iterative methods for sparse linear systems. SIAM Philadelpha, PA
3. Bruaset AM (1995) A survey of preconditioned iterative methods. Longman Scientific & Technical, Harlow, Essex
4. Chen K (2005) Matrix preconditioning techniques and applications. Cambridge University Press, Cambridge

Software
1. Chow E. Parasails, https://computation.llnl.gov/casc/parasails/parasails.html
2. Barnard S, Bröker O, Grote M, Hagemann M. SPAI and Block SPAI, http://www.computational.unibas.ch/software/spai
3. Huckle T, Kallischko A, Sedlacek M. MSPAI, http://www5.in.tum.de/wiki/index.php/MSPAI

Bibliography
1. Alleon G, Benzi M, Giraud L (1997) Sparse approximate inverse preconditioning for dense linear systems arising in computational electromagnetics. Numer Algorith 16(1):1–15
2. Barnard S, Grote M (1999) A block version of the SPAI preconditioner. Proceedings of the 9th SIAM conference on Parallel Processing for Scientific Computing, San Antonio, TX
3. Barnard ST, Clay RL (1997) A portable MPI implementation of the SPAI preconditioner in ISIS++. In: Heath M, et al (eds) Proceedings of the eighth SIAM conference on parallel processing for scientific computing, Philadelphia, PA

4. Benson MW, Frederickson PO (1982) Iterative solution of large sparse linear systems arising in certain multidimensional approximation problems. Utilitas Math 22:127–140
5. Bröker O, Grote M, Mayer C, Reusken A (2001) Robust parallel smoothing for multigrid via sparse approximate inverses. SIAM J Scient Comput 23(4):1396–1417
6. Bröker O, Grote M (2002) Sparse approximate inverse smoothers for geometric and algebraic multigrid. Appl Num Math 41(1):61–80
7. Chan TFC, Mathew TP (1992) The interface probing technique in domain decomposition. SIAM J Matrix Anal Appl 13(1):212–238
8. Chan TF, Tang WP, Wan WL (1997) Wavelet sparse approximate inverse preconditioners. BIT 37(3):644–660
9. Chow E (2000) A priori sparsity patterns for parallel sparse approximate inverse preconditioners. SIAM J Sci Comput 21(5):1804–1822
10. Cosgrove JDF, D´iaz JC, Griewank A (1992) Approximate inverse preconditionings for sparse linear systems. Int J Comput Math 44:91–110
11. Demko S, Moss WF, Smith PW (1984) Decay rates of inverses of band matrices. Math Comp 43:491–499
12. Gould NIM, Scott JA (1995) On approximate-inverse preconditioners. Technical Report RAL-TR-95-026, Rutherford Appleton Laboratory, Oxfordshire, England
13. Grote MJ, Huckle T (1997) Parallel preconditioning with sparse approximate inverses. SIAM J Sci Comput 18(3):838–853
14. Huckle T (2003) Factorized sparse approximate inverses for preconditioning. J Supercomput 25:109–117
15. Huckle T, Kallischko A (2007) Frobenius norm minimization and probing for preconditioning. Int J Comp Math 84(8):1225–1248
16. Huckle T, Sedlacek M (2010) Smoothing and regularization with modified sparse approximate inverses. Journal of Electrical and Computer Engineering – Special Issue on Iterative Signal Processing in Communications, Appearing (2010)
17. Holland RM, Shaw GJ, Wathen AJ (2005) Sparse approximate inverses and target matrices. SIAM J Sci Comput 26(3):1000–1011
18. Kaporin IE (1994) New convergence results and preconditioning strategies for the conjugate gradient method. Numer Linear Algebra Appl 1:179–210
19. Kolotilina LY, Yeremin AY (1993) Factorized sparse approximate inverse preconditionings I: Theory. SIAM J Matrix Anal Appl 14(1):45–58
20. Kolotilina LY, Yeremin AY (1995) Factorized sparse approximate inverse preconditionings II: Solution of 3D FE systems on massively parallel computers. Inter J High Speed Comput 7(2):191–215
21. Tang W-P (1999) Toward an effective sparse approximate inverse preconditioner. SIAM J Matrix Anal Appl 20(4):970–986
22. Tang WP, Wan WL (2000) Sparse approximate inverse smoother for multigrid. SIAM J Matrix Anal Appl 21(4):1236–1252
23. Zhang J (2002) A sparse approximate inverse technique for parallel preconditioning of general sparse matrices. Appl Math Comput 130(1):63–85

Spanning Tree, Minimum Weight

David A. Bader[1], Guojing Cong[2]
[1]Georgia Institute of Technology, Atlanta, GA, USA
[2]IBM, Yorktown Heights, NY, USA

Definition

Given an undirected connected graph G with n vertices and m edges, the minimum-weight spanning tree (MST) problem consists in finding a spanning tree with the minimum sum of edge weights. A single graph can have multiple MSTs. If the graph is not connected, then it has a minimum spanning forest (MSF) that is a union of minimum spanning trees for its connected components. MST is one of the most studied combinatorial problems with practical applications in VLSI layout, wireless communication, and distributed networks, recent problems in biology and medicine such as cancer detection, medical imaging, and proteomics.

With regard to any MST of graph G, two properties hold: *Cycle property*: the heaviest edge (edge with the maximum weight) in any cycle of G does not appear in the MST. *Cut property*: if the weight of an edge e of any cut C of G is smaller than the weights of other edges of C, then this edge belongs to all MSTs of the graph.

When all edges of G are of unique weights, the MST is unique. When the edge weights are not unique, they can be made unique by numbering the edges and break ties using the edge number.

Sequential Algorithms

Three classical sequential algorithms, Prim, Kruskal, and Borůvka, are known for MST. Each algorithm grows a forest in stages, adding at each stage one or more tree edges, whose membership in the MST is guaranteed by the cut property. They differ in how the tree edges are chosen and the order that they are added.

Prim starts with one vertex and takes a greedy approach in growing the tree. In each step, it always maintains a connected tree by choosing the edge of the smallest weight that connects the current tree to a vertex that is outside the tree.

Kruskal starts with isolated vertices. As the algorithm progresses, multiple trees may appear, and eventually they merge into one.

Borůvka selects for each vertex the incident edge of the smallest weight as a tree edge. It then compacts the graph by contracting each connected component into a super-vertex. Note that finding the tree edges can be done in parallel for each vertices. Borůvka's algorithm lends itself naturally to parallelization.

These algorithms can easily be made to run in $O(m \log n)$ time. Better complexities can be achieved with Prim's algorithm if Fibonacci heap is used instead of binary heap.

Graham and Hell [14] gave a good introduction for the history of MST algorithms up to 1985. More complex algorithms with better asymptotic run times have since been proposed. For example, Gabow et al. designed an algorithm that runs in almost linear time, i.e., $O(m \log \beta(m, n))$, where $\beta(m, n) = \min\{i | \log^{(i)} n \leq m/n\}$. Karger, Klein, and Tarjan presented a randomized linear-time algorithm to find minimum spanning trees. This algorithm uses the random sampling technique together with a linear time verification algorithm (e.g., King's verification algorithm). Pettie and Ramachandran presented an optimal MST algorithm that runs in $O(T^*(m, n))$, where T^* is the minimum number of edge-weight comparisons needed to determine the solution.

Moret and Shapiro [20] presented a comprehensive experimental study on the performance MST algorithms. Prim's algorithm with binary heap is found in general to be a fast solution. Katriel et al. [19] have developed a pipelined algorithm that uses the cycle property and provide an experimental evaluation on the special-purpose NEC SX-5 vector computer.

Cache-oblivious MST is presented by Arge et al. [2]. Their algorithm is based on a cache-oblivious priority queue that supports *insertion*, *deletion*, and *deletemin* operations in $O\left(\frac{1}{B} \log_{M/B} \frac{N}{B}\right)$ amortized memory transfers, where M and B are the memory and block transfer sizes. The cache-oblivious implementation of MST runs in $O(sort(m) \log \log(n/c) + c)$ memory transfers ($c = m/B$). The MST algorithm combines two phases: Borůvka and Prim.

The memory access behavior of some MST algorithms are characterized in [11].

Parallel Algorithms

Fast theoretical parallel MST algorithms also exist in the literature. Pettie and Ramachandran [21] designed a randomized, time-work optimal MST algorithm for the EREW PRAM, and using EREW to QSM and QSM to BSP emulations from [13], mapped the performance onto QSM and BSP models. Cole et. al. [7, 8] and Poon and Ramachandran [22] earlier had randomized linear-work algorithms on CRCW and EREW PRAM. Chong et al. [5] gave a deterministic EREW PRAM algorithm that runs in logarithmic time with a linear number of processors. On the BSP model, Adler et al. [1] presented a communication-optimal MST algorithm.

Most parallel and some fast sequential MST algorithms employ the Borůvka iteration. Three steps characterize a Borůvka iteration: *find-min*, *connect-components*, and *compact-graph*.

1. *find-min*: for each vertex v label the incident edge with the smallest weight to be in the MST.
2. *connect-components*: identify connected components of the induced graph with edges found in Step 1.
3. *compact-graph*: compact each connected component into a single supervertex, remove self-loops and multiple edges; and relabel the vertices for consistency.

The Borůvka algorithm iterates until no new tree edges can be found. After each Borůvka iteration, the number of vertices in the graph is reduced at least by half. Some algorithms invoke several rounds of the Borůvka iterations to reduce the input size (e.g., [1]) and/or to increase the edge density (e.g., [18]).

Implementation of Parallel Borůvka

Many of the fast theoretic MST algorithms are considered impractical for input of realistic size because they are too complicated and have large constant factors hidden in the asymptotic complexity. Complex MST algorithms are hard to implement and usually do not achieve good parallel speedups on current architectures. Most existing implementations are based on the Borůvka algorithm.

For a Borůvka iteration, *Find-min* and *connect-components* are simple and straightforward to implement. The *compact-graph* step performs bookkeeping that is often left as a trivial exercise to the reader. JáJá [16] describes a compact-graph algorithm for dense inputs. For sparse graphs, though, the compact-graph step often is the most expensive step in the Borůvka iteration. Implementations and data structures for parallel Borůvka on shared-memory machines are described in [3].

Edge List Representation

This implementation of Borůvka's algorithm (designated **Bor-EL**) uses the edge list representation of graphs, with each edge (u, v) appearing twice in the list for both directions (u, v) and (v, u). An elegant implementation of the compact-graph step sorts the edge list (using an efficient parallel sample sort [15]) with the supervertex of the first endpoint as the primary key, the supervertex of the second endpoint as the secondary key, and the edge weight as the tertiary key. When sorting completes, all of the self-loops and multiple edges between two supervertices appear in consecutive locations and can be merged efficiently using parallel prefix-sums.

Adjacency List Representation

With the adjacency list representation, each entry of an index array of vertices points to a list of its incident edges. The compact-graph step first sorts the vertex array according to the supervertex label, then concurrently sorts each vertex's adjacency list using the supervertex of the other endpoint of the edge as the key. After sorting, the set of vertices with the same supervertex label are contiguous in the array, and can be merged efficient. This approach is designated as **Bor-AL**.

Both **Bor-EL** and **Bor-AL** achieve the same goal that self-loops and multiple edges are moved to consecutive locations to be merged. **Bor-EL** uses one call to sample sort, while **Bor-AL** calls a smaller parallel sort and then a number of concurrent sequential sorts.

Flexible Adjacency List Representation

The flexible adjacency list augments the traditional adjacency list representation by allowing each vertex to hold multiple adjacency lists instead of just a single one; in fact, it is a linked list of adjacency lists. During initialization, each vertex points to only one adjacency list. After the connect-components step, each vertex appends its adjacency list to its supervertex's adjacency list by sorting together the vertices that are labeled with the same supervertex. The compact-graph step is simplified, allowing each supervertex to have self-loops and multiple edges inside its adjacency list. Thus, the compact-graph step now uses a smaller parallel sort plus several pointer operations instead of costly sortings and memory copies, while the find-min step gets the added responsibility of filtering out the self-loops and multiple edges. This approach is designated as **Bor-FAL**.

Figure 1 illustrates the use of the flexible adjacency list for a 6-vertex input graph. After one Borůvka iteration, vertices 1, 2, and 3 form one supervertex, and vertices 4, 5, and 6 form a second supervertex. Vertex labels 1 and 4 represent the supervertices and receive the adjacency lists of vertices 2 and 3, and vertices 5 and 6, respectively. Vertices 1 and 4 are relabeled as 1 and 2. Note that most of the original data structure is kept intact. Instead of relabeling vertices in the adjacency list, a separate lookup table is maintained that holds the

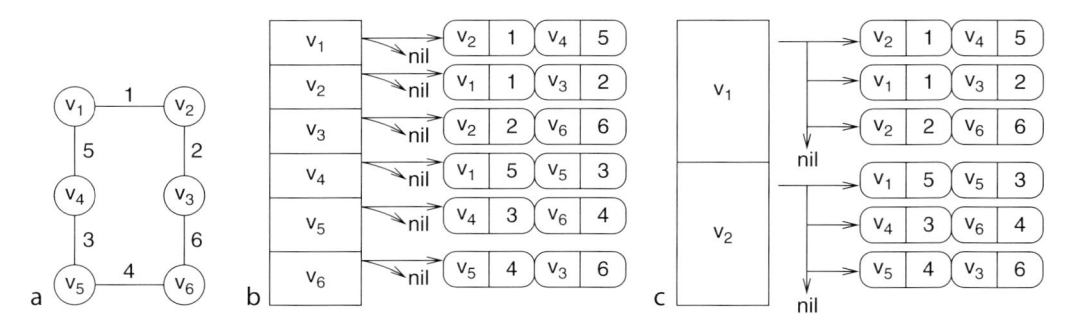

Spanning Tree, Minimum Weight. Fig. 1 Example of flexible adjacency list representation. (**a**) Input graph. (**b**) Initialized flexible adjacency list. (**c**) Flexible adjacency list after one iteration

supervertex label for each vertex. The find-min step uses this table to filter out self-loops and multiple edges.

Analysis of Implementations

Helman and JáJá's SMP complexity model [15] provides a reasonable framework for the realistic analysis that favors cache-friendly algorithms by penalizing noncontiguous memory accesses. Under this model, there are two parts to an algorithm's complexity: M_E, the memory access complexity and, T_C, the computation complexity. The M_E term is the number of noncontiguous memory accesses, and the T_C term is the running time. The M_E term recognizes the effect that memory accesses have over an algorithm's performance. Parameters of the model includes the problem size n and the number of processors p.

For a sparse graph G with n vertices and m edges, as the algorithm iterates, the number of vertices decreases by at least half in each iteration, so there are at most $\log n$ iterations for all of the Borůvka variants.

Hence, the complexity of **Bor-EL** is given as, where c and z are constants related to cache size and sampling ratio [15].

$$T(n,p) = \langle M_E\ ;\ T_C \rangle$$
$$= \left\langle \left(\frac{8m + n + n\log n}{p} + \frac{4mc\log(2m/p)}{p\log z}\right)\log n\ ;\right.$$
$$\left. O\left(\frac{m}{p}\log m \log n\right)\right\rangle.$$

As in each iteration these **Bor-AL** and **Bor-EL** compute similar results in different ways, it suffices to compare the complexity of the first iteration. For **Bor-AL**, the complexity of the first iteration is

$$T(n,p) = \langle M_E;\ T_C \rangle$$
$$= \left\langle \left(\frac{8n + 5m + n\log n}{p}\right.\right.$$
$$\left.+ \frac{2nc\log(n/p) + 2mc\log(m/n)}{p\log z}\right);$$
$$\left. O\left(\frac{n}{p}\log m + \frac{m}{p}\log(m/n)\right)\right\rangle.$$

While for **Bor-EL**, the complexity of the first iteration is

$$T(n,p) = \langle M_E;\ T_C \rangle$$
$$= \left\langle \left(\frac{8m + n + n\log n}{p} + \frac{4mc\log(2m/p)}{p\log z}\right);\right.$$
$$\left. O\left(\frac{m}{p}\log m\right)\right\rangle.$$

Bor-AL is a faster algorithm than **Bor-EL**, as expected, since the input for **Bor-AL** is "bucketed" into adjacency lists, versus **Bor-EL** that is an unordered list of edges, and sorting each bucket first in **Bor-AL** saves unnecessary comparisons between edges that have no vertices in common. The complexity of **Bor-EL** can be considered to be an upper bound of **Bor-AL**.

In **Bor-FAL**, n reduces at least by half while m stays the same. Compact-graph first sorts the n vertices, then assigns $O(n)$ pointers to append each vertex's adjacency list to its supervertex's. For each processor, sorting takes $O\left(\frac{n}{p}\log n\right)$ time, and assigning pointers takes $O(n/p)$ time assuming each processor gets to assign roughly the same amount of pointers. Updating the lookup table costs each processor $O(n/p)$ time. With **Bor-FAL**, to find the smallest weight edge for the supervertices, all the m edges will be checked, with each processor covering $O(m/p)$ edges. The aggregate running time is $T_C(n,p)_{fm} = O(m\log n/p)$, and the memory access complexity is $M_E(n,p)_{fm} = m/p$. For the finding connected component step, each processor takes $T_{cc} = O\left(n\log\frac{n}{p}\right)$ time, and $M_E(n,p)_{cc} \leq 2n\log n$. The complexity for the whole Borůvka's algorithm is

$$T(n,p) = T(n,p)_{fm} + T(n,p)_{cc} + T(n,p)_{cg}$$
$$\leq \left\langle \frac{8n + 2n\log n + m\log n}{p} + \frac{4cn\log(n/p)}{p\log z}\ ;\right.$$
$$\left. O\left(\frac{m+n}{p}\log n\right)\right\rangle$$

A Hybrid Parallel MST Algorithm

An MST algorithm has been proposed in [3] that marries Prim's algorithm (known as an efficient sequential algorithm for MST) with that of the naturally parallel Borůvka approach. In this algorithm, essentially each processor simultaneously runs Prim's algorithm from different starting vertices. A tree is said to be *growing* when there exists a lightweight edge that connects the tree to a vertex not yet in another tree, and *mature* otherwise. When all of the vertices have been incorporated into mature subtrees, the algorithm contracts each subtree into a supervertex and call the approach recursively until only one supervertex remains. When the problem size is small enough, one processor solves the remaining problem using the best sequential MST algorithm.

This parallel MST algorithm possesses an interesting feature: when run on one processor the algorithm behaves as Prim's, and on n processors becomes Borůvka's, and runs as a hybrid combination for $1 < p < n$, where p is the number of processors. Each of p processors in the algorithm finds for its starting vertex the smallest-weight edge, contracts that edge, and then finds the smallest-weight edge again for the contracted supervertex. It does not find all the smallest-weight edges for all vertices, synchronize, and then compact as in the parallel Borůvka's algorithm. The algorithm adapts for any number p of processors in a practical way for SMPs, where p is often much less than n, rather than in parallel implementations of Borůvka's approach that appear as PRAM emulations with p coarse-grained processors that emulate n virtual processors.

Implementation with Fine-Grained Locks

Most parallel graph algorithms are designed without locks. Indeed it is hard to measure contention for these algorithms. Yet proper use of locks can simplify implementation and improve performance. Cong and Bader [10] presented an implementation of Borůvka's algorithm (**Bor-spinlock**) that uses locks and avoids modifying the input data structure. In **Bor-spinlock**, the *compact-graph* step is completely eliminated.

The main idea is that instead of compacting connected components, for each vertex there is now an associated label *supervertex* showing to which supervertex it belongs. In each iteration, all the vertices are partitioned as evenly as possible among the processors. Processor p finds the adjacent edge with smallest weight for a supervertex v'. As the graph is not compacted, the adjacent edges for v' are scattered among the adjacent edges of all vertices that share the same supervertex v', and different processors may work on these edges simultaneously. Now the problem is that these processors need to synchronize properly in order to find the edge with the minimum weight. Figure 2 illustrates the specific problem for the MST case.

On the top in Fig. 2 is an input graph with six vertices. Suppose there are two processors P_1 and P_2. Vertices 1, 2, and 3 are partitioned on to processor P_1, and vertices 4, 5, and 6 are partitioned on to processor P_2. It takes two iterations for Borůvka's algorithm to find the MST. In the first iteration, the *find-min* step of **Bor-spinlock** labels < 1, 5 >, < 5, 3 >, < 2, 6 >, and < 6, 4 >,

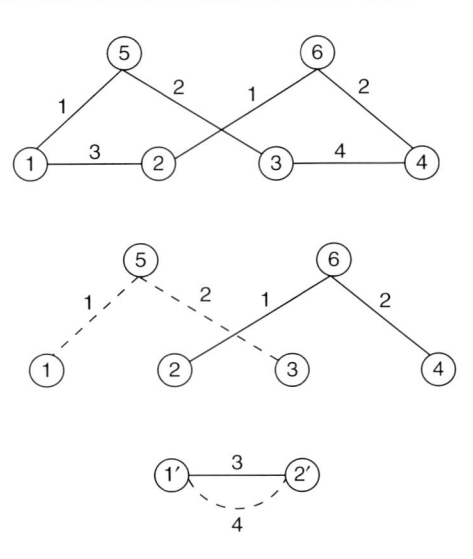

Spanning Tree, Minimum Weight. Fig. 2 Example of the race condition between two processors when Borůvka's algorithm is used to solve the MST problem

to be in the MST. *Connected-components* finds vertices 1, 3, and 5 in one component, and vertices 2, 4, and 6 in another component. The MST edges and components are shown in the middle of Fig. 2. Vertices connected by dashed lines are in one component, and vertices connected by solid lines are in the other component. At this time, vertices 1, 3, and 5 belong to supervertex $1'$, and vertices 2, 4, and 6 belong to supervertex $2'$. In the second iteration, processor P_1 again inspects vertices 1, 2, and 3, and processor P_2 inspects vertices 4, 5, and 6. Previous MST edges < 1, 5 >, < 5, 3 >, < 2, 6 >, and < 6, 4 > are found to be edges inside supervertices and are ignored. On the bottom of Fig. 2 are the two supervertices with two edges between them. Edges < 1, 2 > and < 3, 4 > are found by P_1 to be the edges between supervertices $1'$ and $2'$, edge < 3, 4 > is found by P_2 to be the edge between the two supervertices. For supervertex $2'$, P_1 tries to label < 1, 2 > as the MST edge, while P_2 tries to label < 3, 4 >. This is a race condition between the two processors, and locks are used in **Bor-spinlock** to ensure correctness.

In addition to locks and barriers, recent development in transactional memory provides a new mechanism for synchronization among processors. Kang and Bader implemented minimum spanning forest algorithms with transactional memory [17]. Their implementation achieved good scalability on some current architectures.

Implementation on Distributed-Memory Machines

Partitioned global address space (PGAS) languages such as UPC and X10 [4, 23] have been proposed recently that present a shared-memory abstraction to the programmer for distributed-memory machines. They allow the programmer to control the data layout and work assignment for the processors. Mapping shared-memory graph algorithms onto distributed-memory machines is straightforward with PGAS languages.

Figure 3 shows both the SMP implementation and UPC implementation of parallel Borůvka. The two implementations are also almost identical. The differences are shown in underscore. Performance wise, straightforward PGAS implementation for irregular graph algorithms does not usually achieve high performance due to the aggregate startup cost of many small messages. Cong, Almasi, and Saraswat presented their study in optimizing the UPC implementation of graph algorithm in [9]. They apply communication coalescing together with other techniques for improving the performance. The idea is to merge the small messages to/from a processor into a single, large message. As all operations in each step of a typical PRAM algorithm are parallel, reads and writes can be scheduled in an order such that communication coalescing is possible. After communication coalescing, these data can be accessed in one communication round where one processor sends at most one message to another processor.

Experimental Results

Chung and Condon [6] implement parallel Borůvka's algorithm on the TMC CM-5. On a 16-processor machine, for geometric, structured graphs with 32,000 vertices and average degree 9 and graphs with fewer vertices but higher average degree, their code achieves a relative parallel speedup of about 4, on 16-processors, over the sequential Borůvka's algorithm, which was already 2–3 times slower than their sequential Kruskal

```
grafted = 0;
upc_forall(1=0; l<m; 1++; i)
{
    i = El[1].v1; w = El[1].w;
    j = El[1].v2;
    i = D[i]; j = D[j];
    if(i!=j ){
        upc_lock(lock_array[i]);
        if(Min[i] > w) {
            Min[i] = w;
            Min_ind[i] = j;
            grafted = 1;
        }
        upc_unlock(lock_array[i]);
    }
}
upc_barrier;
grafted = all_reduce_i(grafted, UPC_MAX);
if(grafted ==0) break;

upc_forall(i=0; i<n; i++; i)
    if(Min_ind[i]!=-1)
        D[i]=Min_ind[i];
upc_barrier;

upc_forall(i=0; i<n; i++; i)
    while(D[i]!=D[D[i]]) D[i]=D[D[i]];
```

```
grafted = 0;
pardo(l,0,m,1)
{
    i = El[1].v1; w = El[1].w
    j = El[1].v2
    i = D[i]; j = D[j];
    if(i!=j ){
        pthread_lock(lock_array[i]);
        if(Min[i]>w) {
            Min[i] = w;
            Min_ind[i]=j;
            grafted=1;
        }
        pthread_unlock(lock_array[i]);
    }
}
node_barrier();
grafted = node_Reduce_i(grafted, MAX, TH);
if(grafted==0) break;

pardo(i,0,n,1)
    if(Min_ind[i]!=-1)
        D[i]=Min_ind[i];
node_Barrier();

pardo(i,0,n,1)
    while(D[i]!=D[D[i]]) D[i]=D[D[i]];
```

Spanning Tree, Minimum Weight. Fig. 3 UPC implementation and SMP implementation of MST: the main loop bodies

algorithm. Dehne and Götz [12] studied practical parallel algorithms for MST using the BSP model. They implement a dense Borůvka parallel algorithm, on a 16-processor Parsytec CC-48, that works well for sufficiently dense input graphs. Using a fixed-sized input graph with 1,000 vertices and 400,000 edges, their code achieves a maximum speedup of 6.1 using 16 processors for a random dense graph. Their algorithm is not suitable for the more challenging sparse graphs.

Bader and Cong presented their studies of parallel MST on symmetric multiprocessors (SMPs) in [3, 10]. Their implementation achieved for the first time good parallel speedups over a wide range of inputs on SMPs. Their Experimental results show that for **Bor-EL** and **Bor-AL** the compact-graph step dominates the running time. **Bor-EL** takes much more time than **Bor-AL**, and only gets worse when the graphs get denser. In contrast the execution time of compact-graph step of **Bor-FAL** is greatly reduced: in the experimental section with a random graph of 1M vertices and 10M edges, it is over 50 times faster than **Bor-EL**, and over 7 times faster than **Bor-AL**. Actually the execution time of the compact-graph step of **Bor-FAL** is almost the same for the three input graphs because it only depends on the number of vertices. As predicted, the execution time of the find-min step of **Bor-FAL** increases. And the connect-components step only takes a small fraction of the execution time for all approaches.

Cong, Almasi and Saraswat presented a UPC implementation of distributed MST in [9]. For input graphs with billions of edges, the distributed implementation achieved significant speedups over the SMP implementation and the best sequential implementation.

Bibliography

1. Adler M, Dittrich W, Juurlink B, Kutyłowski M, Rieping I (1998) Communication-optimal parallel minimum spanning tree algorithms (extended abstract). In: SPAA '98: proceedings of the tenth annual ACM symposium on parallel algorithms and architectures, Puerto Vallarta, Mexico. ACM, New York, pp 27–36
2. Arge L, Bender MA, Demaine ED, Holland-Minkley B, Munro JI (2002) Cache-oblivious priority queue and graph algorithm applications. In: Proceedings of the 34th annual ACM symposium on theory of computing, Montreal, Canada. ACM, New York, pp 268–276
3. Bader DA, Cong G (2006) Fast shared-memory algorithms for computing the minimum spanning forest of sparse graphs. J Parallel Distrib Comput 66:1366–1378
4. Charles P, Donawa C, Ebcioglu K, Grothoff C, Kielstra A, Van Praun C, Saraswat V, Sarkar V (2005) X10: an object-oriented approach to non-uniform cluster computing. In: Proceedings of the 2005 ACM SIGPLAN conference on object-oriented programming systems, languages and applications (OOPSLA), San Diego, CA, pp 519–538
5. Chong KW, Han Y, Lam TW (2001) Concurrent threads and optimal parallel minimum spanning tree algorithm. J ACM 48: 297–323
6. Chung S, Condon A (1996) Parallel implementation of Borůvka's minimum spanning tree algorithm. In: Proceedings of the 10th international parallel processing symposium (IPPS'96), Honolulu, Hawaii, pp 302–315
7. Cole R, Klein PN, Tarjan RE (1996) Finding minimum spanning forests in logarithmic time and linear work using random sampling. In: Proceedings of the 8th annual symposium parallel algorithms and architectures (SPAA-96), Newport, RI. ACM, New York, pp 243–250
8. Cole R, Klein PN, Tarjan RE (1994) A linear-work parallel algorithm for finding minimum spanning trees. In: Proceedings of the 6th annual ACM symposium on parallel algorithms and architectures, Cape May, NJ, ACM, New York, pp 11–15
9. Cong G, Almasi G, Saraswat V (2010) Fast PGAS implementation of distributed graph algorithms. In: Proceedings of the 2010 ACM/IEEE international conference for high performance computing, networking, storage and analysis (SC '10), IEEE Computer Society, Washington, DC, pp 1–11
10. Cong G, Bader DA (2004) Lock-free parallel algorithms: an experimental study. In: Proceeding of the 33rd international conference on high-performance computing (HiPC 2004), Banglore, India
11. Cong G, Sbaraglia S (2006) A study of the locality behavior of minimum spanning tree algorithms. In: The 13th international conference on high performance computing (HiPC 2006), Bangalore, India. IEEE Computer Society, pp 583–594
12. Dehne F, Götz S (1998) Practical parallel algorithms for minimum spanning trees. In: Proceedings of the seventeenth symposium on reliable distributed systems, West Lafayette, IN. IEEE Computer Society, pp 366–371
13. Gibbons PB, Matias Y, Ramachandran V (1997) Can shared-memory model serve as a bridging model for parallel computation? In: Proceedings 9th annual symposium parallel algorithms and architectures (SPAA-97), Newport, RI, ACM, New York pp 72–83
14. Graham RL, Hell P (1985) On the history of the minimum spanning tree problem. IEEE Ann History Comput 7(1):43–57
15. Helman DR, JáJá J (1999) Designing practical efficient algorithms for symmetric multiprocessors. In: Algorithm engineering and experimentation (ALENEX'99), Baltimore, MD, Lecture notes in computer science, vol 1619. Springer-Verlag, Heidelberg, pp 37–56
16. JáJá J (1992) An Introduction to parallel algorithms. Addison-Wesley, New York
17. Kang S, Bader DA (2009) An efficient transactional memory algorithm for computing minimum spanning forest of sparse graphs. In: Proceedings of the 14th ACM SIGPLAN symposium on principles and practice of parallel programming (PPoPP), Raleigh, NC

18. Karger DR, Klein PN, Tarjan RE (1995) A randomized linear-time algorithm to find minimum spanning trees. J ACM 42(2):321–328
19. Katriel I, Sanders P, Träff JL (2003) A practical minimum spanning tree algorithm using the cycle property. In: 11th Annual European symposium on algorithms (ESA 2003), Budapest, Hungary, Lecture notes in computer science, vol 2832. Springer-Verlag, Heidelberg, pp 679–690
20. Moret BME, Shapiro HD (1994) An empirical assessment of algorithms for constructing a minimal spanning tree. In: DIMACS monographs in discrete mathematics and theoretical computer science: computational support for discrete mathematics vol 15, American Mathematical Society, Providence, RI, pp 99–117
21. Pettie S, Ramachandran V (2002) A randomized time-work optimal parallel algorithm for finding a minimum spanning forest. SIAM J Comput 31(6):1879–1895
22. Poon CK, Ramachandran V (1997) A randomized linear work EREW PRAM algorithm to find a minimum spanning forest. In: Proceedings of the 8th international symposium algorithms and computation (ISAAC'97), Lecture notes in computer science, vol 1350. Springer-Verlag, Heidelberg, pp 212–222
23. Carlson WW, Draper JM, Culler DE, Yelick K, Brooks E, Warren K (1999) Introduction to UPC and Language Specification. CCS-TR-99-157. IDA/CCS, Bowie, Maryland

Sparse Approximate Inverse Matrix

▶ SPAI (SParse approximate inverse)

Sparse Direct Methods

ANSHUL GUPTA
IBM T.J. Watson Research Center, Yorktown Heights, NY, USA

Synonyms

Gaussian elimination; Linear equations solvers; Sparse gaussian elimination

Definition

Direct methods for solving linear systems of the form $Ax = b$ are based on computing $A = LU$, where L and U are lower and upper triangular, respectively. Computing the triangular factors of the coefficient matrix A is also known as *LU decomposition*. Following the factorization, the original system is trivially solved by solving the triangular systems $Ly = b$ and $Ux = y$. If A is symmetric, then a factorization of the form $A = LL^T$ or $A = LDL^T$ is computed via *Cholesky factorization*, where L is a lower triangular matrix (unit lower triangular in the case of $A = LDL^T$ factorization) and D is a diagonal matrix. One set of common formulations of LU decomposition and Cholesky factorization for dense matrices are shown in Figs. 1 and 2, respectively. Note that other mathematically equivalent formulations are possible by rearranging the loops in these algorithms. These algorithms must be adapted for sparse matrices, in which a large fraction of entries are zero. For example, if $A[j,i]$ in the division step is zero, then this operation need not be performed. Similarly, the update steps can be avoided if either $A[j,i]$ or $A[i,k]$ ($A[k,i]$ if A is symmetric) is zero.

When A is sparse, the triangular factors L and U typically have nonzero entries in many more locations than A does. This phenomenon is known as *fill-in*, and results in a superlinear growth in the memory and time requirements of a direct method to solve a sparse system with respect to the size of the system. Despite a high memory requirement, direct methods are often used in many real applications due to their generality and robustness. In applications requiring solutions with respect to several right-hand side vectors and the same coefficient matrix, direct methods are often the solvers of choice because the one-time cost of factorization can be amortized over several inexpensive triangular solves.

Discussion

The direct solution of a sparse linear system typically involves four phases. The two computational phases, *factorization* and *triangular solutions* have already been mentioned. The number of nonzeros in the factors and sometimes their numerical properties are functions of the initial permutation of the rows and columns of the coefficient matrix. In many parallel formulations of sparse factorization, this permutation can also have an effect on load balance. The first step in the direct solution of a sparse linear system, therefore, is to apply heuristics to compute a desirable permutation the matrix. This step is known as *ordering*. A sparse matrix can be viewed as the adjacency matrix of a graph. Ordering heuristics typically use the graph view of the matrix

```
1.  begin LU_Decomp (A, n)
2.    for i = 1, n
3.      for j = i + 1, n
4.        A[j, i] = A[j, i]/A[i, i]; /* division step, computes column i of L */
5.      end for
6.      for k = i + 1, n
7.        for j = i + 1, n
8.          A[j, k] = A[j, k] − A[j, i] × A[i, k]; /* update step*/
9.        end for
10.     end for
11.   end for
12. end LU_Decomp
```

Sparse Direct Methods. Fig. 1 A simple column-based algorithm for LU decomposition of an $n \times n$ dense matrix A. The algorithm overwrites A by L and U such that A = LU, where L is unit lower triangular and U is upper triangular. The diagonal entries after factorization belong to U; the unit diagonal of L is not explicitly stored

```
1.  begin Cholesky (A, n)
2.    for i = 1, n
3.      A[i, i] = √A[i, i];
4.      for j = i + 1, n
5.        A[j, i] = A[j, i]/A[i, i]; /* division step, computes column i of L */
6.      end for
7.      for k = i + 1, n
8.        for j = k, n
9.          A[j, k] = A[j, k] − A[j, i] × A[k, i]; /* update step*/
10.       end for
11.     end for
12.   end for
13. end Cholesky
```

Sparse Direct Methods. Fig. 2 A simple column-based algorithm for Cholesky factorization of an $n \times n$ dense symmetric positive definite matrix A. The lower triangular part of A is overwritten by L, such that $A = LL^T$

and label the vertices in a particular order that is equivalent to computing a permutation of the coefficient matrix with desirable properties. In the second phase, known as *symbolic factorization*, the nonzero pattern of the factors is computed. Knowing the nonzero pattern of the factors before actually computing them is useful for several reasons. The memory requirements of numerical factorization can be predicted during symbolic factorization. With the number and locations of nonzeros known before hand, a significant amount of indirect addressing can be avoided during numerical factorization, thus boosting performance. In a parallel implementation, symbolic factorization helps in the distribution of data and computation among processing units. The ordering and symbolic factorization phases are also referred to as preprocessing or analysis steps.

Of the four phases, numerical factorization typically consumes the most memory and time. Many applications involve factoring several matrices with different numerical values but the same sparsity structure. In such cases, some or all of the results of the ordering and symbolic factorization steps can be reused. This is also advantageous for parallel sparse solvers because parallel ordering and symbolic factorization are typically less scalable. Amortization of the cost of these steps over several factorization steps helps maintain the overall scalability of the solver close to that of numerical factorization. The parallelization of the triangular solves is highly dependent on the parallelization of the numerical factorization phase. The parallel formulation of numerical factorization dictates how the factors are distributed among parallel tasks. The subsequent triangular solution steps must use a parallelization scheme that works on this data distribution, particularly in a distributed-memory parallel environment. Given its prominent role in the parallel direct solution of sparse linear system, the numerical factorization phase is the primary focus of this entry.

The algorithms used for preprocessing and factoring a sparse coefficient matrix depend on the properties of the matrix, such as symmetry, diagonal dominance, positive definiteness, etc. However, there are common elements in most sparse factorization algorithms. Two of these, namely, *task graphs* and *supernodes*, are key to the discussion of parallel sparse matrix factorization of all types for both practical and pedagogical reasons.

Task Graph Model of Sparse Factorization

A parallel computation is usually the most efficient when running at the maximum possible level of granularity that ensures a good load balance among all the processors. Dense matrix factorization is computationally rich and requires $O(n^3)$ operations for factoring an $n \times n$ matrix. Sparse factorization involves a much smaller overall number of operations per row or column of the matrix than its dense counterpart. The sparsity results in additional challenges, as well as additional opportunities to extract parallelism. The challenges are centered around finding ways of orchestrating the unstructured computations in a load-balanced fashion and of containing the overheads of interaction between parallel tasks in the face of a relatively small number or operations per row or column of the matrix. The added opportunity for parallelism results from the fact that, unlike the dense algorithms of Figs. 1 and 2, the columns of the factors in the sparse case do not need to be computed one after the other. Note that in the algorithms shown in Figs. 1 and 2, row and column i are updated by rows and columns $1 \ldots i-1$. In the sparse case, column i is updated by a column $j < i$ only if $U[j,i] \neq 0$, and a row i is updated by a row $j < i$ only if $L[i,j] \neq 0$. Therefore, as the sparse factorization begins, the division step can proceed in parallel for all columns i for which $A[i,j] = 0$ and $A[j,i] = 0$ for all $j < i$. Similarly, at any stage in the factorization process, there could be large pool of columns that are ready of the division step. Any unfactored column i would belong to this pool iff all columns $j < i$ with a nonzero entry in row i of L and all rows $j < i$ with a nonzero entry in column i of U have been factored.

A task dependency graph is an excellent tool for capturing parallelism and the various dependencies in sparse matrix factorization. It is a directed acyclic graph (DAG) whose vertices denote tasks and the edges specify the dependencies among the tasks. A task is associated with each row and column (column only in the symmetric case) of the sparse matrix to be factored. The vertex i of the task graph denotes the task responsible for computing column i of L and row i of U. A task is ready for execution if and only if all tasks with incoming edges to it have completed. Task graphs are often explicitly constructed during symbolic factorization to guide the numerical factorization phase. This permits the numerical factorization to avoid expensive searches in order to determine which tasks are ready for execution at any given stage of the parallel factorization process. The task graphs corresponding to matrices with a symmetric structure are trees and are known as *elimination trees* in the sparse matrix literature.

Figure 3 shows the elimination tree for a structurally symmetric sparse matrix and Fig. 4 shows the task DAG for a structurally unsymmetric matrix. Once a task graph is constructed, then parallel factorization (and even parallel triangular solution) can be viewed as the problem of scheduling the tasks onto parallel processes or threads. Static scheduling is generally preferred in a distributed-memory environment and dynamic scheduling in a shared-memory environment. The shape of the task graph is a function of the initial permutation of rows and columns of the sparse matrix, and is therefore determined by the outcome of the ordering phase. Figure 5 shows the elimination tree corresponding to the same matrix as in Fig. 3a, but with a different initial permutation. The structure of the task DAG usually affects how effectively it can be scheduled for parallel factorization. For example, it may be intuitively recognizable to readers that the elimination tree in Fig. 3 is more amenable to parallel scheduling than the tree corresponding to a different permutation of the same matrix in Fig. 5. Figure 6 illustrates that the matrices in Figs. 3 and 5 have the same underlying graph. The only difference is in the labeling of the vertices of the graph, which results in a different permutation of the rows and columns of the matrix, different amount

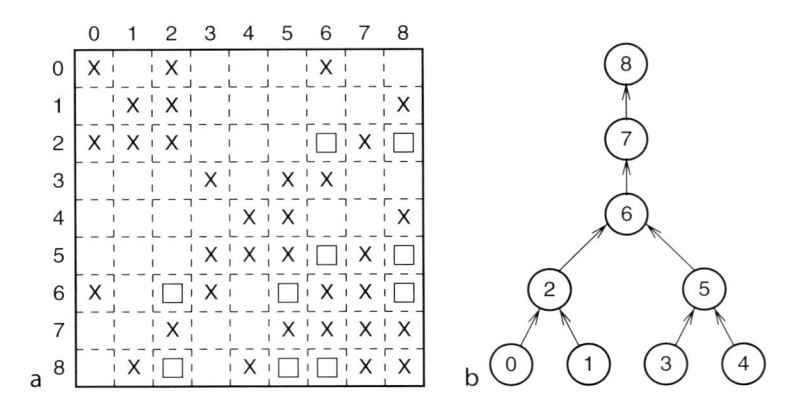

Sparse Direct Methods. Fig. 3 A structurally symmetric sparse matrix and its elimination tree. An X indicates a nonzero entry in the original matrix and a box denotes a fill-in

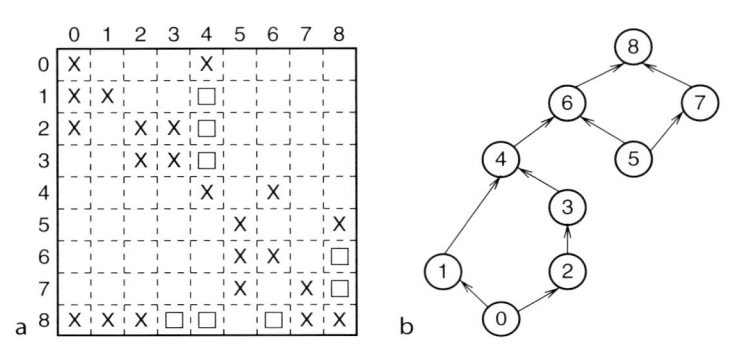

Sparse Direct Methods. Fig. 4 An unsymmetric sparse matrix and the corresponding task DAG. An X indicates a nonzero entry in the original matrix and a box denotes a fill-in

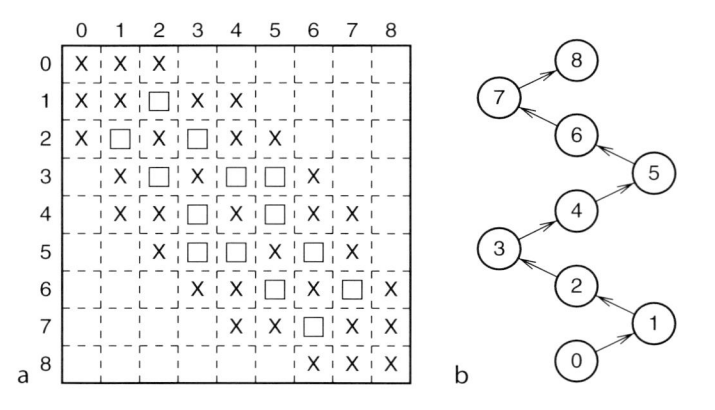

Sparse Direct Methods. Fig. 5 A permutation of the sparse matrix of Fig. 3a and its elimination tree

of fill-in, and different shapes of task graphs. In general, long and skinny task graphs result in limited parallelism and a long critical path. Short and broad task graphs have a high degree of parallelism and shorter critical paths.

Since the shape, and hence the amenability to efficient parallel scheduling of the task graph is sensitive to ordering, heuristics that result in balanced and broad task graphs are preferred for parallel factorization. The best known ordering heuristic in this class is called

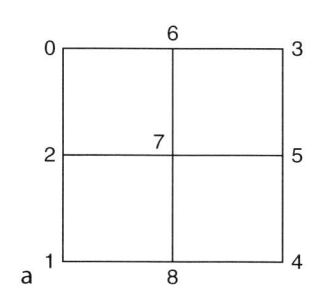

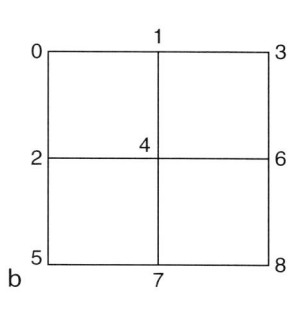

Sparse Direct Methods. Fig. 6 An illustration of the duality between graph vertex labeling and row/column permutation of a structurally symmetric sparse matrix. Grid (**a**), with vertices labeled based on nested dissection, is the adjacency graph of the matrix in Fig. 3a and grid (**b**) is the adjacency graph of the matrix in Fig. 5a

nested dissection. Nested dissection is based on recursively computing balanced bisections of a graph by finding small vertex separators. The vertices in the two disconnected partitions of the graph are labeled before the vertices of the separator. The same heuristic is applied recursively for labeling the vertices of each partition. The ordering in Fig. 3 is actually based on nested dissection. Note that the vertex set 6, 7, 8 forms a separator, dividing the graph into two disconnected components, 0, 1, 2 and 3, 4, 5. Within the two components, vertices 2 and 5 are the separators, and hence have the highest label in their respective partitions.

Supernodes

In sparse matrix terminology, a set of consecutive rows or columns that have the same nonzero structure is loosely referred to as a supernode. The notion of supernodes is crucial to efficient implementation of sparse factorization for a large class of sparse matrices arising in real applications.

Coefficient matrices in many applications have natural supernodes. In graph terms, there are sets of vertices with identical adjacency structures. Graphs like these can be compressed by having one supervertex represent the whole set that has the same adjacency structure. When most vertices of a graph belong to supernodes and the supernodes are of roughly the same size (in terms of the number of vertices in them) with an average size of, say, m, then it can be shown that the compressed graph has $O(m)$ fewer vertices and $O(m^2)$ fewer edges than in the original graph. It can also be shown that an ordering of original graph can be derived from an ordering of the compressed graph, while preserving the properties of the ordering, by simply labeling the vertices of the original graph consecutively in the order of the supernodes of the compressed graph. Thus, the space and the time requirements of ordering can be dramatically reduced. This is particularly useful for parallel sparse solvers because parallel ordering heuristics often yield orderings of lower quality than their serial counterparts. For matrices with highly compressible graphs, it is possible to compute the ordering in serial with only a small impact on the overall scalability of the entire solver because ordering is performed on a graph with $O(m^2)$ fewer edges.

While the natural supernodes in the coefficient matrix, if any, can be useful during ordering, it is the presence of supernodes in the factors that have the biggest impact on the performance of the factorization and triangular solution steps. Although there can be multiple ways of defining supernodes in matrices with an unsymmetric structure, the most useful form involves groups of indices with identical nonzero pattern in the corresponding columns of L and rows of U. Even if there are no supernodes in the original matrix, supernodes in the factors are almost inevitable for matrices in most real applications. This is due to fill-in. Examples of supernodes in factors include indices 6–8 in Fig. 3a, indices 2–3 and 7–8 in Fig. 4a, and indices 4–5 and 6–8 in Fig. 5. Some practitioners prefer to artificially increase the size (i.e., the number of member rows and columns) of supernodes by padding the rows and columns that have only slightly different nonzero patterns, so that they can be merged into the same supernode. The supernodes in the factors are typically detected and recorded as they emerge during symbolic factorization. In the remainder of this chapter, the term supernode refers to a supernode in the factors.

It can be seen from the algorithms in Figs. 1 and 2 that there are two primary computations in a column-based factorization: the division step and the update step. A supernode-based sparse factorization too has the same two basic computation steps, except that these are now matrix operations on row/column blocks corresponding to the various supernodes.

Supernodes impart efficiency to numerical factorization and triangular solves because they permit floating point operations to be performed on dense submatrices instead of individual nonzeros, thus improving memory hierarchy utilization. Since rows and columns in supernodes share the nonzero structure, indirect addressing is minimized because the structure needs to be stored only once for these rows and columns. Supernodes help to increase the granularity of tasks, which is useful for improving computation to overhead ratio in a parallel implementation. The task graph model of sparse matrix factorization was introduced earlier with a task k defined as the factorization of row and column k of the matrix. With supernodes, a task can be defined as the factorization of all rows and columns associated with a supernode. Actual task graphs in practical implementations of parallel sparse solvers are almost always supernodal task graphs.

Note that some applications, such as power grid analysis, in which the basis of the linear system is not a finite-element or finite-difference discretization of a physical domain, can give rise to sparse matrices that incur very little fill-in during factorization. The factors of these matrices may have very small supernodes.

An Effective Parallelization Strategy

The task graphs for sparse matrix factorization have some typical properties that make scheduling somewhat different from traditional DAG scheduling. Note that the task graphs corresponding to irreducible matrices have a distinct root; that is, one node that has no outgoing edges. This corresponds to the last (rightmost) supernode in the matrix. The number of member rows and columns in supernodes typically increases away from the leaves and toward the root of the task graph. The reason is that a supernode accumulates fill-in from all its predecessors in the task graph. As a result, the portions of the factors that correspond to task graph nodes with a large number of predecessors tend to get denser. Due to their larger supernodes, the tasks that are relatively close to the root tend to have more work associated with them. On the other hand, the width of the task graph shrinks close to the root. In other words, a typical task graph for sparse matrix factorization tends to have a large number of small independent tasks closer to the leaves, but a small number of large tasks closer to the root. An ideal parallelization strategy that would match the characteristics of the problem is as follows. Starting out, the relatively plentiful independent tasks at or near the leaves would be scheduled to parallel threads or processes. As tasks complete, other tasks become available and would be scheduled similarly. This could continue until there are enough independent tasks to keep all the threads or processes busy. When the number of available parallel tasks becomes smaller than the number of available threads or processes, then the only way to keep the latter busy would be to utilize more than one of them per task. The number of threads or processes working on individual tasks would increase as the number of parallel tasks decreases. Eventually, all threads or processes would work on the root task. The computation corresponding to the root task is equivalent to factoring a dense matrix of the size of the root supernode.

Sparse Factorization Formulations Based on Task Roles

So far in this entry, the tasks have been defined somewhat ambiguously. There are multiple ways of defining the tasks precisely, which can result in different parallel implementations of sparse matrix factorization. Clearly, a task is associated with a supernode and is responsible for computing that supernode of the factors; that is, performing the computation equivalent to the division steps in the algorithms in Figs. 1 and 2. However, a task does not own all the data that is required to compute the final values of its supernode's rows and columns. The data for performing the update steps on a supernode may be contributed by many other supernodes. Based on the tasks' responsibilities, sparse LU factorization has traditionally been classified into three categories, namely, *left-looking*, *right-looking*, and *Crout*. These variations are illustrated in Fig. 7. The traditional left-looking variant uses nonconforming supernodes made up of columns of both L and U, which are not very

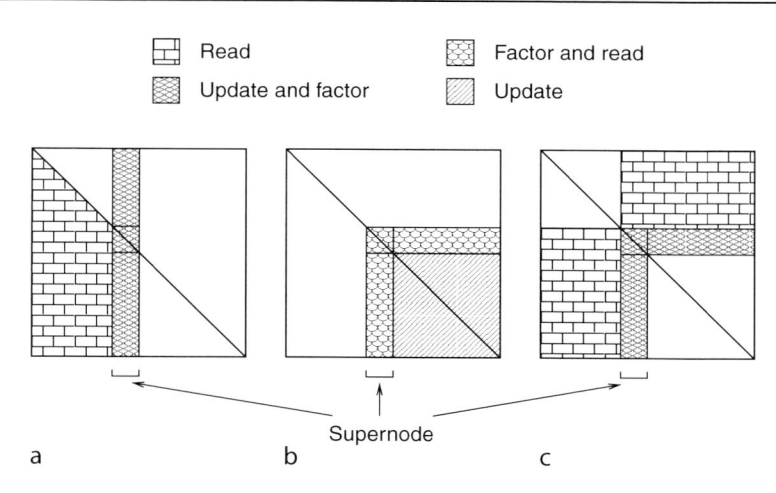

Sparse Direct Methods. Fig. 7 The left-looking (**a**), right-looking (**b**), and Crout (**c**) variations of sparse LU factorization. Different patterns indicate the parts of the matrix that are read, updated, and factored by the task corresponding to a supernode. *Blank portions* of the matrix are not accessed by this task

common in practice. In this variant, a task is responsible for gathering all the data required for its own columns from other tasks and for updating and factoring its columns. The left-looking formulation is rarely used in modern high-performance sparse direct solvers. In the right-looking variation of sparse LU, a task factors the supernode that it owns and performs all the updates that use the data from this supernode. In the Crout variation, a task is responsible for updating and factoring the supernode that it owns. Only the right-looking and Crout variants have symmetric counterparts.

A fourth variation, known as the *multifrontal method*, incorporates elements of both right-looking and Crout formulations. In the multifrontal method, the task that owns a supernode computes its own contribution to updating the remainder of the matrix (like the right-looking formulation), but does not actually apply the updates. Each task is responsible for collecting all relevant precomputed updates and applying them to its supernode (like the Crout formulation) before factoring the supernode. The supernode data and its update contribution in the multifrontal method is organized into small dense matrices called *frontal matrices*. Integer arrays maintain a mapping of the local contiguous indices of the frontal matrices to the global indices of the sparse factor matrices. Figure 8 illustrates the complete supernodal multifrontal Cholesky factorization of the symmetric matrix shown in Fig. 3a. Note that, since rows and columns with indices 6–8 form a supernode, there would be only one task (Fig. 8g) corresponding to these in the supernodal task graph (elimination tree).

When a task is ready for execution, it first constructs its frontal matrix by accumulating contributions from the frontal matrices of its children and from the coefficient matrix. It then factors its supernode, which is the portion of the frontal matrix that is shaded in Fig. 8. After factorization, the unshaded portion (this submatrix of a frontal matrix is called the *update matrix*) is updated based on the update step of the algorithm in Fig. 2. The update matrix is then used by the parent task to construct its frontal matrix.

Note that Fig. 8 illustrates a symmetric multifrontal factorization; hence, the frontal and update matrices are triangular. For general LU decomposition, these matrices would be square or rectangular. In symmetric multifrontal factorization, a child's update matrix in the elimination tree contributes only to its parent's frontal matrix. The task graph for general matrices is usually not a tree, but a DAG, as shown in Fig. 4. Apart from the shape of the frontal and update matrices, unsymmetric pattern multifrontal method differs from its symmetric counterpart in two other ways. First, an update matrix can contribute to more than one frontal matrices. Secondly, the frontal matrices receiving data from an update matrix can belong to the contributing supernode's ancestors (not necessarily parents) in the task graph.

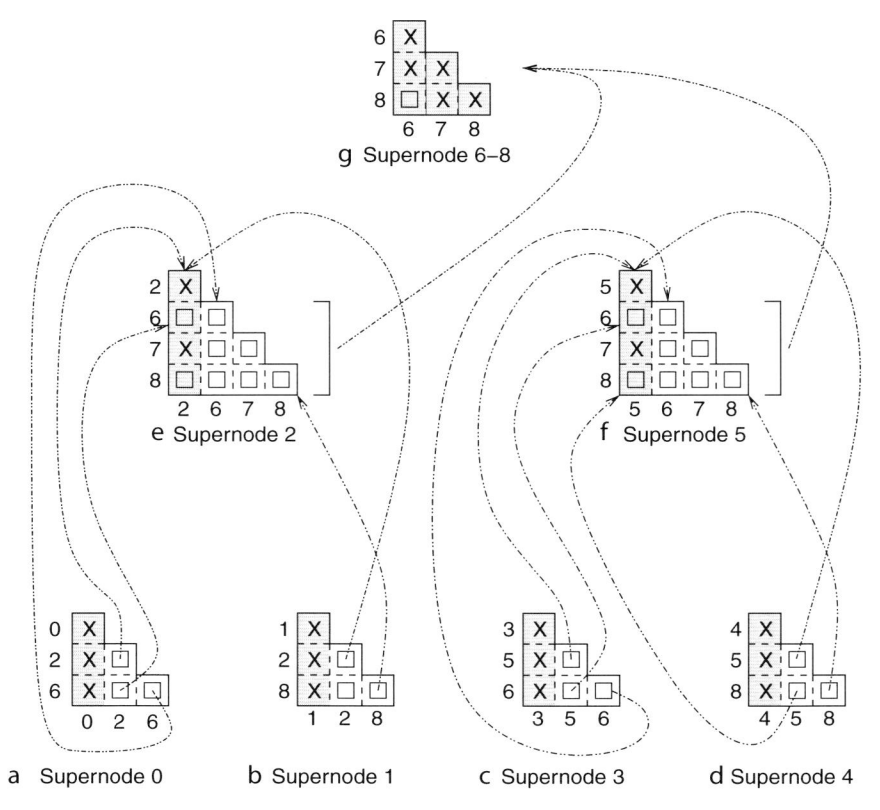

Sparse Direct Methods. Fig. 8 Frontal matrices and data movement among them in the supernodal multifrontal Cholesky factorization of the sparse matrix shown in Fig. 3a

The multifrontal method is often the formulation of choice for highly parallel implementations of sparse matrix factorization. This is because of its natural data locality (most of the work of the factorization is performed in the well-contained dense frontal matrices) and the ease of synchronization that it permits. In general, each supernode is updated by multiple other supernodes and it can potentially update many other supernodes during the course of factorization. If implemented naively, all these updates may require excessive locking and synchronization in a shared-memory environment or generate excessive message traffic in a distributed environment. In the multifrontal method, the updates are accumulated and channeled along the paths from the leaves of the task graph to its root. This gives a manageable structure to the potentially haphazard interaction among the tasks.

Recall that the typical supernodal sparse factorization task graph is such that the size of tasks generally increases and the number of parallel tasks generally diminishes on the way to the root from the leaves. The multifrontal method is well suited for both task parallelism (close to the leaves) and data parallelism (close to the root). Larger tasks working on large frontal matrices close to the root can readily employ multiple threads or processes to perform parallel dense matrix operations, which not only have well-understood data-parallel algorithms, but also a well-developed software base.

Pivoting in Parallel Sparse LDL^T and LU Factorization

The discussion in this entry so far has focussed on the scenario in which the rows and columns of the matrix are permuted during the ordering phase and this permutation stays static during numerical factorization. While this assumption is valid for a large class of practical problems, there are applications that would generate matrices that could encounter a zero or a very small entry on the diagonal during the factorization process.

This will cause the division step of the LU decomposition algorithm to fail or to result in numerical instability. For nonsingular matrices, this problem can be solved by interchanging rows and columns of the matrix by a process known as *partial pivoting*. When a small or zero entry is encountered at $A[i,i]$ before the division step, then row i is interchanged with another row j ($i < j \leq n$) such that $A[j,i]$ (which would occupy the location $A[i,i]$ after the interchange) is sufficiently greater in magnitude compared to other entries $A[k,i]$ ($i < k \leq n, k \neq j$). Similarly, instead of row i, column i could be exchanged with a suitable column j ($i < j \leq n$). In symmetric LDL^T factorization, both row and column i are interchanged simultaneously with a suitable row–column pair to maintain symmetry.

Until recently, it was believed that due to unpredictable changes in the structure of the factors due to partial pivoting, a priori ordering and symbolic factorization could not be performed, and these steps needed to be combined with numerical factorization. Keeping the analysis and numerical factorization steps separate has substantial performance and parallelization benefits, which would be lost if these steps are combined. Fortunately, modern parallel sparse solvers are able to perform partial pivoting and maintain numerical stability without mixing the analysis and numerical steps. The multifrontal method permits effective implementation of partial pivoting in parallel and keeps its effects as localized as possible.

Before computing a fill-reducing ordering, the rows or columns of the coefficient matrix are permuted such that the absolute value of the product of the magnitude of the diagonal entries is maximized. Special graph matching algorithms are used to compute this permutation. This step ensures that the diagonal entries of the matrix have relatively large magnitudes at the beginning of factorization. It has been observed that once the matrix has been permuted this way, in most cases, very few interchanges are required during the factorization process to keep it numerically stable. As a result, factorization can be performed using the static task graph and the static structures of the supernodes of L and U predicted by symbolic factorization. When an interchange is necessary, the resulting changes in the data structures are registered. Since such interchanges are rare, the resulting disruption and the overhead is usually well contained.

The first line of defense against numerical instability is to perform partial pivoting within a frontal matrix. Exchanging rows or columns within a supernode is local, and if all rows and columns of a supernode can be successfully factored by simply altering their order, then nothing outside the supernode is affected. Sometimes, a supernode cannot be factored completely by local interchanges. This can happen when all candidate rows or columns for interchange have indices greater than that of the last row–column pair of the supernode. In this case, a technique known as *delayed pivoting* is employed. The unfactored rows and columns are simply removed from the current supernode and passed onto the parent (or parents) in the task graph. Merged with the parent supernode, these rows and columns have additional candidate rows and columns available for interchange, which increases the chances of their successful factorization. The process of upward migration of unsuccessful pivots continues until they are resolved, which is guaranteed to happen at the root supernode for a nonsingular matrix.

In the multifrontal framework, delayed pivoting simply involves adding extra rows and columns to the frontal matrices of the parents of supernode with failed pivots. The process is straightforward for the supernodes whose tasks are mapped onto individual threads or processes. For the tasks that require data-parallel involvement of multiple threads or processes, the extra rows and columns can be partitioned using the same strategy that is used to partition the original frontal matrix.

Parallel Solution of Triangular Systems

As mentioned earlier, solving the original system after factoring the coefficient matrix involves solving a sparse lower triangular and a sparse upper triangular system. The task graph constructed for factorization can be used for the triangular solves too. For matrices with an unsymmetric pattern, a subset of edges of the task DAG may be redundant in each of the solve phases, but these redundant edges can be easily marked during symbolic factorization. Just like factorization, the computation for the lower triangular solve phase starts at the leaves of the task graph and proceeds toward the root. In the upper triangular solve phase, computation starts at the root and fans out toward the leaves (in other words, the direction of the edges in the task graph is effectively reversed).

Related Entries
▶Dense Linear System Solvers
▶Multifrontal Method
▶Reordering

Bibliographic Notes and Further Reading

Books by George and Liu [6] and Duff et al. [5] are excellent sources for a background on sparse direct methods. A comprehensive survey by Demmel et al. [4] sums up the developments in parallel sparse direct solvers until the early 1990s. Some remarkable progress was made in the development of parallel algorithms and software for sparse direct methods during a decade starting in the early 1990s. Gupta et al. [9] developed the framework for highly scalable parallel formulations of symmetric sparse factorization based on the multifrontal method (see tutorial by Liu [12] for details), and recently demonstrated scalable performance of an industrial strength implementation of their algorithms on thousands of cores [10]. Demmel et al. [3] developed one of the first scalable algorithms and software for solving unsymmetric sparse systems without partial pivoting. Amestoy et al. [1, 2] developed parallel algorithms and software that incorporated partial pivoting for solving unsymmetric systems with (either natural or forced) symmetric pattern. Hadfield [11] and Gupta [7] laid the theoretical foundation for a general unsymmetric pattern parallel multifrontal algorithm with partial pivoting, with the latter following up with a practical implementation [8].

Bibliography

1. Amestoy PR, Duff IS, Koster J, L'Excellent JY (2001) A fully asynchronous multifrontal solver using distributed dynamic scheduling. SIAM J Matrix Anal Appl 23(1):15–41
2. Amestoy PR, Duff IS, L'Excellent JY (2000) Multifrontal parallel distributed symmetric and unsymmetric solvers. Comput Methods Appl Mech Eng 184:501–520
3. Demmel JW, Gilbert JR, Li XS (1999) An asynchronous parallel supernodal algorithm for sparse Gaussian elimination. SIAM J Matrix Anal Appl 20(4):915–952
4. Demmel JW, Heath MT, van der Vorst HA (1993) Parallel numerical linear algebra. Acta Numerica 2:111–197
5. Duff IS, Erisman AM, Reid JK (1990) Direct methods for sparse matrices. Oxford University Press, Oxford, UK
6. George A, Liu JW-H (1981) Computer solution of large sparse positive definite systems. Prentice-Hall, NJ
7. Gupta A (2002) Improved symbolic and numerical factorization algorithms for unsymmetric sparse matrices. SIAM J Matrix Anal Appl 24(2):529–552
8. Gupta A (2007) A shared- and distributed-memory parallel general sparse direct solver. Appl Algebra Eng Commun Comput 18(3):263–277
9. Gupta A, Karypis G, Kumar V (1997) Highly scalable parallel algorithms for sparse matrix factorization. IEEE Trans Parallel Distrib Syst 8(5):502–520
10. Gupta A, Koric S, George T (2009) Sparse matrix factorization on massively parallel computers. In: SC09 Proceedings, ACM, Portland, OR, USA
11. Hadfield SM (1992) On the LU factorization of sequences of identically structured sparse matrices within a distributed memory environment. PhD thesis, University of Florida, Gainsville, FL
12. Liu JW-H (1992) The multifrontal method for sparse matrix solution: theory and practice. SIAM Rev 34(1):82–109

Sparse Gaussian Elimination

▶Sparse Direct Methods
▶SuperLU

Sparse Iterative Methods, Preconditioners for

▶Preconditioners for Sparse Iterative Methods

SPEC Benchmarks

MATTHIAS MÜLLER[1], BRIAN WHITNEY[2]
ROBERT HENSCHEL[3], KALYAN KUMARAN[4]
[1]Technische Universität Dresden, Dresden, Germany
[2]Oracle Corporation, Hillsboro, OR, USA
[3]Indiana University, Bloomington, IN, USA
[4]Argonne National Laboratory, Argonne, IL, USA

Synonyms
SPEC HPC96; SPEC HPC2002; SPEC MPI2007; SPEC OMP2001

Definition

Application-based Benchmarks measure the performance of computer systems by running a set of applications with a well defined configuration and workload.

Discussion

Introduction

The Standard Performance Evaluation Corporation (SPEC [Product and service names mentioned herein may be the trademarks of their respective owners]) is an organization for creating industry-standard benchmarks to measure various aspects of modern computer system performance. SPEC was founded in 1988. In January 1994, the High-Performance Group of the Standard Performance Evaluation Corporation (SPEC HPG) was founded with the mission to establish, maintain, and endorse a suite of benchmarks representative of real-world, high-performance computing applications. Several efforts joined forces to form SPEC HPG and to initiate a new benchmarking venture that is supported broadly. Founding partners included the member organizations of SPEC, former members of the Perfect Benchmark effort, and representatives of area-specific benchmarking activities. Other benchmarking organizations have joined the SPEC HPG committee since its formation.

SPEC HPG has developed various benchmark suites and its run rules over the last few years. The purpose of those benchmarks and their run rules is to further the cause of fair and objective benchmarking of high-performance computing systems. Results obtained with the benchmark suites are to be reviewed to see whether the individual run rules have been followed. Once they are accepted, the results are published on the SPEC web site (http://www.spec.org). All results, including a comprehensive description of the hardware they were produced on, are freely available. SPEC believes that the user community benefits from an objective series of tests which serve as a common reference.

The development of the benchmark suites includes obtaining candidate benchmark codes, putting these codes into the SPEC harness, testing and improving the codes' portability across as many operating systems, compilers, interconnects, runtime libraries as possible, and testing the codes for correctness and scalability.

The codes are put into the SPEC harness. The SPEC harness is a set of tools that allow users of the benchmark suite to easily run the suite, and obtain validated and publishable results. The users then only need to submit the results obtained to SPEC for review and publication on the SPEC web site.

The goals of the run rules of the benchmark suites are to ensure that published results are meaningful, comparable to other results, and reproducible. A result must contain enough information to allow another user to reproduce the result. The performance tuning methods employed when attaining a result should be more than just "prototype" or "experimental" or "research" methods; there must be a certain level of maturity and general applicability in the performance methods employed, e.g., the used compiler optimization techniques should be beneficial for other applications as well and the compiler should be generally available and supported.

Two set of metrics can be measured with the benchmark suite: "Peak" and "Base" metrics. "Peak" metrics may also be referred to as "aggressive compilation," e.g., they may be produced by building each benchmark in the suite with a set of optimizations individually selected for that benchmark, and running them with environment settings individually selected for that benchmark. The optimizations selected must adhere to the set of general benchmark optimization rules. Base optimizations must adhere to a stricter set of rules than the peak optimizations. For example, the "Base" metrics must be produced by building all the benchmarks in the suite with a common set of optimizations and running them with environment settings common to all the benchmarks in the suite.

SPEC HPC96

The efforts of SPEC HPG began in 1994 when a group from industry and academia came together to try and provide a benchmark suite based upon the principles that had started with SPEC. Two of the more popular benchmarks suites at the time were the NAS Parallel Benchmarks and the PERFECT Club Benchmarks. The group built upon the direction these benchmarks provided to produce their first benchmark, SPEC HPC96.

The benchmark SPEC HPC96 came out originally with two components, SPECseis96 and SPECchem96, with a third component SPECclimate available later.

Each of these benchmarks provided a set of rules, code, and validation which allowed benchmarking across a wide variety of hardware, including parallel platforms.

SPECseis96 is a benchmark application that was originally developed at Atlantic Richfield Corporation (ARCO). This benchmark was designed to test computation that was of interest to the oil and gas industry, in particular, time and depth migrations which are used to locate gas and oil deposits.

SPECchem96 is a benchmark based upon the application GAMESS (General Atomic and Molecular Electronic Structure System). This computational chemistry code was used in the pharmaceutical and chemical industries for drug design and bonding analysis.

SPECclimate is a benchmark based upon the application MM5, the PSU/NCAR limited-area, hydrostatic or non-hydrostatic, sigma-coordinate model designed to simulate or predict mesoscale and regional-scale atmospheric circulation. MM5 was developed by the Pennsylvania State University (Penn State) and the University Corporation for Atmospheric Research (UCAR).

SPEC HPC96 was retired in February 2003, a little after the introduction of SPEC HPC2002 and SPEC OMP2001. The results remain accessible on the SPEC web site, for reference purposes.

SPEC HPC2002

The benchmark SPEC HPC2002 was a follow-on to SPEC HPC96. The update involved using newer versions of some of the software, as well as additional parallelism models. The use of MM5 was replaced with the application WRF.

The benchmark was suitable for shared and distributed memory machines or clusters of shared memory nodes. SPEC HPC applications have been collected from among the largest, most realistic computational applications that are available for distribution by SPEC. In contrast to SPEC OMP, they were not restricted to any particular programming model or system architecture. Both shared-memory and message passing methods are supported. All codes of the current SPEC HPC2002 suite were available in an MPI and an OpenMP programming model and they included two data set sizes.

The benchmark consisted of three scientific applications:

SPECenv (WRF) is based on the WRF weather model, a state-of-the-art, non-hydrostatic mesoscale weather model, see http://www.wrf-model.org. The code consists of 25,000 lines of C and 145,000 lines of F90.

SPECseis was developed by ARCO beginning in 1995 to gain an accurate measure of performance of computing systems as it relates to the seismic processing industry for procurement of new computing resources. The code is written in F77 and C and has approximately 25,000 lines.

SPECchem used to simulate molecules ab initio, at the quantum level, and optimize atomic positions. It is a research interest under the name of GAMESS at the Gordon Research Group of Iowa State University and is of interest to the pharmaceutical industry. It consists of 120,000 lines of F77 and C.

The SPEC HPC2002 suite was retired in June 2007. The results remain accessible on the SPEC web site, for reference purposes.

SPEC OMP2001

SPEC's benchmark suite that measures performance using applications based on the OpenMP standard for shared-memory parallel processing. Two levels of workload (OMPM2001 and OMPL2001) characterize the performance of medium and large sized systems. Benchmarks running under SPEC OMPM2001 use up to 1.6 GB of memory, whereas the applications of SPEC OMPL2001 require about 6.4 GB in a 16-thread run.

The SPEC OMPM2001 benchmark suite consists of 11 large application programs, which represent the type of software used in scientific technical computing. The applications include modeling and simulation programs from the fields of chemistry, mechanical engineering, climate modeling, and physics. Of the 11 application programs, 8 are written in Fortran and 3 (AMMP, ART, and EQUAKE) are written in C. The benchmarks require a virtual address space of about 1.5 GB in a 1-processor execution. The rationales for this size were to provide data sets fitting in a 32-bit address space.

SPEC OMPL2001 consists of 9 application programs, of which 7 are written in Fortran and 2 (ART and

EQUAKE) are written in C. The benchmarks require a virtual address space of about 6.4 GB in a 16-processor run. The rationale for this size were to provide data sets significantly larger than those of the SPEC OMPM benchmarks, with a requirement for a 64-bit address space.

The following is a short description of the application programs of OMP2001:

APPLU   Solves five coupled non-linear PDEs on a 3-dimensional logically structured grid, using the Symmetric Successive Over-Relaxation implicit time-marching scheme.

APSI   Lake environmental model, which predicts the concentration of pollutants. It solves the model for the mesoscale and synoptic variations of potential temperature, wind components, and for the mesoscale vertical velocity, pressure, and distribution of pollutants.

MGRID   Simple multigrid solver, which computes a 3-dimensional potential field.

SWIM   Weather prediction model, which solves the shallow water equations using a finite difference method.

FMA3D   Crash simulation program. It simulates the inelastic, transient dynamic response of 3-dimensional solids and structures subjected to impulsively or suddenly applied loads. It uses an explicit finite element method.

ART   (Adaptive Resonance Theory) neural network, which is used to recognize objects in a thermal image. The objects in the benchmark are a helicopter and an airplane.

GAFORT   Computes the global maximum fitness using a genetic algorithm. It starts with an initial population and then generates children who go through crossover, jump mutation, and creep mutation with certain probabilities.

EQUAKE   Is an earthquake-modeling program. It simulates the propagation of elastic seismic waves in large, heterogeneous valleys in order to recover the time history of the ground motion everywhere in the valley due to a specific seismic event. It uses a finite element method on an unstructured mesh.

WUPWISE   (Wuppertal Wilson Fermion Solver) is a program in the field of lattice gauge theory. Lattice gauge theory is a discretization of quantum chromodynamics. Quark propagators are computed within a chromodynamic background field. The inhomogeneous lattice-Dirac equation is solved.

GALGEL   This problem is a particular case of the GAMM (Gesellschaft fuer Angewandte Mathematik und Mechanik) benchmark devoted to numerical analysis of oscillatory instability of convection in low-Prandtl-number fluids. This program is only part of OMPM2001.

AMMP   (Another Molecular Modeling Program) is a molecular mechanics, dynamics, and modeling program. The benchmark performs a molecular dynamics simulation of a protein-inhibitor complex, which is embedded in water. This program is only part of OMPM2001.

SPEC MPI2007

SPEC MPI2007 is SPEC's benchmark suite for evaluating MPI-parallel, floating point, compute-intensive performance across a wide range of cluster and SMP hardware. MPI2007 continues the SPEC tradition of giving users the most objective and representative benchmark suite for measuring and comparing high-performance computer systems.

SPEC MPI2007 focuses on performance of compute intensive applications using the Message-Passing Interface (MPI), which means these benchmarks emphasize the performance of the type of computer processor (CPU), the number of computer processors, the MPI Library, the communication interconnect, the memory architecture, the compilers, and the shared file system.

It is important to remember the contribution of all these components. SPEC MPI performance intentionally depends on more than just the processor. MPI2007 is not intended to stress other computer components such as the operating system, graphics, or the I/O system. Table 1 contains the list of codes, together with information on the benchmark set size, programming language, and application area.

104.milc,142.dmilc   stands for MIMD Lattice Computation and is a quantum chromodynamics (QCD) code for lattice gauge theory with dynamical quarks. Lattice gauge theory involves the study of some of the fundamental constituents of matter, namely

SPEC Benchmarks. Table 1 List of applications in SPEC MPI2007

Benchmark	Suite	Language	Application domain
104.milc	medium	C	Physics: Quantum Chromodynamics (QCD)
107.leslie3d	medium	Fortran	Computational Fluid Dynamics (CFD)
113.GemsFDTD	medium	Fortran	Computational Electromagnetics (CEM)
115.fds4	medium	C/Fortran	Computational Fluid Dynamics (CFD)
121.pop2	medium, large	C/Fortran	Ocean Modeling
122.tachyon	medium, large	C	Graphics: Parallel Ray Tracing
125.RAxML	large	C	DNA Matching
126.lammps	medium, large	C++	Molecular Dynamics Simulation
127.wrf2	medium	C/Fortran	Weather Prediction
128.GAPgeofem	medium, large	C/Fortran	Heat Transfer using Finite Element Methods (FEM)
129.tera_tf	medium, large	Fortran	3D Eulerian Hydrodynamics
130.socorro	medium	C/Fortran	Molecular Dynamics using Density-Functional Theory (DFT)
132.zeusmp2	medium, large	C/Fortran	Physics: Computational Fluid Dynamics (CFD)
137.lu	medium, large	Fortran	Computational Fluid Dynamics (CFD)
142.dmilc	large	C	Physics: Quantum Chromodynamics (QCD)
143.dleslie	large	Fortran	Computational Fluid Dynamics (CFD)
145.lGemsFDTD	large	Fortran	Computational Electromagnetics (CEM)
147.l2wrf2	large	C/Fortran	Weather Prediction

quarks and gluons. In this area of quantum field theory traditional perturbative expansions are not useful and introducing a discrete lattice of space-time points is the method of choice.

107.leslie3d,143.dleslie The main purpose of this code is to model chemically reacting (i.e., burning) turbulent flows. Various different physical models are available in this algorithm. For MPI2007, the program has been set up a to solve a test problem which represents a subset of such flows, namely the temporal mixing layer. This type of flow occurs in the mixing regions of all combustors that employ fuel injection (which is nearly all combustors). Also, this sort of mixing layer is a benchmark problem used to understand physics of turbulent mixing.

LESlie3d uses a strongly conservative, finite-volume algorithm with the MacCormack Predictor-Corrector time integration scheme. The accuracy is fourth-order spatially and second-order temporally.

113.GemsFDTD,145.lGemsFDTD GemsFDTD solves the Maxwell equations in 3D in the time domain using the finite-difference time-domain (FDTD) method. The radar cross section (RCS) of a perfectly conducting (PEC) object is computed. GemsFDTD is a subset of the code GemsTD developed in the General ElectroMagnetic Solvers (GEMS) project.

The core of the FDTD method are second-order accurate central-difference approximations of the Faraday's and Ampere's laws. These central-differences are employed on a staggered Cartesian grid resulting in an explicit finite-difference method. The FDTD method is also referred to as the Yee scheme. It is the standard time-domain method within computational electrodynamics (CEM).

An incident plane wave is generated using so-called Huygens' surfaces. This means that the computational domain is split into a total field part and a scattered field part, where the scattered field part surrounds the total field part. A time-domain near-to-far-field transformation computes the RCS according to Martin and Pettersson. Fast Fourier transforms (FFT) are employed in the post-processing.

145.lGemsFDTD contains extensive performance improvements as compared with 113.GemsFDTD.

115.fds4 is a computational fluid dynamics (CFD) model of fire-driven fluid flow. The software solves numerically a form of the Navier-Stokes equations appropriate for low-speed, thermally driven flow with an emphasis on smoke and heat transport from fires. It uses the block64 test case as dataset. This dataset is similar to ones used to simulate fires in the World Trade Center. The author's agency did the investigation of the collapse.

121.pop2 The Parallel Ocean Program (POP) is a descendant of the Bryan-Cox-Semtner class of ocean models first developed by Kirk Bryan and Michael Cox at the NOAA Geophysical Fluid Dynamics Laboratory in Princeton, NJ, in the late 1960s. POP had its origins in a version of the model developed by Semtner and Chervin. POP is the ocean component of the Community Climate System Model. Time integration of the model is split into two parts. The three-dimensional vertically varying (baroclinic) tendencies are integrated explicitly using a leapfrog scheme. The very fast vertically uniform (barotropic) modes are integrated using an implicit free surface formulation in which a preconditioned conjugate gradient solver is used to solve for the two-dimensional surface pressure.

122.tachyon is a ray tracing program. It implements all of the basic geometric primitives such as triangles, planes, spheres, cylinders, etc. Tachyon is nearly embarrassingly parallel. As a result, MPI usage tends to be much lower as compared to other types of MPI applications. The scene to be rendered is partitioned into a fixed number of pieces, which are distributed out by the master process to each processor participating in the computation. Each processor then renders its piece of the scene in parallel, independent of the other processors. Once a processor completes the rendering of its particular piece of the scene, it waits until the other processors have rendered their pieces of the scene, and then transmits its piece back to the master process. The process is repeated until all pieces of the scene have been rendered.

126.lammps is a classical molecular dynamics simulation code designed to run efficiently on parallel computers. It was developed at Sandia National Laboratories, a US Department of Energy facility, with funding from the DOE. LAMMPS divides 3D space into 3D sub-volumes, e.g., a $P = A \times B \times C$ grid of processors, where P is the total number of processors. It tries to make the sub-volumes as cubic as possible, since the volume of data exchanged is proportional to the surface of the sub-volume.

127.wrf2,147.l2wrf is a weather forecasting code based on the Weather Research and Forecasting (WRF) Model, which is a next-generation mesocale numerical weather prediction system designed to serve both operational forecasting and atmospheric research needs. The code is written in Fortran 90. WRF features multiple dynamical cores, a 3-dimensional variational (3DVAR) data assimilation system, and a software architecture allowing for computational parallelism and system extensibility. Multi-level parallelism support includes distributed memory (MPI), shared memory (OpenMP), and hybrid shared/distributed modes of execution. In the SPEC MPI2007 version of WRF, all OpenMP directives have been switched off. WRF version 2.0.2 is used in the 127.wrf2 benchmark version. WRF version 2.1.2 is used in the benchmark version, 147.l2wrf2.

128.GAPgeofem is a GeoFEM-based parallel finite-element code for transient thermal conduction with gap radiation and very heterogeneous material property. GeoFEM is an acronym for Geophysical Finite Element Methods, and it is a software used on the Japanese Earth Simulator system for the modeling of solid earth phenomena such as mantle-core convection, plate tectonics, and seismic wave propagation and their coupled phenomena. A backward Euler implicit time-marching scheme has been adopted. Linear equations are solved by parallel CG (conjugate gradient) iterative solvers with point Jacobi preconditioning.

129.tera_tf is a three dimensional Eulerian hydrodynamics application using a 2nd order Godunov-type scheme and a 3rd order remapping. It uses mostly point-to-point messages, and some reductions use non-blocking messages. The global domain is a cube, with N cells in each direction, which amounts to a total number of N^3 cells. To set up the problem, one needs to define the number of cells in each direction, and the number of blocks in each direction. Each block corresponds to an MPI task.

130.socorro is a modular, object oriented code for performing self-consistent electronic-structure calculations utilizing the Kohn-Sham formulation of density-functional theory. Calculations are performed using a plane wave basis and either norm-conserving pseudopotentials or projector augmented wave functions. Several exchange-correlation functionals are available for use including the local-density approximation (Perdew-Zunger or Perdew-Wang parameterizations of the Ceperley-Alder QMC correlation results) and the generalized-gradient approximation (PW91, PBE, and BLYP). Both Fourier-space and real-space projectors have been implemented, and a variety of methods are available for relaxing atom positions, optimizing cell parameters, and performing molecular dynamics calculations.

132.zeusmp2 is a computational fluid dynamics code developed at the Laboratory for Computational Astrophysics (NCSA, SDSC, University of Illinois at Urbana-Champaign, UC San Diego) for the simulation of astrophysical phenomena. The program solves the equations of ideal (non-resistive), non-relativistic, hydrodynamics and magnetohydrodynamics, including externally applied gravitational fields and self-gravity. The gas can be adiabatic or isothermal, and the thermal pressure is isotropic. Boundary conditions may be specified as reflecting, periodic, inflow, or outflow.

132.zeusmp2 is based on ZEUS-MP Version 2, which is a Fortran 90 rewrite of ZEUS-MP under development at UCSD (by John Hayes). It includes new physics models such as flux-limited radiation diffusion (FLD), and multispecies fluid advection is added to the physics set. ZEUS-MP divides the computational space into 3D tiles that are distributed across processors. The physical problem solved in SPEC MPI2007 is a 3D blastwave simulated with the presence of a uniform magnetic field along the x-direction. A Cartesian grid is used and the boundaries are "outflow."

137.lu has a rich ancestry in benchmarking. Its immediate predecessor is the LU benchmark in NPB3.2-MPI, part of the NAS Parallel Benchmark suite. It is sometimes referred to as APPLU (a version of which was 173.applu in CPU2000) or NAS-LU. The NAS-LU code is a simplified compressible Navier-Stokes equation solver. It does not perform an LU factorization, but instead implements a symmetric successive over-relaxation (SSOR) numerical scheme to solve a regular-sparse, block lower and upper triangular system.

The code computes the solution of five coupled non-linear PDE's, on a 3-dimensional logically structured grid, using an implicit pseudo-time marching scheme, based on two-factor approximate factorization of the sparse Jacobian matrix. This scheme is functionally equivalent to a nonlinear block SSOR iterative scheme with lexicographic ordering. Spatial discretization of the differential operators are based on a second-order accurate finite volume scheme. It insists on the strict lexicographic ordering during the solution of the regular sparse lower and upper triangular matrices. As a result, the degree of exploitable parallelism during this phase is limited to $O(N^2)$ as opposed to $O(N^3)$ in other phases and its spatial distribution is non-homogenous. This fact also creates challenges during the loop re-ordering to enhance the cache locality.

Related Entries

▶Benchmarks
▶HPC Challenge Benchmark
▶NAS Parallel Benchmarks
▶Perfect Benchmarks

Bibliographic Notes and Further Reading

There are numerous efforts to create benchmarks for different purposes. One of the early application benchmarks are the so-called "Perfect Club Benchmarks"[6], an effort that among others initiated the SPEC High Performance Group (HPG) activities[9]. The goal of SPEC HPG is to create application benchmarks to measure the performance of High Performance Computers. There are also other efforts that share this goal. Often such a collection is assembled during a procurement process. However, it normally is not used outside this specific process, nor does such a collection claim to be representative for a wider community. Two of the collections that are in wider use are the NAS Parallel Benchmarks [5] and the HPC Challenge benchmark [8]. The NAS Parallel Benchmarks (NPB) are a small set of programs designed to help evaluate the performance of parallel supercomputers. The benchmarks, which are derived from computational fluid dynamics (CFD) applications, consist of five kernels and three pseudo-applications. HPCC consists of synthetic kernels measuring different aspects of a parallel system, like CPU, memory subsystem, and interconnect.

Two other benchmarks that consist of applications are the ASCI-benchmarks used in the procurement process of various ASCI-machines. ASCI-Purple [1] consists of nine benchmarks and three stress tests. Its last update was in 2003. The ASCI-Sequoia benchmark [2] is the successor, it consists of 17 applications and synthetic benchmarks, but only seven codes are MPI parallel. A similar collection is the DEISA benchmark suite [7]. It contains 14 codes, but for licensing reasons, three of the benchmarks must be obtained directly from the code authors and placed in the appropriate location within the benchmarking framework.

There are also a number of publications with more details about the SPEC HPG benchmarks. Details of SPEC HPC2002 are available in [10]. Characteristics of the SPEC benchmark suite OMP2001 are described by Saito et al. [14] and Müller et. al [12]. Aslot et al. [3] have presented the benchmark suite. Aslot et al.[4] and Iwashita et al.[11] have described performance characteristics of the benchmark suite. The SPEC High Performance Group published a more detailed description of MPI2007 in [13]. Some performance characteristics are depicted in [15].

Bibliography

1. ASCI-Purple home page (2003) https://asc.llnl.gov/computing_resources/purple/archive/benchmarks
2. ASCI-Sequoia home page. https://asc.llnl.gov/sequoia/benchmarks.
3. Aslot V, Domeika M, Eigenmann R, Gaertner G, Jones WB, Parady B (2001) SPEComp: a new benchmark suite for measuring parallel computer performance. In: Eigenmann R, Voss MJ (eds) WOMPAT'01: workshop on openmp applications and tools. LNCS, vol 2104. Springer, Heidelberg, pp 1–10
4. Aslot V, Eigenmann R (2001) Performance characteristics of the SPEC OMP2001 benchmarks. In: 3rd European workshop on OpenMP, EWOMP'01, Barcelona, Spain, September 2001
5. Bailey D, Harris T, Saphir W, van der Wijngaart R, Woo A, Yarrow M (1995) The NAS parallel benchmarks 2.0. Technical report NAS-95-020, NASA Ames Research Center, Moffett Field, CA. http://www.nas.nasa.gov/Software/NPB
6. Berry M, Chen D, Koss P, Kuck D, Lo S, Pang Y, Pointer, Rolo R, Sameh A, Clementi E, Chin S, Schneider D, Fox G, Messina P, Walker D, Hsiung C, Schwarzmeier J, Lue K, Orszag S, Seidl F, Johnson O, Goodrum R, Martin J (1989) The perfect club benchmarks: effective performance evaluation of supercomputers. Int J High Perform Comp Appl 3(3):5–40
7. DEISA benchmark suite home page. http://www.deisa.eu/science/benchmarking
8. Dongarra J, Luszczek P (2005) Introduction to the hpcchallenge benchmark suite. ICL technical report ICL-UT-05-01, ICL 2005
9. Eigenmann R, Hassanzadeh S (1996) Benchmarking with real industrial applications: the SPEC high-performance group. IEEE Comp Sci & Eng 3(1):18–23
10. Eigenmann R, Gaertner G, Jones W (2002) SPEC HPC2002: the next high-performance computer benchmark. In: Lecture notes in computer science, vol 2327. Springer, Heidelberg, pp 7–10
11. Iwashita H, Yamanaka E, Sueyasu N, van Waveren M, Miura K (2001) The SPEC OMP 2001 benchmark on the Fujitsu PRIMEPOWER system. In: 3rd European workshop on OpenMP, EWOMP'01, Barcelona, Spain, September 2001
12. Müller MS, Kalyanasundaram K, Gaertner G, Jones W, Eigenmann R, Lieberman R, van Waveren M, Whitney B (2004) SPEC HPG benchmarks for high performance systems. Int J High Perform Comp Netw 1(4):162–170
13. Müuller MS, van Waveren M, Lieberman R, Whitney B, Saito H, Kumaran K, Baron J, Brantley WC, Parrott C, Elken T, Feng H, Ponder C (2010) SPEC MPI2007 – an application benchmark suite for parallel systems using MPI. Concurrency Computat: Pract Exper 22(2):191–205
14. Saito H, Gaertner G, Jones W, Eigenmann R, Iwashita H, Lieberman R, van Waveren M, Whitney B (2002) Large system performance of SPEC OMP2001 benchmarks. In: Zima HP, Joe K, Sata M, Seo Y, Shimasaki M (eds) High performance computing, 4th international symposium, ISHPC 2002. Lecture notes in computer science, vol 2327. Springer, Heidelberg, pp 370–379
15. Szebenyi Z, Wylie BJN, Wolf F (2008) SCALASCA parallel performance analyses of SPEC MPI2007 applications. In: Proceedings of the 1st SPEC international performance evaluation workshop (SIPEW). LNCS, vol 5119. Springer, Heidelberg, pp 99–123

SPEC HPC2002

▶SPEC Benchmarks

SPEC HPC96

▶SPEC Benchmarks

SPEC MPI2007

▶SPEC Benchmarks

SPEC OMP2001

▶SPEC Benchmarks

Special-Purpose Machines

▶Anton, a Special-Purpose Molecular Simulation Machine
▶GRAPE
▶JANUS FPGA-Based Machine
▶QCD apeNEXT Machines
▶QCDSP and QCDOC Computers

Speculation

▶Speculative Parallelization of Loops
▶Speculation, Thread-Level
▶Transactional Memory

Speculation, Thread-Level

Josep Torrellas
University of Illinois at Urbana-Champaign, Urbana, IL, USA

Synonyms

Speculative multithreading (SM); Speculative parallelization; Speculative run-time parallelization; Speculative threading; Speculative thread-level parallelization; Thread-level data speculation (TLDS); Thread level speculation (TLS) parallelization; TLS

Definition

Thread-Level Speculation (TLS) refers to an environment where execution threads operate speculatively, performing potentially unsafe operations, and temporarily buffering the state they generate in a buffer or cache. At a certain point, the operations of a thread are declared to be correct or incorrect. If they are correct, the thread commits, merging the state it generated with the correct state of the program; if they are incorrect, the thread is squashed and typically restarted from its beginning. The term TLS is most often associated to a scenario where the purpose is to execute a sequential application in parallel. In this case, the compiler or the hardware breaks down the application into speculative threads that execute in parallel. However, strictly speaking, TLS can be applied to any environment where threads are executed speculatively and can be squashed and restarted.

Discussion

Basic Concepts in Thread-Level Speculation

In its most common use, Thread-Level Speculation (TLS) consists of extracting units of work (i.e., tasks) from a sequential application and executing them on different threads in parallel, hoping not to violate sequential semantics. The control flow in the sequential code imposes a relative ordering between the tasks, which is expressed in terms of predecessor and successor tasks. The sequential code also induces a data dependence relation on the memory accesses issued by the different tasks that parallel execution cannot violate.

A task is *Speculative* when it may perform or may have performed operations that violate data or control dependences with its predecessor tasks. Otherwise, the task is nonspeculative. The memory accesses issued by speculative tasks are called speculative memory accesses.

When a nonspeculative task finishes execution, it is ready to *Commit*. The role of commit is to inform the rest of the system that the data generated by the task is now part of the safe, nonspeculative program state. Among other operations, committing always involves passing the *Commit Token* to the immediate successor task. This is because maintaining correct sequential semantics in the parallel execution requires that tasks commit in order from predecessor to successor. If a task reaches its end and is still speculative, it cannot commit until it acquires nonspeculative status and all its predecessors have committed.

Figure 1 shows an example of several tasks running on four processors. In this example, when task T3 executing on processor 4 finishes the execution, it cannot commit until its predecessor tasks T0, T1, and T2 also finish and commit. In the meantime, depending on

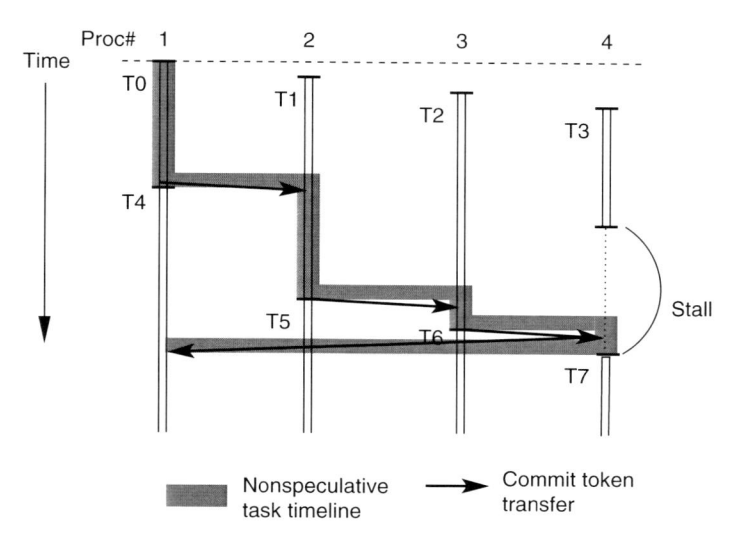

Speculation, Thread-Level. Fig. 1 A set of tasks executing on four processors. The figure shows the nonspeculative task timeline and the transfer of the commit token

the hardware support, processor 4 may have to stall or may be able to start executing speculative task T7. The example also shows how the nonspeculative task status changes as tasks finish and commit, and the passing of the commit token.

Memory accesses issued by a speculative task must be handled carefully. Stores generate *Speculative Versions* of data that cannot simply be merged with the nonspeculative state of the program. The reason is that they may be incorrect. Consequently, these versions are stored in a *Speculative Buffer* local to the processor running the task – e.g., the first-level cache. Only when the task becomes nonspeculative are its versions safe.

Loads issued by a speculative task try to find the requested datum in the local speculative buffer. If they miss, they fetch the correct version from the memory subsystem, i.e., the closest predecessor version from the speculative buffers of other tasks. If no such version exists, they fetch the datum from memory.

As tasks execute in parallel, the system must identify any violations of cross-task data dependences. Typically, this is done with special hardware or software support that tracks, for each individual task, the data that the task wrote and the data that the task read without first writing it. A data-dependence violation is flagged when a task modifies a datum that has been read earlier by a successor task. At this point, the consumer task is *squashed* and all the data versions that it has produced are discarded. Then, the task is re-executed.

Figure 2 shows an example of a data-dependence violation. In the example, each iteration of a loop is a task. Each iteration issues two accesses to an array, through an un-analyzable subscripted subscript. At run-time, iteration J writes A[5] after its successor iteration J+2 reads A[5]. This is a Read After Write (RAW) dependence that gets violated due to the parallel execution. Consequently, iteration J+2 is squashed and restarted. Ordinarily, all the successor tasks of iteration J+2 are also squashed at this time because they may have consumed versions generated by the squashed task. While it is possible to selectively squash only tasks that used incorrect data, it would involve extra complexity. Finally, as iteration J+2 re-executes, it will re-read A[5]. However, at this time, the value read will be the version generated by iteration J.

Note that WAR and WAW dependence violations do not need to induce task squashes. The successor task has prematurely written the datum, but the datum remains buffered in its speculative buffer. A subsequent read from a predecessor task (in a WAR violation) will get a correct version, while a subsequent write from a predecessor task (in a WAW violation) will generate a version that will be merged with main memory before the one from the successor task.

```
for (i=0; i<N; i++) {
    ... = A[L[i]] + ...
    :
    :
    A[K[i]] = ...
}
```

Iteration J   Iteration J+1   Iteration J+2
... = A[4] + ... = A[2] + ... = A[5] + ...
                          RAW violation
   :   :   :
A[5] = ...   A[2] = ...   A[6] = ...

Speculation, Thread-Level. Fig. 2 Example of a data-dependence violation

However, many proposed TLS schemes, to reduce hardware complexity, induce squashes in a variety of situations. For instance, if the system has no support to keep different versions of the same datum in different speculative buffers in the machine, cross-task WAR and WAW dependence violations induce squashes. Moreover, if the system only tracks accesses on a per-line basis, it cannot disambiguate accesses to different words in the same memory line. In this case, false sharing of a cache line by two different processors can appear as a data-dependence violation and also trigger a squash.

Finally, while TLS can be applied to various code structures, it is most often applied to loops. In this case, tasks are typically formed by a set of consecutive iterations.

The rest of this article is organized as follows: First, the article briefly classifies TLS schemes. Then, it describes the two major problems that any TLS scheme has to solve, namely, buffering and managing speculative state, and detecting and handling dependence violations. Next, it describes the initial efforts in TLS, other uses of TLS, and machines that use TLS.

Classification of Thread-Level Speculation Schemes

There have been many proposals of TLS schemes. They can be broadly classified depending on the emphasis on hardware versus software, and the type of target machine.

The majority of the proposed schemes use hardware support to detect cross-task dependence violations that result in task squashes (e.g., [1, 4, 6, 8, 11, 12, 14, 16, 18, 20, 23, 27, 28, 31, 32, 36]). Typically, this is attained by using the hardware cache coherence protocol, which sends coherence messages between the caches when multiple processors access the same memory line. Among all these hardware-based schemes, the majority rely on a compiler or a software layer to identify and prepare the tasks that should be executed in parallel. Consequently, there have been several proposals for TLS compilers (e.g., [9, 19, 33, 34]). Very few schemes rely on the hardware to identify the tasks (e.g., [1]).

Several schemes, especially in the early stages of TLS research, proposed software-only approaches to TLS (e.g., [7, 13, 25, 26]). In this case, the compiler typically generates code that causes each task to keep shadow locations and, after the parallel execution, checks if multiple tasks have updated a common location. If they have, the original state is restored.

Most proposed TLS schemes target small shared-memory machines of about two to eight processors (e.g., [14, 18, 27, 29]). It is in this range of parallelism that TLS is most cost effective. Some TLS proposals have focused on smaller machines and have extended a superscalar core with some hardware units that execute threads speculatively [1, 20]. Finally, some TLS proposals have targeted scalable multiprocessors [4, 23, 28]. This is a more challenging environment, given the longer communication latencies involved. It requires applications that have significant parallelism that cannot be analyzed statically by the compiler.

Buffering and Managing Speculative State

The state produced by speculative tasks is unsafe, since such tasks may be squashed. Therefore, any TLS scheme must be able to identify such state and, when necessary, separate it from the rest of the memory state. For this, TLS systems use structures, such as caches [4, 6, 12, 18, 28], and special buffers [8, 14, 23, 32], or undo logs [7, 11, 36]. This section outlines the challenges in buffering and managing speculative state. A more detailed analysis and a taxonomy is presented by Garzaran et al. [10].

Multiple Versions of the Same Variable in the System

Every time that a task writes for the first time to a variable, a new version of the variable appears in the system. Thus, two speculative tasks running on different processors may create two different versions of the same variable [4, 12]. These versions need to be buffered separately, and special actions may need to be taken so that a reader task can find the correct version out of the several coexisting in the system. Such a version will be the version created by the producer task that is the closest predecessor of the reader task.

A task has at most a single version of any given variable, even if it writes to the variable multiple times. The reason is that, on a dependence violation, the whole task is undone. Therefore, there is no need to keep intermediate values of the variable.

Multiple Speculative Tasks per Processor

When a processor finishes executing a task, the task may still be speculative. If the TLS buffering support is such that the processor can only hold state from a single speculative task, the processor stalls until the task commits. However, to better tolerate task load imbalance, the local buffer may have been designed to buffer state from several speculative tasks, enabling the processor to execute another speculative task. In this case, the state of each task must be tagged with the ID of the task.

Multiple Versions of the Same Variable in a Single Processor

When a processor buffers state from multiple speculative tasks, it is possible that two such tasks create two versions of the same variable. This occurs in load-imbalanced applications that exhibit private data patterns (i.e., WAW dependences between tasks). In this case, the buffer will have to hold multiple versions of the same variable. Each version will be tagged with a different task ID. This support introduces complication to the buffer or cache. Indeed, on an external request, extra comparisons will need to be done if the cache has two versions of the same variable.

Merging of Task State

The state produced by speculative tasks is typically merged with main memory at task commit time; however, it can instead be merged as it is being generated. The first approach is called *Architectural Main Memory* (*AMM*) or *Lazy Version Management*; the second one is called *Future Main Memory (FMM)* or *Eager Version Management*. These schemes differ on whether the main memory contains only safe data (AMM) or it can also contain speculative data (FMM).

In AMM systems, all speculative versions remain in caches or buffers that are kept separate from the coherent memory state. Only when a task becomes nonspeculative can its buffered state be merged with main memory. In a straightforward implementation, when a task commits, all the buffered dirty cache lines are merged with main memory, either by writing back the lines to memory [4] or by requesting ownership for them to obtain coherence with main memory [28].

In FMM systems, versions from speculative tasks are merged with the coherent memory when they are generated. However, to enable recovery from task squashes, when a task generates a speculative version of a variable, the previous version of the variable is saved in a log. Note that, in both approaches, the coherent memory state can temporarily reside in caches, which function in their traditional role of extensions of main memory.

Detecting and Handling Dependence Violations

Basic Concepts

The second aspect of TLS involves detecting and handling dependence violations. Most TLS proposals focus on data dependences, rather than control dependences. To detect (cross-task) data-dependence violations, most TLS schemes use the same approach. Specifically, when a speculative task writes a datum, the hardware sets a Speculative Write bit associated with the datum in the cache; when a speculative task reads a datum before it writes to it (an event called *Exposed Read*), the hardware sets an Exposed Read bit. Depending on the TLS scheme supported, these accesses also cause a tag associated with the datum to be set to the ID of the task.

In addition, when a task writes a datum, the cache coherence protocol transaction that sends invalidations to other caches checks these bits. If a successor task has its Exposed Read bit set for the datum, the successor task has prematurely read the datum (i.e., this is a RAW dependence violation), and is squashed [18].

If the Speculative Write and Exposed Read bits are kept on a per-word basis, only dependences on the same word can cause squashes. However, keeping and maintaining such bits on a per-word basis in caches, network messages, and perhaps directory modules is costly in hardware. Moreover, it does not come naturally to the coherence protocol of multiprocessors, which operate at the granularity of memory lines.

Keeping these bits on a per-line basis is cheaper and compatible with mainstream cache coherence protocols. However, the hardware cannot then disambiguate accesses at word level. Furthermore, it cannot combine different versions of a line that have been updated in different words. Consequently, cross-task RAW and WAW violations, on both the same word and different words of a line (i.e., false sharing), cause squashes.

Task squash is a very costly operation. The cost is threefold: overhead of the squash operation itself, loss of whatever correct work has already been performed by the offending task and its successors, and cache misses in the offending task and its successors needed to reload state when restarting. The latter overhead appears because, as part of the squash operation, the speculative state in the cache is invalidated. Figure 3a shows an example of a RAW violation across tasks i and $i+j+1$. The consumer task and its successors are squashed.

Techniques to Avoid Squashes

Since squashes are so expensive, there are techniques to avoid them. If the compiler can conclude that a certain pair of accesses will frequently cause a data-dependence violation, it can statically insert a synchronization operation that forces the correct task ordering at runtime.

Alternatively, the machine can have hardware support that records, at runtime, where dependence violations occur. Such hardware may record the program counter of the read or writes involved, or the address of the memory location being accessed. Based on this information, when these program counters are reached or the memory location is accessed, the hardware can try one of several techniques to avoid the violation. This section outlines some of the techniques that can be used. A more complete description of the choices is presented by Cintra and Torrellas [5]. Without loss of generality, a RAW violation is assumed.

Based on past history, the predictor may predict that the pair of conflicting accesses are engaged in false sharing. In this case, it can simply allow the read to proceed and then the subsequent write to execute silently, without sending invalidations. Later, before the

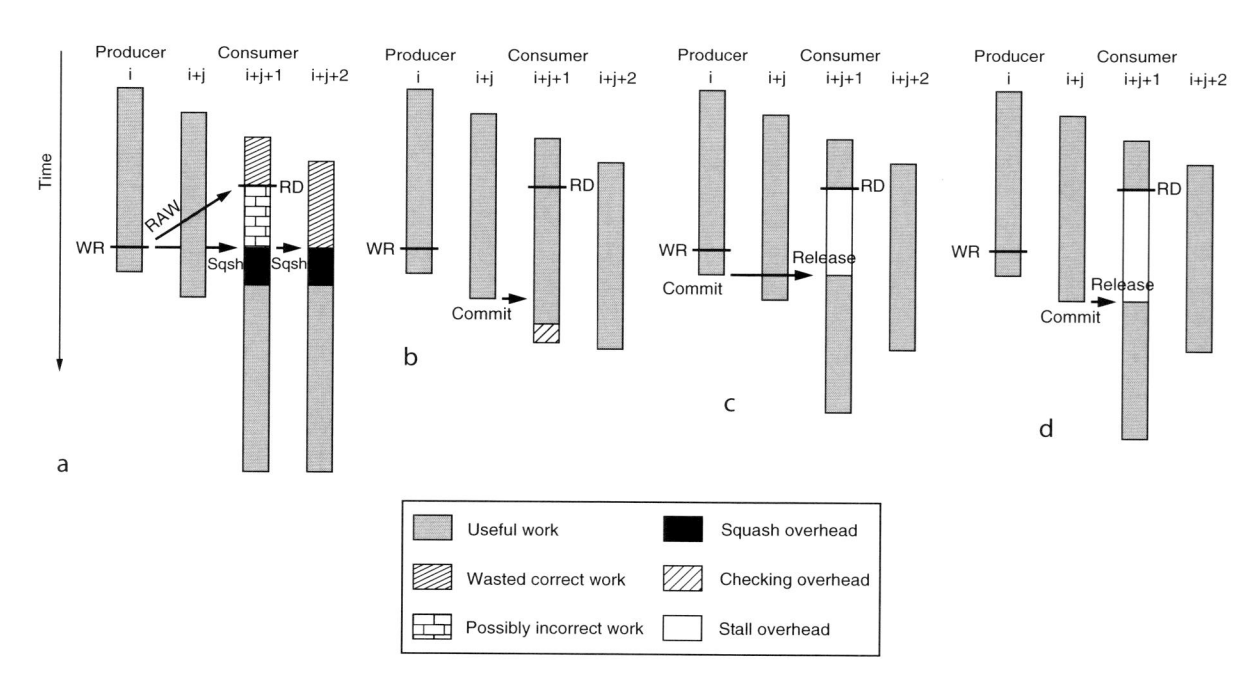

Speculation, Thread-Level. Fig. 3 RAW data-dependence violation that results in a squash (**a**) or that does not cause a squash due to false sharing or value prediction (**b**), or consumer stall (**c** and **d**)

consumer task is allowed to commit, it is necessary to check whether the sections of the line read by the consumer overlap with the sections of the line written by the producer. This can be easily done if the caches have per-word access bits. If there is no overlap, it was false sharing and the squash is avoided. Figure 3b shows the resulting time line.

When there is a true data dependence between tasks, a squash can be avoided with effective use of value prediction. Specifically, the predictor can predict the value that the producer will produce, speculatively provide it to the consumer's read, and let the consumer proceed. Again, before the consumer is allowed to commit, it is necessary to check that the value provided was correct. The timeline is also shown in Fig. 3b.

In cases where the predictor is unable to predict the value, it can avoid the squash by stalling the consumer task at the time of the read. This case can use two possible approaches. An aggressive approach is to release the consumer task and let it read the current value as soon as the predicted producer task commits. The time line is shown in Fig. 3c. In this case, if an intervening task between the first producer and the consumer later writes the line, the consumer will be squashed. A more conservative approach is not to release the consumer task until it becomes nonspeculative. In this case, the presence of multiple predecessor writers will not squash the consumer. The time line is shown in Fig. 3d.

Initial Efforts in Thread-Level Speculation

An early proposal for hardware support for a form of speculative parallelization was made by Knight [16] in the context of functional languages. Later, the Multiscalar processor [27] was the first proposal to use a form of TLS within a single-chip multithreaded architecture. A software-only form of TLS was proposed in the LRPD test [25]. Early proposals of hardware-based TLS include the work of several authors [14, 17, 21, 29, 35].

Other Uses of Thread-Level Speculation

TLS concepts have been used in environments that have goals other than trying to parallelize sequential programs. For example, they have been used to speed up explicitly parallel programs through Speculative Synchronization [22], or for parallel program debugging [24] or program monitoring [37]. Similar concepts to TLS have been used in systems supporting hardware transactional memory [15] and continuous atomic-block operation [30].

Machines that Use Thread-Level Speculation

Several machines built by computer manufacturers have hardware support for some form of TLS – although the specific implementation details are typically not disclosed. Such machines include systems designed for Java applications such as Sun Microsystems' MAJC chip [31] and Azul Systems' Vega processor [2]. The most high-profile system with hardware support for speculative threads is Sun Microsystems' ROCK processor [3]. Other manufacturers are rumored to be developing prototypes with similar hardware.

Bibliography

1. Akkary H, Driscoll M (1998) A dynamic multithreading processor. In: International symposium on microarchitecture, Dallas, November 1998
2. Azul Systems. Vega 3 Processor. http://www.azulsystems.com/products/vega/processor
3. Chaudhry S, Cypher R, Ekman M, Karlsson M, Landin A, Yip S, Zeffer H, Tremblay M (2009) Simultaneous speculative threading: a novel pipeline architecture implemented in Sun's ROCK Processor. In: International symposium on computer architecture, Austin, June 2009
4. Cintra M, Martínez JF, Torrellas J (2000) Architectural support for scalable speculative parallelization in shared-memory multiprocessors. In: International symposium on computer architecture, Vancouver, June 2000, pp 13–24
5. Cintra M, Torrellas J (2002) Eliminating squashes through learning cross-thread violations in speculative parallelization for multiprocessors. In: Proceedings of the 8th High-Performance computer architecture conference, Boston, Feb 2002
6. Figueiredo R, Fortes J (2001) Hardware support for extracting coarse-grain speculative parallelism in distributed shared-memory multiprocesors. In: Proceedings of the international conference on parallel processing, Valencia, Spain, September 2001
7. Frank M, Lee W, Amarasinghe S (2001) A software framework for supporting general purpose applications on raw computation fabrics. Technical report, MIT/LCS Technical Memo MIT-LCS-TM-619, July 2001
8. Franklin M, Sohi G (1996) ARB: a hardware mechanism for dynamic reordering of memory references. IEEE Trans Comput 45(5):552–571

9. Garcia C, Madriles C, Sanchez J, Marcuello P, Gonzalez A, Tullsen D (2005) Mitosis compiler: An infrastructure for speculative threading based on pre-computation slices. In: Conference on programming language design and implementation, Chicago, Illinois, June 2005
10. Garzarán M, Prvulovic M, Llabería J, Viñals V, Rauchwerger L, Torrellas J (2005) Tradeoffs in buffering speculative memory state for thread-level speculation in multiprocessors. ACM Trans Archit Code Optim
11. Garzaran MJ, Prvulovic M, Llabería JM, Viñals V, Rauchwerger L, Torrellas J (2003) Using software logging to support multiversion buffering in thread-level speculation. In: International conference on parallel architectures and compilation techniques, New Orleans, Sept 2003
12. Gopal S, Vijaykumar T, Smith J, Sohi G (1998) Speculative versioning cache. In: International symposium on high-performance computer architecture, Las Vegas, Feb 1998
13. Gupta M, Nim R (1998) Techniques for speculative run-time parallelization of loops. In: Proceedings of supercomputing 1998, ACM Press, Melbourne, Australia, Nov 1998
14. Hammond L, Willey M, Olukotun K (1998) Data speculation support for a chip multiprocessor. In: International conference on architectural support for programming languages and operating systems, San Jose, California, Oct 1998, pp 58–69
15. Herlihy M, Moss E (1993) Transactional memory: architectural support for lock-free data structures. In: International symposium on computer architecture, IEEE Computer Society Press, San Diego, May 1993
16. Knight T (1986) An architecture for mostly functional languages. In: ACM lisp and functional programming conference, ACM Press, New York, Aug 1986, pp 500–519
17. Krishnan V, Torrellas J (1998) Hardware and software support for speculative execution of sequential binaries on a chip-multiprocessor. In: International conference on supercomputing, Melbourne, Australia, July 1998
18. Krishnan V, Torrellas J (1999) A chip-multiprocessor architecture with speculative multithreading. IEEE Trans Comput 48(9):866–880
19. Liu W, Tuck J, Ceze L, Ahn W, Strauss K, Renau J, Torrellas J (2006) POSH: A TLS compiler that exploits program structure. In: International symposium on principles and practice of parallel programming, San Diego, Mar 2006
20. Marcuello P, Gonzalez A (1999) Clustered speculative multithreaded processors. In: International conference on supercomputing, Rhodes, Island, June 1999, pp 365–372
21. Marcuello P, Gonzalez A, Tubella J (1998) Speculative multithreaded processors. In: International conference on supercomputing, ACM, Melbourne, Australia, July 1998
22. Martinez J, Torrellas J (2002) Speculative synchronization: applying thread-level speculation to explicitly parallel applications. In: International conference on architectural support for programming languages and operating systems, San Jose, Oct 2002
23. Prvulovic M, Garzaran MJ, Rauchwerger L, Torrellas J (2001) Removing architectural bottlenecks to the scalability of speculative parallelization. In: Proceedings of the 28th international symposium on computer architecture (ISCA'01), New York, June 2001, pp 204–215
24. Prvulovic M, Torrellas J (2003) ReEnact: using thread-level speculation to debug data races in multithreaded codes. In: International symposium on computer architecture, San Diego, June 2003
25. Rauchwerger L, Padua D (1995) The LRPD test: speculative run-time parallelization of loops with privatization and reduction parallelization. In: Conference on programming language design and implementation, La Jolla, California, June 1995
26. Rundberg P, Stenstrom P (2000) Low-cost thread-level data dependence speculation on multiprocessors. In: Fourth workshop on multithreaded execution, architecture and compilation, Monterrey, Dec 2000
27. Sohi G, Breach S, Vijaykumar T (1995) Multiscalar processors. In: International Symposium on computer architecture, ACM Press, New York, June 1995
28. Steffan G, Colohan C, Zhai A, Mowry T (2000) A scalable approach to thread-level speculation. In: Proceedings of the 27th Annual International symposium on computer architecture, Vancouver, June 2000, pp 1–12
29. Steffan G, Mowry TC (1998) The potential for using thread-level data speculation to facilitate automatic parallelization. In: International symposium on high-performance computer architecture, Las Vegas, Feb 1998
30. Torrellas J, Ceze L, Tuck J, Cascaval C, Montesinos P, Ahn W, Prvulovic M (2009) The bulk multicore architecture for improved programmability. Communications of the ACM, New York
31. Tremblay M (1999) MAJC: microprocessor architecture for java computing. Hot Chips, Palo Alto, Aug 1999
32. Tsai J, Huang J, Amlo C, Lilja D, Yew P (1999) The superthreaded processor architecture. IEEE Trans Comput 48(9):881–902
33. Vijaykumar T, Sohi G (1998) Task selection for a multiscalar processor. In: International symposium on microarchitecture, Dallas, Nov 1998, pp 81–92
34. Zhai A, Colohan C, Steffan G, Mowry T (2002) Compiler optimization of scalar value communication between speculative threads. In: International conference on architectural support for programming languages and operating systems, San Jose, Oct 2002
35. Zhang Y, Rauchwerger L, Torrellas J (1998) Hardware for speculative run-time parallelization in distributed shared-memory multiprocessors. In: Proceedings of the 4th International symposium on high-performance computer architecture (HPCA), Phoenix, Feb 1998, pp 162–174
36. Zhang Y, Rauchwerger L, Torrellas J (1999) Hardware for speculative parallelization of partially-parallel loops in DSM multiprocessors. In: Proceedings of the 5th international symposium on high-performance computer architecture, Orlando, Jan 1999, pp 135–139
37. Zhou P, Qin F, Liu W, Zhou Y, Torrellas (2004) iWatcher: efficient architectural support for software debugging. In: International symposium on computer architecture, IEEE Computer society, München, June 2004

Speculative Multithreading (SM)

▶Speculation, Thread-Level

Speculative Parallelization

▶Speculation, Thread-Level
▶Speculative Parallelization of Loops

Speculative Parallelization of Loops

Lawrence Rauchwerger
Texas A&M University, College Station, TX, USA

Synonyms

Optimistic loop parallelization; Parallelization; Speculative Parallelization; Speculative Run-Time Parallelization; Thread-level data speculation (TLDS); TLS

Definition

Speculative loop (thread) level parallelization is a compiler run-time technique that executes optimistically parallelized loops, verifies the correctness of their execution and, when necessary, backtracks to a safe state for possible re-execution. This technique includes a compiler (static) component for the transformation of the loop for speculative parallel execution as well as a run-time component which verifies correctness and re-executes when necessary.

Discussion

Introduction

The correctness of optimizing program transformations, such as loop parallelization, relies on compiler or programmer analysis of the code. Compiler-performed analysis is preferred because it is more productive and is not subject to human error. However, it usually involves a very complex symbolic analysis which often fails to produce an optimizing transformation. Sometimes the outcome of the code analysis depends on the input values of the considered program block or on computed values, neither of which are available during compilation. Manual code analysis relies on the use of a higher level of semantic analysis which is usually more powerful but not applicable if it depends on run-time computed or input values. To overcome this limitation, the analysis can be (partially) performed at run-time. Run-time analysis can succeed where static analysis fails because it has access to the actual values with which *the program symbolic expressions* are instantiated and thus can make aggressive, instance-specific optimization (e.g., loop parallelization) decisions.

There are essentially two ways of performing the run-time analysis that can (in)validate loop parallelization (and, in general any other optimization):

- Before executing the parallel version of a loop
- During execution of the parallel version of the loop

The analysis that is performed before loop execution can be of various degrees of complexity: from constant time to time proportional to the original loop computation. The parallel execution of a loop before run-time analysis is completed is called speculative (aka optimistic) execution. It represents a speculation because the outcome of the analysis may, in the end, invalidate the (optimistic) parallel execution of the loop (and its results). In this case the state before the speculation has to be restored and the loop is re-executed in a safe manner, e.g., sequentially. Figure 1 shows the global flowchart of the speculative parallelization process.

Fundamentals of Loop Parallelization

A loop can be executed in parallel, without synchronizations, if and only if the desired outcome of the loop does not depend upon the relative execution order of the data accesses across its iterations. This problem has been modeled with the help of data dependence analysis [1, 13, 19, 42, 48]. There are three possible types of dependences between two statements that access the same memory location: *flow* (read after write – RAW), *anti* (write after read – WAR), and *output* (write after write – WAW). Flow dependences express a fundamental relationship about the data flow in the program. Anti and output dependences, also known as memory-related

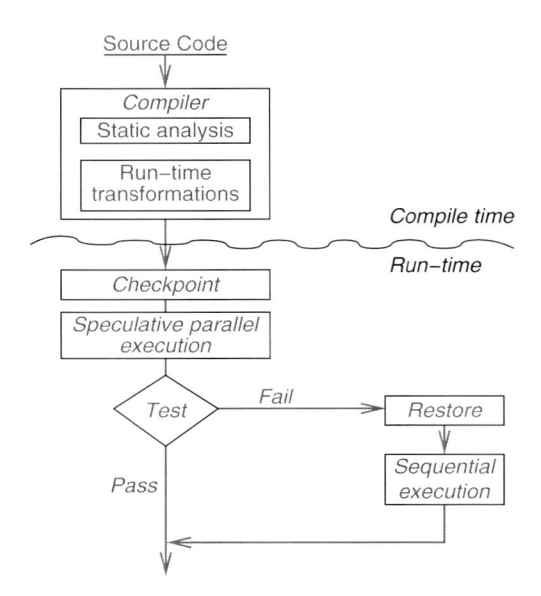

Speculative Parallelization of Loops. Fig. 1 Speculative run-time parallelization

dependences, are caused by the reuse of storage for program variables.

When flow data dependences exist between loop iterations, the loop cannot be executed in parallel because the original (sequential) semantics of the loop cannot be preserved. For example, the iterations of the loop in Fig. 2a must be executed in sequential order because iteration $i+1$ needs the value that is produced in iteration i, for $1 \leq i < n$. The simplest and most desired outcome of the data dependence analysis is when there are no anti, output, or flow dependences. In this case, all the iterations of the loop are independent and can be executed in any order, e.g., concurrently. Such loops are known as DOALL loops. In the absence of flow dependences, which are fundamental to a program's algorithms, the anti and/or output dependences can be removed through *privatization* (or *renaming*) [40], a very effective loop transformation.

Privatization creates, for each processor cooperating on the execution of the loop, private copies of the program variables that can give rise to anti-or output dependences (see, e.g., [2, 16, 17, 38, 39]). Figure 2b exemplifies a loop that can be executed in parallel after applying the privatization transformation: The anti-dependences between statement S2 of iteration i and statement S1 of iteration $i + 1$, for $1 \leq i < n/2$, are removed by privatizing the temporary variable tmp.

This transformation can be applied to a loop variable if it can be proven, statically or dynamically, that every read access to it (e.g., elements of array A) is preceded by a write access to the same variable within the same iteration. Of course, variables that are never written (read only) cannot generate any data dependence. Intuitively, variables are privatizable when they are used as workspace (e.g., temporary variables) *within* an iteration.

A semantically higher level transformation is the parallelization of *reduction* operations. Reductions are operations of the form $x = x \otimes exp$, where $\otimes$ is an associative operator and x does not occur in exp or anywhere else in the loop. A simple, but typical example of a reduction is statement S1 in Fig. 2c. The operator $\otimes$ is exemplified by the + operator, the access to the array $A(:)$ is a *read, modify, write* sequence, and the function performed by the loop is a prefix sum of the values stored in A. This type of reduction is sometimes called an *update* and occurs quite frequently in programs.

A reduction can be readily transformed into a parallel operation using, e.g., a recursive doubling algorithm [12, 15]. When the operator takes the form $x = x + exp$, the values taken by variable x can be accumulated in private storage followed by a global reduction operation. There are also other, less scalable methods that use unordered critical sections [7, 48]. When the operator is also *commutative*, its substitution with a parallel algorithm can be done with fewer restrictions (e.g., dynamic scheduling of DOALL loops can be employed).

Thus, the difficulty encountered by compilers in parallelizing loops with reductions arises not from transforming the loop for parallel execution but from correctly identifying and validating reduction patterns in loops. This problem has been handled at compile time mainly by syntactically pattern matching the loop statements with a template of a generic reduction, and then performing a data dependence analysis of the variable under scrutiny to guarantee that it is not used anywhere else in the loop except in the reduction statement and thus does not cause additional dependences [48].

Compiler Limitation and Run-time Parallelization

In essence, the parallelization of DO (for) loops depends on proving that their memory reference

```
do i=1, n                      do i = 1, n/2                   do i=1, n
   A(K(i)) = A(K(i)) + A(K(i–1))    S1:   tmp = A(2*i)               do j = 1, m
   if (A(K(i)) .eq. 0) then                A(2*i) = A(2*i–1)    S1:      A(j) = A(j) + exp()
       B(i) = A(L(i)                S2    A(2*i–1) = tmp              enddo
   endif                          enddo                         enddo
enddo
       a                              b                              c
```

Speculative Parallelization of Loops. Fig. 2 Examples of representative loops targeted by automatic parallelization

patterns do not carry data dependences or that there are legal transformations that can remove possible data dependences. The burden of proof relies on the static analysis performed by autoparallelizing compilers. However, there are many situations when this is not possible because either symbolic analysis is not powerful enough or the memory reference pattern is input or data dependent. The technique that can overcome such problems is run-time parallelization because, at run-time, all input values are known and the symbolic evaluation of complex expressions is vastly simplified. In this scenario, the compiler generates, conceptually at least, a parallel and a serial version of the loop as well code for the dynamic dependence analysis using the loop's memory references.

If the decision about the serial or parallel character of the loop is (and can be) made before its execution, then the results computed and written by the loop to memory can be considered to be always correct. Such a technique is called "inspector/executor" [31–33] because the memory references are first "inspected" and then executed in a safe manner, whether sequentially or concurrently. In this context, an "inspector" is obtained by extracting a loop slice that generates (and perhaps records) the relevant memory addresses which can then reveal possible loop-carried data dependences. It is important for such "inspectors" to be scalable and not to become serial bottlenecks. If no dependences are found, then the loop can be scheduled (and executed) as a DOALL, i.e., all its iterations can be executed concurrently. If dependences are found, then the "executor" of the loop has to enforce them using ordered synchronizations at the memory or iteration level such that sequential semantics is preserved. A frequently used solution [23, 24, 33] to this problem has been to first construct the loop dependence graph from the memory trace obtained by the inspector and then to use it to compute a parallel execution schedule. Finally, the loop is executed in parallel according to the schedule.

The computation of this execution schedule can also be interleaved with the executor [46]. If the reference pattern does not change within a larger scope than the considered loop, then the schedule can be reused, thus reducing the impact of its overhead. There have been several variations of this technique which were reported in [22].

If a loop is executed in parallel *before* its data dependences are uncovered, then it can cause out of order memory references which may lead to incorrect computation. Such an execution model is called *speculative execution*, also known as *optimistic execution*, because its performance is based on the the optimistic assumption that such dependences do in fact not materialize or are quite infrequent. To ensure that even when dependences may occur, the final computation produces sequentially equivalent results, the speculative execution model includes a *restart* from a safe (correct) state mechanism. Such a mechanism implies either saving state (checkpointing) before its speculative modification or writing into a temporary memory which has to be later merged (committed) into the global state of the program.

For example, the references to array A in the loop in Fig. 2a depend on some input values stored in array K and cannot be statically analyzed by the compiler. An inspector for this loop would analyze the contents of array K and decide whether the loop is parallel and then execute it accordingly. A speculative approach is to execute the loop in parallel while at the same time recording all the references to A. After the loop has ended, the memory trace is checked for data dependences and, if any are found, the results are discarded and the loop is re-executed sequentially or in some other safer mode. Alternatively, the memory references can be checked as they occur ("on-the-fly") and, if dependences are detected the execution can be aborted at that point, the program state repaired and the loop restarted in a safe manner.

There are advantages and disadvantages to using either of the run-time parallelization methods. In the "inspector/executor" approach, the inspector does not modify the program state and thus does not require a restart mechanism with its associated memory overhead. On the other hand, a speculative approach may need to discard its results and restart from a safe state. This implies the allocation of additional memory for checkpointing or buffering state. Inspectors always add to the critical path of the program because they have to be inserted serially before the parallelized loop. Speculative parallelization performs the needed inspection of the memory references *during* the parallel execution almost independently from the actual computation and thus can be almost overlapped with it (assuming available resources). On the other hand, the checkpoint or commit phase introduces some overhead which may add to the critical path. What is perhaps the most important feature of speculative parallelization is its general applicability, even when the memory reference pattern is dependent on the computation of the loop. For example, the code snippet in Fig. 3 shows that the reference to array *NUSED* is dependent on its value which in turn, may have been modified in a different iteration (because the indirection array *IHITS* is not known at compile time).

There are two ways to look at speculation: optimistically assuming that a loop is fully parallel and can be executed as a DOALL or, pessimistically, assuming that the loop has dependences and must be executed as a DOACROSS, i.e., with synchronizations. When a DOALL is expected, then the overhead of the data checking can be done once, after the speculative loop has finished. If, however, dependences are expected, then they need to be detected early so that the resulting incorrect computation can be minimized. Early detection means frequent memory reference checks, well before the speculative loop has finished. These speculative approaches are bridged (transformed into one another) through the variation of the frequency (granularity) of the memory reference checks from once per loop to once per reference.

A related, but different limitation of compilers is their inability to analyze and parallelize most while loops. The reason is twofold:

- The classical loop dependence analysis looks for dependences in a bounded iteration space. However, the upper bound of a while loop can only be conservatively established at compile time which results in overly restrictive decisions, possibly inhibiting parallelization.
- The fully parallel execution of a while loop without data dependences (e.g., do loops with possible premature exits) may not be limited to the original iteration space. Iterations may be executed beyond their sequential upper bound, i.e., "overshoot" and thus incorrectly modify the global state.

A possible solution is to use a speculative parallel execution framework which allows discarding any unnecessary work and its effects. Speculation can also be used to estimate an upper bound of the iteration space of while loops.

DOALL Speculative Parallelization: The LRPD Test

The optimistic version of speculative parallelization executes a loop in parallel and tests *subsequently* if any data dependences could have occurred. If this validation test fails, then the loop is re-executed in a safe manner, starting from a safe state, e.g., sequentially from a previous checkpoint. This approach, known as the *LRPD Test* (Lazy Reduction and Privatization Doall Test), [25, 27] is sketched in the next paragraph. To qualify more loops as parallel, *array privatization* and *reduction parallelization* can be speculatively applied and their validity tested after loop termination.

Consider a do loop for which the compiler cannot statically determine the access pattern of a shared array *A* (Fig. 4a). The compiler allocates the shadow arrays for

```
read (IHITS(:))
do k= 1, LST
    j = IHITS(1,k)
    if (NUSED(j).LE.1) then
        NUSED(j)=NUSED(j) −1
    endif
enddo
```

Speculative Parallelization of Loops. Fig. 3 A loop example where only speculative parallelization is possible: array indexes are computed during loop execution

```
do i=1, 5                doall i=1, 5
    z = A(K(i))              markread(K(i))
    if (B(i) .eq. .true.) then   z = A(K(i))
        A(L(i)) = z +C(i)         if (B(i) .eq. .true.) then
    endif                            markwrite(L(i))
enddo                                A(L(i)) = z +C(i)
                                 endif
        B(1:5) = (1 0 1 0 1)     enddoall
        K(1:5) = (1 2 3 4 1)
        L(1:5) = (2 2 4 4 2)
a                        b
```

PD test	Shadow arrays				tw	tm
	1	2	3	4		
A_w	0	1	0	1	3	2
A_r	1	1	1	1		
A_{np}	1	1	1	1		
$A_w(:) \wedge A_r(:)$	0	1	0	1		
$A_w(:) \wedge A_{np}(:)$	0	1	0	1		

c

Speculative Parallelization of Loops. Fig. 4 Do loop (**a**) transformed for speculative execution, (**b**) the `markwrite` and `markread` operations update the appropriate shadow arrays, (**c**) shadow arrays after loop execution. In this example, the test fails

marking the write accesses, A_w, and the read accesses, A_r, and an array A_{rp}, for flagging non-privatizable elements. The loop is augmented with code (Fig. 4b) that during the speculative execution will mark the shadow arrays every time A is referenced (based on specific rules). The result of the marking can be seen in Fig. 4c. The first time an element of A is written during an iteration, the corresponding element in the write shadow array A_w is marked. If, during any iteration, an element in A is read, but never written, then the corresponding element in the read shadow array A_r is marked. Another shadow array A_{np} is used to flag the elements of A that *cannot* be privatized: An element in A_{np} is marked if, in any iteration, the corresponding element in A has been written only after it has been read.

A *post-execution analysis*, illustrated in Fig. 4c, determines whether there were any cross-iteration dependencies between statements referencing A as follows. If $any(A_w(:) \wedge A_r(:))$ is true, (*any* returns the "OR" of its vector operand's elements, i.e., $any(v(1 : n)) = (v(1) \vee v(2) \vee \ldots \vee v(n))$) then there is at least one flow- or anti-dependence that was not removed by privatizing A (some element is read and written in different iterations). If $any(A_{np}(:))$ is true, then A is not privatizable (some element is read before being written in an iteration). If tw, the total number of writes marked during the parallel execution, is not equal to tm, the total number of marks computed after the parallel execution, then there is at least one output dependence (some element is overwritten); however, if A is privatizable (i.e., if $any(A_{np}(:))$ is false), then these dependencies were removed by privatizing A.

The addition of an A_{rx} field to the shadow structure and some simple marking logic can extend the previous algorithm to validate parallel reductions at run-time [25, 27].

For this speculative technique two *safe restart* methods can be used [21, 25].

- The compiler either generates a checkpoint of all global, modified variables before the starting the speculative loop or does it, on demand, before a variable is modified the first time.

- The compiler generates code to allocate temporary, private storage for the global, modified variables. If the test fails the private storage is de-allocated, else its contents are merged into the global storage.

The data structures used for the checkpointing and shadowing can be appropriately chosen depending on the dense (e.g., arrays) or sparse reference characteristics of the loop (e.g., hash tables, linked lists) [44].

Compiler analysis can reduce the overhead of speculation by establishing equivalence classes (in the data dependence sense) of the interesting memory references and then tracking only one representative per class [44].

The speculative LRPD test has been later modified into the R-LRPD (Recursive LRPD) test [6] to improve its performance for loops with dependences. When a speculative parallel loop is block scheduled, the R-LRPD test can detect the iteration that is the source of the earliest dependence and thus validate the execution of the loop up to it. The remainder of the loop is then speculatively re-executed in a recursive manner until all work has finished, thus guaranteeing, at worst, a serial time complexity.

DOACROSS Speculative Parallelization

If dependences are expected, then speculation should be verified frequently, so that incorrect iterations can be restarted as soon as violations have occurred, thus reducing the overall speculation overhead. Approaches that track dependencies at low level (access/iteration), usually simulate the operation of a cache coherence protocol-based (hardware-based) TLS (Thread Level Speculation). Figure 5 depicts a sliding-window approach: The updates are recorded in per-iteration private storage and are merged (*committed*) to global storage by the oldest executing iteration, referred to as the *master*. Since the master represents a nonspeculative thread, i.e., it cannot be invalidated by any future iteration, its updates are known to be correct and the copy-out operation is safe. Then, the next iteration becomes nonspeculative and can eventually commit its updates, etc.

While implementations are diverse, one approach [4, 28] could be that (1) a read access returns the value written by the closest predecessor iteration (*forwarding*), or the nonspeculative value if no such write exists, and (2) a write access to memory location l signals a flow dependence violation if a successor iteration has read from location l. This behavior is achieved by inspecting the shadow vectors A_w and A_r, which record per-iteration write/read accesses. For example, in Fig. 5, the call of the function validate by iteration

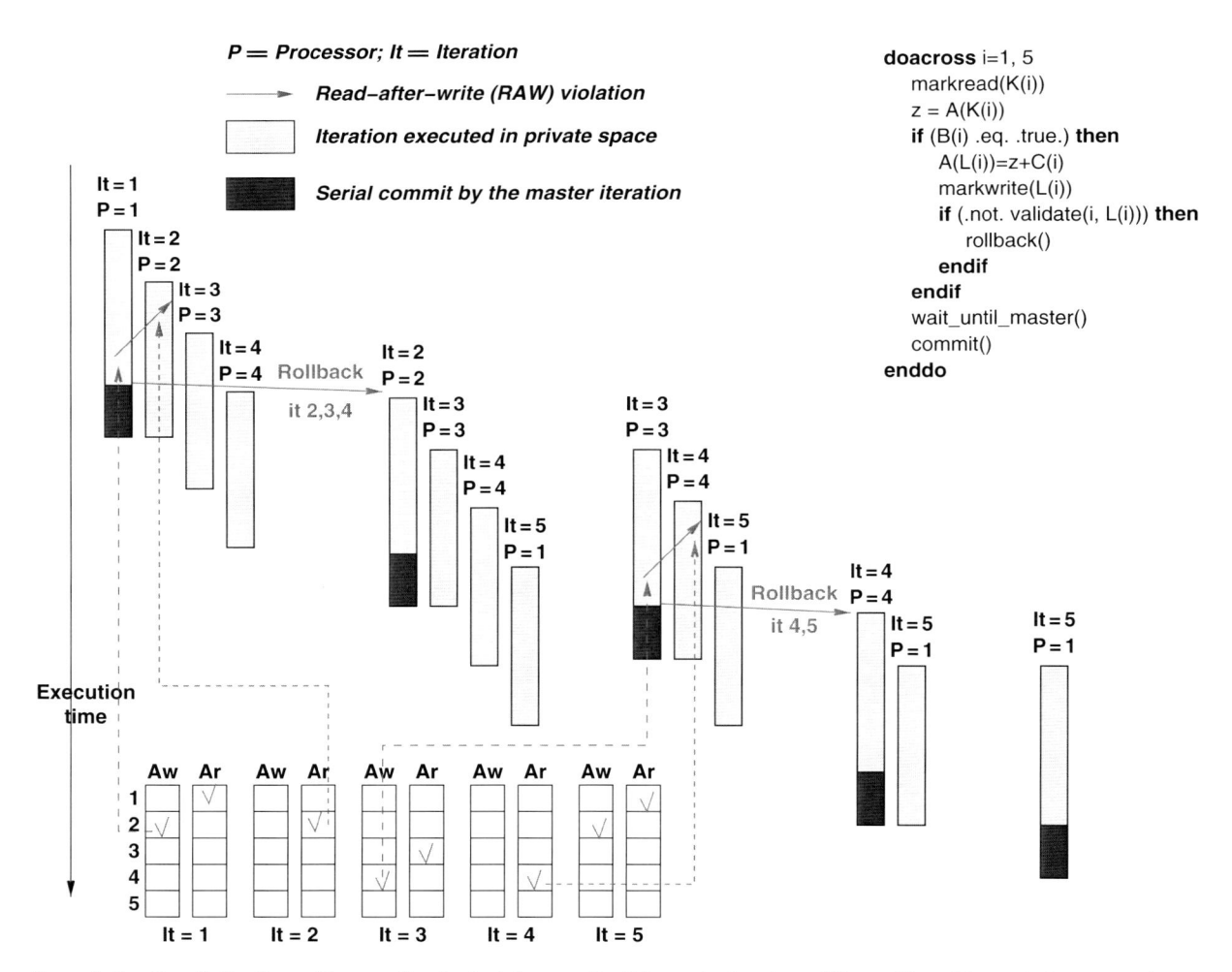

```
doacross i=1, 5
    markread(K(i))
    z = A(K(i))
    if (B(i) .eq. .true.) then
        A(L(i))=z+C(i)
        markwrite(L(i))
        if (.not. validate(i, L(i))) then
            rollback()
        endif
    endif
    wait_until_master()
    commit()
enddo
```

Speculative Parallelization of Loops. Fig. 5 Serial-commit, sliding-window-based Thread Level Speculation execution. Dashed, *red arrows* starting from A_w/A_r represent the source/sink of flow dependences

1, which writes $A[2]$, detects a flow dependence violation because iteration 2 already read $A[2]$. The master is always correct, so iteration 1 commits its updates, but restarts iterations 2, 3, and 4. Similarly, iterations 3 and 4 are the source and sink of another flow dependence violation.

While maintaining per-iteration shadow vectors is prohibitively expensive in many cases, a sliding window of size C will reduce the memory overhead to more manageable levels. In particular, since only C consecutive iterations may execute concurrently, only $O(C)$ sets of shadow vectors need to be maintained, and then recycled.

Speculative DOACROSS methods are best suited for loops with more frequent data dependences because they can detect dependences earlier thus reducing wasted computation. However, verifying the dependence violation for each memory reference can be quite expensive because it requires global synchronizations. Furthermore, the merge (commit) phase is done in iteration order which constitutes a serial bottleneck. Loops with frequent dependences are not candidates for scalable parallelization regardless of the methods used to detect and process them. They cause, aside from lack of parallelism, frequent back tracking which rapidly degrades performance to possible negative levels.

While Loop Speculative Parallelization

While loops and do loops with conditional premature exits arise frequently in practice and techniques for extracting their available parallelism [5, 26] are highly desirable. In the most general form, a while loop can be defined as a loop that includes at least one *recurrence*, a *remainder*, and at least one *termination condition*. The dominating recurrence, which precedes the rest of the computation is called the *dispatching recurrence*, or simply the *dispatcher* (Fig. 6a).

Sometimes the termination conditions form part of one of the recurrences, but they can also occur in the remainder, e.g., *conditional exits* from do loops. Assuming, for simplicity, that the *remainder* is fully parallelizable, there are two potential problems in the parallelization of while constructs:

- *Evaluating the recurrences*. If the recurrences cannot be evaluated in parallel, then the iterations of the loop must be started sequentially, leading in the best case to a pipelined execution.
- *Evaluating the termination conditions*. If the termination conditions (loop exits) cannot be evaluated independently by all iterations, the parallelized while loop could continue to execute beyond the point where the original sequential loop would stop, i.e., it can *overshoot*.

Evaluating the recurrences concurrently. In general, the terms of the dispatcher must be evaluated sequentially, e.g., the pointer chasing when traversing a linked list. Because the values of the dispatcher (the pointer) must be evaluated in sequential order, iteration i of the loop cannot be initiated until the dispatcher for iteration $i - 1$ has been computed (see Fig. 6b). However, if the dispatching recurrence is associative then it can be evaluated in parallel using, e.g., a parallel prefix algorithm (see Fig. 6c). Better yet, when the dispatcher takes the form of an induction, its values can be computed concurrently by evaluating its symbolic form and thus allowing all iterations of the while loop to execute in parallel. A typical example is represented by a do loop (see Fig. 6d, e).

Evaluating the termination conditions in parallel. Another difficulty with parallelizing while loops is that the termination condition (*terminator*) of the loop may be *overshot*, i.e., the loop would continue to execute beyond its sequential (original) counterpart. The *terminator* is defined as *remainder invariant*, or *RI*, if it is only dependent on the dispatcher and values that are computed outside the loop. If it is dependent on some value computed in the loop, then it is considered to be *remainder variant* or *RV*. If the *terminator* is RV, then iterations larger than the last (sequentially) valid iteration could be performed in a parallel execution of the loop, i.e., iteration i cannot decide if the *terminator* is satisfied in the remainder of some iteration $i' < i$. Overshooting may also occur if the dispatcher is an induction, or an associative recurrence, and the *terminator* is RI. An exception in which overshooting would not occur is if the dispatcher is a monotonic function, and the *terminator* is a threshold on this function, e.g., $d(i) = i^2$, and $tc(i) = (d(i) < V)$, where V is a constant, and $d(j)$ and $tc(j)$ denote the dispatcher and the *terminator*, respectively, for the jth iteration. Overshooting can also

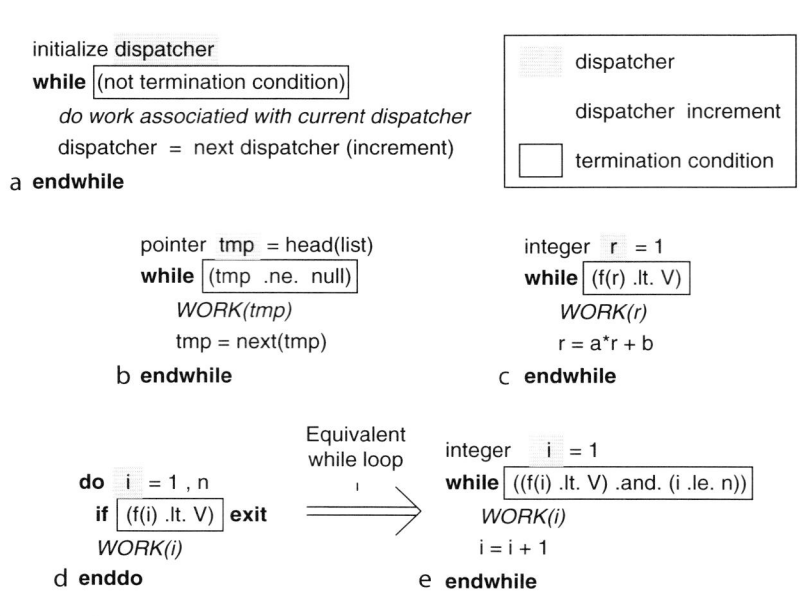

```
                initialize dispatcher
                while (not termination condition)
                    do work associated with current dispatcher
                    dispatcher = next dispatcher (increment)
              a endwhile
```

Legend:
- ░░ dispatcher
- ░░ dispatcher increment
- □ termination condition

```
              pointer tmp = head(list)              integer r = 1
              while (tmp .ne. null)                 while (f(r) .lt. V)
                  WORK(tmp)                             WORK(r)
                  tmp = next(tmp)                       r = a*r + b
            b endwhile                            c endwhile


                                    Equivalent     integer i = 1
                                    while loop     while ((f(i) .lt. V) .and. (i .le. n))
              do i = 1 , n         ==========>         WORK(i)
                  if (f(i) .lt. V) exit                i = i + 1
                  WORK(i)
            d enddo                               e endwhile
```

Speculative Parallelization of Loops. Fig. 6 (**a**) The general structure of `while` loops (**b**) Pointer chasing (**c**) Threshold *terminator* with monotonic *dispatcher* (**d**) `DO` loop with premature exit and (**e**) its equivalent `while` loop

be avoided when the dispatcher is a general recurrence, and the *terminator* is RI. For example, the dispatcher *tmp* is a pointer used to traverse a linked list, and the *terminator* is (*tmp* = *null*) (see Fig. 6b). The parallelization potential of the *dispatcher* is summarized by the taxonomy of `while` loops given in Table 1.

Speculative `while` *loop Parallelization.* Executing a loop outside its intended iteration space may result in undesired global state modification which has to be later undone. Such parallel execution can be regarded as *speculative* and is handled similarly to the previously mentioned speculative `do` loop parallelization.

The effects of *overshooting* in speculative parallel *while* loops can be undone after loop termination by restoring the (sequentially equivalent) correct state from a trace of the time (iteration) stamped memory references recorded during speculative execution. This solution may, however, have a large memory overhead for the time-stamped memory trace.

Alternatively, shared variables can be written into temporary storage, and then copied out only if their time stamps are less than or equal to the last valid iteration. There are various techniques for reducing memory overhead that can take advantage of the specific memory reference pattern, e.g., sparse patterns can be stored in hash tables. Further optimizations include *strip mining* the loop, or using a "sliding window" of iterations whose advance can be throttled adaptively.

An alternative to time-stamping is to attempt to extract a slice from the original `while` loop that can precompute the iteration space. When such a transformation is possible (e.g., traversal of a linked list) then the remainder of the `while` loop can be executed as a `doall`.

While loops with statically unknown cross-iteration dependences. When the data dependences of a `While` loop cannot be conclusively analyzed by a static compiler, the loop parallelization can be attempted by combining the LRPD test (applied to the *remainder* loop) with the techniques for *while* loop parallelization described above.

When it can be determined statically (see the taxonomy Table 1) that the parallelized `while` loop will not overshoot, then the shadow variable tracing instrumentation for the LRPD test can be inserted directly into the `while` loop.

In the more complex case when overshooting may occur (see the taxonomy Table 1) the LRPD test can be combined with the `while` loop parallelization methods by augmenting its shadow arrays with the minimum

Speculative Parallelization of Loops. Table 1 A taxonomy of `while` loops and their dispatcher's potential for parallel execution. In the table, *mono* is monotonic, *OV* is overshoot, *P* is parallel, *N* is no, *Y* is yes, and *pp* means parallelizable with a parallel prefix computation. *RV* is remainder variant and *RI* is remainder invariant

Loop terminator	Dispatcher							
	Induction				Recurrence			
	mono		other		associative		general	
	OV	P	OV	P	OV	P	OV	P
RI	N	Y	Y	Y	Y	Y-pp	N	N
RV	Y	Y	Y	Y	Y	Y-pp	Y	N

iteration that marked each element. The post-execution analysis of the LRPD test has to ignore the shadow array entries with minimum time stamps greater than the last valid iteration.

A special and unwelcome situation arises when the termination condition of the `while` loop is dependent (data or control) upon a variable which has **not** been found by the LRPD test to be independent. The speculative parallel execution of such a `while` loop may incorrectly compute its iteration space, or even worse, the termination condition might never be met (an infinite loop). Such loops are very hard to parallelize efficiently.

In general, `while` loops do not usually lend themselves to scalable parallelization due to their inherent nontrivial recurrence and overshooting potential which is expensive to mitigate.

Speculative Parallelization as a Parallel Programming Paradigm

The speculative techniques presented thus far concern themselves with the automatic transformation of sequential loops into parallel ones. They can validate, at run-time, if an instance of a loop executed in parallel does not have potential dependences and thus has *exactly* the same output as its sequential original. This validation does not, and could not, realistically check if the parallel and sequential execution have the same results. However, it imposes conditions on the memory reference trace which can ensure that the parallel loop respects the same dependence graph as the sequential one. In general, the speculative parallelization presented thus far represents a gamble that its results are equal to those of the sequential execution because it executes the same fine-grain algorithm, i.e., the same fine-grain dependence graph as the sequential original loop. This approach has lent itself well to automatic compiler implementation.

There is, however, a higher semantic level, albeit more complex, use of speculative parallelization. Instead of speculating on the execution of a fine-grain dependence graph (constructed from memory references), the programmer can generate the same results by following the correct execution of a coarser, semantically higher level dependence graph. For example, the nodes of such a coarse graph could represent the methods of a container and the edges the order in which they will be invoked. The programmer may also specify high-level properties of the methods involved. For example, the order of "inquire" type method invocations may be declared as interchangeable (commutative) similar with the `read` operations on an array. Other methods may be required to respect the program order, e.g., *add* and *delete*. In general, the cause-and-effect relation of the operations can be user defined. The result is a partial order of operations, a coarse dependence graph. A speculative parallelization of a program at this level of abstraction will ensure that its execution respects the higher level dependence graph. It implements a more relaxed execution model thus possibly improving performance. The Galois system implements this approach to speculative parallel programming [14]. It is based on two key abstractions: (1) *optimistic iterators* that can iterate over *sets* of iterations in any order and (2) a collection of assertions about properties of methods in class libraries. In addition a run-time scheme can detect and undo potentially unsafe operations due to speculation.

The *set iterator* abstracts the possibility selecting for execution elements of a set of iteration in any serial order (similar to the `DOANY` construct [43]). When an iteration executes it may add new iterations to the iteration space, hence allowing for fully dynamic execution. This is inherently possible because the addition of work can be inserted anywhere in the unordered set without changing the semantics of the loop. The *set iterator* can become an *optimistic iterator* if the generated work can create conflicts at the iteration level. To exploit parallelism, the system relies on the semantic commutativity property of methods which must be declared by the programmer through special class interface method declarations. Finally, when the program executes, the methods are invoked like transactions (in isolation) and the commutativity property of the sequence of invoked methods is asserted. If it fails, then it is possible that operations have been executed in an illegal order and therefore have to be undone. The execution is rolled back using *anti-methods*, i.e., methods that undo the effects of the offending method. For example, an *add* operation can be undone by a *delete* operation. The entire system is reminiscent of Jefferson's Virtual Time system [10].

Speculating about higher level operations using higher level abstractions allows the exploitation of algorithmic parallelism otherwise impossible to exploit at the memory reference level. It requires, however, the user to reason more about the employed algorithm.

Future Directions

Run-time parallelization in general, and speculative parallelization in particular, are likely to be essential techniques for both automatic and manual parallelization. Speculation has its drawbacks: The success rate of speculation is rather unpredictable and thus affects performance in a nondeterministic manner. Speculation may waste resources, including power, when it does not produce a speedup. However, given the ubiquitous parallelism encountered today, it is sometimes the only avenue of performance improvement.

It would be of great benefit if meaningful statistics about the success rate of speculative parallelization could be found. Speculation will continue to be used for manual parallelization of irregular programs [14], at least until good parallel algorithms will be found. In this case, high-level speculation is likely to produce better results and result in more expressive programs!.

Speculative parallelization has been integrated into the Hybrid Analysis compiler framework [29, 30]. This framework seamlessly integrates static and dynamic analysis to extract the minimum sufficient conditions that need to be evaluated at run-time in order to validate a parallel execution of a loop. By carefully staging these sufficient conditions in order of their run-time complexity, the compiler often minimizes the need for a full speculative parallelization, thus reducing the nondeterminism of the code performance.

In conclusion, speculative parallelization is a globally applicable parallelization technique that can make the difference between a fully and a partially parallelized program, i.e., between scalable and non-scalable performance.

Related Entries
▶Debugging
▶Dependences
▶Dependence Analysis
▶Parallelization, Automatic
▶Race Conditions
▶Run Time Parallelization
▶Speculation, Thread-Level

Bibliographic Notes and Further Reading

Speculative run-time parallelization has been first mentioned in the context of processes of parallel discrete event simulations by D. Jefferson [10]. In his *virtual time* concurrent processes are launched asynchronously and are tagged with their logical time stamp. When such processes communicate, they compare time stamps to check if their order respects the logical clock of the program (i.e., if data dependences are not violated). If a violation is detected, then anti-messages will recursively undo the effects of the incorrect computations and restart from a safe point.

The LRPD test, i.e., the speculative parallelization of loops, was introduced in [27]. It has later been modified to parallelize loops with dependences [6]. Compiler optimizations [21, 44] have lowered its overhead. The Hybrid Analysis framework has integrated the LRPD test in a compiler framework [30].

A significant amount of later work [4, 11, 20] has followed the hardware based approach to speculative parallelization presented in [8, 36, 37, 45].

Other related work reduces communication overhead via a master–slave model [47] in which the master executes an optimistic (fast) approximation of the code, while the slaves verify the master's correctness. Another framework [3, 41] exploits method-level parallelism for Java applications. The design space of speculative parallelization has been further widened by allowing tunable memory overhead [18] by mapping more than one memory reference to the same "shadow" structure, but with the penalty of generating false dependence violations.

Software Transactional Memory [9, 35] can be and often is implemented using speculative parallelization techniques.

Debugging of parallel programs in general and detecting memory reference "anomalies" in particular [34] is a related topic to speculative parallelization and data dependence violation detection.

Bibliography

1. Banerjee U (1988) Dependence analysis for supercomputing. Kluwer, Boston
2. Burke M, Cytron R, Ferrante J, Hsieh W (1989) Automatic generation of nested, fork-join parallelism. J Supercomput 2:71–88
3. Chen MK, Olukotun K (1998) Exploiting method level parallelism in single threaded java programs. In: International conference on parallel architectures and compilation techniques PACT'98, IEEE, Paris, pp 176–134
4. Cintra M, Llanos DR (2003) Toward efficient and robust software speculative parallelization on multiprocessors. In: International conference on principle and practice of parallel computing PPoPP'03, ACM, San Diego, pp 13–24
5. Collard J-F (1994) Space-time transformation of while-loops using speculative execution. In: Scalable high performance computing conference, IEEE, Knoxville, pp 429–436
6. Dang F, Yu H, Rauchwerger L (2002) The R-LRPD test: speculative parallelization of partially parallel loops. In: International parallel and distributed processing symposium, Florida
7. Eigenmann R, Hoeflinger J, Li Z, Padua D (1991) Experience in the automatic parallelization of four perfect-benchmark programs. Lecture notes in computer science 589. Proceedings of the fourth workshop on languages and compilers for parallel computing, Santa Clara, pp 65–83
8. Hammond L, Willey M, Olukotun K (1998) Data speculation support for a chip multiprocessor. In: 8th international conference on architectural support for programming languages and operating systems, San Jose, pp 58–69
9. Herlihy M, Shavit N (1995) The art of multiprocessor programming. Morgan Kaufmann, London
10. Jefferson DR (1985) Virtual time. ACM Trans Program Lang Syst 7(3):404–425
11. Kazi IH, Lilja DJ (2001) Coarsed-grained thread pipelining: a speculative parallel execution model for shared-memory multiprocessors. IEEE Trans Parallel Distrib Syst 12(9):952
12. Kruskal C (1986) Efficient parallel algorithms for graph problems. In: Proceedings of the 1986 international conference on parallel processing, University Park, pp 869–876, Aug 1986
13. Kuck DJ, Kuhn RH, Padua DA, Leasure B, Wolfe M (1981) Dependence graphs and compiler optimizations. In: Proceedings of the 8th ACM symposium on principles of programming languages, Williamsburg, pp 207–218
14. Kulkarni M, Pingali K, Walter B, Ramanarayanan G, Bala K, Paul Chew L (2007) Optimistic parallelism requires abstractions. In: Proceedings of the 2007 ACM SIGPLAN conference on programming language design and implementation, PLDI '07, ACM, New York, pp 211–222
15. Thomson Leighton F (1992) Introduction to parallel algorithms and architectures: arrays, trees, hypercubes. Morgan Kaufmann, London
16. Li Z (1992) Array privatization for parallel execution of loops. In: Proceedings of the 19th international symposium on computer architecture, Gold Coast, pp 313–322
17. Maydan DE, Amarasinghe SP, Lam MS (1992) Data dependence and data-flow analysis of arrays. In: Proceedings 5th workshop on programming languages and compilers for parallel computing, New Haven
18. Oancea CE, Mycroft A, Harris T (2009) A lightweight in-place implementation for software thread-level speculation. In: International symposium on parallelism in algorithms and architectures SPAA'09, ACM, Calgary, pp 223–232
19. Padua DA, Wolfe MJ (1986) Advanced compiler optimizations for supercomputers. Commun ACM 29:1184–1201
20. Papadimitriou S, Mowry TC (2001) Exploring thread-level speculation in software: the effects of memory access tracking granularity. Technical report, CMU
21. Patel D, Rauchwerger L (1999) Implementation issues of loop-level speculative run-time parallelization. In: Proceedings of the 8th international conference on compiler construction (CC'99), Amsterdam. Lecture notes in computer science, vol 1575. Springer, Berlin
22. Rauchwerger L (1998) Run-time parallelization: its time has come. Parallel Comput 24(3–4):527. Special issues on languages and compilers for parallel comput
23. Rauchwerger L, Amato N, Padua D (1995) Run-time methods for parallelizing partially parallel loops. In: Proceedings of the 9th ACM international conference on supercomputing, Barcelona, Spain, pp 137–146
24. Rauchwerger L, Amato N, Padua D (1995) A scalable method for run-time loop parallelization. Int J Parallel Prog 26(6):537–576
25. Rauchwerger L, Padua DA (1999) The LRPD test: speculative run-time parallelization of loops with privatization and reduction parallelization. IEEE Trans Parallel and Distrib Syst 10(2):160–180
26. Rauchwerger L, Padua DA (1995). Parallelizing WHILE loops for multi-processor systems. In: Proceedings of 9th international parallel processing symposium, Santa Barbara
27. Rauchwerger L, Padua DA (1995) The LRPD test: speculative run-time parallelization of loops with privatization and reduction parallelization. In: Proceedings of the SIGPLAN 1995 conference on programming language design and implementation, La Jolla pp 218–232
28. Rundberg P, Stenstrom P (2000) Low-cost thread-level data dependence speculation on multiprocessors. In: 4th workshop on multithreaded execution, architecture and compilation, Monterey

29. Rus S, Pennings M, Rauchwerger L (2007) Sensitivity analysis for automatic parallelization on multi-cores. In: Proceedings of the ACM international conference on supercomputing (ICS07), Seattle
30. Rus S, Hoeflinger J, Rauchwerger L (2003) Hybrid analysis: static & dynamic memory reference analysis. Int J Parallel Prog 31(3):251–283
31. Saltz J, Mirchandaney R (1991) The preprocessed doacross loop. In: Schwetman HD (ed) Proceedings of the 1991 international conference on parallel processing, Software, vol II. CRC Press, Boca Raton, pp 174–178
32. Saltz J, Mirchandaney R, Crowley K (1989) The doconsider loop. In: Proceedings of the 1989 international conference on super-computing, Irakleion, pp 29–40
33. Saltz J, Mirchandaney R, Crowley K (1991) Run-time parallelization and scheduling of loops. IEEE Trans Comput 40(5):603–612
34. Schonberg E (1989) On-the-fly detection of access anomalies. In: Proceedings of the SIGPLAN 1989 conference on programming language design and implementation, Portland, pp 285–297
35. Shavit N, Touitou D (1995) Software transactional memory. In: Proceedings of the fourteenth annual ACM symposium on principles of distributed computing, PODC '95, ACM, New York, pp 204–213
36. Sohi GS, Breach SE, Vijayakumar TN (1995) Multiscalar processors. In: 22nd international symposium on computer architecture, Santa Margherita
37. Steffan JG, Mowry TC (1998) The potential for using thread-level data speculation to facilitate automatic parallelization. In: Proceedings of the 4th international symposium on high-performance computer architecture, Las Vegas
38. Tu P, Padua D (1992) Array privatization for shared and distributed memory machines. In: Proceedings 2nd workshop on languages, compilers, and run-time environments for distributed memory machines, Boulder
39. Tu P, Padua D (1993) Automatic array privatization. In: Proceedings 6th annual workshop on languages and compilers for parallel computing, Portland
40. Tu P, Padua D (1995) Efficient building and placing of gating functions. In: Proceedings of the SIGPLAN 1995 conference on programming language design and implementation, La Jolla, pp 47–55
41. Welc A, Jagannathan S, Hosking A (2006) Safe futures for Java. In: International conference object-oriented programming, systems, languages and applications OOP-SLA'06, ACM, New York, pp 439–453
42. Wolfe M (1989) Optimizing compilers for supercomputers. MIT Press, Boston
43. Wolfe M (1992) Doany: not just another parallel loop. In: Proceedings 5th annual workshop on programming languages and compilers for parallel computing, New Haven. Lecture notes in computer science, vol 757. Springer, Berlin
44. Yu H, Rauchwerger L (2000) Run-time parallelization overhead reduction techniques. In: Proceedings of the 9th international conference on compiler construction (CC 2000), Berlin Germany. Lecture notes in computer science vol 1781. Springer, Heidelberg
45. Zhang Y, Rauchwerger L, Torrellas J (1998) Hardware for speculative run-time parallelization in distributed shared-memory multiprocessors. In: Proceedings of the 4th international symposium on high-performance computer architecture (HPCA), Las Vegas, pp 162–174
46. Zhu C, Yew PC (1987) A scheme to enforce data dependence on large multiprocessor systems. IEEE Trans Softw Eng 13(6):726–739
47. Zilles C, Sohi G (2002) Master/slave speculative parallelization. In: International symposium on microarchitecture Micro-35, IEEE, Los Alamitos, pp 85–96
48. Zima H (1991) Supercompilers for parallel and vector computers. ACM Press, New York

Speculative Run-Time Parallelization

▶Speculation, Thread-Level
▶Speculative Parallelization of Loops

Speculative Threading

▶Speculation, Thread-Level

Speculative Thread-Level Parallelization

▶Speculation, Thread-Level

Speedup

▶Metrics

SPIKE

Eric Polizzi
University of Massachusetts, Amherst, MA, USA

Definition

SPIKE is a polyalgorithm that uses many different strategies for solving large banded linear systems in parallel. Existing parallel algorithms and software using direct methods for banded matrices are mostly based on LU factorizations. In contrast, SPIKE uses a novel decomposition method (i.e., DS factorization) to balance communication overhead with arithmetic cost to achieve better scalability than other methods. The SPIKE algorithm is similar to a domain decomposition technique that allows performing independent calculations on each subdomain or partition of the linear system, while the interface problem leads to a reduced linear system of much smaller size than that of the original one. Direct, iterative, or approximate schemes can then be used to handle the reduced system in a different way depending on the characteristics of the linear system and the parallel computing platform.

Discussion

Introduction

Many science and engineering applications, particularly those involving finite element analysis, give rise to very large sparse linear systems. These systems can often be reordered to produce either banded systems or low-rank perturbations of banded systems in which the width of the band is but a small fraction of the size of the overall problem. In other instances, banded systems can act as effective preconditioners to general sparse systems, which are solved via iterative methods.

Direct methods for solving linear systems $AX = F$ are commonly based on the LU decomposition that represents a matrix A as a product of lower and upper triangular matrices $A = LU$. Consequently, solving $AX = F$ can be achieved by solutions of two triangular systems $LG = F$ and $UX = G$. A parallel LU decomposition for banded linear systems has also been proposed by Cleary and Dongarra in [1] for the ScaLAPACK package [2]. The central idea behind the SPIKE algorithm is a different decomposition for banded linear systems, introduced by A. Sameh in the late 1970s [3], which is ideally suited for parallel implementation as it naturally leads to lower communication cost. Several enhancements and variants of the SPIKE algorithm have since been proposed by Sameh and coauthors in [4–11]. In the case when A is a banded matrix as depicted in Fig. 1, SPIKE is using a direct partitioning in the context of parallel processing.

SPIKE relies on the decomposition of a given banded matrix A into the product of a block-diagonal matrix D, and another matrix S which has the structure of an identity matrix with some extra "spikes" (and hence the name of the algorithm). This DS factorization procedure is illustrated in Fig. 2.

Solving $AX = F$ can then be accomplished in two steps:

1. Solution of block-diagonal system $DG = F$. Because D consists of decoupled systems of each of the diagonal block A_i, they can be solved in parallel without requiring any communication between the individual systems.
2. Solution of the system $SX = G$. This system has a wonderful characteristic that it is also decoupled to a large extent. Except for a reduced system (near the interface of each of the identity blocks), the rest are independent from one another. The natural way to tackle this system is to first solve the reduced system via some parallel algorithms that

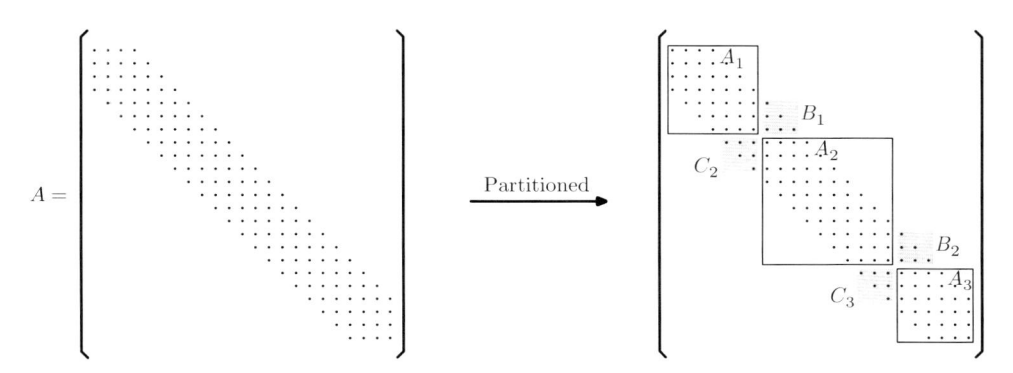

SPIKE. Fig. 1 A banded matrix with a conceptual partition

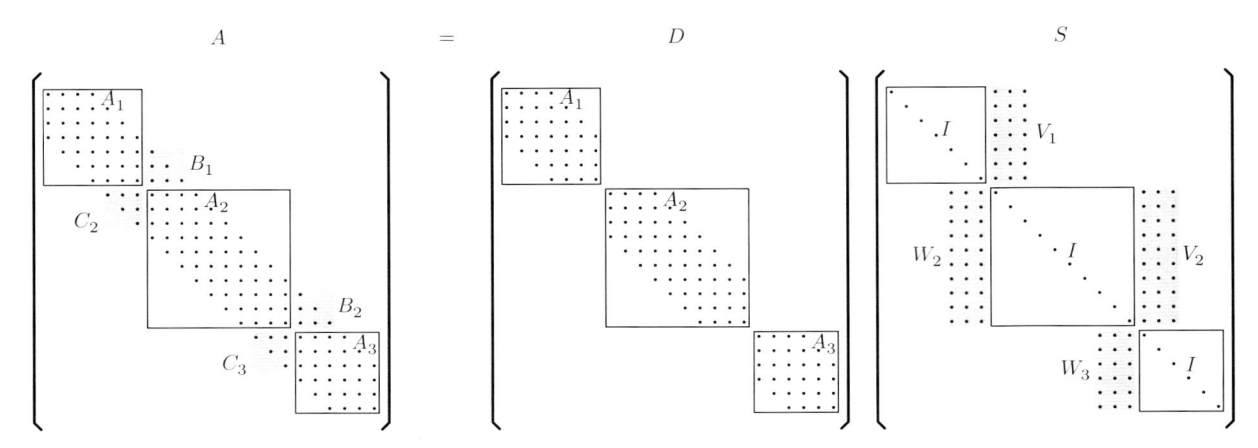

SPIKE. Fig. 2 SPIKE factorization where $A = DS$, $S = D^{-1}A$. The blocks in the block-diagonal matrix D are supposed non-singular

require inter-processor communications, followed by retrieval of the rest of the solution without requiring further inter-processor communications.

The SPIKE Algorithm: Basics

As illustrated in Fig. 1, a $(N \times N)$ banded matrix A can be partitioned into a block tridiagonal form $\{C_j, A_j, B_j\}$, where A_j is the $(n_j \times n_j)$ diagonal block j, and B_j (i.e., C_j) is the $(ku \times ku)$ (i.e., $(kl \times kl)$) right block (i.e., left block). Using p partitions, it comes that n_j is roughly equal to N/p. In order to ease the description of the SPIKE algorithm but without loss of generality, the size off-diagonal blocks are both supposed equal to m ($kl = ku = m$). The size of the bandwidth is then defined by $b = 2m + 1$ where $b \ll n_j$. Each partition j ($j = 1, \ldots, p$) can be associated to one processor or one node allowing multilevel of parallelism. Using the DS factorization illustrated in Fig. 2, the obtained spike matrix S has a block tridiagonal form $\{W_j, I_j, V_j\}$, where I_j is the $(n_j \times n_j)$ identity matrix, V_j and W_j are the $(n \times m)$ right and left spikes. The spikes V_j and W_j are solutions of the following linear systems:

$$A_j V_j = \begin{bmatrix} 0 \\ \vdots \\ 0 \\ B_j \end{bmatrix}, \quad \text{and} \quad A_j W_j = \begin{bmatrix} C_j \\ 0 \\ \vdots \\ 0 \end{bmatrix}. \quad (1)$$

respectively for $j = 1, \ldots, p-1$ and $j = 2, \ldots, p$.

Solving the system $AX = F$ now consists of two steps:

(a) solve $\quad DG = F \quad$ (2)

(b) solve $\quad SX = G. \quad$ (3)

The solution of the linear system $DG = F$ in Step (a) yields the modified right-hand side G needed for Step (b). In case of assigning one partition to each processor, Step (a) is performed with perfect parallelism. To solve $SX = G$ in Step (b), one should observe that the problem can be reduced further by solving a system of much smaller size, which consists of the m rows of S immediately above and below each partitioning line. Indeed, the spikes V_j and W_j can also be partitioned as follows

$$V_j = \begin{bmatrix} V_j^{(t)} \\ V_j' \\ V_j^{(b)} \end{bmatrix} \quad \text{and} \quad W_j = \begin{bmatrix} W_j^{(t)} \\ W_j' \\ W_j^{(b)} \end{bmatrix} \quad (4)$$

where $V_j^{(t)}$, V_j', $V_j^{(b)}$, and $W_j^{(t)}$, W_j', $W_j^{(b)}$, are the top m, the middle $n_j - 2m$ and the bottom m rows of V_j and W_j, respectively. Here,

$$V_j^{(b)} = [0 \quad I_m]V_j; \quad W_j^{(t)} = [I_m \quad 0]W_j, \quad (5)$$

and

$$V_j^{(t)} = [I_m \quad 0]V_j; \quad W_j^{(b)} = [0 \quad I_m]W_j. \quad (6)$$

Similarly, if X_j and G_j are the jth partitions of X and G, it comes

$$X_j = \begin{bmatrix} X_j^{(t)} \\ X_j' \\ X_j^{(b)} \end{bmatrix} \quad \text{and} \quad G_j = \begin{bmatrix} G_j^{(t)} \\ G_j' \\ G_j^{(b)} \end{bmatrix}. \qquad (7)$$

It is then possible to extract from a block tridiagonal reduced linear system (8) of size $2(p-1)m$, which involves only the top and bottom elements of V_j, W_j, X_j, and G_j. As example, the reduced system obtained for the case of four partitions ($p = 4$) is given by

$$\begin{bmatrix} I_m & V_1^{(b)} & & & & & \\ W_2^{(t)} & I_m & & V_2^{(t)} & & & \\ W_2^{(b)} & & I_m & V_2^{(b)} & & & \\ & & W_3^{(t)} & I_m & & V_3^{(t)} & \\ & & W_3^{(b)} & & I_m & V_3^{(b)} & \\ & & & & W_4^{(t)} & I_m \end{bmatrix} \begin{bmatrix} X_1^{(b)} \\ X_2^{(t)} \\ X_2^{(b)} \\ X_3^{(t)} \\ X_3^{(b)} \\ X_4^{(t)} \end{bmatrix} = \begin{bmatrix} G_1^{(b)} \\ G_2^{(t)} \\ G_2^{(b)} \\ G_3^{(t)} \\ G_3^{(b)} \\ G_4^{(t)} \end{bmatrix}.$$

$$(8)$$

Finally, once the solution of the reduced system is obtained, the global solution X can be reconstructed from $X_k^{(b)}$ ($k = 1, \ldots, p-1$) and $X_k^{(t)}$ ($k = 2, \ldots, p$) either by computing

$$\begin{cases} X_1' = G_1' - V_1' X_2^{(t)}, \\ X_j' = G_j' - V_j' X_{j+1}^{(t)} - W_j' X_{j-1}^{(b)}, \quad j = 2, \ldots, p-1 \\ X_p' = G_p' - W_j' X_{p-1}^{(b)}, \end{cases} \qquad (9)$$

or by solving

$$\begin{cases} A_1 X_1 = F_1 - \begin{bmatrix} 0 \\ I_m \end{bmatrix} B_j X_2^{(t)}, \\ A_j X_j = F_j - \begin{bmatrix} 0 \\ I_m \end{bmatrix} B_j X_{j+1}^{(t)} - \begin{bmatrix} I_m \\ 0 \end{bmatrix} C_j X_{j-1}^{(b)}, \quad j = 2, \ldots, p-1 \\ A_p X_p = F_p - \begin{bmatrix} I_m \\ 0 \end{bmatrix} C_j X_{p-1}^{(b)}. \end{cases}$$

$$(10)$$

SPIKE: A Hybrid and Polyalgorithm

Multiple options are available for efficient parallel implementation of the SPIKE algorithm depending on the properties of the linear system as well as the architecture of the parallel platform. More specifically, the following stages of the SPIKE algorithm can be handled in several ways resulting in a polyalgorithm:

1. Factorization of the diagonal blocks A_j. Depending on the sparsity pattern of the matrix and the size of the bandwidth, these diagonal blocks could be considered either as dense or sparse within the band. For the dense banded case, a number of strategies based on the LU decomposition of each A_i can be applied here. This include variants such as LU with pivoting, LU without any pivoting but diagonal boosting, as well as a combination of LU and UL decompositions, either with or without pivoting. For the sparse banded case, it is common to use a sparse direct linear system solver to reorder and then factorize the diagonal blocks. However, solving the various linear systems for A_j can also be achieved using an iterative solver with preconditioner. Finally, each partition in the decomposition can be associated with one or several processors (one node), enabling multilevel parallelism.

2. Computation of the spikes. If the spikes V_j and W_j are determined entirely, the reduced system (8) can be solved explicitly and equation (9) can be used to retrieve the entire solution. In contrast, if equation (10) is used to retrieve the solution, the spikes may not be computed but only for the top and bottom ($m \times m$) blocks of V_j and W_j needed to form the reduced system. It should be noted that the determination of the top and bottom spikes is also not explicitly needed for computing the actions of the multiplications with $W_j^{(t)}$, $W_j^{(b)}$, $V_j^{(t)}$, and $V_j^{(b)}$. These latter can be realized "on-the-fly" using $\begin{pmatrix} I_m & 0 \end{pmatrix} A_j^{-1} \begin{pmatrix} I_m \\ 0 \end{pmatrix} C_j$, $\begin{pmatrix} 0 & I_m \end{pmatrix} A_j^{-1} \begin{pmatrix} I_m \\ 0 \end{pmatrix} C_j$, $\begin{pmatrix} I_m & 0 \end{pmatrix} A_j^{-1} \begin{pmatrix} I_m \\ 0 \end{pmatrix} B_j$, $\begin{pmatrix} 0 & I_m \end{pmatrix} A_j^{-1} \begin{pmatrix} I_m \\ 0 \end{pmatrix} B_j$, respectively.

3. Solution scheme for the reduced system. One of the earliest concerns with the SPIKE algorithm for large number of partitions was to propose a reliable and efficient parallel strategy for solving the reduced

system (8). Krylov subspace-based iterative methods have been the first candidates to fulfill this purpose, while giving to SPIKE its hybrid nature. These iterative methods are often used in conjunction with a block Jacobi preconditioner (i.e., diagonal blocks of the reduced system) if the bottom of the V_j spikes and the top of the W_j spikes are computed explicitly. In turn, the matrix-vector multiplication operations of the iterative technique can be done explicitly or implicitly ("on-the-fly"). In order to enhance robustness and scalability for solving the reduced system, two new highly efficient direct methods have been introduced by Polizzi and Sameh in [10, 11]. These SPIKE schemes, which have been named "truncated scheme" for handling diagonally dominant systems, and "recursive scheme" for non-diagonally dominant systems, are presented in the next sections. Here again, a number of different strategies exists for solving the reduced system.

As mentioned above, and in order to minimize memory references, it is sometimes advantageous to factorize the diagonal blocks A_j using LU without any pivoting but adding a diagonal boosting if a "zero-pivot" is detected. Hence, A is not exactly the product DS and rather takes the form $A = DS + R$, where R represents the correction which, even if nonzero, is by design small in some sense. Outer iterations via Krylov subspace schemes or iterative refinement, are then necessary to obtain sufficient accuracy as SPIKE would act on $M = DS$ (i.e., the approximate SPIKE decomposition for M is used as effective preconditioner).

Finally, a SPIKE-balance scheme has also been proposed by Golub, Sameh, and Sarin in [12], for addressing the case where the block diagonal A_j are nearly singular (i.e., ill-conditioned), and when even the LU decomposition with partial pivoting is expected to fail.

The Truncated SPIKE Scheme for Diagonally Dominant Systems

The truncated SPIKE scheme is an optimized version of the SPIKE algorithm with enhanced use of parallelism for handling diagonally dominant systems. These systems may arise from several science and engineering applications, and are defined if the degree of diagonally dominance, dd, of the matrix A is greater than 1, where dd is given by

$$dd = \min \frac{|A_{i,i}|}{\sum_{j \neq i} |A_{i,j}|}. \quad (11)$$

It is possible to show from equation (1), that the magnitude of the elements of the right spikes V_j decay from bottom to top, while the elements of the left spikes W_j decay in magnitude from top to bottom [13, 14]. Since the size n of A_j is much larger than the size m of the blocks B_j and C_j, the bottom blocks of the left spikes $W_j^{(b)}$ and the top blocks of the right spikes $V_j^{(t)}$ can be approximately set equal to zero. In fact, the zero accuracy machine is ensured to be reached either in the case of a pronounced decay (i.e., high value for dd), or for large ratio n_j/m. Thus, it follows that the off-diagonal blocks of the reduced system (8) are equal to zero, and the solution of this new block-diagonal "truncated" reduced system can be obtained by solving $p - 1$ independent $2m \times 2m$ linear systems in parallel:

$$\begin{bmatrix} I_m & V_j^{(b)} \\ W_{j+1}^{(t)} & I_m \end{bmatrix} \begin{bmatrix} X_j^{(b)} \\ X_{j+1}^{(t)} \end{bmatrix} = \begin{bmatrix} G_j^{(b)} \\ G_{j+1}^{(t)} \end{bmatrix}. \quad (12)$$

These systems can be solved directly using a block-LU factorization, where the solution steps consist of the following: (a) Form $E = I_m - W_{j+1}^{(t)} V_j^{(b)}$, (b) Solve $E X_{j+1}^{(t)} = G_{j+1}^{(t)} - W_{j+1}^{(t)} G_j^{(b)}$ to obtain $X_{j+1}^{(t)}$, (c) Compute $X_j^{(b)} = G_j^{(b)} - V_j^{(b)} X_{j+1}^{(t)}$.

Solving the reduced system via the truncated SPIKE algorithm for diagonally dominant systems demonstrates then linear scalability with the number partitions. The truncated scheme is often associated with an outer-iterative refinement step to increase the solution accuracy.

Within the framework of the truncated scheme, two other major contributions have also been proposed for improving computing performance and scalability of the factorization stage: (a) a LU/UL strategy, and (b) a new unconventional partitioning scheme.

LU/UL Strategy

The truncated scheme facilitates different new options for the factorization step that make possible to avoid the computation of the entire spikes. As illustrated in

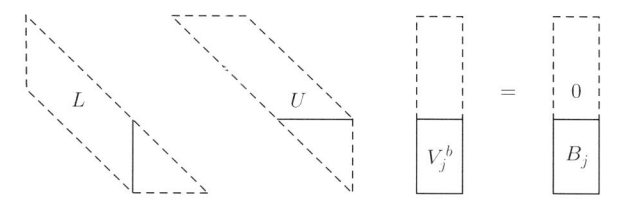

SPIKE. Fig. 3 The bottom of the spike V_j can be computed using only the bottom $m \times m$ blocks of L and U. Similarly, the top of the spike W_j may be obtained if one performs the UL-factorization

Fig. 3, computational solve times can be drastically reduced by using the LU factorization without pivoting on each diagonal block A_j. Obtaining the top block of W_j, however, would still require computing the entire spike with complete forward and backward sweeps. Another approach consists of performing also the UL-factorization of the block A_j without pivoting. Similar to the LU-factorization, this allows obtaining the top block of W_j involving only the top $m \times m$ blocks of the new $\dot{U}$ and $\dot{L}$ matrices. Numerical experiments indicate that the time consumed by this LU/UL strategy is much less than that taken by performing only one LU factorization per diagonal block and generating the entire left spikes.

Unconventional Partitioning Schemes

A new partitioning scheme can be introduced to avoid performing both LU and UL factorization for a given A_j ($j = 2, \ldots, p-1$). This scheme acts on a new parallel distribution of the system matrix, which considers less partition than processors. Practically, if k represents an even number of processors (or nodes in the case of multilevel parallelism), the new number of partitions will be equal to $p = (k+2)/2$. The new block matrices A_j, $j = 1, \ldots, p$ can be associated to the first p processors while processors $p+1$ to k hold another copy of the block matrix A_j, $j = 2, \ldots, p-1$. Figure 4 illustrates the new partitioning of the matrix right-hand side and solution, for the case $k = 4$ and $p = 3$.

The diagonal blocks A_j associated to processors 1 to $p-1$ are then factorized using LU without pivoting, while a UL factorization is used for the diagonal blocks associated with processors p to k. In the example of $k = 4$, $L_j U_j \leftarrow A_j$ for $j = 1, 2$ (processors 1, 2), and $\dot{U}_j \dot{L}_j \leftarrow$ A_j for $j = 2, 3$ (processors 4, 3). As described above using the LU/UL strategy, the $V_j^{(b)}$ ($j = 1, \ldots, p-1$) can be obtained with minimal computational efforts via the LU solve step on processors 1 to $p-1$, while the $W_j^{(t)}$ ($j = 2, \ldots, p$) can be obtained in the similar way but now on different processors using the UL solve step. Using this new partitioning scheme, the size of the partitions does increase but the number of arithmetic operations by partition decreases as well as the size of the truncated reduced system. This scheme achieves better balance between the computational cost of solving the sub-problems and the communication overhead. In addition to increasing scalability results for large number of processors, the scheme also addresses the "bottleneck" of the small number of processors case as described below.

Speed-Up Performances on Small Number of Processors

One of the main focus in the development of parallel algorithms for solving linear systems aims at achieving linear scalability on large number of processors. However, the emergence of multicore computing platforms in these recent years has brought new emphasis for parallel algorithms on achieving net speedup over the corresponding best sequential algorithms on small number of processors/cores. Clearly, parallel algorithms often inherit extensive preprocessing stages with increased memory references or arithmetics, leading to counter-performances on small number of cores. For parallel banded solvers, in particular, four to eight cores may be usually needed to solve linear systems as fast as the best corresponding sequential solver in LAPACK [15]. It is then important to note that the new partitioning scheme for the truncated SPIKE algorithm has also been designed to address this issue while offering a speedup of two from only two cores. While the two-cores (two-partitions) case can take advantage of a single LU or UL factorization for A_1 and A_2, respectively, the efforts to solve the reduced system become minimal (i.e., as compared to a LU decomposition on the overall system, the number of arithmetic operations is essentially divided by two in the SPIKE factorization and solve stages). When the number of cores increases, and without accounting for the communication costs (which are minimal for the truncated scheme), the

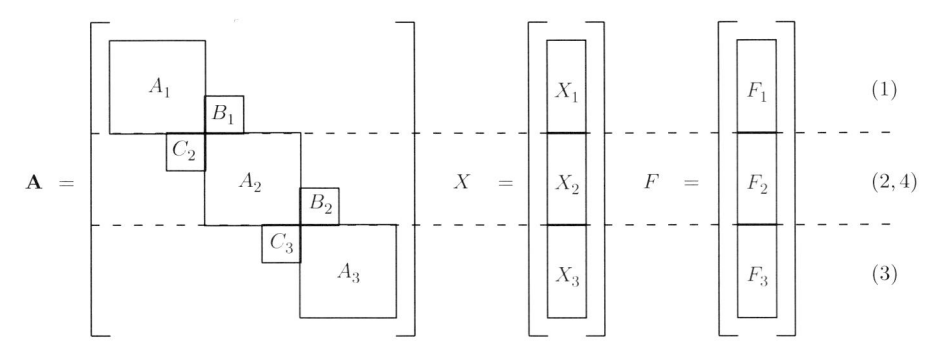

$$\mathbf{A} = \begin{bmatrix} A_1 & & & \\ & B_1 & & \\ C_2 & A_2 & & \\ & & B_2 & \\ & C_3 & A_3 & \end{bmatrix} \quad X = \begin{bmatrix} X_1 \\ \hline X_2 \\ \hline X_3 \end{bmatrix} \quad F = \begin{bmatrix} F_1 \\ \hline F_2 \\ \hline F_3 \end{bmatrix} \quad \begin{array}{c} (1) \\ (2,4) \\ (3) \end{array}$$

SPIKE. Fig. 4 Illustration of the unconventional partitioning of the linear system for the truncated SPIKE algorithm in the case of 4 processors. A_1 is sent to processor 1, A_2 to processors 2 and 4, and A_3 to processor 3.

speedup are expected ideally equal to the number of partitions: ×2 on two cores, ×3 on four cores, ×5 on eight cores, etc. Thereafter, the SPIKE performance will approach linear scalability as the number of cores increases.

The Recursive SPIKE Scheme for Non-Diagonally Dominant Systems

For non-diagonally dominant systems and large number of partitions, solving the reduced system (8) using Krylov subspace iterative method with or without preconditioner may result in high interprocessor communication cost. Interestingly, the truncated scheme for the two-cores (two-partitions) case is as well applicable for non-diagonally dominant systems since the reduced system (12) contains only one diagonal block. It should be noted, however, that this scheme may necessitate outer-refinement steps, since the diagonal boosting used to handle the "zero-pivot" in the *LU* and *UL* factorization stages, are more likely to appear for non-diagonally dominant systems.

For larger number of partitions, a new direct approach named "recursive" scheme has been proposed for solving the reduced system and enhancing robustness, accuracy, and scalability. This recursive scheme consists of successive iterations of the SPIKE algorithm from systems to reduced systems, resulting in better balance between the costs of computation and communication. This scheme assumes that the original number of (conventional) partitions is given by $p = 2^d$ ($d > 1$). The bottom and top blocks of the V_j and W_j spikes are then computed explicitly to form the reduced system. In practice, a modified version of the reduced system is preferred which also includes the top block V_1^t and bottom block W_p^b. For the case $p = 4$, the original reduced system (8) is now represented by the following "reduced spike matrix":

$$\begin{pmatrix} I_m & V_1^{(t)} & & & & & & \\ & I_m & V_1^{(b)} & & & & & \\ W_2^{(t)} & & I_m & & V_2^{(t)} & & & \\ W_2^{(b)} & & & I_m & V_2^{(b)} & & & \\ \hline & & W_3^{(t)} & & I_m & & V_3^{(t)} & \\ & & W_3^{(b)} & & & I_m & V_3^{(b)} & \\ & & & & W_4^{(t)} & & I_m & \\ & & & & W_4^{(b)} & & & I_m \end{pmatrix} \begin{bmatrix} X_1^{(t)} \\ X_1^{(b)} \\ X_2^{(t)} \\ X_2^{(b)} \\ X_3^{(t)} \\ X_3^{(b)} \\ X_4^{(t)} \\ X_4^{(b)} \end{bmatrix} = \begin{bmatrix} G_1^{(t)} \\ G_1^{(b)} \\ G_2^{(t)} \\ G_2^{(b)} \\ G_3^{(t)} \\ G_3^{(b)} \\ G_4^{(t)} \\ G_4^{(b)} \end{bmatrix}.$$

(13)

This reduced spike system matrix contains p partitions with p diagonal block identities. The system can be easily redistributed in parallel using only $p/2$ partitions which are factorized by SPIKE recursively up until obtaining two partitions only. It can be shown [10] that the two partitions case leading to a $2m \times 2m$ linear system presented in (12), constitutes the basic computational kernel of the recursive SPIKE scheme.

The SPIKE Solver: Current and Future Implementation

Since the publications of the first SPIKE algorithm in the late seventies [3, 4], many variations and new schemes have been implemented. In recent years, a comprehensive MPI-Fortran 90 SPIKE package for distributed memory architecture has been developed by the author.

This implementation includes, in particular, all the different family of SPIKE algorithms: recursive, truncated, and on-the-fly schemes. These SPIKE solvers rely on a hierarchy of computational modules, starting with the data locality-rich BLAS level-3, up to the blocked LAPACK [15] algorithms for handling dense banded systems, or up to the direct sparse solver PARDISO [16] for handling sparse banded systems, with SPIKE being on the outermost level of the hierarchy. The package also includes new primitives for banded matrices that make efficient use of BLAS level-3 routines. Those include banded triangular solvers with multiple right-hand sides, banded matrix-matrix multiplications, and LU, UL factorizations with diagonal boosting strategy.

In addition, the large number of options/decision schemes available for SPIKE created the need for the automatic generation of a sophisticated runtime decision tree "SPIKE-ADAPT" that has been developed by Intel. This adaptive layer indicates the most appropriate version of the SPIKE algorithm capable of achieving the highest performance for solving banded systems that are dense within the band. The relevant linear system parameters in this case are system size, number of nodes/processors to be used, bandwidth of the linear system, and degree of diagonal dominance. SPIKE and SPIKE-ADAPT have been regrouped into one package, named "Intel Adaptive Spike-Based Solver," which has been released to the public in June 2008 on the Intel whatif web site [17].

The SPIKE package also includes a SPIKE-PARDISO scheme for addressing banded linear systems with large sparse bandwidth while offering a basic distributed version of the current shared memory PARDISO package. The capabilities and domain applicability of the SPIKE-PARDISO scheme have recently been significantly enhanced by Manguoglu, Sameh, and Schenk in [18] to address general sparse systems. In this approach, a weighted reordering strategy is used to extract efficient banded preconditioners that are solved via SPIKE-PARDISO including new specific PARDISO features for computing the relevant bottom and top tips of the spikes.

While the current parallel distributed SPIKE package does offer HPC users a new and valuable tool for solving large-scale problems arising from many areas in science and engineering, the growing size of the number of cores in compute node forestalls distributed programming model (i.e., MPI) for many users. On the other hand, the scalability of the LAPACK banded algorithms on multicore node or SMP is first and foremost dependent on the threaded capabilities of the underlying BLAS routines. A new implementation of the SPIKE solver recently initiated by the author is concerned with a shared memory programming model (i.e., OpenMP) that can consistently match the LAPACK functions for solving banded systems. This SPIKE Open-MP project is expected to offer high efficient threaded alternatives for solving banded linear systems on current and emerging multicore architectures.

Related Entries
▶BLAS (Basic Linear Algebra Subprograms)
▶Collective Communication
▶Dense Linear System Solvers
▶Linear Algebra, Numerical
▶Load Balancing, Distributed Memory
▶Metrics
▶PARDISO
▶Preconditioners for Sparse Iterative Methods
▶ScaLAPACK

Bibliography Notes and Further Reading
As mentioned in the introduction, the main ideas of the SPIKE algorithm has been introduced in the late 1970s [3, 4], since then, many improvements and variations have been proposed [5–12, 18]. In particular, the highly efficient truncated and recursive schemes for solving the reduced system presented here are discussed in more detail in [10, 11]. All the main SPIKE algorithm variations have been regrouped into a comprehensive MPI-based SPIKE solver package in [17], where the associated SPIKE's user guide contains more detailed information on the capabilities of the different SPIKE schemes and their domain of applicability.

Bibliography
1. Cleary A, Dongarra J (1997) Implementation in ScaLAPACK of divide and conquer algorithms for banded and tridiagonal linear systems. University of Tennessee Computer Science Technical Report, UT-CS-97-358
2. Blackford LS, Choi J, Cleary A, Dazevedo E, Demmel J, Dhillon I, et al (1997) ScaLAPACK users guide. Society for Industrial and Appl. Math, Philadelphia
3. Sameh A (1977) Numerical parallel algorithms: a survey. In: Kuck D, Lawrie D, Sameh A (eds) High speed computer and algorithm organization. Academic, New York, pp 207–228

4. Sameh A, Kuck D (1978) On stable parallel linear system solvers. J ACM 25:81–91
5. Sameh A (1983) On two numerical algorithms for multiprocessors. In: Proceedings of NATO adv res workshop on high-speed comp. Series F: computer and systems sciences, vol 7. Springer, Berlin, pp 311–328
6. Lawrie D, Sameh A (1984) The computation and communication complexity of a parallel banded system solver. ACM Trans Math Software 10(2):185–195
7. Dongarra J, Sameh A (1984) On some parallel banded system solvers. Parallel Comput 1:223–235
8. Berry M, Sameh A (1988) Multiprocessor schemes for solving block tridiagonal linear systems. Int J Supercomput Appl 2(3):37–57
9. Sameh A, Sarin V (1999) Hybrid parallel linear solvers. Int J Comput Fluid Dyn 12:213–223
10. Polizzi E, Sameh A (2006) A parallel hybrid banded system solver: the SPIKE algorithm. Parallel Comput 32(2):177–194
11. Polizzi E, Sameh A (2007) SPIKE: A parallel environment for solving banded linear systems. Comput Fluids 36:113–120
12. Golub G, Sameh V, Sarin V (2001) A parallel balance scheme for banded linear systems. Numer Linear Algebr Appl 8(5):297–316
13. Demko S, Moss WF, Smith PW (1984) Decay rates for inverses of band matrices. Math Comput 43(168):491–499
14. Mikkelsen CCK, Manguoglu M (2008) Analysis of the truncated spike algorithm. SIAM J Matrix Anal Appl 30(4):1500–1519
15. Anderson E, Bai Z, Bischof C, Blackford S, Demmel J, Dongarra J, et al (1999) LAPACK users guide, 3rd edn. Society for Industrial and Appl. Math, Philadelphia
16. Schenk O, Grtner K (2004) Solving unsymmetric sparse systems of linear equations with PARDISO. J Future Gener Comput Syst 20(3):475–487
17. A distributed memory version of the SPIKE package can be obtained from http://software.intel.com/en-us/articles/intel-adaptive-spike-based-solver/
18. Manguoglu M, Sameh A, Schenk O (2009) PSPIKE: a parallel hybrid sparse linear system solver. Lecture notes in computer science, vol 5704. Springer, Berlin, pp 797–808

Spiral

Markus Püschel[1], Franz Franchetti[2], Yevgen Voronenko[2]
[1]ETH Zurich, Zurich, Switzerland
[2]Carnegie Mellon University, Pittsburgh, PA, USA

Definition

Spiral is a program generation system (software that generates other softwares) for linear transforms and an increasing list of other mathematical functions. The goal of Spiral is to automate the development and porting of performance libraries. Linear transforms include the discrete Fourier transform (DFT), discrete cosine transforms, convolution, and the discrete wavelet transform. The input to Spiral consists of a high-level mathematical algorithm specification and selected architectural and microarchitectural parameters. The output is performance-optimized code in a high-level language such as C, possibly augmented with vector intrinsics and threading instructions.

Discussion

Introduction

The advent of computers with multiple cores, SIMD (single-instruction multiple-data) vector instruction sets, and deep memory hierarchies has a dramatic effect on the development of high-performance software. The problem is particularly apparent for functions that perform mathematical computations, which form the core of most data or information processing applications. Namely, on a current workstation, the performance difference between a straightforward implementation of an optimal (minimizing operations count) algorithm and the fastest possible implementation is typically 10–100 times.

As an example, consider Fig. 1, which shows the performance (in gigafloating point operations per second) of four implementations of the discrete Fourier transform for varying input sizes on a quadcore Intel Core i7. Each one uses a fast algorithm with roughly the same operations count. Yet the difference between the slowest and the fastest is 12–35 times. The bottom line is the code from Numerical Recipes [20]. The best standard C code is about five times faster due to memory hierarchy optimizations and constant precomputation. Proper use of explicit vector intrinsics instructions yields another three times. Explicit threading for the four cores, properly done, yields another three times for large sizes.

The plot shows that the compiler cannot perform these optimizations as is true for most mathematical functions. The reason lies in both the compiler's lack of domain knowledge needed for the necessary transformations and the large set of optimization choices with uncertain outcome that the compiler cannot assess. Hence the optimization task falls with the programmer and requires considerable skill. Further, the optimizations are usually platform specific, and hence have to be repeated with every new generation of computers.

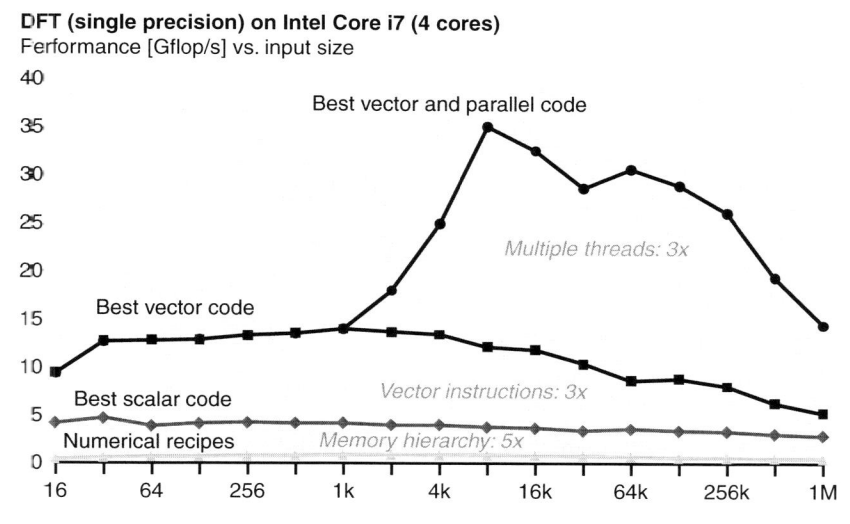

Spiral. Fig. 1 Performance of different implementations of the discrete Fourier transform (DFT) and reason for the performance difference (From [10])

Spiral overcomes these problems by completely automating the implementation and optimization processes for the functions it supports. Complete automation means that Spiral produces source code for a given function given only a very high-level representation of the algorithms for this function and a high-level platform description. After algorithm and platform knowledge are inserted, Spiral can generate various types of code including for fixed and general input size, threaded or vectorized.

The approach taken by Spiral is based on the following key principles:

- Algorithm knowledge for a given mathematical function is represented in the form of *breakdown rules* in a *domain-specific language*. Each rule represents a divide-and-conquer algorithm. The language is based on mathematics, and is declarative and platform independent. These properties enable the mapping to various forms of parallelism from algorithm knowledge that is inserted only once. They also enable the derivation of the library structure for general input size implementations by computing the so-called *recursion step closure*.
- Platform knowledge is organized into *paradigms*. A paradigm is a feature of a platform that requires structural optimization and possibly source code extensions. Examples include shared memory parallelism and SIMD vector processing. Each paradigm consists of a set of *parameterized rewrite rules* and *base cases* expressed in the same language as the algorithm knowledge. The base cases constitute a subset of the domain-specific language that maps well to a paradigm. The rewrite rules interact with the breakdown rules to produce algorithms that are base cases, which means they are structurally optimized for the considered paradigm. Examples of parameters include the SIMD vector length or the cacheline size. Paradigms are designed to be composable.
- Spiral uses *empirical search* to automatically explore choices in a feedback loop. This is done by generating candidate implementations and evaluating their performance. Even though theoretically unsatisfying, search enables further optimization for intricate microarchitectural details that may be unknown or are not well understood.

In summary, Spiral integrates techniques from mathematics, programming languages, compilers, automatic performance tuning, and symbolic computation. The entire Spiral system combines aspects of a compiler, generative programming, and an expert system.

The remainder of this section describes the framework underlying Spiral and the inner workings of the actual system. The presentation focuses on linear transforms; extensions of Spiral beyond transforms are briefly discussed in the end.

Algorithm Representation

Linear transforms. A linear transform is a function

$$x \mapsto Mx,$$

where M is a fixed matrix, x is the input vector, and $y = Mx$ the output vector. Different transforms correspond to different matrices M. For simplicity, M is referred to as transform in the following. Most transforms M are square $n \times n$, which implies that x and y are of length n. Most transforms exist for all $n = 1, 2, \ldots$.

Possibly the most well-known transform is the DFT, defined by the $n \times n$ matrix:

$$\mathrm{DFT}_n = \left[\omega_n^{k\ell}\right]_{0 \leq k, \ell < n}, \omega_n = e^{-2\pi i/n}, \quad i = \sqrt{-1}.$$

Other examples include the discrete Hartley transform,

$$\mathrm{DHT}_n = \left[\cos(2\pi k\ell/n) + \sin(2\pi k\ell/n)\right]_{0 \leq k, \ell < n},$$

the discrete cosine transform (DCT) of type 2,

$$\mathrm{DCT}\text{-}2_n = \left[\cos\left(k\left(\ell + \tfrac{1}{2}\right)\pi/n\right)\right]_{0 \leq k, \ell < n},$$

as well as other types of discrete cosine and sine transforms, the Walsh–Hadamard transform, the real DFT, the discrete wavelet transform, the inverses and other variants of the preceding transforms, and finite impulse response filters.

Fast transform algorithms: SPL. If M is $n \times n$ and has few or no zero entries, then a direct computation of $y = Mx$ requires $O(n^2)$ many operations. However, all the transforms mentioned above have fast algorithms that reduce their complexity below that, typically to $O(n \log(n))$. Every algorithm can be expressed as a factorization of the transform matrix M into a product of sparse matrices. As an example, assume $M = M_1 M_2 M_3 M_4$; then $y = Mx$ can be computed in four steps as

$$t = M_4 x, u = M_3 t, v = M_2 u, y = M_1 v.$$

If the M_i are sufficiently sparse, this reduces the operations count.

The sparse matrices occurring in transform algorithms have a structure that can be formally expressed using basic matrices and matrix operators such as the direct sum and the tensor or Kronecker product. This notation forms the basis for the language SPL (signal processing language) explained next.

Basic matrices include the $n \times n$ identity matrix I_n, diagonal matrices $D_n = \mathrm{diag}(a_0, \ldots, a_{n-1})$, the 2×2 butterfly matrix

$$F_2 = \begin{bmatrix} 1 & 1 \\ 1 & -1 \end{bmatrix},$$

the stride permutation matrix L_k^n, defined for $n = km$ by the underlying permutation

$$\ell_k^n : im + j \mapsto jk + i, \ 0 \leq i < k, \ 0 \leq j < m, \quad (1)$$

and several others.

Matrix operators include the matrix product, the direct sum

$$A \oplus B = \begin{bmatrix} A & \\ & B \end{bmatrix},$$

and the tensor product

$$A \otimes B = \left[a_{k,\ell} B\right]_{0 \leq k, \ell < n}, \quad \text{for } A = \left[a_{k,\ell}\right]_{0 \leq k, \ell < n}.$$

Most important are the tensor products where A or B is the identity:

$$I_n \otimes B = \begin{bmatrix} B & & \\ & \ddots & \\ & & B \end{bmatrix},$$

and, for example,

$$\begin{bmatrix} a & b \\ c & d \end{bmatrix} \otimes I_3 = \begin{bmatrix} aI_3 & bI_3 \\ cI_3 & dI_3 \end{bmatrix} = \begin{bmatrix} a & & & b & & \\ & a & & & b & \\ & & a & & & b \\ c & & & d & & \\ & c & & & d & \\ & & c & & & d \end{bmatrix}.$$

A (partial) description of SPL in Backus–Naur form is provided in Table 1.

Algorithms as SPL breakdown rules. Using SPL, the algorithm knowledge in Spiral is captured by *breakdown rules*. A breakdown rule represents a one-step divide-and-conquer algorithm of a transform. This means the transform is factorized into sparse matrices involving other, typically smaller, transforms.

Spiral. Table 1 A subset of SPL in Backus–Naur form; n, k are positive integers, a_i are real or complex numbers

$$
\begin{aligned}
\langle spl \rangle &::= \langle generic \rangle \mid \langle basic \rangle \mid \langle transform \rangle \mid \\
&\quad \langle spl \rangle \cdots \langle spl \rangle \mid \quad \text{(product)} \\
&\quad \langle spl \rangle \oplus \ldots \oplus \langle spl \rangle \mid \quad \text{(direct sum)} \\
&\quad \langle spl \rangle \otimes \cdots \otimes \langle spl \rangle \mid \quad \text{(tensor product)} \\
&\quad \ldots \\
\langle generic \rangle &::= \mathrm{diag}(a_0, \ldots, a_{n-1}) \mid \ldots \\
\langle basic \rangle &::= I_n \mid L_k^n \mid F_2 \mid \ldots \\
\langle transform \rangle &::= \mathrm{DFT}_n \mid \mathrm{DHT}_n \mid \text{DCT-}2_n \mid \ldots
\end{aligned}
$$

The most well-known example is the general-radix Cooley–Tukey fast Fourier transform (FFT):

$$\mathrm{DFT}_n \to (\mathrm{DFT}_k \otimes I_m) T_m^n (I_k \otimes \mathrm{DFT}_m) L_k^n, \quad n = km, \tag{2}$$

where T_m^n is the diagonal matrix of *twiddle factors*. For $n = 16 = 4 \times 4$, the factorization is visualized in Fig. 2 together with the associated data-flow graph. The smaller DFT_4's are boxes of equal shades of gray.

To terminate the recursion, base cases are needed. For example, for two-powers n, a size two base case is sufficient:

$$\mathrm{DFT}_2 \to F_2. \tag{3}$$

A few points are worth noting about this representation of transform algorithms:

- The representation (2) is *point free*, i.e., the input vector is not present.
- The representation (2) is declarative.
- Since the rule (2) is a matrix equation, it can be manipulated using matrix identities. For example, both sides can be inverted or transposed, to obtain an inverse or transposed transform algorithm.
- A breakdown rule may have degrees of freedom. An example is the choice of k in (2).
- A rule like (2) does not specify how to compute the smaller transforms. This implies that rules have to be applied recursively until an algorithm is completely specified. Because of this and the availability of different rules for the same transform, there is a large set of choices. In other words, the relatively few existing rules yield a very large space of possible algorithms. This makes rules a very efficient representation of algorithm knowledge. For example, for $n = 2^\ell$, (2) alone yields $\Theta(5^\ell / \ell^{3/2})$ different algorithms, all with roughly the same operations count.

Spiral contains about 200 breakdown rules for about 40 transforms, some of which are auxiliary. The most important rules for the DFT, without complete specification, are shown in Table 2. Note the occurrence of auxiliary transforms.

Spiral Program Generation: Overview

The task performed by Spiral is to translate the algorithm knowledge (represented as in Table 2) for a given transform into optimized source code (we assume C/C++) for a given platform.

The exact approach for generating the code depends on the type of code that has to be generated. The most important distinctions are the following:

- *Fixed input size versus general input size*: If the input size is known (e.g., "DFT of size 4" as shown in Table 3a and b), the algorithm to be used and other decisions can be determined at program generation time and can be inlined. The result is a function containing only loops and basic blocks of straightline code. If the input size is not known, it becomes an additional input and the implementation becomes recursive (Table 3c). The actual algorithm, i.e., recursive computation, is now chosen at runtime once the input size is known.
- *Straightline code versus loop code (fixed input size only)*: Straightline code (Table 3a) is only suitable for small sizes, but can be faster, due to reduced overhead and increased opportunities for algebraic simplifications. Loop code (Table 3b) requires additional optimizations that merge redundant loops.
- *Scalar code versus parallel code*: Code that is parallelized for SIMD vector extensions or multiple cores requires specific optimizations and the use of explicit vector intrinsics or threading directives.

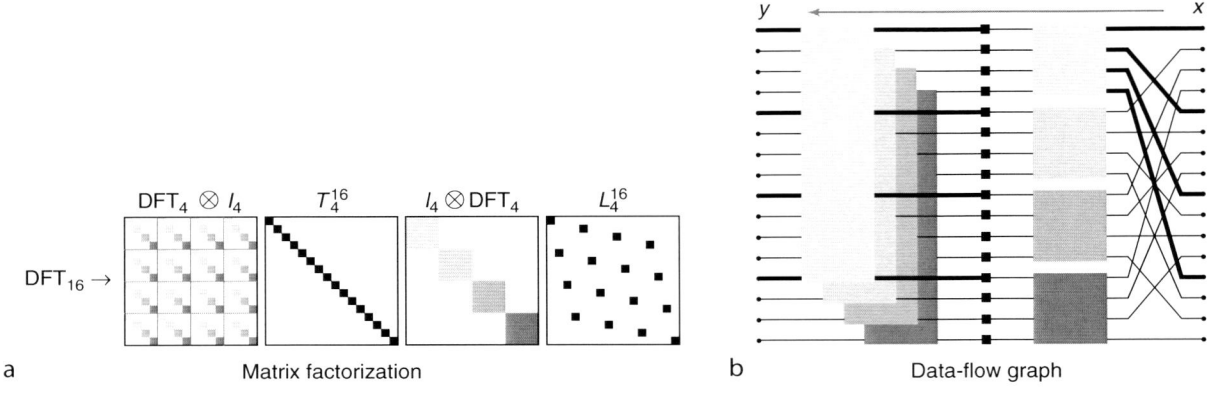

Spiral. Fig. 2 Cooley–Tukey FFT (2) for 16 = 4 × 4 as SPL rule and as (complex) data-flow graph (from *right* to *left*). Some lines are bold to emphasize the strided access of the **DFT**$_4$s (From [10])

Spiral. Table 2 A selection of breakdown rules representing algorithm knowledge for the DFT. rDFT is an auxiliary transform and has two parameters. RDFT is a version of the real DFT

DFT$_n$	$\to$	$(\text{DFT}_k \otimes I_m) T_m^n (I_k \otimes \text{DFT}_m) L_k^n$,	(Cooley–Tukey FFT)	$n = km$
DFT$_n$	$\to$	$V_n^{-1}(\text{DFT}_k \otimes I_m)(I_k \otimes \text{DFT}_m) V_n$,	(Prime-factor FFT)	$n = km$, $\gcd(k,m) = 1$
DFT$_n$	$\to$	$W_n^{-1}(I_1 \oplus \text{DFT}_{p-1}) E_n (I_1 \oplus \text{DFT}_{p-1}) W_n$,	(Rader FFT)	n prime
DFT$_n$	$\to$	$B'_n D_m \text{DFT}_m D'_m \text{DFT}_m D''_m B_n$,	(Bluestein FFT)	$n > 2m$
DFT$_n$	$\to$	$P_{k,2m}^T \left(\text{DFT}_{2m} \oplus \left(I_{k-1} \otimes_i C_{2m} \text{rDFT}_{2m, i/2k} \right) \right) (\text{RDFT}_{2k} \otimes I_m)$,		$n = 2km$
RDFT$_n$	$\to$	$\left(P_{k,m}^T \otimes I_2 \right) \left(\text{RDFT}_{2m} \oplus \left(I_{k-1} \otimes_i D_{2m} \text{rDFT}_{2m, i/2k} \right) \right) (\text{RDFT}_{2k} \otimes I_m)$,		$n = 2km$
rDFT$_{n,u}$	$\to$	$L_m^{2n} \left(I_k \otimes_i \text{rDFT}_{2m,(i+u)/k} \right) (\text{rDFT}_{2k,u} \otimes I_m)$,		$n = 2km$

Spiral. Table 3 Code types

(a) Fixed input size, unrolled	(b) Fixed input size, looped	(c) General input size library, recursive
```void dft_4(cpx *Y, cpx *X){ cpx s, t, t2, t3; t = (X[0] + X[2]); t2 = (X[0] - X[2]); t3 = (X[1] + X[3]); s = _I_*(X[1] - X[3]); Y[0] = (t + t3); Y[2] = (t - t3); Y[1] = (t2 + s); Y[3] = (t2 - s); }```	```void dft_4(cpx *Y, cpx *X){ cpx T[4]; cpx W[2] = {1, _I_}; for(int i = 0; i <= 1; i++) { cpx w = W[i]; T[2*i] = (X[i] + X[i+2]); T[2*i+1] = w*(X[i] - X[i+2]); } for(int j = 0; j <= 1; j++) { Y[j] = T[j] + T[j+2]; Y[2+j] = T[j] - T[j+2]; } }```	```struct dft : public Env{ dft(int n); // constructor void compute(cpx *Y, cpx *X); int _rule, f, n; char *_dat; Env *ch1, *ch2; }; void dft::compute(cpx *Y, cpx *X){ ch2->compute(Y, X, n, f, n, f); ch1->compute(Y, Y, n, f, n, n/f); }```

The program generation process is explained in the next four sections corresponding to four different code types of increasing difficulty. The order matches the historic development, since for each move to the next code type at least one new idea had to be introduced. The types and main ideas (in parentheses) are

- Fixed input size straightline code (SPL, breakdown rules, feedback loop)

- Fixed input size loop code (Σ-SPL, loop merging)
- Fixed input size parallel code (paradigms, tagged rewriting)
- General input size code (recursion step closure, parameterization)

Spiral generates code for fixed input size transforms (first three bullets), as shown in Fig. 3. The input is the transform symbol (e.g., "DFT") and the size (e.g., "128"). The output is a C function that computes the transform ($y = \text{DFT}_{128}\, x$ in this case). Depending on code type, not all blocks in Fig. 3 may be used.

The block diagram for the general input size code is shown later.

Fixed Input Size: Straightline Code

Given as input to Spiral is a transform symbol ("DFT") and the input size. The program generation does not need the parallelization and loop optimization blocks. Further, no Σ-SPL is needed, which means the SPL-to-Σ-SPL block and the Σ-SPL-to-code block are joined to one SPL-to-code block.

Algorithm generation. Spiral uses a rewrite system that recursively applies the breakdown rules (e.g., Table 2) to generate a complete SPL algorithm for the transform. As mentioned before, there are many choices due to the choice of rule and the degree of freedom in some rules (e.g., k in (2)).

SPL to C code and optimization. The SPL expression is then compiled into actual C code using the internal SPL compiler, which recursively applies the translation rules sketched in Table 4.

All loops are unrolled and code-level optimizations are applied. These include array scalarization, constant propagation, and algebraic simplification.

Performance evaluation. The runtime of the resulting code is measured and fed into the search block that controls the algorithm generation.

Search. The search drives a feedback loop that generates and evaluates different algorithms to find the fastest. Dynamic programming has proven to work best in many cases, but other techniques including evolutionary search or bandit-based Monte Carlo exploration have also been studied.

Fixed Input Size: Loop Code

The approach to generating straightline code can also be used to generate loop code (Table 4 yields loops), but the code will be inefficient.

The problem: Loop merging. To illustrate the problem, consider the SPL expression

$$(I_4 \otimes F_2)L_4^8.$$

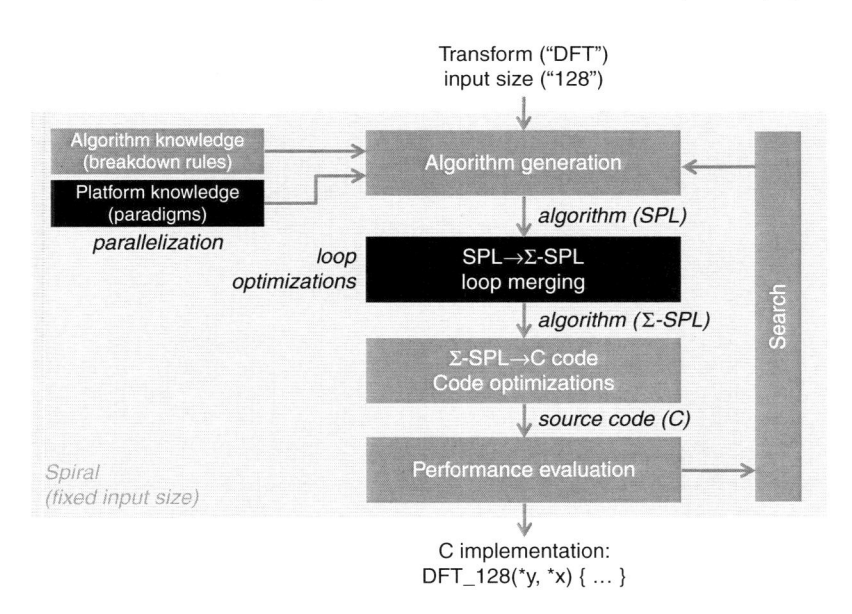

Spiral. Fig. 3 Spiral program generator for fixed input size functions. For straightline code, no Σ-SPL is needed and SPL is translated directly into C code

Spiral. Table 4 Translation of SPL to code. The subscript of A, B specifies the (square) matrix size. `x[b:s:e]` denotes (Matlab style) the subvector of x starting at `b`, ending at `e`, and extracted at stride `s`. D is a diagonal matrix, whose diagonal elements are stored in an array with the same name

SPL expression S	Pseudo code for $y = Sx$
$A_n B_n$	`<code for: t = Bx>` `<code for: y = At>`
$I_m \otimes A_n$	`for (i=0; i<m; i++)` `    <code for: y[i*n:1:i*n+n-1] = A(x[i*n:1:i*n+n-1])>`
$A_m \otimes I_n$	`for (i=0; i<n; i++)` `    <code for: y[i:n:i+m*n-n] = A(x[i:n:i+m*n-n])>`
D_n	`for (i=0; i<n; i++)` `    y[i] = D[i]*x[i];`

L_k^{km}	`for (i=0; i<k; i++)`
	 `    for (j=0; j<m; j++)`
	 `        y[i*m+j] = x[j*k+i];`

F_2	`y[0] = x[0] + x[1];` `y[1] = x[0] - x[1];`

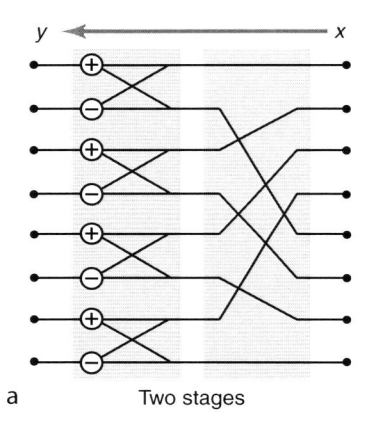

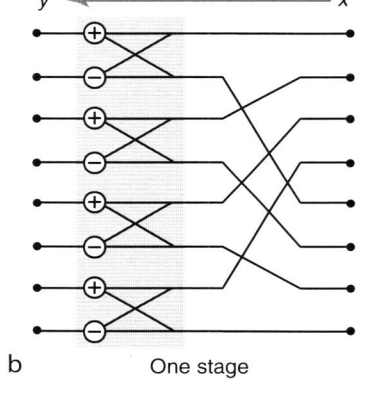

Spiral. Fig. 4 The loop merging problem for $(I_4 \otimes F_2)L_4^8$

The application of Table 4 yields the code visualized in Fig. 4a:

```
// Input: double x[8], output: y[8]
double t[8];
for(int i=0; i<4; i++) {
    for (int j=0; j<2; j++) {
        t[i*2+j] = x[j*4+i];
    }
}
for (int j=0; j<4; j++) {
    y[2*j]   = t[2*j] + t[2*j+1];
    y[2*j+1] = t[2*j] - t[2*j+1];
}
```

This is known to be suboptimal since the permutation (first loop) can be fused with the subsequent computation loop, thus eliminating one pass through the data (Fig. 4b):

```
//Input: double x[8], output: y[8]
for (int j=0; j<4; j++) {
    y[2*j]   = x[j] + x[j+4];
    y[2*j+1] = x[j] - x[j+4];
}
```

This transformation cannot be expressed in SPL and, in the general case, is difficult to perform on C code. To solve this problem, Σ-SPL was developed, an extension of SPL that can express loops. The loop merging is then performed by rewriting Σ-SPL expressions.

Σ-SPL. Σ-SPL adds four basic components to SPL:

1. Index mapping functions
2. Scalar functions
3. Parameterized matrices
4. Iterative sum $\sum$

These are defined next.

An integer interval is denoted by $\mathbb{I}_n = \{0, \ldots, n-1\}$, and an index mapping function f with domain $\mathbb{I}_n$ and range $\mathbb{I}_N$ is denoted by

$$f^{n \to N} : \mathbb{I}_n \to \mathbb{I}_N;\ i \mapsto f(i).$$

An example is the stride function

$$h_{b,s}^{n \to N} : \mathbb{I}_n \to \mathbb{I}_N;\ i \mapsto b + is, \quad \text{for } s|N. \tag{4}$$

Permutations are written as $f^{n \to n} = f^n$, such as the stride permutation in (1).

A scalar function $f : \mathbb{I}_n \to \mathbb{C};\ i \mapsto f(i)$ maps an integer interval to the domain of complex or real numbers, and is abbreviated as $f^{n \to \mathbb{C}}$. Scalar functions are used to describe diagonal matrices.

Σ-SPL adds four types of parameterized matrices to SPL (gather, scatter, permutation, diagonal):

$$G(f^{n \to N}),\ S(f^{n \to N}),\ P(f^n),\ \text{and}\ \mathrm{diag}\left(f^{n \to \mathbb{C}}\right).$$

Their translation into actual code (which also defines the matrices) is shown in Table 5. For example,

$$G(h_{0,1}^{n \to N}) = \begin{bmatrix} 1 & & \\ & \ddots & \\ & & 1 \end{bmatrix},\quad S(h_{0,1}^{n \to N}) = G(h_{0,1})^\top.$$

Spiral. Table 5 Translation of $\sum$-SPL to code

Σ-SPL expression S	Code for y = Sx
$G(f^{n \to N})$	`for(i=0; i<n; i++)` `  y[i] = x[f(i)];`
$S(f^{n \to N})$	`for(i=0; i<n; i++)` `  y[f(i)] = x[i];`
$P(f^n)$	`for(i=0; i<n; i++)` `  y[i] = x[f(i)];`
$\mathrm{diag}\left(f^{n \to \mathbb{C}}\right)$	`for(i=0; i<n; i++)` `  y[i] = f(i)*x[i];`
$\sum_{i=0}^{k-1} A_i$	`for(i=0; i<k; i++)` `  <code for: y = A_i * x>`

Finally, Σ-SPL adds the iterative matrix sum

$$\sum_{i=0}^{n-1} A_i$$

to represent loops. The A_i are restricted such that no two A_i have a nonzero entry in the same row.

The following example shows how $\otimes$ is converted into a sum. A is assumed to be $n \times n$, and domain and range in the occurring stride functions are omitted for simplicity.

$$I_k \otimes A = \begin{bmatrix} A & & \\ & \ddots & \\ & & A \end{bmatrix} = \begin{bmatrix} A & & \\ & & \\ & & \end{bmatrix} + \cdots + \begin{bmatrix} & & \\ & & \\ & & A \end{bmatrix}$$
$$= S(h_{0,1})AG(h_{0,1}) + \ldots$$
$$\quad + S(h_{(k-1)n,1})AG(h_{(k-1)n,1})$$
$$= \sum_{i=0}^{k-1} S(h_{in,1})AG(h_{in,1})$$

Intuitively, the conversion to Σ-SPL makes the loop structure of $y = (I_k \otimes A)x$ explicit. In each iteration i, $G(\cdot)$ and $S(\cdot)$ specify how to read and write a portion of the input and output, respectively, to be processed by A.

Loop merging using Σ-SPL and rewriting. Using Σ-SPL, the loop merging problem identified before in the example $(I_4 \otimes F_2)L_4^8$ is solved by the loop optimization block in Fig. 3 as follows:

$$(I_4 \otimes F_2)L_4^8 \to \left(\sum_{i=0}^{3} S(h_{2i,\,1})F_2 G(h_{2i,\,1})\right) P(\ell_4^8)$$
$$\to \sum_{i=0}^{3} \left(S(h_{2i,\,1})F_2 G(\ell_4^8 \circ h_{2i,\,1})\right)$$
$$\to \sum_{i=0}^{3} \left(S(h_{2i,\,1})F_2 G(h_{i,\,2})\right)$$

The first step translates SPL into Σ-SPL. The second step performs the loop merging by composing the permutation ℓ_4^8 with the index functions of the subsequent gathers. The third step simplifies the resulting index functions. After that, actual C code is generated using Table 5.

Besides the added loop optimizations block in Fig. 3, the program generation for loop code operates iteratively exactly as for straightline code.

Fixed Input Size: Parallel Code

As was illustrated in Fig. 1, for compute functions, compilers usually fail to optimally (or at all) exploit the parallelism offered by a platform. Hence, the task falls with the programmer, who has to leave the standard C programming model and insert explicit threading or OpenMP loops for shared memory parallelism and so-called intrinsics for vector instruction sets. However, doing so in a straightforward way does not necessarily yield good performance.

The problem: Algorithm structure. To illustrate the problem, consider a target platform with four cores that share a cache with a cache block size of two complex numbers.

The first goal is to obtain parallel code with four threads for $I_4 \otimes F_2$ visualized in Fig. 5a. The computation is data parallel; hence, the loop suggested in Table 4 can be replaced, for example, by an OpenMP parallel loop. Note that each processor "owns" as working set exactly one cache block; hence, the parallelization will be efficient.

Now consider again the SPL expression $(I_4 \otimes F_2)L_4^8$ visualized in Fig. 5b. The computation is again data parallel, but the access pattern has changed such that always two processors access the same cache block. This produces false sharing, which triggers the cache coherency protocol and reduces performance. The problem is obviously the permutation L_4^8. Since the rules (e.g., those in Table 2) contain many, and various, permutations, a straightforward mapping to parallel code will yield highly suboptimal performance. To solve this problem inside Spiral, another rewrite system is introduced to restructure algorithms before mapping to parallel code. The restructuring will be different for different forms of parallelism, called paradigms.

Paradigms and tagged rewriting. A *paradigm* in Spiral is a feature of the target platform that requires structural optimization. Typically, a paradigm is a form of parallelism. Examples include shared memory parallelism (SMP) and SIMD parallelism. A paradigm may be parameterized, for example, by the vector length v for SIMD parallelism. In Spiral, a paradigm manifests itself by another rewrite system provided by the additional parallelism block in Fig. 3 (and backend extensions in the Σ-SPL to C code block to produce the actual code).

The goal of the new rewrite system is to structurally optimize a given SPL expression into a form that can be efficiently mapped to a given paradigm. The rewrite system is built from three main components:

- *Tags* encode the paradigm and relevant parameters. Examples include the tags "vec(v)" for SIMD vector extensions and the tag "smp(p,μ)" for SMP. The meaning of the parameters is explained later.
- *Base cases* are SPL constructs that can be mapped well to a given paradigm. As illustrated above, one example is any $I_p \otimes A_n$ for p-way SMP.
- *Tagged rewrite rules* are mathematical identities that translate general SPL expressions toward base cases. An example is the rule (assuming $p|n$)

$$\underbrace{A_m \otimes I_n}_{\text{smp}(p,\mu)} \to \underbrace{L_m^{mn}}_{\text{smp}(p,\mu)} \left(I_p \otimes (I_{n/p} \otimes A_m) \right) \underbrace{L_n^{mn}}_{\text{smp}(p,\mu)}.$$

The rule extracts the p-way parallel loop (base case) $I_p \otimes (I_{n/p} \otimes A_m)$ from $A_m \otimes I_n$. The stride permutations L_m^{mn} and L_n^{mn} are handled by further rewriting.

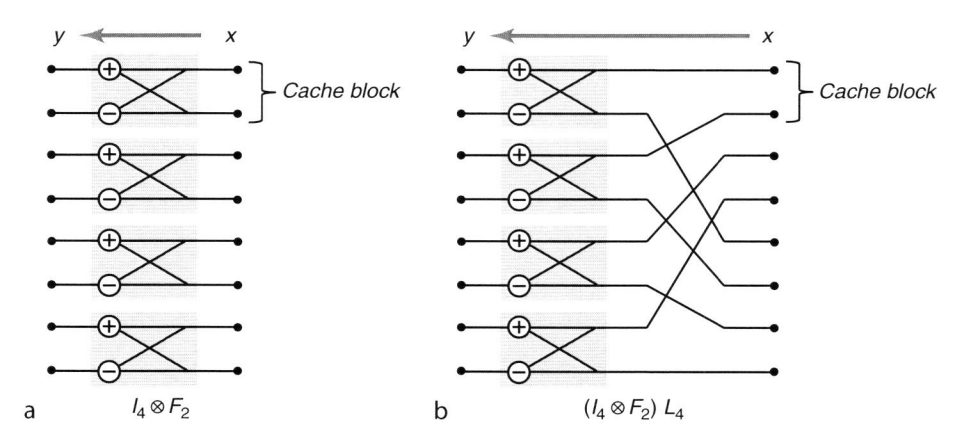

Spiral. Fig. 5 Mapping SPL constructs to four threads. Each thread computes one F_2. Both computations are data parallel, but (**a**) produces no false sharing, whereas (**b**) does

Example: SMP. For SMP, the tag $\text{smp}(p,\mu)$ contains the number of processors p and the cache block size μ. Base cases include $I_p \otimes A_n$ and $P \otimes I_\mu$, where P is any permutation. $P \otimes I_\mu$ moves data in blocks of size μ; hence false sharing is avoided. From these, other base cases can be built recursively as captured by the sketched grammar in Table 6.

Some SMP rewrite rules are shown in Table 7. Note that the rewriting is not unique, and not every sequence of rules terminates. Once all tags disappear, the rewriting terminates.

Example: SIMD. For SIMD, the tag $\text{vec}(\nu)$ contains only the vector length ν. The most important base case is $A_n \otimes I_\nu$, which can be mapped to vector code by generating scalar code for A_n and replacing every operation by its corresponding ν-way vector operation. Other base cases include $L_\nu^{2\nu}$, $L_2^{2\nu}$, and $L_\nu^{\nu^2}$, which are generated automatically from the instruction set [9]. Similar to Table 6, the entire set of vector base cases is specified by a grammar recursively built from the above special constructs.

Parallelization by rewriting. In Spiral, parallelization adds the new parallelization block in Fig. 3. The parallelization rules are applied interleaved with the breakdown rules to generate SPL algorithms that have the right structure for the desired paradigm. For example, for the DFT it may operate as follows:

$$\underbrace{\text{DFT}_{mn}}_{\text{smp}(p,\mu)} \to \underbrace{\left((\text{DFT}_m \otimes I_n) T_n^{mn} (I_m \otimes \text{DFT}_n) L_m^{mn}\right)}_{\text{smp}(p,\mu)}$$

$$\cdots$$

$$\to \underbrace{(\text{DFT}_m \otimes I_n)}_{\text{smp}(p,\mu)} \underbrace{T_n^{mn}}_{\text{smp}(p,\mu)} \underbrace{(I_m \otimes \text{DFT}_n)}_{\text{smp}(p,\mu)} \underbrace{L_m^{nm}}_{\text{smp}(p,\mu)}$$

$$\cdots$$

$$\to \left((L_m^{mp} \otimes I_{n/p\mu}) \otimes I_\mu\right)\left(I_p \otimes (\text{DFT}_m \otimes I_{n/p})\right)$$
$$\left((L_p^{mp} \otimes I_{n/p\mu}) \otimes I_\mu\right) T_m^{mn} \left(I_p \otimes (I_{m/p} \otimes \text{DFT}_n)\right)$$
$$\left(I_p \otimes L_{m/p}^{mn/p}\right) \left((L_p^{pn} \otimes I_{m/p\mu}) \otimes I_\mu\right)$$

First, Spiral applies the breakdown rule (2). Then the parallelization rules transform the resulting SPL expression in several steps. Note how the final expression has only access patterns (permutations) of the form $P \otimes I_\mu$ and all computations are in the form $I_p \otimes A$ (and the diagonal T_m^{mn}). The smaller DFTs can be expanded in different ways, for example, by rewriting for SIMD. Further choices are used for search.

The remaining operation of Spiral including Σ-SPL conversion and search proceeds as before.

General Input Size

An implementation that can compute a transform for arbitrary input size is fundamentally different from one for fixed input size (compare Table 3b and c). If the input size n is fixed, for example, $n = 4$, the computation is

```
(x,y) -> dft_4(y,x)
```

and all decisions such as the choice of recursion until base cases are reached can be made at implementation time. In an equivalent implementation (called library) for general input size n,

```
(n,x,y) -> dft(n,y,x)
```

the recursion is fixed only once the input size is known. Formally, the computation now becomes

```
n -> ((x,y) -> dft(n,y,x))
```

Spiral. Table 6 $\text{smp}(p,\mu)$ base cases in Backus–Naur form; n is a positive integer, a_i are real or complex numbers

⟨smp⟩ ::= ⟨gener c⟩ | ⟨basic⟩ |
⟨smp⟩ · · · · ⟨smp⟩ | (product)
⟨smp⟩ ⊕ . . . ⊕ ⟨smp⟩ | (direct sum)
$I_n \otimes$ ⟨smp⟩ | (tensor product)
. . .
⟨generic⟩ ::= $\text{diag}(a_0,\ldots,a_{n-1})$ | . . .
⟨basic⟩ ::= $I_p \otimes A_n$ | $P \otimes I_\mu$ | . . .

Spiral. Table 7 Examples of $\text{smp}(p,\mu)$ rewrite rules

$\underbrace{AB}_{\text{smp}(p,\mu)}$	$\to$	$\underbrace{A}_{\text{smp}(p,\mu)} \underbrace{B}_{\text{smp}(p,\mu)}$
$\underbrace{A_m \otimes I_n}_{\text{smp}(p,\mu)}$	$\to$	$\underbrace{\left(L_m^{mp} \otimes I_{n/p}\right)\left(I_p \otimes (A_m \otimes I_{n/p})\right)\left(L_p^{mp} \otimes I_{n/p}\right)}_{\text{smp}(p,\mu)}$
$\underbrace{L_m^{mn}}_{\text{smp}(p,\mu)}$	$\to$	$\begin{pmatrix}\underbrace{\left(I_p \otimes L_{m/p}^{mn/p}\right)}_{\text{smp}(p,\mu)} \underbrace{\left(L_p^{pn} \otimes I_{m/p}\right)}_{\text{smp}(p,\mu)} \\ \underbrace{\left(L_n^{2m} \otimes I_{n/p}\right)}_{\text{smp}(p,\mu)} \underbrace{\left(I_p \otimes L_m^{mn/p}\right)}_{\text{smp}(p,\mu)}\end{pmatrix}$
$\underbrace{I_m \otimes A_n}_{\text{smp}(p,\mu)}$	$\to$	$I_p \otimes (I_{m/p} \otimes A_n)$
$\underbrace{(P \otimes I_n)}_{\text{smp}(p,\mu)}$	$\to$	$(P \otimes I_{n/\mu}) \otimes I_\mu$

which is an example of function currying. A C++ implementation is sketched in Table 3c, where the two steps would take the form

```
dft * f = new dft(n); // initialization
f->compute(y, x);     // computation
```

The first step determines the recursion to be taken using search or heuristics, and precomputes the twiddle factors needed for the computation. The second step performs the actual computation. The underlying assumption is that the cost of the first step is amortized by a sufficient number of computations. This model is used by FFTW [15] and the libraries generated by Spiral.

To support the above model, the implementation needs recursive functions. The major problem is that the optimizations introduced before operate in nontrivial ways across function boundaries, thus creating more functions than expected. The challenge is to derive these functions automatically.

The problem: Loop merging across function boundaries. To illustrate the problem, consider the Cooley–Tukey FFT (2). A direct recursive implementation would consist of four steps corresponding to the four matrix factors in (2). Two of the steps would call smaller DFTs:

```
void dft(int n, cpx *y, cpx *x) {
    int k = choose_factor(n);
    int m = n/k;
    cpx *t1 = Permute x with L(n,k);
    // t2 = (I_k tensor DFT_m)*t1
    for(int i=0; i<k; ++i)
        dft(m, t2 + m*i, t1 + m*i);
    // t3 = T^n_m*t2, f() computes
    // diagonal entries of T
    for(int i=0; i<n; ++i)
        t3[i] = f(i) * t2[i];
    // y = (DFT_k tensor I_m)*t3,
    //cannot call dft() recursively,
    //need strided I/O
    for(int i=0; i<m; ++i)
        dft_stride(k, m, y + i, t3 + i);
}
// to be implemented
void dft_stride(int n, int stride,
    cpx *Y, cpx *X);
```

Note how even this simple implementation is not self-contained. A new function `dft_stride` is needed that accesses the input in a stride and produces the output at the same stride (see the data flow in Fig. 2).

However, as explained before, loops should be merged where possible. For fixed size code, Spiral would merge the first loop with the second, and the third loop with the fourth, using Σ-SPL rewriting. The same can be done in the general size recursive implementation, but the merging crosses function boundaries:

```
void dft(int n, cpx *y, cpx *x) {
    int k = choose_factor(n);
    //t1 = (I_k tensor DFT_m)L(n,k)*x
    for(int i=0; i < k; ++i)
        dft_iostride(m, k, 1, t1 + m*i,
            x + m*i);
    // y = (DFT_k tensor I_m) T^n_m
    // diagonal entries of T are now
    // precomputed in precomp_f[]
    for(int i=0; i < m; ++i)
        dft_scaled(k, m, precomp_f[i],
            y + i, t1 + i);
}

// to be implemented
void dft_iostride(int n, int istride,
int ostride, cpx *y, cpx *x);
void dft_scaled(int n, int stride,
cpx *d, cpx *y, cpx *x);
```

Now there are two additional functions: `dft_iostride` reads at a stride and writes at a different stride, and `dft_scaled` first scales the input and then performs a DFT at a stride.

So at least three functions are needed with different signatures. However, the two additional functions are also implemented recursively, possibly spawning new functions. Calling these functions *recursion steps*, the main challenge is to automatically derive the complete set of recursion steps needed, called the "recursion step closure." Further, for each recursion step in the closure, the signature has to be derived.

Recursion step closure by Σ-SPL rewriting. Spiral derives the recursion step closure using Σ-SPL and the same rewriting system that is used for loop merging.

For example, the two additional recursion steps in the optimized implementation above are automatically obtained from (2) as follows. Recursion steps are marked by overbraces.

$$\overbrace{\mathrm{DFT}_n} \to (\overbrace{\mathrm{DFT}_{n/k}} \otimes I_k) T_k^n (I_{n/k} \otimes \overbrace{\mathrm{DFT}_k}) L_{n/k}^n$$

$$\to \left(\sum_{i=0}^{k-1} S(h_{i,k}) \overbrace{\mathrm{DFT}_{n/k}} G(h_{i,k}) \right)$$

$$\mathrm{diag}(f) \left(\sum_{j=0}^{n/k-1} S(h_{jk,1}) \overbrace{\mathrm{DFT}_k} G(h_{jk,1}) \right) P(\ell_{n/k}^n)$$

$$\to \sum_{i=0}^{k-1} S(h_{i,\kappa}) \overbrace{\mathrm{DFT}_{n/k} \mathrm{diag}(f \circ h_{i,k})} G(h_{i,k})$$

$$\sum_{j=0}^{n/k-1} S(h_{j\kappa,\_}) \overbrace{\mathrm{DFT}_k} G(h_{j,n/k})$$

$$\to \sum_{i=0}^{k-1} \overbrace{S(h_{i,k}) \mathrm{DFT}_{n/k} \mathrm{diag}(f \circ h_{i,k}) G(h_{i,k})}$$

$$\sum_{j=0}^{n/k-1} \overbrace{S(h_{j\kappa,\_}) \mathrm{DFT}_k G(h_{j,n/k})} \quad (5)$$

The first step applies the breakdown rule (2). The second step converts to Σ-SPL. The third step performs loop merging as explained before. The fourth step expands the braces to include the context. The two expressions under the braces correspond to the two functions `dft_iostride` and `dft_scaled`. The process is now repeated for the expression under the braces until closure is reached. In this example, only one additional function is needed, i.e., the recursion step closure consists of four mutually recursive functions. The derivation of the recursion steps also yields a Σ-SPL specification of the actual recursion, i.e., their implementation by a recursive function (e.g., (5) for DFT_n).

For the best performance, the braces may be extended to also include the loop represented by the iterative sum. Moving the loop into the function enables better C/C++ compiler optimizations.

If the implementation is vectorized or parallelized, the initial breakdown rules are first rewritten as explained before and then the closure is computed. The size of the closure is typically increased in this case.

Program generation for general input size: Overview. The overall process is visualized in Fig. 6. The input to Spiral is now a (sufficient) set of breakdown rules for a given transform or transforms. The rules are parallelized if desired, using the appropriate paradigms; then the recursion step closure is computed, which also yields the actual recursions.

The resulting recursion steps need base cases for termination. These are generated using the algorithm generation block from the fixed input size Spiral (Fig. 3)

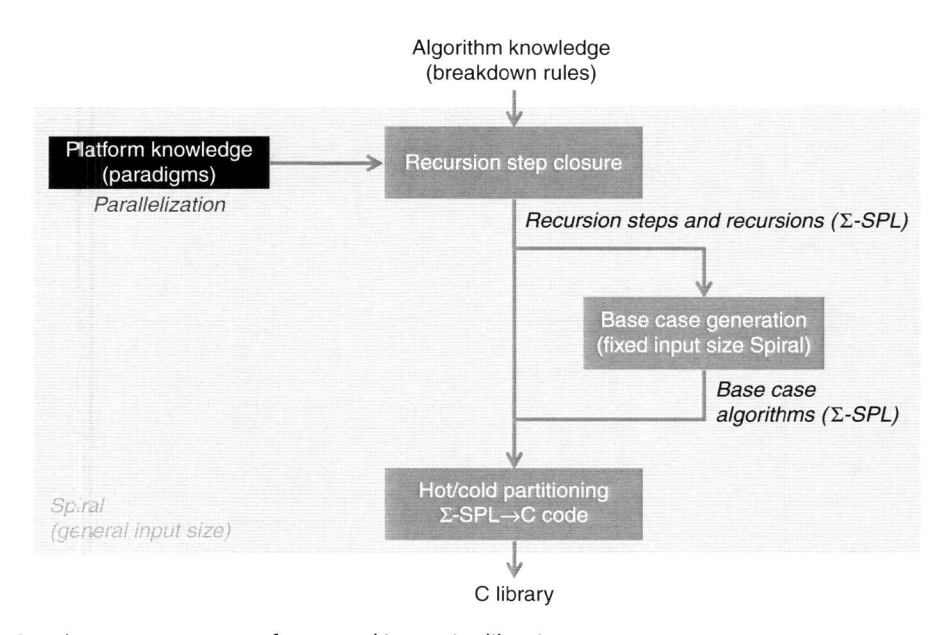

Spiral. Fig. 6 Spiral program generator for general input size libraries

for a range of small sizes (e.g., $n \leq 32$) to improve performance. These, the recursion steps, and the recursions are fed into the final block to generate the final library. Among other junctions, the block performs the *hot/cold partitioning* that determines which parameters in a recursion step are precomputed during initialization and which become parameters of the actual compute function. Finally, the actual code is generated (which now includes recursive functions) and integrated into a common infrastructure to obtain a complete library.

Many details are omitted in this description and are provided in [29, 30].

Extensions

A major question is whether the approach taken by Spiral can be extended beyond the domain of linear transforms, while maintaining both the basic principles outlined in the introduction and the ability to automatically perform the necessary transformations and reasoning. First progress in this direction was made in [7] with the introduction of the operator language (OL). OL generalizes SPL by considering operators that may be nonlinear and may have more than one vector input or output. Important constructs such as the tensor product are generalized to operators. First results on program generation for functions such as radar imaging, Viterbi decoding, matrix multiplication, and the physical layer functions of wireless communication protocols have already been developed.

Related Entries

▶ATLAS (Automatically Tuned Linear Algebra Software)
▶FFT (Fast Fourier Transform)
▶FFTW

Bibliographic Notes and Further Reading

Spiral is based on early ideas on using tensor products to map FFT algorithms to parallel supercomputers [16]. The first paper describing SPL and the SPL compiler is [32]. See also [14] for basic block optimizations for transforms. The first complete basic Spiral system including SPL algorithm generation and search was presented in [23], with a more extensive treatment in [24] and probably the best overview paper [22], which fully develops SPL for a variety of transforms. The path to complete automation in the transform domain continued with Σ-SPL and loop merging [11], the introduction of rewriting systems for SIMD vectorization [8, 13] and base case generation [9], SMP parallelization [12], and distributed memory parallelization [2, 3]. The final step to generating general size, parallel, adaptive libraries was made in [29, 30]. The generated libraries are modeled after FFTW [15], which is written by hand but uses generated basic blocks [14].

The most important extensions of Spiral are the following. Extensions to generate Verilog for field-programmable gate-arrays (FPGAs) are presented in [18, 19]. Search techniques other than dynamic programming are developed in [5, 26]. The use of learning to avoid search was studied in [6, 25]. Finally, [4, 7, 17] make the first steps toward extending Spiral beyond the transform domain including the first OL description. The Spiral project website with more information and all publications is given in [1].

A good introduction to FFTs using tensor products is given in the books [27, 28]. A comprehensive overview of algorithms for Fourier/cosine/sine transforms is given in [21, 31]. A good introduction to mapping FFTs to multicore platforms is given in [10].

Bibliography

1. Spiral project website. www.spiral.net
2. Bonelli A, Franchetti F, Lorenz J, Püschel M, Ueberhuber CW (2006) Automatic performance optimization of the discrete Fourier transform on distributed memory computers. In: International symposium on parallel and distributed processing and application (ISPA), Lecture notes in computer science, vol 4330. Springer, Berlin, pp 818–832
3. Chellappa S, Franchetti F, Püschel M (2009) High performance linear transform program generation for the Cell BE. In: Proceedings of the high performance embedded computing (HPEC), Lexington, 22–23 September 2009
4. de Mesmay F, Chellappa S, Franchetti F, Püschel M (2010) Computer generation of efficient software Viterbi decoders. In: International conference on high performance embedded architectures and compilers (HiPEAC), Lecture notes in computer science, vol 5952. Springer, Berlin, pp 353–368
5. de Mesmay F, Rimmel A, Voronenko Y, Püschel M (2009) Bandit-based optimization on graphs with application to library performance tuning. In: International conference on machine learning (ICML), ACM international conference proceedings series, vol 382. ACM, New York, pp 729–736

6. de Mesmay F, Voronenko Y, Püschel M (2010) Offline library adaptation using automatically generated heuristics. In: International parallel and distributed processing symposium (IPDPS)
7. Franchetti F, de Mesmay F, McFarlin D, Püschel M (2009) Operator language: a program generation framework for fast kernels. In: IFIP working conference on domain specific languages (DSL WC), Lecture notes in computer science, vol 5658. Springer, Berlin, pp 385–410
8. Franchetti F, Püschel M (2002) A SIMD vectorizing compiler for digital signal processing algorithms. In: International parallel and distributed processing symposium (IPDPS). pp 20–26
9. Franchetti F, Püschel M (2008) Generating SIMD vectorized permutations. In: International conference on compiler construction (CC), Lecture notes in computer science, vol 4959. Springer, Berlin, pp 116–131
10. Franchetti F, Püschel M, Voronenko Y, Chellappa S, Moura JMF (2009) Discrete Fourier transform on multicore. IEEE Signal Proc Mag 26(6):90–102
11. Franchetti F, Voronenko Y, Püschel M (2005) Formal loop merging for signal transforms. In: Programming languages design and implementation (PLDI). ACM, New York, pp 315–326
12. Franchetti F, Voronenko Y, Püschel M (2006) FFT program generation for shared memory: SMP and multicore. In: Supercomputing (SC). ACM, New York
13. Franchetti F, Voronenko Y, Püschel M (2006) A rewriting system for the vectorization of signal transforms. In: High performance computing for computational science (VECPAR), Lecture notes in computer science, vol 4395. Springer, Berlin, pp 363–377
14. Frigo M (1999) A fast Fourier transform compiler. In: Proceedings of the programming language design and implementation (PLDI). ACM, New York, pp 169–180
15. Frigo M, Johnson SG (2005) The design and implementation of FFTW3. Proc IEEE 93(2):216–231
16. Johnson J, Johnson RW, Rodriguez D, Tolimieri R (1990) A methodology for designing, modifying, and implementing Fourier transform algorithms on various architectures. IEEE Trans Circ Sys 9:449–500
17. McFarlin D, Franchetti F, Moura JMF, Püschel M (2009) High performance synthetic aperture radar image formation on commodity architectures. Proc SPIE 7337:733708
18. Milder PA, Franchetti F, Hoe JC, Püschel M (2008) Formal datapath representation and manipulation for implementing DSP transforms. In: Design automation conference (DAC). ACM, New York, pp 385–390
19. Nordin G, Milder PA, Hoe JC, Püschel M (2005) Automatic generation of customized discrete Fourier transform IPs. In: Design automation conference (DAC). ACM, New York, pp 471–474
20. Press WH, Flannery BP, Teukolsky SA, Vetterling WT (1992) Numerical recipes in C: the art of scientific computing, 2nd edn. Cambridge University Press, Cambridge
21. Püschel M, Moura JMF (2008) Algebraic signal processing theory: Cooley-Tukey type algorithms for DCTs and DSTs. IEEE Trans Signal Proces 56(4):1502–1521
22. Püschel M, Moura JMF, Johnson J, Padua D, Veloso M, Singer B, Xiong J, Franchetti F, Gacic A, Voronenko Y, Chen K, Johnson RW, Rizzolo N (2005) SPIRAL: code generation for DSP transforms. Proc IEEE (Special Issue on Program Generation, Optimization, and Adaptation) 93(2):232–275
23. Püschel M, Singer B, Veloso M, Moura JMF (2001) Fast automatic generation of DSP algorithms. In: International conference on computational science (ICCS), Lecture notes in computer science, vol 2073. Springer, Berlin, pp 97–106
24. Püschel M, Singer B, Xiong J, Moura JMF, Johnson J, Padua D, Veloso M, Johnson RW (2004) SPIRAL: a generator for platform-adapted libraries of signal processing algorithms. J High Perform Comput Appl 18(1):21–45
25. Singer B, Veloso M (2001) Learning to generate fast signal processing implementations. In: International conference on machine learning (ICML). Morgan Kaufmann, San Francisco, pp 529–536
26. Singer B, Veloso M (2001) Stochastic search for signal processing algorithm optimization. In: Supercomputing (SC). ACM, New York, p 22
27. Tolimieri R, An M, Lu C (1997) Algorithms for discrete Fourier transforms and convolution, 2nd edn. Springer, Berlin
28. Van Loan C (1992) Computational framework of the fast Fourier transform. SIAM, Philadelphia
29. Voronenko Y (2008) Library generation for linear transforms. Ph.D. thesis, Electrical and Computer Engineering, Carnegie Mellon University
30. Voronenko Y, de Mesmay F, Püschel M (2009) Computer generation of general size linear transform libraries. In: International symposium on code generation and optimization (CGO). IEEE Computer Society, Washington, DC, pp 102–113
31. Voronenko Y, Püschel M (2009) Algebraic signal processing theory: Cooley-Tukey type algorithms for real DFTs. IEEE Trans Signal Proces 57(1):205–222
32. Xiong J, Johnson J, Johnson RW, Padua D (2001) SPL: a language and compiler for DSP algorithms. In: Programming languages design and implementation (PLDI). ACM, New York, pp 298–308

SPMD Computational Model

Frederica Darema
National Science Foundation, Arlington, VA, USA

Definition of the Subject

The Single Program – Multiple Data (SPMD) parallel programming paradigm is premised on the concept that all processes participating in the execution of a program work cooperatively to execute that program, but at any given instance different processes may execute different instruction-streams, and act on different data and on different sections in the program, and whereby these processes dynamically self-schedule themselves, according to the program workflow and through synchronization constructs embedded in the application program. SPMD programs comprise of serial, parallel, and replicate sections.

Introduction

The (*SPMD*) Single Program-Multiple Data model [1–6] is premised on the concept that all processes participating in the (parallel) execution of a program work cooperatively to execute this program, but at any given instance, through synchronization constructs embedded in the application program, different processes may execute different instruction-streams, and act on different data and on different sections in the program; thus the name of the model: Single Program – Multiple Data. The model was proposed by the author in January 1984 [1], as a means for expressing and enabling parallel execution of applications on highly parallel MIMD computational platforms. The term "single-program" was used for emphasis on the parallel execution of a given program (i.e., concurrent execution of tasks in a given program), in distinction from the environments of that time, where OS-level concurrent tasks would (concurrently) execute different programs on the multiprocessors of that time (e.g., IBM 3081). The initial motivation for the SPMD model was to enable the expression of the (then) high degrees of parallelism supported by the IBM Research Parallel Processor Prototype (RP3) [7] parallel computer system. The model was first implemented in the Environment for Parallel Execution (EPEX) [2–6] programming environment (one of the first general-purpose parallel programming environments, and of course the first to implement SPMD). This entry is an excerpt of a more comprehensive treatise on the SPMD [8] which puts the motivation for the SPMD in the context of the landscape of the computer platforms and software support of the early- to mid-1980s, and discusses experiences, effectiveness, and impact of the SPMD in expediting adoption of parallelism in that time frame and as it has influenced derivative programming environments in the intervening 25 years.

The SPMD model fostered a new approach to parallel programming, differing than the Fork & Join (or Master–Slave) model predominantly pursued by others at around the 1984 timeframe. In SPMD, all processes that participate in the parallel execution of a program commence execution of the program, and each process is dynamically self-scheduled and selects work-tasks to execute (self-allocated work), based on parallelization directives embedded in the program and according to the program workflow. In the SPMD model, a process represents a separate instantiation of the program, and processes participating in the cooperative execution of a program (also referred to as parallel processes) execute distinct instruction streams in a coordinated way through these embedded parallelization directives (also referred to as synchronization directives). With respect to parallel execution, in general a program consists of sections that are executed by one process (*serial sections*) and sections that can be executed by multiple cooperating processes (i.e., *parallel sections*, that can be executed by several processes in a cooperative and concurrent manner, and *replicate sections*, where the computations are executed by every process; parallel sections may include one or more levels of nested parallel sections). Regardless of the section considered, the beginning and end of serial and of parallel sections (and nested parallel sections) are points of synchronization of the processes (*synchronization points*), that is, points of coordination and control of the execution path of the participating processes. The definition in [1, 2]: "*all processes working together will execute the very same program,*" uses the word "same" to emphasize concurrent execution of a given program by these ("multiple") processes, and not to imply that all these processes execute identical instruction streams (as it has been interpreted by some). In expressing parallelism through the SPMD model, the flow of control is distinguished in two classes: the *parallel* flow of control is the flow of control followed by the processes while executing a serial or a parallel section in the program; the *global flow of control* is the flow of control followed by the processes as they step through the synchronization points of the program, according to the program workflow. In parallel execution with the SPMD model, the participating processes follow a different *parallel flow of control*, but all the processes follow the same *global flow of control*.

Conceptually, the SPMD model has been from the outset a general model, enabling to express parallelism for concurrent execution of distinct instruction streams and allowing application-level parallelization control and dynamic scheduling of work-tasks ready to execute (with process self-scheduling). The model is able to support general MIMD task-level parallelism, including nested parallelism, and is applicable to a range of parallel architectures (those considered at the time the model was proposed and other parallel and distributed architectures that have subsequently appeared) in more efficient and general ways than the then proposed alternate parallel programming models, such as those based on Fork-and-Join, SIMD, and data-parallel and systolic-arrays approaches. In fact SPMD allows combining with and implementing such models as parallel execution models invoked under the SPMD rubric. Applied to parallel architectures supporting shared memory (for example RP3) the SPMD is a global-view programming model. From its inception, SPMD allowed efficient implementations of expressing parallelism, through parallelization directives inserted in the initial serial application programs, the ensuing "parallelized" program compiled with the standard serial compliers. The parallelization directives enabled application-level dynamic scheduling and control of the parallel execution, with efficient runtime implementations, requiring minimal interaction with the OS, avoiding (the heavy) OS level-synchronization overheads, and without requiring new, parallel OS services. These were important considerations in the 1984 time frame, the SPMD showed early-on that it allowed the parallelization of non-trivial programs; many were production-level application programs, for example, from the areas of applied physics, aerospace, and design automation. Thus the *SPMD* expedited adoption of parallelism in the mid-1980s, as the model enabled to determine that it was not difficult to express parallelism, and map and execute such non-trivial applications on parallel machines, and thus exploit parallelism and do so flexibly and adaptively, and with efficiency.

SPMD enabled creating parallel versions of FORTRAN and C programs, and also enabled the parallel execution of such programs without the need for new parallel languages. To date, there are many environments that have implemented *SPMD*, primarily for science and engineering parallel computing, but also for commercial applications. The most widely used today being MPI [9] for distributed multiprocessing systems or *"message-passing"* systems, and later used also for shared memory systems; the predecessor of MPI being PVM [10], which appeared in the late-1980s as one of the first popular implementations of SPMD for "message-passing" systems. The SPMD model through its implementation in MPI is widely used for exploiting today's heterogeneous complex parallel and distributed computational platforms, including computational grids [11], which embody many types of processors, multiple levels of memory hierarchy, and multiple levels of networks and communication, and which may employ a combination of SPMD as well as Fork-and-Join programming environments. Other influential programming environments also based on SPMD include OpenMP [12] for shared-memory parallel programming in FORTRAN, C, and C++; Titanium [13] for parallelization of Java programs; and Split-C [14] and Unified Parallel C (UPC) [15] for parallel execution of C programs.

The SPMD Model

In the SPMD model, a parallel program conceptually consists of serial, parallel (including nested parallel), and replicate sections. The program data are distinguished into application data and synchronization data; synchronization data are shared among the parallel processes, and application data are distinguished into private and into shared data. In the following are discussed how these parallelization aspects are treated in SPMD:

- *Serial sections* are executed by one process (either a designated process, or more generally, and typically, the first one to arrive at that section). The other processes that arrive at this serial section, through the *"serial-section synchronization directives"* are directed to bypass its execution; there, they either wait at the end of the section for its execution to complete, or they may proceed to seek and execute available work-task(s) in subsequent section(s), if that is allowed by the program workflow dependencies (and with appropriate synchronizations imposed – *soft* and *hard* barriers, discussed later on in their EPEX implementation).
- *Parallel sections* are executed concurrently by processes that arrive at the beginning of such a section. These processes, through *"parallel-section synchronization directives"* dynamically self-schedule themselves and get allocated with the next available parallel work-task to execute. As each of these

processes arriving in a parallel section is self-assigned a work - task, and as each process completes its task of work, these processes can seek the next available work-task to execute in that parallel section; or if all work tasks in the parallel section have been allocated to processes, the remaining process(es) can proceed to the end of that parallel section, and either wait there till all the work of the parallel section is completed, or continue-on to the next section of the program or other subsequent sections of the program as allowed by the program workflow dependencies (and with appropriate synchronizations imposed – *soft* and *hard* barriers, discussed later on in their EPEX implementation). Parallel loops in programs are the predominant form of a parallel section and thus major targets of parallel execution; however, SPMD also supports other forms of general task parallelism. Later in this section nested parallelism support in SPMD is discussed.

- *Replicate sections* of the program are sections allowed to be executed by all processes (it is the default mode of execution that was envisioned when the SPMD was first proposed). Such sections involve parts of the computation (typically small portion of the total amount of the computation) and where allowing all processes to replicate the execution of the computation is more efficient than having one process execute the section (while the others wait) and then make the result of the computation available to other processes (as shared data or as communicated messages). This is applicable, for example, where replicate execution avoids: the serialization overhead, the busy-waiting and polling a synchronization semaphore by the other processes (with potential additional overhead due for example contention in this semaphore, and also potential network contention), and the overhead of making the resulting data available to the other process (e.g., in shared memory architectures, potential of contention upon access of the resulting data placed in shared memory; or network contention upon broadcasting the results to the other processes through message passing, in logically distributed, "message-passing" architectures). Especially for message-passing environments, such overheads can be rather high, and in such cases the approach of replicate computations can be a more efficient alternative for certain portions of the computation.

- *Shared and Private Data*: These refer to application data and synchronization data. For parallel machine architectures which support shared as well as private memory, parallelism is expressed by considering two types of data: *shared data* and *private data*; each of the parallel processes having read and write capability on the shared data, while private data are exclusive to each process (and typically the private data of a process would reside in the local memory of the processor on which the process executes). A*pplication shared data* and *synchronization data* are declared as *shared data*. SPMD was originally proposed for architectures supporting a mix of shared and (logically local – private) memory, and the approach followed in the original SPMD implementation was for the default to be the *private data* (to each parallel process); this decision was made (by the author) on the basis that it is easier (especially for the user) to identify the application shared data and the synchronization data, rather than explicitly defining the private data as other approaches have done. For message-passing architectures, where the SPMD was also applied, the *application shared data* are partitioned into per process private data, and "sharing" of such data is effected through "messages" exchanged between parallel processes, as needed during the course of the computation. It is the belief of this author that expressing parallelism through message-passing is more challenging than supporting parallelism through a "shared-memory plus private memory" architecture support, and that is also the case with the kinds of programming models for expressing parallelism (more on this in later discussion on MPI).

- *I/O*: The SPMD model allows general flexibility in handling I/O. Any of the parallel processes executing a parallel program are allowed to perform I/O, and (as discussed later-on in the context of the EPEX programming environment) all processes can have read/write access to any of the parallel program's files. One can argue that the typical approach would be for I/O to be treated as a serial action, although that is not necessarily always so. For example, upon commencing execution of a program, one process typically would be assigned to read the input data file, and perform the program state initialization. However, there are many other instances in the program execution, for example, within parallel sections, where it may be more efficient to allow each process to read data from a file, and as needed write data back into a file. In this case, for flexibility, random-access file structure would be more desirable, than sequential record files; it is then not necessary to attach a file to a given process, which is a possible but more restrictive approach.

In the early implementations of the SPMD, where processes were implemented by heavy-weight mechanisms (such as VMs – Virtual Machines), to enable efficient parallel execution, all processes were created in the beginning of the program execution, and this has been applied to most SPMD implementations since then. Noted, however, that the SPMD model does not preclude by principle the case where additional processes can be created and participate in the program execution; this was allowed through EPEX implemented directives, allowing such additional processes to skip the already executed portion of the entire computation. However, at the time SPMD was proposed and within the systems then available for the implementation of the model, creation of such processes and inheriting program state was expensive, unlike capabilities that were enabled later on, like creation of light-weight threads.

Nesting in SPMD can be implemented by allowing enough processes to enter an (outer) parallel loop, for example, allocate several processes – a group of processes – to a given outer loop iteration, allowing only one of these processes to execute the outer loop portion (for example, with appropriate directives treating it as a "nested serial") and then allow all processes in this group to execute in parallel the inner loop. In fact this author experimented with such approaches, as well as a hybrid of SPMD combined with Fork-and-Join capabilities to implement nesting, but they were never implemented in a production way, due to the overheads of spawning VM/SP virtual processes, but also because in the mid-1980s timeframe the degrees of parallelism in the applications (e.g., dimensionality of the outer parallel loops in a program) exceeded the numbers of processors in the commercial and in the prototype systems of that time, so exploiting nesting was more of an intellectual endeavor rather than a practical need. With threading capabilities, other implementations can be used to support more elegantly execution of nested parallel computations, for example, by each process spawning threads to execute the inner iterations of the loop, like for example in OpenMP. Later in this entry is discussed the need for nested or multilevel threading capabilities, gang scheduling of threads, partially shared data and active data-distribution notions, in the context of multi-level parallelization hierarchies that will be encountered in the emerging and future parallel architectures.

The SPMD model does not restrict how many processes can run on each parallel processor. While often one process executes per processor, there are cases where multiple processes may be spawned to execute per processor, for example, to mask memory latency, shared memory contention, I/O, etc. Also SPMD does not require a given process to be attached to a given processor; however, the typical approach is to bind a process (or a thread to a processor), to avoid cost of migration, context-switch, and better exploitation of (local data) cache; however, there are situations where, as long as there is no thrashing, a process may be moved, for example, to improve performance, and in other cases for fault tolerance or recovery [16, 17].

Other SPMD features are provided as illustrative examples of the EPEX programming environment discussed next.

The EPEX Programming Environment – Implementation of the SPMD Model

The first implementation of SPMD was in the EPEX environment [2–5], initially implemented on IBM multiprocessors like the dual processor IBM/3081 and, later, the six-processor IBM/3090 vector multiprocessor (through MVS/XA [18]). The IBM/3081 through the VM/SP OS [19] supported execution of multiple virtual machines (VMs), running in time-shared mode (on each node of the 3081). This capability was used to simulate parallel execution by a large number of processors working together on a single program, each simulated parallel processor and its local memory (correspondingly for each of the parallel processes) being simulated by a VM (a virtual machine). Although in practice the 3081 hardware supported 2-way parallelism (and the 3090 hardware supported 6-way parallelism), the simulation environment created was used to simulate up to 64 parallel processors; of course, in principle the environment could simulate even higher numbers of processors. To simulate execution on parallel platforms, like RP3, the VM/SP OS support of the Writable Shared Segments (VM/WSS) capability was used, which allowed to establish a portion of the virtual machines' memory as shared across a set of VMs (in read and write modalities); this feature allowed to simulate the shared-memory of a parallel system (like RP3), while the private memory of each virtual machine simulated the local memory of an RP3 processor, and the private memory of the corresponding process. The VM/WSS was also used to emulate message-passing environments, by using the WSS-based (virtual) shared memory as a "mailbox" for messages, and thus allowing to also experiment and to demonstrate the use of SPMD as a model also supporting message-passing parallel computation. These capabilities were used to create a simulation platform for the EPEX programming environment, and were also used for the development of other simulation tools for analysis of execution on various parallel machines with shared-plus-local memory systems as well as for "message - passing" distributed systems. While over the last two decades most parallel systems have been used with MPI (a message-passing environment), it behooves elaborating on shared-plus-local memory systems because the emerging multicore-based architectures are expected to support such memory organizations within the likely set of memory hierarchies.

Initially, parallelization of programs under EPEX was enabled by implementing the "serial," "parallel," and "barrier" parallelization directives through synchronization subroutine calls inserted in the program; the first EPEX implementation was applied to parallelization of FORTRAN programs, and shared data declared explicitly, through FORTRAN Shared COMMON statements. Shortly thereafter, the synchronization subroutine calls were replaced by corresponding parallelization macros, with the development of a preprocessor (source-to-source translator from macros to subroutine calls). Denoting the parallelization directives through macros, and likewise for the declaration of application shared data, allowed converting serial programs to their parallel counterparts, more easily and elegantly. Additional synchronization constructs were also expressed through other appropriate macros. All these parallelization macros inserted in the program were then expanded by the "EPEX Preprocessor" into the parallel program version, by inserting the SPMD parallelization subroutines (specifically referred to here is the EPEX FORTRAN Preprocessor source-to-source translator [20–22]; later a preprocessor for C was also developed [23]). Then the ensuing "parallelized program" was compiled through a standard serial FORTRAN or C compiler. By '87–'88 the SPMD-based EPEX system had been installed in ten IBM sites (including IBM Scientific Centers, such as those in Palo Alto, CA-USA and Rome, Italy), three National and International Labs (LANL, ANL, and CERN); two industrial partners (MartinMarietta and Grumman), and eight universities.

The syntax and utilization of the initial EPEX implementation is presented in [2–5]. The macros implementing SPMD and the EPEX preprocessor are presented in detail in [6, 19–21] which document in more detail the preprocessor–based EPEX environment. Here, for reference, an illustrative sample of the set of the EPEX macros is given with a brief description of their use:

- The traditional FORTRAN DO-loop was designated through the:
  @DO [stmt#|label] index = n1, n2, [n3]
  [CHUNK = chunksize]
  … loop body …
  [stmt#] @ENDO [label] [WAIT | NOWAIT]

  Processes entering the @DO get self-assigned with the next available loop-iteration(s), through synchronization routines utilizing the Fetch-and-Add (F&A) [24] RP3 primitive (implemented in the simulated environment through the Compare&Swap instruction); processes that arrive after all the work in the loop has been allocated or all the work in the loop has been completed proceed to the end of the section (@ENDO); there they may wait for the loop execution to be completed, or proceed to subsequent section(s), as allowed by the program workflow dependencies. The CHUNK option allows processes to get assigned more than one iterations at a time, thus decreasing the overhead of parallelism; the WAIT option requires processes to wait for the execution of the preceding section (in this case the loop body) to be completed before continuing to the next section of the program; the NOWAIT option allowed processes that reach the end of the section to continue execution of subsequent section(s), thus allowing multiple concurrent sections of the program (or subroutines) to be executed concurrently, as allowed by dependencies in the program workflow.

- The serial section is bounded by the @SERBEG and @SEREND macros. The default is for the first process to encounter the @SERBEG to execute the section, the other processes proceed to @SEREND, with [WAIT | NOWAIT] options similar to the ones for a parallel loop. The environment also allows designating a given process to execute a given serial section.
- The @WAITFOR macro can be inserted at any point of the program and designates that processes cannot go beyond that point, until *a logical condition* specified by the argument of the macro is satisfied; for instance, this construct can be used for imposing various kinds of soft barriers – for example, for the processes to wait until execution of the preceding section(s) is completed.
- The @BARRIER macro can be inserted at any point of the program and forces all processes participating in the execution of the program to arrive at that point of the program (hard barrier).
- The parallel processes are endowed with an identity [@MYNUM]; the MYNUM for each process can be a parameterized assignment. This property can be used in several ways: for example, for designating a given process to perform I/O to a file if that is desired, or execute a given section (e.g., a serial section) that can be designated to be executed by a given process (of course in general this is not mandatory, as the default option for a section, and more generally the next available work-task is to be executed on a "first-arrives-executes" basis).
- @SHARED [application shared data: parameters, arrays] allows the user to designate the application shared data; by default all other data of the application are assumed as private to each parallel process; @SHARED [synchronization data] are created automatically by the preprocessor and designated all the shared data used by the synchronization constructs.

A schematic of an example of SPMD execution is shown in Fig. 1.

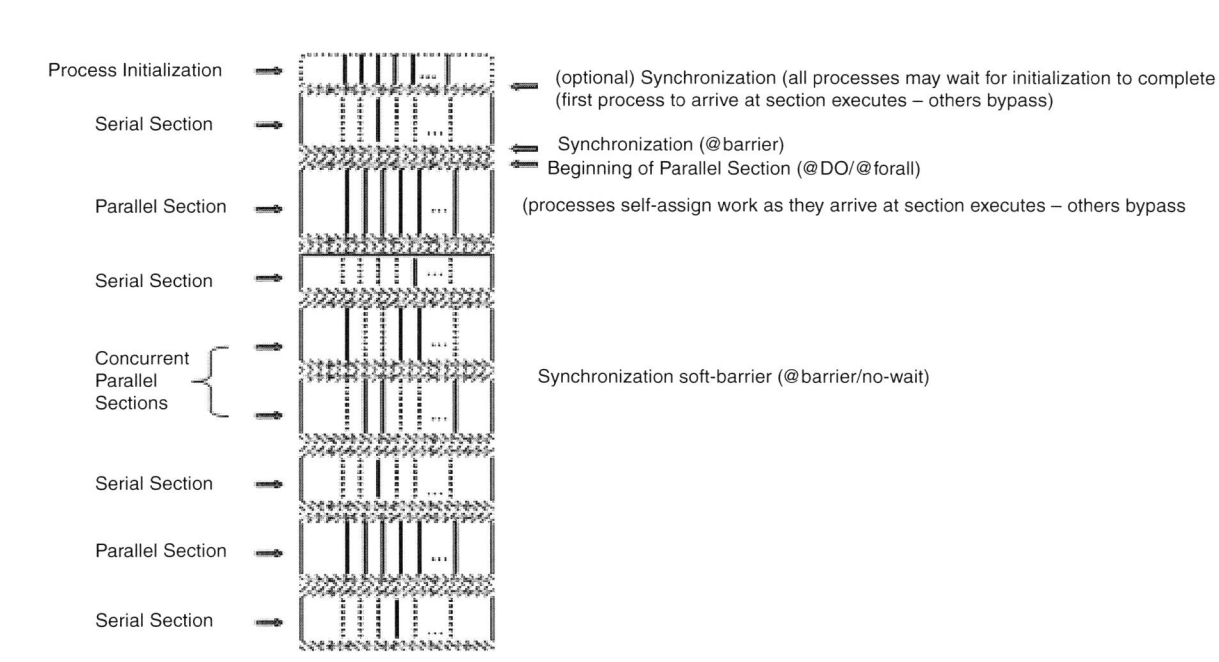

SPMD Computational Model. Fig. 1 Schematic of an example of SMPD MIMD task-parallel execution

- Handling of I/O: In [25, 26] are discussed implementations of ideas for parallel I/O presented in the previous section, which allowed I/O by multiple processes, and not necessarily serializing I/O. A file could be opened, written into and closed, and then made available to other processes. This could be done at the end of a parallel section or at the end of an outmost iteration of the program, depending on the problem needs; such implementations might be enabled via a barrier at the end of the outermost loop, or if no barrier was imposed the file maybe accessed (in read-write mode) by another process (which may need to spin-wait if the file had not been closed by the previous process). The @MYNUM designation allowed to tie a given process to a file if that was desirable. The advent of newer file-systems (such as GPFS [27, 28]) allows more flexible mechanisms for parallel I/O in SPMD programs, and parallel I/O is supported in programming environments, like OpenMP. Furthermore, as mass storage technologies evolve from disk to solid-state and nano-devices, it is possible that parallel I/O could be implemented through other than file-based methods (perhaps something akin to a "DBMS-like" I/O management).

Through the EPEX parallelization directives, the participating processes executing cooperatively the program step through the synchronization points in the program, and are dynamically allocated the next work-task or execution path to take. In that sense all participating processes follow the same global flow of control in the program. In executing serial or parallel sections, each process is allocated the next available work-task, and thus they may execute different instructions at any given time and act on different parts of the program (including potentially different procedures or subroutines), as consistent with the workflow dependencies in the program. A given process may follow a different parallel flow of control during different passes of an outer iteration of the entire program. The synchronization routines provided in EPEX allowed executing outer iterations of the entire program (that is repeated execution of the serial and parallel sections of the program) without necessarily imposing the need for the programmer to introduce explicit blocking at the end of the outer iteration of the program.

The EPEX programming environment allowed to parallelize and simulate the parallel execution of a large number of applications, to understand their characteristics, and assess the efficacy and effectiveness of parallelism. In the 1984 – 1986 time-span, over 40 applications were parallelized with SPMD, and executed in parallel under the EPEX programming environment. The set of these applications (mostly numeric, but also non-numeric) included: Fluid Dynamics (e.g., advanced turbulent-flow programs [29], and shallow water and heart blood-flow problems); Radiation Transport (Discrete Ordinates methods and Monte-Carlo); Design Automation (Chip placement and Routing by Simulated Annealing [30–33]; and Fault simulation); Seismic, Reservoir Modeling, Weather Modeling, Pollution Propagation; Physics Applications (Band Structure, Spin-Lattice, Shell Model); Applied Physics and Chemistry Applications (Molecular Dynamics); Epidemic Spread; Computer Graphics and Image Processing (e.g., ray-tracing); Numerical and non-numeric Libraries (FFTs, Linear Solvers, Eigen-solvers, sorting), etc.

Advancing into the Future: Directions, Opportunities, Challenges, and Approaches

Emerging Computational Platforms and Emerging Applications Systems. Increasingly, large-scale distributed systems are deploying as their building blocks high-performance multicore processors (and in combination with special-purpose processor chips, like GPUs), as are the emerging petaflops and future hexaflops platforms. In fact, it is also conceivable that this kind of heterogeneity of processors will be eventually embedded in the multicore chip itself. Such systems, with 1,000s to 100s of thousands of tightly coupled nodes, will be enabled as Grids-in-a-Box (GiBs). Computational platforms include both high-end systems as well as globally-distributed, meta-computing, heterogeneous, networked and adaptive platforms, ranging from assemblies of networked workstations, to networked supercomputing clusters or combinations thereof, together with their associated peripherals such as storage and visualization systems. All these hardware platforms will have potentially not only multiple levels of processors, but also multiple levels of memory hierarchies (at the cache, main memory and storage levels), and multiple levels of interconnecting networks, with multiple levels of latencies (variable at inter-node and intra-node levels) and bandwidths (differing for different links, differing based on traffic). Moving into the exascale domain, the challenges are augmented as we are faced with prospects of addressing billion-way concurrency, and in the presence of heterogeneity of processing units in a processing node, increasing degrees in the multiple levels of memory hierarchies, and multiple levels of interconnects hierarchies; these are the Grids-in-a-Box, referred to earlier-on, with significantly added complexity, because of the wider range of granularity, needing to expose concurrency from the fine grain to many more levels of coarser grain. The questions range from: how to express parallelism and optimally map and execute applications on such platforms, to how to enable load balancing, and at what level (or levels) is load balancing applied. It becomes evident that static parallelization approaches are inadequate, that one needs programming models that allow expressing parallelism so that it can be exploited dynamically, for load balancing and hiding latency, and for expressing dynamic flow control and synchronization possibly at multiple levels. The ideas of dynamic runtime compiler [34] capabilities discussed below are becoming more imperative.

Furthermore, new application paradigms (e.g., DDDAS – Dynamic Data Driven Applications Systems [35, 36]) that have emerged over the last several years and which entail dynamic on-line integration and feed-back and control between the computations of complex application models and measurement aspects of the application system, leading to *SuperGrids* [37] of integrated computational and instrumentation platforms, as well as other sensory devices and control platforms. In the context of this entry on programming environments and programming models, the implications are that these environments and models will need to support seamlessly execution of applications encompassing dynamically integrated high-end computing with real-time data-acquisition and control components and requirements.

New Programming Environments and Runtime-Support Technologies Such environments require technology approaches which break down traditional barriers in existing software components in the application development support and runtime layers, to deliver QoS in application execution. That is, together with new programming models, new compiler technology is needed, such as the runtime-compiler system (RCS [38]), where part of the compiler becomes embedded in the runtime and where the compiler interacts with the system monitoring and resource managers, as well as performance models of the underlying hardware and software, using such capabilities for optimizing the mapping of the application on the underlying complex platform(s). This runtime-compiler system is aware of the heterogeneity in the underlying architecture of the platforms, such as multi-level hierarchy of processing nodes, memories, and interconnects, with differing architecture, memory organization, and latencies, and will link to appropriately selected components (*dynamic application composition*) to generate consistent code at runtime. Representative examples of developing runtime-compiler capabilities are given in [39] and [40]. Together with the "runtime-compiler" capabilities [33], called for novel approaches and substantial enhancements in computational models to actualize the distributed applications software, including user-provided *assists* to facilitate and enhance the runtime-compiler's ability to analyze task and data dependencies in the application programs, resolve dependencies, and dynamically optimize mapping across a complex set of processing nodes and memory structure of distributed platforms (such as Grids and GiBs, multicore and GPU-based), with multiple levels of processors and processing nodes, interconnects, and memory hierarchies. It is the thesis of this entry that the models needed should facilitate the RCS (runtime compiling system) to map applications, without requiring detailed resource management specifications by the user and without requiring specification of data location (e.g., proximity – or PGAS). Rather the programming models should incorporate advanced concepts such as "*active data-distribution,*" that is the user specifies that these data are candidates for *active or runtime distribution*, and the RCS determines at runtime how to map them, determines partial sharing, copy/move between memory hierarchies, through dynamic adaptive resource management, decoupled execution and data location/placement, memory consistency models, and multithreaded hierarchical concurrency. Such capabilities may be materialized through a hybrid combination of language, library models, development of OS-supported "hierarchical threading" capabilities and partial sharing of data approaches.

In order to adequately support the future parallel systems, it is advocated here that the new software technologies need to adopt a more integrated view of the architectural layers and software components of a computing system (hardware/software co-design), consisting of the applications, the application support environments (languages, compilers, application libraries, linkers, run-time support, security, visualization, etc.), operating systems (scheduling, resource allocation and management, etc), computing platform architectures, processing nodes and network layers, and also support systems encompassing the computational and application measurement systems. Furthermore, such environments need to include approaches for engineering such systems, at the hardware, systems software, and at the applications levels, so that they execute with optimized efficiency with respect to runtime, quality of service, performance, power utilization, fault tolerance, and reliability. Such capabilities require robust software frameworks, encompassing the systems software layers and the application layers and cognizant of the underlying hardware platform resources.

Summary

This entry has provided an overview of the SPMD model, its origin and its initial implementations, its effectiveness and impact in expediting adoption of parallelism in the mid-80s, and its use as a vehicle for exploiting parallel and distributed computational platforms for the intervening 25 years. As we consider what are the possible new parallel programming models for new and future computing platforms, as well as present and emerging compute-, data-intensive, dynamically integrated applications executing on such platforms, it is becoming imperative to advance programming models and programming environments by building from past experiences and opening new directions through synergistic approaches of models, advanced runtime-compiler methods, user assists, multi-level threading OS services, and ensuring that the approaches and technologies developed are created in the context of end-to-end software architectural frameworks.

Acknowledgment

The IBM RP3 Project became the ground for my inspiration and work on the SPMD model; I'm forever grateful for being part of the RP3 team and will always value my collaborations with the RP3 team.

Bibliography

1. Darema-Rogers F (1984) IBM Internal Communication, Jan 1984
2. Darema-Rogers F, George D, Norton VA, Pfister G (1984) A VM parallel environment. Proceedings of the IBM Kingston Parallel Processing Symposium, 27–29 Nov 1984 (IBM Confidential)
3. Darema-Rogers F, George DA, Norton VA, Pfister GF (1985) A VM based parallel environment. IBM research report, RC11225
4. Darema-Rogers F, George DA, Norton VA, Pfister GF (1985) Environment and system interface for VM/EPEX. IBM research report R11381, 9/19/1985
5. Darema-Rogers F, George DA, Norton VA, Pfister GF (1985) Using a single-program-multiple-data model for parallel execution of scientific applications. SIAM Conference on Parallel Processing for Scientific Computing, November, 1985, and IBM research report R11552, 11/19/1985
6. Darema F, George DA, Norton VA, Pfister GF (1988) A single-program-multiple-data computational model for EPEX/FORTRAN. Parallel Comput 7:11–24 (received April 1987 upon publication release by IBM - IBM Technical Disclosure Bulletin 29(9) February 1987)
7. Pfister G et al (1984) The research parallel processor prototype (RP3). Proceedings of the IBM Kingston Parallel Processing Symposium, 27–29 Nov 1984 (IBM Confidential); and Proceedings of the ICPP, August 1985
8. Darema F Historical and future perspectives on the SPMD computational model. – Forthcoming Publication
9. MPI standard – draft released by the MPI Forum. http://www.mcs.anl.gov/Projects/mpi/standard.html
10. PVM – Parallel Visrtual Machine. http://www.csm.ornl.gov/pvm/pvm_home.html
11. Foster I, Kesselman C (eds) (1999) The grid: blueprint for a new computing infrastructure. Morgan Kaufmann
12. OpenMP. http://openmp.org/wp/
13. Yelick KA, Semenzato L, Pike G, Miyamoto C, Liblit B, Krishnamurthy A, Hilfinger PN, Graham SL, Gay D, Colella P, Aiken A (1998) Concurrency: practice and experience. vol 10, No. 11–13, September-November. An earlier version was presented at the Workshop on Java for High-Performance Network Computing, Palo Alto, CA, Feb 1998
14. Culler DE, Arpaci-Dusseau AC, Goldstein SC, Krishnamurthy A, Lumetta S, Eicken T, Yelick KA (1993) Parallel programming in Split-C. SC, pp 262–273
15. El-Ghazawi T, Carlson W, Sterling T, Yelick KA (2005) UPC: distributed shared-memory programming. Wiley, Hoboken
16. Bronevetsky G, Marques D, Pingali K, Stodghill P (2000) Automated application-level checkpointing of MPI programs. ACM SIGPLAN 38(10):84–94
17. Bronevetsky G, Marques D, Pingali K, Szwed P, Schulz M (2004) Application-level checkpointing for shared memory programs. ACM Comp Ar 32(5):235–247
18. George DA MVS/XA EPEX – Environment for parallel execution. IBM research report RC 13158, 9/28/87
19. VM/System Product (VM/SP). http://www-03.ibm.com/ibm/history/exhibits/mainframe/mainframe_PP3081.html (and MVS/XA also supported)

20. Stone JM, Darema-Rogers F, Norton VA, Pfister GF Introduction to the VM/EPEX FORTRAN Preprocessor. IBM research report RC 11407, 9/30/85
21. Stone JM, Darema-Rogers F, Norton VA, Pfister GF The VM/EPEX FORTRAN Preprocessor Reference. IBM research report RC 11408, 9/30/85
22. Bolmarcich T, Darema-Rogers F Tutorial for EPEX/FORTRAN Program Parallelization and Execution. IBM research report RC12515, 2/18/87
23. Whet-Ling C, Norton A (1986) VM/EPEX C preprocessor user's manual. Version 1.0. Technical report RC 12246, IBM T.J. Watson Research Center, Yorktown Heights, NY, October 1986
24. Gottlieb A, Kruskal CP (1981) Coordinating parallel processors: a partial unification. Computer Architecture News, pp 16–24, October 1981
25. Darema-Rogers F I/O capabilities in the VM/EPEX system. IBM research report, RC 12219, 10/9/86
26. Darema F (1987) Applications environment for the IBM research parallel processor prototype (RP3). IBM research report RC 12627, 3/27/87; and Proceedings of the International Conference on Supercomputing (ICS), (published by Springer, Athens, Greece, June 1988
27. GPFS: http://www.almaden.ibm.com/StorageSystems/projects/gpfs
28. Schmuck F, Haskin R (2002) GPFS: a shared-disk file system for large computing clusters. (pdf). Proceedings of the FAST'02 Conference on File and Storage Technologies. USENIX, Monterey, California, USA, pp 231–244. ISBN 1-880446-03-0. http://www.usenix.org/events/fast02/full_papers/schmuck/schmuck.pdf. Accessed 18 Jan 2008
29. ARC3D: Pulliam TH Euler and thin layer navier stokes codes: ARC2D, ARC3D. Computational fluid dynamics, A workshop held at the University of Tennessee Space Institute, UTSI publ. E02-4005-023-84, 1984 {other related application programs parallelized included: SIMPLE and HYDRO-1}
30. Darema-Rogers F, Kirkpatrick S, Norton VA (1987) Parallel techniques for chip placement by simulated annealing. Proceedings of the International Conference on Computer-Aided Design. pp 91–94
31. Darema F, Kirkpatrick S, Norton VA (1987) Simulated annealing on shared memory parallel systems. IBM Journal of R&D 31:391–402
32. Jayaraman R, Darema F Error analysis of parallel simulated annealing techniques. Proceedings of the ICCD'88, Rye, NY, 10/3-5/88
33. Greening D, Darema F Rectangular spatial decomposition methods for parallel simulated annealing. IBM research report, RC14636, 5/2/89, and in the Proceedings of the International Conference on Supercomputing '89. Crete-Greece
34. Darema F (2009) Report on cyberifrastructures of cyber-applications-systems & cyber-systems-software, submitted for external publication
35. DDDAS. www.cise.nsf.gov/dddas
36. DDDAS. www.dddas.org
37. Darema F (2005) Grid computing and beyond: the context of dynamic data driven applications systems. Proc IEEE (Special Issue on Grid Computing) 93(3):692–697
38. Darema F (2000) New software architecture for complex applications development and runtime support. Int J High-Perform Comput (Special Issue on Programming Environments, Clusters, and Computational Grids For Scientific Computing) 14(3)
39. GRADS project. http://www.hipersoft.rice.edu/grads/
40. Adve VS, Sanders WH A compiler-enabled model- and measurement-driven adaptation environment for dependability and performance. – http://www.perform.csl.illinois.edu/projects/newNSFNGS.html, LLVL compiler – http://llvlm.org

SSE

▶AMD Opteron Processor Barcelona
▶Intel Core Microarchitecture, x86 Processor Family
▶Vector Extensions, Instruction-Set Architecture (ISA)

Stalemate

▶Deadlocks

State Space Search

▶Combinatorial Search

Stream Processing

▶Stream Programming Languages

Stream Programming Languages

RYAN NEWTON
Intel Corporation, Hudson, MA, USA

Synonyms

Complex event processing; Event stream processing; Stream processing

Definition

Stream Programming Languages are specialized to the processing of data streams. A key feature of stream programming languages is that they structure programs not as a series of instructions, but as a graph of computation *kernels* that communicate via data streams. Stream programming languages are implicitly parallel and contain data, task, and pipeline parallelism. They offer some of the best examples of high-performance, fully automatic parallelization of implicitly parallel code.

Discussion

Overview

Stream processing is found in many areas of computer science. Accordingly, it has received distinct and somewhat divergent treatments. For example, most work on stream processing in the context of compilers, graphics, and computer architecture has focused on streams with predictable data-rates, such as in digital signal processing (DSP) applications. These can be modeled using *synchronous dataflow*, are deterministic (being a subclass of Kahn process networks), and are especially attractive as parallel programming models. Specialized languages for dataflow programming go at least as far back the SISAL (Streams and Iteration in a Single Assignment Language) in 1983. Somewhat different are *streaming databases* that are concerned with asynchronous (unpredictable) streams of timestamped events. Typical tasks include searching for temporal patterns and relating streams to each other and to data in stored tables, which may be termed "complex event processing."

This entry considers a broad definition of stream processing, requiring only that kernel functions and data streams be the dominant means of computation and communication. This includes both highly restrictive models – statically known, fixed graph and data-rates – and less restrictive ones. More restrictions allow for better performance and more automatic parallelism, whereas less restrictive models handle a broader class of applications.

Even this broad definition has necessarily blurry boundaries. For example, while stream-processing models typically allow only pure *message passing* communication, they can be extended to allow various forms of shared memory between kernel functions. General purpose programming languages equipped with libraries for stream processing are likely to fall into this category, as are streaming databases that include shared, modifiable tables.

Example Programming Models

This entry classifies stream programming designs along two major axes: *Graph Construction Method* and *Messaging Discipline*. The following three fictional programming models will be used to illustrate the design space:

- **StreamStatic**: a language with a statically known, fixed graph of kernel functions, as well as statically known, fixed data-rates on edges.
- **StreamDynamic**: a general purpose language that can manipulate streams as first-class values, constructing and destroying graphs on the fly and allowing arbitrary access to shared memory.
- **StreamDB**: Kernel graphs that are changed dynamically through transactions. Includes shared memory in the form of modifiable tables. More restricted and with different functionality than **StreamDynamic**.

Snippets of code corresponding to these three languages appear in Figs. 1–3, respectively. Kernels, being nothing more than functions, are usually defined in a manner resembling function definitions. In **StreamDynamic** the same language is used for graph construction as for kernel definition, whereas **StreamStatic** employs a distinct notation for graph topologies. Only in **StreamDB** are the definitions of kernels nonobvious. Whenever a new stream is defined from an

```
# metadata: pop 1 push 1
stream out AddAccum(stream in) {
  state { int s = 0; }
  execute() {
    s++;
    out.push(s + in.pop());
  }
}

// A static graph topology, in literal
   textual notation:
IntIn -> AddAccum -> IntOutput;
```

Stream Programming Languages. Fig. 1 A kernel function in StreamStatic might appear as in the above pseudocode, explicitly specifying the amount of data produced and consumed (pushed and popped) by the kernel during each invocation. This particular kernel carries a state that persists between invocations

```
-- Streams and tables coexist
CREATE TABLE Prices (
    Id      string PRIMARY KEY,
    Price   double);
CREATE INPUT STREAM PriceIncrs (
    Id       string,
    Increase double);
-- A 'kernel' is constructed by building new streams from old
CREATE STREAM NormedPriceIncrs AS
    SELECT Id, Increase / 10.0
    FROM PriceIncrs;
-- Table modified based on streaming data:
UPDATE Prices USING NormedPriceIncrs
    SET Price = Prices.Price + NormedPriceIncrs.Increase,
    WHERE Prices.Id == NormedPriceIncrs.Id;
```

Stream Programming Languages. Fig. 2 A pseudocode example of StreamDB code

```
// A function that creates $N$ copies of a kernel
fun pipeline(int n, Function fn, Stream S) {
  if (n==0) return S;
  else pipeline(n-1, fn, map(fn,S));
}

// Graph wiring is implicit in program execution:
pipeline(10, AddAccum, OrigStream)
```

Stream Programming Languages. Fig. 3 A pseudocode example of StreamDynamic code

old one with a SELECT statement, the expressions used in the SELECT statement form the body of a new kernel function. However, in streaming databases, much more functionality is built into the primitive operators, supporting, for example, a variety of windowing and grouping operations on streaming data.

Messaging StreamStatic assumes that each kernel specifies exactly how many inputs it consumes on each inbound edge, and outputs it produces on outbound edges. StreamDynamic instead uses asynchronous event streams and allows *nondeterministic merge*, which interleaves the elements of two streams in the real-time order in which they occur. StreamDB is similar to StreamDynamic, but timestamps all stream elements at their source, and then maintains a deterministic semantics with respect to those explicit timestamps.

Methods for Graph Wiring

Our three fictional languages use different mechanisms for constructing graphs. StreamStatic uses a literal textual encoding of the graph (Fig. 1). StreamDB also uses a direct encoding of a graph in the text of a query, but in the form of named streams with explicit dependencies (Fig. 2). In contrast, in StreamDynamic the graph is implicit, resulting from applying operators such as map to stream objects (Fig. 3).

There are other common graph construction methods not represented in these fictional languages: first, GUI-based construction of graphs, as found in LabView[12] and StreamBase[1]; second, an API for adding edges in a general purpose language, along the lines of "connect(X,Y);". Compared to implicit graph wiring via the manipulation of stream values (as seen in StreamDynamic or in real systems such as FlumeJava[2]), APIs of this kind are more explicit about edges and usually more verbose.

Finally, an advanced technique for constructing stream graphs is *metaprogramming*. Metaprogramming, or staged execution, simply refers to any program that generates another program. In the case of streaming, the most common situation is that a static kernel graph is desired, yet the programmer wishes to use loops and abstraction in the construction of (potentially complex) graphs. Therefore the need for metaprogramming in streaming is analogous to hardware description languages, which also have a static target (logic gates) but need abstraction in the source language.

While it would be possible to write a program to generate the textual graph descriptions used by, for example, StreamStatic, a much more disciplined form of metaprogramming can be provided by stream-processing DSLs (domain specific languages), which can integrate the type-checking of the metalanguage and the target kernel language. Indeed, this is the approach taken by DSLs such as WaveScript[9] and to a lesser extent StreamIt[].

Parallelism in Stream Programs

Once constructed, a kernel graph exposes *pipeline*, *task*, and *data* parallelism. This terminology, used by the StreamIt authors [4] among others, distinguishes between producer/consumer parallelism (pipeline) and kernels lacking that relationship, such as the siblings in a fork-join pattern (task parallelism). Data parallelism in this context refers specifically to the ability to execute a kernel simultaneously on multiple elements in a single stream. Data parallelism is not always possible with a stateful kernel function – equivalent to a loop-carried dependence.

Stream programs expose abundant parallelism. It is the job of a scheduler or program optimizer to manage that parallelism and map it onto hardware. Fully automatic solutions to this problem remain difficult, but less difficult in a restrictive stream programming model than many other programming models. The key advantage is that stream programs define independent kernels with local data access and explicit, predictable communication.

This advantage enables stream programming models like StreamStatic to target a wide range of hardware architectures, including traditional cache-based CPUs (both multicore and vector parallelism), as well as GPUs, and architectures with software-controlled communication, such as the RAW tiled architecture [11] or the Cell processor. For example, the DSL StreamIt[4] (which subsumes StreamStatic) is an example of a programming language that has targeted all these platforms as well as networked clusters of workstations.

Optimization and Scheduling

An effective stream-processing implementation must accomplish three things: adjust granularity, choose between sources of parallelism, and place computations. Granularity here refers to how much data is processed in bulk, as well as whether or not kernels are combined (fused). Second, because stream programs include multiple kinds of parallelism, it is necessary to balance pipeline/task parallelism and data parallelism. Finally, placement and ordering presents a variant of the traditional task-scheduling problem.

Consider the two-kernel pipeline shown in Fig. 4. Even the simple composition of two kernels exposes several trade-offs. Three possible placements of kernels A and B onto four processors are shown in the figure. Placement (a) illustrates a common scenario: fusing kernels and leveraging data parallelism rather than pipeline parallelism. Yet choosing pipeline parallelism (placement (b)) could be preferable if, for example, A and B's combined working sets exceed the cache capacity of a processor. (Note that in a steady state streams provide enough data to keep A and B simultaneously executing – software pipelining.) Finally, placement (c) illustrates another common scenario – a kernel carries state and cannot be parallelized. In this case, kernel B must be executed serially, so it must not be fused with A or it would serialize A.

Note that there is a complicated interplay between batch size, kernel working set, and fusion/placement. One simple model for kernel working set assumes its size is linear in the size of its input x: that is, $mx + k$ where k represents memory that must be read irrespective of batch size. A large k might, for example, suggest the selection of placement (b) in Fig. 4 because if $k = 0$ batch size could be tuned to make placement (a) attractive. But a phase-ordering problem arises: Solving either batch size or fusion/fission independently (rather than simultaneously) can sacrifice opportunities to achieve optimal placement.

A related complication is that while the choices made by a stream-processing system could take place either statically or dynamically, granularity adjustment is more difficult to perform dynamically. For example, while dynamic work-stealing on a shared-memory computer can provide load balance and place kernels onto processors, it cannot deal with fine-grained kernels

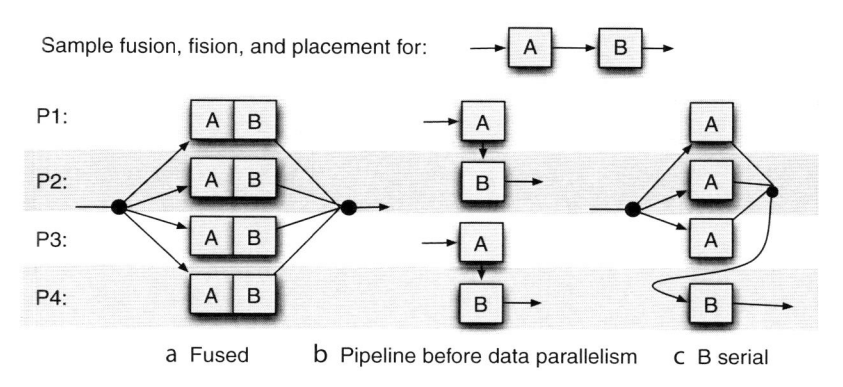

Stream Programming Languages. Fig. 4 Sample placements of two kernels, A and B onto processors P1–P4

(a) Fused (b) Pipeline before data parallelism (c) B serial

that perform only a few FLOPS per invocation. That said, as long as kernels are compiled to handle batches of data, the exact size of batches can be adjusted at runtime.

Program Transformation

If optimizations are performed statically by a compiler, they can take the form of source-to-source transformations. The most important optimizations fall into the following four categories:

- High-level / Algebraic – domain - specific optimizations, for example, canceling an FFT and an inverse FFT (see Haskell [8], WaveScript [9])
- Batch-processing / Execution Scaling – choosing batch size
- Fusion – combining and inlining kernels
- Fission / Data Parallelism – choosing N-ways to split a kernel

StreamStatic, for example, could follow the example of StreamIT and perform fusion, fission, and scaling as source-to-source program transformations, resulting in a number of kernels that match the target number of processors and leaving only a one-to-one placement problem to be solved by a simulated annealing optimization process. To achieve load balance during this process, StreamIt happens to use static work-estimation for kernels, but profiling is another option. In fact, given more dynamic data-rates, as in StreamDynamic and StreamDB, profile-based optimization and auto-tuning techniques are a good way to enable some of the above static program transformations. (WaveScript takes this approach [9].) To our knowledge no systems attempt to apply high-level / algebraic optimizations dynamically.

Algorithms

Dynamic systems along the lines of StreamDynamic tend to use work-stealing, as do most of today's popular task-scheduling frameworks. Further, many streaming databases use heuristics for kernel/operator migration to achieve load balance in a distributed setting. On the other hand, streaming models with fixed data-rates permit static scheduling strategies and much work has focused there. Scheduling predictable stream programs bears some resemblance to the well-studied problem of mapping a coarse-grained task-graph onto a multiprocessor (surveyed in [6]). But there is a notable difference: stream programs run continuously and are usually scheduled for throughput (with some exceptions [10]). Likewise, traditional graph-partitioning methods can be applied, but they do not, in general, capture all the degrees of freedom present in stream programs, whose graphs are not fixed, but are subject to transformations such as data-parallel fission of kernels.

An overview of scheduling work on stream processing specifically can be found in [13], focusing on embedded and real-time uses. The ideal would be an algorithm that simultaneously optimizes all aspects of a streaming program. A recent paper [5] proposed one such system that uses integer linear programming to simultaneously perform fission and processor placement for StreamIt programs.

Data Structures and Synchronization

Static and dynamic scheduling approaches employ different data structures. Dynamic approaches targeting shared memory multiprocessors are likely to rely on concurrent data structures including queues. In contrast, a completely static schedule typically requires no synchronization on data structures. Rather it may repeat a fixed schedule, using a global barrier synchronization at the end of each iteration of the schedule.

Relation to Other Parallel Programming Models

Functional Reactive Programming

Like StreamDynamic, FRP enables general purpose functional programs (usually in Haskell) to manipulate streams of values. FRP in particular deals not with discrete streams of elements, but with semantically continuous *signals*. Sampling of signals is performed by the runtime, or separately from the main definition of programs. Most FRP implementations are not high-performance, but parallel implementations and staged implementations that generate efficient code exist.

Relation to Data-parallel Models

With the increasing popularity of the *MapReduce* paradigm, there is a lot of interest in programming models for massively parallel manipulation of data. The FlumeJava library [2] (built on Google's MapReduce) bears a lot of resemblance to a stream-processing system. The user composes parallel operations on collections, and FlumeJava applies fusion transformations to pipelines of parallel operations. Similar systems like Cascade and Dryad explicitly construct dataflow graphs. These systems have a different application focus, target hardware, and scale than most of the work on stream processing. Further, they focus on batch processing of data in parallel, not on continuous execution.

Relation to Fork-Join Shared-Memory Parallelism

Fork-join parallelism in the form of parallel subroutine calls and parallel loops, as found in Cilk [7] and OpenMP [3], are attractive because of their relative ease of incorporation into legacy codes. In contrast, stream processing requires that a program be factored into kernels and that communication become explicit. Once a program is ported, however, it is perhaps easier to assure that it is correct and deterministic. Stream-processing languages provide a complete programming model encompassing computation and communication. In contrast, fork-join models treat the issues of control-flow and work-decomposition, but do not directly address data decomposition or communication.

Future Directions

This entry has described a family of programming models that have already accomplished a lot. Unfortunately, the systems described above have seen little application to industrial stream-processing problems. Most stream-processing codes are written in general purpose languages without any special support for stream processing. A major future challenge is to increase adoption of the body of techniques developed for stream processing.

Libraries, rather than stream-programming languages may have an advantage in this respect. Further, stream programming systems that are *wide spectrum* may prove desirable in the future – models that can reproduce the best results of more restrictive programming models, while also allowing graceful degradation into more general programming, therefore not confining the user strictly.

Related Entries

▶Cell Processor

Bibliography

1. http://www.streambase.com/
2. Chambers C, Raniwala A, Perry F, Adams S, Henry RR, Bradshaw R, Weizenbaum N (2010) Flumejava: easy, efficient data-parallel pipelines. In: PLDI '10: proceedings of the 2010 ACM SIGPLAN conference on programming language design and implementation. ACM, New York, pp 363–375
3. Dagum L, Menon R (1998) OpenMP: an industry standard API for shared memory programming. IEEE Comp Sci Eng 5(1):46–55
4. Gordon MI, Thies W, Amarasinghe S (2006) Exploiting coarse-grained task, data, and pipeline parallelism in stream programs. SIGOPS Oper Syst Rev 40(5):151–162
5. Kudlur M, Mahlke S (2008) Orchestrating the execution of stream programs on multicore platforms. In: PLDI '08 proceedings of

the 2008 ACM SIGPLAN conference on programming language design and implementation. ACM, New York, pp 114–124
6. Kwok Y-K, Ahmad I (1999) Static scheduling algorithms for allocating directed task graphs to multiprocessors. ACM Comput Surv 31(4):406–471
7. Leiserson CE (2009) The cilk + + concurrency platform. In: DAC '09 proceedings of the 46th annual design automation conference. ACM, New York, pp 522–527
8. Liu H, Cheng E, Hudak P (2009) Causal commutative arrows and their optimization. In: ICFP '09 proceedings of the 14th ACM SIGPLAN international conference on functional programming. ACM, New York, pp 35–46
9. Newton RR, Girod LD, Craig MB, Madden SR, Morrisett JG (2008) Design and evaluation of a compiler for embedded stream programs. In: LCTES '08 proceedings of the 2008 ACM SIGPLAN-SIGBED conference on languages, compilers, and tools for embedded systems. ACM, New York, pp 131–140
10. Pillai PS, Mummert LS, Schlosser SW, Sukthankar R, Helfrich CJ (2009) Slipstream: scalable low-latency interactive perception on streaming data. In: NOSSDAV '09 proceedings of the 18th international workshop on network and operating systems support for digital audio and video. ACM, New York, pp 43–48
11. Taylor MB, Lee W, Miller J, Wentzlaff D, Bratt I, Greenwald B, Hoffmann H, Johnson P, Kim J, Psota J, Saraf A, Shnidman N, Strumpen V, Frank M, Amarasinghe S, Agarwal A (2004) Evaluation of the raw microprocessor: an exposed-wire-delay architecture for ilp and streams. In: ISCA '04 proceedings of the 31st annual international symposium on Computer architecture. IEEE Computer Society, Washington, DC, p 2
12. Travis J, Kring J (2006) LabVIEW for everyone: graphical programming made easy and fun, 3rd edn. Prentice Hall, Upper Saddle River
13. Wiggers MH (2009) Aperiodic multiprocessor scheduling for real-time stream processing applications. Ph.D. thesis, University of Twente, Enschede, The Netherlands

Strong Scaling

▶Amdahl's Law

Suffix Trees

AMOL GHOTING, KONSTANTIN MAKARYCHEV
IBM Thomas. J. Watson Research Center, Yorktown Heights, NY, USA

Synonyms
Position tree

Definition
The suffix tree is a data structure that stores all the suffixes of a given string in a compact tree-based structure. Its design allows for a particularly fast implementation of many important string operations.

Discussion

Introduction
The suffix tree is a fundamental data structure in string processing. It exposes the internal structure of a string in a way that facilitates the efficient implementation of a myriad of string operations. Examples of these operations include string matching (both exact and approximate), exact set matching, all-pairs suffix-prefix matching, finding repetitive structures, and finding the longest common substring across multiple strings [12].

Let A denote a set of characters. Let $S = s_0, s_1, \ldots, s_{n-1}, \$$, where $s_i \in A$ and $\$ \notin A$, denote a $\$$ terminated input string of length $n + 1$. The ith suffix of S is the substring $s_i, s_{i+1}, \ldots, s_{n-1}, \$$. The suffix tree for S, denoted as T, stores all the suffixes of S in a tree structure. The tree has the following properties:

1. Paths from the root node to the leaf nodes have a one-to-one relationship with the suffixes of S. The terminal character $\$$ is unique and ensures that no suffix is a proper prefix of any other suffix. Therefore, there are as many leaf nodes as there are suffixes.
2. Edges spell nonempty strings.
3. All internal nodes, except the root node, have at least two children. The edge for each child node begins with a character that is different from the starting character of its sibling nodes.
4. For an internal node v, let $l(v)$ denote the substring obtained by traversing the path from the root node to v. For every internal node v, with $l(v) = x\alpha$, where $x \in A$ and $\alpha \in A^*$, we have a pointer known as a suffix link to an internal node u such that $l(u) = \alpha$.

An instance of a suffix tree for a string $S = ABCABC\$$ is presented in Fig. 1. Each edge in a suffix tree is represented using the start and end indices of the corresponding substring in S. Therefore, even though a suffix tree represents n suffixes (each with at most n characters) for a total of $\Omega(n^2)$ characters, it only requires $O(n)$ space [31].

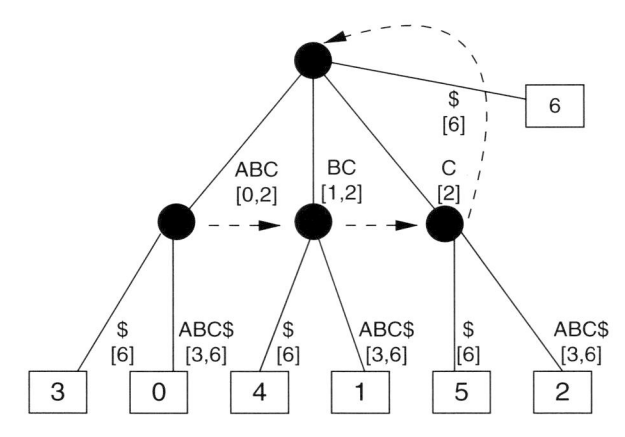

Suffix Trees. Fig. 1 Suffix tree for $S = ABCABC\$$ [0123456]. Internal nodes are represented using circles and leaf nodes are represented using rectangles. Each leaf node is labeled with the index of the suffix it represents. The *dashed arrows* represent the suffix links. Each edge is labeled with the substring it represents and its corresponding edge encoding

Applications

Over the past few decades, the suffix tree has been used for a spectrum of tasks ranging from data clustering [33] to data compression [3]. The quintessential usage of suffix trees is seen in the bioinformatics domain [2, 5, 6, 12, 17, 19, 24] where it is used to effectively evaluate queries on biological sequence data sets. A hallmark of suffix trees is that in many cases it allows one to process queries in time proportional to the size of the query rather than the size of string.

Suffix Tree Construction

Serial Suffix Tree Construction Algorithms

Algorithms due to Weiner [32], McCreight [22], and Ukkonen [31] have shown that suffix trees can be built in linear space and time. These algorithms afford a linear time construction by employing suffix links. Ukkonen's algorithm is more recent and popular because it is easier to implement than the other algorithms. It is an $O(n)$, in-memory construction algorithm. The algorithm is based on the simple, but elegant observation that the suffixes of a string $S_i = s_0, s_1, \ldots, s_i$ can be obtained from the suffixes of string $S_{i-1} = s_0, s_1, \ldots, s_{i-1}$ by catenating symbol s_i at the end of each suffix of S_{i-1} and by adding the empty suffix. The suffixes of the whole string $S = S_n = s_0, s_1, \ldots, s_n$ can then be obtained by first expanding the suffixes of S_0 into the suffixes of S_1 and so on, until the suffixes of S_n are obtained from the suffixes of S_{n-1}. This translates into a suffix tree construction that can be performed by iteratively expanding the leaves of a partially constructed suffix tree. Through the use of suffix links, which provide a mechanism for quickly locating suffixes, the suffix tree can be expanded by simply adding the $(i + 1)$th character to the leaves of the suffix tree built on the previous i characters. The algorithm thus relies on suffix links to traverse through all of the sub-trees in the main tree, expanding the outer edges for each input character.

Parallel Suffix Tree Construction

Parallel suffix tree construction has been extensively studied in theoretical computer science. Apostolico et al. [1], Sühleyman et al. [28], and Hariharan [14] proposed theoretically efficient parallel algorithms for the problem based on the PRAM model. For example, Hariharan [14] showed how to execute McCreight's [22] algorithm concurrently on many processors. These algorithms, however, are designed for the case when the string and the suffix tree fit in main memory. Since the memory accesses of these algorithms exhibit poor locality of reference [8], these algorithms are inefficient when either the string or the suffix tree do not fit in main memory. On many real-world data sets, this is often the case.

The aforementioned problem has been theoretically resolved by Farach-Colton et al. [8]. Farach-Colton et al. [8] proposed a divide-and-conquer algorithm that operates as follows. First, construct a suffix tree for suffixes starting at odd positions. To do so, sort all pairs of characters at positions $2i - 1$ and $2i$ and replace each pair with its index in the sorted list. This gives us a string of length $\lceil n/2 \rceil$ with characters in a bigger alphabet. Recursively construct the suffix tree for this string. The obtained tree is essentially the suffix tree for suffixes starting at odd positions in the original string. Then, given the "odd" suffix tree construct an "even" suffix tree of suffixes starting at even positions. Finally, merge the trees. The details of the Farach-Colton et al. [8] algorithms are very complex, and there have not been any successful implementations. However, the doubling approach has been successfully used in practice for constructing suffix arrays (see [4, 7], and section Suffix Arrays). While the authors do not explicitly provide a parallel algorithm, they indicate that the sort and merge phases do lend themselves to a parallel implementation. While the aforementioned algorithms provide theoretically optimal performance, for most algorithms, memory accesses exhibit poor locality of reference. As a consequence, these algorithms are grossly inefficient when either the tree or the string does not fit in main memory. To tackle this problem, this past decade has seen several research efforts that target large suffix tree construction. Algorithms that have been developed in these efforts can be placed in two categories: ones that require the input string to fit in main memory and ones that do not have this requirement. Many of these efforts only provide and evaluate serial algorithms for suffix tree construction. However, by design, as will be discussed, they do indeed lend themselves to a parallel implementation.

Practical Parallel Algorithms for In-Core Strings

Hunt et al. [13] presented the very first approach to efficiently build suffix trees that do not fit in main memory. The approach drops the use of suffix links in favor of better locality of reference. Typically, the suffix tree is an order of magnitude larger than the string being indexed. As a result, for large input strings, the suffix tree cannot be accommodated in main memory. The method first finds a set of prefixes so as to partition the suffix tree into sub-trees (each prefix corresponds to a sub-tree) that can be built in main memory. The number of times a prefix occurs in a string is used to bound the size of the suffix sub-tree. The approach iteratively increases the size of the prefix until a length is reached where all the suffix sub-trees will fit in memory. Next, for each of these prefixes, the approach builds the associated suffix sub-tree using a scan of the data set. Essentially, for each suffix with the prefix, during insertion, one finds a path in the partially constructed suffix sub-tree that shares the longest common prefix (lcp) with this suffix, and branches from this path when no more matching characters are found. The worst case complexity of the approach is $O(n^2)$, but it exhibits $O(n \log n)$ average case complexity. This algorithm can be parallelized by distributing the prefixes to the different processors in a round-robin fashion and having each processor build one or more suffix sub-trees of the

suffix tree. Kalyanaraman et al. [18] presented a parallel generalized suffix tree construction algorithm that in some ways builds upon Hunt's approach to realize a scalable parallel suffix tree construction. A generalized suffix tree is a suffix tree for not one but a group of strings. While the algorithm was presented in the context of the genome assembly problem, the proposed approach is not tied to genome assembly and can be applied else where. The approach first sorts all suffixes based on their w-length prefixes, where (like Hunt et al.'s approach) w is picked to ensure that the associated suffix sub-trees will fit in main memory. Suffixes with the same prefix are then assigned to the a single bucket. The buckets are then partitioned across the processors such that load is approximately balanced. Each processor then builds a sub-tree of the final suffix tree using a depth-first tree building approach. This is accomplished by sorting all the suffixes in the local bucket and then inserting them in sorted order. The end result in a distributed representation of the generalized suffix tree as a collection of sub-trees.

Japp introduced top-compressed suffix trees [15] that improves upon Hunt's approach by introducing a pre-processing stage to remove the need for repeated scans of the input sequence. Moreover, the author employed partitioning and optimized the insertion of suffixes into partitions using suffix links. The method is based on a new linear time construction algorithm for "sparse" suffix trees, which are sub-trees of the whole suffix tree. The new data structures are called the paged suffix tree (PST) and the distributed suffix tree (DST), respectively. Both tackle the memory bottleneck by constructing sub-trees of the full suffix tree independently and are designed for single processor and distributed memory parallel computing environments, respectively. The standard operations on suffix trees of biological importance are shown to be easily translatable to these new data structures.

Practical Parallel Algorithms for Out-of-Core Strings

The above mentioned parallel algorithms scale well when the input string fits in main memory. Many real-world input strings (like the human genome), however, do not fit in main memory. Researchers have developed a variety of algorithms to handle this situation. The earlier solutions for this problem follow what is known as the partition-and-merge methodology. The approach is illustrated in Fig. 2. ST-MERGE [30], proposed by Tian et al. partitions the input string and constructs a suffix tree for each of these partitions in main memory. These suffix trees are then merged to create the final suffix tree. Merging two suffix trees involves finding matching suffixes in the two trees that share the longest common prefix, reusing this path in the new merged tree, and splitting this path when no more matching characters are found. Suffix link recovery can them be accomplished using a postprocessing step. The approach can be parallelized as follows. During the partition phase, each processor can be assigned block of the input string and it can build a suffix tree for the partition. During the merge phase, a processor can be assigned a pair of suffix trees where it is responsible for merging a pair of trees. One can realize a binary merge tree to build the final suffix tree. TRELLIS [26], due to Phoophakdee and Zaki, is similar in flavor but differs in the following regards. First, the approach finds a set of variable-length prefixes such that the corresponding suffix sub-trees will fit in main memory. Second, it partitions the input string and constructs a suffix tree for each partition in main memory (like ST-MERGE) and stores the sub-trees for each prefix determined in the first step, separately, on disk. Finally, it merges all the sub-trees associated with each prefix to realize the final set of suffix sub-trees. By design, TRELLIS ensures that each of the suffix sub-trees (built using the merge operation) will fit in main memory. TRELLIS can be parallelized using an approach similar to the parallelization of ST-MERGE.

Ghoting and Makarychev [10] studied the performance of the "partition-and-merge" approach for very large input strings and showed that the working set for these algorithms scales linearly with the size of the input string. This results in a lot of *random disk I/O* during the merge phase (the authors of TRELLIS do mention this as well [26]) when indexing strings that do not fit in main memory. One can even argue that for very large strings, the performance of the "partition-and-merge" way will converge to that of Hunt's approach [13], as merging sub-trees in tantamount to inserting suffixes into a partially constructed suffix tree. To address this challenge, Ghoting and Makarychev presented a serial algorithm WAVEFRONT and its parallelization P-WAVEFRONT [10, 11]. P-WAVEFRONT is the first parallel algorithm that can build a suffix tree for an input string that does not fit in main memory. P-WAVEFRONT diverges from the partition-and-merge methodology to suffix tree construction. Leveraging the structure of suffix trees, the algorithm builds a suffix tree by simultaneously tiling accesses to both the input string and the partially constructed suffix tree. Steps for P-WAVEFRONT are presented in Fig. 3. First, an in-network string cache is built by distributing the input strings across all processors in a round-robin fashion. The algorithm assumes that the input string can fit in collective main memory. This step uses collective I/O to ensure efficient reading of the input string. Next, like TRELLIS, a set of variable length prefixes are found in parallel such that the associated suffix sub-trees fit in memory. These prefixes are then distributed across all processors in a round-robin fashion. The following prefix location discovery phase is used to find the location of each prefix being processed using a collective procedure. During this step, each processor is responsible for finding locations of all prefixes (not just its own) in a partition of the input string and these are collective exchanged with other processors such that each processor has locations of its prefix in the entire input string. Finally, the suffix sub-tree for each prefix is built in a tiled and iterative manner by processing a pair of blocks of the input string at a time. The end result is an algorithm that can index very large input strings and at the same time maintain a

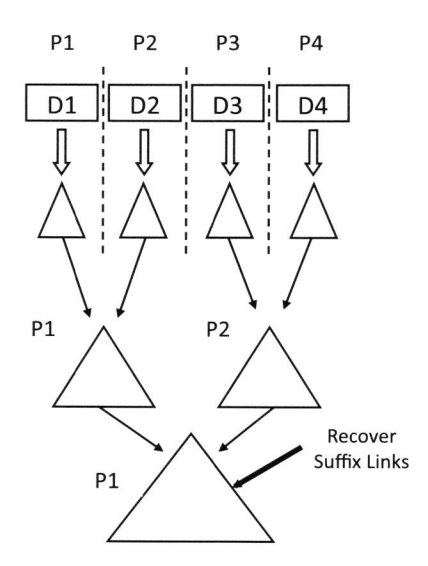

Suffix Trees. Fig. 2 Illustration of the partition and merge approach

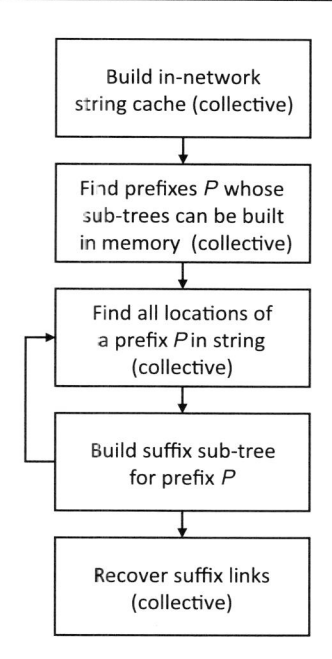

Suffix Trees. Fig. 3 Steps of P-wavefront

bounded working set size and a fixed memory footprint. The proposed methodology was applied to the suffix link recovery process as well, realizing an end-to-end I/O-efficient solution.

Suffix Arrays

Closely related to suffix trees is the suffix array [23]. Suffix array is the alphabetically sorted list of all suffixes of a given string S. For example, the suffix array of the string $S = ABCABC\$$ is as follows

Index	Suffix	lcp
6	$	0
3	ABC$	0
0	ABCABC$	3
4	BC$	0
1	BCABC$	2
5	C$	0
2	CABC$	1

The suffix array only contains pointers to the suffixes in the original string S. Thus, in the example above, the suffix array is the first column of the table, that is, the array $\{6, 3, 0, 4, 1, 5, 2\}$. Given a suffix tree one can obtain a suffix array in linear time by performing a depth-first search (DFS) (see Fig. 1). Suffix arrays are often used instead of suffix trees. The main advantage of suffix arrays is that they have a more compact representation in the memory. Besides the pointers to the suffixes, suffix arrays can also be augmented to contain lengths of the longest common prefixes (lcps) between adjacent strings (see the third column in the example above). In which case, given a suffix array it is easy to reconstruct the suffix tree. Essentially, the longest common prefix corresponds to the lowest common ancestor (lca) in the tree. Relative to suffix trees, the main drawback is that query processing using suffix arrays can be more time consuming as most queries are processed in time that is function of the size of the input string and not the size of the query (as was the case with suffix trees). Researchers have developed several linear time algorithms for directly building suffix arrays without pre-building a suffix tree [16, 21].

Futamura et al. [9] presented the first algorithm for parallel suffix array construction. The approach is similar to the one by Kalyanaraman et al. [18] that was described in section Practicel Parallel Algorithms for In-Core Strings. The approach first partitions the suffixes into buckets based on their w-length prefixes. These buckets are then distributed across the processors, where the suffixes in each bucket are sorted locally to obtain a portion of the suffix array. The final suffix array can then be realized by concatenating these distributed suffix arrays.

Algorithms for constructing suffix arrays in external memory have been extensively studied and compared by Crauser and Ferragina [4] and by Dementiev et al. [7]. Kärkkäinen et al. [21] proposed the DC3 algorithm, which is based on a similar approach as the Farach et al. [8] divide-and-conquer algorithm for suffix trees (see section Parallel Suffix Tree Construction). However, instead of dividing suffixes in the input string into suffixes starting at odd and even positions, it divides them in three groups depending on the remainder of the suffix position modulo 3. Surprisingly, this change significantly simplifies the algorithm. A variant of DC3, called pDC3, has been implemented by Kulla and Sanders [20]. Their study as well as the study of Dementiev et al. [7] indicate that DC3 and pDC3 are currently the most efficient algorithms for constructing suffix arrays.

Related Entries
▶Bioinformatics
▶Genome Assembly

Bibliographic Notes and Further Reading

Research on parallel indexing for sequence/string data sets is still in its infancy. The primary reason for this is that until 2005, sequence data sets were not growing at a rapid pace and most problems could be handled in main memory. However, over the past few years, with advances in sequencing technologies, sequence databases have reached gigantic proportions. For instance, aggressive DNA sequencing efforts have resulted in the GenBank sequence database surpassing the 100 Gbp (one bp (base pair) is one character in the sequence) mark [25], with sequences from over 165, 000 organisms. Further complicating the issue is the fact that researchers not only need the ability to index a single large genome, but a group of large genomes. For example, consider the area of comparative genomics [27] where one is interested in comparing different genomes, be they from the same or different species. Here researchers may be interested in comparing the genomes of individuals that are prone to a specific type of cancer to those that are not susceptible. In this case, we need to efficiently build a suffix tree for a group of large genomes, as and when needed. These trends suggest the parallel indexing technology for sequence data sets will be extremely important in the coming decade.

Much of this entry focused on parallel construction of suffix trees and suffix arrays. We would like to point the reader to Dan Gusfield's book [12] for a larger overview of applications. There has not been much work on parallelization of query processing using suffix trees and suffix arrays.

Another important direction is the design of parallel cache-conscious algorithms for multi-core processors so as to effectively utilize the memory hierarchy on modern processors. Tsirogiannis and Koudas looked at the problem of parallelizing the partition-and-merge approach on chip-multiprocessor architectures [29] and developed a cache-conscious algorithm for suffix tree construction. Such directions will become increasingly important in the near future given the tendency of packing many cores on a single processor.

Bibliography

1. Apostolico A, Iliopoulos C, Landau G, Schieber B, Vishkin U (1988) Parallel construction of a suffix tree with applications. Algorithmica 3(1–4):347–365
2. Bray N, Dubchak I, Pachter L (2003) AVID: a global alignment program. Genome research 13(1):97–102
3. Burrows M, Wheeler D (1994) A block sorting lossless data compression algorithm. Technical report, Digital Equipment Corporation. Palo Alto, California
4. Crauser A, Ferragina P (2008) A theoretical and experimental study on the construction of suffix arrays in external memory. Algorithmica 32(1):1–35
5. Delcher A, Kasif S, Fleischmann R, Peterson J, White O, Salzberg S (1999) Alignment of whole genomes. Nucleic Acids Res 27(11):2369–2376
6. Delcher A, Phillippy A, Carlton J, Salzberg S (2002) Fast algorithms for large-scale genome alignment and comparison. Nucleic Acids Res 30(1)
7. Dementiev R, Kärkkäinen J, Mehnert J, Sanders P (2008) Better external memory suffix array construction. J Exp Algorithmics (JEA) 12:3–4
8. Farach-Colton M, Ferragina P, Muthukrishnan S (2000) On the sorting-complexity of suffix tree construction. J ACM 47(6): 987–1011
9. Futamura N, Aluru S, Kurtz S (2001) Parallel suffix sorting. In: Proceedings 9th international conference on advanced computing and communications. Citeseer, pp 76–81
10. Ghoting A, Makarychev K (2009) Indexing genomic sequences on the IBM Blue Gene. In: SC '09: proceedings of the conference on high performance computing networking, storage and analysis. ACM, New York, pp 1–11
11. Ghoting A, Makarychev K (2009) Serial and parallel methods for I/O efficient suffix tree construction. In: Proceedings of the ACM international conference on management of data. ACM, New York
12. Gusfield D (1997) Algorithms on strings, trees, and sequences: computer science and computational biology. Cambridge University Press, Cambridge
13. Hariharan R (1994) Optimal parallel suffix tree construction. In: Proceedings of the symposium on theory of computing. ACM, New York
14. Hunt E, Atkinson M, Irving R (2001) A database index to large biological sequences. In: Proceedings of 27th international conference on very large databases. Morgan Kaufmann, San Francisco
15. Japp R (2004) The top-compressed suffix tree: a disk resident index for large sequences. In: Proceedings of the bioinformatics workshop at the 21st annual british national conference on databases

16. Kalyanaraman A, Emrich S, Schnable P, Aluru S (2007) Assembling genomes on largescale parallel computers. J Parallel Distr Comput 67(12):1240–1255
17. Kärkkäinen J, Sanders P, Burkhardt S (2006) Linear work suffix array construction. J ACM 53(6):918–936
18. Ko P, Aluru S (2005) Space efficient linear time construction of suffix arrays. J Discret Algorithms 3(2–4):143–156
19. Kulla F, Sanders P (2006) Scalable parallel suffix array construction. In: Recent advances in parallel virtual machine and message passing interface: 13th European PVM/MPI User's Group Meeting, Bonn, Germany, 17–20 September, 2006: proceedings. Springer, New York, p 22
20. Kurtz S, Choudhuri J, Ohlebusch E, Schleiermacher C, Stoye J, Giegerich R (2001) Reputer: the manifold applications of repeat analysis on a genome scale. Nucleic Acids Res 29(22):4633–4642
21. Kurtz S, Phillippy A, Delcher A, Smoot M, Shumway M, Antonescu C, Salzberg S (2004) Versatile and open software for comparing large genomes. Genome Bio 5:(R12)
22. Manber U, Myers G (1990) Suffix arrays: a new method for on-line string searches. In: Proceedings of the first annual ACM-SIAM symposium on discrete algorithms. Society for Industrial and Applied Mathematics, Philadelphia, pp 319–327
23. McCreight E (1976) A space-economical suffix tree construction algorithm. J ACM 23(2)
24. Meek C, Patel J, Kasetty S (2003) Oasis: an online and accurate technique for localalignment searches on biological sequences. In: Proceedings of 29th international conference on very large databases
25. NCBI. Public collections of DNA and RNA sequence reach 100 gigabases, 2005. http://www.nlm.nih.gov/news/press_releases/dna_rna_100_gig.html.
26. Phoophakdee B, Zaki M (2007) Genome-scale disk-based suffix tree indexing. In: Proceedings of the ACM international conference on management of data. ACM, New York
27. Rubin GM, Yandell MD, Wortman JR, Gabor Miklos GL, Nelson CR, Hariharan IK, Fortini ME, Li PW, Apweiler R, Fleischmann W, Cherry JM, Henikoff S, Skupski MP, Misra S, Ashburner M, Birney E, Boguski MS, Brody T, Brokstein P, Celniker SE, Chervitz SA, Coates D, Cravchik A, Gabrielian A, Galle RF, Gelbart WM, George RA, Goldstein LS, Gong F, Guan P, Harris NL, Hay BA, Hoskins RA, Li J, Li Z, Hynes RO, Jones SJ, Kuehl PM, Lemaitre B, Littleton JT, Morrison DK, Mungall C, O'Farrell PH, Pickeral OK, Shue C, Vosshall LB, Zhang J, Zhao Q, Zheng XH, Zhong F, Zhong W, Gibbs R, Venter JC, Adams MD, Lewis S (2000) Comparative genomics of the eukaryotes. Science 287(5461):2204–2215
28. Sahinalp SC, Vishkin U (1994) Symmetry breaking for suffix tree construction. In: STOC '94: proceedings of the twenty-sixth annual ACM symposium on Theory of computing ACM, New York, pp 300–309
29. Tian Y, Tata S, Hankins R, Patel J (2005) Practical methods for constructing suffix trees. VLDB J 14(3):281–299
30. Tsirogiannis D, Koudas N (2010) Suffix tree construction algorithms on modern hardware. In: EDBT '10: Proceedings of the 13th international conference on extending database Technology. ACM, New York, pp 263–274
31. Ukkonen E (1992) Constructing suffix trees on-line in linear time. In: Proceedings of the IFIP 12th work computer congress on algorithms, software, architecture: information processing. North Holland Publishing Co., Amsterdam
32. Weiner P (1973) Linear pattern matching algorithms. In: Proceedings of 14th annual symposium on switch and automata theory. IEEE Computer Society, Washington, DC
33. Zamir O, Etzioni O (1998) Web document clustering: a feasibility demonstration. In: Proceedings of 21st international conference on research and development in information retrieval. ACM, New York

Superlinear Speedup

▶ Metrics

SuperLU

Xiaoye Sherry Li[1], James Demmel[2], John Gilbert[3], Laura Grigori[4], Meiyue Shao[5]
[1]Lawarence Berkeley National Laboratory, Berkeley, CA, USA
[2]University of California at Berkeley, Berkeley, CA, USA
[3]University of California, Santa Barbara, CA, USA
[4]Laboratoire de Recherche en Informatique Universite Paris-Sud 11, Paris, France
[5]Umeå University, Umeå, Sweden

Synonyms
Sparse gaussian elimination

Definition
SuperLU is a general-purpose library for the solution of large, sparse, nonsymmetric systems of linear equations using direct methods. The routines perform LU decomposition with numerical pivoting and solve the triangular systems through forward and back substitution. Iterative refinement routines are provided for improved backward stability. Routines are also provided to equilibrate the system, to reorder the columns to preserve sparsity of the factored matrices, to estimate the condition number, to calculate the relative backward error, to estimate error bounds for the refined solutions,

and to perform threshold-based incomplete LU factorization (ILU), which can be used as a preconditioner for iterative solvers. The algorithms are carefully designed and implemented so that they achieve excellent performance on modern high-performance machines, including shared-memory and distributed-memory multiprocessors.

Discussion

Introduction

SuperLU consists of a collection of three related ANSI C subroutine libraries for solving sparse linear systems of equations $AX = B$. Here A is a square, nonsingular, $n \times n$ sparse matrix, and X and B are dense $n \times nrhs$ matrices, where $nrhs$ is the number of right-hand sides and solution vectors. The LU factorization routines can handle non-square matrices. Matrix A need not be symmetric or definite; indeed, SuperLU is particularly appropriate for matrices with very unsymmetric structure. All three libraries use variations of Gaussian elimination optimized to take advantage of both sparsity and the computer architecture, in particular memory hierarchies (caches) and parallelism [5, 17]. All three libraries can be obtained from the following URL:

http://crd.lbl.gov/~xiaoye/SuperLU/

The three libraries within SuperLU are as follows:

- *Sequential SuperLU* (SuperLU) is designed for sequential processors with one or more levels of caches [3]. Routines for both complete and threshold-based incomplete LU factorizations are provided [20].
- *Multithreaded SuperLU* (SuperLU_MT) is designed for shared-memory multiprocessors, such as multicore, and can effectively use 16–32 parallel processors on sufficiently large matrices in order to speed up the computation [4].
- *Distributed SuperLU* (SuperLU_DIST) is designed for distributed-memory parallel machines, using MPI for interprocess communication. It can effectively use hundreds of parallel processors on sufficiently large matrices [19].

Table 1 summarizes the current status of the software. All the routines are implemented in C, with parallel extensions using Pthreads or OpenMP for

SuperLU. Table 1 SuperLU software status

	Sequential SuperLU	SuperLU_MT	SuperLU_DIST
Platform	Serial	Shared-memory	distributed-memory
Language (with Fortran interface)	C	C + Pthreads or OpenMP	C + MPI
Data type	Real/complex Single/double	Real/complex Single/double	Real/comples Double

shared-memory programming, or MPI for distributed-memory programming. Fortran interfaces are provided in all three libraries.

Overall Algorithm

The kernel algorithm in SuperLU is sparse Gaussian elimination, which can be summarized as follows:

1. Compute a *triangular factorization* $P_r D_r A D_c P_c = LU$. Here D_r and D_c are diagonal matrices to equilibrate the system, and P_r and P_c are *permutation matrices*. Premultiplying A by P_r reorders the rows of A, and postmultiplying A by P_c reorders the columns of A. P_r and P_c are chosen to enhance sparsity, numerical stability, and parallelism. L is a unit lower triangular matrix ($L_{ii} = 1$) and U is an upper triangular matrix. The factorization can also be applied to non-square matrices.

2. Solve $AX=B$ by evaluating $X=A^{-1}B=(D_r^{-1}P_r^{-1}LUP_c^{-1}D_c^{-1})^{-1}B=D_c\left(P_c(U^{-1}(L^{-1}(P_r(D_rB))))\right)$. This is done efficiently by multiplying from right to left in the last expression: Scale the rows of B by D_r. Multiplying $P_r B$ means permuting the rows of $D_r B$. Multiplying $L^{-1}(P_r D_r B)$ means solving $nrhs$ triangular systems of equations with matrix L by substitution. Similarly, multiplying $U^{-1}(L^{-1}(P_r D_r B))$ means solving triangular systems with U.

In addition to exact, or complete, factorization, SuperLU also contains routines to perform incomplete factorization (ILU), in which sparser and so cheaper approximations to L and U are computed, which can be used as a general-purpose preconditioner in an iterative solver.

The simplest implementation, used by the *simple driver* routines in SuperLU and SuperLU_MT, consists of the following steps:

Simple Driver (assumes $D_r = D_c = I$)

1. *Choose P_c to order the columns of A* to increase the sparsity of the computed L and U factors, and hopefully increase parallelism (for SuperLU_MT). Built-in choices are described later.
2. *Compute the LU factorization of AP_c.* SuperLU and SuperLU_MT can perform dynamic pivoting with row interchanges during factorization for numerical stability, computing P_r, L, and U at the same time.
3. *Solve the system* using P_r, P_c, L, and U as described above (where $D_r = D_c = I$).

The simple driver subroutines for double precision real data are called dgssv and pdgssv for SuperLU and SuperLU_MT, respectively. The letter d in the subroutine names means double precision real; other options are s for single precision real, c for single precision complex, and z for double precision complex. SuperLU_DIST does not include this simple driver.

There is also an *expert driver* subroutine that can provide more accurate solutions, compute error bounds, and solve a sequence of related linear systems more economically. It is available in all three libraries.

Expert Driver

1. *Equilibrate* the matrix A, that is, compute diagonal matrices D_r and D_c so that $\hat{A} = D_r A D_c$ is "better conditioned" than A, that is, $\hat{A}^{-1}$ is less sensitive to perturbations in $\hat{A}$ than A^{-1} is to perturbations in A.
2. *Preorder the rows of $\hat{A}$* (SuperLU_DIST only), that is, replace $\hat{A}$ by $P_r \hat{A}$ where P_r is a permutation matrix. This step is called "static pivoting," and is only done in the distributed-memory algorithm, which allows scaling to more processors.
3. *Order the columns of $\hat{A}$*, to increase the sparsity of the computed L and U factors, and increase parallelism (for SuperLU_MT and SuperLU_DIST). In other words, replace $\hat{A}$ by $\hat{A} P_c^T$ in SuperLU and SuperLU_MT, or replace $\hat{A}$ by $P_c \hat{A} P_c^T$ in SuperLU_DIST where P_c is a permutation matrix.
4. *Compute the LU factorization of $\hat{A}$.* SuperLU and SuperLU_MT can perform dynamic pivoting with row interchanges for numerical stability. In contrast, SuperLU_DIST uses the order computed by the preordering step (Step 2), and replaces tiny pivots by larger values for stability; this is corrected by Step 6.
5. *Solve the system* using the computed triangular factors.
6. *Iteratively refine the solution*, again using the computed triangular factors. This is equivalent to Newton's method.
7. *Compute error bounds.* Both forward and backward error bounds are computed.

The expert driver subroutines for double precision real data are called dgssvx, pdgssvx, and pdgssvx for SuperLU, SuperLU_MT, and SuperLU_DIST, respectively.

The driver routines are composed of several lower level computational routines for computing permutations, computing LU factorization, solving triangular systems, and so on. For large matrices, the LU factorization step takes most of the time, although choosing P_c to order the columns can also be time consuming.

Common Features of the Three Libraries

Supernodes in the Factors

The factorization algorithms in all three libraries use unsymmetric supernodes [3], which enable the use of higher level BLAS routines with higher flops-to-byte ratios, and so higher speed. A supernode is a range $(r : s)$ of columns of L with the triangular block just below the diagonal being full, and the same nonzero structure below the triangular block. Matrix U is partitioned rowwise by the same supernodal boundaries. But due to the lack of symmetry, the nonzero pattern of U consists of dense column segments of different lengths.

Sparse Matrix Data Structure

The principal data structure for a matrix is SuperMatrix, defined as a C structure. This structure contains two levels of fields. The first level defines the three storage-independent properties of a matrix: mathematical type, data type, and storage type. The second level points to the actual storage used to store the compressed matrix. Specifically, matrix A is stored in either column-compressed format (aka Harwell–Boeing format), or row-compressed format (i.e., A^T stored in column-compressed format) [1]. Matrices B and X are stored as a single dense matrix of dimension $n \times nrhs$ in column-major order, with output X overwriting input B. In SuperLU_DIST, A and B can be either replicated or distributed across all processes. The factored matrices L and U are stored differently in SuperLU/SuperLU_MT and SuperLU_DIST, to be described later.

Options Input Argument

The options is an input argument to control the behaviour of the libraries. The user can tell the solvers how the linear systems should be solved based on some known characteristics of the system. For example, for diagonally dominant matrices, choosing the diagonal pivots ensures stability; there is no need for numerical pivoting (i.e., P_r can be an identity matrix). In another situation where a sequence of matrices with the same sparsity pattern needs to be factorized, the column permutation P_c (and also the row permutation P_r, if the numerical values are similar) needs to be computed only once, and reused thereafter. In these cases, the solvers' performance can be much improved over using the default parameter settings.

Performance-Tuning Parameters

All three libraries depend on having an optimized BLAS library to achieve high performance [7, 8]. In particular, they depend on matrix–vector multiplication or matrix–matrix multiplication of relatively small dense matrices arising from the supernodal structure. The block size of these small dense matrices can be tuned to match the "sweet spot" of the BLAS performance on the underlying architecture. These parameters can be altered in the inquiry routine sp_ienv.

Example Programs

In the source code distribution, the EXAMPLE/ directory contains several examples of how to use the driver routines, illustrating the following usages:

- Solve a system once
- Solve different systems with the same A, but different right-hand sides
- Solve different systems with the same sparsity pattern of A
- Solve different systems with the same sparsity pattern and similar numerical values of A

Except for the case of one-time solution, all the other examples can reuse some of the data structures obtained from a previous factorization, hence, save some time compared to factorizing A from scratch. The users can easily modify these examples to fit their needs.

Differences Between SuperLU/SuperLU_MT and SuperLU_DIST

Numerical Pivoting

Both sequential SuperLU and SuperLU_MT use *partial pivoting with diagonal threshold*. The row permutation P_r is determined dynamically during factorization. At the jth column, let a_{mj} be a largest entry in magnitude on or below the diagonal of the partially factored A: $|a_{mj}| = \max_{i \geq j} |a_{ij}|$. Depending on a threshold u ($0.0 \leq u \leq 1.0$) selected by the user, the code may use the diagonal entry a_{jj} as the pivot in column j as long as $|a_{jj}| \geq u |a_{mj}|$ and $a_{jj} \neq 0$, or else use a_{mj}. If the user sets $u = 1.0$, a_{mj} (or an equally large entry) will be used as the pivot; this corresponds to the classical partial pivoting. If the user has ordered the matrix so that choosing diagonal pivots is particularly good for sparsity or parallelism, then smaller values of u tend to choose those diagonal pivots, at the risk of less numerical stability. Selecting $u = 0.0$ guarantees that the pivot on the diagonal will be chosen, unless it is zero. The code can also use a user-input P_r to choose pivots, as long as each pivot satisfies the threshold for each column. The backward error bound *BERR* measures how much stability is actually lost.

It is hard to get satisfactory execution speed with partial pivoting on distributed-memory machines, because of the fine-grained communication and the dynamic data structures required. SuperLU_DIST uses a *static pivoting* strategy, in which P_r is chosen before factorization and based solely on the values of the original A, and remains fixed during factorization. A maximum weighted matching algorithm and the code MC64 developed by Duff and Koster [6] is currently employed. The algorithm chooses P_r to maximize the product of the diagonal entries, and chooses D_r and D_c simultaneously so that each diagonal entry of $P_r D_r A D_c$ is ± 1 and each off-diagonal entry is bounded by 1 in magnitude. On the basis of empirical evidence, when this strategy is combined with diagonal scaling, setting very tiny pivots to larger values, and iterative refinement, the algorithm is as stable as partial pivoting for most matrices that have occurred in the actual applications. The detailed numerical experiments can be found in [19].

Sparsity-Preserving Reordering

For unsymmetric factorizations, preordering for sparsity is less understood than that for Cholesky factorization. Many unsymmetric ordering methods use symmetric ordering techniques, either minimum degree or nested dissection, applied to a symmetrized matrix (e.g., $A^T A$ or $A^T + A$). This attempts to minimize certain upper bounds on the actual fills. Which symmetrized matrix to use strongly depends on how the numerical pivoting is performed.

In sequential SuperLU and SuperLU_MT, where partial pivoting is used, an $A^T A$–based ordering algorithm is preferable. This is because the nonzero pattern of the Cholesky factor R in $A^T A = R^T R$ is a superset of the nonzero pattern of the L^T and U in $P_r A = LU$, for any with row interchanges [9]. Therefore, a good symmetric ordering P_c on $A^T A$ that preserves the sparsity of R can be applied to the columns of A, forming $A P_c^T$, so that the LU factorization of $A P_c^T$ is likely to be sparser than that of the original A.

In SuperLU_DIST, an a priori row permutation P_r is computed to form $P_r A$. With fixed P_r, an $(A^T + A)$-based ordering algorithm is preferable. This is because the symbolic Cholesky factor of $A^T + A$ is a much tighter upper bound on the structures of L and U than that of $A^T A$ when the pivots are chosen on the diagonal. Note that after P_c is chosen, a symmetric permutation $P_c (P_r A) P_c^T$ is performed so that the diagonal entries of the permuted matrix remain the same as those in $P_r A$, and they are larger in magnitude than the off-diagonal entries. Now the final row permutation is $P_c P_r$.

In all three libraries, the user can choose one of the following ordering methods by setting the options.ColPerm option:

- NATURAL: Natural ordering
- MMD_ATA: Multiple Minimum Degree [21] applied to the structure of $A^T A$
- MMD_AT_PLUS_A: Multiple Minimum Degree applied to the structure of $A^T + A$
- METIS_ATA: MeTiS [14] applied to the structure of $A^T A$
- METIS_AT_PLUS_A: MeTiS applied to the structure of $A^T + A$
- PARMETIS: ParMeTiS [15] applied to the structure of $A^T + A$
- COLAMD: Column Approximate Minimum Degree [2]
- MY_PERMC: Use a permutation P_c supplied by the user as input

COLAMD is designed particularly for unsymmetric matrices when partial pivoting is needed, and does not require explicitly forming $A^T A$. It usually gives comparable orderings as MMD on $A^T A$, and is faster.

The purpose of the last option MY_PERMC is to be able to reap the results of active research in the ordering methods. Recently, there is much research on the orderings based on graph partitioning. The user can invoke those ordering algorithms separately, and then input the ordering in the permutation vector for P_c. The user may apply them to the structures of $A^T A$ or $A^T + A$. The routines getata() and at_plus_a() in the file get_perm_c.c can be used to form $A^T A$ or $A^T + A$.

Task Ordering

The Gaussian elimination algorithm can be organized in different ways, such as left-looking (fan-in) or right-looking (fan-out). These variants are mathematically equivalent under the assumption that the floating-point operations are associative (approximately true), but they have very different memory access and communication patterns. The pseudo-code for the left-looking blocking algorithm is given in Algorithm 1.

Algorithm 1 *Left-looking Gaussian elimination*

for *block* $K = 1$ to N do
   (1) *Compute* $U(1:K-1, K)$
      (*via a sequence of triangular solves*)
   (2) *Update* $A(K:N, K) \leftarrow A(K:N, K)$
      $- L(1:N, 1:K-1) \cdot U(1:K-1, K)$
      (*via a sequence of calls to GEMM*)
   (3) *Factorize* $A(K:N, K) \rightarrow L(K:N, K)$
      (*may involve pivoting*)
end for

SuperLU and SuperLU_MT use the left-looking algorithm, which has the following advantages:

- In each step, the sparsity changes are restricted within the Kth block column instead of the entire trailing submatrix, which makes it relatively easy to accommodate dynamic compressed data structures due to partial pivoting.
- There are more memory *read* operations than *write* operations in Algorithm 1. This is better for most modern cache-based computer architectures, because write tends to be more expensive in order to maintain cache coherence.

The pseudo-code for the right-looking blocking algorithm is given in Algorithm 2.

Algorithm 2 *Right-looking Gaussian elimination*

   for *block* $K = 1$ **to** N **do**
      (1) *Factorize* $A(K:N,K) \to L(K:N,K)$
         (*may involve pivoting*)
      (2) *Compute* $U(K,K+1:N)$
         (*via a sequence of triangular solves*)
      (3) *Update* $A(K+1:N, K+1:N) \leftarrow$
         $A(K+1:N, K+1:N) - L(K+1:N, K) \cdot$
         $U(K, K+1:N)$
         (*via a sequence of calls to GEMM*)
   end for

SuperLU_DIST uses right-looking algorithm mainly for scalability consideration.

- The sparsity pattern and data structure can be determined before numerical factorization because of static pivoting.
- The right-looking algorithm fundamentally has more parallelism: at step (3) of Algorithm 2, all the GEMM updates to the trailing submatrix are independent and so can be done in parallel. On the other hand, each step of the left-looking algorithm involves operations that need to be carefully sequenced, which requires a sophisticated pipelining mechanism to exploit parallelism across multiple loop steps.

Parallelization and Performance

SuperLU_MT is designed for parallel machines with shared address space, thus there is no need to partition the matrices. Matrices A, L, and U are stored in separate compressed formats. The parallel elimination uses an asynchronous and barrier-free scheduling algorithm to schedule two types of parallel tasks to achieve a high degree of concurrency. One such task is factorizing the independent panels in the disjoint subtrees of the column elimination tree [10]. Another task is updating a panel by previously computed supernodes. The scheduler facilitates the smooth transition between the two types of tasks, and maintains load balance dynamically. In symbolic factorization, a non-blocking algorithm is used to perform depth-first search and symmetric pruning in parallel. The code achieved over tenfold speedups on a number of earlier SMP machines with 16 processors [4]. Recent evaluation shows that SuperLU_MT performs very well on current multi-threaded, multicore machines; it achieved over 20-fold speedup on a 16 core, 128 thread Sun VictoriaFalls [16].

The design of SuperLU_DIST is drastically different from SuperLU/SuperLU_MT. Many design choices were made by the need for scaling to a large process count. The input sparse matrix A is divided by block rows, with each process having one block row represented in a local row-compressed format. This format is user-friendly and is compatible with the input interface of much other distributed-memory sparse matrix software. The factored L and U matrices, on the other hand, are distributed by a two-dimensional block cyclic layout using supernodal structure for block partition. This distribution ensures that most (if not all) processors are engaged in the right-looking update at each block elimination step, and also ensures that interprocess communication is restricted among process row set or column set. The right-looking factorizations use elimination DAGs to identify task and data dependencies, and a one step look-ahead scheme to overlap communication with computation. A distributed parallel symbolic factorization algorithm is designed so that there is no need to gather the entire graph on a single node, which largely increases memory scalability [12]. SuperLU_DIST has achieved 50- to 100-fold speedups with sufficiently large matrices, and over half a Teraflops factorization rate [18].

Future Directions

There are still many open problems in the development of high performance algorithm and software for sparse direct methods. The current architecture trend shows that the Chip Multiprocessor (CMP) will be the basic building block for computer systems ranging from laptops to extreme high-end supercomputers. The core count per chip will quickly increase from four to eight today to tens in the near future. Given the limited per-chip memory and memory bandwidth, the standard parallelization procedure based on MPI would suffer from serious resource contention. It becomes essential to consider a hybrid model of parallelism at the algorithm level as well as the programming level. The quantitative multicore evaluation of SuperLU shows that the left-looking algorithm in `SuperLU_MT` consistently outperforms the right-looking algorithm in `SuperLU_DIST` on a single node of the recent CMP systems, mainly because the former incurs much less memory traffic [16]. One new design is to combine the two algorithms – partitioning the matrix into larger panels, performing left-looking intra-chip elimination and right-looking inter-chip elimination.

A second new direction is to exploit the property of low numerical rank in many discretized operators so that a specialized Gaussian elimination algorithm can be designed. For example, it has been shown recently that *semi-separable structures* occur in the pivoting block and the corresponding Schur complement of each block factorization step. Thus, using the compressed, semi-separable representation throughout the entire factorization leads to an approximate factorization algorithm that has nearly linear time and space complexity [13, 22]. For many discretized elliptic PDEs, this approximation is sufficiently accurate and can be used as an optimal direct solver. For more general problems, the factoriation can be used as an effective preconditioner. Because of its asymptotically lower data volume compared with conventional algorithms, the amount of memory-to-processor and inter-processor communication is smaller, making it more amenable to a scalable implementation.

Another promising area is to extend the new communication avoiding dense LU and QR factorizations to sparse factorizations [11]. In conventional algorithms, the panel factorization of a tall-skinny submatrix requires a sequence of fine-grained message transfers, and often lies on the critical path of parallel execution. The new method employs a divide-and-conquer scheme for this phase, which has asymptotically less communication. This method should also work for sparse matrices. In particular, the new pivoting strategy for LU can replace the static pivoting currently used in `SuperLU`, leading to a more stable and scalable solver.

Related Entries

▶Chaco
▶LAPACK
▶METIS and ParMETIS
▶Mumps
▶PARDISO
▶PETSc (Portable, Extensible Toolkit for Scientific Computation)
▶Preconditioners for Sparse Iterative Methods
▶Reordering
▶ScaLAPACK
▶Sparse Direct Methods

Bibliography

1. Barrett R, Berry M, Chan TF, Demmel J, Donato J, Dongarra J, Eijkhout V, Pozo R, Romine C, van der Vorst H (1994) Templates for the solution of linear systems: building blocks for the iterative methods. SIAM, Philadelphia, PA
2. Davis TA, Gilbert JR, Larimore S, Ng E (2004) A column approximate minimum degree ordering algorithm. ACM Trans Math Softw 30(3):353–376
3. Demmel JW, Eisenstat SC, Gilbert JR, Li XS, Liu JWH (1999) A supernodal approach to sparse partial pivoting. SIAM J Matrix Anal Appl 20(3):720–755
4. Demmel JW, Gilbert JR, Li XS (1999) An asynchronous parallel supernodal algorithm for sparse gaussian elimination. SIAM J Matrix Anal Appl 20(4):915–952
5. Demmel JW, Gilbert JR, Li XS (1999) SuperLU users' guide. technical report LBNL-44289, Lawrence Berkeley National Laboratory, September 1999. http://crd.lbl.gov/~xiaoye/SuperLU/. Last update: September 2007
6. Duff IS, Koster J (1999) The design and use of algorithms for permuting large entries to the diagonal of sparse matrices. SIAM J Matrix Anal Appl 20(4):889–901
7. BLAS Technical Forum (2002) Basic Linear Algebra Subprograms Technical (BLAST) Forum Standard I. Int J High Perform Comput Appl 16:1–111

8. BLAS Technical Forum (2002) Basic Linear Algebra Subprograms Technical (BLAST) Forum Standard II. Int J High Perform Comput Appl 16:115–199
9. George A, Liu J, Ng E (1988) A data structure for sparse QR and LU factorizations. SIAM J Sci Stat Comput 9:100–121
10. Gilbert JR, Ng E (1993) Predicting structure in nonsymmetric sparse matrix factorizations. In: George A, Gilbert JR, Liu JWH (eds) Graph theory and sparse matrix computation. Springer-Verlag, New York, pp 107–139
11. Grigori L, Demmel J, Xiang H (2008) Communication-avoiding Gaussian elimination. In: Supercomputing 08, Austin, TX, November 15–21, 2008.
12. Grigori L, Demmel JW, Li XS (2007) Parallel symbolic factorization for sparse LU with static pivoting. SIAM J Sci Comput 29(3):1289–1314
13. Gu M, Li XS, Vassilevski P (2010) Direction-preserving and schur-monotonic semi-separable approximations of symmetric positive definite matrices. SIAM J Matrix Anal Appl 31(5):2650–2664
14. Karypis G, Kumar V (1998) MeTiS – a software package for partitioning unstructured graphs, partitioning meshes, and computing fill-reducing orderings of sparse matrices – version 4.0. University of Minnesota, September 1998. http://www-users.cs.umn.edu/~karypis/metis/. Accessed 2010
15. Karypis G, Schloegel K, Kumar V (2003) ParMeTiS: Parallel graph partitioning and sparse matrix ordering library – version 3.1. University of Minnesota. http://www-users.cs.umn.edu/~karypis/metis/parmetis/. Accessed 2010
16. Li XS (2008) Evaluation of sparse factorization and triangular solution on multicore architectures. In: Proceedings of VECPAR08 8th international meeting high performance computing for computational science, Toulouse, France, June 24–27, 2008
17. Li XS (Sept 2005) An overview of SuperLU: algorithms, implementation, and user interface. ACM Trans Math Softw 31(3):302–325
18. Li XS (2009) Sparse direct methods on high performance computers. University of California, Berkeley, CS267 Lecture Notes
19. Li XS, Demmel JW (June 2003) SuperLU DIST: a scalable distributed-memory sparse direct solver for unsymmetric linear systems. ACM Trans Math Softw 29(2):110–140
20. Li XS, Shao M (2011) A supernodal approach to imcomplete LU factorization with partial pivoting. ACM Trans Math Softw 37(4)
21. Liu JWH (1985) Modification of the minimum degree algorithm by multiple elimination. ACM Trans Math Softw 11:141–153
22. Xia J, Chandrasekaran S, Gu M, Li XS (2009) Superfast multifrontal method for large structured linear systems of equations. SIAM J Matrix Anal Appl 2008, 31(3):1382–1411

Supernode Partitioning

▶Tiling

Superscalar Processors

WEN-MEI HWU
University of Illinois at Urbana-Champaign, Urbana, IL, USA

Synonyms

Multiple-instruction issue; Out-of-order execution processors

Definition

A superscalar processor is designed to achieve an execution rate of more than one instruction per clock cycle for a single sequential program.

Discussion

Introduction

Superscalar processor design typically refers to a set of techniques that allow the central processing unit (CPU) of a computer to achieve a throughput of more than one instruction per cycle while executing a single sequential program. While there is not a universal agreement on the definition, superscalar design techniques typically include parallel instruction decoding, parallel register renaming, speculative execution, and out-of-order execution. These techniques are typically employed along with complementing design techniques such as pipelining, caching, branch prediction, and multi-core in modern microprocessor designs.

A typical superscalar processor today is the Intel Core i7 processor based on the Nehalem microarchitecture. There are multiple processor cores in a Core i7 design, where each processor core is a superscalar processor. The processor performs parallel decoding on IA (X86) instructions, performs parallel register renaming to map the X86 registers used by these instructions to a larger set of physical registers, performs speculative execution of instructions beyond conditional branch instruction and potential exception causing instructions, and allows instructions to execute out of their program specified order while maintaining the appearance of in-order completion. These techniques are accompanied and supported by pipelining, instruction caching, data caching, and branch prediction in the design of each processor core.

Instruction-Level Parallelism and Dependences

Superscalar processor design assumes the existence of instruction-level parallelism, a phenomenon that multiple instructions can be executed independently of each other at each point in time. Instruction-level parallelism arises due to the fact that instructions in an execution phase of a program often read and write different data, thus their executions do not affect each other.

In Fig. 1, Instruction A is a memory load instruction that forms its address from the contents of register 1 (r1), accesses the data in the address location, and deposits the accessed data into register 2 (r2). Instruction B is a memory load instruction that forms its address by adding value 4 to the contents of register 1 (r1), accesses the data in the address location, and deposits the accessed data into register 3 (r3). Instructions A and B can be executed independently of each other. Neither of their execution results is affected by the other. With sufficient execution resources, a superscalar processor can execute A and B together and achieve an execution rate of more than one instruction per clock cycle.

Note that Instruction C cannot be executed independently of Instruction A or Instruction B. This is because Instruction C uses the data in register 2 (r2) and register 3 (r3) as its input. These data are loaded from memory by Instruction A and Instruction B. That is, the execution of Instruction C *depends* on that of instruction A and Instruction B. Such dependences limit the amount of instruction-level parallelism that exists in a program.

In general, *data dependences* arise in programs due to the way instructions read from and write into register and memory storage locations. Data dependencies occur between instructions in three forms. We use the code example in Fig. 1 to illustrate these forms of data dependences:

1. Data flow dependency: the destination register of Instruction A is the same as one of the source registers of Instruction C, and C follows A in the sequential program order. In this case, a subsequent instruction consumes the execution result of a previous instruction.
2. Data antidependency: one of the source operands of Instruction C is the same as the destination register of Instruction D, and D follows C in the sequential program order. In this case, Instruction C should receive result of Instruction B. However, if Instruction D is executed too soon, C may receive execution result of Instruction D, which is too new. In this case, a subsequent instruction overwrites one of the source registers of a previous instruction.
3. Data output dependency: the destination register of Instruction B is the same as the destination register of Instruction D, and Instruction D follows B in the sequential program order. In this case, a subsequent instruction overwrites the destination register of a previous instruction. If D is executed too soon, its result could be overwritten by Instruction B, leaving a result which is too old in the destination register. Subsequent instructions would be using stale results.

A superscalar processor uses register renaming and out-of-order execution techniques to detect and enhance the amount of instruction-level parallelism between instructions so that it can execute multiple instructions per clock cycle. These techniques ensure that all instructions acquire the appropriate input value in the presence of all the parallel execution activities and data dependences. They also make sure that the output values of instructions are reflected correctly in the processor registers and memory locations.

Register Renaming

Register renaming is a technique that eliminates register antidependences and output dependences in order to increase instruction parallelism. A register renaming mechanism provides a physical or implementation register file that is larger than the architectural register files. For example, the IA (X86) architecture specifies 8 general-purpose registers whereas the register

A	r2 ← Load MEM[r1+0]
B	r3 ← Load MEM[r1+4]
C	r2 ← r2+r3
D	r3 ← Load MEM[r1+8]

Superscalar Processors. Fig. 1 Code example for register access data dependences

renaming mechanism of a superscalar processor typically provides 32 or more physical registers. At any time, each architectural register is mapped to one or more of the physical registers. By mapping, an architectural register is mapped to multiple physical registers, one can eliminate apparent antidependences and output dependences between instructions.

For example, a register renaming mechanism may map architectural register r3 to physical register pr103 for the destination operand of Instruction B and source of Instruction C in Fig. 1. That is, Instruction B will deposit its result to pr103 and Instruction C will fetch its second input operand from pr103. As long as the producer of the data and all the consumers of the data are redirected to the same physical register, the execution results will not be affected.

Let's further assume that architecture register r3 is mapped to physical register pr105 for the destination operand of Instruction D. That is, Instruction D will deposit its execution results to pr105. As long as all subsequent uses of the data produced by Instruction D are redirected to pr105 for their input, their execution results will remain the same.

The reader should see that the antidependence between Instruction C and Instruction D has been eliminated by the register renaming mechanism. Since Instruction C will go to pr103 for its input whereas Instruction D will deposit its result into pr105, Instruction D will no longer overwrite the input for Instruction C no matter how soon it is executed. As a result, we have eliminated a dependence constraint between Instruction C and Instruction D.

The reader should also notice that the output dependence between Instruction B and Instruction D has been eliminated by the register renaming mechanism. Since Instruction B deposits its result into pr103 and Instruction D deposits its result into pr105, B will no longer overwrite the result of D no matter how soon D is executed. As long as subsequent Instructions that use architecture register r3 are also directed to pr105, they will see the updated results rather than stale results even though B could be executed after D.

By eliminating the register antidependence between C and D and output dependence between B and D, Instruction D can now be executed in parallel with Instructions A and B. This increases the level of instruction-level parallelism. This is the reason why register renaming has become an essential mechanism for superscalar processor design.

Speculative Execution

A major limitation on the amount of instruction-level parallelism is uncertainties in program execution sequence. There are two major sources of such uncertainty. The first is conditional and indirect branch instructions. Conditional branches are used to implement control constructs such as if-then-else statements and loops in high-level language programs. Depending on the condition values, the instructions to be executed after a conditional branch can be either from the next sequential location or from a target location specified by the branch offset. Indirect branches use the contents of a register or memory location as the address of the next instruction to execute. Indirect branches are used to implement procedure return statements, case statements, and table-based procedural calls in high-level language programs.

While conditional and indirect branch instructions serve essential purposes in implementing high-level languages, they introduce uncertainties for execution. The classic approach to addressing this problem is branch prediction, where a mechanism is used to predict the next instructions to execute when conditional and indirect branches are encountered during program execution. However, prediction alone is not sufficient. One needs a means to speculatively execute the instructions on the predicted path of execution and recover from any incorrect predictions.

The second source of uncertainty in program execution is exception conditions. Modern computers use exceptions to support the implementation of virtual memory management, memory protection, and rare execution condition handling. For example, the Instruction A in Fig. 1 may trigger a page fault in its execution and require operating system service to bring in its missing load data. The execution needs to be able to resume cleanly after the page fault is handled by the operating system. This requirement means that the instructions after a load instruction, or any instruction that can potentially cause exceptions, cannot change the execution state in a way that prevents the execution from restarting at the exception causing instruction.

Like in the case of branch prediction, one can "predict" that the exception conditions do not occur and assume that the execution will simply continue down the current path. However, one needs a means to recover the state when an exception indeed occurs so that the execution can correctly restart from the exception-causing instruction.

Speculative execution is a mechanism that allows processors to fetch and execute instructions down a predicted path and to recover if the prediction is incorrect. In general, these mechanisms use buffers to keep both the original state and the recent updates to the state. The updated state is used during the speculative execution. The original state is used if the processor needs to recover from an incorrect prediction. Since conditional and indirect branches occur frequently, one in every four to five instructions on average, the level of instruction level parallelism a superscalar processor can exploit would be extremely low without speculative execution. This is why speculative execution has become an essential mechanism in superscalar processor design. The most popular methods for recovering from incorrect branch predictions are reorder buffer (ROB) and checkpointed register file. The most popular method for recovering from exception causing instructions is reorder buffer.

A retirement mechanism in speculative execution attempts to make the effects of instruction execution permanent. An instruction is eligible for retirement when all instructions before it have retired. An eligible instruction is then checked if it has caused any exceptions or incorrect branch prediction. If the instruction does not incur any exception or incorrect branch prediction, it can commit its execution result into an *architectural state*. Otherwise, the instruction triggers a recovery and the state of the processor is restored to a previous architectural state.

The capacity of reorder buffers and checkpoint buffers defines the notion of *instruction window*, a collection of consecutive instructions that are actively processed by a superscalar processor. At any point in time, the instruction window starts with the oldest instruction that has not completed execution and ends with the youngest instruction that has started execution. The larger the instruction window, the more hardware is needed to keep track of the execution status of all instructions in the window and the information needed to recover the processor state if anything goes wrong with the execution of the instructions in the window.

Out-of-Order Execution

In a superscalar processor, instructions are fetched according to their sequential program order. However, this may not be best order of execution. For example, in Fig. 1, Instruction D is fetched after Instruction C. However, Instruction C cannot execute until Instructions B and Instruction D completes their execution. On the other hand, with register renaming, Instruction D does not have any dependence on Instructions A, Instruction B, or Instruction C. Therefore, a superscalar processor "reorders" the execution of Instruction C and Instruction D so that Instruction D can produce results for its consumers as soon as possible.

An out-of-order execution mechanism provides buffering for Instructions that need to wait for their input data so that some of their subsequent instructions can proceed with execution. A popular method used in out-of-order execution is the Tomasulo's Algorithm that was originally used in the IBM 360/91. The method maintains *reservation stations*, hardware buffers that allow the instructions to wait for their input operands.

Brief Early History

The most popular out-of-order execution mechanism in modern superscalar processors is Tomasulo's algorithm [1] designed by Bob Tomasulo and used in the IBM 360/91 floating point unit in 1967. The out-order-execution mechanism was abandoned in later IBM machines partly due to the concern of the problems it introduces to virtual memory management.

The Intel Pentium processor [2] is an early superscalar design that fetches and executes multiple instructions at each clock cycle. It did not employ register renaming or speculative execution and was able to exploit only a very limited amount of instruction-level parallelism.

Register renaming in superscalar processor design started with the Register Alias Table (RAT) by Patt et al. [3]. To this day, the register renaming structure used in Intel superscalar processors are still called RAT.

Simth and Plaszkun proposed reorder buffers and history buffers for recovering from exceptions in highly pipelined processors [4]. Hwu et al. [5] extended the concepts with checkpointing and incorporated these speculative execution mechanisms with Tomasulo's algorithm.

In 1985, Patt et al. [3] proposed a comprehensive superscalar design that incorporates register renaming, speculative execution, out-of-order execution, along with parallel instruction decode and branch prediction. This is the first comprehensive academic design of superscalar processors. In 1987, Sohi and Vijapeyam [6] proposed a unified reservation station design. These designs were later adopted and refined by Intel to create the Pentium Pro Processor, the first commercially successful superscalar processor design [7].

Recent superscalar processors include MIPS R10000, Intel Pentium 4, IBM Power 6, AMD Athlon, and ARM Cortex. Interested readers should refer to Hennessy and Patterson [8] for more detailed treatment and more recent history on superscalar processor design.

Bibliography

1. Tomasulo R (1967) An efficient algorithm for exploiting multiple arithmetic units. IBM J ResDev 11(1):8–24
2. Case B (1993) Intel reveals pentium implementation details. Microprocessor Report 29 Mar 1993
3. Patt Y, Hwu W-M, Shebanow M (1985) HPS, a new microarchitecture: rationale and introduction. In: Proceedings of the 18th annual workshop on microprogramming, Pacific Grove, pp 103–108
4. Smith J, Pleszkun A (1985) Implementation of precise interrupts in pipelined processors. In: Proceedings of the 12th international symposium on computer architecture, Boston
5. Hwu W-M, Patt Y (1987) Checkpoint repair for out-of-order execution machines. In: Proceedings of the 14th international symposium on computer architecture, Pittsburgh
6. Sohi G, Vajapeyam S (1987) Instruction issue logic for high-performance, interruptable pipelined processors. In: Proceedings of the 14th international symposium on computer architecture, New York
7. Colwell R (2005) Pentium chronicles – the people, passion, and politicc behind Intel's Lanmark chips. Wiley-IEEE Computer Society, ISBN 978-0-47-173617-2
8. Hennessy J, Patterson D (2007) Computer architecture – a quantitative approach, 4th edn. Morgan Kauffman, San Francisco, ISBN 978-0-12-370490-0

SWARM: A Parallel Programming Framework for Multicore Processors

DAVID A. BADER[1], GUOJING CONG[2]
[1]Georgia Institute of Technology, Atlanta, GA, USA
[2]IBM, Yorktown Heights, NY, USA

Definition

So**ft**Ware and **A**lgorithms for **R**unning on **M**ulti-core (SWARM) is a portable open-source parallel library of basic primitives for programming multicore processors. SWARM is built on POSIX threads that allows the user to use either the already developed primitives or direct thread primitives. SWARM has constructs for parallelization, restricting control of threads, allocation and deallocation of shared memory, and communication primitives for synchronization, replication and broadcast. Built on these techniques, it contains a higher-level library of multicore-optimized parallel algorithms for list ranking, comparison-based sorting, radix sort, and spanning tree. In addition, SWARM application example codes include efficient implementations for solving combinatorial problems such as minimum spanning tree [3], graph decomposition [8], breadth-first-search [9], tree contraction [10], and maximum parsimony [7].

Motivation

For the last few decades, software performance has improved at an exponential rate, primarily driven by the rapid growth in processing power. However, performance improvements can no longer rely solely on Moore's law. Fundamental physical limitations such as the size of the transistor and power constraints have now necessitated a radical change in commodity microprocessor architecture to multicore designs. Dual and quad-core processors from Intel [13] and AMD [2] are now ubiquitous in home computing. Also, several novel architectural ideas are being explored for high-end workstations and servers [15, 16]. Continued software performance improvements on such novel multicore systems now require the exploitation of concurrency at the algorithmic level. Automatic methods for detecting concurrency from sequential codes, for example with parallelizing compilers, have had only limited success. SWARM was introduced to fully utilize multicore processors.

On multicore processors, caching, memory bandwidth, and synchronization constructs have a considerable effect on performance. In addition to time complexity, it is important to consider these factors for algorithm analysis. SWARM assumes the multicore model that can be used to explain performance on systems such as Sun Niagara, Intel, and AMD multicore chips. Different models [6] are required for modeling heterogeneous multicore systems such as the Cell architecture.

Model for Multicore Architectures

Multicore systems have a number of processing cores integrated on to a single chip [2, 11, 13, 15, 16]. Typically, the processing cores have their own private L_1 cache and share a common L_2 cache [13, 16]. In such a design, the bandwidth between the L_2 cache and main memory is shared by all the processing cores. Figure 1 shows the simplified architectural model.

Multicore Model
The multicore model (MCM) consists of p identical processing cores integrated onto a single chip. The processing cores share an L_2 cache of size C, and the memory bandwidth is σ.

1. *Let $T(i)$ denote the local time complexity of the core i for $i = 1, \ldots, p$. Let $T = \max_i T(i)$.*
2. *Let B be the total number of blocks transferred between L_2 cache and the main memory. The requests may arise out of any processing core.*
3. *Let L be the time required for synchronization between the cores. Let $N_S(i)$ be the total number of synchronizations required on core i for $i = 1, \ldots, p$. Let $N_S = \max_i N_S(i)$.*

Then the complexity under the multicore model can be represented by a triple $\langle T, B \cdot \sigma^{-1}, N_S \cdot L \rangle$. The complexity of an algorithm will be represented by the dominant element in this triple.

The model proposed above is in many ways similar to the Helman-JáJá model for symmetric multiprocessor (SMP) systems [12], with a few important differences. In the case of SMPs, each processor typically has a large L_2 cache and dedicated bandwidth to main memory, whereas in multicore systems, the shared memory bandwidth will be an important consideration. Thus, SWARM explicitly models the cache hierarchy, and count the number of block transfers between the cache and main memory in a manner similar to Aggarwal and Vitter's external memory model [1].

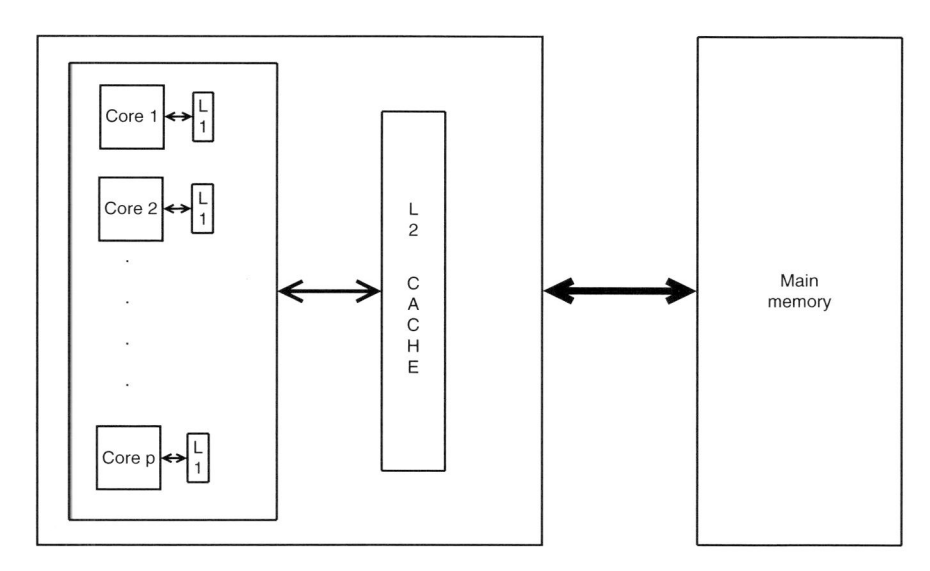

SWARM: A Parallel Programming Framework for Multicore Processors. Fig. 1 Architectural model for multicore systems

SWARM targets three primary issues that affect performance on multicore systems:

1. *Number of processing cores*: Current systems have two to eight cores integrated on a single chip. Cores typically support features such as simultaneous multithreading (SMT) or hardware multithreading, which allow for greater parallelism and throughput. In future designs, up to 100 cores can exist on a single chip.
2. *Caching and memory bandwidth*: Memory speeds have been historically increasing at a much slower rate than processor capacity [14]. Memory bandwidth and latency are important performance concerns for several scientific and engineering applications. Caching is known to drastically affect the efficiency of algorithms even on single processor systems [17, 18]. In multicore systems, this will be even more important due to the added bandwidth constraints.
3. *Synchronization*: Implementing algorithms using multiple processing cores will require synchronization between the cores from time to time, which is an expensive operation in shared memory architectures.

Case Study: Merge Sort

Algorithm 1

In the first algorithm, the input array of length N is equally divided among the p processing cores so that each core gets N/p elements to sort. Once the sorting phase is completed, there are p sorted sub-arrays, each of length N/p. Thereafter the merge phase takes place. A p-way merge over the runs will give the sorted array. Each processor individually sorts its elements using some *cache-friendly* algorithm. This approach does not try to minimize the number of blocks transferred between the L_2 cache and main memory.

Analysis. Since the p processors are all sorting their respective elements at the same time, the L_2 cache will be shared by all the cores during the sorting phase. Thus, if the size of the L_2 cache is C, then effectively each core can use just a portion of the cache with size C/p. Assuming the input size is larger than the cache size, the cache misses will be p times that if only a single core were sorting. Also the bandwidth between the cache and shared main memory is also shared by all the p cores, and this may be a bottleneck.

The time complexity of each processor is:

$$T_c(\text{sort}) = \frac{N}{p} \cdot \log\left(\frac{N}{p}\right)$$

During the merge phase:

$$T_c(\text{merge}) = N \cdot \log(p)$$

$$T_c(\text{total}) = \frac{N}{p} \log\left(\frac{N}{p}\right) + N \log(p)$$

Algorithm 2

This algorithm divides the given array of length N into blocks of size M where M is less that C, the size of the L_2 cache. Each of such N/M blocks is first sorted using all p cores. This is the sorting phase. When the sorting phase is completed, the array consists of N/M runs each of length M. During the merge phase, p blocks are merged at a time. This process is repeated till a single sorted array is arrived. Thus, the merge phase is carried out $\log_p\left(\frac{N}{M}\right)$ times.

Analysis. This algorithm is very similar to the I/O model merge sort [1]. Thus, this algorithm is optimal in terms of transfers between main memory and L_2 cache. However, it will have slightly higher-computational complexity. The p cores sort a total of N/M blocks of size M. Assuming the use of a split-and-merge sort for sorting the block of M elements, thus, during the sorting phase, the time per core is:

$$T_c(\text{sort}) = \frac{N}{M} \cdot \frac{M}{p} \log\left(\frac{M}{p}\right) + \frac{N}{M} \cdot M \log(p)$$
$$= \frac{N}{p} \log\left(\frac{M}{p}\right) + N \log(p) \quad (1)$$

During any merge phase, if blocks of size S are being merged p at a time, the complexity per core is $\frac{N}{Sp} \cdot Sp \log(p) = N \log(p)$. There are $\log_p\left(\frac{N}{M}\right)$ merge phases, thus

$$T_c(\text{merge}) = N \log(p) \cdot \log_p\left(\frac{N}{M}\right)$$

$$T_c(\text{total}) = \frac{N}{p} \log\left(\frac{M}{p}\right) + N \log(p)\left(1 + \log_p\left(\frac{N}{M}\right)\right)$$

Comparison. Algorithm 1 clearly has better time complexity than algorithm 2. However, algorithm 2 is optimal in terms of transfers between L_2 cache and shared main memory. Algorithm analysis using this model captures computational complexity as well as memory performance.

Programming in SWARM

A typical SWARM program is structured as follows:

```
int main (int argc, char **argv)
{
    SWARM_Init(&argc, &argv);
    /* sequential code */
    ....
    ....
    /* parallelize a routine using
    SWARM */
    SWARM_Run(routine);
    /* more sequential code */
    ....
    ....
    SWARM_Finalize();
}
```

In order to use the SWARM library, the programmer needs to make minimal modifications to existing sequential code. After identifying compute-intensive routines in the program, work can be assigned to each core using an efficient multicore algorithm. Independent operations such as those arising in *functional parallelism* or *loop parallelism* can be typically threaded. For functional parallelism, this means that each thread acts as a functional process for that function, and for loop parallelism, each thread computes its portion of the computation concurrently. Note that it might be necessary to apply loop transformations to reduce data dependencies between threads.

SWARM contains efficient implementations of commonly used primitives in parallel programming.

Data parallel. The SWARM library contains several basic "pardo" directives for executing loops concurrently on one or more processing cores. Typically, this is useful when an independent operation is to be applied to every location in an array, for example element-wise addition of two arrays. Pardo implicitly partitions the loop among the cores without the need for coordinating overheads such as synchronization of communication between the cores. By default, pardo uses block partitioning of the loop assignment values to the threads, which typically results in better cache utilization due to the array locations on lefthand side of the assignment being owned by local caches more often than not. However, SWARM explicitly provides both block and cyclic partitioning interfaces for the pardo directive.

```
/* example: partitioning a "for"
    loop among the cores */
pardo(i, start, end, incr) {
    A[i] = B[i] + C[i];
}
```

Control. SWARM control primitives restrict which threads can participate in the context. For instance, the control may be given to a single thread on each core, all threads on one core, or a particular thread on a particular core.

```
THREADS: total number of execution
threads
MYTHREAD: the rank of a thread,
from 0 to THREADS-1
/* example: execute code on
    thread MYTHREAD */
on_thread(MYTHREAD) {
    ....
    ....
}
/* example: execute code on
    one thread */
on_one_thread {
    ....
    ....
}
```

Memory management. SWARM provides two directives SWARM_malloc and SWARM_free that, respectively, dynamically allocate a shared structure and release this memory back to the heap.

```
/* example: allocate a shared array
    of size n */
A=(int*)SWARM_malloc(n*sizeof(int),
TH);
/* example: free the array A */
SWARM_free(A);
```

Barrier. This construct provides a way to synchronize threads running on the different cores.

```
/* parallel code */
```

```
    ....
    ....
/* use the SWARM Barrier for
   synchronization */
SWARM_Barrier();
/* more parallel code */
    ....
    ....
```

Replicate. This primitive uniquely copies a data buffer for each core.

Scan (reduce). This performs a prefix (reduction) operation with a binary associative operator, such as addition, multiplication, maximum, minimum, bitwise-AND, and bitwise-OR. allreduce replicates the result from reduce for each core.

```
/* function signatures */
int SWARM_Reduce_i(int myval,
            reduce_t op,
            THREADED);
double SWARM_Reduce_d(double
            myval,
            reduce_t op,
            THREADED);

/* example: compute global sum,
using
partial local values from each
core */
sum = SWARM_Reduce_d(mySum, SUM,
TH);
```

Broadcast. This primitive supplies each processing core with the address of the shared buffer by replicating the memory address.

```
/* function signatures */
int  SWARM_Bcast_i   (int myval,
                      THREADED);
int* SWARM_Bcast_ip  (int* myval,
                      THREADED);
char SWARM_Bcast_c   (char myval,
                      THREADED);
```

Apart from the primitives for computation and communication, the thread-safe parallel pseudo-random number generator SPRNG [19] is integrated in SWARM.

Algorithm Design and Examples in SWARM

The SWARM library contains a number of techniques to demonstrate key methods for programming on multi-core processors.

- The ***prefix-sum*** algorithm is one of the most useful parallel primitives and is at the heart of several other primitives, such as array compaction, sorting, segmented prefix-sums, and broadcasting; it also provides a simple use of balanced binary trees.
- ***Pointer-jumping*** (or path-doubling) iteratively halves distances in a list or graph. It is used in numerous parallel graph algorithms, and also as a sampling technique.
- Determining the root for each tree node in a rooted-directed forest is a crucial step in handling equivalence classes – such as detecting whether or not two nodes belong to the same component; when the input is a linked list, this algorithm also solves the parallel prefix problem.
- An entire family of techniques of major importance in parallel algorithms is loosely termed ***divide-and-conquer*** – such techniques decompose the instance into smaller pieces, solve these pieces independently (typically through recursion), and then merge the resulting solutions into a solution to the original instance. These techniques are used in sorting, in almost any tree-based problem, in a number of computational geometry problems (finding the closest pair, computing the convex hull, etc.), and are also at the heart of fast transform methods such as the FFT. The pardo primitive in SWARM can be used for implementing such a strategy.
- A variation of the above theme is the ***partitioning strategy***, in which one seeks to decompose the problem into independent subproblems – and thus avoid any significant work when recombining solutions; quicksort is a celebrated example, but numerous problems in computational geometry can be solved efficiently with this strategy (particularly problems involving the detection of a particular configuration in three- or higher-dimensional space).
- Another general technique for designing parallel algorithms is ***pipelining***. In this approach, waves of concurrent (independent) work are employed to achieve optimality.

Built on these techniques, SWARM contains a higher-level library of multicore-optimized parallel algorithms for list ranking, comparison-based sorting, radix sort and spanning tree. In addition, SWARM application example codes include efficient implementations for solving combinatorial problems such as minimum spanning tree [3], graph decomposition [8], breadth-first-search [9], tree contraction [10] and maximum parsimony [7].

Related Entries
▶Cilk
▶OpenMP
▶Parallel Skeletons

History
The SWARM programming framework is a descendant of the symmetric multiprocessor (SMP) node library component of SIMPLE [4].

Bibliography
1. Aggarwal A, Vitter J (1988) The input/output complexity of sorting and related problems. Commun ACM 31:1116–1127
2. AMD Multi-Core Products (2006), http://multicore.amd.com/en/Products/
3. Bader DA, Cong G (2004) A fast, parallel spanning tree algorithm for symmetric multiprocessors (SMPs). In: Proceedings of the international parallel and distributed processing symposium (IPDPS 2004), Santa Fe, NM, April 2004
4. Bader DA, JáJá J (1999) SIMPLE: a methodology for programming high performance algorithms on clusters of symmetric multiprocessors (SMPs). J Parallel Distrib Comput 58(1):92–108
5. Bader DA (2006) SWARM: a parallel programming framework for multicore processors, https://sourceforge.net/projects/multicore-swarm
6. Bader DA, Agarwal V, Madduri K (2007) On the design and analysis of irregular algorithms on the Cell processor: a case study of list ranking. In: Proceedings of the International Parallel and Distributed Processing Symposium (IPDPS 2007), Long Beach, CA
7. Bader DA, Chandu V, Yan M (2006) ExactMP: an efficient parallel exact solver for phylogenetic tree reconstruction using maximum parsimony. In: Proceedings of the 35th International Conference on Parallel Processing (ICPP), Columbus, OH, August 2006
8. Bader DA, Illendula AK, Moret BME, Weisse-Bernstein N (2001) Using PRAM algorithms on a uniform-memory-access shared-memory architecture. In: Brodal GS, Frigioni D, Marchetti-Spaccamela A (eds) Proceedings of the 5th international workshop on algorithm engineering (WAE 2001), volume 2141 of lecture notes in computer science. Springer-Verlag, Århus, Denmark, pp 129–144
9. Bader DA, Madduri K (2006) Designing multithreaded algorithms for breadth-first search and st-connectivity on the Cray MTA-2. In: Proceedings of the 35th international conference on parallel processing (ICPP), IEEE Computer Society, Columbus, OH, August 2006
10. Bader DA, Sreshta S, Weisse-Bernstein N (2002) Evaluating arithmetic expressions using tree contraction: a fast and scalable parallel implementation for symmetric multiprocessors (SMPs). In: Sahni S, Prasanna VK, Shukla U (eds) Proceedings of the 9th international conference on high performance computing (HiPC 2002), volume 2552 of lecture notes in computer science. Bangalore, India, Springer-Verlag, December 2002, pp 63–75
11. Barroso LA, Gharachorloo K, McNamara R, Nowatzyk A, Qadeer S, Sano B, Smith S, Stets R, Verghese B (2000) Piranha: a scalable architecture based on single-chip multi-processing. SIGARCH Comput Archit News 28(2):282–293
12. Helman DR, JáJá J (1999) Designing practical efficient algorithms for symmetric multiprocessors. In: Algorithm engineering and experimentation (ALENEX'99), volume 1619 of lecture notes in computer science, Springer-Verlag, Baltimore, MD, January 1999, pp 37–56
13. Multi-Core from Intel – Products and Platforms (2006) http://www.intel.com/multi-core/products.htm
14. International Technology Roadmap for Semiconductors (2004), http://itrs.net, 2004 update
15. Kahle JA, Day MN, Hofstee HP, Johns CR, Maeurer TR, Shippy D (2005) Introduction to the cell multiprocessor. IBM J Res Dev 49(4/5):589–604
16. Kongetira P, Aingaran K, Olukotun K (2005) Niagara: a 32-way multithreaded Sparc processor. IEEE Micro 25(2):21–29
17. Ladner R, Fix JD, LaMarca A (1999) The cache performance of traversals and random accesses. In: Proceedings of the 10th annual symposium discrete algorithms (SODA-99), ACM-SIAM, Baltimore, MD, pp 613–622
18. Ladner RE, Fortna R, Nguyen B-H (2002) A comparison of cache aware and cache oblivious static search trees using program instrumentation. In: Fleischer R, Meineche-Schmidt E, Moret BME (eds) Experimental algorithms, volume 2547 of lecture notes in computer science, Springer-Verlag, Berlin Heidelberg, pp 78–92
19. Mascagni M, Srinivasan A (2000) Algorithm 806: SPRNG: a scalable library for pseudorandom number generation. ACM Trans Math Softw 26(3):436–461

Switch Architecture

José Flich
Technical University of Valencia, Valencia, Spain

Synonyms
Router architecture

Definition

The switch architecture defines the internal organization and functionality of components in a switch. The switch is in charge of forwarding units of information from the input ports to the output ports.

Discussion

High-performance computing systems, like clusters and massively parallel processors (MPPs), rely on the use of an efficient interconnection network. As the number of end nodes increases to thousands, or even larger sizes, the network becomes a key component since it must provide low latencies and high bandwidth at a moderate cost and power consumption. The basic components of a network are switches/routers, links, and network interfaces. The interconnection network efficiency largely depends on the switch design.

Prior to defining and describing the switch architecture concept, it is worth differentiating between router and switch. Typically, the router is the basic component in a network that forwards messages from a set of input ports to a set of output ports. The router usually negotiates paths and computes the output ports messages need to take. Therefore, the router has some intelligence and adapts to the varying conditions of the network. Indeed, the router concept comes from Wide Area Networks (WANs) where the switching devices must be smart enough to adapt to the varying topological conditions. In high-performance interconnection networks, typically found in cluster cabinets, connecting massively parallel processors, and nowadays even inside a chip, switching devices are also needed. However, differently from the WAN environment, these devices, although have some intelligence and can make critical decisions, they have no capabilities to negotiate the paths and to adapt to the varying conditions. Indeed, usually the topology is expected not to change, thus no need for such negotiation. This is the reason why these devices are also known as switches rather than routers. However, both terms are used with no clear differentiation by the community and thus both become acceptable. This entry is related to switch architecture, although it can be seen also as *router architecture*.

The switch architecture defines the internal organization and functionality of a switch or router. Basically, the switch has a set of input ports where data messages come in and a set of output ports where data messages are delivered. The way internal components are used and connected between them is defined by the switch architecture.

The switch architecture largely depends on the switching technique (see ▶Switching Techniques) used; thus, we may find switch architectures implementing *store and forward switching* that greatly vary from switches implementing *wormhole switching*. Most of the current modern routers and switches, used in high-performance networks, implement *cut-through switching*, or some variant. This entry focuses on such architectures, mainly in wormhole (WH) switches and virtual cut-through (VCT) switches. Although there are basic differences between them, that affect the switch architecture, there are commonalities as both rely on the same form of switching. In the next section, a canonical switch architecture including all the commonalities found in current switches is provided. Then, different components are reviewed and alternative switch organizations are described.

Canonical Switch Architecture

Figure 1 shows the organization of a basic switch architecture. The switch is made up of a set of identical input ports, connected to input physical channels. Each input port uses a link control module to adapt messages coming through the physical channel to the internal switch. Each message is then stored in a buffer at the input port. The buffer can be made of different queues, each one usually associated to a virtual channel. Each message is then routed (computing the appropriate output port to take) at the Routing control unit. Once the output port is computed, the message may cross the internal crossbar of the switch, thus reaching the output port. To do so, the message has to win the access to the output port since different messages may compete for the same port. In addition, the message has to compete to get access to an available virtual channel. Both are resolved by the arbitration unit. Once the access is granted, the message crosses the crossbar and is written at the corresponding queue at the output port. Each message, again, needs to compete with other messages in order to win the access to the physical channel. Prior to reaching the physical channel the message passes through the link controller logic.

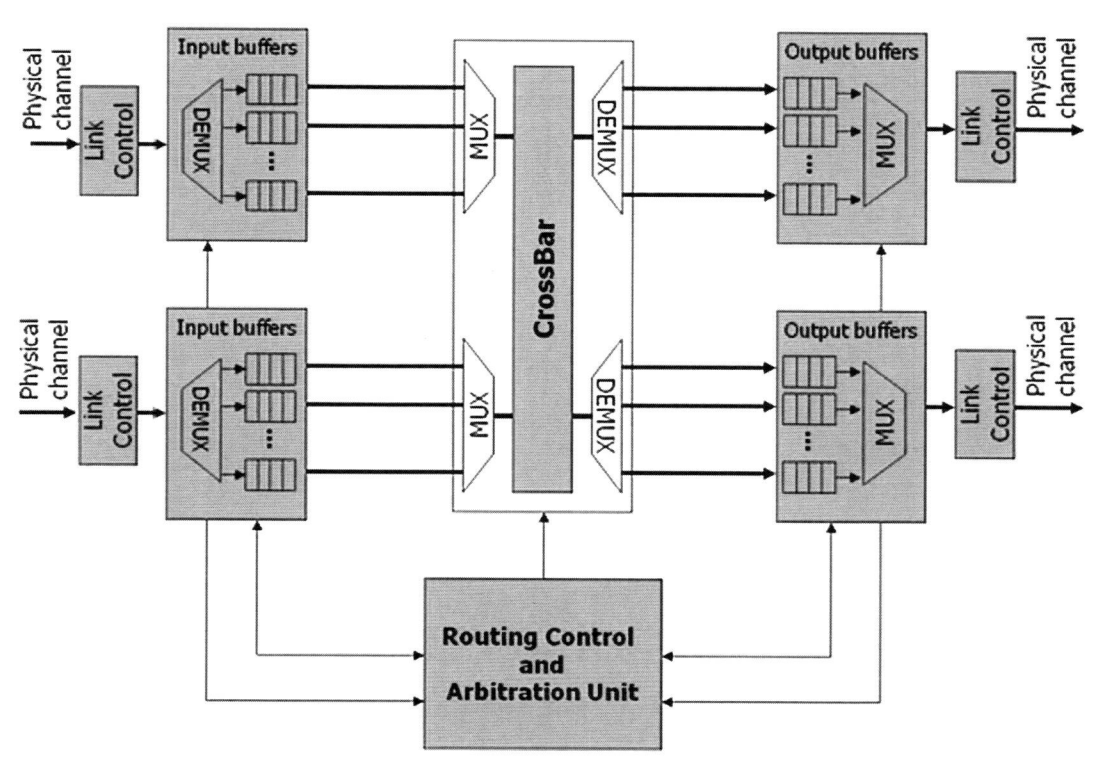

Switch Architecture. Fig. 1 Basic switch architecture

As an alternative view, the resources found in the switch can be divided into two separate blocks: the *data plane (or datapath)* and the *control plane*. Basically, the data plane is the set of resources messages use while being forwarded (storage and movement) through the switch. The control plane is made of the resources used to make decisions at the switch, like the routing control unit and the arbitration unit.

Alternative Switch Architectures

Taking this basic switch architecture as the starting point, several alternative architectures can be derived, some of them better suited for a particular switching mechanism. One of the key issues in the switch architecture is the location of the buffering resources. Regarding this, switch architectures can be classified as:

Output-Queued (OQ) switch architecture. In this architecture buffers only exist at the output ports and thus no buffering exists at the input port. Thus, whenever a message arrives at the switch it must be sent directly to the appropriate output port. An $N \times N$ OQ switch requires only N memories, one per output port. As packets are mapped to the memory associated with the requested output port, HOL blocking is totally eliminated (see ▶Congestion Management Entry); thus, this organization achieves maximum switch efficiency. However, internal speedup is required to handle the worst-case scenario without dropping messages, allowing all the input ports to transmit packets to the same output port at the same time. In particular, output queues must either implement multiple write ports or use a higher clock frequency. A speedup of N is required in OQ switches in the worst case. Unfortunately, providing such internal speedup is not always viable.

Input-Queued (IQ) switch architecture. Buffers only exist at input ports and not at output ports. In this architecture the required internal bandwidth does not increase with the number of ports and the switch can be designed with the same bandwidth as the link. However, a switch designed with this organization may face low performance due to contention/congestion at the output ports. It is well known that such switches achieve only 58% of maximum efficiency under uniformly distributed requests [3]. This is mainly due to the HOL blocking problem. One solution to eliminate the HOL blocking issue in IQ switches is the use of N queues at every input port, mapping the incoming message to a queue associated with the requested output port. This technique is known as Virtual Output Queuing (VOQ) [4]. However, it increases the queue requirements quadratically with the number of ports. Therefore, as the number of ports increases, this solution becomes too expensive.

Combined-Input-Output-Queued (CIOQ) switch architecture. With this organization, the contention/congestion problem found in IQ switches is alleviated or even eliminated, since messages can be also stored at the output side of the switch. In this architecture some moderate internal speedup is used, as the internal bandwidth is higher than the aggregate link bandwidth. A speedup of two is usually enough to compensate the performance drop produced by HOL blocking. Speedup can be implemented by using internal datapaths with higher transmission frequencies or wider transmission paths. However, as the external link bandwidth increases, sustaining the speedup may become difficult.

Buffered-Crossbar (BC) switch architecture. This organization uses a memory at every crossbar crosspoint. An input link is connected to N memories, each one connected to a different output port. By design, the BC organization implements internal speedup, as many inputs can forward a packet to the same output at the same time. Additionally, such memory organization eliminates the HOL blocking (every packet is mapped to the memory associated with the requested output port). As a consequence, the BC organization requires low-cost arbiters per output port. However, the problem with such organization is that the number of memories increases quadratically with the number of ports (N^2), thus limiting scalability.

When focusing on the switching device (the crossbar) different alternatives exist. The solution used in the basic example is the most frequently implemented one, where a crossbar connecting every input to every possible output is used. The crossbar has inherited bandwidth as it is able to connect an input to every output (broadcast communication). There are, however, other solutions, like using a centralized buffer and using a bus.

In addition, the connection of the input ports to the crossbar, and the crossbar to the output ports can be implemented in different ways. In the example multiplexers and demultiplexers are used at both sides of the crossbar. This is done to reduce the crossbar complexity (that increases quadratically with the number of ports). Different alternative configurations arise when these devices are removed from one or both sides of the crossbar. In the case multiplexers are removed, the input speedup of the switch is increased, since different messages can be forwarded through the crossbar from the same input port. If demultiplexers are removed then the output speedup of the switch is increased, since different messages can be written to the same output port at the same time. Obviously, output buffers are required when implementing output speedup.

Input Buffer Organization

An important component of the switch architecture is the buffer organization, mostly when virtual channels are implemented. The way memory resources are assigned to queues will impact on the performance of the switch. This issue is highly related to the flow control protocol (see ▶Flow Control). Buffer partitioning can be designed in several ways. The first one is to combine all the buffers across the entire switch (a single memory). In that case, there is no need for a switching element. The benefit of this approach is the flexibility in dynamically allocating memory across the input ports. The problem, however, is the high memory bandwidth required.

The second way to organize buffers is by partitioning them by physical input ports and dynamically assigning them to virtual channels of the same input port. The third way is to partition the buffers by virtual channel, providing a separate memory for each virtual channel at each port. This, however, may lead to high cost and poor memory utilization.

Another important aspect of buffer organization is the way flits are stored. Such memories require data structures to keep track of where flits are located, and to manage free slots. Two buffer organizations are mostly used: circular buffers and linked lists. Circular buffers are used when memory is statically assigned to a queue (virtual channel) and have low implementation overheads. However, a linked list is used when memory is assigned dynamically and has, in turn, higher implementation overhead.

Pipelined Organization

It is common to design a switch as a pipelined datapath. Such designs allow for high clock frequencies of the switch and, thus, high throughput. On every cycle, a different flit (see ►Flow Control Entry) from the same message may be processed at each stage. Typically, five stages are conceived for the switches:

- Input Buffer (IB) stage, where the flit is stored at the input port of the switch.
- Routing computation (RC) stage, where the output port is computed for the message.
- Switch allocation (SA) stage, where the access to the output port is granted among all the requesting messages. Also, selection of the virtual channel to use is performed.
- Switch transversal (ST) stage, where the flit crosses the crossbar and reaches the output.
- Output Buffer (OB) stage, where the flit is stored at the output port of the switch.

In the ideal case (no contention experienced within the switch) the flit advances through the pipelined switch architecture as shown in Fig. 2. The figure shows the case for a switch implementing virtual cut-through switching where arbitration is performed once per packet.

The first flit is the header flit of the message. At the first cycle the header flit is stored at the input port (IB stage) in a virtual channel. The header includes the identifier of the virtual channel to use. At the second cycle, the header flit is processed at the RC stage so the output port for the message is computed. The output port identifier is associated with the input virtual channel, as this output port will be used by all the flits of the message. At the same cycle the second flit of the message (payload flit) is stored at the input port (IB stage). At the third cycle the SA stage is executed to get access to the requested output port. A valid virtual channel for the message at the next switch is also requested. On success (there is an available virtual channel and the output port is granted) the header flit crosses the crossbar at the next cycle, followed in the following cycles by the rest of payload flits. All the flits use the same virtual channel and output port. Notice also that resources (access to the output port) are granted per message, so flit multiplexing in the crossbar may not occur. Upon crossing the crossbar, the flits are stored at the output port in the corresponding queue (OB stage). The tail flit of a message will have a different treatment since the connection of the input port to the output port will be broken. Notice that the RC and SA stages are performed only once per packet.

A typical wormhole switch architecture differs in some stages. First, it is not common to have a buffer at the output port, thus using an IQ switch approach. Second, virtual channel allocation and port allocation are usually performed in separate stages. Therefore, a new stage appears, referred to as Virtual channel allocation (VA) used only for header flits, and the SA stage only intended for requesting the output port. Also, output port usually is granted flit by flit. Figure 3 shows an example of a five-stage pipelined wormhole switch.

The pipeline design may experience stalls. Stalls may happen due to different reasons (a virtual channel is not available in the SA stage, the RC stage does not find a free output port, ...). In all these cases, the switch must be designed accordingly. Also, the flow control (see ►Flow Control) must be aware of the stalls and thus backpressure the previous switch to avoid buffer overflows. For a detailed analysis of pipelined switches and stall treatments, the reader is referred to [1] (Chapter 16).

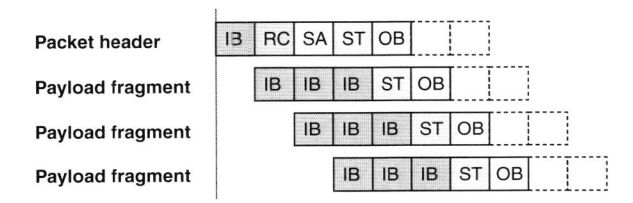

Switch Architecture. Fig. 2 Typical five-stage pipelined switch design for a virtual cut-through switch

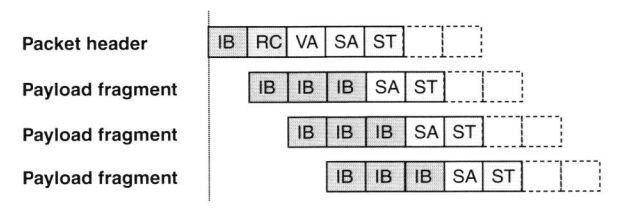

Switch Architecture. Fig. 3 Typical five-stage pipelined switch architecture for a wormhole switch

This basic pipelined architecture can be enhanced with different techniques, most of them trying to reduce the number of stages, thus also reducing the delay of traversing a switch. Routers with three or even two stages can be found in the literature. Also, single-cycle switches are common in some environments, like networks-on-chip (NoCs) for low-end systems-on-chip (SoCs). Obviously, such reduction in the number of stages should be achieved by not incurring in an excessive increase of the cycle time. Two basic procedures exist to reduce the number of stages, the first one by using speculation and performing actions in parallel, and the second one by performing computations ahead of time to remove the operation from the critical path.

Virtual channel allocation can be performed speculatively and in parallel with switch allocation in wormhole switching. Notice that this is done only for header flits. If both resources are obtained (the virtual channel is successfully assigned and the output port is granted) then the wormhole switch saves one cycle. If any of the two fails (or both fail) then the pipeline stalls and at the next cycle the operation is repeated. Figure 4 shows the case.

A further reduction in cycles would be to speculatively send the flit through the crossbar to the output port (ST) at the same time. To achieve this, internal speedup is required. Finally, the output port computation can be performed at the previous switch and stored at the head flit. So, when the flit reaches the next switch the output port to take is already computed and thus, there is no need for the RC stage. In that case, the output port computed for the next switch can be done in parallel with the VA stage, thus further reducing the pipeline depth.

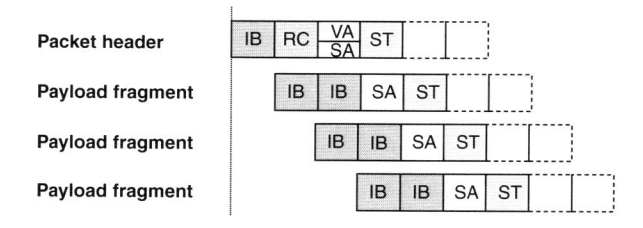

Packet header	IB	RC	VA/SA	ST			
Payload fragment		IB	IB	SA	ST		
Payload fragment			IB	IB	SA	ST	
Payload fragment				IB	IB	SA	ST

Switch Architecture. Fig. 4 Four-stage pipelined wormhole switch design

High-Radix Switch Architectures

As identified in [5], during the last decades, the pin bandwidth of a switch has increased exponentially (from 64 Mb/s of the Torus routing chip in 1986 to the 1Tb/s of the recent Velio 3003). This is due to the increase in the signaling speed and the increase in the number of signals. In this sense, high-radix switches with narrow channels are able to achieve lower packet latencies than low-radix switches with wide channels. The explanation is simple. With high-radix switches the hop count in the network decreases. Additional benefits from high-radix switches are a lower cost and lower power consumption (as the total number of switches and links to build a network is reduced). Following this trend, there are some proposals for high-radix switch architectures, [5–7].

However, designing high-radix switches presents major challenges. The most important one is to keep a high switch efficiency with an affordable cost. The cost of a high-radix switch will largely depend on three key components: memory resources, arbiter logic, and internal connection logic. Depending on the location of memories in the switch, different switch organizations (memory and crossbar capabilities and their interconnects) have been used. In some of them, the number of memories increases quadratically with the number of ports. Also, arbiters and crossbars must cope with more candidates and connections, and for that reason become expensive. As an example, in on-chip networks, the use of high-radix switches is not appropriate due to the increase in power consumption and reduction in switch-operating frequency [8].

Related Entries

▶Flow Control
▶Switching Techniques

Bibliographic Notes and Further Reading

Two basic books exist for interconnection networks. Both describe in detail the concept of switch architecture. The first one, [2] describes a wide range of routers, some with wormhole switching (Intel Teraflops router,

Cray 3TD and 3TE routers, Reliable router and SGI spider), others with virtual cut-through switching (Chaos router, Arctic router, R2 router, Alpha 21364 router), and others with circuit switching (Intel iPSC Direct Connect Module). Also, the book describes the Myrinet switch.

The other book [1], provides as a case study the Alpha 21364 router and the IBM Colony router.

In on-chip networks building an efficient switch is critical. In addition to delay constraints, designing an on-chip switch has also power consumption and area limitations. In [9] basic design rules for building an on-chip router are provided. Also, literature is populated with many switch/router architectures for on-chip networks.

Bibliography

1. Dally W, Towles B (2004) Principles and practices of interconnection networks. Morgan Kaufmann, San Francisco, CA
2. Duato J, Yalamanchili S, Ni N (2002) Interconnection networks: an engineering approach. Morgan Kaufmann, San Francisco, CA
3. Karol MJ et al (1987) Input versus output queueing on a space-division packet switch. IEEE Trans Commun COM-35(12):1347–1356
4. Tamir Y, Frazier GL (1988) High-performance multi-queue buffers for vlsi communications switches. SIGARCH Comput Archit News 16(2):343–354
5. Kim J, Dally WJ, Towles B, Gupta AK (2005) Microarchitecture of a high-radix router. In: 32nd Annual International Symposium on Computer Architecture (ISCA '05), Madison, WI, pp 420–431
6. Scott S, Abts D, Kim J, Dally WJ (2006) The blackwidow high-radix clos network. In: Proceedings of the 33rd Annual International Symposium on Computer Architecture (ISCA), The Washington, DC, June 2006
7. Mora G, Flich J, Duato J, López P, Baydal E, Lysne O (2006) Towards and efficient switch architecture for high-radix switches. In: Proceedings of ANCS 2006, San Jose, CA
8. Pullini A, Angiolini F, Murali S, Atienza D, De Micheli G, Benini G (2007) Bringing NOCs to 65 nm. IEEE Micro 27(5):75–85
9. de Micheli G, Benini L (2006) Networks on chips: technology and tools. Morgan Kaufmann, San Francisco, CA

Switched-Medium Network

▶Buses and Crossbars

Switching Techniques

Sudhakar Yalamanchili
Georgia Institute of Technology, Atlanta, GA, USA

Definition

Switching techniques determine how messages are forwarded through the network. Specifically, these techniques determine how and when buffers and switch ports of individual routers are allocated and released and thereby the timing with which messages or message components can be forwarded to the next router on the destination path.

Discussion

Introduction

This section introduces basic switching techniques used within the routers of multiprocessor interconnection networks. Switching techniques determine *when* and *how* messages are forwarded through the network. These techniques determine the granularity and timing with which resources such as buffers and switch ports are requested and released and consequently determine the blocking behavior of routing protocols that utilize them in different network topologies. As a result, they are key determinants of the deadlock properties of routing protocols. Further, their relationship to flow control protocols and traffic characteristics significantly impact the latency and bandwidth characteristics of the network.

A Generic Router Model

Switching techniques are understood in the context of routers used in multiprocessor interconnection networks. A simple generic router architecture is illustrated in Fig. 1. This router microarchitecture presents to messages a four stage pipeline comprised of the following stages.

- *Input Buffering (IB)*: Message data is received into the input buffer.
- *Route Computation (RC) and Switch Allocation (SA)*: Based on the message destination, a switch output port is computed, requested, and allocated.

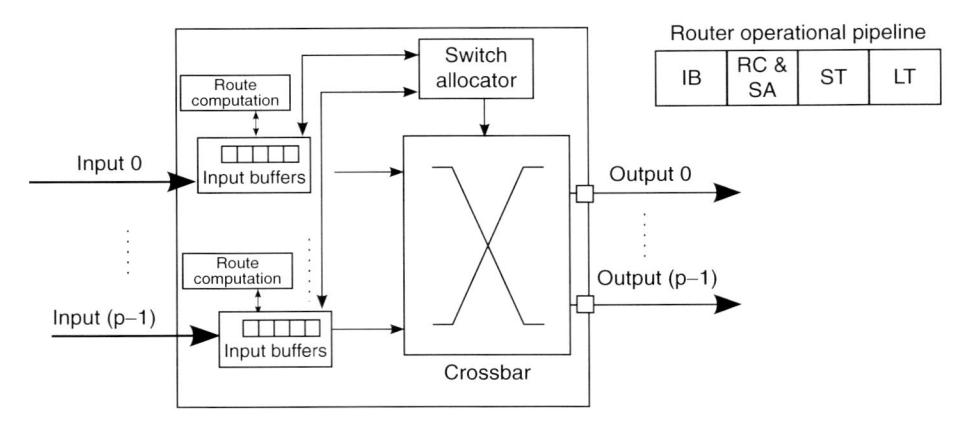

Switching Techniques. Fig. 1 A generic router model

- *Switch Traversal (ST)*: Message data traverses the switch to the output buffer.
- *Link Traversal (LT)*: The message data traverses the link to the next router.

The end-to-end latency experienced by a message depends on how the switching techniques interact with this pipeline. This generic router architecture has been enhanced over the years with virtual channels [1], speculative operation [2, 3], flexible arbiters, effective channel and port allocators [4], deeper pipelines, and a host of buffer management and implementation optimizations (e.g., see [5, 6]). The result has been a range of router designs with different processing pipelines.

For the purposes of this discussion, here it is assumed that all of the pipeline stages take the same time – one cycle. This is adequate to define, distinguish, and compare properties of basic switching techniques. The following section addresses some basic concepts governing the operation and implementation of switching techniques based on the generic router model shown in Fig. 1. The remainder of the section is devoted to a detailed presentation of alternative switching techniques.

Basic Concepts

The performance and behavior of switching techniques are enabled by the low-level flow control protocols used for the synchronized transfer of data between routers. Flow control determines the granularity with which data is moved through the network and consequently when routing decisions can be made, when switching operations can be initiated, and how (at what granularity) data is transferred.

Flow control is the synchronized transfer of a unit of data between a sender and a receiver and ensures the availability of sufficient buffering at the receiver to avoid the loss of data. Selection of the unit of data transfer is based on a few simple concepts. A message is partitioned into fixed-length *packets*. Packets are individually routable units of data and are comprised of control bits packaged as the header and data bits packaged as the body. Packets are typically terminated with some bits for error detection such as a checksum. The header contains destination information used by the routers to select the onward path through the network. The packet as a whole is partitioned into fixed size units corresponding to the unit of transfer across a link or across a router and is referred to as a flow control digit or *flit* [7]. A flit becomes the unit of buffer management for transmission across a physical channel. Many schemes have been developed over the years for flow control including on-off, credit-based, sliding window, and flit reservation. The physical transfer of a flit across a link may in fact rely on synchronized transfers of smaller units of information. For example, consider flit sizes of 4 bytes and a physical channel width of 8 bits. The transfer of a flit across the physical link requires the synchronized transfer of 8-bit quantities referred to as a physical digit or *phit* [4] using phit-level flow control. In contrast to flits which represent units of buffer management, phits correspond to quantities reflecting a specific physical link implementation. Both flit-level and phit-level flow control are atomic in the sense that in the absence of errors, all transfers will complete successfully and are not interleaved with other transfers. While phit sizes between chips or boards tend to be small, e.g., 8–32 bits, phit sizes on-chip can be much larger, e.g., 128 bits. Typical message sizes can range from 8–12 bytes (control messages) to 64–128 bytes (for example cache lines), to much larger sizes in message-passing parallel architectures. The preceding hierarchy of units is illustrated in Fig. 2 along with an example of a packet format [4, 8]. The actual content of a packet header will depend on the specifics of an implementation such as the routing protocol (e.g., destination address), flow control strategy (e.g., credits), use of virtual channels (e.g., virtual channel ID), and fault tolerance strategy (e.g., acknowledgements).

Switching techniques determine when messages are forwarded through the network and differ in the relative timing of flow control operations, route computation, and data transfer. High-performance switching techniques seek as much overlap as possible between these operations while reliable communication protocols may seek less concurrency between these operations in the interest of efficient error recovery. For example, one can wait until the entire packet is received before a request is made for the output port of the router's switch (packet switching). Alternatively, the request can be made as soon as all flits corresponding to the header are received (cut-through switching) but before the rest of the packet has been received.

The remainder of this section will focus on the presentation and discussion of switching techniques under the assumption of a flit-level flow control protocol and a supporting phit-level flow control protocol. It is common to have the flit size the same as the phit size.

Basic Switching Techniques

As one might expect, switching techniques have their roots in traditional digital communication and have evolved over the years to address the unique requirements of multiprocessor interconnection networks. For the purposes of comparison, the no-load latency is computed for an L-bit message. The phit size and flit size are assumed to be equivalent and equal to the physical data channel width of W bits, which is also the width of the internal datapath of the router. The routing header is assumed to be one flit, thus the message size is $L + W$

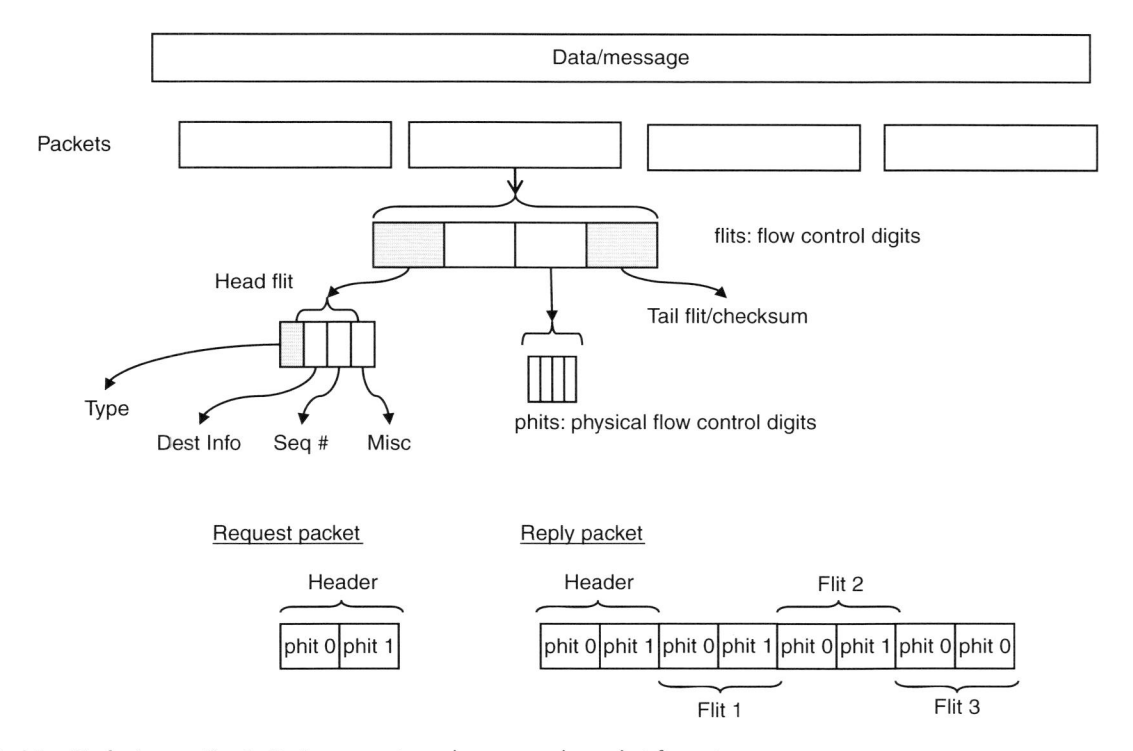

Switching Techniques. Fig. 2 Basic concepts and an example packet format

bits. A router can make a routing decision in one cycle and a flit can traverse a switch or link in one cycle as described with respect to Fig. 1.

Circuit Switching

Circuit switching evolved from early implementations in telephone switching networks. In circuit switching, a physical path from the source network interface to the destination network interface is reserved prior to the transmission of the data. The source injects a routing packet commonly called a probe into the network. The probe is routed to the destination as specified by the routing protocol reserving the physical channels and switch ports along the way. An acknowledgement is returned to the source node to confirm path reservation. Figure 3b shows several circuits that have been set up and one in the process of being set up. While circuits B, C, D have been set up, circuit A is blocked from being set up by circuit B.

The base no-load latency of a circuit-switched message is determined by the sum of the time to set up a path and the time to transmit data. For a circuit that traverses D routers to the destination and operates at B Hz, the no-load message latency can be represented as follows.

$$
\begin{aligned}
t_{circuit} &= t_{setup} + t_{data} \\
t_{setup} &= D[t_{RC} + 2(t_{IB} + t_{ST} + t_{LT})] \\
t_{data} &= \frac{1}{B}\left\lceil \frac{L}{W} \right\rceil
\end{aligned} \quad (1)
$$

The notation in the expression follows the generic router model shown in Fig. 1, and the expression does not include the time to inject the probe into the router at the source (a link traversal) or the time to inject the acknowledgement into the router at the destination. The subscripts correspond to the pipeline stages illustrated in Fig. 1. For example, t_{RC} is the time taken to compute the output port to be traversed by the message at a router. This computation is carried out in the same cycle as the process of requesting and allocating a switch port, and therefore the switch allocation (SA) time is hidden and does not appear in the expression. The terms t_{IB}, t_{ST}, and t_{LT} represent the times for input buffering, switch traversal, and link traversal,

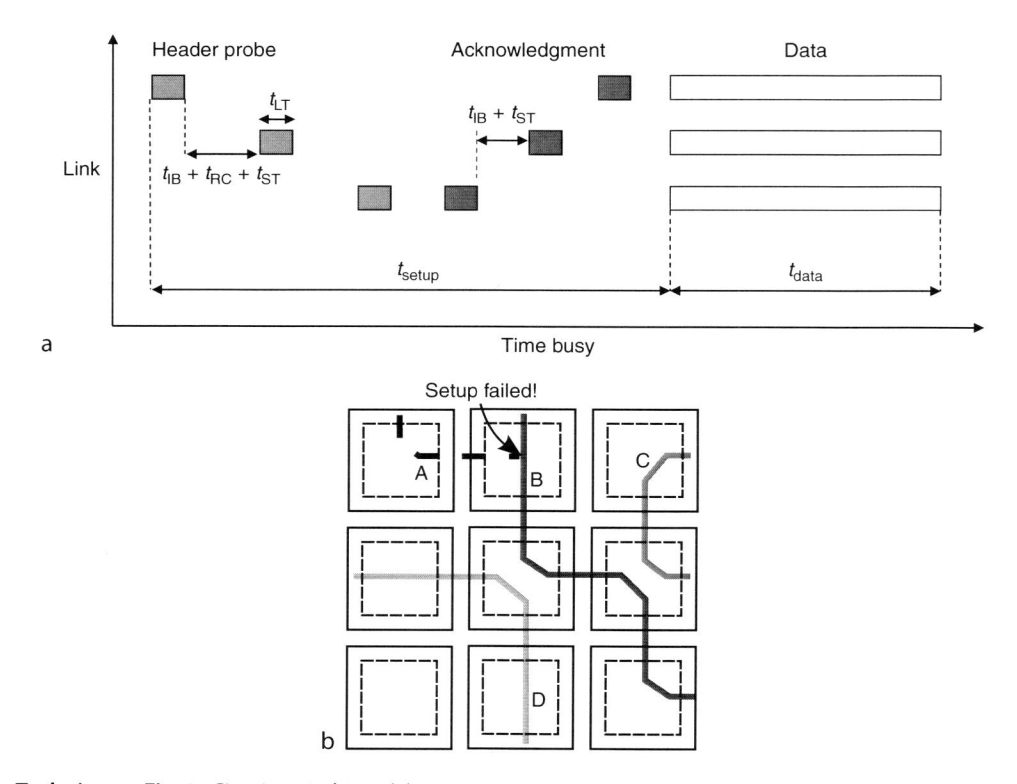

Switching Techniques. Fig. 3 Circuit switching. (**a**) Time-space utilization across two routers, (**b**) an example

respectively, experienced by the probe and the acknowledgement. The factor of 2 in the expression for path setup reflects the forward progress of the probe and the return progress of the acknowledgement – assuming the acknowledgement traverses the same path in the reverse direction. Note the acknowledgements do not have to be routed and therefore do not experience any routing delays at intermediate routers. A time-space diagram in Fig. 3a depicts the setup and operation of a circuit that crosses two routers.

Nominally, the routing probe contains the destination address and additional control bits used by the routing protocol and is buffered at intermediate routers where it is processed to reserve links and set router switch settings. On reaching the destination, an acknowledgement packet is transmitted back to the source. The hardware circuit has been set up and data can be transmitted at the full speed of the circuit. Flow control for data transfer is exercised end-to-end across the circuit and the flow control bandwidth (rate of signaling) should be at least as fast as the transmission speeds to avoid slowing down the hardware circuit. When transmission is complete, a few control bits traversing the circuit from the source release link and switch resources along the circuit. These bits may take the form of a small packet or with suitable channel design and message encoding, may be transmitted as part of the last few bits of the message data. Routing and data transmission functions are disjoint operations where all switches on the source-destination path are set prior to the transmission of any data.

Circuit switching is generally advantageous when messages are infrequent and long compared to the size of the routing probe. It is also advantageous when internode traffic exhibits a high degree of temporal locality. After a path has been set up, subsequent messages to the same destination can be transmitted without incurring the latency of path set-up times. The inter-node throughput is also maximized since once a path has been set up, messages to the destination are not routed and do not block in the network. The disadvantages are the same as those typically associated with most reservation-based protocols. When links and switch ports are reserved for a duration they prevent other traffic from making progress if they need to use any of the resources reserved by the established circuit. In particular, a probe can be blocked during circuit set up while waiting for another circuit to be torn down. The links reserved by the probe up to that point can similarly prevent other circuits from being established.

Wire delays place a practical limit on the speed of circuit switching as a function of system size, motivating the development of techniques to mitigate or eliminate end-to-end wire delay dependencies. One set of techniques evolved around pipelining multiple bits on the wire essentially using a long latency wire as a deeply pipelined transmission medium. Such techniques have been referred to as *wave pipelining* or *wave switching* [9–11]. These techniques maximize wire bandwidth while reducing sensitivity to distance. However, when used in anything other than bit serial channels, pragmatic constraints of signal skew and stable operation across voltage and temperature remain challenges to widespread adoption. Alternatively, both the wire length issue and blocking are mitigated by combining circuit switching concepts with the use of virtual channels. Virtual channel buffers at each router are reserved by the routing probe setting up a pipelined virtual circuit from source to destination in a manner referred to as pipelined circuit switching [12]. This approach increases physical link utilization by enabling sharing across circuits although the available bandwidth to each circuit is now reduced. This approach was also used in the Intel iWarp chip that was designed to support systolic communication through *message pathways*: long-lived communication paths [13]. Rather than set up and remove network paths each time data are to be communicated, paths through the network persist for long periods of time. Special messages called *pathway begin markers* are used to reserve virtual channels (referred to as *logical channels* in iWarp) and set up interprocessor communication paths. On completion of the computation, the paths are explicitly removed by other control messages.

Packet Switching

In circuit switching, routing and data transfer operations are separated. All switches in the path to the destination are set a priori, and all data is transmitted in a burst at the full bandwidth of the circuit. In packet switching, the message data is partitioned into fixed-sized packets. The first few bytes of a packet contain routing and control information and are collectively referred to as the *packet header* while the data is contained in the packet body. Each packet can now be independently routed through the network. Flow control between routers is at the level of a complete packet. A packet cannot be forwarded unless buffer space for a complete packet is available at the next router. A packet is then transferred in its entirety across a link to the input buffer of the next router. Only then is the header information extracted and used by the routing and control unit to determine the candidate output port. The switch can now be set to enable the packet to be transferred to the output port and then stored at the next router before being forwarded. This switching technique is also known as *store-and-forward* (SAF) switching. There is no overlap between flow control, routing operations, and data transfer. Consequently, the end-to-end latency of a packet is proportional to the distance between the source and destination nodes.

An example of packet switching is illustrated in Fig. 4b (links to local processors are omitted for brevity). Note how packets A, B, and C are in the process of being transferred across a link. Each input buffer is partially full pending receipt of the remainder of the packet before being forwarded.

The no-load latency for a packet transmission across D routers can be modeled as follows.

$$t_{packet} = D\left\{t_{RC} + (t_{IB} + t_{ST} + t_{LT})\left\lceil\frac{L+W}{W}\right\rceil\right\} \qquad (2)$$

This expression does not include the time to inject the packet into the network at the source. The expression follows the router model in Fig. 1 where entire packets must traverse the link or switch at each router.

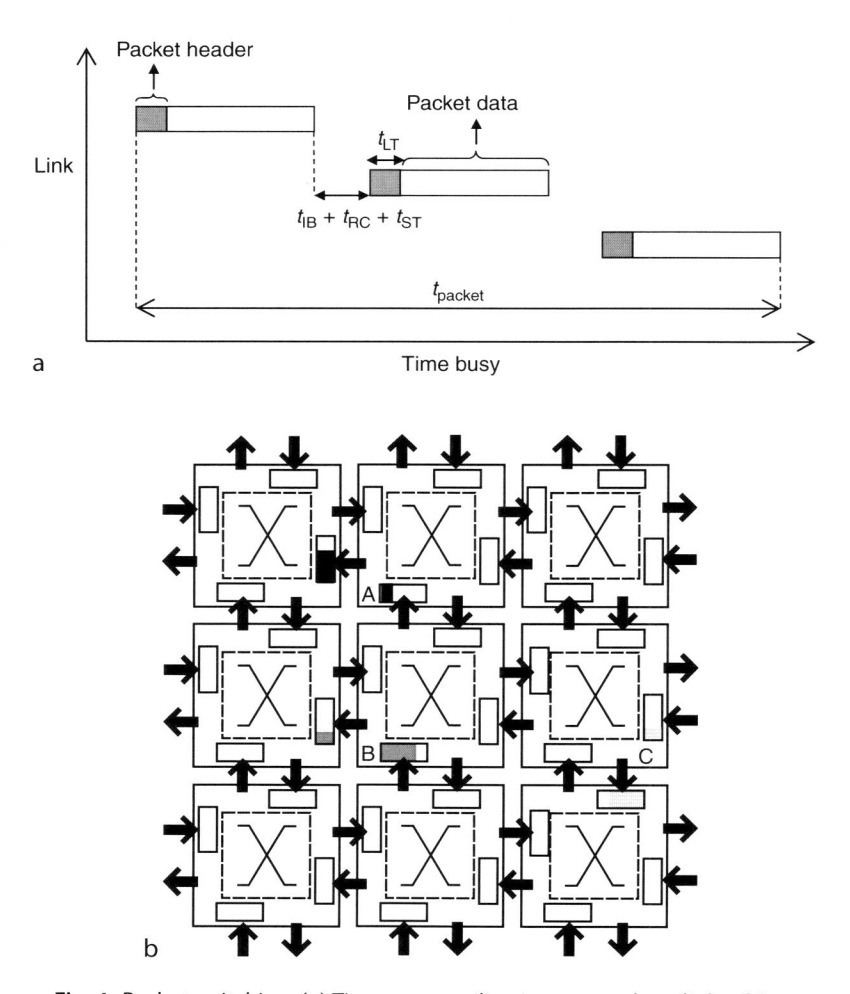

Switching Techniques. Fig. 4 Packet switching. (**a**) Time-space utilization across three links, (**b**) an example

Therefore end-to-end latency is proportional to the distance between the source and destination.

Packet switching evolved from early implementations in data networks. Relative to circuit switching, packet switching is advantageous when the average message size is small. Since packets only hold resources as they are being used, this switching technique can achieve high link utilization and network throughput. Packets are also amenable to local techniques for error detection and recovery since all data and its associated routing information are encapsulated as a single locally available unit. However, the overhead per data bit is higher – each packet must invest in a header reducing energy efficiency as well as the proportion of physical bandwidth that is accessible to actual data transfer. If a message is partitioned into multiple packets and adaptive routing is employed, packets may arrive at the destination out of order necessitating investments in reordering mechanisms. Packet-switched routers have also been designed with dynamically allocated centralized queues rather than keeping the messages buffered at the router input and output resulting in both cost and power advantages.

Virtual Cut-Through (VCT) Switching

Virtual cut-through (VCT) switching is an optimization for packet switching where in the absence of congestion, packet transfer is pipelined. Like the preceding techniques, VCT has its genesis in packet data networks [14]. Flow control is still at the packet level. However, packet transfer is overlapped with flow control and routing operations as follows. Routing can begin as soon as the header bytes of a packet have arrived at the input buffer and before the rest of the packet has been received. In the absence of congestion, switch allocation and switch traversal can proceed and the forwarding of the packet through the switch as well as flow control requests to the next router can begin. Thus, packet transfer can be pipelined through multiple routers. For example, consider a 128 byte packet with an 8 byte header. After the first 8 bytes have been received, routing decisions and switch allocation can be initiated. If the switch output port is available, then the router can begin forwarding bytes to the output port before the remainder of the packet has arrived and can *cut-through* to the next router. In the absence of blocking in the network, the latency for the header to arrive at the destination network interface is proportional to the distance between the source and destination. Thereafter a phit can exit the network every cycle. If the header is blocked on a busy output channel at an intermediate router, the packet is buffered at the router – a consequence of the fact that flow control is at the level of a packet. Thus, at high network loads, VCT switching behaves like packet switching. An example of VCT at work is illustrated in Fig. 5b. Packet A is blocked by packet B. Note that packet A has enough buffer space to be fully buffered at the local router. Packet B can be seen to be spread across multiple routers as it is pipelined through the network.

The no-load latency of a message that successfully cuts through D intermediate routers is captured in the following expression.

$$t_{VCT} = D(t_{IB} + t_{RC} + t_{ST} + t_{LT}) + t_{IB}\left[\frac{L}{W}\right] \quad (3)$$

This expression does not include the time to inject the packet into the network at the source. The first term in the equation is much smaller than the second term (recall that each value of delay is one pipeline cycle). Therefore, under low load conditions, the message latency is approximately proportional to the packet size rather than distance between source and destination. However, when a packet is blocked, the packet is buffered at the router. Thus, at high network loads, the behavior of VCT approximates that of packet switching. At low loads, the performance improves considerably approaching that of wormhole switching which is described next.

Wormhole Switching

The need to buffer complete packets within a router can make it difficult to construct small, compact, and fast routers. In the multiprocessor machines of the 1980s, interconnection networks employed local node memory as storage for buffering blocked packets. This ejection and re-injection of packets incurred significant latency penalties. It was desirable to keep packets in the network. However, there was insufficient buffering within individual routers. Wormhole switching evolved as a small buffer optimization of virtual cut-through where packets were pipelined through routers. The buffers in each router had enough storage for several flits. When a packet header blocks, the message occupies buffers in several routers. For example, consider

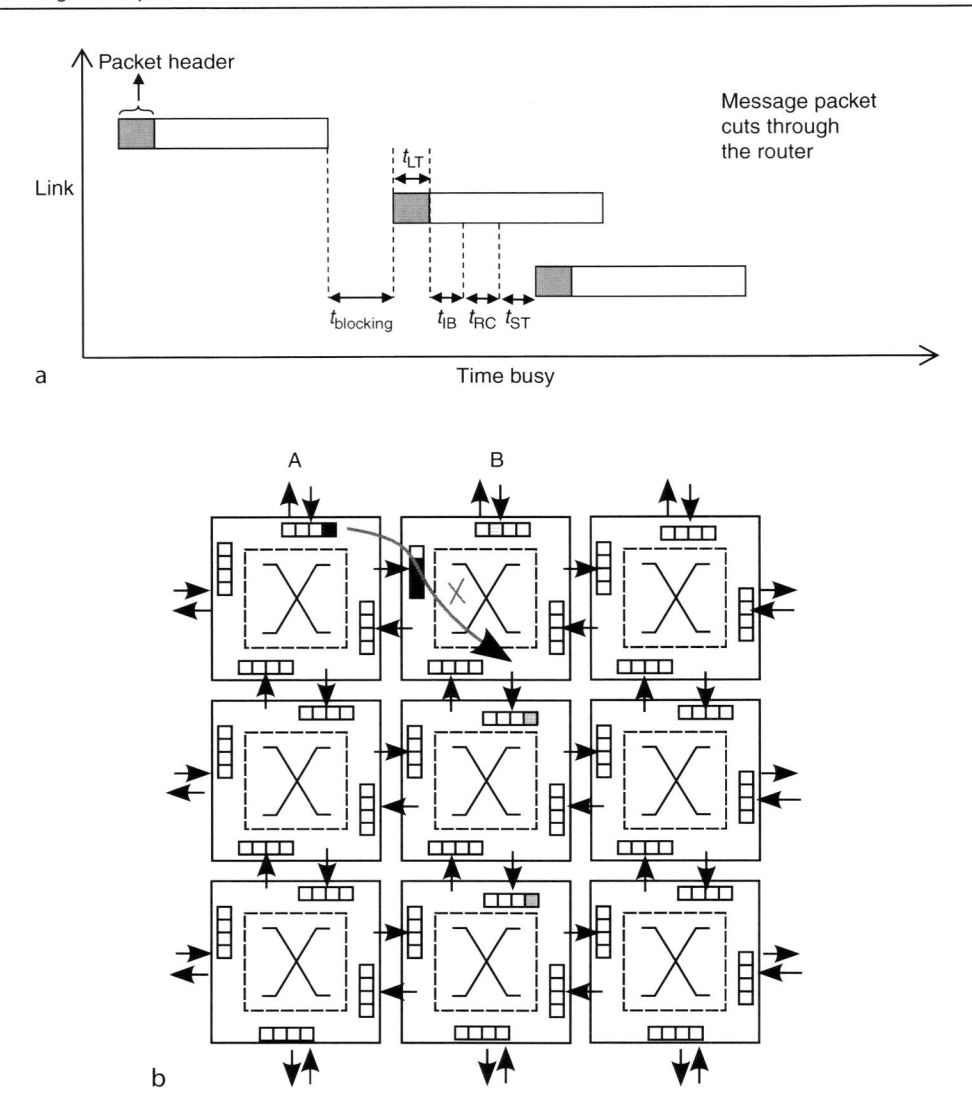

Switching Techniques. Fig. 5 Virtual cut-through switching. (**a**) Time-space utilization across three links, (**b**) an example

the message pattern shown in Fig. 6b with routers with one flit buffers. Message A is blocked by message B and occupies buffers across multiple routers leading to secondary blocking across multiple routers. The time-space diagram illustrates how packets are pipelined across multiple routers significantly reducing the sensitivity of message latency to distance.

When it was introduced [7, 15], the pipelined behavior of wormhole switching led to relatively large reductions in message latency at low loads. Further gains derived from not having to eject messages from the network for storage. The use of small buffers also has two physical consequences. First, smaller buffers lead to lower access latency and shorter pipeline stage time (see Fig. 1). The smaller pipeline delay enables higher clock rates and consequently high bandwidth routers, for example, 5 GHz in today's Intel TeraFlops router [16]. Second, the smaller buffers also reduce static energy consumption which is particularly important in the context of on-chip routers. However, as the offered communication load increases, messages block in place occupying buffers across multiple routers and the links between them. This leads to secondary blocking of messages that share any of these links which in turn propagates congestion further. The disadvantage of wormhole switching is that blocked messages hold physical channel resources. Routing information is only associated with a few header flits. Data flits have no routing information associated with them. Consequently, when a packet is blocked in place, packet transmission cannot be interleaved over a physical link without additional support (such as virtual channels – see Section on Virtual Channels) and physical channels cannot be shared. The result is the rapid onset of saturation as offered load increases. Virtual channel flow control was introduced to alleviate this problem.

The key deadlock issue is that a single message produces dependencies between buffers across multiple routers. Routing protocols must be designed to ensure that such dependencies are not composed across multiple messages to produce deadlocked configurations of messages. Deadlock freedom requirements for deterministic routing protocols are described in [7] while proofs for adaptive routing protocols are described in [17–19].

The base latency of a wormhole-switched message crossing D routers with the flit size equal to the phit size can be computed as follows.

$$t_{wormhole} = D(t_{IB} + t_{RC} + t_{ST} + t_{LT}) + t_{IB}\left\lceil \frac{L}{W} \right\rceil \quad (4)$$

This expression does not include the time to inject flits into the network at the source. After the first flit arrives at the destination, each successive flit is delivered

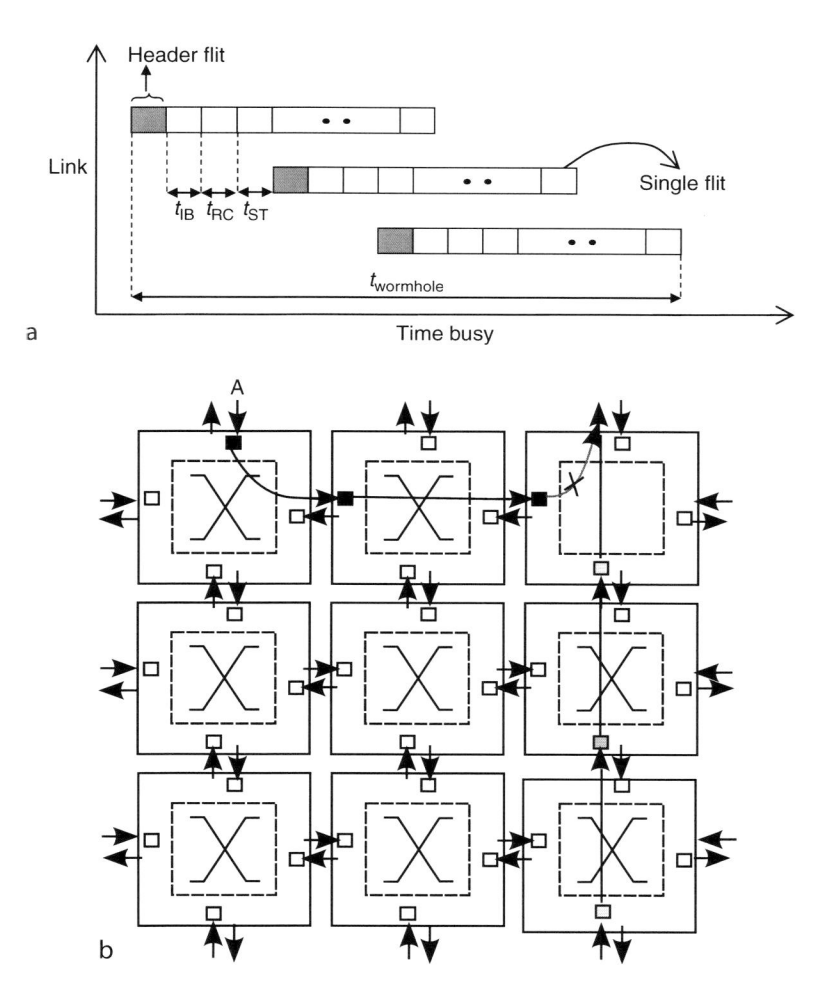

Switching Techniques. Fig. 6 Wormhole switching. (**a**) Time-space utilization across three links, (**b**) an example

in successive clock cycles. Thus, for message sizes that are large relative to the distance between sender and destination, the no-load latency is approximately a function of the message size rather than distance.

Several optimizations have been proposed to further improve the performance of wormhole switching. One example is flit reservation flow control was introduced to improve buffer turn-around time in wormhole switching [20]. Deeply pipelined, high speed routers can lead to low buffer occupancy as a consequence of propagation delays of flits over the link and the latency in receiving and processing credits before the buffer can be reused. Flit reservation is a technique that combines some elements of circuit switching (a priori reservations) to improve performance. A control flit advances ahead of the data flits of a message to reserve buffer and channel resources. Note that router pipeline for data flits is much shorter (they do not experience routing and switch allocation delays). As a result, reservations and transfers can be overlapped and buffer occupancy is significantly increased.

Another example that combines the advantages of wormhole switching and packet switching is *buffered wormhole switching (BWS)*. This was proposed and used in IBM's Power Parallel SP systems [21, 22]. In the absence of blocking, messages are routed through the network using wormhole switching. When messages block, 8-flit *chunks* are constructed at the input port of a switch and buffered in a dynamically allocated centralized router memory freeing up the input port for use by other messages. Subsequently, buffered chunks are transferred to an output port where they are converted to a flit stream for transmission across the physical channel. BWS differs from wormhole switching in that flits are not buffered in place. Rather flits are aggregated and buffered in a local memory within the switch and in this respect BWS is similar to packet switching. The no-load latency of a message routed using BWS is identical to that of wormhole-switched messages.

Virtual Channels

An important interconnection architecture function is the use of virtual channel flow control [1]. Each unidirectional virtual channel across a physical link is realized by an independently managed pair of message buffers. Multiple virtual channels are multiplexed across the physical link increasing link utilization and network throughput. Importantly, routing constraints on the use of virtual channels are commonly used to ensure deadlock freedom. The use of virtual channels decouples message flows from the physical links and their use is orthogonal to the operation of switching techniques. Each switching technique is now employed to regulate the flow of packet data within a virtual channel while constraints on virtual channel usage may govern routing decisions at intermediate routers. The microarchitecture pipeline of the routers now includes an additional stage for virtual channel allocation. Virtual channels have been found to be particularly useful for optimizing the performance of wormhole-switched routers ameliorating the consequences of blocking and thus broadening the scope of application of wormhole switching. A simple example of the operation of virtual channel flow control is illustrated in Fig. 7.

A modified router architecture reflecting the use of virtual channels is shown in Fig. 8. The route computation operation now returns a set of virtual channels that are candidates for forwarding the message (note that the router might be employing adaptive routing). A typical router pipeline is now extended by an extra stage as shown – *virtual channel allocation*. This is implemented prior to requesting an output port of the switch extending the router pipeline of Fig. 1 by one stage.

A Comparison of Switching Techniques

Switching techniques have fundamental differences in their ability to utilize network bandwidth. In packet switching and VCT switching, messages are partitioned into fixed length packets each with its own header. Consequently, the overhead per transmitted data byte of a message is a fixed function of the message length. Wormhole switching supports variable sized messages and consequently overhead per data byte decreases with message size. However, as the network load increases when wormhole-switched messages block, they hold links and resources across multiple routers, wasting physical bandwidth, propagating congestion, and saturating the network at a fraction of the peak. The use of virtual channels in wormhole switching decouples the physical channel from blocked messages improving network utilization but increases the flow control latency across the physical link as well as the complexity of the channel controllers and intra-router switching.

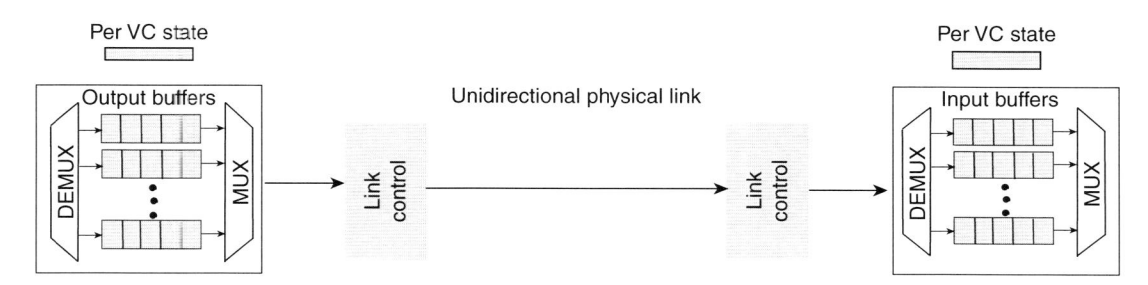

Switching Techniques. Fig. 7 Virtual channel flow control

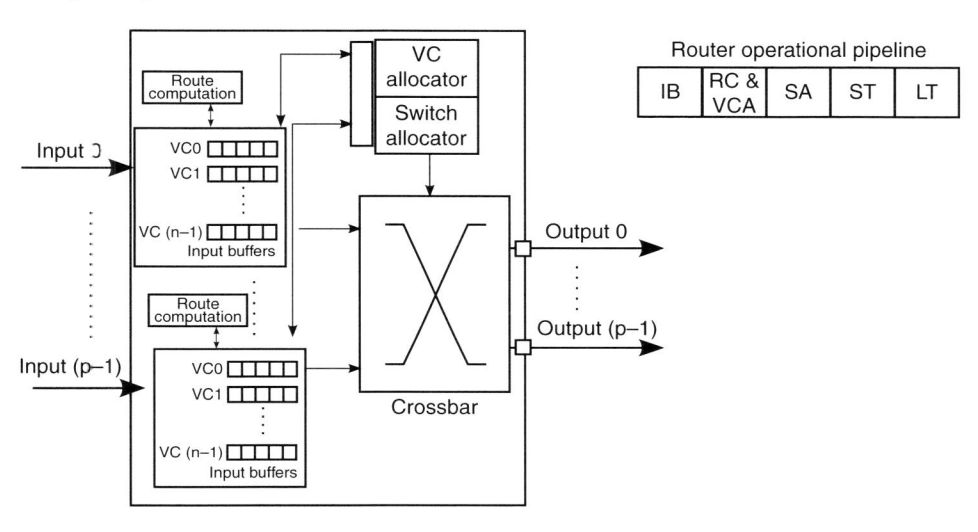

Switching Techniques. Fig. 8 The generic router with virtual channels

In VCT switching and packet switching, packets are fully buffered at each router and therefore traffic consumes network bandwidth in proportion to network load at the expense of increased amount of in-network buffering.

The latency behavior of packets using different switching techniques exhibits distinct behaviors. At low loads, the pipelined behavior of wormhole switching produces superior latency characteristics. However, saturation occurs at lower loads and the variance in packet latency is higher and accentuated with variance in packet length. The latency behavior of packets under packet switching tends to be more predictable since messages are fully buffered at each load. VCT packets will operate like wormhole switching at low loads and approximate packet switching at high loads where blocking will force packets to be buffered at an intermediate node. Consequently, approaches to provide Quality of Service guarantees (QoS) typically utilize VCT or packet switching. Attempting to control QoS when blocked messages are spread across multiple nodes is by comparison much more difficult.

Reliability schemes are shaped by the switching techniques. Alternative topologies and routing algorithms affect the probability of encountering a failed component. The switching technique affects feasible detection and recovery algorithms. For example, packet switching is naturally suited to link level error detection and retransmission since each packet is an independently routable unit. For the same reason, packets may be adaptively routed around faulty regions of the network. However, when messages are pipelined over several links, error recovery and control becomes complicated. Recall that data flits have no routing information. Thus, errors that occur within a message that is spread across multiple nodes can lead to buffers and channel resources that are indefinitely occupied (e.g., link transceiver failures) and can lead to deadlocked message configurations. Thus, link level recovery must be accompanied by some higher level layer recovery protocols that typically operate end-to-end.

Finally, it can be observed that the switching techniques exert a considerable influence on the architecture of the router, and as a result, the network performance. For example, flit level flow control enabled pipelined message transfers as well as the use of small buffers. The combination resulted in higher flow control signaling speeds and small compact router pipeline stages that could be clocked at higher speeds. The use of wormhole switching precluded the need for larger (slower) buffers or costly use of local storage at a node – the message could remain the network. This is a critical design point if one considers that the link bandwidth can often exceed the memory bandwidth. Such architectural advances have amplified the performance gained via clock speed advances over several technology generations. For example, consider the difference in performance between the Cosmic cube network [23] that operated at 5 MHz and produced message latencies approaching hundreds of microseconds to milliseconds while the most recent TeraFlops chip from Intel operating at 5 GHz produces latencies on the order of nanoseconds. While performance has increased almost 5 orders of magnitude, the clock speeds have only increased by about 3 orders of magnitude. Much of this performance differential can be attributed to switching techniques and associated microarchitecture innovations that accompany their implementation.

Related Entries
▶Collective Communication, Network Support for
▶Congestion Management
▶Flow Control
▶Interconnection Networks
▶Networks, Fault-Tolerant
▶Routing (Including Deadlock Avoidance)

Bibliographic Notes and Further Reading
Related topics such as flow control and deadlock freedom are intimately related to switching techniques. A combined coverage of fundamental architectural, theoretical, and system concepts and a distillation of key concepts can also be found in two texts [4, 8]. More advanced treatments of these and related topics can be found in papers in most major systems and computer architecture conferences with the preceding texts contributing references to many seminal papers in the field.

Acknowledgments
Assistance and feedback from Mitchelle Rasquinha, Dhruv Choudhary, and Jeffrey Young are gratefully acknowledged.

Bibliography
1. Dally WJ (1992) Virtual-channel flow control. IEEE Trans Parallel Distrib Syst 3(2):194–205
2. Peh L-S, Dally WJ (2001) A delay model for router microarchitectures. IEEE Micro 21:26–34
3. Peh L-S, Dally WJ (2001) A delay model and speculative architecture for pipelined routers. In: Proceedings of the 7th international symposium on high-performance computer architecture, Nuevo Leone
4. Dally WJ, Towles B (2004) Principles and practices of interconnection networks. Morgan Kaufman, San Francisco
5. Choi Y, Pinkston TM (2004) Evaluation of queue designs for true fully adaptive routers. J Parallel Distrib Comput 64(5):606–616
6. Mullins R, West A, Moore S (2004) Low-latency virtual-channel routers for on-chip networks. In: Proceedings of the 31st annual international symposium on computer architecture, Munchen
7. Dally WJ, Seitz CL (1987) Deadlock-free message routing in multiprocessor interconnection networks. IEEE Trans Comput C-36(5):547–553
8. Duato J, Yalamanchili S, Ni L (2003) Interconnection networks: an engineering Approach. Morgan Kaufmann, San Francisco
9. Flynn M (1995) Computer architecture: pipelined and parallel processor design. Jones & Bartlett, Boston, pp 63–140
10. Duato J et al (1996) A high performance router architecture for interconnection networks. In: Proceedings of the 1996 international conference on parallel processing, Bloomington, vol I, August 1996, pp 61–68
11. Scott SL, Goodman JR (1994) The impact of pipelined channels on k-ary n-cube networks. IEEE Trans Parallel Distrib Syst 5(1):2–16
12. Gaughan PT et al (1996) Distributed, deadlock-free routing in faulty, pipelined, direct interconnection networks. IEEE Trans Comput 45(6):651–665
13. Borkar S et al (1988) iWarp: an integrated solutionto high-speed parallel computing. In: Proceedings of supercomputing '88, Orlando, November 1988, pp 330–339
14. Kermani P, Kleinrock L (1979) Virtual cut-through: a new computer communication switching technique. Comp Networks 3(4):267–286
15. Dally WJ, Seitz CL (1986) The torus routing chip. J Distrib Comput 1(3):187–196
16. Hoskote Y, Vangal S, Singh A, Borkar N, Borkar S (2007) A 5-GHz mesh interconnect for a teraflops processor. IEEE Micro 27(5):51–61

17. Duato J (1993) A new theory of deadlock-free adaptive routing in wormhole networks. IEEE Trans Parallel Distrib Syst 4(12): 1320–1331
18. Duato J (1995) A necessary and sufficient condition for deadlock-free adaptive routing in wormhole networks. IEEE Trans Parallel Distrib Syst 6(10):1055–1067
19. Duato J (1996) A necessary and sufficient condition for deadlock-free routing in cut-through and store-and-forward networks. IEEE Trans Parallel Distrib Syst 7(8):841–854
20. Peh L-S, Dally WJ (2000) Flit reservation flow control. In: Proceedings of the 6th international symposium on high-performance computer architecture, Toulouse, France, January 2000, pp 73–84
21. Stunkel CB et al (1994) Architecture and implementation of vulcan. In: Proceedings of the 8th international parallel processing symposium, Cancun, Mexico, pp 266–274
22. Stunkel CB et al (1994) The SP1 high-performance switch. In: Proceedings of the scalable high performance computing conference, Knoxville, pp 150–157
23. Seitz C (1985) The cosmic cube. Commun ACM 28(1):22–23

Symmetric Multiprocessors

▶ Shared-Memory Multiprocessors

Synchronization

MICHAEL L. SCOTT
University of Rochester, Rochester, NY, USA

Synonyms
Fences; Multiprocessor synchronization; Mutual exclusion; Process synchronization

Definition
Synchronization is the use of language or library mechanisms to constrain the ordering (interleaving) of instructions performed by separate threads, to preclude orderings that lead to incorrect or undesired results.

Discussion
In a parallel program, the instructions of any given thread appear to occur in sequential order (at least from that thread's point of view), but if the threads run independently, their sequences of instructions may interleave arbitrarily, and many of the possible interleavings may produce incorrect results. As a trivial example, consider a global counter incremented by multiple threads. Each thread loads the counter into a register, increments the register, and writes the updated value back to memory. If two threads load the same value before either stores it back, updates may be lost:

```
                       c == 0
Thread 1:                              Thread 2:
    r1 := c
                                           r1:= c
    ++r1
                                           ++r1
    c := r1
                                           c := r1
                       c == 1
```

Synchronization serves to preclude invalid thread interleavings. It is commonly divided into the subtasks of *atomicity* and *condition synchronization*. Atomicity ensures that a given sequence of instructions, typically performed by a single thread, appears to all other threads as if it had executed indivisibly – not interleaved with anything else. In the example above, one would typically specify that the load-increment-store instruction sequence should execute atomically.

Condition synchronization forces a thread to wait, before performing an operation on shared data, until some desired precondition is true. In the example above, one might want to wait until all threads had performed their increments before reading the final count.

While it is tempting to suspect that condition synchronization subsumes atomicity (make the precondition be that no other thread is currently executing a conflicting operation), atomicity is in fact considerably harder, because it requires *consensus* among all competing threads: they must all agree as to which will proceed and which will wait. Put another way, condition synchronization delays a thread until some locally observable condition is seen to be true; atomicity is a property of the system as a whole.

Like many aspects of parallel computing, synchronization looks different in shared-memory and message-passing systems. In the latter, synchronization is generally subsumed in the message-passing methods; in a shared-memory system, it typically employs a separate set of methods.

Shared-memory implementations of synchronization can be categorized as *busy-wait* (*spinning*), or *scheduler-based*. The former actively consume processor cycles until the running thread is able to proceed. The latter deschedule the current thread, allowing the processor to be used by other threads, with the expectation that future activity by one of those threads will make the original thread runnable again. Because it avoids the cost of two context switches, busy-wait synchronization is typically faster than scheduler-based synchronization when the expected wait time is short and when the processor is not needed for other purposes. Scheduler-based synchronization is typically faster when expected wait times are long; it is *necessary* when the number of threads exceeds the number of processors (else quantum-long delays or even deadlock can occur). In the typical implementation, busy-wait synchronization is built on top of whatever hardware instructions execute atomically. Scheduler-based synchronization, in turn, is built on top of busy-wait synchronization, which is used to protect the scheduler's own data structures (see entries on *Scheduling Algorithms* and on *Processes, Tasks, and Threads*).

Hardware Primitives

In the earliest multiprocessors, *load* and *store* were the only memory-access instructions guaranteed to be atomic, and busy-wait synchronization was implemented using these. Modern machines provide a variety of atomic *read-modify-write* (RMW) instructions, which serve to *update* a memory location atomically. These significantly simplify the implementation of synchronization. Common RMW instructions include:

Test-and-set (l) sets the Boolean variable at location l to *true*, and returns the previous value.

Swap (l, v) stores the value v to location l and returns the previous value.

Atomic-ϕ (l, v) replaces the value o at location l with $\phi(o, v)$ for some simple arithmetic function ϕ (add, sub, and, etc.).

Fetch-and-ϕ (l, v) is like atomic-ϕ, but also returns the previous value.

Compare-and-swap (l, o, n) inspects the value v at location l, and if it is equal to o, replaces it with n. In either case, it returns the previous value, from which one can deduce whether the replacement occurred.

Load-linked (l) **and store-conditional** (l, v). The first of these returns the value at location l and "remembers" l. The second stores v to l if l has not been modified by any other processor since a previous load-linked by the current processor.

These instructions differ in their expressive power. Herlihy has shown [9] that compare-and-swap (CAS) and load-linked / store-conditional (LL/SC) are *universal* primitives, meaning, informally, that they can be used to construct a *non-blocking* implementation of any other RMW operation. The following code provides a simple implementation of fetch-and-ϕ using CAS.

```
val old := *l;
loop
    val new := phi(old);
    val found := CAS(l, old, new);
    if (old == found) break;
    old := found;
```

If the test on line 5 of this code fails, it must be because some other thread successfully modified *l. The system as a whole has made forward progress, but the current thread must try again.

As discussed in the entry on Non-blocking Algorithms, this simple implementation is *lock-free* but not *wait-free*. There are stronger (but slower and more complex) non-blocking implementations in which each thread is guaranteed to make forward progress in a bounded number of its own instructions.

NB: In any distributed system, and in most modern shared memory systems, instructions executed by a given thread are not, in general, guaranteed to be seen in sequential order by other threads, and instructions of any two threads are not, in general, guaranteed to be seen in the same order by all of their peers. Modern processors typically provide so-called *fence* or *barrier* instructions (not to be confused with the barriers discussed under Condition Synchronization below) that force previous instructions of the current thread to be seen by other threads before subsequent instructions of the current thread. Implementations of synchronization methods typically include sufficient fences that if synchronization method s_1 in thread t_1 occurs before synchronization method s_2 in thread t_2, then all instructions that precede s_1 in t_1 will appear in t_2 to have occurred before any of its own instructions that follow s_2. For more information, see the entry on Memory Models. The remainder of the discussion here assumes that memory is *sequentially consistent*, that is, that instructions appear to interleave in some global total order that is consistent with program order in every thread.

Atomicity

A multi-instruction operation is said to be *atomic* if appears to occur "all at once" from every other thread's point of view. In a sequentially consistent system, this means that the program behaves as if the instructions of the atomic operation were contiguous in the global instruction interleaving. More specifically, in any system, intermediate states of the atomic operation should never be visible to other threads, and actions of other threads should never become visible to a given thread in the middle of one of its own atomic operations.

The most straightforward way to implement atomicity is with a *mutual-exclusion (mutex) lock* – an abstract object that can be *held* by at most one thread at a time. In standard usage, a thread invokes the *acquire* method of the lock when it wishes to begin an atomic operation and the *release* method when it is done. *Acquire* waits (by spinning or rescheduling) until it is safe for the operation to proceed. The code between the acquire and release (the body of the atomic operation) is known as a *critical section*.

Critical sections that conflict with one another (typically, that access some common location, with at least one section writing that location) must be protected by the same lock. Programming discipline commonly ensures this property by associating data with locks. A thread must then acquire locks for all the data accessed in a critical section. It may do so all at once, at the beginning of the critical section, or it may do so incrementally, as the need for data is encountered. Considerable care may be required to ensure that locks are acquired in the same order by all critical sections, to avoid deadlock. All locks are typically held until the end of the critical section. This *two-phase locking* (all acquires occur before any releases) ensures that the global set of critical section executions remains *serializable*.

Relaxations of Mutual Exclusion

So-called *reader–writer locks* increase concurrency by observing that it is safe for more than one thread to read a location concurrently, so long as no thread is modifying that location. Each critical section is classified as either a reader or a writer of the data associated with a given lock. The *reader_acquire* method waits until there is no concurrent writer of the lock; the *writer_acquire* method waits until there is no concurrent reader *or* writer.

In a standard reader–writer lock, a thread must know, when it first reads a location, whether it will ever need to write that location in the current critical section. In some contexts it may be possible to relax this restriction. The Linux kernel, for example, provides a *sequence lock* mechanism that allows a reader to *abort* its peers and upgrade to writer status. Programmers are required to follow a restrictive programming discipline that makes critical sections "restartable," and checks, before any write or "dangerous" read, to see whether a peer's upgrade has necessitated a restart.

For data structures that are almost always read, and very occasionally written, several operating system kernels provide some variant of a mechanism known as *RCU* (originally an abbreviation for read-copy update). RCU divides execution into so-called *epochs*. A writer creates a new copy of any data structure it needs to update. It replaces the old copy with the new, typically using a single CAS instruction. It then waits until the end of the current epoch to be sure that all readers that might have been using the old copy have completed their critical sections (at which point it can reclaim the old copy, or perform other actions that depend on the visibility of the update). The advantage of RCU, in comparison to locks, is that it imposes *zero overhead* in the read-only case.

For more general-purpose use, *transactional memory* (TM) allows arbitrary operations to be executed atomically, with an underlying implementation based on *speculation* and *rollback*. Originally proposed [10] as a hardware assist for lock-free data structures – sort of a multi-word generalization of LL/SC – TM has seen a flurry of activity in recent years, and several hardware and software implementations are now widely available. Each keeps track of the memory locations accessed by transactions (would-be atomic operations). When two concurrent transactions are seen to conflict, at most one is allowed to *commit*; the others *abort*, "roll back," and try again, using a fully automated, transparent analogue of the programming discipline required by sequence locks. For further details, see the separate entry on TM.

Fairness

Because they sometimes force multiple threads to wait, synchronization mechanisms inevitably raise issues of *fairness*. When a lock is released by the current holder, which waiting thread should be allowed to acquire it? In a system with reader–writer locks, should a thread be allowed to join a group of already-active readers when writers are already waiting? When transactions conflict in a TM system, which should be permitted to proceed, and which should wait or abort?

Many answers are possible. The choice among conflicting threads may be arbitrary, random, first-come-first-served (FIFO), or based on some other notion of priority. From the point of view of an individual thread, the resulting behavior may range from potential *starvation* (no progress guarantees) to some sort of proportional share of system run time. Between these extremes, a thread may be guaranteed to run eventually if it is continuously ready, or if it is ready infinitely often. Even given the possibility of starvation, the system as a whole may be *livelock-free* (guaranteed to make forward progress) as a result of algorithmic guarantees or pseudo-random heuristics. (Actual livelock is generally considered unacceptable.) Any starvation-free system is clearly livelock free.

Simple Busy-Wait Locks

Several early locking algorithms were based on only loads and stores, but these are mainly of historical interest today. All required $\Omega(tn)$ space for t threads and n locks, and $\omega(1)$ (more-than-constant) time to arbitrate among threads competing for a given lock.

In modern usage, the simplest constant-space, busy-wait mutual exclusion lock is the *test-and-set (TAS)*

lock, in which a thread acquires the lock by using a test-and-set instruction to change a Boolean flag from false to true. Unfortunately, spinning by waiting threads tends to induce extreme contention for the lock location, tying up bus and memory resources needed for productive work. On a cache-coherent machine, better performance can be achieved with a "test-and-test-and-set" (TATAS) lock, which reduces contention by using ordinary load instructions to spin on a value in the local cache so long as the lock remains held:

```
type lock = Boolean;

proc acquire(lock *l):
    while (test-and-set(l))
        while (*l) /* spin */ ;

proc release(lock *l):
    *l := false;
```

This lock works well on small machines (up to, say, four processors).

Which waiting thread acquires a TATAS lock at release time depends on vagaries of the hardware, and is essentially arbitrary. Strict FIFO ordering can be achieved with a *ticket lock*, which uses fetch-and-increment (FAI) and a pair of counters for constant space and (per-thread) time. To acquire the lock, a thread atomically performs an FAI on the "next available" counter and waits for the "now serving" counter to equal the value returned. To release the lock, a thread increments its own ticket, and stores the result to the "now serving" counter. While arguably fairer than a TATAS lock, the ticket lock is more prone to performance anomalies on a multiprogrammed system: if any waiting thread is preempted, all threads behind it in line will be delayed until it is scheduled back in.

Scalable Busy-Wait Locks

On a machine with more than a handful of processors, TATAS and ticket locks scale poorly, with time per critical section growing linearly with the number of waiting threads. Anderson [1] showed that exponential backoff (reminiscent of the Ethernet contention-control algorithm) could substantially improve the performance of TATAS locks. Mellor-Crummey and Scott [17] showed similar results for linear backoff in ticket locks (where a thread can easily deduce its distance from the head of the line).

To eliminate contention entirely, waiting threads can be linked into an explicit queue, with each thread spinning on a separate location that will be modified when the thread ahead of it in line completes its critical section. Mellor-Crummey and Scott showed how to implement such queues in total space $O(t + n)$ for t threads and n locks; their *MCS lock* is widely used in large-scale systems. Craig [4] and, independently, Landin and Hagersten [16] developed an alternative *CLH lock* that links the queue in the opposite direction and performs slightly faster on some cache-coherent machines. Auslander et al. developed a variant of the MCS lock that is API-compatible with traditional TATAS locks [3]. Kontothanassis et al. [14] and He et al. [8] developed variants of the MCS and CLH locks that avoid performance anomalies due to preemption of threads waiting in line.

Scheduler-Based Locks

A busy-wait lock wastes processor resources when expected wait times are long. It may also cause performance anomalies or deadlock in a multiprogrammed system. The simplest solution is to *yield* the processor in the body of the spin loop, effectively moving the current thread to the end of the scheduler's ready list and allowing other threads to run. More commonly, *scheduler-based locks* are designed to *deschedule* the waiting thread, moving it (atomically) from the ready list to a separate queue associated with the lock. The release method then moves one waiting thread from the lock queue to the ready list. To minimize overhead when waiting times *are* short, implementations of scheduler-based synchronization commonly spin for a small, bounded amount of time before invoking the scheduler and yielding the processor. This strategy is often known as *spin-then-wait*.

Condition Synchronization

It is tempting to assume that busy-wait condition synchronization can be implemented trivially with a Boolean flag: a waiting thread spins until the flag is true; a thread that satisfies the condition sets the flag to true. On most modern machines, however, additional fence instructions are required both in the satisfying thread, to ensure that its prior writes are visible to other threads, and in the waiting thread, to ensure that its subsequent reads do not occur until after the spin completes. And even on a sequentially consistent machine, special steps are required to ensure that the compiler does not violate the programmer's expectations by reordering instructions within threads.

In some programming languages and systems, a variable may be made suitable for condition synchronization by labeling it `volatile` (or, in C++'0X, `atomic<>`). The compiler will insert appropriate fences at reads and writes of `volatile` variables, and will refrain from reordering them with respect to other instructions.

Some other systems provide special *event* objects, with methods to set and await them. Semaphores and monitors, described in the following two subsections, can be used for both mutual exclusion and condition synchronization.

In systems with dynamically varying concurrency, the *fork* and *join* methods used to create threads and to verify their completion can be considered a form of condition synchronization. (These are, in fact, the principal form of synchronization in systems like Cilk and OpenMP.)

Barriers

One form of condition synchronization is particularly common in data-parallel applications, where threads iterate together through a potentially large number of algorithmic phases. A *synchronization barrier*, used to separate phases, guarantees that no thread continues to phase $n + 1$ until all threads have finished phase n.

In most (though not all) implementations, the barrier provides a single method, composed internally of an *arrival* phase that counts the number of threads that have reached the barrier (typically via a log-depth tree) and a *departure* phase in which permission to continue is broadcast back to all threads. In a so-called *fuzzy barrier* [6], these arrival and departure phases may be separate methods. In between, a thread may perform any instructions that neither depend on the arrival of other threads nor are required by other threads prior to their departure. Such instructions can serve to "smooth out" phase-by-phase imbalances in the work assigned to different threads, thereby reducing overall wait time. Wait time may also be reduced by an *adaptive barrier* [7, 19], which completes the arrival phase in constant time after the arrival of the final thread.

Unfortunately, when t threads arrive more or less simultaneously, no barrier implementation using ordinary loads, stores, and RMW instructions can complete the arrival phase in less than $\Omega(\log t)$ time. Given the importance of barriers in scientific applications, some supercomputers have provided special near-constant-time hardware barriers. In some cases the same hardware has supported a fast *eureka* method, in which one thread can announce an event to all others in constant time.

Semaphores

First proposed by Dijkstra in 1965 [5] and still widely used today, *semaphores* support both mutual exclusion and condition synchronization. A *general semaphore* is a nonnegative counter with an initial value and two methods, known as **V** and **P**. The **V** method increases the value of the semaphore by one. The **P** method waits for the value to be positive and then decreases it by one. A *binary semaphore* has values restricted to zero and one (it is customarily initialized to one), and serves as a mutual exclusion lock. The **P** method acquires the lock; the **V** method releases the lock. Programming discipline is required to ensure that **P** and **V** methods occur in matching pairs.

The typical implementation of semaphores pairs the counter with a queue of waiting threads. The **V** method checks to see whether the counter is currently zero. If so, it checks to see whether any threads are waiting in the queue and, if there are, moves one of them to the ready list. If the counter is already positive (in which case the queue is guaranteed to be empty) or if the counter is zero but the queue is empty, **V** simply increments the counter. The **P** method also checks to see whether the counter is zero. If so, it places the current thread on the queue and calls the scheduler to yield the processor. Otherwise it decrements the counter.

General semaphores can be used to represent resources of which there is a limited number, but more than one. Examples include I/O devices, communication channels, or free or full slots in a fixed-length buffer. Most operating systems provide semaphores as part of the kernel API.

Monitors

While semaphores remain the most widely used scheduler-based shared-memory synchronization mechanism, they suffer from several limitations. In particular, the association between a binary semaphore (mutex lock) and the data it protects is solely a matter of convention, as is the paired usage of **P** and **V** methods. Early experience with semaphores, combined with the development of language-level abstraction mechanisms in the 1970s, led several developers to suggest building higher-level synchronization abstractions into programming languages. These efforts culminated in the definition of *monitors* [12], variants of which appear in many languages and systems.

A monitor is a data abstraction (a module or class) with an implicit mutex lock and an optional set of *condition variables*. Each *entry* (method) of the monitor automatically acquires and releases the mutex lock; entry invocations thus exclude one another in time. Programmers typically devise, for each monitor, a program-specific *invariant* that captures the mutual consistency of the monitor's state (data members – fields). The invariant is assumed to be true at the beginning of each entry invocation, and must be true again at the end.

Condition variables support a pair of methods superficially analogous to **P** and **V**; in Hoare's original formulation, these were known as *wait* and *signal*. Unlike **P** and **V**, these methods are *memory-less*: a signal invocation is a no-op if no thread is currently waiting.

For each reason that a thread might need to wait within a monitor, the programmer declares a separate condition variable. When it waits on a condition, the thread releases exclusion on the monitor. The programmer must thus ensure that the invariant is true immediately prior to every wait invocation.

Semantic Details

The details of monitors vary significantly from one language to another. The most significant issues, discussed in the paragraphs below, are commonly known as the *nested monitor problem* and the modeling of signals as *hints vs. absolutes*. More minor issues include language syntax, alternative names for signal and wait, the modeling of condition variables in the type system, and the prioritization of threads waiting for conditions or for access to the mutex lock.

The nested monitor problem arises when an entry of one monitor invokes an entry of another monitor, and the second entry waits on a condition variable. Should the wait method release exclusion on the outer monitor? If it does, there is no guarantee that the outer monitor will be available again when execution is ready to resume in the inner call. If it does not, the programmer must take care to ensure that the thread that will perform the matching signal invocation does not need to go through the outer monitor in order to reach the inner one. A variety of solutions to this problem have been proposed; the most common is to leave the outer monitor locked.

Signal methods in Hoare's original formulation were defined to transfer monitor exclusion directly from the signaler to the waiter, with no intervening execution. The purpose of this convention was to guarantee that the condition represented by the signal was still true when the waiter resumed. Unfortunately, the convention often has the side effect of inducing extra context switches, and requires that the monitor invariant be true immediately prior to every signal invocation. Most modern monitor variants follow the lead of Mesa [15] in declaring that a signal is merely a hint, and that a waiting process must double-check the condition before continuing execution. In effect, code that would be written

```
if (!condition)
    cond_var.wait();
```

in a Hoare monitor is written

```
while (!condition)
    cond_var.wait();
```

in a Mesa monitor. To make it easier to write programs in which a condition variable "covers" a set of possible conditions (particularly when signals are hints), many monitor variants provide a *signal-all* or *broadcast* method that awakens all threads waiting on a condition, rather than only one.

Message Passing

In a system in which threads interact by exchanging messages, rather than by sharing variables, synchronization is generally implicit in the *send* and *receive* methods. A receive method typically blocks until an appropriate message is available (a matching send has been performed). Blocking semantics for send methods vary from one system to another:

Asynchronous send – In some systems, a sender continues execution immediately after invoking a send method, and the underlying system takes responsibility for delivering the message. While often desirable, this behavior complicates the delivery of failure notifications, and may be limited by finite buffering capacity.

Synchronous send – In other systems – notably those based on Hoare's Communicating Sequential Processes (CSP) [13] – a sender waits until its message has been received.

Remote-invocation send – In yet other systems, a send method has both ingoing and outcoming parameters; the sender waits until a reply is received from its peer.

Distributed Locking

Libraries, languages, and applications commonly implement higher-level distributed locks or transactions on top of message passing. The most common lock implementation is analogous to the MCS lock: acquired requests are sent to a *lock manager* thread. If the lock is available, the manager responds directly; otherwise it forwards the request to the last thread currently waiting in line. The release method sends a message to the manager or, if a forwarding request has already been received, to the next thread in line for the lock. Races in which the manager forwards a request at the same time the last lock holder sends it a release are trivially resolved by statically choosing one of the two (perhaps the lock holder) to inform the next thread in line. Distributed transaction systems are substantially more complex.

Rendezvous and Remote Procedure Call

In some systems, a message must be received explicitly by an already existing thread. In other systems, a thread is created by the underlying system to handle each arriving message. Either of these options – *explicit* or *implicit receipt* – can be paired with any of the three send options described above. The combination of remote-invocation send with implicit receipt is often called *remote procedure call* (RPC). The combination of remote-invocation send with explicit receipt is known as *rendezvous*. Interestingly, if all shared data is encapsulated in monitors, one can model – or implement – each monitor with a *manager* thread that executes entry calls one at a time. Each such call then constitutes a rendezvous between the sender and the monitor.

Related Entries
▶Actors
▶Cache Coherence
▶Concurrent Collections Programming Model
▶Deadlocks
▶Memory Models
▶Monitors, Axiomatic Verification of
▶Non-Blocking Algorithms
▶Path Expressions
▶Processes, Tasks, and Threads
▶Race Conditions
▶Scheduling Algorithms
▶Shared-Memory Multiprocessors
▶Transactions, Nested

Bibliographic Notes
The study of synchronization began in earnest with Dijkstra's "Cooperating Sequential Processes" monograph of 1965 [5]. Andrews and Schneider provide an excellent survey of synchronization mechanisms circa 1983 [2]. Mellor-Crummey and Scott describe and compare a variety of busy-wait spin locks and barriers, and introduce the MCS lock [17]. More extensive coverage of synchronization can be found in Chapter 12 of Scott's programming languages text [18], or in the recent texts of Herlihy and Shavit [11] and Taubenfeld [20].

Bibliography
1. Anderson TE (Jan 1990) The performance of spin lock alternatives for shared-memory multiprocessors. IEEE Trans Parallel Distr Sys 1(1):6–16
2. Andrews GR, Schneider FB (Mar 1983) Concepts and notations for concurrent programming. ACM Comput Surv 15(1):3–43
3. Auslander MA, Edelsohn DJ, Krieger OY, Rosenburg BS, Wisniewski RW (2003) Enhancement to the MCS lock for increased functionality and improved programmability. U.S. patent application 20030200457, submitted 23 Oct 2003
4. Craig TS (Feb 1993) Building FIFO and priority-queueing spin locks from atomic swap. Technical Report 93-02-02, University of Washington Computer Science Department
5. Dijkstra EW (Sept 1965) Cooperating sequential processes. Technical report, Technological University, Eindhoven, The Netherlands. Reprinted in Genuys F (ed) Programming Languages, Academic Press, New York, 1968, pp 43–112. Also available at www.cs.utexas.edu/users/EWD/transcriptions/EWD01xx/EWD123.html.
6. Gupta R (Apr 1989) The fuzzy barrier: a mechanism for high speed synchronization of processors. Proceedings of the 3rd International Conference on Architectural Support for Programming Languages and Operating Systems, Boston, MA, pp 54–63
7. Gupta R, Hill CR (June 1989) A scalable implementation of barrier synchronization using an adaptive combining tree. Int J Parallel Progr 18(3):161–180
8. He B, Scherer III WN, Scott ML (Dec 2005) Preemption adaptivity in time-published queuebased spin locks. Proceeding of the 2005 International Conference on High Performance Computing, Goa, India
9. Herlihy MP (Jan 1991) Wait-free synchronization. ACM Trans Progr Lang Syst 13(1):124–149
10. Herlihy MP, Moss JEB (1993) Transactional memory: architectural support for lock-free data structures. Proceedings of the 20th International Symposium on Computer Architecture, San Diego, CA, May 1993 pp 289–300
11. Herlihy MP, Shavit N (2008) The Art of Multiprocessor Programming. Morgan Kaufmann, Burlington, MA
12. Hoare CAR (Oct 1974) Monitors: an operating system structuring concept. Commun ACM 17(10):549–557
13. Hoare CAR (Aug 1978) Communicating sequential processes. Commun ACM 21(8):666–677
14. Kontothanassis LI, Wisniewski R, Scott ML (Feb 1997) Scheduler-conscious synchronization. ACM Trans Comput Sys 15(1):3–40
15. Lampson BW, Redell DD (Feb 1980) Experience with processes and monitors in Mesa. Commun ACM 23(2):105–117
16. Magnussen P, Landin A, Hagersten E (Apr 1994) Queue locks on cache coherent multiprocessors. Proceedings of the 8th International Parallel Processing Symposium, Cancun, Mexico, pp 165–171
17. Mellor-Crummey JM, Scott ML (Feb 1991) Algorithms for scalable synchronization on sharedmemory multiprocessors. ACM Trans Comput Syst 9(1):21–65
18. Scott ML (2009) Programming Language Pragmatics, 3rd edn. Morgan Kaufmann, Burlington, MA
19. Scott ML, Mellor-Crummey JM (Aug 1994) Fast, contention-free combining tree barriers. Int J Parallel Progr 22(4):449–481
20. Taubenfeld G (2006) Synchronization Algorithms and Concurrent Programming. Prentice Hall, Upper Saddle River

System Integration

▶Terrestrial Ecosystem Carbon Modeling

System on Chip (SoC)

▶ SoC (System on Chip)
▶ VLSI Computation

Systems Biology, Network Inference in

Jaroslaw Zola[1], Srinivas Aluru[1,2]
[1]Iowa State University, Ames, IA, USA
[2]Indian Institute of Technology Bombay, Mumbai, India

Synonyms
Gene networks reconstruction; Gene networks reverse-engineering

Definition
Inference of gene regulatory networks, also called reverse-engineering of gene regulatory networks, is a process of characterizing, either qualitatively or quantitatively, regulatory mechanisms in a cell or an organism from observed expression data.

Discussion

Introduction
Biological processes in every living organism are governed by complex interactions between thousands of genes, gene products, and other molecules. Genes that are encoded in the DNA are transcribed and translated to form multiple copies of gene products including proteins and various types of RNAs. These gene products coordinate to execute cellular processes – sometimes by forming supramolecular complexes (e.g., ribosome), or by acting in a concerted fashion, e.g., in biochemical or metabolic pathways. They also regulate the expression of genes, often through binding to cis-regulatory sequences upstream of the coding region of the genes, to calibrate gene expression depending on the endogenous and exogenous stimuli carried by, e.g., small molecules.

Gene regulatory networks are conceptual representations of interactions between genes in a cell or an organism. They are depicted as graphs with vertices corresponding to genes and edges representing regulatory interactions between genes (see Fig. 1). Overall, gene regulatory networks are mathematical models to explain the observed gene expression levels. Network inference, or reconstructing, is the process of identifying the underlying network from multiple observations of gene expressions (outputs of the network). To infer a gene network, one relies on experimental data from high-throughput technologies such as microarrays, quantitative polymerase chain reaction, or short-read sequencing, which measure a snapshot of all gene expression levels under a particular condition or in a time series.

Information Theoretic Approaches
Consider a set of n genes $\{g_1, g_2, \ldots, g_n\}$, where for each gene a set of m expression measurements is given. One can represent expression of gene i (g_i) as a random variable $X_i \in \mathcal{X}$, $\mathcal{X} = \{X_1, \ldots, X_n\}$, with marginal probability p_{X_i} derived from some unknown joint probability characterizing the entire system. This random variable is described by observations $\{x_{i,1}, \ldots, x_{i,m}\}$, where $x_{i,j}$ corresponds to the expression level of g_i under condition j. The vector $\langle x_{i,1}, x_{i,2}, \ldots, x_{i,m} \rangle$ is called profile of g_i. Given a profile matrix $Y_{n \times m}$, $Y[i,j] = x_{i,j}$, one can formulate network inference problem as that of finding a model that best explains the data in Y.

Such formulated problem can be approached using a variety of methods, including Bayesian networks [21] and Gaussian graphical models [20]; one class of methods that has been widely adopted uses the concept of mutual information. These methods [15] operate under the assumption that correlation of expression implies coregulation, and proceed in two main phases: First significant dependencies (connection between two genes) or independencies (lack of connections) are determined by means of computing mutual information for every pair of genes. Then, identification and removal of indirect interactions (e.g., when two genes are coregulated by a third) is performed.

Mutual information is arguably the best measure of correlation between two random variables, and is defined based on entropy $\mathcal{H}$ in the following way:

$$\mathcal{I}(X_i; X_j) = \mathcal{H}(X_i) + \mathcal{H}(X_j) - \mathcal{H}(X_i, X_j),$$

where entropy $\mathcal{H}$ is given by:

$$\mathcal{H}(X) = -\sum p_X(x) \log p_X(x),$$

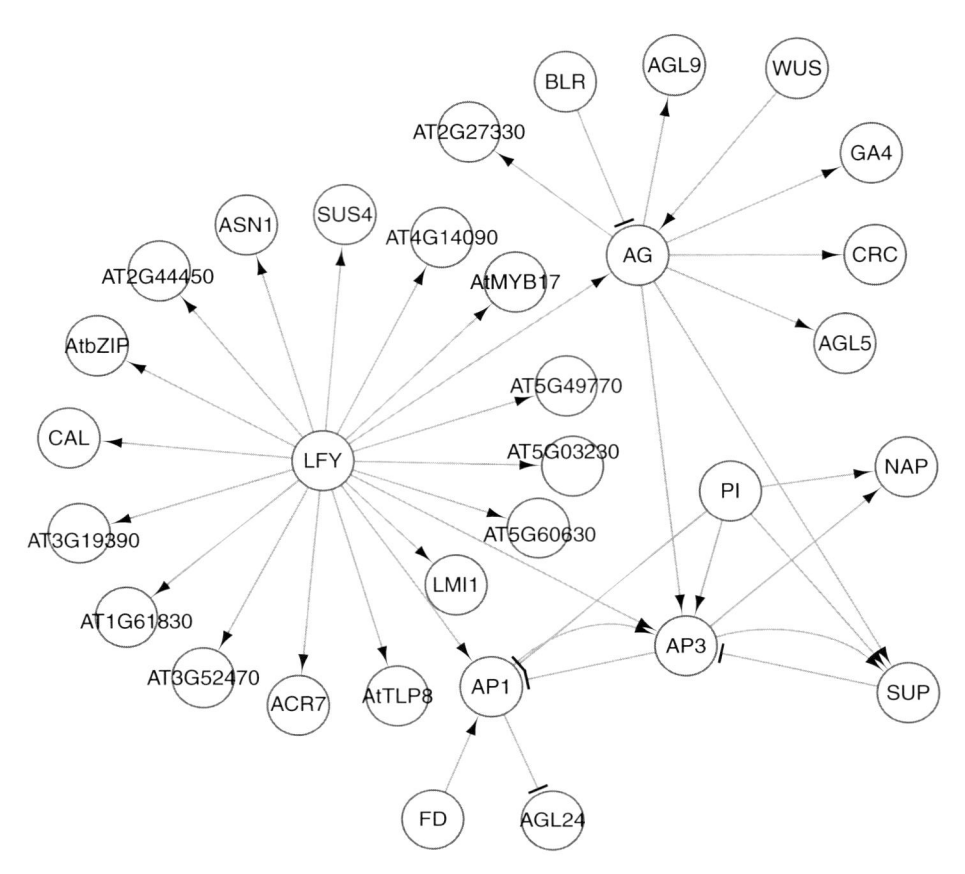

Systems Biology, Network Inference in. Fig. 1 Example gene regulatory network. Nodes represent genes, *"T"-edges* denote regulation in which a source gene represses expression of the target gene. *Arrow-edges* denote regulation in which a source gene induces expression of the target gene

and p_X defines the probability distribution of X, and $\sum$ is replaced by integral if X is continuous. Mutual information is a symmetric, nonnegative function, and is equal to zero if and only if two random variables are independent.

Application of mutual information for gene network inference poses two significant challenges. As the probability distribution of the random variable describing a gene is unknown, it has to be estimated from the expression profile. Consequently, gene comparison becomes more difficult because even independent expression profiles can result in mutual information greater than zero (owing to sampling and estimation errors). This in turn requires some mechanism to decide if the given mutual information estimate is statistically significant. The second challenge is due to the fact that a typical genome-level network covers thousands of genes, and hence "all-pairs" comparison adds considerably to computational requirements. In practice, several mutual information estimators are available that offer different precision to complexity ratios (e.g., Gaussian kernel estimator, B-spline estimator), and complex statistical techniques are employed to decide if observed mutual information implies dependency.

Although all information theoretic approaches for reverse-engineering depend on "all-pairs" mutual information kernel executed in the first stage, they differ in how they identify indirect interactions in the second stage. For example, in relevance networks [4] the second stage is omitted, in ARACNe [3] and TINGe [22, 23] the Data Processing Inequality concept is used, while CLR algorithm [6] depends on estimates of a likelihood of obtained mutual information values. Some other methods extend mutual information into conditional mutual information or augment it with feature selection techniques.

Parallel Information Theoretic Approach

Reverse engineering of regulatory networks using mutual information is compute and memory intensive especially if whole-genome (i.e., covering all genes of an organism) networks are considered. Memory consumption arises from the $\Theta(nm)$ size of input data, and from the $\Theta(n^2)$ dense initial network generated in the first phase of the reconstruction algorithm. Adding to this is complexity of mutual information estimators, which for Gaussian kernel estimator for instance is $O(m^2)$. Taking into account that the number of genes typically considered is in the thousands, and at the same time genome-level inference requires that the number of observations m is large, the problem becomes prohibitive for sequential computers.

In [23], Zola et al. proposed a parallel information theory-based inference method that efficiently exploits multiple levels of parallelism inherent to mutual information computations and uses a generalized scheme for pairwise computation scheduling. The method has been implemented in the MPI-based software package called TINGe (Tool Inferring Networks of Genes), along with a version that supports the use of cell accelerators.

The algorithm proceeds in three stages. In the first stage, input expression profiles are rank-transformed and mutual information is computed for each of the $\binom{n}{2}$ pairs of genes, and q randomly chosen permutations per pair. Rank transformation substitutes a gene expression profile with a permutation of $\langle 1, \ldots, m \rangle$ by replacing a gene expression with its rank among all gene expressions within the same expression profile. It has been shown that mutual information is invariant under this transformation [5]. By applying it the algorithm can reduce the total number of mutual information estimations between gene expression vectors and their random permutations [22]. In the second phase, the threshold value above which mutual information is considered to signify dependence is computed, and edges below this threshold are discarded. The threshold is computed by finding the element with rank $(1-\varepsilon) \cdot q \cdot \binom{n}{2}$ among $q \cdot \binom{n}{2}$ values contributed by permutations generated in the earlier stage, where ε is specifies the desired statistical significance of the corresponding permutation test. Finally, in the third stage data processing inequality is applied with the consequence that if g_i interacts with g_k via some other gene g_j then $\mathcal{I}(X_i; X_k) \leq \min(\mathcal{I}(X_i; X_j), \mathcal{I}(X_j; X_k))$.

The algorithm represents gene network using the standard adjacency matrix $D_{n \times n}$. The input and output data are distributed row-wise among p processors. Each processor stores up to $\lceil \frac{n}{p} \rceil$ consecutive rows of matrix Y and the same number of consecutive rows from matrix D. Matrix D is then partitioned into $p \times p$ blocks of submatrices which are computed in $\lceil \frac{p+1}{2} \rceil$ iterations, where in iteration i processor with rank j computes submatrix $D_{j,(j+i) \bmod p}$. To implement the second stage a simple reduction operation is used to find the threshold value followed by pruning of matrix D. Finally, removing of indirect interactions is performed based on streaming of matrix D in $p-1$ communication rounds, where in iteration i only processors with ranks lower than $p-i$ participate in communication and computation.

In their method, Zola et al. use B-spline mutual information estimator which is implemented to take advantage of SIMD extensions of modern processors. However, any mutual information estimator could be used. Furthermore, they report modification of the first stage of the algorithm that enables execution on cell heterogeneous processors. The method has been used to reconstruct a 15,222 network of the model plant *Arabidopsis thaliana* from 3,137 microarray experiments in 30 minutes on a 2,048 core IBM Blue Gene/L, and in 2 h and 25 min on a 8-node QS20 cell blade cluster.

Approaches Based on Bayesian Networks

Bayesian networks are a class of graphical models that represent probabilistic relationships among random variables of a given domain. Formally, a Bayesian network is a pair (N, P), where P is the joint probability distribution and N is a directed acyclic graph, with vertices representing random variables and edges corresponding to "parent – child" relationship between variables, which encodes the Markov assumption that a node is conditionally independent from its non-descendants, given its parents in N. Under this assumption one can represent the joint probability as a product of conditional probabilities:

$$P(X_1, \ldots, X_n) = \prod_i P(X_i | \pi_i),$$

where π_i is a set of parents of X_i in N. Given a set of realizations (observations) of random variables one can learn a structure of the Bayesian network that best fits the observed data.

Bayesian networks have been widely employed for reverse-engineering of gene regulatory networks [8, 18, 21]. Following the same formalization as for information theoretic approaches described above, the problem of gene network inference becomes that of learning the structure of the corresponding Bayesian network. Nodes of the network are random variables assigned to genes $\mathcal{X} = \{X_1, \ldots, X_n\}$, expression profiles are realizations of those variables, and a Bayesian network learned from such data represents a gene regulatory network, where π_i is interpreted as a set of regulators of gene g_i. In order to learn the structure of a Bayesian network, a statistically motivated scoring function that evaluates the posterior probability of a network given the input data is typically assumed: $Score(N) = \log P(N|Y)$. To find the optimal network efficiently such a function should be decomposable into individual score contributions $s(X_i, \pi_i)$, i.e.:

$$Score(N) = \sum_i s(X_i, \pi_i).$$

A major difficulty in Bayesian network structure learning is the super exponential search space in the number of random variables – for a set of n variables there exist $\frac{n! 2^{\frac{n}{2}(n-1)}}{r \cdot z^n}$ possible directed acyclic graphs, where $r \approx 0.57436$ and $z \approx 1.4881$.

Parallel Exact Structure Learning

Even assuming that the cost of evaluating scoring function is negligible, exhaustive enumeration of all possible network structures remains prohibitive. Although heuristics have been proposed to tackle the problem, e.g., based on simulated annealing, oftentimes reconstructing the optimal network is advantageous as it enables more meaningful conclusions.

Nikolova et al. [17] proposed an elegant parallel exact algorithm for learning Bayesian networks that builds on top of earlier sequential methods [18]. In this approach a network is represented as a permutation of nodes where each node is preceded by its parents. The algorithm identifies the optimal ordering, and a corresponding optimal network, using a dynamic programming approach that operates on the lattice formed on the power set of $\mathcal{X}$ by the partial order "set inclusion." The lattice is organized into $n + 1$ levels, where level $l \in [0, n]$ contains all subsets of size l, and a node at level l has l incoming and $n - l$ outgoing edges. At each node of the lattice $(n - l)$ evaluations of individual scores s have to be performed as a part of dynamic programming search, which next have to be communicated along outgoing edges.

The key component of the approach by Nikolova et al. is the observation that dynamic programming lattice forms an n-dimensional hypercube that can be decomposed on $p = 2^k$ processors into 2^{n-k} k-dimensional hypercubes, each mapping to p processors. These hypercubes can be processed in a pipelined fashion that provides a work optimal algorithm.

The reported method has been used to reverse-engineer regulatory networks using synthetic data with up to 30 genes and 500 microarray observations, and applying Minimum Description Length principle [11] as a scoring function. To reconstruct a network for the largest data it took 1 h and 30 min on 1,024 processors of an IBM BlueGene/L.

Approaches Based on Differential Equations

Under several simplifying assumptions the dynamics of a gene's expression can be modeled as a function of abundance of all other genes and the rate of degradation:

$$\dot{x}_i = f_i(\mathbf{x}) - \lambda(x_i),$$

where f_i is called input function of gene i, x_i is expression of gene i, vector $\mathbf{x}$ represents expression levels of all genes, and λ describes the rate of degradation. One can further assume that input functions are linear and in such cases the dynamics of the entire system can be represented as:

$$\dot{\mathbf{x}} = A \cdot \mathbf{x},$$

where $A_{n \times n}$ is a matrix describing influences of genes on each other (including rates of degradation), i.e., $A[i, j]$ represents the influence of gene g_j on g_i. Consequently by solving such system of equations one would obtain the underlying gene network represented by matrix A. Unfortunately finding the solution requires a large number of measurements of **x** and **ẋ** since otherwise the system is greatly underdetermined. At the same time obtaining representative measurements is experimentally very challenging and sometimes infeasible.

To overcome this limitation, and to enable linearization of systems with nonlinear gene input functions, Gardner et al. [9] proposed an approach in which m perturbation experiments (i.e., experiments in which expression of selected genes is affected in a controlled way) are performed, and resulting expression profiles are used to write the following system of differential equations:

$$\dot{Y} = AY + U,$$

which at steady state gives:

$$AY = -U.$$

Here $Y_{n \times m}$ is a matrix describing expression of all genes in all experiments, i.e., $Y[i,j]$ describes expression of gene i under perturbation j, and matrix $U_{n \times m}$ represents the effect of perturbations on every gene in all m experiments. Because in the majority of cases $m < n$ and the resulting system remains underdetermined, Gardner et al. assumed that each gene can have at most k regulatory inputs (which is biologically plausible), and then applied multiple regression for every possible combination of k regulators, choosing the one that best fits the data to approximate A.

Parallelization of Multiple Regression Algorithms

The approach of Gardner et al., named Network Identification by Multiple Regression, is computationally prohibitive for networks with more than a few dozen genes as it is infeasible to consider all $\binom{n}{k}$ combinations of regulators, especially that for each gene and each combination of regulators the following expression must be evaluated

$$\hat{\mathbf{a}}_i = -\mathbf{u}_i Z^T (ZZ^T)^{-1},$$

to find the combination for which $\hat{\mathbf{a}}_i$ minimizes the sum squared errors with respect to the observed data. Here, $\mathbf{u}_i$ represents row of matrix U for gene i, and Z consists of k rows selected from Y that correspond to k selected regulator genes.

In [10], Gregoretti et al. describe parallel implementation of the algorithm that replaces the exact enumeration of all combinations of regulators with a greedy search heuristic that starts with d best candidate regulators that are next iteratively combined with other genes to form the final set of regulators. Furthermore, they observe that it is possible to obtain $\hat{\mathbf{a}}_i$ by solving the system of linear equations $S\mathbf{a}_i = -\mathbf{r}$, where S is the symmetric submatrix of YY^T of k rows and columns that correspond to the considered regulators, and $\mathbf{r}$ is the i-th row of Y^T. Because S is positive definite the Cholesky factorization can be used to efficiently solve this system. In practice, the implementation uses the PPSV routine, which has multiple parallel implementations. Finally, searching for regulators of a gene can be performed independently for every gene. Consequently, in the parallel version each of p processors is assigned at most $\lceil \frac{n}{p} \rceil$ genes for which it executes the search heuristic.

The main limitation of the multiple regression algorithm is that it requires perturbation data as an input. Because in many cases such data is not available, Gregoretti et al. used synthetic data consisting of 2,500 genes with a single perturbation experiment for each gene. This data has been analyzed on a cluster with 100 nodes, each with dual core Itanium2 processor, and with Quadrics ELAN 4 interconnect in approximately 3 h and 25 min.

Future Directions

The problem of reverse engineering gene regulatory networks is one of many in the broad area of computational systems biology, and parallel processing only recently attracted attention of systems biology researchers. Together with the rapid progress in high-throughput biological technologies one can expect accumulation of massive and diverse data, which will enable more complex and realistic models of regulation. Most likely these models will be evolving such as to enable *in silico* simulation of biological systems, which is one of the goals of the emerging field of synthetic biology. Consequently, parallel processing in its various flavors, ranging from accelerators and multicore processors to clusters, grids, and clouds, will be necessary to tackle the resulting computational complexity.

Bibliographic Notes and Further Reading

The textbook by Alon [1] and articles by Kitano [12, 13] and Murali and Aluru [16] provide a good general introduction to systems biology. A brief overview of existing approaches and challenges in gene networks inference can be found in [2, 14]. In [7] Friedman gives an introduction to using graphical models for network inference, and Meyer et al. review information theoretic approaches in [15]. The "Dialogue for Reverse Engineering Assessments and Methods" project [19] provides a robust set of benchmark data that can be used to assess the quality of inference methods, and it is a good source of information about developments in the area of networks reconstruction.

Bibliography

1. Alon U (2006) An Introduction to Systems Biology: Design Principles of Biological Circuits. Chapman & Hall/CRC, Boca Raton
2. Bansal M, Belcastro V, Ambesi-Impiombato A, di Bernardo D (2007) How to infer gene networks from expression profiles. Mol Syst Biol 3:78
3. Basso K, Margolin AA, Stolovitzky G, Klein U, Dalla-Favera R, Califano A (2005) Reverse engineering of regulatory networks in human B cells. Nat Genet 37(4):382–390
4. Butte AJ, Kohane IS (2000) Mutual information relevance networks: functional genomic clustering using pairwise entropy measurements. In Pacific Symposium on Biocomputing, pp 418–429
5. Cover TM, Thomas JA (2006) Elements of Information Theory, 2nd edn. Wiley, New York
6. Faith JJ, Hayete B, Thaden JT, Mogno I, Wierzbowski J, Cottarel G, Kasif S, Collins JJ, Gardner TS (2007) Large-scale mapping and validation of *Escherichia coli* transcriptional regulation from a compendium of expression profiles. PLoS Biol 5(1):e8
7. Friedman N (2004) Inferring cellular networks using probabilistic graphical models. Science 303:799–805
8. Friedman N, Linial M, Nachman I, Pe'er D (2000) Using Bayesian networks to analyze expression data. J Comput Biol 7:601–620
9. Gardner TS, di Bernardo D, Lorenz D, Collins JJ (2003) Inferring genetic networks and identifying compound mode of action via expression profiling. Science 301(5629):102–105
10. Gregoretti F, Belcastro V, di Bernardo D, Oliva G (2010) A parallel implementation of the network identification by multiple regression (NIR) algorithm to reverse-engineer regulatory gene networks. PLoS One 5(4):e10979
11. Grunwald PD (2007) The Minimum Description Length Principle. MIT Press, Cambridge
12. Kitano H (2002) Computational systems biology. Nature 420(6912):206–210
13. Kitano H (2002) Systems biology: a brief overview. Science 295(5560):1662–1664
14. Margolin A, Califano A (2007) Theory and limitations of genetic network inference from microarray data. Ann N Y Acad Sci 1115:51–72
15. Meyer PE, Kontos K, Lafitte F, Bontempi G (2007) Information-theoretic inference of large transcriptional regulatory networks. EURASIP J Bioinform Syst Biol 2007:79879
16. Murali TM, Aluru S (2009) Algorithms and Theory of Computation Handbook, chapter Computational Systems Biology. Chapman & Hall/CRC, Boca Raton
17. Nikolova O, Zola J, Aluru S (2009) A parallel algorithm for exact Bayesian network inference. In IEEE Proceedings of the International Conference on High Performance Computing (HiPC 2009), pp 342–349
18. Ott S, Imoto S, Miyano S (2004) Finding optimal models for small gene networks. In Pacific Symposium on Biocomputing, pp 557–567
19. Prill RJ, Marbach D, Saez-Rodriguez J, Sorger PK, Alexopoulos LG, Xue X, Clarke ND, Altan-Bonnet G, Stolovitzky G (2010) Towards a rigorous assessment of systems biology models: the DREAM3 challenges. PLoS One 5(2):e9202
20. Schafer J, Strimmer K (2005) An empirical Bayes approach to inferring large-scale gene association networks. Bioinformatics 21(6):754–764
21. Yu J, Smith V, Wang PP, Hartemink AJ, Jarvis ED (2004) Advances to Bayesian network inference for generating causal networks from observational biological data. Bioinformatics 20(18):3594–3603
22. Zola J, Aluru M, Aluru S (2008) Parallel information theory based construction of gene regulatory networks. In Proceedings of the International Conference on High Performance Computing (HiPC 2008). LNCS, vol 5375, pp 336–349
23. Zola J, Aluru M, Sarje A, Aluru S (2010) Parallel information-theory-based construction of genome-wide gene regulatory networks. IEEE Trans Parallel Distributed Syst 21(12):1721–1733

Systolic Architecture

▶Systolic Arrays

Systolic Arrays

JAMES R. REINDERS
Intel Corporation, Hillsboro, OR, USA

Synonyms

Instruction systolic arrays; Processor arrays; Systolic architecture; Wavefront arrays

Definition

A *Systolic Array* is a collection of processing elements, called cells, that implements an algorithm by rhythmically computing and transmitting data from cell to cell using only local communication. Cells of a Systolic Array are arranged and connected in a regular pattern with a design that emphasizes a balance between computational and communicational capabilities. Systolic Arrays have proven particularly effective for real-time applications in signal and image processing.

Systolic Algorithms are algorithms specifically designed to make effective use of Systolic Arrays. Systolic Algorithms have also been shown to make particularly efficient use of many general-purpose parallel computers.

The name *Systolic Arrays* derives from an analogy with the regular pumping of blood by the heart. Systolic, in medical terms, refers to the phase of blood circulation in which the pumping chambers of the heart, ventricles, are contracting forcefully and therefore blood pressure is at its highest.

Discussion

Background: Motivated by Emergence of VLSI

Systolic Arrays, first described in 1978 by H. T. Kung and Charles E. Leiserson, were originally described as a systematic approach to take advantage of rapid advances in VLSI technology and coping with difficulties present in designing VLSI systems. The simplicity and regularity of Systolic Arrays lead to a cheaper VLSI implementation as well as higher chip density.

Systolic Arrays were originally proposed for VLSI implementation of some matrix operations that were shown to have efficient solutions thereafter known as Systolic Algorithms. Systolic Algorithms support high degrees of concurrency while requiring only simple, regular communication and control, which in turn allows for efficient implementation in hardware.

Early VLSI offered high degrees of integration but no speed advantage over the decade-old TTL technology. While tens of thousands of gates could be integrated on a single chip, it appeared that computational speed would only come from the concurrent use of many processing elements. In 1982, H. T. Kung wrote, "Since the technological trend clearly indicates a diminishing growth rate for component speed, any major improvement in computation speed must come from the concurrent use of many processing elements."

Furthermore, large-scale designs were pushing the limits of the methodologies of the day. It was observed at the time that the general practice of ad hoc designs for VLSI systems was not contributing to sufficient accumulation of experiences, and errors were often repeated. By providing general guidelines, the concept of a Systolic Array, a general methodology emerged for mapping high-level computations into hardware structures.

Cost-effectiveness emerged as a chief concern with special-purpose systems; costs need to be low enough to justify construction of any device with limited applicability. The cost of special-purpose systems can be greatly reduced if a limited number of simple substructures or building blocks, such as a cell, can be reused repeatedly for the overall design.

The VLSI implications of Systolic Array designs proved to be substantial. Spatial locality divides the time to design a chip by the degree of regularity. Locality avoids the need for long and therefore high capacitive wires, temporal regularity and synchrony reduces control issues, pipelinability yields performance, I/O closeness holds down I/O bandwidth, and modularity allows for parameterized designs.

Special-purpose systems pushed the limits of technology in order to achieve the performance needed to justify their cost. Systolic Arrays embraced VLSI circuit technology to achieve high performance via parallelism, honoring the scarcity of power and resistive delay by using a communication topology devoid of long inter-processor wires. Such communication topologies require chip area that is only linear in the number of processors. Systolic Arrays also embraced the design economics of special-purpose processors by reusing a limited number of cell designs.

Systolic Arrays proved especially well suited for processing data from sensor devices as an attached processor. Stringent time requirements of real-time signal processing and large-scale scientific computation strongly favor special-purpose devices that can be built in a cost-effective and reliable fashion because they deliver the performance needed.

Concept

Unlike general-purpose processors, a Systolic Array is characterized by its regular data flow. Typically, two or more data streams flow through a Systolic Array in various speeds and directions. The crux of the Systolic Array approach is that once a stream of data is formed, it can be used effectively by each processing element it passes. A higher computational throughput is therefore achieved as compared with a general-purpose processor in which its computational speed may be limited by the I/O bandwidth. When a complex algorithm can be decomposed to fine-grained, regular operations, each operation will then be simpler to implement.

A Systolic Array consists of a set of interconnected cells, each capable of performing at least simple computational operations, and communicating only with cells in close proximity. Simple, regular communication and control structures offer substantial advantages over complicated ones in both design and implementation. Many shapes for an "array" are possible, and have been proposed including triangular, but simple two-dimensional meshes, or tori, have dominated as Systolic Arrays have trended to become more general because of the flexibility and simplicity of meshes and tori (Fig. 1).

Systolic Arrays are specifically designed to address the communication requirements of parallel computer systems by placing an emphasis on strong connections between computation and communication in order to achieve both balance and scaling. Systolic Arrays directly address the importance of the communication system for scalable parallel systems by providing direct paths between the communication system and the computational units. Systolic Algorithms address the need for "balanced algorithms" to best utilize parallelism.

In a Systolic Array, data flows from the computer memory in a rhythmic fashion, passing through many processing cells before it returns to memory, much as blood circulates into and out of the heart. The system works like an assembly line where many people work on the same automobile at different times and many cars are assembled simultaneously. The network for the flow of data can offer different degrees of parallelism, and data flow itself may be at different speeds and multiple directions. Traditional pipelined systems flow only results, whereas a Systolic Array flow includes inputs and partial results.

The essential characteristic of a Systolic Array is an emphasis on balance between computational and communicational capabilities, and the scalability of practical parallel systems. The features of Systolic Arrays, in pursuit of this emphasis on balance and scalability, are generally as follows:

- Spatial regularity and locality: the variety of processing cells is limited, and connections are limited to nearby processors. Cells are not connected via shared busses, which would not scale due to contention. There is neither global broadcasting nor global memory.
- Temporal regularity and synchrony: each cell acts as a finite state transducer. Cells do not need to execute the same program.
- Pipelinability: a design of N cells will exhibit a linear speedup O(N).
- I/O closeness: only cells on the boundaries of the array have access to "the outside world" to perform I/O.
- Modularity/scaling: a larger array can handle a larger instance of a problem than the smaller version of which it is an extension. Replacing a processing cell with an array of cells offers a higher computation throughput without increasing memory bandwidth. This realization of parallelism offers the advantages

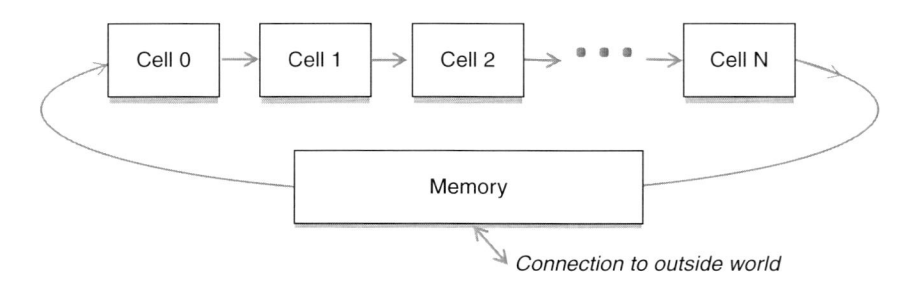

Systolic Arrays. Fig. 1 Simple linear systolic array configuration of both increased performance from increased concurrency and increased designer productivity from component reuse.

Synchronous global clocking is not a requirement of Systolic Arrays despite it being a property of many early implementations. Systolic Arrays are distinguished by their pursuit of both balance and scaling with a design emphasis on strong connections between computation and communication in order to achieve both.

Importance of Interconnect Design

A central issue for every parallel system is how the computational nodes of a parallel computer communicate with other nodes. There are problems that have been dubbed "embarrassingly parallel," where little or no communication is necessary between the multiple processors performing subsets of the problem. For those applications, the computation speed alone will determine the speed of execution on a parallel system. There are numerous important problems that are not embarrassingly parallel, in which communication plays a critical role in determining the effective speed of execution as well as the degree to which the problem can scale to utilize parallelism.

The exploration of "balanced algorithms" looked to find algorithms that scale without bounds. Such algorithms are marked by a constant ratio of computation to communication steps. These algorithms became known as "Systolic Algorithms." While Systolic Algorithms can be mapped to a wide range of hardware, it was found that these algorithms tended to rely on finer and finer-grained communication as machine sizes increased. To efficiently deal with this fine-grained parallelism, communication with little to no overhead is needed.

Systolic Arrays accomplish this goal by providing a method to directly couple computation to communication. In such machines, the design will seek to match the communicational capabilities to the computational capabilities of the machine.

Systolic Arrays are one approach to addressing the communication requirements of parallel systems. Systolic Arrays acknowledge the importance of the communication system for scalable parallel systems and provide direct paths between the communication system and the computational units. The key concepts behind a Systolic Array are the balance between computational and communicational capabilities, and the scalability of practical parallel systems. A balanced design minimizes inefficiencies as measured by underutilization of portions of a system due to stalls and bottlenecks. A scalable design allows for expanding performance by increasing the number of computational nodes in a system. Regularity, an often-noted characteristic of a Systolic Array, is a consequence of the scalability goal and not itself part of the definition of a Systolic Array. Another advantage of regularity is that the system can be scaled by repeating a common subsystem design, a benefit to designers that has reinforced use of regularity as a way to accomplish scalability.

The Systolic Array approach initially led to very rigidly synchronous hardware designs that, while elegant, proved overly constraining for many programming solutions. While balance is desirable, the tight coupling of systolic systems is not always desirable. Designs of more programmable Systolic Arrays worked to preserve the benefits of systolic communication while generalizing the framework to allow for more application diversity.

With tight coupling, any stall in communication will stall computation and vice versa. For many applications, a looser coupling that allowed coupling at a level of data blocks instead of individual data elements was advantageous. Looser coupling also leads to increased ability to overlap communication and computation in practice. As a result, the idea of Systolic Arrays evolved from an academic concept to realization in microprocessors such as the CMU/Intel iWarp.

Variations

Increasing the degree of independence of individual processors in an array adds complexity for flexibility and affects the efficiency and performance of an array. One design consideration is whether individual processors have a local control store or a design where instructions were delivered via the processor interconnects to be executed upon arrival. The latter was sometimes referred to as an Instruction Systolic Array (ISA). Synchronous broadcasting of instructions to an array, as opposed to the flow of instructions via the interconnect, would be inconsistent with the goals of Systolic Array designs because it would introduce long paths and the associated delays. Processors with individual control stores have been referred to as *programmable* Systolic Arrays, and therefore incur some overhead for the initial loading of the control stores.

As a design methodology for VLSI, silicon implementations were generally hard coded to a large degree once a design was determined. The resulting array performed a fixed function and offered no ability to be loaded with a new algorithm for other functions. Such designs could be optimized to offer the most efficient implementations with the least flexibility for future changes by customizing the cells and the connection networks. More flexible designs offered more design reuse, and thereby offered the opportunity to amortize development costs over multiple uses in exchange for some loss of efficiency, increase in silicon size and generally some loss of array performance.

The most flexible implementations of Systolic Arrays were machines developed principally for academic and research purposes to host the exploration and demonstration of Systolic Algorithms. The Warp and iWarp machines, developed under the guidance of H. T. Kung at Carnegie Mellon University, were such machines.

Systolic Algorithms

Systolic Arrays have garnered substantial attention in the development of Systolic Algorithms, which have proven to be efficient at creating solutions suited to the demands of real-time systems in terms of reliability and the ability to meet stringent time constraints. Development of error detections and fault tolerance in Systolic Algorithms has also received substantial attention.

Systolic Algorithms are among the most efficient class of algorithms for massively parallel implementation. A systolic algorithm can be thought of as having two major parts: a cell program and a data flow specification. The cell program defines the local operations of each processing element, while the data flow describes the communication network and its use (Fig. 2).

One nice property of a Systolic Algorithm is that each processor communicates only with a few other processors. It is thus suitable for implementation on a cluster of computers in which we seek to avoid costly global communication operations. Systolic Algorithms require preservation of data ordering within a stream but do not require that streams of data proceed in lockstep as they would have in the earliest hardware implementations of Systolic Arrays.

A Systolic Algorithm will make multiple uses of each input data item, make extensive use of concurrency, rely on only a few simple cell types, and utilize simple and regular data and control flows. Bottlenecks to computational speedups are often caused by limited system memory bandwidths, known as von Neumann bottlenecks, rather than limited processing capabilities (Fig. 3).

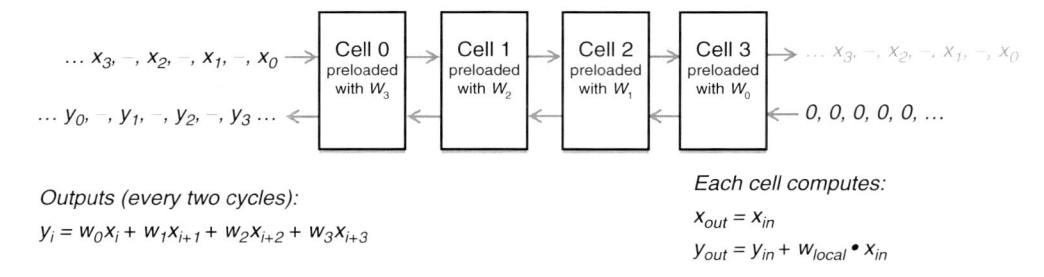

Systolic Arrays. Fig. 2 Systolic array implementation for a convolution product

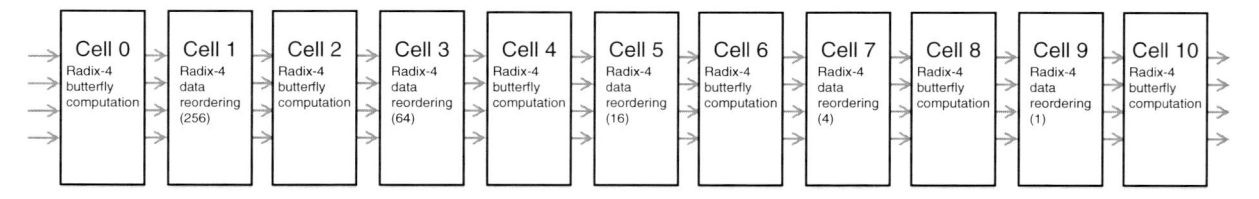

Outputs (every two cycles):
$y_i = w_0 x_i + w_1 x_{i+1} + w_2 x_{i+2} + w_3 x_{i+3}$

Each cell computes:
$x_{out} = x_{in}$
$y_{out} = y_{in} + w_{local} \cdot x_{in}$

Systolic Arrays. Fig. 3 Systolic array implementation for a 4096-point FFT

Systolic Algorithms have been shown to have wide applicability. They utilize a computational model for a wide range of parallel processing structures not limited to the initially targeted special-purpose needs, and which offer efficient operations on parallel computers in general, not just special-purpose designs. For instance, linear algebra algorithms and FFT algorithms are computationally demanding, especially when high throughput rates are expected, and they display a high degree of regularity. These algorithms are ideal candidates for parallel implementation via Systolic Algorithms.

Systolic Array Machines

The Colossus Mark II, built in 1944, has been cited as the first digital computer known to have used a technique similar to Systolic Arrays.

In 1978, H. T. Kung and Charles E. Leiserson published their concept of Systolic Arrays. They made systematic use of ideas that were already present in older architectural paradigms in order to respond to the new challenges posed by VLSI technology. This sparked much interest and many designs for Systolic Arrays. While there have been many designs, only a handful have been actually built and put into use. Here is a brief review of key systems in chronological order.

The earliest Systolic Arrays were introduced as a straightforward way to create scalable, balanced, systems for special-purpose computations, by directly embodying a systolic algorithm in the hardware design. These early Systolic Arrays were very limited in applications because the algorithm was expressed in efficient and special-purpose designs. Changing an algorithm implemented as a Systolic Array may be difficult or impossible without redesigning the hardware, particularly the communication interconnects. More general processors used in parallel have been shown to be able to perform a broad range of applications, but are often too large, too slow, or too expensive due to inefficiencies imposed by communication overhead.

Systolic Convolution Chip

The systolic convolution chip was created at CMU in 1979 to solve finite-sized two-dimensional convolutions. All nodes in a system performed the same operation while data flowed through the systems in a completely regular synchronous manner (Fig. 4).

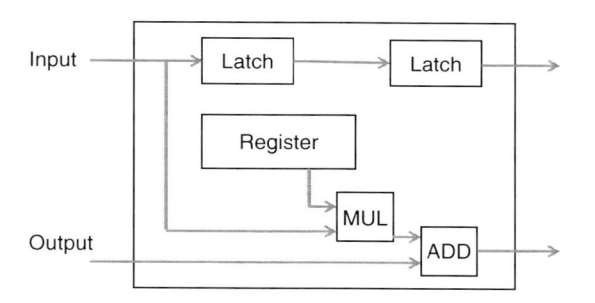

Systolic Arrays. Fig. 4 2-D convolution systolic system cell architecture

ESL Systolic Processor

A Systolic Array to compute convolutions and other signal processing computations was designed and implemented at ESL and operational by 1982. Seven nodes fit on a board measuring 37 cm by 40 cm using discrete high-performance components with each node capable of ten million operations per second. Up to five boards could be linked together in a system, which was attached to a VAX 11/780 host machine. Accessing the capabilities of the Systolic Array from a high-level language was a key innovation of this Systolic Array. A Fortran program viewed capabilities as a function to call with information on the kernel to execute the input data and where to store the output data. The ESL systolic processor was able to greatly expand the application domain for which it was suited by including local memory to hold more kernel elements and a control unit to create addresses to access data from memory. This systolic system could perform 1-D and 2-D convolutions, matrix multiplication, and Fourier and cosine transforms (Fig. 5).

NOSC Systolic Array Test Bed

A programmable Systolic Array, formed using standard off-the-shelf Intel 8051 microprocessors, was built by the Naval Ocean Systems Center (NOSC) from 1981 to 1983. The microprocessor operated as the control unit, while a separate arithmetic unit on the board consumed and output data. The arithmetic processor was directly connected to the communication ports so as to tightly link computations and communications. The NOSC test bed contained 64 nodes arranged in an 8×8 grid. Each node fits on a 6×24-cm board. Each node in the system is connected to five other nodes. The

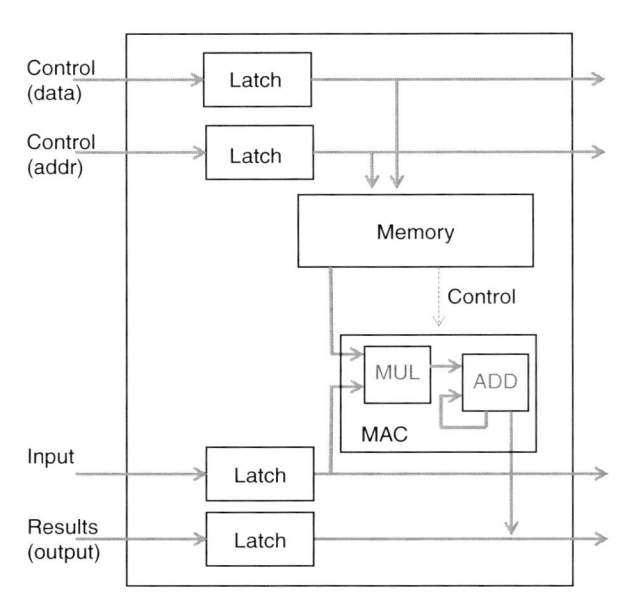

Systolic Arrays. Fig. 5 ESL systolic cell architecture

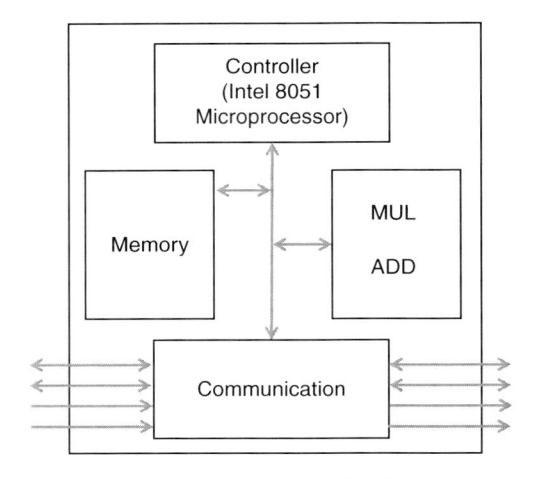

Systolic Arrays. Fig. 6 NOSC test bed cell architecture

topology allows for direct implementation of several key Systolic Algorithms such as matrix multiplication by a hexagonal array.

All programming was done in assembly language. Node performance was about 24 K FLOPs for a total performance of 1.5 MFlop for the system. The machine was a test bed for software development, and the design could not extend beyond 64 nodes. NOSC research into Systolic Arrays spanned a number of machines from 1979 to 1991 including the Systolic Array Processor (SAP), the Systolic Linear Algebra Parallel Processor (SLAPP), the Video Analysis Transputer Array (VATA), and the High-Speed Systolic Array Processor (HISSAP) test bed. Subsequent algorithm development moved to iWarp and on to general-purpose machines (Fig. 6).

Programmable Systolic Chip (PSC)

A programmable Systolic Array chip designed at CMU led to a functional nine-node system in 1984. The architecture of the PSC was similar to the NOSC Systolic Array but was organized around three buses instead of one, cells had three input and output ports to attach to other cells. All programming was in assembly language. The machine was used for low-level image processing computations (Fig. 7).

Geometric Arithmetic Processor (GAPP)

The NCR GAPP programmable Systolic Array is a mesh-connected single-bit cell that communicates directly with neighbors to the North, East, South, and West. It was first implemented as a medium-scale integration (MSI) breadboard in 1982 for a 6 × 12 cell array. GAPP I was a PLA-based 3 × 6 cell chip, GAPP II was a 6 × 12 cell in 3-^-m CMOS, and finally a version in two-micron CMOS clocked at 10 MHz with 30 MB/s input and 30 MB/s output bandwidth was sold as NCR45CG72 and could perform 28 million eight-bit additions per second. The use of one-bit data paths and one-bit registers minimize the size of a single cell. Local memory on a node was only 128 bits. The machine broadcast long instruction words to control the machine in pure lockstep SIMD. Programming was originally done in STOIC, a variant of Forth, but later development of an "Ada-like" language compiler eased programming to create important libraries of commonly used functions. VAX, IBM PC-AT, and Sun 3 workstation host support existed. Military and space systems leveraged GAPP for use in image processing, and the construction of the largest array of processing elements of their generation (82,944 processing cells in one system reported in 1988) (Fig. 8).

Warp and iWarp

The Warp project (1984–1993) was a series of increasingly general-purpose programmable Systolic Array

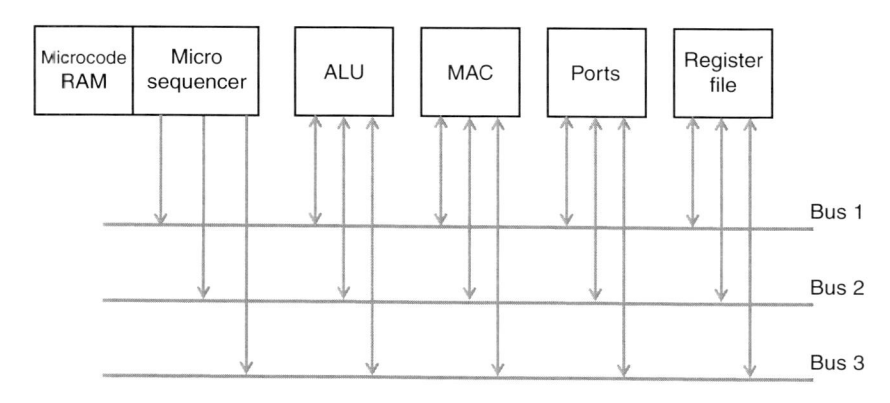

Systolic Arrays. Fig. 7 PSC cell architecture

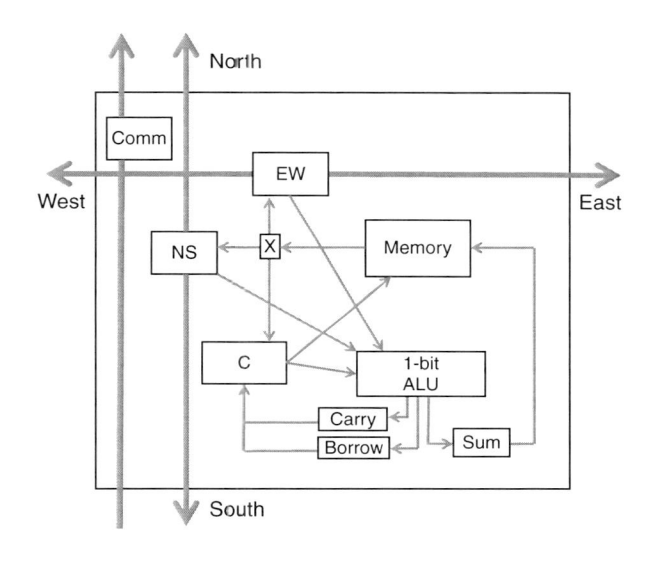

Systolic Arrays. Fig. 8 Geometric arithmetic cell architecture

systems and related software, created by Carnegie Mellon University (CMU) and developed in conjunction with industrial partners G.E., Honeywell, and Intel with funding from the US Defense Advanced Research Projects Agency (DARPA) (see Warp and iWarp). Warp was a highly programmable Systolic Array computer with a linear array of ten or more cells, capable of performing ten million single-precision floating-point operations per second (10 MFLOPS). A ten-cell machine had a peak performance of 100 MFLOPS. The iWarp machines doubled this performance, delivering 20 MFLOPS single-precision and supporting double-precision floating point at half the performance.

iWarp was based on a full custom VLSI component integrating a 700,000 transistor LIW microprocessor, a network interface, and a switching node into one single chip of $1.2 \times 1.2\ cm$ silicon. The processor dissipated up to 15 watts and was packaged in a ceramic pin grid array with 280 pins. Intel marketed the iWarp with the tag line "Building Blocks for GigaFLOPs." The standard iWarp machines configuration arranged iWarp nodes in a $2m \times 2n$ torus. All iWarp machines included the "back edges" and, therefore, were tori.

Warp and iWarp were programmed using high-level languages and domain-specific program generators. About 20 Warp machines were built, and more than 1,500 iWarp processors were manufactured. Warp and iWarp handled a large number of image and signal processing algorithms (Figs. 9 and 10).

Future Directions

Faced with relatively little growth in transistor speeds coupled with ever-expanding transistor densities in the late 1970s and early 1980s, the use of transistors for many forms for parallelism, from multiple cells to LIW, were urgently explored. Investigations in Systolic Arrays gave rise to fruitful exploration of Systolic Algorithms. Transistor speeds did finally explode, which helped divert interest from parallelism including Systolic Arrays and Systolic Algorithms.

By 2005, once again clock speed gains dramatically slowed, while transistor densities continued growing in accord with Moore's Law as much as they had at the dawn of VLSI. Hardware parallelism, this time as multicore processors, and parallel programming have

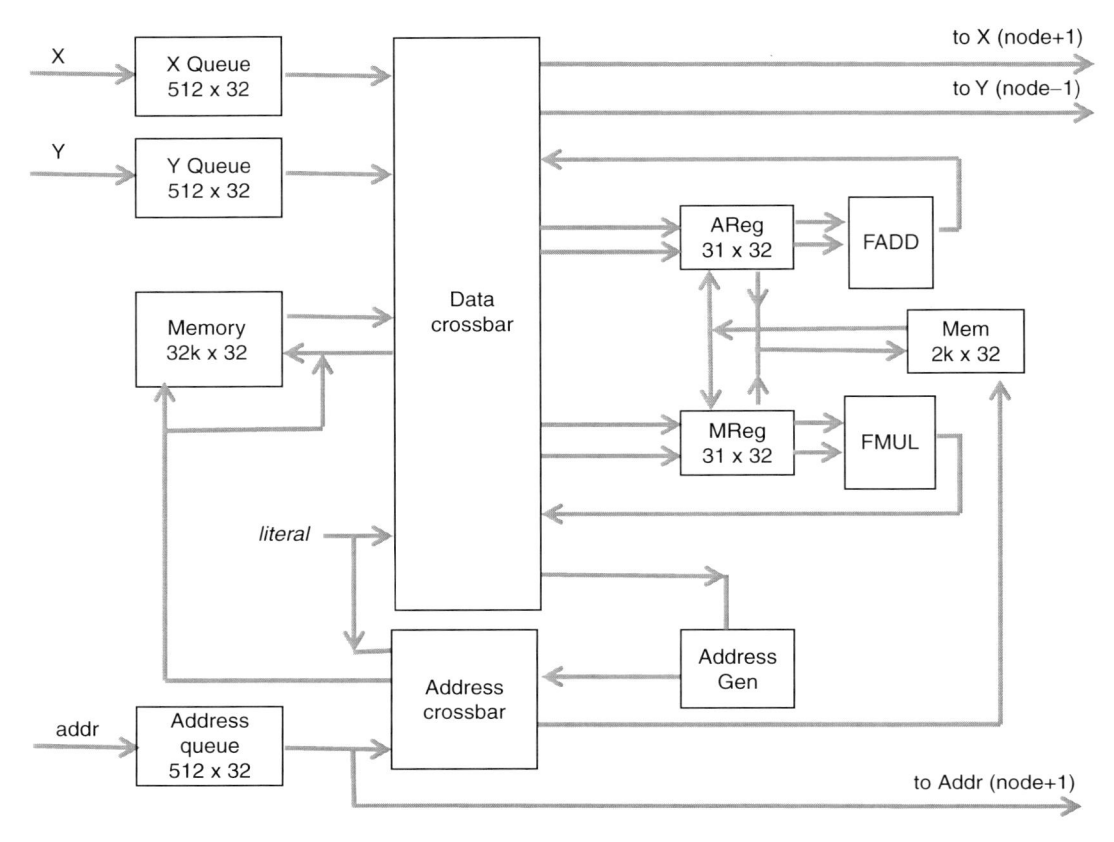

Systolic Arrays. Fig. 9 PC-warp cell architecture

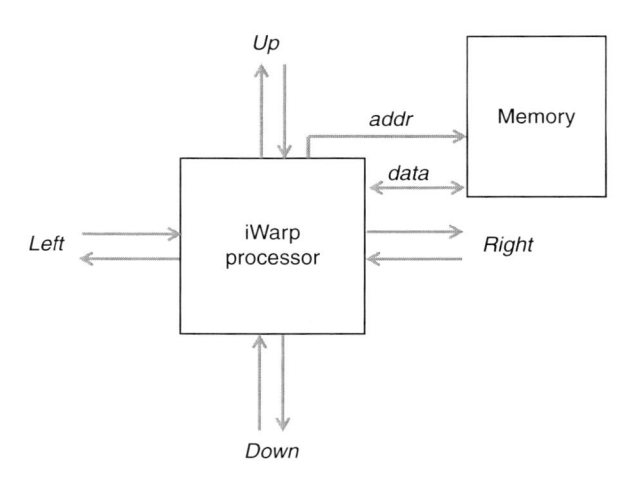

Systolic Arrays. Fig. 10 iWarp cell architecture

once again found widespread interest. Single processor designs have become the cells in multicore and many core processor designs, and interconnect debates are being revisited. Interconnection of many processor cores faces the same challenges Systolic Arrays worked to solve the first time the industry found transistor density on the rise without transistor performance moving nearly as quickly, and Systolic Algorithms proved their usefulness via programmability.

Related Entries
▶ VLIW Processors
▶ Warp and iWarp

Bibliographic Notes and Further Reading

Application-specific solutions, like the early Systolic Arrays, continue today in the annual *IEEE International Conference on Application-specific Systems, Architectures and Processors*. This conference traces its origins back to the International Workshop on Systolic Arrays, first organized in 1986. It later developed into the International Conference on Application-Specific

Array Processors. With its current title, it was organized for the first time in Chicago, USA, in 1996.

Systolic Arrays were first described in 1978 by H. T. Kung and Charles E. Leiserson [3, 4]. VLSI designs took serious note of the concept and the design principles [4, 6]. Digital systems operating in a synchronous fashion utilizing a central clock predated the description of Systolic Arrays and VLSI by many years, the earliest such machine has been cited as the Colossus [3] built in 1944. Additional reading about actual realizations of Systolic Arrays are available[1, 7–13].

Bibliography

1. Cloud EL (1988) Frontiers of massively parallel computation. In: Proceedings of the 2nd symposium on the frontiers of massively parallel computation. Fairfax, VA, pp 373–381
2. Cragon HG (2003) From fish to colossus: how the German Lorenz cipher was broken at Bletchley park. Cragon Books, Dallas, ISBN: 0-9743045-0-6
3. Frank GA, Greenawalt EM, Kulkarni AV (1982) A systolic processor for signal processing. In: Proceedings of AFIPS '82, June 7–10. ACM, New York, pp 225–231
4. Fisher AL, Kung HT, Monier LM, Dohi Y (1983) Architecture of the PSC: a programmable systolic chip. In: Proceedings of the 10th annual international symposium on computer architecture (ISCA '83), Stockholm, Sweden. ACM, New York, Vol 11, Issue 3, pp 48–53
5. Gross T, O'Hallaron DR (1998) iWarp: anatomy of a parallel computing system. MIT Press, Cambridge, MA, 488 p
6. Kung HT, Leiserson CE (1978) Systolic arrays (for VLSI). In: Duff IS, Stewart GW (eds) Proceedings of sparse matrix proceedings 1978. Society for Industrial and Applied Mathematics (SIAM), Philadelphia, PA, pp 256–282
7. Kung HT, Song SW (1981) A systolic 2-D convolution chip. In: Proceedings of 1981 IEEE computer society workshop on computer architecture for pattern analysis and image database management, 11–13 Nov 1981, Hot Springs, Virginia, pp 159–160
8. Kung HT (1982) Why systolic architectures? IEEE Comput 15(1):37–46
9. Kung SY (1988) VLSI array processors. Prentice Hall, Upper Saddle River
10. Mead C, Conway L (1980) Chap. 8, Highly concurrent systems. In: Introduction to VLSI systems. Addison-Westey series in computer science, Addison-Wesley, Menlo Park, CA, pp 263–332
11. Tirpak FM Jr (1991) Software development on the high-speed systolic array processor (HISSAP): lessons learned. Technical report 1429. Naval Ocean Systems Center, San Diego, CA

T

Task Graph Scheduling

YVES ROBERT
Ecole Normale Supérieure de Lyon, France

Synonyms
DAG scheduling; Workflow scheduling

Definition
Task Graph Scheduling is the activity that consists in mapping a task graph onto a target platform. The task graph represents the application: Nodes denote computational tasks, and edges model precedence constraints between tasks. For each task, an assignment (choose the processor that will execute the task) and a schedule (decide when to start the execution) are determined. The goal is to obtain an efficient execution of the application, which translates into optimizing some objective function, most usually the total execution time.

Discussion

Introduction
Task Graph Scheduling is the activity that consists in mapping a task graph onto a target platform. The task graph is given as input to the scheduler. Hence, scheduling algorithms are completely independent of models and methods used to derive task graphs. However, it is insightful to start with a discussion on how these task graphs are constructed.

Consider an application that is decomposed into a set of computational entities, called *tasks*. These tasks are linked by *precedence constraints*. For instance, if some task T produces some data that is used (read) by another tasks T', then the execution of T' cannot start before the completion of T. It is therefore natural to represent the application as a *task graph*: The task graph is a DAG (Directed Acyclic Graph), whose nodes are the tasks and whose edges are the precedence constraints between tasks.

The decomposition of the application into tasks is given to the scheduler as input. Note that the task graph may be directly provided by the user, but it can also be determined by some parallelizing compiler from the application program. Consider the following algorithm to solve the linear system $Ax = b$, where A is an $n \times n$ nonsingular lower triangular matrix and b is a vector with n components:

for $i = 1$ **to** n **do**
    Task $T_{i,i}$: $x_i \leftarrow b_i/a_{i,i}$
    for $j = i + 1$ **to** N **do**
        Task $T_{i,j}$: $b_j \leftarrow b_j - a_{j,i} \times x_i$
    end
end

For a given value of i, $1 \leq i \leq n$, each task $T_{i,*}$ represents some computations executed during the i-th iteration of the external loop. The computation of x_i is performed first (task $T_{i,i}$). Then, each component b_j of vector b such that $j > i$ is updated (task $T_{i,j}$). In the original sequential program, there is a total precedence order between tasks. Write $T <_{seq} T'$ if task T is executed before task T' in the sequential code. Then:

$$T_{1,1} <_{seq} T_{1,2} <_{seq} T_{1,3} <_{seq} \cdots <_{seq} T_{1,n} <_{seq}$$
$$T_{2,2} <_{seq} T_{2,3} <_{seq} \cdots <_{seq} T_{n,n}.$$

However, there are independent tasks that can be executed in parallel. Intuitively, independent tasks are tasks whose execution orders can be interchanged without modifying the result of the program execution. A necessary condition for tasks to be independent is that they do not update the same variable. They can read the same value, but they cannot write into the same memory location (otherwise there would be a race condition and the result would be nondeterministic). For instance, tasks $T_{1,2}$ and $T_{1,3}$ both read x_1 but modify distinct components of b, hence they are independent.

This notion of independence can be expressed more formally. Each task T has an input set $\text{In}(T)$ (read values) and an output set $\text{Out}(T)$ (written values). In the example, $\text{In}(T_{i,i}) = \{b_i, a_{i,i}\}$ and $\text{Out}(T_{i,i}) = \{x_i\}$. For $j > i$, $\text{In}(T_{i,j}) = \{b_j, a_{j,i}, x_i\}$ and $\text{Out}(T_{i,j}) = \{b_j\}$. Two tasks T and T' are not independent (write $T \bot T'$) if they share some written variable:

$$T \bot T' \Leftrightarrow \begin{cases} \text{In}(T) \cap \text{Out}(T') & \neq \emptyset \\ \text{or } \text{Out}(T) \cap \text{In}(T') & \neq \emptyset \\ \text{or } \text{Out}(T) \cap \text{Out}(T') & \neq \emptyset \end{cases}$$

For instance, tasks $T_{1,1}$ and $T_{1,2}$ are not independent because $\text{Out}(T_{1,1}) \cap \text{In}(T_{1,2}) = \{x_1\}$; therefore $T_{1,1} \bot T_{1,2}$. Similarly, $\text{Out}(T_{1,3}) \cap \text{Out}(T_{2,3}) = \{b_3\}$, and hence $T_{1,3}$ and $T_{2,3}$ are not independent; hence $T_{1,3} \bot T_{2,3}$.

Given the dependence relation $\bot$, a partial order $\prec$ can be extracted from the total order $\prec_{seq}$ induced by the sequential execution of the program. If two tasks T and T' are dependent, that is, $T \bot T'$, they are ordered according to the sequential execution: $T \prec T'$ if both $T \bot T'$ and $T \prec_{seq} T'$. The precedence relation $\prec$ represents the dependences that must be satisfied to preserve the semantics of the original program; if $T \prec T'$, then T was executed before T' in the sequential code, and it has to be executed before T' even if there are infinitely many resources, because T and T' share a written variable. In terms of order relations, $\prec$ is defined more accurately, as the transitive closure of the intersection of $\bot$ and $\prec_{seq}$, and captures the intrinsic sequentiality of the original program. Note that transitive closure is needed to track dependence chains. In the example, $T_{2,4} \bot T_{4,4}$ and $T_{4,4} \bot T_{4,5}$, hence a path of dependences from $T_{2,4}$ to $T_{4,5}$, while $T_{2,4} \bot T_{4,5}$ does not hold.

A directed graph is drawn to represent the dependence constraints that need to be enforced. The vertices of the graph denote the tasks, while the edges express the dependence constraints. An edge $e : T \rightarrow T'$ in the graph means that the execution of T' must begin only after the end of the execution of T, whatever the number of available processors. Transitivity edges are not drawn, as they represent redundant information; only predecessor edges are shown. T is a predecessor of T' if $T \prec T'$ and if there is no task T'' in between, that is, such that $T \prec T''$ and $T'' \prec T'$. In the example, predecessor relationships are as follows (see Fig. 1):

- $T_{i,i} \prec T_{i,j}$ for $1 \leq i < j \leq n$
  (the computation of x_i must be done before updating b_j at step i of the outer loop).
- $T_{i,j} \prec T_{i+1,j}$ for $1 \leq i < j \leq n$
  (updating b_j at step i of the outer loop is done before reading it at step $i + 1$).

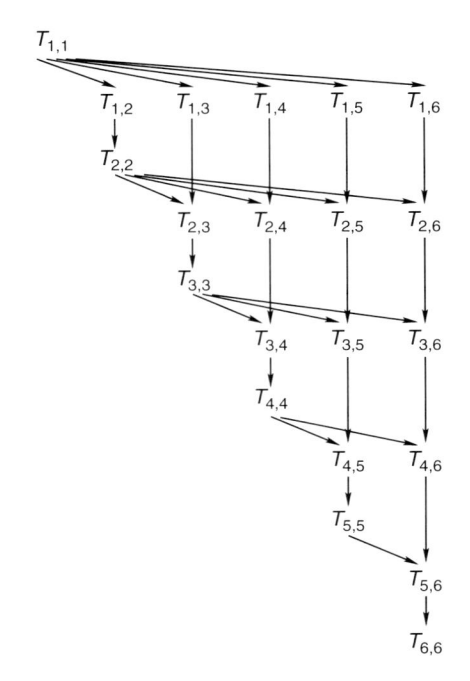

Task Graph Scheduling. Fig. 1 Task graph for the triangular system ($n = 6$)

In summary, this example shows how an application program can be decomposed into a task graph, either manually by the user, or with the help of a parallelizing compiler.

Fundamental Results

Traditional scheduling assumes that the target platform is a set of p identical processors, and that no communication cost is paid. Fundamental results are presented in this section, but only two proofs are provided, that of Theorem 1, an easy result on the efficiency of a schedule, and that of Theorem 4, Graham's bound on list scheduling.

Definitions

Definition 1 *A task graph is a directed acyclic vertex-weighted graph $G = (V, E, w)$, where:*

- *The set V of vertices represents the tasks (note that V is finite).*
- *The set E of edges represents precedence constraints between tasks:*
  $e = (u, v) \in E$ *if and only if* $u < v$.
- *The weight function $w : V \longrightarrow \mathbb{N}^*$ gives the weight (or duration) of each task. Task weights are assumed to be positive integers.*

For the triangular system (Fig. 1), it can be assumed that all tasks have equal weight: $w(T_{i,j}) = 1$ for $1 \leq i \leq j \leq n$. On a contrary, a division could be considered as more costly than a multiply-add, leading to a larger weight for diagonal tasks $T_{i,i}$.

A schedule σ of a task graph is a function that assigns a start time to each task.

Definition 2 *A schedule of a task graph $G = (V, E, w)$ is a function $\sigma : V \longrightarrow \mathbb{N}^*$ such that $\sigma(u) + w(u) \leq \sigma(v)$ whenever $e = (u, v) \in E$.*

In other words, a schedule must preserve the *dependence constraints* induced by the precedence relation $<$ and embodied by the edges of the dependence graph; if $u < v$, then the execution of u begins at time $\sigma(u)$ and requires $w(u)$ units of time, and the execution of v at time $\sigma(v)$ must start after the end of the execution of u. Obviously, if there was a cycle in the task graph, no schedule could exist, hence the restriction to acyclic graphs (DAGs).

There are other constraints that must be met by schedules, namely, *resource constraints*. When there is an infinite number of processors (in fact, when there are as many processors as tasks), the problem is *with unlimited processors*, and denoted $Pb(\infty)$. When there is only a fixed number p of available processors, the problem is *with limited processors*, and denoted $Pb(p)$. In the latter case, an allocation function $\text{alloc} : V \longrightarrow \mathcal{P}$ is required, where $\mathcal{P} = \{1, \ldots, p\}$ denotes the set of available processors. This function assigns a target processor to each task. The resource constraints simply specify that no processor can be allocated more than one task at the same time. This translates into the following conditions:

$$\text{alloc}(T) = \text{alloc}(T') \Rightarrow \begin{cases} \sigma(T) + w(T) \leq \sigma(T') \\ \text{or } \sigma(T') + w(T') \leq \sigma(T). \end{cases}$$

This condition expresses the fact that if two tasks T and T' are allocated to the same processor, then their executions cannot overlap in time.

Definition 3 *Let $G = (V, E, w)$ be a task graph.*

1. *Let σ be a schedule for G. Assume σ uses at most p processors (let $p = \infty$ if the processors are unlimited). The makespan $MS(\sigma, p)$ of σ is its total execution time:*

$$MS(\sigma, p) = \max_{v \in V}\{\sigma(v) + w(v)\} - \min_{v \in V}\{\sigma(v)\}.$$

2. *$Pb(p)$ is the problem of determining a schedule σ of minimal makespan $MS(\sigma, p)$ assuming p processors (let $p = \infty$ if the processors are unlimited). Let $MS_{opt}(p)$ be the value of the makespan of an optimal schedule with p processors:*

$$MS_{opt}(p) = \min_{\sigma} MS(\sigma, p).$$

If the first task is scheduled at time 0, which is a common assumption, the expression of the makespan can be reduced to $MS(\sigma, p) = \max_{v \in V}\{\sigma(v) + w(v)\}$. Weights extend to paths in G as usual; if $\Phi = (T_1, T_2, \ldots, T_n)$ denotes a path in G, then $w(\Phi) = \sum_{i=1}^{n} w(T_i)$. Because schedules respect dependences, the following easy bound on the makespan is readily obtained:

Proposition 1 *Let $G = (V, E, w)$ be a task graph and σ a schedule for G with p processors. Then, $MS(\sigma, p) \geq w(\Phi)$ for all paths Φ in G.*

The last definition introduces the notions of speedup and efficiency for schedules.

Definition 4 *Let $G = (V, E, w)$ be a task graph and σ a schedule for G with p processors:*

1. *The speedup is the ratio $s(\sigma, p) = \frac{Seq}{MS(\sigma, p)}$, where $Seq = \sum_{v \in V} w(v)$ is the sum of all task weights (Seq is the optimal execution time $MS_{opt}(1)$ of a schedule with a single processor).*
2. *The efficiency is the ratio $e(\sigma, p) = \frac{s(\sigma, p)}{p} = \frac{Seq}{p \times MS(\sigma, p)}$.*

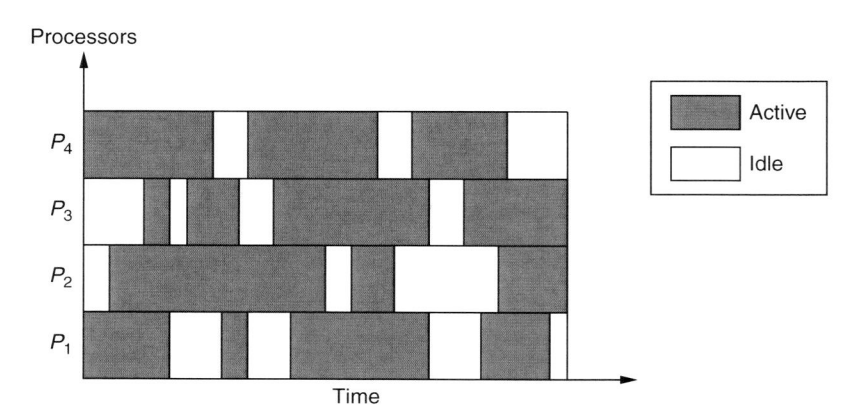

Task Graph Scheduling. Fig. 2 Active and idle processors during execution

Theorem 1 *Let $G = (V, E, w)$ be a task graph. For any schedule σ with p processors,*

$$0 \leq e(\sigma, p) \leq 1.$$

Proof Consider the execution of σ as illustrated in Fig. 2 (this is a fictitious example, not related to the triangular system example). At any time during execution, some processors are active, and some are idle. At the end, all tasks have been processed. Let Idle denote the cumulated idle time of the p processors during the whole execution. Because Seq is the sum of all task weights, the quantity Seq + Idle is equal to the area of the rectangle in Fig. 2, that is, the product of the number of processors by the makespan of the schedule: Seq + Idle = $p \times \text{MS}(\sigma, p)$. Hence, $e(\sigma, p) = \frac{\text{Seq}}{p \times \text{MS}(\sigma, p)} \leq 1$. □

Solving Pb(∞)

Let $G = (V, E, w)$ be a given task graph and assume unlimited processors. Remember that a schedule σ for G is said to be *optimal* if its makespan $\text{MS}(\sigma, \infty)$ is minimal, that is, if $\text{MS}(\sigma, \infty) = \text{MS}_{opt}(\infty)$.

Definition 5 *Let $G = (V, E, w)$ be a task graph.*

1. *For $v \in V$, $PRED(v)$ denotes the set of all immediate predecessors of v, and $SUCC(v)$ the set of all its immediate successors.*
2. *$v \in V$ is an entry (top) vertex if and only if $PRED(v) = \emptyset$.*
3. *$v \in V$ is an exit (bottom) vertex if and only if $SUCC(v) = \emptyset$.*
4. *For $v \in V$, the top level $tl(v)$ is the largest weight of a path from an entry vertex to v, excluding the weight of v.*
5. *For $v \in V$, the bottom level $bl(v)$ is the largest weight of a path from v to an output vertex, including the weight of v.*

In the example of the triangular system, there is a single entry vertex, $T_{1,1}$, and a single exit vertex, $T_{n,n}$. The top level of $T_{1,1}$ is 0, and $tl(T_{1,2}) = tl(T_{1,1}) + w(T_{1,1}) = 1$. The value of $T_{2,3}$ is

$$tl(T_{2,3}) = \max\{w(T_{1,1}) + w(T_{1,2}) + w(T_{2,2}), w(T_{1,1}) + w(T_{1,3})\} = 3$$

because there are two paths from the entry vertex to $T_{2,3}$.

The top level of a vertex can be computed by a traversal of the DAG; the top level of an entry vertex is 0, while the top level of a non-entry vertex v is

$$tl(v) = \max\{tl(u) + w(u); u \in PRED(v)\}.$$

Similarly, $bl(v) = \max\{bl(u); u \in SUCC(v)\} + w(v)$ (and $bl(v) = w(v)$ for an exit vertex v). The top level of a vertex is the earliest possible time at which it can be executed, while its bottom level represents a lower bound of the remaining execution time once starting its execution. This can be stated more formally as follows.

Theorem 2 *Let $G = (V, E, w)$ be a task graph and define σ_{free} as follows:*

$$\forall v \in V, \ \sigma_{free}(v) = tl(v).$$

Then, σ_{free} is an optimal schedule for G.

From Theorem 2:

$$\text{MS}_{opt}(\infty) = \text{MS}(\sigma_{free}, \infty) = \max_{v \in V}\{tl(v) + w(v)\}.$$

Hence, $\text{MS}_{opt}(\infty)$ is simply the maximal weight of a path in the graph. Note that σ_{free} is not the only optimal schedule.

Corollary 1 *Let $G = (V, E, w)$ be a directed acyclic graph. $Pb(\infty)$ can be solved in time $O(|V| + |E|)$.*

Going back to the triangular system (Fig. 1), because all tasks have weight 1, the weight of a path is equal to its length plus 1. The longest path is

$$T_{1,1} \to T_{1,2} \to T_{2,2} \to \cdots \to T_{n-1,n-1} \to T_{n,-1,n} \to T_{n,n},$$

whose weight is $2n - 1$. Not as many processors as tasks are needed to achieve execution within $2n-1$ time units. For example, only $n - 1$ processors can be used. Let $1 \leq i \leq n$; at time $2i - 2$, processor P_1 starts the execution of task $T_{i,i}$, while at time $2i - 1$, the first $n - i$ processors P_1, P_2, ..., P_{n-i} execute tasks $T_{i,j}$, $i + 1 \leq j \leq n$.

NP-completeness of Pb(p)

Definition 6 *The decision problem $Dec(p)$ associated with $Pb(p)$ is as follows. Given a task graph $G = (V, E, w)$, a number of processors $p \geq 1$, and an execution bound $K \in \mathbb{N}^*$, does there exist a schedule σ for G using at most p processors, such that $MS(\sigma, p) \leq K$? The restriction of $Dec(p)$ to independent tasks (no dependence, that is, when $E = \emptyset$) is denoted Indep-tasks(p). In both problems, p is arbitrary (it is part of the problem instance). When p is fixed a priori, say $p = 2$, problems are denoted as $Dec(2)$ and Indep-tasks(2).*

Well-known complexity results are summarized in the following theorem.

Theorem 3
- *Indep-tasks(2) is NP-complete but can be solved by a pseudo-polynomial algorithm. Moreover, $\forall \varepsilon > 0$, Indep-tasks(2) admits a $(1+\varepsilon)$-approximation whose complexity is polynomial in $\frac{1}{\varepsilon}$.*
- *Indep-tasks(p) is NP-complete in the strong sense.*
- *$Dec(2)$ (and hence $Dec(p)$) is NP-complete in the strong sense.*

List Scheduling Heuristics

Because $Pb(p)$ is NP-complete, heuristics are used to schedule task graphs with limited processors. The most natural idea is to use greedy strategies: At each instant, try to schedule as many tasks as possible onto available processors. Such strategies deciding *not to deliberately keep a processor idle* are called *list scheduling* algorithms. Of course, there are different possible strategies to decide which tasks are given priority in the (frequent) case where there are more free tasks than available processors. But a key result due to Graham [10] is that any list algorithm can be shown to achieve at most twice the optimal makespan.

Definition 7 *Let $G = (V, E, w)$ be a task graph and let σ be a schedule for G. A task $v \in V$ is free at time t (note $v \in FREE(\sigma, t)$) if and only if its execution has not yet started ($\sigma(v) \geq t$) but all its predecessors have been executed ($\forall u \in PRED(v)$, $\sigma(u) + w(u) \leq t$).*

A list schedule is a schedule such that no processor is deliberately left idle; at each time t, if $|FREE(\sigma, t)| = r \geq 1$, and if q processors are available, then $\min(r, q)$ free tasks start executing.

Theorem 4 *Let $G = (V, E, w)$ be a task graph and assume there are p available processors. Let σ be any list schedule of G. Let $MS_{opt}(p)$ be the makespan of an optimal schedule. Then,*

$$MS(\sigma, p) \leq \left(2 - \frac{1}{p}\right) MS_{opt}(p).$$

It is important to point out that Theorem 4 holds for *any* list schedule, regardless of the strategy to choose among free tasks when there are more free tasks than available processors.

Lemma 1 *There exists a dependence path Φ in G whose weight $w(\Phi)$ satisfies*

$$Idle \leq (p - 1) \times w(\Phi),$$

where Idle is the cumulated idle time of the p processors during the whole execution of the list schedule.

Proof Define the ancestors of a task are its predecessors, the predecessors of its predecessors, and so on. Let T_{i_1} be a task whose execution terminates at the end of the schedule:

$$\sigma(T_{i_1}) + w(T_{i_1}) = MS(\sigma, p).$$

Let t_1 be the largest time smaller than $\sigma(T_{i_1})$ and such that there exists an idle processor during the time interval $[t_1, t_1 + 1]$ (let $t_1 = 0$ if such a time does not exist).

Why is this processor idle? Because σ is a list schedule, no task is free at t_1, otherwise the idle processor would start executing a free task. Therefore, there must be a task T_{i_2} that is an ancestor of T_{i_1} and that is being executed at time t_1; otherwise T_{i_1} would have been started at time t_1 by the idle processor. Because of the definition of t_1, it is known that all processors are active between the end of the execution of T_{i_2} and the beginning of the execution of T_{i_1}.

Then, start the construction again from T_{i_2} so as to obtain a task T_{i_3} such that all processors are active between the end of T_{i_3} and the beginning of T_{i_2}. Iterating the process, one ends up with r tasks $T_{i_r}, T_{i_{r-1}}, \ldots, T_{i_1}$ that belong to a dependence path Φ of G and such that all processors are active except perhaps during their execution. In other words, the idleness of some processors can only occur during the execution of these r tasks, during which at least one processor is active (the one that executes the task). Hence, Idle $\leq (p-1) \times \sum_{j=1}^{r} w(T_{i_j}) \leq (p-1) \times w(\Phi)$. □

Proof Going back to the proof of Theorem 4, recall that $p \times \mathrm{MS}(\sigma, p) = \mathrm{Idle} + \mathrm{Seq}$, where $\mathrm{Seq} = \sum_{v \in V} w(v)$ is the sequential time, that is, the sum of all task weights (see Fig. 2). Now take the dependence path Φ constructed in Lemma 1: $w(\Phi) \leq \mathrm{MS}_{opt}(p)$, because the makespan of any schedule is greater than the weight of all dependence paths in G (simply because dependence constraints are met). Furthermore, $\mathrm{Seq} \leq p \times \mathrm{MS}_{opt}(p)$ (with equality only if all p processors are active all the time). Putting this together:

$$p \times \mathrm{MS}(\sigma, p) = \mathrm{Idle} + \mathrm{Seq} \leq (p-1)w(\Phi) + \mathrm{Seq}$$
$$\leq (p-1)\mathrm{MS}_{opt}(p) + p\mathrm{MS}_{opt}(p)$$
$$= (2p-1)\mathrm{MS}_{opt}(p),$$

which proves the theorem. □

Fundamentally, Theorem 4 says that any list schedule is within 50% of the optimum. Therefore, list scheduling is guaranteed to achieve half the best possible performance, regardless of the strategy to choose among free tasks.

Proposition 2 *Let $\mathrm{MS}_{list}(p)$ be the shortest possible makespan produced by a list scheduling algorithm.*

The bound

$$\mathrm{MS}_{list}(p) \leq \frac{2p-1}{p} \mathrm{MS}_{opt}(p)$$

is tight.

Note that implementing a list scheduling algorithm is not difficult, but it is somewhat lengthy to describe in full detail; see Casanova et al. [3].

Critical Path Scheduling

A widely used list scheduling technique is *critical path scheduling*. The selection criterion for free tasks is based on the value of their bottom level. Intuitively, the larger the bottom level, the more "urgent" the task. The *critical path* of a task is defined as its bottom level and is used to assign priority levels to tasks. Critical path scheduling is list scheduling where the priority level of a task is given by the value of its critical path. Ties are broken arbitrarily.

Consider the task graph shown in Fig. 3. There are eight tasks, whose weights and critical paths are listed in Table 1. Assume there are $p = 3$ available processors and let Q be the priority queue of free tasks. At $t = 0$, Q is initialized as $Q = (T_3, T_2, T_1)$. These three tasks are executed. At $t = 1$, T_8 is added to the queue: $Q = (T_8)$. There is one processor available, which starts the execution of T_8. At $t = 2$, the four successors of T_2 are added to the queue: $Q = (T_5, T_6, T_4, T_7)$. Note that ties have been broken arbitrarily (using task indices in this case). The available processor picks the first task T_5 in Q. Following this scheme, the execution goes on up to $t = 10$, as summarized in Fig. 4.

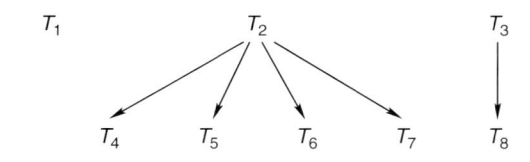

Task Graph Scheduling. Fig. 3 A small example

Task Graph Scheduling. Table 1 Weights and critical paths for the task graph in Fig. 3

Tasks	T_1	T_2	T_3	T_4	T_5	T_6	T_7	T_8
Weights	3	2	1	3	4	4	3	6
Critical paths	3	6	7	3	4	4	3	6

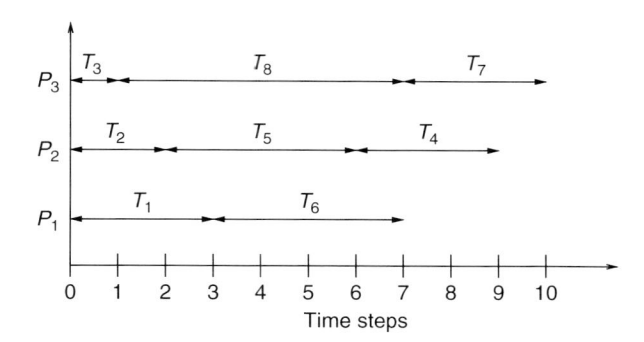

Task Graph Scheduling. Fig. 4 Critical path schedule for the example in Fig. 3

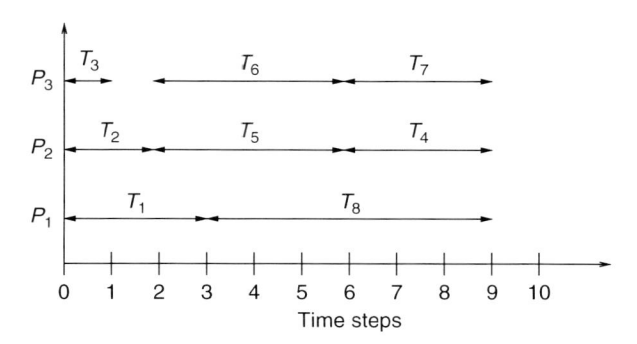

Task Graph Scheduling. Fig. 5 Optimal schedule for the example in Fig. 3

Note that it is possible to schedule the graph in only 9 time units, as shown in Fig. 5. The trick is to leave a processor idle at time $t = 1$ deliberately; although it has the highest critical path, T_8 can be delayed by two time units. T_5 and T_6 are given preference to achieve a better load balance between processors. The schedule shown in Fig. 5 is optimal, because Seq = 26, so that three processors require at least $\left\lceil \frac{26}{3} \right\rceil = 9$ time units. This small example illustrates the difficulty of scheduling with a limited number of processors.

Taking Communication Costs into Account

The Macro-Dataflow Model

Thirty years ago, communication costs have been introduced in the scheduling literature. Because the performance of network communication is difficult to model in a way that is both precise and conducive to understanding the performance of algorithms, the vast majority of results hold for a very simple model, which is as follows.

The target platform consists of p identical processors that are part of of a fully connected clique. All interconnection links have same bandwidth. If a task T communicates data to a successor task T', the cost is modeled as

$$\text{cost}(T, T') = \begin{cases} 0 & \text{if } \mathsf{alloc}(T) = \mathsf{alloc}(T') \\ c(T, T') & \text{otherwise,} \end{cases}$$

where $\mathsf{alloc}(T)$ denotes the processor that executes task T, and $c(T, T')$ is defined by the application specification. The time for communication between two tasks running on the same processor is negligible. This so-called *macro-dataflow* model makes two main assumptions: (i) communication can occur as soon as data are available and (ii) there is no contention for network links. Assumption (i) is reasonable as communication can overlap with (independent) computations in most modern computers. Assumption (ii) is much more questionable. Indeed, there is no physical device capable of sending, say, 1,000 messages to 1,000 distinct processors, at the same speed as if there were a single message. In the worst case, it would take 1,000 times longer (serializing all messages). In the best case, the output bandwidth of the network card of the sender would be a limiting factor. In other words, assumption (ii) amounts to assuming infinite network resources. Nevertheless, this assumption is omnipresent in the traditional scheduling literature.

Definition 8 *A communication task graph (or commTG) is a direct acyclic graph $G = (V, E, w, c)$, where vertices represent tasks and edges represent precedence constraints. The computation weight function is $w : V \longrightarrow \mathbb{N}^*$ and the communication cost function is $c : E \longrightarrow \mathbb{N}^*$. A schedule σ must preserve dependences, which is written as*

$$\forall e = (T, T') \in E, \begin{cases} \sigma(T) + w(T) \leq \sigma(T') \\ \qquad \text{if } \mathsf{alloc}(T) = \mathsf{alloc}(T') \\ \sigma(T) + w(T) + c(T, T') \leq \sigma(T') \\ \qquad \text{otherwise.} \end{cases}$$

The expression of resource constraints is the same as in the no-communication case.

Complexity and List Heuristics with Communications

Including communication costs in the model makes everything difficult, including solving Pb(∞). The intuitive reason is that a trade-off must be found between allocating tasks to either many processors (hence balancing the load but communicating intensively) or few processors (leading to less communication but less parallelism as well). Here is a small example, borrowed from [9].

Consider the commTG in Fig. 6. Task weights are indicated close to the tasks within parentheses, and communication costs are shown along the edges, underlined. For the sake of this example, two non-integer communication costs are used: $c(T_4, T_6) = c(T_5, T_6) = 1.5$. Of course, every weight w and cost c could be scaled to have only integer values. Observe the following:

- On the one hand, if all tasks are assigned to the same processor, the makespan will be equal to the sum of all task weights, that is, 13.
- On the other hand, with unlimited processors (no more than seven processors are needed because there are seven tasks), each task can be assigned to a different processor. Then, the makespan of the ASAP schedule is equal to 14. To see this, it is important to point out that once the allocation of tasks to processors is given, the makespan is computed easily: For each edge $e : T \to T'$, add a virtual node of weight $c(T, T')$ if the edge links two different processors ($\mathsf{alloc}(T) \neq \mathsf{alloc}(T')$), and do nothing otherwise. Then, consider the new graph as a DAG (without communications) and traverse it to compute the length of the longest path. Here, because all tasks are allocated to different processors, a virtual node is added on each edge. The longest path is $T_1 \to T_2 \to T_7$, whose length is $w(T_1) + c(T_1, T_2) + w(T_2) + c(T_2, T_7) + w(T_7) = 14$.

There is a difficult trade-off between executing tasks in parallel (hence with several distinct processors) and minimizing communication costs. In the example, it turns out that the best solution is to use two processors, according to the schedule in Fig. 7, whose makespan is equal to 9. Using more processors does not always lead to a shorter execution time. Note that dependence constraints are satisfied in Fig. 7. For example, T_2 can start at time 1 on processor P_1 because this processor executes T_1, hence there is no need to pay the communication cost $c(T_1, T_2)$. By contrast, T_3 is executed on processor P_2, hence it cannot be started before time 2 even though P_2 is idle: $\sigma(T_1) + w(T_1) + c(T_1, T_3) = 0 + 1 + 1 = 2$.

With unlimited processors, the optimization problem becomes difficult: Pb(∞) is NP-complete in the strong sense. Even the problem in which all task weights and communication costs have the same (unit) value, the so-called UET-UCT problem (unit execution time-unit communication time), is NP-hard [13].

With limited processors, list heuristics can be extended to take communication costs into account, but Graham's bound does not hold any longer. For instance, the *Modified Critical Path (MCP)* algorithm proceeds as follows. First, bottom levels are computed using a pessimistic evaluation of the longest path, accounting for each potential communication (this corresponds to the allocation where there is a different processor per task).

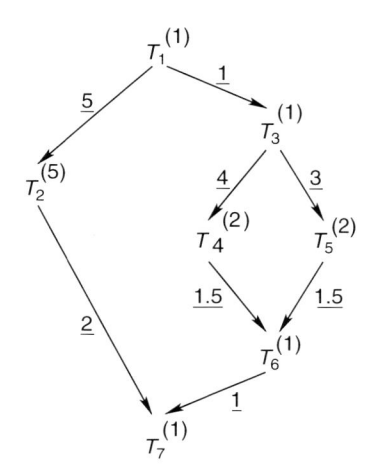

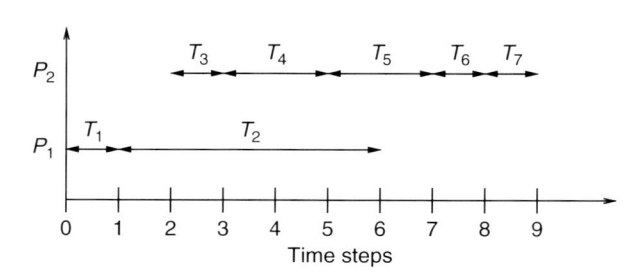

Task Graph Scheduling. Fig. 6 An example commTG

Task Graph Scheduling. Fig. 7 An optimal schedule for the example

These bottom levels are used to determine the priority of free tasks. Then each free task is assigned to the processor that allows its earliest execution, given previous task allocation decisions. It is important to explain further what "previous task allocation decisions" means. Free tasks from the queue are processed one after the other. At any moment, it is known which processors are available and which ones are busy. Moreover, for the busy processors, it is known when they will finish computing their currently allocated tasks. Hence, it is always possible to select the processor that can begin executing the task soonest. It may well be the case that a currently busy processor is selected.

Extension to Heterogeneous Platforms

This section explains how to extend list scheduling techniques to heterogeneous platforms, that is, to platforms that consist of processors with different speeds and interconnection links with different bandwidths. Key differences with the homogeneous case are outlined.

Given a commTG with n tasks $T_1, \ldots, T_n$, the goal is to schedule it on a platform with p heterogeneous processors $P_1, \ldots, P_p$. There are now many parameters to instantiate:

- **Computation costs**: The execution cost of T_i on P_q is modeled as w_{iq}. Therefore, an $n \times p$ matrix of values is needed to specify all computation costs. This matrix comes directly for the specific scheduling problem at hand. However, when attempting to evaluate competing scheduling heuristics over a large number of synthetic scenarios, one must generate this matrix. One can distinguish two approaches. In the first approach one generates a *consistent* (or *uniform*) matrix with $w_{iq} = w_i \times \gamma_q$, where w_i represents the number of operations required by T_i and γ_q is the inverse of the speed of P_q (in operations per second). With this definition the relative speed of the processors does not depend on the particular task they execute. If instead some processors are faster for some tasks than some other processors, but slower for other tasks, one speaks of an *inconsistent* (or *nonuniform*) matrix. This corresponds to the case in which some processors are specialized for some tasks (e.g., specialized hardware or software).
- **Communication costs**: Just as processors have different speeds, communication links may have different bandwidths. However, while the speed of a processor may depend upon the nature of the computation it performs, the bandwidth of a link does not depend on the nature of the bytes it transmits. It is therefore natural to assume *consistent* (or *uniform*) links. If there is a dependence $e_{ij} : T_i \to T_j$, if T_i is executed on P_q and T_j executed on P_r, then the communication time is modeled as

$$\text{comm}(i,j,q,r) = \text{data}(i,j) \times v_{qr},$$

where $\text{data}(i,j)$ is the data volume associated to e_{ij} and v_{qr} is the communication time for a unit-size message from P_q to P_r (i.e., the inverse of the bandwidth). Like in the homogeneous case, let $v_{qr} = 0$ if $q = r$, that is, if both tasks are assigned the same processor. If one wishes to generate synthetic scenarios to evaluate competing scheduling heuristics, one then must generate two matrices: one of size $n \times n$ for data and one of size $p \times p$ for v_{qr}.

The main list scheduling principle is unchanged. As before, the priority of each task needs to be computed, so as to decide which one to execute first when there are more free tasks than available processors. The most natural idea is to compute averages of computation and communication times, and use these to compute priority levels exactly as in the homogeneous case:

- $\overline{w_i} = \frac{\sum_{q=1}^{p} w_{iq}}{p}$, the *average* execution time of T_i.
- $\overline{\text{comm}_{ij}} = \text{data}(i,j) \times \frac{\sum_{1 \leq q, r \leq p, q \neq r} v_{qr}}{p(p-1)}$, the *average* communication cost for edge $e_{ij} : T_i \to T_j$.

The last (but important) modification concerns the way in which tasks are assigned to processors: Instead of assigning the current task to the processor that will *start* its execution first (given all already taken decisions), one should assign it to the processor that will *complete* its execution first (given all already taken decisions). Both choices are equivalent with homogeneous processors, but intuitively the latter is likely to be more efficient in the heterogeneous case. Altogether, this leads to the list heuristic called HEFT, for *Heterogeneous Earliest Finish Time* [19].

Workflow Scheduling

This section discusses *workflow scheduling*, that is, the problem of scheduling a (large) collection of identical task graphs rather than a single one. The main idea is to pipeline the execution of successive instances. Think of a sequence of video images that must be processed in a pipelined fashion: Each image enters the platform and follows the same processing chain, and a new image can enter the system while previous ones are still being executed. This section is intended to give a flavor of the optimization problems to be solved in such a context. It restricts to simpler problem instances.

Consider "chains," that is, applications structured as a sequence of stages. Each stage corresponds to a different computational task. The application must process a large number of data sets, each of which must go through all stages. Each stage has its own communication and computation requirements: It reads an input from the previous stage, processes the data, and outputs a result to the next stage. Initial data are input to the first stage and final results are obtained as the output from the last stage. The pipeline operates in synchronous mode: After some initialization delay, a new task is completed every period. The period is defined as the longest "cycle-time" to operate a stage, and it is the inverse of the throughput that can be achieved.

For simplicity, it is assumed that each stage is assigned to a single processor, that is in charge of processing all instances (all data sets) for that stage. Each pipeline stage can be viewed a sequential task that may write some global data structure, to disk or to memory, for each processed data set. In this case, tasks must always be processed in a sequential order within a stage. Moreover, due to possible local updates, each stage must be mapped onto a single processor. For a given stage, one cannot process half of the tasks on one processor and the remaining half on another without maintaining global information, which might be costly and difficult to implement. In other words, a processor that is assigned a stage will execute the operations required by this stage (input, computation, and output) for all the tasks fed into the pipeline.

Of course, other assumptions are possible: some stages could be replicated, or even data-parallelized. The reader is referred the bibliographical notes at the end of the chapter for such extensions.

Objective Functions

An important metric for parallel applications that consists of many individual computations is the *throughput*. The throughput measures the aggregate rate of data processing; it is the rate at which data sets can enter the system. Equivalently, the inverse of the throughput, defined as the *period*, is the time interval required between the beginning of the execution of two consecutive data sets. The period minimization problem can be stated informally as follows: Which stage to assign to which processor so that the largest period of a processor is kept minimal?

Another important metric is derived from makespan minimization, but it must be adapted. With a large number of data sets, the total execution time is less relevant, but the execution time for each data set remains important, in particular for real-time applications. One talks of *latency* rather than of makespan, in order to avoid confusion. The latency is the time elapsed between the beginning and the end of the execution of a given data set, hence it measures the response time of the system to process the data set entirely.

Minimizing the latency is antagonistic to maximizing the throughput. In fact, assigning all application stages to the fastest processor (thus working in a fully sequential way) would suppress all communications and accelerate computations, thereby minimizing the latency, but achieving a very bad throughput. Conversely, mapping each stage to a different processor is likely to decrease the period, hence increase the throughput (work in a fully pipelined manner), but the resulting latency will be high, because all interstage communications must be accounted for in this latter mapping. Trade-offs will have to be found between these criteria.

How to deal with several objective functions? In traditional approaches, one would form a linear combination of the different objectives and treat the result as the new objective to optimize for. But it is not natural for the user to maximize a quantity like $0.7T + 0.3L$, where T is the throughput and L the latency. Instead, one is more likely to fix a throughput T, and to search for the best latency that can be achieved while enforcing T? One single criterion is optimized, under the condition that a threshold is enforced for the other one.

Period and Latency

Consider a pipeline with n stages $\mathcal{S}_k$, $1 \leq k \leq n$, as illustrated in Fig. 8. Tasks are fed into the pipeline and processed from stage to stage, until they exit the pipeline after the last stage. The k-th stage $\mathcal{S}_k$ receives an input from the previous stage, of size b_{k-1}, performs a number of w_k operations, and outputs data of size b_k to the

Task Graph Scheduling. Fig. 8 The application pipeline

next stage. The first stage $\mathcal{S}_1$ receives an initial input of size b_0, while the last stage $\mathcal{S}_n$ returns a final result of size b_n.

The target platform is a clique with p processors P_u, $1 \leq u \leq p$, that are fully interconnected (see Fig. 9). There is a bidirectional link $\text{link}_{u,v} : P_u \leftrightarrow P_v$ with bandwidth $B_{u,v}$ between each processor P_u and P_v. The literature often enforces more realistic communication models for workflow scheduling than for Task Graph Scheduling. For the sake of simplicity, a very strict model is enforced here: A given processor can be involved in a single communication at any time unit, either a send or a receive. Note that independent communications between distinct processor pairs can take place simultaneously. Finally, there is no overlap between communications and computations, so that all the operations of a given processor are fully sequentialized. The speed of processor P_u is denoted as W_u, and it takes X/W_u time units for P_u to execute X operations. It takes $X/B_{u,v}$ time units to send (respectively, receive) a message of size X to (respectively, from) P_v.

The mapping problem consists in assigning application stages to processors. For *one-to-one mappings*, it is required that each stage $\mathcal{S}_k$ of the application pipeline be mapped onto a distinct processor $P_{\text{alloc}(k)}$ (which is possible only if $n \leq p$). The function **alloc** associates a processor index to each stage index. For convenience, two fictitious stages $\mathcal{S}_0$ and $\mathcal{S}_{n+1}$ are created, assigning $\mathcal{S}_0$ to P_{in} and $\mathcal{S}_{n+1}$ to P_{out}.

What is the period of $P_{\text{alloc}(k)}$, that is, the minimum delay between the processing of two consecutive tasks? To answer this question, one needs to know to which processors the previous and next stages are assigned. Let $t = \text{alloc}(k-1)$, $u = \text{alloc}(k)$, and $v = \text{alloc}(k+1)$. P_u needs $b_{k-1}/B_{t,u}$ time units to receive the input data from P_t, w_k/W_u time units to process it, and $b_k/B_{u,v}$ time units to send the result to P_v, hence a cycle-time of $b_{k-1}/B_{t,u} + w_k/W_u + b_k/B_{u,v}$ time units for P_u. These three steps are serialized (see Fig. 10 for an illustration). The *period* achieved with the mapping is the maximum of the cycle-times of the processors, which corresponds to the rate at which the pipeline can be activated.

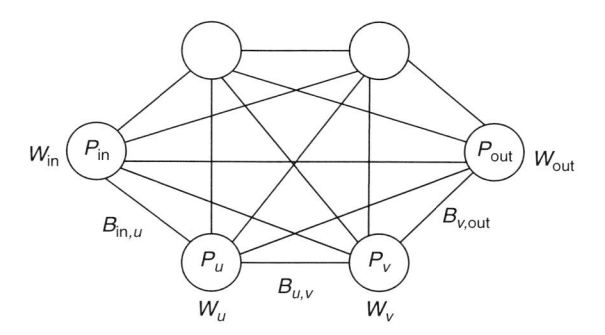

Task Graph Scheduling. Fig. 9 The target platform

In this simple instance, the optimization problem can be stated as follows: Determine a one-to-one allocation function $\text{alloc} : [1, n] \to [1, p]$ (augmented with $\text{alloc}(0) = \text{in}$ and $\text{alloc}(n+1) = \text{out}$) such that

$$T_{\text{period}} = \max_{1 \leq k \leq n} \left\{ \frac{b_{k-1}}{B_{\text{alloc}(k-1), \text{alloc}(k)}} + \frac{w_k}{W_{\text{alloc}(k)}} + \frac{b_k}{B_{\text{alloc}(k), \text{alloc}(k+1)}} \right\}$$

is minimized.

Natural extensions are *interval mappings*, in which each participating processor is assigned an interval of consecutive stages. Note that when $p < n$ interval mappings are mandatory. Intuitively, assigning several consecutive tasks to the same processor will increase its computational load, but will also decrease communication. The best interval mapping may turn out to be a one-to-one mapping, or instead may utilize only a very small number of fast computing processors interconnected by high-speed links. The optimization problem associated to interval mappings is formally expressed as follows. The intervals achieve a partition of the original set of stages $\mathcal{S}_1$ to $\mathcal{S}_n$. One searches for a partition of $[1, \ldots, n]$ into m intervals $I_j = [d_j, e_j]$ such that $d_j \leq e_j$ for $1 \leq j \leq m$, $d_1 = 1$, $d_{j+1} = e_j + 1$ for $1 \leq j \leq m-1$, and $e_m = n$. Recall that the function $\text{alloc} : [1, n] \to [1, p]$ associates a processor index to each stage index. In a one-to-one mapping, this function was a one-to-one

Task Graph Scheduling. Fig. 10 An example of one-to-one mapping with three stages and processors. Each processor periodically receives input data from its predecessor (★), performs some computation (■), and outputs data to its successor (△). Note that these operations are shifted in time from one processor to another. The cycle-time of P_1 and P_2 is 5 while that of P_3 is 4, hence $T_{period} = 5$

assignment. In an interval mapping, for $1 \leqslant j \leqslant m$, the whole interval I_j is mapped onto the same processor $P_{\text{alloc}(d_j)}$, that is, for $d_j \leqslant i \leqslant e_j$, $\text{alloc}(i) = \text{alloc}(d_j)$. Also, two intervals cannot be mapped to the same processor, that is, for $1 \leqslant j, j' \leqslant m$, $j \neq j'$, $\text{alloc}(d_j) \neq \text{alloc}(d_{j'})$. The period is expressed as

$$T_{\text{period}} = \max_{1 \leqslant j \leqslant m} \left\{ \frac{\mathsf{b}_{d_j-1}}{B_{\text{alloc}(d_j-1),\text{alloc}(d_j)}} + \frac{\sum_{i=d_j}^{e_j} \mathsf{w}_i}{W_{\text{alloc}(d_j)}} + \frac{\mathsf{b}_{e_j}}{B_{\text{alloc}(d_j),\text{alloc}(e_j+1)}} \right\}$$

Note that $\text{alloc}(d_j - 1) = \text{alloc}(e_{j-1}) = \text{alloc}(d_{j-1})$ for $j > 1$ and $d_1 - 1 = 0$. Also, $e_j + 1 = d_{j+1}$ for $j < m$, and $e_m + 1 = n + 1$. It is still assumed that $\text{alloc}(0) = \text{in}$ and $\text{alloc}(n + 1) = \text{out}$. The optimization problem is then to determine the mapping that minimizes T_{period}, over all possible partitions into intervals, and over all mappings of these intervals to the processors.

The latency of an interval mapping is computed as follows. Each data set traverses all stages, but only communications between two stages mapped on the same processors take zero time units. Overall, the latency is expressed as

$$T_{\text{latency}} = \sum_{1 \leqslant j \leqslant m} \left\{ \frac{\mathsf{b}_{d_j-1}}{B_{\text{alloc}(d_j-1),\text{alloc}(d_j)}} + \frac{\sum_{i=d_j}^{e_j} \mathsf{w}_i}{W_{\text{alloc}(d_j)}} \right\} + \frac{\mathsf{b}_n}{B_{\text{alloc}(n),\text{alloc}(n+1)}}$$

The latency for a one-to-one mapping obeys the same formula (with the restriction that each interval has length 1). Just as for the period, there are two minimization problems for the latency, with one-to-one and interval mappings.

It goes beyond the scope of this entry to assess the complexity of these period/latency optimization problems, and of their bi-criteria counterparts. The aim was to provide the reader with a quick primer on workflow scheduling, an activity that borrows several concepts from Task Graph Scheduling, while using more realistic platform models, and different objective functions.

Related Entries
▶Loop Pipelining
▶Modulo Scheduling and Loop Pipelining
▶Scheduling Algorithms

Recommended Reading
Without communication costs, pioneering work includes the book by Coffman [5]. The book by El-Rewini et al. [7] and the IEEE compilation of papers [15] provide additional material. On the theoretical side, Appendix A5 of Garey and Johnson [8] provides a list of NP-complete scheduling problems. Also, the book by Brucker [2] offers a comprehensive overview of many complexity results.

The literature with communication costs is more recent. See the survey paper by Chrétienne and Picouleau [4]. See also the book by Darte et al. [6], where many heuristics are surveyed. The book by Sinnen [16] provides a thorough discussion on communication models. In particular, it describes several extensions for modeling and accounting for communication contention.

Workflow scheduling is quite a hot topic with the advent of large-scale computing platforms. A few representative papers are [1, 11, 17, 18].

Modern scheduling encompasses a wide spectrum of techniques: divisible load scheduling, cyclic scheduling, steady-state scheduling, online scheduling, job scheduling, and so on. A comprehensive survey is available in the book [14]. See also the handbook [12].

Most of the material presented in this entry is excerpted from the book by Casanova et al. [3].

Bibliography

1. Benoit A, Robert Y (2008) Mapping pipeline skeletons onto heterogeneous platforms. J Parallel Distr Comput 68(6):790–808
2. Brucker P (2004) Scheduling algorithms. Springer, New York
3. Casanova H, Legrand A, Robert Y (2008) Parallel algorithms. Chapman & Hall/CRC Press, Beaumont, TX
4. Chrétienne P, Picouleau C (1995) Scheduling with communication delays: a survey. In: Chrétienne P, Coffman EG Jr, Lenstra JK, Liu Z (eds) Scheduling theory and its applications. Wiley, Hoboken, NJ, pp 65–89
5. Coffman EG (1976) Computer and job-shop scheduling theory. Wiley, Hoboken, NJ
6. Darte A, Robert Y, Vivien F (2000) Scheduling and automatic parallelization. Birkhaüser, Boston
7. El-Rewini H, Lewis TG, Ali HH (1994) Task scheduling in parallel and distributed systems. Prentice Hall, Englewood Cliffs
8. Garey MR, Johnson DS (1991) Computers and intractability, a guide to the theory of NP-completeness. WH Freeman and Company, New York
9. Gerasoulis A, Yang T (1992) A comparison of clustering heuristics for scheduling DAGs on multiprocessors. J Parallel Distr Comput 16(4):276–291
10. Graham RL (1996) Bounds for certain multiprocessor anomalies. Bell Syst Tech J 45:1563–1581
11. Hary SL, Ozguner F (1999) Precedence-constrained task allocation onto point-to-point networks for pipelined execution. IEEE Trans Parallel Distr Syst 10(8):838–851
12. Leung JY-T (ed) (2004) Handbook of scheduling: algorithms, models, and performance analysis. Chapman and Hall/CRC Press, Boca Raton
13. Picouleau C (1995) Task scheduling with interprocessor communication delays. Discrete App Math 60(1–3):331–342
14. Robert Y, Vivien F (eds) (2009) Introduction to scheduling. Chapman and Hall/CRC Press, Boca Raton
15. Shirazi BA, Hurson AR, Kavi KM (1995) Scheduling and load balancing in parallel and distributed systems. IEEE Computer Science Press, San Diego
16. Sinnen O (2007) Task scheduling for parallel systems. Wiley, Hoboken
17. Spencer M, Ferreira R, Beynon M, Kurc T, Catalyurek U, Sussman A, Saltz J (2002) Executing multiple pipelined data analysis operations in the grid. Proceedings of the ACM/IEEE supercomputing conference. ACM Press, Los Alamitos
18. Subhlok J, Vondran G (1995) Optimal mapping of sequences of data parallel tasks. Proceedings of the 5th ACM SIGPLAN symposium on principles and practice of parallel programming. ACM Press, San Diego, pp 134–143
19. Topcuoglu H, Hariri S, Wu MY (2002) Performance-effective and low-complexity task scheduling for heterogeneous computing. IEEE Trans Parallel Distr Syst 13(3):260–274

Task Mapping, Topology Aware

▶ Topology Aware Task Mapping

Tasks

▶ Processes, Tasks, and Threads

TAU

SAMEER SHENDE, ALLEN D. MALONY, ALAN MORRIS, WYATT SPEAR, SCOTT BIERSDORFF
University of Oregon, Eugene, OR, USA

Synonyms

TAU performance system®; Tuning and analysis utilities

Definition

The TAU Performance System® is an integrated suite of tools for instrumentation, measurement, and analysis of parallel programs with particular focus on large-scale, high-performance computing (HPC) platforms. TAU's objectives are to provide a flexible and interoperable framework for performance tool research and development, and robust, portable, and scalable set of technologies for performance evaluation on high-end computer systems.

Discussion

Introduction

Scalable parallel systems have always evolved together with the tools used to observe, understand, and optimize their performance. Next-generation parallel computing environments are guided to a significant degree by what is known about application performance on current machines and how performance factors might be influenced by technological innovations. State-of-the-art performance tools play an important role in helping to understand application performance, diagnose performance problems, and guide tuning decisions on modern parallel platforms. However, performance tool technology must also respond to the growing complexity of next-generation parallel systems in order to help deliver the promises of high-end computing (HEC).

The TAU project began in the early 1990s with the goal of creating a performance instrumentation, measurement, and analysis framework that could produce robust, portable, and scalable performance tools for use in all parallel programs and systems over several technology generations. Today, the TAU Performance System® is a ubiquitous performance tools suite for shared-memory and message-passing parallel applications written in multiple programming languages (e.g., C, C++, Fortran, OpenMP, Java, Python, UPC, Chapel) that can scale to the largest parallel machines available.

TAU Design

TAU is of a class of performance systems based on the approach of *direct performance observation*, wherein execution *actions* of performance interest are exposed as *events* to the performance system through direct insertion of instrumentation in the application, library, or system code, at locations where the actions arise. In general, the actions reflect an occurrence of some execution state, most commonly as a result of a code location being reached (e.g., entry in a subroutine). However, it could also include a change in data. The key point is that the observation mechanism is direct. Generated events are made visible to the performance system in this way and contain implicit meta information as to their associated action. Thus, for any *performance experiment* using direct observation, the performance events of interest must be decided and necessary instrumentation done for their generation. Performance measurements are made of the events during execution and saved for analysis. Knowledge of the events is used to process the performance data and interpret the analysis results.

The TAU framework architecture, shown in Fig. 1, separates the functional concerns of a direct performance observation approach into three primary layers – *instrumentation*, *measurement*, and *analysis*. Each layer uses multiple modules which can be configured in a flexible manner under user control. This design makes it possible for TAU to target alternative models of parallel computation, from shared-memory multi-threading to distributed memory message passing to mixed-mode parallelism [17]. TAU defines an abstract computation model for parallel systems that captures general architecture and software execution features and can be mapped to existing complex system types [16].

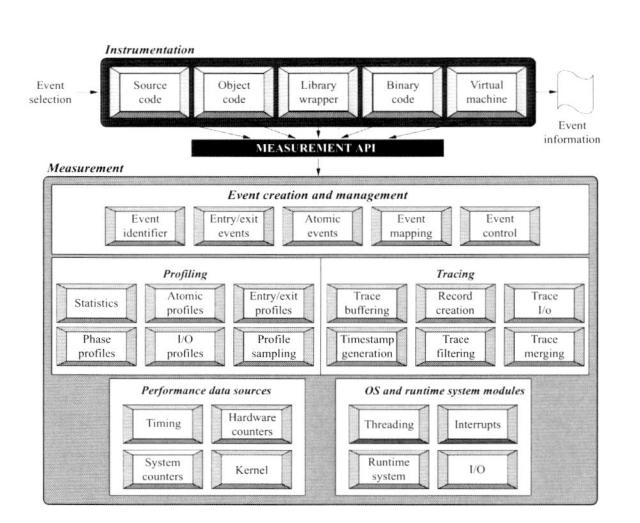

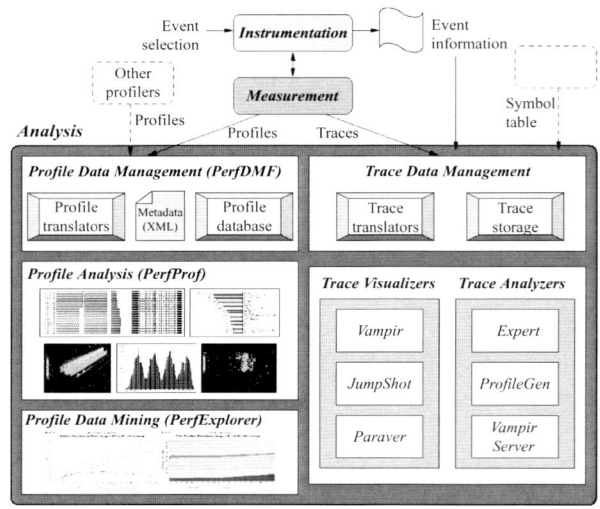

TAU. Fig. 1 TAU architecture: instrumentation and measurement (*left*), analysis (*right*)

TAU's design has proven to be robust, sound, and highly adaptable to generations of parallel systems. The framework architecture has allowed new components to be added that have extended the capabilities of the TAU toolkit. This is especially true in areas concerning kernel-level performance integration [11, 14], performance monitoring [10, 12, 13], performance data mining [6], and GPU performance measurement [8].

TAU Instrumentation

The role of the instrumentation layer in direct performance observation is to insert code (a.k.a. *probes*) to make performance events visible to the measurement layer. Performance events can be defined and instrumentation inserted in a program at several levels of the program transformation process. In fact, it is important to realize that a complete performance view may require contribution of event information across code levels [15]. For these reasons, TAU supports several instrumentation mechanisms based on the code type and transformation level: source (manual, preprocessor, library interposition), binary/dynamic, interpreter, and virtual machine. There are multiple factors that affect the choice of what level to instrument, including accessibility, flexibility, portability, concern for intrusion, and functionality. It is not a question of what level is "correct" because there are trade-offs for each and different events are visible at different levels. TAU is distinguished by its broad support for different instrumentation methods and their use together.

TAU supports two general classes of events for instrumentation using any method: *atomic* events and *interval* events. An atomic event denotes a single action. Instrumentation is inserted at a point in the program code to expose an atomic action, and the measurement system obtains performance data associated with the action where and when it occurs. An interval event is a pair of events: *begin* and *end*. Instrumentation is inserted at two points in the code, and the measurement system uses data obtained from each event to determine performance for the interval between them (e.g., the time spent in a subroutine from entry (beginning of the interval) to exit (end of the interval)). In addition to the two general events classes, TAU allows events to be selectively enabled / disabled for any instrumentation method.

TAU Measurement

The TAU performance measurement system is a highly robust, scalable infrastructure portable to all HPC platforms. As shown in Fig. 1, TAU supports the two dominant methods of measurement for direct performance observation – parallel *profiling* and *tracing* – with rich access to performance data through portable timing facilities, integration with hardware performance counters, and user-level information. The choice of measurement method and performance data is made independently of the instrumentation decisions. This allows multiple performance experiments to be conducted to gain different performance views for the same set of events. TAU also provides unique support for novel performance mapping [15], runtime monitoring [10, 12, 13], and kernel-level measurements [11, 14].

TAU's measurement system has two core capabilities. First, the *event management* handles the registration and encoding of events as they are created. New events are represented in an *event table* by instantiating a new *event record*, recording the *event name*, and linking in storage allocated for the event performance data. The event table is used for all atomic and interval events regardless of their complexity. Event type and context information are encoded in the event names. The TAU event-management system hashes and maps these names to determine if an event has already occurred or needs to be created. Events are managed for every thread of execution in the application. Second, a runtime representation, called the *event callstack*, captures the nesting relationship of interval performance events. It is a powerful runtime measurement abstraction for managing the TAU performance state for use in both profiling and tracing. In particular, the event callstack is key for managing execution context, allowing TAU to associate this context to the events being measured.

Parallel profiling in TAU characterizes the behavior of every application thread in terms of its aggregate performance metrics. For interval events, TAU computes *exclusive* and *inclusive* metrics for each event. The TAU profiling system supports several profiling variants. The standard type of profiling is called *flat profiling*, which shows the exclusive and inclusive performance of each event but provides no other performance information about events occurring when an interval is active (i.e., nested events). In contrast, TAU's *event path profiling* can capture performance data with respect to event nesting relationships. It is also interesting to observe performance data relative to an execution *state*. The structural, logical, and numerical aspects of a computation can be thought of as representing different execution *phases*. TAU supports an interface to create (*phase events*) and to mark their entry and exit. Internally in the TAU measurement system, when a phase, P, is entered, all subsequent performance will be measured with respect to P until it exits. When phase profiles are recorded, a separate parallel profile is generated for each phase.

TAU implements robust, portable, and scalable parallel tracing support to log events in time-ordered tuples containing a time stamp, a location (e.g., node, thread), an identifier that specifies the type of event, event-specific information, and other performance-related data (e.g., hardware counters). All performance events are available for tracing. TAU will produce a trace for every thread of execution in its modern trace format as well as in OTF [7] and EPILOG [9] formats. TAU also provides mechanisms for online and hierarchical trace merging [3].

TAU Analysis

As the complexity of measuring parallel performance increases, the burden falls on analysis and visualization tools to interpret the performance information. As shown in Fig. 1, TAU includes sophisticated tools for parallel profile analysis and performance data mining. In addition, TAU leverages advanced trace analysis technologies from the performance tool community, primarily the Vampir [2] and Scalasca [18] tools. The following focuses on the features of the TAU profiling tools.

TAU's parallel profile analysis environment consists of a framework for managing parallel profile data, *PerfDMF* [5], and TAU's parallel profile analysis tool, *ParaProf* [1]. The complete environment is implemented entirely in Java. The performance data management framework (PerfDMF) in TAU provides a common foundation for parsing, storing, and querying parallel profiles from multiple performance experiments. It builds on robust SQL relational database engines and must be able to handle both large-scale performance profiles, consisting of many events and threads of execution, as well as many profiles from multiple performance experiments. To facilitate performance analysis development, the PerfDMF architecture includes a well-documented data-management API to abstract query and analysis operation into a more programmatic, non-SQL form.

TAU's parallel profile analysis tool, *ParaProf* [1], is capable of processing the richness of parallel profile information produced by the measurement system, both in terms of the profile types (flat, callpath, phase, snapshots) as well as scale. ParaProf provides the users with a highly graphical tool for viewing parallel profile data with respect to different viewing scopes and presentation methods. Profile data can be input directly from a PerfDMF database and multiple profiles can be analyzed simultaneously. ParaProf can show parallel profile information in the form of bargraphs, callgraphs, scalable histograms, and cumulative plots. ParaProf is also capable of integrating multiple performance profiles for the same performance experiment but using different performance metrics for each. ParaProf uses scalable histogram and three-dimensional displays for larger datasets.

To provide more sophisticated performance analysis capabilities, we developed support for parallel performance data mining in TAU. *PerfExplorer* [4, 6] is a framework for performance data mining motivated by our interest in automatic parallel performance analysis and by our concern for extensible and reusable performance tool technology. PerfExplorer is built on PerfDMF and targets large-scale performance analysis for single experiments on thousands of processors and for multiple experiments from parametric studies. PerfExplorer uses techniques such as clustering and dimensionality reduction to manage large-scale data complexity.

Summary

The TAU Performance System® has undergone several incarnations in pursuit of its primary objectives of flexibility, portability, integration, interoperability, and scalability. The outcome is a robust technology suite that has significant coverage of the performance problem solving landscape for high-end computing. TAU follows a direct performance observation methodology since it is based on the observation of effects directly associated with the program's execution, allowing performance data to be interpreted in the context of the computation. Hard issues of instrumentation scope and measurement intrusion have to be addressed, but these have been aggressively pursued and the technology enhanced in several ways during TAU's lifetime. TAU is still evolving, and new capabilities are being added to the tools suite. Support for whole-system performance analysis, model-based optimization using performance expectations and knowledge-based data mining, and heterogeneous performance measurement are being pursued.

Related Entries
▶Metrics
▶Performance Analysis Tools

Bibliography

1. Bell R, Malony A, Shende S (2003) A portable, extensible, and scalable tool for parallel performance profile analysis. In: European conference on parallel computing (EuroPar 2003), Klagenfurt
2. Brunst H, Kranzlmüller D, Nagel WE (2004) Tools for scalable parallel program analysis – Vampir NG and DeWiz. In: Distributed and parallel systems, cluster and grid computing, vol 777. Springer, New York
3. Brunst H, Nagel W, Malony A (2003) A distributed performance analysis architecture for clusters. In: IEEE international conference on cluster computing (Cluster 2003), pp 73–83. IEEE Computer Society, Los Alamitos
4. Huck KA, Malony AD (2005) Perfexplorer: a performance data mining framework for large-scale parallel computing. In: High performance networking and computing conference (SC'05). IEEE Computer Society, Los Alamitos
5. Huck K, Malony A, Bell R, Morris A (2005) Design and implementation of a parallel performance data management framework. In: International conference on parallel processing (ICPP 2005). IEEE Computer Society, Los Alamitos
6. Huck K, Malony A, Shende S, Morris A (2008) Knowledge support and automation for performance analysis with PerfExplorer 2.0. J Sci Program 16(2–3):123–134 (Special issue on large-scale programming tools and environments)
7. Knüpfer A, Brendel R, Brunst H, Mix H, Nagel WE (2006) Introducing the Open Trace Format (OTF). In: International conference on computational science (ICCS 2006). Lecture notes in computer science, vol 3992. Springer, Berlin, pp 526–533
8. Mayanglambam S, Malony A, Sottile M (2009) Performance measurement of applications with GPU acceleration using CUDA. In: Parallel computing (ParCo), Lyon
9. Mohr B, Wolf F (2003) KOJAK – a tool set for automatic performance analysis of parallel applications. In: European conference on parallel computing (EuroPar 2003). Lecture notes in computer science, vol 2790. Springer, Berlin, pp 1301–1304
10. Nataraj A, Sottile M, Morris A, Malony AD, Shende S (2007) TAUoverSupermon: low-overhead online parallel performance monitoring. In: European conference on parallel computing (EuroPar 2007), Rennes
11. Nataraj A, Morris A, Malony AD, Sottile M, Beckman P (2007) The ghost in the machine: observing the effects of kernel operation on parallel application performance. In: High performance networking and computing conference (SC'07), Reno
12. Nataraj A, Malony A, Morris A, Arnold D, Miller B (2008) In search of sweet-spots in parallel performance monitoring. In: IEEE international conference on cluster computing (Cluster 2008), Tsukuba
13. Nataraj A, Malony A, Morris A, Arnold D, Miller B (2008) TAUoverMRNet (ToM): a framework for scalable parallel performance monitoring. In: International workshop on scalable tools for high-end computing (STHEC '08), Kos
14. Nataraj A, Malony AD, Shende S, Morris A (2008) Integrated parallel performance views. Clust Comput 11(1):57–73
15. Shende S (2001) The role of instrumentation and mapping in performance measurement. Ph.D. thesis, University of Oregon
16. Shende S, Malony A (2006) The TAU parallel performance system. Int J Supercomput Appl High Speed Comput 20(2, Summer):287–311 (ACTS collection special issue)
17. Shende S, Malony AD, Cuny J, Lindlan K, Beckman P, Karmesin S (1998) Portable profiling and tracing for parallel scientific applications using C++. In: SIGMETRICS symposium on parallel and distributed tools, SPDT'98, Welches, pp 134–145
18. Wolf F et al (2008) Usage of the SCALASCA toolset for scalable performance analysis of large-scale parallel applications. In: Proceedings of the second HLRS parallel tools workshop, Stuttgart. Lecture notes in computer science. Springer, Berlin

TAU Performance System®

▶TAU

TBB (Intel Threading Building Blocks)

▶Intel® Threading Building Blocks (TBB)

Tensilica

▶Green Flash: Climate Machine (LBNL)

Tera MTA

BURTON SMITH
Microsoft Corporation, Redmond, WA, USA

Synonyms

Cray MTA; Cray XMT; Horizon

Definition

The MTA (for Multi-Threaded Architecture) is a highly multithreaded scalar shared-memory multiprocessor architecture developed by Tera Computer Company (renamed Cray Inc. in 2000) in Seattle, Washington. Work began in 1985 at The Institute for Defense Analyses Center for Computing Sciences on a closely related predecessor (Horizon), and development of both hardware and software was continuing at Cray Inc. as of 2010.

Discussion

Introduction

The Tera MTA [1] is in many respects a direct descendant of the Denelcor HEP computer [2]. Like the HEP, the MTA is a scalar shared-memory system equipped with full/empty bits at every 64-bit memory location and multiple protection domains to permit multiprogramming within a processor. However, the MTA introduced a few innovations including VLIW instructions without any register set partitioning, additional ILP via dependence data encoded in each instruction, two-phase blocking synchronization, unlimited data breakpoints, speculative loads, division and square root to full accuracy using iterative methods, operating system entry via procedure calls, traps that never change privilege, and no interrupts at all.

Software developed for the MTA introduced its share of novel ideas as well, including a user-mode runtime responsible for synchronization and work scheduling, negotiated resource management between the user-mode runtime and the operating system, an operating system that returns control to the user-mode runtime when the call blocks, a compiler for Fortran and C++ that parallelizes and restructures a wide variety of loops including those whose inter-iteration dependences require a parallel prefix computation, and dynamic scheduling of loop nests having mixed rectangular, triangular, and skyline loop bounds.

Beginnings

While spending the summer of 1984 as an intern at Denelcor, UC Berkeley graduate student Stephen W. Melvin invented a scheme for organizing a register file in a fine-grain multi-threaded processor to let VLIW instructions enjoy multiple register accesses per instruction while preserving a flat register address space within each hardware thread. The idea was simple: organize the register file into multiple banks with each bank containing all of the registers for an associated subset of the hardware threads; let each issued instruction use multiple cycles to read and write its associated bank as many times as necessary to implement the instruction; and have the instruction issue logic refrain from issuing from threads associated with currently busy banks. From this beginning, an architectural proposal emerged that was whimsically referred to as "Vulture" and was later known as the "HEP array processor". Denelcor envisioned heterogeneous systems with second-generation HEP processors sharing memory with processors based on this new VLIW idea.

Denelcor filed for Chapter 7 bankruptcy in mid-1985 whereupon its CTO, Burton J. Smith, joined the Supercomputing Research Center (now called the Center for Computing Sciences) of the Institute for Defense Analyses (IDA) in Maryland. His plan was to further evaluate the merits of the multithreaded VLIW ideas. It had already become clear that code generation and optimization for such a processor was only slightly more difficult than for the HEP but the resulting performance was potentially much higher. The design that resulted from collaborations on this topic at IDA over the years 1985–1987 was known as *Horizon* and was described in a series of papers presented at Supercomputing'88 [3, 4].

Horizon instructions were 64 bits wide and typically contained three operations: a memory reference (M) operation, an arithmetic or logic (A) operation, and a control (C) operation which did branches but could also do some arithmetic and logic. As many as ten five-bit register references might appear in any single instruction. The memory reference semantics were derived from those of the HEP but added data trap bits to implement data break points (watchpoints) and possibly other things. The A operations included fused multiply-adds for both integer and floating point arithmetic and a rich variety of operations on vectors and matrices of bits. Branches were encoded compactly as an opcode, an eight-bit condition mask, a two-bit condition code number specifying one of the four most recently generated three-bit condition codes, and two bits naming a branch target register that had been preloaded with the branch address. Most A- and C-operations emitted a condition code as an optional side-effect.

Horizon increased ILP beyond three with an idea known as *explicit-dependence lookahead*, replacing the usual register reservation scheme. Intel would later employ a kindred concept for encoding dependence information within instructions in the Itanium architecture, calling it *explicitly parallel instruction computing* (EPIC). The Horizon version included in every instruction an explicit 3-bit unsigned integer, the *lookahead* that bounded from below the number of instructions separating this instruction from later ones that might depend on it. Subsequent instructions within the bound could overlap with the current instruction. To implement this scheme, every hardware thread was equipped with a three-bit *flag* counter, incremented when the thread is selected to issue its next instruction, and an array of eight three-bit *lock* counters. On instruction issue, the lock counter subscripted by the lookahead plus the flag (mod 8) is incremented; when the instruction fully retires, that same lock is decremented. A thread is permitted to issue its next instruction when the lock subscripted by its flag is zero. Instruction instances were thus treated very much like operations in a static data flow machine. As a further refinement, branches were available to terminate lookahead along the unlikely control flow direction, potentially increasing ILP along the likelier one.

Tera

Early in 1988, Smith and a colleague, James E. Rottsolk, decided to start a company to build general-purpose parallel computer systems based on the Horizon concepts. They named the new company *Tera*, acquired initial funding from private investors and from the Defense Advanced Research Projects Agency (DARPA), and began to search for a suitable home. In August 1988, Seattle, Washington was chosen and Tera began recruiting engineers. The University of Washington helped the company in its early days.

Languages

The Tera language strategy [5] was to add directives and pragmas to Fortran and C++ to guide compiler loop parallelization and provide performance and compatibility with existing vector processors. A consistency model strongly resembling release consistency was adopted based on acquire and release synchronization points to let the compiler cache values in registers and restructure code aggressively. Basically, memory references could not move backward over acquires or forward over releases. Only the built-in synchronization based on full/empty bits was permitted at first; later, volatile variable references were made legal (but deprecated) for synchronization. A *future* statement borrowed from Multilisp [6] was introduced in both Fortran and C++ to support task parallelism as well as divide-and-conquer data parallelism. It uses the full/empty bits to synchronize completion of the future with its invoker. The body of the future appears in-line and can reference variables in its enclosing environment.

Compiler Optimization

The MTA compilers can automatically parallelize a variety of loops [7]. Consider the example below:

```
void sort(int *src, int *dst, int nitems, int nvals) {
   int i, j, t1[nvals], t2[nvals];
   for (j = 0; j< nvals; j++) {
      t1[j] = 0;}
   for (i = 0; i< nitems; i++) {
      t1[src[i]]++;}              //atomic update
   t2[0] = 0;
   for (j = 1; j<nvals; j++) {
      t2[j] = t2[j-1] + t1[j-1];}  //parallel prefix
   $t2 = (sync int *) t2;
   #pragma tera assert parallel
   for (i = 0; i<nitems; i++) {
      dst[$t2[src[i]]++] = src[i];}
}
```

All four loops are parallelized by the MTA compiler. Updates like the one in the second loop are automatically made atomic using full/empty bits if and as necessary. The third loop is an example of a *parallel prefix computation* [8] (also called a *parallel scan*) which the compiler can automatically parallelize as long as the internal state of the accumulating prefix is bounded [9]. The fourth loop will not be parallelized automatically by the compiler and requires a pragma and explicit use of full/empty bits via the *sync* type qualifier.

To achieve as high a level of ILP as the instruction set can afford, software pipelining [10] is exploited by distributing loops based on estimates of register pressure and then unrolling and packing to obtain a good schedule. Experiments at both IDA and Tera led to a modification of the lookahead scheme to overlap only memory references. Software pipelining was further enabled by implementing speculative loads. A *poison* bit is associated with every register in the thread, and memory protection violations can optionally be made to poison the destination register instead of raising an exception. Any instruction that attempts to use a poisoned value will trap instead. The speculative load feature allows prefetching in a software pipeline without having to "unpeel" final iterations to prevent accesses beyond mapped memory. In any case the instruction can be reattempted if the cause of the protection violation is remediable.

Nests of parallelizable "for" loops may vary in iterations per loop, sometimes dynamically, making them hard to execute efficiently. The MTA compiler schedules these nests as a whole, even when inner loops have bounds that depend on outer iteration variables. First, code is generated to compute the total number of (inner loop) iterations of the whole nest. Functions are then generated to compute the iteration number of each loop from the total iteration count. Finally, code is generated to dynamically schedule the loop nest by having each worker thread acquire a "chunk" of total iterations using a variant of guided self-scheduling [11], reconstruct the iteration variable bindings, and then jump into the loop nest to iterate until the chunk is consumed.

User-Level Runtime

A user-level runtime environment was developed to help implement the language features and schedule fine-grain parallel tasks. The Horizon architecture was modified to make full/empty synchronization operations lock the location and generate a user-level trap after a programmable limit on the number of synchronization retry attempts is exceeded. The runtime trap handler saves the state of the blocked task, initializes a queue of blocked tasks containing this one as its first element, and places a pointer to this new queue in the still-locked full/empty location. It then sets a trap bit and unlocks the location so that subsequent references of any kind will trap immediately. In this way the tasks that arrive later either block, joining the queue of waiting tasks right away, or dequeue a waiting task immediately. The retry limit is set to match the time needed to save and later restore the task state, making this scheme within a factor of two of optimal. When memory references are frequent, the retry rate is throttled to be much less than that for new memory references, and if the processor is not starved for hardware threads the polling cost becomes almost negligible and the retry limit can be increased substantially.

When formerly blocked tasks are unblocked, they are enqueued in a pool of runnable tasks. Since these tasks are equipped with a stack and may have additional memory associated with them, they are run in preference to tasks associated with future statements that have not yet run. Still, the number of blocked tasks can be substantial. To reduce memory waste, stacks are organized as linked lists of fixed-size blocks. Automatic arrays and other things that must be contiguously allocated are stored in the heap. Interprocedural analysis is used to avoid most stack bounds checks.

Another modification to the Horizon architecture comprised instructions to allocate multiple hardware threads. Each protection domain has an operating system-imposed limit on the number of hardware threads in the domain and a *reservation* which can be increased (or decreased) by one of the new instructions [12]. One of them reserves a variable number, from zero up to a maximum specified as an argument, depending on availability. The other instruction either reserves the requested amount or none at all. In either case, the number of additional hardware threads actually allocated is returned in a register so a loop can be used to initiate them. The primary motivation for this reservation capability was to accommodate rapidly varying quantities of parallelism found in short parallel loops. Hardware threads can be materialized and put to work quickly when such opportunities are encountered.

Operating System

Since the MTA's operating system (OS) plays no role in user-level thread synchronization and allocates but does not micromanage the dynamic quantity of hardware threads, the usual OS invocation machinery (trapping) was rejected in favor of procedure calls. A protection ring-crossing instruction guarantees only valid OS entry points are called. The operating system can allocate its own stack space when and if necessary. If an OS call ultimately blocks, the hardware thread is returned to user level via a runtime entry point that associates the continuation of the original user computation with a "cookie" supplied by the OS. When the original OS call completes, the appropriate cookie is passed to the user runtime so it can unblock the user-level continuation. As a result, the operating system executes in parallel with the user-level program. This scheme was invented independently [13] at the University of Washington and is referred to as *scheduler activations*.

When an illegal operation is attempted, a trap to the user-level trap handler occurs. If OS intervention is required, the trap handler calls the OS to service the trap. To evict a process from a protection domain, all of its hardware threads are made to trap in response to an OS-generated signal. The OS also has the ability to kill all hardware threads in a protection domain.

Memory Mapping

The MTA has a large virtual data address space, making high-performance memory address translation challenging. To address this issue, segmentation is used instead of paging, with a 48-bit virtual address comprising a 20-bit segment number and a 28-bit offset. Contiguous allocations of memory larger than 256 MB can use multiple segments. Segment size granularity is 8 KB. Each protection domain has base and limit registers that define its own range of segment numbers. A segment map entry specifies minimum privilege levels for loads and stores, and whether physical addresses are to be *distributed* across the multiple memory banks of the system by "scrambling" the address bits [14]. When memory is distributed in this fashion there are virtually no bank conflicts due to strided accesses. Program memory, as addressed by the program counters, is handled differently using a paging scheme with 4 KB pages. The program space is mapped to data space via a non-distributed (i.e., local) segment.

Arithmetic

The instruction set supports the usual variety of two's complement and unsigned integers and both 32- and 64-bit IEEE 754 floating point. Division for signed and unsigned integers [15] along with floating point division and square root all use Newton's method but nevertheless implement full accuracy and correct semantics. Excepting these few operations, denormalized arithmetic is fully supported in hardware. High-precision integer arithmetic is abetted by a 128-bit unsigned integer multiply instruction and the ability to propagate carry bits easily. There is also support for a 128-bit floating point format using pairs of 64-bit floats; the smaller value is insignificant with respect to the larger, thereby yielding 106 bits of significand precision or more. The existence of a fused multiply-add makes this format relatively inexpensive to implement and use, but instruction modifications were needed to mitigate a variety of pathologies. A true 128-bit IEEE format would doubtless be preferable.

MTA-1 and MTA-2

The MTA-1 was a water-cooled system built from Gallium Arsenide logic. To provide adequate memory bandwidth, the processors sparsely populated a 3D toroidal mesh interconnection network. As an example, 512 routing nodes were required for 64 processors. To make network wiring implementable, one-third of the mesh links were elided. The first and only MTA-1 system was delivered to the San Diego Supercomputer Center in June 1999.

The MTA-2 was a major improvement in manufacturability over the MTA-1. It used CMOS logic and had an interconnection network based on notions from group theory [16]. It was first delivered in 2002 to the US Naval Research Laboratory in Washington, DC. A few other MTA-2 systems were built before deliveries of the Cray XMT (*q.v.*) began in 2007.

Related Entries

▶Cray MTA
▶Cray XMT
▶Data Flow Computer Architecture
▶Denelcor HEP
▶EPIC Processors
▶Futures
▶Interconnection Networks
▶Latency Hiding
▶Little's Law
▶Memory Wall
▶MIMD (Multiple Instruction, Multiple Data) Machines

▶ Modulo Scheduling and Loop Pipelining
▶ Multilisp
▶ Multi-Threaded Processors
▶ Networks, Direct
▶ Networks, Multistage
▶ Processes, Tasks, and Threads
▶ Processors-in-Memory
▶ Shared-Memory Multiprocessors
▶ SPMD Computational Model
▶ Synchronization
▶ Ultracomputer, NYU
▶ VLIW Processors

Bibliography

1. Alverson R, Callahan D, Cummings D, Koblenz B, Porterfield A, Smith B (1990) The Tera computer system. In: Proceedings of the 1990 international conference on supercomputing, Amsterdam
2. Smith BJ (1981) Architecture and applications of the HEP multiprocessor computer system. Proc SPIE Real-Time Signal Process IV 298:241–248
3. Kuehn JT, Smith BJ (1988) The Horizon supercomputing system: architecture and software. In: Proceedings of the 1988 ACM/IEEE conference on supercomputing, Orlando
4. Thistle MR, Smith BJ (1988) A processor architecture for Horizon. In: Proceedings of the 1988 ACM/IEEE conference on supercomputing, Orlando
5. Callahan D, Smith B (1990) A future-based parallel language for a general-purpose highly-parallel computer. In: Selected papers of the second workshop on languages and compilers for parallel computing, Irvine
6. Halstead RH (1985) MultiLisp: a language for concurrent symbolic computation. ACM T Program Lang Syst 7(4):501–538
7. Alverson G, Briggs P, Coatney S, Kahan S, Korry R (1997) Tera hardware-software cooperation. In: Proceedings of supercomputing, San Jose
8. Ladner RE, Fischer MJ (1980) Parallel prefix computation. J ACM 27(4):831–838
9. Callahan D (1991) Recognizing and parallelizing bounded recurrences. In: Proceedings of the fourth workshop on languages and compilers for parallel computing, Santa Clara
10. Lam M (1988) Software pipelining: an effective scheduling technique for VLIW machines. In: Proceedings of the ACM SIGPLAN 88 conference on programming language design and implementation, Atlanta
11. Polychronopoulos C, Kuck D (1987) Guided self-scheduling: a practical scheduling scheme for parallel supercomputers. IEEE T Comput C-36(12):1425–1439
12. Alverson G, Alverson R, Callahan D, Koblenz B, Porterfield A, Smith B (1992) Exploiting heterogeneous parallelism on a multithreaded multiprocessor. In: Proceedings of the 1992 international conference on supercomputing, Washington, DC
13. Anderson T, Bershad B, Lazowska E, Levy H (1992) Scheduler activations: effective kernel support for the user-level management of parallelism. ACM T Comput Syst 10(1):53–79
14. Norton A, Melton E (1987) A class of Boolean linear transformations for conflict-free power-of-two stride access. In: Proceedings of the international conference on parallel processing, St. Charles, IL
15. Alverson R (1991) Integer division using reciprocals. In: Proceedings of the 10th IEEE symposium on computer arithmetic, Grenoble
16. Akers S, Krishnamurthy B (1989) A group-theoretic model for symmetric interconnection networks. IEEE T Comput C-38(4):555–566
17. Alverson G, Kahan S, Korry R, McCann C, Smith B (1995) Scheduling on the Tera MTA. In: Proceedings of the first workshop on job scheduling strategies for parallel processing, Santa Barbara. Lecture Notes in Computer Science 949:19–44

Terrestrial Ecosystem Carbon Modeling

Dali Wang[1], Daniel Ricciuto[1], Wilfred Post[1], Michael W. Berry[2]
[1]Oak Ridge National Laboratory, Oak Ridge, TN, USA
[2]The University of Tennessee, Knoxville, TN, USA

Synonyms

Carbon cycle research; System integration; Terrestrial ecosystem modeling; Uncertainty quantification

Definition

A Terrestrial Ecosystem Carbon Model (TECM) is a category of process-based ecosystem models that describe carbon dynamics of plants and soils within global terrestrial ecosystems. A TECM generally uses spatially explicit information on climate/weather, elevation, soils, vegetation, and water availability as well as soil- and vegetation-specific parameters to make estimates of important carbon fluxes and carbon pool sizes in terrestrial ecosystems.

Discussion

Introduction

Terrestrial ecosystems are a primary component of research on global environmental change. Observational and modeling research on terrestrial ecosystems at the global scale, however, has lagged behind their counterparts for oceanic and atmospheric systems, largely because of the unique challenges associated with the tremendous diversity and complexity of terrestrial ecosystems. There are eight major types of terrestrial ecosystem: tropical rain forest, savannas, deserts, temperate grassland, deciduous forest, coniferous forest, tundra, and chaparral. The carbon cycle is an important mechanism in the coupling of terrestrial ecosystems with climate through biological fluxes of CO_2. The influence of terrestrial ecosystems on atmospheric CO_2 can be modeled via several means at different timescales to incorporate several important processes, such as plant dynamics, change in land use, as well as ecosystem biogeography. Over the past several decades, many terrestrial ecosystem models (see the "▶Model Developments" section) have been developed to understand the interactions between terrestrial carbon storage and CO_2 concentration in the atmosphere, as well as the consequences of these interactions. Early TECMs generally adapted simple box-flow exchange models, in which photosynthetic CO_2 uptake and respiratory CO_2 release are simulated in an empirical manner with a small number of vegetation and soil carbon pools. Demands on kinds and amount of information required from global TECMs have grown. Recently, along with the rapid development of parallel computing, spatially explicit TECMs with detailed process-based representations of carbon dynamics become attractive, because those models can readily incorporate a variety of additional ecosystem processes (such as dispersal, establishment, growth, mortality, etc.) and environmental factors (such as landscape position, pest populations, disturbances, resource manipulations, etc.), and provide information to frame policy options for climate change impact analysis.

Key Components of TECM

1. Fundamental terrestrial ecosystem carbon dynamics

Terrestrial carbon processes can be described by an exchange between four major compartments: (1) foliage where photosynthesis occurs; (2) structural material, including roots and wood; (3) surface detritus or litter; and (4) soil organic matter (including peat). Nearly all life on Earth depends (directly or indirectly) on photosynthesis, in which carbon dioxide and water are used, and oxygen is released. The majority of the carbon in the living vegetation of terrestrial ecosystems is found in woody material, which constitutes a major carbon reservoir in the carbon cycle. Detritus refers to leaf litter and other organic matter on or below the soil surface. Dead woody material, often called coarse woody debris, is a large component of the surface detritus in forest ecosystems. Detritus is typically colonized by communities of microorganisms which act to decompose (or remineralize) the material. Transformation and translocation of detritus is the source of soil organic matter, another major component in the global carbon cycle. Globally three times as much carbon is stored in soils as in the atmosphere with peatlands contributing a third of this. Thus even relatively small changes in soil C stocks might contribute significantly to atmospheric CO_2 concentrations and thus global climate change. The soil carbon pool is vulnerable to impacts of human activity especially agriculture. A simplified scheme of carbon cycle dynamics is shown in Fig. 1.

2. Terrestrial carbon observations and experiments

Early research generally focused on determining characteristics of individual plants and small soil samples, often in a laboratory setting. This type of research continues today and provides a wealth of information that is used to develop and to parameterize TECMs. However, successful modeling of the carbon cycle also requires understanding the structure and response of entire ecosystems. Observation networks involving ecosystems have expanded greatly in the past two decades. One important development for in situ monitoring of ecosystem-level carbon exchange has been the establishment of flux towers that use the eddy covariance method. Atmospheric CO_2 concentration measurements using satellites, tall towers, and aircraft provide information about carbon dioxide fluxes over a larger scale. Finally, remote sensing products provide important information about changes in land use and vegetation characteristics (e.g., total leaf area) that can be used to either drive or validate TECMs. While these observations are important for characterizing the carbon cycle at present, they do not provide information about how the carbon cycle may change in the future as a result of climate change. In order to address those challenging questions, several large-scale ecosystem-level experiments have been conducted to mimic possible

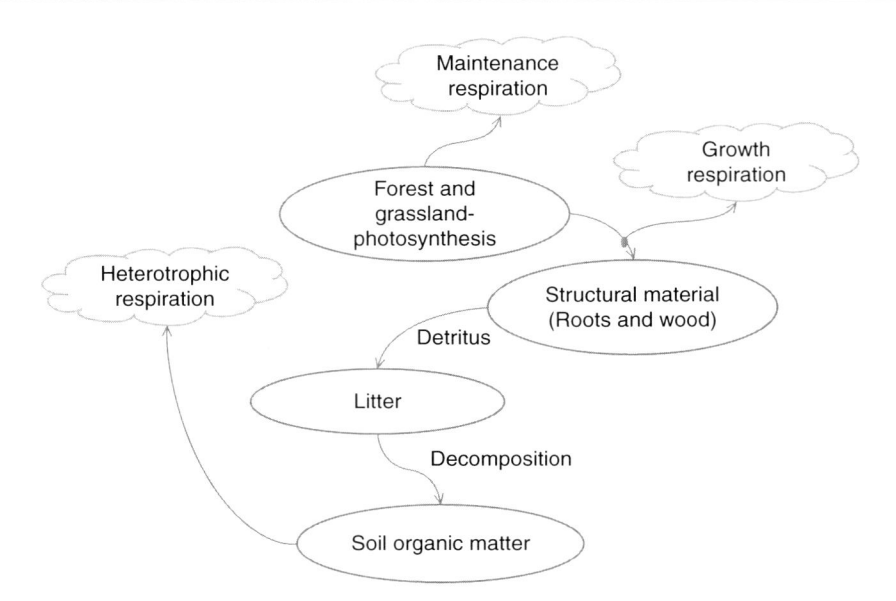

Terrestrial Ecosystem Carbon Modeling. Fig. 1 Simplified schematic of the carbon dynamics (photosynthesis, autotrophic respiration, allocation, and heterotrophic respiration) within a typical TECM model

future conditions (such as rising CO_2 concentrations, potential future precipitation patterns and the future temperature scenarios) and associated impacts and mitigation options for terrestrial ecosystems. Figure 2 illustrates some of these carbon observation systems and experiments.

3. Terrestrial ecosystem carbon model developments

In the early 1970s, several process-based conceptual models were developed to study the primary productivity of the biosphere and the uptake of anthropogenic CO_2 emissions. Early box models were improved in the 1980s to include more spatially explicit ecological representations of terrestrial ecosystems along with a significant push to understand the relationships between climatic measurements and properties of ecosystem processes. The concept of biomes was used to categorize terrestrial ecosystems using several climatically and geographically related factors (i.e., plant structure, leaf types, and climate), instead of the traditional classification by taxonomic similarity. In the 1990s, rapid developments of general circulation models and scientific computing, along with the increasing availability of remote sensing data (from satellites), led to the development of land-surface models. These models used satellite images to obtain information about the spatial distribution of surface properties (such as vegetation type, phenology, and density) along with spatially explicit forcing from numerical weather prediction reanalysis or coupled general circulation models (e.g., temperature and precipitation) to improve prediction and enhance the model representation of land-atmosphere water and energy interactions within global climate models. Recently, emphasis has been focused on improving the predictive capacity of climate models at the decadal to century scale through a better characterization of carbon cycle feedbacks with climate. For example, several TECMs are incorporating nutrient cycles and shifts in vegetation distribution, in response and a potential feedback to climate change.

The Contributions of Parallel Computing to TECM Developments

The contributions of parallel computing to the TECM can be classified into three separate categories: (1) model construction, (2) model integration, and (3) model behavior controls.

As more processes are incorporated into TECMs to replace simple empirical relationships, computational demands have increased. Since these processes are very

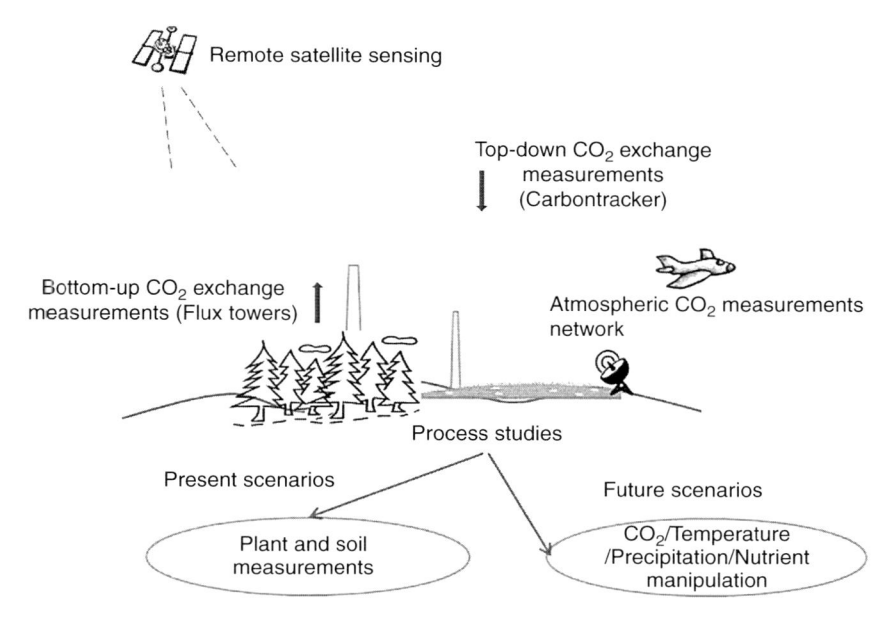

Terrestrial Ecosystem Carbon Modeling. Fig. 2 Illustrated carbon observations and experiments

sensitive to environmental heterogeneity inherent in spatial patterns of temperature, radiation, precipitation, soil characteristics, etc., increased spatial resolution improved simulation accuracy. A new class of models is becoming more widespread for global scale TECMs. This class, instead of using a traditional system of differential equations, is agent-based and requires a fine grid spatial representation to represent the competition for resources among the coexisting agents. This approach dramatically increases the computational demand, but is more compatible with experimental and observational data and population scale vegetation change processes. Parallel computing has enabled models to be constructed with these additional complexities.

Over several decades of research, TECMs have dramatically changed in structure and in the amount and kind of information required and produced making model integration a challenge. In addition, these models are now being incorporated into climate models to form Earth System Models (ESMs). From a parallel computing perspective, there is huge demand from the modeling community to develop a parallel model coupling framework (Earth System Modeling Frame (ESMF) is one of these kinds of efforts) to enable further parallel model developments and validations.

Instead of rewriting a package *wrapper* for each component, memory-based IO staging systems may provide an alternative method for fast and seamless coupling. There are two basic methods to provide climate forcing information for a TECM, from observation data or coupling to a global climate model simulation. Currently, model simulation can provide global data, but only at low spatial resolutions. Observation datasets are available at those fine resolutions, and can be used for validation over observed time frames at those observation stations. However, further research and parallel computing will be needed for gap-filling and downscaling those observation datasets for global terrestrial ecosystem carbon modeling.

One consequence of TECM complexity is the increasing demand for better methodologies that can exploit ever-increasing rich datastreams and thereby improve model behavior (e.g., the ecosystem model's sensitivity to the model parameters, and software structure). Quantitative methods need to be established to determine model uncertainty and reduce uncertainty through model-data analysis. As computers become larger and larger in the number of CPU cores, not necessarily faster and faster at the single CPU core level, we envision that ultrascale software designs for systematic uncertainty quantification for TECM will became one research area which will require the full advantage of parallel computing and statistics.

As our understanding of the global carbon cycle improves, high fidelity, process-based models will continue to be developed, and the increasing complexity of these ecosystem model systems will require that parallel computing play an increasingly important role. We have explained several key components of terrestrial ecosystem carbon modeling, and have classified three categories that parallel computing can play significant contributions to the TECM developments. It is our view that parallel computing will increasingly be an integral part of modern terrestrial ecosystem modeling efforts, which require solid, strong partnerships between the high-performance computing community and the carbon cycle science community. Through such partnerships these two communities can share a common mission to advance our understanding of global change using computational sciences.

Related Entries
▶Analytics, Massive-Scale
▶Computational Sciences
▶Exascale Computing

Bibliographic Notes and Further Reading

As mentioned in the model development section, terrestrial carbon modeling started in the early 1970s [1, 2], when beta-factor concept was developed to account for CO_2 fertilization using a nonspatial representation of terrestrial carbon dynamics. In 1975, Lieth described a model (MIAMI, the first gridded model) [3] to estimate the primary productivity of the biosphere. A carbon accounting model was developed at Marine Biological Laboratory (MBL) at Woods Hole to track carbon fluxes associated with land-use change. Along with the success of International Biological Program, spatially distributed compartment models representing different ecosystem types responding to local environmental conditions were developed. Widely used examples include the Terrestrial Ecosystem Model (www.mbl.edu/eco42/) at MBL, and CENTURY (www.nrel.colostate.edu/projects/century/) at Colorado State University. As satellite measurements of basic terrestrial properties became available, several models were developed that utilized this information directly, including the Ames-Stanford Approach (CASA) (geo.arc.nasa.gov/sge/casa/bearth.html) and Biome-BGC (www.ntsg.umt.edu/models/bgc/). In the 1990s, land surface components of climate models incorporated an aspect of terrestrial carbon cycling, namely photosynthesis, for the purpose of providing a mechanistic model of latent heat exchange with the atmosphere. The Simple Biosphere (SiB) biophysical model [4] and Biosphere-Atmosphere Transfer Scheme (BATS) [5] at National Center for Atmospheric Research (NCAR), and STOMATE [6] at Laboratoire des Sciences du Climat et de l'Environnement (LSCE) are examples. Later at NCAR, additional components of terrestrial carbon cycle were included in the Land Surface Model (LSM) (www.cgd.ucar.edu/tss/lsm/). The Community Land Model (CLM-CN) (www.cgd.ucar.edu/tss/clm/) is the successor of LSM and is being further developed as a community-based model. Agent-based models at the global scale, a class of what are called Dynamic Global Vegetation Models (DGVM), have been developed independently because of their data and computation demands. Developments in parallel computer systems are making incorporation of such dynamics plausible for earth system models. HYBRID [7] was an early experimental model, and now prototypes exist for the NCAR CCSM land surface CLM-CN which is based on the Lund-Postdam-Jena (LPJ) model [8] and called CLM-CN-DV. Evolved from the Ecosystem Demography (ED) model [9, 10], ENT [11] is another Dynamic Global Terrestrial Ecosystem Model (DGTEM), being coupled with NASA's GEOS-5 General Circulation Models.

Observation networks involving ecosystems have expanded greatly in the past two decades. AmeriFlux (public.ornl.gov/ameriflux/) is an effort to use flux towers to monitor ecosystem-level carbon exchange with atmosphere. Since 1990, more than 400 such flux towers have been established on six continents representing every major biome. First established in Mauna Loa in 1958, the CO_2 measurements have become a global operation. Inversion techniques are used to infer the pattern of CO_2 fluxes required to produce the observed CO_2 concentrations; one such product using this technique is CarbonTracker (www.esrl.noaa.gov/gmd/ccgg/carbontracker/), which provides weekly flux estimates that can be compared against output from process-based TECMs. Currently, a variety of remote sensing products (such as Moderate Resolution Imaging Spectroradiometer (MODIS)) are available to either drive or validate TECMs.

Several experiments have been conducted or initiated to understand potential climate change impacts. The Free-Air CO_2 Enrichment (FACE) (public.ornl.gov/face/global_face.shtml) experiment has been running for over a decade at several sites in different biomes to study the potential effects of higher CO_2 concentration. The Throughfall Displacement Experiment (TDE) (tde.ornl.gov/) used elaborate systems to alter the amount of precipitation that is available to an ecosystem. A new experiment has been initiated at Oak Ridge National Laboratory to assess the responses of northern peatland ecosystems to increased temperature and exposures to elevated atmospheric CO_2 concentrations (mnspruce.ornl.gov).

More information on terrestrial ecosystem carbon modeling can be found in books devoted to this subject [12, 13].

Bibliography

1. Bacastow RB, Keeling CD (1973) Atmospheric carbon dioxide and radiocarbon in the natural carbon cycle: II. Changes from AD 1700 to 2070 as deduced from a geochemical model. In: Woodwell GM, Pecan EV (eds) Carbon and the biosphere. CONF-720510. National Technical Information Service, Springfield, Virginia, pp 86–135
2. Emanuel WR, Killough GG, Post WM, Shugart HH (1984) Modeling terrestrial ecosystems in the global carbon cycle with shifts in carbon storage capacity by land-use change. Ecology 65(3): 970–983
3. Lieth H (1975) Modeling the primary productivity of the world. In: Lieth H, Wittaker RH (eds) Primary productivity of the biosphere, ecological studies, vol 14. Springer-Verlag, New York, pp 237–283
4. Sellers JP, Randell DA, Collatz GJ, Berry JA, Field CB, Dazlich DA, Zhang C, Collelo GD, Bounua L (1996) A revised land surface parametrization (SiB 2) for atmospheric GCMs. Part I: model formulation. J Climate 9:676–705
5. Dickinson R, Henderson-sellers A, Kennedy P (1993) Biosphere-atmosphere transfer scheme (BATS) version as coupled to the NCAR community climate model. Technical report, National Center for Atmospheric Research
6. Ducoudré N, Laval K, Perrier A (1993) SECHIBA, a new set of parametrizations of the hydrologic exchanges at the land/atmosphere interface within the LMD atmospheric general circulation model. J Climate 6(2):248–273
7. Friend AD, Stevens AK, Knox RG, Cannell MGR (1997) A process-based, terrestrial biosphere model of ecosystem dynamics (Hybrid v3.0). Ecol Model 95:249–287
8. Prentice IC, Heimann M, Sitch S (2000) The carbon balance of the terrestrial biosphere: ecosystem models and atmospheric observations. Ecol Appl 10:1553–1573
9. Moorcroft P, Hurtt GC, Pacala SW (2001) A method for scaling vegetation dynamics: the ecosystem demography model (ED). Ecol Monogr 71(4):557–586
10. Govindarajan S, Dietze MC, Agarwal PK, Clark JS (2004) A scalable simulator for forest dynamics. In: Proceedings of the twentieth annual symposium on computational geometry SCG 04, Brooklyn, NY, pp 106–115, doi:10.1145/997817.997836
11. Yang W, Ni-Meister W, Kiang NY, Moorcroft P, Strahler AH, Oliphant A (2010) A clumped-foliage canopy radiative transfer model for a Global Dynamic Terrestrial Ecosystem Model II: Comparison to measurements. Agricultural and Forest Meteorology, 150(7):895–907, doi:10.1016/j.agrformet.2010.02.008
12. Trabalka JR, Reichle DE (ed) (1986) The changing carbon cycle: a global analysis. Springer-Verlag, Berlin
13. Field CB, Raupach MR (ed) (2004) The global carbon cycle: integrating human, climate, and the natural world. Island, Washington, DC

Terrestrial Ecosystem Modeling

▶ Terrestrial Ecosystem Carbon Modeling

The High Performance Substrate

▶ HPS Microarchitecture

Theory of Mazurkiewicz-Traces

▶ Trace Theory

Thick Ethernet

▶ Ethernet

Thin Ethernet

▶ Ethernet

Thread Level Speculation (TLS) Parallelization

▶ Speculation, Thread-Level

Thread-Level Data Speculation (TLDS)

▶ Speculative Parallelization of Loops
▶ Speculation, Thread-Level

Thread-Level Speculation

▶ Speculative Parallelization of Loops
▶ Speculation, Thread-Level

Threads

▶ Processes, Tasks, and Threads

Tiling

FRANÇOIS IRIGOIN
MINES ParisTech/CRI, Fontainebleau, France

Synonyms

Blocking; Hyperplane partitioning; Loop blocking; Loop tiling; Supernode partitioning

Definition

Tiling is a program transformation used to improve the spatial and/or temporal memory locality of a loop nest by changing its iteration order, and/or to reduce its synchronization or communication overhead by controlling the granularity of its parallel execution. Tiling adds some control overhead because the number of loops is doubled, and reduces the amount of parallelism available in the outermost loops. The n initial loops are replaced by n outer loops used to enumerate the tiles and n inner loops used to execute all the iterations within a tile.

Discussion

Introduction

Tiling is useful for most recent parallel computer architectures, with shared or distributed memory, since they all rely on locality to exploit their memory hierarchies and on parallelism to exploit several cores. It is also useful for heterogeneous architectures with hardware accelerators, and for monoprocessors with caches. Unlike many loop transformations, tiling is not a unimodular transformation. Iterations that are geometrically close in the loop nest iteration set are grouped in so-called *tiles* to be executed together atomically. Tiles are also called blocks when their edges are parallel to the axes or more generally when their facets are orthogonal to the base vectors. For instance, the parallel stencil written in C:

```
for(i1=1;i1<n;i1++)
   for(i2=1;i2<m;i2++)
     a[i1][i2] = 0.2*(b[i1-1][i2]
                +b[i1][i2]
                +b[i1+1][i2]
                +b[i1][i2-1]
                +b[i1][i2+1])
```

can be transformed into:

```
#pragma omp parallel for
for(t1=1;t1<n;t1+=b1)
#pragma omp parallel for
  for(t2=1;t2<m;t2+=b2)
    // tile code
    for(i1=t1;i1<min(t1+b1, n);i1++)
      for(i2=t2;i2<min(t2+b2, m);i2++)
        a[i1][i2] = 0.2*(b[i1-1][i2]
                   +b[i1][i2]
                   +b[i1+1][i2]
                   +b[i1][i2-1]
                   +b[i1][i2+1])
```

where `t1` and `t2` are tile coordinates and `b1` and `b2` are the tile or block sizes.

Initially, this tiling transformation was called loop blocking by Allen & Kennedy and tiling by Wolfe [32, 33] before it was extended to slanted tiles under the name of supernode partitioning by Irigoin and Triolet [21]. Wolfe suggested to use systematically the

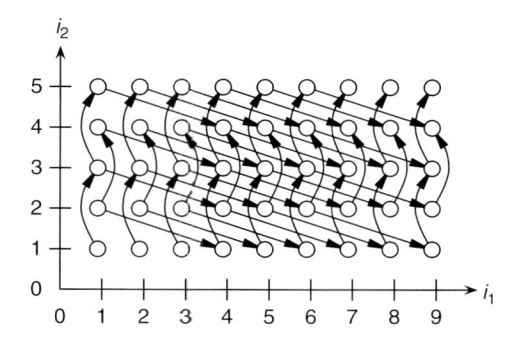

Tiling. Fig. 1 Iteration space with dependence vectors

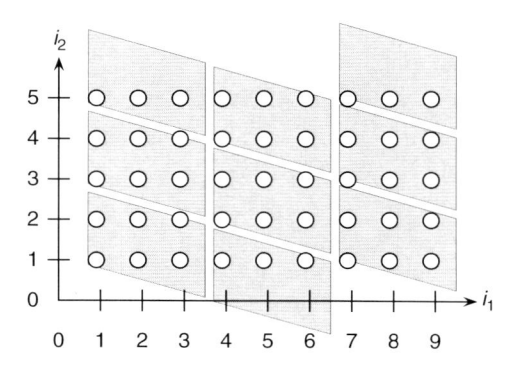

Tiling. Fig. 2 Tiled iteration set

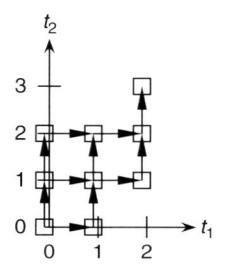

Tiling. Fig. 3 Iteration set for tiles, with tile dependence vectors

name tiling as it is short and easy to understand. He uses it in his textbook about program transformations [34]. But loop blocking is still used because it is a proper subset of tiling: see, for instance, Allen and Kennedy [4].

Slanted tiles can be used with these sequential Fortran loops taken from Xue [35]

```
do i1 = 1, 9
  do i2 = 1, 5
    a(i1,i2) = a(i1,i2-2)+a(i1-3,i2+1)
  enddo
enddo
```

whose 2-D iteration set and dependence vectors are shown in Fig. 1 (All figures are taken or derived from Figure 4.1, page 103, of Xue [35] by courtesy of the publisher. Some were adapted or derived to fit the notations used in this entry.). These two loops can be transformed into

```
do t1 = 0, 2
  do t2 = max(it-1,0), (it+4)/2
    do i1 = 3*t1+1, 3*t1+3
      do i2 = max(-t1+2*t2+1,1),
              min((-t1+6*t2+9)/3,5)
        a(i1,i2) = a(i1,i2-2)
                  +a(i1-3,i2+1)
      enddo
    enddo
  enddo
enddo
```

using slanted tiles with vectors $(3,-1)$ and $(0,2)$ shown in Fig. 2. The sets of integer points in each tile are not slanted in this case, but they are not horizontally aligned as shown by the *grey* areas. The tile iteration set is shown in Fig. 3. Note that Fortran allows negative array indices, which makes references to a(1,-1) and a(-2,2) possibly legal.

Mathematically speaking, this grouping/blocking is a partition of the loop iteration space that induces a renumbering and a reordering of the iterations. This reordering should not modify the program semantics. Hence, several issues are linked to tiling as to any other program transformations: Why should tiling be considered? What are the legal tilings for a given loop nest? How is an optimal tiling chosen? How is the transformed code generated?

Motivations for Tiling

Tiling has several positive impacts. Depending on the target architecture, it reduces the synchronization overhead, the communication overhead, the cache coherency traffic, the number of external memory accesses, and the amount of memory required to execute a loop nest in an accelerator or a scratch pad memory, or the number of cache misses. Thus, the execution time and/or the energy used to execute the loop nest are reduced, or the execution with a small memory is made possible.

Tiling also has two possibly negative impacts. The control overhead is increased, if only because the number of loops is doubled, and the amount of parallelism degree is smaller at the tile level because the initial parallelism is partly transferred within each tile and traded for locality and communication and synchronization overheads. The control overhead depends on the code generation phase, especially when partial tiles are needed to cover the boundaries of the iteration set.

Tile selection depends on the target architecture. For shared memory multiprocessors, including multicores, the primary bottleneck is the memory bandwidth and tiling is used to improve the cache hit ratio by reducing the memory footprint, that is, the set of live variables that should be kept in cache, and to reduce the cache coherency traffic. Some array references in the initial code must exhibit some spatial and/or temporal locality for tiling to be beneficial.

Tiling can be applied again, recursively or hierarchically, to increase locality at the different cache levels (L0, L1, L2, L3,…) and even at the register level by using very small tiles compatible with the number of registers. These register tiles are fully unrolled to exploit the registers. The tiling of tiles is also known as multilevel tiling. Tiling can also be used to increase locality at the virtual memory page level as shown in 1969 by McKeller and Coffman in [24].

For vector multiprocessors, the size of the tiles must be large enough to use the vector units efficiently, but small enough for their memory footprint to fit in the local cache, which is one of many trade-offs encountered in tile selection.

For distributed memory multiprocessors, tiling is used to generate automatically distributed code. The tiles are mapped on the processors and the processors communicate data on or close to the tile boundaries. Let p be the edge length of a n-dimensional tile. The idea is to compute $O(p^n)$ values and exchange only $O(p^{n-1})$ values so as to overlap the computation with communication although computations are faster than communications. The amount of memory on each processor is supposed large enough not to be a constraint, but the value of p is adjusted to trade parallelism against communication and synchronization overheads. As mentioned above, these large tiles can be tiled again if locality or parallelism is an issue at the elementary processor level.

Heterogeneous processors using hardware accelerators, FPGA- or GPGPU- based, require the same kind of trade-offs. Either large tiles must be executed on the accelerator to benefit from its parallel architecture, or small tiles only are possible because of the limited local memory, but in both cases communications between the host and the accelerator must take place asynchronously during the computation. Tiling is used to meet the local memory or vector register size constraints, and to generate opportunities for asynchronous transfers overlapped with the computation.

Multiprocessors System-on-Chip (MPSoC) designed for embedded processing may combine some local internal memories, a.k.a. scratchpad memories, and a global external memory, which make them distributed systems with a global memory. Tiling is used to meet the local memory constraints, but communications between the processors or between the processors and the external global memory must be generated. Other transformations, such as *loop fusion* and *array contraction* (see ▶Parallelization, Automatic), are used in combination with tiling to reduce the communication and the execution time. A combination of loop fusion and loop distribution may give a better result than the tiling of fused loops, at least when the scratchpad memory is very small.

Tiling can also be applied to multidimensional arrays instead of loop nests. This approach is used by *High-Performance Fortran* (see ▶High Performance Fortran (HPF)). The code generation is derived from the initial code and from mapping constraints, based, for instance, on the *owner-computes* rule: the computation must be located where the result is stored. This idea may also be applied to speed up array IOs and out-of-core computations.

Finally, tiling can be applied to more general spaces and sets. For instance, Griebl [15] use the ▶*Polyhedron Model* to map larger pieces of code to a unique space of large dimension. Sequences of loops can be mapped onto such a space and be tiled globally.

Because of the many machine architectures that can benefit from tiling, numerous papers have been published on the subject. It is important to check what kind of architecture is targeted before reading or comparing them.

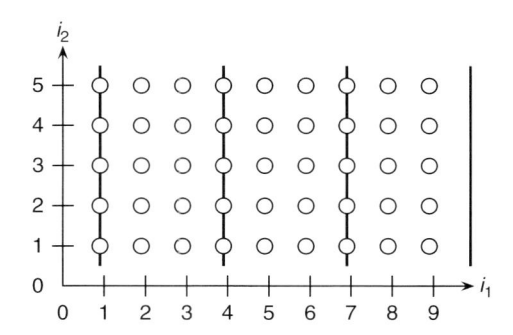

Tiling. Fig. 4 First hyperplane partitioning with $h_1 = \left(\frac{1}{3}, 0\right)$ and $o = (1,1)$

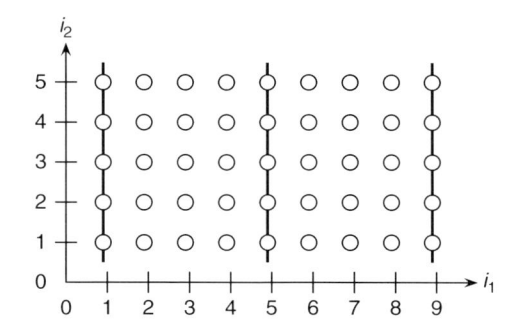

Tiling. Fig. 5 Same hyperplane partitioning with a smaller $h_1 = \left(\frac{1}{4}, 0\right)$

Legality of Tiling

The general definition and legality of tiling were introduced by Irigoin and Triolet who gave sufficient legality conditions in [21]. Necessary conditions were added later by Xue [35].

The basic idea is to use parallel hyperplanes defined by a normal vector h to slice the iteration space Z^n, where n is the number of nested loops, to obtain a partition. The partition of a set E is a set P of nonempty subsets of E, whose two-by-two intersection is always empty and whose union is equal to e. Each slice is mathematically speaking a part (there is no agreement about the naming of elements of P: part, block or cell are used. We chose to use *part*) and two iteration vectors j_1 and j_2 belong to the same part if $\lfloor h.(j_1 - o) \rfloor = \lfloor h.(j_2 - o) \rfloor$, where . denotes the scalar product, $\lfloor\ \rfloor$ the floor function, and o is an offset vector. For instance, using the normal vector $h = \left(\frac{1}{3}, 0\right)$ and the offset $o = (1,1)$, the iteration set of Fig. 1 is partitioned in three parts shown in Fig. 4. Because of this definition, the slices, or parts become larger when the norm of h decreases (see Fig. 5). To make sure that the parts can be executed one after the other, dependence cycles between two parts must be avoided. For instance, the diagonal partition in Fig. 6 creates a cycle between the two subsets. Iteration $(2,1)$ must be executed before iteration $(2,3)$, so the left subset must be executed before the right subset, but iteration $(1,2)$ must be executed before iteration $(4,1)$, which is incompatible.

Cycles between subsets are avoided if each dependence vector d in the loop nest meets the condition $h.d \geq 0$. This condition does depend neither on $\|h\|$, the norm of h, nor on the iteration set, which makes

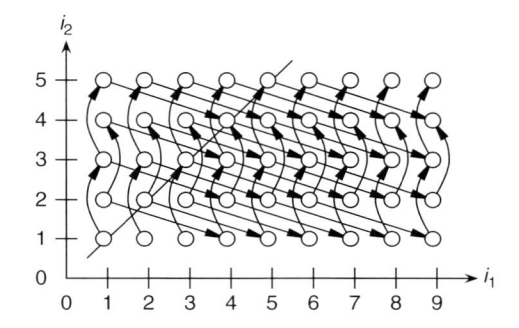

Tiling. Fig. 6 Dependence cycle between two parts

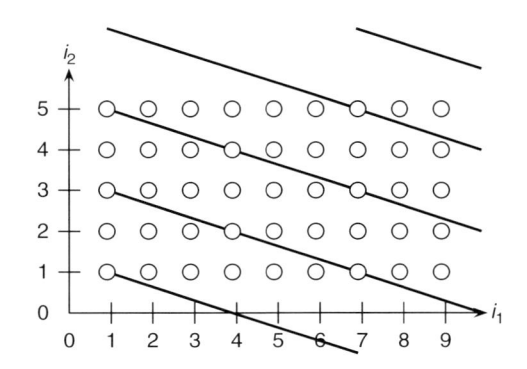

Tiling. Fig. 7 Second hyperplane partitioning with $h_2 = \left(\frac{1}{6}, \frac{1}{2}\right)$ and $o = (1,1)$

all such legal tilings scalable to meet the different needs enumerated above.

Several hyperplane partitionings $h_1, h_2, \ldots$ can be combined to increase the number of parts and reduce their sizes (see Figs. 7 and 8). The vectors $h_1, h_2, \ldots$ are usually grouped (Xue [35] uses H to denote the transposed matrix of H, that is, the h vectors are transformed into affine forms) together in a matrix, H. When the

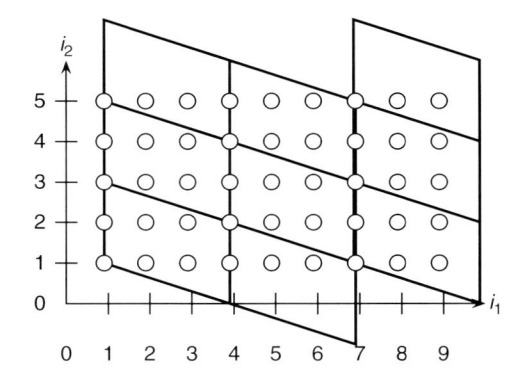

Tiling. Fig. 8 Combined 2-D hyperplane partitioning

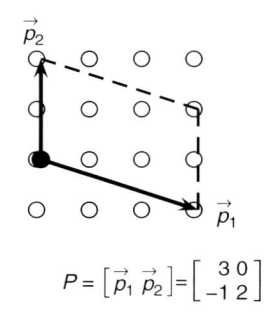

$$P = \begin{bmatrix} \vec{p}_1 & \vec{p}_2 \end{bmatrix} = \begin{bmatrix} 3 & 0 \\ -1 & 2 \end{bmatrix}$$

Tiling. Fig. 9 Partitioning or clustering matrix

number of different hyperplane families h_i used is equal to the number of nested loops n and when the h_i are linearly independent vectors, the part sizes are bounded, regardless of the iteration set, and all parts of the iteration space are equal up to a translation if H^{-1} is an integer matrix. However, the parts of the iteration set L may differ because of the loop boundaries. See, for instance, tile $(2,3)$, the upper right tile in Fig. 2, which contains only three iterations.

The transpose of H^{-1}, the partitioning matrix P, contains the edges of the tile and its determinant is the number of iterations within each tile. So P (Fig. 9) is easier to visualize than H (Fig. 10). Note that $det(P) = 6$, which is the maximum number of iterations within one tile, as can be seen on Fig. 2.

A tiling H is defined by the number of hyperplane sets used, by the directions of the normal vectors h_i and by their relative norms, that is, the tile shape, and by the number of iterations within a tile, that is, the tile size. The tile shape is defined when $det(H) = 1$. The tile size is controlled by a scaling coefficient. The tiling origin is another parameter impacting mostly the code generation, but also the execution time. Often, a

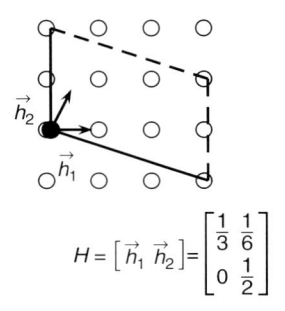

$$H = \begin{bmatrix} \vec{h}_1 & \vec{h}_2 \end{bmatrix} = \begin{bmatrix} \frac{1}{3} & \frac{1}{6} \\ 0 & \frac{1}{2} \end{bmatrix}$$

Tiling. Fig. 10 Hyperplane matrix H

tiling selection is decomposed into the selection of a shape and the selection of a size and finally the choice of an offset.

The legality conditions are summed up by $H^T R \geq 0$, where R is a matrix made of the *rays of a convex cone* containing all possible dependence vectors d, because the condition $h.d \geq 0$ is convex. The computation of R by a dependence test is explained by Irigoin and Triolet [21] and the dependence cone is one of many approximations of the dependence vector set. When dependences are *uniform* (see ▶Dependences), R can be built directly with the dependence vectors. The valid hyperplanes h belong to another cone, dual of R.

A necessary and sufficient condition, $\lfloor H^T d \rfloor \succeq 0$, was introduced by Xue [35] in 1997, where $\succeq$ is the lexicographic order, but it does not bring any practical improvement over the previous sufficient condition. Xue also provided an exact legality test based on integer programming and using information about the iteration set $L(j)$, that is, the loop bounds of the initial loop nest.

Note also that the subset of tilings such that $det(H) = 1$ is the set of unimodular transformations and that $H^T d \geq 0$ is their legality condition (see ▶Loop Nest Parallelization).

Tile Selection and Optimal Tiling

Tile selection requires some choice criterion, and optimal tile selection some cost function. The cost function is obviously dependent on the target machine, which makes many optimal tilings possible since many target architectures can benefit from tiling. Also, if the cost function is the execution time, the tiling per se is only part of the compilation scheme. The execution time of one tile depends on the scheduling of the local iterations, for instance because each processor has some vector capability. It also depends on the tiles previously executed on the same processor, whether a cache or a local memory is used, that is, it depends on the *mapping* of tiles on processor. And finally, the total execution time of the tiled nest depends on the schedule and on the mapping of the tiles on the logical or physical resources, threads, or cores.

In other words, any optimal tiling is optimal with respect to a cost function modeling the execution time or the energy for a given target. Models used to derive analytical optimal solutions often assume that the execution and the communication times are respectively proportional to the computation and communication volumes, which is not realistic, especially with multicores, superword parallelism, and several levels of cache memories. Models may also assume that the number of processors available (because of multicore and multi-threaded architectures, the definition of *processor*, virtual or physical, is not well defined. Here, the processor is not a chip, but rather the total number of physical threads in a multicore or the total number of user processes running simultaneously in the machine) is greater than the number of tiles that can be executed simultaneously, which simplifies the mapping of tiles on processors.

When the target architecture has some kind of implicit vector capability, for instance when the cache lines are loaded, a partial tiling with $rank(H) < n$, that is, a set of hyperplane partitionings, may be more effective than a full tiling. Tiles are not longer bounded by the hyperplanes, but they remain bounded by the initial loop nest iteration set.

Because the execution time of real machine becomes more and more complex with the number of transistors used, iterative compilation is used when performance is key. The code is compiled and executed with different tile sizes and the best tile size is retained. Symbolic tiling is useful to speed up the process.

Some decisions can be made at run time. For instance, Rastello et al. [25] use run-time scheduling to speed-up the execution. Note that they overlap the computations and the communications related to *one* tile, which somehow breaks the tile atomicity constraint.

Tiled Code Generation

As for tiling optimality, tile code generation depends on the target machine. A parallel machine requires the mapping and the parallel execution of the tiles. A distributed memory machine also requires communication generation. A processor with a memory hierarchy and/or a vector capability requires loop optimization at the tile level. The minimal requirement is that all iterations of the initial loop nest are performed by the tiled nest.

Let vector j be an iteration of loop nest L, t a tile coordinate, and l the local coordinate of an iteration within a tile t. Since no redundant computations are added by hyperplane partitioning, the relationship between j and (t, l) is a one-to-one mapping from the initial set of iterations $L(j)$ to the new iteration set $T(t, l)$. Ancourt and Irigoin [5] show that an affine relationship can be built between j and (t, l) and that the new loop bounds for t and l can be derived from this relationship and from L when the matrix H is numerically known and when L is a parametric polyhedron, that is, when the loop bounds are affine functions of loop indices and parameters. To simplify array subscript expressions, the code may be generated using t and j instead of t and l. This optimization is used in the code examples given above.

This loop nest generation is sufficient for shared memory machines, although it is better to generate several versions of the tile code, one for the full tiles, and several ones for the partial tiles on the iteration set boundaries, in order to reduce the average control overhead. Multilevel tiling is also used to reduce the overhead due to partial tiles on the boundaries (see the top left and top right tiles in Fig. 2).

This does not specify the mapping of tiles onto threads or cores when the tile parallelism is greater than the number of processors. But locality-aware scheduling lets tiles inherit data from other tiles previously executed on the same thread as suggested by Xue and Huang in [37] who minimize the number of partitioning hyperplanes, that is, the rank of H.

Parametric tiling does not require H to be numerically known at compile time. The tile size, if not the tile shape, can be adjusted at run time or optimized dynamically. A technique is proposed by Renganarayanna et al. [28] for multilevel tiling, and another one by Hartono et al. [18, 23].

Note that parallelism within tiles or across tiles is obtained by *wavefronting*, a unimodular loop transformation (see ▶Loop Nest Parallelization), unless the initial loop nest is fully parallel, in which case cone R is empty or reduced to $\{0\}$. For instance, the tiles $(1,0)$ and $(1,0)$ on Fig. 3 can be computed in parallel.

Applicability

Tiling and hyperplane partitioning are defined for perfectly nested loops only, but many algorithms, including matrix multiply, are made of non-perfectly nested loops. It is possible to move all non-perfectly nested statements into the loop nest body by adding guards (a.k.a. statement sinking), but these guards must then be carefully moved or removed when the tile code is generated. The issue is tackled directly by Ahmed et al. [3] and Griebl [15, 16], who avoid statement sinking by mapping all statement in another space (see ▶Polyhedron Model) and by applying transformations, including tiling, on this space before code generation, and by Hartono et al. [18] who use a polyhedral representation of the code to generate multilevel tilings of imperfectly nested loops. See the Polyhedron Model entry for more information about the mapping of a piece of code onto a polyhedral space.

Tiling can also be applied to loop nests containing commutative and associative reductions, but this does not fit the general legality condition $HR \geq 0$.

Tiling can be applied by the programmer. For instance, 3-D tiling improved with array padding has been used to optimize 3-D PDE solvers and 3-D stencil codes. Tiling has been used to optimize some instances of dynamic programming, the resolution of the heat equation, and even some sparse computations. Because tiling is difficult to apply by hand, source-to-source tilers have been developed.

Finally, Guo et al. suggest in [17] to support tiling at the programming language level, using hierarchically tiled arrays (HTA) to keep the code readable, while letting the programmer be in control.

Related Loop Transformations

The partitioning matrix $P = \left(H^T\right)^{-1}$ can be built step-by-step by a combination of loop skewing, or more generally any unimodular loop transformations, strip-minings (1-D tiling), and loop interchanges. Loop skewing is a unimodular transformation used to change the iteration coordinates and to make loop blocking legal because the new loop nest obtained is *fully permutable*.

In other words, the P matrix is replaced by the product of a diagonal matrix Λ, which defines a rectangular tiling, a.k.a. loop blocking, and of $\frac{1}{det(P)}P$, and the tiling by a sequence of easier transformations. This is advocated by Allen & Kennedy in their textbook [4]. Reducing tiling to blocking via basis changes, for example, using a Smith normal form of H, is also often used to optimize the tile shape and size, but some of the tile shape problem remains and the constraints of the iteration set L usually become more complex.

Strip-mining is a 1-D tiling, a degenerated case of hyperplane partitioning. It is used to adapt the parallelism available to the hardware resources, for instance vector registers.

Loop interchange is a unimodular transformation. Like all unimodular transformations, it is an extreme case of tiling with no tiling effect because $det(H) = 1$, that is, each tile contains only one element. It is often used to increase locality.

Loop unroll-and-jam first unrolls an outer loop by some factor k, that is, it is a strip-mining followed by a full unroll of the new loop. Then, the replicated innermost loops are fused (jammed). This is equivalent to a rectangular hyperplane partitioning with blocking factors $(k, 1, 1, \ldots)$, followed by an unrolling of the tile loop. Unroll-and-jam can be applied to several outer loops with several factors, which again is equivalent to a rectangular tiling with the same factors followed by an unrolling of the tile loops. Unroll-and-jam is used to increase locality and is effective like tiling if some references exhibit temporal locality along outer loops.

Tiling is designed to forbid redundant computations. However, overlap between tiles can reduce communications at the expense of additional computation. Data overlaps are also used to compile ▶HPF (High-Performance Fortran) using the owner compute rule.

Finally, tiling is also related to the partitioning of ▶systolic arrays, used to fit a large parametric size iteration set on a fixed-size chip.

Future Directions

Although tiling is a powerful transformation by itself, and quite complex to use, it does not include some other key transformations such as loop fusion or loop peeling. Furthermore, the loop body is handled as a unique statement although it may contain sequences, tests, and loops.

So more complex code transformations were advocated in 1991 by Wolf and Lam [31] to optimize parallelism and locality. More recently, Griebl [15] and Bondhugula et al. [8] use the polyhedral framework (see ▶Polyhedron Model) to handle each elementary statement individually, at least within static control pieces of code. This is also attempted within gcc with the Graphite plug-in.

Otherwise, it is possible to move away from the complexity of tiling by replacing it with sequences of simpler transformations, including hyperplane partitioning. The difficulty is then to decide which sequence leads to an optimal or at least to a well-performing code.

In case the execution time of each iteration is different or even very different, the tile equality constraint could be lifted up to obtain a nonuniform partitioning. This has already been done in the 1-D case. In such cases, strip-mining is replaced by more complex partitions to map the parallel iterations onto the processors. The larger partitions are executed first to reduce the imbalance between processors at the end without increasing the control overhead at the beginning (see ▶Nested loops scheduling).

Related Entries
▶Code Generation
▶Dependences
▶Dependence Abstractions
▶Dependence Analysis
▶Distributed-Memory Multiprocessor
▶HPF (High Performance Fortran)
▶Locality of Reference and Parallel Processing
▶Loop Nest Parallelization
▶Parallelization, Automatic
▶Polyhedron Model
▶Shared-Memory Multiprocessors
▶Systolic Arrays
▶Unimodular Transformations

Bibliographic Notes and Further Reading
The best reference about tiling is the book written by Xue [35]. It provides the necessary background on linear algebra and program transformations. It starts with rectangular tilings before moving to slanted, that is, parallelepiped, tilings. Code generation for distributed memory machines and tiling optimizations are finally addressed.

Tile size optimization is addressed explicitly by Coleman and McKinley [12] to eliminate cache capacity, self-interference, and cross-interference misses, that is, for locality improvement.

For shared memory machines, Högstedt et al. [20] introduce the concepts of *idle time* and *rise* for a tiling, and optimal tile shape for a multiprocessor with a memory hierarchy. They propose an algorithm to select an non-rectangular optimal tile shape for a shared memory multiprocessor, with enough processors to use all parallelism available. They assume that the tile execution time is proportional to its volume. Rastello and Robert [26] provide a closed form for the tile shape that minimizes the number of cache misses during the execution of a rectangular tile for a given cache size and for parallel loops, that is, without tiling legality constraints. They also provide a heuristic to optimize the same function for any shape of tiles.

For distributed memory machines, the contributions to the quest for analytic solutions are numerous. Boulet et al. [10] carefully include a question mark in their paper title, *(Pen)-ultimate tiling?*. Hodzic and Shang give several closed forms for the size and the relative side lengths [19]. Xue [36] uses communication/computation overlap and provides a closed form for the optimal tile size.

Tile shapes are restrained to orthogonal shapes by Andonov et al. [7] in order to find an optimal solution. For 2-D iteration spaces, using the BSP model and an unbounded number of processors, Andonov et al. [6] provide closed forms for the optimal tiling parameters and the optimal number of processors.

Agarwal et al. [1, 2] introduce a method for deriving an optimal hyperparallelepiped tiling of iteration spaces for minimal communication in multiprocessors with caches and for distributed shared-memory multiprocessors. More recently, Bondhugula et al. [9] tile sequences of imperfectly nested loops for locality and parallelism. They use an analytical model and integer linear optimization.

Carter et al. introduce hierarchical tiling for superscalar machines [11], but the tuning is handmade. Renganarayanna and Rajopadhye [27] determine optimal tile sizes with a BSP-like model. Strzodka et al. [29] use multilevel tiling to speed up stencil computations by optimizing simultaneously locality, parallelism and vectorization.

For distributed memory machines, communication code must be generated too. See Ancourt [5], Tang [30], Xue [35], Chapter 6 and 7, and finally Goumas et al. [14], who generate MPI code automatically.

Goumas et al. propose [13] a tile code generation algorithm for parallelepiped tiles. This can be used for general tiles thanks to changes of basis.

Bibliography

1. Agarwal A, Kranz D, Natarajan V (1993) Automatic partitioning of parallel loops for cache-coherent multiprocessors. In: International conference on parallel processing (ICPP), Syracuse University, Syracuse, NY, 16–20 August 1993, vol 1, pp 2–11
2. Agarwal A, Kranz DA, Natarajan V (September 1995) Automatic partitioning of parallel loops and data arrays for distributed shared-memory multiprocessors. IEEE Trans Parallel Distrib Syst 6(9):943–962
3. Ahmed N, Mateev N, Pingali K (2000) Synthesizing transformations for locality enhancement of imperfectly-nested loop nests. In: Proceedings of the 14th international conference on supercomputing, Santa Fe, 8–11 May 2000, pp 141–152
4. Allen R, Kennedy K (2002) Optimizing compilers for modern architectures: a dependence-based approach. Morgan-Kaufmann. San Francisco, pp 477–491
5. Ancourt C, Irigoin F (1991) Scanning polyhedra with DO loops. In: Third ACM symposium on principles and practice of parallel programming, Williamsburg, VA, pp 39–50
6. Andonov R, Balev S, Rajopadhye S, Yanev N (July 2001) Optimal semi-oblique tiling. In: Proceedings of the 13th annual ACM symposium on parallel algorithms and architectures, Crete Island, pp 153–162
7. Andonov R, Rajopadhye SV, Yanev N (1998) Optimal orthogonal tiling. In: Proceedings of the fourth international Euro-Par conference on parallel processing, Southampton, 1–4 Sept 1998, pp 480–490
8. Bondhugula U, Baskaran M, Krishnamoorthy S, Ramanujam J, Rountev A, Sadayappan P (2008) Automatic transformations for communication-minimized parallelization and locality optimization in the polyhedral model. In: Proceedings of the joint European conferences on theory and practice of software 17th international conference on compiler construction, Budapest, Hungary, 29 March–6 April 2008
9. Bondhugula U, Hartono A, Ramanujam J, Sadayappan P (June 2008) A practical automatic polyhedral parallelizer and locality optimizer. In: PLDI 2008. ACM SIGPLAN Not 43(6)
10. Boulet P, Darte A, Risset T, Robert Y (1996) (Pen)-ultimate tiling? Integr: VLSI J 17:33–51
11. Carter L, Ferrante J, Hummel SF (1995) Hierarchical tiling for improved superscalar performance. In: Proceedings of the ninth international symposium on parallel processing, Santa Barbara, 25–28 April 1995, pp 239–245
12. Coleman S, McKinley KS (June 1995) Tile size selection using cache organization and data layout. In: PLDI'95; ACM SIGPLAN Not 30(6):279–290
13. Goumas G, Athanasaki M, Koziris N (2002) Automatic code generation for executing tiled nested loops onto parallel architectures. In: Proceedings of the 2002 ACM symposium on applied computing, Madrid, Spain, 11–14 March 2002
14. Goumas G, Drosinos N, Athanasaki M, Koziris N (November 2006) Message-passing code generation for non-rectangular tiling transformations. Parallel Computing 32(10): 711–732
15. Griebl M (July 2001) On tiling space-time mapped loop nests. In: Proceedings of the 13th annual ACM symposium on parallel algorithms and architectures, Crete Island, pp 322–323
16. Griebl M (June 2004) Automatic parallelization of loop programs for distributed memory architectures. Habilitation thesis, Department of Informatics and Mathematics, University of Passau. http://www.fim.uni-passau.de/cl/publications/docs/Gri04.pdf
17. Guo J, Bikshandi G, Fraguela BB, Garzaran MJ, Padua D (2008) Programming with tiles. In: Proceedings of the 13th ACM SIGPLAN symposium on principles and practice of parallel programming, Salt Lake City, UT, USA, 20–23 Feb 2008
18. Hartono A, Manikandan Baskaran M, Bastoul C, Cohen A, Krishnamoorthy S, Norris B, Ramanujam J, Sadayappan P (2009) Parametric multi-level tiling of imperfectly nested loops. In: Proceedings of the 23rd international conference on supercomputing, Yorktown Heights, NY, USA, 8–12 June 2009
19. Hodzic E, Shang W (December 2002) On time optimal supernode shape. IEEE Trans Parallel Distrib Syst 13(12):1220–1233
20. Högstedt K, Carter L, Ferrante J (March 2003) On the parallel execution time of tiled loops. IEEE Trans Parallel Distrib Syst 14(3):307–321
21. Irigoin F, Triolet R (1988) Supernode partitioning. In: Fifteenth annual ACM symposium on principles of programming languages, San Diego, CA, pp 319–329
22. Jiménez M, Llabería JM, Fernández A (July 2002) Register tiling in nonrectangular iteration spaces. ACM Trans Program Lang Syst 24(4):409–453
23. Manikandan Baskaran M, Hartono A, Tavarageri S, Henretty T, Ramanujam J, Sadayappan P (2010) Parameterized tiling revisited. In: CGO'10: proceedings of the eighth annual IEEE/ACM international symposium on code generation and optimization, pp 200–209
24. McKeller AC, Coffman EG (1969) The organization of matrices and matrix operations in a paged multiprogramming environment. Commun ACM 12(3):153–165
25. Rastello F, Rao A, Pande S (February 2003) Optimal task scheduling at run time to exploit intra-tile parallelism. Parallel Comput 29(2):209–239
26. Rastello F, Robert Y (May 2002) Automatic partitioning of parallel loops with parallelepiped-shaped tiles. IEEE Trans Parallel Distrib Syst 13(5):460–470
27. Renganarayana L, Rajopadhye S (2004) A geometric programming framework for optimal multi-level tiling. In: Proceedings of the 2004 ACM/IEEE conference on supercomputing, Pittsburgh, PA, 6–12 Nov 2004, p 18

28. Renganarayanan L, Kim D, Rajopadhye S, Strout MM (June 2007) Parameterized tiled loops for free. In: PLDI'07, ACM SIGPLAN Not 42(6)
29. Strzodka R, Shaheen M, Pajak D, Seidel H-P (2010) Cache oblivious parallelograms in iterative stencil computations. In: ICS'10: proceedings of the 24th ACM international conference on supercomputing, Tsukuba, Japan, pp 49–59
30. Tang P, Xue J (2000) Generating efficient tiled code for distributed memory machines. Parallel Comput 26(11):1369–1410
31. Wolf ME, Lam MS (October 1991) A loop transformation theory and an algorithm to maximize parallelism. IEEE Trans Parallel Distrib Syst 2(4):452–471
32. Wolfe MJ (1987) Iteration space tiling for memory hierarchies. In: Rodrigue G (ed) Parallel processing for scientific computing. SIAM, Philadelphia, pp 357–361
33. Wolfe MJ (1989) More iteration space tiling. In: Proceedings of the 1989 ACM/IEEE conference on supercomputing, Reno, NV, 12–17 Nov 1989, pp 655–664
34. Wolfe MJ (1995) High performance compilers for parallel computing. Addison-Wesley Longman, Boston
35. Xue J (2000) Loop tiling for parallelism. Kluwer, Boston
36. Xue J, Cai W (June 2002) Time-minimal tiling when rise is larger than zero. Parallel Comput 28(6):915–939
37. Xue J, Huang C-H (December 1998) Reuse-driven tiling for improving data locality. Int J Parallel Program 26(6):671–696

Titanium

Katherine Yelick[1], Susan L. Graham[2], Paul Hilfinger[2], Dan Bonachea[3], Jimmy Su[2], Amir Kamil[2], Kaushik Datta[2], Phillip Colella[2], Tong Wen[2]
[1]University of California at Berkeley and Lawrence Berkeley National Laboratory, Berkeley, CA, USA
[2]University of California, Berkeley, CA, USA
[3]Lawrence Berkeley National Laboratory, Berkeley, CA, USA

Definition

Titanium is a parallel programming language designed for high-performance scientific computing. It is based on Java™ and uses a Single Program Multiple Data (SPMD) parallelism model with a Partitioned Global Address Space (PGAS).

Discussion

Introduction

Titanium is an explicitly parallel dialect of Java™ designed for high-performance scientific programming [14, 15]. The Titanium project started in 1995, at a time when custom supercomputers were losing market share to PC clusters. The motivation was to create a language design and implementation that would enable portable programming for a wide range of parallel platforms by striking an appropriate balance between expressiveness, user-provided information about concurrency and memory locality, and compiler and runtime support for parallelism. The goal was to design a language that could be used for high performance on some of the most challenging applications, such as those with adaptivity in time and space, unpredictable dependencies, and sparse, hierarchical, or pointer-based data structures.

The strategy was to build on the experience of several Partitioned Global Address Space (PGAS) languages, but to design a higher-level language offering object orientation with strong typing and safe memory management in the context of applications requiring high performance and scalable parallelism. Titanium uses Java as the underlying base language, but is neither a strict superset nor subset of that language. Titanium adds general multidimensional arrays, support for extending the value types in the language, and an unordered loop construct. In place of Java threads, which are used for both program structuring and concurrency, Titanium uses a static thread model with a partitioned address space to allow for locality optimizations.

Titanium's Parallelism Model

Titanium uses a Single Program Multiple Data (SPMD) parallelism model, which is familiar to users of message-passing models. The following simple Titanium program illustrates the use of built-in methods **Ti.numProcs()** and **Ti.thisProc()**, which query the environment for the number of threads (or processes) and the index within that set of the executing thread. The example prints these indices in arbitrary order. The number of Titanium threads need not be equal to the number of physical processors, a feature that is often useful when debugging parallel code on single-processor machines. However, high-performance runs typically use a one-to-one mapping between Titanium threads and physical processors.

```
class HelloWorld {
  public static void main (String [] argv) {
```

```
        System.out.println("Hello from proc " +
            Ti.thisProc() + " out of " + Ti.numProcs());
    }
}
```

Titanium supports Java's synchronized blocks, which are useful for protecting asynchronous accesses to shared objects. Because many scientific applications use a bulk-synchronous style, Titanium also has a barrier-synchronization construct, **Ti.barrier()**, as well as a set of collective communication operations to perform broadcasts, reductions, and scans. A novel feature of Ti- tanium's parallel execution model is that barriers must be textually aligned in the program – not only must all threads reach a barrier before any one of them may proceed, but they must all reach the same textual barrier. For example, the following program is not legal in Titanium:

```
if (Ti.thisProc() == 0) Ti.barrier();
    //illegal barrier
else Ti.barrier();//illegal barrier
```

Aiken and Gay developed the static analysis the compiler uses to enforce this alignment restriction, based on two key concepts [1]:

- A *single method* is one that must be invoked by all threads collectively. Only single methods can execute barriers.
- A *single-valued expression* is an expression that is guaranteed to take on the same sequence of values on all processes. Only single-valued expressions may be used in conditional expressions that affect which barriers or single-method calls get executed.

The compiler automatically determines which methods are single by finding barriers or (transitively) calls to other single methods. Single-valued expressions are required in statements that determine the flow of control to barriers, ensuring that the barriers are executed by all threads or by none. Titanium extends the Java type system with the single qualifier. Variables of single-qualified type may only be assigned values from single-valued expressions. Literals and values that have been broadcast are simple examples of single-valued expressions. The following example illustrates these concepts. Because the loop contains barriers, the expressions in the for-loop header must be single-valued. The compiler can check that property statically, since the variables are declared single and are assigned from single-valued expressions.

```
int single allTimestep = 0;
int single allEndTime = broadcast
    inputTimeSteps from 0;
for (; allTimestep < allEndTime;
    allTimestep)++{
    < read values belonging to other threads >
    Ti.barrier();
    < compute new local values >
    Ti.barrier();
}
```

Barrier analysis is entirely static and provides compile-time prevention of barrier-based deadlocks. It can also be used to improve the quality of concurrency analysis used in optimizations. Single qualification on variables and methods is a useful form of program design documentation, improving readability by making replicated quantities and collective methods explicitly visible in the program source and subjecting these properties to compiler enforcement.

Titanium's Memory Model

The two basic mechanisms for communicating between threads are accessing shared variables and sending messages. Shared memory is generally considered easier to program, because communication is one-sided: Threads can access shared data at any time without interrupting other threads, and shared data structures can be directly represented in memory. Titanium is based on a Partitioned Global Address Space (PGAS) model, which is similar to shared memory but with an explicit recognition that access time is not uniform. As shown in Fig. 1, memory is partitioned such that each partition has affinity to one thread. Memory is also partitioned orthogonally into private and shared memory, with stack variables living in private memory, and heap objects, by default, living in the shared space. A thread may access any variable that resides in shared space, but has fast access to variables in its own partition. Objects created by a given thread will reside in its own part of the memory space.

Titanium statically makes an explicit distinction between local and global references: A local reference must refer to an object within the same thread partition, while a global reference may refer to either a remote or

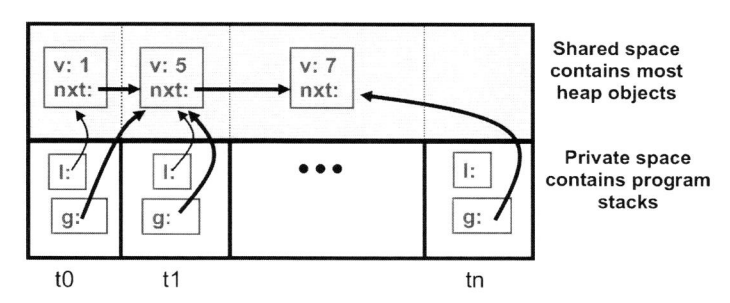

Titanium. Fig. 1 Titanium's partitioned global address space memory model

local partition. In Fig. 1, instances of **l** are local references, whereas **g** and **nxt** are global references and can therefore cross partition boundaries. The motivation for this distinction is performance. Global references are more general than local ones, but they often incur a space penalty to store affinity information and a time penalty upon dereference to check whether communication is required. References in Titanium are global by default, but may be designated local using the local type qualifier. The compiler performs type inference to automatically label variables as local [10].

The partitioned memory model is designed to scale well on distributed memory platforms without the need for caching of remote data and the associated coherence protocols. Titanium also runs well on shared memory multiprocessors and uniprocessors, where the partitioned-memory model may not correspond to any physical locality on the machine and the global references generally incur no overhead relative to local ones. Naively written Titanium programs may ignore the partitioned-memory model and, for example, allocate all data structures in one thread's shared memory partition or perform fine-grained accesses on remote data. Such programs would run correctly on any platform but would likely perform poorly on a distributed memory platform. In contrast, a program that carefully manages its data-structure partitioning and access behavior in order to scale well on distributed memory hardware is likely to scale well on shared memory platforms as well. The partitioned model provides the ability to start with a functional, shared memory style code and incrementally tune performance for distributed memory hardware by reorganizing the affinity of key data structures or adjusting access patterns in program bottlenecks to improve communication performance.

Titanium Arrays

Java arrays do not support sub-array objects that are shared with larger arrays, nonzero base indices, or true multidimensional arrays. Titanium retains Java arrays for compatibility, but adds its own multidimensional array support, which provides the same kinds of sub-array operations available in Fortran 90. Titanium arrays are indexed by integer tuples known as points and built on sets of points, called domains. The design is taken from that of a language for Finite Different Calculations, FIDIL, designed by Colella and Hilfinger [7]. Points and domains are first-class entities in Titanium – they can be stored in data structures, specified as literals, passed as values to methods, and manipulated using their own set of operations. For example, NAS multigrid (MG) benchmark requires a 256^3 grid. The problem has periodic boundaries, which are implemented using a one-deep layer of surrounding ghost cells, resulting in a 258^3 grid. Such a grid can be constructed with the following declaration:

```
double [3d] gridA
   = new double [[-1,-1,-1]:[256,256,256]];
```

The 3D Titanium array **gridA** has a rectangular index set that consists of all points [i, j, k] with integer coordinates such that $-1 \leq i, j, k \leq 256$. Titanium calls such an index set a rectangular domain of Titanium type **RectDomain**, since all the points lie within a rectangular box. Titanium also has a type **Domain** that represents an arbitrary set of points, but Titanium arrays can only be built over **RectDomains**. Titanium arrays may start at an arbitrary base point, as the example with a [−1, −1, −1] base shows. In this example, the grid was designed to have space for ghost regions, which are all the points that have either −1 or 256 as a coordinate. On machines with hierarchical memory systems, **gridA** resides in memory with affinity to exactly one process, namely the process that executes the above statement. Similarly, objects reside in a single logical memory space for their entire lifetime (there is no transparent migration of data), though they are accessible from any process in the parallel program.

The power of Titanium arrays stems from array operators that can be used to create alternative views of an array's data, without an implied copy of the data. While this is useful in many scientific codes, it is especially valuable in hierarchical grid algorithms like Multigrid and Adaptive Mesh Refinement (AMR). In a Multigrid computation on a regular mesh, there is a set of grids at various levels of refinement, and the primary computations involve sweeping over a given level of the mesh performing nearest neighbor computations (called stencils) on each point. To simplify programming, it is common to separate the interior computation from computation at the boundary of the mesh, whether those boundaries come from partitioning the mesh for parallelism or from special cases used at the physical edges of the computational domain. Since these algorithms typically deal with many kinds of boundary operations, the ability to name and operate on sub-arrays is useful.

Domain Calculus

Titanium's domain calculus operators support sub-arrays both syntactically and from a performance standpoint. The tedious business of index calculations and array offsets has been migrated from the application code to the compiler and runtime system. For example, the following Titanium code creates two blocks that are logically adjacent, with a boundary of ghost cells around each to hold values from the adjacent block. The shrink operation creates a view of **gridA** by shrinking its domain on all sides, but does not copy any of its elements. Thus, **gridAInterior** will have indices from [0, 0, 0] to [255, 255, 255] and will share corresponding elements with **gridA**. The **copy** operation in the last line updates one plane of the ghost region in **gridB** by copying only those elements in the intersection of the two arrays. Operations on Titanium arrays such as **copy** are not opaque method calls to the Titanium compiler. The compiler recognizes and treats such operations specially, and thus can apply optimizations to them, such as turning blocking operations into non-blocking ones.

```
double [3d] gridA =
 new double [[-1,-1,-1]:[256,256,256]];
double [3d] gridB =
 new double [[-1,-1,256]:[256,256,512]];
//define interior without creating a copy
double [3d] gridAInterior = gridA.shrink(1);
//update overlapping ghost cells
   from neighboring block
//by copying values from gridA to gridB
gridB.copy(gridAInterior);
```

The above example appears in a NAS MG implementation in Titanium [4], except that **gridA** and **gridB** are themselves elements of a higher-level array structure. The copy operation as it appears here performs contiguous or noncontiguous memory copies, and may perform interprocessor communication when the two grids reside in different processor memory spaces. The use of a global index space across distinct array objects (made possible by the arbitrary index bounds of Titanium arrays) makes it easy to select and copy the cells in the ghost region, and is also used in the more general case of adaptive meshes.

Unordered Loops, Value Types, and Overloading

The *foreach* construct provides an unordered looping construct designed for iterating through a multidimensional space. In the foreach loop below, the point **p** plays the role of a loop index variable.

```
foreach (p in gridAInterior.domain()) {
  gridB[p] = applyStencil(gridAInterior, p);
}
```

The **applyStencil** method may safely refer to elements that are one point away from **p**, since the loop is over the interior of a larger array.

This one loop concisely expresses an iteration over a multidimensional domain that would correspond to a multi-level loop nest in other languages. A common class of loop bounds and indexing errors is avoided by having the compiler and runtime system automatically manage the iteration boundaries for the multidimensional traversal. The foreach loop is a purely serial iteration construct – it is not a data-parallel construct. In addition, if the order of loop execution is irrelevant to a computation, then using a foreach loop to traverse the points in a domain explicitly allows the compiler to reorder loop iterations to maximize performance – for instance, by performing automatic cache blocking and tiling optimizations [12]. It also simplifies bounds-checking elimination and array access strength-reduction optimizations.

The Titanium immutable class feature provides language support for defining application-specific primitive types (often called "lightweight" or "value" classes), allowing the creation of user-defined unboxed objects, analogous to C structs. Immutables provide efficient support for extending the language with new types which are manipulated and passed by value, avoiding pointer-chasing overheads which would otherwise be associated with the use of tiny objects in Java.

One compelling example of the use of immutables is for defining a Complex number class, which was used in a Titanium implementation of the NAS FT benchmark.

Titanium also allows for operator overloading, a feature that was strongly desired by application developers on the team, and was used in the FT example to simplify the expressions on complex values.

Distributed Arrays

Titanium also supports the construction of distributed array data structures, which are built from local pieces rather than declared as distributed types. This reflects the design emphasis on adaptive and sparse data structures in Titanium, rather than the simpler "regular array" computations that could be supported with simpler flat arrays. The general pointer-based distribution mechanism combined with the use of arbitrary base indices for arrays provides an elegant and powerful mechanism for shared data.

The following code is a portion of the parallel Titanium code for a multigrid computation. It is run on every processor and creates the **blocks3D distributed** array, which can access any processor's portion of the grid.

```
Point< 3 > startCell =
myBlockPos * numCellsPerBlockSide;
Point< 3 > endCell = startCell + (numCellsPerBlock
   Side - [1,1,1]);
double [3d] myBlock =
new double[startCell:endCell];
//"blocks" is used to create "blocks3D" array
double [1d] single [3d] blocks =
  new double [0:(Ti.numProcs()-1)] single [3d];
blocks.exchange(myBlock);
//create local "blocks3D" array
double [3d] single [3d] blocks3D =
  new double [[0,0,0]:numBlocksInGridSide -
     [1,1,1]]single [3d];
//map from "blocks" to "blocks3D" array
foreach (p in blocks3D.domain())
  blocks3D[p] = blocks[procForBlockPosition(p)];
```

Each processor computes its start and end indices by performing arithmetic operations on **Points**. These indices are used to create a local **myBlock** array. Every processor also allocates its own 1D array **blocks**. Then, by combining the **myBlock** arrays using the exchange operation, **blocks** becomes a distributed data structure. As shown in Fig. 2, the exchange operation performs an all-to-all broadcast and stores each processor's contribution in the corresponding element of its local blocks array. To create a more natural mapping, a 3D processor array is used, with each element containing a reference to a particular local block. By using global indices in the local block – meaning that each block has a different set of indices that overlap only in the area of ghost regions – the copy operations described above can be used to update the ghost cells. The generality of Titanium's distributed data structures is not fully utilized in the example of a uniform mesh, but in an adaptive block structured mesh, a union of rectangles can be used to

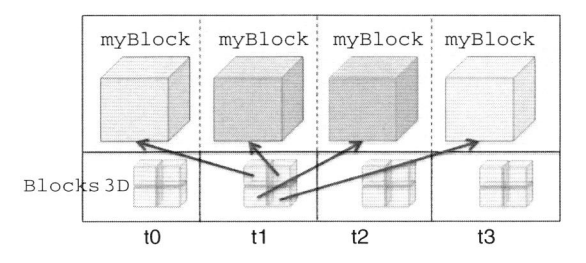

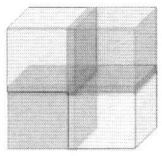

Titanium. Fig. 2 Distributed 3D array in titanium's PGAS address space. The pointers in the blocks3D array are shown only for thread t1 for simplicity

fill a spatial area, and the global indexing and global address space used to simplify much more complicated ghost region updates.

Implementation Techniques and Research

The Titanium compiler translates Titanium code into C code, and then hands that code off to a C compiler to be compiled and linked with the Titanium runtime system and, in the case of distributed memory back ends, with the GASNet communication system [5]. The choice of C as a target was made to achieve portability, and produces reasonable performance without the overhead of a virtual machine. GASNet is a one-sided communication library that is used within a number of other PGAS language implementations, including Co-Array Fortran, Chapel, and multiple UPC implementations. GASNet is itself designed for portability, and it runs on top of Ethernet (UDP) and MPI, but there are optimized implementations for most of the high-speed networks that are used in clusters and supercomputers designs. Titanium can also run on shared memory systems using a runtime layer based on POSIX Threads, and on combinations of shared and distributed memory by combining this with GASNet. Titanium, like Java, is designed for memory safety, and the Titanium runtime system includes the Boehm-Weiser garbage collector for shared memory code. To handle distributed memory environments, the runtime system tracks references that leak to remote nodes, but also adds a scalable region-based memory management concept to the language along with compiler analysis [5].

Aggressive program analysis is crucial for effective optimization of parallel code. In addition to serial loop optimizations [12] and some standard optimizations to reduce the size and complexity of generate C code, the compiler performs a number of novel analyses on parallelism constructs. For example, information about what sections of code may operate concurrently is useful for many optimizations and program analyses. In combination with alias analysis, it allows the detection of potentially erroneous race conditions, the removal of unnecessary synchronization operations, and the ability to provide stronger memory consistency guarantees. Titanium's textually aligned barriers divide the code into independent phases, which can be exploited to improve the quality of concurrency analysis. The single-valued expressions are also used to improve concurrency analysis on branches. These two features allow a simple graph encoding of the concurrency in a program based on its control-flow graph. We have developed quadratic-time algorithms that can be applied to the graph in order to determine all pairs of expressions that can run concurrently.

Alias analysis identifies pointer variables that may, must, or cannot reference the same object. The Titanium compiler uses alias analysis to enable other analyses (such as locality and sharing analysis), and to find places where it is valid to introduce restrict qualifiers in the generated C code, enabling the C compiler to apply more aggressive optimizations. The Titanium compiler's alias analysis is a Java derivative of Andersen's points-to analysis with extensions to handle multiple threads. The modified analysis is only a constant factor slower than the sequential analysis, and its running time is independent of the number of runtime threads.

Application Experience

A number of benchmarks and larger applications have been written in Titanium, starting with some of the NAS Benchmarks [4]. In addition, Yau developed a distributed matrix library that supports blocked-cyclic layouts and implemented Cannon's Matrix Multiplication algorithm, Cholesky and LU factorization (without pivoting). Balls and Colella built a 2D version of their Method of Local Corrections algorithm for solving the Poisson equation for constant coefficients over an infinite domain [2]. Bonachea, Chapman, and Putnam built a Microarray Optimal Oligo Selection Engine for selecting optimal oligonucleotide sequences from an entire genome of simple organisms, to be used in microarray design. The most ambitious efforts have been applications frameworks for Adaptive Mesh Refinement (AMR) algorithms and Immersed Boundary Method simulations [6] by Tong Wen and Ed Givelberg, respectively. In both cases, these application efforts have taken a few years and were preceded by implementations of Titanium codes for specific problem instances, e.g., AMR Poisson by Luigi Semenzato, AMR gas dynamics [11] by Peter McCorquodale and Immersed Boundaries for simulation of the heart by Armando Solar-Lezama and cochlea by Ed Givelberg, with various optimization and analysis efforts by Sabrina Merchant, Jimmy Su, and Amir Kamil.

The performance results show good scalability on the applications problems on up to hundreds of separate distributed memory nodes, and performance that is in some cases comparable to applications written in C++ or FORTRAN with message passing. The compiler is a research prototype and does not have all of the static and dynamic optimizations one would expect from a commercial compiler, but even serial running-time comparisons show competitive performance. No formal productivity studies involving humans have been done, but a variety of case studies have shown that the global address space combined with a powerful multi-dimensional array abstraction and the data abstraction support derived from Java leads to code that is elegant and concise.

Related Entries

▶Coarray Fortran
▶PGAS (Partitioned Global Address Space) Languages
▶UPC

Bibliography

1. Aiken A, Gay D (1998) Barrier inference. In: Principles of programming languages, San Diego, CA
2. Balls GT, Colella P (2002) A finite difference domain decomposition method using local corrections for the solution of Poisson's equation. J Comput Phys 180(1):25–53
3. Bonachea D (2002) GASNet specification. Technical report CSD-02-1207, University of California, Berkeley
4. Datta K, Bonachea D, Yelick K (2005) Titanium performance and potential: an NPB experimental study. In: 18th international workshop on languages and compilers for parallel computing (LCPC). Hawthorne, NY, October 2005
5. Gay D, Aiken A (2001) Language support for regions. In: SIGPLAN conference on programming language design and implementation. Washington, DC, pp 70–80
6. Givelberg E, Yelick K Distributed immersed boundary simulation in titanium. http://titanium.cs.berkeley.edu, 2003
7. Hilfinger PN, Colella P (1989) FIDIL: a language for scientific processing. In: Grossman R (ed) Symbolic computation: applications to scientific computing. SIAM, Philadelphia, pp 97–138
8. Kamil A, Yelick K (2007) Hierarchical pointer analysis for distributed programs. Static Analysis Symposium (SAS), Kongens Lyngby, Denmark, August 22–24, 2007
9. Kamil A, Yelick K (2010) Enforcing textual alignment of collectives using dynamic checks. In: 22nd international workshop on languages and compilers for parallel computing (LCPC), October 2009. Also appears in Lecture notes in computer science, vol 5898. Springer, Berlin, pp 368–382. DOI: 10.1007/978-3-642-13374-9
10. Liblit B, Aiken A (2000) Type systems for distributed data structures. In: The 27th ACM SIGPLAN-SIGACT symposium on principles of programming languages (POPL), Boston, January 2000
11. McCorquodale P, Colella P (1999) Implementation of a multilevel algorithm for gas dynamics in a high-performance Java dialect. In: International parallel computational fluid dynamics conference (CFD'99)
12. Pike G, Semenzato L, Colella P, Hilfinger PN (1999) Parallel 3D adaptive mesh refinement in Titanium. In: 9th SIAM conference on parallel processing for scientific computing, San Antonio, TX, March 1999
13. Su J, Yelick K (2005) Automatic support for irregular computations in a high-level language. In: 19th International Parallel and Distributed Processing Symposium (IPDPS)
14. Yelick K, Hilfinger P, Graham S, Bonachea D, Su J, Kamil A, Datta K, Colella P, Wen T (2007) Parallel languages and compilers: perspective from the titanium experience. Int J High Perform Comput App 21:266–290
15. Yelick K, Semenzato L, Pike G, Miyamoto C, Liblit B, Krishnamurthy A, Hilfinger P, Graham S, Gay D, Colella P, Aiken A (1998) Titanium: a high-performance Java dialect. Concur: Pract Exp 10:825–836

Web Documentation Bibliography

GASNet Home Page. http://gasnet.cs.berkeley.edu/
Titanium Project Home Page at http://titanium.cs.berkeley.edu.

TLS

▶Speculation, Thread-Level
▶Speculative Parallelization of Loops

TOP500

Jack Dongarra, Piotr Luszczek
University of Tennessee, Knoxville, TN, USA

Definition

TOP500 is a list of 500 fastest supercomputers in the world ranked by their performance achieved from running the LINPACK Benchmark. The list is assembled twice a year and officially presented at two supercomputing conferences: one in Europe and one in the USA. This list has been put together since 1993.

Discussion

Statistics on high-performance computers are of major interest to manufacturers, users, and potential users. These people wish to know not only the number of systems installed, but also the location of the various supercomputers within the high-performance computing community and the applications for which a computer system is being used. Such statistics can facilitate the establishment of collaborations, the exchange of data and software, and provide a better understanding of the high-performance computer market.

Statistical lists of supercomputers are not new. Every year since 1986, Hans Meuer has published system counts of the major vector computer manufacturers, based principally on those at the Mannheim Supercomputer Seminar. In the early 1990s, a new definition of supercomputer was needed to produce meaningful statistics. After experimenting with metrics based on processor count in 1992, the idea was born at the University of Mannheim to use a detailed listing of installed systems as the basis. In early 1993, Jack Dongarra was convinced to join the project with the LINPACK benchmark. A first test version was produced in May 1993. Today the TOP500 list is compiled by Hans Meuer of the University of Mannheim, Germany, Jack Dongarra of the University of Tennessee, Knoxville, and Erich Strohmaier and Horst Simon of NERSC/Lawrence Berkeley National Laboratory.

New statistics are required that reflect the diversification of supercomputers, the enormous performance difference between low-end and high-end models, the increasing availability of massively parallel processing (MPP) systems, and the strong increase in computing power of the high-end models of workstation suppliers (SMP).

To provide a new statistical foundation, the authors of the TOP500 decided in 1993 to assemble and maintain a list of the 500 most powerful computer systems. The list is updated twice a year. The first of these updates always coincides with the International Supercomputer Conference in June (submissions are accepted until April 15), the second one is presented in November at the IEEE Super Computer Conference in the USA (submissions are accepted until October 1st). The list is assembled with the help of high-performance computer experts, computational scientists, and manufacturers.

In the present list (called the TOP500), computers are ranked by their performance on the LINPACK Benchmark. The list is freely available at http://www.top500.org/ where users can create additional sublists and statistics out of the TOP500 database on their own.

The main objective of the TOP500 list is to provide a ranked list of general-purpose systems that are in common use for high-end applications. A general-purpose system is expected to be able to solve a range of scientific problems.

The TOP500 list shows the 500 most powerful commercially available computer systems known. To keep the list as compact as possible, only a part of the information is shown:

- Nworld – Position within the TOP500 ranking
- Manufacturer – Manufacturer or vendor
- Computer – Type indicated by manufacturer or vendor
- Installation Site – Customer
- Location – Location and country
- Year – Year of installation/last major update
- Field of Application
- #Proc. – Number of processors (Cores)
- Rmax – Maximal LINPACK performance achieved
- Rpeak – Theoretical peak performance
- Nmax – Problem size for achieving Rmax
- N1/2 – Problem size for achieving half of Rmax

In the TOP500 List table, the computers are ordered first by their Rmax value. In the case of equal performances (Rmax value) for different computers, a choice was made to order by Rpeak. For sites that have the same computer, the order is by memory size and then alphabetically.

Method of Solution

In an attempt to obtain uniformity across all computers in performance reporting, the algorithm used in solving the system of equations ($Ax = b$, for a dense matrix A) in the benchmark procedure must conform to LU factorization with partial pivoting. In particular, the operation count for the algorithm must be $2/3\, n^3 + O(n^2)$ double point floating point operations (Rmax value is computed by dividing this count by the time taken to solve). Here a floating point operation is an addition or multiplication of 64-bit operands. This excludes the use of a fast matrix multiply algorithm like "Strassen's

Method" or algorithms which compute a solution in a precision lower than full precision (64 bit floating point arithmetic) and refine the solution using an iterative approach. This is done to provide a comparable set of performance numbers across all computers. Submitters of the results are free to implement their own solution as long as the above criteria are met. A reference implementation of the benchmark called HPL (High Performance LINPACK) is provided at: http://www.netlib.org/benchmark/hpl/. In addition to satisfying the rules, HPL also verifies the result with a numerical check of the obtained solution.

Restrictions

The main objective of the TOP500 list is to provide a ranked list of general-purpose systems that are in common use for high-end applications. The authors of the TOP500 reserve the right to independently verify submitted LINPACK Benchmark [1] results, and exclude systems from the list, which are not valid or not general purpose in nature. A system is considered to be of general purpose if it is able to be used to solve a range of scientific problems. Any system designed specifically to solve the LINPACK benchmark problem or have as its major purpose the goal of a high TOP500 ranking will be disqualified. The systems in the TOP500 list are expected to be persistent and available for use for an extended period of time. In that period, it is allowed to submit new results which will supersede any prior submissions. Thus, an improvement over time is allowed. The TOP500 authors will reserve the right to deny inclusion in the list if it is suspected that the system violates these conditions.

The TOP500 List keepers can be reached by sending email to info at top500.org.

The TOP500 list can be found at www.top500.org.

Related Entries

▶ Benchmarks
▶ HPC Challenge Benchmark
▶ LINPACK Benchmark
▶ Livermore Loops

Bibliography

1. Dongarra JJ, Luszczek P, Petitet A (2003) The LINPACK benchmark: past, present, and future. Concurr Comput Pract Exp 15:1–18

Topology Aware Task Mapping

ABHINAV BHATELE
University of Illinois at Urbana-Champaign, Urbana, IL, USA

Synonyms

Graph embedding; MPI process mapping

Definition

Topology aware task mapping refers to the mapping of communicating parallel objects, tasks, or processes in a parallel application on nearby physical processors to minimize network traffic, by considering the communication of the objects or tasks and the interconnect topology of the machine.

Discussion

Introduction

Processors in modern supercomputers are connected together using a variety of interconnect topologies: meshes, tori, fat-trees, and others. Increasing size of the interconnect leads to an increased sharing of resources (network links and switches) among messages and hence network contention. This can potentially lead to significant performance degradation for certain classes of parallel applications. Sharing of links can be avoided by minimizing the distance traveled by messages on the network. This is achieved by mapping communicating objects or tasks on nearby physical processors on the network topology and is referred to as topology aware task mapping. Topology aware mapping is a technique to minimize communication traffic over the network and hence optimize performance of parallel programs. It is becoming increasingly relevant for obtaining good performance on current supercomputers.

The general mapping problem is known to be NP-hard [1, 2]. Apart from parallel computing, topology aware mapping also has applications in graph embedding in mathematics and VLSI circuit design. The problem of embedding one graph on another while minimizing some metric has been well studied in mathematics. Layout of VLSI circuits to minimize length of the longest wire is another problem that requires mapping of one grid on to another. However, the problems to be tackled are different in several aspects in parallel computing from mathematics or circuit layout. For example, in VLSI, the size of the host graph can be larger than that of the guest graph whereas, in parallel computing, typically, the host graph is equal to or smaller than the guest graph.

Research on topology aware mapping in parallel computing began in the 1980s with a paper by Bokhari [1]. Work in this area has primarily involved the development of heuristics that target different mapping scenarios. Heuristics typically provide close to optimal solutions in a reasonable time. Arunkumar et al. [3] categorize various heuristic techniques into – deterministic, randomized, and random start heuristics. Over the years, specific techniques better suited for certain architectures were developed – for hypercubes and array processors in the 1980s and meshes and tori in the 1990s. In the recent years, developers of certain parallel applications have also developed application specific mapping techniques to map their codes on to modern supercomputers [4–6].

Prior to a survey of the various heuristic techniques for task mapping, a brief description of the existing interconnect topologies and the kinds of communication graphs that are prevalent in parallel applications is essential.

Interconnect Topologies

Various common and radical topologies have been deployed in supercomputers, ranging from hypercubes to fat-trees to three-dimensional tori and meshes. They can be divided into two categories:

1. *Direct networks*: In direct networks, each processor is connected to a few other processors directly. A message travels from source to destination by going through several links connecting the processors. Hypercubes, tori, meshes, etc., are all examples of direct networks (see Figs. 1 and 2). Several modern supercomputers currently have a three-dimensional (3D) mesh or torus interconnect topology. IBM Blue Gene/L and Blue Gene/P machines are 3D tori built from blocks of a torus of size $8 \times 8 \times 8$ nodes. Cray XT machines (XT5 and XE6) are also 3D tori. The primary difference between IBM and Cray machines is that on IBM machines, each allocated job partition

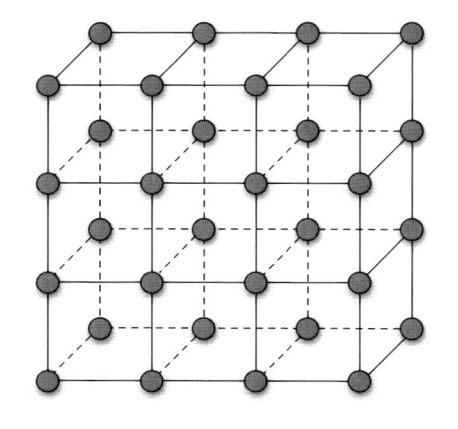

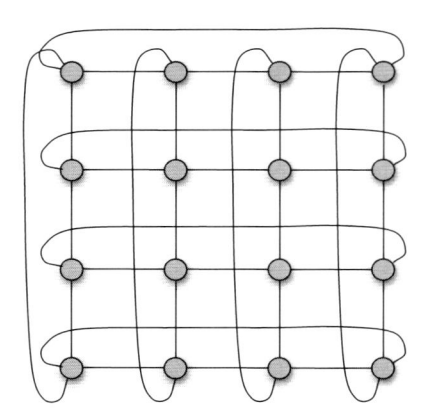

Topology Aware Task Mapping. Fig. 1 A three-dimensional mesh and a two-dimensional torus

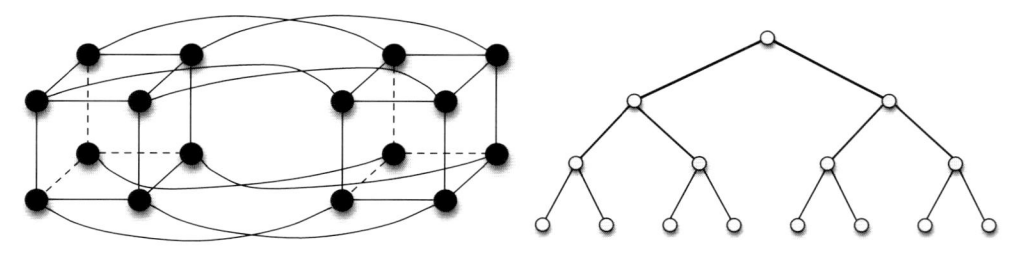

Topology Aware Task Mapping. Fig. 2 A four-dimensional hypercube and a three-level fat-tree network

is a contiguous mesh or torus. However, on Cray machines, nodes are randomly selected for a job and do not constitute a complete torus.
2. *Indirect networks*: Indirect networks have switches which route the messages to the destination. No two processors are connected directly and messages always have to go through switches to reach their destination. Fat-tree networks are examples of indirect networks (see Fig. 2). Infiniband, IBM's Federation interconnect and SGI Altix machines are examples of fat-tree networks. LANL's RoadRunner also has a fat-tree network.

Some of these networks benefit from topology aware task mapping more than others. A significant percentage of the parallel machines in the 1980s had a hypercube interconnect and hence, much of the research then was directed toward such networks. More recent work involves optimizing applications on 3D meshes and tori.

Communication Graphs

Tasks in parallel applications can interact in a variety of ways in terms of the specific communication partners, number of communicators, global versus localized communication, etc. All applications can be classified into a few different categories based on different parameters governing the communication patterns:

Static versus dynamic communication: Depending on whether the communication graph of the application changes at runtime, graph can be classified as static or dynamic. If the communication graph is static, topology aware mapping can be done offline and used for the entirety of the run. If the communication is dynamic, periodic remapping depending on the changes in the communication graph are required. Several categories of parallel applications such as Lattice QCD, Ocean Simulations, and Weather Simulations have a stencil-like communication pattern that does not change during the run. On the other hand, molecular dynamics and cosmological simulations have dynamic communication patterns.

Regular versus irregular communication: Communication in a parallel application can be regular (structured) or irregular (unstructured). An example of regular communication is a five-point stencil-like application where every task communicates with four of its neighbors. When no specific pattern can be attributed to the communication graph, it is classified as irregular or unstructured. Unstructured grid computations are examples of applications with irregular communication graphs.

Point-to-point versus collective communication: Some applications primarily use point-to-point messages with minimal global communication. Others, however use collective operations such as broadcasts, reductions, and all-to-alls between all or a subset of processors. Different mapping algorithms are required to optimize different types of communication patterns.

Parallel applications can also be classified into computation bound or communication bound depending on the relative amount of communication involved. A large body of parallel applications spend a small portion of their overall execution time doing communication. Such applications will typically be unaffected by topology aware mapping. Communication-bound latency-sensitive applications benefit most in terms of performance from topology aware task mapping.

The Mapping Process

An algorithm for mapping of tasks in an application requires two inputs – the communication graph of an application and the machine topology of the allocated job partition. Given these two inputs, the aim is to map communicating objects or tasks close to one another on nearby physical processors. The success of a mapping algorithm is evaluated in terms of minimizing or maximizing some function which correlates well with the contention on the network or actual application performance.

Objective Functions

Mapping algorithms aim at minimizing some metric referred to as an objective function which should be chosen carefully. A good objective function is one that does an accurate evaluation of a mapping solution in terms of yielding better performance. Objective functions are also important to compare the optimality of different mapping solutions. Several objective functions which have been used for different mapping algorithms are listed below:

- Overlap between guest and host graph edges: One metric to determine the quality of the mapping is

the number of edges in the guest graph which fall on the host graph. This metric is referred to as the cardinality of the mapping by Bokhari [1]. The mapping which yields the highest cardinality is the best.
- Maximum dilation: This metric is used for architectures and applications where the longest edge in the communication graph determines the performance. In other words, the message that travels the maximum number of hops or links on the network determines the overall performance [7, 8].

$$\text{Maximum dilation} = \max_{i=1}^{n} |d_i| \quad (1)$$

The mapping which leads to the smallest dilation for any edge in the guest graph on the processor interconnect is the best.
- Hop-bytes: This is the weighted sum of all edges in the communication graph multiplied by their dilation on the processor graph as per the mapping algorithm [9, 10].

$$\text{Hop-bytes} = \sum_{i=1}^{n} d_i \times b_i \quad (2)$$

where d_i is the number of hops or links traveled by the message on the network and b_i is the size of the message in bytes.

Hop-bytes is a measure of the total communication traffic on the network and hence, an approximate indication of the contention. A smaller value for hop-bytes indicates less contention on the network. Average hops per byte is another way of expressing the same metric,

$$\text{Average hops per byte} = \frac{\sum_{i=1}^{n} d_i \times b_i}{\sum_{i=1}^{n} b_i} \quad (3)$$

The last two objective functions, maximum dilation and hop-bytes, are typically used today and are applicable in different scenarios. The choice of one over the other depends upon the parallel application and the architecture for which the mapping is being performed.

Heuristic Techniques for Mapping

Owing to the general applicability of mapping in various fields, a huge body of work exists targeting this problem. Many techniques used for solving combinatorial optimization problems can be used for obtaining solutions to the mapping problem. Simulated annealing, genetic algorithms, and neural network–based heuristics are examples of such physical optimization techniques. Other heuristic techniques are recursive partitioning, pairwise exchanges, and clustering and geometry-based mapping. Arunkumar et al. [3] categorize various heuristic techniques into – deterministic, randomized, and random start heuristics. The following sections discuss some of the mapping techniques classified into these categories.

Deterministic Heuristics

In this class, the choice of search path is deterministic and typically a fixed search strategy is used taking the domain-specific knowledge about the parallel application into account. Yu et al. [11] present folding and embedding techniques to obtain deterministic solutions for mapping of two- and three-dimensional grids on to 3D mesh topologies. Their topology mapping library provides support for MPI virtual topology functions on IBM Blue Gene machines. Bhatele [12] uses domain-specific knowledge and communication patterns of parallel application for heuristic techniques such as "affine transformation" inspired mapping and guided graph traversals to map on to 3D tori. The mapping library developed as a result can map application graphs that are regular (n-dimensional grids) as well as those that are irregular. Several application developers such as those of Blue Matter [4], Qbox [5], and OpenAtom [6] have developed application specific mapping algorithms to map tasks on to processor topologies. Recursive graph partitioning–based strategies which partition both the application and processor graph for mapping also fall under this category [13]. Algorithms using deterministic algorithms are typically the fastest among the three categories.

Randomized Heuristics

This category of solutions does not depend on domain-specific knowledge and uses search techniques that are randomized, yielding different solutions in successive executions. Neural networks, genetic algorithms, and simulated annealing–based heuristics are example of this class. Bokhari's algorithm of pairwise exchanges accompanied by probabilistic jumps also falls under this category.

In genetic algorithm–based heuristics [3], possible mapping solutions are first encoded in some manner and a random population of such patterns is generated. Then different genetic operators such as crossover and mutation are applied to derive new generations from old ones. Certain criteria are used to estimate the fitness of a selection and unfit solutions are rejected. Given a termination rule, the best solution among the population is taken to be the solution at termination.

Obtaining an exact solution to the mapping problem is difficult and iterative algorithms tend to produce solutions that are not globally optimal. The technique of simulated annealing provides a mechanism to escape local optima and hence is a good fit for mapping problems. The most important considerations for a simulated annealing algorithm are deciding a good objective function and an annealing schedule. This technique has been used for processor and link assignment by Midkiff et al. [14] and Bhanot et al. [15].

Random Start Heuristics

In some algorithms, a random initial mapping is chosen and then improved iteratively. Such solutions fall under the category of *random start* heuristics. Techniques such as pairwise exchanges and recursive partitioning fall under this category.

The technique of pairwise exchanges that starts from an initial assignment, is a simple brute force method which has been used with different variations to tackle the mapping problem [7]. The basic idea is simple: An objective function or metric to be optimized is selected and then an initial mapping of the guest graph on the host graph is determined. Then, a pair of nodes is chosen, either randomly or based on some selection criteria and their mappings are interchanged. If the metric or objective function becomes better, the exchange is preserved and the process is repeated, until some termination criterion is achieved.

Another technique in this class is task clustering followed by cluster allocation. In the clustering phase, tasks are clustered into groups equal to the number of processors using recursive min-cut algorithms. Then these clusters are allocated to the processors by starting with a random assignment and iteratively improving it by local exchanges. The first phase aims at minimizing intercluster communication without comprising load balancing while the second phase aims at minimizing inter-processor communication. This is especially useful for models such as Charm++ where the number of tasks is much larger than the number of processors.

Future Directions

The emergence of new architectures and network topologies requires modifying existing algorithms and developing new ones to suit them. As an example, the increase in number of cores per node adds another dimension to the network topology and should be taken into account. Algorithms also need to be developed for new parallel applications. There is a growing need for runtime support in the form of an automated mapping framework that can map applications intelligently on to the processor topology. This will reduce the burden on application developers to map individual applications and will also help reuse algorithms across similar communication graphs. Bhatele et al. [16] are making some efforts in this direction. There is an increasing demand for support in the MPI runtime for mapping of MPI virtual topology functions [11].

The increase in size of parallel machines and in the number of threads in a parallel program requires parallel and distributed techniques for mapping. Gathering the entire communication graph on one processor and applying sequential centralized techniques will not be feasible in the future. Hence, an effort should be made towards developing strategies which are distributed, scalable, and can be run in parallel. Hierarchical multilevel graph partitioning techniques are one such effort in this direction.

Related Entries

▶Cray XT3 and Cray XT Series of Supercomputers
▶Cray XT4 and Seastar 3-D Torus Interconnect
▶Graph Partitioning
▶Hypercubes and Meshes
▶IBM Blue Gene Supercomputer
▶Infiniband
▶Interconnection Networks
▶Load Balancing, Distributed Memory
▶Locality of Reference and Parallel Processing
▶Processes, Tasks, and Threads
▶Routing (Including Deadlock Avoidance)
▶Space-Filling Curves
▶Task Graph Scheduling

Bibliographic Notes and Further Reading

Bokhari [1] wrote one of the first papers on task mapping for parallel programs. A good discussion of the various objective functions used for comparing mapping algorithms can be found in [7]. Fox et al. [17] divide the various mapping algorithms into physical optimization and heuristic techniques. Arunkumar et al. [3] provide another classification into deterministic, randomized, and random start heuristics.

Application developers attempting to map their parallel codes can gain insights from mapping algorithms developed by individual application groups [4–6]. Bhatele and Kale have been developing an automatic mapping framework for mapping of Charm++ and MPI applications to the processor topology [12]. They are also developing techniques for parallel and distributed topology aware mapping.

Bibliography

1. Bokhari SH (1981) On the mapping problem. IEEE Trans Comput 30(3):207–214
2. Kasahara H, Narita S (1984) Practical multiprocessor scheduling algorithms for efficient parallel processing. IEEE Trans Comput 33:1023–1029
3. Arunkumar S, Chockalingam T (1992) Randomized heuristics for the mapping problem. Int J High Speed Comput (IJHSC) 4(4):289–300
4. Fitch BG, Rayshubskiy A, Eleftheriou M, Ward TJC, Giampapa M, Pitman MC (2006) Blue matter: approaching the limits of concurrency for classical molecular dynamics. In: SC'06: Proceedings of the 2006 ACM/IEEE conference on Supercomputing, Tampa, ACM Press, New York, 11–17 Nov 2006
5. Gygi F, Draeger EW, Schulz M, Supinski BRD, Gunnels JA, Austel V, Sexton JC, Franchetti F, Kral S, Ueberhuber C, Lorenz J (2006) Large-scale electronic structure calculations of high-Z metals on the blue gene/L platform. In: SC'06: Proceedings of the 2006 ACM/IEEE conference on Supercomputing, ACM Press, New York
6. Bhatelé A, Bohm E, Kalé LV (2011) Optimizing communication for Charm++ applications by reducing network contention. Concurr Comput 23(2):211–222
7. Lee S-Y, Aggarwal JK (1987) A mapping strategy for parallel processing. IEEE Trans Comput 36(4):433–442
8. Berman F, Snyder L (1987) On mapping parallel algorithms into parallel architectures. J Parallel Distrib Comput 4(5):439–458
9. Ercal F, Ramanujam J, Sadayappan P (1988) Task allocation onto a hypercube by recursive mincut bipartitioning. In: Proceedings of the 3rd conference on Hypercube concurrent computers and applications, ACM Press, New York, pp 210–221
10. Agarwal T, Sharma A, Kalé LV (2006) Topology-aware task mapping for reducing communication contention on large parallel machines, In: Proceedings of IEEE International Parallel and Distributed Processing Symposium 2006, Rhodes Island, 25–29 Apr 2006. IEEE, Piscataway
11. Yu H, Chung I-H, Moreira J (2006) Topology mapping for blue gene/L supercomputer. In: SC'06: Proceedings of the 2006 ACM/IEEE conference on Supercomputing, Tampa, 11–17 Nov 2006. ACM, New York, p 116
12. Bhatele A (2010) Automating topology aware mapping for supercomputers. Ph.D. thesis, Dept. of Computer Science, University of Illinois. http://hdl.handle.net/2142/16578 (August 2010)
13. Kernighan BW, Lin S (1970) An efficient heuristic procedure for partitioning graphs. Bell Syst Tech J 49(1):291–307
14. Bollinger SW, Midkiff SF (1988) Processor and link assignment in multicomputers using simulated annealing. In: 1988 ICPP, vol 1, Aug 1988, pp 1–7
15. Bhanot G, Gara A, Heidelberger P, Lawless E, Sexton JC, Walkup R (2005) Optimizing task layout on the blue gene/L supercomputer. IBM J Res Dev 49(2/3):489–500
16. Bhatele A, Gupta G, Kale LV, Chung I-H (2010) Automated mapping of regular communication graphs on mesh interconnects. In: Proceedings of International Conference on High Performance Computing & Simulation (HiPCS) 2010, Caen, 28 June–2 July 2010. IEEE, Piscataway
17. Mansour N, Ponnusamy R, Choudhary A, Fox GC (1993) Graph contraction for physical optimization methods: a quality-cost tradeoff for mapping data on parallel computers. In: ICS'93: Proceedings of the 7th International Conference on Supercomputing, Tokyo, 19–23 July 1993. ACM, New York, pp 1–10

Torus

▶Networks, Direct

Total Exchange

▶Allgather

Trace Scheduling

STEFAN M. FREUDENBERGER
Zürich, Switzerland

Definition

Trace scheduling is a global acyclic instruction scheduling technique in which the scheduling region consists of a linear acyclic sequence of basic blocks embedded in the control flow graph. Trace scheduling differs from other global acyclic scheduling techniques by allowing the scheduling region to be entered after the first instruction.

Trace scheduling was the first global instruction scheduling technique that was proposed and successfully implemented in both research and commercial compilers. By demonstrating that simple microcode operations could be statically compacted and scheduled on multi-issue hardware, trace scheduling provided the basis for making large amounts of instruction-level parallelism practical. Its first commercial implementation demonstrated that commercial codes could be statically compiled for multi-issue architectures, and thus greatly influenced and contributed to the performance of superscalar architectures. Today, the ideas of trace scheduling and its descendants are implemented in most compilers.

Discussion

Introduction

Global scheduling techniques are needed for processors that expose instruction-level parallelism (ILP), that is, processors that allow multiple operations to execute simultaneously. This situation may independently arise for two reasons: either because a processor issues more than a single operation during each clock cycle, or because a processor allows issuing independent operations while deeply pipelined operations are still executing. The number of independent operations that need to be found for an ILP processor is a function of both the number of operations issued per clock cycle, and the latency of operations, whether computational or memory. The latency of computational operations depends upon the design of the functional units. The latency of memory operations depends upon the design and latencies of caches and main memory, as well as on the availability of prefetch and cache-bypassing operations. Global scheduling techniques are needed for these processors because the number of independent operations available in a typical basic block is too small to fully utilize their available hardware resources. By expanding the scheduling region, more operations become available for scheduling. Global scheduling techniques differ from other global code motion techniques (such as loop-invariant code motion or partial redundancy elimination) because they take into account the available hardware resources (such as available functional units and operation issue slots).

Instruction scheduling techniques can be broadly classified based on the region that they schedule, and whether this region is cyclic or acyclic. Algorithms that schedule only single basic blocks are known as *local scheduling* algorithms; algorithms that schedule multiple basic blocks at once are known as *global scheduling* algorithms. Global scheduling algorithms that operate on entire loops of a program are known as *cyclic scheduling* algorithms, while methods that impose a scheduling barrier at the end of a loop body are known as *acyclic scheduling* algorithms. Global scheduling regions include regions consisting of a single basic block as a "degenerate" form of region, and acyclic schedulers may consider entire loops but, unlike cyclic schedulers, stop at the loops' back edges (a back edge points to an ancestor in a depth-first traversal of the control flow graph; it captures the flow from one iteration of the loop to the start of the next iteration).

All scheduling algorithms can benefit from hardware support. When control-dependent operations that can cause side effects move above their controlling branch, they need to be either executed conditionally so that their effects only arise if the operation is executed in the original program order, or any side effects must be delayed until the point at which the operation would have been executed originally.

Hardware techniques to support this include *predication* of operations, implicit or explicit *register renaming*, and mechanisms to suppress or delay exceptions in order to prevent an incorrect exception to be signaled. Predication of operations controls whether the side effects of the predicated operations become visible to the program state through an additional predicate operand. The predicate operand can be implicit (such as the conditional execution of operations in branch delay slots depending on the outcome of the branch condition) or explicit (through an additional machine register operand); in the latter case, the predicate operand could simply be the same predicate that controls the conditional branch on which the operation was control-dependent in the original flow graph (in which case the predicated operation could move just above a single conditional branch). Register renaming refers to the technique where additional machine registers are used to hold the results of an operation until the point where the operation would have occurred in the original program order.

Global scheduling algorithms principally consist of two phases: *region formation* and *schedule construction*. Algorithms differ in the shape of the region and the global code motions permitted during scheduling. Depending on the region and the allowed code motions, *compensation code* needs to be inserted at appropriate places in the control flow graph to maintain the original program semantics; depending on the code motions allowed during scheduling, compensation code needs to be inserted during the scheduling phase of the compiler.

Trace scheduling allows traces to be entered after the first operation and before the last operation. This complicates the determination of compensation code because the location of *rejoin points* cannot be done before a trace has been scheduled. This leads to the following overall trace scheduling loop:

```
while (unscheduled operations remain)
{
        select trace T
        construct schedule for T
        bookkeeping -
           determine rejoin points to T
           generate compensation code
}
```

The remainder of this entry first discusses region formation and schedule construction in general and as it applies to trace scheduling, and then compares trace scheduling to other acyclic global scheduling techniques. Cyclic scheduling algorithms are discussed elsewhere.

Region Formation – Trace Picking

Traces were the first global scheduling region proposed, and represent contiguous linear paths through the code (Fig. 1). More formally, a trace consists of the operations of a sequence of basic blocks $B_0, B_1, \ldots, B_n$ with the properties that:

- Each basic block is a predecessor of the next in the sequence (i.e., for each $k = 0, \ldots, n-1$, B_k is a predecessor of B_{k+1}, and B_{k+1} is a successor of B_k in the control flow graph).

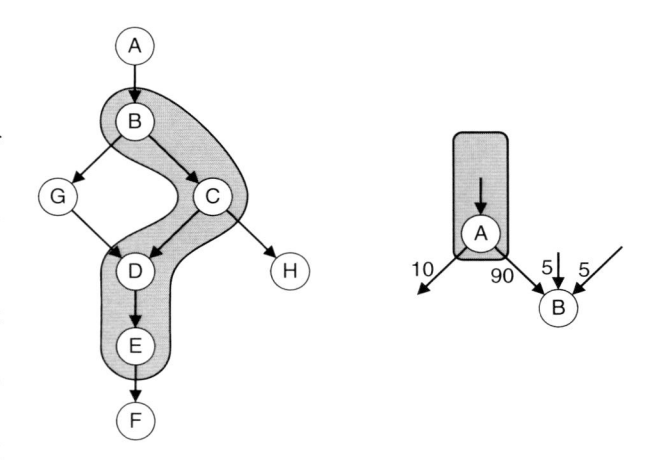

Trace Scheduling. Fig. 1 Trace selection. The *left* diagram shows the selected trace. The *right* diagram illustrates the mutual-most-likely trace picking heuristic: assume that A is the last operation of the current trace, and that B is one of A's successors. Here B is the most likely successor of A, and A is the most likely predecessor of B

- For any j, k there is no path $B_j \to B_k \to B_j$ except for those that include B_0 (i.e., the code is cycle free, except that the entire region can be part of some encompassing loop).

Note that this definition does not exclude forward branches within the region, nor control flow that leaves the region and reenters it at a later point. This generality has been controversial in the research community because many felt that the added complexity of its implementation was not justified by its added benefit and has led to several alternative approaches that are discussed below.

Of the many ways in which one can form traces, the most popular algorithm employs the following simple trace formation algorithm:

- Pick the as-yet unscheduled operation with the largest expected execution frequency as the seed operation of the trace.
- Grow the trace both forward in the direction of the flow graph as well as backward, picking the *mutually most-likely* successor (predecessor) operation to the currently last (first) operation on the trace.
- Stop growing a trace when either no mutually most-likely successor (predecessor) exists, or when some heuristic trace length limit has been reached.

The mutually most-likely successor S of an operation P is the operation with the properties that:

- S is the most likely successor of P;
- P is the most likely predecessor of S.

For this definition, it is immaterial whether the likelihood that S follows P (P precedes S) is based on available profile data collected during earlier runs of the program, has been determined by a synthetic profile, or is based on source annotations in the program. Of course, the more benefit is derived from having picked the correct trace, the greater is the penalty when picking the wrong trace.

Trace picking is the region formation technique used for trace scheduling. Other acyclic region formation techniques and their relationship to trace scheduling are discussed below.

Region Enlargement

Trace selection alone typically does not expose enough ILP for the instruction scheduler of a typical ILP processor. Once the limit on the length of a "natural" trace has been reached (e.g., the entire loop body), *region-enlargement* techniques can be employed to further increase the size of the region, albeit at the cost of a larger code size for the program. Many enlargement techniques exploit the fact that programs iterate and grow the size of a region by making extra copies of highly iterated code, leading to a larger region that contains more ILP.

These code-replicating techniques have been criticized by advocates of other approaches, such as cyclic scheduling and loop-level parallel processing, because comparable benefits to larger schedule regions may be found using other techniques. However, no study appears to exist that quantifies such claims.

The simplest and oldest region-enlargement technique is *loop unrolling* (Fig. 2): to unroll a loop, duplicate its body several times, change the targets of the back edges of each copy but the last to point to the header of the next copy (so that the back edges of the last copy point back to the loop header of the first copy). Variants of loop unrolling include pre-/post-conditioning of a loop by k for counted *for* loops with unknown loop bounds (leading to two loops: a "fixup loop" that executes up to k iterations; and a "main loop" that is unrolled by k and has its internal exits removed; the fixup loop can precede or follow the main loop), and loop peeling by the expected small iteration count. When the iteration count of the fixup loop of a p-conditioned loop is small (which it typically is), the fixup loop is completely unrolled.

Typically, loop unrolling is done before region formation so that the enlarged region becomes available

Original loop	Unrolled by 4	Pre-conditioned by 4	Post-conditioned by 4
L: if ... goto E	L: if ... goto E	if ... goto L	L: if ... goto X
body	body	body	body
goto L	if ... goto E	if ... goto L	body
E:	body	body	body
	if ... goto E	if ... goto L	goto L
	body	body	X: if ... goto E
	if ... goto E	L: if ... goto E	body
	body	body	if ... goto E
	goto L	body	body
	E:	body	if ... goto E
		body	body
		goto L	E:
		E:	

Trace Scheduling. Fig. 2 Simplified illustration of variants of loop unrolling. "if" and "goto" represent the loop control operations; "body" represents the part of the loop without loop-related control flow. In the general case (e.g., a *while* loop) the loop exit tests remain inside the loop. This is shown in the second column ("unrolled by 4"). For counted loops (i.e., *for* loops), the compiler can condition the unrolled loop so that the loop conditions can be removed from the main body of the loop. Two variants of this are shown in the two rightmost columns. Modern compilers will typically precede the loop with a zero trip count test and place the loop condition at the bottom of the loop. This removes the unconditional branch from the loop

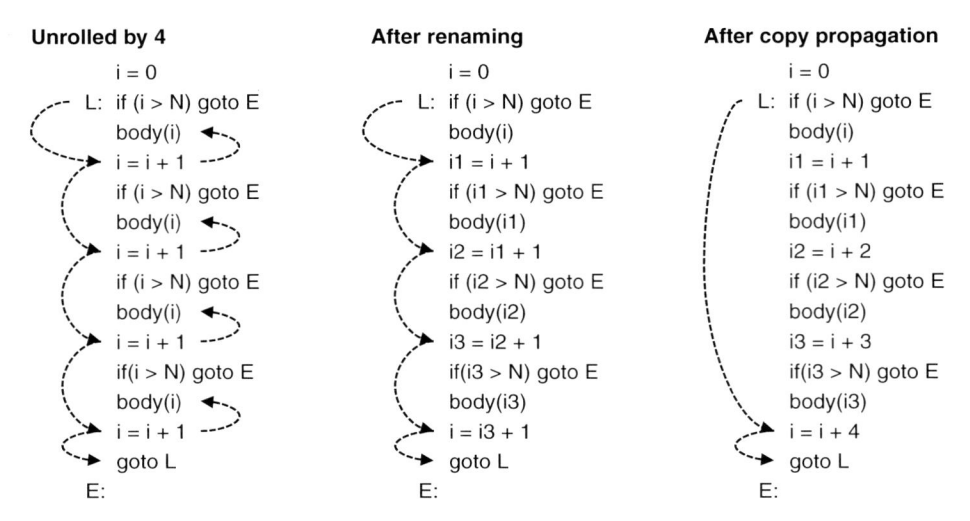

Unrolled by 4	After renaming	After copy propagation
i = 0	i = 0	i = 0
L: if (i > N) goto E	L: if (i > N) goto E	L: if (i > N) goto E
body(i)	body(i)	body(i)
i = i + 1	i1 = i + 1	i1 = i + 1
if (i > N) goto E	if (i1 > N) goto E	if (i1 > N) goto E
body(i)	body(i1)	body(i1)
i = i + 1	i2 = i1 + 1	i2 = i + 2
if (i > N) goto E	if (i2 > N) goto E	if (i2 > N) goto E
body(i)	body(i2)	body(i2)
i = i + 1	i3 = i2 + 1	i3 = i + 3
if(i > N) goto E	if(i3 > N) goto E	if(i3 > N) goto E
body(i)	body(i3)	body(i3)
i = i + 1	i = i3 + 1	i = i + 4
goto L	goto L	goto L
E:	E:	E:

Trace Scheduling. Fig. 3 Typical induction variable manipulations for loops. Downward arrows represent flow dependences; upward arrows represent anti dependences. Only the critical dependences are shown

to the region selector. This is done to keep the region selector simpler but may lead to phase-ordering issues, as loop unrolling has to guess the "optimal" unroll amount. At the same time, when loops are unrolled before region formation then the resulting code can be scalar optimized in the normal fashion; in particular height-reducing transformations that remove dependences between the individual copies of the unrolled loop body can expose a larger amount of parallelism between the individual iterations (Fig. 3). Needless to say, if no parallelism between the iterations exists or can be found, loop unrolling is ineffective.

Loop unrolling in many industrial compilers is often rather effective because a heuristically determined small amount of unrolling is sufficient to fill the resources of the target machine.

Region Compaction – Instruction Scheduler

Once the scheduling region has been selected, the instruction scheduler assigns functional units of the target machine and time slots in the instruction schedule to each operation of the region. In doing so, the scheduler attempts to minimize an objective cost function while maintaining program semantics and obeying the resource limitations of the target architecture. Often, the objective cost function is the expected execution time, but other objective functions are possible (for example, code size and energy efficiency could be part of an objective function).

The semantics of a program defines certain sequential constraints or *dependences* that must be maintained by a valid execution. These dependences preclude some reordering of operations within a program. The data flow of a program imposes *data dependences*, and the control flow of a program imposes *control dependences*. (Note the difference between control flow and control dependence: block B is control dependent on block A if A precedes B along some path, but B does not postdominate A. In other words, the result of the control decision made in A directly affects whether or not B is executed.)

There are three types of data dependences: *read-after-write* dependences (also called *RAW*, *flow*, or *true* dependences), *write-after-read* dependences (also called *WAR* or *anti* dependences), and *write-after-write* dependences (also called *WAW* or *output* dependences). The latter two types are also called *false* dependences because they can be removed by renaming.

There are two types of control dependences: *split* dependences may prevent operations from moving below the exit of a basic block, and *join* dependences may prevent operations from moving above the entrance to a basic block. Control dependence does not constrain the relative order of operations within a basic block but rather expresses constraints on moving operations between basic blocks.

Both data and control dependences represent ordering constraints on the program execution, and hence induce a partial ordering on the operations. Any partial ordering can be represented as a *directed acyclic graph* (DAG), and DAGs are indeed often used by scheduling algorithms. Variants to the simple DAG are the *data dependence graph* (DDG), and the *program dependence graph* (PDG). All these graphs represent operations as nodes and dependences as edges (some graphs only express data dependences, while others include both data and control dependences).

Code Motion Between Adjacent Blocks

Two fundamental techniques, predication and speculation, are employed by schedulers (or earlier phases) to transform or remove control dependence. While it is sometimes possible to employ either technique, they represent independent techniques, and usually one is more natural to employ in a given situation. Speculation is used to move operations above a branch that is highly weighted in one direction; predication is used to collapse short sequences of alternative operations following a branch that is nearly equally likely in each direction. Predication can also play an important role in software pipelining.

Speculative code motion (or *code hoisting* and sometimes *code sinking*) moves operations above control-dominating branches (or below joins for sinking). In principle, this transformation does not always maintain the original program semantics, and in particular it may change the exception behavior of the program. If an operation may generate an exception and the exception recovery model does not allow speculative exceptions to be dismissed (ignored), then the compiler must generate recovery code that raises the exception at the original program point of the speculated operation. Unlike predication, speculation actually removes control dependences, and thus potentially reduces the length of the critical path of execution. Depending on the shape and size of recovery code, and if multiple operations are speculated, the addition of recovery code can lead to a substantial amount of code.

Predication is a technique where with hardware support operations have an additional input operand, the predicate operand, which determines whether any effects of executing the operations are seen by the program execution. Thus, from an execution point of view, the operation is conditionally executed under the control of the predicate input. Hence changing a control-dependent operation to its predicated equivalent that depends on a predicate that is equivalent to the condition of the control dependence turns control dependence into data dependence.

Trace Compaction

There are many different scheduling techniques, which can broadly be classified by features into cycle versus operation scheduling, linear versus graph-based, cyclic versus acyclic, and greedy versus backtracking. However, for trace scheduling itself the scheduling technique employed is not of major concern; rather, trace scheduling distinguishes itself from other global acyclic scheduling techniques by the way the scheduling region is formed, and by the kind of code motions permitted during scheduling. Hence these techniques will not be described here, and in the following, a greedy graph-based technique, namely list scheduling, will be used.

Compensation Code

During scheduling, typically only a very small number of operations can be moved freely between basic blocks without changing program semantics. Other operations may be moved only when additional *compensation code* is inserted at an appropriate place in order to maintain original program semantics. Trace scheduling is quite general in this regard. Recall that a trace may be entered after the first instruction, and exited before the last instruction. In addition, trace scheduling allows operations in the region (trace) to move freely during scheduling relative to entries (join points) to and exits (split points) from the current trace. A separate *bookkeeping* step restores the original program semantics after trace compaction through the introduction of compensation code. It is this freedom of code motion during scheduling, and the introduction of compensation code between the scheduling of individual regions, that represents a major difference between trace scheduling and other acyclic scheduling techniques.

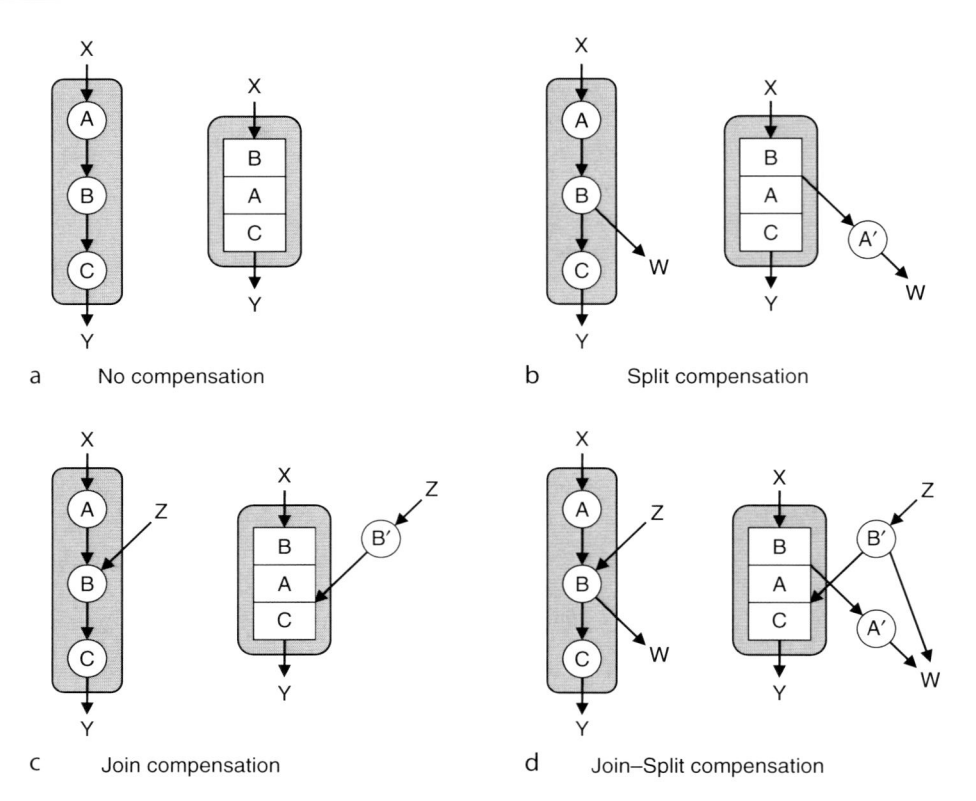

Trace Scheduling. Fig. 4 Basic scenarios for compensation code. In each diagram, the *left* part shows the selected trace, the *right* part shows the compacted code where operation B has moved above operation A

Since trace scheduling allows operations to move above join points as well as below split points (conditional branches) in the original program order, the bookkeeping process includes the following kinds of compensation. Note that a complete discussion of all the intricacies of compensation code is well beyond the scope of this entry; however, the following is a list of the simple concepts that form the basis of many of the compensation techniques used in compilers.

No compensation (Fig. 4a). If the global motion of an operation on the trace does not change the relative order of operations with respect to split and join points, no compensation code is needed. This covers the situation when an operation moves above a split, in which case the operation becomes *speculative*, and requires compensation depending on the recovery model of exceptions: in the case of *dismissible speculation*, no compensation code is needed; in the case of *recovery speculation*, the compiler has to emit a recovery block to guarantee the timely delivery of exceptions for correctly speculated operations.

Split compensation (Fig. 4b). When an operation A moves below a split operation B (i.e., a conditional branch), a copy of A (called A') must be inserted on the off-trace split edge. When multiple operations move below a split operation, they are all copied on the off-trace edge in source order. These copies are unscheduled, and hence will be picked and scheduled later during the trace scheduling of the program.

Join compensation (Fig. 4c). When an operation B moves above a join point A, a copy of B (called B') must be copied on the off-trace join edge. When multiple operations move above a join point, they are all copied on the off-trace edge in source order.

Join–Split compensation (Fig. 4d). When splits are allowed to move above join points, the situation becomes more complicated: when the split is copied on the rejoin edge, it must account for any split compensation and therefore introduce additional control paths with additional split copies.

These rules define the compensation code required to correctly maintain the semantics of the original

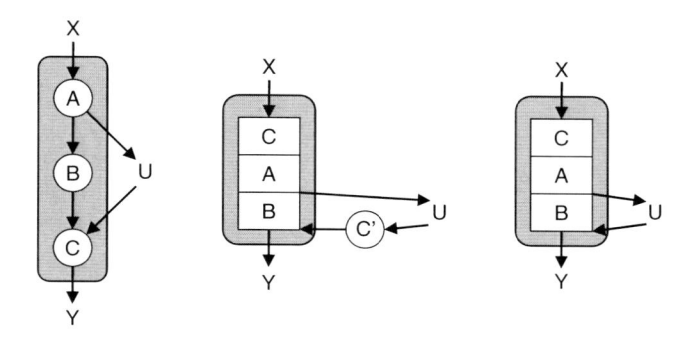

Trace Scheduling. Fig. 5 Compensation copy suppression. The *left* diagram shows the selected trace. The *middle* diagram shows the compacted code where operation C has moved above operation A together with the normal join compensation. The *right* diagram shows the result of compensation copy suppression assuming that C is available at Y

program. The following observations can be used to heuristically control the amount of compensation code that is generated.

To limit split compensation, the Multiflow Trace Scheduling compiler [12], the first commercial compiler to implement trace scheduling, required that all operations that precede a split on the trace precede the split on the schedule. While this limits the amount of available parallelism, the intuitive explanation is that a trace represents the most likely execution path; the on-trace performance penalty of this restriction is small; and off-trace the same operations would have to be executed in the first place. Multiflow's implementation excluded memory-store operations from this heuristic because in Multiflow's Trace architecture stores were unconditional and hence could not move above splits; they were allowed to move below splits to avoid serialization between stores and loop exits in unrolled loops. The Multiflow compiler also restricted splits to remain in source order. Not only did this reduce the amount of compensation code, it also ensured that all paths created by compensation code are subsets of paths (possibly rearranged) in the flow graph before trace scheduling.

Another observation concerns the possible suppression of compensation copies [8] (Fig. 5): sometimes an operation C that moves above a join point following an operation B actually moves to a position on the trace that dominates the join point. When this happens, and the result of C is still available at the join point, no copy of C is needed. This situation often arises when loops with internal branches are unrolled. Without copy suppression, such loops can generate large amounts of redundant compensation code.

Bibliographic Notes and Further Reading

The simplest form of a scheduling region is a region where all operations come from a single-entry single-exit straight-line piece of code (i.e., a basic block). Since these regions do not contain any internal control flow, they can be scheduled using simple algorithms that maintain the partial order given by data dependences. (For simplicity, it is best to require that operations that could incur an exception must end their basic block, allowing the exception to be caught by an exception handler.)

Traces and trace scheduling were the first region-scheduling techniques proposed. They were introduced by Fisher [6, 7] and described more carefully in Ellis' thesis [4]. By demonstrating that simple microcode operations could be statically compacted and scheduled on multi-issue hardware trace scheduling provided the basis for making VLIW machines practical. Trace scheduling was implemented in the Multiflow compiler [12]; by demonstrating that commercial codes could be statically compiled for multi-issue architectures, this work also greatly influenced and contributed to the performance of superscalar architectures. Today, ideas of trace scheduling and its descendants are implemented in most compilers (e.g., GCC, LLVM, Open64, Pro64, as well as commercial compilers).

Trace scheduling inspired several other global acyclic scheduling techniques. The most important linear acyclic region-scheduling techniques are presented next.

Superblocks

Hwu and his colleagues on the IMPACT project have developed a variant of trace scheduling called *superblock scheduling*. Superblocks are traces with the added restriction that the superblock must be entered at the top [2, 3]. Hence superblocks can be joined only before the first or after the last operation in the superblock. As such, superblocks are single-entry, multiple-exit traces.

Since superblocks do not contain join points, scheduling a superblock cannot generate any join or join–split compensation. By also prohibiting motion below splits, superblock scheduling avoids the need of generating compensation code outside the schedule region, and hence does not require a separate bookkeeping step. With these restrictions, superblock formation can be completed before scheduling starts, simplifying its implementation.

Superblock formation often includes a technique called *tail duplication* to increase the size of the superblock: tail duplication copies any operations that follow a rejoin in the original control flow graph and that are part of the superblock into the rejoin edge, thus effectively lowering the rejoin point to the end of the superblock. This is done at superblock formation time, before any compaction takes place [11].

A variant of superblock scheduling that allows speculative code motion is sentinel scheduling [14].

Hyperblocks

A different approach to global acyclic scheduling also originated with the IMPACT project. *Hyperblocks* are superblocks that have eliminated internal control flow using predication [13]. As such, hyperblocks are single-entry, multiple-exit traces (superblocks) that use predication to eliminate internal control flow.

Treegions

Treegions [9, 10] consist of the operations from a list of basic blocks $B_0, B_1, \ldots, B_n$ with the properties that:

- For each $j > 0$, B_j has exactly one predecessor.
- For each $j > 0$, the predecessor B_i of B_j is also on the list, where $i < j$.

Hence, treegions represent trees of basic blocks in the control flow graph. Since treegions do not contain any side entrances, each path through a treegion yields a superblock. Like superblock compilers, treegion compilers employ tail duplication and other region-enlarging techniques. More recent work by Zhou and Conte [16, 17] shows that treegions can be made quite effective without significant code growth.

Nonlinear Regions

Nonlinear region approaches include percolation scheduling [1] and DAG-based scheduling [15]. Trace scheduling-2 [5] extends treegions by removing the restriction on side entrances. However, its implementation proved so difficult that its proposer eventually gave up on it, and no formal description or implementation of it is known to exist.

Related Entries

▶ Modulo Scheduling and Loop Pipelining

Bibliography

1. Aiken A, Nicolau A (1988) Optimal loop parallelization. In: Proceedings of the SIGPLAN 1988 conference on programming language design and implementation, June 1988, pp 308–317
2. Chang PP, Warter NJ, Mahlke SA, Chen WY, Hwu WW (1991) Three superblock scheduling models for superscalar and super-pipelined processors. Technical Report CRHC-91-29. Center for Reliable and High-Performance Computing, University of Illinois at Urbana-Champaign
3. Chang PP, Mahlke SA, Chen WY, Warter NJ, Hwu WW (1991) IMPACT: an architectural framework for multiple-instruction-issue processors. In: Proceedings of the 18th annual international symposium on computer architecture, May 1991, pp 266–275
4. Ellis JR (1985) Bulldog: a compiler for VLIW architectures. PhD thesis, Yale University
5. Fisher JA (1993) Global code generation for instruction-level parallelism: trace scheduling-2. Technical Report HPL-93-43. Hewlett-Packard Laboratories
6. Fisher JA (1981) Trace scheduling: a technique for global microcode compaction, IEEE Trans Comput, July 1981, 30(7):478–490
7. Fisher JA (1979) The optimization of horizontal microcode within and beyond basic blocks. PhD dissertation. Technical Report COO-3077-161. Courant Institute of Mathematical Sciences, New York University, New York, NY

8. Freudenberger SM, Gross TR, Lowney PG (1994) Avoidance and suppression of compensation code in a trace scheduling compiler, ACM Trans Program Lang Syst, July 1994, 16(4):1156–1214
9. Havanki WA (1997) Treegion scheduling for VLIW processors. MS thesis. Department of Electrical and Computer Engineering, North Carolina State University, Raleigh, NC
10. Havanki WA, Banerjia S, Conte TM (1998) Treegion scheduling for wide issue processors. In: Proceedings of the fourth international symposium on high-performance computer architecture, February 1998, pp 266–276
11. Hwu WW, Mahlke SA, Chen WY, Chang PP, Warter NJ, Bringmann RA, Ouellette RG, Hank RE, Kiyohara T, Haab GE, Holm JG, Lavery DM (May 1993) The superblock: an effective technique for VLIW and superscalar compilation. J Supercomput, 7(1–2):229–248
12. Lowney PG, Freudenberger SM, Karzes TJ, Lichtenstein WD, Nix RP, O'Donnell JS, Ruttenberg JC (1993) The Multiflow trace scheduling compiler, J Supercomput, May 1993, 7(1-2):51–142
13. Mahlke SA, Lin DC, Chen WY, Hank RE, Bringmann RA (1992) Effective compiler support for predicated execution using the hyperblock. In: Proceedings of the 25th annual international symposium on microarchitecture, 1992, pp 45–54
14. Mahlke SA, Chen WY, Bringmann RA, Hank RE, Hwu WW, Rau BR, Schlansker MS (1993) Sentinel scheduling: a model for compiler-controlled speculative execution, ACM Trans Comput Syst, November 1993, 11(4):376–408
15. Moon SM, Ebcioglu K (1997) Parallelizing nonnumerical code with selective scheduling and software pipelining, ACM Trans Program Lang Syst, November 1997, 19(6):853–898
16. Zhou H, Conte TM (2002) Code size efficiency in global scheduling for ILP processors. In: Proceedings of the sixth annual workshop on the interaction between compilers and computer architectures, February 2002, pp 79–90
17. Zhou H, Jennings MD, Conte TM (2001) Tree traversal scheduling: a global scheduling technique for VLIW/EPIC processors. In: Proceedings of the 14th annual workshop on languages and compilers for parallel computing, August 2001, pp 223–238

Trace Theory

Volker Diekert[1], Anca Muscholl[2]
[1]Universität Stuttgart FMI, Stuttgart, Germany
[2]Université Bordeaux 1, Talence, France

Synonyms

Partial computation; Theory of Mazurkiewicz-traces

Definition

Trace Theory denotes a mathematical theory of free partially commutative monoids from the perspective of concurrent or parallel systems. Traces, or equivalently, elements in a free partially commutative monoid, are given by a sequence of letters (or atomic actions). Two sequences are assumed to be equal if they can be transformed into each other by equations of type $ab = ba$, where the pair (a, b) belongs to a predefined relation between letters. This relation is usually called *partial commutation* or *independence*. With an empty independence relation, that is, without independence, the setting coincides with the classical theory of words or strings.

Discussion

Introduction

The analysis of sequential programs describes a run of a program as a sequence of atomic actions. On an abstract level such a sequence is simply a string in a free monoid over some (finite) alphabet of letters. This purely abstract viewpoint embeds program analysis into a rich theory of combinatorics on words and a theory of automata and formal languages. The approach has been very fruitful from the early days where the first compilers have been written until now where research groups in academia and industry develop formal methods for verification.

Efficient compilers use autoparallelization, which provides a natural example of independence of actions resulting in a partial commutation relation. For example, let $a; b; c; a; d; e; f$ be a sequence of arithmetic operations where:

$(a)\ x := x + 2y,\quad (b)\ x := x - z,\quad (c)\ y := y \cdot 5z$

$(d)\ w := 2w,\quad (e)\ z := y \cdot z,\quad (f)\ z := x + y \cdot w.$

A concurrent-read-exclusive-write protocol yields a list of pairs of independent operations (a, d), (a, e), (b, c), (b, d), (c, d), and (d, e), which can be performed concurrently or in any order. The sequence can therefore be performed in four parallel steps $\{a\}; \{b, c\}; \{a, d, e\}; \{f\}$, but as d commutes with a, b, c the result of $a; b; c; a; d; e; f$ is equal to $a; d; b; c; a; e; f$, and two processors are actually enough to guarantee minimal parallel execution time, since another possible schedule is $\{a, d\}; \{b, c\}; \{a, e\}; \{f\}$. Trace theory yields a tool to do such (data-independent) transformations automatically.

Parallelism and concurrency demand for specific models, because a purely sequential description is neither accurate nor possible in all cases, for example, if asynchronous algorithms are studied and implemented. Several formalisms have been proposed in this context. Among these models there are Petri nets, Hoare's CSP and Milner's CCS, event structures, and branching temporal logics. The mathematical analysis of Petri nets is however quite complicated and much of the success of Hoare's and Milner's calculus is due to the fact that it stays close to the traditional concept of sequential systems relying on a unified and classical theory of words. Trace theory follows the same paradigm; it enriches the theory of words by a very restricted, but essential formalism to capture the main aspects of parallelism: In a static way a set I of independent letters (a, b) is fixed, and sequences are identified if they can be transformed into each other by using equations of type $ab = ba$ for $(a, b) \in I$. In computer science this approach appeared for the first time in the paper by Keller on *Parallel Program Schemata and Maximal Parallelism* published in 1973. Based on the ideas of Keller and the behavior of elementary net systems, Mazurkiewicz introduced in 1977 the notion of *trace theory* and made its concept popular to a wider computer science community. Mazurkiewicz's approach relies on a graphical representation for a trace. This is a node-labeled directed acyclic graph, where arcs are defined by the dependence relation, which is by definition the complement of the independence relation I.

Thereby, a concurrent run has an immediate graphical visualization, which is obviously convenient for practice. The picture of the two parallel executions $\{a\}; \{b, c\}; \{a, d, e\}; \{f\}$ and $\{a, d\}; \{b, c\}; \{a, e\}; \{f\}$ can be depicted as follows, which represents (the Hasse diagrams of) isomorphic labeled partial orders:

$$
\begin{array}{c}
a \to b \to a \qquad\qquad a \to b \to a \\
\searrow \times \searrow \qquad\qquad \searrow \times \searrow \\
c \to e \to f \qquad d \quad c \to e \to f \\
\nearrow\quad d
\end{array}
$$

Moreover, the graphical representation yields immediately a correct notion of *infinite trace*, which is not clear when working with partial commutations. In the following years it became evident that trace theory indeed copes with some important phenomena such as *true concurrency*. On the other hand it is still close to the classical theory of word languages describing sequential programs. In particular, it is possible to transfer the notion of finite sequential state control to the notion of asynchronous state control. This important result is due to Zielonka; it is one of the highlights of the theory. There is a satisfactory theory of recognizable languages relating finite monoids, rational operations, asynchronous automata, and logic. This leads to decidability results and various effective operations. Moreover, it is possible to develop a theory of asynchronous Büchi automata, which enables in trace theory the classical automata theory-based approach to automated verification.

Mathematical Definitions and Normal Forms

Trace theory is founded on a rigorous mathematical approach. The underlying combinatorics for partial commutation were studied in mathematics already in 1969 in the seminal Lecture Notes in Mathematics *Problèmes combinatoires de commutation et réarrangements* by Cartier and Foata. The mathematical setting uses a finite alphabet Σ of letters and the specification of a symmetric and irreflexive relation $I \subseteq \Sigma \times \Sigma$, called the *independence* relation. Conveniently, its complement $D = \Sigma \times \Sigma \subseteq I$ is called the *dependence* relation. The dependence relation has a direct interpretation as graph as well. For the dependency used in the first example above it looks as follows:

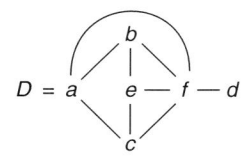

$$
D = a \quad \begin{array}{c} b \\ | \\ e - f - d \\ | \\ c \end{array}
$$

The intended semantics is that independent letters commute, but dependent letters must be ordered. Taking $ab = ba$ with $(a, b) \in I$ as defining relations one obtains a quotient monoid $\mathbb{M}(\Sigma, I)$, which has been called *free partial commutative monoid* or simply *trace monoid* in the literature. The elements are finite (Mazurkiewicz-)traces. For $I = \emptyset$, traces are just words in Σ^*; for a full independence relation, that is, $D = \mathrm{id}_\Sigma$, traces are vectors in some $\mathbb{N}^k$, hence Parikh-images of words. The general philosophy is that the extrema Σ^* and $\mathbb{N}^k$ are well understood (which is far from being true), but the interesting and difficult problems arise when $\mathbb{M}(\Sigma, I)$ is neither free nor commutative.

For effective computations and the design of algorithms appropriate normal forms can be used. For the *lexicographic* normal form it is assumed that the alphabet Σ is totally ordered, say $a < b < c < \cdots < z$. This defines a lexicographic ordering on Σ^* exactly the same way words are ordered in a standard dictionary. The lexicographic normal form of a trace is the minimal word in Σ^* representing it. For example, if I is given by $\{(a, d), (d, a), (b, c), (c, a)\}$, then the trace defined by the sequence $badacb$ is the congruence class of six words:

$$\{baadbc, badabc, bdaabc, baadcb, badacb, bdaacb\}.$$

Its lexicographic normal form is the first word $baadbc$. An important property of lexicographic normal forms has been stated by Anisimov and Knuth. A word is in lexicographic normal form if and only if it does not contain a *forbidden pattern*, which is a factor bua where $a < b \in \Sigma$ and the letter a commutes with all letters appearing in $bu \in \Sigma^*$. As a consequence, the set of lexicographic normal forms is a regular language.

The other main normal is due to Foata. It is a normal form that encodes a maximal parallel execution. Its definition uses *steps*, where a step means here a subset $F \subseteq \Sigma$ of pairwise independent letters. Thus, a step requires only one parallel execution step. A step F yields a trace by taking the product $\Pi_{a \in F} a$ over all its letters in any order. The *Foata normal form* is a sequence of steps $F_1 \cdots F_k$ such that $F_1, \ldots, F_k$ are chosen from left to right with maximal cardinality. The sequence $\{a, d\}; \{b, c\}; \{a, e\}; \{f\}$ above has been the Foata normal form of $abcadef$.

The graphical representation of a trace due to Mazurkiewicz can be viewed as a third normal form. It is called the *dependence graph representation*; and it is closely related to the Foata normal form. Say a trace t is specified by some sequence of letters $t = a_1 \cdots a_n$. Each index $i \in V = \{1, \ldots, n\}$ is labeled by the letter a_i. Finally, arcs $(i, j) \in E$ are introduced if and only if both $(a_i, a_j) \in D$ and $i < j$. In this way an acyclic directed graph $G(t)$ is defined which is another unique representation of t. The information about t is also contained in the induced partial order (i.e., the transitive closure of $G(t)$ or in its Hasse-diagram (i.e., removing all transitive arcs from $G(t)$).

Computation of Normal Forms

There are efficient algorithms that compute normal forms in polynomial time. A very simple method uses a stack for each letter of the alphabet Σ. An input word is scanned from right to left, so the last letter is read first. When processing a letter a it is pushed on its stack and a marker is pushed on the stack of all the letters b ($b \neq a$), which do not commute with a. Once the word has been processed its lexicographic normal form, the Foata normal form, and the Hasse-diagram of the dependence graph representation can be obtained straightforwardly. For example, the sequence $a; b; c; a; d; e; f$ (with a dependence relation as depicted above) yields stacks as follows:

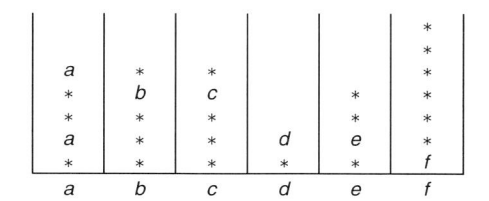

a					*
*	*	*			*
*	b	c		*	*
*	*	*		*	*
a	*	*	d	*	*
*	*	*	*	e	*
*	*	*	*	*	f
a	b	c	d	e	f

Regular Sets

A fundamental concept in formal languages is the notion of a *regular set*. Kleene's Theorem says that a regular set can be specified either by a finite deterministic (resp. nondeterministic) automaton DFA (resp. NFA) or, equivalently, by a regular expression. Regular expressions are also called *rational expressions*. They are defined inductively by saying that every finite set denotes a rational expression and if R, S is rational, then $R \cup S$, $R \cdot S$, and R^* are rational expressions, too. The semantics of a rational expression is defined in any monoid M since the semantics of $R \cup S$, $R \cdot S$ is obvious, and R^* can be viewed as the union $\bigcup_{k \in \mathbb{N}} R^k$. For *star-free* expressions one does not allow the star-operation, but one adds complementation, denoted, for example, by $\overline{R}$ with the semantics $M \setminus R$.

In trace theory a direct translation of Kleene's Theorem fails, but it can be replaced by a generalization due to Ochmański. If (a, b) is a pair of independent letters, then $(ab)^*$ is a rational expression, but due to $ab = ba$ it represents all strings with an equal number of a's and b's which is clearly not regular. With three pairwise independent letters $(abc)^*$ is not even context-free. A general formal language theory distinguishes between recognizable and rational sets. A subset L of a trace monoid is called *recognizable*, if its closure is a regular word language. Here the closure refers to all words in Σ^*, which represent some trace in L. A subset L is called *rational*, if L can be specified by some regular (and hence rational) expression. Using the algebraic notion of homomorphism this can be rephrased as follows. Let φ be the canonical homomorphism of Σ^* onto $\mathbb{M}(\Sigma, I)$, which simply means the interpretation of a string as its trace. Now, L is recognizable if and only if $\varphi^{-1}(L)$ is a regular word language, and L is rational if and only if $L = \varphi(K)$ for some regular word language K. As a consequence of Kleene's Theorem all recognizable trace languages are rational, but the converse fails as soon as there is a pair of independent letters, that is, the trace monoid is not free.

Given a recognizable trace language L, the corresponding word language $\varphi^{-1}(L)$ is accepted by some NFA (actually some DFA), which satisfies the so-called *I-diamond property*. This means whenever it holds $(a, b) \in I$ and a state p leads to a state q by reading the word ab, then it is in state p also possible to read ba and this leads to state q, too. NFAs satisfying the I-diamond property accept closed languages only. Therefore they capture exactly the notion of recognizability for traces.

It has been shown that the concatenation of two recognizable trace languages is recognizable, in particular *star-free languages* (i.e., given by star-free expressions) are recognizable. However, the example $(ab)^*$ above shows that the star-operation leads to non-recognizable sets as soon as the trace monoid is not free. Métivier and Ochmański have introduced a restricted version where the star-operation is allowed only when applied to languages L where all traces $t \in L$ are connected. This means the dependence graph $G(t)$ is connected or, equivalently, there is no nontrivial factorization $t = uv$ where all letters in u are independent of all letters in v. A theorem shows that L^* is still recognizable, if L is connected (i.e., all $t \in L$ are connected) and recognizable. Ochmański's Theorem yields also the converse: A trace language L is recognizable if and only if it can be specified by a rational expression where the star-operation is restricted to connected subsets. As word languages are always connected this is a proper generalization of the classical Kleene's Theorem. Yet another characterization of recognizable trace languages is as follows: They are in one-to-one correspondence with regular subsets inside the regular set LexNF $\subseteq \Sigma^*$ of lexicographic normal forms. The correspondence associates with $L \subseteq \mathbb{M}(\Sigma, I)$ the set $K = \varphi^{-1}(L) \cap$ LexNF. A rational expression for K is a rational expression for L, where the star-operation is restricted to connected languages.

Decidability Questions

The Star Mystery
The *Star Problem* is to decide for a given recognizable trace language $L \subseteq \mathbb{M}(\Sigma, I)$ whether L^* is recognizable. It is not known whether the star problem is decidable, even if it is restricted to finite languages L. The surprising difficulty of this problem has been coined as the *star mystery* by Ochmański. It has been shown by Richomme that the Star Problem is decidable, if (Σ, I) does not contain any C_4 (cycle of four letters) as an induced subgraph.

Undecidability Results for Rational Sets

For rational languages (unlike as for recognizable languages) some very basic problems are known to be undecidable. The following list contains undecidable decision problems, where the input for each instance consists of an independence alphabet (Σ, I) and rational trace languages $R, T \subseteq \mathbb{M}(\Sigma, I)$ specified by rational expressions.

- **Inclusion** question: Does $R \subseteq T$ hold?
- **Equality** question: Does $R = T$ hold?
- **Universality** question: Does $R = \mathbb{M}(\Sigma, I)$ hold?
- **Complementation** question: Is $\mathbb{M}(\Sigma, I) \setminus R$ a rational?
- **Recognizability** question: Is R recognizable?
- **Intersection** question: Does $R \cap T = \emptyset$ hold?

On the positive side, if I is transitive, then all six problems above are decidable. This is also a necessary condition for the first five problems in the list. Transitivity of the independence alphabet means in algebraic terms that the trace monoid is a free product of free and free commutative monoids, like, for example, $\{a, b\}^* * \mathbb{N}^3$.

The intersection problem is simpler. It is known that the problem Intersection is decidable if and only if (Σ, I)

is a transitive forest. It is also well known that transitive forests are characterized by forbidden induced subgraphs C_4 and P_4 (cycle and path, resp., of four letters).

Asynchronous Automata

Whereas recognizable trace languages can be defined as word languages accepted by DFAs or NFAs with I-diamond property, there is an equivalent distributed automaton model called *asynchronous automata*. Such an automaton is a parallel composition of finite-state processes synchronizing over shared variables, whereas a DFA satisfying the I-diamond property is still a device with a centralized control. An asynchronous automaton $\mathcal{A}$ has, by definition, a distributed finite state control such that independent actions may be performed in parallel. The set of global states is modeled as a direct product $Q = \prod_{p \in P} Q_p$, where the Q_p are states of the local component $p \in P$ and P is some finite index set (a set of processors). For each letter $a \in \Sigma$ there is a *read domain* $R(a) \subseteq P$ and a *write domain* $W(a) \subseteq P$ where for simplicity $W(a) \subseteq R(a)$. Processors p and q share a variable a if and only if $p, q \in R(a)$. The transitions are given by a family of partially defined functions δ_p, where each processor p reads the status in the local components of its read domain and changes states in local components of its write domain. Accordingly to the read-and-write-conflicts being allowed, four basic types are distinguished:

- Concurrent-Read-Exclusive-Write (*CREW*), if $R(a) \cap W(b) = \emptyset$ for all $(a, b) \in I$.
- Concurrent-Read-Owner-Write (*CROW*), if $R(a) \cap W(b) = \emptyset$ for all $(a, b) \in I$ and $W(a) \cap W(b) = \emptyset$ for all $a \neq b$.
- Exclusive-Read-Exclusive-Write (*EREW*), if $R(a) \cap R(b) = \emptyset$ for all $(a, b) \in I$.
- Exclusive-Read-Owner-Write (*EROW*), if $R(a) \cap R(b) = \emptyset$ for all $(a, b) \in I$ and $W(a) \cap W(b) = \emptyset$ for all $a \neq b$.

The local transition functions $(\delta_p)_{p \in P}$ give rise to a partially defined transition function on global states $\delta : (\prod_{p \in P} Q_p) \times \Sigma \longrightarrow \prod_{p \in P} Q_p$.

If $\mathcal{A}$ is of any of the four types above, then the action of a trace $t \in \mathbb{M}(\Sigma, I)$ on global states is well defined. This allows to see an asynchronous automaton as an I-diamond DFA. There are effective translations from one model to the other. The most compact versions can be obtained by a CREW model, therefore it is of prior practical interest.

Zielonka has shown in his thesis (published in 1987) the following deep theorem in trace theory: Every recognizable trace language can be accepted by some finite asynchronous automaton. The proof of this theorem is very technical and complicated. Moreover, the original construction was doubly exponential in the size of an I-diamond automaton for the language L. Therefore, it is part of ongoing research to simplify its construction, in particular since efficient constructions are necessary to make the result applicable in practice. The best result to date is due to Genest et al. They provide a construction where the size of the obtained asynchronous automaton is polynomial in the size of a given DFA and simply exponential in the number of processes. They also show that the construction is optimal within the class of automata produced by Zielonka-type constructions, which yields a nontrivial lower bound on the size of asynchronous automata.

A rather direct construction of asynchronous automata is known for triangulated dependence alphabets, which means that all chordless cycles are of length 3. For example, complete graphs and forests are triangulated.

Infinite Traces

The theory of infinite traces has its origins in the mid-1980s when Flé and Roucairol considered the problem of serializability of iterated transactions in data bases. A suitable definition of an infinite trace uses the dependence graph representation due to Mazurkiewicz. Just as in the finite case an infinite sequence $t = a_1 a_2 \cdots$ of letters yields an infinite node-labeled acyclic directed graph $G(t)$, where now each $i \in V = \mathbb{N}$ is labeled by the letter a_i, and again arcs $(i, j) \in E$ are introduced if and only if both $(a_i, a_j) \in D$ and $i < j$. It is useful to consider finite and infinite objects simultaneously as an infinite trace may split into connected components where some of them might be finite. The notion of *real trace* has been introduced to denote either a finite or an infinite trace. If $t_1, t_2, \ldots$ is (finite or infinite) sequence of finite traces, then the product $t_1 t_2 \cdots$ is a well-defined real trace. It is a finite trace if almost all t_i are empty and an infinite trace otherwise. In particular, one can define the ω-product L^ω for every set L of finite traces and one enriches the set of rational expressions by this operation.

The set $\mathbb{R}(\Sigma, I)$ of real traces can be embedded into a monoid of *complex traces* where the *imaginary* component is a subset of Σ. This alphabetic information is necessary in order to define an associative operation of concatenation. (Over complex traces L^ω is defined for all subsets L.)

Many results from the theory of finite traces transfer to infinite traces according to the same scheme as for finite and infinite words.

Logics

MSO and First-Order Logic

Formulae in monadic second-order logic (MSO) are built up upon first-order variables $x, y, \ldots$ ranging over vertices and second-order variables $X, Y, \ldots$ ranging over subsets of vertices. There are Boolean constants *true* and *false*, the logical connectives $\vee, \wedge, \neg$, and quantification $\exists, \forall$ for the first- and second-order variables. In addition there are four types of atomic formulae:

$$x \in X, x = y, (x, y) \in E, \text{ and } \lambda(x) = a.$$

A first-order formula is a formula without any second-order variable. A *sentence* is a closed formula, that is, a formula without free variables. The semantics of an MSO-sentence is defined for every node-labeled graph $[V, E, \lambda]$ (here: V = set of vertices, E = set of edges, $\lambda : V \to \Sigma$ = vertex labeling). Identifying a trace t with its dependence graph $G(t)$, the truth value of $t \vDash \psi$ is therefore well defined for every sentence ψ. The trace language defined by a sentence ψ is $L(\psi) = \{t \in \mathbb{R}(\Sigma, I) \mid t \vDash \psi\}$. It follows a notion of first-order and second-order definability of trace languages.

Temporal Logic

Linear temporal logic, LTL, can be inductively defined inside first order as formulae with one free variable, as soon as the transitive closure $(x, y) \in E^*$ is expressible in first order (as it is the case for trace monoids). There are no quantifiers, but all Boolean connectives. The atomic formulae are $\lambda(x) = a$. If $\varphi(x), \psi(x)$ are LTL-formulae, then $\text{EX}\,\varphi(x)$ and $(\varphi \cup \psi)(x)$ are LTL-formulae. In temporal logic $(x, y) \in E^*$ means that y is in the future of the node x. The semantics of $\text{EX}\,\varphi(x)$ is *exists next*, thus $\varphi(y)$ holds for a direct successor of x. The semantics of $(\varphi \cup \psi)(x)$ reflects an *until operator*, it says that in the future of x there is some z that satisfies $\psi(z)$ and all y in the future of x but in the strict past of z satisfy $\varphi(y)$. Hence, condition φ holds until ψ becomes true. There are dual past-tense operators, but they do not add expressivity.

For LTL one can also give a syntax without any free variable and a *global semantics* where the evaluation is based on the prefix relation of traces. The local semantics as defined above is for traces a priori expressively weaker, but it was shown that both, the global and local LTL have the same expressive power as first-order logic. This was done by Thiagarajan and Walukiewicz in 1998 for global LTL and by Diekert and Gastin in 2006 for local LTL, respectively. Both results extend a famous result of Kamp from words to traces. The complexity of the satisfiability problem (or model checking) is however quite different. In global semantics it is nonelementary, whereas in local semantics it is in PSPACE (= class of problems solvable on a Turing machine in polynomial space.)

Fragments

For various applications fragments of first-order logics suffice. This has the advantage that simpler constructions are possible and that the complexity of model checking is possibly reduced. A prominent fragment is first-order logic with at most two names for variables. Two-variable logics capture the core features of XML navigational languages like XPath. Over words and over traces two variable logic $\text{FO}^2[E]$ can be characterized algebraically via the variety of monoids DA (referring to the fact that regular $\mathcal{D}$-classes are aperiodic semigroups), in logic by *Next-Future* and *Yesterday-Past* operators, and in terms of rational expressions via unambiguous polynomials. It turns out that the satisfiability problem for two-variable logic is NP-complete (if the independence alphabet is not part of the input). The extension of these results from words to traces is due to Kufleitner.

Logics, Algebra, and Automata

The connection between logic and recognizability uses algebraic tools from the theory of finite monoids. If $h : \mathbb{M}(\Sigma, I) \to M$ is a homomorphism to a finite monoid M and $L \subseteq \mathbb{R}(\Sigma, I)$ is a set of real traces, then one says that h recognizes L, if for all $t \in L$ and factorizations $t = t_1 t_2 \cdots$ into finite traces t_i the following inclusion holds: $h^{-1}(t_1) h^{-1}(t_2) \cdots \subseteq L$. This allows to speak of *aperiodic languages* if some recognizing monoid is aperiodic. A monoid M is *aperiodic*, if for all $x \in M$ there is some $n \in \mathbb{N}$ such that $x^{n+1} = x^n$. A deep result states that a language is first-order definable if and only if it is recognized by a homomorphism to a finite aperiodic monoid. Algebraic characterizations lead to decidability of fragments. For example, it is decidable whether a recognizable language is aperiodic or whether it can be expressed in two-variable first-order logic.

Another way to define recognizability is via Büchi automata. A Büchi automaton for real traces is an I-diamond NFA with a set of final states F and a set of repeated states R. It accepts a trace if the run stops in F or if repeated states are visited infinitely often. If its transformation monoid is aperiodic it is called aperiodic, too. There is also a notion of asynchronous (cellular) Büchi automaton, and it is known that every I-diamond Büchi automaton can be transformed into an equivalent asynchronous cellular Büchi automaton.

The main result connecting logic, recognizability, rational expressions, and algebra can be summarized by saying that the following statements in the first block (second block resp.) are equivalent for all trace languages $L \subseteq \mathbb{R}(\Sigma, I)$:

MSO definability:

1. L is definable in monadic second-order logic.
2. L is recognizable by some finite monoid.
3. L is given as a rational expression where the star is restricted to connected languages.
4. L is accepted by some asynchronous Büchi automaton.

First-order definability:

1. L is definable in first-order logic.
2. L is definable in LTL (with global or local semantics).
3. L is recognizable by some finite and aperiodic monoid.
4. L is star-free.

Automata-Based Verification

The automata theoretical approach to verification uses the fact that systems and specifications are both modeled with finite automata. More precisely, a system is given as a finite transition system $\mathcal{A}$, which is typically realized as an NFA without final states. So, the system allows finite and infinite runs. The specification is written in some logical formalism, say in the linear temporal logic LTL. So the specification is given by some formula φ, and its semantics $L(\varphi)$ defines the runs that obey the specification. Model checking means to verify the inclusion $L(\mathcal{A}) \subseteq L(\varphi)$. This is equivalent to $L(\mathcal{A}) \cap L(\neg\varphi) = \emptyset$. Once an automaton $\mathcal{B}$ with $L(\mathcal{B}) = L(\neg\varphi)$ has been constructed, standard methods yield a product automaton for $L(\mathcal{A}) \cap L(\mathcal{B})$. The check for emptiness becomes a reachability problem in directed graphs.

A main obstacle is the combinatorial explosion when constructing the automaton $\mathcal{B}$. But this works in practice nevertheless reasonable well, because typical specifications are simple enough to be understood (hopefully) by the designer, so they are short. From a theoretical viewpoint the complexity of model checking for MSO and first order is nonelementary, but for (local) LTL is still in PSPACE. This approach is mostly applied and very successful where runs can be modeled as sequences. Trace theory provides the necessary tools to extend these methods to asynchronous systems. A first step in this direction has been implemented in the framework of *partial order* reduction. Another application of trace theory is the analysis of communication protocols.

Traces and Asynchronous Communication

Trace automata like asynchronous ones model concurrency in the same spirit as Petri nets, using shared variables. A more complex model arises when concurrent processes cooperate over unbounded, fifo communication channels.

A *communicating automaton* is defined over a set P of processes, together with point-to-point communication channels $Ch \subseteq \{(p,q) \in P^2 \mid p \neq q\}$. It consists of a tuple of NFAs $\mathcal{A}_p$, one for each process $p \in P$. Each NFA $\mathcal{A}_p$ has a set of local states Q_p and transition relation $\delta_p \subseteq Q_p \times \Sigma_p \times Q_p$. The set Σ_p of local actions of process p consists of send-actions $p!q(m)$ (of message m to process q, $(p,q) \in Ch$) and receive-actions $p?r(m)$ (of message m from process r, $(r,p) \in Ch$), respectively. The semantics of such an automaton is defined through configurations consisting of a tuple of local states (one for each process) and a tuple of word contents (one for each channel). In terms of partial orders the semantics of runs corresponds to *message sequence charts*

(*MSCs*), a graphical notation for fifo message exchange. In contrast with asynchronous automata, communicating automata have an infinite state space and are actually Turing powerful; thus, most algorithmic questions about them are undecidable.

The theory of recognizable trace languages enjoys various nice results known from word languages, for example, in terms of logics and automata. Since communicating automata are Turing powerful, one needs restrictions in order to obtain, for example, logical characterizations. A natural restriction consists in imposing bounds on the size of the channels. Such bounds come in two versions, namely, as *universal* and *existential* bounds, respectively. The existential version of channel bounds is optimistic and considers all those runs that can be rescheduled on bounded channels. The universal version is pessimistic and considers only those runs that, independent of the scheduling, can be executed with bounded channels. Thus, communicating automata with an universal channel bound are finite state, whereas with an existential channel bound they are infinite state systems.

Kuske proposed an encoding of runs of communicating automata with bounded channels into trace languages. Using this encoding, the set of runs (MSCs) of a communicating automaton is the projection of a recognizable trace language (for a universal bound), respectively the set of MSCs generated by the projection of a recognizable trace language (for an existential bound). This correspondence has the same flavor as the distinction between recognizable and rational trace languages, respectively.

The logic MSO over MSCs is defined with an additional binary message-predicate relating matching send and receive events. Henriksen et al. and Genest et al., respectively, have shown that the equivalence between MSO and automata extends to communicating automata with universal and existential channel bound, respectively. Another equivalent characterization exists in terms of MSC-graphs, similar to star-connected expressions for trace languages. These expressiveness results are complemented by decidable instances of the model-checking problem.

Related Entries

▶Asynchronous Iterative Algorithms
▶CSP (Communicating Sequential Processes)
▶Formal Methods–Based Tools for Race, Deadlock, and Other Errors
▶Multi-Threaded Processors
▶Parallel Computing
▶Parallelization, Automatic
▶Peer-to-Peer
▶Petri Nets
▶Reordering
▶Synchronization
▶Trace Scheduling
▶Verification of Parallel Shared-Memory Programs, Owicki-Gries Method of Axiomatic

Bibliographic Notes and Further Reading

Trace theory has its origin in enumerative combinatorics when Cartier and Foata found a new proof of the MacMahon Master Theorem in the framework of partial commutation by combining algebraic and bijective ideas [2]. The Foata normal form was defined in this Lecture Note. In computer science the key idea to use partial commutation as tool to investigate parallel systems was laid by Keller [10], but it was only by the influence of the technical report of Mazurkiewicz [11] when these ideas were spread to a wider computer science community, in particular to the Petri-net community. It was also Mazurkiewicz who coined the notion *Trace theory* and who introduced the notion of dependence graphs as a visualization of traces. The characterization of lexicographic normal forms by forbidden pattern is due to Anisimov and Knuth [1].

The investigation of recognizable (regular, rational resp.) languages is central in the theory of traces. The characterization of recognizable languages in terms of star-connected regular expressions is due to Ochmański [13]. The notion of *asynchronous automaton* is due to Zielonka. The major theorem showing that all recognizable languages can be accepted by asynchronous automata is his work (built on his thesis) [15]. The research on asynchronous automata is still an important and active area. The best constructions so far are due to Genest et al., where also nontrivial lower bounds were established [8].

The theory of infinite traces has its origin in the mid-1980s. A definition of a real trace as a prefix-closed and directed subset of real traces and its characterization by dependence graphs is given in a survey by

Mazurkiewicz [12]. The theory of recognizable real trace languages has been initiated by Gastin in 1990. The generalization of the Kleene–Büchi–Ochmański Theorem to real traces is due to Gastin, Petit, and Zielonka [7]. Diekert and Muscholl gave a construction for deterministic asynchronous Muller automata accepting a given recognizable real trace language.

Ebinger initiated the study of LTL for traces in his thesis in 1994. But it took quite an effort until Diekert and Gastin were able to show that LTL (in local semantics) has the same expressive power as first-oder logic [3]. The advantage of a local LTL is that model checking in PSPACE, whereas in its global semantics it becomes nonelementary by a result of Walukiewicz [14]. The PSPACE-containment has been shown for a much wider class of logics by Gastin and Kuske [6]. Diekert, Horsch, and Kufleitner [4] give a survey on fragments of first-order logic in trace theory. The Büchi-like equivalence between automata and MSO for existentially bounded communicating automata has been shown by Genest, Kuske, and Muscholl [9]. The translation from MSO into automata uses the equivalence for trace languages, but needs some additional, quite technical construction specific to communicating automata.

Very much of the material used in the present discussion can be found in The Book of Traces, which was edited by Diekert and Rozenberg [5]. The book surveys also a notion of *semi-commutation* (introduced by Clerbout and Latteux), and it provides many hints for further reading. Current research efforts concentrate on the topic of distributed games and controller synthesis for asynchronous automata.

Bibliography

1. Anisimov AV, Knuth DE (1979) Inhomogeneous sorting. Int J Comput Inf Sci 8:255–260
2. Cartier P, Foata D (1969) Problèmes combinatoires de commutation et réarrangements. Lecture notes in mathematics, vol 85. Springer, Heidelberg
3. Diekert V, Gastin P (2006) Pure future local temporal logics are expressively complete for Mazurkiewicz traces. Inf Comput 204:1597–1619. Conference version in LATIN 2004, LNCS 2976: 170–182, 2004
4. Diekert V, Horsch M, Kufleitner M (2007) On first-order fragments for Mazurkiewicz traces. Fundamenta Informaticae 80:1–29
5. Diekert V, Rozenberg G (eds) (1995) The book of traces. World Scientific, Singapore
6. Gastin P, Kuske D (2007) Uniform satisfiability in pspace for local temporal logics over Mazurkiewicz traces. Fundam Inf 80(1–3): 169–197
7. Gastin P, Petit A, Zielonka WL (2007) An extension of Kleene's and Ochmański's theorems to infinite traces. Theoret Comput Sci 125:167–204, x
8. Genest B, Gimbert H, Muscholl A, Walukiewicz I (2010) Optimal Zielonka-type construction of deterministic asynchronous automata. In: Abramsky S, Gavoille C, Kirchner C, Meyer auf der Heide F, Spirakis PG (eds) ICALP (2). Lecture notes in computer science, vol 6199. Springer, pp 52–63
9. Genest B, Kuske D, Muscholl A (2006) A Kleene theorem and model checking algorithms for existentially bounded communicating automata. Inf Comput 204:926–956. http://dx.doi.org/10.1016/j.ic.2006.01.005;DBLP, http://dblp.uni-trier.de
10. Keller RM (1973) Parallel program schemata and maximal parallelism I. Fundamental results. J Assoc Comput Mach 20(3):514–537
11. Mazurkiewicz A (1977) Concurrent program schemes and their interpretations. DAIMI Rep. PB 78, Aarhus University, Aarhus
12. Mazurkiewicz A (1987) Trace theory. In: Brauer W et al. (eds) Petri nets, applications and relationship to other models of concurrency. Lecture notes in computer science, vol 255. Springer, Heidelberg, pp 279–324
13. Ochmański E (Oct 1985) Regular behaviour of concurrent systems. Bull Eur Assoc Theor Comput Sci (EATCS) 27:56–67
14. Walukiewicz I (1998) Difficult configurations – on the complexity of LTrL. In: Larsen KG, et al. (eds) Proceedings of the 25th International Colloquium Automata, Languages and Programming (ICALP'98), Aalborg (Denmark). Lecture notes in computer science, vol 1443. Springer, Heidelberg, pp 140–151
15. Zielonka WL (1987) Notes on finite asynchronous automata. R.A.I.R.O. Informatique Théorique et Applications 21:99–135

Tracing

▶Performance Analysis Tools
▶Scalasca
▶TAU

Transactional Memories

MAURICE HERLIHY
Brown University, Providence, RI, USA

Synonyms

Locks; Monitors; Multiprocessor synchronization

Introduction

Transactional memory (TM) is an approach to structuring concurrent programs that seeks to provide better scalability and ease-of-use than conventional approaches based on locks and conditions. The term is commonly used to refer to ideas that range from programming language constructs to hardware architecture. This entry will survey how transactional memory affects each of these domains.

The major chip manufacturers have, for the time being, given up trying to make processors run faster. Moore's law has not been repealed: Each year, more and more transistors fit into the same space, but their clock speed cannot be increased without overheating. Instead, attention has turned toward *chip multiprocessing* (CMP), in which multiple computing cores are included on each processor chip. In the medium term, advances in technology will provide increased parallelism, but not increased single-thread performance. As a result, system designers and software engineers can no longer rely on increasing clock speed to hide software bloat. Instead, they must learn to make more effective use of increasing parallelism.

This adaptation will not be easy. Conventional programming practices typically rely on combinations of locks and conditions, such as monitors [1], to prevent threads from concurrently accessing shared data. Locking makes concurrent programming possible because it allows programmers to reason about certain code sections as if they were executed atomically. Nevertheless, the conventional approach suffers from a number of shortcomings.

First, programmers must decide between *coarse-grained* locking, in which a large data structure is protected by a single lock, and *fine-grained* locking, in which a lock is associated with each component of the data structure. Coarse-grained locking is relatively easy to use, but permits little or no concurrency, thereby preventing the program from exploiting multiple cores. By contrast, fine-grained locking is substantially more complicated because of the need to ensure that threads acquire all necessary locks (and only those, for good performance), and because of the need to avoid deadlock when acquiring multiple locks. Such designs are further complicated because the most efficient engineering solution may be platform dependent, varying with different machine sizes, workloads, and so on, making it difficult to write code that is both scalable and portable.

Second, locking provides poor support for code composition and reuse. For example, consider a lock-based queue that provides atomic enq() and deq() methods. Ideally, it should be easy to transfer an item atomically from one queue to another, but such elementary composition simply does not work. It is necessary to lock both queues at the same time to make the transfer atomic. If the queue methods synchronize internally, then there is no way to acquire and hold both locks simultaneously. If the queues export their locks, then modularity and safety are compromised, because the integrity of the objects depends on whether their users follow *ad hoc* conventions correctly.

Finally, such basic issues as the mapping from locks to data, that is, which locks protect which data, and the order in which locks must be acquired and released, are all based on convention, and violations are notoriously difficult to detect and debug. For these and other reasons, today's software practices make concurrent programs too difficult to develop, debug, understand, and maintain.

The Transactional Model

A *transaction* is a sequence of steps executed by a single thread. Transactions are *atomic*: Each transaction either commits (it takes effect) or aborts (its effects are discarded). Transactions are linearizable [2]: They appear to take effect in a one-at-a-time order. Transactional memory supports a computational model in which each thread announces the start of a transaction, executes a sequence of operations on shared objects, and then tries to commit the transaction. If the commit succeeds, the transaction's operations take effect; otherwise, they are discarded.

Sometimes we refer to these transactions as *memory transactions*. Memory transactions satisfy the same formal serializability and atomicity properties as the transactions used in conventional database systems, but they are intended to address different problems.

Unlike database transactions, memory transactions are short-lived activities that access a relatively small number of objects in primary memory. Database transactions are *persistent*: When a transaction commits, its changes are backed up on a disk. Memory transactions need not be persistent, and involve no explicit disk I/O.

To illustrate why memory transactions are attractive from a software engineering perspective, consider the problem of constructing a concurrent FIFO queue that permits one thread to enqueue items at the tail of the queue at the same time another thread dequeues items from the head of the queue, at least while the queue is non-empty. Any problem so easy to state, and that arises so naturally in practice, should have an easily devised, understandable solution. In fact, solving this problem with locks is quite difficult. In 1996, Michael and Scott published a clever and subtle solution [3]. It speaks poorly for fine-grained locking as a methodology that solutions to such simple problems are challenging enough to be publishable.

By contrast, it is almost trivial to solve this problem using transactions. Figure 1 shows how the queue's enqueue method might look in a language that provides direct support for transactions. It consists of little more than enclosing sequential code in a transaction

```
class Queue<T> {
  QNode head;
  Qnode tail ;
  public void enq(T x) {
    atomic {
      Qnode q = new Qnode(x);
      if ( tail == null) {   // empty queue
        head = tail = q;
      } else {
        tail .next = q;
        tail = q;
      }
    }
  }
  public T deq() {
    atomic {
      if (head == null)
        retry ;
      T item = head.item;
      head = head.next;
      if (head == null)
        tail = null;
      return item;
    }
  }
  ...
}
```

Transactional Memories. Fig. 1 Transactional queue code fragment

```
atomic {
  x = q0.deq ();
} orElse {
  x = q1.deq ();
}
```

Transactional Memories. Fig. 2 The orElse statement: waiting on multiple conditions

block. In practice, of course, a complete implementation would include more details (such as how to respond to an empty queue), but even so, this concurrent queue implementation is a remarkable achievement: It is not, by itself, a publishable result.

Conditional synchronization can be accomplished in the transactional model by means of the retry construct [4]. As illustrated in Fig. 1, if a thread attempts to dequeue from an empty queue, it executes retry, which rolls back the partial effects of the atomic block, and re-executes that block later when the object's state has changed. The retry construct is attractive because it is not subject to the *lost wake-up* bug that can arise using monitor conditions.

Transactions also admit compositions that would be impossible using locks and conditions. Waiting for one of several conditions to become *true* is impossible using objects with internal monitor condition variables. A novel aspect of retry is that such composition becomes easy. Figure 2 shows a code snippet illustrating the orElse statement, which joins two or more code blocks. Here, the thread executes the first block. If that block calls retry, then that subtransaction is rolled back, and the thread executes the second block. If that block also calls retry, then the orElse as a whole pauses, and later reruns each of the blocks (when something changes) until one completes.

Motivation

TM is commonly used to address three distinct problems: first, a simple desire to make highly concurrent data structures easy to implement; second, a more ambitious desire to support well-structured large-scale concurrent programs; and third, a pragmatic desire to make conventional locking more concurrent. Here is a survey of each area.

Lock-Free Data Structures

A data structure is *lock-free* if it guarantees that infinitely often *some* method call finishes in a finite number of steps, even if some subset of the threads halt in arbitrary places. A data structure that relies on locking cannot be lock-free because a thread that acquires a lock and then halts can prevent non-faulty threads from making progress.

Lock-free data structures are often awkward to implement using today's architectures which typically rely on *compare-and-swap* for synchronization. The *compare-and-swap* instruction takes three arguments, and *address a*, an *expected* value *e*, and an *update* value *u*. If the value stored at *a* is equal to *e*, then it is atomically replaced with *u*, and otherwise it is unchanged. Either way, the instruction sets a flag indicating whether the value was changed.

Often, the most natural way to define a lock-free data structure is to make an atomic change to several fields. Unfortunately, because *compare-and-swap* allows only one word (or perhaps a small number of contiguous words) to be changed atomically, designers of lock-free data structures are forced to introduce complex multistep protocols or additional levels of indirection that create unwelcome overhead and conceptual complexity. The original TM paper [5] was primarily motivated by a desire to circumvent these restrictions.

Software Engineering

TM is appealing as a way to help programmers structure concurrent programs because it allows the programmer to focus on what the program should be doing, rather than on the detailed synchronization mechanisms needed. For example, TM relieves the programmer of tasks such as devising specialized locking protocols for avoiding deadlocks, and conventions associating locks with data.

A number of programming languages and libraries have emerged to support TM. These include Clojure [6], .Net [7], Haskell [4]. Java [8, 9], C++ [10], and others.

Several groups have reported experiences converting programs from locks to TM. The TxLinux [11] project replaced most of the locks in the Linux kernel with transactions. Syntactically, each transaction appears to be a lock-based critical section, but that code is executed speculatively as a transaction (see Section 3.3). If an I/O call is detected, the transaction is rolled back and restarted using locks. Using transactions primarily as an alternative way to implement locks minimized the need to rewrite and restructure the original application.

Damron et al. [12] transactionalized the Berkeley DB lock manager. They found the transformation more difficult than expected because simply changing critical sections into atomic blocks often resulted in a disappointing level of concurrency. Critical sections often shared data unnecessarily, usually in the form of global statistics or shared memory pools. Later on, we will see other work that reinforces the notion the need to avoid *gratuitous conflicts* means that concurrent transactional programs must be structured differently than concurrent lock-based programs.

Pankratius et al. [13] conducted a user study where twelve students, working in pairs, wrote a parallel desktop search engine. Three randomly chosen groups used a compiler supporting TM, and three used conventional locks. The best TM group were much faster to produce a prototype, the final program performed substantially better, and they reported less time spent on debugging. However, the TM teams found performance harder to predict and to tune. Overall, the TM code was deemed easier to understand, but the TM teams did still make some synchronization errors.

Rossbach et al. [14] conducted a user study in which 147 undergraduates implemented the same programs using coarse-grained and fine-grained locks, monitors, and transactions. Many students reported they found transactions harder to use than coarse-grain locks, but slightly easier than fine-grained locks. Code inspection showed that students using transactions made many fewer synchronization errors: Over 70% of students made errors with fine-grained locking, while less than 10% made errors using transactions.

Lock Elision

Transactions can also be used as a way to implement locking. In *lock elision* [15], when a thread requests a lock, rather than waiting to acquire that lock, the thread starts a speculative transaction. If the transaction commits, then the critical section is complete. If the transaction aborts because of a synchronization conflict, then the thread can either retry the transaction, or it can actually acquire the lock.

Here is why lock elision is attractive. Locking is conservative: A thread must acquire a lock if it *might* conflict with another thread, even if such conflicts are rare. Replacing lock acquisition with speculative execution enhances concurrency if actual conflicts are rare. If conflicts persist, the thread can abandon speculative execution and revert to using locks. Lock elision has the added advantage that it does not require code to be restructured. Indeed, it can often be made to work with legacy code.

Azul Systems [16] has a JVM that uses (hardware) lock elision for contended Java locks, with the goal of accelerating "dusty deck" Java programs. The run-time system keeps track of how well the hardware transactional memory (HTM) is doing, and decides when to use lock elision and when to use conventional locks. The results work well for some applications, modestly well for others, and poorly for a few. The principal limitation seems to be the same as observed by Damron et al. [12]: many critical sections are written in a way that introduces gratuitous conflicts, usually by updating performance counters. Although these are not real conflicts, the HTM has no way to tell. Rewriting such code can be effective, but requires abandoning the goal of speeding up "dusty deck" programs.

Hardware Transactional Memory

Most hardware transactional memory (HTM) proposals are based on straightforward modifications to standard multiprocessor cache-coherence protocols. When a thread reads or writes a memory location on behalf of a transaction, that cache entry is flagged as being transactional. Transactional writes are accumulated in the cache or write buffer, but are not written back to memory while the transaction is active. If another thread invalidates a transactional entry, a data conflict has occurred, that transaction is aborted and restarted. If a transaction finishes without having had any of its entries invalidated, then the transaction commits by marking its transactional entries as valid or as dirty, and allowing the dirty entries to be written back to memory in the usual way.

One limitation of HTM is that in-cache transactions are limited in size and scope. Most hardware transactional memory proposals require programmers to be aware of platform-specific resource limitations such as cache and buffer sizes, scheduling quanta, and the effects of context switches and process migrations. Different platforms provide different cache sizes and architectures, and cache sizes are likely to change over time. Transactions that exceed resource limits or are repeatedly interrupted will never commit. Ideally, programmers should be shielded from such complex, platform-specific details. Instead, TM systems should provide full support even for transactions that cannot execute directly in hardware.

Techniques that substantially increase the size of hardware transactions include signatures [17] and permissions-only caches [18]. Other proposals support (effectively) unbounded transactions by allowing transactional metadata to overflow caches, and for transactions to migrate from one core to another. These proposals include TCC [19], VTM [20], OneTM [18], UTM [21], TxLinux [11], and LogTM [17].

Software Transactional Memory

Software transactional memory (STM) is an alternative to direct hardware support for TM. STM is a software system that provides programmers with a transactional model through a library or compiler interface. In this section, we describe some of the questions that arise when designing an STM system. Some of these questions concern *semantics*, that is, how the STM behaves, and other concern *implementation*, that is, how the STM is structured internally.

Weak vs Strong Isolation

How should threads that execute transactions interact with threads executing non-transactional code? One possibility is *strong isolation* [22] (sometimes called *strong atomicity*), which guarantees that transactions are atomic with respect to non-transactional accesses. The alternative, *weak isolation* (or *weak atomicity*), makes no such guarantees. HTM systems naturally provide strong atomicity. For STM systems, however, strong isolation may be too expensive.

The distinction between strong and weak isolation leaves unanswered a number of other questions about STM behavior. For example, what does it mean for an unhandled exception to exit an atomic block? What does I/O mean if executed inside a transaction? One appealing approach is to say that transactions behave as if they were protected by a *single global lock* (SGL) [19, 23, 24].

One limitation of the SGL semantics is that it does not specify the behavior of *zombie* transactions: transactions that are doomed to abort because of synchronization conflicts, but continue to run for some duration before the conflict is discovered. In some STM implementations, zombie transactions may see an inconsistent state before aborting. When a zombie aborts, its effects are rolled back, but while it runs, observed inconsistencies could provoke it to pathological behavior that may be difficult for the STM system to protect against, such as dereferencing a null pointer or entering an infinite loop. *Opacity* [25] is a correctness condition that guarantees that all uncommitted transactions, including zombies, see consistent states.

I/O and System Calls

What does it mean for a transaction to make a system call (such as I/O) that may affect the outside world? Recall that transactions are often executed speculatively, and a transaction that encounters a synchronization conflict may be rolled back and restarted. If a transaction creates a file, opens a window, or has some other external side effect, then it may be difficult or impossible to roll everything back.

One approach is to allow *irrevocable* transactions [11, 18, 26] that are not executed speculatively, and so never need to be undone. An irrevocable transaction cannot explicitly abort itself, and only one such transaction can run at a time, because of the danger that multiple irrevocable transactions could deadlock.

An alternative approach is to provide a mechanism to escape from the transactional system. Escape actions [27] and open nested transactions citeNi07 allow a thread to execute statements outside the transaction system, scheduling application-specific commit and abort handlers to be called if the enclosing transaction commits or aborts. For example, an escape action might create a file, and register a handler to abort that file if the transaction aborts. Escape mechanisms can be misused, and often their semantics are not clearly defined. Using open nested transactions, for example, care must be taken to ensure that abort handlers do not deadlock.

Exploiting Object Semantics

STM systems typically synchronize on the basis of *read/write conflicts*. As a transaction executes, it records the data items it read in a *read set*, and the data items it wrote in a *write set*. Two transactions *conflict* if one transaction's read or write set intersects the other's write set. Conflicting transactions cannot both commit. Synchronizing via read/write conflicts has one substantial advantage: it can be done automatically without programmer participation. It also has a substantial disadvantage: It can severely and unnecessarily restrict concurrency for certain shared objects. If these objects are subject to high levels of contention (that is, they are "hot-spots"), then the performance of the system as a whole may suffer.

This problem can be addressed by open nested transactions, as described above in Section 5.2, but open nested transactions are difficult to use correctly, and lack the expressive power to deal with certain common cases [28].

Another approach is to use type-specific synchronization and recovery to exploit concurrency inherent in an object's high-level specification. One such mechanism is *transactional boosting* [28], which allows thread-safe (but non-transactional) object implementations to be transformed into highly concurrent transactional implementations by allowing method calls to proceed in parallel as long as their high-level specifications are *commutative*.

Eager vs Lazy Update

There are two basic ways to organize transactional data. In an *eager* update system, data objects are modified in place, and each transaction maintains an *undo log* allowing it to undo its changes if it aborts. The dual approach is *lazy* (or deferred) update, where each transaction computes optimistically on its local copy of the data, installing the changes if it commits, and discarding them if it aborts. An eager system makes committing a transaction more efficient, but makes it harder to ensure that zombie transactions see consistent states.

Eager vs Lazy Conflict Detection

STM systems differ according to when they detect conflicts. In *eager* conflict detection schemes, conflicts are detected before they arise. When one transaction is about to create a conflict with another, it may consult a contention manager, defined below, to decide whether to pause, giving the other transaction a chance to finish, or to proceed and cause the other to abort. By contrast, a *lazy* conflict detection scheme detects conflicts when a transaction tries to commit. Eager detection may abort transactions that could have committed lazily, but lazy detection discards more computation, because transactions are aborted later.

Contention Managers

In many STM proposals, conflict resolution is the responsibility of a *contention manager* [29] module. Two transactions *conflict* if they access the same object and one access is a write. If one transaction discovers it is about to conflict with another, then it can pause, giving the other a chance to finish, or it can proceed, forcing the other to abort. Faced with this decision, the transaction consults a contention management module that encapsulates the STM's conflict resolution policy.

The literature includes a number of contention manager proposals [29–32], ranging from exponential backoff to priority-based schemes. Empirical studies have shown that the choice of a contention manager algorithm can affect transaction throughput, sometimes substantially.

Visible vs Invisible Reads

Early STM systems [29] used either *invisible reads*, in which each transaction maintains per-read metadata to be revalidated after each subsequent read, or *visible reads*, in which each reader registers its operations in shared memory, allowing a conflicting writer to identify when it is about to create a conflict. Invisible read schemes are expensive because of the need for repeated validation, while visible read schemes were complex, expensive, and not scalable.

More recent STM systems such as TL2 [33] or SKYSTM [34] use a compromise solution, called *semi-visible reads*, in which read operations are tracked imprecisely. Semi-visible reads conservatively indicate to the writer that a read-write conflict might exist, avoiding expensive validation in the vast majority of cases.

Privatization

It is sometimes useful for a thread to *privatize* [35] a shared data structure by making it inaccessible to other threads. Once the data structure has been privatized, the owning thread can work on the data structure directly, without incurring synchronization costs. In principle, privatization works correctly under SGL semantics, in which every transaction executes as if it were holding a "single global lock." Unfortunately, care is required to ensure that privatization works correctly. Here are two possible hazards. First, the thread that privatizes the data structure must observe all changes made to that data by previously committed transactions, which is not necessarily guaranteed in an STM system where updates are lazy. Second, a doomed ("zombie") transaction must not be allowed to perform updates to the data structure after it has been privatized.

Bibliographic Notes and Further Reading

The most comprehensive TM survey is the book *Transactional Memory* by Larus and Rajwar [23]. Of course, this area changes rapidly, and the best way to keep up with current developments is to consult the the *Transactional Memory Online* web page at: http://www.cs.wisc.edu/trans-memory/.

Bibliography

1. Hoare CAR (1974) Monitors: an operating system structuring concept. Commun ACM 17(10):549–557
2. Herlihy MP, Wing JM (1990) Linearizability: a correctness condition for concurrent objects. ACM T Progr Lang Sys 12(3):463–492
3. Michael MM, Scott ML (1996) Simple, fast, and practical non-blocking and blocking concurrent queue algorithms. In: PODC, Philadelphia. ACM, New York, pp 267–275
4. Harris T, Marlow S, Peyton-Jones S, Herlihy M (2005) Composable memory transactions. In: PPoPP '05: Proceedings of the tenth ACM SIGPLAN symposium on principles and practice of parallel programming, Chicago. ACM, New York, pp 48–60
5. Herlihy M, Moss JEB (May 1993) Transactional memory: architectural support for lock-free data structures. In: International symposium on computer architecture, San Diego
6. Hickey R (2008) The clojure programming language. In: DLS '08: Proceedings of the 2008 symposium on dynamic languages, Paphos. ACM, New York, pp 1–1
7. Microsoft Corporation. Stm.net. http://msdn.microsoft.com/en-us/devlabs/ee334183.aspx
8. Korland G Deuce STM. http://www.deucestm.org/
9. S. Microsystems. DSTM2. http://www.sun.com/download/products.xml?id=453fb28e
10. Intel Corporation. C++ STM compiler. http://software.intel.com/en-us/articles/intel-c-stm-compiler-prototype-edition-20/
11. Rossbach CJ, Hofmann OS, Porter DE, Ramadan HE, Aditya B, Witchel E (2007) TxLinux: using and managing hardware transactional memory in an operating system. In: SOSP '07: Proceedings of twenty-first ACM SIGOPS symposium on operating systems principles, Stevenson. ACM, New York, pp 87–102

12. Damron P, Fedorova A, Lev Y, Luchangco V, Moir M, Nussbaum D (2006) Hybrid transactional memory. In: ASPLOS-XII: Proceedings of the 12th international conference on architectural support for programming languages and operating systems, Boston. ACM, New York, pp 336–346
13. Pankratius V, Adl-Tabatabai A-R, Otto F (Sept 2009) Does transactional memory keep its promises? Results from an empirical study. Technical Report 2009-12, University of Karlsruhe
14. Rossbach CJ, Hofmann OS, Witchel E (Jun 2009) Is transactional memory programming actually easier? In: Proceedings of the 8th annual workshop on duplicating, deconstructing, and debunking (WDDD), Austin
15. Rajwar R, Goodman JR (2001) Speculative lock elision: enabling highly concurrent multithreaded execution. In: MICRO 34: Proceedings of the 34th annual ACM/IEEE international symposium on microarchitecture, Austin. IEEE Computer Society, Washington, DC, pp 294–305
16. Click C (Feb 2009) Experiences with hardware transactional memory. http://blogs.azulsystems.com/cliff/2009/02/and-now-some-hardware-transactional-memory-comments.html
17. Yen L, Bobba J, Marty MR, Moore KE, Volos H, Hill MD, Swift MM, Wood DA (2007) LogTM-SE: decoupling hardware transactional memory from caches. In: HPCA '07: Proceedings of the 2007 IEEE 13th international symposium on high performance computer architecture, Phoenix. IEEE Computer Society, Washington, DC, pp 261–272
18. Blundell C, Devietti J, Lewis EC, Martin M (Jun 2007) Making the fast case common and the uncommon case simple in unbounded transactional memory. In: International symposium on computer architecture, San Diego
19. Hammond L, Carlstrom BD, Wong V, Hertzberg B, Chen M, Kozyrakis C, Olukotun K (2004) Programming with transactional coherence and consistency (TCC). ACM SIGOPS Oper Syst Rev 38(5):1–13
20. Rajwar R, Herlihy M, Lai K (Jun 2005) Virtualizing transactional memory. In: International symposium on computer architecture, Madison
21. Ananian CS, Asanović K, Kuszmaul BC, Leiserson CE, Lie S (Feb 2005) Unbounded transactional memory. In: Proceedings of the 11th international symposium on high-performance computer architecture (HPCA'05), San Franscisco, pp 316–327
22. Blundell C, Lewis EC, Martin MMK (Jun 2005) Deconstructing transactions: the subtleties of atomicity. In: Fourth annual workshop on duplicating, deconstructing, and debunking, Wisconsin
23. Larus J, Rajwar R (2007) Transactional memory (Synthesis lectures on computer architecture). Morgan & Claypool, San Rafael
24. Menon V, Balensiefer S, Shpeisman T, Adl-Tabatabai A-R, Hudson RL, Saha B, Welc A (2008) Single global lock semantics in a weakly atomic STM. SIGPLAN Notices 43(5):15–26
25. Guerraoui R, Kapalka M (2008) On the correctness of transactional memory. In: PPoPP '08: Proceedings of the 13th ACM SIGPLAN symposium on principles and practice of parallel programming, Salt Lake City. ACM, New York, pp 175–184
26. Welc A, Saha B, Adl-Tabatabai A-R (2008) Irrevocable transactions and their applications. In: SPAA '08: Proceedings of the twentieth annual symposium on parallelism in algorithms and architectures, Munich. ACM, New York, pp 285–296
27. Moravan MJ, Bobba J, Moore KE, Yen L, Hill MD, Liblit B, Swift MM, Wood DA (2006) Supporting nested transactional memory in logTM. SIGPLAN Notices 41(11):359–370
28. Herlihy M, Koskinen E (2008) Transactional boosting: a methodology for highly-concurrent transactional objects. In: PPoPP '08: Proceedings of the 13th ACM SIGPLAN symposium on principles and practice of parallel programming, Salt Lake City. ACM, New York, pp 207–216
29. Herlihy M, Luchangco V, Moir M, Scherer W (Jul 2003) Software transactional memory for dynamic-sized data structures. In: Symposium on principles of distributed computing, Boston
30. Guerraoui R, Herlihy M, Pochon B (2005) Toward a theory of transactional contention managers. In: PODC '05: Proceedings of the twenty-fourth annual ACM symposium on principles of distributed computing, Las Vegas. ACM, New York, pp 258–264
31. Scherer WN III, Scott ML (Jul 2004) Contention management in dynamic software transactional memory. In: PODC workshop on concurrency and synchronization in java programs, St. John's
32. Attiya H, Epstein L, Shachnai H, Tamir T (2006) Transactional contention management as a non-clairvoyant scheduling problem. In: PODC '06: Proceedings of the twenty-fifth annual ACM symposium on principles of distributed computing, Denver. ACM, New York, pp 308–315
33. Dice D, Shalev O, Shavit N (2006) Transactional locking II. In: Proceedings of the 20th international symposium on distributed computing, Stockholm
34. Lev Y, Luchangco V, Marathe V, Moir M, Nussbaum D, Olszewski M (2009) Anatomy of a scalable software transactional memory. In: TRANSACT 2009, Raleigh
35. Spear MF, Marathe VJ, Dalessandro L, Scott ML (2007) Privatization techniques for software transactional memory. In: PODC '07: Proceedings of the twenty-sixth annual ACM symposium on principles of distributed computing, Portland. ACM, New York, pp 338–339

Transactions, Nested

J. Eliot B. Moss
University of Massachusetts, Amherst, MA, USA

Synonyms

Multi-level transactions; Nested spheres of control

Definition

Nested Transactions extend the traditional semantics of transactions by allowing meaningful nesting of one or more child transactions within a parent transaction. Considering the traditional ACID properties of transactions, atomicity, consistency, isolation, and durability, a child transaction possesses these properties in a relative way, such that a parent transaction effectively provides a universe within which its children act similarly to ordinary transactions in a non-nested system. In parallel computation, the traditional property of durability in the face of various kinds of system failures may not be required.

Discussion

Transactions

Transactions are a way of guaranteeing atomicity of more or less arbitrary sequences of code in a parallel computation. Unlike locks, which identify computations that may need serialization according to the identity of held and requested locks, transaction serialization is based on the specific data accessed by a transaction while it runs. In some cases, it is possible usefully to pre-declare the maximal set of data that a transaction might access, but it is not possible in general. Transactions *specify semantics*, while locks express an implementation of serialization. The usual semantics of transactions are that concurrent execution of a collection of transactions must be equivalent to execution of those transactions one at a time, in some order. This property is called *serializability*.

The ACID properties capture transaction semantics in a slightly different way. *Atomicity* requires that transactions are all-or-nothing: Either all of a transaction's effects occur, or the transaction fails and has no effect. *Consistency* requires that each transaction take the state of the world from one consistent state to another. *Isolation* requires that no transaction perceive any state in the middle of execution of another transaction. *Durability* requires that the effects of any transaction, once the transaction is accepted by the system, not disappear.

In general, in parallel computing, as opposed to database systems where transactions had their origins, the consistency and durability properties are often less important. Consistency may be ignored in that most commonly there are no explicitly stated consistency constraints and no mechanism to enforce them. However, a correct transaction system is still required not to leave effects of partially executed or failed transactions. Durability is often ignored in that a parallel computing system may have no permanent state. If the system has distributed memory, then it may achieve significant durability by keeping multiple copies of data in different units of the distributed memory. Of course, parallel systems can also use one or more nonvolatile copies to achieve durability, according to a system's durability requirements.

It is important to distinguish transactions from concurrency-safe data structures. A concurrency-safe data structure generally offers a guarantee of *linearizability*: If two actions on the data structure by different threads overlap in their execution, then the effect is as if the actions are executed in one order or the other. That is, a set of concurrent actions by different threads appears to occur in some linear order. This is *similar* to serializability, but what transactions and serializability add is the possibility for a given thread to execute a whole *sequence* of actions $a_1, a_2, ..., a_n$ without any intervening actions of other threads. A concurrency-safe data structure guarantees only that the individual a_i execute correctly as defined by the data type, but permits actions of other threads to interleave between the a_i.

In discussing transactions and their nesting, some additional terms will be useful. Transactions are said to *commit* (succeed) or *abort* (fail). They may fail for many reasons, one of them being serialization conflicts with other transactions. Transactional concurrency control may be *pessimistic*, also called early conflict detection, or *optimistic*, also called late conflict detection. Pessimistic conflict detection usually employs some kind of locks, while optimistic generally uses some kind of version numbers or timestamps on data and transactions to determine conflicts. It is even possible to maintain multiple versions so as to allow more transactions to commit, while still enforcing serializability. In general, locking schemes require some kind of deadlock avoidance or detection protocol. However, if a set of transactions is in deadlock, the system has a way out: It can abort one of the transactions to break the deadlock. Thus, deadlock is not a fatal problem as it is when using just locks for synchronization.

A system may update data *in place*, which requires an *undo log* to support removing the effects of a failed transaction. Alternatively, a system may create *new copies* of data, and install them only if a transaction commits, which in general requires a *redo log*. Updating in-place requires early conflict detection if the system guarantees that a transaction will not see effects of other uncommitted transactions. It is possible to allow such effects to be visible, but serializability then requires that the observing transaction commit only if the transaction it observed also commits. However, the system must still prevent two transactions from observing each other's effects, since then they cannot be serialized. More advanced models have also been explored but are not discussed here.

Semantics of Nesting

The simplest motivation for nesting is to make it easy to compose software components into larger systems. If a library routine uses transactions, and the programmer wishes to use that routine within an application transaction, then there will be nesting of transaction begin/end pairs. One can simply treat this as one large transaction, effectively ignoring the inner transaction begin/end pairs. However, it is also possible to attribute transactional semantics to them, as follows.

Consider a transaction T and a transaction U contained with it, i.e., whose begin and end are between the begin and end of T. T is a *parent* transaction and U a *child transaction* or *subtransaction* of T. If T is not contained within any enclosing transaction, it is *top-level*. Only proper nesting of begin/end transaction pairs is legal, so a top-level transaction and subtransactions at all depths form a tree.

Conflict semantics of non-nested transactions extend to nested transactions straightforwardly in terms of relationships in the forest of transaction trees. If action A conflicts with action B when executed by two different non-nested transactions T1 and T2, then A conflicts with B in the nested setting if neither of T1 and T2 is an ancestor of the other. Why is there no conflict in the case where, say, T1 is an ancestor of T2? It is because T1 is providing an environment or universe *within which* additional transactions can run, compete, and be serialized.

It is simplest, however, to envision nesting where a parent does not execute actions directly, but rather always creates a child transaction to perform them. Alternatively, a parent might perform actions directly, but only when it has no active subtransactions. This model leads to serializability among the subtransactions of any given transaction T. However, as viewed from outside of the transaction tree that includes T and its descendants, T and its subtransactions form a single transaction that must itself be serializable with transactions outside of T.

As with non-nested transactions, a nested transaction can fail (abort). In that case, it is as if the failing transaction, and all of its descendants, never ran. Thus, commit of a child transaction is not final, but only relative to its parent, while abort of the parent *is* final and aborts all descendants, even those that have (provisionally) committed.

Example Closed Nesting Implementation Approach

Consider adding support for nesting to a non-nested transaction implementation that employs in-place update and early conflict detection based on locking. As each transaction runs, it accumulates a set of locks and a list of undos. If the transaction aborts, the system applies the transaction's undos (in reverse order) and then discards the transaction's locks. Note that a transaction T can be granted a lock L provided that the only conflicting holders of L are ancestors of T. Also note that discarding a child's lock does not discard any ancestor's lock on the same item. If a child transaction commits, then the system adds the child's locks to those held by the parent, and appends the child's undo list to that of the parent. If a top-level transaction commits, the system simply discards its held locks and its undo list. Moss [5, 6] described this protocol. It is also possible to devise timestamp-based approaches, possibly supporting late conflict detection, as articulated by Reed [10].

Notice that these nesting schemes use the same set of possible actions at each level of nesting. They provide *temporal grouping* of actions, and in a distributed system can also be used for *spatial grouping* within temporal groups.

Motivations for Closed Nesting

There are two primary advantages of closed nesting. One is that failure of a child does not require immediate failure of its parent. Thus, if a transaction desires to execute an action that has higher than usual likelihood of causing failure, it can execute that action within a child transaction and avoid immediate failure of itself should the action cause an abort. In a centralized system aborts might most likely be caused by conflicts with other transactions, but in a decentralized system, failure of a remote node or communication link is also possible. Thus, remote calls are natural candidates to execute as subtransactions. If a child does fail, the parent can retry it, which may often make sense, or the parent can perform some alternate action. For example, in a distributed system, if one node of a replicated database is down, the parent could try another one.

A possibly stronger motivation for closed nesting is safe transaction execution when the application desires to exploit concurrency *within* a transaction. It is easy to see this by considering that if there is concurrency within a transaction, then proper semantics and synchronization or serialization within the transaction present the same issues that led to proposing transaction mechanisms in the first place. Even if, at first blush, it appears that the space of data that concurrent actions might update is disjoint, and thus that there can be no conflict, that property can be a delicate one, and difficult to enforce in complex software systems having many layers. For example, transaction T at node A might make apparently disjoint concurrent remote calls to nodes B and C. However, B and C, unknown to T, use a common service at node D, and should have their actions properly serialized there. If the work at B and C is not performed in distinct concurrent child transactions of T, the work at D might not be properly serialized

Open Nesting

While closed nested transactions indeed support safe concurrency within transactions, and also offer limited recoverability from partial failure, they have a significant limitation: Transactions that are "big," either in terms of how long they run or the volume of data they access, tend to conflict with other transactions. While this cannot always be avoided, many conflicts are *false conflicts* at the level of application semantics. For example, consider a transaction T that adds a number of new records to a data structure organized as a B-tree. *Logically* speaking, if other transactions do not access these records or otherwise inquire directly or indirectly about their presence or absence in the data structure, then they do not conflict with T. However, straightforward mechanisms for guaranteeing safe transactional access to the B-tree might acquire locks on B-tree nodes and hold them until T commits. Thus, other transactions could be locked out of whole nodes of the tree, even though they are not (logically) affected by the changes T is making.

The solution discovered in the context of databases applies also to the case of parallel computing. It is to make a distinction between different *levels of semantics*, and requires recognizing certain data as being part of a coherent and distinct data abstraction. For example, in the case of a B-tree, each B-tree node is part of a given B-tree, and should be visible and manipulated only by actions on that B-tree. That is, the B-tree nodes are *encapsulated* within their owning B-tree. This allows B-tree actions to apply conflict management and undo or redo to B-tree nodes, during execution of those actions, and for the system to switch to *abstract* concurrency control and *abstract* undo or redo once a B-tree action is complete.

How does this solve the problem? The concurrency control and undo/redo on B-tree nodes allows safe concurrent (transactional) execution of B-tree actions themselves. This could also be achieved by non-transactional locking, lock-free or wait-free algorithms, or any other means that guarantees linearizability, but open nesting is generally taken to refer to the recursive use of transaction-like mechanisms, while wrapping a not necessarily transactional data type with abstract concurrency control and recovery is called *transactional boosting* [4]. More significantly, though, the conflicts between full B-tree *actions* will be much fewer than the (internal, temporary) conflicts on B-tree nodes during those actions. For example, looking up record r_1 and adding record r_2 do not conflict logically, but if they lie in the same B-tree node, there will be a (physical) conflict on that node. While open nesting is by no means restricted to use with such collection data types, it is certainly very useful in allowing higher concurrency for them.

An Example Open Nesting Protocol

A fleshed-out example protocol for open nesting may be helpful to build understanding. This example uses in-place update and employs locks for early conflict detection, but other protocols are possible for other approaches to update and conflict detection. For understanding the protocol, a specific example data structure is instructive. Consider a Set abstraction implemented using a linked list. Suppose it supports actions add(x) and remove(x) to manipulate whether x is in the set, size() to return the set's cardinality, and contains(x) to test whether x is in the set.

Suppose the items a, b, and c have been added to the set in that order, and that add appends new elements to the end (since it must scan to the end anyway in order to avoid entering duplicates). Assume these elements are committed and there are no transactions pending against the set. Now suppose that a transaction adds a new member d and continues with other work. During the add operation, the transaction observes a, b, and c and the list links, then it creates a new list node containing d and modifies c's link to refer to the new node. Suppose that another transaction concurrently queries whether the set contains e. At the physical level this contains query conflicts with the uncommitted add, because the query will read the link value in c's list node, etc. Likewise a transaction that tries to remove b will conflict with both the add and the contains actions because it will try to modify the link in a's node, to unchain b's node from the list. To guarantee correct manipulation of the list each operation can acquire transactional locks on list nodes, acquiring an exclusive (X) mode lock when modifying a node and a share (S) mode lock when only observing it. Two S mode locks on the same object do not conflict, but all other mode combinations conflict. The pointer to the first node is likewise protected with the same kind of locks. This locking protocol works fine for closed nesting, but it is easy to see that it leads to many needless conflicts.

Open nesting requires identifying the *abstract* conflicts between operations. This example protocol uses *abstract locks*. These locks include an S and X mode lock for each possible element of the set, and an additional lock with modes Read (R) and Modify (M) for the cardinality of the set. Two R mode locks do not conflict, and two M mode locks also do not conflict, but R and M mode conflict with each other. Here is a table showing the abstract locks acquired by each action on a Set:

add(x)	X mode on x; M mode on cardinality
remove(x)	X mode on x; M mode on cardinality
contains(x)	S mode on x
size()	R mode on cardinality

This can be refined to acquire only an S mode lock on x if add or remove does not actually change the membership of the set, and in that case also not to acquire the M mode lock on the cardinality.

Assuming that each action on the set is run as an open nested transaction, then before an action completes it must acquire the specified abstract locks. If it cannot do that, it is in conflict and some transaction must be aborted. Once the action is complete *and* holds the abstract locks, the nested transaction commits and releases the lower-level locks on list nodes. The parent transaction will hold the abstract locks until it itself commits. Similar to closed nesting, if an uncommitted open nested transaction aborts, it can simply unwind back to where it started and try again. Often such cases arise because of temporary conflicts on the physical data structure. However, if the conflict is because of an abstract lock, then retry is not likely to help – either other transactions need to complete or abort to get out of this transaction's way, or this transaction needs to abort higher up in the nested transaction tree.

Abstract locks are just one way of implementing detection of abstract conflicts. In general what is required is an encoding of *abstract conflict predicates* into conflict checking code. These conflict predicates indicate which actions on a data type conflict with other actions. Here is an example table for Set:

	add(y)	remove(y)	contains(y)	size()
add(x)	x = y	x = y	x = y	true
remove(x)	x = y	x = y	x = y	true
contains(x)	x = y	x = y	false	false
size()	true	true	false	false

In this table, the left action is considered to have been performed by one transaction, and the right action is requested by another. The entry in the table indicates the condition under which the new request conflicts with the older, not yet committed, action. The table above is expressed in terms of the operations and their arguments. However, it is possible to refine these predicates if they can refer to the *state* of the set. In general this might include the state after the first operation as well as the state before it. The refined table below uses references to the state S before the first operation:

	add(y)	remove(y)	contains(y)	size()
add(x)	$x = y \wedge x \notin S$	x = y	$x = y \wedge x \notin S$	$x \notin S$
remove(x)	x = y	$x = y \wedge x \in S$	$x = y \wedge x \in S$	$x \in S$
contains(x)	$x = y \wedge x \notin S$	$x = y \wedge x \in S$	false	false
size()	$y \notin S$	$y \in S$	false	false

Open nesting involves more than just conflict detection. Until an open nested action commits, aborting it works like aborting a closed nested action: Simply apply its (lower level) undos in reverse order and release its (lower level) locks. However, once an open nested action commits, it does not work to undo it using the list of lower level undos it accumulated while it ran. The lower level undos are guaranteed to work properly only if the lower level locks are still held. To undo a *committed* open nested action, the system applies an *abstract undo*, also called an *inverse* or *compensating action*. Here is a table of inverses for actions on the Set abstraction; a — entry means that no inverse is needed (the action did not change the state):

Action	add(x)	remove(x)	contains(x)	size()
Inverse	if $x \notin S$ then remove(x)	if $x \in S$ then add(x)	—	—

Notice that the appropriate inverse can depend on the state in which the original action ran. If add or remove does not actually change the state, then they can simply omit adding an inverse.

These inverses are added to the parent transaction's undo list, to apply if the parent transaction needs to abort. The abstract concurrency control will guarantee that these inverses still make sense when they are applied. They should be run as open nested transactions, and if they fail, it will only be because of temporary conflicts on the physical data structure, so they should simply be retried until they succeed.

Coarse-Grained Transactions

Transactions at the more abstract level, employing abstract concurrency control, and, if using in-place update, abstract undos, can be more generally termed *coarse-grained transactions*. As previously noted, the individual actions need not be run as transactions under a transaction mechanism – all that is required is that they are linearizable. However, using a transaction mechanism does offer the advantage of being able to abort and retry an action in case of conflict, while other approaches must guarantee absence of conflict. Thus, if the system does not use nested transactions to implement the actions, then, if using in-place update, it will need to acquire abstract locks *before* running the action. This implies that it cannot base the lock acquisition on the state of the data abstraction or on the result of the action. However, if executing the action reveals that the originally acquired abstract lock is stronger than necessary, the implementation can then downgrade the lock.

As noted before, the underlying implementation might use non-transactional locks to synchronize (for example, one mutual exclusion lock on the whole data structure will work, at the cost of reduced concurrency), or might use lock-free, obstruction-free, or wait-free techniques to obtain linearizability.

Upon first consideration, in-place updates may appear more complicated, since they require specifying, implementing, tracking, and applying undos. However, providing new copies of an abstract data structure has its own problems. One difficulty is being clear as to what needs to be copied. A second problem is cost. To reduce cost, a coarse-grained transaction implementation might use *Bloom filters*, which record and examine an ongoing transaction's changes in a side data structure, private to the transaction. Transactions must also record additional information even for read-only actions, in order to check for conflicts later.

Correct Abstract Concurrency Control

The tables above gave conflict predicates without indicating how to derive or verify them. A conflict predicate is *safe* if the actions commute when the predicate is false. [Some make a distinction between actions moving to the left and to the right, but in most practical cases actions either commute (move both ways) or they do not (neither way).] Two actions commute if executing them in either order allows them to return the same results, and also does not affect the outcome of any future actions. Assuming that all relevant aspects of the state are observable, then this can be rephrased as: Actions commute if, when executed in either order, they produce the same results and the same final state.

There are some subtleties lurking in this definition. First, the "same state" means the same *abstract* state. For example, in the case of Set implemented as a linked list, the abstract state consists in what elements are in, and not in, the set. The order in which the members occur on the linked list does not matter. Therefore, even though add(x) and add(y) result in a different linked list when executed in the opposite order, *abstractly* there is no difference. Thus it is important to have clarity about what the abstract state *is*.

Second, interfaces vary in what they reveal. For example, add(x) might return nothing, not revealing whether x was previously in the set. As far as concurrency control goes, the less revealing interface reduces conflicts: two transactions could both do add(x) without conflict as perceived via this interface.

Third, if the system uses undos, then the undo added to a transaction's undo list is part of the result to consider when determining conflicts. So, if x is not initially in a set, and then two transactions each invoke add(x), even if the add actions return no result, the actions conflict since the undo for the first one is remove(x) and the undo for the second is "do nothing." In this respect, late conflict detection sometimes allows more concurrency. However, in general it requires making a copy (at least an effective copy) of the data structure, and if any transaction commits changes to the data structure while transaction T is running, T's actions must be redone on the primary copy of the data structure rather than directly installing the new state that T constructed.

Fourth, certain non-mutating operations entail concurrency control obligations that may at first seem surprising. For example, if x is not in a set and transaction T runs the query contains(x), the set must guarantee that any other transaction that adds x will conflict with T. Thus, if the system uses abstract locking, contains(x) must in this case lock the *absence* of x. Hence, an abstract lock is not necessarily a lock attached to some piece of the original data structure. (In some database implementations the locks are mixed with the actual records, and the system creates a new record for a lock like this, a record that goes away at the end of the transaction. This is called a *phantom record*.) A similar case occurs with an ordered set abstraction when a call to getNextHigher(x) returns y: The transaction must lock the fact that the ordered set has no value between x and y. Thus, read-only actions still require checking and recording, and this applies equally to late conflict detection as to early detection.

Extended Semantics

Another use for open nesting is to break out of strict serializability (at the programmer's risk, of course). It is sometimes useful, even necessary, to keep some effects of a transaction even if it is aborted. For example, in processing a commercial transaction, a system might discover that the credit card presented is on a list of stolen cards. While most effects of the purchase should be undone, information about the attempted use of the card should go to a log that will definitely *not* be undone. This is easy to do by giving the log action's inverse as "do nothing." (This is harder to do in a system that is not doing in-place updates, and would require a special notation.) In this way open nesting can be abused to achieve irrevocable effects. Similarly, a programmer can understate conflict predicates and allow communication between transactions. The "extended semantics" of open nesting abused in these ways may depend on the underlying implementation.

Nesting in Transactional Memory

Both closed and open nesting have been proposed for use with transactional memory (TM), for both software (STM) and hardware (HTM) approaches. The primary difficulty in implementing closed nesting for TM is its more complex conflict rule. It no longer suffices to check for equality or inequality of transaction identifiers – the test must distinguish an ancestor transaction from a non-ancestor. (This assumes that only transactions that are currently leaves of the transaction tree can execute.) HTM designs must also deal with the reality that hardware resources are always limited, and thus, there may be hard limits on the nesting depth, for example. HTM will also not be aware of abstract locks and abstract concurrency control; they will always be implemented in software. However, the number of conflict checks required for abstract concurrency control is strictly less than for physical units such as words or cache lines.

It is particularly more complex to check for conflict between concurrent subtransactions running under nested TM. However, if a transaction has at most one child at once, and only leaf transactions can execute, then the implementation is only slightly more complex than for non-nested transactions. Because the transaction tree in this case consists of a single line of descent from a top-level transaction, it is called *linear nesting*. Linear nesting admittedly forgoes one of the strong advantages of nesting, namely concurrent sibling subtransactions, but it retains partial rollback and thus remains potentially more useful than non-nested transactions.

Bibliographic Notes and Further Reading

The early exposition of nested transactions is marked by Davies [2], Reed [10], and Moss [5, 6]. Open nesting (also called *multi-level transactions*) was articulated by Beeri et al. [1], Moss et al. [8], and Weikum and Schek [11]. Nested transactions for hardware transactional memory are explored in Yen et al. [12] and Moss and Hosking [7], and Ni et al. [9] describe a prototype that supports open nesting in software transactional memory. Transactional boosting was introduced by Herlihy and Koskinen [4]. Gray and Reuter [3] provide comprehensive coverage of transaction processing concepts and techniques.

Bibliography

1. Beeri C, Bernstein PA, Goodman N (1983) A concurrency control theory for nested transactions. In: Proceedings of the ACM Symposium on Principles of Distributed Computing. ACM Press, New York, pp 45–62
2. Davies CT Jr (1973) Recovery semantics for a DB/DC system. In: ACM '73 Proceedings of the ACM Annual Conference. ACM, New York, pp 136–141. doi: http://doi.acm.org/10.1145/800192.805694
3. Gray J, Reuter A (1993) Transaction processing: concepts and techniques. Data Management Systems. Morgan Kaufmann, Los Altos, CA
4. Herlihy M, Koskinen E (2008) Transactional boosting: a methodology for highly-concurrent transactional objects. In: Chatterjee S, Scott ML (eds) Proceedings of the 13th ACM SIGPLAN Symposium on Principles and Practice of Parallel Programming, PPOPP 2008, Salt Lake City, UT, 20–23 Feb 2008. ACM, New York, pp 207–216, ISBN 978-1-59593-795-7
5. Moss JEB (1985) Nested transactions: an approach to reliable distributed computing. PhD thesis, Massachusetts Institute of Technology, Cambridge, MA (Also published as MIT Laboratory for Computer Science Technical Report 260)
6. Moss JEB (1985) Nested transactions: an approach to reliable distributed computing. MIT Press, Cambridge, MA
7. Moss JEB, Hosking AL (2006) Nested transactional memory: model and architecture sketches. Sci Comput Progr 63: 186–201
8. Moss JEB, Griffeth ND, Graham MH (1986) Abstraction in recovery management. In: Proceedings of the ACM Conference on Management of Data. Washington, DC. ACM SIGMOD, ACM Press, New York, pp 72–83
9. Ni Y, Menon V, Adl-Tabatabai AR, Hosking AL, Hudson RL, Moss JEB, Saha B, and Shpeisman T (2007) Open nesting in software transactional memory. In: ACM SIGPLAN 2007 Symposium on Principles and Practice of Parallel Programming, San Jose, CA. ACM, New York, pp 68–78
10. Reed DP (1978) Naming and synchronization in a decentralized computer system. PhD thesis, Massachusetts Institute of Technology, Cambridge, MA (Also published as MIT Laboratory for Computer Science Technical Report 205)
11. Weikum G, Schek HJ (1992) Concepts and applications of multilevel transactions and open nested transactions. Morgan Kaufmann, Los Altos, CA, pp 515–553, ISBN 1-55860-214-3
12. Yen L, Bobba J, Marty MR, Moore KE, Volos H, Hill MD, Swift MM, Wood DA (2007) LogTM-SE: decoupling hardware transactional memory from caches. In: Proceedings of the 13th International Conference on High-Performance Computer Architecture (HPCA-13 2007), 10–14 February 2007, Phoenix, Arizona, USA, IEEE Computer Society, Washington, DC, pp 261–272

Transpose

▶ All-to-All

TStreams

▶ Concurrent Collections Programming Model

Tuning and Analysis Utilities

▶ TAU

U

Ultracomputer, NYU

ALLAN GOTTLIEB
New York University, New York, NY, USA

Definition

The NYU Ultracomputer is a class of highly parallel, shared-memory multiprocessors featuring two innovations: the *fetch-and-add* process coordination primitive, and a hardware method to *combine* (nearly simultaneous) *memory references* directed at the same location. These references can be loads, stores, or fetch-and-adds. The combining procedure generalizes to fetch-and-phi for any associative operator phi, for example, max or min.

Combining often enables all simultaneous memory requests from many processors to be completed in essentially the time required for just one such request. This property, together with the power of fetch-and-add/phi, has enabled construction of coordination algorithms with the important property of imposing no serialization beyond that specified in the problem itself. For example, fetch-and-add-based readers-writers algorithms, during periods of no writer activity, can satisfy multiple requests in essentially constant time. Similarly, fetch-and-add-based queue algorithms, during periods when the queue is neither full nor empty, can satisfy multiple inserts and deletes in essentially constant time. Such implementations are sometimes called "bottleneck free."

The Ultracomputer project constructed a few small-scale prototype implementations, the largest being a fully functional 16-processor prototype with a processor-to-memory interconnection network whose full-custom VLSI switches successfully combined memory references, including fetch-and-adds.

Implemented software included two generations of the Unix operating system tailored to run on the multiprocessor. The first version required nearly all kernel activity to occur on one processor; the second was itself a parallel program that made extensive use of locally developed, highly parallel (aka scalable) process coordination algorithms. All the software was compiled by the locally developed port of GCC (the GNU Compiler Collection, formerly the GNU C Compiler).

Discussion

Early History

The NYU Ultracomputer project was launched in 1979 when Jack Schwartz wrote a highly influential paper [14] itself entitled *Ultracomputers*. However, the primary architecture described in that paper is not what became the NYU Ultracomputer. Instead, influenced by the Burroughs proposal for NASA's Numerical Aerodynamic Simulation Facility, Schwartz and his NYU colleagues increased their consideration of shared-memory MIMD (Multiple Instruction stream Multiple Data stream) designs. This lead to the discovery of both fetch-and-add together with several effective process coordination algorithms using this primitive, and the hardware design enabling nearly simultaneous fetch-and-adds to be combined into a single memory operation.

In fact fetch-and-add had been discovered previously. Dijkstra [4] considered essentially the same primitive and showed that the natural fetch-and-add implementation of a semaphore had a fatal race condition. The NYU group, ignorant of this earlier work, not only found the same primitive but also implemented essentially the same flawed semaphore, thinking it was correct. However, they subsequently discovered the same race condition, and found another semaphore implementation, which they proved correct.

Fetch-and-Add (and Friends)

Fetch-and-add is essentially an indivisible add to memory operation. Its format is F&A(X, v), where X is an integer variable and v is an integer value. This function

David Padua (ed.), *Encyclopedia of Parallel Computing*, DOI 10.1007/978-0-387-09766-4,
© Springer Science+Business Media, LLC 2011

with side effects is defined to both return the (old) value of X and replace the memory value of X by $X+v$. That is, F&A(X, v) *fetches X and adds v* to it.

Simultaneous fetch-and-add's directed at the same integer variable X, are required to satisfy the *serialization principle* (cf. Eswaran et al. [6]), meaning that their effect must be the same as if they were executed serially in some unspecified order. That is, fetch-and-add is *atomic*.

Fetch-and-ϕ and Replace-Add

The fetch-and-add function can easily be generalized to fetch-and-ϕ, where ϕ is a binary operator. For example fetch-and-max(X, v) would return the old value of X while atomically setting $X := \max(X, v)$. As shall be seen below, the ability to combine simultaneous fetch-and-ϕ's requires that ϕ be associative.

The early versions of fetch-and-add actually used a slightly different function Replace-add(X, v) which returned the new (incremented) version of X. Thus, it was an atomic version of ++X rather than X++. For an invertible function such as addition, there is little to choose between the two variants since

F&A(X, v) is equivalent to
Replace-Add (X, v)-v
Replace-Add(X, v) is equivalent to
F&A(X, v)+v

However, when generalizing to non-invertible ϕ's such as max, the fetch-and- version is superior to the replace- version since there is no analogue of the first equivalence for *max*. This observation becomes especially important when simultaneous fetch-and-$\phi(X, v)$'s are performed on the same variable X.

A Fetch-and-Add Semaphore

Perhaps the simplest coordination algorithm is the busy-waiting, binary semaphore (aka. spin-lock) used to enforce mutual exclusion for critical sections.

```
loop
  P(S)
  critical section
  V(S)
end loop
```

The idea behind a fetch-and-add-based semaphore S is to treat S as an integer variable, letting $S = 1$ represent "open" and $S \leq 0$ represent "closed." S is then atomically incremented and decremented with fetch-and-add.

A successful P(S) operation finds $S = 1$. It executes F&A($S, -1$) receiving 1 and setting S to 0. The V(S) operation executes F&A($S, +1$) thereby undoing the effect of its successful P.

But what about an unsuccessful P(S), one that finds $S < 1$ when it does F&A($S, -1$)? The unsuccessful P(S) simply does F&A($S, +1$) to undo its decrement and tries again, hoping that some V(S) will have occurred in the interim.

Code implementing this (faulty) pair of algorithms is presented in Section Code Examples; the corresponding functions are named NaiveP(S) and V(S). These two functions are essentially the same code that Dijkstra correctly criticized for having a fatal race condition in which no process is in the critical section, but several process continually try and fail to enter. For example, consider the following scenario, beginning with the semaphore initially open (i.e., $S = 1$) and three processes A, B, and C arriving at NaiveP(S).

Assume all three execute the F&A($S, -1$) simultaneously and the serial order effected is A, B, C. Thus A receives +1 and enters the critical section. B and C receive 0 and –1, respectively; they each add back a 1 and retry. As long as A is inside the critical section (i.e., has not executed V(S)), S remains less than 1 correctly preventing B and C from succeeding.

When A does execute V(S), its initial decrement is undone and either B or C should be able to succeed. Indeed, if both B and C have just executed F&A($S, +1$), the semaphore will be restored to its initial value of +1 and the next process to execute F&A($S, -1$) will receive +1 and succeed. However, this may never happen since the following endless scenario may occur instead.

Assume that, after A increments S, both B and C are at their increment instruction (at this point $S = -1$). Suppose that the effected serialization is that B increments and then decrements prior to C executing. The result is that S moves to 0 and then back to –1, and B receives 0 from F&A($S, -1$); thus B was not successful. Now the same sequence can occur for C, and then again for B, etc.

Although this race condition is quite unlikely to occur for three processes, it is *possible*, and becomes steadily more probable as the number of processes increases.

If `NaiveP(S)` is replaced by `TrueP(S)` also from the section Code Examples, the race is no longer possible. Indeed, using `TrueP(S)`, a correct implementation of `P(S)`, Gottlieb et al. [11] proved that if, at time T, $N > 0$ processes are executing the `P(S)-V(S)` loop above and no process ceases execution, then there is a time $t > T$ when exactly one process is executing its critical section.

At first glance, `TrueP(S)` appears to simply add a redundant test to `NaiveP(S)`. As just shown, however, the extra test is needed. In fact the resulting test-decrement-retest paradigm has proved fruitful for other algorithms as well (Gottlieb et al. [11]). Tighter coding of several of these algorithms can be found in [7] and application to a highly parallel version of Unix can be found in [5].

The Ultracomputer Architecture

The basic Ultracomputer design is that of a symmetric multiprocessor, that is, there are multiple processors sharing a central memory. Although the memory can be packaged together with the processors, the prototype hardware did not do this and neither do the diagrams in this article. Figure 1 in the Section Diagrams shows the basic block diagram with multiple processors connected to multiple memory modules.

The Processors

The Ultracomputer processors are fairly standard; the primary novelty is that they can issue fetch-and-add instructions. The prototype hardware used AMD 29000 microprocessors with locally developed support hardware to implement fetch-and-add.

The Memory Modules

The memory modules were also straightforward. An adder was included at each module to enable fetch-and-add.

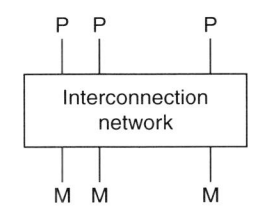

Ultracomputer, NYU. Fig. 1 Ultracomputer block diagram

The Interconnection Network

The primary novelty of the hardware design is the ability of the interconnection network to combine (nearly) simultaneous requests to the same memory location, in particular, the ability to combine multiple fetch-and-add operations into a single memory operation.

The Topology The interconnection topology used was an $N \times N$ Ω-Network composed of 2×2 crossbar switches. See Fig. 2 for an example with $N = 8$ and, for the moment ignore the colors. The very left and right columns contain 0–7 written in binary, they correspond to the eight processors and memory modules; the rectangles are bidirectional crossbar switches that can connect either left port with either right port; and the inter-column wires implement the so-called shuffle map.

Consider the red wire. Counting from zero it connects the third horizontal line on the left to the fifth on the right. Note that $3 = 011$, $5 = 101$, and $RightRotate(011) = 101$. That is the defining property of the shuffle map; it holds for all the wires.

To see that any of the eight far left ports can be connected to any of eight far right, first note that any crossbar can connect xyz to either $xy0$ or $xy1$, that is, each crossbar can determine the low-order bit of the right-hand row independent of the low-order bit of the left-hand row. So any column can "correct" the low-order bit and the shuffle map ensures that each successive column operates on a new low-order bit. Thus, after $logN$ columns and shuffles, the message is at the desired row.

When traversed "backward" (i.e., from right to left), the network can again correct the low-order bit in each column, but now gets the next low-order bit via the inverse shuffle, which corresponds to a left rotate. Thus, each of the processors can access each memory module and vice versa.

Now consider the blue lines in Fig. 2. They show the paths from each processor to memory module number 2. Note that $2 = 010$ and that every path successively exits switch ports 0, 1, and 0. Thus the Ω-network is the superposition of N trees, one rooted at each memory module. It is also the superposition of N other trees, one rooted at each processor.

It will be important for combining to note that the network has a *unique* path π from a given processor to a

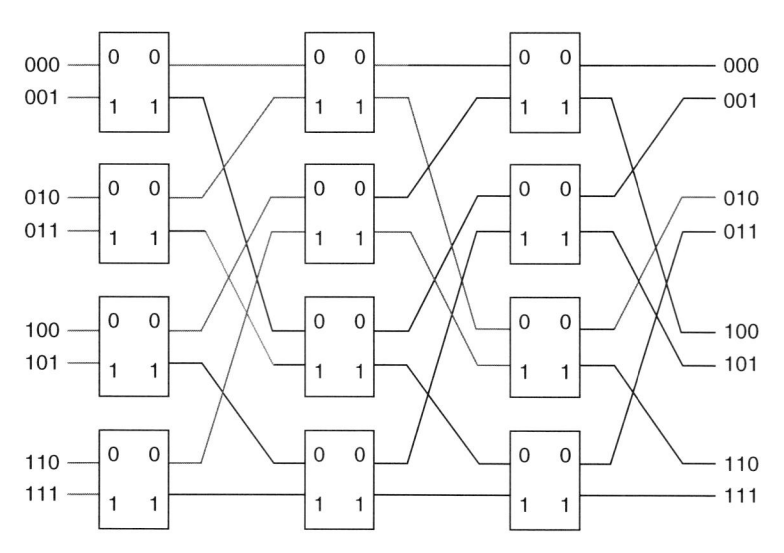

Ultracomputer, NYU. Fig. 2 8 × 8 Omega network

given memory module and that the (unique) path from that memory to that processor is just the reverse of π. It is possible to use a network with multiple paths but then forward request must generate enough information to ensure that the reply traverses the reverse path.

The Switches As mentioned, each Ultracomputer switch is a 2 × 2 crossbar. The switches are buffered so that if two requests entering the left side wish to exit the same right-side port, one is stored at the switch (assuming the available buffer space has not been exhausted). In addition to providing the throughput advantages of buffered switches, buffering is essential for the chosen combining implementation.

Combining Loads and Stores

It is fairly easy to see how to combine two loads or two stores that are directed at the same memory location and are present in a single switch at the same time. For two loads, the switch sends one forward and retains the other. When the memory response arrives, two replies are sent back, one for each request.

For two stores, the switch again sends just one forward. When this store is performed at memory, the effect is as if the non-forwarded store was executed immediately before. When the memory acknowledgment for the forwarded store arrives, the switch acknowledges both requests. It is important for program

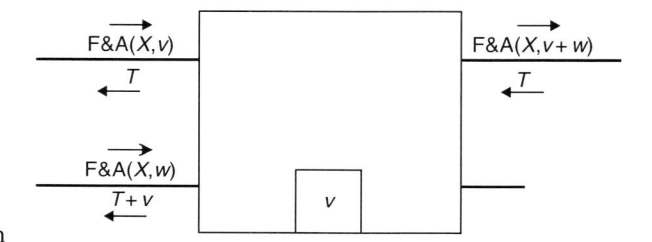

Ultracomputer, NYU. Fig. 3 Combining two fetch-and-adds

semantics not to acknowledge either request before the memory acknowledgment has arrived.

Note that combined loads and combined stores appear to the next stage switch just like ordinary loads and stores and thus can be further combined. In the best case, each processor can issue a request to the same memory location and all N requests will be combined along the tree to the memory module so that only a single request need be serviced at the memory itself.

Combining Fetch-and-Adds

Combining fetch-and-adds is not as easy as combining loads or stores [13]. Figure 3 in section Diagrams shows the actions performed when F&A (X, v) meets F&A (X, w) at a switch. The switch computes the sum $v + w$, transmits the combined request F&A $(X, v+w)$, and stores the value v in its local memory. Eventually, a value T will be returned to the switch in response to

F&A(X, v+w). At this point, the switch returns T to satisfy the request F&A(X, v), returns $T + v$ to satisfy the request F&A(X, w), and deletes v from its local memory.

If the combined request F&A(X, v+w) was not itself combined, then T is simply X. In this case, the values returned are X and $X+v$ which is consistent with the serialization order "F&A(X, v) followed immediately by F&A(X, w)." The memory location has been incremented to $X + (v + w)$. By the associativity of addition, this value equals $(X + v) + w$, which is again consistent with "F&A(X, v) followed immediately by F&A(X, w)."

It is not hard to apply this argument recursively and see that, thanks to associativity, if combined requests are further combined while on their way to memory, the results returned to each requesting processor are consistent with some serialization of the constituent fetch-and-adds. For example, Fig. 4 shows four fetch-and-adds with increments 1, 2, 4, and 8 being combined and de-combined to achieve the serialization order F&A(X, 8), F&A(X, 4), F&A(X, 1), F&A(X, 2).

Combining Heterogeneous Requests

Having seen how to combine loads, stores, and fetch-and-adds, it is natural to ask if the switch can combine two *different* request types. Since load X can be viewed as F&A(X, 0), the only heterogeneous case that need be considered is combining a fetch-and-add with a store, which can be combined as follows.

When F&A(X, v) meets Store(X, w), the switch transmits Store(w+v) and remembers w. When the acknowledgment of this "combined" store is received, the switch acknowledges the original store, returns w to satisfy F&A(X, v), and deletes w from its local memory. These actions have the same effect as "Store(X, w) followed immediately by F&A(X, v)."

Combining Switch Design

As shown above, the physical combining of memory requests occurs at the network switches. The first externally available description of combining switches was [15], a later description can be found in [2], and a detailed description together with analysis and simulation results occurs in Dickey's thesis [3].

A block diagram of a single 2×2 switch is shown in Fig. 5. Unlike previous diagrams in which lines represented bidirectional data flow, each line in this figure is unidirectional. The processors would be to the left and memory to the right.

In terms of the combining description given in section Combining Fetch-and-Adds, F&A(X, v) meets F&A(X, w) in the Combining Queue associated with the right-side port on the path to X. The value v

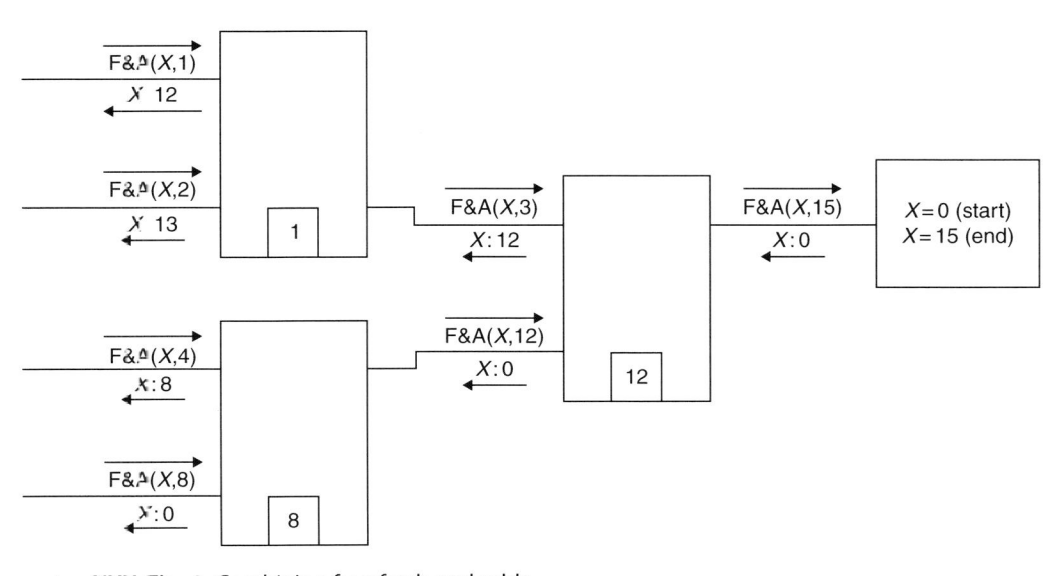

Ultracomputer, NYU. Fig. 4 Combining four fetch-and-adds

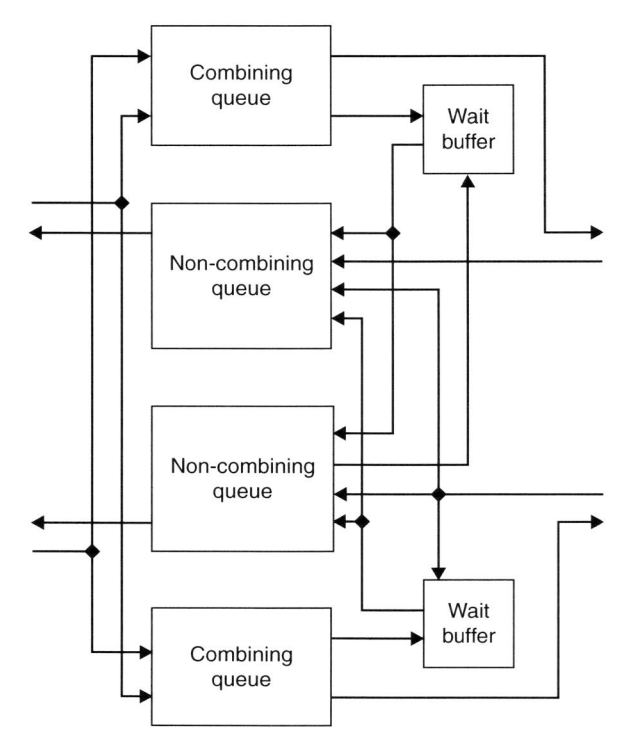

Ultracomputer, NYU. Fig. 5 2 × 2 Switch

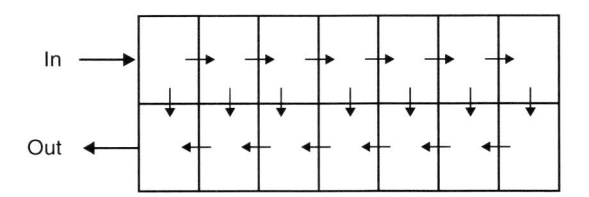

Ultracomputer, NYU. Fig. 6 2 × 2 Systolic queue

is stored in the Wait Buffer, together with additional information identifying the requests. The eventual response from memory is compared with entries in the Wait Buffer and matching entries are sent to the Non-combining Queue(s) associated with left-side port(s) on the paths to the processors that issued the original requests.

There are challenges designing each of the components and in partitioning the design to meet the constraints imposed by the low pin-count chip packages available at the time. However, the most interesting component is likely the enhanced systolic queue used to implement the combining queue, so that component is described in more detail.

(Semi-)Systolic (Combining) Queues Before turning our attention to the actual queue designs, note that Fig. 5 shows combining queues with two inputs. Designs of this kind were studied, but the actual implementation of the two-input queues consisted of two one-input queues followed by a two-input multiplexer (see Ref. [3] for a detailed comparison).

Systolic Queues The point of departure for the NYU combining queue, was the systolic (non-combining) queue design of Guibas and Liang [12], the basic idea of which is shown in Fig. 6. This queue implementation is called systolic since communication within the queue is local, unlike a solution using a RAM with head and tail pointers. Avoiding global signals is advantageous for VLSI.

Items enter the *In* row and exit the *Out* row. If the output destination can always accept an item, then only the first column is used. In a single cycle, an item enters *In*, goes to the first column, and then drops to the bottom row, from which it exits on the subsequent cycle.

More interesting is the behavior when the downstream queue is full and blocks the current queue. In this case the item will find that it cannot go down (since that slot is full and the current occupant cannot leave) and it remains in the top row. In the next cycle, the item in question again moves right and then moves down, providing the correspond slot is available. Thus, if downstream remains full, the current queue will itself become full as all columns become occupied.

As the careful reader will have noticed, the single cycle referred to above is (internal to the queue) divided into two subcycles, one each for horizontal and vertical motion.

The NYU designs for both the non-combining queues just described and the combining queues to be described next used two global control signals *in_moving* and *out_moving* and thus are properly called quasi- or semi-systolic. The global signals can be precomputed at the expense of an extra column to accept an incoming message from each predecessor after the switch announces that it is full. The signals can be implemented efficiently as qualified clocks (see Ref. [3]).

The semi-systolic design used in the implementation permits insertions and deletions to occur every

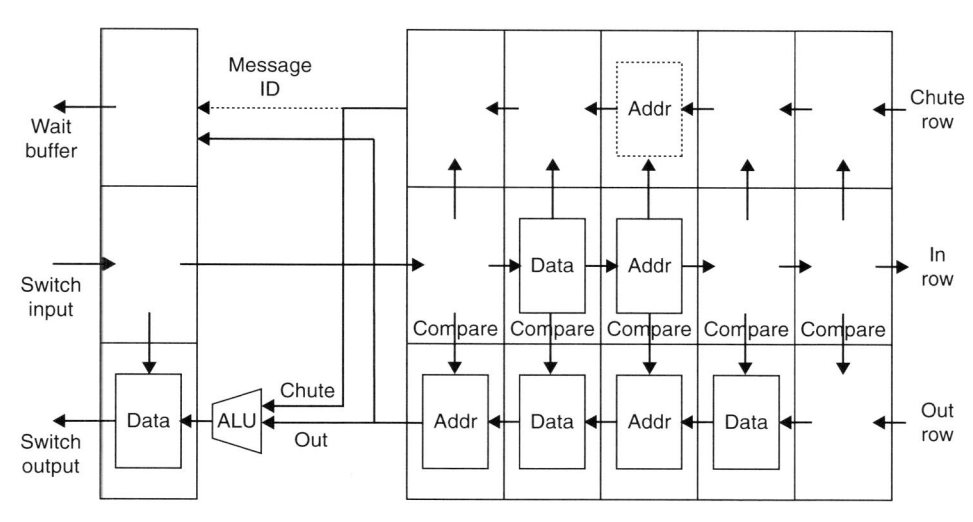

Ultracomputer, NYU. Fig. 7 2 × 2 Combining queue

cycle, an important property that is not supported by the purely systolic design of [12].

Semi-Systolic Combining Queues The key observation enabling a variation of the systolic queues to support combining is that as an item moves left along *Out*, it passes directly under all subsequent items as they move right along *In*. When one item is directly above another, local logic can compare them and determine if they are destined for the same address. (Since both *In* and *Out* can move during the same cycle, it would appear that items can pass by without having a chance for comparison. However, all Ultracomputer memory references use an even number of packets, the first of which contains the address. Thus, with some extra logic, the system can assure that "address packets" are vertically adjacent at the end of a cycle.)

Figure 7, adapted from [3], is a block diagram of the Ultracomputer combining queue. When this diagram is compared to Fig. 6, the non-combining queue, three additions become apparent: the new *Chute* row, the comparators between the *In* and *Out* rows, and the "stuff on the left." Each is discussed in turn.

When combinable messages are detected (one traversing *Out*, the other *In*), the message traversing *In* is moved to the *Chute*. As a result it will never be moved to *Out* and will not be sent to the memory. For example, Fig. 7 shows this event occurring in column 3. The *Chute* moves in synchrony with *Out* and thus both the message traversing *Out* and the corresponding message traversing *Chute* will leave their respective rows together.

If the needed slot in *Chute* is already full when combinable messages are detected, the second combining opportunity is lost. (The *Out* message has already been combined with another message from *In*.) Thus, having only one *Chute* supports only pairwise combining in a single switch. As noted above, these pairwise combined messages can themselves combine as they pass through subsequent switches. Adding a second *Chute* (together with enhancing the ALU to accept three inputs, and other changes) would permit three-way combining within a switch.

The comparators between the *In* and *Out* rows detect references to the same address. As mentioned previously, while the address packet of a message traverses *Out*, it will sit directly below all address packets traversing *In*. When the comparator in a column detects equal addresses in the *In* and *Out* rows, logic in the column moves the address packet (and subsequently the remaining packets) to the *Chute* (unless this chute slot is full due to a previous combine, as described earlier in this section.).

The logic on the left is essentially an extra column, *without* the comparators, together with an ALU needed to sum the increments when two fetch-and-adds are combined. The lack of a comparator in this leftmost column does mean that some combining opportunities are lost. It was omitted to prevent the increased cycle time that would result from one column implementing both addition and comparison.

When a combined message moves from the rectangular array of cells to the left-side logic, the memory address plus some identifying information is stored in the wait buffer. If the operation was fetch-and-add, the *Out*-row increment is also stored. This enables the eventual memory response to be decomposed into responses for the two originating requests.

Code Examples

```
procedure NaiveP(S) -- faulty
  implementation of P(S)
  OK := False;
  repeat
    if F&A(S,-1) > 0
      OK := True;
    else
      F&A(S,+1);
    end if;
  until OK;
end NaiveP;


procedure V(S) -- correct
  implementation
  F&A(S,+1);
end V;


procedure TrueP(S) -- correct
  implementation
  OK := False;
  repeat
    if S > 0 then
      if F&A(S,-1) > 0 then
        OK := True;
      else
        F&A(S,+1);
      end if;
    end if;
  until OK;
end P;
```

Related Entries

▶ Buses and Crossbars
▶ Cedar Multiprocessor
▶ Flynn's Taxonomy
▶ Interconnection Networks
▶ Memory Models
▶ MIMD (Multiple Instruction, Multiple Data) Machines
▶ Networks, Multistage
▶ Non-Blocking Algorithms
▶ Nonuniform Memory Access (NUMA) Machines
▶ Parallel Computing
▶ PRAM (Parallel Random Access Machines)
▶ Reduce and Scan
▶ Scan for Distributed Memory, Message-Passing Systems
▶ Shared-Memory Multiprocessors
▶ Switch Architecture
▶ Switching Techniques
▶ Synchronization

Bibliographic Notes and Further Reading

Perhaps the most polished account of the NYU Ultracomputer can be found in the book by Almasi and Gottlieb [1]. More information, plus an extensive bibliography, can be found in [8]. An early Ultracomputer paper [10] was selected to appear in a collection of ISCA papers together with a retrospective on the project [9].

Bibliography

1. Almasi G, Gottlieb A (1994) Highly parallel computing, 2nd edn. Benjamin/Cummings, Redwood City
2. Dickey S, Kenner R, Snir M (1986) An implementation of a combining network for the NYU ultracomputer. Ultracomputer Note 93, NYU
3. Dickey SR (1994) Systolic combining switch designs. PhD thesis, NYU, May 1994
4. Dijkstra EW (1972) Hierarchical orderings of sequential processes. In: Hoare CAR, Perrot RH (eds) Operating systems techniques. Academic Press, New York
5. Edler J (1995) Practical structures for parallel operating systems. PhD thesis, NYU, May 1995
6. Eswaran KP, Gray JN, Lorie RA, Traiger IL (Nov 1976) The notion of consistency and predicate locks in a database system. Commun ACM 19(11):624–633
7. Freudenthal E (2003) Comparing and improving centralized and distributed techniques for coordinating massively parallel shared-memory systems. PhD thesis, NYU, May 2003
8. Gottlieb A (1987) An overview of the NYU ultracomputer project. In: Dongarra JJ (ed) Experimental parallel computing architectures. North Holland, Amsterdam, pp 25–95
9. Gottlieb A (1998) A personal retrospective on the NYU ultracomputer. In: Sohi GS (ed) 25 years of the international symposia

on computer architecture (selected papers), Barcelona, ACM, New York, pp 29–31
10. Gottlieb A, Grishman R, Kruskal CP, McAuliffe KP, Rudolph L, Snir M (1982) The NYU ultracomputer|designing a MIMD shared memory parallel machine. In: International symposium on computer architecture, Austin, Apr 1982, pp 27–42
11. Gottlieb A, Lubachevsky BD, Rudolph L (Apr 1983) Basic techniques for the efficient coordination of very large numbers of cooperating sequential processors. Trans Program Lang Syst 5(2):164–189
12. Guibas LJ, Liang F (1982) Systolic stacks, queues, and counters. In: MIT conference on research in VLSI, Cambridge, pp 155–162
13. Rudolph LS (1982) Software structures for ultraparallel computing. PhD thesis, NYU, Feb 1982
14. Schwartz JT (Oct 1980) Ultracomputers. ACM Toplas 2(4):484–521
15. Snir M, Solworth J (1984) The ultraswitch—a VLSI network node for parallel processing. Ultracomputer Note 39, NYU, Jan 1984

Uncertainty Quantification

▶ Terrestrial Ecosystem Carbon Modeling

Underdetermined Systems

▶ Linear Least Squares and Orthogonal Factorization

Unified Parallel C

▶ UPC

Unimodular Transformations

UTPAL BANERJEE
University of California at Irvine, Irvine, CA, USA

Definition

A *Unimodular Transformation* is a general loop transformation based on a unimodular matrix. It changes a perfect nest of sequential loops into a similar nest with the same set of iterations executing in a different sequential order.

Discussion

Introduction

This essay gives the basic introduction to Unimodular Transformations. More advanced results on this topic are given in the essay ▶ *Loop Nest Parallelization* in this encyclopedia, where other transformations are considered as well.

The program model is a perfect nest **L** of m sequential loops. An *iteration* of **L** is an instance of the body of **L**. The program consists of a certain set of iterations that are to be executed in a certain sequential order. This execution order imposes a *dependence structure* on the set of iterations, based on how they access different memory locations. A loop in **L** *carries a dependence* if the dependence between two iterations is due to the unfolding of that loop. A loop can *run in parallel* if it carries no dependence.

A *unimodular matrix* is a square integer matrix with determinant 1 or −1. An $m \times m$ unimodular matrix **U** can be used to transform **L** into a perfect nest **L**′ of m loops, with the same set of iterations executing in a different sequential order. This is a *unimodular transformation*. The new nest **L**′ is *equivalent* to the old nest **L** (i.e., they give the same results), if whenever an iteration depends on another iteration in **L**, the first iteration is executed after the second in **L**′. If a loop in **L**′ carries no dependence, then that loop can run in parallel. It turns out that a unimodular transformation always exists, such that **L**′ is equivalent to **L** and all loops in **L**′, except possibly one, can run in parallel.

There is a section on mathematical preliminaries to prepare the reader for what comes next. It is followed by a section on basic concepts. The general unimodular transformation is then explained in detail by examples. Finally, some important special features of special unimodular transformations like loop permutation and loop skewing are pointed out.

Mathematical Preliminaries

For basic Linear Algebra concepts used in this essay, see any standard text. The set of real numbers is denoted by **R** and the set of integers by **Z**. For any positive integer m, $\mathbf{R}^m$ denotes the m-dimensional vector space over **R** consisting of all real m-vectors, where vector addition and scalar multiplication are defined coordinate-wise in the usual way. The zero vector $(0, 0, \ldots, 0)$ is written as **0**.

The subset of $\mathbf{R}^m$ consisting of all integer m-vectors is denoted by $\mathbf{Z}^m$.

Lexicographic Order

For $1 \leq \ell \leq m$, define a relation $<_\ell$ in $\mathbf{Z}^m$ as follows: If $\mathbf{i} = (i_1, i_2, \ldots, i_m)$ and $\mathbf{j} = (j_1, j_2, \ldots, j_m)$ are vectors in $\mathbf{Z}^m$, then $\mathbf{i} <_\ell \mathbf{j}$ if

$$i_1 = j_1,\ i_2 = j_2,\ \ldots,\ i_{\ell-1} = j_{\ell-1},\ \text{and}\ i_\ell < j_\ell.$$

The *lexicographic order* $<$ in $\mathbf{Z}^m$ is then defined by requiring that $\mathbf{i} < \mathbf{j}$, if $\mathbf{i} <_\ell \mathbf{j}$ for some ℓ in $1 \leq \ell \leq m$. The notation $\mathbf{i} \leq \mathbf{j}$ means either $\mathbf{i} < \mathbf{j}$ or $\mathbf{i} = \mathbf{j}$. Note that $\leq$ is a total order in $\mathbf{Z}^m$.

The associated relations $>$ and $\geq$ are defined in the usual way: $\mathbf{j} > \mathbf{i}$ means $\mathbf{i} < \mathbf{j}$, and $\mathbf{j} \geq \mathbf{i}$ means $\mathbf{i} \leq \mathbf{j}$. ($\geq$ is also a total order in $\mathbf{Z}^m$.) An integer vector $\mathbf{i}$ is *positive* if $\mathbf{i} > \mathbf{0}$, *nonnegative* if $\mathbf{i} \geq \mathbf{0}$, and *negative* if $\mathbf{i} < \mathbf{0}$.

For $x \in \mathbf{R}$, the value of $\operatorname{sgn}(x)$ is 1, -1, or 0, according as $x > 0$, $x < 0$, or $x = 0$, respectively. The *direction vector* of a vector $(i_1, i_2, \ldots, i_m) \in \mathbf{Z}^m$ is the vector of signs: $(\operatorname{sgn}(i_1), \operatorname{sgn}(i_2), \ldots, \operatorname{sgn}(i_m))$. Note that a vector is positive (negative) if and only if its direction vector is positive (negative).

For more details on lexicographic order, see [4].

Fourier's Method of Elimination

Fourier's method of elimination can be used to decide if a system of linear inequalities in real variables has a solution [12]. Consider a set of n inequalities in m real variables $x_1, x_2, \ldots, x_m$, of the form

$$a_{1j}x_1 + a_{2j}x_2 + \cdots + a_{mj}x_m \leq c_j \qquad (1 \leq j \leq n), \qquad (1)$$

where the a_{ij}'s and the c_j's are real constants. To solve this system, eliminate the variables one at a time in the order: $x_m, x_{m-1}, \ldots, x_1$. If an inequality $c \leq 0$ turns up during the elimination process where c is a positive constant, then the system has no solution. Otherwise, the final result is a system of inequalities of the form:

$$b_i(x_1, x_2, \ldots, x_{i-1}) \leq x_i \leq B_i(x_1, x_2, \ldots, x_{i-1})$$
$$(1 \leq i \leq m), \qquad (2)$$

where each b_i is either $-\infty$ or the maximum of a set of linear functions of $x_1, x_2, \ldots, x_{i-1}$, and each B_i is either ∞ or the minimum of a set of linear functions of $x_1, x_2, \ldots, x_{i-1}$. In this case, $b_1 \leq B_1$. The set of all real solutions $(x_1, x_2, \ldots, x_m)$ to (1) is given by (2): Pick any x_1 such that $b_1 \leq x_1 \leq B_1$, then pick any x_2 such that $b_2(x_1) \leq x_2 \leq B_2(x_1)$, and so on.

For the purpose of finding loop limits after a unimodular transformation, Fourier's method is extended to check for any integer solutions to a system of the form (1), where the coefficients a_{ij}'s and c_j's are integer constants. If (1) has no real solution, then obviously it has no integer solution. Assume then (1) has a set of real solutions $(x_1, x_2, \ldots, x_m)$ given by (2). The set of all integer solutions $(z_1, z_2, \ldots, z_m)$ to (1) is then given by

$$\alpha_i(z_1, z_2, \ldots, z_{i-1}) \leq z_i \leq \beta_i(z_1, z_2, \ldots, z_{i-1})$$
$$(1 \leq i \leq m), \qquad (3)$$

where α_i and β_i are defined by $\alpha_i(z_1, z_2, \ldots, z_{i-1}) = \lceil b_i(z_1, z_2, \ldots, z_{i-1}) \rceil$ and $\beta_i(z_1, z_2, \ldots, z_{i-1}) = \lfloor B_i(z_1, z_2, \ldots, z_{i-1}) \rfloor$ for each i. If $\alpha_1 > \beta_1$, then there is no integer solution. Otherwise, proceed by enumeration: Take any integer z_1 such that $\alpha_1 \leq z_1 \leq \beta_1$, then check if there is an integer z_2 such that $\alpha_2(z_1) \leq z_2 \leq \beta_2(z_1)$, and so on.

The process described above is illustrated by the following example. For a detailed description of Fourier's method including an algorithm, see [4].

Example 1 Consider the system of linear inequalities

$$\left.\begin{aligned} 2x_1 - 11x_2 &\leq 3 \\ -3x_1 + 2x_2 &\leq -5 \\ x_1 + 3x_2 &\leq 4 \\ -2x_1 &\leq -3. \end{aligned}\right\} \qquad (4)$$

Rearrange the inequalities so that the ones with a positive coefficient for x_2 are at the top; they are followed by the ones where the coefficient for x_2 is negative; and then come the inequalities where x_2 is absent:

$$\left.\begin{aligned} -3x_1 + 2x_2 &\leq -5 \\ x_1 + 3x_2 &\leq 4 \\ 2x_1 - 11x_2 &\leq 3 \\ -2x_1 &\leq -3. \end{aligned}\right\} \qquad (5)$$

Divide each of the first three inequalities by the corresponding coefficient of x_2:

$$\left.\begin{array}{rcl} -\frac{3}{2}x_1 + x_2 & \leq & -\frac{5}{2} \\ \frac{1}{3}x_1 + x_2 & \leq & \frac{4}{3} \\ -\frac{2}{11}x_1 + x_2 & \geq & -\frac{3}{11}. \end{array}\right\}$$

Note how the direction of the third inequality is reversed after division, as the coefficient of x_2 in it was negative. Isolate x_2 in this system to get

$$\left.\begin{array}{rcl} x_2 & \leq & \frac{3}{2}x_1 - \frac{5}{2} \\ x_2 & \leq & -\frac{1}{3}x_1 + \frac{4}{3} \\ \frac{2}{11}x_1 - \frac{3}{11} & \leq & x_2. \end{array}\right\}$$

Thus, when x_1 is given, x_2 must satisfy

$$b_2(x_1) \leq x_2 \leq B_2(x_1), \tag{6}$$

where

$$b_2(x_1) = \frac{2}{11}x_1 - \frac{3}{11}$$
$$B_2(x_1) = \min\left(\frac{3}{2}x_1 - \frac{5}{2}, -\frac{1}{3}x_1 + \frac{4}{3}\right).$$

Now, eliminate x_2 by setting each of its lower bounds less than or equal to each of its upper bounds:

$$\left.\begin{array}{rcl} \frac{2}{11}x_1 - \frac{3}{11} & \leq & \frac{3}{2}x_1 - \frac{5}{2} \\ \frac{2}{11}x_1 - \frac{3}{11} & \leq & -\frac{1}{3}x_1 + \frac{4}{3}. \end{array}\right\}$$

Simplify these inequalities and bring in the last member of (5):

$$\left.\begin{array}{rcl} -\frac{29}{22}x_1 & \leq & -\frac{49}{22} \\ \frac{17}{33}x_1 & \leq & \frac{53}{33} \\ -2x_1 & \leq & -3. \end{array}\right\}$$

There is no inequality where x_1 is absent. Rearrange the system so that the single inequality with a positive coefficient for x_1 goes to the top:

$$\left.\begin{array}{rcl} \frac{17}{33}x_1 & \leq & \frac{53}{33} \\ -\frac{29}{22}x_1 & \leq & -\frac{49}{22} \\ -2x_1 & \leq & -3. \end{array}\right\}$$

Divide each inequality by the corresponding coefficient of x_1 (and reverse the direction if that coefficient is negative):

$$\left.\begin{array}{rcl} x_1 & \leq & \frac{53}{17} \\ x_1 & \geq & \frac{49}{29} \\ x_1 & \geq & \frac{3}{2}. \end{array}\right\}$$

The minimum value of x_1 is $\max\left(\frac{49}{29}, \frac{3}{2}\right)$ or $\frac{49}{29}$, and the maximum value is $\frac{53}{17}$. Since the range

$$\frac{49}{29} \leq x_1 \leq \frac{53}{17} \tag{7}$$

is nonempty, the original system (4) has a real solution. All solutions have the form (x_1, x_2), where x_1 is a real number in the range (7) and x_2 satisfies (6) for that value of x_1. Clearly, $(x_1, x_2) = \left(2, \frac{1}{2}\right)$ is one such solution.

Next, explore if (4) has an integer solution. The set of all integer vectors (z_1, z_2) satisfying the four inequalities in (4) is given by

$$\alpha_1 \leq z_1 \leq \beta_1$$
$$\alpha_2(z_1) \leq z_2 \leq \beta_2(z_1),$$

where

$$\alpha_1 = \left\lceil \frac{49}{29} \right\rceil = 2 \quad \text{and} \quad \beta_1 = \left\lfloor \frac{53}{17} \right\rfloor = 3,$$

$$\alpha_2(z_1) = \left\lceil \frac{2}{11}z_1 - \frac{3}{11} \right\rceil \quad \text{and}$$
$$\beta_2(z_1) = \left\lfloor \min\left(\frac{3}{2}z_1 - \frac{5}{2}, -\frac{1}{3}z_1 + \frac{4}{3}\right) \right\rfloor.$$

The only possible values of z_1 are 2 and 3. It is easy to show that for either value of z_1, a corresponding integral value for z_2 does not exist. Thus, there are real solutions to the system of inequalities (4), but no integer solutions.

Unimodular Matrices

An $m \times m$ real matrix $\mathbf{A} = (a_{rt})$ represents a linear mapping of $\mathbf{R}^m$ into itself that maps a vector $\mathbf{x} = (x_1, x_2, \ldots, x_m)$ into the vector $\mathbf{xA} = (y_1, y_2, \ldots, y_m)$, where

$$y_t = \sum_{r=1}^{m} a_{rt} x_r \qquad (1 \le t \le m).$$

This mapping is a bijection (one-to-one and onto) if and only if $\mathbf{A}$ is invertible, that is, $\det \mathbf{A} \ne 0$.

A *unimodular matrix* is a square integer matrix whose determinant is 1 or -1. The product of two unimodular matrices is unimodular. A unimodular matrix is invertible and its inverse is also unimodular. Thus, an $m \times m$ unimodular matrix $\mathbf{U}$ maps each integer vector $\mathbf{x} \in \mathbf{R}^m$ into an integer vector $\mathbf{xU} \in \mathbf{R}^m$, and for each integer vector $\mathbf{y} \in \mathbf{R}^m$, there is a unique integer vector $\mathbf{x} \in \mathbf{R}^m$ such that $\mathbf{y} = \mathbf{xU}$. In other words, an $m \times m$ unimodular matrix defines a bijection of $\mathbf{Z}^m$ onto itself. See [4, 11] for detailed discussions on unimodular matrices.

For any m, the $m \times m$ unit matrix is unimodular. More unimodular matrices can be easily constructed from a unit matrix by elementary row (or column) operations. One gets a *reversal matrix* by multiplying a row of a unit matrix by -1, an *interchange matrix* by interchanging two rows of a unit matrix, and a *skewing matrix* by adding an integer multiple of one row to another row. These are called the *elementary matrices*. The 3×3 matrices

$$\begin{pmatrix} 1 & 0 & 0 \\ 0 & -1 & 0 \\ 0 & 0 & 1 \end{pmatrix}, \begin{pmatrix} 0 & 1 & 0 \\ 1 & 0 & 0 \\ 0 & 0 & 1 \end{pmatrix}, \text{ and } \begin{pmatrix} 1 & 0 & 3 \\ 0 & 1 & 0 \\ 0 & 0 & 1 \end{pmatrix}$$

are examples of a reversal, an interchange, and a skewing matrix, respectively. Elementary matrices are all unimodular. And each unimodular matrix can be expressed as the product of a finite number of elementary matrices. (See Lemma 2.3 in [4].)

A *permutation* of a finite set is a one-to-one mapping of the set onto itself. A permutation matrix is any matrix that can be obtained by permuting the columns (or rows) of a unit matrix. More formally, a *permutation matrix* is a square matrix of 0's and 1's, such that each row has exactly one 1 and each column has exactly one 1. An interchange matrix is a permutation matrix. A product of interchange matrices is clearly a permutation matrix. The converse is also true: every permutation matrix can be expressed as a finite product of interchange matrices. In fact, every permutation matrix can be expressed as a finite product of interchange matrices each of which interchanges two adjacent columns (or rows). A permutation matrix is unimodular. (See Sect. 2.5 in [4].)

Let $\mathbf{U}$ denote any $m \times m$ permutation matrix. For $1 \le i \le m$, let $\pi(i)$ denote the number of the row containing the unique 1 in column i. Then, the function $\pi : i \mapsto \pi(i)$ is a permutation of the set $\{1, 2, \ldots, m\}$, and it completely specifies the matrix $\mathbf{U}$. For any m-vector $\mathbf{x} = (x_1, x_2, \ldots, x_m)$, one has

$$\mathbf{xU} = \left(x_{\pi(1)}, x_{\pi(2)}, \ldots, x_{\pi(m)}\right). \qquad (8)$$

Basic Concepts

The program model is a perfect nest of loops $\mathbf{L} = (L_1, L_2, \ldots, L_m)$ shown in Fig. 1. For $1 \le r \le m$, the index variable I_r of L_r runs from p_r to q_r in steps of 1, where p_r and q_r are integer-valued linear functions of $I_1, I_2, \ldots, I_{r-1}$. The *index vector* of the loop nest is $\mathbf{I} = (I_1, I_2, \ldots, I_m)$. An *index point* or *index value* of the nest is a possible value of the index vector, that is, a vector $\mathbf{i} = (i_1, i_2, \ldots, i_m) \in \mathbf{Z}^m$ such that $p_r \le i_r \le q_r$ for $1 \le r \le m$. The subset $\mathcal{R}$ of $\mathbf{Z}^m$ consisting of all index points is the *index space* of the loop nest. During sequential execution of the nest, the index vector traverses the entire index space in the lexicographic order.

The *body* of the loop nest $\mathbf{L}$ is denoted by $H(\mathbf{I})$. A given index value $\mathbf{i}$ defines a particular *instance* $H(\mathbf{i})$ of $H(\mathbf{I})$, which is an *iteration* of $\mathbf{L}$. The program of Fig. 1 consists of the set of iterations $\{H(\mathbf{i}) : \mathbf{i} \in \mathcal{R}\}$, and they are executed sequentially in such a way that an iteration $H(\mathbf{i})$ comes before an iteration $H(\mathbf{j})$ if and only if $\mathbf{i} < \mathbf{j}$.

There is *dependence between* two distinct iterations $H(\mathbf{i})$ and $H(\mathbf{j})$ if there is a memory location that is referenced (read or written) by both. (Sometimes, it may be required that at least one of the references be a "write.") Suppose there is dependence between $H(\mathbf{i})$ and $H(\mathbf{j})$.

$$\begin{array}{ll} L_1: & \textbf{do } I_1 = p_1, q_1 \\ L_2: & \textbf{do } I_2 = p_2, q_2 \\ \vdots & \qquad \vdots \\ L_m: & \textbf{do } I_m = p_m, q_m \\ & \qquad H(\mathbf{I}) \end{array}$$

Unimodular Transformations. Fig. 1 Loop nest $\mathbf{L}$

Then $H(\mathbf{j})$ *depends on* $H(\mathbf{i})$ if $H(\mathbf{j})$ is executed after $H(\mathbf{i})$, that is, if $\mathbf{i} < \mathbf{j}$.

If $H(\mathbf{j})$ depends on $H(\mathbf{i})$, then $\mathbf{d} = \mathbf{j} - \mathbf{i}$ is a *(dependence) distance vector* of the loop nest. Since $\mathbf{i} < \mathbf{j}$, a distance vector is necessarily positive. To keep matters simple, it is assumed that each distance vector $\mathbf{d}$ is *uniform* in the sense that whenever $\mathbf{i}$ and $\mathbf{i}+\mathbf{d}$ are two index points, the iteration $H(\mathbf{i} + \mathbf{d})$ depends on the iteration $H(\mathbf{i})$. Let N denote the total number of distinct distance vectors. Then the *distance matrix* of $\mathbf{L}$ is an $N \times m$ matrix $\mathbf{D}$ whose rows are the distance vectors. The distance matrix is unique up to a permutation of its rows.

If $\mathbf{d}$ is a distance vector of $\mathbf{L}$, then the direction vector of $\mathbf{d}$ is a *(dependence) direction vector* of the loop nest. A direction vector of $\mathbf{L}$ is necessarily positive. The *direction matrix* of $\mathbf{L}$ is a matrix Δ with m columns whose rows are the direction vectors. The direction matrix is unique up to a permutation of its rows.

A loop L_r in the nest $\mathbf{L}$, where $1 \le r \le m$, *carries a dependence* if there is a distance vector $\mathbf{d}$ with $\mathbf{d} >_r 0$. A loop can *run in parallel* if it carries no dependence. According to this definition, a trivial loop with a single iteration can run in parallel. This is helpful in avoiding special cases.

Let $\mathbf{U}$ denote an $m \times m$ unimodular matrix. The image of $\mathcal{R}$ under $\mathbf{U}$ is the set $\{\mathbf{IU} : \mathbf{I} \in \mathcal{R}\}$. By using Fourier's method of elimination, one can get a suitable description for this image. Note that the index space $\mathcal{R}$ consists of all integer m-vectors $\mathbf{I} = (I_1, I_2, \ldots, I_m)$ that satisfy the system of inequalities:

$$p_r \le I_r \le q_r \qquad (1 \le r \le m), \qquad (9)$$

where p_r and q_r are integer-valued linear functions of $I_1, I_2, \ldots, I_{r-1}$. Let $\mathbf{K} = \mathbf{IU}$, so that $\mathbf{I} = \mathbf{KU}^{-1}$. If $\mathbf{K} = (K_1, K_2, \ldots, K_m)$ and $\mathbf{U}^{-1} = (v_{tr})$, then $I_r = \sum_{t=1}^{m} v_{tr} K_t$ for each r. Replacing each I_r in (9) with the corresponding expression in $K_1, K_2, \ldots, K_m$, one gets a system of linear inequalities in $K_1, K_2, \ldots, K_m$. Fourier's method then yields an equivalent system of inequalities of the following type:

$$\alpha_r \le K_r \le \beta_r \qquad (1 \le r \le m), \qquad (10)$$

where α_r and β_r are integer-valued functions of $K_1, K_2, \ldots, K_{r-1}$. The image of $\mathcal{R}$ under $\mathbf{U}$ consists of all integer m-vectors $\mathbf{K} = (K_1, K_2, \ldots, K_m)$ that satisfy (10).

The loop nest $\mathbf{L}'$ of Fig. 2, where $H'(\mathbf{K}) = H(\mathbf{KU}^{-1})$, defines the *unimodular transformation* of the loop nest $\mathbf{L}$

$$\begin{aligned} L'_1: &\quad \mathbf{do}\ K_1 = \alpha_1, \beta_1 \\ L'_2: &\quad \mathbf{do}\ K_2 = \alpha_2, \beta_2 \\ \vdots &\qquad \vdots \\ L'_m: &\quad \mathbf{do}\ K_m = \alpha_m, \beta_m \\ &\qquad H'(\mathbf{K}) \end{aligned}$$

Unimodular Transformations. Fig. 2 Loop nest $\mathbf{L}'$

induced by the unimodular matrix $\mathbf{U}$. The transformed program has the same set of iterations as the original program, executing in a different sequential order. Two iterations $H(\mathbf{i})$ and $H(\mathbf{j})$ in the original nest $\mathbf{L}$ become iterations $H'(\mathbf{k})$ and $H'(\mathbf{l})$, respectively, in the transformed nest $\mathbf{L}'$, where $\mathbf{k} = \mathbf{iU}$ and $\mathbf{l} = \mathbf{jU}$. In $\mathbf{L}$, $H(\mathbf{i})$ precedes $H(\mathbf{j})$ if $\mathbf{i} < \mathbf{j}$. But in $\mathbf{L}'$, $H'(\mathbf{k})$ precedes $H'(\mathbf{l})$ if $\mathbf{k} < \mathbf{l}$, that is, if $\mathbf{iU} < \mathbf{jU}$. The loop nest $\mathbf{L}'$ is *equivalent* to $\mathbf{L}$, if whenever $H(\mathbf{j})$ depends on $H(\mathbf{i})$ in $\mathbf{L}$, $H'(\mathbf{k})$ precedes $H'(\mathbf{l})$ in $\mathbf{L}'$, that is, $\mathbf{iU} < \mathbf{jU}$. The transformation $\mathbf{L} \Rightarrow \mathbf{L}'$ is *valid* if $\mathbf{L}'$ is equivalent to $\mathbf{L}$.

Theorem 1 *The transformation* $\mathbf{L} \Rightarrow \mathbf{L}'$ *induced by a unimodular matrix* $\mathbf{U}$ *is valid if and only if* $\mathbf{dU} > \mathbf{0}$ *for each distance vector* $\mathbf{d}$ *of* $\mathbf{L}$.

Proof The "if" Part. Suppose $\mathbf{dU} > \mathbf{0}$ for each distance vector $\mathbf{d}$ of $\mathbf{L}$. Let an iteration $H(\mathbf{j})$ depend on an iteration $H(\mathbf{i})$. Since $\mathbf{j} - \mathbf{i}$ is a distance vector of $\mathbf{L}$, one gets $\mathbf{jU} - \mathbf{iU} = (\mathbf{j} - \mathbf{i})\mathbf{U} > \mathbf{0}$. Hence, $\mathbf{iU} < \mathbf{jU}$. Therefore, $\mathbf{L}'$ is equivalent to $\mathbf{L}$, and the transformation $\mathbf{L} \Rightarrow \mathbf{L}'$ is valid.

The "only if" Part. Suppose the transformation $\mathbf{L} \Rightarrow \mathbf{L}'$ is valid. Let $\mathbf{d}$ denote any distance vector of $\mathbf{L}$. There exist index points $\mathbf{i}$ and $\mathbf{j}$ of $\mathbf{L}$, such that $\mathbf{d} = \mathbf{j} - \mathbf{i}$ and the iteration $H(\mathbf{j})$ depends on the iteration $H(\mathbf{i})$. By hypothesis, $\mathbf{iU} < \mathbf{jU}$, so that $\mathbf{dU} = \mathbf{jU} - \mathbf{iU} > \mathbf{0}$. ∎

Corollary 1 *If the transformation* $\mathbf{L} \Rightarrow \mathbf{L}'$ *by a unimodular matrix* $\mathbf{U}$ *is valid, then the distance vectors of* $\mathbf{L}'$ *are the vectors* $\mathbf{dU}$ *where* $\mathbf{d}$ *is any distance vector of* $\mathbf{L}$.

Proof There is dependence between two iterations $H'(\mathbf{k})$ and $H'(\mathbf{l})$ of $\mathbf{L}'$ if and only if there is dependence between the iterations $H(\mathbf{i})$ and $H(\mathbf{j})$ of $\mathbf{L}$, where $\mathbf{k} = \mathbf{iU}$ and $\mathbf{l} = \mathbf{jU}$. Since $\mathbf{l} - \mathbf{k} = (\mathbf{j} - \mathbf{i})\mathbf{U}$, the distance vectors of $\mathbf{L}'$ are vectors of the form $\pm \mathbf{dU}$ where $\mathbf{d}$ is a distance vector of $\mathbf{L}$. Now a distance vector has to be positive. Since $\mathbf{dU} > \mathbf{0}$ for each $\mathbf{d}$ (Theorem 1), it follows that the distance vectors of $\mathbf{L}'$ are precisely the vectors $\mathbf{dU}$. ∎

Parallelization by Unimodular Transformation

The goal of this section is to explain by examples how a loop nest can be transformed by a unimodular matrix, such that the innermost or outermost loops in the transformed program can run in parallel. Detailed algorithms are given in the essay *Loop Nest Parallelization* in this encyclopedia.

Example 2 (Inner Loop Parallelization) Consider a nest **L** of two loops:

L_1:   **do** $I_1 = 0, 3$
L_2:   **do** $I_2 = 0, 3$
$H(\mathbf{I})$: $A(I_1, I_2) = A(I_1 - 1, I_2) + A(I_1, I_2 - 1)$

The index space $\mathcal{R}$ of **L** is given by

$$\mathcal{R} = \{(I_1, I_2) : 0 \leq I_1 \leq 3,\ 0 \leq I_2 \leq 3\}.$$

The index space and the dependence between iterations are shown in Fig. 3. The only distance vectors of **L** are $(1, 0)$ and $(0, 1)$. Each of the two loops carries a dependence, and hence cannot run in parallel.

Let $\mathbf{U} = (u_{rt})$ denote any 2×2 unimodular matrix. Let the unimodular transformation of **L** induced by **U** result in a loop nest $\mathbf{L}' = (L'_1, L'_2)$. By Theorem 1, $\mathbf{L}'$ is equivalent to **L** if $(1,0)\mathbf{U} > (0,0)$ and $(0,1)\mathbf{U} > (0,0)$. Assume $\mathbf{L}'$ is equivalent to **L**. Then, by Corollary 1 to Theorem 1, the distance vectors of $\mathbf{L}'$ are $(1,0)\mathbf{U}$ and $(0,1)\mathbf{U}$. The inner loop L'_2 of $\mathbf{L}'$ can run in parallel if it carries no dependence, that is, if $(1,0)\mathbf{U} >_2 (0,0)$ and $(0,1)\mathbf{U} >_2 (0,0)$ are both false. Thus, to get an equivalent nest $\mathbf{L}'$ whose inner loop can run in parallel, one must have $(1,0)\mathbf{U} >_1 (0,0)$ and $(0,1)\mathbf{U} >_1 (0,0)$, that is, $(u_{11}, u_{12}) >_1 (0,0)$ and $(u_{21}, u_{22}) >_1 (0,0)$, or $u_{11} > 0$ and $u_{21} > 0$.

A simple unimodular matrix **U** that fits these constraints, and its inverse are shown below:

$$\mathbf{U} = \begin{pmatrix} 1 & 0 \\ 1 & 1 \end{pmatrix} \quad \text{and} \quad \mathbf{U}^{-1} = \begin{pmatrix} 1 & 0 \\ -1 & 1 \end{pmatrix}.$$

The equation $(I_1, I_2) = (K_1, K_2)\mathbf{U}^{-1}$ gives $I_1 = K_1 - K_2$ and $I_2 = K_2$. Since $0 \leq I_1 \leq 3$ and $0 \leq I_2 \leq 3$, one gets the inequalities $0 \leq K_1 - K_2 \leq 3$ and $0 \leq K_2 \leq 3$ that lead to the ranges (by Fourier's method):

$$\left.\begin{array}{rcl} 0 \leq K_1 \leq 6 \\ \max(0, K_1 - 3) \leq K_2 \leq \min(3, K_1). \end{array}\right\}$$

Thus, the given program **L** is equivalent to the loop nest $\mathbf{L}'$:

L'_1:   **do** $K_1 = 0, 6$
L'_2:   **do** $K_2 = \max(0, K_1 - 3),\ \min(3, K_1)$
$H'(\mathbf{K}) : A(K_1 - K_2, K_2) = A(K_1 - K_2 - 1, K_2)$
                            $+ A(K_1 - K_2, K_2 - 1)$

where the new body $H'(\mathbf{K})$ is obtained from $H(\mathbf{I})$ by replacing I_1 with $K_1 - K_2$ and I_2 with K_2. The index space of the transformed loop nest $\mathbf{L}'$ is shown in Fig. 5. The distance vectors of $\mathbf{L}'$ are $(1, 0)$ and $(1, 1)$. The inner loop L'_2 can now run in parallel since it carries no dependence.

In Fig. 4, consider the set of 7 parallel lines $I_1 + I_2 = c$, where $0 \leq c \leq 6$. They correspond to the 7 values of K_1. On any given line, the index points correspond to the values of K_2 for a fixed K_1. Executing L'_1 sequentially and L'_2 in parallel means that these lines are taken sequentially from $c = 0$ to $c = 6$, while iterations for index points on each given line are executed in parallel. Since the lines appear to constitute a "wave" through the index space of **L**, the name *wavefront method* is often given to this process of executing a loop nest.

In the essay ▶*Loop Nest Parallelization*, a general algorithm is given that finds a valid unimodular transformation for any given loop nest such that all but

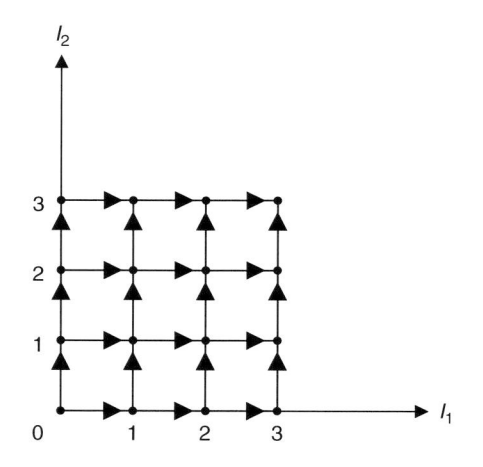

Unimodular Transformations. Fig. 3 Index space of **L**

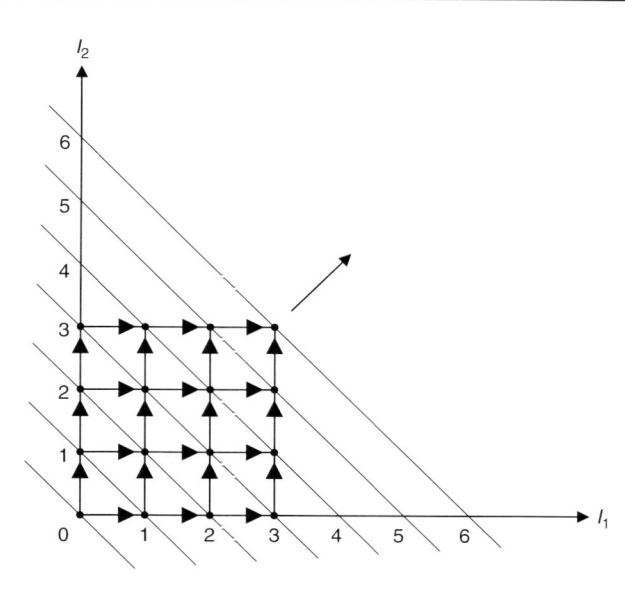

Unimodular Transformations. Fig. 4 Wave through the index space of **L**

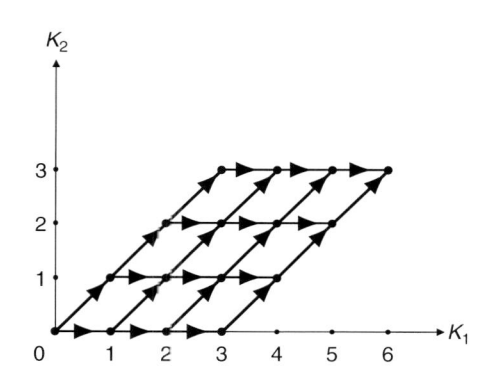

Unimodular Transformations. Fig. 5 Index space of **L'** in Example 2

Let $\mathbf{U} = (u_{rt})$ denote any 2×2 unimodular matrix. Let the unimodular transformation of **L** induced by **U** result in a loop nest $\mathbf{L'} = (L'_1, L'_2)$. By Theorem 1, **L'** is equivalent to **L** if $(2,4)\mathbf{U} \succ (0,0)$ and $(3,6)\mathbf{U} \succ (0,0)$. Assume **L'** is equivalent to **L**. Then, by Corollary 1 to Theorem 1, the distance vectors of **L'** are $(2,4)\mathbf{U}$ and $(3,6)\mathbf{U}$. The outer loop L'_1 of **L'** can run in parallel if it carries no dependence, that is, if $(2,4)\mathbf{U} \succ_1 (0,0)$ and $(3,6)\mathbf{U} \succ_1 (0,0)$ are both false. Thus, to get an equivalent nest **L'** whose outer loop can run in parallel, one must have $(2,4)\mathbf{U} \succ_2 (0,0)$ and $(3,6)\mathbf{U} \succ_2 (0,0)$. The conditions on the elements of **U** are then

$$\left.\begin{array}{r} 2u_{11} + 4u_{21} = 0 \\ 2u_{12} + 4u_{22} > 0 \\ 3u_{11} + 6u_{21} = 0 \\ 3u_{12} + 6u_{22} > 0. \end{array}\right\}$$

A simple unimodular matrix **U** that fits these constraints, and its inverse are shown below:

$$\mathbf{U} = \begin{pmatrix} -2 & 1 \\ 1 & 0 \end{pmatrix} \quad \text{and} \quad \mathbf{U}^{-1} = \begin{pmatrix} 0 & 1 \\ 1 & 2 \end{pmatrix}.$$

The limits on I_1 and I_2 are given by $5 \leq I_1 \leq 100$ and $16 \leq I_2 \leq 80$. Since

$$(I_1, I_2) = (K_1, K_2)\mathbf{U}^{-1} = (K_2, K_1 + 2K_2),$$

the constraints in terms of K_1 and K_2 are

$$5 \leq K_2 \leq 100$$
$$16 \leq K_1 + 2K_2 \leq 80.$$

By Fourier's method of elimination, one gets

$$-184 \leq K_1 \leq 70$$
$$\lceil \max(5, 8 - K_1/2) \rceil \leq K_2 \leq \lfloor \min(100, 40 - K_1/2) \rfloor.$$

Thus, the given program **L** is equivalent to the loop nest **L'**:

$L'_1:$ do $K_1 = -184, 70$
$L'_2:$ do $K_2 = \lceil \max(5, 8 - K_1/2) \rceil,$
                $\lfloor \min(100, 40 - K_1/2) \rfloor$
$H'(\mathbf{K}): X(K_2, K_1 + 2K_2) = X(K_2 - 2, K_1 + 2K_2 - 4)$
                         $+ X(K_2 - 3, K_1 + 2K_2 - 6)$

the outermost loop in the transformed nest can run in parallel. See also Remark 2.

Example 3 (Outer Loop Parallelization) Consider the loop nest **L**:

$L_1:$ do $I_1 = 5, 100$
$L_2:$ do $I_2 = 16, 80$
     $H(\mathbf{I}):$ $X(I_1, I_2) = X(I_1 - 2, I_2 - 4)$
                         $+ X(I_1 - 3, I_2 - 6)$

The only distance vectors of **L** are $(2, 4)$ and $(3, 6)$. Since the outer loop carries a dependence, it cannot run in parallel.

where the new body $H'(\mathbf{K})$ is obtained from $H(\mathbf{I})$ by replacing I_1 with K_2 and I_2 with $K_1 + 2K_2$. The distance vectors of $\mathbf{L}'$ are $(0, 2)$ and $(0, 3)$. The outer loop L'_1 can now run in parallel since it carries no dependence.

In general, if the rank of the distance matrix for $\mathbf{L}$ is ρ, then a unimodular matrix $\mathbf{U}$ can always be found such that the outermost $(m - \rho)$ loops $L'_1, L'_2, \ldots, L'_{m-\rho}$ of $\mathbf{L}'$ can run in parallel. Using inner loop parallelization techniques on top of this, one may get an equivalent loop nest where all loops except $L'_{m-\rho+1}$ can run in parallel. Details are given in the essay ▶ Loop Nest Parallelization.

There are some special unimodular transformations that can be handled more easily than a general transformation. They are described next.

Loop Permutation

Again, the model program is the loop nest $\mathbf{L}$ of Fig. 1, and the transformation of $\mathbf{L}$ induced by a unimodular matrix $\mathbf{U}$ results in the loop nest $\mathbf{L}'$ of Fig. 2. Let $\mathbf{U}$ denote a permutation matrix. Then the transformation $\mathbf{L} \Rightarrow \mathbf{L}'$ is a *loop permutation*. If π is the corresponding permutation of the set $\{1, 2, \ldots, m\}$, then the index vector $\mathbf{K} = (K_1, K_2, \ldots, K_m)$ of $\mathbf{L}'$ is given by $K_r = I_{\pi(r)}$ for $1 \leq r \leq m$. (See (8).)

One important feature of loop permutations is that their validity can be determined from a knowledge of direction vectors alone. This is quite useful since the number of direction vectors is never more (and often less) than the number of distance vectors, and they may be easier to compute and store than distance vectors.

Theorem 2 *Let $\mathbf{U}$ denote an $m \times m$ permutation matrix and π the corresponding permutation of the set $\{1, 2, \ldots, m\}$. The loop permutation $\mathbf{L} \Rightarrow \mathbf{L}'$ induced by $\mathbf{U}$ is valid, if and only if for each direction vector $\sigma = (\sigma_1, \sigma_2, \ldots, \sigma_m)$ of $\mathbf{L}$, the vector $(\sigma_{\pi(1)}, \sigma_{\pi(2)}, \ldots, \sigma_{\pi(m)})$ is positive.*

Proof The "if" Part. Suppose the condition holds. Let $\mathbf{d} = (d_1, d_2, \ldots, d_m)$ denote a distance vector of $\mathbf{L}$. Let σ be the direction vector of $\mathbf{d}$. Since $\sigma_i = \text{sgn}(d_i)$, it follows that $\left(\text{sgn}(d_{\pi(1)}), \text{sgn}(d_{\pi(2)}), \ldots, \text{sgn}(d_{\pi(m)})\right)$ is positive. This means $\left(d_{\pi(1)}, d_{\pi(2)}, \ldots, d_{\pi(m)}\right) > \mathbf{0}$, that is, $\mathbf{dU} > \mathbf{0}$. (See (8).) Hence the transformation $\mathbf{L} \Rightarrow \mathbf{L}'$ is valid by Theorem 1.

The "only if" Part can be proved similarly. ∎

Corollary 1 *If the loop permutation $\mathbf{L} \Rightarrow \mathbf{L}'$ is valid, then the direction vectors of $\mathbf{L}'$ are the vectors $(\sigma_{\pi(1)}, \sigma_{\pi(2)}, \ldots, \sigma_{\pi(m)})$, where $(\sigma_1, \sigma_2, \ldots, \sigma_m)$ is any direction vector of $\mathbf{L}$.*

A direction vector $(\sigma_1, \sigma_2, \ldots, \sigma_m) > \mathbf{0}$ prevents the loop permutation defined by a permutation π of $\{1, 2, \ldots, m\}$ if $(\sigma_{\pi(1)}, \sigma_{\pi(2)}, \ldots, \sigma_{\pi(m)}) < \mathbf{0}$. A very useful permutation is the interchange of two loops L_r and L_{r+1} in $\mathbf{L}$, where $1 \leq r < m$. The only direction vectors that would prevent it have the form $(0, 0, \ldots, 0, 1, -1, *, *, \ldots, *)$, where there are $(r - 1)$ zeros in the front and "$*$" indicates any member of the set $\{0, 1, -1\}$. Algorithm 2.1 in [5] shows how to find all direction vectors that prevent the permutation of a loop nest $\mathbf{L}$ defined by any given permutation π of $\{1, 2, \ldots, m\}$.

Remark 1 Loop permutation is often used to achieve a desirable memory access pattern. A few comments are made here about inner and outer loop parallelization using permutation (see [5]). Let $1 \leq r \leq m$. Note that the loop L_r carries a dependence if and only if there is a direction vector of the form $(0, 0, \ldots, 0, 1, *, \ldots, *)$ with $(r - 1)$ leading zeros. Consider these special cases:

1. Column r of the direction matrix Δ has only 0's. By a suitable loop permutation, L_r can be moved inward or outward to any position, and it can run in parallel there. (When a loop moves, its limits may change.)
2. Column r of Δ has only 0's and 1's. Then L_r can move outward to any position.
3. Column r of Δ has only 1's. Then L_r can move outward to any position. If it is made the outermost loop, then no other loop in $\mathbf{L}'$ will carry a dependence and each inner loop can run in parallel.
4. L_r carries no dependence. Then L_r can move inward to any position where it can run in parallel. (Even when L_r carries a dependence, it may still be possible to move it inward to a position where it runs in parallel.)
5. If there is no -1 in the direction matrix Δ, then every permutation of the nest $\mathbf{L}$ is valid.

Loop Skewing

Let a and b denote two integers such that $1 \leq a < b \leq m$. Let $\mathbf{U}$ denote the matrix obtained from the $m \times m$ unit matrix by replacing the 0 on row a and column b with an integer z. Then $\mathbf{U}$ is a skewing matrix and unimodular. The transformation $\mathbf{L} \Rightarrow \mathbf{L}'$ induced by $\mathbf{U}$ is a *skewing* of the loop L_b by the loop L_a with skewing factor z. (More precisely, it is an *upper* skewing.) The index vector $\mathbf{K}$ of $\mathbf{L}'$ is given by

$$\mathbf{K} = \mathbf{IU} = (I_1, \ldots, I_a, \ldots, I_{b-1}, I_b + zI_a, I_{b+1}, \ldots, I_m).$$

Theorem 3 *Let $1 \leq a < b \leq m$. A skewing of the loop L_b in the nest $\mathbf{L}$ by the loop L_a is always valid.*

Proof Let $\mathbf{d} = (d_1, d_2, \ldots, d_m)$ denote any distance vector of $\mathbf{L}$. Then

$$\mathbf{dU} = (d_1, d_2, \ldots, d_{b-1}, d_b + zd_a, d_{b+1}, \ldots, d_m).$$

Since $\mathbf{d} > \mathbf{0}$, it follows that $(d_1, d_2, \ldots, d_{b-1}) \geq \mathbf{0}$. If $(d_1, d_2, \ldots, d_{b-1}) > \mathbf{0}$, then $\mathbf{dU} > \mathbf{0}$. Suppose $(d_1, d_2, \ldots, d_{b-1}) = \mathbf{0}$. Then $d_a = 0$ since $1 \leq a < b$. Hence, $\mathbf{dU} = (0, 0, \ldots, 0, d_b, d_{b+1}, \ldots, d_m) = \mathbf{d} > \mathbf{0}$. Now apply Theorem 1. ∎

Corollary 1 *After a skewing of a loop L_b by a loop L_a with a skewing factor z, the distance vectors of the transformed nest $\mathbf{L}'$ are vectors of the form $(d_1, d_2, \ldots, d_{b-1}, d_b + zd_a, d_{b+1}, \ldots, d_m)$, where $(d_1, d_2, \ldots, d_m)$ is any distance vector of $\mathbf{L}$.*

Remark 2 Let $\mathbf{d} = (d_1, d_2, \ldots, d_m)$ be a distance vector of $\mathbf{L}$. Since $\mathbf{d}$ is positive, it must be of the form $\mathbf{d} = (0, \ldots, 0, d_a, d_{a+1}, \ldots, d_m)$ where $1 \leq a \leq m$ and $d_a > 0$. Suppose there is a b such that $a < b \leq m$ and $d_b < 0$. Then skewing of the loop L_b by the loop L_a with the positive skewing factor $\lceil -d_b/d_a \rceil$ will change $\mathbf{d}$ into a distance vector $(d_1, d_2, \ldots, d_{b-1}, d_b', d_{b+1}, \ldots, d_m)$, where $d_b' \geq 0$. For a given distance vector $\mathbf{d}$ with a leading element d_a, it is possible to skew all such loops L_b in one step via a single unimodular matrix that is the product of a number of skewing matrices.

By systematically considering all distance vectors of the above type and applying loop skewing repeatedly, it is thus possible to find a loop nest $\mathbf{L}'$ equivalent to $\mathbf{L}$ such that the distance matrix $\mathbf{D}'$ of $\mathbf{L}'$ has all nonnegative entries. Furthermore, by a slight extension, one can make column m of $\mathbf{D}'$ a vector of positive integers. Then column m of the direction matrix $\mathbf{\Delta}'$ of $\mathbf{L}'$ will be a column of 1's. By Remark 1.3, the innermost loop L_m' of $\mathbf{L}'$ can be made the outermost loop to create an equivalent program where all the $(m-1)$ inner loops can run in parallel. See the example below.

Example 4 Consider a loop nest $\mathbf{L} = (L_1, L_2, L_3)$ with the distance matrix

$$\mathbf{D} = \begin{pmatrix} 0 & 2 & -4 \\ 2 & -3 & 5 \\ 0 & 0 & 2 \end{pmatrix}.$$

By applying loop skewing repeatedly and a loop permutation at the end, $\mathbf{D}$ can be transformed into the form described in Remark 2:

$$\begin{aligned}
&\begin{pmatrix} 0 & 2 & -4 \\ 2 & -3 & 5 \\ 0 & 0 & 2 \end{pmatrix} \begin{pmatrix} 1 & 0 & 0 \\ 0 & 1 & 2 \\ 0 & 0 & 1 \end{pmatrix} \begin{pmatrix} 1 & 2 & 1 \\ 0 & 1 & 0 \\ 0 & 0 & 1 \end{pmatrix} \begin{pmatrix} 1 & 0 & 0 \\ 0 & 1 & 1 \\ 0 & 0 & 1 \end{pmatrix} \begin{pmatrix} 0 & 1 & 0 \\ 0 & 0 & 1 \\ 1 & 0 & 0 \end{pmatrix} \\
&= \begin{pmatrix} 0 & 2 & 0 \\ 2 & -3 & -1 \\ 0 & 0 & 2 \end{pmatrix} \begin{pmatrix} 1 & 2 & 1 \\ 0 & 1 & 0 \\ 0 & 0 & 1 \end{pmatrix} \begin{pmatrix} 1 & 0 & 0 \\ 0 & 1 & 1 \\ 0 & 0 & 1 \end{pmatrix} \begin{pmatrix} 0 & 1 & 0 \\ 0 & 0 & 1 \\ 1 & 0 & 0 \end{pmatrix} \\
&= \begin{pmatrix} 0 & 2 & 0 \\ 2 & 1 & 1 \\ 0 & 0 & 2 \end{pmatrix} \begin{pmatrix} 1 & 0 & 0 \\ 0 & 1 & 1 \\ 0 & 0 & 1 \end{pmatrix} \begin{pmatrix} 0 & 1 & 0 \\ 0 & 0 & 1 \\ 1 & 0 & 0 \end{pmatrix} \\
&= \begin{pmatrix} 0 & 2 & 2 \\ 2 & 1 & 2 \\ 0 & 0 & 2 \end{pmatrix} \begin{pmatrix} 0 & 1 & 0 \\ 0 & 0 & 1 \\ 1 & 0 & 0 \end{pmatrix} \\
&= \begin{pmatrix} 2 & 0 & 2 \\ 2 & 2 & 1 \\ 2 & 0 & 0 \end{pmatrix}
\end{aligned}$$

The index vector of the loop nest transforms as follows:

$$(I_1, I_2, I_3) \Rightarrow (I_1, I_2, I_3 + 2I_2) \Rightarrow (I_1, I_2 + 2I_1, I_3 + 2I_2 + I_1)$$
$$\Rightarrow (I_1, I_2 + 2I_1, I_3 + 3I_2 + 3I_1) \Rightarrow (I_3 + 3I_2 + 3I_1, I_1, I_2 + 2I_1)$$
$$= (K_1, K_2, K_3),$$

where (K_1, K_2, K_3) is the index vector of the final loop nest. Thus, $(I_1, I_2, I_3) = (K_2, -2K_2 + K_3, K_1 + 3K_2 - 3K_3)$. Limits for K_1, K_2, K_3 can be computed from the limits for I_1, I_2, I_3 by Fourier's method in the usual way. The two inner loops of the final nest do not carry a dependence, and hence they can run in parallel.

Related Entries

▶ Code Generation
▶ Parallelization, Automatic
▶ Loop Nest Parallelization
▶ Parallelism Detection in Nested Loops, Optimal

Bibliographic Notes and Further Reading

Research on unimodular transformations goes back to Leslie Lamport's paper [9] in 1974, although he did not use this particular term. This essay is based on the theory of unimodular transformations as developed in the author's books on loop transformations [4, 5]. The general theory grew out of the theory of unimodular transformations of double loops described in [3]. (Watch for some notational differences between those references and the current essay.) The paper by Michael Wolf and Monica Lam [13] covers many aspects of unimodular transformations in detail. See also Michael Dowling [7], Erik H. D'Hollander [6], and François Irigoin and Rémi Triolet [8].

Loop interchange has been studied extensively by Michael Wolfe [15, 16], and by Randy Allen and Ken Kennedy [1, 2]. Implementation of the wavefront method by loop skewing and interchange was discussed by Wolfe in [14]. The same technique is described in a general setting in [13].

Wei Li and Keshav Pingali [10] discuss a loop transformation framework based on the class of nonsingular matrices (that includes unimodular matrices).

Bibliography

1. Allen R, Kennedy K (Oct 1987) Automatic translation of FORTRAN programs to vector form. ACM Trans Program Lang Syst 9(4):491–542
2. Allen R, Kennedy K (Oct 2001) Optimizing compilers for modern architectures. Morgan Kaufmann, San Francisco
3. Banerjee U (1990) Unimodular transformations of double loops. In: Proceedings of the third workshop on languages and compilers for parallel computing, Irvine, 1–3 Aug 1990. Available as Nicolau A, Gelernter D, Gross T, Padua D (eds) (1991) Advances in languages and compilers for parallel computing. The MIT Press, Cambridge, pp 192–219
4. Banerjee U (1993) Loop transformations for restructuring compilers: the foundations. Kluwer Academic, Norwell
5. Banerjee U (1994) Loop transformations for restructuring compilers: loop parallelization. Kluwer Academic, Norwell
6. D'Hollander EH (July 1992) Partitioning and labeling of loops by unimodular transformations. IEEE Trans Parallel Distrib Syst 3(4):465–476
7. Dowling ML (Dec 1990) Optimal code parallelization using unimodular transformations. Parallel Comput 16(2–3):157–171
8. Irigoin F, Triolet R (1989) Dependence approximation and global parallel code generation for nested loops. Cosnard M et al. (eds) Parallel distrib algorithms. Elsevier (North-Holland), New York, pp 297–308
9. Lamport L (Feb 1974) The parallel execution of DO loops. Commun ACM 17(2):83–93
10. Li W, Pingali K (Apr 1994) A singular loop transformation framework based on non-singular matrices. Int J Parallel Program 22(2):183–205
11. Schrijver A (Oct 1987) Theory of linear and integer programming. Wiley, New York
12. Williams HP (Nov 1986) Fourier's method of linear programming and its dual. The American Mathematical Monthly 93(9):681–695
13. Wolf ME, Lam MS (Oct 1991) A loop transformation theory and an algorithm to maximize parallelism. IEEE Trans Parallel Distrib Syst 2(4):452–471
14. Wolfe M (Aug 1986) Loop skewing: the wavefront method revisited. Int J Parallel Program 15(4):279–293
15. Wolfe M (1986) Advanced loop interchanging. In: Proceedings of the 1986 international conference on parallel processing, St. Charles, 19–22 Aug 1986, pp 536–543. IEEE Computer Society Press, Los Angeles
16. Wolfe MJ (1989) Optimizing supercompilers for supercomputers. The MIT Press, Cambridge

Universal VLSI Circuits

▶ Universality in VLSI Computation

Universality in VLSI Computation

GIANFRANCO BILARDI[1], GEPPINO PUCCI[2]
[1]University of Padova, Padova, Italy
[2]Università of di Padova, Padova, Italy

Synonyms

Area-universal networks; Universal VLSI circuits

Definition

A VLSI circuit $U(A)$ is said to be *area-universal* if it can be configured to emulate every VLSI circuit of a given area A. If $U(A)$ has area A_U, then it has *blowup* $\alpha = A_U/A$. If any circuit with area-time bounds (A, T) is emulated by $U(A)$ in time $T_U \leq \sigma T$, then $U(A)$ has *slowdown* σ. Clearly, smaller blowup and smaller slowdown reflect a better quality of a universal circuit. An analogous formulation enables the study of area-universal general-purpose routing. The broad goal of research on area-universality is to characterize blowup/slowdown trade-offs, that is, what is the minimum blowup achievable for any given slowdown.

Discussion

Models of VLSI Computation

The VLSI model of computation (see Article [1] of this Encyclopedia) was formulated in the late seventies to capture the resource trade-offs of computation by large-scale integrated circuits. In this model, a computational engine is an interconnection of basic Boolean gates and storage elements (flip-flops), with a specified space layout defining the geometric placement of these building blocks (*nodes*) and of their interconnections (*wires*). Although the details of the model were developed with integrated circuit technology in mind, the spirit of the model is quite general and captures constraints that apply to any reasonable physical computing device. These key physical constraints can be stated as follows.

P1 – *Principle of information density*. There is a lower bound to the amount of space required to store a bit.
P2 – *Principle of bandwidth density*. There is an upper bound to the amount of information that can be transmitted through a unit of surface in a unit of time.
P3 – *Principle of computation delay*. There is a lower bound to the time necessary to compute a Boolean function of a given constant number of inputs.
P4 – *Principle of communication delay*. There is an upper bound to the speed at which information can travel.

The bounds stated by the above principles are assumed to be fixed positive constants. Any given technology typically comes to within constant factors of these bounds and technological progress aims, by and large, to an improvement of these factors.

Most of the research on VLSI computing has been based on Thompson's model [2], which does not actually include principle P4, as it assumes that information can be transmitted in constant time along a wire, irrespective of its length. The rationale was that, in the VLSI systems of the time, transmission delays did not add substantially to computation delays. An alternate VLSI model, including principle P4, was proposed by Chazelle and Monier [3]. A detailed study of how the predicted development of silicon technology would have impacted the choice between the two models was carried out by Bilardi, Pracchi, and Preparata in [4], indicating (correctly, in retrospective) that the Thompson model would prove to be a reasonable approximation for a decade or more, at least with reference to single-chip systems. Furthermore, even when not applicable to the entire computing system, Thompson's model still leads to valuable insights on the design of sufficiently small regions of the system. In this entry, VLSI universality will be discussed in the regime where communication delays are negligible. In the complementary regime, governed by principle P4, computing systems do exhibit different behaviors, with signifcant impact on machine organization and algorithm design, as discussed by Bilardi and Preparata in [5].

The Question of Universality

Many studies have utilized the VLSI model of computation to explore area-time trade-offs in special-purpose computing. Given a target problem, the objective is to determine, for any achievable computation time T, the minumum area A such that there is a VLSI circuit that can be laid out in area A and can solve the problem in time T. The area-time trade-off has been determined for several key problems. For example, the cumulative product of N elements drawn from a semigroup of fixed size can be computed in area $A = \Theta(N/T)$, where $\Omega(\log N) \leq T \leq O(N)$. For the addition of two N-bit numbers, the area becomes $A = \Theta((N/T)\log(N/T))$, where $\Omega(\log N) \leq T \leq O(N)$. Finally, the integer multiplication of two N-bit numbers, the sorting of n integer keys of $2\log n$ bits each (hence $N = 2n\log n$ input bits overall), and the n-point Discrete Fourier Transform in the ring of the integers modulo m (hence $N = n\log m$ input bits overall), are all problems which feature optimal circuits of area $A = \Theta(N^2/T^2)$, where $\Omega(\log N) \leq T \leq O(\sqrt{N})$. The designs achieving the optimal area-time performance are typically based on different topologies for different problems, or even for different computation times concerning the same problem. Thus, a variety of interconnection topologies have been exploited for various operations, including *meshes* of various dimensions, the *tree*, the *shuffle-exchange*, the *cube connected cycles* and its *pleated* version, the *mesh-of-trees*, and several others. This state of affairs seems to lead to an unwelcome conclusion: if the optimal execution of different computations requires different architectures, then no architecture is universally good, and general-purpose computing is inherently suboptimal. Is this conclusion really warranted? The theory of area-time universality in VLSI is a way to address this fundamental question.

To be specific and quantitative, the question for the case of circuits can be formulated as follows (the adaptation to routers will be discussed at the end of the next section). A VLSI circuit $U(A)$ is *area-universal* if it can be programmed to emulate every circuit of a given area A. If $U(A)$ has area A_U, then its *blowup* is $\alpha = A_U/A$. If any circuit with area-time bounds (A, T) is emulated by U_A in time $T_U \leq \sigma T$, then $U(A)$ has *slowdown* σ. Clearly, smaller blowup and smaller slowdown reflect a better quality of a universal circuit. The general goal is to characterize the blowup–slowdown trade-off, that is, what is the minimum blowup achievable for any given slowdown.

In the VLSI model, the basic processing elements are Boolean gates with a fixed number, say q, of inputs and outputs. If the unit of length is chosen to reflect the feature size of the technology, then the area of an elementary gate is a small, integer constant. It is straightforward to design a q-universal gate of constant area a_q, programmable to compute any Boolean function of q inputs and outputs, in constant time τ_q. A universal circuit $U(A)$ can then be conceived as a set of A universal gates connected by a routing network programmable to simulate the interconnection of any specific circuit to be emulated. Since the universal Boolean gates contribute a constant factor both to the blowup and to the slowdown, the pivotal issue is the area-time performance of the routing network. Although a general permutation network could easily be adapted for the purpose, it would result in an inefficient solution. In fact, a data exchange that can be realized in unit time by a set of wires laid out in area A is considerably more constrained than a general permutation. To be area-time efficient, a router must take advantage of such constraints, which are formulated quantitatively in the next section.

Bandwidth and Area

A key insight of the theory of VLSI layout is that the area of a graph is closely related to how well such graph can be embedded into a binary tree. This insight is systematically and beautifully developed by Bhatt and Leighton in [6]. Below, the results relevant to the present discussion are reviewed and cast in the unifying terminology of graph embedding.

In an embedding, each vertex $v \in V$ of a *guest* graph $G = (V, E)$ is mapped onto a node $\phi(v) \in W$ of a *host* graph $H = (W, D)$, and each edge $(a, b) \in E$ of G is mapped onto a path $\psi(a, b)$ joining node $\phi(a)$ to node $\phi(b)$ in tree H. The *load* $\ell(w)$ of a host node $w \in W$ is the number of guest vertices mapped onto w. The *dilation* $d(a, b)$ of a guest edge $(a, b) \in E$ is the length (number of edges) of the corresponding host path $\psi(a, b)$. The *congestion* $c(u, w)$ of a host edge $(u, w) \in D$ is the number of guest edges whose corresponding path includes edge (u, w). Good embeddings are characterized by small values of load, dilation, and congestion.

A two-dimensional VLSI layout of a graph G, for simplicity assumed throughout of degree 4, can be defined as an embedding of G into a rectangular grid, subject to three constraints: (1) the load of each grid node is at most one; (2) the congestion of each grid egde is at most one; and (3) the grid path associated with a guest edge (a, b) can only traverse grid nodes of zero load, except for $\phi(a)$ and $\phi(b)$. It turns out that a good layout of graph G leads rather straightforwardly to a good embedding of G in a binary tree; it is also the case that a good layout can be obtained from a good tree embedding, although the process is more subtle. Intuitively, searching for a good tree embedding is easier than searching for a good grid layout, due to the removal of constraints (1), (2), and (3) above and to the fact that a tree embedding is uniquely determined by vertex placement, if simple paths (which are unique for any choice of their endpoints) are used for hosting edges. The price to pay for the simplification is that, even if the given tree embedding is optimal, the area of the resulting layout may be suboptimal by up to two logarithmic factors.

A tree embedding can be obtained from a layout as follows. By simple transformations that increase the area by at most a constant factor, the layout is made to fit a $\sqrt{A} \times \sqrt{A}$ square grid, where $\sqrt{A}$ is an integer power of two. Next, each grid vertex is labeled with a pair of integer coordinates (i, j), with $i, j = 0, \ldots, \sqrt{A} - 1$. The grid vertices are labeled so that vertex $(0, 0)$ is the north-west corner of the grid, thus i increases eastward and j increases southward. Let $H = (W, D)$ be a complete, ordered binary tree of A leaves, numbered $0, \ldots,$

$A - 1$, from left to right. The tree embedding is based on the *shuffle-major* one-to-one correspondence that associates grid vertex (i, j) with leaf k of tree H, where the binary representation of k is obtained from those of $i \equiv (i_{(\log A)/2-1} \ldots i_0)$ and $j \equiv (j_{(\log A)/2-1} \ldots j_0)$ as $k = shm(i, j) \equiv (j_{(\log A)/2-1} i_{(\log A)/2-1} \ldots j_1 i_1 j_0 i_0)$. Then, each node of the tree is naturally associated with the region of the grid matched to its descendant leaves. This association can be understood as a recursive decomposition, with the root corresponding to the entire layout, the left and the right children of the root, respectively, corresponding to the west and to the east halves of the layout, the four grandchildren of the root corresponding, from left to right, to the north-west, south-west, north-east, and south-east quadrants, and so on. With the preceeding setup, a layout of a graph $G = (V, E)$ naturally induces an embedding of G in H where (1) a vertex v of G placed at vertex (i, j) of the grid is mapped onto leaf $\phi(v) = shm(i, j)$ of H and (2) an edge (a, b) is mapped onto the unique simple tree path from $\phi(a)$ to $\phi(b)$.

In the resulting embedding, the load is one for the leaves and zero for the internal nodes. Furthermore, edges have dilation at most $2 \log A$. Finally, the congestion C_q of a tree edge joining a node w at level $q + 1$ to its parent u (at level q) is at most $3\sqrt{2}\sqrt{A/2^q}$ at even levels ($q = 0(root), 2, \ldots, \log A - 2$) and is at most $4\sqrt{A/2^q}$, at odd levels ($q = 1, 3, \ldots, \log A - 1$), since C_q cannot exceed the perimeter of the layout region corresponding to node w, as the layout of all the edges of G congesting tree edge (w, u) must cross the boundary of said region. A graph G is said to have *tree-area* $\tilde{A}$ if $\tilde{A}$ is the minimum value such that G admits a tree embedding with the properties just derived for graphs of area $\tilde{A}$. From a tree-embedding of area $\tilde{A}$, a grid layout of area $A = O(\tilde{A} \log^2 \tilde{A})$ can be constructed in polynomial time [6]. The procedure is subtle and exploits some powerful combinatorial lemmas. A variant of the procedure also yields a more sophisticated embedding of G in H satisfying the following properties. The load of any node at level q if at most $\lambda\sqrt{A/2^q}$; the congestion of any edge joining a node w at level $q + 1$ to its parent is al most $\gamma\sqrt{A/2^q}$; and the dilation of any edge is at most 4, where λ and γ are suitable constants. The developments of [6] revolve around the concept of minimum $\sqrt{2}$-*bifurcator* of a graph G, denoted by F and related to the tree area as $F = \Theta\left(\sqrt{\tilde{A}}\right)$.

Most machines meant for general-purpose computing consist of a set of processing elements that can exchange messages via a routing network. In this context, it becomes interesting to compare machines with the same type of processing elements, but with different routers. Analogously to the question raised in the previous subsection for circuits, one can ask how well a given general-purpose router $R(A)$ can deliver messages, compared to *any* router G of area A. To this end, it is useful to define the *load factor* λ of a given set of messages, whose sources and destinations (called *terminals*) are placed in a square region of area A, as the maximum over all the edges of the tree H (defined above) of the ratio between the number of messages with source and destination on opposite sides of an edge, and the congestion value C_q associated with that edge. It has to be observed that λ is a lower bound to the routing time of a message set for any network that can be laid out in a square region of area A. Therefore, the quality of a universal VLSI router is conveniently captured by its blowup and by its routing time, expressed as a function of λ and A.

Universal Fat-Tree Architectures

Most efficient area-universal networks proposed in the literature exhibit a treelike structure, with the bandwidth of child-to-parent channels growing going from the leaves toward the root. Informally, these networks are called *fat-trees*. Usually, the leaves of a fat-tree act as processing elements (in universal circuits) or as terminals (in universal routers) and the subnetworks located at the internal nodes perform a mere switching role. However, in a few notable cases, internal nodes also play an active role.

Typically, the bandwidth between a node and its parent doubles every other level, going from constant at the N leaves to $\sqrt{N}$ at the root. Alll variants of fat-trees considered in the literature have layout area $O(N \log^2 N)$. In [7], Bilardi and Bay define the class of *channel-sufficient* fat-trees, as those where the maximum number of edge-disjoint paths connecting any two sets of leaves comes within a constant factor of the largest value compatible with the node-to-parent bandwidths. Graphs in this class, which contains all fat-trees proposed in the literature, are shown to require area $\Omega(N \log^2 N)$. When targeting universality for area A, if a fat-tree with $N = \Theta(A)$ leaves is chosen, then the area becomes $\Theta(A \log^2 A)$, resulting in a blowup $\alpha = \Theta(\log^2 A)$.

The first efficient universal fat-tree was proposed by Leiserson in [8]. Its internal nodes are realized as partial concentrators of constant depth, whence the name of *Concentrator Fat-Tree* (CFT). On a CFT, a message set of load factor $\lambda \le 1$ can be routed in time $O(\log A)$, hence, as an area-universal circuit, the CFT exhibits slowdown $\sigma = O(\log A)$. The authors of [8] also devise an off-line decomposion of an arbitrary message set of load factor λ into $O(\lambda \log A)$ message sets of load factor smaller than 1. Thus, as an area-universal router, the CFT exhibits a routing time of $O(\lambda \log^2 A)$.

Routing time on the CFT has been subsequently improved by Greenberg and Leiserson in [9] and by Leighton et al. in [10], with randomized, online algorithms. Concentrators are powerful routing components, but setting their switches is achieved by computing bipartite graph matchings, for which area-time efficient, deterministic algorithms are not known. For this reason, two new fat-trees that do not make use of partial concentrators, namely, the *pruned butterfly* and the *sorting fat-tree*, have been introduced by Bay and Bilardi in [11] for online, deterministic routing. Finally, a variant of the CFT, called *Fat-Pyramid*, was proposed by Greenberg in [12] to achieve good blowup and slowdown in a VLSI model where the cost to transmit a bit over a wire is a (quite) general function of the wire length, ranging between constant and linear time.

In the context of universal circuits, the *Meshed CFT* has been considered, both by Leighton et al. in [10] and by Bay and Bilardi in [13]. The Meshed CFT consists of $O(A/\log^2 A)$ meshes of size $O(\log A \times \log A)$, connected to the leaves of a CFT with root bandwidth $O(\sqrt{A}/\log A)$; the total area is $O(A)$. In [10], the routing required to simulate a circuit makes use of standard permutation routing techniques on the mesh combined with a sophisticated randomized technique on the CFT. When evaluating the area requirements of the resulting circuit in the bit model, the mesh nodes require $\Theta(\log \log A)$ bits apiece to encode switching decisions, pushing the total area to $O(A \log \log A)$. The $O(\log \log A)$ blowup is avoided in [13] by a specialized routing approach that makes crucial use of the fact that the permutations to be routed in the meshes are not arbitrary, but arise from a layout. In both designs,

in spite of the reduced root bandwdth ($O\left(\sqrt{A}/\log A\right)$ against $O\left(\sqrt{A}\right)$ of the original CFT), the routing time remains $O(\log A)$, thanks to a careful pipelining of $O(\log A)$ message waves along the tree. In [13], it is also shown that the entire transformation of a given circuit layout into the meshed CFT configuration needed to simulate it can be computed in (optimal) sequential time $O(A)$. Whether a universal circuit of area $O(A)$ can achieve sublogarithmic slowdown remains an open question. As a corollary of a more general result, Bilardi et al. in [14] have shown that any universal circuit which employs an embedding of the guest circuit for its simulation must incur a slowdown of $\Omega\left(\sqrt{\log A}/\log \log A\right)$. It is instead possible to achieve sublogarithmic and even constant slowdown with a substantial blowup, as established by Bhatt, Bilardi, and Pucci in [15]. Their construction makes crucial use of the constant-dilation tree-embedding discussed in Chapter 3 and of a redundant-computation technique. A slowdown of $O(\log \log A)$ was also achieved by Kaklamanis, Krizanc, and Rao in [16], with a multi-fat-tree network targeted to the simulation of planar circuits, and a with butterfly network, targeted to the simulation of circuits with a number of nodes suitably sublinear in the area. The butterfly approach suffers a larger blouwp than the one achieved in [15] for the same slowdown, even for the restricted class of circuits that it can handle; however, the techniques of [16] are different from those employed in [15] and could have other significant applications.

A summary of the main characteristics of the universal designs discussed above is displayed in Table 1. For the sake of uniformity and comparison, in the table as well as in the preceding discussion, all results have been translated to a common framework. In particular, layouts are taken to be two dimensional, with area and time evaluated in Thompson's model. Also, the family of simulated routers (respectively, circuits) is assumed to be all those admitting layouts within area A. All routing times, except that of [10], apply to messages of $b = O(\log A)$ bits, although they remain unchanged if $b = O(1)$. Features of a design that do not fit into the outlined common framework are explicitly reported and marked with symbol "⊖" if they represent a restriction, and with symbol "⊕" if they represent an enhancement.

Finally, it is interesting to observe that a universal router naturally yields a universal circuit, by first

Universality in VLSI Computation. Table 1 Each table entry refers to a specific universal (router or circuit) design. The following features are displayed: (a) the topology; (b) the mode of operation (only for routers), that is, whether or not the universal router requires preprocessing to be configured for the simulation (off-line vs. online design), and whether or not the routing algorithm makes use of random bits (randomized vs. deterministic design); (c) the area blowup; (d) the routing time for universal routers (as a function of the load factor λ of the message set to be routed), or, alternatively, the slowdown of the simulation for universal circuits; and (e) the corresponding scientific reference

Universal routers				
Topology	Mode	Blowup	Routing time	Ref
Concentrator Fat-Tree (CFT)	off/det	$O(\log^2 A)$	$O(\lambda \log^2 A)$	[8]
CFT	on/rand	$O(\log^2 A)$	$O(\lambda \log A +$ $+ \log^2 A \log \log A)$	[9]
CFT (⊖:word model)	on/rand	$O(\log^2 A)$	$O(\lambda + \log A)$	[10]
Pruned Butterfly	on/det	$O(\log^2 A)$	$O(\lambda \log^2 A)$	[11]
Sorting FT (⊖: constant-degree message sets)	on/det	$O(\log^2 A)$	$O(\lambda \log A + \log^2 A)$	[11]
Fat Pyramid (⊖:$O(A/\log A)$ terminals)	off/det	$O(1)$	$O(\lambda + \log A)$ (⊕:general delay model)	[12]
Universal circuits				
Topology		Blowup	Slowdown	Ref
CFT		$O(\log^2 A)$	$O(\log A)$	[8]
Meshed CFT		$O(\log \log A)$	$O(\log A)$	[10]
Meshed CFT		$O(1)$	$O(\log A)$	[13]
Multi-Computation FT (parametric design) (⊕: simulates circuits with $\sqrt{A}$-bifurcator)		$O(A^\epsilon)$	$O(1/\epsilon)$ $4 \log \log A / \log A \leq \epsilon \leq 1$	[15]
Multi-FT (⊖: planar guest circuits only)		$O(\log^2 A)$	$O(\log \log A)$	[16]
Butterfly (parametric design) (⊖: $O\left(\sqrt{A^{1+\epsilon}} \log A\right)$ nodes)		$O(A^\epsilon)$	$O(1/\epsilon + \log \log A)$ $0 < \epsilon < 1, \epsilon$ constant	[16]

matching the terminals of the host router with the computing elements of the guest circuit according to the tree embedding induced by the guest's layout, and then hardwiring the routing decisions relative to the message set induced by the guest's proximity structure. The slowdown of the resulting universal circuit is obtained by setting $\lambda = 1$ in the formula for the routing time. The blowup could increase, due to the area needed to store the hardwired routing decisions, although the increase is often negligible. The resulting performance metrics tend to be inferior to those of explictly designed universal circuits. On the positive side, the class of simulated circuits typically includes all those of tree-area A (or, equivalently, with bifurcator $F = O(\sqrt{A})$), which is a larger family than all circuits with a layout of area A. A similar observation applies to the planar circuit simulator of [16], which is able to simulate all planar graphs with $O(A)$ nodes, some of which are know to have area $\omega(A)$.

Conclusions

Research on VLSI universality has demonstrated the viability of universal circuits and routers featuring area and time performances which are only a few logarithmic factors away from those exhibited by specialized devices of a stipulated area budget. This line of work has provided significant insight on several important technological issues. Regarding circuits, universal designs provide theoretical grounding to the compelling practical evidence that Field-Programmable

Gate Arrays (FPGAs) are indeed a viable and cost-effective option for the design of highly configurable, general-purpose integrated circuits and may offer considerable savings at the cost of a modest degradation in performance for a vast number of applications. On the other hand, the inevitable slowdowns incurred by such devices could be undesirable for specific, mission-critical computations, for which the development of specialized circuitry is most appropriate. The legacy of area-universal routing is instead related to the emergence of a number of successful commercial fat-treelike interconnection networks for parallel machines including the Thinking Machines CM-5, the Quadrics CS2, and the IBM RS/6000 SP.

Related Entries
▶Models of Computation, Theoretical
▶VLSI Computation

Bibliographic Notes and Further Reading
The following bibliography lists most relevant references on area-universality. For a more comprehensive introduction on research on the VLSI model of computation, the reader is referred to Jeffrey D. Ullman's book: *Computational Aspects of VLSI*, Computer Science Press, Rockville MD, 1984.

Bibliography
1. Preparata FP. VLSI computation. In: Encyclopedia of parallel computing. Springer
2. Thompson CD (1980) A complexity theory for VLSI. Ph.D. thesis, Tech. Rep. CMUCS- 80-140, Dept. of Computer Science, Carnegie-Mellon University, Pittsburgh
3. Chazelle B, Monier L (1981) A model of computation for VLSI with related complexity results. In: Proceedings of the 13th ACM symposium on theory of computing, Milwaukee, pp 318–325
4. Bilardi G, Pracchi M, Preparata FP (1982) A critique of network speed in VLSI models of computation. IEEE J Solid-St Circ SC-17(4):696–702
5. Bilardi G, Preparata FP (1995) Horizons of parallel computation. J Parallel Distr Com 27(2):172–182
6. Bhatt SN, Leighton FT (1984) A framework for solving VLSI graph layout problems. J Comput Syst Sci 28:300–343
7. Bilardi G, Bay PE (1994) An area lower bound for a class of fat-trees. In: Proceedings of the second European symposium on algorithms, Utrecht, pp 413–423
8. Leiserson CE (1985) Fat-trees: universal networks for hardware-efficient supercomputing. IEEE T Comput C-34(10):892–900
9. Greenberg RI, Leiserson CE (1989) Randomized routing on fat-trees. In: Micali S (ed) Randomness and computation. JAI Press, Greenwich, pp 345–374
10. Leighton FT, Maggs BM, Ranade AG, Rao S (1994) Randomized routing and sorting on fixed-connection networks. J Algorithm 17(1):157–205
11. Bay PE, Bilardi G (1995) Deterministic on-line routing on area-universal networks. J ACM 42(3):614–640
12. Greenberg RI (1994) The fat-pyramid and universal parallel computation independent of wire delay. IEEE T Comput 43(12):1358–1364
13. Bay PE, Bilardi G (1993) An area-universal VLSI circuit. In: Proceedings of the 1993 symposium on integrated systems, Seattle, pp 53–67
14. Bilardi G, Chaudhuri S, Dubhashi DP, Mehlhorn K (1994) A lower bound for area-universal graphs. Inform Process Lett 51(2):101–105
15. Bhatt SN, Bilardi G, Pucci G (2008) Area-time tradeoffs for universal VLSI circuits. Theor Comput Sci 408(2–3):143–150
16. Kaklamanis C, Krizanc D, Rao S (1993) Universal emulations with sublogarithmic slowdown. In: Proceedings of the 34th IEEE symposium on foundations of computer science, Palo Alto, pp 341–350

UPC

WILLIAM CARLSON[1], PHILLIP MERKEY[2]
[1]Institute for Defense Analyses, Bowie, MD, USA
[2]Michigan Technological University, Houghton, MI, USA

Synonyms
Unified parallel C

Definition
UPC, Unified Parallel C, is a parallel programming language which is derived from the C language. It supports the Partitioned Global Address Space (PGAS) programming model.

Discussion

Introduction
UPC is a strict superset of the C programming language in the sense that any legal C program is a legal UPC program. It extends the C memory and execution model, and implements the Partitioned Global Address Space (PGAS) programming model. UPC adds several

new type-qualifiers to describe the sharing and consistency models of objects (e.g., variables, structures, and arrays). It also adds some new keywords to control the synchronization of the parallel threads (e.g., activities) within the UPC runtime environment. The driving goal behind UPC is to maintain the C aesthetic in a parallel programming language and model: users have a high degree of affinity with the machine they are programming; there are minimal runtime checks and restrictions; and programs are portable to a wide variety of parallel platforms.

As it is entirely possible to write in many programming styles within the C programming model and language, UPC makes no demands on programmers to conform to a particular parallel programming style. For example, UPC programs have been written in the styles of dynamic work queues; message queues; fine- and coarse-grained shared memory; fine- and coarse-grained distributed memory, lock- and barrier-based synchronized; synchronization-free "Monte Carlo"; and "embarrassing parallel." UPC compilers strive to render each of these styles as efficiently as can be, but cannot prevent users from writing programs in a style that does not match a particular system's performance profile. For example, it is possible to write a fine-grained, lock-based shared-memory program in UPC and run it on a system with no native support for such features. Performance of such attempts will be predictably horrid. Conversely, running such a program on a well-equipped system may be delightful.

UPC is implemented by a variety of compilers and runtime systems. These include both open-source-based compilers and runtimes as well as proprietary ones. Together these implementations allow users to run UPC on almost every significant parallel system in service today. It is important to note that this includes systems which have native support for shared memory and those whose physical interconnection is based on message passing paradigms. In addition, UPC support is planned for all future products of the main vendors of HPC systems. On all of these systems, UPC offers competitive performance to other parallel programming models, as well as the productivity offered by the C programming model and a shared-memory programming paradigm. Links to a variety of these implementations are provided in the Compiler section of the Bibliography.

Parallelism Model

UPC uses the SPMD (Single Program Multiple Data) execution model and the PGAS (Partitioned Global Address Space) model of memory. In UPC, these models are so intertwined that it is difficult to discuss them independently. This article will first describe the execution model with the understanding that the threads operate within the context of the yet to be defined PGAS memory model.

Each instance of execution is called a *thread*. A UPC programmer typically thinks of a thread as a sequential program which shares some data with some number of other threads. The two keywords MYTHREAD and THREADS are expressions with a value of type int that provide a unique thread index for each thread and the total number of threads, respectively. UPC threads are statically declared, heavy-weight threads whose execution span the life of the whole program. There is no mechanism within UPC to spawn or kill threads. Where and how the threads are executed in hardware is determined by the system, not the language. UPC programs are usually executed via a system-dependent "parallel run" command, sometimes called upcrun. Arguments to such a command control the number of threads that will execute and can pass parameters to the runtime system to best suit a particular system.

Instruction-driven synchronization is provided by barriers and locks. The upc_barrier statement provides a "split-phase" barrier: upc_notify followed by upc_wait. These functions are *collective* functions in the sense that they must be called by all threads. The upc_notify/upc_wait pair implements a barrier because no thread can return from the call to upc_wait until all threads have called the upc_notify. The split-phase barrier requires that no globally sensitive code, including other collectives, be executed between the upc_notify and upc_wait. It provides a mechanism to reduce barrier overhead by allowing local or non-globally sensitive work to be placed between the two phases. An extreme instance of this is the bulk-synchronous model in which all "computation" is placed between the notify and wait while all data interaction ("communication") is placed between the wait and the following notify.

Locks in UPC are provided by the functions upc_lock, upc_lock_attempt, and upc_unlock along with library functions to allocate locks.

These operate on objects of type `upc_lock_t`, an opaque type for a shared object which takes on one of two states, *locked* or *unlocked*. Since locks can be allocated, a programmer can use them in a number of ways. For example, one could make an association between a lock and a section of code to provide instruction-driven synchronization like a critical section. If one allocated enough locks to associate individual locks with shared objects or subsets of object, one could use them for data-driven synchronization like atomic or transactional memory operations. Again, UPC defines the semantics, but makes no assumptions about the performance characteristics.

Memory Model

UPC pairs the SPMD execution model with a compatible PGAS memory model. The notion of affinity in UPC captures the locality between processors and memory that exists on most parallel architectures.

Figure 1 shows that memory in UPC is segmented into private and shared. For each thread, *private* memory has precisely the same semantics as in C programs. Private memory for one thread cannot be addressed by any other thread. This is the extreme case of memory locality. The ability to use private memory is important because it allows the explicit description of thread level concurrency and the associated scaling of processor to memory bandwidth; the importation of normal C functions on a thread by thread bases; and the explicit expression of the lack synchronization required among different threads acting on their own private objects.

Shared memory is declared via the keyword type-qualifier `shared` or is allocated by a library function defined to create a shared object. UPC logically partitions shared memory into equivalence classes based on threads. This relationship is referred to as *affinity*. The affinity of shared objects is defined by cyclically assigning blocks of objects to threads. The default block size of one corresponds to the standard cyclic distribution. The other extreme is the standard block distribution that has only one block per thread.

The fact that shared objects are assigned affinity in a known pattern allows programmers and compilers to exploit the performance characteristics of private memory for some uses of the shared objects. The `upc_forall` loop construct does precisely this. The command has the form:

```
upc_forall(init;condition;
   increment;affinity)
```

This is the familiar `for` loop except that the bodies of the loop are only executed by the threads that match the affinity field. If the affinity field is an integer, the thread which is congruent to that integer, modulo `THREADS`, is the thread that executes the loop body. If the affinity field is a shared address, then the thread with affinity to the object at that address is the thread that executes the loop. It is important to note that this construct is not a "fork-join" based parallel loop, nor does it impose synchronization before, during, or after the loop. It does not express parallelism, it expresses locality. In addition to being a useful idiom for programmers that can be optimized by compilers, it is a suggestive abstraction that ties the execution model to a PGAS memory model for a two-level memory hierarchy. Generalizations of `upc_forall` may be useful for deeper memory hierarchies.

The memory consistency model for UPC also facilitates performance by eliminating unrequested synchronization. Every memory reference for a shared object is either *strict* or *relaxed*. One can set the default behavior for all objects in a program by including either the header file `<upc_strict.h>` or `<upc_relaxed.h>` at the beginning of the program. One can override the default behavior for a particular object with use of the reference type-qualifier `strict` or `relaxed`. Finally, one can control the behavior a particular use of an object with a compiler pragma.

Strict references are sequentially consistent and *relaxed* references provide a weak consistency. The key

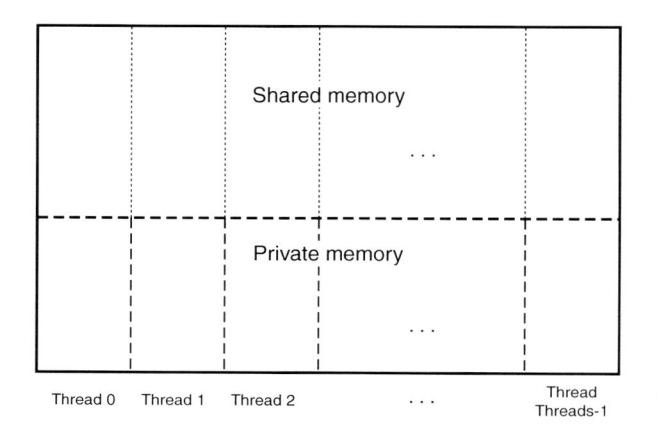

UPC. Fig. 1 UPC Memory model

is the interaction of the two. The strict references lay down a sequentially consistent grid of references that provides fenced regions in which the ordering of relaxed references can be somewhat arbitrary. That is, strict accesses always appear (to all threads) to have executed in program order with respect to other strict accesses, and in a given execution all threads observe the effects of strict accesses in a manner consistent with a single, global total order over the strict operations. Any sequence of purely relaxed shared accesses issued by a given thread may appear to be reordered relative to program order, and different threads need not agree upon the order in which such accesses appeared to have taken place. The only exception to the previous statement is that two relaxed accesses issued by a given thread to the same memory location where at least one is a write will always appear to all threads to have executed in program order. When a thread's program order dictates a set of relaxed operations followed by a strict operation, all threads will observe the effects of the prior relaxed operations made by the issuing thread (in some order) before observing the strict operation. Similarly, when a thread's program order dictates a strict access followed by a set of relaxed accesses, the strict access will be observed by all threads before any of the subsequent relaxed accesses by the issuing thread. Consequently, code blocks containing only relax operations are open to all serial compiler optimization techniques and strict operations can be used to synchronize the execution of different threads by preventing the apparent reordering of relaxed operations contained within the grid of strict operation.

An Example Program

The following UPC code implements a fairly standard algorithm to illustrate a Monte Carlo technique for calculating the mathematical constant Pi. It does so by determining what percentage of random values in a unit rectangle fall within a unit quarter-circle and multiplying by four. It is a parallel algorithm in that any number of parallel actors can make contributions to the accumulations of "tries" and "hits."

```
#include <upc.h>
static shared int tries;
static shared int hits;
double pi(int count) {
  int i;
  for (i=0; i<count; i++) {
    tries++;
    double x = drand48();
    double y = drand48();
    if (x*x+y*y <= 1.0)
      hits++;
  }
  double a = (double) hits/ tries;
  return (4.0*a);
}
```

The only changes from a standard C program required to make this a parallel program are the addition of the shared keyword to the two accumulators. In this very simple version of the code, there is no synchronization required. Any thread calling the function will use the values of tries and hits that all threads have completed by the point it completes its loop. Of course this will result in threads returning different values of Pi, but it is important to note that the algorithm itself is nondeterministic, so the writer of this code decided that added synchronization was unnecessary. Note that this function could be called any number of times by any group of threads, each time a "better" answer would be returned (assuming of course that the implementation of drand48() is a good random number generator!). If the writer wanted to ensure that all threads returned the same value, a upc_barrier statement could be added before the return statement, but this would then require that all threads call pi() collectively.

This simple version may not scale very well to large numbers of threads on some systems as they will "fight" over the shared variables and each access to these is a remote access, which are generally more expensive than local accesses, sometimes dramatically so on large systems. A second version, given in the following code, would be "faster" on many systems.

```
#include <upc.h>
static shared int tries [THREADS];
static shared int hits [THREADS];
double pi(int count) {
  int i;
  for (i=0; i<count; i++) {
    tries[MYTHREAD] ++;
    double x = drand48();
    double y = drand48();
    if (x*x+y*y <= 1.0)
      hits [MYTHREAD] ++;
  }
  int t_tries=0, t_hits=0;
  for (i=0; i<THREADS;i++) {
```

```
    t_tries += tries[i];
    t_hits += hits[i];
  }
  double a = (double) t_hits/ t_tries;
  return (4.0*a);
}
```

Here the program will likely run faster and scale better as any reasonable implementation of UPC will know that (due to affinity) all accesses in the first loop are effectively local. It maintains the characteristic of a loosely synchronized program. If the writer wished a more strictly synchronized program, than version two, a barrier could be inserted before the second loop. In fact, the writer could use the collective function upc_all_reduce() to avoid writing that second loop. Using the provided collective function could also increase performance, as it may be implemented with a more clever algorithm than the simple loop above. But the writer of this code did not want to "over-synchronize."

A savvy reader of this article may notice that the second program also eliminates race conditions that the first code contained relative to the parallel increments of the shared variables. It is a philosophical question whether race conditions are "good" or "bad." Understanding them, using them or avoiding them is a programming choice. It could be argued that for this algorithm, one would obtain better results by not preventing the race. Following the general C philosophy, UPC takes no position on whether race conditions are "good" or "bad," but it does provide mechanisms to manage them. If the programmer wanted to avoid the nondeterministic effects of the race condition, she could surround the shared accesses with a pair of upc_lock()/upc_unlock() routines. This would likely result in an even less scalable program. If available, she could also use atomic operations. Atomic increment operations are available on some machines and are, in fact, faster than usual read from memory, update, and write back cycle. Hence, the compiler or the runtime system may choose to use the atomic update for the sake of performance and incidentally avoid the race condition.

Applications

Like C, UPC is a high-level language that is designed to give programmers control of the machine without imposing one particular paradigm. The following sketches what a program might look like if UPC were used to implement a few of the most popular parallelization strategies.

Consider the master/slave model of parallelism. If one uses a upc_lock to protect a shared work queue, all the threads could execute as slave tasks. Each thread in turn: obtains the lock, takes the next assignment and updates the work queue, then releases the lock and executes the slave task. The process repeats until the work queue is empty. There are minor details in starting the process and terminating the process, but the shared work queue allows one to use a master/slave model without the need of a master thread.

Again, the programmer can chose the appropriate amount of synchronization. If the size of the task is large compared to modifying the work queue, then conflicts at the critical section are probably low and the lock overhead is probably tolerable. If the application has a large Amdahl fraction because of the conflicts at the critical section, one could remove that overhead at the expense of the redundant work caused by not using a lock.

A number of applications are commonly identified as applications that use blocking point-to-point communication to exchange objects and synchronize threads. These include applications like Fast Fourier Transforms, most codes that use domain decomposition, non-continent sorts, and dense linear algebra. These have well-known distributed-memory implementations. Since UPC has a well-defined data layout scheme, forming partnerships between threads (the equivalent of picking send/receive pairs) and the use of explicit messages can be avoided by using standard (albeit sometimes messy) pointer arithmetic and simple assignment statements on shared variables. The second version of the Pi program above is a trivial example of a UPC version of such a program. The first loop use of affinity on a shared array is effectively using private variables on each thread. The difference between message passing and shared memory is illustrated in the second loop. UPC programs can "receive" the values "on" another thread with a simple read statement without interrupting its work flow. This one-sided communication does not require synchronization, so synchronization is a choice.

Often these applications work "in phases" or with an outer loop. The outer loop commonly executes a compute phase and then a communication phase. The synchronization at this level would be instruction driven. Depending on the application this can be an exact fit for the bulk-synchronous programming model or in other cases the communication can essentially disappear. If threads only write to objects for which they have affinity, there can be no race conditions and computation phase can be asynchronous. If the communication phase must wait until the computation is completed, a split-phase barrier as described above would yield a bulk-synchronous implementation. In addition, if the algorithm enjoys sufficient reuse of off-affinity references one could use upc_memcpy to make private copies of shared objects to improve performance in the next computation phase. In many cases the communication phase is unnecessary as the communication will be accomplished by interweaving off-affinity references with the computation. The relaxed consistency model then allows one to overlap (via prefetching or caching) these off-affinity references with the ongoing computation. On some systems this can essentially hide the communication costs.

UPC does not impose a synchronization model, a preferred granularity, or parallelization technique. Therefore, the UPC programmer is free to match applications, algorithm choices, and implementation to a given architecture in order to maximize performance.

UPC History

UPC is the direct descendant of three C language extensions developed in the 1990s: Split-C [4], PCP [1], and AC [2]. Each of these languages had implementations on several platforms of the day and was the result of several years of experimentation. In 1996, the principal contributors to these languages met at UC-Berkeley and designed UPC. Its initial implementation was completed in 1997 for the Cray T3-E system by Carlson and Draper. The first published specification was [3]. The UPC consortium was formed in May 2000 and is open to all interested parties. The consortium controls the specification which stands at version 1.2, published in May 2005.

Related Entries

▶Coarray Fortran

▶PGAS (Partitioned Global Address Space) Languages

Biographical Notes and Further Reading

Textbook

Tarek El-Ghazawi, William Carlson, Thomas Sterling, Katherine Yelick, UPC: Distributed Shared-Memory Programming, John Wiley & Sons, Hoboken, New Jersey, 2005.

Web Documentation

UPC Documentation, http://upc.gwu.edu/documentation.html
UPC Wiki, https://upc-wiki.lbl.gov/index.php

Compilers

IBM XL UPC Compilers, http://www.alphaworks.ibm.com/tech/upccompiler
HP UPC, http://h30097.www3.hp.com/upc/
Intrepid Technology, Inc, http://www.intrepid.com/
GCC UPC, http://www.gccupc.org/

Research Efforts

UPC@Berkeley, http://upc.lbl.gov
UPC@Florida, http://www.hcs.ufl.edu/upc
UPC@GWU, http://upc.gwu.edu
UPC@MTU, http://upc.mtu.edu

Bibliography

1. Brooks E, Warren K (1995) Development and evaluation of an efficient parallel programming methodology, spanning uniprocessor, symmetric shared-memory multi-processor, and distributed-memory massively parallel architectures, poster session at Supercomputing '95, San Diego, CA, 3–8 December 1995
2. Carlson WW, Draper JM (1995) Distributed data access in AC. Proceedings of the Fifth ACM SIGPLAN Symposium on Principles and Practice of Parallel Programming (PPOPP), Santa Barbara, CA, 19–21 July 1995, pp 39–47
3. Carlson WW, Draper JM, Culler DE, Yelick K, Brooks E, Warren K (1999) Introduction to UPC and language specification, CCS-TR-99-157. IDA/CCS, Bowie

4. Culler DE, Dusseau A, Goldstein SC, Krishnamurthy A, Lumetta S, von Eicken T, Yelick K (1993) Parallel programming in split-C. In: Proceedings of Supercomputing '93, Portland, OR, 15–19 November 1993, pp 262–273

Use-Def Chains

▶Dependence Abstractions

Vampir

HOLGER BRUNST, ANDREAS KNÜPFER
Technische Universität Dresden, Dresden, Germany

Synonyms

Vampir 7; VampirServer; VampirTrace; Vampir NG; VNG

Definition

In the scope of HPC, the name Vampir denotes a software framework that addresses the performance monitoring, visualization, and analysis of concurrent software programs by means of a technique referred to as event tracing. Originally, VAMPIR was an acronym for "**V**isualization and **A**nalysis of **MPI R**esources." Today, the framework no longer addresses MPI programs only. Support for many different programing paradigms and performance data sources has been included over time.

The framework consists of a monitor and a visualization component, which are sometimes independently referred to as VampirTrace and Vampir. The monitor component attaches to a running software program and records timed status information about the invocation of program subroutines, the usage of communication interfaces, and the utilization of system resources.

Discussion

Monitoring

The monitoring component (VampirTrace) is used for recording the event traces during a program run. This process involves two steps, the instrumentation step and the runtime recording step [2, 3].

The former modifies the target executable by inserting measurement points that later on allow the detection of runtime events. The latter step handles the runtime events as they occur. This includes collecting events and attributes of events as well as buffering and storing the event data stream.

Supported Paradigms and Languages

VampirTrace currently supports event tracing for the programing languages C, C++, Fortran, and Java. It works for sequential programs as well as for parallel programs using MPI, OpenMP, POSIX Threads, GPUs, the Cell Broadband Engine, or hybrid combinations of them.

Instrumentation

Instrumentation is the modification of the target program in order to detect predefined runtime events. It is inserting monitoring probes on different levels and in different ways:

Source code: On the source code level either manually or automatically with the help of source-to-source translation tools. This may take place during the software development as permanent part of the code or as a preprocessing step during compilation.

Compiler: By compilers with specific command line switches and interfaces. This is supported by most relevant compilers today, including the GNU compiler collection, the OpenUH compilers, and the commercial compilers from Intel, Pathscale, PGI, SUN, IBM, and NEC.

Re-linking: Re-linking with a wrapper library that includes instrumentation. Typically, the wrapper library will refer to the original library for the provided functionality.

Binary: By binary rewriting of a ready executable either in a file or a memory image.

In VampirTrace, different instrumentation techniques can be combined for different types of events. For convenience, the complex internal instrumentation details are hidden in compiler wrappers. The compiler wrappers can be used like regular compiler commands. They refer to underlying compilers but perform all instrumentation activities and/or add instrumentation command line options.

Runtime Recording

The runtime recording library receives events from the instrumentation layer. It is responsible for collecting the events together with related attributes. Then it stores them as event records in a memory buffer which is written to a file eventually.

Below, the most important types of events are listed. They are recorded with a high-resolution time stamp and a location identifier specifying the process or thread. Furthermore, there are additional type-specific attributes.

- **Enter/leave**: Entering to or returning from a subroutine call. This is used for instrumented subroutines in the user code as well as for MPI calls, POSIX I/O calls, or LIBC calls.
- **Send/receive**: Sending or receiving of point-to-point messages both for the blocking and the non-blocking versions. This is modeled according to the MPI standard but can be used for alternative message-passing models.
- **Begin/end collective communication**: Begin and end of an MPI collective communication operation. They are present at every rank participating in an MPI collective operation.
- **Begin/end of I/O operation**: Begin and end of an I/O operation.
- **Counter sample**: Provides the current value of a performance counter.

Timers and Timer Synchronization Precise timing plays an important role for event tracing. Therefore, VampirTrace supports a wide range of generic and platform specific high-precision timers that have a resolution of up to a single CPU clock tick.

VampirTrace provides its own timer synchronization mechanism because most high precision timers in parallel environments are asynchronous. During trace collection, only local timer values are recorded. In addition, synchronization information is collected, which allow the conversation from local time stamps to globally synchronized time stamps in a post-processing step.

Performance Counters VampirTrace supports a number of sources for performance counters. Firstly, it can read hardware performance counters via the PAPI library, SUN Solaris CPC counters, and NEC SX counters. Secondly, it allows to record memory allocation statistics, I/O throughput statistics, and arbitrary counter values provided by the program.

Profiling As an alternative mode, VampirTrace supports profiling, which delivers a concise statistic summary instead of a detailed trace file.

Open Trace Format

The standard trace file format of VampirTrace is the Open Trace Format (OTF). It is developed and maintained by ZIH, Technische Universität Dresden in cooperation with the University of Oregon and the Lawrence Livermore National Lab.

Visualization

The visualization component of Vampir displays the runtime behavior of parallel programs. It visualizes event traces gathered by the monitoring component VampirTrace. The Vampir tool translates trace file data into a variety of graphical representations that give developers detailed insights into performance issues of their parallel program. Vampir allows to quickly browse large performance data sets by means of interactive zooming and scrolling. The detection and explanation of unexpected or incorrect performance behavior is straightforward due to the exact rendering of the program flow. Vampir supports two general display types for the illustration of trace data: timeline and chart views [1, 4].

Timelines

A timeline view shows detailed event-based information for arbitrary time intervals. It graphically presents the chain of events of monitored processes on a horizontal time axis. Detailed information about subroutine invocation, communication, synchronization, and hardware counter events is provided. Vampir currently features three different timeline types: master timeline, process timeline, and counter-data timeline. Figure 1 shows the three different timeline types on the left-hand side from top to bottom.

Master Timeline The master timeline consists of a collection of rows which represent individual processes.

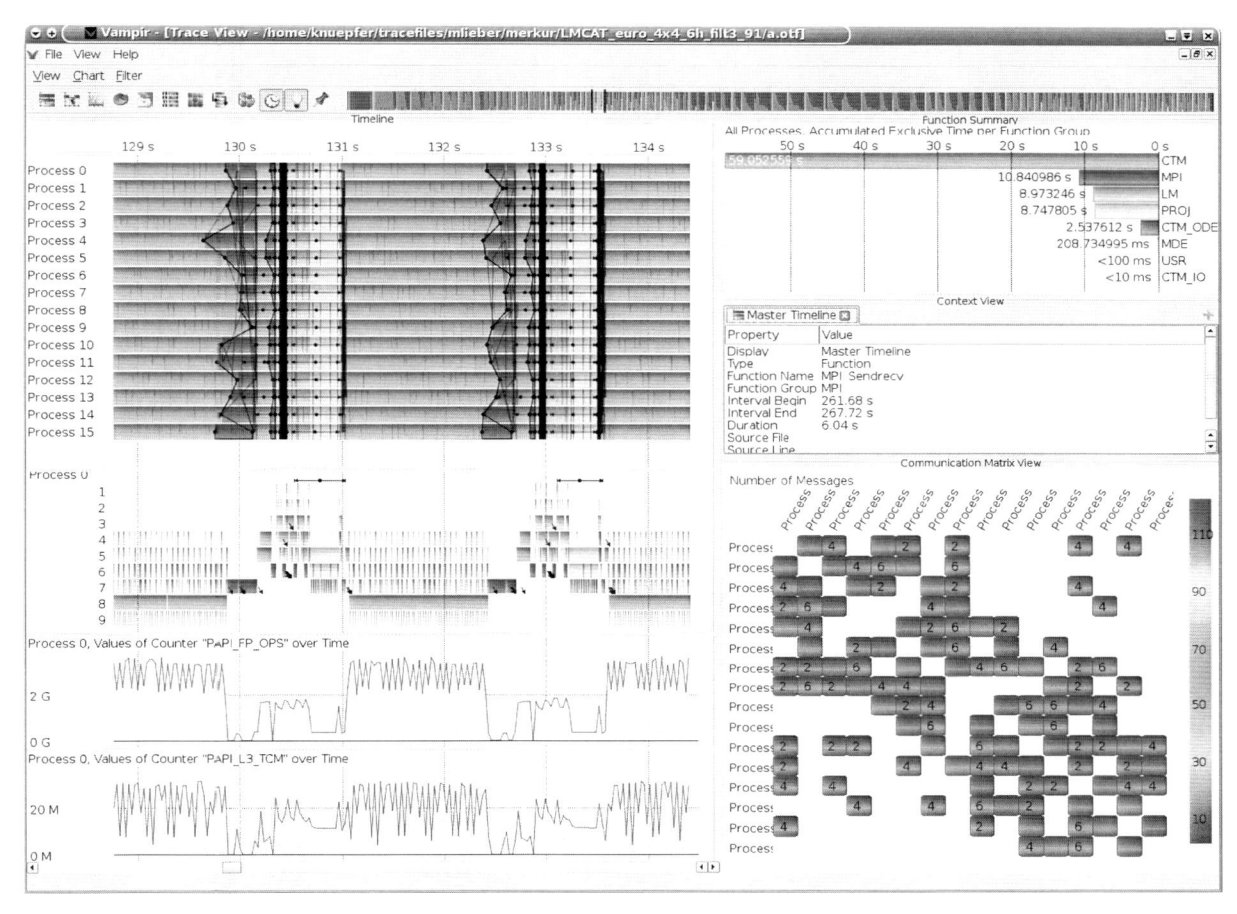

Vampir. Fig. 1 Vampir GUI with the most important displays: the small *Navigation Timeline* (*top*), the *Master Timeline* (*upper left*), the *Process Timeline* (*middle left*), two *Counter Timelines* (*bottom left*), the *Function Summary* (*upper right*), the *Context View* below (*middle left*), and the *Communication Matrix View* (*bottom right*)

All timelines are equipped with a horizontal timescale. Likewise, timelines provide the names of the depicted processes on the left. Color-coding is used to identify specific program actions. In this example, "dark" sections identify MPI communication and synchronization. This color-coding is customizable and depends on the user and the contents of the recorded trace file.

Process Timeline The process timeline resembles the master timeline but has a slight difference. In this case, the different vertical levels represent the different stack levels of subroutine calls. The main routine begins at the topmost level, a respective subroutine call is depicted a level below, and so forth. If a subroutine is completed, the graphical representation of the calling routine continues one level above.

Counter Data Timeline The counter timeline shows recorded performance counter values of the processes with a scale on the left-hand side. The display gives the minimum, average, and maximum values if the individual fluctuations are too tiny to distinguish.

Zooming All timeline displays allow zooming in time to look at details within the huge amounts of data. The zoom intervals of all timelines are aligned such that zooming in one of the displays will update all others to the same time interval.

Charts

In addition to the timeline displays, there are chart displays that provide summarized performance metrics computed from the corresponding event data. Again, the chart displays are connected to the zoom interval of the timeline views. The summary information always relates to the current zoom interval, i.e., the statistics are constraint to the current contents of the timeline views.

Function Summary The function summary gives a profile (statistics) about subroutine calls, either as number of calls or inclusive/exclusive timing for individual subroutines or for classes of subroutines. It provides different graphical representations.

Communication Matrix View The communication matrix provides statistics about point-to-point messages between sender and receiver processes in a two-dimensional matrix with a color legend. It can report message counts, data volumes, timing, and speed. This display can also be zoomed to a subset of senders/receivers or coarsened to groups of processes.

Call Tree The call tree display presents caller and callee relations between subroutines in the current zoom interval.

Context View Finally, the context view shows individual detail information for a selected event (by mouse click), e.g., subroutine calls or messages.

Editions

The Vampir performance data browser is available for all major platforms, including Unix, Microsoft Windows, and Apple Mac OS X–based systems. Three different product editions are available. "Vampir-Light," "Vampir-Standard," and "Vampir-Professional" address the needs of small, midsize, and large institutions. These three editions mainly differ in terms of the supported platform size and pricing. In addition to the above editions, a feature and time-restricted copy of Vampir is available for students and evaluation purposes.

History

In 1992, the development of the Vampir performance visualization tool was started by Wolfgang E. Nagel and Alfred Arnold at the Center for Applied Mathematics (ZAM) of Research Center Jülich in Germany. In these early times, it was still called *PARvis*. When the software became a commercial product in 1996, its name was changed to the acronym VAMPIR (visualization and analysis of MPI resources) in order to underline its focus at that time, which was the visualization of MPI parallel programs. The German company *Pallas GmbH* became the commercial distributor for the software in 1996. In 1998, the design responsibilities for the Vampir software tool moved from Research Center Jülich to the Center for High Performance Computing of Technische Universität Dresden due to the relocation of its founder Wolfgang E. Nagel. Between the years 2004 and 2005, the software was temporarily distributed by the Intel Corporation under the label *Intel Trace Analyzer*. Since 2005, the original software is available again under its most prominent name *Vampir* and can be obtained from Technische Universtät Dresden and GWT-TUD GmbH which are colocated in Dresden.

Future Directions

Motivated by the changing requirements and needs of parallel software developers, the Vampir tool suite is under constant development. The tapping and processing of new performance data sources, namely, hardware accelerators and energy meters is an active field of research. A customizable event data mining engine and the comparison of successive trace runs are under investigation. Furthermore, the overall scalability of the tool suite will be improved in the near future by means of compression techniques that are based on pattern detection algorithms, which allow the elimination of redundant information [5].

Credits
We would like to acknowledge Vampir's original inventors, Prof. Wolgang E. Nagel and Alfred Arnold. Furthermore, we would like to acknowledge the financial support from the Bundesministerium für Bildung und Forschung, the European Union, and other government sponsors. Finally, we would like to acknowledge Forschungszentrum Jülich, Indiana University, and Oak Ridge National Laboratory, in particular Bernd Mohr, Craig Stewart and Rainer Keller.

Licenses and Other Software
VampirTrace and OTF come under a BSD Open Source license. They are also included as default components in the Open MPI distribution from version 1.3, in the Sun

Cluster Tools from version 8.2, and in the Open Speed Shop package from version 1.9.

Related Entries
▶Performance Analysis Tools

Bibliographic Notes and Further Reading

1. For more information about product releases of Vampir, please visit http://www.vampir.eu
2. For more information about VampirTrace, please visit http://www.tu-dresden.de/zih/vampirtrace
3. For more information about the Open Trace Format (OTF), please visit http://www.tu-dresden.de/zih/otf
4. For more information about Vampir related research, please visit http://www.tu-dresden.de/zih/ptools

Bibliography

1. Nagel WE, Arnold A, Weber M, Hoppe H-Chr, Solchenbach K (1996) VAMPIR: visualization and analysis of MPI resources. Supercomput J 1(12):69–80. SARA, Amsterdam
2. Müller M, Knüpfer A, Jurenz M, Lieber M, Brunst H, Mix H, Nagel WE (2007) Developing scalable applications with Vampir, VampirServer and VampirTrace. In: Parallel computing: architectures, algorithms and applications, Adv Parallel Comput 15:637–644. IOS Press, Amsterdam. ISBN 978-1-58603-796-3
3. Knüpfer A, Brunst H, Doleschal J, Jurenz M, Mickler LH, Müller M, Nagel WE (2008) The Vampir performance analysis tool-set. In: Tools for high performance computing. Springer, Berlin, pp 139–155. ISBN 978-3-540-68561-6
4. Brunst H (2008) Integrative concepts for scalable distributed performance analysis and visualization of parallel programs. Dissertation, Technische Universität Dresden. ISBN 978-3-8322-6990-6
5. Knüpfer A (2009) Advanced memory data structures for scalable event trace analysis. Dissertation, Technische Universität Dresden, Suedwestdeutscher Verlag fuer Hochschulschriften. ISBN 978-3-838-10943-5

Vampir 7
▶Vampir

Vampir NG
▶Vampir

VampirServer
▶Vampir

VampirTrace
▶Vampir

Vector Extensions, Instruction-Set Architecture (ISA)

VALENTINA SALAPURA
IBM Research, Yorktown Heights, NY, USA

Synonyms
Data-parallel execution extensions; Media extensions; Multimedia extensions; SIMD (Single Instruction, Multiple Data) Machines; SIMD extensions; SIMD ISA

Definition
Instruction-Set Architecture (ISA) vector extensions extend instruction-set architectures with instructions which operate on multiple data packed into vectors in parallel.

Discussion
Instruction-set architecture vector extensions or vector instructions are SIMD instructions. SIMD stands for "Single Instruction stream, Multiple Data stream," and it is a technique used to exploit data level parallelism.

SIMD architectures apply operations to a fixed number of bits in a single logical computation. These bits are generally spatially local (i.e., a set of successive bits) and can represent a variable number of distinct data elements. The number of elements in a SIMD vector is a direct relationship of the total SIMD register size and the number of bits per data element – one can generally fit 16 8-bit (byte) elements in a 128-bit SIMD register, providing for a 16-way parallel operation on bytes, but only 4 32-bit data elements can fit in the same register, providing a maximal 4-way parallel operation on 32-bit (word) elements.

The maximal speedup available by applying a SIMD architecture to a problem is bounded by both the maximal number of elements in the SIMD vector register and the computational efficiency of the SIMD algorithm. Computational efficiency is a measure of the effective utilization of the elements available within the SIMD register. If a SIMD register can contain 4 elements, but only 2 of the elements contain data that are used in the computational algorithm, then the computational efficiency of that SIMD algorithm is 50% (i.e., 2 out of 4). Combining the maximum parallelism with the computational efficiency gives a rough measure of the overall speedup.

History

There are two distinct types of architectures captured by the classification "vector architecture" which is used today to describe instructions which operate on multiple data values simultaneously. The term was initially coined when traditional vector processors were in common use. Vector-processing facilities operated on multiple data items stored in a vector register containing a large number of vector elements ordered sequentially in the vector register. A single instruction (e.g., a vector add) would indicate that the successive elements of each source operand register would be added together and placed into a third vector register. This process necessarily specified a set of multiple data items (in this case tuples) on which the same instruction operation (i.e., add) was to be performed. An example of such vector processors is the Cray X-MP from the early 1980s.

Modern vector architectures also operate on vectors of data, but do so in a more time-parallel fashion. Vector length is typically held to be quite short, usually dependent on the size of the vector elements, and generally not exceeding 16 elements. These SIMD architectures generally fix the total capacity of a vector register (in terms of bits) to a well-defined constant value (typically 128 bits) and allow a varying number of elements per vector based on the bit-size representation of the element data type (e.g., 16 8-bit byte elements, or 4 32-bit word elements). This architecture facility is referred to as "SIMD architecture," and qualify with "short/parallel vector SIMD" when necessary.

The first architecture to include short parallel vector SIMD instructions was the Intel i860 [1]. These instructions were targeted at 3D graphics acceleration. Vectors had a data width of 64 bits and were stored in the floating-point registers. Processing was performed on vectors of eight 8-bit elements, four 16-bit elements, or two 24-bit or 32-bit elements, by a dedicated graphics processing unit.

Subsequently, several other architectures were extended with a SIMD facility to support graphics processing: as an example, the HP Precision Architecture's MAX facility was targeted at speeding up MPEG decompression, achieving the first real-time software-based decoding of MPEG video streams. Unlike the separate i860 facility, the HP MAX facility shared the data path of the main integer pipeline and stored four 8-bit elements of data in the integer (general purpose) register file. Based on this choice, key operations such as vector byte add could be achieved simply by breaking the carry chain between the bytes of the normal 32-bit integer data path, resulting in only minor incremental cost to support this "subword" SIMD facility [2].

Architects chose a different route for the IBM Power Architecture Vector Multimedia Extension facility. The Power Architecture vector facility (also known as AltiVec) added a dedicated SIMD vector register file with 32 128-bit registers, and a rich set of operation primitives and data types ranging from 4-bit pixels, 8-bit, 16-bit, 32-bit integers, to 32-bit (IEEE 754 single-precision) floating point. Execution commonly occurs in four execution pipelines, one dedicated to simple integer operations (add/subtract/logical), one for complex integer operations (multiply, multiply-add), one for floating-point operation, and one for permute (data formatting) operations [3].

Starting with Power 7, a new vector-scalar extension (VSX) integrates the floating point and VMX register files to offer a single 64-entry register file for scalar and vector computation while retaining binary compatibility with legacy applications.

Several application-domain specific SIMD facilities are provided for the Power Architecture, including GameCube's processing of two single-precision floating-point data elements in a single 64-bit double-precision floating-point register, Motorola's SPE, and BlueGene's "Double-Hummer" 2-wide double-precision floating-point elements in paired floating-point registers.

The Intel x86/AMD64 architecture has several distinct SIMD facilities. The MMX facility supports integer data formats in eight 64-bit registers, which "overlay" the traditional FPU register stack. The 3DNow! extensions add single precision floating-point operations. A third SIMD facility (SSE) includes an eight-entry 128-bit register file and also provides scalar floating-point operations to serve as both a new floating-point facility and a SIMD architecture.

The Cell Synergistic Processor Architecture is a new architecture built from the ground up around short parallel vector SIMD processing. A single 128-entry 128-bit register file stores both scalar and vector data, and SIMD data paths provide the computation capabilities for both scalar and SIMD processing. The SPU supports a repertoire of 8-bit, 16-bit, and 32-bit integer operations, and 32-bit and 64-bit floating-point operations [4].

Area Efficiency

As processor designs have become increasingly complex, ISA vector extensions have become more attractive by delivering increased performance for a range of workloads. Unlike traditional ILP extraction in microprocessors which require to fetch, decode, issue, and complete more instructions to increase compute performance, vector extensions increase the compute capability *per instruction*. Thus, while ILP performance techniques require scaling up of all parts of the processor, such as instruction fetch bandwidth, instruction issue bandwidth, global completion tables or reorder buffers, the amount of register file and data cache ports and, hence, register file size, as well as execution units, vector instructions can increase performance by replicating execution units operating in lockstep and ensure adequate data delivery by widening register files and implementing wide data cache and register file ports. In contrast, instruction processing capabilities, such as the number of instructions fetched, decoded, renamed, issued, and completed remains independent of the number of operations completed by a single instruction.

In addition to the attractive area efficiency, vector extensions are comparatively easier to verify than many other performance techniques, as such designs increase the dataflow content of a design by replicating execution units. The dataflow of these execution units can in turn by verified in a modular fashion at the individual dataflow level.

Power and Energy Efficiency

Vector extensions have also become increasingly attractive in the power-constrained design space in which modern microprocessor designs must be implemented. From a power- and energy-efficiency perspective, reduced area consumption directly translates into a reduction in power and energy use.

Beyond the power and energy benefits associated with area reduction, the performance increase offered by exploiting data parallelism with vector extension can also be translated into using more efficient operating points.

By exploiting the increased performance potential offered by vector extensions to operate microprocessors in a more power-efficient regime, power and energy efficiency can be dramatically improved. Because performance $perf = \text{ops/cycle}^* f$, any increase in ops/cycle can be offset by a commensurate reduction in operating frequency. Following the power equation

$$P = CV^2 f$$

(here P is power, C capacitance, V voltage, and f operating frequency), and the observation

$$f \sim\sim V$$

any increase in processing performance can be used as a cubic reduction in power due to the $V^2 f$ factor. On the other hand, the capacitance C will only rise modestly as the number of execution units is increased.

Salapura et al. study energy efficiency of the Blue-Gene system and contains a discussion of power efficiency of SIMD architectures based on power/performance characterization of BlueGene workloads [5].

Software Enablement

Programmers can exploit vector capabilities provided by vector ISA extensions in several different ways.

Compiler Supported Exploitation

Compiler support is the single most important enabler, and yet also the biggest obstacle, to ensure the reach of vector architectures beyond the traditional graphics and high-performance compute kernels.

In this approach, application is written without any vector architecture in mind. The compiler detects parts of the code with data parallelism and generates the code which takes advantage of SIMD capabilities for the target architecture. As advantage, data parallelism in applications can be exploited to achieve higher performance, the application is portable, and the usage of vector unit and vector instructions is transparent to the programmer. This approach requires compiler support, developed libraries, and middleware for the target vector architecture to exploit the vector capabilities.

Usage of Intrinsics

To overcome the limitations of compilers commonly in use today, SIMD instructions are often generated directly using intrinsics, a form of inline assembly. This approach requires the programmer to map the algorithm to the sequence of assembly instructions, but it allows the compiler to perform register allocation and instruction scheduling. When using compiler intrinsics, the programmer gives directions to the compiler on which variables to perform the specified vector operation for the target vector architecture.

As a result, the code is optimized for the particular vector architecture, and it exploits vector capabilities efficiently and achieves high performance. As a disadvantage, the application developer has to be familiar with the vector instructions of the target architecture and to be able to use them efficiently. The resulting code is also typically not portable to any other vector architecture.

To port the code to some other vector architecture, compiler intrinsic for the vector instructions specified in the original code have to be replaced to match the new target vector architecture. Alternatively, the vector intrinsics from the first architecture can be mapped to the equivalent vector operation or sequence of vector operations of the second target architecture. This task can be facilitated by using translation libraries.

To date, widespread adoption of SIMD-based computing has been hampered by low programmer productivity due to the need for low-level programming to exploit the SIMD ISA.

Limitations

While exploiting vector architectures with intrinsics allows more efficient exploitation, the speedup attainable with vector architectures is often limited. Some of these limitations causing a program not to achieve performance increase when using vector processing are listed here.

Sequential Code

The applications with data level parallelism gain the largest performance improvement when using vector unit. Not all applications can benefit from vector processing. For example, in a widely cited study performed at the University of California at Berkeley [6] finite-state machine (FSM)-based algorithms associated with text processing were identified as particularly challenging to leverage the parallelism that modern processors have made available. In these algorithms, a loop iterates over a pointer-based linked list. The current element has to be read in order to determine the memory location of the next memory element.

Data Formatting

Layout of data in memory impacts performance of vector architectures. If data are laid out in the memory in the consecutive memory locations, data can be loaded into vector registers. Otherwise, data need to be formatted until they are in a format suitable for vector processing. This manipulation introduces overhead which diminishes or eliminates performance increase of vector processing. Applications that operate on non-contiguous memory location will not experience the same speedup due to SIMD.

The overhead due to formatting requires additional formatting instructions and increases register pressure in order to keep values in the register file as they are being formatted. Reduced number of registers can in turn reduce the effectiveness of compiler optimizations.

As of today, no processor provides hardware support for loading from or storing to non-contiguous memory locations by using some form of SIMD gather/scatter instructions.

Another data formatting factor which impacts performance of vector architectures is data alignment. An aligned reference means that the desired data reside at an address that is a multiple of the vector register size. Contiguous data are unaligned when they are not physically located at addresses that are multiple of the SIMD data width. For example, vector loads on Power 6 or on Cell PPU/SPU can only load data that start at addresses that start at addresses which are aligned at 16-byte boundaries.

The compiler attempts to position data at aligned addresses, but the data address cannot be always determined at compile time, for example, when address calculation uses a result from previous operations. To ensure that data are aligned, an alignment sequence can be used. This sequence loads all necessary data, and some additional data, and then formats it accordingly to use only data dictated by the application. This introduces overhead and, in turn, reduces the performance advantage of using vector instructions. In the cases there is a large number of misaligned streams, performance speedup will be minimal due to increased instruction bandwidth and register pressure [7].

Recent vector architectures provide hardware support for loading contiguous memory locations that are not aligned at multiple of the vector length of the vector unit. Frequently, such loads are inefficient and have significantly higher latency compared to vector loads of aligned data. Inefficient hardware implementation may simply shift the software overhead to the hardware.

Exemplary ISA Vector Extensions
AltiVec and VMX

AltiVec is a floating-point and integer SIMD instruction-set architecture designed by the IBM, Motorola (the Motorola semiconductor division is now operating independently as Freescale Semiconductor), and Apple between 1996 and 1998.

AltiVec is implemented in a number or PowerPC processors. The first implementation of AltiVec was in Motorola's G4 PowerPC. IBM implements AltiVec in a number of IBM processors, in IBM's PowerPC 970 (also called G5 by Apple) and Power 6 processors. Since Freescale owns a trademark for AltiVec, the system is also referred to as IBM Vector Multimedia Extension VMX by IBM, and Velocity Engine by Apple. AltiVec was the first SIMD instruction set to gain widespread acceptance by programmers. Apple was the primary customer to adopt AltiVec in PowerPC-based Mac PCs.

AltiVec/VMX architects a dedicated set of vector register file with 32 128-bit registers that can represent 16 8-bit signed or unsigned characters, eight 16-bit signed or unsigned shorts, four 32-bit integers, or four 32-bit floating-point single precision variables. AltiVec supports a special RGB "pixel" data type and provides cache-control instructions intended to minimize cache pollution when working on streams of data.

Most AltiVec instructions take three register operands, and there is a small number of four operand instructions. The four operand instructions include merged floating-point and integer multiply-add instructions, which is very important in achieving high floating-point performance, and a vector permute instruction. Another very useful four operand instruction is the permute instruction. It allows to take any byte of either of two input vectors, as specified in the third vector, and place it in the resulting vector. This allows for complex data manipulations in a single instruction and is very useful in a number of applications, ranging from image processing to cryptography.

AltiVec is a standard part of the Power ISA v.2.03 [8] and later specifications.

VMX128 is a modified version of VMX for the Xenon processor (used in Microsoft's XBox 360). It architects 128 registers and adds support for sum-across operations, where all the vector elements in a single vector register are added together to generate a single sum. These are application-specific operations for accelerating 3D graphics and game physics.

The Blue Gene/L and BlueGene/P supercomputers use a double-precision floating-point SIMD unit. This unit uses 128-bit vector registers to contain two double-precision floating-point values, and the scalar and vector registers share the same register file.

MMX

MMX is a SIMD instruction set designed by Intel and implemented in the Pentium processor in 1997.

MMX used 64-bit vector data, which were stored in the floating-point registers. Processing was performed on vectors of eight 8-bit elements, four 16-bit elements, or two 32-bit elements by a dedicated graphics processing unit. The mapping of MMX registers onto floating-point registers made difficult to use floating-point and SIMD data in the same application, and required mode switching. MMX provided only integer operations [9].

AMD designed an extension to the x86 instruction set with the 3DNow! instruction set. 3DNow! added floating-point support to MMX SIMD instructions. This first implementation of 3DNow! instruction set was in the AMD's K6-2 processor in 1998.

SSE

Streaming SIMD Extensions (SSE) is a SIMD instruction set extension of the x86 architecture. SSE was designed by Intel and introduced in 1999. The first SSE implementations were in Intel's Pentium III processors and later in AMD's Athlon XP and Duron processors.

SSE uses a separate set of vector registers and general purpose registers. It has eight 128-bit registers that can represent sixteen 8-bit bytes or characters, eight 16-bit short integers, four 32-bit integers, or four 32-bit floating-point single precision variables, or two 64-bit integers or two 64-bit double-precision floating-point numbers. SSE includes integer and floating-point instructions. Unlike MMX instruction set, SSE does not reuse the floating-point registers but implements separate registers for SIMD. This allows interleaving of SSE and scalar floating-point operations without having to switch between the two modes.

Since the introduction of SSE, SSE has gone through several revisions (SSE, SSE2, SSE3, SSE4). SSE2 was introduced in Pentium 4 processors in 2002. SSE2 adds new instructions for double-precision (64-bit) floating point. SSE3 was introduced in new Pentium 4 chips in 2004. SSE3 adds the capability to work horizontally in a register such as instructions to add and subtract the multiple values stored within a single register. SSE4 was introduced in the Intel Core processor in 2006.

Cell SPE

The Cell Synergistic Processor Architecture (SPE) instruction set is designed by IBM, Sony, and Toshiba. It is implemented in IBM's Cell BE processor for Sony's PlayStation 3 in 2006 and in PowerXCell 8i processor by IBM in 2008.

The Cell SPE architecture implements a single 128-entry 128-bit register file for storing both scalar and vector data and supports both scalar and SIMD processing. The SPE can perform four single precision, or two double-precision floating-point operations, sixteen 8-bit integer, eight 16-bit integer, or four 32-bit integer operations.

Many architectures separate scalar registers and execution units from SIMD registers and execution units. Some applications (for example, as text processing) require frequent data movement between the two sets of registers. The movement of data between vector and general purpose registers is achieved by storing data from one set of registers and loading it in the another registers. This type of transfer incurs a significant delay often wiping out any performance gains that might be gotten from exploiting SIMD data parallelism.

Cell SPE architects a unified register file for storing both short vector and scalar values, and it reuses its execution units for both scalar and vector processing. Scalar values are stored in the leftmost slot of the vector register, the so-called "preferred slot." The unified register file makes data sharing between scalar and SIMD vector operations straightforward and incurs no delay.

VSX

VSX (Vector-Scalar Extension) is a new SIMD instruction set designed by IBM. It is first implemented in IBM's Power 7 processor in 2009 and described in Power ISA v2.06 [10].

VSX implements 64 SIMD registers and includes instructions for double-precision floating point, decimal floating point, and vector execution. VSX implements a unified register file, where floating-point registers and VMX/AltiVec vector registers are mapped to the VSX vector registers. VSX SIMD floating-point operations use 64 128-bit vector registers (32 of them overlayed on top of the VMX registers, and 32 overlaid on top of the scalar floating-point registers) [11].

VSX implements the concept of "preferred slot," as introduced in Cell's SPE, where the leftmost element of a register can be used as both scalar and vector element. The data from the merged vector-scalar floating-point registers are used for scalar and vector floating-point processing, as well as for vector integer processing. Furthermore, VSX introduces double-precision floating-point vector operations to increase parallelism in double-precision floating-point processing.

Bibliography

1. Kohn L, Margulis N (1989) Introducing the Intel i860 64-bit microprocessor. IEEE Micro 9(4):15–30
2. Lee R (1997) Effectiveness of the MAX-2 multimedia extensions for PA-RISC 2.0 processors. HotChips IX, Palo Alto, 24–26 August 1997
3. Diefendorff K, Dubey P, Hochsprung R, Scales H (2000) AltiVec extension to PowerPC accelerates media processing. IEEE Micro 20(2):85–95

4. Gschwind M, Hofstee P, Flachs B, Hopkins M, Watanabe Y, Yamazaki T (2006) Synergistic processing in cell's multicore architecture. IEEE Micro 26(2):10–24
5. Salapura V, Walkup R, Gara A (2006) Exploiting workload parallelism for performance and power optimization in BlueGene. IEEE Micro 26(5):67–81
6. Asanovic K, Bodik R, Catanzaro BC, Gebis JJ, Husbands P, Keutzer K, Patterson DA, Plishker WL, Shalf J, Williams SW, Yelick KA (2006) The landscape of parallel computing research: a view from Berkeley. Technical Report, UCB/EECS-2006-183, EECS Department, University of California, Berkeley
7. Eichenberger A, Wu P, O'Brien K (2004) Vectorization for SIMD architectures with alignment constraints. In: Programming language design and implementation. ACM, New York
8. Power ISA v.2.03, Power.org, 2006-08-29. http://www.power.org/resources/downloads/PowerISA_203.Public.pdf
9. Peleg A, Weiser U (1996) MMX technology extension to the Intel architecture. IEEE Micro 16(4):42–50
10. Power ISA Version 2.06. Power.org. 2009-02-10. http://www.power.org/resources/downloads/PowerISA_V2.06_PUBLIC.pdf
11. Gschwind M, Olsson B (2009) Multi-addressable register file. Patent Application US-20090198966, Aug 2009

Vectorization

▶ FORGE
▶ Parallelization, Automatic
▶ Parafrase

Verification of Parallel Shared-Memory Programs, Owicki-Gries Method of Axiomatic

▶ Owicki-Gries Method of Axiomatic Verification

View from Berkeley

▶ Green Flash: Climate Machine (LBNL)

Virtual Shared Memory

▶ Software Distributed Shared Memory

VLIW Processors

Joseph A. Fisher[1], Paolo Faraboschi[2], Cliff Young[3]
[1]Miami Beach, FL, USA
[2]Hewlett Packard, Sant Cugat del Valles, Spain
[3]D. E. Shaw Research, New York, NY, USA

Definition

VLIW (*Very Long Instruction Word*) is a CPU architectural style that offers large amounts of irregular instruction-level parallelism (ILP) by overlapping the execution of multiple machine-level operations within a single flow of control. In a VLIW, the instruction-level parallelism is visible in the machine-level program and must be exposed and arranged before programs run; this complex job is done using sophisticated compiler technology, with little, if any, help from the programmer. A classic organization of a VLIW instruction consists of many individual operations bundled together into a long instruction word, with one such word issued each processor cycle. VLIW processors are used extensively in high-performance embedded applications, and have found some success as high-performance servers.

Discussion

VLIW architectures offer large amounts of instruction-level parallelism by arranging a parallel execution pattern in advance of the running of the program. The parallelism is carried out among multiple machine-level operations, typically RISC-style, within a single flow of control. In a VLIW, a single program counter is used to determine the instruction stream, and instructions (each of which might itself include multiple operations) are fetched and dispatched one at a time with no rearrangements of their order done in the hardware. The execution arrangement is orchestrated in advance of the running of the program. The hardware simply fetches, decodes, and issues the wide instructions in an in-order fashion, preserving the order that the compiler had previously established.

Unlike vector architectures which require code with a regular form of parallelism where the same operation is applied to parallel data, VLIW parallelism does not rely upon such regular patterns being identified and presented to special execution units. The identification and then choreography of "irregular" parallelism can be extremely complex, and since VLIWs must look like ordinary processors to the user, sophisticated compiler technology is required for a VLIW to be effective. This effect is so strong that VLIW architectures are often co-designed with a matching compiler technology.

The "very long" instructions are what inspired the name VLIW, which provides a good mnemonic device for the key architectural characteristics. There is, however, no requirement that a VLIW actually have "long instructions." Rather, the key defining characteristic is that the single-stream ILP is exposed in the program, and thus planned in advance, rather than organized on-the-fly while the program runs. Operations might instead be statically scheduled to be issued rapid-fire, while several previous operations are still in flight. Such an architecture style, sometimes called *superpipelining*, has the same key characteristics as one with actual long instructions, differing only in implementation details, and can be considered as a form of VLIW where statically scheduled parallel instructions overlap over time.

VLIWs are often juxtaposed with Superscalar architectures, since both have the goal of rearranging the instruction stream to effect a speedup via the parallel execution of simple operations on multiple functional units. The two design styles differ fundamentally in when and by what mechanism the rearrangement is done: whether beforehand at compile time (VLIW), or via specialized hardware operating each cycle while the program runs (Superscalar).

Real implementations have interpreted the "Very" in VLIW in rather different ways, depending on the target domain, the available circuit, and compiler technology. For example, in high performance computing, the Multiflow Trace architecture (a 1984–1990 mini-supercomputer) could issue up to 28 operations per cycle. In the embedded space, the vast majority of VLIW architectures to date issue between 4 and 8 operations per cycle.

Two techniques that combine architectural support with compiler transformations, speculative execution and predicated execution, offer complementary methods to increase instruction-level parallelism in ILP processors. In *speculative execution*, the compiler moves operations above conditional branches that dominate the original location of the operation. Because the branch is conditional, this code motion is a gamble: if the compiler guesses right, the program runs faster; if not, the program will have wasted execution resources. Care must be taken to suppress side effects (e.g., memory stores or exceptions) that would change the semantics of the program if the speculated operation is incorrectly executed. In *predicated execution*, the instruction-set architecture of the machine supports additional input registers to operations that conditionally enable or disable (viz., predicate) the operation. Compiler optimizations can then choose to predicate operations from different control paths and fuse those paths into a single flow of control. Predication can reduce branch-related pipeline penalties and enable further scalar optimizations, but it comes at the cost of a more complicated implementation and potentially increased instruction fetch bandwidth when the operations from all fused paths must be fetched. These two techniques are covered by other articles in this encyclopedia, and will not be discussed in more detail in this article.

VLIW Implementation

A classic VLIW implementation might have instruction encodings that look like the following, from the Multiflow Trace 7/300 (1987–1990) (Fig. 1).

The Trace 7/300 issues seven operations per clock cycle: one branch, two integer operations, two memory operations (either of which can optionally be an integer operation instead), and two floating operations. A machine-level program is a sequence of such instructions, as shown below, with one instruction issued per clock cycle, unless the CPU stalls (Fig. 2).

Classic VLIW execution unit hardware usually consists of several execution functional units, several register banks and paths to memory arranged in a crossbar for unrestricted access to all in any cycle, as shown below. Implementation realities will often make such rich connection not scalable beyond a certain number of fully connected units, because of the non-linear relationship between the number of execution units and the area and complexity of the register file and the bypass (forwarding) logic. Sometimes functional units can be arranged to only be connected to a subset of the register banks – for example, two identical integer ALUs might each address a different register bank. In this case, the partitioned-register architecture is referred to as a *clustered VLIW* – successfully dealing with clustered register banks is a compiler research topic of its own.

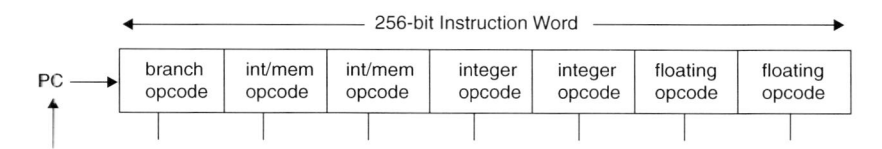

VLIW Processors. Fig. 1 A possible encoding of a 256-bit wide VLIW instruction composed of 7 operations

VLIW Processors. Fig. 2 A machine-level program with one instruction issued per clock cycle, unless the CPU stalls

The two figures below show the block diagrams of (unclustered and clustered) VLIW architectures (Fig. 3).

Benefits of VLIW

The VLIW design style exists to provide effective high performance, with little if any programmer intervention, and without great hardware cost. A VLIW usually requires less hardware than other ILP approaches (such as superscalar or dataflow) to high performance, since the choreography of parallelism is done in advance and there is no need for hardware to rearrange the instruction execution sequence at run time.

The absence of rearrangement hardware, running every cycle, has broad implications for performance, cost, and power:

- A faster clock is possible (since there is less to do each cycle).
- There is less hardware, thus a lower silicon cost.

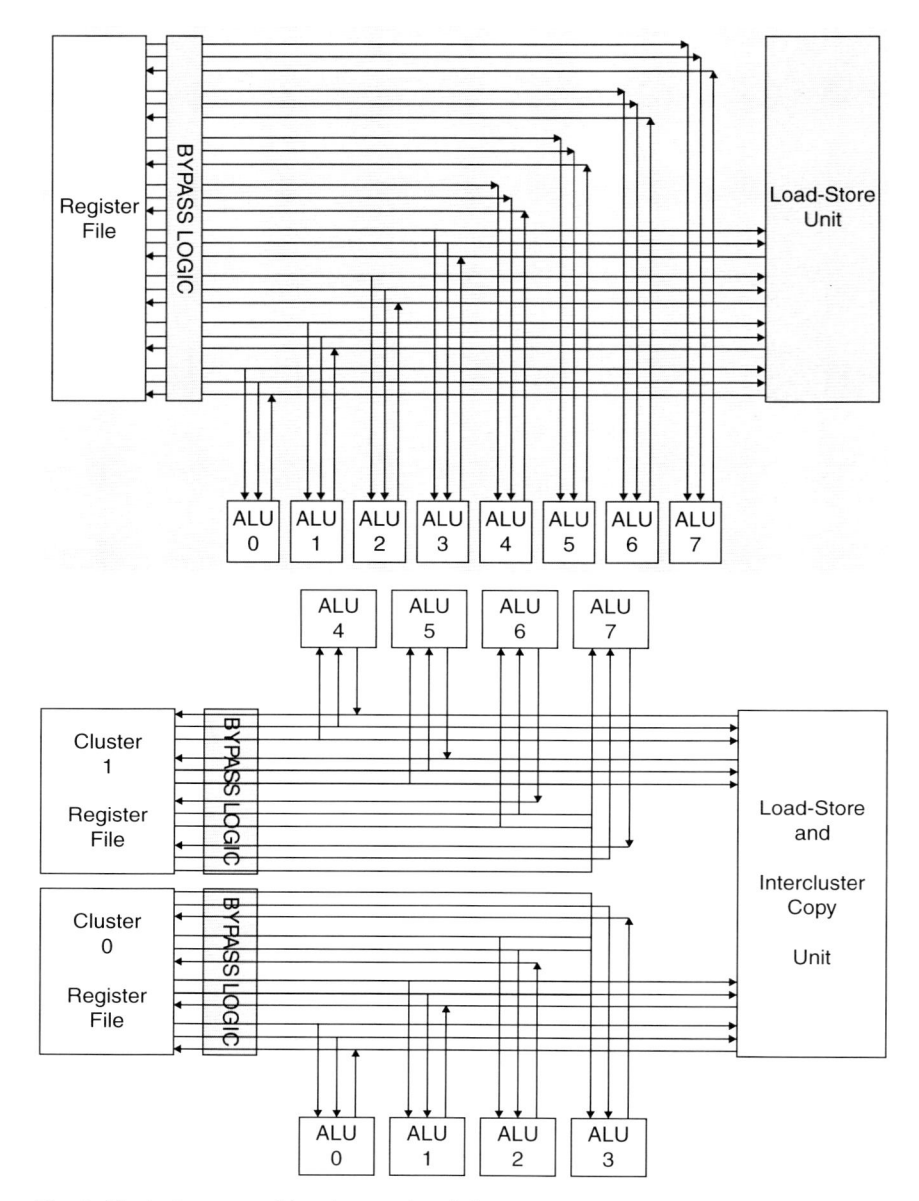

VLIW Processors. Fig. 3 Block diagrams of (unclustered and clustered) VLIW architecture

- Less power is used.
- Far more ILP is practical, since the additional hardware needed to rearrange computations tends to grow exponentially with the amount of ILP available.

A result of this is that ILP in the range of 4–8 operations issued per cycle is common in VLIWs. The Multiflow Trace 28/300 offered 28 operations issued per cycle, and for some heavily computational code was able to sustain a large fraction of complete utilization.

These advantages exist primarily in comparison to superscalar architectures, the closest equivalent form of parallelism. When compared to other forms of parallelism, both VLIW and superscalar architectures have the advantage that the computing paradigm does not change, that is, parallel processes and regular structures do not have to be identified in the code. To the programmer, both are much like "normal" scalar processors.

Object-Code Compatibility

The greatest shortcoming in VLIW's use as "ordinary" computers lies in its defining characteristic. Old programs will not run correctly on new machines where either the set of hardware resources or the number of cycles to perform an operation (i.e., its *latency*) has changed vs. what the compiler assumed when it generated the original object code. The exact computation to be carried out, and the machine on which to execute it, is visible in a VLIW binary program. Thus, a new implementation of a VLIW architecture is not likely to be object-code compatible with an old one, which represents a major flaw in VLIW's use as a general-purpose computer. One consequence of this shortcoming is that VLIWs have found far greater success in the embedded computing world, where object-code compatibility is far less of a factor than on general purpose computers such as desktops or servers.

If an architecture is not changed dramatically, there are several techniques that can help solve this problem, individually or in combination:

- If the new architecture is in some sense a superset of the old one, then the system can be designed to allow the old programs to run on a limited portion of the hardware, corresponding to the old architecture. Eventually, the code may be recompiled to get greater performance on the new architecture. This upward compatibility was used by Multiflow, where the system that issued 14 operations at a time could run code compiled for the system that issued 7. It is also used, in a different manner, in the Intel IA-64 where the compiler generates code assuming a superset of the resources are available, and each implementation may choose to only execute some operations in parallel.
- If the incompatibility results largely from changed latencies, then programs can carry information about their assumptions, and mode switches built into the CPU can enforce the correct timings (delaying any instruction issue when a component operation cannot be guaranteed to have finished).
- The system can statically change old programs into new ones that follow the new architectural assumptions at the time the program is loaded.
- The system can dynamically change old programs into new ones that follow the new architectural assumptions while the program is running. This only makes sense if the translations can be cached and reused repeatedly. For example, the x86-compatible Transmeta processors (2000–2005) used a similar dynamic binary translation technology to generate VLIW instructions from a stream of x86 instructions on the fly.

Other Perceived Disadvantages of VLIW

Dynamic Code Behavior

Often compilers cannot predict the behavior of a program, most importantly in branch direction and in memory latency. A VLIW, having had its execution laid out in advance, can't adjust to these dynamic changes.

- To ameliorate the problem of unpredictable branch directions, a compiler uses static branch prediction to assume that the more likely branch will be taken, and inserts code to correct the program behavior when this is wrong. The development of these techniques (Trace Scheduling was the first) greatly increased the potential for ILP in ordinary programs. Short, hard-to-predict branches can also be eliminated through various forms of predication (also known as conditional, or guarded, execution).
- To ameliorate the problem of unpredictable memory latency, VLIWs often include decoupled register fetch mechanisms, and other dynamic features.

The designers of VLIW architectures have been careful to regard the VLIW design style not as a dogma, but rather as a design principle, to guide decisions but not mandate them. When dynamic features have been desirable, designers have felt free to use them. For example, the use of register scoreboarding reduces code size by removing the need for no-op operations. Dynamic branch prediction reduces the misprediction penalty by prefetching instructions among the most likely path. Stall-on-use memory techniques help ameliorate the L1 cache miss penalty when the compiler can schedule the consumer of a memory operation later than the shortest latency without impacting performance.

Code Size

A VLIW can offer a great deal of parallelism, but most sections of code will only use a portion of what is offered. Code outside the dense inner loops will often use only a very small part of what is offered. While performance improvements in such sections of code are very valuable, and VLIWs tend to do comparatively well there, most instructions still contain only a few operations to be carried out. That leaves many fields of the long instruction word blank, or filled with no-ops. Left untreated, this would cause programs to occupy an undesirably large amount of memory.

Every modern VLIW, from the 1980s forward, has dealt with this problem in some way. Sophisticated code compression techniques have been developed that bring a VLIW's code size down to the size of uncompressed RISC programs. Compression appears at every level of the instruction memory hierarchy, though typically the greatest degree of decompression is done as the instruction cache is filled.

Compiler Sophistication and Compile Time

The job of arranging a VLIW's parallelism, which falls to the compiler, is difficult to engineer and time-consuming to run. While this is true, it is a fallacy to think of these effects as an undesirable quality of the VLIW design style, especially when that is compared to superscalars. The actual scheduling phase of a VLIW compiler, while complex, is fairly well understood and need not take a lot of compile time.

The hard part of the compiling process is doing the code rearrangements to expose the parallelism in the first place, including the branch prediction mentioned above. All of this is a function of the available instruction-level parallelism, not of the style of architecture that exploits it. The reason VLIW architectures require "heroic compilers" is that they offer so much ILP. If it were practical to build a superscalar architecture with that much ILP, it would require an equivalently heroic compiler.

Dealing with Exceptions

Any system that does as much rearranging of a program as a VLIW does must deal with preserving the original program semantics in the face of exceptions. Even worse, rearranging programs by speculating the execution of an instruction before a controlling branch may cause excepting operations to execute, when they would not have executed at all in the original program's sequential order. A vast body of technology, too much to give justice to here, has grown to address this problem, including the concepts of "dismissible loads" and "delayed exceptions."

Important VLIW Systems

Startup Computer Companies in the 1980s

The first commercial VLIW systems were small supercomputers:

- The Trace 7/200, and its successors, introduced in 1987 by the startup Multiflow Computer
- The Cydra-5, introduced in 1987 by the startup Cydrome

About 120 Multiflow Traces were sold, most into mechanical, chemical, and electronic simulation environments. Despite Multiflow's initial success, neither company survived beyond 1990.

First VLIW Microprocessor

After 9 years of design, the Philips Life-1 (later renamed the TriMedia) was introduced in 1996, and was the first commercially successful VLIW Microprocessor. Eventually, the division of Philips that produced the TriMedia became the private company NXP Semiconductors, which still designs and builds VLIW microprocessors, the latest being the PNX1005, used in digital TVs and other digital audio and video products, as well as in cellular handsets and other applications.

Other Modern VLIW Microprocessors

Today's most important VLIW microprocessors, and their main uses, include:

- The STMicroelectronics ST231 (used extensively in digital video and printing and scanning)
- The Texas Instruments C6x family (used extensively in cellular basestations and smartphones, and in-home entertainment)
- The Fujitsu FR-V (used in digital cameras)

Although companies do not generally release volumes for individual parts, ST has reported that over 70 million ST231 cores were shipped by April, 2009, and Texas Instruments report that over 80% of all cellular base stations contain VLIW processors. VLIW processors have been used successfully in products such as hearing aids, graphics boards, and network communications devices.

There are also numerous "Fabless" (Intellectual-Property-Based) VLIW Designs commercially available from CEVA, Silicon Hive, Tensilica, and others. These processors are generally found as the high-performance core or cores in a larger system-on-a-chip.

VLIW in Processors for General Purpose Use

During the decade of the 1990s, two prominent efforts were made to use VLIW in desktops, notebooks, and servers.

- Transmeta used a VLIW processor as the underlying engine to run an emulator of the Intel x86. However, Intel and AMD's strength in the marketplace, and the complexity of setting up a high-volume manufacturing operation was too much of a barrier for the excellent cost/performance characteristics of this product to overcome.
- Intel's Itanium processor family borrows many characteristics from VLIWs, while adding many new complex features of its own. Intel refers to the design style of that family as "EPIC" (explicitly parallel instruction computing). The Itanium borrows many design artifacts from the Cydra-5, and founders of both Cydrome and Multiflow were involved in the initial design at HP Labs. While the Itanium is the fourth most popular server architecture today, it has not met industry projections for its volume, as its lack of compatibility and its ineffective early implementations have greatly limited its growth.

VLIW was Motivated by Compiler Techniques

The Trace Scheduling compiler algorithm was put forward by Joseph Fisher [1] at the Courant Institute of New York University in 1979. Trace scheduling was designed to solve the "horizontal microcode compaction problem" by eliminating the restriction that overlapping operations must originate from the same basic block of straight-line code. No practical algorithm to do so had been put forward before that. The basic idea in trace scheduling has two steps. First, select code originating in a large region (typically many basic blocks). Second, compact operations from the entire region as if it were one big basic block (which often contains a lot of ILP), possibly adding extra operations to maintain the semantics of the program, despite the violence done to the flow of control.

Given that Trace Scheduling made far more ILP available, Fisher predicted that general-purpose systems like today's VLIWs made sense, coining the term Instruction-level Parallelism for the kind of parallel processing [2]. While at Yale University, Fisher then defined and named the VLIW design style in 1981, publishing his thoughts in 1983 [3]. By January of 1987, Multiflow Computer, a company started by Fisher and members of his Yale University group, delivered high-performance commercial VLIWs to customers.

During that same period, software pipelining began to mature. Software pipelining is a compiler technique (originally, it was sometimes done by hand) to speed up inner loops. It does this by rearranging the loop so that operations from multiple iterations are computed within the same revised inner loop. Code is placed before (prologue) and after (epilogue) the new loop to preserve the program semantics, by starting the first iteration(s) and completing the last one(s).

Software pipelining was done by hand on early computers containing some ILP, and was carried out via simple pattern matching by the Fortran compiler for the CDC-6600 as early as the 1960s. By the early 1980s, the Floating Point Systems Fortran compiler could software pipeline a loop consisting of a single basic block [4, 5]. In 1981, Bob Rau [6] described a more scientific version of software pipelining, using the term "Modulo Scheduling." His work helped lead to an early interest in VLIWs, and Rau went on to start Cydrome, which, along with Multiflow, pioneered VLIWs.

Modulo Scheduling researchers all favored "rotating registers," as found in the FPS systems. Rotating registers change their addresses to match the code iterations in modulo scheduled loop. These have been shown to not be necessary, and whether they are beneficial is still controversial. They are found in the Itanium and (in a more restricted form) in the TI C6x.

Precursors of VLIWs

During the 1960s and 1970s, three different architectural trends led the way toward VLIWs.

1. *High-performance general-purpose scientific computers.* These were the supercomputers of their day. The best examples are the CDC-6600 and the IBM 360/91, which was preceded by the IBM research processor Stretch. They derived ILP by performing several arithmetic operations simultaneously, in a manner arranged by the hardware (like today's

superscalars). Although the hardware could identify independent operations and schedule their issuance, practitioners quickly realized that a compiler could place operations close enough to each other in the machine-level program that the hardware, with its limited visibility, could overlap them more effectively. Because these systems typically overlapped only 2 or 3 operations, the compiler's rearrangement only needed to span short sections of straight-line code in the source program.

These systems were general-purpose ILP CPUs. Primitive software pipelining and basic block instruction scheduling both originated in this environment. Researchers working on these systems, convinced by flawed experiments that available ILP was limited to a factor of 2 or 3 times speedup, never pushed the superscalar aspects of their technology farther.

2. *Attached signal processors, or "array processors."* In the 1970s, and perhaps earlier, engineers and scientists built hardware that resembled VLIW, called attached signal processors, or "array processors." The most famous of these were the Floating Point Systems AP-120b (introduced in 1975) and FPS-164 (introduced in 1980), though there were many others, offered by Numerix, Mercury, CDC and Texas Instruments, among others. Although they evoke today's VLIWs, they were typically built to compute a particular inner loop very effectively, and were thus very idiosyncratic, and their parallelism was almost always specified by hand, rather than via compiling. Circuits are still built in this style, and are called DSPs (Digital Signal Processors).

3. *Horizontal microcode.* Microcode is an RISC-like level of code, sometimes found hard wired in a CPU to emulate the true, more complex, machine-level architecture. Since the emulator is a single program, running all the time, it was straightforward to build "horizontal microcode," in which several of the pieces of hardware run in parallel. This again resembles the hardware structure of VLIW.

In the latter two domains, compiling was regarded as desirable, but only as an afterthought. It was never very effective, but research into compiling in those domains led to the compiler breakthroughs that enabled VLIW.

Related Entries

▶Cydra 5
▶Dependence Analysis
▶Instruction-Level Parallelism
▶Modulo Scheduling and Loop Pipelining
▶Multiflow Computer
▶Speculation
▶Trace Scheduling

Bibliography

1. Fisher JA (1979) The optimization of horizontal microcode within and beyond basic blocks: an application of processor scheduling with resources. Ph.D. dissertation, Technical Report COO-3077-161. Courant Mathematics and Computing Laboratory, New York University, New York
2. Fisher JA (1981) Trace scheduling: a technique for global microcode compaction. IEEE T Comput 30(7):478–490
3. Fisher JA (1983) Very long instruction word architectures and the ELI-512. In: Proceedings of the 10th annual international symposium on computer architecture, Stockholm, Sweden, 13–17 June 1983, pp 140–150
4. Charlesworth A (1981) An approach to scientific array processing: the architectural design of the AP-120b/FPS-164 family. IEEE Comput 14(3):18–27
5. Touzeau RF (1984) A FORTRAN compiler for the FPS-164 scientific computer. In: Proceedings of ACM SIGPLAN' 84 symposium on compiler construction, Montreal, pp 48–57
6. Rau BR, Glaeser CD (198) Some scheduling techniques and an easily schedulable horizontal architecture for high performance scientific computing. In: Proceedings of the 14th annual microprogramming workshop, IEEE Press, Piscataway, pp 183–197
7. Fisher JA, Faraboschi P, Young C (2005) Embedded computing – a VLIW approach to architecture, compiler, and tools. Morgan Kaufmann, San Francisco

VLSI Algorithmics

▶VLSI Computation

VLSI Computation

FRANCO P. PREPARATA
Brown University, Providence, RI, USA

Synonyms

Application-specific integrated circuits; VLSI algorithmics

Definition

VLSI Computation (computation within the Very-Large-Scale-Integrated technology) concerns the analysis of the computations realized by large integrated networks, whereby the traditional distinction between networks and computations disappears (each network is "dedicated" to the execution of a particular algorithm). Specific algorithms realized by such circuits are evaluated in terms of their efficient use of the integrated technology.

Discussion

Historical Background

Switching networks, the basic constituents of digital systems, were traditionally realized by interconnecting discrete electrical components, such as transistors, resistors, capacitors, etc., by means of conducting wires.

Transistors, the fundamental switching elements, were initially realized by appropriately modifying ("doping") different portions of the surface of a piece of semiconductor material. A key innovation occurred in the late 1950s of the past century, when it was realized that conducting wires could also be implemented on the same surface, either by deposition of metal or by modification of the semiconductor. The consequence was that several distinct transistors could be fabricated on the *same* piece of material, along with appropriate interconnecting wires. This discovery ushered in the era of integrated circuits, initially as interconnections of a few gates, called *micrologics*. The technology progressed rapidly by reducing the dimensions of the individual transistor and therefore increasing the number of transistors realizable within a fixed area of material. In those days (1965) *Moore's law* was formulated, the empirical observation that the number of transistors that could be placed on an individual integrated circuit would double approximately every two years.

In a few years it was possible to bring to market extremely simple processors, entirely realized on a single plate of semiconductor (the *chip*) and acting on operands of very few bits (4 or 8). The progression, however, was extremely rapid: by the late 1970s, the computer science and engineering community became fully aware of a mature technology of large-scale integrated circuits, and for the theoretical component of this community a new model of computation emerged: the discipline of VLSI computation was therefore established within the scope of computer science research and became the theoretical underpinning of massive parallel computation. Although today parallel computation research pursues different directions, VLSI computation remains a rich theoretical acquisition.

A Model of VLSI Computation

A paramount theoretical issue is the formulation of the computation model to be adopted. The computation model defines the framework within which performance is to be evaluated; it defines the nature of the usable resources and their respective costs. As is typical of all models, we expect the VLSI model to be reasonably simple to facilitate mathematical treatment, but sufficiently faithful to the physical reality to provide an adequate level of confidence to predictions based on the model. This goal calls here for a review, albeit extremely sketchy, of the technology.

The fundamental element of a widely used, but by no means exclusive, VLSI technology is the Metal-Oxide-Semiconductor (MOS) transistor (other technologies can be treated analogously). Its geometry is illustrated in Fig. 1. In Fig. 1a a thin silicon wafer is selectively doped, by diffusion of appropriate atoms, into a p-type *substrate* and two n-type electrodes called *source* and *drain*, separated by a gap called *channel*. On top of this gap a third electrode, called *gate*, is created by depositing an (insulating) oxide layer and a conducting layer on top of it. A voltage applied to the gate creates a conducting channel between source and drain. The control exerted by the gate is the hallmark of the transistor.

Revealing is the top view of the device (Fig. 1b). Here the transistor may be viewed simply as a (horizontal) strip comprising source and drain "crossed" by a (vertical) strip containing the gate. Similarly, a wire joining different electrodes appears as a strip of conducting material on the surface of the chip. The conclusion is that a VLSI circuit is described by the geometry of an interconnection of strips, representing devices and wires.

We can now elucidate the abstraction process leading from technology to model. The model assumptions can be subdivided into three groups:

1. Network layout on the semiconductor chip.

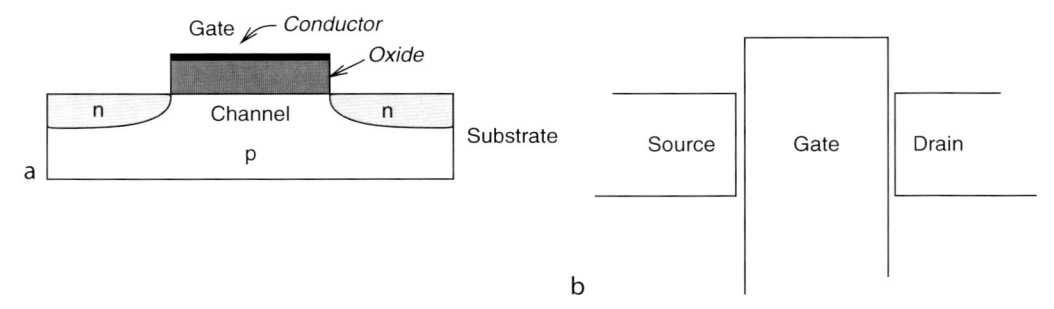

VLSI Computation. Fig. 1 Geometry of the MOS transistor

The physical layout of a VLSI circuit must be as compact as possible. However, manufacturing must guarantee the integrity of the circuit, that is, the layout must comply with *design rules* for transistors and wires (to avoid accidental interruption a wire cannot be too narrow, to avoid shorts two wires cannot be laid out too close to each other). Therefore, the design rules for the layout strips mainly concern widths and separations, and are expressed in terms of a technology-independent parameter λ called *feature size*, typically expressing the sum of the width of a wire and its separation from adjacent layout items (The decrease of λ is a measure of technological progress: in fact λ has decreased by nearly two orders of magnitude since the late 1970s). Another important parameter is the number ν of usable layers, a parameter that over the years has grown appreciably over its original value (of just 2). However, VLSI technology is essentially two-dimensional. The fundamental reason, beside ease of manufacturing, is heat dissipation: as λ decreases, higher clock speed and shorter transistor switching times are attainable. This results in higher production of heat, which must be dissipated in a medium in contact with the chip surface.

The area of an integrated circuit is obviously the sum of the areas of its transistors, its wires, and its input/output pads. We shall later see the dominant role of wire area in fast circuits.

2. Timing of signal transmission from device to device.

The elementary action involved in timing considerations is the switching of a transistor and the propagation of its output signal to another transistor. In a simplified view, this action is the cascade of switching time and propagation time. The latter, due to the finiteness of the speed of light, clearly grows with the length of the wire. However, in compact circuits switching time dominates propagation time, and this circumstantial evidence was used originally to axiomatize that the time of an elementary action is constant (independent of the wire layout length).

3. Input/output protocols.

To be honest with respect to the use of area, each input is assumed to be read just *once* (denoted *time-determinate*) and in just *one pad* (denoted *place-determinate*), so that it remains stored within the chip. In addition, each input and output is uniquely identified by its time of use and by its place of occurrence. This provision excludes trivial algorithms, where one could claim sorting just by the order in which randomly permuted inputs are read out as outputs.

We can therefore summarize the model discussed above as follows:

- VLSI networks are synchronous boolean machines with the following features, presented here as the axioms of the model:
  - Axiom 1. Wires have minimum width λ, transistors have minimum area $C_T \lambda^2$, I/O pads have minimum area $C_P \lambda^2$ (C_T, C_P are technological parameters).
  - Axiom 2. The time of an elementary action is constant (synchronicity).
  - Axiom 3. Inputs are read once and in one place. Input/outputs are time- and place-determinate.

For its simplicity, this VLSI model belongs to the best computer science tradition of machine models. Its salient features dispense with details and aim to capture the essentials of the technology. As we shall discuss later, its soft spot is the timing assumption (Point 2 above).

Area-Time Trade-offs

The primary concern of the design of algorithms is to establish bounds on the resources used by a computational task. In the context of VLSI the crucial resources are computation time (number of time units) and circuit size (area). Here, as in any other area of algorithmic research, we try to find intrinsic relationships between resources (in the form of lower bounds), and then design algorithms that possibly achieve these bounds.

The relation between time and area is based on the evaluation of the flow of information required for the correct execution of a computation. Specifically, we wish to identify sections (lines) in the chip through which a given flow of information is required by the computation. Two types of sections can be identified:

1. Input/output boundary
2. Internal sections

The boundary trivially defines its required flow, as information proportional to the problem size, conventionally n. More subtle is the analysis of the internal flow.

Assume, for simplicity, that the input bits are stored uniformly within the two-dimensional chip domain. A *balanced bisection* is a curve that divides the domain, and correspondingly the input set, into two parts of about the same size. Assume also that a computational argument shows that I bits must be exchanged through the bisection to correctly complete the computation. Then, if d is the length of the bisection, the number w of wires crossing the bisection satisfies $w \leq vd/\lambda$; in clocked operation, at least I/w clock cycles (time units) are required. All we need is to relate length d to the chip area A. Simple arguments show that $A \geq d^2/2$, so that, denoting T the number of time units, we conclude

$$T \geq \frac{I\lambda}{v\sqrt{2A}} \quad \text{or} \quad AT^2 \geq cI^2$$

for some technological constant c. This important relationship exhibits a trade-off between area and time: it gives formal substance to the intuitive expectation that, for a given problem, faster VLSI circuits have larger size.

As we shall see in the next section, several important problems are covered by this analysis.

It is worth mentioning that, according to the preceding analysis, as we increase T the area A correspondingly decreases. There are problems, like the sorting of very long keys, where the area may become too small to store the data, that is, it becomes *saturated*. When saturated information is the mechanism limiting performance, optimal circuits have an area growing with $1/T$ rather than $1/T^2$.

Finally, the outlined bisection-width analysis applies to a class of computations (a large and significant one) where the internal information flow depends upon the entire input set. However, there are other significant problems that are not covered by this rubric. These are the computations where subsets of the output variables depend upon subsets of the input variables, so that, for any such pair of (input,output) subsets, no variable can be output before all variables of the corresponding input set have been stored in the network. Moreover, the boolean circuit computing the output variables has depth at least logarithmic in the size of ts input set. In other words, each input must remain stored for some time within the chip, that is, the flow of information is being slowed down. This behavior, dubbed *computational friction*, is characterized as the following area-time trade-off:

$$\frac{AT}{\log A} \geq c''I.$$

VLSI Architectures and Algorithms

The preceding section outlines, in a very succinct form, the intrinsic limitations placed by the VLSI technology on computations realized by networks. A crucial feature of VLSI computation is the potential of being able to select, for any given application, the targeted computation time and to attempt to design a network realizing it. So, at one end of the spectrum we have sequential circuits, and the other the fastest parallelizations.

The objective of this section is to consider classes of important computations, to describe their VLSI implementations, and to compare their performance with the lower-bounds developed in the previous section.

Preliminarily, we must complete the definition of VLSI machine model with the notions of "architecture" and "algorithm."

1. Architecture
   - An *architecture* is a graph $G = (V, E)$, whose nodes V are modules and whose edges E are (bundles of) wires.
   - The *diameter* of an architecture is the maximum of the lengths of the shortest path between any two of its modules. (A large diameter is $\Theta(\sqrt{(A)})$, a small diameter is $\Theta(\log A)$.)
   - A *module* is the elementary component of an architecture. It could be as simple as a transistor or as complex as a microprocessor. The structure of the module is assumed independent of the size of the network.
   - Operation is *synchronous*, that is, clocked.
2. Algorithm
   - $X = \{x_1, \ldots, x_n\}$ are *variables* and $K = \{k_1, \ldots, k_m\}$ are *constants*.
   - A *parallel step* σ is a collection of assignments
   $$\sigma = \{x_i \leftarrow f_j(X \cup K) | i = 1 \ldots n, f_j \in \mathcal{F}\}$$
   where $\mathcal{F}$ is a set of functions for which hardware is duly provided in the network. The semantics is that all assignments in set σ are simultaneously executed.
   - A *parallel computation* is a time sequence
   $$\sigma_1 \sigma_2 \ldots \sigma_p$$
   - A *parallel algorithm* is a procedure executed as a parallel computation.

A most significant achievement of research in VLSI computation has been the identification of a few fundamental interconnections (networks) and of their natural association with classes of computations. Most interesting architectures results from the composition of such interconnections. Even more revealing is the identification of classes of computations matched to each of such architectures. Such classes are unified not by superficial similarity of applications, but by the communication patterns, or data exchanges, implied by their algorithms. Such fundamental interconnections are discussed next.

Meshes

Meshes are the simplest architectures. Although higher-dimensional constructions are conceivable, dimensions 1 (array), 2 (grids or meshes, for short), and 3 (three-dimensional grids) have practical value. The array is a chain of modules, where each module communicates, typically, with its adjacent modules. The mesh is a network whose modules are conventionally placed at the vertices of a regular tiling (triangular, square, etc.) of the plane. The most natural mesh, and the one discussed hereafter, is the rectangular $n \times m$ planar grid, whose modules are placed at points of integer coordinates and each communicates with its four adjacent modules (see Fig. 2a).

A typical use of meshes is as *systolic networks*. The qualifier "systolic" suggests that data is fed to the network in waves to be processed in pipeline fashion. A useful illustration is provided by matrix multiplication, that is, the computation $C = AB$ (A, B, and C are square matrices of dimension n). The network is an $n \times n$ square mesh, whose simple modules (inner-product modules, see Fig. 2b) keep stored one operand z (initialized to 0), receive inputs x and y from their upstream neighbors, perform the update $z \leftarrow z + x \cdot y$, and supply the updated z to their downstream neighbors. Inputs enter the network as waves from the left (A) and from the top (B): these waves, however, are not the conventional rows and columns, but cross-diagonals, that is, vectors whose components have identical sums of their two indices. The product appears stored in the mesh at the completion of the systolic flow. The network has $O(n^2)$ area and the computation is completed in n steps, so that $AT^2 = O(n^4)$. Since the corresponding area-time lower-bound is $\Omega(n^4)$, this systolic network provides an optimal implementation. Note that the diameter of this network is $O(\sqrt{N})$, where N is the number of its modules.

Systolic implementations have been proposed for a variety of other problems, such as matrix-vector multiplication, open convolution, integer multiplication, solution of lower-triangular linear systems, etc. The

VLSI Computation. Fig. 2 (**a**) A two-dimensional mesh; (**b**) inner-product module

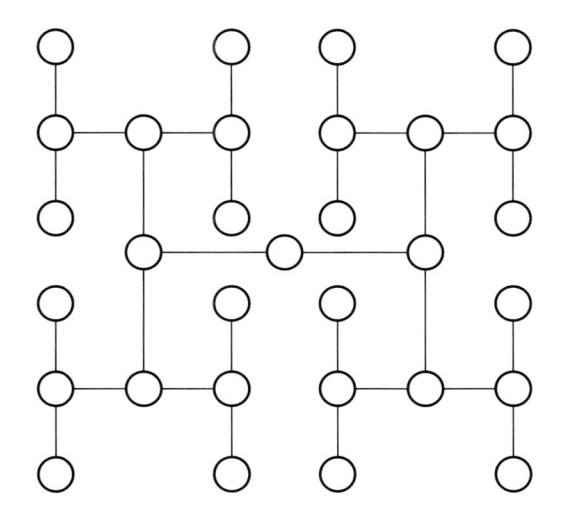

VLSI Computation. Fig. 3 The H-tree layout of a 16-leaf tree network

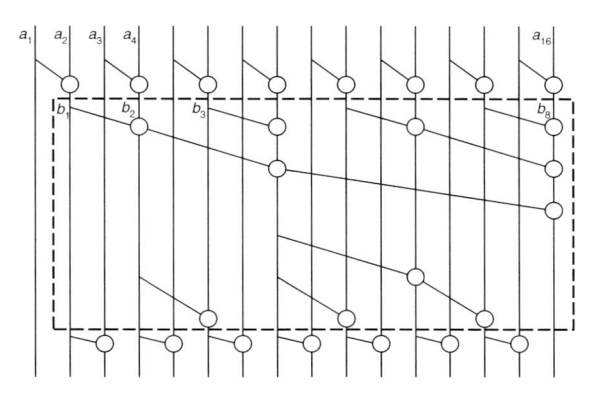

VLSI Computation. Fig. 4 A circuit for prefix computation

resulting algorithms are, in general, simple and elegant; however, none of these appears to be area-time optimal.

We shall return to meshes as simulators of other more complex architectures.

Tree-Based Networks

The basic interconnection is represented by a rooted full binary tree. The standard planar layout of a tree with $n = 2^j$ leaves for j even has the shape of a square of side-length L_j and is denoted H-tree by its typical appearance (see Fig. 3). Denoting L_0 the side-length of a module, we have the simple recurrence $L_j = 2L_{j-2} + L_0$, yielding $L_j = L_0 2^{j/2}$, that is $A = O(n)$; as is intuitive, a bound of the same order is achievable by deploying larger modules as we proceed from the leaves to the root. To be noted is that a tree network has small (logarithmic) diameter.

An important application of tree networks is the implementation of semigroup prefix computations, frequently referred to as "scans." The operations are, typically, AND, OR, MAX, MIN, ADD, etc., generically denoted here as "$*$". We are given a sequence $a_1, a_2, \ldots, a_n$ and wish to compute the prefixes $a_1, a_1 * a_2, a_1 * a_2 * a_3, \ldots, a_1 * a_2 * \ldots * a_n$ (n a power of 2, for simplicity) Sequentially, this is trivially doable in time $O(n)$ with constant area. What is the performance of a fastest (logarithmic time) implementation? Figure 4 supplies the answer: The recursive box is a prefix computer for the sequence $b_1, b_2, \ldots, b_{n/2}$ where $b_i = a_{2i-1} * a_{2i}$. We recognize that the explicit part of the diagram consists of the leafward two levels of two binary trees traversed in opposite directions (in addition, the bottom one misses its leftmost edge), so that we conclude that prefixes can be computed by two back-to-back tree networks. Such network can be realized with the previously described H-tree layout, and we reach the conclusion that the network area is $O(n)$ and the number of steps is $O(\log n)$. Lower-bound considerations show that prefix computations are governed by

$$\frac{AT}{\log A} = \Omega(n)$$

Since $AT/\log A = O(n \log n / \log n) = O(n)$, the described implementation is area-time optimal. (Note that the sequential implementation is also optimal.)

Prefix computations include binary addition, comparison-exchange, sorting of long keys, etc.

Hypercubic Networks

A hypercubic network is generated by an iterative construction technique called *dimensional duplication*, where the basic network is a single module H_0 (indexed by the integer 0) and H_j is obtained by duplicating H_{j-1} and connecting pairs of homologous modules indexed $(i, 2^{j-1} + i)$ for $i = 0, \ldots, 2^{j-1} - 1$. Obviously, H_j is a j-dimensional hypercube, and each of its modules is connected to j other modules, that is, the module type depends on the parameter j. This feature violates an assumption of the model (modules independent of network size), so that the hypercube cannot be viewed as a VLSI architecture in the narrow sense.

Module j stores operand $T[j]$ and is provided with arithmetic capabilities. Hypercubic networks support the *recursive combination* paradigm, executed by the call ALGORITHM$(0, 2^m - 1)$ of the following procedure:

ALGORITHM$(l, l + 2^h - 1)$
if $(h > 1)$ **then**
    ALGORITHM$(l, l + 2^{h-1} - 1)$,
    ALGORITHM$(l + 2^{h-1}, l + 2^h - 1)$
    foreach $l \leq j \leq l + 2^{h-1} - 1$
        pardo $(T[j], T[j + 2^{h-1}]) \leftarrow$ OPER$(T[j], T[j + 2^{h-1}])$

Specialization of the operation OPER yields algorithms for such diverse applications as merging, Fast-Fourier-Transform, convolution, permutations, integer multiplication, etc. The paradigm handles one hypercube dimension at a time (parameter h) in a fixed order, and is also referred to as "normal" and "ASCEND-DESCEND."

Due to its nonstandard modules the hypercube does not lend itself to scalable VLSI layouts, because for very large size n the outdegree of the modules may be unrealizable. However, there exist effective emulators of the hypercube which have standard VLSI layouts. Significantly, since the computations considered obey the bound $AT^2 = \Omega(n^2)$, these emulators are found to be area-time optimal. Two of these emulators, the linear array and the mesh, have large diameters (respectively, $O(n)$ and $O(\sqrt{n})$); two more emulators, the shuffle-exchange and the cube-connected cycles, have $O(\log n)$ diameter. The diameter, of course, determines the computation time.

Composite Architectures

The previous basic architectures have different diameters and are therefore targeted to different computation times. Interestingly enough, these architectures can be combined in a variety of ways, both to solve different classes of problems and to achieve a full range of computation times. The typical composite structure is a network of modules that are themselves complex VLSI architectures.

To illustrate this philosophy we consider an area-time optimal emulator of the hypercube. We begin with the emulation of normal algorithms by means of a linear array. The key activity to be emulated is

foreach $(0 \leq j \leq 2^{h-1} - 1)$
    pardo $(T[j], T[j + 2^{h-1}]) \leftarrow$ OPER$(T[j], T[j + 2^{h-1}])$

The operands are stored in the array $T[0, 2^h - 1]$. The above operation can be executed in the array if operands $T[j]$ and $T[j + 2^{h-1}]$ are brought to reside in adjacent modules. This is achieved by the following algorithm executed on the array:

for $s = 0$ **to** $2^{h-1} - 1$
    foreach $0 \leq i \leq s$
        $U \leftarrow 2^{h-1} - 1 - s$
        pardo $(T[U + 2i], T[U + 2i + 1])$
            $\leftarrow$ EXCHANGE$(T[U + 2i], T[U + 2i + 1])$

The overall time required by these rearrangements in processing the h dimensions is clearly $O(n)$, so the array *per se* is not area-time optimal. However, suppose we partition the n operands into n/k sets of size k and assign each set to a distinct linear array to process the lowest $\log k$ dimensions as outlined above. In order to process the remaining $\log n - \log k$ dimensions, these arrays are closed by an end-around edge, and are interconnected as a hypercube (where in each array different dimensions are handled by different modules). The resulting modules have outdegree 4 regardless of n. The resulting composite architecture, called the *cube-connected cycles*, is an emulator of the hypercube. It runs in time $T = O(k)$ and can be laid out in area $O(n^2/k^2)$, so that it is area-time optimal. Since k can be chosen between $\Omega(\log n)$ and $O(\sqrt{n})$, this is an explicit example of area-time trade-off.

A Critical Comment

Research on VLSI computation was prompted by a technological revolution and developed in the 1980s under the shadow of a funding policy that promoted massive parallel computing. A sufficiently simple model became established, unleashing a volume of research that elucidated important relationships between computations and parallel architectures.

As mentioned before, the Achilles' heel of the VLSI model is its second axiom concerning timing. It was soon realized that with reference to the scalability of VLSI architectures, the finiteness of the speed of light and the inability to indefinitely reduce the size of the devices invalidate the timing axiom. It happens that small-diameter networks (notably trees and hypercubes) have maximum wire length growing nearly as the square-root of the network area. In a technology where the physical limits are approached (*limiting technology*) only meshes are truly scalable architectures.

However, it must be mentioned that as this entry is written (2009), the approaching physical limits have revived interest in parallel computations, although along directions different from massive parallel computing.

Bibliographic Notes and Further Reading

The origins of the theory of VLSI computation can be roughly traced back to the appearance in the late 1970s of a book by Mead and Conway [1], a somewhat simplified presentation of the technology, which enormously stimulated the algorithmic community. At about the same time, C. Thompson [2] presented the VLSI computation model and the area-time approach, and shortly thereafter J.D. Ullman [3] framed the emerging research area in the language of the theoretical community.

The literature on VLSI computation is enormous. A comprehensive reference is the authoritative text by F. T. Leighton [4], which presents a scholarly compendium of the computational/architectural aspect of VLSI at a time (1992) when research interest was beginning to wane. The interested reader is encouraged to consult this source.

Suffice it to mention here: systolic networks were introduced by H.T. Kung and C.E. Leiserson [5], the shuffle-exchange network was discussed in [2], and the cube-connected-cycles in [6]. The notion of computational friction was proposed in [7]. The implications of the physical limitations are analyzed in [8].

Bibliography

1. Mead C, Conway L (1980) Introduction to VLSI systems. Addison-Wesley, Reading, MA
2. Thompson C (1980) A complexity theory for VLSI. Ph.D thesis, C.S. Department, Carnegie-Mellon University
3. Ullman JD (1984) Computational aspects of VLSI. Computer Science Press, Rockville, MD
4. Leighton FT (1992) Introduction to parallel algorithms and architectures: arrays-trees-hypercubes, Morgan Kaufmann Publishers, San Mateo, CA
5. Kung HT, Leiserson CE (1978) Systolic arrays for VLSI. Sparse Matrix Proc. 1978–79, SIAM, pp 256–282
6. Preparata FP, Vuillemin J (1981) The cube-connected-cycles: a versatile network for parallel computation. Commun ACM 24(5):300–309
7. Bilardi G, Preparata FP (1986) Area-time lower-bound techniques with applications to sorting. Algorithmica 1(1):65–91
8. Bilardi G, Preparata FP (1995) Horizons of parallel computation. J Parallel Distrib Comput 27:172–182

VNG

▶Vampir

W

Warp and iWarp

JAMES R. REINDERS
Intel Corporation, Hillsboro, OR, USA

Definition

The Warp project was a series of increasingly general-purpose programmable systolic array systems and related software. The project was created by Carnegie Mellon University (CMU) and developed in conjunction with industrial partners G.E., Honeywell, and Intel with funding from the U.S. Defense Advanced Research Projects Agency (DARPA). There were three distinct machine designs known as the WW-Warp, PC-Warp, and iWarp. Each successive design was made increasingly general-purpose by increasing memory capacity and relaxing the tight synchronization between processors. A two-cell prototype of WW-Warp was completed in June 1985, the first WW-Warp in February 1986, the first PC-Warp in April 1987, and the first iWarp system in March 1990. iWarp systems were produced and sold by Intel in 1992 and 1993 to universities, government agencies, and industrial research laboratories. Signal and image processing were the target applications for the Warp program, a natural fit for systolic arrays. The Warp program produced pioneering work on software pipelining support in compilers to utilize the LIW capabilities of the cells (processors).

The name Warp referred to warp factors used by the Star Trek TV series to induce very high velocities in anticipation of the new Star Trek episodes, known as "Star Trek: Next Generation," which appeared in the fall of the year that PC-Warp became operational. iWarp added "i" for *integrated* for the VLSI version and was adopted before Intel was selected as recipient of the contract to design and manufacture it. Intel, at the time, used "i" as a prefix on many product names.

Discussion

Introduction

Systolic Arrays, first described in 1978 by H. T. Kung and Charles E. Leiserson, were originally conceived as a systematic approach to utilize rapid advances in electronics, known as Very-Large-Scale-Integrated (VLSI) technology, and coping with inherent difficulties present in designing VLSI systems. The systolic array concept proved to be successful at taking advantage of this evolution and led also to advancements in software models for utilizing hardware parallelism.

At the same time, instruction-level parallelism was attracting considerable interest for utilizing the rapidly expanding capabilities of VLSI. The use of explicitly scheduled instructions in the form of long instruction word (LIW) design was of interest to H. T. Kung and his team.

In 1983, H. T. Kung, at Carnegie Mellon University, started the Warp program with a desire to investigate the many hardware, software, and application aspects of systolic array processing. Over the course of a following decade, the program yielded research results, publications, and advancements in general-purpose systolic hardware design, compiler design, and systolic software algorithms.

At first, Warp was conceived as a limited prototype to be used by the vision group at CMU for low-level vision operations that were simple and highly regular (1D or 2D convolutions, edge detection operators, etc.). As work progressed, opportunities for more complex uses for Warp machines were proposed.

As the Warp design came together, the Strategic Computing Initiative (SCI) was looking for high-performance computing platforms to tackle specific problems, one of which was the development of an Autonomous Land Vehicle (ALV). It was decided to place the CMU prototype Warp machine (two cells) onboard the CMU ALV. The ALV program would need more than one Warp, and H. T. Kung decided to pursue

David Padua (ed.), *Encyclopedia of Parallel Computing*, DOI 10.1007/978-0-387-09766-4,
© Springer Science+Business Media, LLC 2011

funding from the SCI program. Through the support of DARPA, and working with industrial partners, a series of three Warp machines were produced over the span of a decade. Since using VLSI was the inspiration for the systolic array concept, it was natural for H. T. Kung to guide the Warp project from an idea, to a wire-wrapped prototype, to a printed circuit card implementation, and finally to a VLSI implementation. In 1986, while the first wire-wrapped prototype of a 10-cell machine was being delivered and the printed circuit version was being designed, Intel was selected to be the industrial partner for the integrated circuit implementation of Warp.

Consistent with the desire to harness leaps in VLSI and heavily influenced by a deep interest in signal and image processing, the use of LIW in the hardware and software was a key area of investigation as well. The Warp program focused specifically on developing a compiler scheduling technique of software pipelining as a key technique to utilize LIW. This contrasted with work by Joseph (Josh) Fisher at Yale University and Multiflow Computer Inc., which focused on developing a compiler scheduling technique of trace scheduling to utilize LIW. Neither effort resulted in hardware that benefited significantly from employing both compiler scheduling techniques together. Later, the Itanium project at HP and Intel included engineers formerly of both the Multiflow and the Warp projects. The Itanium design included hardware designed to be able to utilize both trace scheduling and software pipelining.

Complementing the development of the machines, software research and development was a big part of the Warp program. Advances in compiler techniques for software pipelining, as well as advances in systolic programming and programming models, were made as part of the Warp program.

All Warp and iWarp machines were Systolic Arrays, so they consisted of a set of interconnected cells, each capable of performing at least simple computational operations and communicating only with cells in close proximity. Warp machines were simple linear configurations, while iWarp machines were organized as 2-D arrays with the edges wrapping around to form a torus. In both cases, programming could generally be described in terms of streaming data through the array for processing as it passed through cell. In the simplest example, every cell could be programmed to read a data element, add one to it, and send the result along to the next cell. Such a program on any of the Warp systems would be written roughly as sendf(receivef()+ 1.0) and compile to a single instruction that executed in a single cycle, thereby highlighting the tight coupling of computation and communication. A stream of data sent through a machine thus programmed would emerge with every element of the stream incremented by N, where N was the number of cells in the machine. Many systolic algorithms have been developed to take advantage of the parallelism of such a system.

The Warp program focused on practical realizations of systolic array concepts in order to facilitate advanced software research on real-world applications of the machine. This started when the first hand-built two-cell Warp machine, which was designed to solve vision problems, was quickly pressed into service in a real-world challenge in the CMU ALV. This early focus on vision and signal processing, coupled with a desire to solve real problems for researchers outside computer architecture research, lead to four defining characteristics for the Warp program.

1. **Systolic communications: Efficient fine-grained communications**.

   Internode communication is the most fundamental and key issue in the design of a parallel computer because the communication system directly impacts the mapping of an application onto the computer. The exploration of "balanced algorithms" at CMU, led by H. T. Kung starting in the mid-1970s, looked to find algorithms that scale without bounds. Communication with little to no overhead is needed to efficiently deal with the fine-grained parallelism that such algorithms tend to utilize as machine sizes grow. Systolic arrays accomplish this goal by providing a method to directly couple computation to communication. This was true in Warp and iWarp machines. This principle is an important consideration in "balanced" system design to allow high-performance systems to have applicability on a broader set of algorithms.

2. **Systolic design advantages coupled with general programmability**.

   The systolic array approach initially led to very rigidly synchronous hardware designs that were elegant yet proved overly constraining for many programming solutions. Each successive generation of the Warp program offered increased programmability by relaxing prior rigid synchronization design constraints and increasing cell autonomy by changes including notable increases in cell memory capacity.

3. **Long instruction word (LIW) designs with optimizing compilers.**
   The cells of all Warp machines utilized LIW (or VLIW, *Very Long Instruction Word*) and invested in compiler technology to utilize the LIW capabilities, including extensive research and publishing focused on developing software pipelining techniques.

4. **Early prototypes for software developers.**
   While inspired by VLSI opportunities, the Warp project focused on developing early prototype systems using a low-risk approach of combining MSI and LSI parts in a relatively conservative design instead of an immediate leap to VLSI. This led to functional hardware that provided a reliable platform for rich software investigations early in the program. Learnings from the prototypes were then implemented into a VLSI version that in turn could draw on the benefits of several years of software development on the early prototypes.

The Warp Machines

Warp and iWarp machines were a series of increasingly general-purpose systolic array processors, created by Carnegie Mellon University (CMU), in conjunction with industrial partners G.E. (Syracuse, New York), Honeywell (Minneapolis, Minnesota) and Intel (Hillsboro, Oregon), and funded by the U.S. Defense Advanced Research Projects Agency (DARPA).

There were three distinct machine designs known as the WW-Warp (Wire Wrap Warp), PC-Warp (Printed Circuit Warp), and iWarp (integrated circuit Warp, conveniently also a play on the "i" for Intel).

Each successive generation became increasingly general-purpose by increasing memory capacity and loosening the coupling between processors. Only the original WW-Warp forced a truly lock step sequencing of stages, which severely restricted its programmability but was in a sense the purest "systolic array" design.

Warp machines were attached to Sun workstations (UNIX based). Software development work for all models of Warp machines were done on Sun workstations (Figs. 1 and 2).

The WW-Warp and PC-Warp machines were systolic array computers with a linear array generally of ten or more cells, each of which is a programmable processor capable of performing ten million single-precision floating-point operations per second (10 MFLOPS). A ten-cell machine had a peak performance of 100 MFLOPS. The iWarp machines doubled this performance, delivering 20 MFLOPS of single precision and supporting a double-precision floating point at half that performance.

A two-cell prototype of WW-Warp was completed at Carnegie Mellon in June 1985. Two essentially identical WW-Warp machines, each with ten identical boards (nodes) plus an address generator I/O board, were produced in 1986. The system from G.E. was delivered in February 1986; the system from Honeywell was delivered in June 1986. G.E. became the sole industrial partner for the PC-Warp machine construction. Significant redesign work was done to generalize the systolic array before production of the PC-Warp. The first PC-Warp was delivered by G.E. in April 1987. About twenty production machines of the PC-Warp were produced and sold by G.E. during 1987–1988. The PC-Warp machine sold for $350,000 without the Sun workstation. Each cell (node board) in a PC-Warp consumed about 100 W of power.

In 1986, Intel was selected, as a result of competitive bidding, to be the industrial partner for the integrated circuit implementation of Warp. The first iWarp system, a twelve-node system, became operational in March 1990. Additional steppings of the chip resulted in the final C-Step part that improved the clock rate, beyond the 16 MHz project target, to 20 MHz and worked out most errata. About 39 machines, with more than 1,500 processors combined, were produced and sold by Intel in 1992 and 1993 to universities, government agencies, and industrial research laboratories. The largest system assembled was a 512-processor machine, and one 256-processor machine was made for CMU. Typical production systems were 64-processor systems. The high-speed static memory and the high-performance low-latency communication system proved to be a well-suited target for research efforts and many "proof-of-concept" applications.

The iWarp machines were based on a full-custom VLSI component integrating a 700,000 transistor LIW microprocessor, a network interface and a switching

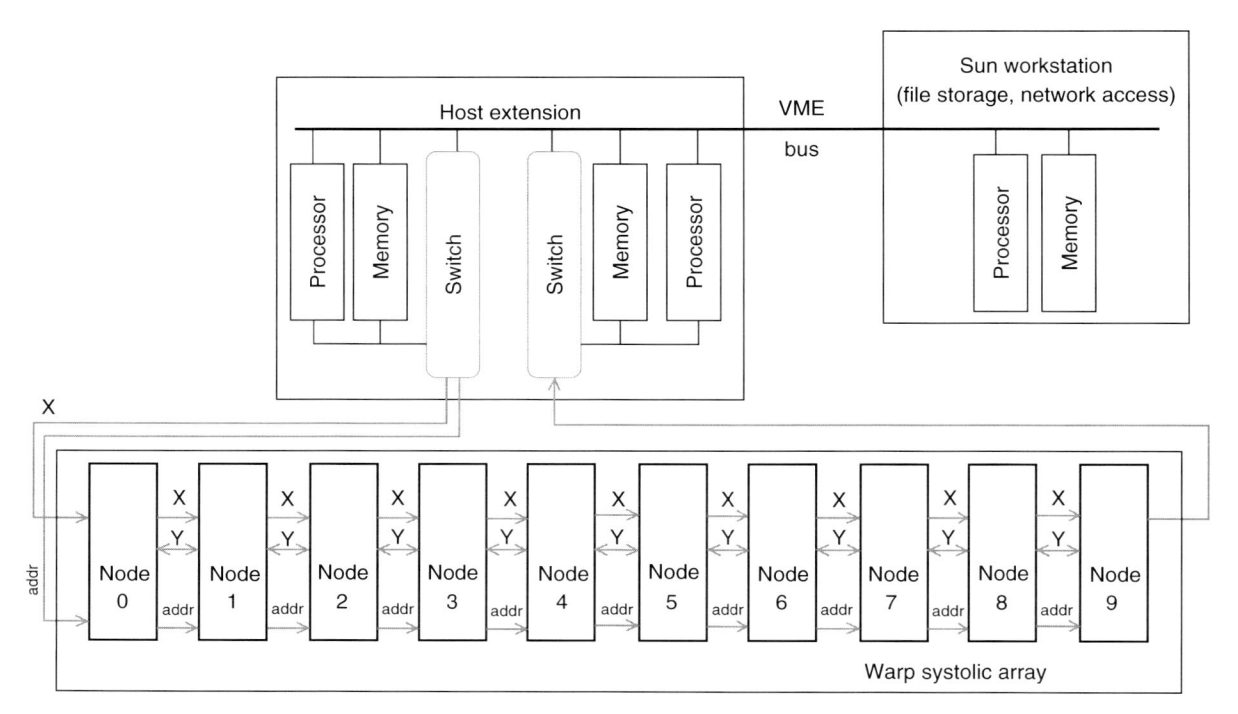

Warp and iWarp. Fig. 1 PC-Warp system architecture

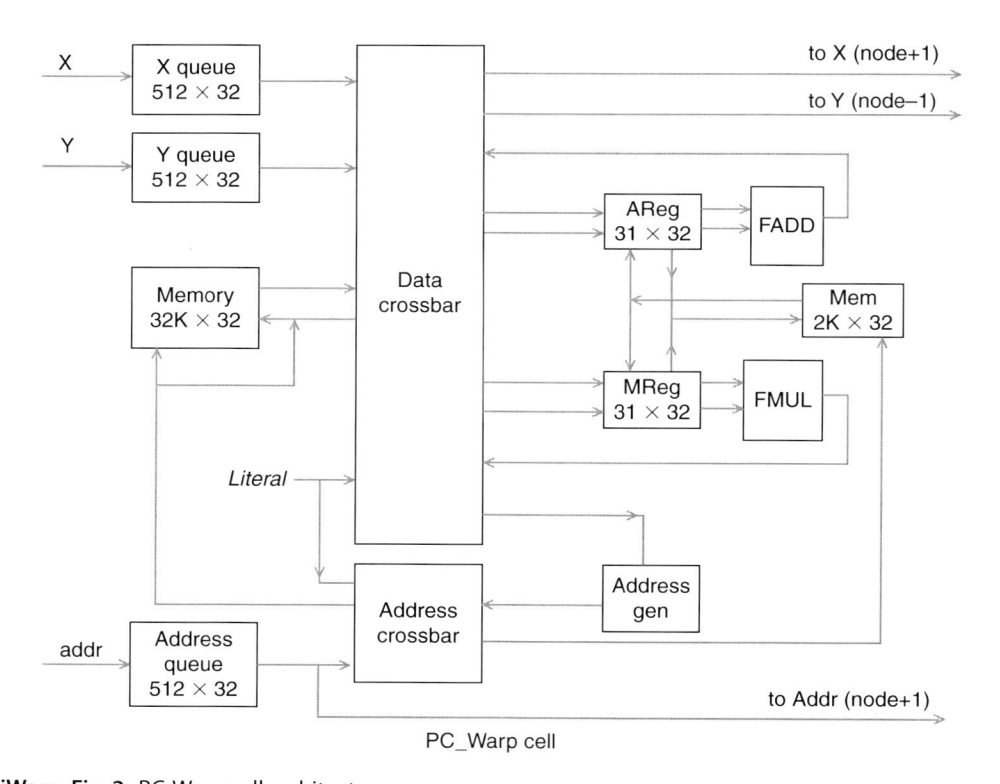

Warp and iWarp. Fig. 2 PC-Warp cell architecture

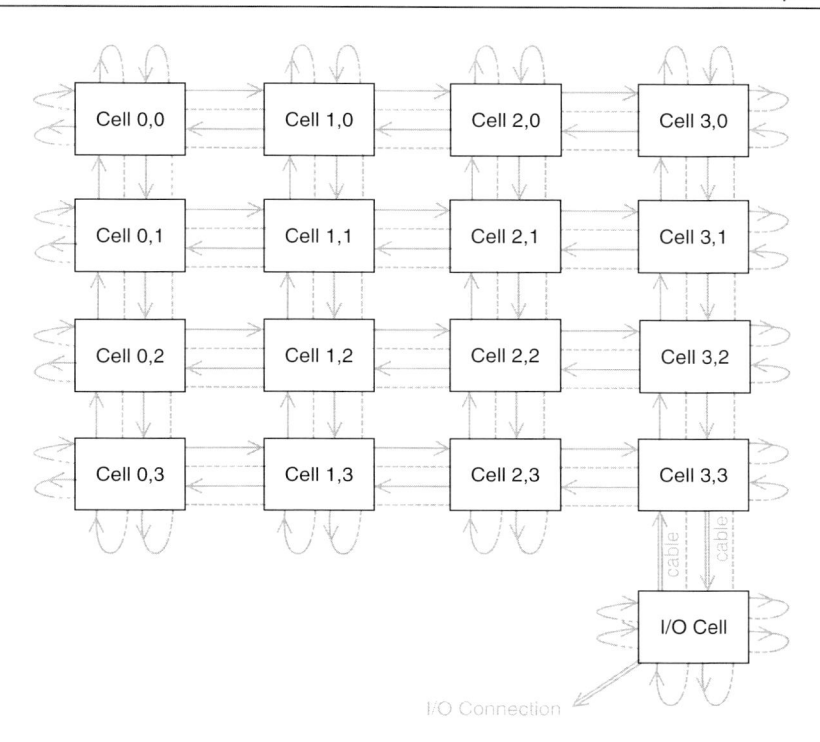

Warp and iWarp. Fig. 3 iWarp system architecture

node, into one single chip of 1.2 cm × 1.2 cm silicon. The processor dissipated up to 15 W and was packaged in a ceramic pin grid array with 280 pins. Intel marketed the iWarp with the tagline "Building Blocks for GigaFLOPs."

The iWarp processor was designed specifically for the Warp project, utilized LIW format instructions, and featured tightly integrated communications with the computational processor. The standard iWarp machines configuration arranged iWarp nodes in a 2m × 2n torus. All iWarp machines included the "back edges" and, therefore, were tori (Figs. 3 and 4).

Programmability increased in each successive generation within the Warp program. In the WW-Warp design, all addresses for data accesses were created on the interface cell, which preceded the first computational cell, and passed along as data on the communication channels. Each WW-Warp cell was technically an independent SIMD machine with local instructions, but the whole design had an underlying assumption that cells would be identically programmed in a very rigid Single-Instruction-Multiple-Data (SIMD) fashion. The lack of ability to locally create data access addresses,

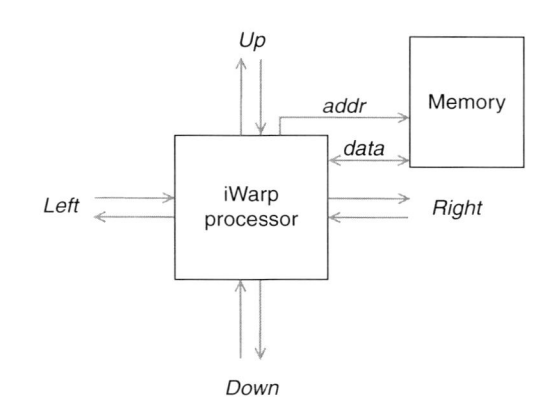

Warp and iWarp. Fig. 4 iWarp cell architecture

in particular, helped ensure such rigid programming. The SIMD program preceded as a wave through the machine in which cells were skewed in their execution, as opposed to operating in a global lock step, as data and addresses streamed through the machine. The tight coupling of the cells meant that if a cell sent data into a full input queue, the data was lost. This tight coupling made it impossible for the compiler to support a pipeline programming mode in practice.

The very rigid clocking of the WW-Warp was relaxed in PC-Warp by the increasing intracell buffering, introducing intracell flow control, as well as the addition of address generation units on individual cells for local address generation capabilities. With added hardware flow control and a local controller, cells were no longer tightly coupled and could operate independently. Direct coupling of neighboring cells on PC-Warp still had no allowance for data to bypass the computational unit of a cell. Only a programmed operation could move data through a PC-Warp cell because of the direct coupling of communication to the functional units in the cell. iWarp introduced a communication agent on the cell to allow for data to pass through a cell without the need to interact with the computational units.

The design of iWarp was oriented toward preserving the benefits of systolic communication while generalizing the framework to allow for more application diversity. iWarp maintained the systolic feature of connections for low overhead communication, while providing for a broad range of applications by making those connections programmable. In iWarp, physical communication channels were augmented with virtual communications channels that allowed logical communication channels to be established over the same physical hardware to add great flexibility in the programming models.

The iWarp processor was a 32-bit Reduced-Instruction-Set-Computing (RISC) design with a 96-bit LIW instruction that, unlike the Intel i860 processor, had no performance penalty for transitioning between long and short instructions in an instruction stream. The final, C-stepping, of the processor was clocked at 20 MHz. The processor had 20 MIPS integer performance, supported full IEEE floating-point compliance for 32- and 64-bit operations with performance of 20 MFLOPs and ten MFLOPs, respectively. Processors were grouped four on a double-height Eurocard PC board (23 cm × 28 cm). Sixteen of these quad-processor boards fit in a 19-inch rack along with a clock board, and four racks could be placed in a single modified iPSC cabinet (156.5 cm × 53.5 cm × 65 cm deep). Up to four cabinets could be connected together.

WW-Warp and PC-Warp utilized their long instructions to route communication inputs directly to arithmetic units, and outputs of arithmetic units directly to the communication outputs for a node. In iWarp, some of the register file was mapped to communication so that a communications input from a neighbor was represented as a register read, and a register write sent data to a neighbor. In all these machines, the communications were matched precisely to the computational capabilities of the machine.

The interconnect capabilities of an iWarp processor were through four 20 MB/s full duplex links. The hardware supported up to 20 logical (virtual) channels that were freely configurable across all four directions and used two pools. Communications were clocked at 40 MHz.

Each successive generation of the Warp program also increased the available memory on each cell. The original WW-Warp design had a very limited 2K program memory but also had little use for large memory modules because the rigidly synchronous design did not encourage use of local storage nor large programs. The relaxation of the rigid connections led to algorithms that benefitted from more local storage so the PC-Warp design had 8X the program store and more memory on each cell. Further relaxing in turn demanded more memory, and the iWarp design initially offered high performance with very limited static memory modules. The creation of a daughter card supporting 16 Mb of dynamic memory greatly increased available memory, for both the application and the resident operating code, and proved very popular. Memory access latency was 100 ns static and 200 ns dynamic. Memory access bandwidth was 160 MB/s. The iWarp processor included eight programmable direct memory access (DMA) agents for data spooling to communication channels.

Systems built from iWarp processors could range from four iWarp processors to 1,024 processors in a 2n × 2m torus. The typical system was 64 cells in an 8 × 8 torus for a total 1.2 GFlop/s peak performance. Measured sustained performance of 64 cells for dense matrix multiply was 1150 MFlop/s, sparse matrix multiply was 400 MFlop/s, and FFT was 700 MFlop/s (Photos 1–4).

Compilers

Multiple compilers associated with the Warp program explored exploitation of both cell programming and array level programming.

Warp and iWarp. Photo 1 The iWarp processor, die exposed

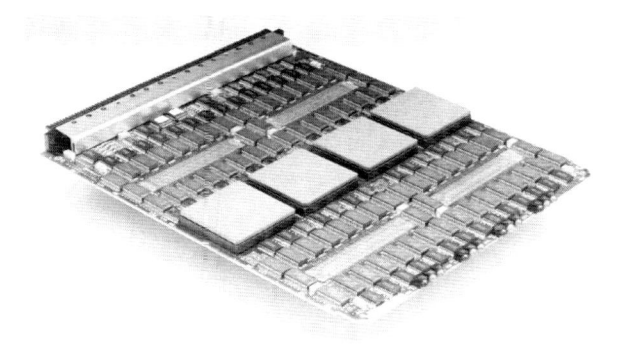

Warp and iWarp. Photo 2 The iWarp quad-cell board (Four processor, memory, communication)

Warp and iWarp. Photo 3 Sixty-four iWarp cells mounted in a 19-inch rack (1.2 GFLOPs)

The cells of all Warp machines utilized LIW (or VLIW, very long instruction word). The WW-Warp and PC-Warp used VLIW to directly send commands to every unit on the board in every cycle, using the VLIW 272-bit wide instructions. The iWarp processor utilized a 96-bit LIW instruction with several possible encoding formats to control integer and floating-point operations in parallel. For instruction compaction, iWarp allowed 32-bit RISC instructions to be freely mixed with the 96-big LIW instructions. The Warp program invested in compiler technology to utilize the LIW capabilities, including extensive research and publishing on software pipelining techniques.

A research compiler, for a language known as "W2," targeted all three machines and was the only compiler for the WW-Warp and PC-Warp, while it served as an early compiler during development of the iWarp. The production compiler for iWarp was a C and Fortran compiler based on the AT&T pcc2 compiler for UNIX with extensive modifications and extensions for systolic programming and exploitation of LIW via software pipelining.

The W2 compiler was written in Common LISP and ran on Sun Workstations. The W2 language was a restrictive procedural language similar in syntax to Pascal or C, and designed to specify a kernel of computation to be spread across the computation array as well as specify the data input and output sufficiently for the compiler to generate the code to feed the input stream and to recover the output stream.

The initial focus was on producing code for both the interface cells and the computational cells of the WW-Warp machine. The PC-Warp allowed more general programming by providing for local address generation that permitted a more general programming of each cell so the W2 language and compiler evolved to support

Warp and iWarp. Photo 4 The iWarp system cabinet containing four racks (256 cells)

more general programming. Once operational with creating the proper control code for the machine, the W2 compiler focus took on software pipelining to fully utilize the combination of tightly coupled communication capabilities with the LIW instruction design. Monica Lam's Ph.D. work "A Systolic Array Optimizing Compiler" covers the results in detail, including methods to software pipeline loops to any depth of nesting. The W2 compiler for PC-Warp was taken on by G.E. in 1987, and CMU focused work on a port of the W2 compiler to iWarp.

It was initially believed that programs for the W2 compiler would typically be "half a page" in length. This was consistent with systolic arrays up to that point. The generalization of PC-Warp saw programs 20X the originally anticipated norm, and automatic program generation systems stretched this even further. Developers of applications for the PC-Warp often requested a more robust compiler for a full and standard language.

The production compiler for iWarp was a C and Fortran compiler based on the AT&T pcc2 compiler for UNIX. HCR Corporation of Toronto, under contract to Intel, provided the initial port of pcc2 for iWarp along with HCR's own global optimizer technology for pcc2. The compilers went on to be extensively modified and extended by Intel and CMU, and were mostly used by developers directly. However, they were also targeted by special frontends, including cfront (for C++), oxygen compiler (for a variant of Fortran77), and the Fx compiler (for a variant of HPF).

Several research compilers also produced code for iWarp, including the retargeted W2 compiler, a code generator for cmcc (a C compiler for research into optimizations at CMU), and a backend for the Stanford SUIF compiler (under the guidance of Prof. Monica Lam).

With the advent of High Performance Fortran (HPF) research, CMU's Fx project was born to explore HPF style investigations on the iWarp platform. Significant energy at CMU in compiler research went into the Fx compiler.

Domain-specific or "application" compilers were an area of interest at CMU. Parallel program generators for iWarp were directed toward specific application domains and included the Apply project (for image processing) and the AL project (for scientific computing).

Applications

One Warp system was installed in the NavLab, a GM van converted by researchers in the Robotics Institute at Carnegie Mellon University. The NavLab was a laboratory for research in autonomous road following, and a Warp machine (as well as a number of workstations) was installed in the van. The Warp machine turned out to be a good engine for neural net learning. It also performed a variety of other vision and planning tasks. A Warp machine remained in the NavLab until 1989, when the van caught fire after the air conditioning system leaked liquid onto the computers.

Several NSF grand challenge problems were investigated.

An iWarp machine had successful sea trials on a U.S. Navy submarine.

Warp's Influence on the Industry

The W2 compiler pioneered software pipelining for LIW. The Warp compiler projects provided extensive investigations into software pipelining, including nested software pipelining, and published solutions. These have become an important and popular compiler optimization for most modern computers.

After iWarp, Intel continued work on interconnect chips derived from the iWarp design. The world's first TeraFLOP computer, ASCI Red built for Sandia National Labs by Intel, utilized a variant of the logical channels developed first for iWarp.

iWarp was the first Intel project that utilized workstations for simulations and mask generation, and worked to move Intel's design tools into this environment for the first time. Future generations of Intel chip designs moved away from mainframes following the lead of the iWarp project.

Related Entries
▶ Systolic Arrays
▶ VLIW Processors

Bibliographic Notes and Further Reading

The first papers mentioning Warp that appeared in 1984 focused on machine vision and not the machine. Papers specifically about the Warp machines appeared in 1986 as the first machines were delivered with a pretty complete overview in 1987 [1]. A retrospective on Warp provides insights into the key lessons of Warp [2]. Monica Lam's May 1987 Ph.D. dissertation focused largely on the pioneering work on software pipelining and was later published as a book [3]. A detailed book on iWarp and the experiences of the project from the perspective of two CMU researchers was published in 1998 [8].

Bibliography

1. Annaratone M, Arnould E, Gross T, Kung HT, Lam M, Menzilcioglu O, Webb J (1987) The warp computer: architecture, implementation and performance. IEEE Trans Comput C-36(12): 1523–1538
2. Gross T, Lam M (1998) Retrospective: a retrospective on the warp machines. In: ISCA '98: 25 years of the international symposia on computer architecture (selected papers). IEEE, Los Alamitos, pp 42–45
3. Lam MS (1989) A systolic array optimizing compiler. Kluwer Academic, Dordrecht
4. Borkar S, Cohn R, Cox G, Gleason S, Gross T (1988) iWarp: an integrated solution of high-speed parallel computing. In: Proceedings of the 1988 ACM/IEEE conference on supercomputing, 12–17 Nov 1988, Orlando, Florida, pp 330–339
5. Adl-Tabatabai A-R, Gross T, Lueh G-Y, Reinders J (1993) Modeling Instruction-Level Parallelism for Software Pipelining. In: Proceedings of the IFIP WG10.3 working conference on architectures and compilation techniques for fine and medium grain parallelism, Orlando, pp 321–330
6. Borkar S, Cohn R, Cox G, Gross T, Kung HT, Lam M, Levine M, Moore B, Moore W, Peterson C, Susman J, Sutton J, Urbanski J, Webb J (1990) Supporting systolic and memory communication in iWarp. In: Proceedings of the 17th annual international symposium on computer architecture, Seattle, Washington, pp 70–81
7. Intel Corp (1991) iWarp microprocessor (Part Number 318153). Technical information, Order Number 281006, Hillsboro, OR
8. Gross T, O'Hallaron DR (1998) iWarp: anatomy of a parallel computing system. MIT, Cambridge, MA, p 488

Wavefront Arrays

▶ Systolic Arrays

Weak Scaling

▶ Gustafson's Law

Whole Program Analysis

▶ FORGE

Work-Depth Model

▶ Models of Computation, Theoretical

Workflow Scheduling

▶ Task Graph Scheduling

Z

Z-Level Programming Language

►ZPL

ZPL

BRADFORD CHAMBERLAIN
Cray Inc., Seattle, WA, USA

Synonyms

Z-level programming language

Definition

ZPL is a parallel programming language that was developed at the University of Washington between 1992 and 2005. ZPL was a contemporary of High Performance Fortran (HPF), targeting a similar class of applications by supporting data parallel computations via operations on global-view arrays distributed between a set of distinct processor memories. ZPL distinguished itself from HPF by providing a less ambiguous execution model, support for first-class index sets, and a syntactic performance model that supported the ability to trivially identify and reason about communication.

Discussion

Foundations

ZPL was initially developed by Lawrence Snyder and Calvin Lin at the University of Washington who strove to design a parallel programming language from first principles. To this end, the ZPL effort began by identifying abstract machine and programming models that would serve as the parallel equivalents of the von Neumann machine model and the imperative-procedural programming model used in traditional sequential computing.

For a machine model, ZPL built upon Snyder's *CTA* or *Candidate Type Architecture*, defined as "a finite set of sequential computers connected in a fixed, bounded degree graph, with a global controller." [13]. In contrast to theoretical models like the PRAM, the CTA was designed to serve as a more practical machine model for realistic parallel architectures. At the same time, the CTA was intentionally vague about the parameterization of the target architecture's capabilities due to the high degree of variation from one parallel system to another, combined with the fact that the complexity in such models often failed to add value to an end-user. The main point of the CTA was that locality matters: remote accesses are more expensive than local accesses and therefore need to be avoided whenever possible.

In terms of its programming model, ZPL built on Lin et al.'s *Phase Abstractions* programming model [12] which defined three levels of specification for parallel programming, named the X, Y, and Z levels. The phase abstractions define the X level as representing Multiple-Instruction Multiple-Data (MIMD) programming in which the programmer is writing code from the point of view of a single sequential processor. The Y level deals with logical topology and specifies the virtual communication channels across which the processors communicate and interact with one another. Finally the Z level describes the high-level data parallel computations in which all of the processors execute similar instructions to cooperatively implement a single logical operation.

It is this final level that gave ZPL its full – though in practice, rarely used – name: the *Z-level Programming Language*. ZPL was originally designed to be the data parallel component of a broader language named Orca C that spanned the X, Y, and Z levels defined by the phase abstractions. However, as ZPL matured, rather than making it part of a larger sublanguage, it was extended to support increasingly rich modes of parallel computation, ultimately including "X level" per-processor computation in its final years [9].

Theoretical foundations aside, from the programmer's view, traditional ZPL computations provided a conceptual single-threaded model of computation in which each statement could be thought of as executing to completion before the next began. In reality, the data parallel statements resulted in concurrent execution across all processors in a loosely coupled manner, but the typical programmer could be completely unaware of such details apart from the performance benefits that resulted.

In terms of its implementation, the ZPL compiler generated a single-threaded Single-Program Multiple-Data (SPMD) executable that implemented the computation and communication required to realize the user's data parallel program. The ZPL compiler took a source-to-source compilation approach for the purposes of portability, translating the user's source down to C code that would then be compiled using a platform-specific C compiler. Communication was implemented in terms of a novel API called *the Ironman interface* [4] that separated the semantics of what data needed to be communicated, and when, from architecture-specific capabilities like shared memory, two-sided message passing, one-sided puts and gets, or even distinct communication threads potentially running on coprocessors. The result was a highly portable compiler that could often match the performance of a hand-coded MPI program and even outperform it on architectures that preferred a different style of communication than two-sided message passing [1, 2, 9].

Primary Concepts: Regions, Arrays, and Directions

Perhaps the key feature of ZPL was its choice to support the notion of a distributed index set using a first-class language concept known as the *region*. Index sets are important for data parallel programming due to their role in defining data structures and iteration spaces. The distribution of these index sets between distinct processors plays a crucial role in dividing parallel work between compute resources while also establishing clear realms of locality. Most traditional languages have failed to provide abstractions for index sets, requiring the programmer to express them using collections of scalar values for each processor and array dimension. In contrast, ZPL's regions support distributed index sets as a high-level language concept. From ZPL's early stages, regions could be named and initialized. Over time they were extended to support assignment and to serve as function arguments while also being made more compatible with other types – for instance by supporting the ability to create arrays of regions or region fields within data structures.

As a sample use of regions, the following code declares an $m \times n$ region and then uses it to declare an array of floating point values:

```
region R = [1..m, 1..n];
var A: [R] float;
```

In addition to declaring arrays, regions also serve the purpose of scoping statements or groups of statements to provide the indices over which array expressions should be evaluated. For example, the following assignments to *A* are prefixed by region scopes that control which elements of arrays *A* and *Index2* are referenced. The initial region scope causes the first assignment to zero out the whole array *A* since it was declared over region *R*; the next restricts the second assignment to *A*'s *j*th row, causing those elements to take on the value of their column index, represented by the built-in virtual array *Index2*:

```
[R]        A := 0;
[j, 1..n]  A := Index2;
```

Another early ZPL concept was the *direction*, which was essentially a named offset vector. Like regions, directions were initially limited to named constants, but like regions they became increasingly general and first-class as the language progressed.

Region bounds were often defined in terms of *configuration variables* – variables which are given an initial value that can be overridden on the executable's command-line via compiler-generated argument parsing hooks. In addition to explicitly declaring regions in terms of their upper and lower bounds as in the example above, programmers could also create regions by applying a series of *prepositional operators* to existing regions. These operators typically combined the base region with a direction to create a new region. For example, the *of* operator creates regions that describe boundary conditions by using the offset vector to define a region that borders the base region. In contrast, the *by* operator uses its direction to compute a strided subset of its base region.

Using regions, arrays, and directions, a programmer could fairly easily write simple data parallel computations such as the following Jacobi iteration which iteratively replaces an array's elements with the average of its

```
 1  program jacobi;

 3  config var
 4    n        : integer = 1000;      -- problem size
 5    epsilon  : float   = 0.0001;    -- convergence factor

 7  region
 8    R    = [1..n,   1..n  ];        -- index set for problem
 9    BigR = [0..n+1, 0..n+1];        -- same, but with borders

11  direction
12    north = [-1,  0];               -- cardinal directions
13    east  = [ 0,  1];
14    south = [ 1,  0];
15    west  = [ 0, -1];

17  procedure jacobi();
18  var
19    A, Temp : [BigR] float;         -- compute arrays
20    delta   :        float;
21    [R] begin                       -- default region scope

23      A := 0.0;                     -- initialization of array interior
24      [north of R] A := 0.0;        -- and boundary conditions
25      [east  of R] A := 0.0;
26      [west  of R] A := 0.0;
27      [south of R] A := 1.0;

29      repeat                        -- main loop
30        Temp := (A@north + A@east + A@south + A@west) / 4.0;
31        delta := max<< abs(A-Temp); -- compute convergence
32        A := Temp;
33      until delta < epsilon;

35      writeln(A);
36  end;
```

nearest neighbors. This continues until the largest difference between elements across any two iterations is less than a convergence value, *epsilon*:

Array Operators and the WYSIWYG Performance Model

In order to support more interesting computations than purely element-wise operations, ZPL supports a number of *array operators* that alter the way an array reference's enclosing region scope provides its indices. For example, the @-*operator*, seen in line 30 of the Jacobi example above translates the region's index set by the given offset before applying it to the array. Thus, A@north refers to the index set [0..n-1, 1..n] rather than the default [1..n, 1..n] as specified by the enclosing region scope [R] on line 21. Similarly, the reduction operator (<<) used in line 31 collapses values specified by that same region scope [R] by generating the maximum value computed by the *promotion* of the scalar abs() function and subtraction operator across array elements.

Other primary ZPL operators include the flood operator (>>) which replicates subarrays of values, the scan operator (||) which computes parallel prefix operations, and the remap operator (#) which supports bulk random access to an array's elements using whole-array indexing expressions. In addition, ZPL supports *wrap* and *reflect* operators that support common boundary conditions on regular grids and a variation on the @-operator to support loop-carried array references [6].

ZPL's semantics require that any two array references within a single statement must be distributed identically, ensuring that like-indexed elements are colocated within a single processor's memory (the remap operator is the one exception to this rule for reasons that we will return to in a few paragraphs). The impact of this rule is that all communication within a ZPL program can be identified and classified by the presence of its array operators.

In particular, if a statement contains no array operators, since all of its array expressions are described by the same region scope and aligned, it will be implemented without communication, resulting in an embarrassingly parallel execution (or perhaps "pleasingly parallel"). In contrast, the application of an array operator implies that the enclosing region scope's index set is transformed in some way for that array reference, requiring communication to bring the array's elements into alignment with the enclosing region scope's index set. For example, since the @-operator implies a translation of the region scope's indices, a translation of array elements in the opposite direction is required to align the indices with those described by the enclosing region scope.

In addition to signaling the need for communication, each array operator also implies a particular style of communication for its array's elements. For example, given ZPL's default block-distributed regions, the @-operator implies nearest neighbor point-to-point communication, while the flood and reduction operators imply broadcasts or reductions of array values across the dimensions of the virtual processor grid for which the operation is being computed.

Because the remap operator can express an arbitrary shuffling of array values, it potentially requires all-to-all communication to bring elements into alignment with the enclosing region scope [10]. This is the reason that an array expression indexed by the remap operator is exempt from the requirement that it be aligned with other arrays in the statement: since remaps can result in arbitrary communication patterns, it hardly matters whether the array argument is aligned with the statement's region scope or not. To this end, remap serves as the operator for bringing distinctly distributed arrays into alignment or for performing operations across arrays of differing rank.

The impact of these semantics was profound, since it permitted ZPL programmers to trivially and visually identify communication within their programs, to classify that communication, and to approximate its cost for a given architecture. As a result, the development team called this property ZPL's *What You See is What You Get* or *WYSIWYG performance model* [3]. Equally important, this syntactic identification of communication also simplified the job of implementing ZPL by making the compiler analysis required to identify and insert communication trivial. For this reason, the WYSIWYG performance model probably served as the biggest differentiator between ZPL and HPF, whose language definition made communication impossible for the programmer to reason about in a portable manner, either syntactically or semantically. Moreover, HPF compilers tended to require complex index analyses to identify common patterns like the vectorizable nearest-neighbor communications that were clearly identified in ZPL via the presence of an @-operator.

Advanced ZPL

By the late 1990s, the original scope of ZPL had largely been implemented, yet the language remained too restricted to take on more interesting parallel computations such as those represented by the NAS Parallel Benchmarks (NPB) or various scientific applications being undertaken in other departments at the University of Washington. To this end, the ZPL team began working on evolving ZPL, referring to the original feature set as *classic ZPL* and the new extensions as *advanced ZPL*. Over time, the classic versus advanced distinction faded and the name ZPL was ultimately used to describe the full set of features developed within the project.

Several of the features attributed to advanced ZPL stemmed from the evolution of the region from a simple named constant to a first-class language concept, as mentioned previously. In particular, the ability to modify a region's index set and to create arrays of regions supported the ability to describe sparse and hierarchical index sets and arrays [1, 5, 7]. Other changes involved adding the concept of processor-specific values and array dimensions to the language, permitting the user to break out of ZPL's traditional single-threaded data parallel programming model and write computations on a processor-by-processor basis. Another extension promoted the representation of the virtual processor grid to a first-class concept, permitting arrays to be redistributed by reshaping the set of processors to which they were mapped. This led to a proposed taxonomy of distributions to extend ZPL's traditional support for block-decomposed regions [9].

Status, Evaluation, and Influence

Several versions of ZPL were released to the public in a binary format during the late 1990s. Thereafter, ZPL was released as open source under the MIT license with the final release occurring in April of 2004. Shortly thereafter, Steve Deitz – the last member of the ZPL team – graduated, at which point the project went on permanent hiatus. At the time of this writing, ZPL remains available for download, but is not actively being developed or supported.

ZPL had a number of limitations that prevented it from ever being broadly adopted. Perhaps chief among these was its support for only a single level of data parallelism (and toward the end, a form of SPMD task parallelism). While this represents a very important common case in parallel computing, real-world applications typically have several different types of parallelism composed in various ways that are richer than ZPL's restricted data parallelism was able to express. Another drawback to ZPL was its use of distinct array types and operations to refer to data parallel computations vs. local, serial array computations. This distinction was crucial to its WYSIWYG performance model but ultimately resulted in a fair amount of frustration and confusion among users, particularly when the same logical computation would have to be written multiple times using distinct concepts to support both distributed and non-distributed arrays. The resulting failure to reuse code was well justified, but frustrating in practice. Finally, ZPL's decision to focus on data parallelism to the exclusion of modern language concepts like object-oriented programming or even modern syntax presented challenges to adoption by a broader or more mainstream programming community.

None of this is to suggest that ZPL was an unsuccessful language. On the contrary, in the (admittedly biased) opinion of this author, it represents the model of a successful academic project in that it picked its target – namely, data parallelism supporting the ability to reason about communication and locality – and focused on it to the exclusion of non-research distractions that were clearly orthogonal and could be dealt with later, such as the aforementioned lack of object-oriented capabilities or modern syntactic constructs. In doing so, ZPL made a number of significant contributions including the introduction of the region concept, the WYSIWYG performance model, and the identification of useful abstractions for representing processor sets and distributed arrays and index sets.

Perhaps the biggest indicator of ZPL's success was its influence on the next generation of parallel languages, represented most notably by the High Productivity Computing Systems (HPCS) phase III languages – Cray's Chapel and IBM's X10. Both of these languages adopted the notion of a distributed first-class index set (Chapel's *domain* and X10's *region*) while adapting it to deal with some of ZPL's limitations and generalizing its use to support a more general class of parallel computations.

Related Entries
▶ Array Languages
▶ Chapel (Cray Inc. HPCS Language)
▶ HPF (High Performance Fortran)
▶ PRAM (Parallel Random Access Machines)

Bibliographic Notes and Further Reading

For an introduction to ZPL and the ZPL project that is both more technical and colorful than this one, the reader is referred to Lawrence Snyder's *The Design and Development of ZPL*, published in the History of Programming Languages Conference, 2007 [15]. Another reasonable technical overview would be a workshop paper published toward the end of the ZPL project that served as somewhat of a "greatest hits" overview of the language at the time that the High Performance Computing community was starting to focus increasingly on end-user productivity [2].

For a reference to the language, the most definitive guide is Snyder's *A Programmer's Guide to ZPL* [14]. However, it comes with the important caveat that the language continued to evolve after the book's publication, and as a result many of the advanced ZPL directions were never captured in a comprehensive book or specification. The dissertations by Chamberlain and Deitz fill in some of the gaps by each starting with an overview of ZPL's capabilities in their second chapters [1, 9]. These descriptions were intentionally incomplete, yet provide a good sense of where the language ended up. These dissertations also provide descriptions of a number of important design and implementation details in ZPL. Chamberlain's thesis describes the WYSIWYG communication model, the Ironman interface, the runtime descriptors used for regions and arrays, and the extensions to support sparse and hierarchical regions. Deitz's dissertation covers support for processor-local data and computation, the first-class representation of processor grids and resulting redistribution machinery, and the proposed distribution taxonomy mentioned previously.

The most important historical foundations of the language come in the form of descriptions of the CTA and phase abstractions [12, 13]. While the dissertations cited above and by other members of the ZPL project are often the best reference for the final work covered in this entry, stand-alone conference papers that may be more approachable due to their size exist for a number of the topics described here including the Ironman interface [4], WYSIWYG performance model [3], wavefront computations [6], hierarchical regions [5], and sparse regions [7].

Though not the focus of this entry, compiler optimizations were also a crucial part of ZPL's ability to achieve good performance, and a number of papers detail optimizations made to improve the performance of communication [8, 10] and computation [11].

Bibliography

1. Chamberlain BL (2001) The design and implementation of a region-based parallel language. Ph.D. thesis, University of Washington, Nov 2001. http://www.cs.washington.edu/homes/brad/cv/pubs/degree/thesis.html
2. Chamberlain BL, Choi S-E, Deitz SJ, Snyder L (2004) The high-level parallel language ZPL improves productivity and performance. In: Proceedings of the IEEE internationals workshop on productivity and performance in high-end computing, Madrid, 2004
3. Chamberlain BL, Choi S-E, Lewis EC, Lin C, Snyder L, Weathersby WD (1998) ZPL's WYSIWYG performance model. In: Proceedings of the IEEE workshop on high-level parallel programming models and supportive environments, Orlando, 1998
4. Chamberlain BL, Choi S-E, Snyder L (1997) A compiler abstraction for machine independent parallel communication generation. In: Proceedings of the workshop on languages and compilers for parallel computing, Minneapolis, 1997
5. Chamberlain BL, Deitz SJ, Snyder L (2000) A comparative study of the NAS MG benchmark across parallel languages and architectures. In: Proceedings of the ACM international conference on supercomputing, Santa Fe, 2000
6. Chamberlain BL, Lewis EC, Snyder L (1999) Array language support for wavefront and pipelined computations. In: Proceedings of the workshop on languages and compilers for parallel computing, La Jolla, 1999
7. Chamberlain BL, Snyder L (2001) Array language support for parallel sparse computation. In: Proceedings of the ACM international conference on supercomputing, Sorrento, 2001
8. Choi S-E, Snyder L (1997) Quantifying the effects of communication optimizations. In: Proceedings of the IEEE international conference on parallel processing, Bloomington, 1997
9. Deitz SJ (2005) High-level programming language abstractions for advanced and dynamic parallel computations. Ph.D thesis, University of Washington, Feb 2005. http://www.cs.washington.edu/projects/zpl/papers/data/Deitz05Thesis.pdf
10. Deitz SJ, Chamberlain BL, Choi S-E, Snyder L (2003) The design and implementation of a parallel array operator for the arbitrary remapping of data. In: Proceedings of the ACM conference on principles and practice of parallel programming, San Diego, 2003
11. Deitz SJ, Chamberlain BL, Snyder L (2001) Eliminating redundancies in sum-of-product array computations. In: Proceedings of the ACM international conference on supercomputing, Sorrento, 2001
12. Lin C (1992) The portability of parallel programs across MIMD computers. Ph.D. thesis, University of Washington, Department of Computer Science and Engineering
13. Snyder L (1995) Experimental validation of models of parallel computation. In: Hofmann A, van Leeuwen J (eds), Computer science today. Lecture notes in computer science, vol 1000. Springer, Berlin, pp 78–100
14. Snyder L (1999) Programming guide to ZPL. MIT, Cambridge
15. Snyder L (2007) The design and development of ZPL. In: HOPL III: Proceedings of the third ACM SIGPLAN conference on history of programming languages, San Diego. ACM, New York, pp 8-1–8-37

List of Entries

Ab Initio Molecular Dynamics
Access Anomaly
Actors
Affinity Scheduling
Ajtai–Komlós–Szemerédi Sorting Network
AKS Network
AKS Sorting Network
Algebraic Multigrid
Algorithm Engineering
Algorithmic Skeletons
All Prefix Sums
Allen and Kennedy Algorithm
Allgather
All-to-All
All-to-All Broadcast
Altivec
AMD Opteron Processor Barcelona
Amdahl's Argument
Amdahl's Law
AMG
Analytics, Massive-Scale
Anomaly Detection
Anton, A Special-Purpose Molecular Simulation Machine
Application-Specific Integrated Circuits
Applications and Parallelism
Architecture Independence
Area-Universal Networks
Array Languages
Array Languages, Compiler Techniques for
Asynchronous Iterations
Asynchronous Iterative Algorithms
Asynchronous Iterative Computations
ATLAS (Automatically Tuned Linear Algebra Software)
Atomic Operations
Automated Empirical Optimization
Automated Empirical Tuning
Automated Performance Tuning
Automated Tuning
Automatically Tuned Linear Algebra Software (ATLAS)
Autotuning
Backpressure
Bandwidth-Latency Models (BSP, Logp)
Banerjee's Dependence Test
Barnes-Hut
Barriers
Basic Linear Algebra Subprograms (BLAS)
Behavioral Equivalences
Behavioral Relations
Benchmarks
Beowulf Clusters
Beowulf-Class Clusters
Bernstein's Conditions
Bioinformatics
Bisimilarity
Bisimulation
Bisimulation Equivalence
Bitonic Sort
Bitonic Sorting Network
Bitonic Sorting, Adaptive
BLAS (Basic Linear Algebra Subprograms)
Blocking
Blue CHiP
Blue CHiP Project
Blue Gene/L
Blue Gene/P
Blue Gene/Q
Branch Predictors
Brent's Law
Brent's Theorem
Broadcast
BSP
BSP (Bulk Synchronous Parallelism)
Bulk Synchronous Parallelism (BSP)
Bus: Shared Channel
Buses and Crossbars
Butterfly
C*
Cache Affinity Scheduling

Cache Coherence
Cache-Only Memory Architecture (COMA)
Caches, NUMA
Calculus of Mobile Processes
Carbon Cycle Research
Car-Parrinello Method
CDC 6600
Cedar Multiprocessor
CELL
Cell Broadband Engine Processor
Cell Processor
Cell/B.E.
Cellular Automata
Chaco
Chapel (Cray Inc. HPCS Language)
Charm++
Checkpoint/Restart
Checkpointing
Checkpoint-Recovery
CHiP Architecture
CHiP Computer
Cholesky Factorization
Cilk
Cilk Plus
Cilk++
Cilk-1
Cilk-5
Cilkscreen
Cluster File Systems
Cluster of Workstations
Clusters
CM Fortran
Cm* - The First Non-Uniform Memory Access Architecture
CML
CM-Lisp
CnC
Coarray Fortran
Code Generation
Collect
Collective Communication
Collective Communication, Network Support For
COMA (Cache-Only Memory Architecture)
Combinatorial Search
Commodity Clusters
Communicating Sequential Processes (CSP)
Community Atmosphere Model (CAM)
Community Climate Model (CCM)
Community Climate System Model
Community Climate System Model (CCSM)
Community Earth System Model (CESM)
Community Ice Code (CICE)
Community Land Model (CLM)
Compiler Optimizations for Array Languages
Compilers
Complete Exchange
Complex Event Processing
Computational Biology
Computational Chemistry
Computational Models
Computational Sciences
Computer Graphics
Computing Surface
Concatenation
Concurrency Control
Concurrent Collections Programming Model
Concurrent Logic Languages
Concurrent ML
Concurrent Prolog
Configurable, Highly Parallel Computer
Congestion Control
Congestion Management
Connected Components Algorithm
Connection Machine
Connection Machine Fortran
Connection Machine Lisp
Consistent Hashing
Control Data 6600
Coordination
Copy
Core2-Duo / Core2-Quad Processors
COW
Crash Simulation
Cray MTA
Cray Red Storm
Cray SeaStar Interconnect
CRAY T3E
Cray Vector Computers
Cray XMT
Cray XT Series
Cray XT3
Cray XT3 and Cray XT Series of Supercomputers
Cray XT4
Cray XT4 and Seastar 3-D Torus Interconnect

Cray XT5
Cray XT6
Critical Race
Critical Sections
Crossbar
CS-2
CSP (Communicating Sequential Processes)
Cyclops
Cyclops-64
Cydra 5
DAG Scheduling
Data Analytics
Data Centers
Data Distribution
Data Flow Computer Architecture
Data Flow Graphs
Data Mining
Data Race Detection
Data Starvation Crisis
Dataflow Supercomputer
Data-Parallel Execution Extensions
Deadlock Detection
Deadlocks
Debugging
DEC Alpha
Decentralization
Decomposition
Deep Analytics
Denelcor HEP
Dense Linear System Solvers
Dependence Abstractions
Dependence Accuracy
Dependence Analysis
Dependence Approximation
Dependence Cone
Dependence Direction Vector
Dependence Level
Dependence Polyhedron
Dependences
Detection of DOALL Loops
Determinacy
Determinacy Race
Determinism
Deterministic Parallel Java
Direct Schemes
Distributed Computer
Distributed Hash Table (DHT)

Distributed Logic Languages
Distributed Memory Computers
Distributed Process Management
Distributed Switched Networks
Distributed-Memory Multiprocessor
Ditonic Sorting
DLPAR
Doall Loops
Domain Decomposition
DPJ
DR
Dynamic Logical Partitioning for POWER Systems
Dynamic LPAR
Dynamic Reconfiguration
Earth Simulator
Eden
Eigenvalue and Singular-Value Problems
EPIC Processors
Erlangen General Purpose Array (EGPA)
ES
Ethernet
Event Stream Processing
Eventual Values
Exact Dependence
Exaflop Computing
Exaop Computing
Exascale Computing
Execution Ordering
Experimental Parallel Algorithmics
Extensional Equivalences
Fast Fourier Transform (FFT)
Fast Multipole Method (FMM)
Fast Poisson Solvers
Fat Tree
Fault Tolerance
Fences
FFT (Fast Fourier Transform)
Fast Algorithm for the Discrete Fourier Transform (DFT)
FFTW
File Systems
Fill-Reducing Orderings
First-Principles Molecular Dynamics
Fixed-Size Speedup
FLAME
Floating Point Systems FPS-120B and Derivatives
Flow Control

Flynn's Taxonomy
Forall Loops
FORGE
Formal Methods–Based Tools for Race, Deadlock, and Other Errors
Fortran 90 and Its Successors
Fortran, Connection Machine
Fortress (Sun HPCS Language)
Forwarding
Fujitsu Vector Computers
Fujitsu Vector Processors
Fujitsu VPP Systems
Functional Decomposition
Functional Languages
Futures
GA
Gather
Gather-to-All
Gaussian Elimination
GCD Test
Gene Networks Reconstruction
Gene Networks Reverse-Engineering
Generalized Meshes and Tori
Genome Assembly
Genome Sequencing
3GIO
Glasgow Parallel Haskell (GpH)
Global Arrays
Global Arrays Parallel Programming Toolkit
Gossiping
GpH (Glasgow Parallel Haskell)
GRAPE
Graph Algorithms
Graph Analysis Software
Graph Partitioning
Graph Partitioning Software
Graphics Processing Unit
Green Flash: Climate Machine (LBNL)
Grid Partitioning
Gridlock
Group Communication
Gustafson's Law
Gustafson–Barsis Law
Half Vector Length
Hang
Harmful Shared-Memory Access
Haskell
Hazard (in Hardware)
HDF5
HEP, Denelcor
Heterogeneous Element Processor
Hierarchical Data Format
High Performance Fortran (HPF)
High-Level I/O Library
High-Performance I/O
Homology to Sequence Alignment, From
Horizon
HPC Challenge Benchmark
HPF (High Performance Fortran)
HPS Microarchitecture
HT
HT3.10
Hybrid Programming With SIMPLE
Hypercube
Hypercubes and Meshes
Hypergraph Partitioning
Hyperplane Partitioning
HyperTransport
IBM Blue Gene Supercomputer
IBM Power
IBM Power Architecture
IBM PowerPC
IBM RS/6000 SP
IBM SP
IBM SP1
IBM SP2
IBM SP3
IBM System/360 Model 91
IEEE 802.3
Illegal Memory Access
Illiac IV
ILUPACK
Impass
Implementations of Shared Memory in Software
Index
InfiniBand
Instant Replay
Instruction-Level Parallelism
Instruction Systolic Arrays
Intel Celeron
Intel Core Microarchitecture, x86 Processor Family
Intel® Parallel Inspector
Intel® Parallel Studio
Intel® Thread Profiler

Intel® Threading Building Blocks (TBB)
Interactive Parallelization
Interconnection Network
Interconnection Networks
Internet Data Centers
Inter-Process Communication
I/O
iPSC
Isoefficiency
JANUS FPGA-Based Machine
Java
JavaParty
Job Scheduling
k-ary n-cube
k-ary n-fly
k-ary n-tree
Knowledge Discovery
KSR
LANai
Languages
LAPACK
Large-Scale Analytics
Latency Hiding
Law of Diminishing Returns
Laws
Layout, Array
LBNL Climate Computer
libflame
Libraries, Numerical
Linda
Linear Algebra Software
Linear Algebra, Numerical
Linear Equations Solvers
Linear Least Squares and Orthogonal Factorization
Linear Regression
LINPACK Benchmark
Linux Clusters
*Lisp
Lisp, Connection Machine
Little's Law
Little's Lemma
Little's Principle
Little's Result
Little's Theorem
Livermore Loops
Load Balancing
Load Balancing, Distributed Memory
Locality of Reference and Parallel Processing
Lock-Free Algorithms
Locks
Logarithmic-Depth Sorting Network
Logic Languages
LogP Bandwidth-Latency Model
Loop Blocking
Loop Nest Parallelization
Loop Tiling
Loops, Parallel
LU Factorization
Manycore
MapReduce
MasPar
Massively Parallel Processor (MPP)
Massive-Scale Analytics
Matrix Computations
Maude
Media Extensions
Meiko
Memory Consistency Models
Memory Models
Memory Ordering
Memory Wall
MEMSY
Mesh
Mesh Partitioning
Message Passing
Message Passing Interface (MPI)
Message-Passing Performance Models
METIS and ParMETIS
Metrics
Microprocessors
MILC
MIMD (Multiple Instruction, Multiple Data) Machines
MIMD Lattice Computation
MIN
ML
MMX
Model Coupling Toolkit (MCT)
Models for Algorithm Design and Analysis
Models of Computation, Theoretical
Modulo Scheduling and Loop Pipelining
Molecular Evolution
Monitors
Monitors, Axiomatic Verification of
Moore's Law

MPI (Message Passing Interface)
MPI-2 I/O
MPI-IO
MPP
Mul-T
Multicomputers
Multicore Networks
Multiflow Computer
Multifrontal Method
Multi-Level Transactions
Multilisp
Multimedia Extensions
Multiple-Instruction Issue
Multiprocessor Networks
Multiprocessor Synchronization
Multiprocessors
Multiprocessors, Symmetric
MultiScheme
Multistage Interconnection Networks
Multi-Streamed Processors
Multi-Threaded Processors
Mumps
MUMPS
Mutual Exclusion
Myri-10G
Myricom
Myrinet
NAMD (NAnoscale Molecular Dynamics)
NAnoscale Molecular Dynamics (NAMD)
NAS Parallel Benchmarks
N-Body Computational Methods
nCUBE
NEC SX Series Vector Computers
NESL
Nested Loops Scheduling
Nested Spheres of Control
NetCDF I/O Library, Parallel
Network Adapter
Network Architecture
Network Interfaces
Network Obliviousness
Network of Workstations
Network offload
Networks, Direct
Networks, Fault-Tolerant
Networks, Multistage
NI (Network Interface)
NIC (Network Interface Controller or Network Interface Card)
Node Allocation
Non-Blocking Algorithms
Nondeterminator
Nonuniform Memory Access (NUMA) Machines
NOW
NUMA Caches
Numerical Algorithms
Numerical Libraries
Numerical Linear Algebra
NVIDIA GPU
NWChem
Omega Calculator
Omega Library
Omega Project
Omega Test
One-to-All Broadcast
Open Distributed Systems
OpenMP
OpenMP Profiling with OmpP
OpenSHMEM - Toward a Unified RMA Model
Operating System Strategies
Optimistic Loop Parallelization
Orthogonal Factorization
OS Jitter
OS, Light-Weight
Out-of-Order Execution Processors
Overdetermined Systems
Overlay Network
Owicki-Gries Method of Axiomatic Verification
Parafrase
Parallel Communication Models
Parallel Computing
Parallel I/O Library (PIO)
Parallel Ocean Program (POP)
Parallel Operating System
Parallel Prefix Algorithms
Parallel Prefix Sums
Parallel Random Access Machines (PRAM)
Parallel Skeletons
Parallel Tools Platform
Parallelism Detection in Nested Loops, Optimal
Parallelization
Parallelization, Automatic
Parallelization, Basic Block
Parallelization, Loop Nest

ParaMETIS
PARDISO
PARSEC Benchmarks
Partial Computation
Particle Dynamics
Particle Methods
Partitioned Global Address Space (PGAS) Languages
PASM Parallel Processing System
Path Expressions
PaToH (Partitioning Tool for Hypergraphs)
Partitioning Tool for Hypergraphs (PaToH)
PC Clusters
PCI Express
PCIe
PCI-E
PCI-Express
Peer-to-Peer
Pentium
PERCS System Architecture
Perfect Benchmarks
Performance Analysis Tools
Performance Measurement
Performance Metrics
Periscope
Personalized All-to-All Exchange
Petaflop Barrier
Petascale Computer
Petri Nets
PETSc (Portable, Extensible Toolkit for Scientific Computation)
PGAS (Partitioned Global Address Space) Languages
Phylogenetic Inference
Phylogenetics
Pi-Calculus
Pipelining
Place-Transition Nets
PLAPACK
PLASMA
PMPI Tools
Pnetcdf
Point-to-Point Switch
Polaris
Polyhedra Scanning
Polyhedron Model
Polytope Model
Position Tree
POSIX Threads (Pthreads)

Power Wall
PRAM (Parallel Random Access Machines)
Preconditioners for Sparse Iterative Methods
Prefix
Prefix Reduction
Problem Architectures
Process Algebras
Process Calculi
Process Description Languages
Process Synchronization
Processes, Tasks, and Threads
Processor Allocation
Processor Arrays
Processors-in-Memory
Profiling
Profiling with OmpP, OpenMP
Program Graphs
Programmable Interconnect Computer
Programming Languages
Programming Models
Prolog
Prolog Machines
Promises
Protein Docking
Pthreads (POSIX Threads)
PVM (Parallel Virtual Machine)
QCD apeNEXT Machines
QCD (Quantum Chromodynamics) Computations
QCD Machines
QCDSP and QCDOC Computers
QsNet
Quadrics
Quantum Chemistry
Quantum Chromodynamics (QCD) Computations
Quicksort
Race
Race Conditions
Race Detection Techniques
Race Detectors for Cilk and Cilk++ Programs
Race Hazard
Radix Sort
Rapid Elliptic Solvers
Reconfigurable Computer
Reconfigurable Computers
Reconstruction of Evolutionary Trees
Reduce and Scan
Relaxed Memory Consistency Models

Reliable Networks
Rendezvous
Reordering
Resource Affinity Scheduling
Resource Management for Parallel Computers
Rewriting Logic
Ring
Roadrunner Project, Los Alamos
Router Architecture
Router-Based Networks
Routing (Including Deadlock Avoidance)
R-Stream Compiler
Run Time Parallelization
Runtime System
Scalability
Scalable Coherent Interface (SCI)
ScaLAPACK
Scalasca
Scaled Speedup
Scan for Distributed Memory, Message-Passing Systems
Scan, Reduce and
Scatter
Scheduling
Scheduling Algorithms
SCI (Scalable Coherent Interface)
Semantic Independence
Semaphores
Sequential Consistency
Server Farm
Shared Interconnect
Shared Virtual Memory
Shared-Medium Network
Shared-Memory Multiprocessors
SHMEM
SIGMA-1
SIMD (Single Instruction, Multiple Data) Machines
SIMD Extensions
SIMD ISA
Single System Image
Singular-Value Decomposition (SVD)
Sisal
Small-World Network Analysis and Partitioning (SNAP) Framework
SNAP (Small-World Network Analysis and Partitioning) Framework

SoC (System on Chip)
Social Networks
Software Autotuning
Software Distributed Shared Memory
Sorting
Space-Filling Curves
SPAI (SParse Approximate Inverse)
Spanning Tree, Minimum Weight
Sparse Approximate Inverse Matrix
Sparse Direct Methods
Sparse Gaussian Elimination
Sparse Iterative Methods, Preconditioners for
SPEC Benchmarks
SPEC HPC2002
SPEC HPC96
SPEC MPI2007
SPEC OMP2001
Special-Purpose Machines
Speculation
Speculation, Thread-Level
Speculative Multithreading (SM)
Speculative Parallelization
Speculative Parallelization of Loops
Speculative Run-Time Parallelization
Speculative Threading
Speculative Thread-Level Parallelization
Speedup
SPIKE
Spiral
SPMD Computational Model
SSE
Stalemate
State Space Search
Stream Processing
Stream Programming Languages
Strong Scaling
Suffix Trees
Superlinear Speedup
SuperLU
Supernode Partitioning
Superscalar Processors
SWARM: A Parallel Programming Framework for Multicore Processors
Switch Architecture
Switched-Medium Network
Switching Techniques
Symmetric Multiprocessors

Synchronization
System Integration
System on Chip (SoC)
Systems Biology, Network Inference in
Systolic Architecture
Systolic Arrays
Task Graph Scheduling
Task Mapping, Topology Aware
Tasks
TAU
TAU Performance System®
TBB (Intel Threading Building Blocks)
Tensilica
Tera MTA
Terrestrial Ecosystem Carbon Modeling
Terrestrial Ecosystem Modeling
The High Performance Substrate
Theory of Mazurkiewicz-Traces
Thick Ethernet
Thin Ethernet
Thread Level Speculation (TLS) Parallelization
Thread-Level Data Speculation (TLDS)
Thread-Level Speculation
Threads
Tiling
Titanium
TLS
TOP500
Topology Aware Task Mapping
Torus
Total Exchange
Trace Scheduling
Trace Theory
Tracing
Transactional Memories

Transactions, Nested
Transpose
TStreams
Tuning and Analysis Utilities
Ultracomputer, NYU
Uncertainty Quantification
Underdetermined Systems
Unified Parallel C
Unimodular Transformations
Universal VLSI Circuits
Universality in VLSI Computation
UPC
Use-Def Chains
Vampir
Vampir 7
Vampir NG
VampirServer
VampirTrace
Vector Extensions, Instruction-Set Architecture (ISA)
Vectorization
Verification of Parallel Shared-Memory Programs, Owicki-Gries Method of Axiomatic
View from Berkeley
Virtual Shared Memory
VLIW Processors
VLSI Algorithmics
VLSI Computation
VNG
Warp and iWarp
Wavefront Arrays
Weak Scaling
Whole Program Analysis
Work-Depth Model
Workflow Scheduling
Z-Level Programming Language
ZPL

Printed by Books on Demand, Germany